Introduction to Programming WITH JAVA

A Problem Solving Approach

John S. Dean
Park University

Raymond H. Dean
University of Kansas

Boston Burr Ridge, IL Dubuque, IA New York San Francisco St. Louis
Bangkok Bogotá Caracas Kuala Lumpur Lisbon London Madrid Mexico City
Milan Montreal New Delhi Santiago Seoul Singapore Sydney Taipei Toronto

The McGraw·Hill Companies

INTRODUCTION TO PROGRAMMING WITH JAVA: A PROBLEM SOLVING APPROACH

Published by McGraw-Hill, a business unit of The McGraw-Hill Companies, Inc., 1221 Avenue of the Americas, New York, NY 10020.

This book is printed on acid-free paper.

1 2 3 4 5 6 7 8 9 0 DOC/DOC 0 9 8

ISBN 978–0–07–304702–7
MHID 0–07–304702–3

Global Publisher: *Raghothaman Srinivasan*
Director of Development: *Kristine Tibbetts*
Developmental Editor: *Heidi Newsom*
Executive Marketing Manager: *Michael Weitz*
Senior Project Manager: *Kay J. Brimeyer*
Lead Production Supervisor: *Sandy Ludovissy*
Designer: *Laurie B. Janssen*
Cover image: ©*Don Palmer, Kansas Flint Hills*
Compositor: *Newgen*
Typeface: *10/12 Times Roman*
Printer: *R. R. Donnelley Crawfordsville, IN*

Figure 1.1: *Mouse: © BigStock Photos; Keyboard, Scanner, and Printer: © PhotoDisc/Getty Images; Monitor: © Brand X/Punchstock;* Figure 1.2: *Motherboard, CPU chip, and main memory chips: © BigStock Photos;* Figure 1.4: *Diskette: © BrandX/Jupiter Images; Compact disc: © Getty Royalty Free; Hard disk and USB flash drive: © BigStock Photos*

Library of Congress Cataloging-in-Publication Data

Dean, John, 1962–
Introduction to programming with Java : a problem solving approach / John Dean, Ray Dean.—1st ed.
p. cm.
Includes index.
ISBN 978–0–07–304702–7 — ISBN 0–07–304702–3 (hard copy : alk. paper) 1. Java (Computer program language) I. Dean, Ray, 1936– II. Title.
QA76.73.J38D4265 2008
005.13′3—dc22

2007037978

www.mhhe.com

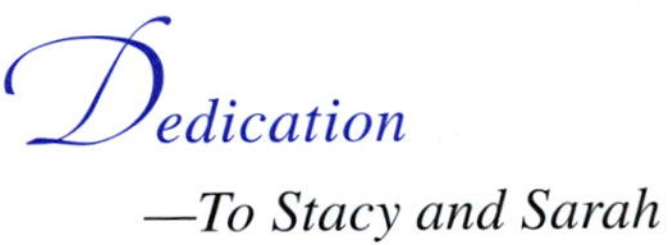
Dedication
—To Stacy and Sarah

About the Authors

John Dean is the Department Chair of the Information and Computer Science Department at Park University. He earned an M.S. degree in computer science from the University of Kansas. He is Sun Java certified and has worked in industry as a software engineer and project manager, specializing in Java and various Web technologies—JavaScript, JavaServer Pages, and servlets. He has taught a full range of computer science courses, including Java programming and Java-based Web programming.

Raymond Dean is a Professor Emeritus, Electrical Engineering and Computer Science, University of Kansas. He earned an M.S. degree from MIT and a Ph.D. degree from Princeton University, and he is a senior member of IEEE. He has published numerous scientific papers and has 21 U.S. patents. He is currently a research scientist with The Land Institute's Climate and Energy Program, which advocates comprehensive energy conservation and replacement of fossil and nuclear fuel consumption with wind power and electrical-energy storage.

Contents

Preface

In this book, we lead you on a journey into the fun and exciting world of computer programming. Throughout your journey, we'll provide you with lots of problem-solving practice. After all, good programmers need to be good problem solvers. We'll show you how to implement your problem solutions with Java programs. We provide a plethora of examples, some short and focused on a single concept, some longer and more "real world." We present the material in a conversational, easy-to-follow manner aimed at making your journey a pleasant one. When you're done with the book, you should be a proficient Java programmer.

Our textbook targets a wide range of readers. Primarily, it targets students in a standard college-level "Introduction to Programming" course or course sequence where no prerequisite programming experience is assumed.

In addition to targeting students with no prerequisite programming experience, our textbook also targets industry practitioners and college-level students who have some programming experience and want to learn Java. This second set of readers can skip the early chapters on general programming concepts and focus on the features of Java that differ from the languages that they already know. In particular, since C++ and Java are so similar, readers with a C++ background should be able to cover the textbook in a single three-credit-hour course. (But let us reiterate for those of you with no programming experience: You should be fine. No prerequisite programming experience is required.)

Finally, our textbook targets high school students and readers outside of academia with no programming experience. This third set of readers should read the entire textbook at a pace determined on a case-by-case basis.

Textbook Cornerstone #1: Problem Solving

Being able to solve problems is a critical skill that all programmers must possess. We teach programmatic problem solving by emphasizing two of its key elements—algorithm development and program design.

Emphasis on Algorithm Development

In Chapter 2, we immerse readers into algorithm development by using pseudocode for the algorithm examples instead of Java. In using pseudocode, students are able to work through non-trivial problems on their own without getting bogged down in Java syntax—no need to worry about class headings, semicolons, braces, and so on.[1] Working through non-trivial problems enables students to gain an early appreciation for creativity, logic, and organization. Without that appreciation, Java students tend to learn Java syntax with a rote-memory attitude. But with that appreciation, students tend to learn Java syntax more quickly and effectively because they have a motivational basis for learning it. In addition, they are able to handle non-

[1] Inevitably, we use a particular style for our pseudocode, but we repeatedly emphasize that other pseudocode styles are fine as long as they convey the intended meaning. Our pseudocode style is a combination of free-form description for high-level tasks and more specific commands for low-level tasks. For the specific commands, we use natural English words rather than cryptic symbols. We've chosen a pseudocode style that is intuitive, to welcome new programmers, and structured, to accommodate program logic.

trivial Java homework assignments fairly early because they have prior experience with similarly non-trivial pseudocode homework assignments.

In Chapter 3 and in later chapters, we rely primarily on Java for algorithm-development examples. But for the more involved problems, we sometimes use high-level pseudocode to describe first-cut proposed solutions. Using pseudocode enables readers to bypass syntax details and focus on the algorithm portion of the solution.

Emphasis on Program Design

Problem solving is more than just developing an algorithm. It also involves figuring out the best implementation for the algorithm. That's program design. Program design is extremely important and that's why we spend so much time on it. We don't just present a solution. We explain the thought processes that arise when coming up with a solution. For example, we explain how to choose between different loop types, how to split up a method into multiple methods, how to decide on appropriate classes, how to choose between instance and class members, and how to determine class relationships using inheritance and composition. We challenge students to find the most elegant implementations for a particular task.

We devote a whole chapter to program design—Chapter 8, Software Engineering. In that chapter, we provide in-depth looks at coding-style conventions, modularization, and encapsulation. Also in the chapter, we describe alternative design strategies—top-down, bottom-up, case-based, and iterative enhancement.

Problem-Solving Sections

We often address problem solving (algorithm development and program design) in the natural flow of explaining concepts. But we also cover problem solving in sections that are wholly devoted to it. In each problem-solving section, we present a situation that contains an unresolved problem. In coming up with a solution for the problem, we try to mimic the real-world problem-solving experience by using an iterative design strategy. We present a first-cut solution, analyze the solution, and then discuss possible improvements to it. We use a conversational trial-and-error format (e.g., "What type of layout manager should we use? We first tried the `GridLayout` manager. That works OK, but not great. Let's now try the `BorderLayout` manager."). This casual tone sets the student at ease by conveying the message that it is normal, and in fact expected, that a programmer will need to work through a problem multiple times before finding the best solution.

Additional Problem-Solving Mechanisms

We include problem-solving examples and problem-solving advice throughout the text (not just in Chapter 2, Chapter 8, and the problem-solving sections). As a point of emphasis, we insert a problem-solving box, with an icon and a succinct tip, next to the text that contains the problem-solving example and/or advice.

We are strong believers in learning by example. As such, our textbook contains a multitude of complete program examples. Readers are encouraged to use our programs as recipes for solving similar programs on their own.

Textbook Cornerstone #2: Fundamentals First

Postpone Concepts That Require Complex Syntax

We feel that many introductory programming textbooks jump too quickly into concepts that require complex syntax. In using complex syntax early, students get in the habit of entering code without fully understanding it or, worse yet, copying and pasting from example code without fully understanding the example code. That can lead to less-than-ideal programs and students who are limited in their ability to solve a wide variety of problems. Thus, we prefer to postpone concepts that require complex syntax. We prefer to introduce such concepts later on when students are better able to fully understand them.

As a prime example of that philosophy, we cover the simpler forms of GUI programming early (in an optional graphics track), but we cover the more complicated forms of GUI programming late. Specifically, we postpone event-driven GUI programming until the end of the book. This is different from some other Java textbooks, which favor early full immersion into event-driven GUI programming. We feel that strategy is a mistake because proper event-driven GUI programming requires a great deal of programming maturity. By covering it at the end of the book, our readers are better able to fully understand it.

Tracing Examples

To write code effectively, it's imperative to understand code thoroughly. We've found that step-by-step tracing of program code is an effective way to ensure thorough understanding. Thus, in the earlier parts of the textbook, when we introduce a new programming structure, we often illustrate it with a meticulous trace. The detailed tracing technique we use illustrates the thought process programmers employ while debugging. It's a printed alternative to the sequence of screen displays generated by debuggers in IDE software.

Input and Output

In the optional GUI-track sections and in the GUI chapters at the end of the book, we use GUI commands for input and output (I/O). But because of our emphasis on fundamentals, we use console commands for I/O for the rest of the book.[2] For console input, we use the `Scanner` class. For console output, we use the standard `System.out.print`, `System.out.println`, and `System.out.printf` methods.

Textbook Cornerstone #3: Real World

More often than not, today's classroom students and industry practitioners prefer to learn with a hands-on, real-world approach. To meet this need, our textbook includes:

- compiler tools
- complete program examples
- practical guidance in program design
- coding-style guidelines based on industry standards
- UML notation for class relationship diagrams
- practical homework-project assignments

Compiler Tools

We do not tie the textbook to any particular compiler tool—you are free to use any compiler tool(s) that you like. If you do not have a preferred compiler in mind, then you might want to try out one or more of these:

- Java2 SDK toolkit, by Sun
- TextPad, by Helios

[2] We cover GUI I/O early on with the `JOptionPane` class. That opens up an optional door for GUI fans. If readers are so inclined, they can use `JOptionPane` to implement all of our programs with GUI I/O rather than console I/O. To do so, they replace all console I/O method calls with `JOptionPane` method calls.

- Eclipse, by the Eclipse Foundation
- Netbeans, backed by Sun
- BlueJ, by the University of Kent and Deaken University

To obtain the above compilers, visit our textbook Web site at http://www.mhhe.com/dean, find the appropriate compiler link(s), and download away for free.

Complete Program Examples

In addition to providing code fragments to illustrate specific concepts, our textbook contains lots of complete program examples. With complete programs, students are able to (1) see how the analyzed code ties in with the rest of a program, and (2) test the code by running it.

Coding-Style Conventions

We include coding-style tips throughout the textbook. The coding-style tips are based on Sun's coding conventions (http://java.sun.com/docs/codeconv/) and industry practice. In Appendix 5, we provide a complete reference for the book's coding-style conventions and an associated example program that illustrates the conventions.

UML Notation

The Universal Modeling Language (UML) has become a standard for describing the entities in large software projects. Rather than overwhelm beginning programmers with syntax for the entire UML (which is quite extensive), we present a subset of the UML. Throughout the textbook, we incorporate UML notation to pictorially represent classes and class relationships. For those interested in more details, we provide additional UML notation in Appendix 7.

Homework Problems

We provide homework problems that are illustrative, practical, and clearly worded. The problems range from easy to challenging. They are grouped into three categories—review questions, exercises, and projects. We include review questions and exercises at the end of each chapter, and we provide projects on our textbook's Web site.

The review questions tend to have short answers and the answers are in the textbook. The review questions use these formats: short-answer, multiple-choice, true/false, fill-in-the-blanks, tracing, debugging, write a code fragment. Each review question is based on a relatively small part of the chapter.

The exercises tend to have short to moderate-length answers, and the answers are not in the textbook. The exercises use these formats: short-answer, tracing, debugging, write a code fragment. Exercises are keyed to the highest prerequisite section number in the chapter, but they sometimes integrate concepts from several parts of the chapter.

The projects consist of problem descriptions whose solutions are complete programs. Project solutions are not in the textbook. Projects require students to employ creativity and problem-solving skills and apply what they've learned in the chapter. These projects often include optional parts, which provide challenges for the more talented students. Projects are keyed to the highest prerequisite section number in the chapter, but they often integrate concepts from several preceding parts of the chapter.

An important special feature of this book is the way it specifies project problems. "Sample sessions" show the precise output generated for a particular set of input values. These sample sessions include inputs that represent typical situations and sometimes also extreme or boundary situations.

Academic-Area Projects

To enhance the appeal of projects and to show how the current chapter's programming techniques might apply to different areas of interest, we take project content from several academic areas:

- Computer Science and Numerical Methods
- Business and Accounting
- Social Sciences and Statistics
- Math and Physics
- Engineering and Architecture
- Biology and Ecology

The academic-area projects do not require prerequisite knowledge in a particular area. Thus, instructors are free to assign any of the projects to any of their students. To provide a general reader with enough specialized knowledge to work a problem in a particular academic area, we sometimes expand the problem statement to explain a few special concepts in that academic area.

Most of the academic-area projects do not require students to have completed projects from earlier chapters; that is, the projects do not build on each other. Thus, instructors are free to assign projects without worrying about prerequisite projects. In some cases, a project repeats a previous chapter's project with a different approach. The teacher may elect to take advantage of this repetition to dramatize the availability of alternatives, but this is not necessary.

Project assignments can be tailored to fit readers' needs. For example:

- For readers outside of academia—
  Readers can choose projects that match their interests.

- When a course has students from one academic area—
  Instructors can assign projects from the relevant academic area.

- When a course has students with diverse backgrounds—
  Instructors can ask students to choose projects from their own academic areas, or
  Instructors can ignore the academic-area delineations and simply assign projects that are most appealing.

To help you decide which projects to work on, we've included a "Project Summary" section after the preface. It lists all the projects by chapter, and for each project, it specifies:

- The associated section within the chapter
- The academic area
- The length and difficulty
- A brief description

After using the "Project Summary" section to get an idea of which projects you might like to work on, see the textbook's Web site for the full project descriptions.

Organization

In writing this book, we lead readers through three important programming methodologies: structured programming, object-oriented programming (OOP), and event-driven programming. For our structured programming coverage, we introduce basic concepts such as variables and operators, `if` statements, and loops. For our OOP coverage, we start by showing readers how to call pre-built methods from Sun's Java Application Programming Interface (API) library. We then introduce basic OOP concepts such as classes, objects, instance variables, and instance methods. Next, we move on to more advanced OOP concepts—class variables, arrays, and inheritance. Chapters on exception handling and files provide a transition into event-driven graphical user interface (GUI) programming. We cover event-driven GUI programming in earnest in the final two chapters.

The content and sequence we promote enable students to develop their skills from a solid foundation of programming fundamentals. To foster this fundamentals-first approach, our book starts with a minimum set of concepts and details. It then gradually broadens concepts and adds detail later. We avoid overloading early chapters by deferring certain less-important details to later chapters.

GUI Track

Many programmers find GUI programming to be fun. As such, GUI programming can be a great motivational tool for keeping readers interested and engaged. That's why we include graphics sections throughout the book, starting in Chapter 1. We call those sections our "GUI track." For readers who do not have time for the GUI track, no problem. Any or all of the GUI track sections may be skipped as they cover material that is independent of later material.

Chapter 1

In Chapter 1, we first explain basic computer terms—what are the hardware components, what is source code, what is object code, and so on. We then narrow our focus and describe the programming language we'll be using for the remainder of the book—Java. Finally, we give students a quick view of the classic bare-bones "Hello World" program. We explain how to create and run the program using minimalist software—Microsoft's Notepad text editor and Sun's command-line Software Development Kit (SDK) tools.

Chapter 2

In Chapter 2, we present problem-solving techniques with an emphasis on algorithmic design. In implementing algorithm solutions, we use generic tools—flowcharts and pseudocode—with pseudocode being given the greatest weight. As part of our algorithm-design explanation, we describe structured programming techniques. In order to give students an appreciation for semantic details, we show how to trace algorithms.

Chapters 3–5

We present structured programming techniques using Java in Chapters 3–5. Chapter 3 describes sequential programming basics—variables, input/output, assignment statements, and simple method calls. Chapter 4 describes non-sequential program flow—`if` statements, `switch` statements, and loops. In Chapter 5 we explain methods in more detail and show readers how to use pre-built methods in the Java API library. In all three chapters, we teach algorithm design by solving problems and writing programs with the newly introduced Java syntax.

Chapters 6–8

Chapter 6 introduces the basic elements of OOP in Java. This includes implementing classes and implementing methods and variables within those classes. We use UML class diagrams and object-oriented tracing techniques to illustrate these concepts.

Chapter 7 provides additional OOP details. It explains how reference variables are assigned, tested for equality, and passed as arguments to a method. It covers overloaded methods and constructors.

While the art of program design and the science of computerized problem-solving are developed throughout the textbook, in Chapter 8, we focus on these aspects in the context of OOP. This chapter begins with an organized treatment of programming style. It includes recommendations on how to use methods to further the goal of encapsulation. It describes the major programming paradigms—top-down design, bottom-up design, using pre-written software for low-level modules, and prototyping.

Chapter 9

Some Java textbooks teach how to implement class members before they teach how to implement instance members. With that approach, students learn to write class members inappropriately, and that practice is hard to break later on when instance members are finally covered. Proper programming practice dictates that programmers (beginning programmers certainly included) should implement instance members more often than class members. Thus, we teach how to implement instance members early on, and we postpone how to implement class members until Chapter 9.

Chapter 10

In Chapter 10, we describe different ways to store related data. We present array basics and several important array applications—searching, sorting, and histogram construction. We present more advanced array concepts using two-dimensional arrays and arrays of objects. Finally, we look at a more powerful form of an array—an `ArrayList`.

Chapter 11

Early on, students need to be immersed in problem-solving activities. Covering too much syntax detail early can detract from that objective. Thus, we initially gloss over some less-important syntax details and come back to those details later on in Chapter 11. Chapter 11 provides more details on items such as these:

- the `byte` and `short` primitive types
- the Unicode character set
- type promotions
- postfix versus prefix modes for the increment and decrement operators
- the conditional operator
- short-circuit evaluation

Chapters 12–13

We describe class relationships in Chapters 12 and 13. We spend two full chapters on class relationships because the subject matter is so important. We take the time to explain class relationship details in depth and provide numerous examples. In Chapter 12, we discuss aggregation, composition, and inheritance. In Chapter 13, we discuss more advanced inheritance-related details such as the `Object` class, polymorphism, `abstract` classes, and interfaces.

Chapters 14–15

We cover exception handling in Chapter 14 and files in Chapter 15. We cover exception handling prior to files because file-handling code utilizes exception handling; for example, opening a file requires that you check for an exception.

Chapters 16–17

We cover event-driven GUI programming at the end of the book in Chapters 16 and 17. By learning event-driven GUI programming late, students are better able to grasp its inherent complexities.

Appendices

Most of the appendices cover reference material, such as the ASCII character set and the operator precedence table. But the last two appendices cover advanced Java material—recursion and multithreading.

Subject-Matter Dependencies and Sequence-Changing Opportunities

We've positioned the textbook's material in a natural order for someone who wants fundamentals first and also wants an early introduction to OOP. We feel that our order is the most efficient and effective order for learning how to become a proficient OOP programmer. Nonetheless, we realize that different readers have different content-ordering preferences. To accommodate those different preferences, we've provided some built-in flexibility. Figure 0.1 illustrates that flexibility by showing chapter dependencies and, more importantly, chapter non-dependencies. For example, the arrow between Chapter 3 and Chapter 4 means that Chapter 3 must be read prior to Chapter 4. And the lack of an arrow between Chapters 1 and 2 means that Chapter 1 may be skipped.

Here are some sequence-changing opportunities revealed by Figure 0.1:

- Readers can skip Chapter 1 (Introduction to Computers and Programming).
- For an earlier introduction to OOP, readers can read the OOP overview section in Chapter 6 after reading Chapter 1. And they can learn OOP syntax and semantics in Chapter 6 after finishing Java basics in Chapter 3.
- For additional looping practice, readers can learn about arrays in Chapter 10 after finishing loops in Chapter 4.
- Readers can skip Chapter 15 (Files).

Note Figure 0.1's dashed arrow that connects Chapter 3 to Chapter 15. We use a dashed arrow to indicate that the connection is partial. Some readers may wish to use files early on for input and output (I/O). Those readers should read Chapter 3 for Java basics and then immediately jump to Chapter 15, Sections 15.3 and 15.4 for text-file I/O. With a little work, they'll then be able to use files for all their I/O needs throughout the rest of the book. We say "with a little work" because the text-file I/O sections contain some code that won't be fully understood by someone coming directly from Chapter 3. To use the text-file I/O code, they'll need to treat it as a template. In other words, they'll use the code even though they probably won't understand some of it.

To support content-ordering flexibility, the book contains "hyperlinks." A hyperlink is an optional jump forward from one place in the book to another place. The jumps are legal in terms of prerequisite knowledge, meaning that the jumped-over (skipped) material is unnecessary for an understanding of the later material. We supply hyperlinks for each of the non-sequential arrows in Figure 0.1. For example, we supply hyperlinks that go from Chapter 1 to Chapter 6 and from Chapter 3 to Chapter 11. For each hyperlink tail end (in the earlier chapter), we tell the reader where they may optionally jump to. For each hyperlink target end (in the later chapter), we provide an icon at the side of the target text that helps readers find the place where they are to begin reading.

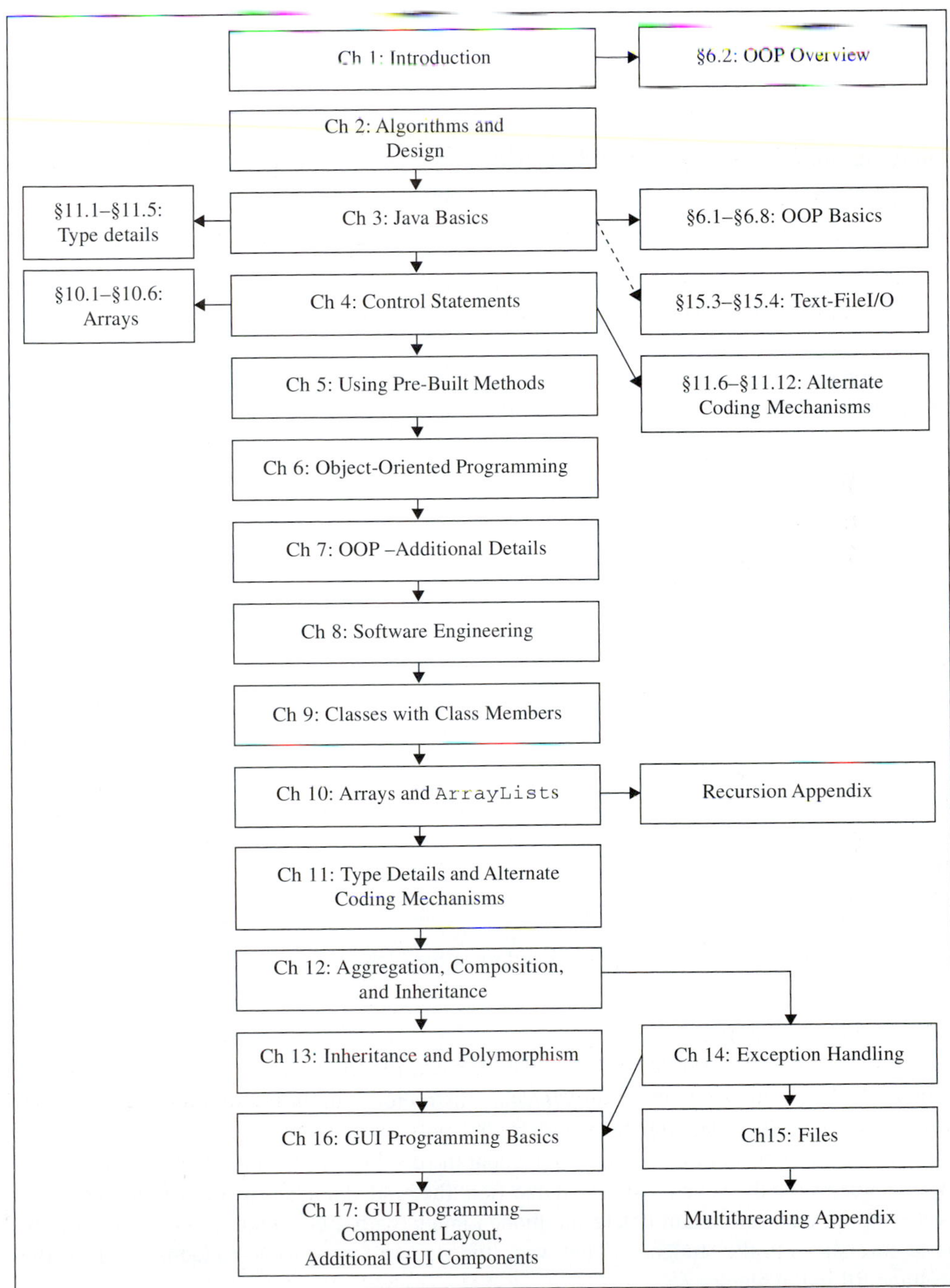

Figure 0.1 Chapter dependencies

Pedagogy

Icons

Program elegance.
Indicates that the associated text deals with a program's coding style, readability, maintainability, robustness, and scalability. Those qualities comprise a program's elegance.

Problem solving.
Indicates that the associated text deals with problem-solving issues. Comments associated with icon attempt to generalize highlighted material in the adjacent text.

Common errors.
Indicates that the associated text deals with common errors.

Hyperlink target.
Indicates the target end of a hyperlink.

Program efficiency.
Indicates that the associated text refers to program-efficiency issues.

Student Resources

At the textbook Web site, http://www.mhhe.com/dean, students (and also teachers) can view and download these resources:

- Links to compiler software—for Sun's Java2 SDK toolkit, Helios's TextPad, Eclipse, NetBeans, and BlueJ
- TextPad tutorial
- Eclipse tutorials
- Textbook errata
- All textbook example programs and associated resource files

Instructor Resources

At the textbook Web site, http://www.mhhe.com/dean, instructors can view and download these resources:

- Customizable PowerPoint lecture slides with hidden notes
  - Hidden notes provide comments that supplement the displayed text in the lecture slides.
  - For example, if the displayed text asks a question, the hidden notes provide the answer.
  - As an option, instructors can delete the hidden notes (with a convenient macro) before distributing the lecture slides to the students. (That way, students are forced to go to lecture to hear the sage on the stage fill in the blanks. ☺)
- Exercise solutions
- Project solutions
- Test bank materials

Acknowledgments

Anyone who has written a textbook can attest to what a large and well-orchestrated team effort it requires. Such a book can never be the work of only one person or even a few. We are deeply indebted to the team at McGraw-Hill Higher Education who have shown continued faith in our writing and invested generously in it.

It was a pleasure to work with Alan Apt during the book's two-year review period. He provided excellent guidance on several large design issues. We are grateful for the tireless efforts of Rebecca Olson. Rebecca did a tremendous job organizing and analyzing the book's many reviews. Helping us through the various stages of production were Project Manager Kay Brimeyer and Designer Laurie Janssen. We would also like to thank the rest of the editorial and marketing team, who helped in the final stages: Raghu Srinivasan, Global Publisher; Kristine Tibbetts, Director of Development; Heidi Newsom, Editorial Assistant; and Michael Weitz, Executive Marketing Manager.

All the professionals we have encountered throughout the McGraw-Hill organization have been wonderful to work with, and we sincerely appreciate their efforts.

We would like to acknowledge with appreciation the numerous and valuable comments, suggestions, and constructive criticisms and praise from the many instructors who have reviewed the book. In particular,

William Allen, *Florida Institute of Technology*
Robert Burton, *Brigham Young University*
Priscilla Dodds, *Georgia Perimeter College*
Jeanne M. Douglas, *University of Vermont*
Dr. H.E. Dunsmore, *Purdue University*
Deena Engel, *New York University*
Michael N. Huhns, *University of South Carolina*
Ibrahim Imam, *University of Louisville*
Andree Jacobson, *University of New Mexico*
Lawrence King, *University of Texas, Dallas*
Mark Llewellyn, *University of Central Florida*
Blayne E.Mayfield, *Oklahoma State University*
Mary McCollam, *Queen's University*
Hugh McGuire, *Grand Valley State University*
Jeanne Milostan, *Vanderbilt University*
Shyamal Mitra, *University of Texas, Austin*
Benjamin B.Nystuen, *University of Colorado, Colorado Springs*
Richard E. Pattis, *Carnegie Mellon University*
Tom Stokke, *University of North Dakota*
Ronald Taylor, *Wright State University*
Timothy A.Terrill, *University at Buffalo, The State University of New York*
Ping Wu, *Dell Inc*

We would also like to thank colleagues Wen Hsin, Kevin Burger, John Cigas, Bob Cotter, Alice Capson, and Mark Adams for helping with informal quick surveys and Barbara Kushan, Ed Tankins,

Mark Reith, and Benny Phillips for class testing. And a special debt of gratitude goes to colleague and grammarian nonpareil Jeff Glauner, who helped with subtle English syntax nuances.

Finally, thanks to the students. To the ones who encouraged the initial writing of the book, and to the ones who provided feedback and searched diligently for mistakes in order to earn bonus points on the homework. In particular, thank you Aris Czamanske, Malallai Zalmai, Paul John, Joby John, Matt Thebo, Josh McKinzie, Carol Liberty, Adeeb Jarrah, and Virginia Maikweki.

Sincerely,
John and Ray

Project Summary

One of the special features of this text is the diversity of its projects. Project subject matter spans six broad academic areas, as this short table shows:

abbreviation	description	easy	moderate	difficult	total
CS	Computer Science and Numerical Methods	14	12	6	32
Business	Business and Accounting	10	10	3	23
Sociology	Social Sciences and Statistics	7	7	5	19
Math & Phys	Math and Physics	9	5	3	17
Engineering	Engineering and Architecture	3	7	5	15
Biol & Ecol	Biology and Ecology	0	2	4	6
	totals	**43**	**43**	**26**	**112**

The abbreviation in the first column above will be used in a larger table below as a brief identification of a particular academic area. The four right-side columns in the above table indicate the number of projects in various categories. Of course, the highest number of projects (32) occurs in the area of computer science and numerical methods. The 26 easy and moderate CS projects are typical CS introductory programming problems. The 6 difficult CS projects provide gentle introductions to some advanced topics like link list operations, database operations, and simulated annealing.

In addition, there are 23 projects in business and accounting, which include miscellaneous financial calculations, simple bookkeeping problems, and cost-accounting applications. There are 19 projects in social sciences and statistics, which include applications in sociology and political science, as well as general experience. There are 17 projects in math and physics, which include applications in both classical and chaotic mechanics. There are 15 projects in engineering and architecture, which include applications in heating ventilating and air conditioning (HVAC), electrical circuits, and structures. Finally, there are 6 projects in biology and ecology, which include realistic growth and predator-prey simulations. Although we've associated each project with one primary academic area, many of these projects can fit into other academic areas as well.

Because many of these projects apply to disciplines outside the field of computer science, we do not expect that the average reader will already know about all of these "other" topics. Therefore, in our problem statements we usually take considerable time to explain the topic as well as the problem. And we often explain how to go about solving the problem—in layman's terms. Therefore, working many of these projects will be like implementing computer solutions for customers who are not programmers themselves but understand their subject matter and know what they want you (the programmer) to do for them. They will explain their problem and how to go about solving it. But then they will expect you to create the program that actually solves that problem.

Because our project explanations frequently take considerable printed space, instead of putting them in the book itself, we put them on our Web site:

http://www.mhhe.com/dean

The following table provides a summary of what's on that Web site. This table lists all of the book's projects in a sequence that matches the book's sequence. The first column identifies the first point in the book at which you should be able to do the project, by chapter and section, in the form: ChapterNumber.SectionNumber. The second column is a unique project number for the chapter in question. The third column identifies the project's primary academic area with an abbreviation that's explained in the shorter table above. The fourth column indicates the approximate number of pages of code that our solution contains. The fifth column indicates the difficulty relative to where you are in your study of Java. For example, you can see that what we call "easy" involves progressively more pages of code as you progress through the book. The last two columns provide a title and brief description of each project.

Project Summary

Ch./Sec	Proj.	Academic Area	Sol. Pages	Difficulty	Title	Brief Description
2.7	1	Business	0.6	easy	Annual Bonus–(Flowchart)	Draw a flowchart for an algorithm that computes an annual bonus.
2.7	2	Business	0.3	easy	Annual Bonus—(Pseudocode)	Write pseudocode for an algorithm that computes an annual bonus.
2.7	3	Business	0.6	easy	Number of Stamps—(Flowchart)	Draw a flowchart for an algorithm that calculates the number of stamps needed for an envelope. Use one stamp for every five sheets of paper.
2.7	4	Business	0.3	easy	Number of Stamps—(Pseudocode)	Write pseudocode for an algorithm that calculates the number of stamps needed for an envelope. Use one stamp for every five sheets of paper.
2.7	5	Biol & Ecol	0.5	moderate	Five Kingdoms—(Pseudocode)	Write pseudocode for an algorithm that identifies a biological kingdom from a set of characteristics.
2.7	6	Math & Phys	0.6	easy	Speed of Sound—(Flowchart)	Draw a flowchart for an algorithm that provides the speed of sound in a particular medium.
2.7	7	Math & Phys	0.4	easy	Speed of Sound—(Pseudocode)	Write pseudocode for an algorithm that provides the speed of sound in a particular medium.
2.7	8	Business	0.6	moderate	Stock Market Return—(Flowchart)	Draw a flowchart for an algorithm that prints the type of market and its probability given a particular rate of return.
2.7	9	Business	0.4	moderate	Stock Market Return—(Pseudocode)	Write pseudocode for an algorithm that prints the type of market and its probability given a particular rate of return.
2.8	10	Business	0.3	moderate	Bank Balance—(Pseudocode)	Write pseudocode for an algorithm that determines the number of years until a growing bank balance reaches a million dollars.
2.9	11	Engineering	1.0	moderate	Loop Termination by User Query—(Flowchart)	Draw a flowchart for an algorithm that calculates the overall miles per gallon for a series of miles and gallons user inputs.

Ch./Sec	Proj.	Academic Area	Sol. Pages	Difficulty	Title	Brief Description
2.9	12	Engineering	0.5	easy	Loop Termination by User Query—(Pseudocode)	Write pseudocode for an algorithm that calculates the overall miles per gallon for a series of miles and gallons user inputs.
2.9	13	Engineering	0.4	moderate	Loop Termination by Sentinal Value—(Pseudocode)	Write pseudocode for an algorithm that calculates the overall miles per gallon for a series of miles and gallons user inputs.
2.9	14	Engineering	0.3	easy	Loop Termination by Counter—(Pseudocode)	Write pseudocode for an algorithm that calculates the overall miles per gallon for a series of miles and gallons user inputs.
2.10	15	CS	0.4	moderate	Average Weight—(Pseudocode)	Write pseudocode for an algorithm that determines average weight for a group of items.
3.2	1	CS	NA	easy	Hello World Experimentation	Experiment with the `Hello.java` program to learn the meanings of typical compile-time and runtime error messages.
3.3	2	CS	NA	moderate	Research	Study Sun's Java Coding Conventions.
3.3	3	CS	NA	moderate	Research	Study Appendix 5 "Java Coding-Style Conventions."
3.16 3.23	4	Engineering	2.5	difficult	Truss Analysis	Given the load in the center of a bridge and the weights of all truss members, compute the compression or tension force in each truss member.
3.17	5	CS	1.0	easy	Sequence of Commands	Trace a sequence of commands and write a program that executes those commands.
3.17 3.23	6	CS	1.7	moderate	Computer Speed	Given a simple set of hardware and software characteristics, write a program that estimates the total time to run a computer program.
3.17 3.23	7	Engineering	2.7	moderate	HVAC Load	Calculate the heating and cooling loads for a typical residence.
3.17 3.23	8	Sociology	3.5	difficult	Campaign Planning	Write a program to help organize estimates of votes, money, and labor.
3.22	9	CS	1.0	easy	String Processing	Trace a set of string processing operations and write a program that implements them.
3.23	10	CS	1.2	easy	Swapping	Trace an algorithm that swaps the values in two variables, and write a program that implements that algorithm.
3.23	11	Math & Phys	1.0	easy	Circle Parameters	Write a program that generates and prints circle-related values.

(*continued*)

Project Summary						
Ch./Sec	**Proj.**	**Academic Area**	**Sol. Pages**	**Difficulty**	**Title**	**Brief Description**
3.23	12	Sociology	0.4	easy	One-Hundredth Birthday	Write a program that prompts the user for his/her birthday month, day, and year and prints the date of the user's one-hundredth birthday.
4.3	1	Math & Phys	1.7	easy	Stopping Distance	Write a program which determines whether a vehicle's tailgating distance is safe, given the speed of the vehicle, the vehicle's tailgating distance, and a formula that gives the distance required to stop the vehicle.
4.3 4.9	2	Engineering	1.9	easy	Column Safety	Write a program that determines whether a structural column is thick enough to support the column's expected load.
4.3	3	Business	1.1	easy	Economic Policy	Write a program that reads in growth rate and inflation values and outputs a recommended economic policy.
4.8	4	Business	2.0	moderate	Bank Balance	Write a program that determines the number of years until a growing bank balance reaches a million dollars.
4.9 4.12	5	CS	2.6	difficult	Game of NIM	Implement the game of NIM. Start the game with a user-specified number of stones in a pile. The user and the computer take turns removing either one or two stones from the pile. The player who takes the last stone loses.
4.12	6	Math & Phys	1.0	easy	Triangle	Write a program that generates an isosceles triangle made of asterisks, given user input for triangle size.
4.12	7	Sociology	0.8	easy	Mayan Calendar	Implement an algorithm that determines the number of Tzolkins and the number of Haabs in one Calendar Round.
4.12	8	CS	0.9	easy	Input Validation	Implement an algorithm that repeatedly prompts for inputs until they fall within an acceptable range and computes the average of valid inputs.
4.14	9	Business	2.6	moderate	Tax Preparation	Write a program that calculates customers' income taxes using the following rules: • The amount of taxes owed equals the taxable income times the tax rate. • Taxable income equals gross income minus $1,000 for each exemption. • The taxable income cannot be less than zero.

Project Summary						
Ch./Sec	Proj.	Academic Area	Sol. Pages	Difficulty	Title	Brief Description
4.14	10	CS	1.7	moderate	Text Parsing	Write a program that converts words to Pig Latin.
5.3	1	Math & Phys	1.2	easy	Trigonometric Functions	Write a demonstration program that asks the user to select one of three possible inverse functions, arcsin, arccos, or arctan, and input a trigonometric ratio. It should generate appropriate output, with diagnostics.
5.3	2	Math & Phys	0.7	easy	Combining Decibels	Determine the acoustical power level produced by the combination of two sound sources.
5.5	3	CS	1.5	moderate	Variable Name Checker	Write a program that checks the correctness of a user-entered variable name, i.e., whether it is: (1) illegal, (2) legal, but poor style, or (3) good style. Assume that "good style" variable names use letters and digits only, and use a lowercase letter for the first character.
5.6	4	CS	1.0	moderate	Phone Number Dissector	Implement a program that reads phone numbers, and for each phone number, it displays the phone number's three components—country code, area code, and local number.
5.6	5	CS	1.1	difficult	Phone Number Dissector—robust version	Implement a more robust version of the above phone number program. Allow for shortened phone numbers—phone numbers that have just a local digit group and nothing else, and phone numbers that have just a local digit group and an area code and nothing else.
5.8	6	Business	1.0	moderate	Net Present Value Calculation	Write a program that computes the net present value of a proposed investment, given a discount rate and an arbitrary set of future cash flows.
6.4	1	Biol & Ecol	1.5	moderate	Plant Germination Observation	Write a program that: (1) creates an object called `tree` from the `MapleTree` class; (2) calls a `plant` method to record the planting of the seed; (3) calls a `germinate` method to record the first observation of a seedling and record its height; (4) calls a `dumpData` method to display the current values of all instance variables.

(continued)

Project Summary						
Ch./Sec	Proj.	Academic Area	Sol. Pages	Difficulty	Title	Brief Description
6.4	2	Business	0.5	easy	Bank Account	Given the code for a `BankAccount` class, provide a driver that tests that class by instantiating an object and calling its methods—`setCustomer`, `setAccountNum`, and `printAccountInfo`.
6.8	3	Math & Phys	1.5	moderate	Logistic Equation	Exercise the logistic equation: nextX = presentX + r × presentX × (1 − presentX), where presentX = (present x) / (maximum x), and r is a growth factor.
6.9	4	Math & Phys	0.9	easy	Circle	Given the code for a `CircleDriver` class, write a `Circle` class that defines a `radius` instance variable, a `setRadius` method, and a `printAndCalculateCircleData` method that uses the circle's radius to calculate and print the circle's diameter, circumference, and area.
6.10	5	Engineering	2.0	moderate	Digital Filter	Given a formula for a "Chebyshev second-order low-pass" filter or a "Butterworth second-order low-pass" filter, with appropriate parameter values, write a program that asks the user to supply a sequence of raw input values and generates the corresponding filtered output.
6.10	6	Sociology	3.1	difficult	Vending Machine	Write a program that mimics the operations of a vending machine. The program should read amounts of money inserted into the vending machine, ask the user to select an item, and then print the change that's returned to the user.
6.12	7	Math & Phys	1.1	easy	Rectangle	Implement a `Rectangle` class that defines a rectangle with length and width instance variables, mutator and accessor methods, and a `boolean isSquare` method.
6.12	8	Biol & Ecol	4.0	difficult	Predator-Prey Dynamics	Write a program that models a species that could be either predator or prey or both. Run a simulation that includes predators, prey, and limited renewable sustenance for the prey.
6.13	9	Math & Phys	2.1	moderate	Guitar Mechanics	Write a program that simulates the motion of a plucked guitar string.

Project Summary						
Ch./Sec	Proj.	Academic Area	Sol. Pages	Difficulty	Title	Brief Description
7.5 7.9	1	CS	3.5	difficult	Linked List	Given the code for a driver, implement a `Recipe` class that creates and maintains a linked list of recipes. The problem assignment specifies all instance variables and methods in UML class diagrams.
7.7	2	CS	2.5	easy	Automobile Description	Use method-call chaining to help display properties of automobiles.
7.7 7.9	3	Biol & Ecol	4.6	difficult	Carbon Cycle	Given the code for a driver, write a pair of classes for a program that models the carbon cycle in an ecosystem. Use two generic classes. One class, `Entity`, defines things. The other class, `Relationship`, defines interactions.
7.8	4	CS	1.4	easy	IP Address	Implement an `IpAddress` class that stores an IP address as a dotted-decimal string and as an array of four octet `int`s.
7.9	5	Math & Phys	4.5	moderate	Fraction Handler	Given the `main` method of a driver class, write a `Fraction` class. Include the following instance methods: `add`, `multiply`, `print`, `printAsDouble`, and a separate accessor method for each instance variable.
7.10	6	Engineering	2.8	moderate	Electric Circuit	Write branch and node classes for lumped-circuit elements. A branch carries current through a resistor in series with an inductor. A node holds voltage on a capacitor connected to a common ground. Driver code is provided in the problem assignment.
7.10	7	Business	5.1	difficult	Cost Accounting	Write an object-oriented program that demonstrates cost accounting in a manufacturing plant.
7.10	8	Sociology	6.4	difficult	Political Campaign	Write a program to help organize estimates of votes, money, and labor. This is an object-oriented version of Project 8 in Chapter 3.
8.4	1	CS	1.6	easy	Input Validation	Implement an algorithm that repeatedly prompts for inputs until they fall within an acceptable range and computes the average of valid inputs. This is an object-oriented version of Project 8 in Chapter 4.

(*continued*)

Project Summary						
Ch./Sec	**Proj.**	**Academic Area**	**Sol. Pages**	**Difficulty**	**Title**	**Brief Description**
8.4	2	Engineering	4.0	difficult	HVAC Load	Calculate the heating and cooling loads for a typical residence. This is an object-oriented version of Project 7 in Chapter 3.
8.6	3	Sociology	2.6	moderate	Elevator Control	Write a program that mimics the operations of the inside of an elevator. The program should simulate what happens when the user chooses to go to a particular floor and when the user pulls the fire alarm.
8.9	4	CS	2.0	easy	Prototype Restructuring	Consider the NestedLoopRectangle program in Figure 4.17 in Section 4.12 to be a prototype. Using top-down methodology, restructure it into OOP format.
9.3	1	Sociology	2.7	easy	Person Class	Define a class that simulates the creation and display of `Person` objects.
9.4	2	Sociology	2.7	moderate	Homework Scores	Write a program that handles homework scores. Use instance variables for actual and maximum points on a particular homework, and use class variables for actual total and maximum total points on all homeworks combined.
9.3	3	Sociology	3.9	difficult	Political Approval Rating	Write a program that determines the mean and standard deviation of statistical samples.
9.4	4	Engineering	5.7	difficult	Solar Input for HVAC and Solar Collectors	Write a program that keeps track of where the sun is and determines how much solar energy penetrates a glass window of any orientation, at any place and time.
9.6	5	Business	2.7	moderate	Net Present Value Calculation	Write a program that computes the net present value of a proposed investment, given a discount rate and an arbitrary set of future cash flows. This is an OOP version of Project 6 in Chapter 5.
9.7	6	Math & Phys	7.0	difficult	Three-Body Problem	Write a program to model the three-body problem in which two equally sized moons circle the earth in different orbits. This illustrates chaotic dynamic motion.
10.4	1	Biol & Ecol	5.0	difficult	Demographic Projections	Write a program that projects future world population and average individual wealth as a function of fertility rates and resource extraction rates, and includes effects of governmental taxation and spending.

Project Summary						
Ch./Sec	Proj.	Academic Area	Sol. Pages	Difficulty	Title	Brief Description
10.6	2	CS	3.3	moderate	Dice-Throwing Simulator	Write a program that simulates the rolling of a pair of dice and prints a histogram showing the frequencies of possible results.
10.6	3	CS	5.1	difficult	Simulated Annealing—the Traveling Salesman Problem	Write a program that uses simulated annealing to solve the intractable problem of finding the shortest itinerary that visits all of the world's major cities exactly one time.
10.7	4	Sociology	2.1	easy	Party Guest List	Write a program that creates a `Party` object, adds guests to the party, and prints party information.
10.9	5	Sociology	2.7	easy	Vowel Counter	Write a program that counts the number of uppercase and lowercase vowels in user-entered lines of text and prints a summary report of vowel counts.
10.9	6	Math & Phys	7.6	difficult	Solution of Simultaneous Algebraic Equations	Write a program that loads a set of simultaneous algebraic equations into two-dimensional arrays and solves the equations by Lower-Upper Decomposition.
10.9	7	Math & Phys	2.5	moderate	Linear Regression	Write a program that computes a linear regression by fitting a straight line to a series of random data.
10.10	8	Business	3.4	moderate	Purchase Vouchers	Write a program that creates business vouchers that record purchases, displays current voucher information, and records payments for those purchases.
10.11	9	Sociology	1.1	easy	Deck of Cards	Write a class that uses an `ArrayList` to hold a deck of cards.
10.13	10	Business	1.9	easy	Bookstore	Write a program that models the storing and retrieving of books based on title.
11.13	1	Biol & Ecol	5.5	difficult	Game of Spawn	Model a "game" that simulates reproduction and growth in a rectangular grid of cells. An X indicates life. A dead cell comes to life when it has exactly three living neighbor cells. A living cell remains alive only when surrounded by two or three living neighbor cells.
11.3	2	CS	0.7	easy	ASCII Table	Write a program that prints the 128-character ASCII table. It should print the table in eight tab-separated columns.

(continued)

Project Summary						
Ch./Sec	**Proj.**	**Academic Area**	**Sol. Pages**	**Difficulty**	**Title**	**Brief Description**
11.7	3	CS	0.8	easy	Circular Queue	A given program implements a circular-array queue. Rewrite the `isFull`, `remove`, and `showQueue` methods by replacing conditional operators, embedded assignments, and embedded increment operators with simpler, more understandable code.
11.7	4	Math & Phys	4.1	moderate	Polynomial Interpolation	Fit a polynomial to points on either side of a pair of points in an array of data and use that to estimate the value at a position between the pair of points.
11.9	5	CS	1.4	moderate	Bitwise Operations	Use arithmetic and logical shifting to display the binary values of numbers.
11.11	6	CS	3.5	moderate	Heap Sort	Use the heap-sort algorithm to sort data. (This is a robust in-place sorting algorithm with a computational complexity of NLogN.)
12.2	1	Business	1.7	easy	Savings Accounts	Compute and display savings account balances that accumulate with compound interest.
12.4	2	Math & Phys	13.4	difficult	Statistics Functions	Write a program that generates values for the Gamma, Incomplete Gamma, Beta, Incomplete Beta, and Binomial statistical functions.
12.5	3	Business	3.3	easy	Car Program	Using inheritance, write a program that keeps track of information about new and used cars.
12.10	4	Sociology	16.4	difficult	Game of Hearts	Write a program that simulates a basic game of hearts with an arbitrary number of players. Give all players an identical set of good strategies which optimize the chance of winning.
13.7	1	Business	9.0	difficult	Grocery Store Inventory	Write an inventory program that keeps track of various kinds of food items. Use different methods in an `Inventory` class to process heterogeneous objects representing generic and branded food items. Store the objects together in a common `ArrayList`.

Project Summary						
Ch./Sec	**Proj.**	**Academic Area**	**Sol. Pages**	**Difficulty**	**Title**	**Brief Description**
13.7	2	Engineering	8.7	difficult	Electric Circuit Analysis	Write a program that calculates the steady-state currents in a two-loop electric circuit that has an arbitrary combination of discrete resistors, inductors, capacitors, and voltage sources in the legs of the circuit. Include methods to perform addition, subtraction, multiplication, and division of complex numbers—numbers that have real and imaginary parts.
13.8	3	Business	5.4	moderate	Payroll	Use polymorphism to write an employee payroll program that calculates and prints the weekly payroll for a company. Assume three types of employees—hourly, salaried, and salaried plus commission. Assume each type of employee gets paid using a different formula. Use an abstract base class.
13.8	4	Business	2.9	moderate	Bank Accounts	Write a bank account program that handles bank account balances for an array of bank accounts. Use two types of bank accounts, checking and savings, derived from an abstract class named `BankAccount`.
14.4	1	Sociology	4.0	moderate	Body Mass Index	Write a program that prompts the user for height and weight values and displays the associated body mass index.
14.5	2	CS	6.4	difficult	Storage and Retrieval of Objects in an Array	Search for a match with the key value in a relational table, using two different search algorithms, a sequential search and a hashed search.
14.9	3	CS	2.5	moderate	Date Formatting	Create a class named `Date` that stores date values and prints out the date in either a numeric format or an alphabetic format. Use a separate class to handle all exceptions.
14.9	4	CS	5.5	difficult	Input Utility	Write a utility class that reads inputs from the keyboard and parses the following datatypes: `String`, `char`, `double`, `float`, `long`, and `int`. It should do input approximately like `Scanner` does.

(continued)

Project Summary						
Ch./Sec	**Proj.**	**Academic Area**	**Sol. Pages**	**Difficulty**	**Title**	**Brief Description**
15.4	1	Engineering	3.7	moderate	Road Use Survey	Model traffic flowing on a highway past a particular place, store observations, and read file later for analysis.
15.4	2	Sociology	2.9	easy	Mail Merge	Write a program that reads a form letter from a text file and modifies custom fields.
15.5 15.9	3	CS	5.0	moderate	File Converter	Write a program that changes whitespace in text files.
15.8	4	CS	1.5	easy	Appending Data to an Object File	Implement code needed to append data to an object file.
16.12	1	Engineering	4.1	moderate	Animated Garage Door	Write a program that simulates the operation of an automatic garage door and its controls and visually display its position as it operates.
16.14	2	Sociology	3.0	moderate	Color Memorization	Write a program that tests the user's ability to memorize a sequence of colors.
16.14	3	Business	8.7	difficult	Grocery Inventory GUI	Write a GUI version of the Grocery Store Inventory project in Chapter 13.
16.15	4	Sociology	4.2	moderate	Word Order Game	Create a simple interactive game that helps kids practice their alphabetic skills.
16.16	5	Business	3.8	moderate	Airline Reservations	Write a GUI program that assigns seats on airline flights.
17.3	1	CS	1.7	easy	Changing Color and Alignment	Write an interactive program that modifies the color and position of buttons in a GUI window.
17.6	2	CS	1.9	easy	Click Tracker	Write an interactive program that modifies the borders and labels of buttons in a GUI window.
17.7	3	Sociology	3.4	moderate	Tic-Tac-Toe	Create an interactive Tic-Tac-Toe game.
17.10	4	Sociology	4.3	moderate	Word Order Game, revisited	Modify Chapter 16's Word Order Game program so it uses a layout manager.
17.10	5	Engineering	7.5	difficult	Thermal Diffusion in a Ground-Source Heat Pump's Well	Write a program that calculates temperatures in the earth around a ground-source heat pump's well. Display results in a color-coded plot of temperature as a function of distance from well center and time of year.

CHAPTER 1

Introduction to Computers and Programming

Objectives

- Describe the various components that make up a computer.
- List the steps involved in program development.
- Know what it means to write algorithms using pseudocode.
- Know what it means to write programs with programming language code.
- Understand source code, object code, and the compilation process.
- Describe how bytecode makes Java portable.
- Become familiar with Java's history—why it was initially developed, how it got its name, and so forth.
- Enter, compile, and run a simple Java program.

Outline

1.1 Introduction

This book is about problem-solving. Specifically, it is about creating solutions to problems through a set of precisely stated instructions. We call such a set of instructions (when in a format that can be entered into and executed on a computer) a *program.* To understand what a program is, think about the following situation.

Suppose you manage a department store, and you don't know when to restock the shelves because you have difficulty keeping track of inventory. The solution to the problem is to write a set of instructions that keeps track of items as they arrive at your store and as they are purchased. If the instructions are correct and in a format that is understood by a computer, you can enter the instructions as a program, run the program, and enter item-arrival and item-purchase data as they occur. You can then retrieve inventory information from the computer any time you need it. That accurate and easily accessible knowledge enables you to restock your shelves effectively, and you are more likely to turn a profit.

The first step to learning how to write programs is to learn the background concepts. In this chapter, we teach background concepts. In subsequent chapters, we use the background concepts in explaining the really good stuff—how to program.

We start this chapter by describing the various parts of a computer. We then describe the steps involved in writing a program and in running a program. Next, we narrow our focus and describe the programming language we'll be using for the remainder of the book—Java. We present step-by-step instructions on how to enter and run a real Java program, so that you'll be able to gain some hands-on experience early on. We finish the chapter with an optional GUI-track section that describes how to enter and run a graphical user interface (GUI) program.

1.2 Hardware Terminology

A *computer system* is all the components that are necessary for a computer to operate and the connections between those components. There are two basic categories of components—*hardware* and *software*. Hardware refers to the physical components associated with a computer. Software refers to the programs that tell a computer what to do. For now, let's focus on hardware.

Our description of a computer's hardware provides you with the information you'll need as a beginning programmer. (A *programmer* is a person who writes programs.) After you master the material here, if you decide you want more, go to Webopedia's Web site at http://www.webopedia.com/ and enter `hardware` in the search box.

The Big Picture

Figure 1.1 shows the basic hardware components in a computer system. It shows input devices at the left (keyboard, mouse, and scanner), output devices at the right (monitor and printer), storage devices at the bottom, and the CPU and main memory in the center. The arrows in Figure 1.1 represent connections between the components. For example, the arrow from the keyboard to the CPU-main memory represents a cable (a connecting wire) that transmits information from the keyboard to the CPU and main memory. Throughout this section, we explain the CPU, main memory, and all the devices in Figure 1.1.

Input and Output Devices

There are different definitions of an *input device,* but usually the term refers to a device that transfers information into a computer. Remember—information going into a computer is input. For example, a keyboard is an input device because when a person presses a key, the keyboard sends information into the computer (it tells the computer which key was pressed).

There are different definitions of an *output device,* but usually the term refers to a device that transfers information out of a computer. Remember—information going out of a computer is output. For example, a

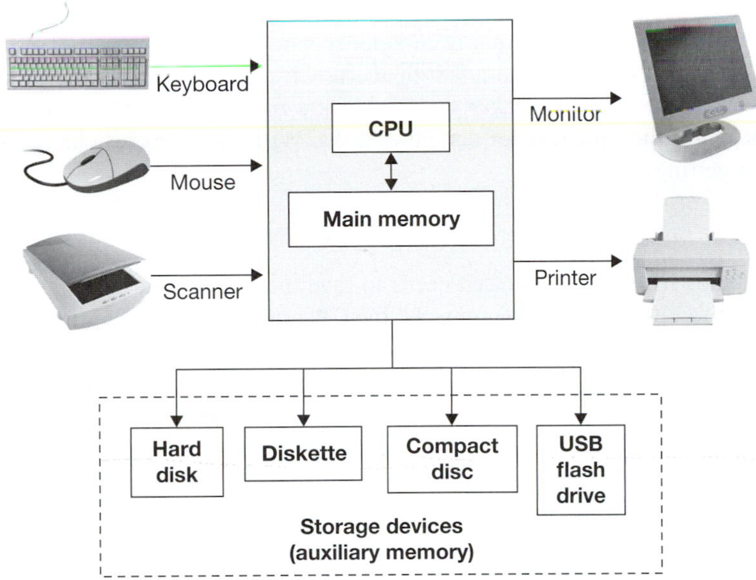

Figure 1.1 A simplified view of a computer

monitor (also called a *display* or a *screen*) is an output device because it displays information going out from the computer.

Central Processing Unit

The *central processing unit* (CPU), often referred to as the *processor* or *microprocessor,* can be considered the computer's brain. As with a biological brain, the CPU splits its time between two basic activities—thinking and managing the rest of its system. The "thinking" activities occur when the CPU reads a program's instructions and executes them. The "managing its system" activities occur when the CPU transfers information to and from the computer system's other devices.

Here's an example of a CPU's thinking activities. Suppose you have a program that keeps track of a satellite's position in its orbit around the earth. Such a program contains quite a few mathematical calculations. The CPU performs those mathematical calculations.

Here's an example of a CPU's managing-its-system activities. Suppose you have a job application program. The program displays boxes in which a person enters his/her name, phone number, and so on. After entering information, the person uses his/her mouse and clicks a Done button. For such a program, the CPU manages its system as follows. To display the initial job application form, the CPU sends information to the monitor. To gather the person's data, the CPU reads information from the keyboard and mouse.

If you're thinking about buying a computer, you'll need to judge the quality of its components. To judge the quality of its components, you need to know certain component details. For CPUs, you should know the popular CPUs and the range of typical CPU speeds. We present the following CPUs and CPU speeds with hesitation because such things change in the computer world at a precipitous rate. By presenting such details, we're dating our book mercilessly. Nonetheless, we forge ahead. . . .

As of September, 2007:

- Popular CPUs—Core 2 Duo (manufactured by Intel), Athlon 64 (manufactured by AMD).
- Current CPU speeds—anywhere from 2.5 GHz up to 3.8 GHz.

What is *GHz* you ask? GHz stands for *gigahertz*. *Giga* means billion and *hertz* is a unit of measure that deals with the number of times that something occurs per second. A 2.5 GHZ CPU uses a clock that ticks 2.5 billion times per second. That's fast, but a 3.8 gigahertz CPU is even faster—it uses a clock that ticks 3.8 billion times per second. A CPU's clock speed provides a rough measure for how fast the CPU gets things done. Clock ticks are the initiators for computer tasks. With more clock ticks per second, there are more opportunities for getting tasks done.

Main Memory

When a computer executes instructions, it often needs to save intermediate results. For example, in calculating the average speed for 100 speed measurements, the CPU needs to calculate the sum of all the speed values prior to dividing by the number of measurements. The CPU calculates the sum by creating a storage area for it. For each speed value, the CPU adds the value to the sum storage area. Think of memory as a collection of storage boxes. The sum is stored in one of memory's storage boxes.

There are two categories of memory—*main memory* and *auxiliary memory*. The CPU works more closely with main memory. Think of main memory as a storage room next to the boss's office. The boss is the CPU, and he/she stores things in the storage room's storage boxes whenever the need arises. Think of auxiliary memory as a warehouse that's across the street from the boss's building. The boss uses the warehouse to store things, but doesn't go there all that often. We'll consider auxiliary memory details in the next subsection. For now, we'll focus on main memory details.

The CPU relies on main memory a lot. It's constantly storing data in main memory and reading data from main memory. With this constant interaction, it's important that the CPU and main memory are able to communicate quickly. To ensure quick communication, the CPU and main memory are physically close together. They are both constructed on *chips*, and they both plug into the computer's main circuit board, the *motherboard*. See Figure 1.2 for a picture of a motherboard, a CPU chip, and main memory chips.

Figure 1.2 Motherboard, CPU chip, and main memory chips

Main memory contains storage boxes, and each storage box contains a piece of information. For example, if a program stores our last name, Dean, it uses eight storage boxes: one for the first half of D, one for the second half of D, one for the first half of e, one for the second half of e, and so on. After storing the four letters, the program will probably need to retrieve them at some point later on. For information to be retrievable, it must have an address. An *address* is a specifiable location. A postal address uses street, city, and zip code values to specify a location. A computer address uses the information's position within main memory to specify a location. Main memory's first storage box is at the zero position, so we say it's at address 0. The second storage box is at the one position, so we say it's at address 1. See Figure 1.3. It shows Dean stored in memory starting at address 50,000.

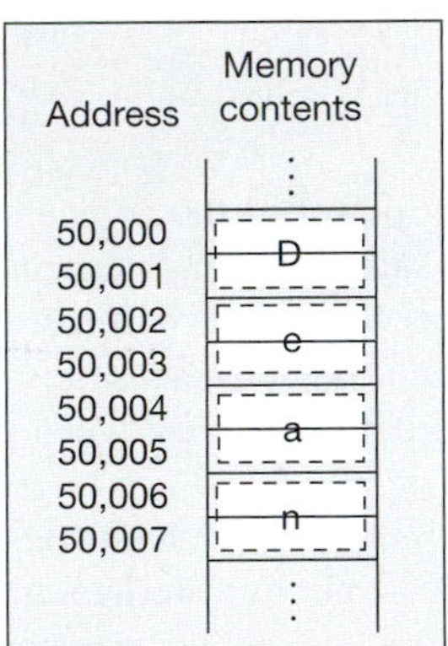

Figure 1.3 The characters D, e, a, n stored in memory starting at address 50,000

It's important to understand the formal terminology when talking about the size of main memory. Suppose you're buying a computer and you want to know how big a computer's main memory is. If you ask a sales person how many "storage boxes" it contains, you'll probably get a perplexed look. What you need to do is ask about its *capacity*—that's the formal term for its size. If you ask for the main memory's capacity, the salesperson will say something like, "It's one *gigabyte*." You already know that giga means billion. A *byte* refers to the size of one storage box. So a one gigabyte capacity main memory holds one billion storage boxes.

Let's describe storage boxes in more detail. You know that storage boxes can hold characters, like the letter D. But computers aren't very smart—they don't understand the alphabet. They only understand 0's and 1's. So computers map each alphabet character to a series of sixteen 0's and 1's. For example, the letter D is 00000000 01000100. So in storing the letter D, main memory actually stores 00000000 01000100. Each of the 0's and 1's is called a *bit*. And each of the eight-bit groupings is called a byte.

Are you wondering why computers use 0's and 1's? Computers understand only high-energy signals versus low-energy signals. When a computer generates a low-energy signal, that's a 0. When a computer generates a high-energy signal, that's a 1.

You know that computers store characters as 0's and 1's, but did you know that computers also store numbers as 0's and 1's? Formally, we say that computers use the *binary number system*. The binary number system uses just two digits, 0 and 1, to represent all numbers. For example, computers store the number 19 as 32 bits, 00000000 00000000 00000000 00010011. The reason those 32 bits represent 19 is that each 1-value bit represents a power of 2. Note that there are three 1-value bits. They are at positions 0, 1, and 4, where the positions start at 0 from the right side. A bit's position determines its power of two. Thus, the rightmost bit, at position 0, represents 2 raised to the power 0, which is 1 ($2^0 = 1$). The bit at position 1 represents

2 raised to the power 1, which is 2 ($2^1 = 2$). And the bit at position 4 represents 2 raised to the power 4, which is 16 ($2^4 = 16$). Add the three powers and you get 19 ($1 + 2 + 16 = 19$). Voila!

Be aware that main memory is often referred to as *RAM*. RAM stands for *random access memory*. Main memory is considered "random access" because data can be directly accessed at any address (i.e., at a "random" address). That's in contrast to some storage devices where data is accessed by starting at the very beginning and stepping through all the data until the target data is reached.

Once again, if you're buying a computer, you'll need to judge the quality of its components. For the main memory/RAM component, you'll need to know whether its capacity is adequate. As of September, 2007, typical main memory capacities range from 512 MB up to 3 GB. *MB* stands for megabyte, where *mega* is one million. *GB* stands for gigabyte.

Auxiliary Memory

Main memory is *volatile,* which means that data is lost when power to the computer goes off. You might ask if data is lost when power goes off, how can anyone save anything permanently on a computer? The answer is something you do (or should do) frequently. When you perform a save command, the computer makes a copy of the main memory data you're working on and stores the copy in auxiliary memory. Auxiliary memory is *nonvolatile,* which means that data is not lost when power to the computer goes off.

One advantage of auxiliary memory over main memory is that it's nonvolatile. Another advantage is that its cost per unit storage is much less than main memory's cost per unit storage. A third advantage is that it is more *portable* than main memory (i.e., it can be moved from one computer to another more easily).

The disadvantage of auxiliary memory is that its *access time* is quite a bit slower than main memory's access time. Access time is the time it takes to locate a single piece of data and make it available to the computer for processing.

Auxiliary memory comes in many different forms, the most common of which are hard disks, diskettes, compact discs, and USB flash drives. Those devices are called *storage media* or simply *storage devices.* Figure 1.4 shows pictures of them.

The most popular types of compact discs can be grouped as follows:

- CD-Audio—for storing recorded music, usually referred to as just "CD" (for compact disc).
- CD-ROM, CD-R, CD-RW—for storing computer data and recorded music.
- DVD, DVD-R, DVD-RW—for storing video, computer data, and recorded music.

The "ROM" in CD-ROM stands for read-only memory. *Read-only* memory refers to memory that can be read from, but not written to. Thus, you can read a CD-ROM, but you can't change its contents. With CD-Rs, you can write once and read as many times as you like. With CD-RWs, you can write and read as often as you like.

DVD stands for "Digital Versatile Disc" or "Digital Video Disc." DVDs parallel CD-ROMs in that you can read from them, but you can't write to them. Likewise, DVD-Rs and DVD-RWs parallel CD-Rs and CD-RWs in terms of their reading and writing capabilities.

USB flash drives are fast, have high storage capacity, and are particularly portable. They are portable because they are the size of a person's thumb and they can be *hot swapped* into virtually any computer. (Hot swapping is when you plug a device into a computer while the computer is on.) The "USB" in USB flash drive stands for Universal Serial Bus, and it refers to a particular type of connection. More specifically, it

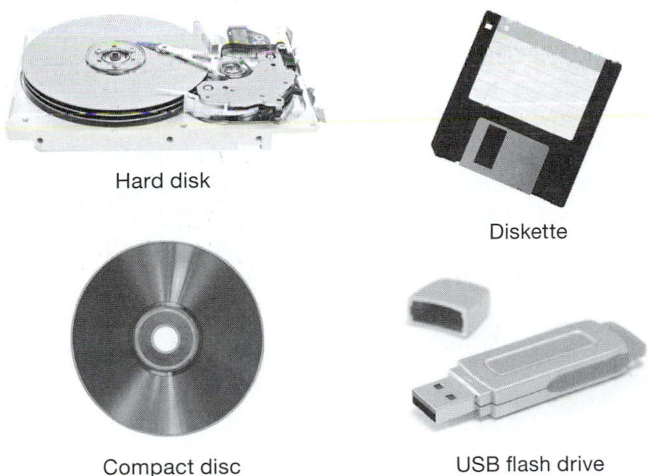

Figure 1.4 Hard disk, diskette, compact disc, and USB flash drive

refers to a particular type of connection wire and connection socket. A flash drive uses that type of connection, and therefore it's called a *USB flash drive*. By the way, many computer devices use USB connections, and they are all hot swappable.

Different storage devices have different storage capacities. As of September, 2007:

- Typical hard disks have a capacity range from 80 GB up to 1 TB (*TB* stands for terabyte, where *tera* is one trillion).
- Typical diskettes have a capacity of 1.44 MB.
- Typical CD-ROMs, CD-Rs, and CD-RWs have a capacity of 700 MB.
- Typical DVDs, DVD-Rs, and DVD-RWs have a capacity range from 4.7 GB up to 8.5 GB.
- Typical USB flash drives have a capacity range from 128 MB up to 64 GB.

A *drive* is a mechanism that enables the computer system to access (read from and write to) data on a storage device. A *disk drive* is a drive for a hard disk, diskette, or compact disc. A disk drive rotates its disk very fast, and one or more *heads* (electronic sensors) access the disk's data as it spins past.

To specify the storage media on which the data resides, you'll need to use the storage media's drive letter followed by a colon. In computers using some version of Microsoft Windows, diskette drives are regularly referred to as `A:`, hard disk drives are usually referred to as `C:` or `D:`, compact disc drives are usually referred to as `D:` or `E:`., and USB flash drives are usually referred to as `E:` or `F:`.

In copying data, you'll actually copy what's known as a *file*, which is a group of related instructions or a group of related data. For example, (1) a program is a file that holds a set of instructions, and (2) a Word document is a file that holds text data created by Microsoft Word.

Common Computer-Hardware Vocabulary

When buying a computer or when talking about computers with your computer friends, you'll want to make sure to understand the vernacular—the terms that people use in everyday speech as opposed to the terms found in textbooks—so that you will be able to understand what's going on. When a computer-savvy person refers to a computer's memory by itself, the person typically means main memory—the computer's RAM. When someone refers to a computer's *disk space,* the person typically means the capacity of the computer's hard disk. When someone refers to computer by itself, the person usually means the box that contains the CPU, the main memory, the hard disk drive and its associated hard disk, and the diskette drive. I/O devices, although they're part of a computer system, are typically not considered to be part of the computer. Instead, they are considered to be *peripheral devices* because they are on the periphery of the computer. When someone says *floppy* or *floppy disk,* they mean a removable diskette.

Why is the term "floppy" used for a diskette? If you've got a diskette lying around, cut open the diskette's hard plastic case. You'll see that the storage media inside is flexible, or floppy. Be aware that in cutting open the diskette case, you'll destroy the diskette. Make sure the diskette doesn't contain your homework. We don't want you to get a bad grade on your homework and tell your teacher "The authors made me do it!"

Pace of Computer Improvements

For as long as memory and CPU components have been around, manufacturers of these devices have been able to improve their products' performances at a consistently high rate. For example, RAM and hard disk capacities double approximately every two years. CPU speeds also double approximately every two years.

An *urban legend* is a story that spreads spontaneously in various forms and is popularly believed to be true. The following exchange is a classic Internet urban legend that comments on the rapid pace of computer improvements.[1] Although the exchange never took place, the comments, particularly the first one, are relevant.

At a recent computer expo (COMDEX), Bill Gates reportedly compared the computer industry with the auto industry and stated, "If GM had kept up with the technology like the computer industry has, we would all be driving $25.00 cars that got 1,000 miles to the gallon."

In response to Bill's comments, General Motors issued a press release stating:

If GM had developed technology like Microsoft, we would all be driving cars with the following characteristics:

1. For no reason whatsoever, your car would crash twice a day.
2. Every time they repainted the lines in the road, you would have to buy a new car.
3. Occasionally your car would die on the freeway for no reason. You would have to pull over to the side of the road, close all of the windows, shut off the car, restart it, and reopen the windows before you could continue. For some reason you would simply accept this.
4. Occasionally, executing a maneuver such as a left turn would cause your car to shut down and refuse to restart, in which case you would have to reinstall the engine.
5. Macintosh would make a car that was powered by the sun, was reliable, five times as fast and twice as easy to drive—but would run on only five percent of the roads.
6. The oil, water temperature, and alternator warning lights would all be replaced by a single "This Car Has Performed an Illegal Operation" warning light, and the car would not work.
7. Occasionally, for no reason whatsoever, your car would lock you out and refuse to let you in until you simultaneously lifted the door handle, turned the key and grabbed hold of the radio antenna.
8. The airbag system would ask "Are you sure?" before deploying.

[1] Snopes.com, *Rumor Has It,* on the Internet at http://www.snopes.com/humor/jokes/autos.asp (visited March 15, 2007).

1.3 Program Development

As mentioned earlier, a program is a set of instructions that can be used to solve a problem. Often, a program contains many instructions, and the instructions are rather complicated. Therefore, developing a successful program requires some effort. It requires careful planning, careful implementation, and ongoing maintenance. Here is a list of typical steps involved in the program development process:

- Requirements analysis
- Design
- Implementation
- Testing
- Documentation
- Maintenance

Requirements analysis is determining the program's needs and goals. *Design* is writing a rough outline of the program. *Implementation* is writing the program itself. *Testing* is verifying that the program works. *Documentation* is writing a description of what the program does. *Maintenance* is making improvements and fixing errors later on. The steps are ordered in a reasonable sequence in that you'll normally perform requirements analysis first, design second, and so on. But some of the steps should be performed throughout the development process rather than at one particular time. For example, you should work on the documentation step throughout the development process, and you should work on the testing step during and after the implementation step and also after the maintenance step. Be aware that you'll often need to repeat the sequence of steps as needs arise. For example, if one of the program's goals changes, you'll need to repeat all of the steps in varying degrees.

We discuss the requirements analysis step and the design step in this section. We discuss the design step in detail in Chapter 2, and we illustrate it with examples throughout the book. We discuss the implementation step in this chapter's "Source Code" section, and we illustrate it with examples throughout the book. We discuss the testing step in Chapter 8. We discuss the documentation step starting in Chapter 3 and illustrate it with examples throughout the book. We discuss the maintenance step in Chapter 8 and illustrate it with examples throughout the book.

Requirements Analysis

The first step in the program development process is a requirements analysis, where you determine the needs and goals of your program. It's important that the programmer thoroughly understands the customer's wishes. Unfortunately, it's all too common for programmers to produce programs only to find out later that the customer wanted something different. This unfortunate circumstance can often be blamed on imprecise communication between the customer and the programmer at the beginning of the project. If a customer and programmer rely solely on a verbal description of the proposed solution, it's easy to omit important details. Later on, those omitted details can be a problem when the customer and programmer realize that they had different assumptions about how the details would be implemented.

To aid the up-front communication process, the customer and programmer should create *screen shots* of data-entry screens and output reports. A screen shot is a picture of what the computer screen looks like. To create screen shots, you can write short programs that print data-entry screens with hypothetical input, and you can write short programs that print reports with hypothetical results. As a quicker alternative, you can create screen shots with the help of drawing software or, if you're a decent artist, with pencil and paper.

Program Design

After the requirements analysis step, the second step is program design, where you write a draft of your program and focus on the basic logic, not the wording details. More specifically, you write instructions that are coherent and logically correct, but you don't worry about missing minor steps or misspelling words. That sort of program is referred to as an *algorithm*. For example, a cake recipe is an algorithm. It contains instructions for solving the problem of baking a cake. The instructions are coherent and logically correct, but they don't contain every minor step, like covering your hands with pot holders prior to removing the cake from the oven.

Pseudocode

In writing an algorithm, you should focus on organizing the flow of the instructions, and you should try to avoid getting bogged down in details. To facilitate that focus, programmers often write an algorithm's instructions using *pseudocode*. Pseudocode is an informal language that uses regular English terms to describe a program's steps. With pseudocode, precise computer *syntax* is not required. Syntax refers to the words, grammar, and punctuation that make up a language. Pseudocode syntax is lenient: Pseudocode must be clear enough so that humans can understand it, but the words, grammar, and punctuation don't have to be perfect. We mention this leniency in order to contrast it with the precision required for the next phase in a program's development. In the next section, we'll cover the next phase, and you'll see that it requires perfect words, grammar, and punctuation.

Example—Using Pseudocode to Find Average Miles Per Hour

Suppose you are asked to write an algorithm that finds the average miles per hour value for a given car trip. Let's step through the solution for this problem. To determine the average miles per hour, you'll need to divide the total distance traveled by the total time. Let's assume that you have to calculate the total distance from two given locations. To determine the total distance, you'll need to take the ending-point location, called "ending location," and subtract the starting-point location, called "starting location," from it. Let's assume that you have to calculate the total time in the same manner, subtracting the starting time from the ending time. Putting it all together, the pseudocode for calculating average miles per hour looks like this:

```
Calculate ending location minus starting location.
Put the result in total distance.
Calculate ending time minus starting time.
Put the result in total time.
Divide total distance by total time.
```

At this point, some readers might want to learn about a relatively advanced form of program development—object-oriented programming, or OOP as it's commonly called. OOP is the idea that when you're designing a program you should first think about the program's components (objects) rather than the program's tasks. You don't need to learn about OOP just yet, and you're not properly prepared to learn about OOP implementation details, but if you're interested in a high-level overview, you can find it in Chapter 6, Section 2.

1.4 Source Code

In the early stages of a program's development, you write an algorithm using pseudocode. Later, you translate the pseudocode to *source code*. Source code is a set of instructions written in a programming language.

Programming Languages

A *programming language* is a language that uses specially defined words, grammar, and punctuation that a computer understands. If you try to run pseudocode instructions on a computer, the computer won't understand them. On the other hand, if you try to run programming language instructions (i.e., source code) on a computer, the computer will understand them.

Just as there are many spoken languages in the world (English, Chinese, Hindi, etc.), there are many programming languages as well. Some of the more popular programming languages are VisualBasic, C++, and Java. Each programming language defines its own set of syntax rules. In this book, we'll focus on the Java programming language. If you write your program in Java, you must follow Java's syntax rules precisely in terms of words, grammar, and punctuation. If you write Java source code using incorrect syntax (e.g., you misspell a word or forget a semicolon), and you try to run such source code on a computer, the computer won't be able to understand it.

Example—Using Java to Find Average Miles Per Hour

Continuing with the earlier example where you wrote pseudocode to find the average miles per hour value for a given car trip, let's now translate the pseudocode into Java source code. In the table below, the pseudocode at the left translates into the Java source code at the right. Thus, the first two pseudocode instructions translate into the single Java source code instruction at their right.

Pseudocode	Java Source Code
Calculate ending location minus starting location. Put the result in total distance.	`distanceTotal = locationEnd - locationStart;`
Calculate ending time minus starting time. Put the result in total time.	`timeTotal = timeEnd - timeStart;`
Divide total distance by total time.	`averageMPH = distanceTotal / timeTotal;`

Programmers normally refer to Java source code instructions as Java *statements*. For Java statements to work, they must use precise syntax. For example, as shown above, Java statements must (1) use a `-` for subtraction, (2) use a / for division, and (3) have a semicolon at their right side. The precision required by Java statements contrasts with the flexibility of pseudocode. Pseudocode allows any syntax, as long as it is understandable by a person. For example, in pseudocode, it would be acceptable to represent subtraction with a `-` or the word "subtract." Likewise, it would be acceptable to represent division with a / or a ÷ or the word "divide."

Skipping the Pseudocode Step

Initially, programming language code will be harder for you to understand than pseudocode. But after gaining experience with a programming language, you may become so comfortable with it that you're able to skip the pseudocode step entirely and go right to the second step where you write the program using programming language code.

For larger programs, we recommend that you do not skip the pseudocode step. Why? Because with larger programs, it's important to first focus on the big picture because if you don't get that right, then nothing else matters. And it's easier to focus on the big picture if you use pseudocode where you're not required to worry about syntax details. After implementing a pseudocode solution, it's relatively easy to convert the pseudocode to source code.

1.5 Compiling Source Code into Object Code

After writing a program, you'll want to have a computer perform the tasks specified by the program. Getting that to work is normally a two-step process: (1) Perform a compile command. (2) Perform a run command. When you perform a *compile* command, you tell the computer to translate the program's source code to code that the computer can run. When you perform a *run* command, you tell the computer to run the translated code and perform the tasks specified by the code. In this section, we describe the translation process.

The computer contains a special program called a *compiler* that's in charge of the translation process. If you submit source code to a compiler, the compiler translates it to code that the computer can run. More formally, the compiler compiles the source code and produces *object code* as the result.[2] Object code is a set of binary-format instructions that can be directly run by a computer to solve a problem. An object-code instruction is made up of all 0's and 1's because computers understand only 0's and 1's. Here's an example of an object-code instruction:

```
0100001111101010
```

This particular object-code instruction is referred to as a *16-bit instruction* because each of the 0's and 1's is called a bit, and there are 16 of them. Each object-code instruction is in charge of only a simple computer task. For example, one object-code instruction might be in charge of copying a single number from some place in main memory to some place in the CPU. There's no need for general-purpose computer programmers to understand the details of how object code works. That's the computer's job, not the programmer's job.

Programmers sometimes refer to object code as *machine code*. Object code is called machine code because it's written in binary and that's what a computer "machine" understands.

1.6 Portability

In Section 1.2's "Auxiliary Memory" subsection, we said that auxiliary memory is more portable than main memory because it can be moved from one computer to another fairly easily. In that context, portability referred to hardware. Portability can also refer to software. A piece of software is *portable* if it can be used on many different types of computers.

Portability Problem with Object Code

Object code is not very portable. As you now know, object code is comprised of binary-format instructions. Those binary-format instructions are intimately tied to a particular type of computer. If you have object code that was created on a type X computer, then that object code can run only on a type X computer. Like-

[2] Most compilers produce object code, but not all. As you'll see in the next section, Java compilers produce an intermediate form of instructions. At a later time, that intermediate form of instructions is translated into object code.

wise, if you have object code that was created on a type Y computer, then that object code can run only on a type Y computer.[3]

So what's all the fuss about portability? Who cares that object code is not very portable? Software manufacturers care. If they want to sell a program that runs on different computer types, they typically have to compile their program on the different computer types. That produces different object-code files, and they then sell those files. Wouldn't it be easier if software manufacturers could provide one form of their program that runs on all types of computers?

Java's Solution to the Portability Problem

The inventors of Java attempted to address the inherent lack of portability in object code by introducing the *bytecode* level between the source code and object code levels. Java compilers don't compile all the way down to object code. Instead, they compile down to bytecode, which possesses the best features of both object code and source code:

- Like object code, bytecode uses a format that works closely with computer hardware, so it runs fast.
- Like source code, bytecode is generic, so it can be run on any type of computer.

How can bytecode be run on any type of computer? As a Java program's bytecode runs, the bytecode is translated into object code by the computer's bytecode interpreter program. The bytecode interpreter program is known as the *Java Virtual Machine,* or *JVM* for short. Figure 1.5 shows how the JVM translates bytecode to object code. It also shows how a Java compiler translates source code to bytecode.

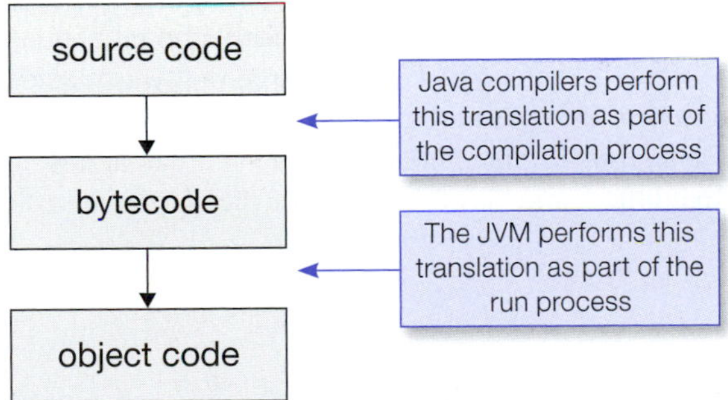

Figure 1.5 How a Java program is converted from source code to object code

To run Java bytecode, a computer must have a JVM installed on it. Fortunately, installing a JVM is straightforward. It's a small program, so it doesn't take up much space in memory. And it's easy to obtain—anyone can download a JVM for free from the Internet. In Section 1.8, we explain how to download a JVM and install it on your own computer.

[3] There are about 15 or so different computer types that are in common use today. Those 15 computer types correspond to 15 categories of CPUs. Each CPU category has its own distinct *instruction set.* An instruction set defines the format and meanings of all the object-code instructions that work on a particular type of CPU. A full discussion of instruction sets is beyond the scope of this book. If you'd like to learn more, see Wikipedia's Web site at http://en.wikipedia.org/ and enter "instruction set" in the search box.

Why Is the Bytecode Interpreter Program Called a "Java Virtual Machine"?

We'll now explain the origin of the name "Java Virtual Machine." For programs written with most programming languages, the CPU "machine" runs the program's compiled code. For programs written in Java, the bytecode interpreter program runs the program's compiled code. So with Java, the bytecode interpreter program acts like a CPU machine. But the bytecode interpreter is just a piece of software, not a piece of hardware like a real CPU. Thus, it's a virtual machine. And that's why Java designers decided to call the bytecode interpreter program a Java virtual machine.

1.7 Emergence of Java

Home-Appliance Software

In the early 1990s, putting intelligence into home appliances was thought to be the next "hot" technology. Examples of intelligent home appliances include coffee pots controlled by a computer and televisions controlled by an interactive programmable device. Anticipating a strong market for such items, Sun Microsystems in 1991 funded a team of researchers to work on the secretive "Green Project" whose mission was to develop software for intelligent home appliances.

An intelligent home appliance's intelligence comes from its embedded processor chips and the software that runs on those processor chips. Appliance processor chips change often because engineers continually find ways to make them smaller, less expensive, and more powerful. To accommodate the frequent turnover of new chips, the software that runs on them should be extremely flexible.

Originally, Sun planned to use C++ for its home-appliance software, but it soon realized that C++ wasn't sufficiently portable. Rather than write C++ software and fight C++'s inherent portability problems, Sun decided to develop a whole new programming language for its home-appliance software.

Sun's new language was originally named Oak (for the tree that was outside project leader James Gosling's window), but it turned out that Oak was already being used as the name of another programming language. As the story goes, while a group of Sun employees was on break at a local coffee shop, they came up with the name "Java." They liked the name "java" because of the significant role caffeine plays in the lives of software developers. ☺

World Wide Web

When the market for intelligent home-appliance software proved to be less fertile than anticipated, Sun almost pulled the plug on its Java project during the prerelease development phase. Fortunately for Sun (and for all of today's Java lovers), the World Wide Web exploded in popularity. Sun realized that the Web's growth could fuel demand for a language like Java, so Sun decided to continue with its Java development efforts. Those efforts bore fruit when they presented Java's first release at the May 1995 SunWorld Conference. Soon thereafter, Netscape, the world's most popular browser manufacturer at the time, announced its intention to use Java in its browser software. With support from Netscape, Java started with a bang and it's been going strong ever since.

The Web relies on Web pages being downloaded and run on many different types of computers. To work in such a diverse environment, Web page software must be extremely portable. You're probably thinking, Java to the rescue! Actually, that would be a bit of an exaggeration. The Web didn't need rescuing—the Web was doing reasonably well even before Java came into the picture, thank you very much. But Java was able to add some much-needed functionality to plain old blah Web pages.

Plain old blah Web pages? Prior to Java, Web pages were limited to one-way communication with their users. Web pages sent information to users, but users did not send information to Web pages. More specifically, Web pages displayed information for users to read, but users did not enter data for Web pages to process. When the Web community figured out how to embed Java programs inside Web pages, that opened the door to more exciting Web pages. Java-embedded Web pages are able to read and process user input, and that provides users with a more enjoyable, interactive experience.

Java Today

Today, programmers use Java in many different environments. They still embed Java programs in Web pages, and those programs are called *applets.* The initial popularity of applets helped Java grow into one of the leading programming languages in the world. Although applets still play a significant role in Java's current success, some of the other types of Java programs are coming close to surpassing applets in terms of popularity, and some have already surpassed applets in terms of popularity.

To help with the small talk at your next Java social event, we'll provide brief descriptions of some of the more popular uses for Java. An applet is a Java program that's embedded in a Web page. A *servlet* is a Java program that supports a Web page, but it runs on a different computer than the Web page. A *JavaServer Page* (JSP) is a Web page that has fragments of a Java program (as opposed to a complete Java program, like an applet) embedded in it. An advantage of servlets and JSPs over applets is that servlets and JSPs lead to Web pages that display more quickly. A *Micro Edition* (ME) *Java application* is a Java program that runs on a limited-resource device, for example, a device that has a limited amount of memory. Examples of limited-resource devices are consumer appliances such as mobile phones and television set-top boxes. A *Standard Edition* (SE) *Java application* is a Java program that runs on a standard computer—a desktop or a laptop. In this book, we focus on SE Java applications as opposed to the other types of Java programs because SE Java applications are the most general purpose and they provide the best environment for learning programming concepts.

1.8 First Program—Hello World

Earlier you learned what it means to compile and run a Java program. But learning by reading only goes so far. It's now time to learn by doing. In this section, you'll enter a Java program into a computer, compile the program, and run it. What fun!

Development Environments

There are different ways to enter a Java program into a computer. You can use an integrated development environment, or you can use a plain text editor. We'll briefly describe the two options.

An *integrated development environment* (IDE) is a rather large piece of software that allows you to enter, compile, and run programs. The entering, compiling, and running are all part of a program's development, and those three functions are integrated together into one environment. Thus, the name "integrated development environment." Some IDEs are free and some are quite expensive. We provide tutorials for several popular IDEs on the book's Web site.

A *plain text editor* is a piece of software that allows you to enter text and save your text as a file. Plain text editors know nothing about compiling or running a program. If you use a plain text editor to enter a program, you'll need to use separate software tools to compile and run your program. Note that *word processors,* like Microsoft Word, can be called text editors, but they're not plain text editors. A word processor allows you to enter text and save your text as a file. But the saved text is not "plain." When a word processor saves text to a file, it adds hidden characters that provide formatting for the text like line height, color, etc.

And those hidden characters create problems for Java programs. If you attempt to enter a program into a computer using a word processor, your program won't compile successfully and it certainly won't run.

Different types of computers have different plain text editors. For example, computers that use Windows have a plain text editor called Notepad. Computers that use UNIX or Linux have a plain text editor called vi. Computers that use Mac OS X have a plain text editor called TextEdit. Note: Windows, UNIX, Linux, and Mac OS X are *operating systems.* An operating system is a collection of programs whose purpose is to help run the computer system. In running the computer system, the operating system manages the transfer of information between computer components.

For the rest of this section, we'll describe how you can enter, compile, and run a program using free, bare-bones tools. You'll use a plain text editor for entering your program, and you'll use simple software tools from Sun for compiling and running your program. If you have no interest in using such bare-bones tools, and you prefer instead to stick exclusively with an IDE, then refer to the IDE tutorials on the book's Web site and feel free to skip the rest of this section. If you're unsure what to do, we encourage you to try out the bare-bones tools. They're free and they don't require as much memory as the IDEs. They serve as a standard baseline that you should be able to use on almost all computers.

Entering a Program into a Computer

We'll now describe how you can enter a program into a computer using Notepad, the plain text editor that comes with all versions of Microsoft Windows.

Move your mouse cursor on top of the Start button at the bottom-left corner of your Windows desktop. Click the Start button. (When we ask you to "click" an item, we want you to move your mouse on top of the item and press the left mouse button.) That should cause a menu to appear. On the menu, move your mouse on top of the Programs option. That should cause another menu to appear. On that menu, move your mouse on top of the Accessories option. That should cause another menu to appear. On that menu, click on the Notepad option. That should cause the Notepad text editor to appear.

In the newly opened Notepad text editor, enter the source code for your first program. More specifically, click somewhere in the middle of the Notepad window and then enter the seven lines of text that are shown in Figure 1.6. When you enter the text, be sure to type the letters with uppercase and lowercase exactly as shown. For example, enter `Hello` with an uppercase `H` and lowercase `e`, `l`, `l`, and `o`. Use spaces, not tabs, for indentations. Your entered text comprises the source code for what is known as the Hello World program. The Hello World program is the traditional first program for all programming students. It simply prints a hello message. In Chapter 3, we'll describe the meaning behind the words in the Hello World source code. In this chapter, we're more interested in hands-on experience, and we show you how to enter, compile, and run the Hello World program.

After entering the source code into the Notepad window, you'll need to save your work by storing it in a file. To save your source code in a file, click the File menu in the top-left corner of the Notepad window. That should cause a menu to appear. On the menu, select the Save As option. That should cause a Save As *dialog box* to appear. A dialog box is a small window that performs one task. For this dialog box, the task is to save a file.

Note the File name: box at the bottom of the dialog box. That's where you'll enter the name of your file. But first, you should create a *directory* to store your file in. A directory, also called a *folder,* is an organizational entity that contains a group of files and other directories.[4] Move your mouse cursor over the down

[4] In the Windows and Macintosh worlds, people tend to use the term "folder." In the UNIX and Linux worlds, people tend to use the term "directory." As you'll see in Chapter 15, Sun uses the term "directory" as part of the Java programming language. We like to follow Sun, and we therefore use the term "directory" rather than "folder."

```
public class Hello
{
  public static void main(String[] args)
  {
    System.out.println("Hello, world!");
  }
}
```

Figure 1.6 The Notepad text editor with the Hello World program entered into it

arrow (▾) that's at the top center of the Save As dialog box. That should cause a directory tree to appear under the down arrow's box. In the directory tree, move your mouse on top of the C: icon if you'd like to save on your hard drive, or move your mouse on top of the E: or F: icon if you'd like to save on your USB flash drive. Click the appropriate drive letter icon. That should cause the clicked drive letter icon to appear in the Save in: box next to the down arrow. Verify that your Save As dialog box now looks similar to the Save As dialog box in Figure 1.7. In particular, note the F: drive in Figure 1.7's Save in: box. Your Save in: box may be different, depending on what drive letter you clicked.

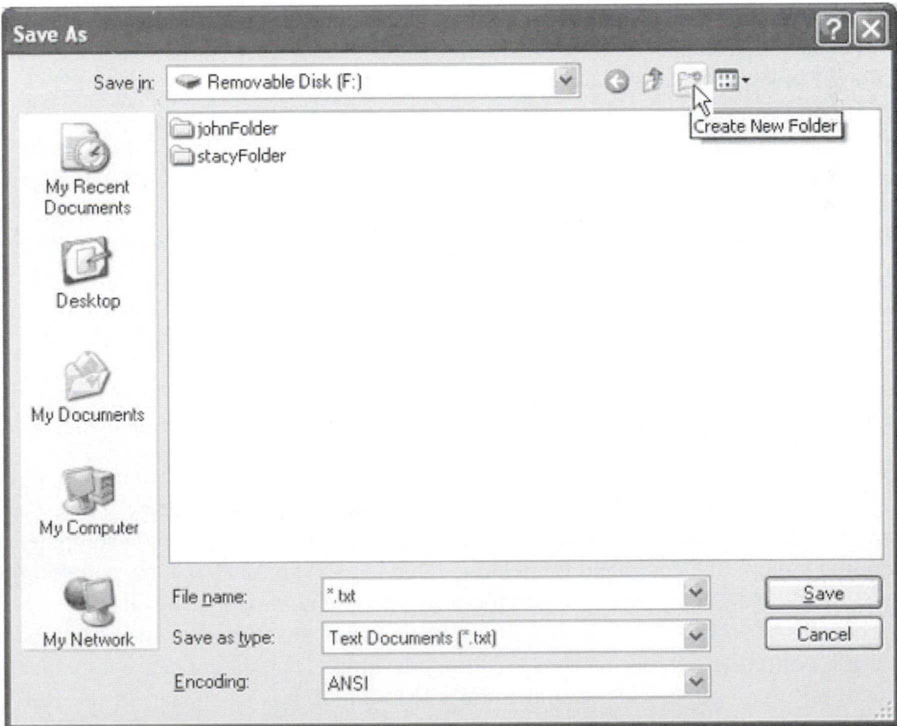

Figure 1.7 Notepad's Save As dialog box with user about to create a new folder

As shown in Figure 1.7, move your mouse cursor over the Create New Folder icon near the top-right corner of the Save As dialog box. Click the icon. That should cause a new directory to appear in the directory tree. The name of the new directory is `New Folder` by default. The `New Folder` name should be selected/highlighted. Enter `myJavaPgms`, and as you do so, `myJavaPgms` should overlay the `New Folder` name. Click the Open button in the bottom-right corner of the dialog box. That should cause the new `myJavaPgms` directory to appear in the Save in: box.

Enter `"Hello.java"` in the File name: box at the bottom of the dialog box. You must enter `"Hello.java"` exactly as shown below:

Don't forget the quotes, the uppercase H, and the lowercase subsequent letters. Click the Save button in the bottom-right corner of the dialog box. That should cause the Save As dialog box to disappear, and the top of the Notepad window should now say Hello.java. Shut down Notepad by clicking on the X in the top-right corner of the Notepad window.

Installing a Java Compiler and the JVM

In the previous subsection, you entered the Hello World program and saved it to a file. Yeah! Normally, the next step would be to compile the file. Remember what compiling is? That's when a compiler translates a source code file into a bytecode file. For our Hello World program, the compiler will translate your `Hello.java` source code file into a `Hello.class` bytecode file. If you're working in a school's computer lab, chances are pretty good that your computer already has a Java compiler installed on it. If your computer does not have a Java compiler installed on it, you'll need to install it now in order to complete the hands-on portion of this section.

Normally, if someone is interested in installing the Java compiler (to compile Java programs), they are also interested in installing the JVM (to run Java programs). To make the installation easier, Sun bundles the Java compiler together with the JVM. Sun calls the bundled software the *Java Development Kit,* or *JDK* for short.

To install the JDK on your computer, you should follow the installation instructions on the book's Web site. Go to http://www.mhhe.com/dean and click on the JDK Installation Instructions link. Read the instructions and install the JDK accordingly. In particular, follow the instructions that describe how to set the PATH variable permanently.

Compiling a Java Program

We'll next describe how you can compile a program using a *command prompt window* (also called a *console*). A command prompt window allows you to enter operating system instructions where the instructions are in the form of words. The words are referred to as *commands.* For example, on a computer that runs the Windows operating system, the command for deleting a file is `del` (for delete). On a computer that runs the UNIX or Linux operating system, the command for deleting a file is `rm` (for remove).

To open a command prompt window on a computer that runs the Windows operating system, click the Start button at the bottom-left corner of your Windows desktop. That should cause a menu to appear. On the menu, click the Run... option. That should cause a Run dialog box to appear. In the Run dialog box's

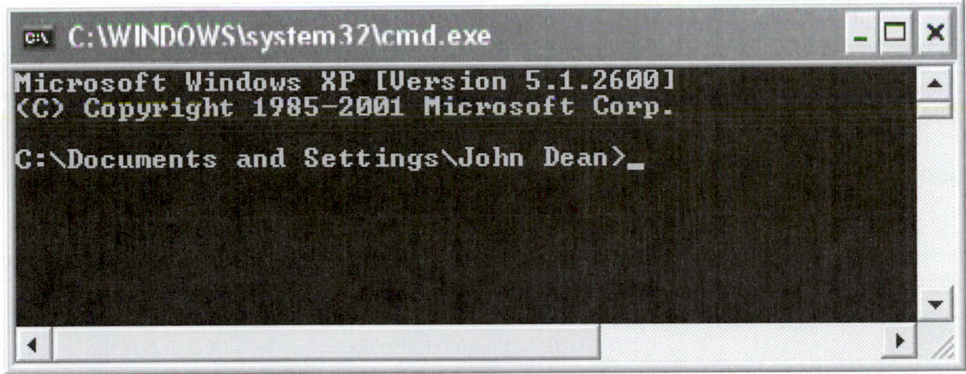

Figure 1.8 A command prompt window when it first opens up

Open: box, type cmd (cmd stands for "command") and click the OK button. That should cause a command prompt window to appear. Figure 1.8 shows the newly opened command prompt window.

In Figure 1.8, note this line:

```
C:\Documents and Settings\John Dean>
```

That's a *prompt*. In general, a prompt tells you to do something. For a command prompt window, the prompt tells you to enter a command. Very soon, you'll enter commands in your actual command prompt window. But first, note the text at the left of the > symbol. The text `C:\Documents and Settings\John Dean` forms the *path* to the current directory. A path specifies the location of a directory. More specifically, a path starts with a drive letter and contains a series of one or more slash-separated directory names. In our example, `C:` refers to the hard drive, `Documents and Settings` refers to the `Documents and Settings` directory that's on the hard drive, and `John Dean` refers to the `John Dean` directory that's contained within the `Documents and Settings` directory.

To compile your Hello World program, you'll need to go first to the drive and directory where it resides. Suppose your command prompt window's prompt indicates that your current drive is C:, and you saved `Hello.java` on F:. Then you'll need to change your drive to F:. To do so, enter `f:` in your command prompt window.

To change to the Hello World program's directory, enter this `cd` command (cd stands for change directory):

```
cd \myJavaPgms
```

Now you're ready to compile your program. Enter this `javac` command (javac stands for java compile):

```
javac Hello.java
```

In entering that command, if your command prompt window displays an error message, refer to Figure 1.9 for possible solutions. If your command prompt window displays no error messages, that indicates success. More specifically, it indicates that the compiler created a bytecode file named `Hello.class`. To run the `Hello.class` file, enter this `java` command:

```
java Hello
```

The compilation error message says something like this:	Explanation:
`'javac' is not recognized`	All three error messages indicate that the computer doesn't understand the `javac` command because it can't find the javac compiler program. The error is probably due to the PATH variable being set improperly. Review the JDK installation instructions and reset the PATH variable accordingly.
`javac: command not found`	
`bad command or filename`	
`Hello.java:` *number*`:` *text*	There is a syntax error in the `Hello.java` source code. The specified *number* provides the approximate line number in `Hello.java` where the error occurs. The specified *text* provides an explanation for the error. Review the contents of the `Hello.java` file and make sure that every character is correct and uses the proper case (lowercase, uppercase).

Figure 1.9 Compilation errors and explanations

Your command prompt window should now display your program's output—`Hello, world!` See Figure 1.10. It shows the command prompt window after completing the steps described above.

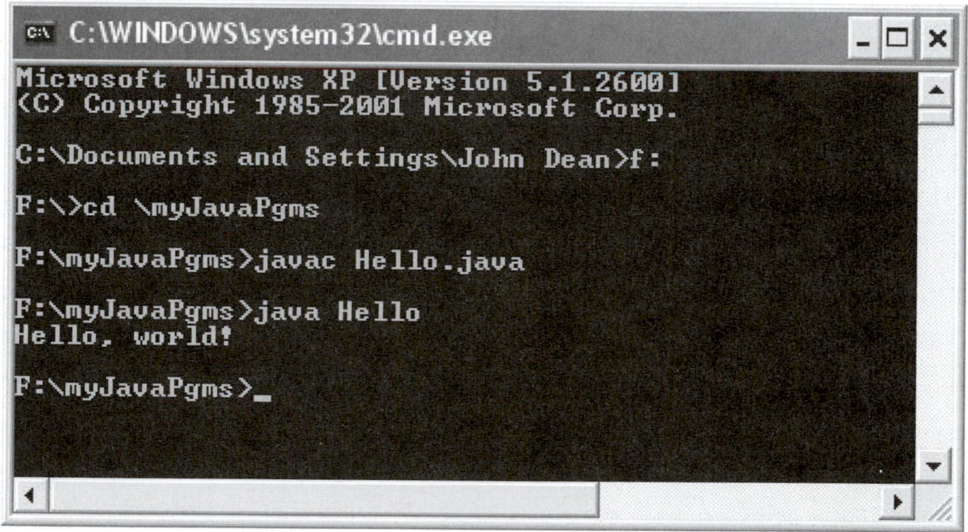

Figure 1.10 Compiling and running the Hello World program

1.9 GUI Track: Hello World (Optional)

This section is the first installment of our optional graphical user interface (GUI) track. In each GUI-track section, we provide a short introduction to a GUI concept. For example, in this section, we describe how to display a message in a GUI window. In another GUI track section, we describe how to draw lines and shapes. For readers who do not have time for the GUI track, no problem. Any or all of the GUI track sections may be skipped as they cover material that is independent of later material. Note that we cover hard-core GUI material in earnest at the end of the book in Chapters 16 and 17. The GUI material in Chapters 16 and 17 is independent of the GUI material in the GUI track, so, once again, it's OK to skip the GUI track. But why skip it? GUI programming is sooooo much fun!

In this section, we present a GUI version of the Hello World program. We'll start by showing you the program's output:

A *GUI program* is defined as a program that uses graphical tools for its interface. This program is indeed a GUI program because it uses these graphical tools for its interface: a title bar (the bar at the top of the window), a close-window button (the "X" in the top-right corner), an OK button, and an i icon. Here's how the tools work: If you drag the title bar with your mouse, the window moves. If you click the close-window button or the OK button, the window closes. The i icon is a visual cue that indicates the nature of the window—the i stands for "information" since the window simply displays information.

See Figure 1.11. The dashed boxes indicate code that differs from the code in the previous section's `Hello` program. For now, don't worry about the meaning of the program's code. We'll explain it later on. For now, the goal is to give you some fun and valuable hands-on experience.

Go ahead and enter the program code into a text editor. If you need a refresher on how to do that, see the previous section. This time, save your source code file with the name `HelloGUI.java` instead of `Hello.java`. When saving `HelloGUI.java`, make sure you spell the filename with capitals for *H, G, U,* and *I* since that's how `HelloGUI` is spelled in your program's third line. Next, you'll want to compile and run the program. Once again, if you need a refresher, see the previous section.

```
import javax.swing.JOptionPane;

public class HelloGUI
{
  public static void main(String[] args)
  {
    JOptionPane.showMessageDialog(null, "Hello, World!");
  }
}
```

The dashed boxes indicate code that differs from the code in the previous section's `Hello` program.

Figure 1.11 GUI version of the Hello World program

Summary

- A computer system is all the components that are necessary for a computer to operate and the connections between those components. More specifically, a computer system consists of the CPU, main memory, auxiliary memory, and I/O devices.
- Programmers write algorithms as first attempt solutions for programming problems.
- Algorithms are written with pseudocode—similar to programming language code except that precise syntax (words, grammar) isn't required.
- Source code is the formal term for programming language instructions.
- Object code is a set of binary-encoded instructions that can be directly executed by a computer.
- Most non-Java compilers compile from source code to object code.
- Java compilers compile from source code to bytecode.
- As a Java program runs, the Java Virtual Machine translates the program's bytecode to object code.
- Originally, Sun developed Java for use in home appliance software.
- To expedite development, Java programmers often use integrated development environments, but you can use a plain text editor and command prompt window.

Review Questions

§1.2 Hardware Terminology

1. What do the following abbreviations mean?
  a) I/O
  b) CPU
  c) RAM
  d) GHz
  e) MB

2. Identify two important computer input devices.

3. Identify two important computer output devices.

4. Assertions:
  a) Main memory is faster than auxiliary memory. (T / F)
  b) Auxiliary memory is volatile. (T / F)
  c) The first position in main memory is at address 1. (T / F)
  d) The CPU is considered to be a peripheral device. (T / F)
  e) Hot swapping is when you plug a device into a computer while the computer is on. (T / F)

§1.3 Writing Algorithms Using Pseudocode

5. What is an algorithm?

6. What is pseudocode?

§1.4 Translating Pseudocode into Programming Language Code

7. Syntax rules are more lenient for which type of code—pseudocode or programming language code?

§1.5 Compiling Source Code into Object Code

8. What happens when you compile a program?

9. What is object code?

§1.6 Portability

10. What is a Java Virtual Machine?

§1.7 Emergence of Java

11. List five different types of Java programs.

Exercises

1. [after §1.2] For each of the following items, determine whether it is associated with main memory or auxiliary memory.
   - **a)** floppy disk main or auxiliary?
   - **b)** RAM main or auxiliary?
   - **c)** hard disk main or auxiliary?
   - **d)** CD-RW main or auxiliary?
2. [after §1.2] What is a bit?
3. [after §1.2] What is a byte?
4. [after §1.2] What type of computer component does `C:` usually refer to?
5. [after §1.2] For each of the following computer system components, identify parallel components in a bear's biological system.
   - **a)** CPU
   - **b)** input devices
   - **c)** output devices
6. [after §1.2] What is "Moore's Law"? You won't find the answer to the question in the book, but you can find it on the Internet. (*Hint:* Gordon Moore was one of the founders of Intel.)
7. [after §1.3] This question is not very specific, so don't worry about whether your solution conforms to some prescribed answer. Just do whatever seems reasonable to you.

   Using pseudocode in the form of short statements, provide an algorithm for a bear that describes the steps involved in gathering honey. If a certain step or a group of steps is to be repeated, use an if statement and an arrow to show the repetition. For example, your algorithm might include something like this:

```
<statement>  <──────────┐
<statement>             │
<statement>             │
.                       │
.                       │
<statement>             │
If still hungry, repeat ┘
```

8. [after §1.5] Humans generally prefer to work with source code rather than object code because source code is easier to understand than object code. So why is object code necessary?
9. [after §1.6] Most programming languages compile down to object code. Java compiles down to bytecode. What is the primary benefit of bytecode over object code?
10. [after §1.6] What does the Java Virtual Machine do?
11. [after §1.7] What was the original name for the Java programming language?
12. [after §1.8] On a computer whose operating system is a recent version of Microsoft Windows, invoke Start > Programs > Accessories > Command Prompt. Navigate to the directory that has the `Hello.java` source code. Enter `dir Hello.*` to list all files starting with "Hello". If this list includes `Hello.class`, delete that file by entering `del Hello.class`. Enter `javac Hello.java` to compile the source code. Again enter `dir Hello.*` and verify that the bytecode file, `Hello.class`, has been created. Now you can enter `java Hello` to execute the compiled program. Enter `type Hello.java` and type `Hello.class` to get a feeling for how bytecode differs from source code.

13. [after §1.8] Experiment with the `Hello.java` program to learn the meanings of typical compilation and runtime error messages:
    a) Omit the final / from the header block.
    b) Omit any part of the argument in the parentheses after `main`.
    c) Omit the semicolon from the end of the output statement.
    d) One at a time, omit the braces—{ and }.
    e) Try using lowercase, `$`, _, or a number for the first character in the class name.
    f) Make the program filename different from the class name.
    g) Change `main` to `Main`.
    h) One at a time, try omitting `public`, `static`, and `void` from before `main`.

14. [after §1.8] Learn how to use TextPad by working your way through the "Getting Started with TextPad" tutorial on the book's Web site. Submit hardcopy of the source code for your Countdown program (i.e., print your program from within TextPad). Note that you're not required to submit source code for your Hello World program or submit output for either program.

Review Question Solutions

1. What do the following abbreviations mean?
    a) I/O: input/output devices.
    b) CPU: central processing unit or processor.
    c) RAM: random access memory or main memory.
    d) GHz: Gigahertz = billions of cycles per second.
    e) MB: MegaBytes = millions of bytes, where one byte is 8 bits, and one bit is the answer to a single yes/no question.

2. The keyboard and a mouse are the two most obvious examples of input devices. Another possible input device is a telephone modem.
3. The display screen and a printer are the two most obvious examples of important output devices. Other examples are a telephone modem and speakers.
4. Assertions:
    a) True. Main memory is physically closer to the processor, and the bus that connects the main memory to the processor is faster than the bus that connects the auxiliary memory to the processor. Main memory is also more expensive and therefore usually smaller.
    b) False. When power goes off, main memory loses its information, while auxiliary memory does not. An unexpected power failure might corrupt information in auxiliary memory, however.
    c) False. The first position in main memory is at address 0.
    d) False. The CPU is considered to be part of the computer itself; it's not a peripheral device.
    e) True. Hot swapping is when you plug a device into a computer while the computer is on.

5. An algorithm is a step-by-step procedure for solving a problem.
6. Pseudocode is an informal language that uses regular English terms to describe a program's steps.
7. Syntax rules are more lenient for pseudocode (as opposed to programming language code).
8. Most compilers convert source code to object code. Java compilers convert source code to bytecode.
9. Object code is the formal term for binary-format instructions that a processor can read and understand.
10. A Java Virtual Machine (JVM) is an interpreter that translates Java bytecode into object code.
11. Five different types of Java Programs are applets, servlets, JSP pages, micro edition applications, and standard edition applications.

CHAPTER 2

Algorithms and Design

Objectives

- Learn how to write an informal text description of what you want a computer program to do.
- Understand how a flowchart describes what a computer program does.
- Become familiar with the standard well-structured control patterns.
- Learn how to structure conditional executions.
- Learn how to structure and terminate looping operations, including nested loops.
- Learn how to "trace through" a program's sequence of operation.
- See how you can describe program operation at different levels of detail.

Outline

2.1 Introduction

As indicated in Chapter 1, writing a computer program involves two basic activities: (1) figuring out what you want to do and (2) writing code to do it. You might be tempted to skip the first step and jump immediately to the second step—writing code. Try to resist that urge. Jumping immediately into the code often results in bad programs that work poorly and are hard to fix because poor organization makes them hard to understand. Therefore, for all but the very simplest problems, it's best to start by thinking about what you want to do and then organize your thoughts.

As part of the organization process, you'll want to write an *algorithm*.[1] An algorithm is a sequence of instructions for solving a problem. It's a recipe. When specifying an algorithm, two formats are common:

1. The first format is a natural-language outline called *pseudocode*, where the prefix "pseudo-" means "fictitious or pretended," so it's not "real" code. Pseudocode, like real code, is composed of one or more *statements*. A statement is the equivalent of a natural language "sentence." If the sentence is simple, the corresponding statement usually appears on one line, but if the sentence is complex, the statement may be spread out over several lines. Statements can be nested inside each other, as in an outline. We'll use the term "statement" a lot, and you'll get a better appreciation for it as we go along.
2. The second format is an arrangement of boxes and arrows that help you visually step through the algorithm. The most detailed form of boxes and arrows is called a *flowchart*. The boxes in a flowchart typically contain short statements that are similar to pseudocode statements.

This chapter shows you how to apply pseudocode and flowcharts to a fundamental set of standard programming problems—problems that appear in almost all large programs. The chapter also shows you how to *trace* an algorithm—step through it one statement at a time—to see what it's actually doing. Our goal is to give you a basic set of informal tools which you can use to describe what you want a program to do. The tools help you organize your thinking before you start writing the actual program. Tracing helps you figure out how an algorithm (or completed program) actually works. It helps you verify correctness and identify problems when things are not right.

2.2 Output

The first problem to consider is the problem of displaying a program's final result—its output. This may sound like something to consider last, so why consider it first? The output is what the *end user*—the client, the person who eventually uses the program—wants. It's the goal. Thinking about the output first keeps you from wasting time solving the wrong problem.

Put yourself in user's place.

Hello World Algorithm

In Chapter 1, we showed you a Java program that generated "Hello, world!" output on the computer screen. Now we'll revisit that problem, but focus on the algorithm, not the program. You may recall that Chapter 1's Hello World program was seven lines long. Figure 2.1 shows the Hello World algorithm—it contains just one line, a pseudocode print statement. The point of an algorithm is to show the steps necessary to solve a problem without getting bogged down in syntax details. The Hello World algorithm does just that. It shows a simple print statement, which is the only step needed to solve the Hello World problem.

Figure 2.1's "Hello, world!" message is a string literal. A *string* is a generic term for a sequence of characters. A *string literal* is a string whose characters are written out explicitly and enclosed in quotation marks. If you print a string literal, you print the characters literally as they appear in the command. So Figure 2.1's algorithm prints the characters H, e, l, l, o, comma, space, w, o, r, l, d, and !.

[1] Ninth century Persian mathematician Muhammad ibn Musa al-Khwarizmi is considered to be the father of algebra. The term *algorithm* comes from Algoritmi, which is the Latin form of his shortened name, al-Khwarizmi.

```
print "Hello, world!"
```

Figure 2.1 Hello World algorithm that prints the message "Hello, world!"

Rectangle Algorithm

For the next example, suppose you want to display the area of a particular rectangle. First consider what you want the program to do. In Figure 2.2, look at the `area = 40` line under Output. That shows what you want the output to look like.

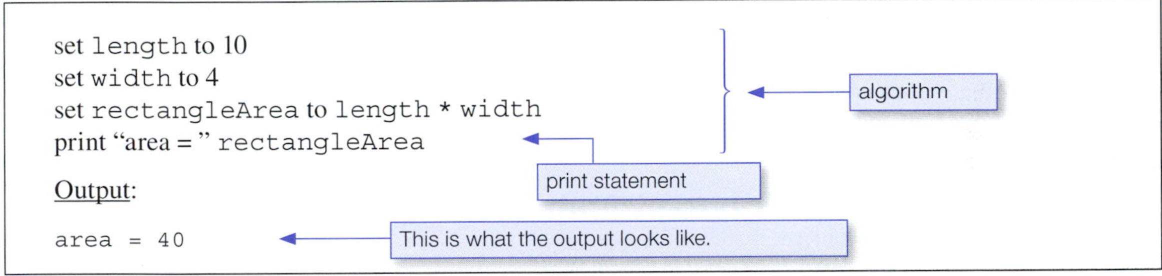
set length to 10
set width to 4
set rectangleArea to length * width
print "area = " rectangleArea
Output:
area = 40
algorithm
print statement
This is what the output looks like.

Figure 2.2 Rectangle algorithm that prints the area of a rectangle

The top part of Figure 2.2 is the algorithm for calculating a rectangle's area. Note that some of the words, like `length` and `width`, appear with monospace font. *Monospace font* is when each character's width is uniform. We use monospace font to indicate that something is a variable. A *variable* is a container that holds a value. The algorithm's first two lines assign 10 and 4 to `length` and `width`, respectively. That means that the `length` variable contains the value 10 and the `width` variable contains the value 4. The third line describes two operations: First compute the area by multiplying `length` times `width`. (The * is the multiplication "times" symbol.) Then assign the result (the product) to the variable, `rectangleArea`. The fourth line prints two items – the string literal "area =" and the value of the `rectangleArea` variable. When a variable appears in a print statement, the print statement prints the value stored inside the variable. `rectangleArea` contains 40, so the print statement prints the value 40. Figure 2.2's output shows the desired display.

2.3 Variables

Now let's consider variables in more detail. Figure 2.2's Rectangle algorithm has three variables—`length`, `width`, and `rectangleArea`. In `rectangleArea`, notice how we run together the two words, "rectangle" and "area," and notice how we start the second word with a capital letter. We do this to help you develop good habits for later Java coding, which does not permit any spaces in a variable name. Although it's not necessary for pseudocode, in Java, it's good style to begin a variable name with a lowercase letter, as in `rectangleArea`. If the name is a combination of several words, in Java you must remove the space(s) between multiple words in a single name, and you should begin all words after the first

one with an uppercase letter to make the combination readable. This is called *camelCase*, because of the bump(s) in the middle. Again, it's not necessary for pseudocode, but it's a good habit to develop. Here are two more examples that show how to name variables with camelCase:

Description	A Good Variable Name
sports team name	`teamName`
weight in grams	`weightInGrams`

Variables can hold different *types* of data. Which type of data would the `teamName` variable probably hold—a number or a string? It would probably be used to hold a string (e.g., "Jayhawks" or "Pirates"). Which type of data would the `weightInGrams` variable probably hold—a number or a string? It would probably be used to hold a number (e.g., 12.5). It's relatively easy for a human to determine the type of a named variable by just thinking about the name, but this kind of thinking is very difficult for a computer. So in a real Java program, we must tell the computer the type of each data item.

However, since pseudocode is designed strictly for humans and not computers, in pseudocode we don't bother with type specification. Notice that Figure 2.2's pseudocode representation of a Rectangle program does not contain any mention of data type. Pseudocode ignores data type so that focus can be kept on the algorithm's essence—its instructions.

2.4 Operators and Assignment Statements

The previous section described variables by themselves. Now let's consider relationships between variables by looking at operators and assignments.

Here is the third statement from Figure 2.2's Rectangle algorithm:

```
set rectangleArea to length * width
```

As indicated earlier, the `*` symbol is the multiplication operator. The other common arithmetic operators are + for addition, - for subtraction, and / for division. These should be familiar to everyone. The `length` and `width` variables are *operands*. In mathematics and again in programming, an operand is an entity (e.g., a variable or a value) that is operated on by an operator. The `length` and `width` variables are operands because they are operated on by the `*` operator.

When we say "set `variableA` to `x`," we mean "put the value of `x` into `variableA`" or "assign the value of `x` to `variableA`." So the set `rectangleArea` to `length * width` statement puts the product of `length` times `width` into the `rectangleArea` variable. A picture is worth a thousand words. See Figure 2.3—it visually describes what the statement does.

rectangleArea length width

40 ← (10 * 4)

Figure 2.3 Assignment (or "set") operation represented by left-pointing arrow

Figure 2.3 includes a pair of parentheses not shown in the pseudocode statement. You could put these parentheses in the pseudocode if you wanted, but most people expect the multiplication operation to have a higher *precedence* (occur sooner) than the assignment operation, so we did not bother including parentheses in this particular pseudocode statement.

Figure 2.3 shows that each of the three variables is a container that holds a value. Figure 2.3 also visually suggests that assignment goes in a right-to-left direction. Assignment in our pseudocode has no directionality, but in Chapter 3, you'll see that assignment in Java code actually does go right to left. So if you are a person who likes to visualize things, visualize assignment going right to left, as Figure 2.3 suggests.

2.5 Input

In the preceding Rectangle algorithm, the algorithm itself supplied the values for the `length` and `width` variables. We did it that way to make the introductory discussion as simple as possible. Sometimes this is an appropriate strategy, but in this particular case, it's silly, because the algorithm solves the problem only for one particular set of values. To make the algorithm more general, instead of having the algorithm supply the values for `length` and `width`, you should have the *user* (the person who runs the program) supply the values. When a user supplies a value(s) for a program, that's called *user input,* or just *input.* Figure 2.4 presents an improved Rectangle algorithm, where input `length` and input `width` perform user input operations.

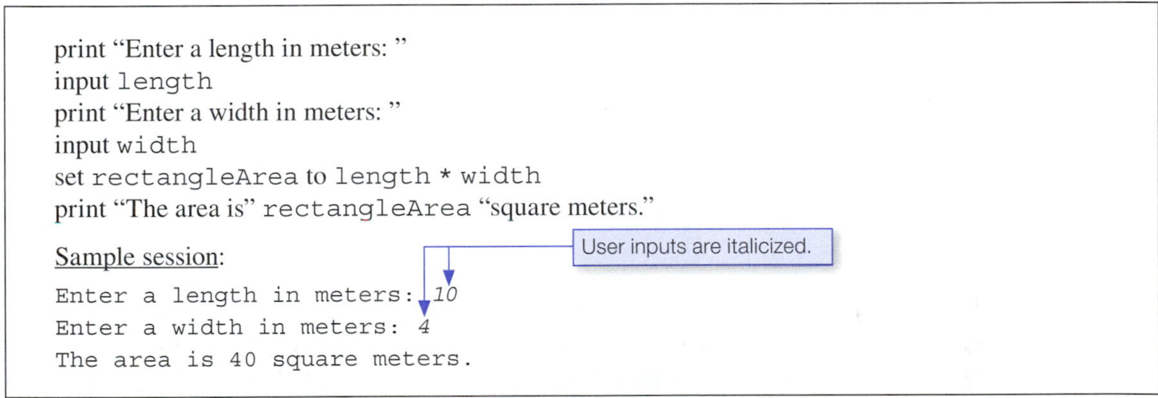

```
print "Enter a length in meters: "
input length
print "Enter a width in meters: "
input width
set rectangleArea to length * width
print "The area is" rectangleArea "square meters."

Sample session:
Enter a length in meters: 10
Enter a width in meters: 4
The area is 40 square meters.
```


Figure 2.4 Rectangle algorithm that gets length and width values from a user

Note the first two `print` statements in Figure 2.4—they're called *prompts* because they tell (or prompt) the user what to enter. Without prompts, most users would be left with an unpleasant sensation and the puzzling question, "What do I do now?"

Throughout the book, we provide *sample sessions* as a means of showing what happens when an algorithm or program is run with a typical set of inputs. When there is space, we include the sample session in the figure with the algorithm or program that generates it. Can you identify the user-input values in the sample session in Figure 2.4? Our convention is to italicize sample session input values to distinguish them from output. Thus, *10* and *4* are user-input values.

Write what you'll do and how you'll do it.

The combination of a pseudocode algorithm and a sample session represents a convenient and efficient way to specify a simple algorithm or program. The sample session shows the format of desired inputs and outputs. It also shows representative input and output numerical values, which allow a programmer to verify that his/her completed program actually behaves as required. In many of the book's projects (projects are on the Web site), we provide some combination of pseudocode and sample session to specify the problem we are asking you to solve.

2.6 Flow of Control and Flowcharts

In the preceding sections, we described various statements—print statements, assignment statements, and input statements—and we focused on the mechanics of how each statement works. Now it's time to focus on the relationships between statements. More specifically, we'll focus on *flow of control*. Flow of control is the order in which program statements are executed. In our discussion of flow of control, we'll refer to both algorithms and programs. Flow of control concepts apply equally to both.

Flow of control is best explained with the help of flowcharts. Flowcharts are helpful because they are pictures. As such, they help you to "see" an algorithm's logic. A flowchart uses two basic symbols: (1) rectangles, which contain commands like print, assign, and input, and (2) diamonds, which contain yes/no questions. At each diamond, the flow of control splits. If the answer is "yes," flow goes one way. If the answer is "no," flow goes another way.

The dashed boxes in Figure 2.5 show three standard structures for flow-of-control—a sequential structure, a conditional structure, and a looping structure. The flowchart on the left—the sequential structure—is a picture of the Rectangle algorithm described in Figure 2.2. *Sequential structures* contain statements that are executed in the sequence/order in which they are written; for example after executing a statement, the computer executes the statement immediately below it. *Conditional structures* contain a yes/no question, and the answer to the question determines whether to execute the subsequent block of statements or skip it. *Looping structures* also contain a yes/no question, and the answer to the question determines whether to repeat the loop's block of statements or move on to the statements after the loop.

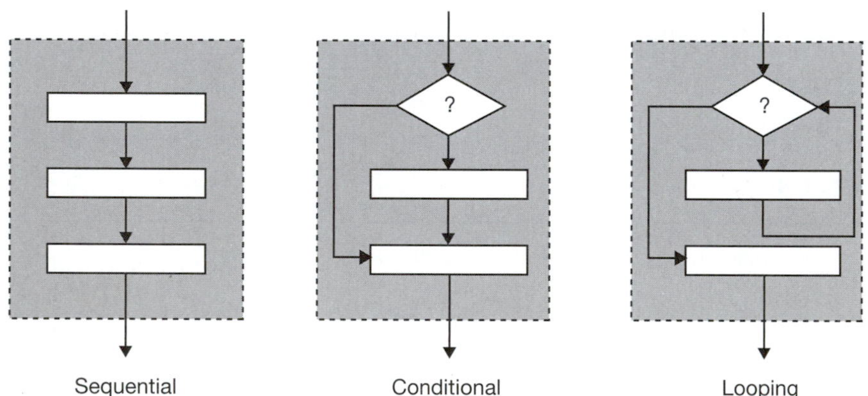

Figure 2.5 Well-structured flow of control

Structured programming is a discipline that requires programs to limit their flow of control to sequential, conditional, or looping structures. A program is considered to be well structured if it can be decomposed into the patterns in Figure 2.5. You should strive for well-structured programs because they tend to be easier to understand and work with. To give you an idea of what not to do, see Figure 2.6. Its flow of control is bad because there are two points of entry into the loop, and when you're inside the loop, it's hard to know what's happened in the past. When a program is hard to understand, it's error-prone and hard to fix. Code that implements an algorithm like this is sometimes called *spaghetti code* because when you draw a flowchart of the code, the flowchart looks like spaghetti. When you see spaghetti, untangle it!

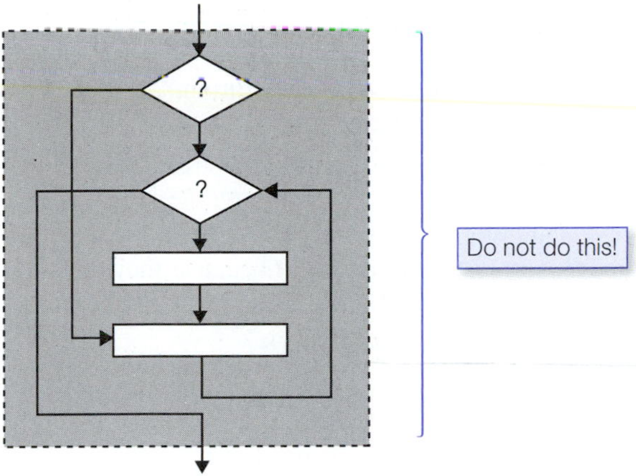

Figure 2.6 Poorly structured flow of control

In addition to standardizing sequential, conditional, and looping control structures, structured programming also splits up large problems into smaller sub-problems. In Java, we put the solution to each sub-problem in a separate block of code called a *method*. We'll discuss methods in Chapter 5, but for now, we'll focus on the three control structures shown in Figure 2.5.

2.7 if Statements

In previous sections describing print, assignment, and input statements, you saw examples of the sequential control structure on the left side of Figure 2.5. Now let's consider the conditional control structure in the center of Figure 2.5. In going through a sequence of steps, sometimes you get to a "fork in the road," at which point you must choose which way to go. The choice you make depends on the situation. More specifically, it depends on the answer to a question. When a program has a fork in the road, programmers use an *if statement* to implement the fork. The if statement asks a question and the answer to the question tells the algorithm which way to go. More formally, the if statement contains a *condition*. A condition is a question whose answer is either yes or no. The answer to the condition's question determines which statement executes next. Here are three forms for the if statement:

"if"
"if, else"
"if, else if"

Now let's look at each of these three forms separately.

"if"

First, suppose you want to do either one thing or nothing at all. In that case, you should use the simple "if" form of the if statement. Here is its format:

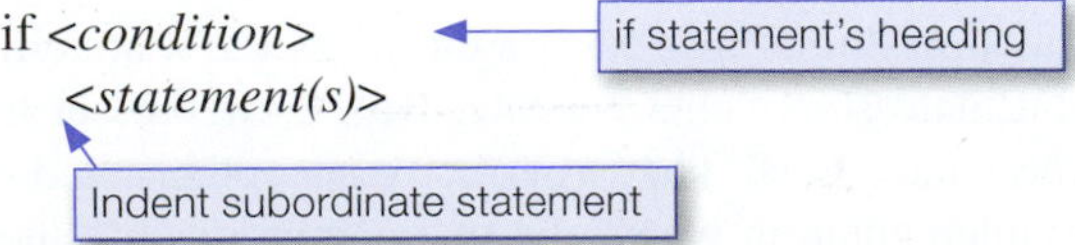

Note the angled brackets "<>" that surround "condition" and "statement(s)." Throughout the book, we use the italics and angled bracket notation for items that require a description. Thus, when you see "<*condition*>," it tells you that an actual condition, not the word "condition," is supposed to follow the word "if." Likewise, when you see "<*statement(s)*>," it tells you that one or more actual statements, not the word "statement(s)," is supposed to go underneath the if statement's heading.

In the above if statement illustration, note how <*statement(s)*> is indented. Pseudocode emulates a natural-language outline by using indentation to show encapsulation or subordination. The statements under an if statement's heading are subordinate to the if statement because they are considered to be part of the larger, encompassing if statement. Since they are subordinate, they should be indented.

Here's how the simple "if" form of the if statement works:

- If the condition is true, execute all subordinate statements, that is, execute all indented statements immediately below the "if."
- If the condition is false, jump to the line after the last subordinate statement, that is, jump to the first un-indented statement below the "if."

Let's put these concepts into practice by showing you an if statement in the context of a complete algorithm. Figure 2.7's Shape algorithm prompts the user for a shape. If the user enters "circle," the algorithm prompts for a radius, calculates the area of a circle using that radius, and prints the resulting area. Finally, regardless of whether the user entered "circle" or not, the algorithm prints a friendly end-of-algorithm message.

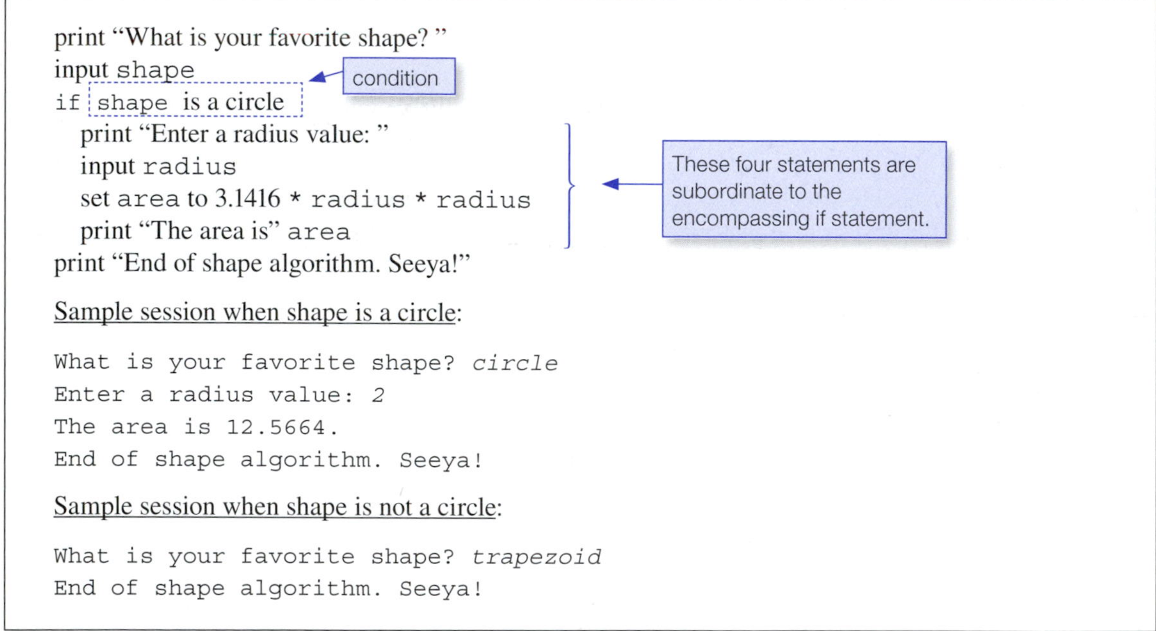

print "What is your favorite shape? "
input shape
if shape is a circle
print "Enter a radius value: "
input radius
set area to 3.1416 * radius * radius
print "The area is" area
print "End of shape algorithm. Seeya!"
condition
These four statements are subordinate to the encompassing if statement.
Sample session when shape is a circle:
What is your favorite shape? circle
Enter a radius value: 2
The area is 12.5664.
End of shape algorithm. Seeya!
Sample session when shape is not a circle:
What is your favorite shape? trapezoid
End of shape algorithm. Seeya!

Figure 2.7 Shape algorithm that calculates a circle's area if the user's favorite shape is a circle

You should take note of several items in the Shape algorithm. "`shape` is a circle" is the if statement's condition. It controls whether the if statement's subordinate statements execute. Note how the set `area` command and subsequent print command are separate statements. That's perfectly acceptable and quite common, but you should be aware of an alternative implementation where the two commands are merged into one statement:

```
print "The area is " (3.1416 * radius * radius)
```

In this case, we put parentheses around the mathematical calculation to emphasize that we want the computer to print the result of the calculation, rather than individual variable values. You can always use parentheses to specify that operations inside the parentheses should be done before operations outside the parentheses.

"if, else"

Now for the second form of the if statement—the "if, else" form. Use the "if, else" form if you want to do either one thing or another thing. Here is its format:

```
if <condition>
   <statement(s)>
else
   <statement(s)>
```

And here's how the "if, else" form of the if statement works:

- If the condition is true, execute all statements subordinate to the "if," and skip all statements subordinate to the "else."
- If the condition is false, skip all statement(s) subordinate to the "if," and execute all statements subordinate to the "else."

Here's an example that uses the "if, else" form of the if statement:

```
if grade is greater than or equal to 60
   print "Pass"
else
   print "Fail"
```

Note how we indent the print "Pass" statement since it is subordinate to the if condition. Note how we indent the print "Fail" statement since it is subordinate to the "else."

"if, else if"

The "if, else" form of the if statement addresses situations in which there are exactly two possibilities. But what if there are more than two possibilities? For example, suppose that you want to print one of five possible letter grades for a particular numerical score. You can do it by using the "if, else if" form of the if statement to establish parallel paths:

```
if grade is greater than or equal to 90
   print "A"
else if grade is greater than or equal to 80
   print "B"
else if grade is greater than or equal to 70
   print "C"
else if grade is greater than or equal to 60
   print "D"
else
   print "F"
```

What happens if the grade is 85? The print "A" statement is skipped, and the print "B" statement is executed. Once one of the conditions is found to be true, then the rest of the entire if statement is skipped. So the third, fourth, and fifth print statements are not executed.

What happens if all of the conditions are false? If all of the conditions are false, then the subordinate statement under "else" is executed. So if the grade is 55, print "F" is executed. Note that you're not required to have an "else" with the "if, else if" statement. If you don't have an "else" and all of the conditions are false, then no statements are executed.

if Statement Summary

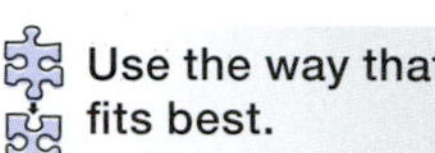

Use the first form ("if") for problems where you want to do one thing or nothing. Use the second form ("if, else") for problems where you want to do either one thing or another thing. Use the third form ("if, else if") for problems where there are three or more possibilities.

Practice Problem with Flowchart and Pseudocode

Let's practice what you've learned about if statements by presenting a flowchart and having you write the corresponding pseudocode for an algorithm that cuts a CEO's excessively large salary in half. Figure 2.8 presents the flowchart.

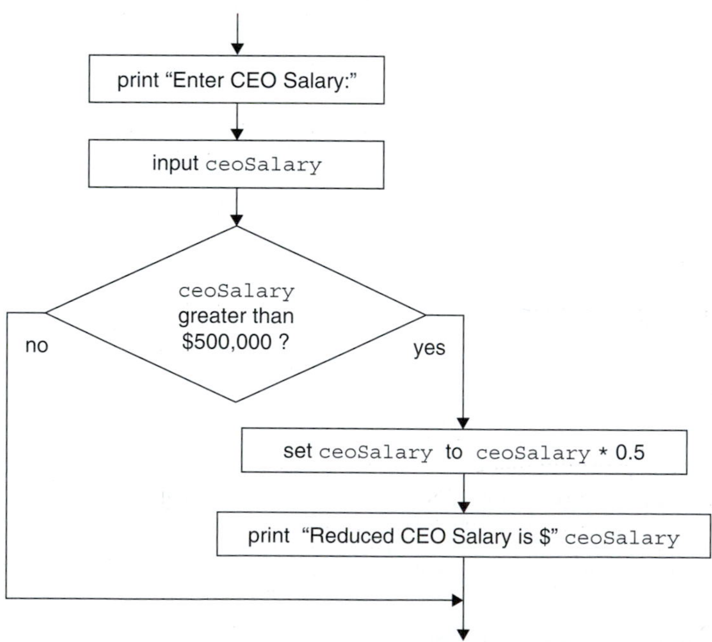

Figure 2.8 Flowchart for reducing CEO salaries

In flowcharts, we omit the word "if" from the condition in diamonds and add a question mark to turn the condition into a question. The question format fits well with the "yes" and "no" on the exiting arrows.

If the condition is true, the answer to the question is "yes." If the condition is false, the answer to the question is "no." Given the flowchart in Figure 2.8, try to write a pseudocode version of the cut-CEO-salary-in-half algorithm. When you're done, compare your answer to our answer:

Practice writing a pseudocode algorithm.

```
print "Enter CEO Salary: "
input ceoSalary
if ceoSalary is greater than 500000
   set ceoSalary to ceoSalary * 0.5
   print "Reduced CEO Salary is $" ceoSalary
```

Practice Problems with Pseudocode Only

Everybody knows the saying, a picture is worth a thousand words. This may be true, but compare the space consumed by and the effort to construct Figure 2.8's flowchart with the space consumed by and the effort to write the corresponding pseudocode. Pictures help you get started, but text is more efficient once you know what you're doing. So now let's try skipping the flowchart and going immediately to pseudocode.

First, let's write an algorithm that prints "No school!" if the temperature is below 0 degrees. Which if statement form should you use for this problem? Since the problem description says to do either something or nothing, you should use the simple "if" form:

```
print "Enter a temperature: "
input temperature
if temperature is less than 0
   print "No school!"
```

Next, let's write an algorithm that prints "warm" if the temperature is above 50 degrees and prints "cold" otherwise. Which if statement form should we use? Since the problem description says to do one thing or another thing, you should use the "if, else" form:

```
print "Enter a temperature: "
input temperature
if temperature is greater than 50
   print "warm"
else
   print "cold"
```

Finally, let's write an algorithm that prints "hot" if the temperature is above 80 degrees, prints "OK" if it's between 50 and 80 degrees, and prints "cold" if it's less than 50 degrees. For this problem, it's appropriate to use the "if, else if" form, like this:

```
print "Enter a temperature: "
input temperature
if temperature is greater than 80
   print "hot"
else if temperature greater than or equal to 50
   print "OK"
else
   print "cold"
```

2.8 Loops

We've now discussed two of the three structures in Figure 2.5—sequential structures and conditional structures. Let's now discuss the third structure—*looping structures*. Looping structures repeat the execution of a particular sequence of statements. If you need to execute a block of code many times, you could, of course, repeatedly write the code wherever you need it. However, that leads to redundancy, which is something you want to avoid in a computer program, because it opens the door to inconsistency. It's better to write the code once and then reuse it. The simplest way to reuse a block of code is to go back up to before where that block starts, and run through it again. That's called a *loop*. Every loop has a condition that determines how many times to repeat the loop. Think of driving through western Kansas and seeing a sign for "Prairie Dog Town." Your kids demand that you take the prairie-dog drive-through tour. The decision about how many times to repeat the tour parallels the condition in a loop statement.

A Simple Example

Suppose you want to print "Happy birthday!" 100 times. Rather than writing 100 print "Happy birthday!" statements, wouldn't it be better to use a loop? Figure 2.9 presents a solution to the Happy birthday algorithm in the form of a flowchart with a loop. The flowchart implements the looping logic with an arrow that goes from "set `count` to `count + 1`" back up to the "`count` less than or equal to 100?" condition.

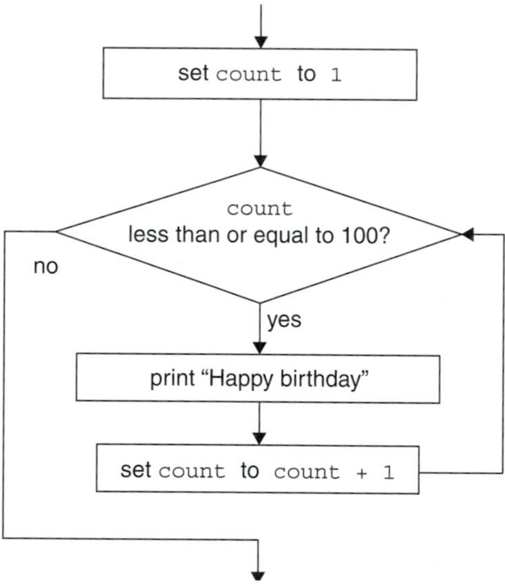

Figure 2.9 Flowchart for our Happy Birthday algorithm

In a loop you'll often use a count variable that keeps track of the number of times the loop has repeated. You can either count up or count down. The Happy birthday flowchart counts up.

In the last operation, instead of saying "set `count` to `count` + 1," you could have said something like "increment `count` by one." We chose to use this "set" wording to reinforce a way of thinking that corresponds to how a computer updates a variable's value. Go back and review the thinking associated with Figure 2.3. First the computer performs a mathematical calculation using existing variable values. In Figure 2.3, the calculation involved two variables, `length` and `width`, that were different from the variable being updated, `rectangleArea`. In Figure 2.9 the calculation involves the variable being updated, `count`. After the computer completes the calculation, it assigns the result of the calculation to the variable being updated. This assignment overwrites the old value and replaces it with a new value. Thus, when it computes count + 1, the computer uses the old value of count. Then (in the subsequent assignment) it changes the value in count to the new value.

In practice, all loops should have some kind of termination. That is, they should stop executing at some point. A loop that counts up normally uses a maximum value as a termination condition. For example, Figure 2.9's loop continues as long as count is less than or equal to 100, and it terminates (stops looping) when count reaches 101. A loop that counts down normally uses a minimum value as a termination condition. For example, a loop might start with count equal to 100 and continue as long as count is greater than zero. Then the loop would terminate when count reached zero.

When a loop's condition compares a counter variable to a maximum value, the question often arises about whether to use "less than or equal to" or just "less than." Likewise, when a loop's condition compares a counter variable to a minimum value, the question often arises about whether to use "greater than or equal to" or just "greater than." There are no absolute answers to those questions. Sometimes you'll need to do it one way, and sometimes you'll need to do it the other way—it depends on the situation. For example, look again at the decision condition in Figure 2.9's Happy birthday algorithm. Suppose you used "less than." Then, when count equaled 100, you would quit before printing the last (100th) "Happy birthday!" Therefore, in this case you should use "less than or equal to." If you mistakenly used "less than," that would be an *off-by-one error.* Such errors are called "off by one" because they occur when you execute a loop one more time than you should or one less time than you should. To avoid off-by-one errors, you should always double check the borderline cases for your algorithms' loops.

The while Loop

Most popular programming languages have several different types of loops. Although it may be awkward, theoretically, there's always a way to convert any one type of loop to any other type of loop. So, for simplicity and brevity, in this discussion of algorithms we'll consider only one type of loop and look at the other types when we get into the details of the Java language. The type of loop we'll consider now is a very popular one, the while loop, which has this format:

```
while <condition>
   <statement(s)>
```

This format should look familiar because it's similar to the if statement's format. The condition is at the top, and the subordinate statements are indented. The subordinate statements, which are inside the loop, are called the loop's *body*. The number of times that a loop repeats is called the number of *iterations.* It's possible for a loop to repeat forever, which is called an *infinite loop*. It's also possible for a loop to repeat zero times. There's no special name for the zero-iteration occurrence, but it's important to be aware that this sometimes happens. For an example, let's see how Figure 2.9's Happy birthday flowchart looks when it's presented as pseudocode with a while loop. This is shown in Figure 2.10.

```
set count to 1
while count is less than or equal to 100
   print "Happy birthday!"
   set count to count + 1
```

Figure 2.10 Pseudocode for another Happy Birthday algorithm

Here's how the while loop works:

- If the condition is true, execute all of the loop's subordinate statements, and then jump back to the loop's condition.
- When the loop's condition finally becomes false, jump to below the loop, that is, the first statement after the loop's last subordinate statement, and continue execution there.

2.9 Loop Termination Techniques

In this section we describe three common ways to terminate loops:

- Counter

  Use a counter variable to keep track of the number of iterations.

- User query

  Ask the user if he/she wants to continue. If the user responds yes, then execute the body of the loop. After each pass through the subordinate statements in the loop, ask the user again if he/she wants to continue.

- Sentinel value

  When a loop includes a data-input statement, identify a special value (a *sentinel value*) that is outside the normal range of input, and use it to indicate that looping should terminate. For example, if the normal range of input is positive numbers, the sentinel value could be a negative number like 21. Here's how you do it: Continue to read in values and execute the loop until the entered value equals the sentinel value, and then stop the looping. In the real world, a sentinel is a guard who lets people continue to pass until the enemy arrives. So a program's sentinel value is like a human sentinel—it allows the loop to continue or not.

Counter Termination

Figure 2.10's Happy birthday algorithm is a good example of using a counter to terminate a looping operation. We should point out, however, that the normal place for a computer to start counting is 0, rather than one. If we use the standard start-at-zero convention, Figure 2.10's pseudocode changes to this:

```
set count to 0
while count is less than 100
   print "Happy birthday!"
   set count to count + 1
```

Notice that as we change the initial count value from 1 to 0, we also change condition comparison from "less than or equal to" to "less than." This will produce the same 100 iterations, but this time, the count values will be 0, 1, 2, . . . 98, 99. Each time you create a counter loop, it's important to assure yourself that the number of iterations will be exactly what you want. Because you can start with numbers different than one, and because the termination condition can employ different comparison operators, it's sometimes hard to be sure about the total number of iterations you'll get. Here's a handy trick to give you more confidence:

To check a loop's terminal condition, temporarily change the terminal condition to produce what you think will be exactly one iteration. For example, in this most recent pseudocode version of the Happy birthday algorithm (where the initial count is zero), change the final count from 100 to 1. Then ask yourself, "How many print operations will occur?" In this case, the initial count is 0. The first time the condition is tested, the condition is "0 is less than 1," which is true. So the condition is satisfied and the loop's subordinate statements execute. Since the final statement in the loop increments the count to 1, the next time the condition is tested, the condition is "1 is less than 1," which is false. So the condition is not satisfied, and looping terminates. Since using 1 in the loop condition produces one iteration, you can have confidence that using 100 in the loop condition will produce 100 iterations.

Simplify the problem to check its essence.

User Query Termination

To understand user query termination, consider an algorithm which repeatedly asks a user for numbers and calculates and prints the squares of the input values. This activity should continue as long as the user answers "y" to a "Continue?" prompt.

Figure 2.11 displays this algorithm as pseudocode. Within the while loop body, the first statement prompts the user to enter a number, the third statement does the computation, and the fourth statement prints the result. The query "Continue? (y/n)" and the corresponding input come just before the end of the body. This loop always executes at least one time, because we assign "y" to the continue variable before the loop begins.

```
set continue to "y"
while continue equals "y"
   print "Enter a number: "
   input num
   set square to num * num
   print num " squared is " square
   print "Continue? (y/n): "
   input continue
```

Figure 2.11 Print Squares algorithm that uses a query loop

Suppose that you want to give the user the opportunity to quit before entering even one number to square. You can do that by replacing the first statement:

```
set continue to "y"
```

with these two statements:

```
print "Do you want to print a square? (y/n): "
input continue
```

This provides the user the option to enter "n" so that no squares will be computed.

Sentinel Value Termination

To understand sentinel value termination, consider an algorithm that reads in bowling scores repeatedly until a sentinel value of −1 is entered. Then, the algorithm prints the average score.

Mull it over. Often, you should spend time just thinking about a problem's solution before writing anything down. And you should think first about the solution at a high level, without worrying about all the details. With that said, we encourage you to set the book aside now and think about the steps needed in the Bowling Score algorithm.

Are you done thinking? If so, compare your thoughts to this high-level description:

Read in scores repeatedly and find the sum of all the scores.
Then, when −1 is entered, divide the sum by the number of scores entered.

There are two details in this high-level description that you now need to address. First, you need to think about how to find the sum of all the scores. Before asking for any input, and before any looping, assign an initial value of zero to a `totalScore` variable. In other words, *initialize* it to zero. Then, in the same loop which repeatedly asks the user for the next score, right after inputting that score, add it to the `totalScore` variable to accumulate the scores as they come in. This way, after all the scores are in, the `totalScore` variable will already contain the sum of all scores.

The sum of all scores is useful because the goal is to determine the average score, and to compute an average you need the sum. But to compute an average you also need the total number of items, and that's not known ahead of time. How can you keep track of the number of scores entered so far? Initialize and accumulate a `count` variable while you initialize and update the `totalScore` variable. Note that just one loop does all three activities (inputting, updating `totalScore`, and updating `count`). We chose −1 as a sentinel value for a Bowling Score algorithm because it's a value that would never be a valid bowling-score entry. But any negative number would work as the sentinel value.

Figure 2.12 illustrates the algorithm solution for this problem. Note how the prompt messages say "(−1 to quit)." That is necessary because without it, the user wouldn't know how to quit. In general, always provide enough prompting information so that the user knows what to do next and knows how to quit.

```
set totalScore to 0
set count to 0
print "Enter score (−1 to quit): "
input score
while score is not equal to −1
   set totalScore to totalScore + score
   set count to count + 1
   print "Enter score (−1 to quit): "
   input score
set avg to totalScore / count
print "Average score is " avg
```

Figure 2.12 Bowling Score algorithm using a sentinel-value loop

What would you expect to happen if the user enters −1 as the very first input? That causes the loop body to be skipped, and the `count` variable never gets updated from its original initialized value, zero. When the set `average` statement attempts to calculate the average score, it divides `totalScore` by `count`. Since `count` is zero, it divides by zero. As you may recall from your math courses, division by zero creates problems. If an algorithm divides by zero, the result is undefined. If a Java program divides by zero, the computer prints a cryptic error message and then immediately shuts down the program. Since the Bowling

Score algorithm allows for the possibility of division by zero, it is not very *robust*. To be robust, it should behave in a way that a typical user would consider to be both sensible and courteous, even when the input is unreasonable. To make it more robust, replace the last two statements in Figure 2.12's algorithm with an `if` statement like this:

```
if count is not equal to 0
   set avg to totalScore / count
   print "Average score is " avg
else
   print "No entries were made."
```

Using this `if` statement enables the program to tell the user why a normal output was not produced, and it avoids the problems inherent with division by zero.

2.10 Nested Looping

In the preceding two sections, we presented algorithms where each algorithm contained one loop. As you proceed through the book and as you proceed through your programming career, you'll find that most programs contain more than one loop. If a program has loops that are independent (i.e., the first loop ends before the second loop begins), then the program's flow should be reasonably straightforward. On the other hand, if a program has a loop inside a loop, then the program's flow can be harder to understand. In this section, we'll try to make you comfortable with a *nested loop*, which is the formal term for an inner loop that's inside an outer loop.

Suppose you're asked to write an algorithm that plays multiple games of "Find the largest number." In each game, the user enters a series of nonnegative numbers. When the user enters a negative number, the algorithm prints the largest number in the series and asks the user if he/she wants to play another game.

Think about what type of loops should be used.

Before writing anything down, you should think about a very important question: What types of loops should be used? You'll need an outer loop that continues as long as the user says that he/she wants to play another game. What type of loop should that be—counter loop, user-query loop, or sentinel value loop? You'll need an inner loop that plays one game by reading in numbers until a negative number is input. What type of loop should that be—counter loop, user-query loop, or sentinel value loop? Have you attempted to answer the questions? If so, read on. If not, stop and think.

The outer loop should be a user-query loop. The inner loop should be a sentinel value loop, where the sentinel value is any negative number. Now look at the algorithm for this problem in Figure 2.13. Note that the algorithm does indeed use a user-query outer loop—at the bottom of the loop, the user is prompted to continue, and at the top of the loop, the response is checked. Note that the algorithm does indeed use a sentinel value inner loop—the loop terminates when the user enters a negative number.

The inner loop's logic is nontrivial and deserves special attention. Before examining the code itself, think about the goal and the solution at a high level. The goal is to read in a series of numbers where the last number is negative and then print the largest number. Suppose the input sequence is 7, 6, 8, 3, 4, −99.

How would a human do it?

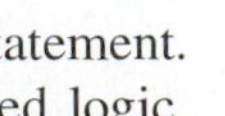

After each new number is entered, the algorithm should ask the question: Is the new number bigger than the previous biggest number? If the new number is bigger, the new number is the new "champion," that is, the new biggest number. Note that the preceding question started with the word "if." That's a good indication that you can implement that logic with an if statement. Find the if statement in Figure 2.13's inner loop and verify that it implements the aforementioned logic.

```
set continue to "y"
while continue equals "y"
   set biggest to −1
   print "Enter a number (negative to quit): "
   input num
   while num is greater than or equal to 0
      if num is greater than biggest
         set biggest to value of num
      print "Enter a number (negative to quit): "
      input num
   if biggest is not equal to −1
      print "The Biggest number entered was " biggest
   print "Play another game? (y/n): "
   input continue
```

inner loop

outer loop

Figure 2.13 Algorithm that plays multiple games of "Find the largest number"

You'll see that the if statement checks the new number to see if it is bigger than the previous biggest number, and if it is bigger, then the new number is assigned into the `biggest` variable. That assignment crowns the new number as the new champion.

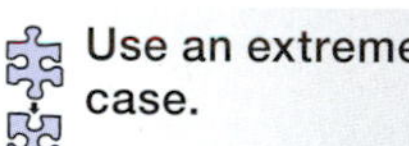

Use an extreme case.

Note the set `biggest` to −1 initialization at the top of the outer loop. What's the point of initializing biggest to −1? Initialize the champion variable (biggest) with a starting value that will automatically lose the first time a new number is compared to it. You know that −1 will lose to the first number in a find-the-largest-number contest because the contests are limited to nonnegative numbers and nonnegative numbers are always greater than −1. After the first input replaces `biggest`'s −1 initial value, subsequent inputs may or may not replace `biggest`'s value, depending on the size of the input number and the size of `biggest`.

2.11 Tracing

Dig into details.

Up until now we have focused on design. Now let's look at *analysis*—breaking up of a whole into its parts. In the present context, that means going through the details of an already-existing algorithm. The analysis technique we'll use is called *tracing*, where you essentially pretend that you're the computer. You step through an algorithm (or a program) line by line and carefully record everything that happens. In the early parts of this book we'll use tracing to illustrate programming details we're trying to explain. Tracing gives you a way to make sure that you really understand newly learned programming mechanisms. Tracing also gives you a way to verify whether an existing algorithm or Java code is correct, or whether it has *bugs*.

What are bugs? One of the early digital computers, the Harvard Mark II, used mechanical relays rather than transistors, and programmers programmed by changing electrical connections. As the story goes,[2] even though all the electrical connections were right, the computer kept making a mistake. Finally the programmer discovered a moth squeezed between the contacts of one of the relays. Apparently, the moth had been squashed when the relay contacts closed, and the moth's dead body was interrupting the proper flow of electricity

[2] http://www.faqs.org/docs/jargon/B/bug.html

between those contacts. After the programmer pulled the moth out—"debugged" the computer program—the computer gave the right answer. When you're tracing an algorithm or program to find software bugs, you may sometimes feel like one of these old timers crawling around inside the CPU, looking for moths.

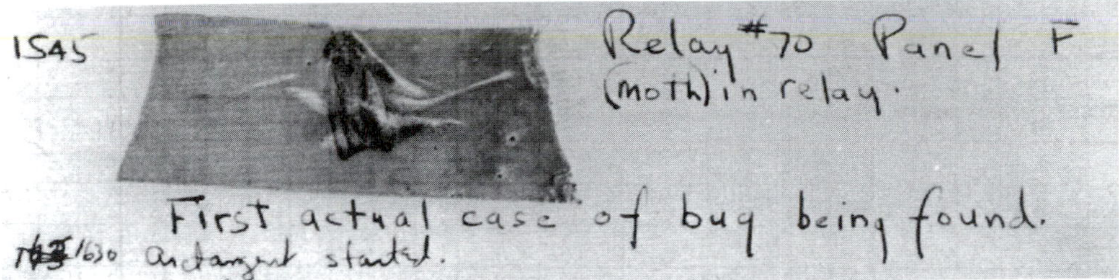

Short-Form Tracing

We present two tracing forms—a short form, described in this subsection, and a long form, described in the next subsection. The short-form tracing procedure is commonly used in industry and in classrooms. It works well in a dynamic environment, where you can move back and forth between pseudocode (or Java code, later) and a trace listing, and fill information in as you go. You may see your teacher go through this dynamic operation on a whiteboard. For example, here's an algorithm that prints the Happy-birthday song:

```
print "What is your name? "
input name
set count to 0
while count is less than 2
   print "Happy birthday to you."
   set count to count + 1
print "Happy birthday, dear " name "."
print "Happy birthday to you."
```

Here's what the short-form trace looks like after the trace is complete:

input	name	count	output
~~Arjun~~	Arjun	~~0~~	What is your name?
		~~1~~	Happy birthday to you.
		2	Happy birthday to you.
			Happy birthday, dear Arjun.
			Happy birthday to you.

The above trace listing has four columns—input, name, count, and output. The input column shows hypothetical input for the algorithm. The output column shows what the algorithm produces when the algorithm runs with the given input. The name and count columns show the values stored in the `name` and `count` variables. In this example, we started with the input value "Arjun." Then we stepped through the code, one line at a time. In stepping through the code, we added values under the name, count, and output columns, and we crossed out old `count` values as they were overwritten by new `count` values. Figure 2.14 describes the general procedure.

Trace setup:

- If there is input, provide a column heading labeled input.
- Provide a column heading for each variable.
- Provide a column heading labeled output.

Trace the program by executing the algorithm one line at a time, and for each line, do this:

- For an `input` statement, cross off the next input value under the input column heading.
- For an assignment statement, update a variable's value by writing the new value under the variable's column heading. If there are already values under the column heading, insert the new value below the bottom value and cross off the old value.
- For a `print` statement, write the printed value under the output column heading. If there are already values under the output column heading, insert the new printed value below the bottom of the output column.

Figure 2.14 Short-form tracing procedure

Short-form tracing works well in a live interactive context, but it does not work as well in a static context like the pages of a printed book. That's because in a book, the short-form tracing does not portray the dynamics of the updating process very well. With our simple Happy birthday algorithm, you may have been able to visualize the dynamics. But for more involved algorithms, a short-form trace listing on the page of a book just "blows through" the details it needs to highlight. Therefore, in this book, we'll use a long-form tracing procedure that keeps better track of each step as the process unfolds.

Long-Form Tracing

With the long-form tracing procedure, there's an added emphasis on keeping track of where you are in the algorithm. To implement that emphasis, (1) you need to have a separate row in the tracing table for each step that's executed in the algorithm, and (2) for each row in the tracing table, you need to provide a line number that tells you the row's associated line in the algorithm. For an example, see the long-form happy birthday trace in Figure 2.15.

Figure 2.15's long-form trace looks somewhat like the previous short-form trace, with a few notable exceptions. The input column has been moved above the main part of the tracing table. In its place is the line# column, which holds line numbers in the algorithm that correspond to rows in the tracing table. Notice the two 5, 6 line number sequences. That shows how the trace "unrolls" the loop and repeats the sequence of statements within the loop for each loop iteration.

Using a Trace To Find a Bug

It's time for you to get your money's worth from all this tracing talk. We'll provide you with an algorithm and it's up to you to determine whether it works properly. More specifically, trace the algorithm to determine whether each step produces reasonable output. If it produces faulty output, find the algorithm's bug and fix the algorithm.

Check each step.

Suppose that Park University's Student Housing office wrote the algorithm shown in Figure 2.16. The algorithm is supposed to read in the names of freshmen and assign each freshman to one of two dormitories. Freshmen with names that begin with A through M are assigned to Chestnut Hall and freshmen with names

```
1 print "What is your name? "
2 input name
3 set count to 0
4 while count is less than 2
5    print "Happy birthday to you."
6    set count to count + 1
7 print "Happy birthday, dear " name "."
8 print "Happy birthday to you."
```

input
Arjun

line#	name	count	output
1			What is your name?
2	Arjun		
3		0	
5			Happy birthday to you.
6		1	
5			Happy birthday to you.
6		2	
7			Happy birthday, dear Arjun.
8			Happy birthday to you.

Figure 2.15 Happy Birthday trace—long form

```
1 print "Enter last name (q to quit): "
2 input lastName
3 while lastName is not equal to q
4    if lastName's first character is between A and M
5       print lastName " is assigned to Chestnut Hall."
6    else
7       print lastName " is assigned to Herr House."
```

input
Ponce
Galati
Aidoo
Nguyen
q

line#	lastName	output

Figure 2.16 Freshmen dormitory assignment algorithm and trace setup

that begin with N through Z are assigned to Herr House. Using the trace setup provided in Figure 2.16, try to either complete the trace or get to a point in the trace where you've identified a problem.

Have you finished working on the trace? If so, compare your answer to this:

line#	lastName	output
1		Enter last name (q to quit):
2	Ponce	
7		Ponce is assigned to Herr House.
7		Ponce is assigned to Herr House.
7		Ponce is assigned to Herr House.
⋮		⋮

The trace points out a problem—the algorithm repeatedly prints Ponce's dorm assignment, but no one else's.

There appears to be an infinite loop. Can you identify the bug? The trace shows that `lastName` gets the first input value, Ponce, but it never gets any other input values. Referring back to Figure 2.16, you can see that the algorithm prompts for the last name above the loop, but not inside the loop. Therefore, the first input value is read in, but no others. The solution is to add another last name prompt inside the while loop, at its bottom. Here is the corrected algorithm:

```
print "Enter last name (q to quit): "
input lastName
while lastName is not equal to q
   if lastName's first character is between A and M
      print lastName "is assigned to Chestnut Hall."
   else
      print lastName "is assigned to Herr House."
   print "Enter last name (q to quit): "
   input lastName
```

We encourage you to trace the corrected algorithm on your own, and you'll find that all four freshmen are assigned to appropriate dorms. Yeah!

Software Development Tools

Most software development tools temporarily label each line of code with a line number to help identify the locations of programming errors. Those line numbers are not actually part of the code, but when they are available, you can use them as identifiers in the *line#* column of a long-form trace. Many software development tools also include a *debugger* that enables you to step through a program one line at a time as it executes. The debugger enables you to look at variable values as you go. Our tracing procedure emulates a debugger's step-by-step type of evaluation. Experience with the tracing used in this book will make it easier for you to understand what an automated debugger is telling you.

2.12 Other Pseudocode Formats and Applications

Pseudocode comes in many different varieties. In this section, we describe several pseudocode variations and the inherent differences between them.

Formal Pseudocode

The following Bowling Scores algorithm uses a more formal pseudocode:

```
totalScore ← 0
count ← 0
print "Enter score (−1 to quit): "
input score
while (score ≠ −1)
{
  totalScore ← totalScore + score
  count ← count + 1
  print "Enter score (−1 to quit): "
  input score
}
avg ← totalScore / count
print "Average score is " + avg
```

This formal variation of pseudocode uses special symbols to make operations stand out more dramatically. The left-pointing arrow (←) represents the right-to-left assignment illustrated previously in Figure 2.3. The ≠ says "is not equal to" more succinctly than words say it. The curly braces emphasize the subordinate nature of the statements in the body of the `while` loop. Later you'll see that Java requires such curly braces whenever the body of an if statement or loop includes more than one subordinate statement. The + in the last line indicates that the two printed items are different types ("Average score is " is a string literal and `avg` is a variable).

Up until now we have used pseudocode, flowcharts, and traces to describe algorithm logic fairly precisely. That precision corresponds closely to the precision found in individual Java-code statements. These algorithmic descriptions have been giving you an informal *implementation view* of a desired program. The final Java code for that program is a formal implementation view of the program. The people who care most about and see implementation views of programs are the programmers who write those programs.

High-Level Pseudocode

Since pseudocode is so flexible, you can also use it to describe algorithms at a higher, more macroscopic level—with more abstraction. The trick is to ignore the details of subordinate operations and just describe and keep track of inputs to and outputs from those subordinate operations. This strategy presents the "big picture" as seen by the outside world. It looks at the "forest" rather than the "trees." It helps keep you on the right track—so you don't solve the wrong problem!

For example, the following Bowling Scores algorithm uses a more high-level pseudocode than what you've seen in the past:

Input all scores.
Compute average score.
Print the average score.

This high-level description presents only the major features, not all the details. It indicates what the program is supposed to do, but not how to do it.

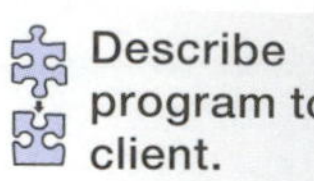

Describe program to client.

Sometimes it's appropriate to think about programs differently from how programmers think about programs. Suppose all you want to do is use somebody else's program, and you don't really care how it's written. In that case, you would be a user or a *client*, and what you would need is a client view of the program. The high-level pseudocode immediately above is an example of an informal *client view* of a desired program. A formal client view of that program would typically include a description of how to use the program and examples of actual input and output. Later, you'll see many "client views" of Java code that has already been written and is free for you to use as part of any program you write.

It's useful to keep in mind these two alternate views of a typical computer program. You'll want to be able to switch back and forth between a client view (when you're acting as or communicating with an end user of a program), and an implementation view (when you're designing and writing the program).

2.13 Problem Solving: Asset Management (Optional)

In this section, we ask you to think about a real-world managerial problem at a fairly abstract level. Imagine that you are the Information-Technology (IT) specialist working in the government of a small city. The head of that city's water department respects your organizational skills and has asked you to come to a city council meeting and lead a discussion of how you might set up a computer program to help the council manage the assets of that city's water system.

First, you suggest that the city-council members help you come up with an overall sequence of steps. On a blackboard, you'll write high-level pseudocode for the "program." To avoid jargon, you'll just call this high-level pseudocode a "to-do list."

After some discussion, the council members agree on—and you list—the following overall steps:[3]

1. Make an inventory of all water system assets.
2. Prioritize those assets.
3. Schedule future changes, replacements, and additions to those assets.
4. Prepare a long-range budget.

This high-level pseudocode is just four sequential steps, like the sequential steps in the left-hand picture in Figure 2.5.

The council thanks you for your help, and for the next meeting, they ask you to flesh out this list with enough detail to show how you plan to implement each of the four steps. They don't want to see a bunch of computer code. They just want to see how you'd proceed—to get a feeling for the difficulty of the project.

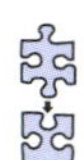

Translate client view into server view.

Back in your office, you create an informal implementation view of the problem. This view is sometimes called a *programmer view* or the *server view*, because the programmer's implementation provides a service to the client. For step 1, you identify seven variables: `assetName`, `expectedLife`, `condition`, `serviceHistory`, `adjustedLife`, `age`, and `remainingLife`. For each asset, you'll have to ask someone in the water department to provide appropriate input for each of the first six variables. Then your program will calculate a value for the last variable. You'll have to repeat this for each significant asset. So here's an abbreviated pseudocode description of the implementation of step 1:

[3] These four steps and their subsequent elaboration are based on recommendations in *Asset Management: A Handbook for Small Water Systems*, Office of Water (4606M) EPA 816-R-03-016, www.epa.gov/safewater, September, 2003.

```
set more to 'y'
while more is equal to 'y'
   input assetName
   input expectedLife
   input condition
   input serviceHistory
   input adjustedLife
   input age
   set remainingLife to adjustedLife - age
   print "Another asset? (y/n): "
   input more
```

This algorithm does not include prompts for the individual variables. Some of these variables may have multiple components, and you may wish to establish and enforce certain conventions for what input values will be acceptable. For example, `condition` and `serviceHistory` may each have several subordinate components. You'll deal with all those details later.

For step 2, you have five variables: `assetName`, `remainingLife`, `importance`, `redundancy`, and `priority`. The `assetName` and `remainingLife` variables are the same as two of the variables used for step 1, so you won't need to input those again. But wait! If this is a separate loop, you'll still have to identify each asset to make sure the new values are being associated with the right asset. You could do this by asking the user to re-enter the `assetName`, or you could do it by looping through all the existing assets and printing out each name just before asking for the required additional information for that asset. The second strategy is easier for the user, so you pick it. Here's an abbreviated pseudocode description of the implementation of step 2:

```
while another asset exists
   print assetName
   input importance
   input redundancy
   input priority
```

Again, the algorithm does not include prompts, and it does not establish and enforce input conventions. You'll deal with those details later.

For step 3, you identify five variables: `assetName`, `activity`, `yearsAhead`, `dollarCost`, and `annualReserve`. Again, `assetName` is already in the system, so again, you can identify it by printing it out. But in scheduling things, the council members will want to deal with the most important things first, so before you start going through the assets, you'll want the program to sort them by `priority`. The sorting operation might be a little tricky. But if you're lucky, someone else already will have written code for that popular computer task, and you'll be able to use it instead of "reinventing the wheel."

The `activity`, `yearsAhead`, and `dollarCost` are inputs, and you'll want the program to compute `annualReserve` as `dollarCost` / `yearsAhead`. After computing the annual reserve for each individual asset, you'll want the program to add it to a `totalAnnualReserve` variable, and after the loop you'll want it to print the final value of `totalAnnualReserve`. Here's an abbreviated pseudocode description of the implementation of step 3:

```
sort assets by priority
set totalAnnualReserve to 0
while another asset exists
   print assetName
   input activity
   input yearsAhead
   input dollarCost
   set annualReserve to dollarCost / yearsAhead
   set totalAnnualReserve to totalAnnualReserve + annualReserve
print totalAnnualReserve
```

Again, the algorithm does not include prompts. You'll deal with all those details later.

For step 4, you identify the three variables, `totalAnnualReserve`, `currentNetIncome`, and `additionalIncome`. For this you need to get someone in the accounting department to provide a value for `currentNetIncome`. Then have the program subtract it from the `totalAnnualReserve` computed in step 3 to obtain the `additionalIncome` required to make the plan work. Oh yes! If the answer comes out negative, you'll want it to just print zero to indicate that your city won't have to come up with any additional income. Here's a pseudocode description of the implementation of step 4:

```
input currentNetIncome
set additionalIncome to currentNetIncome − totalAnnualReserve
if additionalIncome is less than 0
   set additionalIncome to 0
print "Additional income needed = " additionalIncome
```

OK, that's probably enough preparation for next week's city council meeting. At least you'll be able to give the council members a reasonable feeling for the amount of work required.

Summary

- Use pseudocode to write informal descriptions of algorithms. Use understandable names for variables. Indent subordinate statements.
- When your program needs an input, provide an informative prompt to tell the user what kind of information to supply.
- A flowchart provides a visual picture of how the elements of a program are related and how control flows through those elements as the program executes.
- There are three basic well-structured flow-of-control patterns—sequential, conditional, and looping.
- You can implement conditional execution using the three forms of the if statement: "if," "if, else," and "if, else if."
- Provide all loops with some kind of terminating condition such as counter, user query, or sentinel value.
- Use a nested loop if there's a need to repeat something during each iteration of an outer loop.
- Use tracing to (1) obtain an intimate understanding of what an algorithm does and (2) debug programs that have logical errors.
- Use more abstract language to describe larger and more complex programming operations succinctly.

Review Questions

§2.2 Output

1. Describe what this statement does:

    print "user name = " `userName`

§2.3 Variables

2. Provide an appropriate variable name for a variable that holds the total number of students.

§2.4 Operators and Assignment Statements

3. Write a line of pseudocode that tells the computer to assign `distance` divided by `time` into a `speed` variable.

§2.5 Input

4. Write a line of pseudocode that tells the computer to put a user entry into a variable called `height`.

§2.6 Flow of Control and Flowcharts

5. What are the three types of control flow described in this chapter?
6. Looping is appropriate whenever the next thing done is something previously done. (T / F)

§2.7 if Statements

7. Consider the following pseudocode:

    if it is night, set `speedLimit` to 55;
    otherwise, set `speedLimit` to 65.

    Suppose the value of the variable, `night`, is "false." After this code runs, what should be the value of the variable, `speedLimit`?
8. The above pseudocode does not have the exact form suggested in the text. Is that OK?
9. Draw a flowchart that implements this logic:
    If the temperature is greater than 10°C and it's not raining, print "walk." Otherwise, print "drive."
10. Provide a solution to the previous problem in the form of pseudocode.

§2.8 Loops

11. Where is a `while` loop's terminating decision made?
12. When a `while` loop terminates, what executes next?
13. Is it possible for a `while` loop to have an infinite number of iterations?
14. Is it possible for a `while` loop to have zero iterations?

§2.9 Loop Termination Techniques

15. What are the three loop termination techniques described in this chapter?
16. A *sentinel value* is used to do which of the following?
    a) Specify the first value printed.
    b) Print an error message.
    c) Signal the end of input.

§2.10 Nested Looping

17. How does the form of pseudocode we use in most of this chapter differentiate an inner loop from an outer loop?

§2.11 Tracing

18. Which of the following is true?

a) Tracing shows sequence of execution.
b) Tracing helps you debug a program.
c) Tracing highlights errors in loop initialization and termination.
d) All of the above.

19. Trace the following Bowling Score algorithm (taken from Section 2.9). Use the setup shown below the algorithm.

```
 1 set totalScore to 0
 2 set count to 0
 3 print "Enter score (-1 to quit): "
 4 input score
 5 while score is not equal to -1
 6   set totalScore to totalScore + score
 7   set count to count + 1
 8   print "Enter score (-1 to quit): "
 9   input score
10 set avg to totalScore / count
11 print "Average score is " avg
```

Trace setup:

<u>input</u>
94
104
114
−1

line#	score	totalScore	count	avg	output

Exercises

1. [after §2.5] Write pseudocode for an algorithm that (1) asks the user to input the length of the side of a square, (2) computes the square's area, and (3) prints the square's area. Use the following sample session.

<u>Sample session</u>:

The italics signify user input.

```
Enter length of side of square in meters: 15
The area of the square is 225 square meters.
```

2. [after §2.8] What is an infinite loop?

3. [after §2.8] Given the following pseudocode, circle the statements that are considered to be within the body of the while loop:

```
input time
while time is less than 8
  print time
  set time to time + 1
```

4. [after §2.9] In exercise 3, suppose the user's input for `time` is 3. How many lines of output will the algorithm generate?

5. [after §2.11] Trace the following algorithm. The book presents two ways to do tracing—a short form and a long form. To give you a head start, the setup for the short form and also the long form are given below. For your answer, pick one setup and use it. Skip the other setup.

```
1  set y to 0
2  input x
3  while x is not equal to y
4     set y to value of x
5     input x
6     set x to x + y
7     print "x = " x
8     print "y  = " y
```

Short-form setup:

input	x	y	output
2			
3			
4			
0			

Long-form setup:

input
2
3
4
0.

line#	x	y	output

6. [after §2.11] Trace the following algorithm. The book presents two ways to do tracing—a short form and a long form. To give you a head start, the setup for the short form and also the long form are given below. For your answer, pick one setup and use it. Skip the other setup.

```
1  set num to 2
2  set count to 1
3  while count is less than 5
4    set count to count * num
5    if count / 2 is less than 2
6      print "Hello"
7    else
8      while count is less than 7
9         set count to count + 1
10   print "The count is" count "."
```

Short-form setup:

num	count	output

Long-form setup:

line#	num	count	output

Review Question Solutions

1. The statement prints what is in quotation marks literally, and then prints the current value of the variable `userName`.
2. `totalNumberOfStudents`
3. Pseudocode that tells the computer to assign distance divided by time into a speed variable:
   set `speed` to `distance / time`
4. Pseudocode statement:
   input `height`
5. The three types of control flow discussed in Chapter 2 are sequential, conditional, and looping.
6. True. Looping is appropriate whenever the next thing done is something previously done.
7. After the code executes, the value of the variable, `speedLimit`, should be 65.
8. Yes. It's OK because it's only pseudocode, and it conveys the meaning unambiguously. However, if it were supposed to be code the computer could compile, the syntax would have to conform exactly to prescribed rules for a particular programming language like Java.
9. Flowchart that implements walk/drive logic:

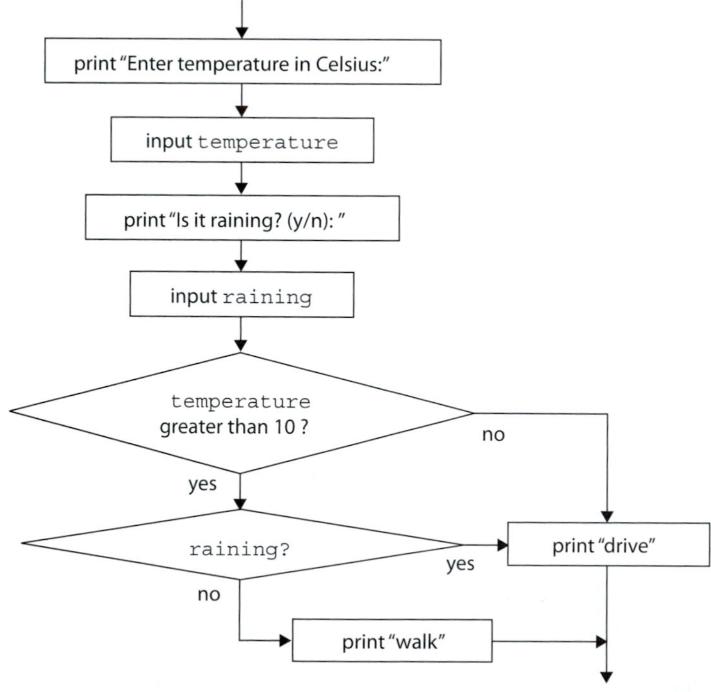

10. Provide a solution to the previous problem in the form of pseudocode.

```
print "Enter temperature in Celsius: "
input temperature
print "Is it raining? (y/n): "
input raining
```

```
if temperature is greater than 10
  if raining equals "n"
    print "walk"
else
  print "drive"
```

11. A while loop's terminating decision is made at the beginning of the loop.

12. After a while loop terminates, the next thing to execute is the first statement after the end of the loop.

13. Yes.

14. Yes.

15. The three loop termination techniques described in this chapter are: counter, user query, and sentinel value.

16. A sentinel value is used to: c) signal the end of input.

17. The inner loop is entirely inside the outer loop. The entire inner loop is shifted to the right compared to the outer loop.

18. d) All of above. Tracing shows sequence of execution, helps debug, and highlights initialization and termination errors.

19. Bowling Score algorithm trace:

input
94
104
114
−1

line#	score	totalScore	count	avg	output
1		0			
2			0		
3					Enter score (-1 to quit):
4	94				
6		94			
7			1		
8					Enter score (-1 to quit):
9	104				
6		198			
7			2		
8					Enter score (-1 to quit):
9	114				
6		312			
7			3		
8					Enter score (-1 to quit):
9	-1				
10				104	
11					Average score is 104

CHAPTER 3

Java Basics

Objectives

- Write simple Java programs.
- Learn about style issues such as comments and readability.
- Declare, assign, and initialize variables.
- Understand primitive data types—integer, floating point, and character.
- Understand reference variables.
- Use the `String` class's methods for string manipulation.
- Use the `Scanner` class for user input.
- Optionally, learn about GUI input and output with the `JOptionPane` class.

Outline

3.1 Introduction

In solving a problem, it's best to spend time first thinking about what you want to do and organizing your thoughts. In Chapter 2, you focused on the thinking and organizing by writing pseudocode algorithm solutions for given problem descriptions. In this chapter, you'll take the next step—you'll focus on writing solutions using a real programming language, Java. By using a real programming language, you'll be able to run your program on a computer and produce results on a computer screen.

As you progress through this chapter, you'll find that much of Java's code parallels pseudocode. The primary difference is the precise syntax required for Java. Pseudocode syntax is lenient: Pseudocode must be clear enough so that humans can understand it, but the spelling and grammar need not be perfect. Programming-code syntax is stringent: It must be perfect in terms of spelling and grammar. Why? Because regular programming code is read by computers, and computers are not able to understand instructions unless they're perfect.

Since this chapter is your first real taste of Java, we'll stick to the basics. We'll present Java syntax that's needed for simple *sequential-execution* programs. A sequential-execution program is one in which all the program's statements are executed in the order in which they are written. As we write such programs, we'll show you output, assignment, and input statements. In addition, we'll describe data types and arithmetic operations. Toward the end of the chapter, we'll present a few slightly more advanced topics—type casting and string methods—that will add important functionality without adding much complexity. Let us begin the Java journey.

3.2 "I Have a Dream" Program

In this section, we present a simple program that prints a single line of text. In the next several sections, we'll analyze the different components of the program. The analysis may be a bit dry, but bear with us. It's important to understand the program's components because all future programs will use those same components. In the rest of the chapter, we'll introduce new concepts that enable us to present more substantial programs.

See Figure 3.1. It shows a program that prints "I have a dream!"[1] In the upcoming sections, we'll refer to it as the Dream program. The program contains comments for human readers and instructions for the computer to execute. We'll analyze the comments first, and then we'll move on to the instructions. You can use this tiny program as a common starting point for all other Java programs. Enter it, run it, and see what it does. Modify it, run it again, and so on, until you have what you need.

Start every program with this code's structure.

[1] Dr. Martin Luther King presented his famous "I have a dream" speech on the steps of the Lincoln Memorial as part of an August 28, 1963 civil rights march on Washington D.C. The speech supported desegregation and helped spur passage of the 1964 Civil Rights Act.

```
/*******************************************
* Dream.java
* Dean & Dean
*
* This program prints "I have a dream."
*******************************************/

public class Dream
{
  public static void main(String[] args)
  {
    System.out.println("I have a dream!");
  }
} // end class Dream
```


Figure 3.1 Dream program

3.3 Comments and Readability

In the real world, you'll spend a lot of your time looking at and fixing other people's code. And other people will spend a lot of their time looking at and fixing your code after you've moved on to something else. With all this looking at other people's code going on, everyone's code needs to be understandable. One key to understanding is good comments. *Comments* are words that humans read but the compiler[2] ignores.

One-Line-Comment Syntax

There are two types of comments—one-line comments and block comments. If your comment text is short enough to fit on one line, use a one-line comment. One-line comments start with two slashes. Here's an example:

```
} // end class Dream
```

The compiler ignores everything from the first slash to the end of the line. So in the above line, the compiler pays attention only to the right brace (}) and ignores the rest of the line. Why is the comment helpful? If you're viewing a long piece of code on a computer screen and you've scrolled to the bottom of the code, it's nice to see a description of the code (e.g., `end class Dream`) without having to scroll all the way back up to the beginning of the code.

Block-Comment Syntax

If your comment text is too long to fit on one line, you can use multiple one-line comments, but it's a bit of a pain to retype the //'s for every line. As an alternative, you can use a block comment. Block comments start with an opening /* and end with a closing */. Here's an example:

[2] A compiler, defined in Chapter 1, is a special program that converts a source-code program into an executable program. An executable program is a program that the computer can execute directly.

```
/*
The following code displays the androids in a high-speed chase,
wreaking havoc on nearby vehicles.
*/
```

The compiler ignores everything between the first slash and the last slash.

Prologue

A prologue is a special example of a block comment. You should put a prologue at the top of every one of your programs. It provides information about the program so that a programmer can quickly glance at it and get an idea of what the program is all about. To make is stand out, it's common to enclose the prologue in a box of asterisks. Here's the `Dream` program's prologue:

the start of the block comment

```
/*******************************************
* Dream.java
* Dean & Dean
*
* This program prints "I have a dream."
*******************************************/
```

the end of the block comment

Note that the opening `/*` and the closing `*/` blend in with the other asterisks. That's OK. The compiler still recognizes the `/*` and `*/` as the start and end points of the block comment.

Include these items in your program's prologue section:

- a line of `*`'s
- filename
- programmer's name
- a line with a single `*` at its left
- program description
- a line of `*`'s

Readability and Blank Lines

We say that a program is *readable* if a programmer can easily understand what the program does. Comments are one way to improve a program's readability. Another way to improve a program's readability is to use blank lines. How are blank lines helpful? Isn't it easier to understand several short, simple recipes rather than a single long, complicated recipe? Likewise, it's easier to understand small chunks of code rather than one large chunk of code. Using blank lines allows you to split up large chunks of code into smaller chunks of code. In a prologue, we insert a blank line to separate the filename-author section from the description section. Also, we insert a blank line below the prologue to separate it from the rest of the program.

By the way, computers don't care about readability; they just care about whether a program works. More specifically, computers skip all comments, blank lines, and contiguous space characters. Since computers don't care about readability, your computer would be perfectly happy to compile and execute this Dream program:

```
public class Dream{public static void
main(String[]args){System.out.println("I have a dream!");}}
```

But a person trying to read the program would probably be annoyed because of the program's poor readability.

3.4 The Class Heading

So far, we've focused on code that the computer ignores—comments. Now let's talk about code that the computer pays attention to. Here's the first non-comment line in the Dream program:

```
public class Dream
```

That line is called a *class heading* because it's the heading for the definition of the program's *class*. What's a class? For now, think of a class simply as a container for your program's code.

Let's examine the three words in the class heading. First, the last word—`Dream`. `Dream` is the name of the class. The compiler allows the programmer to choose any name for the class, but in the interest of making your code readable, you should choose a word(s) that describes the program. Since the Dream program prints "I have a dream," `Dream` is a reasonable class name.

The first two words in the class heading, `public` and `class`, are *reserved words*. Reserved words, also called *keywords*,[3] are words that are defined by the Java language for a particular purpose. They cannot be redefined by a programmer to mean something else. That means programmers cannot use reserved words when choosing names in their programs. For example, we were able to choose `Dream` for the class name because Dream is not a reserved word. We would not have been allowed to choose `public` or `class` for the class name.

So what are the meanings of the `public` and `class` reserved words? The word `class` is a marker that signifies the beginning of the class. For now, with our simple one-class programs, the word `class` also signifies the beginning of the program.

The word `public` is an *access* modifier—it modifies the class's permissions so that the class is accessible by the "public." Making the class publicly accessible is crucial so that when a user attempts to run it, the user's run command will be able to find it.

There are certain coding conventions that most programmers follow. We list such conventions in our "Java Coding-Style Conventions" appendix. Throughout the book, when we refer to "standard coding conventions," we're referring to the coding conventions found in the appendix. Standard coding conventions dictate that class names start with an uppercase first letter; thus, the *D* in the `Dream` class name is uppercase. Java is *case-sensitive,* which means that the Java compiler distinguishes between lowercase and uppercase letters. Since Java is case-sensitive, the filename should also start with an uppercase first letter.

3.5 The `main` Method's Heading

We've talked about the class heading. Now it's time to talk about the heading that goes below the class heading—the `main` method heading. In starting a program, the computer looks for a `main` method heading, and execution begins with the first statement after the `main` method heading. The `main` method heading must have this form:

```
public static void main(String[] args)
```

Let's start our analysis of the `main` method heading by explaining the word `main` itself. So far, all you know about `main` is that in starting a program, the computer looks for it. But `main` is more than that; it's a Java *method.* A Java method is similar to a mathematical function. A mathematical function takes arguments, performs a calculation, and returns an answer. For example, the sin(x) mathematical function

[3] In Java, reserved words and keywords are the same. But in some programming languages, there is a subtle difference. In those languages, both terms refer to words that are defined by the programming language, but keywords can be redefined by the programmer, and reserved words cannot be redefined by the programmer.

takes the x argument, calculates the sine of the given x angle, and returns the calculated sine of x. Likewise, a Java method may take arguments, will perform a calculation, and may return an answer.

The rest of the main heading contains quite a few mysterious words whose explanations may be confusing at this point. In later chapters, when you're better prepared, we'll explain the words in detail. For now, it's OK to treat the main method heading as a line of text that you simply copy and paste under the class heading. We realize that some of you may be uncomfortable with that. For you folks, the rest of this section explains main method heading details.

Explanation of `main` Method Heading Details

We'll now explain the three reserved words at the left of the main method heading—public static void. As previously mentioned, the word public is an access modifier—it grants permissions so that main is accessible by the "public." Since main is the starting point for all Java programs, it must be publicly accessible.

While public specifies who can access the main method (everyone), the word static specifies how to access the main method. With a non-static method, you must do some extra work prior to accessing it.[4] On the other hand, a static method can be accessed immediately, without doing the extra work. Since main is the starting point for all Java programs, it must be immediately accessible, and therefore it requires the word static.

Now for the third reserved word in the main heading—void. Remember that a method is like a mathematical function—it calculates something and returns the calculated value. Well actually, a Java method sometimes returns a value and sometimes returns nothing. void indicates that a method returns nothing. Since the main method returns nothing, we use void in the main method's heading.

Now for the (String[] args) portion of the main heading. Remember that a mathematical function takes arguments. Likewise the main method takes arguments.[5] Those arguments are represented by the word args. In Java, if you ever have an argument, you need to tell the computer what type of value the argument can hold. In this case, the argument's type is defined to be String[], which tells the computer that the args argument can hold an array of strings. The square brackets, [], indicate an array. An *array* is a structure that holds a collection of elements of the same type. In this case String[] is an array that holds a collection of strings. A *string* is a sequence of characters. You'll learn more about strings later in this chapter in Section 3.22, and you'll learn about arrays in Chapter 10.

3.6 Braces

In the Dream program, we inserted opening braces, {, below the class heading and below the main heading, and we inserted closing braces, }, at the bottom of the program. Braces identify groupings for humans and for the computer. They must come in pairs—whenever you have an opening brace, you'll need an associated closing brace. In the Dream program, the top and bottom braces group the contents of the entire class, and the interior braces group the contents of the main method. For readability's sake, you should put an opening brace on a line by itself in the same column as the first character of the previous line. Look at the following code fragment and note how the opening braces are positioned correctly.

[4] To access a non-static method (more formally called an instance method), you must first instantiate an object. We describe object instantiation in Chapter 6.

[5] Although the main method takes arguments, it's rare for the main method to use those arguments. The book's programs do not use the main method's arguments.

```
public class Dream
{
  public static void main(String[] args)
  {
    System.out.println("I have a dream!");
  }
} // end class Dream
```

The first brace is positioned immediately below the first character in the class heading, and the second brace is positioned immediately below the first character in the `main` heading. For readability's sake, you should put a closing brace on a line by itself in the same column as its partner opening brace. Look at the above code fragment and note how the closing braces are positioned correctly.

3.7 `System.out.println`

In the Dream program, the `main` method contains this one statement:

```
System.out.println("I have a dream!");
```

The `System.out.println` statement tells the computer to print something. The word `System` refers to the computer. `System.out` refers to the output part of the computer system—the computer's monitor. The word `println` (pronounced "print line") refers to the Java `println` method that's in charge of printing a message to the computer screen. The above statement would normally be referred to as a `println` method call. You *call* a method when you want to execute it.

The parentheses after `println` contain the message that is to be printed. The above statement prints this message on a computer screen:

```
I have a dream!
```

Note the double quotes in `System.out.println("I have a dream!");` To print a group of characters (e.g., I, space, h, a, v, e, . . .), you need to group them together. As you learned in Chapter 2, the double quotes are in charge of grouping together characters to form a string literal.

Note the semicolon at the end of `System.out.println("I have a dream!");` A semicolon in the Java language is like a period in natural language. It indicates the end of a statement. You'll need to put a semicolon at the end of every `System.out.println` statement.

You'll be calling the `System.out.println` method a lot, so you might want to try to memorize its wording. To help with your memorization, think of it as an acronym—"Sop" for `System`, `out`, and `println`. Don't forget that the *S* is uppercase and the rest of the command is lowercase.

The `System.out.println` method prints a message and then moves to the beginning of the next line. That means that if there is another `System.out.println` method call, it starts its printing on the next line. The upcoming example illustrates what we're talking about.

An Example

In our Dream program, we print just one short line—"I have a dream!" In our next example, we print multiple lines of varying lengths. See Figure 3.2's Sayings program and its associated output. Note how each of the three `println` method calls produces a separate line of output. Note how the second `println` method call is too long to fit on one line, so we split it just to the right of the left parenthesis. The third `println`

```
/*********************************************************************
* Sayings.java
* Dean & Dean
*
* This program prints several sayings.
*********************************************************************/

public class Sayings
{
  public static void main(String[] args)
  {
    System.out.println("The future ain't what it used to be.");
    System.out.println(
      "Always remember you're unique, just like everyone else.");
    System.out.println("If you are not part of the solution," +
      " you are part of the precipitate.");
  } // end main
} // end class Sayings
```

This connects/concatenates the split-apart strings.

Output:

```
The future ain't what it used to be.
Always remember you're unique, just like everyone else.
If you are not part of the solution, you are part of the precipitate.
```

Figure 3.2 Sayings program and its associated output

method call is longer than the second `println` method call and as such, it could not fit on two lines if it was split after the left parenthesis. In other words, this does not work:

```
System.out.println(
  "If you are not part of the solution, you are part of the pr
```

Not enough room.

Thus, we split the third `println` method call in the middle of the string that is to be printed. To split a string literal, you need to put opening and closing quotes around each of the two split-apart substrings, and you need to insert a + between the substrings. See the quotes and the + in Figure 3.2's third `println` method call.

3.8 Compilation and Execution

Up to this point in the chapter, you've been exposed only to the theory behind Java code (the theory behind the Dream program's code and the theory behind the Sayings program's code). To gain a more complete appreciation for code, you need to enter it on a computer, compile it, and run it. After all, learning how to program requires lots of hands-on practice. It's a "contact sport"! We've provided several tutorials on the book's Web site that step you through the compilation and execution of a few simple Java programs. We recommend that you now take the time to work your way through one or more of those tutorials. The rest of this section covers some basic concepts related to compilation and execution. Be aware that we cover these concepts plus additional details in the tutorials.

After entering a program's source code on a computer, save it in a file whose name is comprised of the class name plus a `.java` extension. For example, since the Dream program's class name is `Dream`, its source-code filename must be `Dream.java`.

After saving a program's source code in an appropriately named file, create Java bytecode[6] by submitting the source code file to a Java compiler. In compiling the source code, the compiler generates a bytecode program file whose name is comprised of the class name plus a `.class` extension. For example, since the Dream program's class name is `Dream`, its bytecode filename will be `Dream.class`.

The next step after creating the bytecode program file is to run it. To run a Java program, submit the bytecode program file to the Java Virtual Machine (JVM).

3.9 Identifiers

So far in this chapter, you've learned Java by looking at code. Eventually, you'll need to learn it by writing your own code. When you do so, you'll need to pick out names for your program components. Java has certain rules for naming your program components. We'll look at those rules now.

An *identifier* is the technical term for a program component's name—the name of a class, the name of a method, and so on. In our Dream program, `Dream` was the identifier for the class name, and `main` was the identifier for the method name.

Identifiers must consist entirely of letters, digits, dollar signs (`$`), and/or underscore (`_`) characters. The first character must not be a digit. If an identifier does not follow these rules, your program won't compile.

Coding-convention rules are narrower than compiler rules when it comes to identifiers. Coding conventions suggest that you limit identifiers to just letters and digits. Do not use dollar signs, and (except for named constants—to be described later) do not use underscores. They also suggest that you use lowercase for all your identifier letters except:

- Start class names with an uppercase letter. For example, our `Dream` class starts with an uppercase D.
- Run together the words in a multiple-word identifier, using an uppercase letter for the first letter in the second word, third word, and so on. For example, if a method prints a favorite color, an appropriate method name would be `printFavoriteColor`.

Perhaps the most important coding-convention identifier rule is the one that says identifiers must be descriptive. Returning to the example of a method that prints a favorite color, `printFavoriteColor` is plenty descriptive. But how about `favColor`? Nope, not good enough. Some programmers like to use abbreviations (like "fav") in their identifiers. That works OK sometimes, but not all that often. We recommend staying away from abbreviations unless they're standard. Using complete and meaningful words in identifiers promotes self documentation. A program is *self-documenting* if the code itself explains the meaning, without needing a manual or lots of comments.

If you break a coding-conventions rule, it won't affect your program's ability to compile, but it will detract from your program's readability. Suppose you have a `sngs` method that prints a list of the week's top

[6] Bytecode, defined in Chapter 1, is a binary-encoded version of the source code. The computer cannot execute source code, but it can execute bytecode.

40 songs. Even though `sngs` might work, you should rename it to something like `printTop40Songs` to improve your program's readability.

3.10 Variables

To this point, our programs haven't done a whole lot; they've just printed a message. If you want to do more than that, you'll need to be able to store values in variables. A Java variable can hold only one type of value. For example, an integer variable can hold only integers and a string variable can hold only strings.

Variable Declarations

How does the computer know which type of data a particular variable can hold? Before a variable is used, its type must be declared in a *declaration statement.*

Declaration statement syntax:

<type> <list-of-variables-separated-by-commas>;

Example declarations:

```
int row, col;
String firstName;   // student's first name
String lastName;    // student's last name
int studentId;
```

In each declaration statement, the word at the left specifies the type for the variable or variables at the right. For example, in the first declaration statement, `int` is the type for the `row` and `col` variables. Having an `int` type means that the `row` and `col` variables can hold only integers (`int` stands for integer). In the second declaration statement, `String` is the type for the `firstName` variable. Having a `String` type means that the `firstName` variable can hold only strings.

Have you noticed that we sometimes spell string with an uppercase S and we sometimes spell it with a lowercase s? When we use "string" in the general sense, to refer to a sequence of characters, we use a lowercase s. In Java, `String` is a data type that happens to be a class name also. As you now know, coding conventions dictate that class names begin with an uppercase letter. Thus, the `String` class/data type begins with an uppercase S. So when we refer to `String` as a data type, in code and in conversational text, we use an uppercase S.

When you declare a variable(s), don't forget to put a semicolon at the end of the declaration statement. When you declare more than one variable with one declaration statement, don't forget to separate the variables with commas.

Style Issues

The compiler will accept a variable declaration anywhere in a block of code, as long as it's above where the variable is used. However, in the interest of readability, you should normally put your declarations at the top of the `main` method. That makes them easy to find.

Although it may waste some space, we recommend that you normally declare only one variable per declaration statement. That way, you'll be able to provide a comment for each variable (and you should normally provide a comment for each variable).

We do make exceptions to these recommendations. Note how these `row` and `col` variables are declared together with one declaration statement:

```
int row, col;
```

That's acceptable because they are intimately related. Note that the `row` and `col` variables are declared without a comment. That's acceptable because `row` and `col` are standard names that all programmers should understand. It would be overkill to include a comment like this:

```
int row, col;       // row and col hold row and column index numbers
```

Note how this `studentId` variable is declared without a comment:

```
int studentId;
```

That's acceptable because the `studentId` name is so completely descriptive that everyone should be able to understand it. It would be overkill to include a comment like this:

```
String studentId;  // a student's ID value
```

Variable names are identifiers. Thus, when you name your variables, you should follow the identifier rules covered earlier. The `studentId` variable is well named—it uses all lowercase letters except for the first letter in its second word, `Id`.

One final recommendation for your variable declarations: Try to align your comments such that they all begin in the same column. For example, note how the `//`'s are in the same column:

```
String lastName;        // student's last name
String firstName;       // student's first name
```

3.11 Assignment Statements

You now know how to declare a variable in Java. After declaring a variable, you'll want to use it, and the first step in using a variable is to put a value inside of it. We'll now consider the assignment statement, which allows you to assign/put a value into a variable.

Java Assignment Statements

Java uses the single equal sign (=) for assignment statements. See Figure 3.3's BonusCalculator program. In particular, note the `salary = 50000;` line. That's an example of a Java assignment statement. It assigns the value 50000 into the variable `salary`.

In the BonusCalculator program, note the blank line below the declaration statements. In accordance with the principles of good style, you should insert blank lines between logical chunks of code. A group of declaration statements is usually considered to be a logical chunk of code, so you should normally insert a blank line below your bottom declaration statement.

Let's analyze the code fragment's `bonusMessage` assignment statement. Note the `*` operator. The `*` operator performs multiplication. Note the + operator. If a + operator appears between a string and something else (e.g., a number or another string), then the + operator performs *string concatenation*. That means that the JVM appends the item at the right of the + to the item at the left of the +, forming a new string. In our example, the mathematical expression, `.02 * salary`, is evaluated first since it's inside parentheses. The JVM then appends the result, 100000, to "Bonus = $", forming the new string "Bonus = $100000".

```
/*************************************************************
* BonusCalculator.java
* Dean & Dean
*
* This program calculates and prints a person's work bonus.
*************************************************************/

public class BonusCalculator
{
  public static void main(String[] args)
  {
    int salary;              // person's salary
    String bonusMessage;     // specifies work bonus

    salary = 50000;
    bonusMessage = "Bonus = $" + (.02 * salary);
    System.out.println(bonusMessage);
  } // end main
} // end class BonusCalculator
```

Figure 3.3 BonusCalculator program

In the `bonusMessage` assignment statement, note the parentheses around `.02 * salary`. Although the parentheses are not required by the compiler, we prefer to include them here because they improve the code's readability. They improve readability by making it clear that the math operation (.02 × salary) is separate from the string concatenation operation. Use of discretionary parentheses to enhance clarity is an art. Sometimes it's helpful, but don't get carried away. If you use parentheses too often, your code can look cluttered.

In the `salary` assignment statement, note the 50000. You might be tempted to insert a comma in 50000 to make it read better; that is, you might be tempted to enter 50,000. If you do insert the comma, your program will not compile successfully. In Java programs, numbers are not allowed to have commas. Unfortunately, this makes it easy to accidentally enter the wrong number of zeros in a large number. Count those zeros!

Tracing

As part of a program's presentation, we'll sometimes ask you to trace the program. Tracing forces you to understand program details thoroughly. And understanding program details thoroughly is important for writing good programs. To set up a trace, provide a column heading for each variable and for output. Then execute each statement, starting with the first statement in `main`. For declaration statements, write a ? in the declared variable's column, indicating that the variable exists, but it doesn't have a value yet. For assignment statements, write the assigned value in the variable's column. For a print statement, write the printed value in the output column.[7]

[7] If you'd like a more detailed discussion of tracing, see Chapter 2, Section 2.11.

For your first Java trace, we'll make things easy. Rather than asking you to do a trace on your own, we just ask you to study the completed trace in Figure 3.4. But please do study it. Make sure you understand how all the column values get filled in.[8]

```
1  int salary;
2  String bonusMessage;
3
4  salary = 50000;
5  bonusMessage = "Bonus = $" + (.02 * salary);
6  System.out.println(bonusMessage);
```

line#	salary	bonusMessage	output
1	?		
2		?	
4	50000		
5		Bonus = $1000	
6			Bonus = $1000

Figure 3.4 Calculating a bonus—code fragment and its associated trace

3.12 Initialization Statements

A declaration statement specifies a data type for a particular variable. An assignment statement puts a value into a variable. An initialization statement is a combination of the declaration and assignment statements—it specifies a data type for a variable, and it puts a value into that variable.

The Java language is *strongly typed,* meaning that all variable types are fixed. Once a variable is declared, it cannot be redeclared. Therefore, you can have only one declaration statement for a particular variable. Likewise, since an initialization statement is a specialized form of a declaration statement, you can have only one initialization statement for a particular variable.

Here's the syntax for an initialization statement:

```
<type> <variable> = <value>;
```

And here are some initialization examples:

```
String name = "John Doe"; // student's name
int creditHours = 0;      // student's total credit hours
```

The `name` variable is declared to be a `String` type, and it's given the initial value of "John Doe."[9] The `creditHours` variable is declared to be an `int` and it's given the initial value of 0.

[8] If you run the code fragment on a computer, you'll see a .0 at the end of the output (`Bonus = 1000.0`). The .0 should make sense when you learn about mixed expressions and promotion later in this chapter.

[9] John Doe is commonly used as a filler in the United States and Great Britain when a person's real name is unknown. We use it here as a default value for a student's name. It serves as an indication that the student's real name has not yet been filled in.

Here's an alternative way to do the same thing using declaration and assignment statements (instead of using initialization statements):

```
String name;              // student's name
int creditHours;          // student's total credit hours

name = "John Doe";
creditHours = 0;
```

It's OK to use either technique—initialization or declaration/assignment. You'll see it done both ways in the real world. Initialization has the benefit of compactness. Declaration/assignment has the benefit of leaving more room in the declaration for a comment.

3.13 Numeric Data Types—int, long, float, double

Integers

We've already mentioned one Java numeric data type—`int`. We'll now discuss numeric types in more detail. Variables that hold whole numbers (e.g., 1000, −22) should normally be declared with the `int` data type or the `long` data type. A whole number is a number with no decimal point and no fractional component.

An `int` uses 32 bits of memory. A `long` uses 64 bits of memory (twice as many bits as an `int`). The range of values that can be stored in an `int` variable is approximately −2 billion to +2 billion. The range of values that can be stored in a `long` variable is approximately -9×10^{18} to $+9 \times 10^{18}$. Here's an example that declares `studentId` to be an `int` variable and `satelliteDistanceTraveled` to be a `long` variable:

```
int studentId;
long satelliteDistanceTraveled;
```

If you attempt to store a really big number (a number over 2 billion) in an `int` variable, you'll get an "integer number too large" error when you compile your program. So to be safe, why shouldn't you just always declare your integer variables as type `long` rather than type `int`? An `int` takes up less storage in memory. And using less storage means your computer will run faster because there's more free space. So in the interest of speed/efficiency, use an `int` rather than a `long` for a variable that holds values less than 2 billion.[10] If you're not sure whether a variable will hold values greater than 2 billion, play it safe and use a `long`. If you want the greatest possible precision in financial calculations, convert everything to cents, and use `long` variables to hold all values.

Floating-Point Numbers

In Java, numbers that contain a decimal point (e.g., 66. and −1234.5) are called *floating-point* numbers. Why? Because a floating-point number can be written with different forms by shifting (floating) its decimal point. For example, the number −1234.5 can be written equivalently as -1.2345×10^3. See how the decimal point has "floated" to the left in the second version of the number?

There are two types for floating-point numbers—`float` and `double`. A `float` uses 32 bits of memory. A `double` uses 64 bits of memory. A `double` is called a "double" because it uses twice as many bits as a `float`.

[10] The suggestion to use an `int` for efficiency reasons is valid, but be aware that the speed difference is only occasionally noticeable. It's only noticeable if you've got lots of `long` numbers and you've got a small amount of available memory, such as when you're running a program on a personal digital assistant (PDA).

Here's an example that declares `gpa` as a `float` variable and `cost` as a `double` variable:

```
float gpa;
double cost;
```

The `double` data type is used much more often than the `float` data type. You should normally declare your floating-point variables to be `double` rather than `float` because (1) `double` variables can hold a wider range of numbers[11] and (2) `double` variables can store numbers with greater precision. Greater precision means more significant digits. You can rely on 15 significant digits for a `double` variable but only 6 significant digits for a `float` variable.

Six significant digits may seem like a lot, but for many cases, six significant digits are not enough. With only six significant digits, accuracy errors can creep into `float`-based programs whenever there's a mathematical operation (addition, multiplication, etc.). If such a program performs a significant number of mathematical operations, then the accuracy errors become nontrivial. So as a general rule, use `double` rather than `float` for programs that perform a significant number of floating-point mathematical operations. And since accuracy is particularly important with money, scientific measurements, and engineering measurements, use `double` rather than `float` for calculations that involve those items.

Assignments Between Different Types

You've learned about assigning integer values into integer variables and floating-point values into floating-point variables, but you haven't learned about assignments where the types are different.

Assigning an integer value into a floating-point variable works just fine. Note this example:

```
double bankAccountBalance = 1000;
```

Assigning an integer value into a floating-point variable is like putting a small item into a large box. The `int` type goes up to approximately 2 billion. It's easy to fit 2 billion into a `double` "box" because a `double` goes all the way up to 1.8×10^{308}.

On the other hand, assigning a floating-point value into an integer variable is like putting a large item into a small box. By default, that's illegal.[12] For example, this generates an error:

```
int temperature = 26.7;
```

Since 26.7 is a floating-point value, it cannot be assigned into the `int` variable, `temperature`. That should make sense when you realize that it's impossible to store .7, the fractional portion of 26.7, in an `int`. After all, `int` variables don't store fractions; they store only whole numbers.

This statement also generates an error:

```
int count = 0.0;
```

The rule says that it's illegal to assign a floating-point value into an integer variable. 0.0 is a floating-point value. It doesn't matter that the fractional portion of 0.0 is insignificant (it's .0); 0.0 is still a floating-point value, and it's always illegal to assign a floating-point value into an integer variable. That type of error is known as a *compile-time error* or *compilation error* because the error is identified by the compiler during the compilation process.

Later in the book, we provide additional details about integer and floating-point data types. You don't need those details now, but if you can't wait, you can find the details in Chapter 11, Section 11.2.

[11] A `float` variable can store positive values between 1.2×10^{-38} and $3.4 \times 10^{+38}$ and negative values between $-3.4 \times 10^{+38}$ and -1.2×10^{-38}. A `double` variable can store positive values between 2.2×10^{-308} and $1.8 \times 10^{+308}$ and negative values between $-1.8 \times 10^{+308}$ and -2.2×10^{-308}.

[12] Although such an assignment is normally illegal, you can do it if you add some code. Specifically, you can do it if you add a cast operator. We'll describe cast operators later in this chapter.

3.14 Constants

We've used numeric and string values in our examples, but we haven't given you the formal name for them. Numeric and string values are called *constants*. They're called constants because their values are fixed—they don't change. Here are some examples:

Integer Constants	Floating-Point Constants	String Constants
`8`	`-34.6`	`"Hi, Bob"`
`-45`	`.009`	`"yo"`
`2000000`	`8.`	`"dog"`

For a constant to be a floating-point constant, it must contain a decimal point, but numbers to the right of the decimal point are optional. Thus, 8. and 8.0 represent the same floating-point constant.

What is the default type for integer constants—`int` or `long`? You'd probably guess `int` since integer sounds like `int`. And that guess is correct — the default type for an integer constant is `int`. So the above integer examples (8, −45, and 2000000) are all `int` constants.

What is the default type for floating-point constants—`float` or `double`? Although you might be tempted to say `float`, after the discussion in the previous section, it should not surprise you that Java's default for floating-point constants is `double`. 

Try to identify the compile-time errors in this code fragment:

```
float gpa = 2.30;
float mpg;
mpg = 28.6;
```

The 2.30 and 28.6 constants both default to type `double`, which uses 64 bits. The 64 bits can't squeeze into the 32-bit `gpa` and `mpg` variables so this code generates "possible loss of precision" error messages.

There are two possible solutions for these types of errors. The easiest solution is to use double variables instead of float variables all the time. Here's another solution: Explicitly force the floating-point constants to be `float` by using an `f` or `F` suffix, like this:

Use a larger data type 

```
float gpa = 2.30f;
float mpg;
mpg = 28.6F;
```

Two Categories of Constants

Constants can be split into two categories—hard-coded constants and named constants. The constants we've covered so far can be referred to as hard-coded constants. A *hard-coded constant* is an explicitly specified value. Hard-coded constants are also called *literals*. "Literal" is a good, descriptive term because literals refer to items that are interpreted literally; for example, 5 means 5, "hello" means "hello." In the following statement, the forward slash (/) is the division operator, and `299792458.0` is a hard-coded constant (or literal):

```
propagationDelay = distance / 299792458.0;
```

Assume that this code fragment is part of a program that calculates delays in messages carried through space. What's the meaning behind the value `299792458.0`? Not very obvious, eh? Read on.

In space, message signals travel at the speed of light. Since time = distance / velocity, the time it takes a message signal to travel from a satellite equals the satellite's distance divided by the speed of light. Thus, in the code fragment, the number `299792458.0` represents the speed of light.

The above code fragment is somewhat confusing. The meaning behind the hard-coded constant 299792458.0 may be clear to science techies, but it isn't very clear to the rest of us. For a better solution, use a named constant.

Named Constants

A *named constant* is a constant that has a name associated with it. For example, in this code fragment, SPEED_OF_LIGHT is a named constant:

```
final double SPEED_OF_LIGHT = 299792458.0; // in meters/sec
. . .
propagationDelay = distance / SPEED_OF_LIGHT;
```

As you should be able to discern from this code fragment, a named constant is really a variable. Now there's an oxymoron—a constant is a variable. Note how SPEED_OF_LIGHT is declared to be a double variable, and it's initialized to the value 299792458.0. How is the SPEED_OF_LIGHT initialization different from initializations that you've seen in the past? The word final appears at the left.

The reserved word final is a *modifier*—it modifies SPEED_OF_LIGHT so that its value is fixed or "final." And being fixed is the whole point of a named constant. Thus, all named constants use the final modifier. The final modifier tells the compiler to generate an error if your program ever tries to change the final variable's value at a later time.

Standard coding conventions suggest that you capitalize all characters in a named constant and use an underscore to separate the words in a multiple-word named constant. Example: SPEED_OF_LIGHT. The rationale for the uppercase is that uppercase makes things stand out. And you want named constants to stand out because they represent special values.

Named Constants Versus Hard-Coded Constants

Not all constants should be named constants. For example, if you need to initialize a count variable to 0, use a hard-coded 0 like this:

```
int count = 0;
```

So how do you know when to use a hard-coded constant versus a named constant? Use a named constant if it makes the code easier to understand. The above count initialization is clear the way it is now. If you replace the 0 with a named constant (e.g., int count = COUNT_STARTING_VALUE), it does not improve the clarity, so stick with the hard-coded constant. On the other hand, this code is unclear:

```
propagationDelay = distance / 299792458.0;
```

By replacing 299792458.0 with a SPEED_OF_LIGHT named constant, it does improve the clarity, so switch to the named constant.

There are two main benefits of using named constants:

1. Named constants make code more self-documenting, and therefore more understandable.
2. If a programmer ever needs to change a named constant's value, the change is easy—find the named constant initialization at the top of the method and change the initialization value. That implements the change automatically everywhere within the program. There is no danger of forgetting to change one of many occurrences of some constant value. There is consistency.

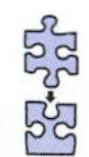
Make it easy to change.

An Example

Let's put what you've learned about constants into practice by using them within a complete program. In Figure 3.5's TemperatureConverter program, we convert a Fahrenheit temperature value to a Celsius temperature value. Note the two named constant initializations at the top of the program: (1) the `FREEZING_POINT` named constant gets initialized to 32.0 and (2) the `CONVERSION_FACTOR` named constant gets initialized to 5.0 / 9.0. Usually, you'll want to initialize each named constant to a single hard-coded constant. For example, `FREEZING_POINT`'s initialization value is 32.0. But be aware that it's legal to use a constant expression for a named constant initialization value. For example, `CONVERSION_FACTOR`'s initialization value is 5.0 / 9.0. That expression is considered to be a constant expression because constant values are used, not variables.

```
/*******************************************************************
* TemperatureConverter.java
* Dean & Dean
*
* This program converts a Fahrenheit temperature to Celsius
*******************************************************************/

public class TemperatureConverter
{
  public static void main(String[] args)
  {
    final double FREEZING_POINT = 32.0;
    final double CONVERSION_FACTOR = 5.0 / 9.0;
    double fahrenheit = 50;    // temperature in Fahrenheit
    double celsius;            // temperature in Celsius

    celsius = CONVERSION_FACTOR * (fahrenheit - FREEZING_POINT);
    System.out.println(fahrenheit + " degrees Fahrenheit = " +
      celsius + " degrees Celsius.");
  } // end main
} // end class TemperatureConverter
```

Output:

```
50.0 degrees Fahrenheit = 10.0 degrees Celsius.
```

Figure 3.5 TemperatureConverter program and its output

In the TemperatureConverter program, this statement performs of the conversion:

```
celsius = CONVERSION_FACTOR * (fahrenheit - FREEZING_POINT);
```

By using named constants, `CONVERSION_FACTOR` and `FREEZING_POINT`, we're able to embed some meaning into the conversion code. Without named constants, the statement would look like this:

```
celsius = 5.0 / 9.0 * (fahrenheit - 32.0);
```

The 5.0 / 9.0 may be distracting to some readers. They may spend time wondering about the significance of the 5.0 and the 9.0. By using a `CONVERSION_FACTOR` named constant, we tell the reader "Don't worry about it; it's just a conversion factor that some scientist came up with." If someone who is unfamiliar with the Fahrenheit scale reads the above statement, they won't know the significance of the 32.0. Using a `FREEZING_POINT` named constant makes things clearer.

3.15 Arithmetic Operators

We've talked about numbers for a while now—how to declare numeric variables, how to assign numbers, and how to work with numeric constants. In addition, we've shown a few examples of using numbers in mathematical expressions. In this section and the next two sections, we study expressions in more depth. An *expression* is a combination of operands and operators that performs a calculation. Operands are variables and constants. An operator is a symbol, like + or -, that performs an operation. In this section, we'll look at arithmetic operators for numeric data types. Later, we'll look at operators for other data types.

Addition, Subtraction, and Multiplication

Java's +, -, and * arithmetic operators should be familiar to you. They perform addition, subtraction, and multiplication, respectively.

Floating-Point Division

Java performs division differently depending on whether the numbers/operands being divided are integers or whether they're floating-point numbers. Let's first discuss floating-point division.

When the Java Virtual Machine (JVM) performs division on floating-point numbers, it performs "calculator division." We call it "calculator division" because Java's floating-point division works the same as division performed by a standard calculator. For example, if you enter this on your calculator, what is the result?

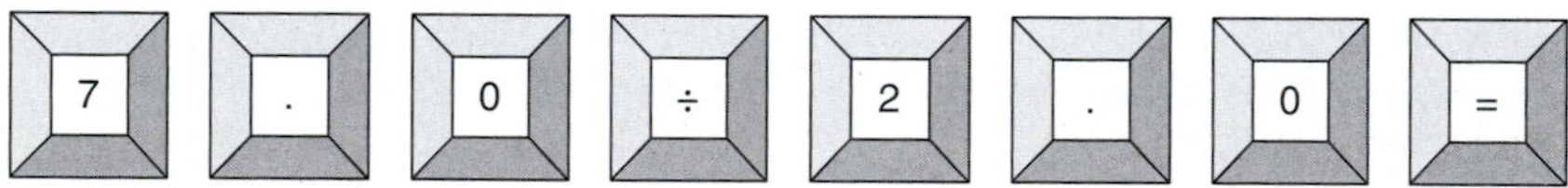

The result is 3.5. Likewise, this line of Java code prints 3.5:

```
System.out.println(7.0 / 2.0);
```

Note that calculators use the ÷ key for division and Java uses the / character.

To explain arithmetic operators, we'll need to evaluate lots of expressions. To simplify that discussion, we'll use the ⇒ symbol. It means "evaluates to." Thus, this next line says that 7.0 / 2.0 evaluates to 3.5:

7.0 / 2.0 ⇒ 3.5

This next line asks you to determine what 5 / 4. evaluates to:

5 / 4. ⇒ ?

5 is an `int` and 4. is a `double`. This is an example of a *mixed expression*. A mixed expression is an expression that contains operands with different data types. `double` values are considered to be more complex than `int` values because `double` values contain a fractional component. Whenever there's a mixed expression, the JVM temporarily *promotes* the less complex operand's type so that it matches the more complex operand's type, and then the JVM applies the operator. In the 5 / 4. expression, the JVM promotes 5 to a

double and then performs floating-point division on the two floating-point values. The expression evaluates to 1.25.

Integer Division

When the JVM performs division on integers, it performs "grade school division." We call it grade school division because Java's integer division works the same as the division you did by hand in grade school. Remember how you calculated two values for each division operation? You calculated a quotient and also a remainder. Likewise, Java has the ability to calculate both a quotient and a remainder when integer division is called for. But Java doesn't calculate both values simultaneously. If Java's / operator is used, then the quotient is calculated. If Java's % operator is used, then the remainder is calculated. The % operator is more formally called the *modulus* operator. Note these examples:

$7 / 2 \Rightarrow 3$

$7 \% 2 \Rightarrow 1$

These correspond to the equivalent grade school arithmetic notation:

```
  3   <---- quotient
2 |7
 -6
  1   <---- remainder
```

We'll give you many expression evaluation problems like this. As a sanity check, we recommend that you verify at least some of the calculated results by executing the expressions on a computer. To execute the expressions, embed the expressions into print statements, embed the print statements into a test program, and run the test program. For example, to execute the above expressions, use the TestExpressions program in Figure 3.6.

Print details to see what computer does.

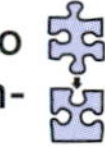

```
public class TestExpressions
{
  public static void main(String[] args)
  {
    System.out.println("7 / 2 = " + (7 / 2));
    System.out.println("7 % 2 = " + (7 % 2));
    System.out.println("8 / 12 = " + (8 / 12));
    System.out.println("8 % 12 = " + (8 % 12));
  } // end main
} // end class TestExpressions
```

Output:

```
7 / 2 = 3
7 % 2 = 1
8 / 12 = 0
8 % 12 = 8
```

Figure 3.6 TestExpressions program and its output

Figure 3.6 also illustrates these additional examples:

8 / 12 ⇒ 0
8 % 12 ⇒ 8

Here is the corresponding grade school arithmetic notation:

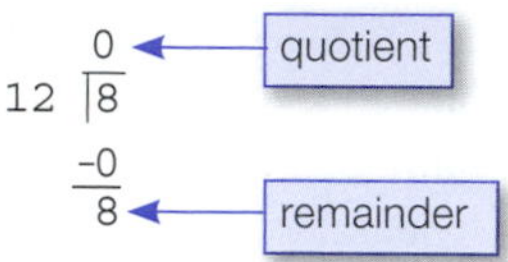

3.16 Expression Evaluation and Operator Precedence

In the above examples, the expressions were pretty basic—they each contained only one operator—so they were fairly easy to evaluate. Expressions are sometimes fairly complicated. In this section, we discuss how to evaluate those more complicated expressions.

Average Bowling Score Example

Suppose you'd like to calculate the average bowling score for three bowling games. Would this statement work?

```
bowlingAverage = game1 + game2 + game3 / 3;
```

The code looks reasonable. But it's not good enough to rely on your sense of what looks reasonable. To be a good programmer, you need to be sure. The code you should be focusing on is the expression on the right side: `game1 + game2 + game3 / 3`. More specifically, you should be asking yourself, "Which operator executes first—the left addition operator or the division operator?" To answer that question, we turn to the operator precedence table.

Operator Precedence Table

The key to understanding complicated expressions is to understand the operator precedence shown in Figure 3.7. Please study Figure 3.7's operator precedence table now.

The operator precedence table might need some clarification. The groups at the top have higher precedence than the groups at the bottom. That means that if one of the top operators appears in an expression along with one of the bottom operators, then the top operator executes first. For example, if * and + both appear in the same expression, then the * operator executes before the + operator (because the * operator's group is higher in the table than the + operator's group). If parentheses appear within an expression, then the items inside the parentheses execute before the items that are outside the parentheses (because parentheses are at the very top of the table).

If an expression has two or more operators in the same group (from Figure 3.7's groups), then apply the operators from left to right. In mathematics, that's referred to as *left-to-right associativity*. In Java, that means that operators appearing at the left should be executed before operators appearing at the right. For example, since the * and / operator are in the same group, if * and / both appear in the same expression and / appears further to the left than * within that expression, division is performed before multiplication.

1. grouping with parentheses:
   (<*expression*>)
2. unary operators:
   ```
   +x
   -x
   (<type>) x
   ```
3. multiplication and division operators:
   ```
   x * y
   x / y
   x % y
   ```
4. addition and subtraction operators:
   ```
   x + y
   x - y
   ```

precedence.

Figure 3.7 Abbreviated operator precedence table (see Appendix 2 for the complete table)
Operator groups at the top of the table have higher precedence than operator groups at the bottom of the table. All operators within a particular group have equal precedence, and they evaluate left to right.

The operators in the second-from-the-top group are *unary operators*. A unary operator is an operator that applies to just one operand. The unary + operator is cosmetic; it does nothing. The unary - operator (negation) reverses the sign of its operand. For example, if the variable x contains a 6, then -x evaluates to a negative 6. The (<*type*>) operator represents the cast operators. We'll get to cast operators later in this chapter.

Average Bowling Score Example Revisited

Let's return to the average bowling score example and apply what you've learned about operator precedence. Does the following statement correctly calculate the average bowling score for three bowling games?

```
bowlingAverage = game1 + game2 + game3 / 3;
```

No. The operator precedence table says that the / operator has higher priority than the + operator, so division is performed first. After the JVM divides game3 by 3, the JVM adds game1 and game2. The correct way to calculate the average is to add the three game scores first and then divide the sum by 3. In other words, you need to force the + operators to execute first. The solution is to use parentheses like this:

```
bowlingAverage = (game1 + game2 + game3) / 3;
```

Expression Evaluation Practice

Let's do some expression evaluation practice problems to ensure that you really understand this operator precedence material. Given these initializations:

Hand calculation helps your understanding.

```
int a = 5, b = 2;
double c = 3.0;
```

What does the following expression evaluate to?

```
(c + a / b) / 10 * 5
```

Here's the solution:

```
1. (c + a / b) / 10 * 5 ⇒
2. (3.0 + 5 / 2) / 10 * 5 ⇒
3. (3.0 + 2) / 10 * 5 ⇒
4. 5.0 / 10 * 5⇒
5. 0.5 * 5 ⇒
6. 2.5
```

In solving expression evaluation problems, we recommend that you show each step of the evaluation process so your solution is easy to follow. In the above solution, we show each step, and we also show line numbers. There's normally no need to show line numbers, but we do it here to help with our explanation. From line 1 to line 2, we replace variables with their values. From line 2 to line 3, we evaluate the highest priority operator, the / inside the parentheses. From line 3 to line 4, we evaluate the next highest priority operator, the + inside the parentheses. Study the remaining lines on your own.

Let's do one more expression evaluation practice problem. Given these initializations:

```
int x = 5;
double y = 3.0;
```

What does the following expression evaluate to?

```
(0 % x) + y + (0 / x)
```

Here's the solution:

```
(0 % x) + y + (0 / x) ⇒
(0 % 5) + 3.0 + (0 / 5) ⇒
0 + 3.0 + (0 / 5) ⇒
0 + 3.0 + 0 ⇒
3.0
```

Perhaps the trickiest part of the above solution is evaluating 0 % 5 and 0 / 5. They both evaluate to 0. This grade school arithmetic notation shows why:

```
   0  ◄── quotient
5 |0
  -0
   0  ◄── remainder
```

3.17 More Operators: Increment, Decrement, and Compound Assignment

So far, we've covered Java math operators that correspond to operations found in math books—addition, subtraction, multiplication, and division. Java provides additional math operators that have no counterparts in math books. In this section, we'll talk about the increment, decrement, and compound assignment operators.

Increment and Decrement Operators

It's fairly common for a computer program to count the number of times something occurs. For example, have you ever seen a Web page that displays the number of "visitors"? The number of visitors is tracked by a program that counts the number of times the Web page has been loaded on someone's Web browser. Since counting is such a common task for programs, there are special operators for counting. The increment operator (++) counts up by 1. The decrement operator (--) counts down by 1.

Here's one way to increment the variable *x*:

```
x = x + 1;
```

And here's how to do it using the increment operator:

```
x++;
```

The two techniques are equivalent in terms of their functionality. Experienced Java programmers almost always use the second form rather than the first form. And proper style suggests using the second form. So use the second form.

Here's one way to decrement the variable *x*:

```
x = x - 1;
```

And here's how to do it using the decrement operator:

```
x--;
```

Once again, you should use the second form.

Compound Assignment Operators

Let's now discuss five of Java's *compound assignment* operators: +=, -=, *=, /=, and %=.

The += operator updates a variable by adding a specified value to the variable. Here's one way to increment x by 3:

```
x = x + 3;
```

And here's how to do it using the += operator:

```
x += 3;
```

The two techniques are equivalent in terms of their functionality. Experienced Java programmers almost always use the shorter second form rather than the longer first form. And proper style suggests using the second form. So use the second form.

Look for shortcuts.

The -= operator updates a variable by subtracting a specified value from the variable. Here's one way to decrement + by 3:

```
x = x - 3;
```

And here's how to do it using the -= operator:

```
x -= 3;
```

Once again, you should use the second form.

The *=, /=, and %= operators parallel the += and -= operators so we won't bore you with detailed explanations for those remaining three operators. But we do encourage you to study the *=, /=, and %= examples shown below:

```
x += 3;        ≡    x = x + 3;
x -= 4;        ≡    x = x - 4;
x *= y;        ≡    x = x * y;
x /= 4;        ≡    x = x / 4;
x %= 16;       ≡    x = x % 16;
x *= y + 1;    ≡    x = x * (y + 1);
```

The examples show assignment operator statements on the left and their equivalent long-form statements on the right. The ≡ symbol means "is equivalent to." It's better style to use the forms on the left rather than the forms on the right, but don't ignore the forms on the right. They show how the assignment operators work.

The bottom example is the only one in which the compound assignment operator uses an expression rather than a single value; that is, the expression to the right of the *= assignment operator is y + 1, rather than just 1. For cases like these, the compound assignment form is somewhat confusing. Therefore, for these cases, it's acceptable style-wise to use the equivalent long form rather than the compound assignment form.

Why are the +=, -=, *=, /=, and %= operators called compound assignment operators? Because they compound/combine a math operation with the assignment operation. For example, the += operator performs addition and assignment. The addition part is obvious, but what about the assignment part? The += does indeed perform assignment because the variable at the left of the += is assigned a new value.

3.18 Tracing

To make sure that you really understand the increment, decrement, and compound assignment operators, let's trace a program that contains those operators. Earlier in the chapter, we showed a trace, but the trace was for a very limited code fragment—the code fragment contained two assignment statements and that was it. In this section, we present a more complicated trace.

See the TestOperators program and associated trace table in Figure 3.8. In particular, look at the first three lines under the heading in the trace table. They contain the variables' initial values. For variables declared as part of an initialization, their initial value is the initialization value. For variables declared without an initialization, we say their initial value is *garbage* because its actual value is unknown. Use a question mark to indicate a garbage value.

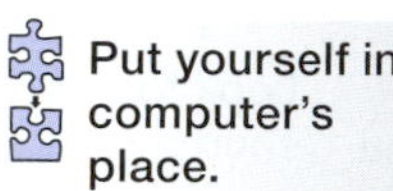
Put yourself in computer's place.

We suggest you cover up the bottom part of the trace, and try to complete the trace on your own. When you're done, compare your answer to Figure 3.8's trace table.

There are different modes for the increment and decrement operators—prefix mode and postfix mode. Later in the book, we explain the modes and provide details on how they work within the context of a trace. You don't need those details now, but if you can't wait, you can find the details in Chapter 11, Section 11.5.

3.19 Type Casting

We've now described simple arithmetic operators (+, -, *, /, %), increment and decrement operators (++, --), and compound assignment operators (+=, -=, *=, /=, %=). In this section, we'll discuss yet another operator, the cast operator.

```
1   public class TestOperators
2   {
3     public static void main(String[] args)
4     {
5       int x;
6       int y = 2;
7       double z = 3.0;
8
9       x = 5;
10      System.out.println("x + y + z = " + (x + y + z));
11      x += y;
12      y++;
13      z--;
14      z *= x;
15      System.out.println("x + y + z = " + (x + y + z));
16    } // end main
17  } // end class TestOperators
```

Trace:

line#	x	y	z	output
5	?			
6		2		
7			3.0	
9	5			
10				x + y + z = 10.0
11	7			
12		3		
13			2.0	
14			14.0	
15				x + y + z = 24.0

Figure 3.8 TestOperators program and its trace

Cast Operator

In writing a program, you'll sometimes need to convert a value to a different data type. The cast operator can be used to perform that sort of conversion. Here's the syntax:

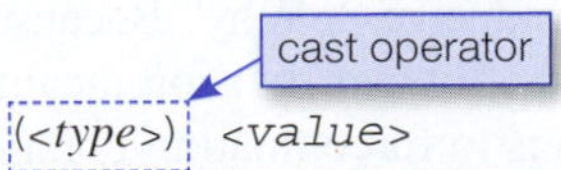

As shown above, a cast operator consists of a data type inside parentheses. You should place a cast operator at the left of the value that you'd like to convert.

Suppose you've got a variable named `interest` that stores a bank account's interest as a `double`. You'd like to extract the dollars portion of the interest and store it in a variable of type `int` that is named `interestInDollars`. To do that, use the `int` cast operator like this:

```
interestInDollars = (int) interest;
```

The `int` cast operator returns the whole number portion of the casted value, truncating the fractional portion. Thus, if `interest` contains the value 56.96, after the assignment, `interestInDollars` contains the value 56. Note that the cast operation does not change the value of `interest`. After the assignment, `interest` still contains 56.96.

Use Parentheses to Cast an Expression

If you ever need to cast more than just a single value or variable, then make sure to put parentheses around the entire expression that you want to cast. Note this example:

```
double interestRate;
double balance;
int interestInDollars;
. . .
interestInDollars = (int) (balance * interestRate);
```

Parentheses are necessary here

In the `interestInDollars` assignment, `balance * interestRate` is the formula for calculating interest. This code fragment performs basically the same operation as the previous one-line code fragment. It extracts the dollars portion of the interest and stores it in an `int` variable named `interestInDollars`. The difference is that the interest this time is in the form of an expression, `balance * interestRate`, rather than in the form of a simple variable, `interest`. Since we want the cast operator to apply to the entire expression, we need to put parentheses around `balance * interestRate`.

In the above code fragment, what would happen if there were no parentheses around the expression, `balance * interestRate`? The cast would then apply only to the first thing at its right, `balance`, rather than the entire expression. That should make sense when you look at the operator precedence table. The operator precedence table shows that the cast operator has very high precedence. So without the parentheses, the cast operator would execute prior to the multiplication operator, and the cast would thus apply only to `balance`. And that leads to an incorrect calculation for interest in dollars.

Use a Floating-Point Cast to Force Floating-Point Division

Suppose you've got a variable named `earnedPoints` that stores a student's earned grade points for a semester's worth of classes. Suppose you've got a variable named `numOfClasses` that stores the number of classes taken by the student. The student's grade point average (GPA) is calculated by dividing earned points by number of classes. In the following statement, `earnedPoints` and `numOfClasses` are `int`s and `gpa` is a `double`. Does the statement correctly calculate the student's GPA?

```
gpa = earnedPoints / numOfClasses;
```

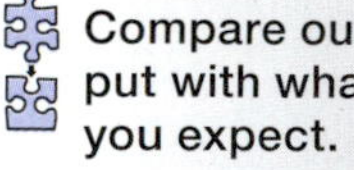
Compare output with what you expect.

Suppose `earnedPoints` holds 14 and `numOfClasses` holds 4. You'd like `gpa` to get a value of 3.5 (because 14 ÷ 4 = 3.5). But alas, `gpa` gets a value of 3. Why? Because the `/` operator performs integer division on its two `int` operands. Integer division means the quotient is returned. The quotient of 14 ÷ 4 is 3. The solution is to force floating-point division by introducing the cast operator. Here's the corrected code:

```
gpa = (double) earnedPoints / numOfClasses;
```

After casting earnedPoints to a double, the JVM sees a mixed expression and promotes numOfClasses to a double. Then floating-point division takes place.

For this example, you should not put parentheses around the earnedPoints / numOfClasses expression. If you did so, the / operator would have higher precedence than the cast operator, and the JVM would perform division (integer division) prior to performing the cast operation.

Later in the book, we provide additional details about type conversions. You don't need those details now, but if you can't wait, you can find the details in Chapter 11, Section 11.4.

3.20 char Type and Escape Sequences

In the past, when we've stored or printed text, we've always worked with groups of text characters (strings), not with individual characters. In this section, we'll use the char type to work with individual characters.

char Type

If you know that you'll need to store a single character in a variable, use a char variable. Here's an example that declares a char variable named ch and assigns the letter *A* into it.

```
char ch;
ch = 'A';
```

Note the 'A'. That's a char literal. char literals must be surrounded by single quotes. That syntax parallels the syntax for string literals—string literals must be surrounded by double quotes.

What's the point of having a char type? Why not just use one-character strings for all character processing? Because for applications that manipulate lots of individual characters, it's more efficient (faster) to use char variables, which are simple, rather than string variables, which are more complex. For example, the software that allows you to view Web pages has to read and process individual characters as they're downloaded onto your computer. In processing the individual characters, it's more efficient if they're stored as separate char variables rather than as string variables.

String Concatenation with char

Remember how you can use the + symbol to concatenate two strings together? You can also use the + symbol to concatenate a char and a string. What do you think this code fragment prints?

```
char first, middle, last;      // a person's initials

first = 'J';
middle = 'S';
last = 'D';
System.out.println("Hello, " + first + middle + last + '!');
```

Here's the output:

```
Hello, JSD!
```

Escape Sequences

Usually, it's easy to print characters. Just stick them inside a System.out.println statement. But some characters are hard to print. We use *escape sequences* to print hard-to-print characters such as the tab character. An escape sequence is comprised of a backslash (\) and another character. See Java's most popular escape sequences in Figure 3.9.

`\t`	move the cursor to the next tab stop
`\n`	newline—go to first column in next line
`\r`	return to first column in current line
`\"`	print a literal double quote
`\'`	print a literal single quote
`\\`	print a literal backslash

Figure 3.9 Common escape sequences

If you print the tab character (`\t`), the computer screen's cursor moves to the next tab stop. The computer screen's cursor is the position on the screen where the computer prints next. If you print the newline character (`\n`), the computer screen's cursor moves to the beginning of the next line.

Here's an example of how you could print two column headings, BALANCE and INTEREST, separated by a tab, and followed by a blank line:

```
System.out.println("BALANCE" + '\t' + "INTEREST" + '\n');
```

Note that escape sequences are indeed characters, so to print the tab and newline characters, we've surrounded them with single quotes.

Normally the compiler interprets a double quote, a single quote, or a backslash as a *control character*. A control character is in charge of providing special meaning to the character(s) that follows it. The double quote control character tells the computer that the subsequent characters are part of a string literal. Likewise, the single quote control character tells the computer that the subsequent character is a `char` literal. The backslash control character tells the computer that the next character is to be interpreted as an escape sequence character.

But what if you'd like to print one of those three characters as is and bypass the character's control functionality? To do that, preface the control character (double quote, single quote, backslash) with a backslash. The initial backslash turns off the subsequent character's control functionality and thus allows the subsequent character to be printed as is. If that doesn't make sense, all you really have to know is this:

To print a double quote, use `\"`.

To print a single quote, use `\'`.

To print a backslash, use `\\`.

Suppose you'd like to print this message:

```
"Hello.java" is stored in the c:\javaPgms folder.
```

Here's how to do it:

```
System.out.println('\"' + "Hello.java" + '\"' +
  " is stored in the c:" + '\\' + "javaPgms folder.");
```

Embedding an Escape Sequence within a String

Write a print statement that generates this heading for a computer-specifications report:

```
HARD DISK SIZE      RAM SIZE ("MEMORY")
```

Specifically, your print statement should generate a tab, a HARD DISK SIZE column heading, two more tabs, a RAM SIZE ("MEMORY") column heading, and then two blank lines. Here's one solution:

```
System.out.println('\t' + "HARD DISK SIZE" + '\t' + '\t' +
  "RAM SIZE (" + '\"' + "MEMORY" + '\"' + ")" + '\n' + '\n');
```

That's pretty cluttered. Fortunately, there's a better way. An escape sequence is designed to be used like any other character within a string of text, so it's perfectly acceptable to embed escape sequences within strings and omit the +'s and the single quotes. For example, here's an alternative solution for the PC specifications report heading problem where the +'s and single quotes have been removed:

Look for shortcuts.

```
System.out.println("\tHARD DISK SIZE\t\tRAM SIZE (\"MEMORY\")\n\n");
```

Everything is now all within just one string literal. By omitting the +'s and single quotes, the clutter is reduced and that makes everyone happy. (Exception—author John's preschoolers love clutter and would thus abhor this second solution.)

Origin of the Word "Escape" for Escape Sequences

Why is the word "escape" used for escape sequences? The backslash forces an "escape" from the normal behavior of a specified character. For example, if `t` is in a print statement, the computer normally prints `t`. If `\t` is in a print statement, the computer escapes from printing `t`; instead it prints the tab character. If the double quote character (`"`) is in a print statement, the computer normally treats it as the start or end of a string literal. If `\"` is in a print statement, the computer escapes from the start/end string behavior; instead the computer prints the double quote character.

Later in the book, we present relatively advanced syntax details that pertain to the `char` type. You don't need those details now, but if you can't wait, you can find the details in Chapter 11, Section 11.3.

3.21 Primitive Variables Versus Reference Variables

Throughout the chapter, we've defined and discussed various types of variables—`String`, `int`, `long`, `float`, `double`, and `char` variables. It's now time to step back and get a big-picture view of the two different categories of variables in Java—primitive variables and reference variables.

Primitive Variables

A *primitive variable* stores a single piece of data. It's helpful to think of a primitive variable's data item as being inherently indivisible. More formally, we say that it's "atomic" because, like an atom, it's a basic "building block" and it cannot be broken apart.[13] Primitive variables are declared with a *primitive type,* and those types include:

`int, long`	(integer types)
`float, double`	(floating-point types)
`char`	(character type)

[13] The word "atom" comes from the Greek *a-tomos* and means indivisible. In 1897, J. J. Thomson discovered one of the atom's components—the electron—and thus dispelled the notion of an atom's indivisibility. Nonetheless, as a holdover from the original definition of atom, the term "atomic" still refers to something that is inherently indivisible.

There are additional primitive types (`boolean`, `byte`, `short`), which we'll get to in Chapters 4 and 11, but for most situations these five primitive types are sufficient.

Reference Variables

Whereas a primitive variable stores a single piece of data, a *reference variable* stores a memory location that points to a collection of data. This memory location is not a literal memory address, like a street address. It's a coded abbreviation, like a post-office box number. However, for everything you can do in Java, the value in a reference variable acts exactly like a literal memory address, so we'll pretend it is one. We said a reference variable's "address" points to a collection of data. More formally, it points to an *object*. You'll learn about object details in Chapter 6, but for now, just realize that an object is a collection of related data wrapped in a protective shell. To access an object's data, you need to use a reference variable (or *reference* for short) that points to the object.

String variables are examples of reference variables. A string variable holds a memory address that points to a string object. The string object holds the data—the string's characters.

Reference variables are declared with a *reference type*. A reference type is a type that provides for the storage of a collection of data. `String` is a reference type, and it provides for the storage of a collection of characters. So in the following example, declaring `name` with a `String` reference type means that `name` points to the collection of characters T, h, a, n, h, space, N, g, u, y, e, n.

```
String name = "Thanh Nguyen";
```

`String` is just one reference type from among a multitude of reference types. Classes, arrays, and interfaces are all considered to be reference types. You'll learn about arrays in Chapter 10 and interfaces in Chapter 13. You'll learn about class details in Chapter 6, but for now, it's good enough to know that a class is a generic description of the data in a particular type of object. For example, the `String` class describes the nature of the data in string objects. More specifically, the `String` class says that each string object can store zero or more characters and the characters are stored in a sequence.

An Example

Let's look at an example that uses primitive variables and reference variables. In this code fragment, we declare variables that keep track of a person's basic data:

```
int ssn;        // social security number
String name;    // person's name
Calendar bday; // person's birthday
```

As you can tell by the `int` and `String` data types, `ssn` is a primitive variable and `name` is a reference variable. In the third line, `Calendar` is a class. That tells us that `bday` is a reference variable. The `Calendar` class allows you to store date information such as year, month, and day.[14] Since `bday` is declared with the `Calendar` class, `bday` is able to store year, month, and day data items.

3.22 Strings

We've used strings for quite a while now, but we've stored them and printed them and that's it. Many programs need to do more with strings than just store and print. For example, Microsoft Office programs

[14] Explaining the `Calendar` class in depth is beyond the scope of this chapter. If you want an in-depth explanation, go to Sun's Java documentation Web site (http://java.sun.com/javase/6/docs/api/) and search for `Calendar`.

(Word, Excel, PowerPoint) all include text search and text replace capabilities. In this section, we describe how Java provides that sort of string-manipulation functionality in the `String` class.

String Concatenation

As you know, strings are normally concatenated with the + operator. Note that strings can also be concatenated with the += compound assignment operator. In the following example, if the `animal` string references "dog" originally, it references "dogfish" after the statement is executed:

```
animal += "fish";
```

We recommend that you now go through a trace to make sure you thoroughly understand string concatenation. See the code fragment in Figure 3.10. Try to trace the code fragment on your own prior to looking at the solution.

Put yourself in computer's place.

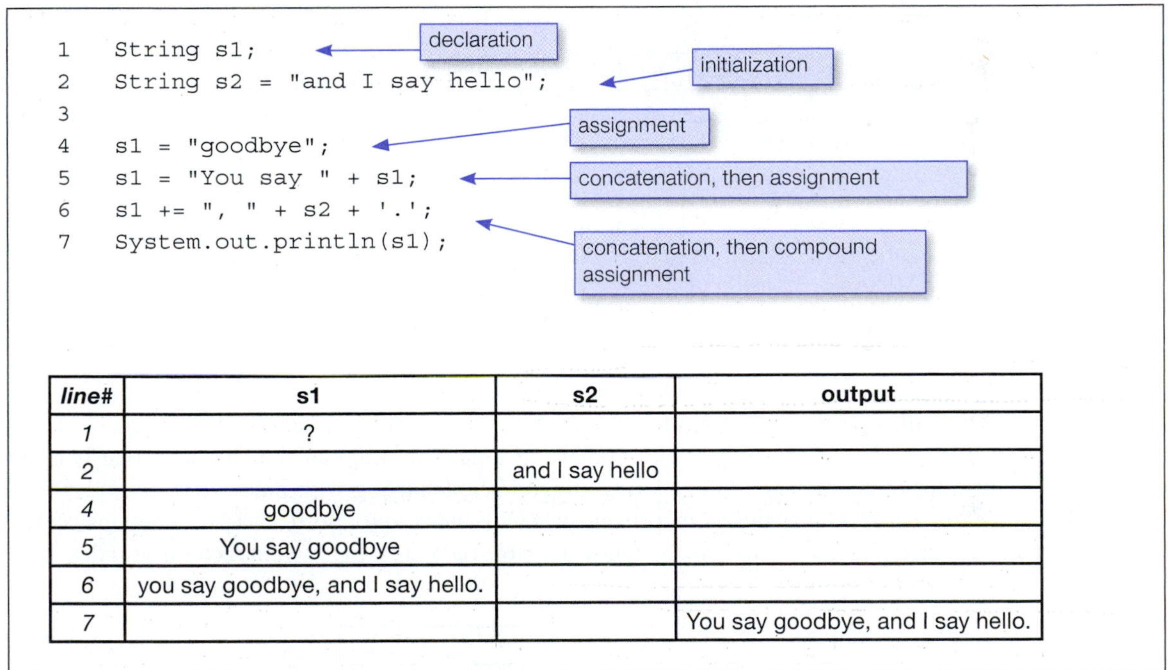

```
1   String s1;
2   String s2 = "and I say hello";
3
4   s1 = "goodbye";
5   s1 = "You say " + s1;
6   s1 += ", " + s2 + '.';
7   System.out.println(s1);
```


line#	s1	s2	output
1	?		
2		and I say hello	
4	goodbye		
5	You say goodbye		
6	you say goodbye, and I say hello.		
7			You say goodbye, and I say hello.

Figure 3.10 Code fragment and associated trace for string concatenation illustration

String Methods

In the previous section, we defined an object to be a collection of data. An object's data is normally protected, and, as such, it can be accessed only through special channels. Normally, it can be accessed only through the object's methods. A string object stores a collection of characters, and a string object's characters can be accessed only through its `charAt` method. In the remainder of this section, we'll describe the `charAt` method as well as three other popular string methods—`length`, `equals`, and `equalsIgnoreCase`. These methods, as well as many about other string methods, are defined in the `String` class.

If you'd like to learn more about the `String` class and all of its methods, visit Sun's Java documentation Web site, http://java.sun.com/javase/6/docs/api/, and follow links that take you to the `String` class.

Get help from the source.

The `charAt` Method

Suppose you initialize a string variable, `animal`, with the value "cow". The `animal` variable then points to a string object that contains three data items—the three characters 'c', 'o', and 'w'. To retrieve a data item (i.e., a character), call the `charAt` method. `charAt` stands for character at. The `charAt` method returns a character at a specified position. For example, if `animal` calls `charAt` and specifies the third position, then `charAt` returns 'w' because 'w' is the third character in "cow".

So how do you call the `charAt` method? Let us answer that question by comparing a `charAt` method call to a method call that you're already comfortable with—the `println` method call. See Figure 3.11.

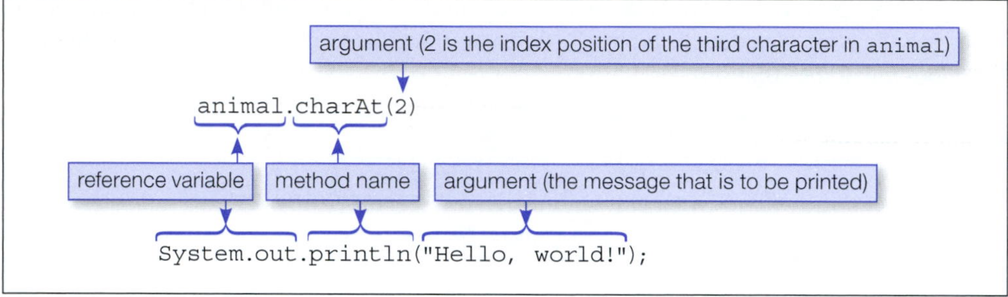

Figure 3.11 Comparison of `charAt` method call to `println` method call

In Figure 3.11, note how the `charAt` method call and the `println` method call both use this syntax:

<reference-variable> . *<method-name>* (*<argument>*)

In the `charAt` call, `animal` is the reference variable, `charAt` is the method name and 2 is the argument. The argument is the tricky part. The argument specifies the *index* of the character that is to be returned. The positions of characters within a string are numbered starting with index zero, not index one. For emphasis, we say again! The positions in a string start with index zero. So if `animal` contains "cow," what does `animal.charAt(2)` return? As the following table indicates, the 'w' character is at index 2, so `animal.charAt(2)` returns 'w.'

index:	0	1	2
"cow" string's characters:	c	o	w

If you call `charAt` with an argument that's negative or that's equal to or greater than the string's length, your code will compile OK, but it won't run properly. For example, suppose you run this program:

```
public class Test
{
  public static void main(String[] args)
  {
    String animal = "sloth";
    System.out.println("Last character: " + animal.charAt(5));
  }
}
```

inappropriate index

Since `sloth`'s last index is 4, not 5, the JVM prints an error message. More specifically, it prints this:

```
Exception in thread "main"
java.lang.StringIndexOutOfBoundsException:
  String index out of range: 5
  at java.lang.String.charAt(String.java:558)
  at Test.main(Test.java:6)
```

The 5 refers to the specified index; it is "out of range."

The 6 refers to the line number in the program where the error occurred.

At first, such error messages are intimidating and depressing, but eventually you'll learn to love them. Well, maybe not quite love them, but you'll learn to appreciate the information they provide. They provide information about the type of error and where the error occurred. Try to view each error message as a learning opportunity! At this point, don't worry about understanding all the details in the above error message. Just focus on the two callouts and the lines that they refer to.

Ask: What is computer trying to tell me?

The above error is an example of a *runtime error*. A runtime error is an error that occurs while a program is running, and it causes the program to terminate abnormally. Said another way, it causes the program to *crash*.

The `length` Method

The `length` method returns the number of characters in a particular string. What does this code fragment print?

```
String s1 = "hi";
String s2 = "";
System.out.println("number of characters in s1 = " + s1.length());
System.out.println("number of characters in s2 = " + s2.length());
```

Since `s1`'s string contains two characters ('h' and 'i'), the first print statement prints this:

```
number of characters in s1 = 2
```

`s2` is initialized with the `""` value. The `""` value is commonly known as the *empty string*. An empty string is a string that contains no characters. Its length is zero. The second print statement prints this:

```
number of characters in s2 = 0
```

In calling the `charAt` method, you need to insert an argument (an index value) in the method call's parentheses. For example, `animal.charAt(2)`. On the other hand, in calling the `length` method, there's no need to insert an argument in the method call's parentheses. For example, `s1.length()`. You may be thinking "With no argument, why bother with the parentheses?" In calling a method, you always need parentheses, even if they're empty. Without the parentheses, the compiler won't know that the method call is a method call.

The `equals` Method

To compare two strings for equality, it's necessary to step through the characters in both strings and compare same-positioned characters, one at a time. Fortunately, you don't have to write code to do that rather tedious comparison operation every time you want to see if two strings are equal. You just have to call the equals method, and it does the tedious comparison operation automatically, behind the scenes. More succinctly, the equals method returns true if two strings contain the exact same sequence of characters. It returns false otherwise.

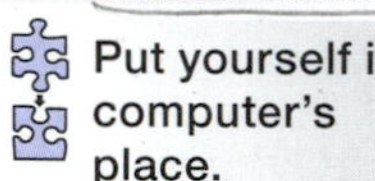

Put yourself in computer's place.

We recommend that you now go through a trace to make sure you thoroughly understand the equals method. See the code fragment in Figure 3.12. Try to trace the code fragment on your own prior to looking at the solution.

```
1   String animal1 = "Horse";
2   String animal2 = "Fly";
3   String newCreature;
4
5   newCreature = animal1 + animal2;
6   System.out.println(newCreature.equals("HorseFly"));
7   System.out.println(newCreature.equals("horsefly"));
```

line#	animal 1	animal 2	newCreature	output
1	Horse			
2		Fly		
3			?	
5			HorseFly	
6				true
7				false

Figure 3.12 Code fragment that illustrates the equals method and its associated trace

Since newCreature contains the value "HorseFly", the equals method returns a value of true when newCreature is compared to "HorseFly". On the other hand, when newCreature is compared to lowercase "horsefly", the equals method returns a value of false.

The equalsIgnoreCase Method

Sometimes, you might want to disregard uppercase versus lowercase when comparing strings. In other words, you might want "HorseFly" and "horsefly" to be considered equal. To test for case-insensitive equality, call the equalsIgnoreCase method.

What does this code fragment print?

```
System.out.println("HorseFly".equalsIgnoreCase("horsefly"));
```

Since equalsIgnoreCase considers "HorseFly" and "horsefly" to be equal, the code fragment prints true.

3.23 Input—the Scanner Class

Programs are normally a two-way street. They produce output by displaying something on the computer screen, and they read input from the user. Up to this point, all our Java programs and code fragments have gone just one way—they've displayed something on the screen, but they haven't read any input. With no input, our programs have been rather limited. In this section, we'll discuss how to get input from a user. With input, we'll be able to write programs that are much more flexible and useful.

Ask: What if?

Suppose you're asked to write a program that calculates earnings for a retirement fund. If there's no input, your program must make assumptions about contribution amounts, years before retirement, and so on. Your program then calculates earnings based on those assumptions. Bottom line: Your no-input program calculates earnings for one specific retirement-fund plan. If input is used, your program asks the user to supply contribution amounts, years before retirement, and so forth. Your program then calculates earnings based on those user inputs. So which version of the program is better—the no-input version or the input version? The input version is better because it allows the user to plug in what-if scenarios. What happens if I contribute more money? What happens if I postpone retirement until I'm 90?

Input Basics

Sun provides a pre-built class named `Scanner`, which allows you to get input from either a keyboard or a file. We describe file input in Chapter 15. Prior to that, when we talk about input, you should assume that we're talking about keyboard input.

The `Scanner` class is not part of the core Java language. So if you use the `Scanner` class, you need to tell the compiler where to find it. You do that by importing the `Scanner` class into your program. More specifically, you need to include this `import` statement at the top of your program (right after your prologue section):

```
import java.util.Scanner;
```

We describe `import` details (like what is `java.util`?) in Chapter 5. For now, suffice it to say that you need to import the `Scanner` class in order to prepare your program for input.

There's one more thing you need to do to prepare your program for input. Insert this statement at the top of your `main` method:

```
Scanner stdIn = new Scanner(System.in);
```

The `new Scanner(System.in)` expression creates an object. As you now know, an object stores a collection of data. In this case, the object stores characters entered by a user at a keyboard. The `stdIn` variable is a reference variable, and it gets initialized to the address of the newly created `Scanner` object. After the initialization, the `stdIn` variable allows you to perform input operations.

With the above overhead in place, you can read and store a line of input by calling the `nextLine` method like this:

```
<variable> = stdIn.nextLine();
```

Let's put what you've learned into practice by using the `Scanner` class and the `nextLine` method call in a complete program. See the FriendlyHello program in Figure 3.13. The program prompts the user to enter his/her name, saves the user's name in a `name` variable, and then prints a greeting with the user's name embedded in the greeting.

In the FriendlyHello program, note the "Enter your name: " print statement. It uses a `System.out.print` statement rather than a `System.out.println` statement. Remember what the "ln" in `println` stands for? It stands for "line." The `System.out.println` statement prints a message and then moves the screen's cursor to the next line. On the other hand, the `System.out.print` statement prints a message and that's it. The cursor ends up on the same line as the printed message (just to the right of the last printed character).

```
/*******************************************************************
* FriendlyHello.java
* Dean & Dean
*
* This program displays a personalized Hello greeting.
*******************************************************************/

import java.util.Scanner;

public class FriendlyHello
{
  public static void main(String[] args)
  {
    Scanner stdIn = new Scanner(System.in);
    String name;
    System.out.print("Enter your name: ");
    name = stdIn.nextLine();
    System.out.println("Hello " + name + "!");
  } // end main
} // end class FriendlyHello
```

These two statements create a keyboard-input connection.

This gets a line of input.

Figure 3.13 FriendlyHello program

So why did we bother to use a `print` statement instead of a `println` statement for the "Enter your name:" prompt? Because users are used to entering input just to the right of a prompt message. If we used `println`, then the user would have to enter input on the next line. One additional item: We inserted a colon and a blank space at the end of the prompt. Once again, the rationale is that that's what users are used to.

Input Methods

In the FriendlyHello program, we called the `Scanner` class's `nextLine` method to get a line of input. The `Scanner` class contains quite a few other methods that get different forms of input. Here are some of those methods:

`nextInt()`	Skip leading whitespace until an `int` value is found. Return the `int` value.
`nextLong()`	Skip leading whitespace until a `long` value is found. Return the `long` value.
`nextFloat()`	Skip leading whitespace until a `float` value is found. Return the `float` value.
`nextDouble()`	Skip leading whitespace until a `double` value is found. Return the `double` value.
`next()`	Skip leading whitespace until a token is found. Return the token as a `String` value.

The above descriptions need some clarification:

1. What is leading whitespace?
   Whitespace refers to all characters that appear as blanks on a display screen or printer. This includes the space character, the tab character, and the newline character. The newline character is generated with the enter key. *Leading whitespace* refers to whitespace characters that are at the left side of the input.

2. What happens if the user provides invalid input?
   The JVM prints an error message and stops the program. For example, if a user enters 45g or 45.0 in response to a `nextInt()` call, the JVM prints an error message and stops the program.
3. The `next` method looks for a token. What is a token?
   Think of a *token* as a word since the `next` method is usually used for reading in a single word. But more formally, a *token* is a sequence of non-whitespace characters. For example, "gecko" and "B@a!" are tokens. But "Gila monster" is not a token because of the space between "Gila" and "monster."

Examples

To make sure you understand `Scanner` methods, study the programs in Figures 3.14 and 3.15. They illustrate how to use the `nextDouble`, `nextInt`, and `next` methods. Pay particular attention to the sample sessions. The sample sessions show what happens when the programs run with typical sets of input. In

```
/*************************************************************
* PrintPO.java
* Dean & Dean
*
* This program calculates and prints a purchase order amount.
*************************************************************/

import java.util.Scanner;

public class PrintPO
{
  public static void main(String[] args)
  {
    Scanner stdIn = new Scanner(System.in);
    double price;   // price of purchase item
    int qty;        // number of items purchased

    System.out.print("Price of purchase item: ");
    price = stdIn.nextDouble();
    System.out.print("Quantity: ");
    qty = stdIn.nextInt();
    System.out.println("Total purchase order = $" + price * qty);
  } // end main
} // end class PrintPO
```

Sample session:

```
Price of purchase item: 34.14
Quantity: 2
Total purchase order = $68.28
```

Figure 3.14 PrintPO program that illustrates `nextDouble()` and `nextInt()`

Figure 3.14, note the italics for `34.14` and `2`. In Figure 3.15, note the italics for `Malallai Zalmai`. We italicize input values in order to distinguish them from the rest of the program. Be aware that the italicization is a pedagogical technique that we use for clarification purposes in the book. Input values are not really italicized when they appear on a computer screen.

```
/*********************************************************************
* PrintInitials.java
* Dean & Dean
*
* This program prints the initials for a user-entered name.
*********************************************************************/

import java.util.Scanner;

public class PrintInitials
{
  public static void main(String[] args)
  {
    Scanner stdIn = new Scanner(System.in);
    String first;  // first name
    String last;   // last name

    System.out.print(
      "Enter your first and last name separated by a space: ");
    first = stdIn.next();
    last = stdIn.next();
    System.out.println("Your initials are " +
      first.charAt(0) + last.charAt(0) + ".");
  } // end main
} // end class PrintInitials
```

<u>Sample session</u>:

```
Enter first and last name separated by a space: Malallai Zalmai
Your initials are MZ.
```

Figure 3.15 PrintInitials program that illustrates `next()`

A Problem with the `nextLine` Method

The `nextLine` method and the other `Scanner` methods don't play well together. It's OK to use a series of `nextLine` method calls in a program. It's also OK to use a series of `nextInt`, `nextLong`, `nextFloat`, `nextDouble`, and `next` method calls in a program. But if you use the `nextLine` method and the other `Scanner` methods in the same program, be careful. Here's why you need to be careful.

The `nextLine` method is the only method that processes leading whitespace. The other methods skip it. Suppose you have a `nextInt` method call and the user types `25` and then presses the enter key. The `nextInt` method call reads the 25 and returns it. The `nextInt` method call does not read in the enter key's newline character. Suppose that after the nextInt method call, you have a nextLine method call. The nextLine method call does not skip leading whitespace, so it's stuck with reading whatever is left over from the previous input call. In our example, the previous input call left the enter key's newline character. Thus, the nextLine call is stuck with reading it. Uh oh.

What happens if the nextLine method reads a newline character? It quits because it's done reading a line (the newline character marks the end of a line, albeit a very short line). So the nextLine method call doesn't get around to reading the next line, which is probably the line that the programmer intended it to read.

One solution to this nextLine problem is to include an extra nextLine method call whose sole purpose is to read in the leftover newline character. Another solution is to use one Scanner reference variable for nextLine input (e.g., stdIn1) and another Scanner reference variable for other input (e.g., stdIn2). But for the most part, we'll try to steer clear of the problem altogether. We'll try to avoid nextLine method calls that follow one of the other Scanner method calls.

As you progress through the book, you'll see that input from the computer keyboard and output to the computer screen is all the I/O you need to solve a vast array of complex problems. But if you have a large amount of input, it might be easier and safer to use a simple text processor to write that input once into a file and then reread it from that file each time you rerun the program. And if you have a large amount of output, it might be easier to analyze the output if it's stored in an output file. You don't need to use files now, but if you can't wait, you can find the details in Chapter 15, Sections 15.3 and 15.4. At this time you probably won't be able to understand many of the details in those later sections of the book. But if you just consider the little program in Figure 15.2 to be a recipe, it will show you how to output to a file anything you can output to the computer screen. Likewise, if you just consider the little program in Figure 15.5 to be a recipe, it will show you how to input from a file anything you can input from the keyboard.

At this point, some readers might want to apply what they've learned to an object-oriented programming (OOP) context. OOP is the idea that programs should be organized into objects. You're not required to learn about OOP just yet, but if you can't wait, you can find such details in Chapter 6, Sections 6.1 through 6.8.

3.24 GUI Track: Input and Output with JOptionPane (Optional)

This section is the second installment of our optional graphical user interface (GUI) track. In each GUI track section, we provide an introduction to a GUI concept. In this section, we describe how to implement rudimentary input/output (I/O) in a GUI window.

Up to this point in the chapter, we've used *console windows* for displaying input and output. In this section, we use *GUI windows*. What's the difference? A console window is a window that can display text only. A GUI window is a window that can display not only text, but also graphical items like buttons, text boxes, and pictures. For an example, see Figure 3.16's GUI window. It displays text (an installation message), a button (an OK button), and a picture (a circled i icon).

Figure 3.16's window is a specialized type of window. It's called a *dialog box*. A dialog box performs just one specific task. Figure 3.16's dialog box performs the task of displaying information (the *i* in the i icon stands for "information"). In later GUI track sections and again in Chapters 16 and 17, we'll use general-purpose standard windows. But for now, we'll stick with dialog boxes.

The JOptionPane Class and Its showMessageDialog Method

In order to display a dialog box, you need to use the JOptionPane class. The JOptionPane class is not part of the core Java language. So if you use the JOptionPane class, you need to tell the compiler where

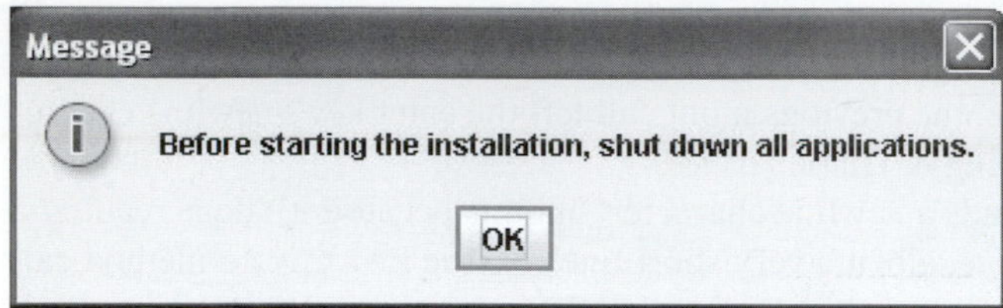

Figure 3.16 A dialog box that displays installation information

to find it. You do that by importing the `JOptionPane` class into your program. More specifically, you need to include this `import` statement at the top of your program:

```
import java.util.JOptionPane;
```

See the InstallationDialog program in Figure 3.17. It produces the dialog box shown in Figure 3.16. The InstallationDialog program's code should look familiar. At the top, it has the `JOptionPane import` statement. Then it has the standard class heading, standard `main` method heading, and braces. What's new is the `JOptionPane.showMessageDialog` method call.

```
/*********************************************************
* InstallationDialog.java
* Dean & Dean
*
* This program illustrates JOptionPane's message dialog.
*********************************************************/

import javax.swing.JOptionPane;

public class InstallationDialog
{
  public static void main(String[] args)
  {
    JOptionPane.showMessageDialog(null,
      "Before starting the installation, " +
      "shut down all applications.");
  }
} // end class InstallationDialog
```

Figure 3.17 InstallationDialog program

The `showMessageDialog` method displays a message in a dialog box. Here's the syntax for calling the `showMessageDialog` method:

```
JOptionPane.showMessageDialog(null, <message>)
```

The `showMessageDialog` method takes two arguments. The first argument specifies the position of the dialog box on the computer screen. We'll keep things simple and go with the default position, which is the center of the screen. To go with the default position, specify `null` for the first argument. The second argument specifies the message that appears in the dialog box.

Input Dialog Box

Note that a dialog box is often referred to simply as a *dialog*. Both terms are acceptable. There are several types of `JOptionPane` dialogs. We consider two of them—the message dialog for output and the input dialog for input. We've already described the message dialog. That's what `showMessageDialog` produces. We'll now look at the input dialog.

The input dialog displays a prompt message and an input box. The top four dialogs in Figure 3.18 are input dialogs. These display a question mark icon as a visual cue that the dialog is asking a question and waiting for user input. Clicking OK processses the value entered. Clicking Cancel closes the dialog box without processing.

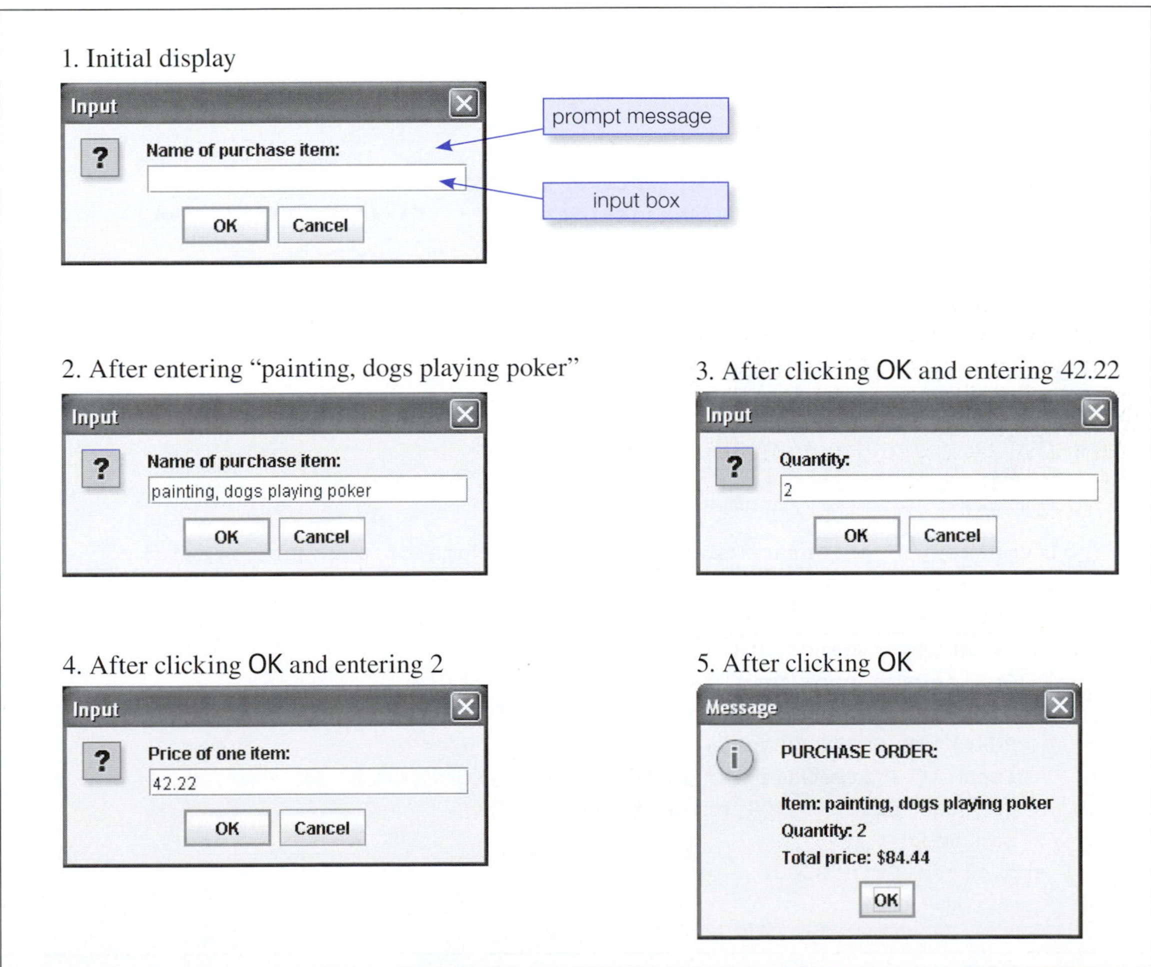

Figure 3.18 Sample session for PrintPOGUI program

The purpose of the input dialog is to read a user-entered value and store it in a variable. To read text values, call `showInputDialog` like this:

```
<string-variable> = JOptionPane.showInputDialog(<prompt-message>);
```

To read in a number, you need to call `showInputDialog` and then convert the read-in string to a number. More specifically, to read an `int` value, do this:

```
<int-variable> = Integer.parseInt(JOptionPane.showInputDialog) (<prompt-message>);
```

And to read a `double` value, do this:

```
<double-variable> = Double.parseDouble(JOptionPane.showInputDialog
                      (<prompt-message>));
```

Now look at Figure 3.19. It shows how to use these new statements to produce Figure 3.18's displays.

```
/*********************************************************************
* PrintPOGUI.java
* Dean & Dean
*
* This program calculates and prints a purchase order report.
*********************************************************************/

import javax.swing.JOptionPane;

public class PrintPOGUI
{
  public static void main(String[] args)
  {
    String itemName; // name of purchase item
    double price;    // price of purchase item
    int qty;         // number of items purchased

    itemName = JOptionPane.showInputDialog("Name of purchase item:");
    price = Double.parseDouble(
      JOptionPane.showInputDialog("Price of one item:"));
    qty = Integer.parseInt(
      JOptionPane.showInputDialog("Quantity:"));
    JOptionPane.showMessageDialog(null,
      "PURCHASE ORDER:\n\n" +
      "Item: " + itemName + "\nQuantity: " + qty +
      "\nTotal price: $" + price * qty);
  } // end main
} // end class PrintPOGUI
```

Figure 3.19 PrintPOGUI program

Integer.parseInt converts the read-in string to an int value, and Double.parseDouble converts the read-in string to a double value. Integer and Double are wrapper classes. parseInt and parseDouble are wrapper class methods. We'll describe wrapper classes and their methods in Chapter 5.

I/O for the Remainder of the Book

For the GUI track sections and for the GUI chapters at the end of the book, we'll of course use GUI windows for I/O. But for the remainder of the book, we'll use console windows. We use console windows for the remainder of the book because that leads to simpler programs. Simpler programs are important so we can cut through clutter and focus on newly introduced material. But if you've decided that you love all things GUI and you can't get enough of it, feel free to convert all our console-window programs to GUI-window programs. To do so, replace all of our output code with showMessageDialog calls, and replace all of our input code with showInputDialog calls.

Summary

- Comments are used for improving a program's readability/understandability.
- The System.out.println method prints a message and then moves the screen's cursor to the next line. The System.out.print method prints a message and leaves the cursor on the same line as the printed message.
- Variables can hold only one type of data item and that type is defined with a variable declaration statement.
- An assignment statement uses the = operator, and it puts a value into a variable.
- An initialization statement is a combination of a declaration statement and an assignment statement. It declares a variable's type and also gives the variable an initial value.
- Variables that hold whole numbers should normally be declared with the int data type or the long data type.
- Variables that hold floating-point numbers should normally be declared with the double data type. If you're sure that a variable is limited to small floating-point numbers, it's OK to use the float data type.
- Named constants use the final modifier.
- There are two types of integer division. One type finds the quotient (using the / operator). The other type finds the remainder (using the % operator).
- Expressions are evaluated using a set of well-defined operator precedence rules.
- The cast operator allows you to return a different-data-type version of a given value.
- Use an escape sequence (with a backslash) to print hard-to-print characters such as the tab character.
- A reference variable stores a memory address that points to an object. An object is a collection of related data wrapped in a protective shell.
- The String class provides methods that can be used for string processing.
- The Scanner class provides methods that can be used for input.

Review Questions

§3.2 "I Have a Dream" Program

1. What does this chapter's Dream.java program do?
2. What are the filename extensions for Java source code and bytecode, respectively?

§3.3 Comments and Readability

3. Why does source code have comments?

§3.4 The Class Heading

4. For a file with a `public` class, the program's filename must match the program's class name except that the filename has a `.java` extension added to it. (T / F)
5. Standard coding conventions dictate that class names start with a lowercase first letter. (T / F)
6. In Java, the case of a character does matter. (T / F)

§3.5 The `main` Method's Heading

7. A program's start-up method, `main`, should be in a class that is `public`. (T / F)
8. The `main` method itself must be `public`. (T / F)
9. From your memory alone (don't look for the answer in the book), write the `main` method heading.

§3.6 Braces

10. Identify two types of groupings that must be enclosed in braces.

§3.7 `System.out.println`

11. From your memory alone (don't look for the answer in the book), write the statement that tells the computer to display this string of text:

```
Here is an example
```

§3.9 Identifiers

12. List all of the types of characters that may be used to form an identifier.
13. List all of the types of characters that may be used as the first character of an identifier.

§3.10 Variables

14. You should abbreviate variable names by omitting vowels, in order to save space. (T / F)
15. Why is it good practice to use a separate line to declare each separate variable?

§3.11 Assignment Statements

16. There must be a semicolon after every assignment statement. (T / F)

§3.12 Initialization Statements

17. Initialization "kills two birds with one stone". What are the "two birds"?

§3.13 Numeric Data Types—`int, long, float, double`

18. The most appropriate type to use for financial accounting is ____________.
19. For each statement, specify true or false:
    a) `1234.5` is a floating-point number. (T / F)
    b) `1234` is a floating-point number. (T / F)
    c) `1234.` is a floating-point number. (T / F)
20. If you try to assign an `int` value into a `double` variable, the computer automatically makes the conversion without complaining, but if you try to assign a `double` value into an `int` variable, the compiler generates an error. Why?

§3.14 Constants

21. For each statement, specify true or false:
    a) `0.1234` is a `float`. (T / F)
    b) `0.1234f` is a `float`. (T / F)

c) `0.1234` is a `double`. (T / F)
d) `1234.0` is a `double`. (T / F)

22. What modifier specifies that a variable's value is fixed/constant?

§3.15 Arithmetic Operators

23. What is the remainder operator?

24. Write the following mathematical expressions as legal Java expressions:

a. $\frac{3x-1}{x^2}$

b. $\frac{1}{2}+\frac{1}{xy}$

§3.16 Expression Evaluation and Operator Precedence

25. Assume this:

```
int m = 3, n = 2;
double x = 7.5;
```

Evaluate the following expressions:

a) `(7 - n) % 2 * 7.5 + 9`
b) `(4 + n / m ) / 6.0 * x`

§3.17 More Operators: Increment, Decrement, .and Compound Assignment

26. Write the shortest Java statement that increments `count` by one.

27. Write the shortest Java statement that decrements `count` by 3.

28. Write the shortest Java statement that multiplies `number` by `(number - 1)` and leaves the product in `number`.

§3.18 Tracing

29. What does it mean if a variable contains garbage?

30. In a trace listing, what are line numbers for?

§3.19 Type Casting

31. Write a Java statement that assigns the `double` variable, `myDouble`, to the `int` variable, `myInteger`.

§3.20 `char` Type and Escape Sequences

32. What's wrong with the following initialization?

```
char letter = "y";
```

33. If we try to put a quotation mark (") somewhere inside a string literal to be printed, the computer interprets the quotation mark as the end of the string literal. How can we overcome this problem and force the computer to recognize the quotation mark as something we want to print?

34. When describing the location of a file or directory, computers use directory paths. In Windows environments, use the backslash character (\) to separate directories and files within a directory path. If you need to print a directory path within a Java program, how should you write the backslash character?

§3.21 Primitive Variables Versus Reference Variables

35. The type name for a primitive type is not capitalized, but the type name for a reference type is usually capitalized. (T / F)

36. List the primitive types this chapter describes, in the following categories:

a) Integer numbers.
b) Floating point numbers.
c) Individual text characters and special symbols.

§3.22 Strings

37. What two operators perform string concatenation, and what's the difference between the operators?
38. What method can be used to retrieve a character at a specified position within a string?
39. What two methods can be used to compare strings for equality?

§3.23 Input—the `Scanner` class

40. What is whitespace?
41. Write the statement that you must put before any other code to tell the compiler that you will be using the `Scanner` class.
42. Write the statement that creates a connection between your program and the computer's keyboard.
43. Write a statement that inputs a line of text from the keyboard and puts it into a variable named `line`.
44. Write a statement that inputs a `double` number from the keyboard and puts it into a variable named `number`.

Exercises

1. [after §3.3] Illustrate the two ways to provide comments in a Java program by writing the following as a comment in both formats:
   `This a very long comment with lots of useless and unnecessary words that force us to use multiple lines to include it all.`
   When using the block syntax, minimize your use of asterisks.
2. [after §3.5] Why does `public static void Main(String[] args)` generate an error?
3. [after §3.6] What are braces used for?
4. [after §3.8] What program is in charge of
   a) Reading Java source code and creating bytecode?
   b) Executing bytecode?
5. [after §3.9] To enhance readability of an identifier that's comprised of several words, use periods between the words. (T / F)
6. [after §3.10] For each of the below variable names, indicate (with y or n) whether it's legal and whether it uses proper style. Note: You may skip the style question for illegal variable names since style is irrelevant in that case.

	legal (y/n)?	proper style (y/n)?
a) `_isReady`		
b) `3rdName`		
c) `num of wheels`		
d) `money#on#hand`		
e) `taxRate`		
f) `SeatNumber`		

7. [after §3.10] You don't need a semicolon after a variable declaration. (T / F)
8. [after §3.13] If we just write a floating point number without specifying its type, what type does the computer assume it is?
9. [after §3.14] How would you specify the square root of two as a named constant? Use 1.41421356237309 for your named constant's value.
10. [after §3.15] Write the following mathematical expressions as legal Java expressions:
    a) $\left(\frac{3-k}{4}\right)^2$

b) $\frac{9x - (4.5 + y)}{2x}$

11. [after §3.16] Assume this:

```
int a = 9;
double b = 0.5;
int c = 0;
```

Evaluate each of the following expressions by hand. Show your work, using a separate line for each evaluation step. Check your work by writing and executing a program that evaluates these expressions and outputs the results.

a) `a + 3 / a`
b) `25 / ((a - 4) * b)`
c) `a / b * a`
d) `a % 2 - 2 % a`

12. [after §3.19] Type Casting:
Assume the following declarations:

```
int integer;
double preciseReal;
float sloppyReal;
long bigInteger;
```

Rewrite those of the following statements which would generate a compile-time error using an appropriate cast that makes the error go away. Do not provide a cast for any statement which the compiler automatically promotes.

a) `integer = preciseReal;`
b) `bigInteger = sloppyReal;`
c) `preciseReal = integer;`
d) `sloppyReal = bigInteger;`
e) `integer = sloppyReal;`
f) `bigInteger = preciseReal;`
g) `sloppyReal = integer;`
h) `preciseReal = bigInteger;`
i) `integer = bigInteger;`
j) `sloppyReal = preciseReal;`
k) `preciseReal = sloppyReal;`
l) `bigInteger = integer;`

13. [after §3.20] Assuming that tab stops are 4 columns apart, what output does the following statement generate?

```
System.out.println("\"pathName:\"\n\tD:\\myJava\\Hello.java");
```

14. [after §3.21] Reference types begin with an uppercase letter. (T / F)

15. [after §3.22] Assume that you have a string variable named `myName`. Provide a code fragment that prints `myName`'s third character.

16. [after §3.22] What does this code fragment print?

```
String s = "hedge";
s += "hog";
System.out.println(s.equals("hedgehog"));
System.out.println((s.length()-6) + " " + s.charAt(0) + "\'s");
```

Review Question Solutions

1. It generates the output:
```
I have a dream!
```
2. The Java source code extension is `.java`. The bytecode extension is `.class`.
3. Source code has comments to help Java programmers recall or determine how a program works. (Comments are ignored by the computer, and they are not accessible to ordinary users.) The initial comment block includes the file name as a continuous reminder to the programmer. It contains program authors, for help and reference. It may include date and version number to identify context. It includes a short description to facilitate rapid understanding. Punctuation comments like `// end class` *<class-name>* help keep a reader oriented. Special comments identify variables and annotate obscure formulas.
4. True. If a file has a `public` class, the filename must equal this class name.
5. False. Class names should start with an uppercase first letter.
6. True. Java is case sensitive. Changing the case of any letter creates a completely different identifier.
7. True.
8. True. Otherwise, the startup procedure cannot be accessed.
9. `public static void main(String[] args)`
10. One must use braces for (1) all the contents of a class and (2) all the contents of a method.
11. `System.out.println("Here is an example");`
12. Upper-case characters, lower-case characters, numbers, underscore, and dollar sign.
13. Upper-case characters, lower-case characters, underscore, and dollar sign. No numbers.
14. False: In source code, saving space is not as important as good communication. Weird abbreviations are hard to say and not as easy to remember as real words.
15. If each variable is on a separate line, each variable has space at the right for an elaborating comment.
16. True.
17. Variable declaration and assigning a value into the variable.
18. Type `double`, or type `long`, with value in cents.
19. **a)** True; **b)** False; **c)** True
20. Assigning an integer value into a floating point variable is like putting a small object into a large box. The `int` type goes up to approximately 2 billion. It's easy to fit 2 billion into a `double` "box" because a `double` goes all the way up to 1.8×10^{308}. On the other hand, assigning a floating point value into an integer variable is like putting a large object into a small box. By default, that's illegal.
21. **a)** False; **b)** True; **c)** True; **d)** True
22. The `final` modifier specifies that a variable's value is fixed/constant.
23. The remainder operator is a percent sign: `%`.
24. Write the following mathematical expressions as legal Java expressions:
    a) (3 * x − 1) / (x * x)
    b) 1.0 / 2 + 1.0 / (x * y)
    or
    .5 + 1.0 / (x * y)

25. Expression evaluation:

a)
```
(7 - n) % 2 * 7.5 + 9 ⇒
5 % 2 * 7.5 + 9 ⇒
1 * 7.5 + 9 ⇒
7.5 + 9 ⇒
16.5
```

b)
```
(4 + n / m) / 6.0 * x ⇒
(4 + 2 / 3) / 6.0 * 7.5 ⇒
(4 + 0) / 6.0 * 7.5 =>
4 / 6.0 * 7.5 ⇒
0.6666666666666667 * 7.5 ⇒
5.0
```

26. `count++;`

27. `count -= 3;`

28. `number *= (number - 1);`

29. For variables declared without an initialization, the initial value is referred to as *garbage* because its actual value is unknown. Use a question mark to indicate a garbage value.

30. Line numbers tell you which statement in the code generates the current trace results.

31. `myInteger = (int) myDouble;`

32. The variable, `letter`, is of type `char`, but the double quotes in `"y"` specify that the initial value has type `String`, so the types are incompatible. It should be written:
`char letter = 'y';`

33. To print a double quotation mark, put a backslash in front of it, that is, use `\"`.

34. To print a backslash, use two backslashes, that is, use `\\`.

35. True.

36. List the primitive types this chapter describes, in the following categories:

a) Integer numbers: `int`, `long`
b) Floating point numbers: `float`, `double`
c) Individual text characters and special symbols: `char`

37. The + and += operators perform *concatenation*. The + operator does not update the operand at its left. The += operator does update the operand at its left.

38. The `charAt` method can be used to retrieve a character at a specified position within a string.

39. The equals and `equalsIgnoreCase` methods can be used to compare strings for equality.

40. Whitespace = the characters associated with the spacebar, the tab key, and the enter key.

41. `import java.util.Scanner;`

42. `Scanner stdIn = new Scanner(System.in);`

43. `line = stdIn.nextLine();`

44. `number = stdIn.nextDouble();`

CHAPTER 4

Control Statements

Objectives

- Learn how to use `if` statements to alter a program's sequence of execution.
- Become familiar with Java's comparison and logical operators, and learn how to use them to describe complex conditions.
- Learn how to use the `switch` statement to alter a program's sequence of execution.
- Recognize repetitive operations, understand the various kinds of looping that Java supports, and learn how to select the most appropriate type of loop for each problem that requires repetitive evaluation.
- Be able to trace a looping operation.
- Learn how and when to nest a loop inside another loop.
- Learn how to use `boolean` variables to make code more elegant.
- Learn how to validate input data.
- Optionally, learn how to simplify complicated logical expressions.

Outline

4.1 Introduction

In Chapter 3, we kept things simple and wrote pure sequential programs. In a pure sequential program, statements execute in the sequence/order in which they are written; that is, after executing a statement, the computer executes the statement that immediately follows it. Pure sequential programming works well for trivial problems, but for anything substantial, you'll need the ability to execute in a nonsequential fashion. For example, if you're writing a recipe-retrieval program, you probably don't want to print all of the program's recipes one after another. You'll want to execute the chocolate chip cookie print statements if the user indicates an affinity for chocolate chip cookies, and you'll want to execute the crab quiche print statements if the user indicates an affinity for crab quiche. That sort of functionality requires the use of *control statements*. A control statement controls the order of execution of other statements. In Chapter 2 you used pseudocode if and while statements to control the order of execution within an algorithm. In this chapter, you'll use Java `if` and `while` statements, plus a few additional Java statements, to control the order of execution within a program.

In controlling the order of execution, a control statement uses a condition (a question) to decide which way to go. We start Chapter 4 with an overview of Java conditions. We then describe Java's control statements—the `if` statement, the `switch` statement, the `while` loop, the `do` loop, and the `for` loop. Along the way, we describe Java's logical operators `&&`, `||`, and `!`, which are needed when dealing with more complicated conditions. We conclude the chapter with several loop-related concepts—nested loops, input validation, and `boolean` variables. Good stuff!

4.2 Conditions and Boolean Values

In Chapter 2's flowcharts, we used diamond shapes to represent logical decision points—points where control flow went either one way or another. Into those diamonds we inserted various abbreviated questions like, "`ceoSalary` greater than $500,000?" and "`count` less than or equal to 100?" Then we labeled alternate paths away from those diamonds with "yes" or "no" answers to those questions. In Chapter 2's pseudocode, we used "if" and "while" clauses to describe logical conditions. Examples included: "if `shape` is a circle," "if `grade` is greater than or equal to 60," and "while `score` is not equal to −1." We considered pseudocode conditions to be either "true" or "false."

Informal condition expressions like these are fine for flowcharts and pseudocode, but when you start writing real Java code, you must be precise. The computer interprets each "if" condition or loop condition as a two-way choice. What are the two possible values recognized by Java? They are the Java values `true` and `false`. These values, `true` and `false`, are called *Boolean values*, after George Boole, a famous 19th century logician. Throughout the rest of this chapter, you'll see `if` statements and loop statements where *conditions* appear as little fragments of code within a pair of parentheses, like this:

```
if (<condition>)
{
    . . .
}

while (<condition>)
{
    . . .
}
```

Whatever is in the places marked by *<condition>* always evaluates to either `true` or `false`.

Typically, each condition involves some type of comparison. With pseudocode, you can use words to describe the comparisons, but in real Java code, you must use special *comparison operators*. Comparison operators (also called equality and relational operators) are like mathematical operators in that they link adjacent operands, but instead of combining the operands in some way, they compare them. When a mathematical operator combines two numbers, the combination is a number like the operands being combined. But when a comparison operator compares two numbers, the result is a different type. It is not a number like the operands being compared. It is a Boolean truth value—either `true` or `false`.

Here are Java's comparison operators:

```
==, !=, <, >, <=, >=
```

The == operator tests whether two values are equal. Notice that this symbol uses two equals signs! This is different from the single equals sign that we all use instinctively to represent equality. Why does Java use two equals signs for equality in a comparison? It's because Java already uses the single equals sign for assignment, and context is not enough to distinguish assignment from equality. Do not try to use a single = for comparison! The Java compiler will not like it.

The != operator tests whether two values are unequal. As you'd expect, the < operator tests whether a value on the left is less than a value on the right. The > operator tests whether a value on the left is greater than a value on the right. The <= operator tests whether a value on the left is less than or equal to a value on the right. The >= operator tests whether a value on the left is greater than or equal to a value on the right. The result of any one of these tests is always either `true` or `false`.

4.3 `if` Statements

Now, let's look at a simple example of the condition in an `if` statement. Here's a simple `if` statement that checks a car's temperature gauge value and prints a warning if the temperature is above 215 degrees:

condition

```
if (temperature > 215)
{
  System.out.println("Warning! Engine coolant is too hot.");
  System.out.println("Stop driving and allow engine to cool.");
}
```

The condition uses the > operator to generate a `true` value if the temperature is above 215 degrees or a `false` value if it is not. The subordinate statements execute only if the condition generates a `true` value.

Syntax

In the above example, note the parentheses around the condition. Parentheses are required whenever you have a condition, regardless of whether it's for an `if` statement, a `while` loop, or some other control structure. Note the braces around the two subordinate print statements. Use braces to surround statements that are logically inside something else. For example, braces are required below the `main` method's heading and at the bottom of the `main` method because the statements inside the braces are logically inside the `main` method. Likewise, you should use braces to surround the statements that are logically inside an `if` statement. To emphasize the point that statements inside braces are logically inside something else, you should always indent statements that are inside braces. Since this is so important, we'll say it again: Always indent when you're inside braces!

When an `if` statement includes two or more subordinate statements, you must enclose the subordinate statements in braces. Said another way, you must use *a block*. A block, also called a *compound statement,* is a set of zero or more statements surrounded by braces. A block can be used anywhere a standard statement can be used. If you don't use braces for the `if` statement's two subordinate statements, the computer considers only the first statement to be subordinate to the `if` statement. When there is supposed to be just one subordinate statement, you're not required to enclose it in braces, but we recommend that you do so anyway. That way, you won't get into trouble if you come back later and want to insert additional subordinate statements at that point in your program. 

Three Forms of the `if` Statement

There are three basic forms for an `if` statement:

- "if"—use when you want to do one thing or nothing.
- "if, else"—use when you want to do one thing or another thing.
- "if, else if"—use when there are three or more possibilities.

Chapter 2 presented pseudocode versions of these forms. Figures 4.1, 4.2, and 4.3 show Java forms.

```
if (<condition>)
{
  <statement(s)>
}
```

<if-condition>
true
false
<statement(s)>
<following-statement>

Figure 4.1 Syntax and semantics for the simple "if" form of the `if` statement

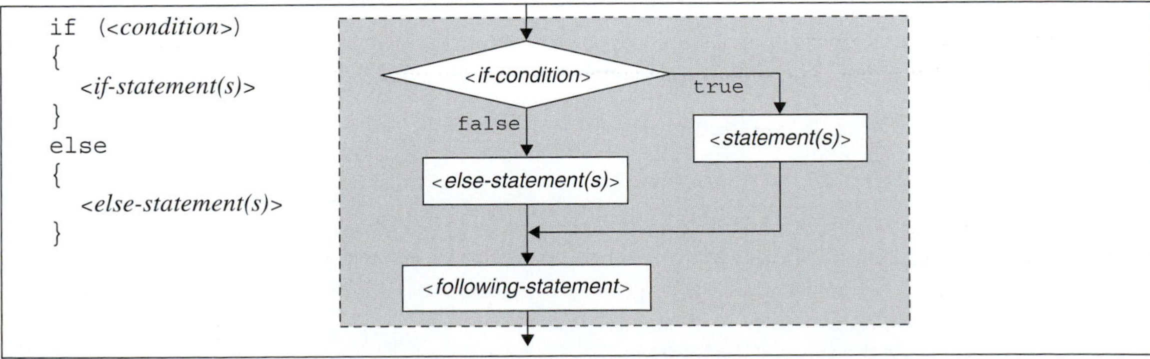

Figure 4.2 Syntax and semantics for the "if, else" form of the `if` statement

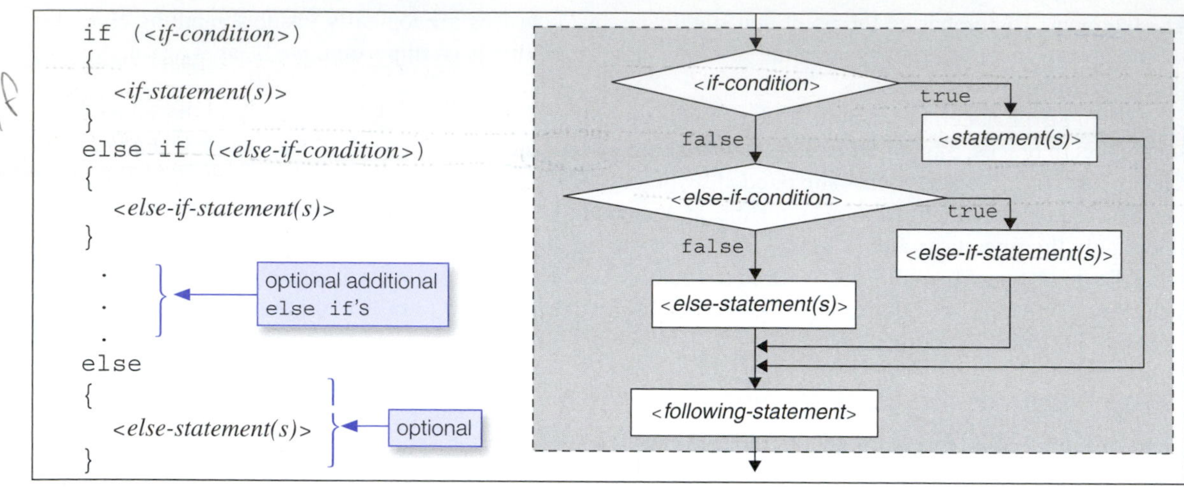

Figure 4.3 Syntax and semantics for the "if, else if" form of the `if` statement

Take several minutes and examine Figures 4.1, 4.2, and 4.3. The figures show the syntax and semantics for the three forms of the Java `if` statement. The *semantics* of a statement is a description of how the statement works. For example, Figure 4.1's flowchart illustrates the semantics of the "if" form of the `if` statement by showing the flow of control for different values of the `if` statement's condition.

Most of what you see in the `if` statement figures should look familiar since it parallels what you learned in Chapter 2. But the "if, else if" form of the `if` statement deserves some extra attention. You may include as many "else if" blocks as you like—more "else if" blocks for more choices. Note that the "else" block is optional. If all the conditions are `false` and there's no "else" block, none of the statement blocks is executed. Here's a code fragment that uses the "if, else if" form of the `if` statement to troubleshoot iPod[1] problems:

```
if (iPodProblem.equals("no response"))
{
  System.out.println("Unlock iPod's Hold switch.");
}
else if (iPodProblem.equals("songs don't play"))
{
  System.out.println("Use iPod Updater to update your software.");
}
else
{
  System.out.println("Visit http://www.apple.com/support.");
}
```

[1] The iPod is a portable media player designed and marketed by Apple Computer.

Practice Problem

Now let's put what you've learned into practice by using the `if` statement within a complete program. Suppose you're asked to write a sentence-tester program that checks whether a user entered line ends with a period. Your program should print an error message if the last character in the line is not a period. In writing the program, use a sample session as a guide. Note that the italicized Mahatma Gandhi quote is a user-entered input value.

Use desired output to specify problem.

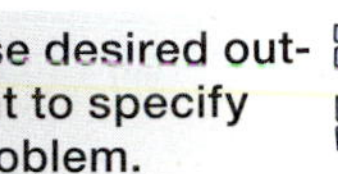

Sample session:

```
Enter a sentence:
Permanent good can never be the outcome of violence.
```

Another sample session:

```
Enter a sentence:
Permanent good can never be the outcome of
Invalid entry - your sentence is not complete!
```

As your first step in implementing a solution, use pseudocode to generate an informal outline of the basic logic:

```
print "Enter a sentence: "
input sentence
if sentence's last character is not equal to '.'
  print "Invalid entry – your sentence is not complete!"
```

Note the simple "if" form of the `if` statement. That's appropriate because there's a need to do something (print an invalid entry message) or nothing. Why nothing? Because the problem description does not say to print anything for user entries that are legitimate sentences. In other words, the program should skip what's in the `if` statement if you finish the sentence properly. Now we suggest that you try writing the Java code to implement this algorithm. You'll need to use a couple of the `String` methods described near the end of Chapter 3. When you're ready, look at the `SentenceTester` solution in Figure 4.4.

How does the SentenceTester program determine whether the last character is a period? Suppose the user enters "Hello." In that case, what value would be assigned to the `lastCharPosition` variable? `String`'s `length` method returns the number of characters in a string. The number of characters in "Hello." is six. Since the first position is zero, `lastCharPosition` would get assigned a value of (6 − 1) or 5. Why do we want `lastCharPosition`? We need to see if the last character in the user-entered value is a period. To do so, we use `lastCharPosition` as the argument in a `charAt` method call. `String`'s `charAt` method returns the character at a specified index position within a string. The index position of the period in "Hello." is 5, and the `if` condition checks whether the user-entered value's last character is a period.

4.4 && Logical Operator

Up to this point, all of our `if` statement examples have used simple conditions. A simple condition evaluates directly to either `true` or `false`. In the next three sections, we introduce you to logical operators, like the "and" operator (`&&`) and the "or" operator (`||`), which make it possible to construct *compound* conditions. A compound condition is a conjunction (either an "anding" or an "oring") of two or more conditions. When

```
/*******************************************************************
* SentenceTester.java
* Dean & Dean
*
* This program checks for period at the end of line of input.
*******************************************************************/

import java.util.Scanner;

public class SentenceTester
{
  public static void main(String[] args)
  {
    Scanner stdIn = new Scanner(System.in);
    String sentence;
    int lastCharPosition;

    System.out.println("Enter a sentence:");
    sentence = stdIn.nextLine();
    lastCharPosition = sentence.length() - 1;
    if (sentence.charAt(lastCharPosition) != '.')
    {
      System.out.println(
        "Invalid entry - your sentence needs a period!");
    }
  } // end main
} // end class SentenceTester
```

This condition checks for proper termination.

Figure 4.4 SentenceTester program

you have a compound condition, each part of the compound condition evaluates to either `true` or `false`, and then the parts combine to produce a composite `true` or `false` for the whole compound condition. The combining rules are what you might expect: When you "and" two conditions together, the combination is `true` only if the first condition is true and the second condition is true. When you "or" two conditions together, the combination is `true` if the first condition is `true` or the second condition is `true`. You'll see plenty of examples as the chapter progresses.

&& Operator Example

Let's begin our discussion of logical operators with an example that uses the && operator. (Note: `&&` is pronounced "and"). Suppose you want to print "OK" if the temperature is between 50 and 90 degrees and print "not OK" otherwise:

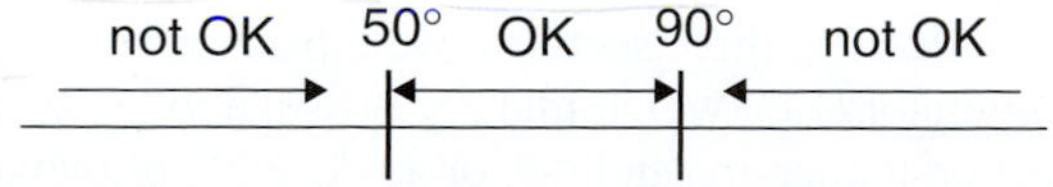

Here's a pseudocode description of the problem:

if temp ≥ 50 and ≤ 90
  print "OK"
else
  print "not OK"

Notice that the pseudocode condition uses ≥ and ≤ rather than > and <. The original problem specification says to print "OK" if the temperature is between 50 and 90 degrees. When people say "between," they usually, but not always, mean to include the end points. Thus, we assumed that the 50 and 90 end points were supposed to be included in the OK range, and we chose to use ≥ and ≤ accordingly. But in general, if you're writing a program and you're unsure about the end points for a particular range, you should not assume. Instead, you should ask the customer what he/she wants. The end points are important.

Think about where boundary values go.

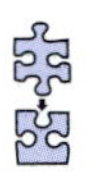

See Figure 4.5. It shows the Java implementation for the temperature-between-50-and-90 problem. In Java, if both of two criteria must be met for a condition to be satisfied (e.g., `temp >= 50` and `temp <= 90`), then separate the two criteria with the && operator. As indicated by Figure 4.5's first callout, if both criteria use the same variable (e.g., `temp`), you must include the variable on both sides of the &&. Note the use of >= and <=. In pseudocode, it's OK to use ≥, ≤, or even the words "greater than or equal to," and "less than or equal to." But in Java, you must use >= and <=.

```
if ((temp >= 50) && (temp <= 90))
{
  System.out.println("OK");
}
else
{
  System.out.println("not OK");
}
```

temp must be repeated

Use <=, not ≤.

Figure 4.5 Java implementation for the temperature-between-50-and-90 problem

Operator Precedence

In Figure 4.5, note the parentheses around each of the two temperature comparisons. They force evaluation of the comparisons before evaluation of the &&. What would happen if we omitted those inner parentheses? To answer that sort of question, you need to refer to an operator precedence table. Appendix 2 provides a complete operator precedence table, but most of the cases you'll encounter are covered by the abbreviated precedence table in Figure 4.6. All operators within a particular numbered group have equal precedence, but operators at the top of the figure (in groups 1, 2, . . .) have higher precedence than operators at the bottom of the figure (in groups . . . 7, 8).

Figure 4.6 shows that the comparison operators >= and <= have higher precedence than the logical operator &&. Thus, the >= and <= operations execute before the && operation—even if the inner parentheses in the condition in Figure 4.5 are omitted. In other words, we could have written Figure 4.5's condition more simply, like this:

1. grouping with parentheses:
   (<*expression*>)
2. unary operators:
   ```
   +x
   -x
   (<type>) x
   x++
   x--
   !x
   ```
3. multiplication and division operators:
   ```
   x * y
   x / y
   x % y
   ```
4. addition and subtraction operators:
   ```
   x + y
   x - y
   ```
5. less than and greater than relational operators:
   ```
   x < y
   x > y
   x <= y
   x >= y
   ```
6. equality operators:
   ```
   x == y
   x != y
   ```
7. "and" logical operator:
   ```
   x && y
   ```
8. "or" logical operator:
   ```
   x || y
   ```

Figure 4.6 Abbreviated operator precedence table (see Appendix 2 for complete table)
The operator groups at the top of the table have higher precedence than the operator groups at the bottom of the table. All operators within a particular group have equal precedence. If an expression has two or more same-precedence operators, then within that expression ones on the left are executed before ones on the right.

```
if (temp >= 50 && temp <= 90)
```

You may include these extra parentheses or not, as you wish. We included them in Figure 4.5 to emphasize the order of evaluation in this initial presentation, but in the future we will often omit them to minimize clutter.

Another Example

For another example, consider commercial promotions at sports events. Suppose the local Yummy Burgers restaurant is willing to provide free French fries to all fans at a basketball game whenever the home team wins and scores at least 100 points. The problem is to write a program that prints the following message whenever that condition is satisfied:

"Fans: Redeem your ticket stub for a free order of French fries at Yummy Burgers."

Figure 4.7 shows the framework. Within the figure, note where it says *<insert code here>*. Before looking ahead at the answer, see if you can provide the inserted code on your own.

```
/*********************************************************************
* FreeFries.java
* Dean & Dean
*
* This program reads points scored by the home team and the
* opposing team and determines whether the fans win free
* french fries.
*********************************************************************/

import java.util.Scanner;

public class FreeFries
{
  public static void main(String[] args)
  {
    Scanner stdIn = new Scanner(System.in);
    int homePts;       // points scored by home team
    int opponentPts;   // points scored by opponents

    System.out.print("Home team points scored: ");
    homePts = stdIn.nextInt();
    System.out.print("Opposing team points scored: ");
    opponentPts = stdIn.nextInt();

    <insert-code-here>

  } // end main
} // end class FreeFries
```

Sample session:

```
Home team points scored: 103
Opposing team points scored: 87
Fans: Redeem your ticket stub for a free order of French fries at Yummy
Burgers.
```

Figure 4.7 FreeFries program with "and" condition

Here's what you should insert:

homePts must be repeated

```
if (homePts > opponentPts && homePts >= 100)
{
  System.out.println("Fans: Redeem your ticket stub for" +
    " a free order of French fries at Yummy Burgers.");
}
```

4.5 || Logical Operator

Now let's look at the complement to the "and" operator—the "or" operator. Assume that you have a variable named `response` that contains (1) a lowercase or uppercase "q" if the user wants to quit or (2) some other character if the user wants to continue. Write a code fragment that prints "Bye" if the user enters either a lowercase or uppercase "q." Using pseudocode, you'd probably come up with something like this for the critical part of the algorithm:

```
if response equals "q" or "Q"
   print "Bye"
```

Note the "or" in the `if` statement's condition. That works fine for pseudocode, where syntax rules are lenient, but for Java, you must use || for the "or" operation, not "or." (Note: || is pronounced "or") To enter the || operator on your computer, look for the vertical bar key on your keyboard and press it twice. Here's a tentative Java implementation of the desired code fragment:

```
Scanner stdIn = new Scanner(System.in);
String response;

System.out.print("Enter q or Q: ");
response = stdIn.nextLine();
if (response == "q" || response == "Q")
{
  System.out.println("Bye");
}
```

When inserted in a `main` method, this compiles, but it does not "work"!

Note that the `response` variable appears twice in the `if` statement's condition. That's necessary because if both sides of an || condition involve the same variable, you must repeat the variable.

The callout indicates that something is wrong. What is it? If you insert this code fragment into a valid program shell, the program compiles and runs. But when a user responds to the prompt by dutifully entering either "q" or "Q," nothing happens. The program does not print "Bye." Why not? Should we have used interior parentheses in the "if" condition? Figure 4.6 shows that the == operator has a higher precedence than the || operator, so what we did was OK. The problem is something else.

⚠ Don't Use == to Compare Strings

The problem is with the `response == "q"` and `response == "Q"` expressions. We'll focus on the `response == "q"` expression. The `response` string variable and the "q" string literal both hold memory addresses that point to string objects; they don't hold string objects themselves. So when you use ==, you're comparing the memory addresses stored in the `response` string variable and the "q" string literal. If the `response` string variable and the "q" string literal contain different memory addresses (i.e., they point to different string objects), then the comparison evaluates to `false`, even if both string objects contain the same sequence of characters. The following picture shows what we're talking about. The arrows represent memory addresses. Since they point to two different objects, `response == "q"` evaluates to `false`.

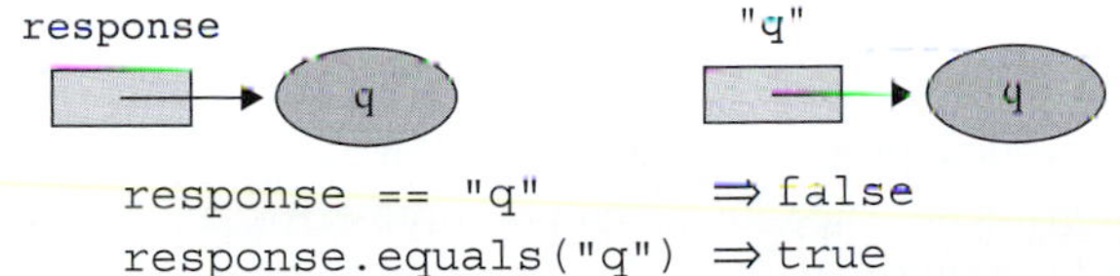

So what can you do to solve this problem? In Chapter 3, you learned to use the `equals` method to test strings for equality. The `equals` method compares the string objects pointed to by the memory addresses. In the above picture, the string objects hold the same sequence of characters, q and q, so the method call, `response.equals("q")`, returns `true`, which is what you want. Here's the corrected code fragment:

```
if (response.equals("q") || response.equals("Q"))
{
  System.out.println("Bye");
}
```

Or as a more compact alternative, use the `equalsIgnoreCase` method like this:

```
if (response.equalsIgnoreCase("q"))
{
  System.out.println("Bye");
}
```

A third alternative is to use the `String` class's `charAt` method to convert the string input into a character and then use the == operator to compare that character with the character literals, 'q' and 'Q':

```
char resp = response.charAt(0);
if (resp == 'q' || resp == 'Q')
{
  System.out.println("Bye");
}
```

These implementations are not trivial translations from the pseudocode that specified the algorithm. It's important to organize your thoughts before you start writing Java code. But even very good preparation does not eliminate the need to keep thinking as you proceed. Details matter also!

The devil is in the details.

Errors

We made a big deal about not using == to compare strings because it's a very easy mistake to make and it's a hard mistake to catch. It's easy to make this mistake because you use == all the time when comparing primitive values. It's hard to catch this mistake because programs that use == for string comparison compile and run with no reported errors. No reported errors? Then why worry? Because although there are no reported errors, there are still errors—they're called logic errors.

A *logic error* occurs when your program runs to completion without an error message, and the output is wrong. Logic errors are the hardest errors to find and fix because there's no error message glaring at you, telling you what you did wrong. To make matters worse, using == for string comparison generates a logic error only some of the time, not all of the time. Because the logic error occurs only some of the time, programmers can be lulled into a false sense of confidence that their code is OK, when in reality it's not OK.

Be careful. Test every aspect.

There are three main categories of errors—compile-time errors, runtime errors, and logic errors. A compile-time error is an error that is identified by the compiler during the compilation process. A runtime error is an error that occurs while a program is running and it causes the program to terminate abnormally. The compiler generates an error message for a compile-time error, and the Java Virtual Machine (JVM) generates an error message for a runtime error. Unfortunately, there are no error messages for a logic error. It's up to the programmer to fix logic errors by analyzing the output and thinking carefully about the code.

4.6 ! Logical Operator

Now it's time to consider the logical "not" operator (!). Assume that you have a `char` variable named `resp` that contains (1) a lowercase or uppercase 'q' if the user wants to quit or (2) some other character if the user wants to continue. This time, the goal is to print "Let's get started. . . ." if `resp` contains anything other than a lowercase or uppercase "q." You could use an "if, else" statement with an empty "if" block like this:

```
if (resp == 'q' || resp == 'Q')
{ }
else
{
  System.out.println("Let's get started. . . .");
  . . .
```

But this is not very *elegant.* Programmers often use the term elegant to describe code that is well written and has "beauty." More specifically, elegant code is easy to understand, easy to update, robust, reasonably compact, and efficient. The above code's empty "if" block is inelegant because it's not compact. If you ever have an empty "if" block with a nonempty "else" block, you should try to rewrite it as just an "if" block with no "else" block. The trick is to invert the `if` statement's condition. In the above example, that means testing for the absence of lowercase or uppercase 'q' rather than the presence of lowercase or uppercase 'q.' To test for the absence of lowercase or uppercase 'q,' use the `!` operator.

The `!` operator changes `true` values into `false` values and vice versa. This true-to-false, false-to-true toggling functionality is referred to as a "not" operation, and that's why the `!` operator is called the "not" operator. Since we want to print "Let's get started. . . ." if the above `if` statement's condition is not true, we insert `!` at the left of the condition like this:

```
if (!(resp == 'q' || resp == 'Q'))
{
  System.out.println("Let's get started. . . .");
  . . .
```

Note that the `!` is inside one set of parentheses and outside another set. Both sets of parentheses are required. The outer parentheses are necessary because the compiler requires parentheses around the entire condition. The inner parentheses are also necessary because without them, the `!` operator would operate on the `resp` variable instead of on the entire condition. Why? Because the operator precedence table (Figure 4.6) shows that the `!` operator has higher precedence than the == and || operators. The way to force the == and || operators to be executed first is to put them inside parentheses.

Don't confuse the `!` (not) operator with the `!=` (inequality) operator. The `!` operator returns the opposite value of the given expression (a true expression returns `false` and a `false` expression returns `true`). The `!=` operator asks a question—are the two expressions unequal?

4.7 switch Statement

The switch statement works similarly to the "if, else if" form of the if statement in that it allows you to follow one of several paths. But a key difference between the switch statement and the if statement is that the switch statement's determination of which path to take is based on a single value. (With an if statement, the determination of which path to take is based on multiple conditions, one for each path.) Having the determination based on a single value can lead to a more compact, more understandable implementation. Think of driving on Route 1 along the California coastline and coming to a junction with alternate routes through and around a city. The different routes are better at certain times of the day. If it's 8 AM or 5 PM, you should take the outer business loop to avoid rush-hour traffic. If it's 8 PM, you should take the coastal bluffs route to appreciate the scenic sunset view. If it's any other time, you should take the through-the-city route because it is the most direct and fastest. Using a single value, time of day, to determine the route parallels the decision-making process in a switch statement.

Syntax and Semantics

Study the switch statement's syntax in Figure 4.8. When executing a switch statement, control jumps to the case constant that matches the controlling expression's value, and the computer executes all subsequent statements up to a break statement. The break statement causes control to exit from the switch statement (to below the closing brace). If there are no case constants that match the controlling expression's value, then control jumps to the default label (if there is a default label) or out of the switch statement if there is no default label.

Usually, break statements are placed at the end of every case block. That's because you normally want to execute just one case block's subordinate statement(s) and then exit the switch statement. However, break statements are not required. Sometimes you want to omit them, and being able to omit them  is a special feature of the switch construct. But accidentally forgetting to include a break statement that should be included is a common error. If there's no break at the bottom of a particular case block, control flows through subsequent case constants and executes all subordinate statements until a break statement

```
switch (<controlling expression>)
{
  case <constant>:
    <statement(s)>;    }
    break;             }
  case < constant>:
    <statement(s)>;    }    optional
    break;             }
  . . .
  default:
    <statement(s)>;    }
} // end switch
```

Figure 4.8 `switch` statement's syntax

is reached. If there's no `break` at the bottom of the last `case` block, control flows through to the subordinate statements in the `default` block (if there is a `default` block).

Referring to Figure 4.8, take note of these details:

- There must be parentheses around the controlling expression.
- The controlling expression must evaluate to either an `int` or a `char`.[2] It's illegal to use a Boolean value, a `long`, a floating point value, or a string value as the controlling expression.
- Although it's common for the controlling expression to consist of a single variable, it can consist of a more complicated expression as well—multiple variables, operators, and even method calls are allowed—provided the expression evaluates to an `int` or a `char`.
- There must be braces around the `switch` statement's body.
- There must be a colon after each `case` constant.
- Even though statements following the `case` constants are indented, braces ({ }) are unnecessary. That's unusual in Java—it's the only time where you don't need braces around statements that are logically inside something else.
- It's good style to include `// end switch` after the `switch` statement's closing brace.

ZIP Code Example

To exercise your understanding of the `switch` statement, write a program that reads in a ZIP Code and uses the first digit to print the associated geographic area. Here's what we're talking about:

If ZIP Code begins with	Print this message
0, 2, 3	*<zip>* `is on the East Coast.`
4-6	*<zip>* `is in the Central Plains area.`
7	*<zip>* `is in the South.`
8-9	*<zip>* `is in the West.`
other	*<zip>* `is an invalid ZIP Code.`

[2] Actually, a controlling expression can also evaluate to a `byte`, a `short`, or an *enum type*. We discuss `byte` and `short` types in Chapter 12. Enum types are beyond the scope of this book, but if you want to learn about them on your own, see http://java.sun.com/docs/books/tutorial/java/javaOO/enum.html.

The first digit of a U.S. postal ZIP Code identifies a particular geographic area within the United States. ZIP Codes that start with 0, 2, or 3 are in the east, ZIP Codes that start with 4, 5, or 6 are in the central region, and so on.[3] Your program should prompt the user for his/her ZIP Code and use the first character of the entered value to print the user's geographical region. In addition to printing the geographical region, your program should *echo print* the user's ZIP Code. (Echo print means print out an input exactly as it was read in.) Here's an example of what the program should do:

<u>Sample session</u>:

```
Enter a ZIP Code: 56044
56044 is in the Central Plains area.
```

Use client's view to specify program.

That's the client's view of the program. Now let's look at the implementation view of the program—the problem solution. It's shown in Figure 4.9.

Look at the controlling expression, `(zip.charAt(0))`. This evaluates to the first character in `zip`. As an alternative, you could have started by reading the first character into a separate variable (for example, `firstChar`), and then inserted that variable into the controlling expression. But because the first character was needed only at one point, the code is made more compact by embedding the `zip.charAt(0)` method call directly in the controlling expression's parentheses.

The `switch` statement compares the character in its controlling expression with each of the `case` constants until it finds a match. Since the controlling expression's `charAt` method returns a `char` value, the `case` constants must all be `char`s. Therefore, the `case` constants must have single quotes around them. If you don't use single quotes—if you use double quotes or no quotes—you'll get a compile-time error. The `switch` statement is not very flexible!

As previously mentioned, it's a common error to accidentally omit a `break` statement at the end of a `switch` statement's `case` block. For example, suppose you did this in the ZipCode program:

```
case '4': case '5': case '6':
  System.out.println(
    zip + " is in the Central Plains area.");
case '7':
  System.out.println(zip + " is in the South.");
  break;
```

Note that there's no longer a `break` statement at the end of the case 4, 5, 6 block. The following sample session illustrates what happens. With an input of 56044, the `switch` statement searches for a '5' and stops when it reaches the `case '5':` label. Execution begins there and continues until it reaches a `break` statement. So it flows through the `case '6':` label and prints the Central Plains message. The flow then continues into the `case: '7':` block and inappropriately prints the South message.

<u>Sample session</u>:

```
Enter a ZIP Code: 56044
56044 is in the Central Plains area.
56044 is in the South.          <---- error!
```

[3] http://www.nass.usda.gov/census/census97/zipcode/zipcode.htm.

```
/*************************************************************
* ZipCode.java
* Dean & Dean
*
* This program identifies geographical region from ZIP code.
*************************************************************/

import java.util.Scanner;

public class ZipCode
{
  public static void main(String[] args)
  {
    Scanner stdIn = new Scanner(System.in);
    String zip;  // user-entered ZIP code

    System.out.print("Enter a ZIP Code: ");
    zip = stdIn.nextLine();

    switch (zip.charAt(0))
    {
      case '0': case '2': case '3':
        System.out.println(zip + " is on the East Coast.");
        break;
      case '4': case '5': case '6':
        System.out.println(
          zip + " is in the Central Plains area.");
        break;
      case '7':
        System.out.println(zip + " is in the South.");
        break;
      case '8': case '9':
        System.out.println(zip + " is in the West.");
        break;
      default:
        System.out.println(zip + " is an invalid ZIP Code.");
    } // end switch
  } // end main
} // end class ZipCode
```

Figure 4.9 Using a `switch` statement to find geographical region from ZIP Code

`switch` Statement Versus "if, else if" Form of the `if` Statement

Now you know that the `switch` statement allows you to do one or more things from a list of multiple possibilities. But so does the "if, else if" form of the `if` statement, so why would you ever use a `switch` statement? Because the `switch` statement provides a more elegant solution (cleaner, better-looking organization) for certain kinds of problems.

Now for the opposite question: Why would you ever use the "if, else if" form of the `if` statement rather than the `switch` statement? Because `if` statements are more flexible. With a `switch` statement, each test (i.e., each `case` label) is limited to an exact match with an `int` or `char` constant. With an `if` statement, each test can be a full-blooded expression, complete with operators, variables, and method calls.

In a nutshell, when you need to do one thing from a list of multiple possibilities:

- Use a `switch` statement if you need to match an `int` or `char` value.
- Use an `if` statement if you need more flexibility.

4.8 while Loop

There are two basic categories of control statements—forward branching statements and looping statements. The `if` statement and `switch` statement implement *forward branching* functionality (so named because the decisions cause control to "branch" to a statement that is ahead of the current statement). The `while` loop, `do` loop, and `for` loop implement looping functionality. We describe the `while` loop in this section and the `do` and `for` loops in the next two sections. But first an overview of loops in general.

Don't duplicate code. Use a loop.

In solving a particular problem, one of the first and most important things to think about is whether there are any repetitive tasks. Repetitive tasks should normally be implemented with the help of a loop. For some problems, you can avoid a loop by implementing the repetitive tasks with consecutive sequential statements. For example, if you are asked to print "Happy Birthday!" 10 times, you could implement a solution with 10 consecutive print statements. But such a solution would be a poor one. A better solution is to insert a single print statement inside a loop that repeats ten times. The loop implementation is better because it's more compact. Also, updating is easier and safer because the updated code appears in only one place. For example, if you need to change "Happy Birthday!" to "Bon Anniversaire!" (happy birthday in French), then it's only a matter of changing one print statement inside a loop rather than updating 10 separate print statements.

while Loop Syntax and Semantics

Now let's look at the simplest kind of loop, the `while` loop. Figure 4.10 shows the syntax and semantics of the `while` loop. The syntax for the `while` loop looks like the syntax for the `if` statement except that the word `while` is used instead of the word `if`. Don't forget the parentheses around the condition. Don't forget the braces, and don't forget to indent the subordinate statements they enclose.

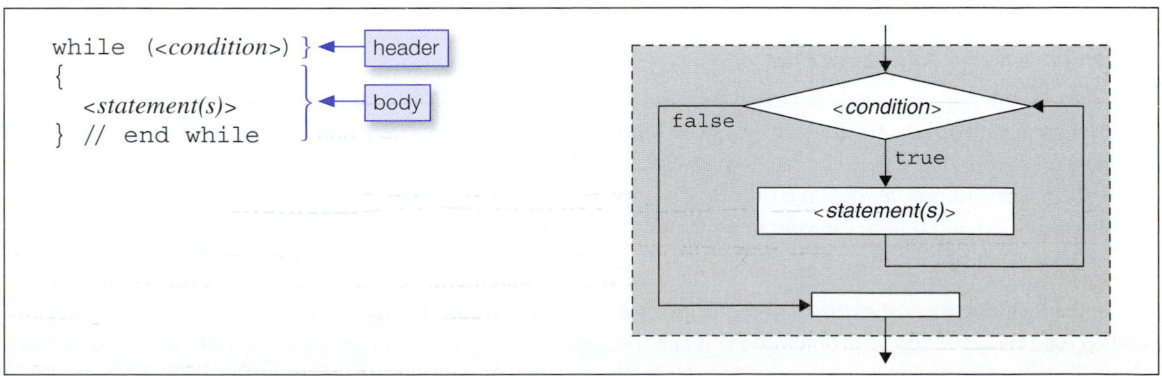

Figure 4.10 Syntax and semantics for the `while` loop

A `while` loop's condition is the same as an `if` statement's condition. It typically employs comparison and logical operators, and it evaluates to `true` or `false`. Here's how the `while` loop works:

1. Check the `while` loop's condition.
2. If the condition is `true`, execute the `while` loop's body (the statements that are inside the braces), jump back to the `while` loop's condition, and repeat step 1.
3. If the condition is `false`, jump to below the `while` loop's body and continue with the next statement.

Example

Now let's consider an example—a program that creates a bridal gift registry. More specifically, the program repeatedly prompts the user for two things—a gift item and the store where the gift can be purchased. When the user is done entering gift and store values, the program prints the bridal registry list. Study this sample session:

Sample session:

```
Do you wish to create a bridal registry list? (y/n): y
Enter item: candle holder
Enter store: Sears
Any more items? (y/n): y
Enter item: lawn mower
Enter store: Home Depot
Any more items? (y/n): n

Bridal Registry:
candle holder - Sears
lawn mower - Home Depot
```

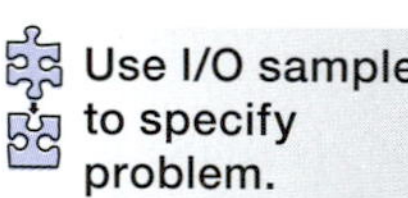

Use I/O sample to specify problem.

That's the problem specification. Our solution appears in Figure 4.11. As you can tell by the `while` loop's `more == 'y'` condition and the query at the bottom of the loop, the program employs a user-query loop. The initial query above the `while` loop makes it possible to quit without making any passes through the loop. If you want to force at least one pass through the loop, you should delete the initial query and initialize `more` like this:

```
char more = 'y';
```

The BridalRegistry program illustrates several peripheral concepts that you'll want to remember for future programs. Within the `while` loop, note the += assignment statements, repeated here for your convenience:

```
registry += stdIn.nextLine() + " - ";
registry += stdIn.nextLine() + "\n";
```

The += operator comes in handy when you need to incrementally add to a string variable. The BridalRegistry program stores all the gift and store values in a single `String` variable named `registry`. Each new gift and store entry gets concatenated to the `registry` variable with the += operator.

At the top and bottom of the BridalRegistry program's `while` loop, note the `nextLine` and `charAt` method calls, repeated here for your convenience:

```
more = stdIn.nextLine().charAt(0);
```

The method calls are *chained* together by inserting a dot between them. The `nextLine()` method call reads a line of input from the user and returns the input as a string. That string then calls the `charAt(0)`, which returns the string's first character. Note that it's acceptable and fairly common to chain multiple method calls together like this.

```
/****************************************************************
* BridalRegistry.java
* Dean & Dean
*
* This makes entries in a bridal registry.
****************************************************************/

import java.util.Scanner;

public class BridalRegistry
{
  public static void main(String[] args)
  {
    Scanner stdIn = new Scanner(System.in);
    String registry = "";
    char more;

    System.out.print(
      "Do you wish to create a bridal registry list? (y/n): ");
    more = stdIn.nextLine().charAt(0);

    while (more == 'y')
    {
      System.out.print("Enter item: ");
      registry += stdIn.nextLine() + " - ";
      System.out.print("Enter store: ");
      registry += stdIn.nextLine() + "\n";
      System.out.print("Any more items? (y/n): ");
      more = stdIn.nextLine().charAt(0);
    } // end while

    if (!registry.equals(""))
    {
      System.out.println("\nBridal Registry:\n" + registry);
    }
  } // end main
} // end BridalRegistry class
```

Figure 4.11 BridalRegistry program with `while` loop and user-query terrmination

Infinite Loops

Suppose you're trying to print the numbers 1 through 10. Will the following code fragment work?

```
int x = 0;
while (x < 10)
{
  System.out.println(x + 1);
}
```

The while loop body does just one thing—it prints 1 (since 0 + 1 is 1). It does not update x's value (since there's no assignment or increment statement for x). With no update for x, the while loop's condition (x < 10) always evaluates to true. That's an example of an *infinite loop*. The computer executes the statements in the loop body over and over—forever. When you have an infinite loop, the computer seems to freeze or "hang up."

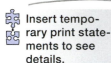

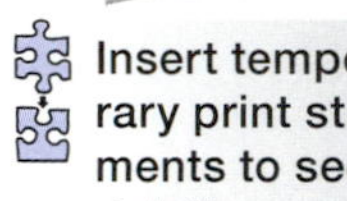

Sometimes, what seems to be an infinite loop is just an extremely inefficient algorithm that takes a long time to finish. In either of these cases, you can figure out what's happening by inserting into the loop a diagnostic statement that prints a value you think should be changing in a certain way. Then run the program and watch what happens to that value.

4.9 do Loop

Now let's consider a second type of Java loop—the do loop. A do loop is appropriate when you're sure that you want the loop body to be repeated at least one time. Because the do loop matches the way most computer hardware performs looping operations, it is slightly more efficient than the other types of loops. Unfortunately, its awkwardness makes it prone to programming error, and therefore some programmers don't like to use it. But at the very least, you need to be aware of it.

Syntax and Semantics

Figure 4.12 shows the do loop's syntax and semantics. Note that the do loop's condition is at the bottom. This contrasts with the while loop, where the condition is at the top. Having the condition tested at the bottom is how the do loop guarantees that the loop executes at least one time. Note the semicolon at the right of the condition. That's required by the compiler, and omitting it is a common error. Finally, note that the while part is on the same line as the closing brace—that's good style. It's possible to put while (<*condition*>); on the line after the closing brace, but that would be bad style because it would look like you're trying to start a new while loop.

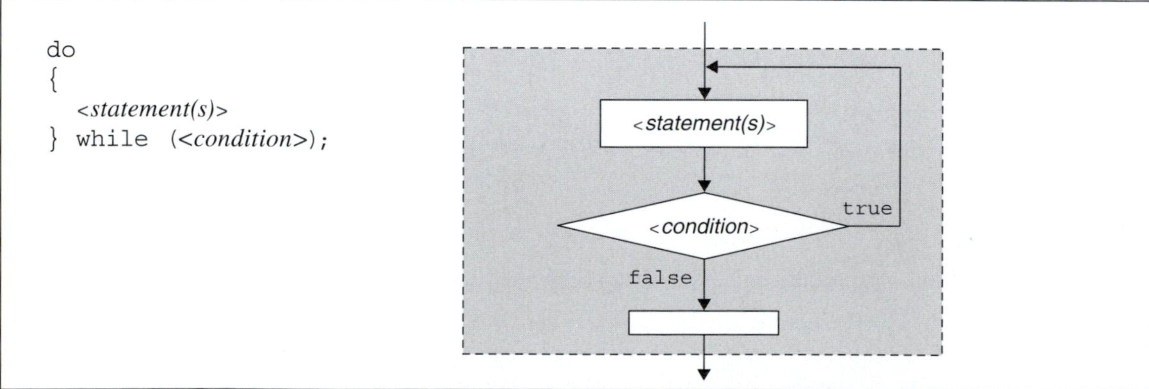

Figure 4.12 Syntax and semantics for the do loop

Here's how the do loop works:

1. Execute the do loop's body.
2. Check the final condition.
3. If the condition is `true`, jump back to the top of the do loop and repeat step 1.
4. If the condition is `false`, continue with the statement immediately below the loop.

Practice Problem

Now let's illustrate the do loop with an example problem. Suppose you're asked to write a program that prompts the user to enter length and width dimensions for each room in a proposed house so that total floor space can be calculated for the entire house. After each length/width entry, ask the user if there are any more rooms. When there are no more rooms, print the total floor space.

How many repeats?

To solve this problem, first ask whether a loop is appropriate. Does anything need to be repeated? Yes, you'll want to read in dimensions repeatedly, so a loop is appropriate. To determine the type of loop, ask yourself: Will you always need to execute the read-in-the-dimensions loop body at least once? Yes, every house must have at least one room, so you'll need to read in at least one set of dimensions. Thus, it's appropriate to use a do loop for this problem. Now that you've thought through the looping issues, you're ready to put pencil to paper and write down your solution. Go for it.

When you're done working out a solution on your own, look at our solution in Figure 4.13. Did you prompt for length and width values within your do loop and then add the length times width product to a total floor space variable? Did you then prompt the user for a continue decision?

Compare the loop-termination technique used in the FloorSpace program with the loop-termination technique used in the BridalRegistry program in Figure 4.11. In the BridalRegistry program, we needed two user queries—one before the start of the loop and one within the loop just before its end. In the FloorSpace program, we need only one user query—within the loop just before its end. The do loop requires that there be at least one pass, but if this is acceptable, it requires fewer lines of code than the `while` loop.

Before leaving the FloorSpace program, take note of a style feature. Do you see the blank lines above and below the do loop? It's good style to separate logical chunks of code with blank lines. Since a loop is a logical chunk of code, it's nice to surround loops with blank lines unless the loop is very short, that is, less than about four lines.

4.10 for Loop

Now let's consider a third type of loop—the `for` loop. A `for` loop is appropriate when you know the exact number of loop iterations before the loop begins. For example, suppose you want to perform a countdown from 10, like this:

Sample session:

```
10 9 8 7 6 5 4 3 2 1 Liftoff!
```

In your program, you'll need to print 10 numbers, and you should print each number with the help of a print statement inside a loop. Since the print statement should execute 10 times, you know the exact number of iterations for the loop, 10. Therefore, you should use a `for` loop.

```
/*************************************************************
* FloorSpace.java
* Dean & Dean
*
* This program calculates total floor space in a house.
*************************************************************/

import java.util.Scanner;

public class FloorSpace
{
  public static void main(String[] args)
  {
    Scanner stdIn = new Scanner(System.in);
    double length, width;         // room dimensions
    double floorSpace = 0;        // house's total floor space
    char response;                // user's y/n response

    do
    {
      System.out.print("Enter the length: ");
      length = stdIn.nextDouble();
      System.out.print("Enter the width: ");
      width = stdIn.nextDouble();
      floorSpace += length * width;
      System.out.print("Any more rooms? (y/n): ");
      response = stdIn.next().charAt(0);
    } while (response == 'y' || response == 'Y');

    System.out.println("Total floor space is " + floorSpace);
  } // end main
} // end class FloorSpace
```

Figure 4.13 Using a do loop to calculate total floor space

For another example, suppose you want to find the factorial of a user-entered number, like this:

Sample session:

```
Enter a whole number: 4
4! = 24
```

For 4 factorial, you need to multiply the values 1 through 4: 1 × 2 × 3 × 4 = 24. The three ×'s indicate that three multiplications are necessary. So 4 factorial requires three loop iterations. For the general case, where you need to find the factorial for a user-entered number, store the user-entered number in a `count` variable. Then multiply the values 1 through `count` like this:

1 * 2 * 3 * . . . * `count`

`count` - 1 number of *'s

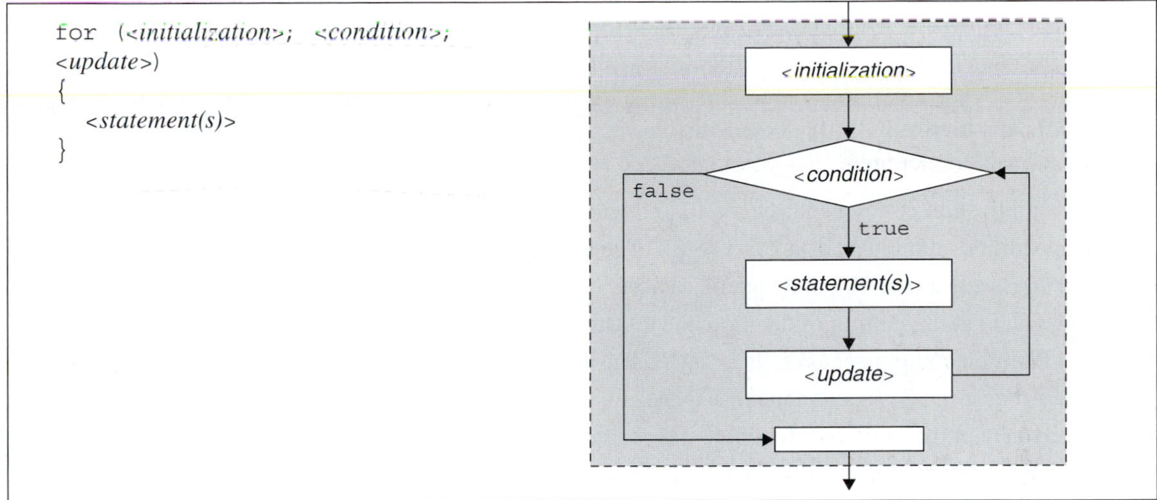

Figure 4.14 Syntax and semantics for the `for` loop

The `*`'s indicate that `count - 1` multiplications are necessary. So `count` factorial requires `count - 1` loop iterations. Since you know the number of iterations for the loop (`count - 1`), use a `for` loop.

Syntax and Semantics

Figure 4.14 shows the `for` loop's syntax and semantics. The `for` loop header does a lot of work. So much work that it's split into three components—the *initialization*, *condition*, and *update* components. The following list explains how the `for` loop uses the three components. As you read the list, refer to Figure 4.14's flowchart to get a better idea of what's going on.

1. Initialization component
   Before the first pass through the body of the loop, execute the initialization component.
2. Condition component
   Before each loop iteration, evaluate the condition component:
   - If the condition is `true`, execute the body of the loop.
   - If the condition is `false`, terminate the loop (exit to the statement below the loop's closing brace).
3. Update component
   After each pass through the body of the loop, return to the loop header and execute the update component. Then, recheck the continuation condition in the second component, and if it's satisfied, go through the body of the loop again.

Countdown Example

Here is a code fragment for the countdown example mentioned at the start of this section:

```
for (int i=10; i>0; i--)
{
  System.out.print(i + " ");
}
System.out.println("Liftoff!");
```

Note that the same variable, i, appears in all three components of the for loop header. That variable is given a special name. It's called an *index variable*. Index variables in for loops are often, but not always, named i for "index." Index variables often start at a low value, increment up, and then stop when they reach a threshold set by the condition component. But in the above example, the index variable does just the opposite. It starts at a high value (10), decrements down, and then stops when it reaches the threshold of 0. Let's informally trace the example:

The initialization component assigns 10 to the index, i.

The condition component asks "Is i > 0?" The answer is yes, so execute the body of the loop.

Print 10 (because i is 10), and append a space.

Since you're at the bottom of the loop, the update component decrements i from 10 to 9.

The condition component asks "Is i > 0?" The answer is yes, so execute the body of the loop.

Print 9 (because i is 9) and append a space.

Since you're at the bottom of the loop, the update component decrements i from 9 to 8.

The condition component asks "Is i > 0?" The answer is yes, so execute the body of the loop.

Repeat the previous printing and decrementing until you print 1.

. . .

After printing 1, since you're at the bottom of the loop, decrement i from 1 to 0.

The condition component asks "Is i > 0?" The answer is no, so quit the loop, drop down to the first statement after the closing brace, and print "Liftoff!"

Alternatively, we could have implemented the solution with a while loop or a do loop. Why is the for loop preferable? With a while loop or a do loop, you'd need two extra statements to initialize and update the count variable. That would work OK, but using a for loop is more elegant.

Factorial Example

Now, let's make sure you really understand how the for loop works by studying a formal trace of the second example mentioned at the start of this section—the calculation of a factorial. Figure 4.15 shows the factorial-calculation code listing and its associated trace. Note the input column in the top-left corner of the trace. You didn't have input in Chapter 3's trace examples, so input is worth mentioning now. When the program reads an input value, you copy the next input from the input column into the next row under the variable to which the input is assigned. In this case, when you get to number = stdIn.nextInt(), you copy the 4 from the input column to the next row in the number column.

This trace shows that the 8, 10 sequence repeats three times, so there are indeed three iterations, as expected. Suppose you entered number = 0. Does the program work for that extreme case? The loop header initializes int i=2 and then immediately tests to see if i<=number. Since this condition is false, the loop terminates before it starts, and the code prints the initial value of factorial, which is 1.0. That's correct, since 0 factorial does indeed equal 1.

What about the other extreme case—when the input value is very large? The factorial of a number increases much more rapidly than the number itself increases. If we had declared factorial to be of type int, then input values greater than 12 would cause the factorial variable to overflow, and the output value would be horribly wrong! That's why we declared factorial to be of type double. A double has more precision than an int, and it gives approximately correct answers even when its precision is inadequate. This makes the program more robust, because it fails more *gracefully*. That is, when it fails, it fails just a little bit, not a lot.

Little mistakes are better than big ones.

```
1  Scanner stdIn = new Scanner(System.in);
2  int number;
3  double factorial = 1.0;
4
5  System.out.print("Enter a whole number: ");
6  number = stdIn.nextInt();
7
8  for (int i=2; i<=number; i++)
9  {
10   factorial *= i;
11 }
12
13 System.out.println(number + "! = " + factorial);
```

Declare `for` loop index variables within the `for` loop header.

input

4

line#	number	factorial	i	output
2	?			
3		1.0		
5				Enter a whole number:
6	4			
8			2	
10		2.0		
8			3	
10		6.0		
8			4	
10		24.0		
8			5	
13				4! = 24.0

Figure 4.15 Code fragment that illustrates factorial calculation plus its associated trace

Scope of `for` Loop Index

In the `for` loop examples presented so far, the loop's index variable (`i`) is initialized (declared and given an initial value) in the `for` loop header. This limits the *scope* or recognizable range of the index variable to the `for` loop itself. In other words, whenever a variable is declared in the `for` loop header, it exists and can be recognized and used only by code that is within the body of that `for` loop. For example, if you tried to use the value of the `i` index variable in the print statement that followed the final brace of the `for` loop in Figure 4.15, the compiler would say "cannot find symbol. . . variable i."

Sometimes, variables used in a loop need to have a scope beyond the loop's scope. The above Factorial program illustrates what we're talking about. The `factorial` variable must be available for the print statement after the end of the loop, so it must be declared outside the loop. Since it is also needed in the loop, it must be declared before the loop, so we declare it at the beginning of the method with the other variables whose scopes extend throughout the method.

4.11 Solving the Problem of Which Loop to Use

Now, let's compare the various kinds of loops.

The do loop's decision point is at the bottom of the loop. That's in contrast to the while and for loops, where the decision point is at the top of the loop. When the decision point is at the top of the loop, the decision stands out more and the code is therefore less prone to programming error.

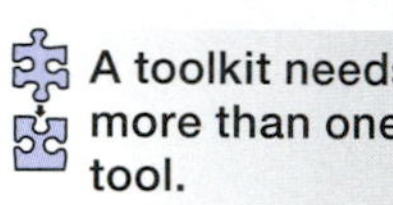
A toolkit needs more than one tool.

With programming, as in life, there are usually many different ways to accomplish the same thing. For example, for a problem that requires repetition, you can actually use any of the three loops to solve any repetition problem. Even though that's the case, you should strive to make your programs elegant, and that means choosing the most appropriate loop even though any loop could be made to work.

Flexibility makes programming fun if you like to be creative. But if you're just starting out, that flexibility can lead to confusion. In Figure 4.16, we provide a table that attempts to alleviate some of that confusion. It suggests a way to choose an appropriate type of loop and how to get started with that loop's code. We use angled brackets around text to indicate that the enclosed text is a description of code, not actual code. Thus, in using Figure 4.16's do loop and while loop templates, you'll need to replace *<prompt—do it again (y/n?)>* with actual code. For example, for a game program, you might use this actual code:

```
System.out.print("Do you want to play another game (y/n)? ");
response = stdIn.nextLine().charAt(0);
```

Loop Type	When to Use	Template

for loop:	When you know, prior to the start of the loop, how many times you want to repeat the loop.	for (i=0; i<max; i++)
		{
		  <statements>
		}

do loop:	When you always need to do the repeated thing at least one time.	do
		{
		  <statements>
		  <prompt - do it again (y/n)?>
		} while (*<response == 'y'>*);

while loop:	When looping is "event driven"; that is, you loop until some special condition changes.	*<prompt - do it (y/n)?>*
		while (*<response == 'y'>*)
		{
		  <statements>
		  <prompt - do it again (y/n)?>
		}

Figure 4.16 Choosing the right loop and getting started with the loop's code

When figuring out which loop to use, it's best to think about the loops in the order of appearance in Figure 4.16. Why? Note how the `for` loop uses the fewest lines, the `do` loop uses the next fewest lines, and the `while` loop uses the most lines. Thus, the `for` loop is the most compact and the `do` loop is the next most compact. But the `while` loop is more popular than the `do` loop because its condition is at the beginning of the loop, which makes it easier to find. Although you may wish to avoid the `do` loop because of its relatively awkward structure, in general, you should use the loop that's most appropriate for your particular problem.

When deciding how to write loop code, you can use the templates shown in Figure 4.16 as starting points. Be aware that in writing loop code, you have to do more than just copy code from Figure 4.16. You need to adapt the code to your particular problem. For example, in writing a `for` loop, it's common to use `i=0` for the initialization component, and that's why the `for` loop template's initialization component shows `i=0`. However, if some other initialization component is more appropriate, like `count=10`, then use the more appropriate code.

4.12 Nested Loops

A *nested loop* is a loop that's inside another loop. You'll see nested loops quite often in real-world programs. In this section, we discuss some of the common characteristics inherent to nested loops.

Suppose you're asked to write a program that prints a rectangle of characters where the user specifies the rectangle's height, the rectangle's width, and the character's value.

Sample session:

```
Enter height: 4
Enter width: 3
Enter character: <
<<<
<<<
<<<
<<<
```

Select the best tool for the job. 

To figure out the loops, you first need to think about what needs to be repeated. So, . . . what needs to be repeated? You need to print rows of characters repeatedly. What type of loop should you use to print the rows repeatedly? First try to use a `for` loop. The test for a `for` loop is whether you know the number of times you'll need to repeat the loop. Do you know the number of times you'll need to repeat this loop? Yes, the user enters the height, you can use that entered value to determine the number of rows, and that tells you the number of times to repeat the loop. Therefore, you should use a `for` loop to print successive rows.

Now that you know how to print multiple rows, you need to know how to print an individual row. Do you need to repeat anything when printing an individual row? Yes, you need to print characters repeatedly. So what type of loop should you use for that? Use another `for` loop because you can use the user's width entry to determine the number of characters to be printed.

So there you go—you need two `for` loops. Should you put one loop right after the other? No! You need to nest the second loop, the one that prints an individual row, inside the first loop. That should make sense if you word the goal carefully—"Print multiple rows and within each row, print a sequence of characters." The key word is "within." That tells you to insert the second `for` loop inside the first `for` loop's braces.

Using this discussion as a guideline, now write a complete program solution. When you're done, compare your answer to the NestedLoopRectangle program in Figure 4.17.

```
/****************************************************************
* NestedLoopRectangle.java
* Dean & Dean
*
* This program uses nested looping to draw a rectangle.
****************************************************************/

import java.util.Scanner;

public class NestedLoopRectangle
{
  public static void main(String[] args)
  {
    Scanner stdIn = new Scanner(System.in);
    int height, width;          // rectangle's dimensions
    char printCharacter;

    System.out.print("Enter height: ");
    height = stdIn.nextInt();
    System.out.print("Enter width: ");
    width = stdIn.nextInt();
    System.out.print("Enter character: ");
    printCharacter = stdIn.next().charAt(0);

    for (int row=1; row<=height; row++)
    {
      for (int col=1; col<=width; col++)
      {
        System.out.print(printCharacter);
      }
      System.out.println();
    }
  } // end main
} // end class NestedLoopRectangle
```

Use `print` here, to stay on same line.

Use `println` here, to move to new line.

Figure 4.17 Program that uses nested loops to draw a rectangle

Note how we use the `print` method for the print statement inside the inner loop to keep subsequent printed characters on the same line. Then after the inner loop finishes, we use a separate `println` method to go to the next line.

For most problems where you're dealing with a two-dimensional picture like this rectangle example, you'll want to use nested `for` loops with index variables named `row` and `col` (`col` is short for column). Why? It makes code more understandable. For example, in the first `for` loop header, the `row` variable goes from 1 to 2 to 3, and so on, and that corresponds perfectly with the actual rows printed by the program. However, be aware that it's also common for nested `for` loops to use index variables named `i` and `j`. Why `i` and `j`? Because `i` stands for "index," and `j` comes after `i`.

In the NestedLoopRectangle program, there are two levels of nesting, but in general there may be any number of nesting levels. Each level adds another dimension to the problem. Our NestedLoopRectangle program is quite symmetrical. Both loops are the same type (they're both `for` loops), and both loops do the same kind of thing (they both print something). In general, however, nested loops do not have to be the same type, and they do not have to do the same kinds of things.

4.13 boolean Variables

The conditions that appear in `if` statements and loops all evaluate to either `true` or `false`. We described these Boolean values in Section 4.2. Java also allows us to define a `boolean` variable, which is a variable that can hold a Boolean value. To declare a `boolean` variable, specify `boolean` for the variable's type, like this:

```
boolean upDirection;
```

In this section, we describe when to use `boolean` variables in general, and we provide a program that uses `boolean` variables, including the `upDirection` variable shown above.

When to Use a boolean Variable

Programs often need to keep track of the state of some condition. You can use a `boolean` variable to keep track of any two-way *state*—a yes/no, up/down, on/off attribute of some entity. For example, if you're writing a program that simulates the operations of an electronic garage door opener, you'll need to keep track of the state of the garage door's direction—is the direction up or down? You need to keep track of the direction "state" because the direction determines what happens when the garage door opener's button is pressed. If the direction state is up, then pressing the garage door button causes the direction to switch to down. If the direction state is down, then pressing the garage door button causes the direction to switch to up.

`boolean` variables are good at keeping track of the state of some condition when the state has one of two values. For example:

Values for the state of a garage door opener's direction	Comparable values for a `boolean` variable named `upDirection`
up	`true`
down	`false`

Garage Door Opener Example

The following code skeleton illustrates how the `upDirection` variable works:

```
boolean upDirection = true;
do
{
  . . .
  upDirection = !upDirection;
  . . .
} while (<user presses the garage door opener button>);
```

The `boolean upDirection = true;` statement tells the program to start in the down/closed position and go up when the garage door opener is first pressed. Each iteration of the loop represents what happens when the user presses the garage door opener button. The `upDirection = !upDirection` statement implements the garage door opener's toggling operation. If `upDirection` holds the value `true`, this statement changes it to `false`, and vice versa.

Now let's look at the `upDirection` variable in the context of a complete GarageDoor program. In the program, each push of the Enter key on the computer keyboard simulates a push of the garage door opener button. The first push makes the door move upward. The second push makes the door stop. The third push makes the door move downward. The fourth push makes the door stop. And so forth, until the user enters 'q' to make the program quit. Note this client view for the GarageDoor program:

Sample session:

```
GARAGE DOOR OPENER SIMULATOR

Press Enter, or enter 'q' to quit:
moving up
Press Enter, or enter 'q' to quit:
stopped
Press Enter, or enter 'q' to quit:
moving down
Press Enter, or enter 'q' to quit:
stopped
Press Enter, or enter 'q' to quit: q
```

Figure 4.18 contains an implementation view of this program—the code. In the program, verify that `upDirection` is used as previously discussed. Note that there's a second `boolean` variable, `inMotion`. The `upDirection` `boolean` variable keeps track of the state of going up or down. That one state variable would be good enough if pressing a garage door opener button always generated an up or down motion. But as shown in the sample session, that's not the case. Half the time, pressing the garage door opener causes the garage door to stop moving. Here's the key point: If the door is moving, the door stops, and if the door is stopped, the door starts moving. We keep track of whether the garage door is currently moving with the help of a second state variable, `inMotion`. The `inMotion` state variable toggles (goes from `false` to `true` or vice versa) at each button push, whereas the `upDirection` state variable toggles only when the door is stopped—at every other button push.

Note how we use the `inMotion` and `upDirection` `boolean` variables by themselves as conditions for `if` statements:

```
if (inMotion)
{
  if (upDirection)
  {
    . . .
```

In the past, you used relational operators within your conditions (e.g., ==, <=) But the only rule for a condition is that it needs to evaluate to `true` or `false`. A `boolean` variable is either `true` or `false`, so using a `boolean` variable by itself for a condition is legal. Actually, using a `boolean` variable by itself for a

```
/*********************************************************************
* GarageDoor.java
* Dean & Dean
*
* This simulated operation of a garage door.
*********************************************************************/

import java.util.Scanner;

public class GarageDoor
{
  public static void main(String[] args)
  {
    Scanner stdIn = new Scanner(System.in);
    String entry;                    // user's entry - enter key or q
    boolean upDirection = true;      // Is the current direction up?
    boolean inMotion = false;        // Is garage door currently moving?

    System.out.println("GARAGE DOOR OPENER SIMULATOR\n");

    do
    {
      System.out.print("Press Enter, or enter 'q' to quit: ");
      entry = stdIn.nextLine();

      if (entry.equals(""))          // pressing Enter generates ""
      {
        inMotion = !inMotion;        // button toggles run state
        if (inMotion)
        {
          if (upDirection)
          {
            System.out.println("moving up");
          }
          else
          {
            System.out.println("moving down");
          }
        }
        else
        {
          System.out.println("stopped");
          upDirection = !upDirection;  // direction reverses at stop
        }
      } // end if entry = ""
    } while (entry.equals(""));
  } // end main
} // end GarageDoor class
```

! operator toggles motion every time

! operator toggles direction when stopped

Figure 4.18 GarageDoor program

condition is often considered to be elegant. For example, the above `if` conditions are more elegant than the following functionally equivalent `if` conditions:

```
if (inMotion == true)
{
  if (upDirection == true)
  {
    . . .
```

The GarageDoor program is *user-friendly* because it requires a minimum amount of user input. A given user entry serves one of two purposes. The simplest kind of entry (pressing the Enter key) simulates pushing the button on a garage door opener. Any other entry (not just a 'q' entry) terminates the looping process. Whenever a special data value (in this case anything except a plain Enter) tells a program to stop looping, we say we're using a *sentinel value* to terminate the looping process. Because the program imposes a minimum burden on the user in terms of input, and because the code is relatively concise and efficient, it's appropriate to call this an elegant implementation.

4.14 Input Validation

In the previous section, you learned to use a `boolean` variable to keep track of a two-way state. In this section, you'll learn to use a `boolean` variable for a particularly common two-way state—the state of a user's input in terms of whether it's valid or invalid.

Input validation is when a program checks a user's input to make sure it's valid, that is, correct and reasonable. If it's valid, the program continues. If it's invalid, the program enters a loop that warns the user about the erroneous input and then prompts the user to re-enter.

In the GarageDoor program, note how the program checks for an empty string (which indicates the user wants to continue). If the string is not empty, it assumes that the user entered a 'q', but it doesn't check specifically for a 'q'. Consequently, it does not deal well with the possibility that the user accidentally hits another key before pressing the Enter key. It interprets that input as a quit command instead of a mistake.

To make the program more robust, you should provide input validation. There are several possible ways to do this. One of the simplest ways is to insert a `while` loop whose condition and's together all bad possibilities and whose body warns the user about the erroneous input and then prompts the user to re-enter. For the GarageDoor program in Figure 4.18, input validation is provided by the code fragment in Figure 4.19.

```
while (!entry.equals("") && !entry.equalsIgnoreCase("q"))
{
  System.out.println("Invalid entry.");
  System.out.print("Press Enter, or enter 'q': ");
  entry = stdIn.nextLine();
}
```

Figure 4.19 Input validation loop to insert after the input statement in Figure 4.18

Where should you insert this code fragment? You want to validate the input right after the input is entered. So to make the GarageDoor program more robust, you should insert the above code fragment into Figure 4.18 immediately after this statement:

```
entry = stdIn.nextLine();
```

Running the modified program produces the following sample session:

Sample session:

```
GARAGE DOOR OPENER SIMULATOR

Press Enter, or enter 'q' to quit:
moving up
Press Enter, or enter 'q' to quit: stop
Invalid entry.
Press Enter, or enter 'q':
stopped
Press Enter, or enter 'q' to quit: q
```

invalid entry

corrected entry

Optional Forward References

At this point, some readers might want to learn about arrays. An array is a collection of related items of the same type. Array manipulations require the use of loops. As such, arrays provide a means for readers to gain further practice with the material presented in Chapter 4, specifically the loop material. You're not required to learn about arrays just yet, but if you can't wait, you can read about arrays in Chapter 10, Sections 10.1 through 10.6.

Later in the book, we present relatively advanced syntax details that pertain to control statements. For example, embedding an assignment expression in a loop header or using a `break` statement to break out of a loop. You're not required to learn those details just yet, but if you can't wait, you can read about them in Chapter 11, Sections 11.6 through 11.12.

4.15 Problem Solving with Boolean Logic (Optional)

The conditions for if statements and loops can sometimes get complicated. For a better understanding of complicated conditions, we'll now look at the logic that comprises a condition. Learning how to manipulate logic should help you to (1) simplify condition code and (2) debug logical problems. What we'll be talking about is known as *Boolean logic* or *Boolean algebra.*

Make the logic as clean as possible.

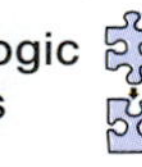

The building blocks for Boolean logic are things that you've already seen—the logical operators `&&`, `||`, and `!`. You've seen how the logical operators work when applied to comparison-operator conditions. For example, this code (which uses the `&&` operator in conjunction with the `>=` and `<=` comparison operators) probably already makes sense to you:

```
(temp >= 50.0 && temp <= 90.0)
```

Boolean Algebra Basic Identities

Sometimes, however, a logical expression is harder to understand. This is particularly true when it includes several "not" (`!`) operators. To gain a better understanding of what the code means and is supposed to do, it's sometimes helpful to transform the logical expression to another form. Boolean algebra provides a special set of formulas called *basic identities,* which anyone can use to make transformations. These basic identities are listed in Figure 4.20. The precedence of the various operators is the precedence given in Figure 4.6. That is, `!` has highest precedence, `&&` has next highest precedence, `||` has the lowest precedence. The ⟷ symbol means equivalence; that is, whatever is on the left side of the double arrow can be replaced by whatever is on the right side, and vice versa.

```
1.   !!x ⟷ x

2.   x || false ⟷ x
3.   x && true ⟷ x

4.   x || true ⟷ true
5.   x && false ⟷ false

6.   x || x ⟷ x
7.   x && x ⟷ x

8.   x || !x ⟷ true
9.   x && !x ⟷ false

10.  x || y ⟷ y || x                           } commutation
11.  x && y ⟷ y && x

12.  x || (y || z) ⟷ (x || y) || z             } association
13.  x && (y && z) ⟷ (x && y) && z

14.  x && (y || z) ⟷ x && y || x && z          } distribution
15.  x || y && z ⟷ (x || y) && (x || z)

16.  !(x || y) ⟷ !x && !y                      } DeMorgan
17.  !(x && y) ⟷ !x || !y
```

Figure 4.20 Basic identities of Boolean algebra
You can use these identities in any combination to change the form of any conditional expression.

The first 13 identities are relatively straightforward, and you should be able to satisfy yourself of their validity by just thinking about them. Likewise, you shouldn't have to memorize them. You should be able to use them instinctively. For example, *commutation* means you can switch the order without changing anything, and *association* means you can move the parentheses without changing anything. The last four identities are more mysterious, and some of them might even seem unreasonable at first. For example, *distribution* is a kind of shuffling, and *DeMorgan's theorem* says you can negate everything and exchange all and's and or's.

Proving the Boolean Identities

Now that you've seen the basic identities, let's see how to prove them. The proof technique is to write a program that compares two arbitrary logical expressions for all possible values of the `boolean` variables they contain. If the two expressions evaluate to the same truth values for all possible variable values, they are logically equivalent. Figure 4.21 contains a program that does just that for the special case of the expressions on either side of basic identity 16 in Figure 4.20.

It's straightforward to modify the TruthTable program in Figure 4.21 to test any of the other basic identities in Figure 4.20. In fact, you can modify the program to test any prospective logical equivalence. To test a different equivalence, substitute the left and right sides of the prospective equivalence for the expressions assigned to `result1` and `result2`, respectively.

```
/*************************************************************
* TruthTable.java
* Dean & Dean
*
* This proves equivalence of two boolean expressions
*************************************************************/

public class TruthTable
{
  public static void main(String[] args)
  {
    boolean x = false;
    boolean y = false;
    boolean result1, result2;

    System.out.println("x\ty\tresult1\tresult2");
    for (int i=0; i<2; i++)
    {
      for (int j=0; j<2; j++)
      {
        result1 = !(x || y);
        result2 = !x && !y;
        System.out.println(x + "\t" + y +
          "\t" + result1 + "\t" + result2);
        y = !y;
      } // end for j
      x = !x;
    } // end for i
  } // end main
} // end TruthTable class
```

To test the equivalence of any two `boolean` expressions, substitute them for these two (shaded) expressions.

Sample output:

```
x       y       result1 result2
false   false   true    true
false   true    false   false
true    false   false   false
true    true    false   false
```

Figure 4.21 Program that generates a truth table for two logical expressions
If `result1` and `result2` values are the same in all rows, the expressions are equivalent.

Applications

There are many ways you can use Boolean identities.

For example, consider the condition in the `if` statement in Figure 4.5, which looked like this:

```
((temp >= 50) && (temp <= 90))
```

Using the standard definition of the not operator, `!`, you can apply ! to each of the above comparison operator conditions and come up with this equivalent condition:

```
(!(temp < 50) && !(temp > 90))
```

You can apply basic identity 16 to the above condition and come up with this equivalent condition:

```
!((temp < 50) || (temp > 90))
```

You can use the above condition as part of a replacement for Figure 4.5's original `if` statement where the `if` and `else` subordinate statements are swapped. Here's the resulting functionally equivalent `if` statement:

```
if ((temp < 50) || (temp > 90))
{
  System.out.println("not OK");
}
else
{
  System.out.println("OK");
}
```

For another example, consider the condition in the `while` loop in Figure 4.19, which looks like this:

```
(!entry.equals("") && !entry.equalsIgnoreCase("q"))
```

You can apply basic identity 16 to the above condition and come up with this equivalent condition:

```
!(entry.equals("") || entry.equalsIgnoreCase("q"))
```

Chapter Summary

- You can alter a program's sequence of execution by using an `if` statement. The choice of which of two alternative paths to take is determined by the truth of the `if` statement's condition.
- Use the "if, else if" form of the `if` statement to choose among three or more alternatives.
- You must use braces around two or more subordinate statements within any part of an `if` statement, and it's advisable to use them even when there is only one subordinate statement.
- A condition's comparison operators (<, >, <=, >=, ==, and `!=`) have higher priority than its "and" (`&&`) and "or" (`||`) logical operators.
- To negate the result of `&&` and/or `||` operations, enclose them in parentheses and precede them with a `!` operator.
- Use a `switch` statement to choose among several alternatives on the basis of integer or character identifiers.
- Use `case` <*number*>: or `case` <*character*>: and a following `break;` to delimit each alternative in a `switch` statement.
- If the condition in a `while` loop's header is `true`, whatever is in the subsequent block executes, and then if the condition is still `true`, that execution repeats.
- A do loop executes its block at least once, and it repeats that execution as long as the condition after the final `while` remains `true`.
- A `for` loop executes its block as long as the condition in the second component of its header remains `true`. The first component in the header initializes a count variable before the first execution, and

the third component in the header updates that count variable after each execution and before the next evaluation of the second component's condition.

- You can perform multidimensional iteration by putting loops inside other loops.
- To avoid duplication and/or clutter, assign complicated logical expressions to `boolean` variables, and use those variables in `if` statement or looping conditions.
- Use input validation to avoid bringing bad data into your programs.
- Optionally, use Boolean logic to simplify the expressions in `if` statement and looping conditions, and use truth tables to verify the equivalence of alternative logical expressions.

Review Questions

§4.2 Conditions and `boolean` Values

1. What are Java's two Boolean values?
2. Provide a list of Java's comparison operators.

§4.3 `if` Statements

3. Provide an `if` statement that implements this logic:
When the water temperature is less than 120°F, turn the heater on by assigning the value "on" to a `heater` string variable. When the water temperature is greater than 140° F, turn the heater off by assigning the value "off" to a `heater` string variable. Don't do anything when the water temperature is between these two temperatures.
4. What is the maximum number of "else if" blocks allowed in an `if` statement that uses the "if, else if" form?

§4.4 `&&` Logical Operator

5. The relational and equality operators have higher precedence than the arithmetic operators. (T / F)

§4.5 `||` Logical Operator

6. Correct the following code fragment so that it executes and outputs `OK` if `a`, an `int` variable, is equal to either 2 or 3:

```
if (a = 2 || 3)
{
  print("OK\n");
}
```

§4.6 `!` Logical Operator

7. What Java operator reverses the truth or falsity of a condition?

§4.7 `switch` Statement

8. What happens if you forget to include `break;` at the end of a block of statements after a particular `case:` label?
9. If you are trying to substitute a `switch` statement for an "if, else" statement, you can use the `if` condition as the controlling expression in the `switch` statement. (T / F)
10. Suppose the controlling expression in a `switch` statement is `(stdIn.next().charAt(0))`, and you want to allow either `'Q'` or `'q'` to produce the same result, which is:
`System.out.println("quitting");`
Write the code fragment for the `case` that produces this result.

§4.8 `while` Loop

11. What must a `while` loop condition evaluate to?

12. Suppose you want to use the user-query technique to terminate a simple `while` loop. Where should you put the user query?

§4.9 do Loop

13. What's wrong with this code fragment?

```
int x = 3;
do
{
  x -= 2;
} while (x >= 0)
```

§4.10 for Loop

14. If you know ahead of time the exact number of iterations through a loop, what type of loop should you use?
15. Implement the following as a `for` loop:

```
int age = 0;
while (age < 5)
{
  System.out.println("Happy Birthday# " + age);
  age = age + 1;
} // end while
```

What output will your equivalent `for` loop generate?

§4.11 Solving the Problem of Which Loop to Use

16. If you know that a loop should be executed at least one time, what type of loop is most appropriate?

§4.12 Nested Loops

17. Construct a template for a `for` loop inside a `for` loop. Use `i` for the outer `for` loop's index variable and use `j` for the inner `for` loop's index variable.

§4.13 Boolean Variables

18. Assume that the variable `OK` has been declared to be of type `boolean`. Replace the following code with an equivalent `for` loop:

```
OK = false;
while (!OK)
{
  <statement(s)>
}
```

§4.15 Problem Solving with Boolean Logic (Optional)

19. Given the logical expression:

```
!(!a || !b)
```

Replace it with an equivalent logical expression that is completely devoid of "not" operations.

Exercises

1. [after §4.3] Whenever you mail a letter, you must decide how much postage to put on the envelope. You like to use this rule of thumb—use one stamp for every five sheets of paper or fraction thereof. For example, if you have 11 sheets of paper, then you use three stamps. To save money, you simply don't mail the letter if an envelope requires more than three stamps.

   Given that the number of sheets is stored in a variable named `numSheets`, write a code fragment that prompts the user and inputs the number of sheets, calculates the number of stamps required, and prints "Use *<number-of-stamps>* stamps" or "Don't mail," where *<number-of-stamps>* is an appropriate integer value.

2. [after §4.8] Given this code fragment:

```
1    double x = 2.1;
2
3    while (x * x <= 50)
4    {
5      switch ((int) x)
6      {
7        case 6:
8          x--;
9          System.out.println("case 6, x= " + x);
10       case 5:
11         System.out.println("case 5, x= " + x);
12       case 4:
13         System.out.println("case 4, x= " + x);
14         break;
15       default:
16         System.out.println("something else, x= " + x);
17     } // end switch
18     x +=2;
19   } // end while
```

Trace the code using either the short form or the long form. To help you get started, here's the trace setup. For the short form, you won't need the line# column.

line#	x	output

3. [after §4.9] The following `main` method is supposed to print the sum of the numbers 1 through 5 and the product of the numbers 1 through 5. Find all the bugs in the program and fix them. Do not add or delete statements. Just fix existing statements. We encourage you to check your work by running test code on a computer.

```
public static void main(String[] args)
{
  int count = 0;
  int sum = 0;
  int product = 0;
  do
  {
    count++;
    sum += count;
    product *= count;
    if (count == 5)
      System.out.println("Sum = " + sum);
      System.out.println("Product = " + product);
  } while (count < 5)
} // end main
```

<u>Intended output</u>:

```
Sum = 15
Product = 120
```

4. [after §4.10] Given this main method:

```
1   public static void main(String[] args)
2   {
3     int i;
4     String debug;
5     for (int i=0; i<3; i++)
6     {
7       switch (i * i)
8       {
9         case 0:
10          debug = "first";
11          break;
12        case 1: case 2:
13          debug = "second";
14        case 3:
15          debug = "third";
16        default:
17          System.out.println("In default");
18      } // end switch
19    } // end for
20    System.out.println("i = " + i);
21  } // end main
```

Trace the code using either the short form or the long form. To help you get started, here's the trace setup. For the short form, you won't need the line# column.

line#	i	debug	output

5. [after §4.10] Given the below program skeleton. Insert code in the *<insert-code-here>* section such that the program prints the product of even integers from 2 to num. You are not required to perform input validation.

```
public class ProductEvenInts
{
  public static void main(String[] args)
  {
    Scanner stdIn = new Scanner(System.in);
    int i, num, product;

    System.out.print("Enter a positive even number: ");
    num = stdIn.nextInt();

    <insert-code-here>

    System.out.println("Product = " + product);
  } // end main
} // end class ProductEvenInts
```

Sample session:

```
Enter a positive even number: 8
Product = 384
```

6. [after §4.12] Given this `main` method:

```
1    public static void main(String[] args)
2    {
3      for (int start=1; start<=5; start+=2)
4      {
5        for (int count=start; count>=1; count--)
6        {
7          System.out.print(count + " ");
8        }
9        System.out.println("Liftoff!");
10     }
11   } // end main
```

Trace the code using either the short form or the long form. To help you get started, here's the trace setup. For the short form, you won't need the line# column.

line#	start	count	output

7. [after §4.13] Given this `main` method:

```
1    public static void main(String[] args)
2    {
3      boolean sheLovesMe = true;
4
5      for (int num=0; num<4; num++)
6      {
7        sheLovesMe = !sheLovesMe;
8      }
9      if (sheLovesMe)
10     {
11       System.out.println("She loves me!");
12     }
13     else
14     {
15       System.out.println("She loves me not!");
16     }
17   } // end main
```

Trace the code using either the short form or the long form. To help you get started, here's the trace setup. For the short form, you won't need the line# column.

line#	sheLovesMe	num	output

8. [after §4.13] Consider the BowlingScores program below.

```
/*************************************************************
* BowlingScores.java
* Dean & Dean
*
* This implements a bowling scores algorithm.
*************************************************************/
```

```
import java.util.Scanner;

public class BowlingScores
{
  public static void main(String[] args)
  {
    Scanner stdIn = new Scanner(System.in);
    int score;
    int totalScore = 0;
    int count = 0;
    double average;

    System.out.print("Enter score (-1 to quit): ");
    score = stdIn.nextInt();

    while (score >= 0)
    {
      totalScore += score;
      count++;
      System.out.print("Enter score (-1 to quit): ");
      score = stdIn.nextInt();
    }

    average = (double) totalScore / count;
    System.out.println("Average score is " + average);
  } // end main
} // end BowlingScores class
```

Modify this program to avoid division by zero. Initialize a `boolean` variable called `more` with `true`, and use it as the `while` loop condition. Eliminate the prompt and input before the loop and move the prompt and input inside the loop to the top of the loop. Use an "if, else" structure in the loop to set `more` to `false` and bypass the normal calculation if the input is negative.

9. [after §4.13] Consider the following code fragment. Without changing the loop type, modify the code as follows. Incorporate an `if` statement in the loop body to prevent printout when the input equals the sentinel value of zero.

```
int x;
do
{
  x = stdIn.nextInt();
  System.out.println("square = " + (x * x));
} while (x != 0);
```

10. [after §4.15] Here's a brainteaser that uses Boolean logic:
You're traveling on a road, and you come to a fork in the road. You know that one path leads to a pot of gold and the other path leads to a dragon. There are two elves at the fork, both of whom know the way to the pot of gold. You know that one elf always tells the truth and the other elf always lies, but you don't know which elf is which. What single question should you ask to figure out the proper path to the pot of gold?

Review Question Solutions

1. Java's Boolean values are `true` and `false`.

2. Java's comparison operators are:

```
==, !=, <, >, <=, >=
```

3. Use an "if, else if" statement, like this:

```
if (temp < 120)
{
  heater = "on";
}
else if (temp > 140)
{
  heater = "off";
}
```

   Do not include a final `else`.

4. There is no limit on the number of "else if" blocks that are allowed.

5. False. The arithmetic operators have higher precedence than the comparison operators.

6. The corrections are underlined:

```
(a == 2 || a == 3)
{
  System.out.print("OK\n");
}
```

7. The `!` operator reverses the truth or falsity of a condition.

8. If you omit the `break`, control flows into the next `case` block, and that `case` block's statements execute also.

9. False. An "if, else" condition evaluates to either `true` or `false`. The controlling expression in a `switch` statement must evaluate to either `int` or `char` (or `byte` or `short`).

10. When more than one identifier produces the same result, concatenate on the same line, if possible, using separate `case` *<identifier>*: for each identifier:

```
case 'Q': case 'q':
  System.out.println("quitting");
```

11. A `while` condition evaluates to either `true` or `false`.

12. The user query should occur just prior to where the termination condition is tested. A `while` loop tests the termination condition at the beginning of the loop. Therefore, the user query should occur just above the top of the loop and also just above the bottom of the loop. If you want the loop to always execute at least once, then omit the user query above the loop and replace it with an assignment that forces the termination condition to be `true`.

13. There is no semicolon after the `while` condition.

14. If you know ahead of time the exact number of iterations through a loop, use a `for` loop.

15. Happy birthday as a `for` loop:

```
for (int age=0; age < 5; age++)
{
  System.out.println("Happy Birthday# " + age);
} // end for
```

Output:

```
Happy Birthday# 0
Happy Birthday# 1
Happy Birthday# 2
Happy Birthday# 3
Happy Birthday# 4
```

16. A do loop is most appropriate in simple situations where there will always be at least one pass.

17. Template for a pair of nested for loops:

```
for (int i=0; i<imax; i++)
{
  for (int j=0; j<jmax; j++)
  {
    <statement(s)>
  } // end for j
} // end for i
```

18. A `for` loop representation of a `while` loop:

```
for (boolean OK=false; !OK;)
{
  <statement(s)>
}
```

19. Given the expression:

```
!(!a || !b)
```

Starting on the left side of basic identity 16 and going to the right side gives this:

```
!!a && !!b
```

Then using basic identity 1 gives this:

```
a && b
```

CHAPTER 5

Using Pre-Built Methods

Objectives

- See what it takes to incorporate Java's pre-built API software into your programs, and become acquainted with Sun's documentation of the API software.
- Use the methods and named constants defined in Java's `Math` class.
- Use the parsing methods in wrapper classes to convert text representations of numbers into numerical format, and learn to use the `toString` methods to go the other way.
- Use methods in the `Character` class to identify and alter character types and formats.
- Use methods in the `String` class to find the first index of a particular character, extract or replace substrings, convert case, and trim leading and trailing whitespaces.
- Format output with the `System.out.printf` method.
- Optionally use the `Random` class to generate non-uniform random-number distributions.
- Optionally see how to draw geometric shapes, display pictures, and display text on a graphics display window and run a Java applet.

Outline

5.1 Introduction

In Chapters 3 and 4, we focused on basic Java programming language constructs—variables, assignments, operators, `if` statements, loops, and so on. We also introduced a more advanced programming technique—calling a method. Method calls provide a lot of "bang for your buck." In other words, they do a lot and require very little work on your part. For example, you get great benefit for little effort when you call the `print` and `println` methods for output, the `next`, `nextLine`, `nextInt`, and `nextDouble` methods for input, and the `charAt`, `length`, `equals`, and `equalsIgnoreCase` methods for string manipulation. In this chapter, we want to expose you to other methods that are already written, already tested, and are readily accessible to all Java programmers.

While this chapter raises your awareness of valuable already-written methods, it also gives you a better feeling for what methods can do in general. And learning what methods can do is an important first step in learning about *object-oriented programming* (OOP). We describe OOP in all its glory in the next chapter, but for now, here's a pared-down explanation: OOP is the idea that programs should be organized into objects. An *object* is a set of related data plus a set of behaviors. For example, a string is an object: A string's "set of related data" is its characters, and its "set of behaviors" is its methods (the `length` method, the `charAt` method, etc.). Each object is an instance of a class. For example, a single string object, "hello," is an instance of the `String` class. This chapter serves as a transition from Java basics in Chapters 3 and 4 to OOP in the remainder of the book. We carry out this transition by showing you how to use pre-built OOP code without having to implement it yourself. More specifically, in this chapter, you learn how to use methods, and in the next chapter, you'll learn how to write your own classes and the methods that go inside those classes.

There are two basic types of methods, *instance methods* and *class methods,* and we provide examples of both in this chapter. Instance methods are methods that are associated with a particular instance of a class. For example, to call the `String` class's `length` method, you have to associate it with a particular string. So in the example below, note how the `firstName` string is associated with the `length` method:

```
firstNameSize = firstName.length();
```

The `firstName` string is an example of a *calling object.* As the name implies, a calling object is an object that calls a method. Whenever you call an instance method, you have to prefix the method name with a calling object and then a dot.

Class methods are methods that are associated with an entire class, not with a particular instance of a class. For example, there's a `Math` class that contains many class methods. Its methods are associated with math in general, not with a particular instance of math (a particular instance of math doesn't even make sense). To call a class method, you prefix the method name with the name of the class that defines it. For example, the `Math` class contains a `round` method that returns the rounded version of a given value. To call the `round` method, you prefix it with `Math` like this:

```
paymentInDollars = Math.round(calculatedEarnings);
```

We start the chapter with an overview of the API library, which is Sun's collection of pre-built classes. We then examine the `Math` class, which provides methods for mathematical calculations. We next turn our attention to the wrapper classes, which encapsulate (wrap up) primitive data types. We then expand on our previous discussion of the `String` class by providing additional string methods. After that, we describe the `printf` method, which provides formatted output functionality. We then discuss the `Random` class, which provides methods for generating random numbers. We end the chapter with an optional GUI track section. In it, we discuss methods provided by the `Graphics` class and describe how to call graphics methods from within a Java applet. Very cool stuff!

5.2 The API Library

When working on a programming problem, you should normally check to see if there are pre-built classes that meet your program's needs. If there are such pre-built classes, then use those classes—don't "reinvent the wheel." For example, user input is a rather complicated task. Java's `Scanner` class handles user input. Whenever you need user input in a program, use the `Scanner` class rather than writing and using your own input class.

There are two primary advantages of using pre-built classes. Using pre-built classes can save you time since you don't have to write the classes yourself. Using pre-built classes can also improve the quality of your programs since the classes have been thoroughly tested, debugged, and scrutinized for efficiency.

Searching API Class Library Documentation

Java's pre-built classes are stored in the *Application Programming Interface (API) class library,* which is more simply known as the API library. You should be able to find documentation for the API library at Sun's Java API Web site:

http://java.sun.com/javase/6/docs/api/

The API library contains tens of thousands of pre-built methods defined in thousands of classes. The classes are organized in almost two hundred groups called *packages* (a package is a group of classes). It's unlikely that you'll be able to memorize the names of all those methods, where they are, and what they do. So how do you locate the particular piece of pre-built software that might be just what you need for your current programming project?

Use available resources. 

Use a textbook (like this textbook ☺) to get you started with selected sample classes and methods. Then go to Sun's Java API Web site and browse. See Figure 5.1. It shows that the Web site's window is partitioned

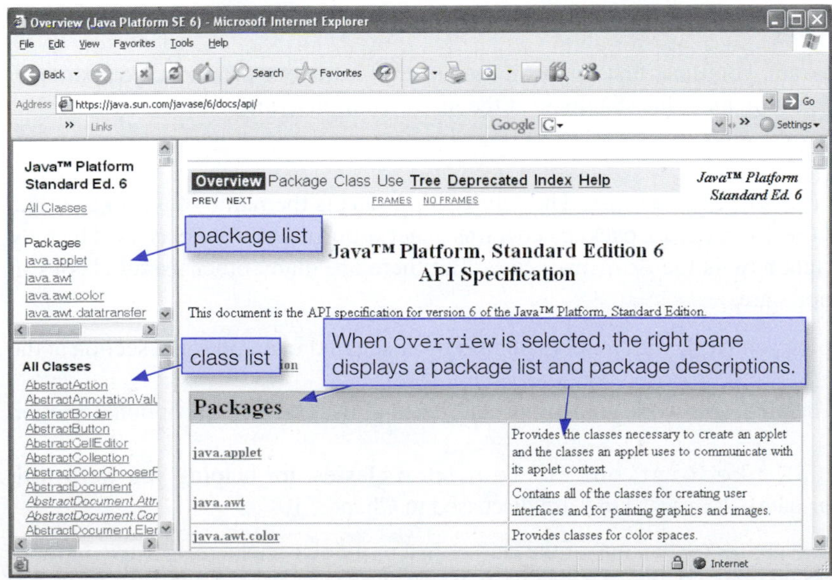

Figure 5.1 Sun's Java API Web site

into three window panes. The top-left pane displays a list of all of Java's packages. The bottom-left pane displays a list of all of Java's classes. The right pane displays a variety of different content, where the type of content depends on what the user specifies.

The Web site provides several ways to look things up:

1. If you hope that the API library contains a method or class that might help with your current programming project, but you're unsure, you'll have to do some browsing. Start by making sure the Overview link at the top of the Web site is selected. When the Overview link is selected, the right window pane displays a list of all the packages and a brief description of each package. If you find a package that looks promising, click the package's name. That causes the right pane to display all the classes within the selected package and a brief description of each class. If you find a class that looks promising, click the class's name. That causes the right pane to display all the methods within the selected class and a brief description of each method. If you find a method that looks promising, click the method's name. That causes the right pane to display the method's complete details.
2. If you know the name of a particular class that you want details on, click anywhere in the bottom-left window pane and press Ctrl+f (hold the control key down and tap the f key). The f stands for "find" and pressing Ctrl+f causes a Find dialog box to appear. Enter the name of the class in the Find dialog box and click the Find Next button. That should cause the class to be found and highlighted in the bottom-left window pane. Click the class and that causes the right window pane to display the class's details.
3. If you know the name of a particular method that you want details on, click the Index link at the top of the window. That causes the right window pane to display the letters of the alphabet. Click the letter that matches the first letter of the method you're interested in. That causes the right window pane to display methods (and other entities, like classes) that begin with the clicked letter. Find the method you're interested in and click it to display all its details.

Using Sun's Java API Web site is like surfing the net, but you're not surfing the whole world. You're just surfing the Java class library. You can do it, and we encourage you to give it a try whenever you're curious.

Using the API Class Library

To use an API class in your program, you must first import it (i.e., load it) into your program. For example, to use the `Scanner` class, you must include this statement at the top of your program:

```
import java.util.Scanner;
```

Note the `java.util` part of `java.util.Scanner`. The `java.util` part is the name of a package. The "`util`" stands for "utility," and the `java.util` package contains general-purpose utility classes. The only `java.util` class you'll need right now is the `Scanner` class. But there are many other useful classes in the `java.util` package. Examples are:

- The `Random` class, for helping you work with random numbers—discussed in an optional section at the end of this chapter.
- The `Calendar` class, for helping you work with times and dates—discussed in an optional section at the end of Chapter 8.
- The `Arrays`, `ArrayList`, `LinkedList`, and `Collections` classes, for helping you work with lists or collections of similar data—`ArrayLists` are discussed in Chapter 10.

If you have a program that needs to use more than one of the classes in a particular package, like two or more of the `util` package classes just mentioned, you can `import` them all at once using a statement like this:

```
import java.util.*;
```

The asterisk is a *wildcard*. In the above statement, the asterisk causes all classes in the `java.util` package to be imported—not just the `Scanner` class. There's no inefficiency in using the wildcard notation. The compiler includes only as much as it needs in the compiled program.

Several classes are so important that the Java compiler automatically imports them for you. These automatically imported classes are in the `java.lang` package, where `lang` stands for "language." In effect, the Java compiler automatically inserts this statement at the top of every Java program:

```
import java.lang.*;
```

Since this is automatic and understood, there's no need to write it explicitly.

The `Math` class is in the `java.lang` package, so there's no need for you to `import` the `Math` class if you want to perform math operations. Likewise, the `System` class is in the `java.lang` package, so there's no need for you to `import` the `System` class if you want to perform a `System.out.println` command.

Headings for API Methods

To use an API class, you don't need to know the internals of the class; you just need to know how to "interface" with it. To interface with a class, you need to know how to use the methods within the class. For example, to perform input, you need to know how to use the `Scanner` class's methods—`next`, `nextLine`, `nextInt`, `nextDouble`, and so on. To use a method, you need to know what type of *arguments* to pass to it and what type of value it *returns*. Arguments are the input you supply to a method when you call it, or ask it to do something for you, and the value it returns is the answer it gives you back.

The standard way to present method-interface information is to show the method's source code heading. For example, here's the source code heading for the `Scanner` class's `nextInt` method:

```
public int nextInt()
```

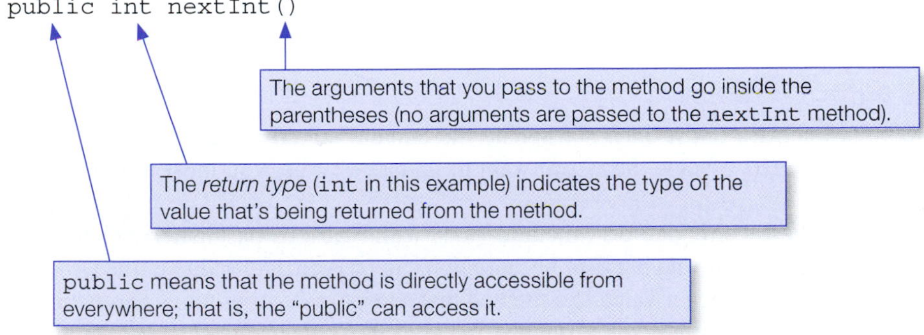

The arguments that you pass to the method go inside the parentheses (no arguments are passed to the nextInt method).
The return type (int in this example) indicates the type of the value that's being returned from the method.
public means that the method is directly accessible from everywhere; that is, the "public" can access it.

In the above `nextInt` heading, the `public` access modifier should look familiar because your `main` method headings all use `public`. We'll discuss `private` methods in Chapter 8. They're accessible only from within the class that defines them. Note that the `nextInt` method returns an `int` value and that it has no arguments inside the parentheses. Here's an example of a Java statement that shows how you might call the `nextInt` method:

```
int days = stdIn.nextInt();
```

5.3 Math Class

The `Math` class is one of the pre-built classes in the always-available `java.lang` package. This class contains methods which implement standard mathematical *functions*. A mathematical function generates a numeric value based on one or more other numeric values. For example, a square root function generates the square root of a given number. Likewise, the `Math` class's `sqrt` method returns the square root of a given number. In addition to providing mathematical methods, the `Math` class also provides two mathematical constants—π (the ratio of a circle's circumference to its diameter) and e (the base of natural logarithms).

Basic `Math` Methods

Let's now look at some of the `Math` class's methods. Throughout the book, when there's a need to present a group of methods from the API library, we'll introduce the methods by showing a list of method headings and associated brief descriptions. Headings for API methods are commonly referred to as *API headings*. Figure 5.2 contains API headings for some of the more popular methods in the `Math` class, with associated brief descriptions.

As you read through Figure 5.2, we hope that you'll find most of the methods to be straightforward. But some items may need clarification. Note the `static` modifier at the left of all the `Math` methods. All the methods in the `Math` class are `static`. The `static` modifier means they are class methods and must be called by prefacing the method's name with the name of the class in which they are defined. For example, here's how you'd call the `abs` method:

Call `Math` methods by prefacing them with `Math` dot.

```
int num = Math.abs(num);
```

The above statement updates `num`'s value, so `num` gets the absolute value of its original value. For example, if `num` starts out with −15, it ends up with 15.

Note that the following statement does not work properly:

```
Math.abs(num);
```

It finds the absolute value of `num`, but it does not update the content stored inside `num`. `Math` methods return a value. They do not update a value. So if you want to update a value, you must use an assignment operator.

In Figure 5.2, note that there's only one `pow` method—one with `double` parameters. There's no `pow` method with `int` parameters. But that's no big deal because you can pass an `int` value to the `pow` method. More generally, it's legal to pass an integer value to a method that accepts a floating-point argument. It's like assigning an integer value into a floating-point variable, discussed in Chapter 3. Let's see how this works within a code fragment. There is an empirical rule called "Horton's Law," which says that the length of a river scales with the area drained by the river in accordance with this formula:

$$\text{length} \approx 1.4\ (\text{area})^{0.6}$$

Here's how you might implement Horton's Law in Java code:

OK to pass an `int (area)`, into `pow`, which accepts `double` arguments.

```
int area = 10000;     // square miles drained
System.out.println("river length = " + 1.4 * Math.pow(area, 0.6));
```

<u>Output</u>:

```
river length = 351.66410041134117
```

```
public static double abs(double num)
```
Returns the absolute value of a `double num`.

```
public static int abs(int num)
```
Returns the absolute value of an `int num`.

```
public static double ceil(double num)
```
Returns the smallest whole number greater than or equal to `num`. `ceil` stands for "ceiling."

```
public static double exp(double power)
```
Returns `E` (base of natural logarithms) raised to the specified `power`.

```
public static double floor(double num)
```
Returns the largest whole number that is less than or equal to `num`.

```
public static double log(double num)
```
Returns the natural logarithm (base `E`) of `num`.

```
public static double log10(double num)
```
Returns the base 10 logarithm of `num`.

```
public static double max(double x, double y)
```
Returns the more positive of the two `double` values, `x` and `y`.

```
public static int max(int x, int y)
```
Returns the more positive of the two `int` values, `x` and `y`.

```
public static double min(double x, double y)
```
Returns the less positive of the two `double` values, `x` and `y`.

```
public static int min(int x, int y)
```
Returns the less positive of the two `int` values, `x` and `y`.

```
public static double pow(double num, double power)
```
Returns `num` raised to the specified `power`.

```
public static double random()
```
Returns a uniformly distributed value between 0.0 and 1.0, but not including 1.0.

```
public static long round(double num)
```
Returns the whole number that is closest to `num`.

```
public static double sqrt(double num)
```
Returns the square root of `num`.

Figure 5.2 API headings and brief descriptions of some of the methods in the `java.lang.Math` class

Note the `round` method in Figure 5.2. How is it different from using an `(int)` type cast operator on a `double` value? The `(int)` operator truncates the fraction, whereas the `round` method rounds up if the fraction is ≥ 0.5.

As shown in Figure 5.2, `Math`'s `random` method returns a uniformly distributed value between 0.0 and 1.0, not including 1.0. "Uniformly distributed" means that there's the same chance of getting any value within the specified range. In other words, if you have a program that calls `random`, the chances are the same for `random` returning 0.317, 0.87, 0.02, or any value between 0.0 and 1.0, not including 1.0.

Why would you want to call the `random` method? If you need to analyze a real-world situation that involves random events, you should consider writing a program that uses the `random` method to model the random events. For example, if you work for a city transportation department, and you're in charge of improving traffic flow at traffic light intersections, you could write a program that uses the `random` method to model the arrival of automobiles at the traffic lights. For each traffic light that you're interested in, you'd set the traffic light's cycle time (e.g., two minutes between each new green signal) and then simulate automobiles arriving at the traffic light at random intervals. You'd run the program so that it simulates one week of traffic flow, and you'd keep track of average wait time for all vehicles. You'd then adjust the traffic light's cycle time (e.g., one minute and forty-five seconds between each new green signal), run the simulation again, and determine which traffic light cycle time produces shorter average wait times.

Let's wrap up the discussion of Figure 5.2's `Math` methods with a complete program example. Suppose you want to calculate the length of the hypotenuse of a right triangle, given the lengths of its base and height, as shown in this picture:

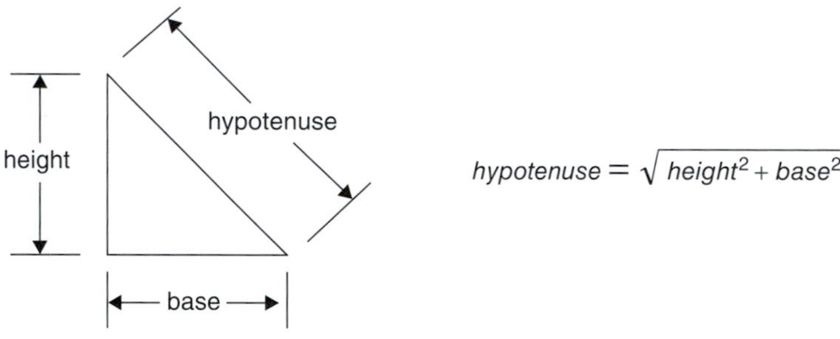

Figure 5.3 contains a simple program that asks the user to provide base and height values. Then it uses `Math`'s `sqrt` method to calculate and print the square root of the sum of the squares. Notice that we did not use the `Math.pow` method to square the base and square the height. For small powers, it's more efficient just to multiply them out.

Trigonometric `Math` Methods

Figure 5.4 contains API headings and descriptions for some of the methods in the `Math` class that can help you solve problems in trigonometry. The `sin`, `cos`, and `tan` methods implement the sine, cosine, and tangent functions, respectively. The `asin`, `acos`, and `atan` methods implement the arcsine, arccosine, and arctangent functions, respectively. The trigonometric and inverse trigonometric functions all use or return angle values as radians, not degrees. Using or assuming degrees is a common programming error. Be careful!

```
/*******************************************************************
* FindHypotenuse.java
* Dean & Dean
*
* This program computes the hypotenuse of a right triangle.
*******************************************************************/

import java.util.Scanner;

public class FindHypotenuse
{
  public static void main(String[] args)
  {
    Scanner stdIn = new Scanner(System.in);
    double base;
    double height;
    double hypotenuse;

    System.out.print("Enter right triangle base: ");
    base = stdIn.nextDouble();
    System.out.print("Enter right triangle height: ");
    height = stdIn.nextDouble();
    hypotenuse = Math.sqrt(base * base + height * height);

    System.out.println("Hypotenuse length = " + hypotenuse);
  } // end main
} // end FindHypotenuse
```

call to `Math` class's `sqrt` method

Sample session:

```
Enter right triangle base: 3.0
Enter right triangle height: 4.0
Hypotenuse length = 5.0
```

Figure 5.3 FindHypotenuse program demonstrates use of one of Java's pre-built math functions

Named Constants

The `Math` class also contains `double` values for two important named constants:

```
PI = 3.14159265358979323846
E = 2.7182818284590452354
```

`PI` and `E` are standard mathematical constants. `PI` is the ratio of a circle's perimeter to its diameter. `E` is Euler's number, the base for natural logarithm calculations. The names `PI` and `E` are in all uppercase characters, because that's standard style for named constants. Constants have fixed values, and if you attempt to assign a value to them, you'll get a compilation error. Just as `Math`'s methods are called class methods, these constants are called *class constants,* and you access them through the `Math` class name. In other words, if you need π, specify `Math.PI`.

```
public static double acos(double ratio)
```
Returns the angle in radians between 0.0 and π whose cosine equals the given value.

```
public static double asin(double ratio)
```
Returns the angle in radians between $-\pi/2$ and $+\pi/2$ whose sine equals the given value.

```
public static double atan(double ratio)
```
Returns the angle in radians between $-\pi/2$ and $+\pi/2$ whose tangent equals the given value.

```
public static double cos(double radians)
```
Returns the cosine of an angle expressed in radians.

```
public static double sin(double radians)
```
Returns the sine of an angle expressed in radians.

```
public static double tan(double radians)
```
Returns the tangent of an angle expressed in radians.

```
public static double toDegrees(double radians)
```
Converts an angle measured in radians to an angle measured in degrees.

```
public static double toRadians(double degrees)
```
Converts an angle measured in degrees to an angle measured in radians.

Figure 5.4 API headings and brief descriptions of some trigonometric methods in the `java.lang.Math` class

Suppose you want to compute the water needed for a 10 centimeter diameter water balloon. Here's the formula for the volume of a sphere:

$$\frac{\pi}{6}diameter^3$$

And here's the code and resulting output for computing the volume of water for the water balloon:

```
double diameter = 10.0;
double volume = Math.PI / 6.0 * diameter * diameter * diameter;
System.out.print("Balloon volume in cubic cm = " + volume);
```

<u>Output</u>:

```
Balloon volume in cubic cm = 523.5987755982989
```

Some of Java's `Math` class methods are extremely helpful when you need to evaluate a non-trivial mathematical function, like raising a floating-point number to a fractional power. Others do simple things you could do yourself. For example, can you think of a primitive way to do the same thing that `Math.round` does? It's pretty easy. Just add `0.5` to your original `double` number and then use a `long` cast operator on that `double` value to end up with a rounded version of the original number. (That's what was done in days of yore.) If it's that easy, why bother to use `Math.round`? Because it makes code more readable! The  expression, `Math.round(number)`, is self-documenting. It's more informative than the odd-looking expression, `((long) (0.5 + number))`.

5.4 Wrapper Classes for Primitive Types

A *wrapper* is a construct that wraps (contains) a primitive data type and converts it to an object with a similar name, so it can be used in a situation where only objects are allowed. Wrapper classes do more than wrapping, however. They also provide some useful class methods and class constants. The java.lang package provides wrapper classes for all of the Java primitive types. Since this package is always available, you don't need to use import to access these classes. Here are the wrapper classes that we'll consider, along with the primitive types they encapsulate:

Wrapper Class	Primitive Type
Integer	int
Long	long
Float	float
Double	double
Character	char

For most wrapper classes, the wrapper class's name is the same as its associated primitive type except that it uses an uppercase first letter. There are two exceptions. The wrapper class for int is Integer, and the wrapper class for char is Character.

Methods

Like the Math class, wrapper classes contain methods and constants. We start with methods. We limit our coverage to just two sets of methods—methods that convert strings to primitives and methods that convert primitives to strings. So when would you need to convert a string to a primitive? For example, when would you need to convert the string "4" to the int 4? If you need to read a value in as a string and then later manipulate the value as a number, you'll need to perform a string-to-number conversion. Later in this section, we'll show a program that reads a value that could be either a number (for a lottery-number choice) or a "q" (for quitting). The program reads the user entry as a string, and if the value is not a "q," then the program converts the user entry to a number.

Now for the other direction—when would you need to convert a primitive to a string? If you need to call a method that takes a string argument and what you've got is a number argument, then you'll need to perform a number-to-string conversion. With graphical user interface (GUI) programs, all numeric output is string based. So to display a number, you need to convert the number to a string prior to calling the GUI display method. With GUI programs, all numeric input is string based, too. So to read a number, you first read the input as a string and then convert the string to a number. You'll see many examples of these processes later, in Chapters 16 and 17.

Here's the syntax for converting strings to primitives and primitives to strings:

Wrapper Class	String → Primitive	Primitive → String
Integer	Integer.parseInt(<*string*>)	Integer.toString(<*#*>)
Long	Long.parseLong(<*string*>)	Long.toString(<*#*>)
Float	Float.parseFloat(<*string*>)	Float.toString(<*#*>)
Double	Double.parseDouble(<*string*>)	Double.toString(<*#*>)

All the number wrapper classes work similarly. So if you understand how to convert from a string to an int, then you'll also understand how to convert from a string to another primitive type. To convert from a string to an int, use int's wrapper class, Integer, to call parseInt. In other words, call Integer.parseInt(*<string>*) and the string's corresponding int is returned. Likewise, to convert from a string to a double, use double's wrapper class, Double, to call parseDouble. In other words, call Double.parseDouble(*<string>*) and the string's corresponding double is returned. Later in this section, we'll show a non-trivial example that uses the wrapper class conversion methods. But first we'll show some trivial examples to get you used to the method-call syntax. Here we use parseInt and parseDouble to convert from strings to primitives:

```
String yearStr = "2002";
String scoreStr = "78.5";
int year = Integer.parseInt(yearStr);
double score = Double.parseDouble(scoreStr);
```

To remember the syntax for the string-to-number method calls, think of *<type>*.parse*<type>* for Integer.parseInt, Long.parseLong, and so on.

To convert from an int to a string, use int's wrapper class, Integer, to call toString. In other words, call Integer.toString(*<int-value>*) and the int value's corresponding string is returned. Likewise, to convert from a double to a string, use double's wrapper class, Double, to call toString. In other words, call Double.toString(*<double-value>*) and the double value's corresponding string is returned. Note this example:

```
int year = 2002;
float score = 78.5;
String yearStr = Integer.toString(year);
String scoreStr = Float.toString(score);
```

About half of the numerical wrapper-class methods are class methods. We're focusing on those methods. Since they're class methods, you call them by prefacing the method call with the wrapper class's name, just as we have done.

Named Constants

The wrapper classes contain more than just methods; they also contain named constants. All the number wrappers provide named constants for minimum and maximum values. The floating-point wrappers also provide named constants for plus and minus infinity and "Not a Number," which is the indeterminate value you get if you try to divide zero by zero. Here's how you access the most important named constants defined in the Integer and Double wrapper classes:

```
Integer.MAX_VALUE
Integer.MIN_VALUE
Double.MAX_VALUE
Double.MIN_VALUE
Double.POSITIVE_INFINITY
Double.NEGATIVE_INFINITY
Double.NaN
```

NaN stands for "not a number."

There are comparable named constants for the Long and Float wrappers.

An Example

Let's put the wrapper and `Math.random` material into practice by showing it in the context of a complete program. Figure 5.5's Lottery program prompts the user to guess a randomly generated number between 0 and the maximum `int` value. The user pays $1.00 for each guess and wins $1,000,000 if the guess is correct. The user enters a "q" to quit.

In the initialization of `winningNumber`, note how the program generates a random winning-number value:

```
winningNumber = (int) (Math.random() * Integer.MAX_VALUE);
```

The starting point is `Math.random()`, a random number between 0.0 and 1.0. The Java Virtual Machine (JVM) then multiplies by `Integer.MAX_VALUE` to expand the range from (0.0 to 1.0) to (0.0 to 2147483647.0). The JVM then performs an `(int)` cast to truncate the fractional component.

Adapt existing software to your needs

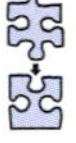

```
/*************************************************************************
* Lottery.java
* Dean & Dean
*
* This program prompts the user to choose a randomly selected number.
*************************************************************************/

import java.util.Scanner;

public class Lottery
{
  public static void main(String[] args)
  {
    Scanner stdIn = new Scanner(System.in);
    String input;
    int winningNumber = (int) (Math.random() * Integer.MAX_VALUE);

    System.out.println("Want to win a million dollars?");
    System.out.println("If so, guess the winning number (a" +
      " number between 0 and " + (Integer.MAX_VALUE - 1) + ").");
    do
    {
      System.out.print(
        "Insert $1.00 and enter your number or 'q' to quit: ");
      input = stdIn.nextLine();
      if (input.equals("give me a hint"))    //  a back door
      {
        System.out.println("try: " + winningNumber);
      }
```

Initialize with scaled random number.

Figure 5.5a Lottery program illustrates use of the `Integer` wrapper class—part A

```
        else if (!input.equals("q"))
        {
          if (Integer.parseInt(input) == winningNumber)
          {
            System.out.println("YOU WIN!");
            input = "q"; // if someone wins, they're forced to quit
          }
          else
          {
            System.out.println(
              "Sorry, good guess, but not quite right.");
          }
        } // end else if
      } while (!input.equals("q"));
      System.out.println("Thanks for playing. Come again!");
    } // end main
  } // end Lottery class
```

The `Integer.parseInt` method converts type from `String` to `int`.

Figure 5.5b Lottery program—part B

Note how the program reads in the user's number guess as a string:

```
input = stdIn.nextLine();
```

By reading the number guess as a string rather than a number, the program can handle the user entering a nonnumerical input, such as "q" for quit or "give me a hint" for a hint. If the user enters "q," the program quits. If the user enters "give me a hint," the program prints the winning number. Big hint, eh? In this case, the hint is really a *backdoor.* A backdoor is a secret technique for gaining access to a program. The Lottery program's backdoor can be used for testing purposes.

If the user does not enter "q" or "give me a hint," the program attempts to convert the user entry to a number by calling `Integer.parseInt`. The program then compares the converted number to the winning number and responds accordingly.

The Lottery program might produce the following output:

Sample session:

```
Want to win a million dollars?
If so, guess the winning number (a number between 0 and 2147483646).
Insert $1.00 and enter your number or 'q' to quit: 66761
Sorry, good guess, but not quite right.
Insert $1.00 and enter your number or 'q' to quit: 1234567890
Sorry, good guess, but not quite right.
Insert $1.00 and enter your number or 'q' to quit: give me a hint
try 1661533855
Insert $1.00 and enter your number or 'q' to quit: 1661533855
YOU WIN!
Thanks for playing. Come again!
```

5.5 Character Class

In the previous section, we mentioned the Character wrapper class, but we didn't explain it. It's time to explain it. Often, you'll need to write programs that manipulate individual characters in a string of text. For example, you might need to read in a phone number and store just the digits, skipping the other characters (dashes, spaces, etc.). To check for digits, use the Character class's isDigit method. Figure 5.6 shows some of the more popular methods in the Character class, including the isDigit method.

Most of Figure 5.6's methods are straightforward, but the toUpperCase and toLowerCase methods may need some clarification. Since the two methods are so similar, we'll clarify only one of the methods, toUpperCase. If you call toUpperCase and pass in a lowercase letter, the method returns the uppercase version of the lowercase letter. But what if you call toUpperCase and pass in an uppercase letter or a nonletter? The method returns the passed-in character, unchanged. And what if you pass in a char variable to toUpperCase instead of a char constant? The method returns the uppercase version of the passed-in char variable, but it does not change the passed-in variable's value.

As evidenced by the static modifiers in Figure 5.6, most of the Character methods are class methods. Since they're class methods, you call them by prefacing the method call with the wrapper class's name. Let's look at an example. Suppose you've got a char variable named middleInitial and you'd like to have its content be converted to an uppercase letter. Here's a first-cut attempt at changing middleInitial's content to an uppercase letter:

```
Character.toUpperCase(middleInitial);
```

```
public static boolean isDigit(char ch)
```
Returns true if the specified character is a numerical digit.

```
public static boolean isLetter(char ch)
```
Returns true if the specified character is a letter of the alphabet.

```
public static boolean isUpperCase(char ch)
```
Returns true if the specified character is an uppercase letter.

```
public static boolean isLowerCase(char ch)
```
Returns true if the specified character is a lowercase letter.

```
public static boolean isLetterOrDigit(char ch)
```
Returns true if the specified character is a letter or a digit.

```
public static boolean isWhitespace(char ch)
```
Returns true if the specified character is any kind of whitespace (blank, tab, newline).

```
public static char toUpperCase(char ch)
```
Returns input character as an uppercase character.

```
public static char toLowerCase(char ch)
```
Returns input character as a lowercase character.

Figure 5.6 API headings and brief descriptions of some of the methods in the Character class

```
/*************************************************************
* IdentifierChecker.java
* Dean & Dean
*
* Check a user entry to see if it's a legal identifier.
*************************************************************/

import java.util.Scanner;

public class IdentifierChecker
{
  public static void main(String[] args)
  {
    Scanner stdIn = new Scanner(System.in);
    String line;            // user entry
    char ch;
    boolean legal = true; // Is entered line a legal identifier?

    System.out.println("This program checks the validity of a" +
      " proposed Java identifier.");
    System.out.print("Enter a proposed identifier: ");
    line = stdIn.nextLine();
    ch = line.charAt(0);
    if (!(Character.isLetter(ch) || ch == '$' || ch == '_'))
    {
      legal = false;
    }
    for (int i=1; i<line.length() && legal; i++)
    {
      ch = line.charAt(i);
      if (!(Character.isLetterOrDigit(ch) || ch == '$' || ch == '_'))
      {
        legal = false;
      }
    }
    if (legal)
    {
      System.out.println(
        "Congratulations, " + line + " is a legal Java identifier.");
    }
    else
    {
      System.out.println(
        "Sorry, " + line + " is not a legal Java identifier.");
    }
  } // end main
} // end class IdentifierChecker
```

Character method calls

Figure 5.7 IdentifierChecker program

That statement compiles and runs, but it does not change middleInitial's content. Here's the proper way to do it: 

```
middleInitial = Character.toUpperCase(middleInitial);
```

The IdentifierChecker program in Figure 5.7 illustrates the character class in the context of a complete program. It uses the Character class's isLetter and isLetterOrDigit methods to check whether the user entry is a legal identifier.

5.6 String Methods

The String class is another one of the classes in the always-available java.lang package. In Chapter 3 you saw several examples of useful methods associated with objects of the String class such as the charAt method, the length method, the equals method, and the equalsIgnoreCase method. In this section, we describe some additional String methods—the String methods shown in Figure 5.8. These String methods do not have the static access modifier, so they are not class methods, and you cannot access them with the class name. They are instance methods and you must access them with a particular string instance. Or said another way, you must access them with a calling-object string.

Lexicographical Ordering of Strings

You know that numbers can be compared to determine which number is greater. Strings can also be compared. When computers compare strings to determine which string is greater, they use *lexicographical ordering.* For the most part, lexicographical ordering is the same as dictionary order. The string "hyena" is greater than the string "hedgehog" because *hyena* comes after *hedgehog* in the dictionary.

The String class's compareTo method compares two strings to determine which is greater. As explained in Figure 5.8, compareTo returns a positive number if the calling string is greater than the argument string, a negative number if the calling string is less than the argument string, and zero if the calling string and argument string are the same. The following code fragment illustrates what we're talking about. It compares YouTube[1] video titles and prints the results of the comparisons. If you run this code fragment, don't be surprised if your first two output values are different from 1 and −14. According to Sun's specification, the first two output values can be any positive number and any negative number, respectively.

```
String youTubeVideo = "Colbert Invades Cuba";
System.out.println(
  youTubeVideo.compareTo("Bad Day at Work") + " " +
  youTubeVideo.compareTo("Colbert Whitehouse Dinner") + " " +
  youTubeVideo.compareTo("Colbert Invades Cuba"));
```

Output:

```
1 -14 0
```

Checking for the Empty String

Previously, you learned that the empty string is a string that contains no characters, and it's represented by two quotes with nothing between them—"". Sometimes you'll need to check a string variable to see whether

[1] YouTube is a popular free video sharing Web site, acquired by Google in October, 2006, which lets users upload, view, and share video clips.

`public String compareTo(String str)`
Returns an integer that indicates the lexicographical ordering of the calling string when compared to the argument string. If the calling string is "greater than" the argument string, a positive number is returned. If the calling string is "less than" the argument string, a negative number is returned. If the calling string equals the argument string, zero is returned.

`public int indexOf(int ch)`
Returns the position of the first occurrence of the specified character.

`public int indexOf(int ch, int fromIndex)`
Returns the position of the first occurrence of the specified character at or after `fromIndex`.

`public int indexOf(String str)`
Returns the start position of the first occurrence of the specified string.

`public int indexOf(String str, int fromIndex)`
Returns the start position of the first occurrence of the specified string at or after `fromIndex`.

`public boolean isEmpty()`
Returns `true` if the calling string is the empty string (`""`). Otherwise, returns `false`.

`public String replaceAll(String target, String replacement)`
Returns a new string with all occurrences of the calling string's `target` replaced by `replacement`.

`public String replaceFirst(String target, String replacement)`
Returns a new string with the first occurrence of the calling string's `target` replaced by `replacement`.

`public String substring(int beginIndex)`
Returns the portion of the calling string from `beginIndex` to the end.

`public String substring(int beginIndex, int afterEndIndex)`
Returns the portion of the calling string from `beginIndex` to just before `afterEndIndex`.

`public String toLowerCase()`
Returns a new string with all characters in the calling string converted to lowercase.

`public String toUpperCase()`
Returns a new string with all characters in the calling string converted to uppercase.

`public String trim()`
Returns a new string with all whitespace removed from the start and end of the calling string.

Figure 5.8 API headings and brief descriptions of some of the methods in the `String` class

it contains the empty string. For example, when reading an input string from a user, you might want to check for the empty string as part of input validation. The following code fragment illustrates:

```
if (userInput.equals(""))
...
```

Since checking for the empty string is such a common need, Sun provides a method to handle that need. The isEmpty method returns true if the calling string contains the empty string and false otherwise. Figure 5.9's program uses the isEmpty method as part of an input validation while loop. The while loop forces the user to enter a non-empty name.

Substring Retrieval

Note the two substring methods in Figure 5.8. The one-parameter substring method returns a string that is a subset of the calling-object string, starting at the beginIndex parameter's position and extending to the end of the calling-object string. The two-parameter substring method returns a string that is a subset of the calling-object string. The returned substring starts at the beginIndex position and extends

```
/*******************************************************************
* StringMethodDemo.java
* Dean & Dean
*
* This program exercises the String class's isEmpty method.
*******************************************************************/

import java.util.Scanner;

public class StringMethodDemo
{
  public static void main(String[] args)
  {
    Scanner stdIn = new Scanner(System.in);
    String name;

    System.out.print("Enter your name: ");
    name = stdIn.nextLine();

    while (name.isEmpty())
    {
      System.out.print("Invalid entry. You must enter your name: ");
      name = stdIn.nextLine();
    }
    System.out.println("Hello, " + name + "!");
  } // end main
} // end StringMethodDemo
```

This checks for the empty string.

Sample session:

```
Enter your name:
Invalid entry. You must enter your name: Virginia Maikweki
Hello, Virginia Maikweki!
```

The user immediately presses Enter here.

Figure 5.9 StringMethodDemo program exercises various String class methods

to the `afterEndIndex-1` position, where `beginIndex` and `afterEndIndex` are the `substring` method's two parameters.

The following code fragment processes a quote from *Candide.*[2] In its `candide.substring(8)` method call, `candide` is the calling object, and 8 is the `beginIndex` parameter value. As you might recall, string indices start at 0. So the 8 refers to `candide`'s ninth character, which is 'c'. Thus, the first `println` statement prints `cultivate our garden`. Note the code fragment's `candide.substring(3,17)` method call. The 3 and 17 refer to `candide`'s fourth and eighteenth characters, which are 'm' and a space. Thus, the second `println` statement prints `must cultivate`.

```
String candide = "we must cultivate our garden";
System.out.println(candide.substring(8));
System.out.println(candide.substring(3,17));
```

Output:

```
cultivate our garden
must cultivate
```

If you want to test the above code fragment or any of the following `String` method code fragments, use Figure 5.9's program as a template. More specifically, replace Figure 5.9's `main` method body with the new code fragment. Then compile and run the resulting program.

Position Determination

Note the one-parameter `indexOf` methods in Figure 5.8. They return the position of the first occurrence of a given character or substring within the calling-object string. If the given character or substring does not appear within the calling-object string, `indexOf` returns −1.

Note the two-parameter `indexOf` methods in Figure 5.8. They return the position of the first occurrence of a given character or substring within the calling-object string, starting the search at the position specified by `indexOf`'s second parameter. If the given character or substring is not found, `indexOf` returns −1.

It's common to use one of the `indexOf` methods to locate a character or substring of interest and then use one of the `substring` methods to extract it. For example, consider this code fragment:[3]

Here's the beginning of the `hamlet2` substring.

```
String hamlet = "To be, or not to be: that is the question;";
int index = hamlet.indexOf(':');
String hamlet2 = hamlet.substring(index + 1);
System.out.println(hamlet2);
```

Output:

```
 that is the question;
```

Notice that the first character printed is a space.

[2] Voltaire, *Candide,* translated by Lowell Bair, Bantam Books, 1959, final sentence.

[3] Shakespeare, *Hamlet,* Act III, Sc. 1.

Text Replacement

Note the `replaceAll` and `replaceFirst` methods in Figure 5.8. The `replaceAll` method searches its calling-object string for `target`, `replaceAll`'s first parameter. It returns a new string, in which all occurrences of `target` are replaced with `replacement`, `replaceAll`'s second parameter. The `replaceFirst` method works the same as `replaceAll` except that only the first occurrence of the searched-for target string is replaced. Here's an example that illustrates both methods:[4]

```
String ladyMacBeth = "Out, damned spot! Out, I say!";
System.out.println(ladyMacBeth.replaceAll("Out", "Expunge"));
ladyMacBeth = ladyMacBeth.replaceFirst(", damned spot", "");
System.out.println(ladyMacBeth);
```

Update the content of the `ladyMacBeth` string variable.

Output:

```
Expunge, damned spot! Expunge, I say!
Out! Out, I say!
```

Note how the second statement prints the Lady MacBeth quote with both occurrences of "Out" replaced by "Expunge," but it does not change the content of the `ladyMacBeth` string object. You can tell that it doesn't change the content of the `ladyMacBeth` string object because the next two statements generate `Out! Out, I say!`, where "Out" is used, not "Expunge." The reason that the second statement's `replaceAll` method does not change content of the `ladyMacBeth` string object is that string objects are *immutable*. Immutable means unchangeable. String methods such as `replaceAll` and `replaceFirst` return a new string, not an updated version of the calling-object string. If you really want to change the content of a string variable, you need to assign a new string object into it. That's what happens in the third statement where the JVM assigns the result of the `replaceFirst` method call into the `ladyMacBeth` variable.

In the Lady MacBeth example, the `replaceFirst` method call deletes the "damned spot" by replacing it with an empty string. Since there is only one occurrence of "damned spot," `replaceAll` would yield the same result as `replaceFirst`. But `replaceFirst` is slightly more efficient and that's why we use it here.

Whitespace Removal and Case Conversion

Note the `trim`, `toLowerCase`, and `toUpperCase` methods in Figure 5.8. The `trim` method removes all whitespace from before and after a calling-object string. The `toLowerCase` method returns a string identical to the calling-object string except that all the characters are lowercase. The `toUpperCase` method returns an uppercase version of the calling-object string. To see how these methods work, suppose we change the previous Hamlet code to this:

```
String hamlet = "To be, or not to be: that is the question;";
int index = hamlet.indexOf(':');
String hamlet2 = hamlet.substring(index + 1);
System.out.println(hamlet2);
hamlet2 = hamlet2.trim();
hamlet2 = hamlet2.toUpperCase();
System.out.println(hamlet2);
```

[4] Shakespeare, *MacBeth*, Act V, Sc. I.

Now the output looks like this:

Output:

```
 that is the question;
THAT IS THE QUESTION;
```

Note how the `trim` method strips the leading space from `hamlet2`'s string. Also note how the `toUpperCase` method returns an all-uppercase version of `hamlet2`.

Insertion

To make an insertion, you must know where you want to make it. If you don't already know the index of where you want the insertion to start, you can find it by using the `indexOf` method with a unique substring argument. Then extract the substring up to that index, concatenate the desired insertion, and concatenate the substring after that index. The following code fragment performs two insertions within a string. More specifically, the code fragment starts with a philosophy espoused by 17th century French mathematician and philosopher Renéé Descartes: "All nature will do as I wish it." It then inserts two strings and transforms the message into a starkly contrasting quote from Charles Darwin: "All nature is perverse & will not do as I wish it." [5]

```
String descartes = "All nature will do as I wish it.";
String darwin;
int index;
index = descartes.indexOf("will");
darwin = descartes.substring(0, index) +
  "is perverse & " +
  descartes.substring(index);
index = darwin.indexOf("do");
darwin = darwin.substring(0, index) +
  "not " +
  darwin.substring(index);
System.out.println(darwin);
```

Output:

```
All nature is perverse & will not do as I wish it.
```

5.7 Formatted Output with the `printf` Method

You've used the `System.out.print` and `System.out.println` methods for quite a while now. They work fine most of the time, but there's a third `System.out` method that you'll want to use every now and

[5]*Charles Darwin's Letters,* edited by Frederick Burkhardt, Cambridge (1996). Charles Darwin started college at the University of Edinburgh in 1825, studying to be a medical doctor like his father. A medical career didn't appeal to him, so he transferred to Cambridge University, where he earned a B.A. in preparation for a career as a country parson. But what he really enjoyed was searching for bugs in the family barn. Right after his graduation, and before he began his first job as a country parson, family connections, a good reference from a college professor, and a pleasant personality gave him the chance to travel around the world as the companion of a brilliant sea captain named Robert FitzRoy (who later invented weather forecasting). This trip launched Darwin's career as one of the most influential scientists of the modern world.

then for formatted output. It's the printf method, where the "f" stands for "formatted." We describe the printf method in this section.

Formatted Output

For most programs, the goal is to calculate something and then display the result. It's important that the displayed result is understandable. If it's not understandable, then no one will bother to use the program, even if it calculates flawlessly. One way to make your displayed results understandable is to format your output. By that, we mean having data columns align properly, having floating-point numbers show the same number of digits after the decimal point, and so on. Note the formatting in the budget report below. The left column is left-aligned. The other columns are right aligned. The numbers show two digits at the right of the decimal point. The numbers show commas between every third digit at the left of the decimal point. And finally, the numbers show parentheses to indicate negativeness.

```
Account                          Actual        Budget      Remaining
-------                          ------        ------      ---------
Office Supplies                1,150.00      1,400.00         250.00
Photocopying                   2,100.11      2,000.00       (100.11)

Total remaining: $149.89
```

The System.out.printf method is in charge of generating formatted output. The printf method has lots of formatting features. We'll keep things simple and explain only a few of the more popular features. We begin our explanation of the printf method by showing you how to generate the "Total remaining" line in the above budget report. Here's the code:

Learn how to use versatile tools.

```
System.out.printf(
  "\nTotal remaining: $%.2f\n", remaining1 + remaining2);
```

(format specifier → %.2f)

The printf method's first argument is known as the *format string*. It contains text that prints as is, plus format specifiers that handle formatted printing. In the above example, "\nTotal remaining: $...\n" is the text that prints as is. And %.2f is the format specifier. Think of a *format specifier* as a hole where you plug in a data item. In the above example, remaining1 + remaining2 is the data item that gets plugged in. If remaining1 holds 250 and remaining2 holds −100.11, the sum is 149.89 and 149.89 gets plugged into the format specifier hole. The format specifier starts with % because all format specifiers must start with %. The format specifier's .2 causes two digits to be displayed after the decimal point. The format specifier's f indicates that the data item is a floating-point number. The example shows only one format specifier. You can have as many format specifiers as you like in a given format string. For each format specifier, you should have a corresponding data item/argument. Here's an illustration of what we're talking about:

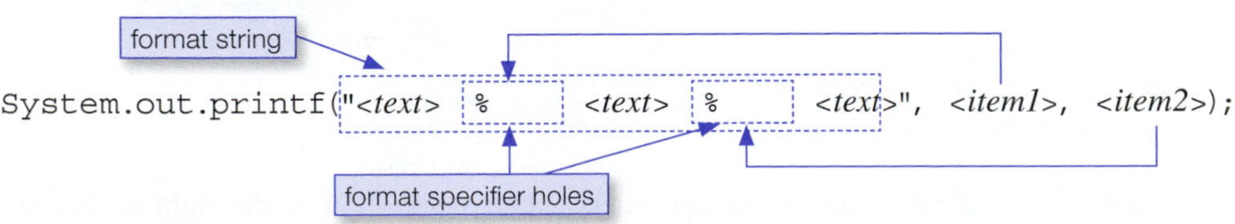

Format Specifier Details

Format specifiers are powerful little critters. We won't try to describe all of their power, but we'll provide enough details to get you up and running. If you come across a formatting issue that you can't resolve with our limited coverage, look up `printf` on Sun's Java API Web site and search for format string details. But be prepared for lots of details. Sun provides a tremendous number of options with the `printf` method.

Here's the syntax for a format specifier:

`%`[*flags*] [*width*] [.*precision*] *conversion-character*

You've already seen the `%` symbol. It indicates the start of a format specifier. The flags, width, precision, and conversion character represent the different parts of a conversion specifier. Each of them specifies a different formatting trait. We'll cover them in right-to-left order. Thus, we'll describe the conversion character first. But before jumping into conversion character details, note the square brackets. They indicate that something is optional. So the flags, width, and precision parts are optional. Only the `%` and the conversion character are required.

Conversion Character

The conversion character tells the JVM the type of data that is to be printed. For example, it might tell the JVM to print a string, or it might tell the JVM to print a floating-point number. Here is a partial list of conversion characters:

- `s` This displays a string.
- `d` This displays a decimal integer (an `int` or a `long`).
- `f` This displays a floating-point number (a `float` or a `double`) with a decimal point and at least one digit to the left of the decimal point.
- `e` This displays a floating-point number (`float` or `double`) in scientific notation.

In explaining each part of a format specifier (conversion character, precision, width, and flags), we'll provide short examples that illustrate the syntax and semantics. After we're done with all the explanations, we'll show a complete program example. Note this code fragment and its associated output:

```
System.out.printf("Planet: %s\n", "Neptune");
System.out.printf("Number of moons: %d\n", 13);
System.out.printf("Orbital period (in earth years): %f\n", 164.79);
System.out.printf(
  "Average distance from the sun (in km): %e\n", 4498252900.0);
```

Ouput:

```
Planet: Neptune
Number of moons: 13
Orbital period (in earth years): 164.790000
Average distance from the sun (in km): 4.498253e+09
```

The `f` and `e` conversion specifiers print six digits by default.

Note that by default, the `f` and `e` conversion specifiers generate six digits at the right of the decimal point.

Precision and Width

The precision part of a format specifier works in conjunction with the f and e conversion characters; that is, it works with floating-point data items. It specifies the number of digits that are to be printed to the right of the decimal point. We'll refer to those digits as the fractional digits. If the data item has more fractional digits than the precision's value, then rounding occurs. If the data item has fewer fractional digits than the precision's value, then zeros are added at the right so the printed value has the specified number of fractional digits.

The width part of a format specifier specifies the minimum number of characters that are to be printed. If the data item contains more than the specified number of characters, then all of the characters are printed. If the data item contains fewer than the specified number of characters, then spaces are added. By default, output values are right aligned, so when spaces are added, they go on the left side.

Note this code fragment and its associated output:

```
System.out.printf("Cows are %6s\n", "cool");
System.out.printf("But dogs %2s\n", "rule");
System.out.printf("PI = %7.4f\n", Math.PI);
```

Ouput

```
Cows are   cool
But dogs rule
PI =  3.1416
```

6 characters

7 characters

In the third statement above, note the %7.4f specifier. It's easy to get fooled by the 7.4. It looks like it might be saying "seven places to the left of the decimal point and four places to the right of the decimal point," but it's actually saying "seven total spaces, with four places to the right of the decimal point." And don't forget that the decimal point is counted as one of those seven total spaces. Math.PI's value is 3.141592653589793, and when it gets printed with four places to the right of the decimal point, it gets rounded to 3.1416.

Flags

As a refresher, here's the syntax for a format specifier:

% [*flags*] [*width*] [.*precision*] *conversion-character*

We've described the conversion, precision, and width parts of a format specifier. It's now time to discuss flags. Flags allow you to add supplemental formatting features, one flag character for each formatting feature. Here's a partial list of flag characters:

- `-` Display the printed value using left justification.
- `0` If a numeric data item contains fewer characters than the width specifier's value, then pad the printed value with leading zeros (i.e., display zeros at the left of the number).
- `,` Display a numeric data item with locale-specific grouping separators. In the United States, that means commas are inserted between every third digit at the left of the decimal point.
- `(` Display a negative numeric data item using parentheses, rather than using a minus sign. Using parentheses for negative numbers is a common practice in the field of accounting.

Let's see how format specifiers work in the context of a complete program. See Figure 5.10's BudgetReport program. Note that we use the same format string for printing the column headers and the column underlines, and the format string is stored in a HEADING_FMT_STR named constant. If you use a format string

```
/*************************************************************
* BudgetReport.java
* Dean & Dean
*
* This program generates a budget report.
*************************************************************/

public class BudgetReport
{
  public static void main(String[] args)
  {
    final String HEADING_FMT_STR = "%-25s%13s%13s%15s\n";
    final String DATA_FMT_STR = "%-25s%,13.2f%,13.2f%(,15.2f\n";
    double actual1 = 1149.999; // amount spent on 1st account
    double budget1 = 1400;     // budgeted for 1st account
    double actual2 = 2100.111; // amount spent on 2nd account
    double budget2 = 2000;     // budgeted for 2nd account
    double remaining1, remaining2; // unspent amounts

    System.out.printf(HEADING_FMT_STR,
      "Account", "Actual", "Budget", "Remaining");
    System.out.printf(HEADING_FMT_STR,
      "-------", "------", "------", "---------");

    remaining1 = budget1 - actual1 ;
    System.out.printf(DATA_FMT_STR,
      "Office Supplies", actual1, budget1, remaining1);
    remaining2 = budget2 - actual2;
    System.out.printf(DATA_FMT_STR,
      "Photocopying", actual2, budget2, remaining2);

    System.out.printf(
      "\nTotal remaining: $%(,.2f\n", remaining1 + remaining2);
  } // end main
} // end class BudgetReport
```


Output:

```
Account                         Actual       Budget      Remaining
-------                         ------       ------      ---------
Office Supplies               1,150.00     1,400.00         250.00
Photocopying                  2,100.11     2,000.00        (100.11)

Total remaining: $149.89
```

Figure 5.10 BudgetReport program and its ouput

in more than one place, it's a good idea to save the format string in a named constant and use the named constant in the `printf` statements. By storing the format string in one common place (in a named constant), you ensure consistency and you make it easier to update the format string in the future.

In the BudgetReport program, note the minus sign in the `HEADING_FMT_STR` and `DATA_FMT_STR` format strings. That left justifies the first column's data. Note the commas in the `DATA_FMT_STR` format string. That causes locale-specific characters (commas in the United States) to appear between every third digit at the left of the decimal point. Note the left parenthesis in the `DATA_FMT_STR` format string. That causes negative numbers to use parentheses instead of a minus sign.

5.8 Problem Solving with Random Numbers (Optional)

This section will show you how to generate random variables that have probability distributions different from the 0.0 to 1.0 uniform distribution assumed in a simple `Math.random` method call.

Using `Math.random` to Generate Random Numbers with Other Probability Distributions

As indicated in Figure 5.2, in Section 5.3, when you need a random number, you can use the `Math.random` method to generate one. Suppose you want a random number from a range that's different from the range 0.0 to 1.0. As we did in the initialization of `winningNumber` in Figure 5.5, you can expand the range to any maximum value by multiplying the random number generated by `Math.random()` by your desired maximum value. You can also offset the range by adding or subtracting a constant. For example, suppose you want to pick a random number that's uniformly distributed in the range between −5.0 and +15.0. Instead of using just plain old `Math.random()`, use this:

```
(20.0 * Math.random()) - 5.0.
```

It's possible to manipulate numbers produced by `Math.random` to get any kind of distribution you want. For example, you can generate any of the distributions shown in Figure 5.11.

Now, let's look at how to generate these five types of random numbers from `Math.random`.

1. The first type (a continuous uniform distribution) is easy. To get a value for a random number, `x`, uniformly distributed in the interval between zero and unity ($0.0 \le x < 1.0$), use a statement like this:

   ```
   double r1 = Math.random();
   ```

   This first type of random number is the basis of all other types of random numbers.

2. For the second type (an offset and expanded continuous uniform distribution), you must have some minimum and maximum values, for example:

   ```
   double minReal = 1.07; // meters for shortest adult human
   double maxReal = 2.28; // meters for tallest adult human
   ```

   Then you shift and expand the basic random number by using a statement like this:

   ```
   double r2 = minReal + Math.random() * (maxReal - minReal);
   ```

3. For the third type (a discrete uniform distribution), you create integer versions of the limits, for example:

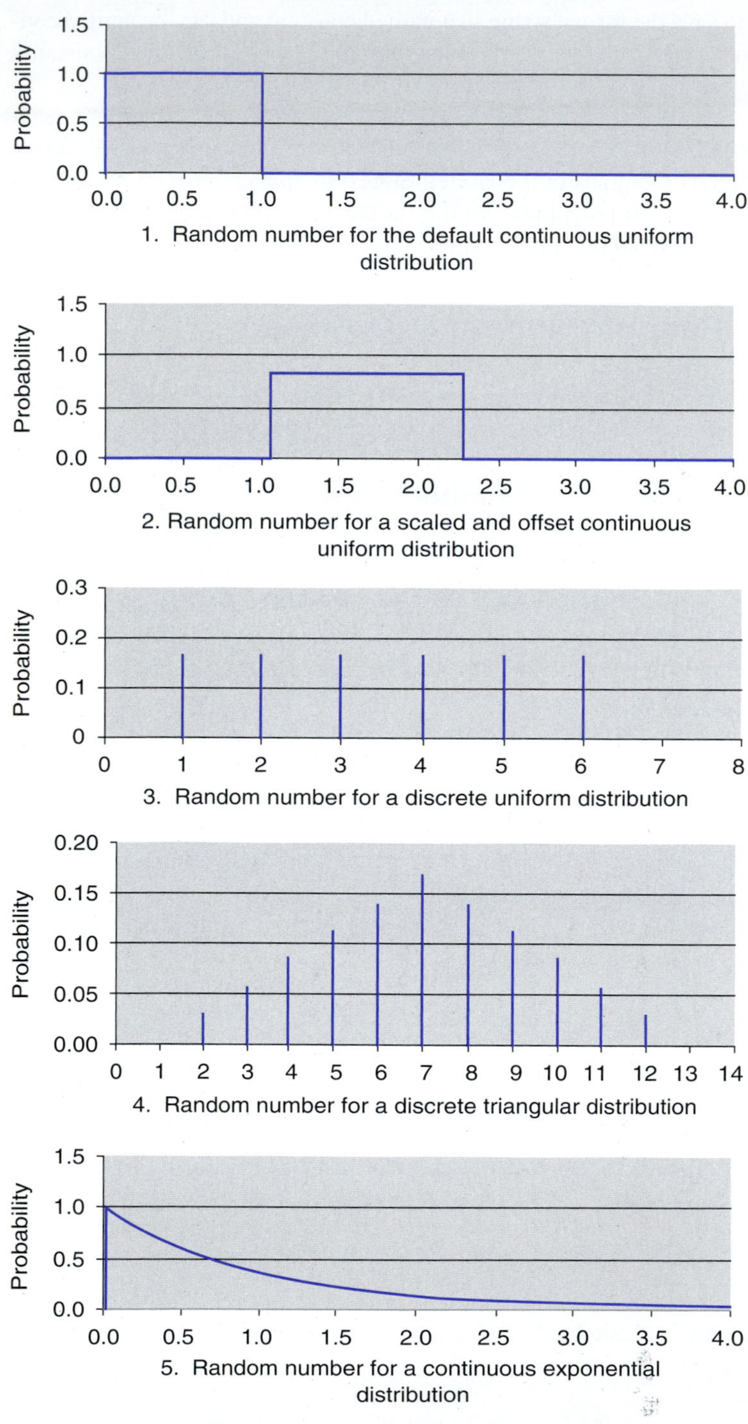

Figure 5.11 Important types of random number distributions

```
int min = 1;                // fewest dots on one die
int max = 6;                // most dots on one die
```

Then you shift and expand the basic random number, sort of like you did for the second type:

```
double r3 = min + (int) (Math.random() * (max - min + 1));
```

This time, you must remember that integer subtraction produces a distance that is one less than the number of integers in the range (6 minus 1 equals 5, not 6), so you have to add 1 to the difference like this (`max - min + 1`). The `double` returned by `Math.random` automatically promotes everything to `double`, so the shifted and expanded range is from 1.0 to 6.99999. The random selection gives equal weight to each of the six intervals above the integers of interest (1, 2, 3, 4, 5, and 6). The final `(int)` cast drops fractions.

4. For the fourth type (a discrete triangular distribution), at first you might think you could just use the third type with min = 2 and max = 12, but that would be wrong. It would generate just as many 2's and 12's as 7's, but the chance of getting a 7 is actually six time higher than getting either a 2 or a 12! The most straightforward way to get the right answer is to call `Math.random` twice, and add the results: 

```
int twoDice = r3 + r3;
```

5. The fifth type of distribution (a continuous exponential distribution) has been included because it's used in models of many important real-world phenomena, like:
   - Inter-arrival time of automobiles at an isolated traffic light.
   - Time between infrequent telephone calls.
   - Time between radioactive emissions from an unstable atom.
   - Time to breakdown of a piece of machinery.
   - Time to failure of a semiconductor device.

   To generate a random variable with a continuous exponential distribution, use a statement like this:

```
double r5 = -Math.log(1.0 - Math.random()) * averageTimeBetweenEvents;
```

The logarithm of zero is −infinity, but that never occurs, because `Math.random` never generates a number as high as `1.0`, so `(1.0 - Math.random())` is never as low as zero.

Using the `Random` class

Although it is possible to get any kind of distribution from `Math.random`, it's not always easy. For example, the algorithm you need to convert `Math.random`'s uniform distribution to a Gaussian (bell-curve) distribution is rather convoluted. So it would be nice to have some pre-built methods that immediately generate random numbers from this and other distributions. The `Random` class in the `java.util` package provides help. Here are API headings for some of the `Random` class methods:

Use the resource that fits best.

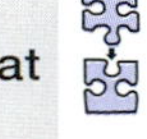

```
public double nextDouble()
public int nextInt()
public int nextInt(int n)
public boolean nextBoolean()
public double nextGaussian()
```

The nextDouble method does essentially the same thing as Math.random does. This distribution appears in the top graph in Figure 5.11. The zero-parameter nextInt method generates random integers uniformly from the entire range of integers, that is, from −2147483648 to +2147483647, inclusive. The one-parameter nextInt method generates random integers uniformly from zero to one less than the parameter value. This distribution is almost like what appears in Figure 5.11's third graph for the special case of n = 7, except zero is allowed also. The nextBoolean method generates random values of true or false. The nextGaussian method generates a double value from a distribution having a mean value of 0.0 and a standard deviation of 1.0.

Notice that the Random class methods do not have the static modifier, so they are not class methods, and you cannot use the Random class name to access these methods. You must create an object first, and then use that object's name to access these methods. To create an object from any class other than the String class, you need to call a *constructor*. A constructor is a special type of method that's in charge of creating and initializing objects. To call a constructor, specify the Java keyword new, the name of the constructor, and then an argument list surrounded by parentheses. For example, see the Random constructor call in Figure 5.12. Note that no arguments are passed to the constructor, so the constructor call's parentheses are empty. Also note how the Random constructor call is assigned to a reference variable named random. The random object then generates two random numbers by calling the nextInt and nextGausssian methods. Due to the Integer.MAX _VALUE argument, nextInt generates a random number between 0 and one less than the maximum integer value. The nextGaussian method generates a random number drawn from a Gaussian distribution having a mean of 5.0 and a standard deviation of 0.8.

Using a Fixed Seed to Freeze a Random Number Sequence

You can call the Random constructor with no arguments, as shown in Figure 5.12, and you can also call it with one argument, where the argument is a *seed*. A seed provides a starting point for the internal state of the random number generator. Suppose you change the body of the main method in Figure 5.12 to this:

```
Random random = new Random(123);

System.out.println(5.0 + 0.8 * random.nextGaussian());
System.out.println(5.0 + 0.8 * random.nextGaussian());
System.out.println(5.0 + 0.8 * random.nextGaussian());
```

Now, if you run the program you'll get this:

Sample session:

```
3.8495605526872745
5.507356060142144
5.1808496102657315
```

If you run the program again, and again, and again, you'll get exactly the same three "random" numbers every time! The 123 seed establishes a starting point, and this determines the "random" sequence precisely. If you pick a different seed, you'll get a different sequence, but that sequence will always be the same as long as you stick with that particular seed. Now you know why the methods in the Random class are not class methods. They need an object to call the methods because the methods need to know some information the object contains—the seed and the current position in the random-number sequence.

```
/*****************************************************************
* RandomTest.java
* Dean & Dean
*
* This program demonstrates methods of the Random class.
*****************************************************************/

import java.util.Random;

public class RandomTest
{
  public static void main(String[] args)
  {
    Random random = new Random();

    System.out.println(random.nextInt(Integer.MAX_VALUE));
    System.out.println(5.0 + 0.8 * random.nextGaussian());
  } // end main
} // end class RandomTest
```

Use `new` to invoke an explicit object constructor.

Sample session:

```
1842579217
4.242694469045554
```

Figure 5.12 RandomTest program uses `Random` class methods to generate random numbers from different distributions

When testing, fix your random numbers.

You can use the deterministic nature of the seeded random-number generator to make your life a lot easier when you are developing and debugging programs that use random numbers.

If you do not use a seeded random number generator, whenever a program generates a random number, what comes out will be a surprise, because it's random! This unpredictability can be quite frustrating when you are trying to develop and test a program that uses random numbers, because every test run produces different numerical values. During development and testing, what you'd like is a fixed set of "random" numbers, which turn out to be exactly the same every time you rerun a program you're testing.

To establish a fixed random-number test set, you could write a simple program that prints a particular set of random numbers. You could copy those particular numbers into assignment statements in your program, that is, hard code them in your program for development and testing. Then, after your program has been tested and verified, you could replace each hard-coded "random number" by a random-number generator that produces a different number every time it's invoked.

But the `Random` class provides a more elegant way to develop programs that have random variables. During development, use its one-parameter constructor with a fixed seed to produce exactly the same sequence of randomly distributed numbers every time you run the program. Then, when all your bugs are fixed, simply delete the seed number from the `Random` constructor in the initialization statement at the beginning of your code, and—*voila*—your random-number generator produces completely different numbers from that time forward.

5.9 GUI Track: Drawing Images, Lines, Rectangles, and Ovals in Java Applets (Optional)

This section shows you how to display images, lines, rectangles, and ovals in a GUI window. The simplest way to do this is to call methods in Java's `Graphics` class from within a Java applet. As you might recall from Chapter 1, an applet is a Java program that's embedded in a Web page. You execute a Java applet by calling it from the Web page's HTML code (HTML is the base language for most Web pages). You can run the Web page by loading it within an Internet browser.

Image Files

Java can handle many kinds of images. Some images are stylized icons. Others are digitized photographs. For example, suppose you have a digitized photograph of a family member, like author John's nephew, Max, shown in Figure 5.13.

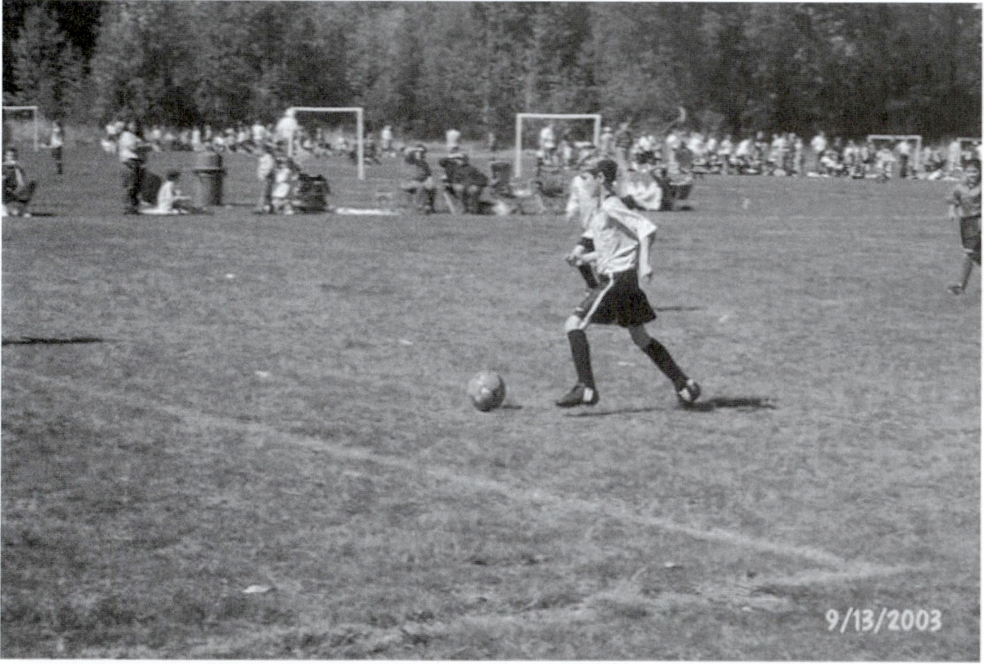

Figure 5.13 A typical image stored in a `.jpg` file

Suppose this photo is stored in a file named `hurricanes.jpg`. "Hurricanes" is the name of Max's soccer team. The extension, ".jpg," is short for JPEG, which stands for Joint Photographic Experts Group. Files with this extension should conform to JPEG standards for digital compression of photographic images. Exact representations of simple drawn images are usually stored in files with a ".gif" extension. GIF stands for Graphics Interchange Format. For simplicity we'll assume that the image file is in the current directory—the same directory that holds the Java program that will display it.

Before you can use a picture in a program, you need to know how big it is—its width and height in numbers of *pixels*. Pixels are the tiny dots of color a computer uses to display something on its screen. Figure 5.14 contains a program you can use to determine the pixel width and pixel height of the contents of an image file. The program imports Java's `Scanner` class to retrieve a keyboard entry of the filename, and it imports Java's `ImageIcon` class to read the image file and determine image properties. After prompting the user for a filename, the program uses that name to create an object we call `icon`, which manages information transfer from the image file—like our `stdIn` object manages information transfer from the keyboard. The `getWidth` and `getHeight` methods return the image's width and height in pixels. This gives the default size of the area required to display the image on a computer screen.

```
/*************************************************************
* ImageInfo.java
* Dean & Dean
*
* This supplies width and height of an image.
*************************************************************/

import java.util.Scanner;
import javax.swing.ImageIcon;

public class ImageInfo
{
  public static void main(String[] args)
  {
    Scanner stdIn = new Scanner(System.in);
    ImageIcon icon;

    System.out.print("Enter image filename: ");
    icon = new ImageIcon(stdIn.nextLine());
    System.out.println("image width = " + icon.getIconWidth());
    System.out.println("image height = " + icon.getIconHeight());
  }
} // end ImageInfo
```

<u>Sample session</u>:

```
Enter image filename: hurricanes.jpg
image width = 640
image height = 427
```

Figure 5.14 ImageInfo program determines the width and height of an image in an image file

Graphics Class Methods

The Java API class called `Graphics` contains several methods for displaying images and geometric shapes. Figure 5.15 presents API headings and descriptions for some of these methods. Notice that these headings do not have `static` modifiers. This means that you must use an object of the `Graphics` class to call all of these methods, just like you must use a `String` object to call most of the methods of the `String` class. This `Graphics` object contains a reference to the window on which things are drawn, and it contains other necessary information like current position of that window on the computer screen, current color, and current font type.

Most of Figure 5.15's methods have pairs of parameters (like `int x, int y`), which indicate x and y coordinates in an image or window. These coordinates are always measured in pixels. The x coordinate is the number of pixels in from the left side of the image or window. The y coordinate is the number of pixels down from the top of the image or window. The x coordinate is like what you probably expect, but the y coordinate might seem funny, because normally we think of y increasing upward. However, in a computer display, y increases downward, because when a computer paints something on a screen, it paints the top line first, the line below second, and so on, in a top-to-bottom sequence.

In a method heading, x and y coordinate parameter names sometimes employ numerical suffixes to distinguish one point from another. In the `drawImage` method's parameters, there is also a character prefix before each coordinate identifier. The d prefix stands for "destination," which means position in the display window. The s prefix stands for "source," which means position in the original image.

Sometimes numbers in a sequence of parameters are not x and y coordinates. Instead, they are width and height, which are coordinate differences. This is the case for the `drawRect` and `fillOval` methods. It's easy to forget which technique a particular method uses to specify width or height. Does it specify positions of upper left and lower right corners, or does it specify position of upper left corner and then width and height? Be careful. This is a common source of GUI programming errors.

```
public boolean drawImage(Image img,
  int dx1, int dy1, int dx2, int dy2,
  int sx1, int sy1, int sx2, int sy2,
  ImageObserver observer)
```

Selects whatever is between `sx1` and `sx2` pixels to the right of the left edge of the source image and between `sy1` and `sy2` pixels below the top of the source image. Scales this selection as required to fit between `dx1` and `dx2` pixels to the right of the left edge of the destination window and between `dy1` and `dy2` below the top of the destination window.

```
public void setColor(Color c)
```

Establishes a specified painting color.

```
public void drawRect(int x, int y, int width, int height)
```

Draws the outline of a rectangle whose upper left corner is `x` pixels to the right of the left side of the window and `y` pixels below the top of the window. Uses most recently set color.

```
public void drawLine(int x1, int y1, int x2, int y2)
```

Draws a straight line from a point `x1` pixels to the right of the left side of the window and `y1` pixels below the top of the window to a point `x2` pixels to the right of the left side of the window and `y2` pixels below the top of the window. Uses most recently set color.

```
public void fillOval(int x, int y, int width, int height)
```

Fills an ellipse bounded by the specified rectangle with the most recently set color.

```
public void drawString(String text, int x, int y)
```

Prints the specified text on a line that starts `x` pixels to the right of the left side of the window and `y` pixels down from the top of the window. Uses the most recently set color.

Figure 5.15 Selected methods from the Java API `Graphics` class

The `drawImage` method copies a rectangular portion of the source image and pastes an expanded or contracted version of it into a specified rectangle in the destination window. The first parameter is a reference to the source image. The second and third parameters are the destination (display window) coordinates of the top left corner of the copied part of the image. The fourth and fifth parameters are the destination coordinates of the bottom right corner of the copied part of the image. The sixth and seventh parameters are the coordinates of the top left corner of the part of the source image to be copied. The eighth and ninth parameters are the coordinates of the bottom right corner of the part of the source image to be copied. The last parameter enables the method to send out current-status information.

The `setColor` method establishes a color to be used in subsequent operations that draw lines or geometric figures or write text. You pass this method an argument like `Color.BLUE`, which identifies one of several named constants defined in the Java API `Color` class. You can find the names of the other named colors in the documentation for the Java API `Color` class. Most of those names are pretty obvious, so as a practical matter, you can just guess and see what happens.

The `drawRect` method draws the border of a rectangle using the most recently set color. The first and second parameters are the coordinates of the top left corner of the rectangle in the display window. The third and fourth parameters are the width and height of the rectangle.

The `drawLine` method draws a straight line between two specified points using the most recently set color. The first and second parameters are the coordinates of the starting point. The third and fourth parameters are the coordinates of the ending point.

The `fillOval` method draws an ellipse in the specified rectangle and fills it with the most recently set color. The parameters are like those for `drawRect`: The first and second parameters are the coordinates of the top left corner of the enclosing rectangle in the display window. The third and fourth parameters are the width and height of the enclosing rectangle, and the width and height of the oval itself.

The `drawString` method prints text at the specified position using the most recently set color. The first parameter is the string to be printed. The second and third parameters are the coordinates of the upper left corner of the string.

Using `Graphics` Methods in a Java Applet

Figure 5.16 provides an example of how you can use the graphics methods in Figure 5.15 to manipulate a photographic image and add your own lines, shapes, and text to it. The overall window in Figure 5.16 is 640 pixels wide and 640 pixels high.

Figure 5.17 shows the Java code needed to render the display in Figure 5.16. The code is all in the body of a method called `paint`. The `paint` method's parameter `g` is used as a prefix on each of the method calls in `paint`. It refers to the `Graphics` object that manages the painting operation. Within `paint`, the first statement retrieves a reference to the source image. The next statement's `drawImage` method employs the source image reference to access the source image.

The `drawImage` method shrinks the `hurricanes.jpg` image in Figure 5.13 to two thirds of its original size and pastes it into the upper left corner of the display window. The `setColor` method sets the current color to blue. The `drawRect` method draws a square around an area of interest. Then four calls to the `drawLine` method draw four straight lines to the corners of where a three-times enlargement of the area of interest will go. Another call to the `drawImage` method pastes an enlarged version of the area of interest at this location. Another call to `drawRect` puts a rectangle around this enlargement. Then the `fillOval` method paints a blue oval in the enlargement, and finally the `drawString` method prints the name "MAX" in the center of this blue oval. Notice how each subsequent operation over-writes or covers all previous operations.

Figure 5.16 Output produced by program in Figure 5.17

The code in Figure 5.17 is very skimpy. For example, it does not include a definition of the `getImage` method. So how can it call that method? As you'll discover in Chapter 12, Java allows any class you define to borrow the methods of another class that's already been defined. In particular, the `GraphicsDemo` class defined in Figure 5.17 borrows the `getImage` method from the already-defined Java API `Applet` class. It does this by appending the clause `extends Applet` to its class heading. Of course, the compiler must know where to find the `Applet` class, so the program must `import` it. It also `imports` the `java.awt` package to provide access to the `Graphics`, `Image`, and `Color` classes used by statements in the `paint` method.

```
/*************************************************************************
* GraphicsDemo.java
* Dean & Dean
*
* This defines a Java applet that displays an image and graphics.
*************************************************************************/

import java.awt.*;        // for Graphics, Image, and Color classes
import java.applet.Applet;

public class GraphicsDemo extends Applet
{
  public void paint (Graphics g)
  {
    Image image =
      this.getImage(getDocumentBase(),"hurricanes.jpg");

    // display smaller complete image in upper left corner of window
    g.drawImage(image, 0, 0, 427, 284,      // destination topL, botR
      0, 0, 640, 427, this);                // source topL, botR

    // establish color of all lines to be drawn
    g.setColor(Color.BLUE);

    // draw rectangle around region to be expanded
    g.drawRect(200, 60, 120, 120);          // topL, width & height

    // draw lines between corners of rectangles
    g.drawLine(200, 60, 240, 240);          // upper left
    g.drawLine(320, 60, 600, 240);          // upper right
    g.drawLine(200, 180, 240, 600);         // lower left
    g.drawLine(320, 180, 600, 600);         // lower right

    // display expanded part of original image
    g.drawImage(image, 240, 240, 600, 600, // destination topL, botR
      300, 90, 480, 270, this);             // source topL, botR

    // draw rectangle around expanded part of image
    g.drawRect(240, 240, 360, 360);         // topL, width & height

    // create BLUE colored oval and write name on it
    g.fillOval(520, 380, 45, 30);           // topL, width & height
    g.setColor(Color.WHITE);                // change color for text
    g.drawString("MAX", 530, 400);          // string & start position
  } // end paint
} // end GraphicsDemo class
```

The `extends Applet` appended to the class heading allows this class to "borrow" the `getImage` method from the already-defined Java API `Applet` class.

Figure 5.17 GraphicsDemo Java applet that illustrates graphics methods listed in Figure 5.15
This applet produces the output shown in Figure 5.16.

Notice that the `getImage` method call has the word `this` as a prefix, and the word `this` also appears in the last argument in the two calls to the `drawImage` method. The next chapter will explain that the special Java term `this` refers to whatever object happened to call the currently executing method. In our GraphicsDemo program, `this` refers to the object that calls the `paint` method, and that object is an instance of the `GraphicsDemo` class defined by the code in Figure 5.17. But where is the code that creates a `GraphicsDemo` object, where is the code that retrieves a reference to the associated `Graphics` object, and where is the code that calls the `paint` method? It's in a separate file. . . .

Applet Execution

Did you notice that there is no `main` method in Figure 5.17? A Java applet is different from a Java application. Because a Java applet does not have a `main` method, it cannot be executed in the normal manner. Typically, it's embedded in another program, such that its code executes when that other program calls it. The primary purpose of a Java applet is to liven up a Web page. So we typically call Java applets from HTML (HyperText Markup Language) programs that define Web pages. Figure 5.18 contains a minimal HTML program that calls the `GraphicsDemo` applet defined in Figure 5.17.

Notice that the part of this HTML code that's specific to our particular applet is all in the fifth line. This identifies the compiled version of the applet, and it specifies the pixel width and pixel height of the window that will hold whatever the applet will display. You can write this HTML code with any primitive text editor, like Microsoft notepad or UNIX vi. Then save it in the same directory as the code that has the compiled version of the applet it drives. For example, in the directory that contains the `GraphicsDemo.class` file. When you save it, give it a name which has the `html` extension, like `graphicsDemo.html`.

You have three alternate ways to run the HTML file (and its associated Java applet):

1. Open a browser like Microsoft's Internet Explorer, navigate to the directory that contains the HTML file, and double click on the HTML filename.
2. Open a Command Prompt Window, navigate to the directory that contains the HTML file, and enter:
   `appletviewer graphicsDemo.html`
3. Select "Run a Java Applet" in your local IDE (Integrated Development Environment), and select the desired HTML filename.

```
<!DOCTYPE html>
<html>
  <head></head>
  <body>
    <applet code="GraphicsDemo.class" width="640" height="640">
    </applet>
  </body>
</html>
```

name of file containing compiled Java applet code

size of display window

Figure 5.18 Code for an HTML file that runs the GraphicsDemo code in Figure 5.17

Summary

- Sun's Java documentation identifies the public interface of all Java API software. It also provides a brief description of what it does and how to use it. The `java.lang` package is always available.
- The `Math` class provides methods that enable you to compute powers and roots, maximums or minimums, angle conversions, and many trigonometric functions. The `random` function generates a random number whose distribution is uniform in the range 0.0 to $0.\overline{9}$ repeating. This class also provides named constant values for PI and E.
- Numerical wrapper classes like `Integer`, `Long`, `Float` and `Double` contain parsing methods like `parseInt` that enable you to convert `String` representations of numbers into numerical format. `MIN_VALUE` and `MAX_VALUE` named constants give maximum and minimum allowable values for the various numerical data types.
- The `Character` class provides methods that tell you whether a character is whitespace, a digit, or letter, and if it's a letter whether it's lowercase or uppercase. Other methods allow you to change case.
- The `String` class's `indexOf` method helps you find the position of a particular character in a string of text. The `substring` method allows you to extract any part of a given string of text. The `replaceAll` and `replaceFirst` methods make substitutions within a string of text. You can make case conversions with the `toLowerCase` and `toUpperCase` methods, and you can use the `trim` method to remove whitespace from either end of a string of text.
- The first argument in the `System.out.printf` method is a format string which enables you to use a special code to specify the output format of text and numbers. For example, to display a `double` number called `price` as dollars and cents with commas between groups of three digits and a zero to the left of the decimal for values less than $1.00, you would write:

  ```
  System.out.printf("$%,04.2f\n", price);
  ```
- Use the `Random` class in the `java.util` package to get various random number distributions or obtain exactly the same list of random numbers every time you run a particular program.
- Use methods in Java API's `Graphics` class to display photographic images, geometric figures, and text in graphics windows.
- To execute a Java applet, create an HTML file that specifies the Java applet, and load the HTML file within a Web browser.

Review Questions

§5.3 Math Class

1. Given these declarations:

   ```
   double diameter = 3.0;
   double perimeter;
   ```

   Provide a statement that assigns the length of a circle's perimeter to the `perimeter` variable. Use the `diameter` variable.
2. What is the name of the class that contains the `abs`, `min`, and `round` methods?
   a) Arithmetic
   b) Math
   c) Number

§5.4 Wrapper Classes for Primitive Types

3. Provide a statement that assigns positive infinity into a `double` variable named `num`.
4. Provide a statement that converts a string variable named `s` to a `long` and assigns the result to a `long` variable named `num`.
5. Provide a statement that converts an `int` variable named `num` to a string and assigns the result to a `String` variable named `numStr`. Use a wrapper class method.

§5.5 Character Class

6. What does the following code fragment print?

```
System.out.println(Character.isDigit('#'));
System.out.println(Character.isWhitespace('\t'));
System.out.println(Character.toLowerCase('B'));
```

§5.6 String Methods

7. Given this declaration:[6]

```
String snyder = "Stick together.\nLearn the flowers.\nGo light.";
```

Write a Java statement that finds the index of the letter 'G' and prints everything in `snyder` from that point on. In other words, it prints `Go light.`

§5.7 Formatted Output with the printf Method

8. Write a format string that handles the display of three data items in three columns. The first column should be 20 spaces wide, and it should print a left-aligned string. The second column should be 10 spaces wide, and it should print a right-aligned integer. The third column should be 16 spaces wide, and it should print a right-aligned floating-point number in scientific format with 6 decimal places. Your format string should cause the screen's cursor to move to the next line after printing the third data item.
9. Provide a format specifier that handles the display of a floating-point data item. It should print a rounded version of the data item with no decimal places. It should insert grouping separators, and it should use parentheses if the number is negative.

§5.8 Problem Solving with Random Numbers (Optional)

10. Write a Java statement that prints a random number for the total number of dots on a roll of a pair of dice.
11. Write a program that prints five random `boolean` values with the seed, `123L`. Then display those values.

Exercises

1. [after §5.3] Write a statement that computes and prints the cube root of a `double` variable named `number`. [*Hint:* look for an appropriate method in Sun's documentation of the `Math` class.]

2. [after §5.3] In probability calculations, we frequently need to compute the value of the factorial of some number n. The factorial of a number `n` (designated `n!`) is given by the formula,
   n! ← n * (n-1) * (n-2) * ... * 3 * 2 * 1.

   When n is a very large number, this is a time-consuming calculation. Fortunately there is a handy formula, called *Stirling's Formula,* which gives a very good approximation to n! whenever n is large. Stirling's formula says:
   $n! \approx (1 + 1/(12n - 1)) * \text{sqrt}(2n\pi) * (n/E)^n$

[6] Gary Snyder, "For the Children" in *Turtle Island,* New Directions (1974).

The symbol π is the ratio of a circle's perimeter to its diameter, and the symbol E is the base of natural logarithms. The actual value of n! is always slightly smaller than the value given by this formula. For this exercise, write a Java code fragment that implements Stirling's formula.

3. [after §5.3] Write a `main` method that asks the user for an angle, θ, in degrees, and prints out the values of sin(θ), cos(θ), and tan(θ).

Sample session:

```
Enter an angle in degrees: 30
sin(deg) = 0.49999999999999994
cos(deg) = 0.8660254037844387
tan(deg) = 0.5773502691896257
```

4. [after §5.3] Provide a statement that prints the length of the hypotenuse of a right triangle whose base is given by the variable `base`, and whose height is given by the variable `height`. In your statement, you must use the `Math` class's `hypot` method. To learn about the `hypot` method, see Sun's Java API Web site.

5. [after §5.3] Given the base-e log, you can always find the log to any other base, with the formula: $\log_{base}(x) = \log_e(x) / \log_e(base)$. For example, a computer scientist might be interested in how many bits are needed to express a given positive integer x in binary. In that case, the total number of bits required is $\log_2(x)$, rounded up to the next higher integer. Write a Java statement that (1) calculates the number of bits required to store variable x's value and (2) assigns that calculated value into an `int` variable named `bits`.

6. [after §5.6] In the following program skeleton, replace <*Insert code here.*> with your own code. *Hint:* Use the variables that are already declared for you (`songs`, `searchText`, `foundIndex`, and `count`). The resulting program should prompt the user for a search string and then display the number of occurrences of the search string in a given list of songs. Study the sample session.

```
import java.util.Scanner;

public class CountSubstringOccurrences
{
  public static void main(String[] args)
  {
    Scanner stdIn = new Scanner(System.in);
    String songs =
      "1. Green Day - American Idiot\n" +
      "2. Jesus Jones - Right Here, Right Now\n" +
      "3. Indigo Girls - Closer to Fine\n" +
      "4. Peter Tosh - Equal Rights\n";

    String searchText; // text that is searched for
    int foundIndex;    // position of where text is found
    int count = 0;     // number of occurrences of search text

    System.out.print("Enter search text: ");
    searchText = stdIn.nextLine();

    <Insert code here.>

    System.out.println("Number of occurrences of \"" +
      searchText + "\": " + count);
  } // end main
} // end class CountSubstringOccurrences
```

Sample session:

```
Enter search text: Right
Number of occurrences of "Right": 3
```

7. [after §5.6] In the following program skeleton, replace <*Insert code here.*> with your own code. *Hint:* Use the variables that are already declared for you (songs, songNum, songIndex, eolIndex, and song). The resulting program should prompt the user for a song number and then extract the song number plus the rest of that string's line from a given list of songs. Study the sample session. You may assume that the user enters a valid song number (no need for input validation).

```
import java.util.Scanner;

public class ExtractLine
{
  public static void main(String[] args)
  {
    Scanner stdIn = new Scanner(System.in);
    String songs =
      "1. Bow Wow - Fresh Azimiz\n" +
      "2. Weezer - Beverly Hills\n" +
      "3. Dave Matthews Band - Crash Into Me\n" +
      "4. Sheryl Crow - Leaving Las Vegas\n";

    String songNum;   // song number that is searched for
    int songIndex;    // position of where song number is found
    int eolIndex;     // position of end of line character
    String song;      // the specified line

    System.out.print("Enter song number: ");
    songNum = stdIn.nextLine();

    <Insert code here.>

    System.out.println(song);
  } // end main
} // end class ExtractLine
```

Sample session:

```
Enter song number: 3
3. Dave Matthews Band - Crash Into Me
```

8. [after §5.7] Given the below program skeleton. Replace the four <*add code here*> items so that the program produces the below output. Try to mimic the output's format precisely, but it's OK if your column widths vary slightly from the shown column widths.

```
public class CarInventoryReport
{
  public static void main(String[] args)
  {
    final String HEADING_FMT_STR = <add code here>;
    final String DATA_FMT_STR = <add code here>;
    String item1 = "Mazda RX-8";
```

```
    int qty1 = 10;
    double price1 = 27999.99;
    String item2 = "MINI Cooper";
    int qty2 = 100;
    double price2 = 23000.25;

    System.out.printf(HEADING_FMT_STR,
      "Item", "Quantity", "Price", "Value");
    System.out.printf(HEADING_FMT_STR,
      "-----", "--------", "------", "------");
    System.out.printf(DATA_FMT_STR, <add code here>);
    System.out.printf(DATA_FMT_STR, <add code here>);
  } // end main
} // end class CarInventoryReport
```

Output:

```
Item                Quantity      Price         Value
-----              ---------     ------        ------
Mazda RX-8                10     28,000       280,000
MINI Cooper              100     23,000     2,300,025
```

9. [after §5.8] Provide a statement that uses `Math.Random` to generate the total number of dots on a rolled pair of dice.

Review Question Solutions

1. `perimeter = Math.PI * diameter;`
2. The class that contains the `abs`, `min`, and `round` methods is: b) `Math`
3. `num = Double.POSITIVE_INFINITY;`
4. `num = Long.parseLong(s);`
5. `numStr = Integer.toString(num);`
6. Here is the code fragment's output:

```
false
true
b
```

7. `System.out.println(snyder.substring(snyder.indexOf('G')));`
8. `"%-20s%10d%16.6e\n"`
   or
   `"%-20s%10d%16e\n"`
   (It's OK to omit the .6 because the e conversion specifier prints 6 decimal places by default.)
9. `"%(,.0f"`
   or
   `"%,(.0f"`
   (The order of flag specifier characters is irrelevant.)

10. Statement that prints the total number of dots on a thrown pair of dice:

```
System.out.println(2 + (int) (6 * (Math.random())) +
  (int) (6 * (Math.random())));
```

11. Program that prints five random boolean values with seed 123L:

```
import java.util.Random;

public class RandomBoolean
{
  public static void main(String[] args)
  {
    Random random = new Random(123L);

    for (int i=0; i<5; i++)
    {
      System.out.println(random.nextBoolean());
    }
  } // end main
} // end RandomBoolean
```

The values are:

```
true
false
true
false
false
```

CHAPTER 6

Object-Oriented Programming

Objectives

- Learn what an object is and how it relates to a class.
- Learn how to encapsulate and access data inside an object.
- Learn how to partition your programs into "driver" and "driven" classes, to create an object of the driven class, and to give the driver a reference to that object.
- Learn the differences between an object's data and data that is local to a method, and learn how to distinguish between those pieces of data when both have the same name.
- Understand implicit initialization (default values) of various kinds of variables.
- Learn how to trace an object-oriented program.
- Learn how to use a UML class diagram.
- Learn how to make a method return a suitable value.
- Learn how values are passed to methods.
- Write methods that get, set, and test the values of an object's data.
- Optionally learn how to improve the speed and accuracy of a simulation.

Outline

6.1 Introduction

As discussed in the Preface, we've written the book with some built-in flexibility in terms of content ordering. Readers who want an early introduction to object-oriented programming (OOP) have the option of reading Sections 6.1 through 6.8 after completing Chapter 3.

Chapter 5 served as a bridge from basic programming language constructs (variables, assignments, operators, `if` statements, loops, etc.) to OOP concepts. We focused primarily on one important aspect of OOP—learning how to use pre-built methods. You used methods associated with an object, like `substring` and `indexOf` for string objects, and you used methods associated with a class, like `abs` and `pow` from the `Math` class. In this chapter, you'll learn how to do more than just use pre-built classes and methods; you'll learn how to write your own classes and methods.

As you'll come to see, OOP makes large programs easier to work with. And making large programs easier to work with is very important because today's computers use lots of very large programs! The tension in learning OOP is that the first OOP programs a student can understand are necessarily small, and they can't show the power of OOP very well. But hang in there. Think of your study of this chapter and most of the next chapter as an investment. By the end of the next chapter, you'll be getting some return on that investment.

In this chapter, we start with an overview of basic OOP terms and concepts. We then step through the design and implementation of a simple OOP program. Typically, OOP design starts with a simple Unified Modeling Language (UML) class diagram, which provides a high-level, pictorial description of what you want the program to model. Then OOP design proceeds to the program's details. We'll show you how to adapt the previously described tracing technique to an OOP environment. We'll show you how to specify method details. In the previous chapter you looked at methods from the outside—with a user or *client* view. Now you'll be looking at methods from the inside—with an implementation or *server* view.

We end the chapter with an optional problem-solving section that introduces you to an important computer application—computer simulation. Computer simulation allows humans to solve problems that are difficult or impossible to solve by hand. We describe a special strategy which enables you to substantially improve both the accuracy and efficiency of computer simulations.

6.2 Object-Oriented Programming Overview

Readers who want a very early OOP overview have the option of reading this section after completing Chapter 1, Section 1.3 (Program Development).

Before OOP, the standard programming technique was *procedural programming*. Procedural programming is so named because the emphasis is on the procedures or tasks that make up a problem solution. You think first about what you want to do—your procedures. In contrast, the OOP programming paradigm invites you to think about what you want the program to represent. You typically respond to this invitation by identifying some things in the world that you want your program to model. Those things might be physical entities or conceptual entities. Once you have identified the things you want to model, you identify their basic properties/attributes. Then you determine what the things can do (their behaviors) or what the things can have done to them. You group each thing's properties and behaviors together into a coherent structure called an object. In writing an OOP program, you define objects, create them, and have them interact with each other.

Objects

An object is:

  a set of related data which identifies the current *state* of the object
\+ a set of *behaviors*.

An object's state refers to the characteristics that currently define the object. For example, if you're writing a program that keeps track of employee salaries, you'd probably want to have employee objects, where an employee object's state consists of the employee's name and current salary.

An object's behaviors refer to the activities associated with the object. Once again, if you're writing a program that keeps track of employee salaries, you'd probably want to define a behavior that adjusts an employee's salary. That type of behavior parallels a real-world behavior—a pay raise or a pay cut. In Java, you implement an object's behaviors as methods. For example, you'd implement the salary adjustment behavior as an `adjustSalary` method. We'll describe method implementation details shortly. But it's important to complete our OOP overview first.

Here are some entities that would make good candidates for objects in an object-oriented program:

Physical Objects	Human Objects	Mathematical Objects
cars in a traffic-flow simulation	employees	points in a coordinate system
aircraft in an air-traffic control system	customers	complex numbers
electrical components in a circuit-design program	students	time

Let's think about the first example object. If a car is considered to be an object in a traffic-flow-simulation program, what is the data stored in each car object? In order to analyze traffic flow, each car's position and speed should be monitored. Therefore, those two pieces of data should be stored as part of a car object's state. And what behaviors are associated with the car objects? You'd need to be able to start the car, stop the car, slow down, and so on. So you'd probably want to implement these methods:

```
start, stop, slowDown
```

An object's behaviors can change an object's state. For example, a car object's `start` method causes the car's position and speed data items to change.

Encapsulation

Objects provide *encapsulation*. In general terms, encapsulation is when something is wrapped up inside a protective covering. When applied to objects, encapsulation means that an object's data are protected by being "hidden" inside the object. With hidden data, how can the rest of the program access an object's data? (*Accessing* an object's data refers to either reading the data or modifying it.) The rest of the program cannot access an object's data directly, but it can access the data with the help of the object's methods. Assuming an object's methods are well written, the methods ensure that data is accessed in an appropriate manner. Returning to the employee-salaries program example, an employee object's salary should be modified only by calling the `adjustSalary` method. The `adjustSalary` method ensures that an employee object's salary is modified appropriately. For example, the `adjustSalary` method prevents an employee object's salary from becoming negative.

See Figure 6.1. It illustrates how an object's methods form the interface between an object's data and the rest of the program.

Benefits of OOP

Now that you have a basic idea of what OOP is, you may be asking yourself what all the hype is about. Why is OOP preferred over procedural programming for most of today's new programs? Here are some benefits of OOP:

- OOP programs have a more natural organization—Since people tend to think about real-world problems in terms of real-world objects, it's easier for people to understand a program that's organized around objects.

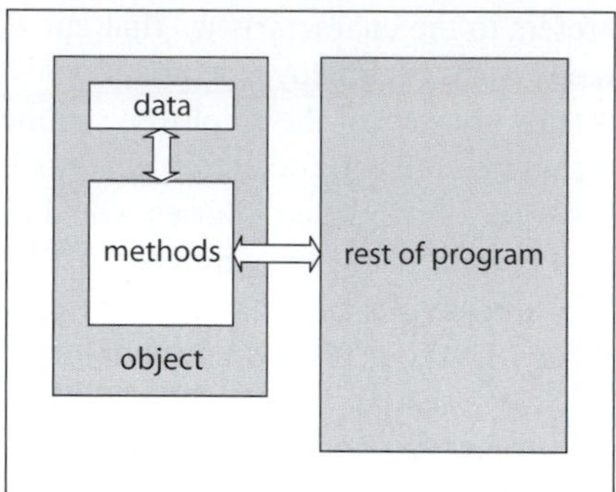

Figure 6.1 To access an object's data, you should use the object's methods as an interface

- OOP makes it easier to develop and maintain large programs—Although switching to OOP programming typically makes a small program more complicated, it naturally partitions things so that the program grows gracefully and does not evolve into a giant mess. Since objects provide encapsulation, bugs (errors) and bug repairs tend to be localized.

The second bullet item needs some clarification. When an object's data can be modified only by using one of that object's methods, it's hard for a programmer to mess up an object's data accidentally. Returning again to the employee-salaries program example, assume the only way to change an employee object's salary is to use its `adjustSalary` method. Then, if there's a bug relating to an employee's salary, the programmer immediately knows where to look for the problem—in the `adjustSalary` method or in one of the calls to the `adjustSalary` method.

Classes

Having discussed objects, it's now time to talk about an intimately related entity—a *class*. We'll start with a broad definition of a class, and we'll refine it later. Broadly speaking, a class is a description of all the objects it defines. As such, it is an *abstraction*—a concept apart from any particular instances. In Figure 6.2, note the three computers on a conveyor belt in a manufacturing plant. The three computers represent objects. The specifications document that hovers above the computers is a blueprint that describes the computers: it lists the computers' components and describes the computers' features. The computer-specification document represents a class. Each object is an instance of its class. Thus, for practical purposes, "object" and "instance" are synonyms.

One class can have any number of objects associated with it. A class can even have zero objects associated with it. This should make sense if you think about the computer-manufacturing example. Isn't it possible to have a blueprint for a computer, but not yet have any computers manufactured from that blueprint?

We'll now present a more complete description of a class. Above, we said that a class is a description for a set of objects. The description consists of:

    a list of variables
\+ a list of methods

Classes can define two types of variables—*class variables* and *instance variables*. And classes can define two types of methods—*class methods* and *instance methods*. Chapter 5 showed you how to use the `Math` class's class methods, and you have been defining a class method called `main` since the beginning. In Chapter 9 we'll show you when it's appropriate to define other class methods and define and use class variables. But it's easy to fall into the trap of defining and using class methods and class variables improp-

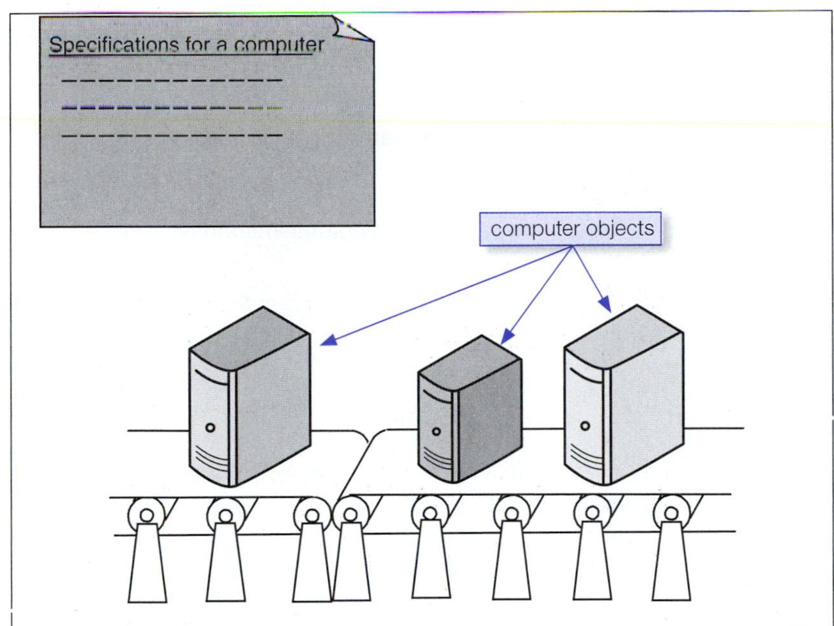

Figure 6.2 Conveyor belt portrayal of the class-objects relationship

erly. We want to keep you away from that trap until after you have developed good OOP habits. Therefore, we focus on instance variables and instance methods throughout this chapter and the next several chapters.

A class's instance variables specify the type of data that an object can store. For example, if you have a class for computer objects, and the `Computer` class contains a `hardDiskSize` instance variable, then each computer object stores a value for the size of the computer's hard disk. A class's instance methods specify the behavior that an object can exhibit. For example, if you have a class for computer objects, and the `Computer` class contains a `printSpecifications` instance method, then each computer object can print a specifications report (the specifications report shows the computer's hard disk size, CPU speed, cost, etc.).

Note the use of the term "instance" in "instance variable" and "instance method." That reinforces the fact that instance variables and instance methods are associated with a particular object instance. For example, each `employee` object would have its own value for a `salary` instance variable, which would be accessed through its `adjustSalary` instance method. That contrasts with class methods. Class methods are associated with an entire class. For example, the `Math` class contains the `round` class method, which is not associated with a particular instance of the `Math` class.

6.3 First OOP Class

In the next several sections, we put what you've learned into practice by implementing a complete OOP program. The program will contain a `Mouse` class, and it will simulate the growth of two `Mouse` objects (we're talking about rodents here, not computer pointing devices). As is customary with OOP programs, we start the implementation process by describing the solution pictorially with a *UML class diagram.* A UML class diagram is a diagrammatic technique for describing classes, objects, and the relationships between them. It is widely accepted in the software industry as a standard for modeling OOP designs. After describing our mouse-simulation solution with a UML class diagram, we will present the Mouse program's source code and walk you through it.

Use UML to specify OOP. 

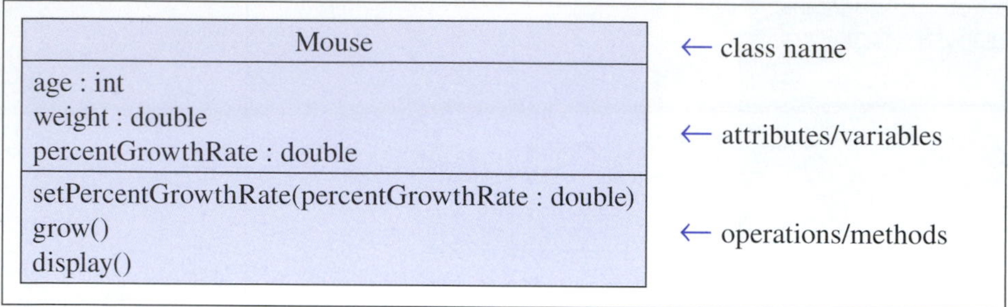

Figure 6.3 Abbreviated UML class diagram for a `Mouse` class

UML Class Diagram

See Figure 6.3. It contains an abbreviated UML class diagram for a `Mouse` class. A UML class diagram box is divided into three parts—class name at the top, *attributes* in the middle, and *operations* at the bottom. With Java programs, attributes equate to variables and operations equate to methods. Henceforth, we'll use the Java terms, variables and methods, rather than the formal UML terms, attributes and operations. Collectively, we refer to a class's variables and methods as the class's *members*. Let's now describe each `Mouse` member.

The `Mouse` class has three instance variables—`age`, `weight`, and `percentGrowthRate`. The `age` instance variable keeps track of how old a `Mouse` object is, in days. The `weight` instance variable keeps track of a `Mouse` object's weight, in grams. The `percentGrowthRate` instance variable is the percentage of its current weight that gets added to its weight each day. If the `percentGrowthRate` is 10 percent and the mouse's current weight is 10 grams, then the mouse gains 1 gram by the next day.

The `Mouse` class has three instance methods—`setPercentGrowthRate`, `grow`, and `display`. The `setPercentGrowthRate` method assigns a specified value to the `percentGrowthRate` instance variable. The `grow` method simulates one day of weight gain for a mouse. The `display` method prints a mouse's age and weight.

Referring to Figure 6.3, note how we specify variable types in a class diagram. The type appears at the right of the variable (e.g., age : int). That's opposite from Java declarations, where we write the type at the left of the variable (e.g., `int age;`)

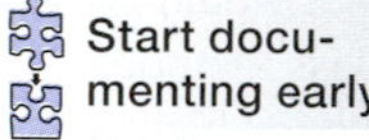
Start documenting early.

Some programmers use UML class diagrams as a means to document programs after they've already been written. That's OK, but it's not how class diagrams were originally intended to be used. We encourage you to start drawing class diagrams as a first step in your solution implementation. The class diagram details provide an outline for your program. Depending on the complexity of the program and your affinity for pseudocode, you may want to code the methods directly with Java or you may want to code the methods first with pseudocode as an intermediate step. For our `Mouse` example, the `Mouse` class's methods are straightforward, so we'll code them directly with Java. Let's now take a look at the `Mouse` class's Java source code.

Mouse Class Source Code

Figure 6.4 shows the `Mouse` class implemented with Java. Note the `Mouse` class's three instance variable declarations for `age`, `weight`, and `percentGrowthRate`. Instance variables must be declared outside all methods, and to make your code more self documenting, you should declare them all at the beginning of the class definition. Instance variable declarations are very similar to variable declarations you've seen in the past: The variable's type goes at the left of the variable, and you can optionally assign an initial value to the variable. Do you remember what it's called when you assign a value to a variable as part of a declara-

```
/*********************************************************************
* Mouse.java
* Dean & Dean
*
* This class models a mouse for a growth simulation program.
*********************************************************************/

public class Mouse
{
  private int age = 0;                  // age of mouse in days
  private double weight = 1.0;          // mouse weight in grams
  private double percentGrowthRate;     // increase per day

  //*************************************************************

  // This method assigns the mouse's percent growth rate.

  public void setPercentGrowthRate(double percentGrowthRate)
  {
    this.percentGrowthRate = percentGrowthRate;
  } // end setPercentGrowthRate

  //*************************************************************

  // This method simulates one day of growth for the mouse.

  public void grow()
  {
    this.weight +=
      (.01 * this.percentGrowthRate * this.weight);
    this.age++;
  } // end grow

  //*************************************************************

  // This method prints the mouse's age and weight.

  public void display()
  {
    System.out.printf("Age = %d, weight = %.3f\n",
      this.age, this.weight);
  } // end display
} // end class Mouse
```


Figure 6.4 Mouse class

tion? That's called an initialization. Note the initializations for age and weight. We initialize age to 0 because newborn mice are zero days old. We initialize weight to 1 because newborn mice weigh approximately 1 gram.

The primary difference between instance variable declarations and variable declarations you've seen in the past is the private access modifier. If you declare a member to be private, then the member can be accessed only from within the member's class and not from the "outside world" (i.e., by code that's outside of the class in which the member resides). Instance variables are almost always declared with the private access modifier because you almost always want an object's data to be hidden. Making an instance variable private gives you control over how its value can be changed. For example, you could assure that a weight is never made negative. Constraining data access is what encapsulation is all about, and it's one of the cornerstones of OOP.

In addition to the private access modifier, there's also a public access modifier. Given the standard definitions of the words "public" and "private," you can probably surmise that public members are easier to access than private members. If you declare a member to be public, then the member can be accessed from anywhere (from within the member's class, and also from outside the member's class). You should declare a method to be public when you want it to be a portal through which the outside world accesses your objects' data. Go back and verify that all three methods in the Mouse class use the public access modifier. When you want a method to help perform a local task only, you should declare it to be private, but we'll delay that consideration until Chapter 8.

Look once again at the Mouse class's instance variable declarations. Note that we initialize age and weight to 0 and 1.0, respectively, but we don't initialize percentGrowthRate. That's because we're comfortable with age = 0 and weight = 1.0 for all newborn Mouse objects, but we're not comfortable with a predefined initial value for percentGrowthRate. Presumably, we'll want to use different percentGrowthRate values for different Mouse objects (mice in a doughnut-eating study might have higher percentGrowthRate values than mice in a cigarette-smoking study).

With no initialization for the percentGrowthRate instance variable, how can you set the growth rate for a Mouse object? You can have the Mouse object call the setPercentGrowthRate method with a growth rate value as an argument. For example, here's how a Mouse object can set its growth rate to 10 (percent):

```
setPercentGrowthRate(10);
```

As you may recall from Chapter 5, a method call's parenthetical values are referred to as *arguments*. Thus, in this example, 10 is an argument. The 10 gets passed into the percentGrowthRate variable in setPercentGrowthRate's heading. A method heading's parenthetical variables are referred to as *parameters*. Thus, in the example shown in Figure 6.4, percentGrowthRate is a parameter. Within the setPercentGrowthRate *method body* (the code between the method's opening and closing braces), the percentGrowthRate parameter is assigned into the percentGrowthRate instance variable. Here's the relevant assignment statement:

```
this.percentGrowthRate = percentGrowthRate;
```

Note the "this dot" in this.percentGrowthRate. The this dot is how you tell the Java compiler that the variable you're referring to is an instance variable. Since the percentGrowthRate variable at the right does not have this dot, the Java compiler knows that that percentGrowthRate refers to the percentGrowthRate parameter, not the percentGrowthRate instance variable. In Figure 6.4's setPercentGrowthRate method, the instance variable and the parameter have the same name. That's a common practice. There's no problem distinguishing between the two variables because the instance variable uses this dot and the parameter does not.

Now, take a look at the Mouse class's display and grow methods. The display method is straightforward; it prints a mouse's age and weight. The grow method simulates one day of weight gain for a mouse. The weight-gain formula adds a certain percentage of the current weight to the current weight. That means that the mouse will continue to grow every day of its life. That's a simple, but not very accurate, portrayal of normal weight gain. We've intentionally kept the weight-gain formula simple in order to avoid getting bogged down in complicated math. In the final section of this chapter, we provide more realistic growth models.

Finally, take a look at the Mouse class's comments. Note the descriptions above each method. Proper style suggests that, above each method, you should have a blank line, a line of asterisks, a blank line, a description of the method, and another blank line. The blank lines and asterisks serve to separate the methods. The method descriptions allow someone who's reading your program to quickly get an idea of what's going on.

6.4 Driver Class

What Is a Driver?

Driver is a common computer term that applies to a piece of software that runs or "drives" something else. For example, a printer driver is a program that is in charge of running a printer. Likewise, a *driver class* is a class that is in charge of running another class.

In Figure 6.5, we present a MouseDriver class. We name the class MouseDriver because it is in charge of driving the Mouse class. We say that the MouseDriver class drives the Mouse class because it creates Mouse objects and then manipulates them. For example, note the gus = new Mouse() and the jaq = new Mouse() statements. That code creates Mouse objects gus and jaq.[1] In addition note the gus.setPercentGrowthRate(growthRate) code. That code manipulates the gus object by updating gus's percentGrowthRate value.

Normally, a driver class consists entirely of a main method and nothing else. The driver class, with its main method, is the starting point for the program. It calls upon the driven class to create objects and manipulate them. The driven class dutifully carries out the object creation and object manipulation requests. Normally, carrying out those tasks is the primary focus of the program, and their implementation requires the majority of the program's code. Thus, driven classes are typically (but not always) longer than driver classes.

Driver classes, such as the MouseDriver class, are in separate files from the classes that they drive. To make them accessible from the outside world, driver classes must be public. Each public class must be stored in a separate file whose name is the same as the class name, so the MouseDriver class must be stored in a file named MouseDriver.java. For MouseDriver's code to find the Mouse class, both classes should be in the same directory.[2]

Reference Variables

In the MouseDriver class, we create Mouse objects, and we refer to those Mouse objects using gus and jaq, where gus and jaq are *reference variables*. The value contained in a reference variable is a "reference" to an object (thus the name reference variable). More precisely, a reference variable holds the address of where an object is stored in memory. For a pictorial explanation, see Figure 6.6. In the figure, the little

[1] Father of two preschool girls, author John Dean is immersed in all things Disney. Gus and Jaq are mice in the Disney classic, *Cinderella*.

[2] We're keeping things simple by telling you to put both classes in the same directory. Actually, the files may be in different directories, but then you'd need to use a package to group together your classes. Appendix 4 describes how to group classes into a package.

```
/*********************************************
* MouseDriver.java
* Dean & Dean
*
* This is a driver for the Mouse class.
*********************************************/

import java.util.Scanner;

public class MouseDriver
{
  public static void main(String[] args)
  {
    Scanner stdIn = new Scanner(System.in);
    double growthRate;
    Mouse gus = new Mouse();
    Mouse jaq = new Mouse();

    System.out.print("Enter % growth rate: ");
    growthRate = stdIn.nextDouble();
    gus.setPercentGrowthRate(growthRate);
    jaq.setPercentGrowthRate(growthRate);
    gus.grow();
    jaq.grow();
    gus.grow();
    gus.display();
    jaq.display();
  } // end main
} // end class MouseDriver
```

the creation of two Mouse objects

Figure 6.5 `MouseDriver` class that drives `Mouse` class in Figure 6.4

boxes immediately to the right of `gus` and `jaq` represent addresses. So `gus`'s little box holds the address of the first object.

Industry OOP Vernacular

Most Java programmers in industry don't use the term reference variable. Instead, they just use the term object. This blurs the distinction between reference variables and objects. For example, in the `MouseDriver` class in Figure 6.5, this statement initializes the `gus` reference variable:

```
Mouse gus = new Mouse();
```

Even though it's a reference variable, most industry Java programmers would refer to `gus` as an object. Despite the common practice of using "object" as a substitute for "reference variable," it's important to know the difference—an object holds a group of data, and a reference variable holds the location where that group of data is stored in memory. Understanding the difference between an object and a reference variable will help you to understand the behavior of Java code.

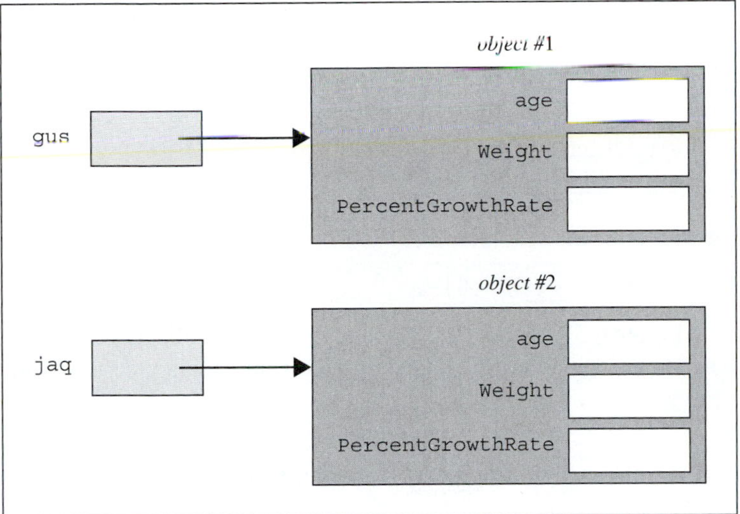

Figure 6.6 Reference variables and objects for the Mouse program in Figures 6.4 and 6.5 The two reference variables on the left, `gus` and `jaq`, contain references that point to the two objects on the right.

Declaring a Reference Variable

You must always declare a variable before you can use it. For example, in order to use an `int` variable named `count`, you must first declare `count` like this:

```
int count;
```

Likewise, in order to use a `gus` reference variable, you must first declare `gus` like this:

```
Mouse gus;
```

As you can see, the process for declaring reference variables mirrors the process for declaring primitive variables. The only difference is that instead of writing a primitive type on the left (e.g., `int`), for reference variables you write a class name on the left (e.g., `Mouse`).

Instantiation and Assigning a Value to a Reference Variable

As you know, the point of a reference variable is to store a reference to an object. But before you can store a reference to an object, you have to have an object. So let's look at object creation.

To create an object, use the `new` operator. For example, to create a `Mouse` object, specify `new Mouse()`. The `new` operator should make sense when you realize that `new Mouse()` creates a new object. The formal term for creating an object is *instantiating* an object. So `new Mouse()` instantiates an object. The term "instantiate" is a verbalized form of the noun "instance." It is computer jargon for "make an instance of a class" or "create an object."

After instantiating an object, you'll normally assign it to a reference variable. For example, to assign a `Mouse` object to the `gus` reference variable, do this:

```
gus = new Mouse();
```

After the assignment, `gus` holds a reference to the newly created `Mouse` object.

Let's review. Here's how we declared a gus reference variable, instantiated a Mouse object, and assigned the object's address to gus:

```
Mouse gus;                    ← declaration
gus = new Mouse();            ← instantiation and assignment
```

Now here's how to do the same thing with only one statement:

```
Mouse gus = new Mouse();      ← initialization
```

The above statement is what appears in Figure 6.5's MouseDriver class. It's an initialization. As mentioned previously, an initialization is when you declare a variable and assign it a value, all in one statement.

Calling a Method

After you instantiate an object and assign its reference to a reference variable, you can call/invoke an instance method using this syntax:

<reference-variable>.*<method-name>*(*<comma-separated-arguments>*);

Here are three example instance method calls from the MouseDriver class:

```
gus.setPercentGrowthRate(growthRate);
gus.grow();
gus.display();
```

Note how the three method calls mimic the syntax template. The first method call has one argument and the next two method calls have zero arguments. If we had a method with two parameters, we'd call it with two arguments separated by a comma.

When a program calls a method, it passes control from the calling statement to the first executable statement in the called method. For example, when the MouseDriver's main method calls the setPercentGrowthRate method with gus.setPercentGrowthRate(growthRate), control passes to this statement in the Mouse class's setPercentGrowthRate method:

```
this.percentGrowthRate = percentGrowthRate;
```

Go back to Figure 6.4's Mouse class and verify that the setPercentGrowthRate method contains the above statement.

After the last statement in any called method executes, control returns to the calling method at the point just after where the call was made. For a pictorial explanation, see Figure 6.7.

6.5 Calling Object, this Reference

Suppose you have two objects that are instances of the same class. For example, gus and jaq refer to two objects that are instances of the Mouse class. And suppose you want the two objects to call the same instance method. For example, you want both gus and jaq to call setPercentGrowthRate. For each method call, the Java Virtual Machine (JVM) needs to know which object to update (if gus calls setPercentGrowthRate, then the JVM should update gus's percentGrowthRate; if jaq calls

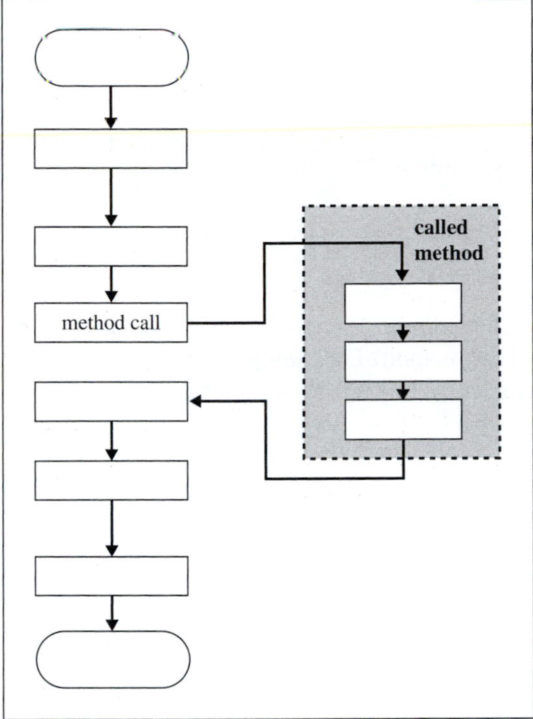

Figure 6.7 Calling a method

setPercentGrowthRate, then the JVM should update jaq's percentGrowthRate). This section describes how the JVM knows which object to update.

Calling Object

As mentioned in Chapter 5, whenever an instance method is called, it is associated with a calling object. You can identify the calling object by looking to the left of the dot in an instance method call statement. Can you identify the calling objects in the following main method?

```
public static void main(String[] args)
{
  Scanner stdIn = new Scanner(System.in);
  double growthRate;
  Mouse gus = new Mouse();

  System.out.print("Enter % growth rate: ");
  growthRate = stdIn.nextDouble();
  gus.setPercentGrowthRate(growthRate);
  gus.grow();
  gus.display();
} // end main
```

The gus object is the calling object for these statements:

```
gus.setPercentGrowthRate(growthRate);
gus.grow();
gus.display();
```

Are there any other calling objects? Yes. The `stdIn` object is a calling object in this statement:

```
growthRate = stdIn.nextDouble();
```

The `this` Reference

It's easy to identify the calling object when you're looking at a method call statement. But what if you're inside the called method—how can you tell what object called the method? For example, when you're looking at the definition of the `Mouse` class in Figure 6.4, can you identify the calling object that called its `grow` method? Here is that method again:

```
public void grow()
{
  this.weight +=
    (0.01 * this.percentGrowthRate * this.weight);
  this.age++;
} // end grow
```

The pronoun `this` (called the *`this` reference*) stands for the calling object, but it doesn't tell you which object that is. Thus, you can't tell what the calling object is just by looking at the method that was called. You must look at what called that method. If the statement that called `grow` was `gus.grow()`, then `gus` is the calling object. Alternately, if the statement that called `grow` was `jaq.grow()`, then `jaq` is the calling object. As you'll see when we do the upcoming trace, you must know which object, `gus` or `jaq`, is the current calling object so that you update the proper object. Within the above `grow` method, note `this.weight` and `this.age`. The `this` reference reminds you that `weight` and `age` are instance variables. Instance variables in which object? In the calling object!

The `setPercentGrowthRate` method in Figure 6.4 provides another example. Here is that method again:

```
public void setPercentGrowthRate(double percentGrowthRate)
{
  this.percentGrowthRate = percentGrowthRate;
} // end setPercentGrowthRate
```

The `this` reference tells you the variable on the left side of this method's lone statement is an instance variable in the calling object. As indicated earlier, the `this` reference in this statement also helps the compiler and a human distinguish the variable on the left side from the variable on the right side. Before the advent of OOP, computer languages did not include `this` dot functionality. Then, the only way the compiler and a human could distinguish between variables in different places that referred to essentially the same thing was to give them similar but slightly different names.

The *ad hoc* (special case) nature of how old-time programmers devised slightly different names made programs confusing and increased programming errors. Java's `this` reference provides a standard way to make the distinction and show the relationship at the same time. You can use exactly the same name to show the relationship and then use `this` dot to make the distinction. So it is no longer necessary to use slightly different names for that purpose, and we recommend against that archaic practice.

To emphasize the meaning and utility of Java's this reference, we will use it with all examples of instance variables up to the end of the next chapter—even when it is not necessary to draw a distinction between an instance variable and a parameter. There is no performance penalty in using this dot, and it provides an immediate indicator to everyone that the variable is an instance variable. Thus, it helps to explain the program; that is, it provides useful self documentation.

6.6 Instance Variables

You've been exposed to instance variables for a while now. You know that an object stores its data in instance variables. You know that an instance method accesses its instance variables by prefacing them with the this reference (e.g., this.weight). In this section, we consider a few more instance variable details. Specifically, we consider default values and persistence.

Default Values for Instance Variables

As implied by the common definition of "default," a variable's *default value* is the variable's value when there's no explicitly assigned initial value; that is, when there's no initialization. Different types of variables have different default values.

There are two integer types that we've covered so far—int and long. Integer-type instance variables are assigned 0 by default. But in the Mouse class, notice that we initialize the age instance variable to 0:

```
private int age = 0;   // age of mouse in days
```

Why bother with the explicit initialization? Wouldn't age be assigned 0 by default even if "= 0" was omitted? Yes, the program would work the same either way. But it's poor practice to depend on hidden default values. By explicitly assigning values to variables, we show our intent. That's a form of self-documenting code.

There are two floating-point types—float and double. Floating-point-type instance variables are assigned 0.0 by default. The Mouse class declares two floating-point instance variables—weight and percentGrowthRate:

```
private double weight = 1.0;         // weight of mouse in grams
private double percentGrowthRate;    // % weight increase per day
```

In this case, we initialize the weight instance variable to 1.0, so the default value doesn't come into play. We do not initialize the percentGrowthRate value, so percentGrowthRate is initialized to 0.0 by default. Didn't we just say that it's poor practice to depend on hidden default values? Yes, but in this case, we're not depending on the default value. In the MouseDriver class, we overlay the percentGrowthRate default value with a custom value by calling setPercentGrowthRate like this:

```
gus.setPercentGrowthRate(growthRate);
```

boolean instance variables are assigned false by default. For example, if you added a boolean instance variable named vaccinated to the Mouse class, vaccinated would be assigned false by default.

Reference-type instance variables are assigned null by default. For example, if you added a String instance variable named breed to the Mouse class, breed would be assigned null by default. Normally, a reference variable holds the address of an object and that address points to an object. The Java designers added null to the language as a way to indicate that a reference variable points to nothing. So the default for a reference-type instance variable is to point to nothing.

Here's a summary of default values for instance variables:

Instance Variable's Type	Default Value
integer	0
floating point	0.0
`boolean`	`false`
reference	`null`

Instance Variable Persistence

Now consider variable *persistence*. Persistence refers to how long a variable's value survives before it's wiped out. Instance variables persist for the duration of a particular object. Thus, if an object makes two method calls, the second called method does not reset the calling object's instance variables to their initialized values. Instead, the object's instance variables retain their values from one method call to the next. For example, in the `MouseDriver` class, `gus` calls `grow` twice. In the first call to `grow`, `gus`'s `age` increments from 0 to 1. In the second call to `grow`, `gus`'s `age` starts out as 1 and increments to 2. `gus`'s `age` retains its value from one `grow` call to the next because `age` is an instance variable.

6.7 Tracing an OOP Program

To reinforce what you've learned so far in this chapter, we'll trace the Mouse program. Remember the tracing procedure we used in prior chapters? It worked fine for programs with only one method—the `main` method. But for OOP programs with multiple classes and multiple methods, you'll need to keep track of which class and which method you're in and which object called that method. In addition, you'll need to keep track of parameters and instance variables. This requires a more elaborate trace table.

In tracing the Mouse program, we'll use a slightly different driver, the `MouseDriver2` class, shown in Figure 6.8. In `MouseDriver2`, we delay the instantiation of the individual mice and assign their growth rates (by calling `setPercentGrowthRate`) immediately after each instantiation. This is better style, because it more closely associates each object's instantiation with its growth rate assignment. However, in changing the driver we "accidentally" forget to call `setPercentGrowthRate` for `jaq`, the second mouse. You can see the effect of this logic error in the output—`jaq` doesn't grow (after the first day, `jaq` still weighs 1 gram). But let's pretend that you don't know why this error occurs and use the trace to help find its cause. Remember—tracing is an effective tool when you need help debugging a program.

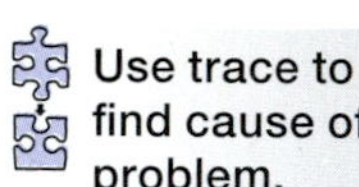
Use trace to find cause of problem.

To perform the trace, in addition to the driver, you'll also need the code for the driven class. For your convenience, we repeat the original driven `Mouse` class in Figure 6.9.

Trace Setup

Figure 6.10 shows the setup. As with the traces in the previous chapters, the input goes in the top-left corner. Unlike the traces in the previous chapters, the headings under the input now require more than one line. The first line of headings shows the class names—`MouseDriver2` and `Mouse`. Under each class name heading, there's a heading for each of the class's methods. In the trace setup, find the `setPercentGrowthRate`, `grow`, and `display` method headings (to save space, we abbreviated `setPercentGrowthRate` and `display` to setPGR and disp, respectively). And under each method-name heading, there's a heading for each of the method's local variables and parameters.

```
/****************************************************
* MouseDriver2.java
* Dean & Dean
*
* This is a driver for the Mouse class.
****************************************************/

import java.util.Scanner;

public class MouseDriver2
{
  public static void main(String[] args)
  {
    Scanner stdIn = new Scanner(System.in);
    double growthRate;
    Mouse gus, jaq;

    System.out.print("Enter % growth rate: ");
    growthRate = stdIn.nextDouble();
    gus = new Mouse();
    gus.setPercentGrowthRate(growthRate);
    gus.grow();
    gus.display();
    jaq = new Mouse();
    jaq.grow();
    jaq.display();
  } // end main
} // end class MouseDriver2
```

This declares reference variables but does not initialize them.

Try to group initialization activities.

There's a logic error here. We "accidentally" forget to initialize the growth rate in jaq.

Sample session:

```
Enter % growth rate: 10
Age = 1, weight = 1.100
Age = 1, weight = 1.000
```

jaq doesn't grow. A bug!

Figure 6.8 MouseDriver2 class that drives Mouse class in Figure 6.9

We'll discuss *local variables* in detail later, but for now, just realize that growthRate (abbreviated to rate in the trace setup), gus, and jaq are considered to be local variables because they're declared and used "locally" within one particular method, the main method. That's different from the age, weight, and percentGrowthRate instance variables, which are declared outside of all methods, at the top of the class. Note that stdIn is another local variable within main, but there's no need to trace it because it's instantiated from an API class, Scanner. There's no need to trace API classes because they've already been traced and tested thoroughly by the good folks at Sun. You can assume that they work properly.

Now let's examine the trace setup's parameters. The setPercentGrowthRate method has two parameters—percentGrowthRate, abbreviated to rate in the trace setup, and the this reference, an implicit parameter. As you may recall, the this reference points to the calling object. For the

```
/*******************************************************************
* Mouse.java
* Dean & Dean
*
* This class models a mouse for a growth simulation program.
*******************************************************************/

public class Mouse
{
  private int age = 0;                  // age of mouse in days
  private double weight = 1.0;          // mouse weight in grams
  private double percentGrowthRate;     // increase per day

  //*****************************************************************

  // This method assigns the mouse's percent growth rate.

  public void setPercentGrowthRate(double percentGrowthRate)
  {
    this.percentGrowthRate = percentGrowthRate;
  } // end setPercentGrowthRate

  //*****************************************************************

  // This method simulates one day of growth for the mouse.

  public void grow()
  {
    this.weight +=
      (.01 * this.percentGrowthRate * this.weight);
    this.age++;
  } // end grow

  //*****************************************************************

  // This method prints the mouse's age and weight.

  public void display()
  {
    System.out.printf(
      "Age = %d, weight = %.3f\n", this.age, this.weight);
  } // end display
} // end class Mouse
```

Figure 6.9 Mouse class repeated from Figure 6.4

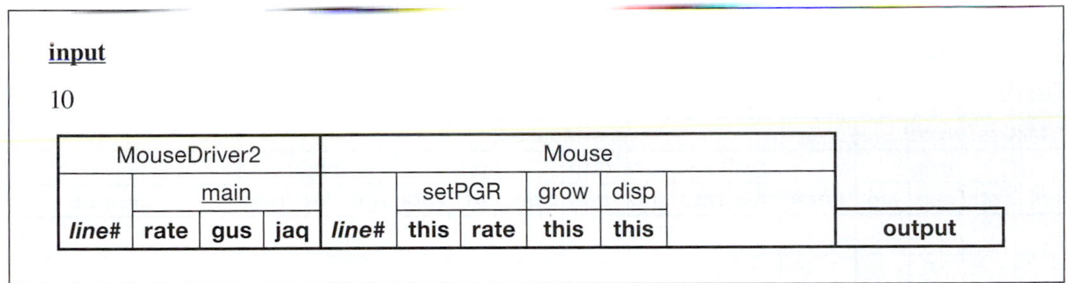

Figure 6.10 Trace setup for the Mouse program

setPercentGrowthRate, grow, and display methods, we include a column for this so the trace can keep track of which object called the method.

Note the vacant area under the Mouse heading. We'll fill in more headings there as we execute the trace.

Trace Execution

Using Figure 6.10's trace setup as a starting point, we'll walk you through the key sections of the trace shown in Figure 6.11. We'll focus on the OOP parts of the trace since those are the parts that are new to you. When starting a method, under the method's local variable headings, write initial values for each of the local variables. Use a question mark for local variables that are uninitialized. In the first three lines of Figure 6.11's trace, note the ?'s for the uninitialized growthRate (abbreviated to rate), gus, and jaq local variables.

When an object is instantiated, under the object's class-name heading, provide a column heading named "obj#", where # is a unique number. Under the obj# heading, provide an underlined column heading for each of the object's instance variables. Under the instance variable headings, write initial values for each of the instance variables. In Figure 6.11's trace, note the obj1 and obj2 column headings and their age, weight, and percentGrowthRate (abbreviated to rate) subheadings. Also note the initial values for the age, weight, and percentGrowthRate instance variables.

When there's an assignment into a reference variable, write obj# under the reference variable's column heading, where obj# matches up with the associated obj# in the object portion of the trace. For example, in Figure 6.11's trace, we created obj1 while tracing the `gus = new Mouse();` statement. Subsequently, we put obj1 under the gus column heading.

When there's a method call, under the called method's this column heading, write the calling object's obj#. In Figure 6.11's trace, note obj1 under setPercentGrowthRate's this heading. If the method call contains an argument, write the argument's value under the called method's associated parameter. In the trace, note the passed-in 10 under the setPercentGrowthRate's percentGrowthRate heading. Inside the method, if there's a this reference, find the obj# under the method's this column heading. Then go to the found obj#'s heading and read or update the obj#'s value accordingly. In Figure 6.9's Mouse class, note this.percentGrowthRate in the setPercentGrowthRate method body. In the trace, note that setPercentGrowthRate's this reference refers to obj1, so obj1's percentGrowthRate is updated accordingly.

When you finish tracing a method, draw a horizontal line under the method's variable values to indicate the end of the method trace and to signify that the values in the method's local variables are wiped out. For example, in the trace, the heavy horizontal line in Mouse line #20 under set PGR indicates the end of the setPercentGrowthRate method, and it signifies that percentGrowthRate's value is wiped out.

input

10

MouseDriver2				Mouse											
	main				setPGR		grow	disp	obj1			obj2			
line#	rate	gus	jaq	*line#*	this	rate	this	this	age	wt	rate	age	wt	rate	output
15	?														
16		?	?												
18															Enter % growth rate:
19	*10.0*														
20															
				10					0						
				11						1.000					
				12							0.0				
20		obj1													
21					obj1	10.0									
				20							10.0				
22							obj1								
				29						1.100					
				31					1						
23								obj1							
				40											Age = 1, weight = 1.100
24															
				10								0			
				11									1.000		
				12										0.0	
24			obj2												
25							obj2								
				29									1.000		
				31								1			
26								obj2							
				40											Age = 1, weight = 1.000

Figure 6.11 Completed trace for the Mouse program

Practice. Now that we've walked you through the new techniques for tracing an OOP program, we encourage you to go back to the trace setup in Figure 6.10 and do the entire trace on your own. Pay particular attention to what happens when `gus` and `jaq` call the `grow` method. Verify that `gus`'s weight increases (as it should) and `jaq`'s weight fails to increase (a bug). When you're done with the trace, compare your answer to Figure 6.11.

Experience with the long-form tracing used in this book will make it easier for you to understand what an automated debugger in an *Integrated Development Environment* (IDE) is telling you. As you step through a program that's running in debug mode under the control of an IDE debugger, when you get to a method call, you have two choices. You can "step into" and go through all the statements in the called method, like we do in Figure 6.11, or you can "step over" and just see what happens after the method returns. In a typical debugging activity, you will use a combination of stepping over and stepping in. For the example problem we have been considering, the sample session in Figure 6.8 tells you that the simulation is OK for the first object. The problem is with the second object. So, the appropriate thing to do is step over the method calls down through line 23 in the `MouseDriver2` class. Then, starting at line 24 in the `MouseDriver2` class, step into the methods calls to zero in on what caused the problem.

Paper trace emulates IDE debugger.

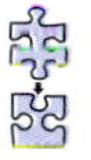

6.8 UML Class Diagrams

The `Mouse` class's `grow` method is not very flexible—it forces the driver to call the `grow` method separately for each day or to provide a `for` loop for each multiple-day simulation. It isn't good style to include such things in a driver. It's better to include multiple-day functionality within the driven class. In this section, we do just that. We present a revised mouse class with a `grow` method that handles any number of days, not just one day.

To specify a second-generation mouse class (Mouse2) and an associated driver class (`Mouse2Driver`), let's create another UML class diagram. The diagram we presented in Figure 6.3 was a pared-down UML class diagram. It did not include all the standard features. This time, in Figure 6.12, we present a UML class diagram that includes all the standard features, plus an extra feature.

Organize.

Figure 6.12's class diagram includes class diagram boxes for both classes—one diagram for the `Mouse2Driver` class and another diagram for the `Mouse2` class. The `Mouse2` class has the same three instance variables as the original `Mouse` class—`age`, `weight`, and `percentGrowthRate`. It also has the same `setPercentGrowthRate` method. But the `getAge` and `getWeight` methods are new and the

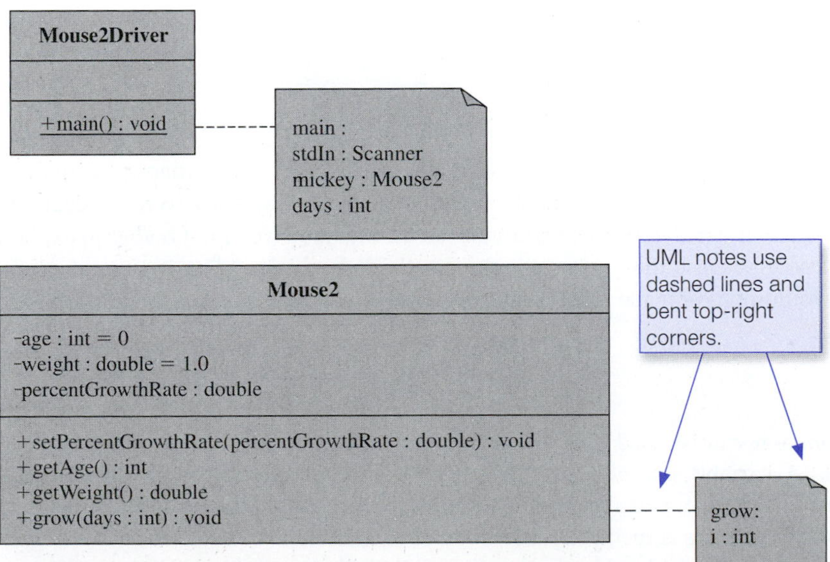

Figure 6.12 A UML class diagram for a second-generation Mouse program

grow method is improved. The getAge method retrieves a mouse's age. Remember the age variable is private, so the only way for the outside world to read a mouse object's age is to use a public method—the getAge method. The getWeight method retrieves a mouse's weight. The grow method simulates a mouse's growth for a specified number of days. Note the days parameter. The number of days is passed into the days parameter and that's how the method knows how many days to simulate.

Here are some of the standard UML class diagram features not found in Figure 6.3 that do appear in Figure 6.12:

- To specify member accessibility, prefix all member specifications with a "-" for private access or a "+" for public access. The instance variables have "-" prefixes, since we want them to be private, and the methods have "+" prefixes, since we want them to be public.
- To specify initialization, append "= <*value*>" to each variable declaration that includes initialization. For example, note the " = 0" after the age instance variable's specification.
- Underline the main method in the MouseDriver class diagram box, since the main method is declared with the static modifier. UML standards suggest that you underline all methods and variables that are declared with the static modifier. As you learned in Chapter 5, the static modifier indicates a class member. You'll learn more about class members in Chapter 9.
- Include a ": <*type*>" suffix with each method. This specifies the type of value that the method returns. All the methods in the Mouse class in Figure 6.4 returned void (nothing), but in Chapter 5 you saw many Java API class methods with return types like int and double, and we'll discuss implementation of such methods later in this chapter.

Figure 6.12 also includes an extra UML class diagram feature. It has *notes* for two of its methods—the main and grow methods. The notes are depicted by the rectangles with the bent top-right corners. Why bent corners? They are supposed to give the impression of a piece of paper with its corner folded, an indication of a hardcopy "note." Including a note in a UML class diagram is purely optional. Usually we won't use them, but this time, we did use them because we wanted to show how you can include local variables in a UML class diagram.

6.9 Local Variables

A *local variable* is a variable that's declared and used "locally" inside a method. That's different from an instance variable, which is declared at the top of a class, outside all methods. As you perhaps now realize, all the variables we defined in chapters prior to this chapter were local variables. They were all declared within main methods, so they were all local variables within the main method. We didn't bother to explain the term "local variable" until now because there were no other methods besides main, and the idea of a variable being local to main wouldn't have made much sense. But the OOP context makes the concept of a local variable more meaningful.

Scope

A local variable has *local scope*—it can be used only from the point at which the variable is declared to the end of the variable's block. A variable's *block* is established by the closest pair of braces that enclose the variable's declaration. Most of the time, you should declare a method's local variables at the top of the method's body. The scope of such variables is then the entire body of the method.

for loop index variables are local variables, but they are special. Their scope rule is slightly different from what is described above. As you know from Chapter 4, you should normally declare a for loop's index variable within the `for` loop's header. The scope of such a variable is the `for` loop's header plus the `for` loop's body.

Method parameters are usually not considered to be local variables, but they are very similar to local variables in that they are declared and used "locally" inside a method. As with local variables, the scope of a method's parameters is limited to within the body of that method.

Let's round out the discussion of scope by comparing local scope to the scope used by instance variables. While variables with local scope can be accessed only within one particular method, instance variables can be accessed by any instance methods within the instance variable's class. Furthermore, if an instance variable is declared with the `public` access modifier, it can be accessed from outside of the instance variable's class (with the help of an instantiated object from the instance variable's class).

`Mouse2Driver` Class

To illustrate local variable principles, we present the Mouse2 program in Figures 6.13 and 6.14. The code includes line numbers to facilitate tracing in an end-of-chapter exercise. The `main` method in the `Mouse2Driver` class has three local variables—`stdIn`, `mickey`, and `days`. These appear in the UML class diagram note at the top of Figure 6.12, and they also appear as declarations in the `main` method in Figure 6.13.

```
/*************************************************************
* Mouse2Driver.java
* Dean & Dean
*
* This is a driver for the Mouse2 class.
*************************************************************/

import java.util.Scanner;

public class Mouse2Driver
{
  public static void main(String[] args)
  {
    Scanner stdIn = new Scanner(System.in)
    Mouse2 mickey = new Mouse2();
    int days;

    mickey.setPercentGrowthRate(10);
    System.out.print("Enter number of days to grow: ");
    days = stdIn.nextInt();
    mickey.grow(days);
    System.out.printf("Age = %d, weight = %.3f\n",
      mickey.getAge(), mickey.getWeight());
  } // end main
} // end class Mouse2Driver
```


Figure 6.13 `Mouse2Driver` class that drives the `Mouse2` class in Figure 6.14

Let's examine Figure 6.13's Mouse2Driver class. In the call to setPercentGrowthRate, note that we pass in a constant, 10, instead of a variable. Normally, you'll use variables for your arguments, but this example shows that it's legal to use constants also. After setting the percent growth rate, we prompt the user for the number of days of simulated growth, and then we pass the days value into the grow method. Then we print mickey's age and weight by embedding getAge and getWeight method calls within a printf statement.

Mouse2 Class

Now look at the Mouse2 class in Figure 6.14. Are there any local variables there? The age, weight, and percentGrowthRate variables are instance variables, not local variables, because they're declared outside of all the methods, at the top of the class. Inside the grow method, we highlight this fact by prefixing each of these instance variables with a this reference. The grow method also includes a local variable—the i in the for loop. Since i is declared within the for loop header, its scope is limited to the for loop block. So you can read and update i only within the for loop. If you try to access i outside the for loop, you'll get a compilation error. This grow method is similar to the previous Mouse program's grow method, but this time we use a for loop to simulate multiple days of growth rather than just one day. The days parameter determines how many times the loop will repeat.

Previously we described the default values for instance variables. Now we'll describe the default values for local variables. Local variables contain *garbage* by default. Garbage means that the variable's value is unknown—it's whatever just happens to be in memory at the time that the variable is created. If a program attempts to access a variable that contains garbage, the compiler generates a compilation error. For example, what would happen if the =0 initialization were removed from the for loop header in the grow method in Figure 6.14? In other words, suppose that for loop was replaced by this:

```
for (int i; i
{
  this.weight +=
    (0.01 * this.percentGrowthRate * this.weight);
}
```

Since i is no longer assigned zero, i contains garbage when the i<days condition is tested. If you tried to compile code with a statement like this, it wouldn't compile, and the compiler would report:

```
variable i might not have been initialized
```

Local Variable Persistence

OK, let's say you do initialize a local variable. How long will it *persist*? A local variable (or parameter) persists only within its scope and only for the current duration of the method (or for loop) in which it is defined. The next time the method (or for loop) is called, the local variable's value resets to the value given it by whatever initialization it gets. The horizontal line drawn in a trace after a method terminates reminds you that method termination converts all the method's local variables into garbage.

6.10 The return Statement

If you look back at our original Mouse class in Figures 6.4 and 6.10, you'll notice that every method heading has a void modifier located at the left of the method name. That means the method does not return any value, and we say "the method has a void return type" or more simply "it's a void method." But recall from

```
/*******************************************************************
* Mouse2.java
* Dean & Dean
*
* This class models a mouse for a growth simulation program.
*******************************************************************/

import java.util.Scanner;

public class Mouse2
{
  private int age = 0;                   // age in days
  private double weight = 1.0;           // weight in grams
  private double percentGrowthRate;      // % daily weight gain

  //*****************************************************************

  public void setPercentGrowthRate(double percentGrowthRate)
  {
    this.percentGrowthRate = percentGrowthRate;
  } // end setPercentGrowthRate

  //*****************************************************************

  public int getAge()
  {
    return this.age;
  }  // end getAge

  //*****************************************************************

  public double getWeight()
  {
    return this.weight;
  } // end getWeight

  //*****************************************************************

  public void grow(int days)
  {
    for (int i=0; i<days; i++)
    {
      this.weight +=
        (0.01 * this.percentGrowthRate * this.weight);
    }
    this.age += days;
  } // end grow
} // end class Mouse2
```

parameter

parameter

local variable

Figure 6.14 Mouse2 class

Chapter 5 that many of the Java API methods return some kind of value, and in each case the type of value returned is indicated by an appropriate return type in the method heading located at the left of the method name.

Returning a Value

If you look at the Mouse2 class in Figure 6.14, you'll see that two of the methods have a return type that is different from void. Here is one of those methods:

```
public int getAge()          // return type
{
  return this.age;           // return statement
} // end getAge
```

The return statement in this method allows you to pass a value from the method back to the place from which the method was called. In this case, the getAge method returns age to Mouse2Driver's printf statement in Figure 6.13. Here is that statement again:

```
System.out.printf("Age = %d, weight = %.3f\n",
  mickey.getAge(), mickey.getWeight());
```

method call

In effect, the JVM "assigns" the return value (this.age) to the method call (mickey.getAge()). To perform a mental trace, imagine that the method call is overlaid by the returned value. So if Mickey's age is 2, then 2 is returned, and you can replace the getAge method call by the value 2.

Whenever a method heading's type is different from void, that method must return a value by means of a return statement, and the type of that value must match the type specified in the method heading. For example, the getAge method heading specifies an int return type. The return statement within the getAge method returns this.age. In Figure 6.14, the age instance variable was declared to be an int, and that matches getAge's int return type, so all is well. It's OK to have an expression following the word return; you aren't limited to just having a simple variable. But the expression must evaluate to the method's return type. For example, would it be legal to use this?

```
return this.age + 1;
```

Yes, because this.age + 1 evaluates to an int type, and that matches getAge's return type.

When a method includes conditional branching (with an if statement or a switch statement), it's possible to return from more than one place in the method. In such cases, all returns must match the type specified in the method heading.

Empty return Statement

For methods with a void return type, it's legal to have an *empty* return statement. The empty return statement looks like this:

```
return;
```

The empty return statement does what you'd expect. It terminates the current method and causes control to be passed back to the calling module at the point that immediately follows the method call. Here's a variation of our previous grow method that uses an empty return statement:

```
public void grow(int days)
{
  int endAge = this.age + days;

  while (this.age < endAge)
  {
    if (this.age >= 100)
    {
      return;       ◄─── empty return statement
    }
    this.weight +=
      .01 * this.percentGrowthRate * this.weight;
    this.age++;
  }  // end while
} // end grow
```

In this variation of the grow method, we cut off the aging process at 100 days—after "adolescence"—by checking age inside the loop and returning when age is greater than or equal to 100. Notice the empty return statement. Since nothing is returned, the method heading must specify void for its return type.

It would be illegal to have an empty return statement and a non-empty return statement in the same method. Why? Empty and non-empty return statements have different return types (void for an empty return statement and some other type for a non-empty return statement). There is no way to specify a type in the heading that simultaneously matches two different return types.

The empty return statement is a helpful statement in that it provides an easy way to exit quickly from a method. However, it does not provide unique functionality. Code that uses an empty return statement can always be replaced by code that is devoid of return statements. For example, here's a return-less version of the previous grow method:

```
public void grow(int days)
{
  int endAge = this.age + days;

  if (endAge > 100)
  {
    endAge = 100;
  }
  while (this.age < endAge)
  {
    this.weight +=
      .01 * this.percentGrowthRate * this.weight;
    this.age++;
  }  // end while
} // end grow
```

return Statement Within a Loop

Programmers in industry often are asked to maintain (fix and improve) other people's code. In doing that, they often find themselves having to examine the loops and, more specifically, the loop termination conditions in the program they're working on. Therefore, it's important that loop termination conditions are clear. Normally, loop termination conditions appear in the standard loop-condition section. For `while` loops, that's the header, for `for` loops, that's the header's second component, and for `do` loops that's the closing. However, a `return` statement inside a loop results in a loop termination condition that's not in a standard location. For example, in the first `grow` method on the previous page the `return` statement is inside an `if` statement and the loop termination condition is consequently "hidden" in the `if` statement's condition.

In the interest of maintainability, you should use restraint when considering the use of a `return` statement inside a loop. Based on the context, if inserting `return` statements inside a loop improves clarity, then feel free to insert. However, if it simply makes the coding chores easier and it does not add clarity, then don't insert. So which `grow` implementation is better—the empty `return` version or the `return`-less version? In general, we prefer the `return`-less version for maintainability reasons. However, because the code in both of our adolescent `grow` methods is so simple, it doesn't make much difference here.

6.11 Argument Passing

In the previous section you saw that when a method finishes, the JVM effectively assigns the return value to the method call. This section describes a similar transfer in the other direction. When a method is called, the JVM effectively assigns the value of each argument in the calling statement to the corresponding parameter in the called method.

Example

Let's examine argument passing by looking at an example—another version of our Mouse program called Mouse3. Here is the code for this new version's driver:

```
public class Mouse3Driver
{
  public static void main(String[] args)
  {
    Mouse3 minnie = new Mouse3();
    int days = 365;

    minnie.grow(days);
    System.out.println("# of days aged = " + days);
  } // end main
} // end class Mouse3Driver
```

The JVM makes a copy of `days`'s value and passes it to the `grow` method.

The `Mouse3Driver` class calls the `grow` method with an argument called `days`, whose value happens to be 365. Then it assigns this value (365) to the parameter called `days` in the `grow` method. The following code shows what happens to the `days` parameter within the `grow` method:

```
public class Mouse3
{
  private int age = 0;                    // age in days
  private double weight = 1.0;            // weight in grams
```

```
  private double percentGrowthRate = 10; // % daily weight gain
  public void grow(int days)
  {
    this.age += days;
    while (days > 0)
    {
      this.weight +=
        .01 * this.percentGrowthRate * this.weight;
      days--;
    }
  } // end grow
} // end class Mouse3
```

The JVM assigns the passed-in value to the days parameter.

The days parameter decrements down to 0.

Within a method, parameters are treated like local variables. The only difference is that a local variable is initialized inside the method, whereas a parameter is initialized by an argument in the method call. As you can see in the above loop body, the `days` parameter decrements down to zero. What happens to the `days` variable in the `main` method in `Mouse3Driver`? Because the two `days` variables are distinct, the `days` variable in the `main` method does not change with the days parameter in the `grow` method. So when `Mouse3Driver` prints its version of `days`, it prints the unchanged value of 365 like this:

```
# of days aged = 365.
```

Pass-By-Value

We say that Java uses *pass-by-value* for its argument-passing scheme. As illustrated by Figure 6.15, pass-by-value means that the JVM passes a copy of the argument's value (not the argument itself) to the parameter. Changing the copy does not change the original.

In `Mouse3Driver` and `Mouse3`, notice that the calling method's argument is called `days` and the `grow` method's parameter is called `days` also. Is the parameter the same variable as the argument? No! They are separate variables separately encapsulated in separate blocks of code. Because these two variables are in separate blocks of code, there is no conflict, and it's OK to give them the same name. Using the same name is natural because these two variables describe the same kind of thing. When names are in different blocks, you don't have to worry about whether they are the same or not. That's the beauty of encapsulation. Big programs would be horrible nightmares if you were prohibited from using the same name in different blocks of code.

Same Name Versus Different Names for Argument-Parameter Pairs

Most of the time, you'll want to use the same name for an argument/parameter pair. But be aware that using different names is legal and fairly common. When it's more natural and reasonable to use different names for an argument/parameter pair, then use different names. The only requirement is that the argument's type must match the parameter's type. For example, in the Mouse3 program, if `num` is an `int` variable, then the following method call successfully passes `num`'s value to the `days int` parameter:

```
minnnie.grow(num);
```

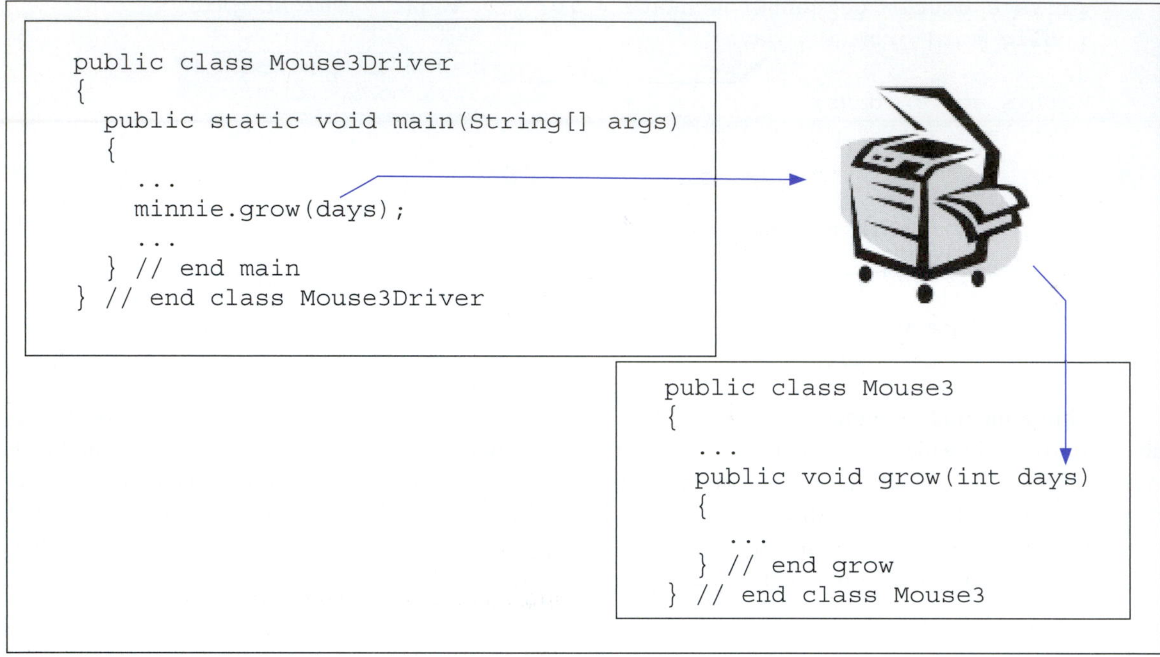

Figure 6.15 Pass-by-value means a copy of the argument's value goes to the corresponding parameter

6.12 Specialized Methods—Accessors, Mutators, Boolean Methods

Let's now discuss some of the common types of specialized methods. You won't be asked to learn any new syntax; you'll just be asked to apply what you've learned so far.

Accessor Methods

An *accessor* is a method that retrieves part of an object's stored data—typically `private` data. Note the following `getAge` and `getWeight` methods (taken from Figure 6.14's `Mouse2` class). They are accessor methods as they retrieve the values of the instance variables, `age` and `weight`, respectively.

```
public int getAge()
{
  return this.age;
} // end getAge

public double getWeight()
{
  return this.weight;
} // end getWeight
```

As evidenced by the `getAge` and `getWeight` methods, accessor methods should be named with a "get" prefix. That's why accessor methods are often called *get methods*.

A method should perform one task. It should be written such that it accomplishes only the one thing that its name implies. For example, a `getAge` method should simply return its object's `age` instance variable value and do nothing else. We mention this notion because there is sometimes a temptation to provide extra functionality to a method to avoid having to implement that functionality elsewhere. One particularly common *faux pas* (a French term meaning error in etiquette) is to add print statements to a method that doesn't need to print. For example, a novice programmer might implement the `getAge` method like this:

```
public int getAge()
{
  System.out.println("Age = " + this.age);   ← inappropriate print statement
  return this.age;
} // end getAge
```

That `getAge` method might work fine for the novice programmer's program, which takes into account the `getAge` method's non-standard print statement. But if later on another programmer needs to work with the program and call the `getAge` method, the new programmer would be surprised to find the non-standard print statement. The new programmer would then either have to (1) accommodate the print statement or (2) remove it from the `getAge` method and check for any ripple effects. To avoid that scenario, you should include print statements in a method only if the purpose of the method is to print something.

The exception to the above rule is that it's acceptable and helpful to temporarily add print statements to methods when you're trying to debug a program. For example, if you think there's something wrong with your `getAge` method, you might want to add the above print statement to verify the correctness of the age value just before `getAge` returns it. If you add such debug print statements, don't forget to remove them later on, once your program is working.

debug with temporary print statements.

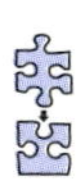

Mutator Methods

A *mutator* is a method that changes or "mutates" an object's state by changing some or all of that object's stored data—typically `private` data. For example, here is the mutator method for setting or changing a mouse's `percentGrowthRate` instance variable:

```
public void setPercentGrowthRate(double percentGrowthRate)
{
  this.percentGrowthRate = percentGrowthRate;
} // end setPercentGrowthRate
```

As evidenced by the `setPercentGrowthRate` method, mutator methods should be named with a "set" prefix. That's why mutator methods are often called *set methods*.

An accessor allows you to read a `private` instance variable. A mutator allows you to update a `private` instance variable. If you provide a `private` instance variable with both an accessor and a simple mutator like the `setPercentGrowthRate` method above, it effectively converts that `private` instance variable into a `public` instance variable, and it breaks the encapsulation of that variable. There's not much danger with having an accessor alone, but having a simple mutator allows an outsider to enter an unreasonable value that may produce erratic program operation. However, if you include constraint checking and perhaps correcting code in your mutators, they can serve as data *filters* that assign only proper data to your `private` instance variables. For example, here's a `setPercentGrowthRate` mutator that filters out growth rates that are less than −100%:

Use mutator to filter input.

```
public void setPercentGrowthRate(double percentGrowthRate)
{
  if (percentGrowthRate < -100)
  {
    System.out.println("Attempt to assign an invalid growth rate.");
  }
  else
  {
    this.percentGrowthRate = percentGrowthRate;
  }
} // end setPercentGrowthRate
```

Our examples will occasionally include some mutator error checking to illustrate this filtering function, but to reduce clutter we'll usually employ the minimal form.

Boolean Methods

A *Boolean method* checks to see whether some condition is true or false. If the condition is true, then true is returned. If the condition is false, then false is returned. To accommodate the boolean returned value, Boolean methods must always specify a boolean return type. A Boolean method name should normally start with "is." For example, here's an isAdolescent method that determines whether a Mouse object is an adolescent by comparing its age value to 100 days:

```
public boolean isAdolescent()
{
  if (this.age <= 100)
  {
    return true;
  }
  else
  {
    return false;
  }
} // end isAdolescent
```

Here's how this code might be shortened:

```
public boolean isAdolescent()
{
  return this.age <= 100;
} // end isAdolescent
```

To show how the shortened method works, we'll plug in sample values. But first, let's get settled on the goal: Whenever age is less than or equal to 100, we want the method to return true to indicate adolescence. If age is 50, what is returned? true (Because the return statement's this age <= 100 expression evaluates to true.) If age is 102, what is returned? false (Because the return statement's this age <= 100 expression evaluates to false.) Plug in any number for age and you'll see that the shortened function does indeed work properly. In other words, the shortened isAdolescent method does indeed return true whenever age is less than or equal to 100.

Are you bothered by the lack of parentheses around the `return` statement's returned expression? With statements that use a condition (`if` statement, `while` statement, etc.), the condition must be surrounded by parentheses. With the `return` statement's returned expression, the parentheses are optional. You'll see it both ways in industry—sometimes parentheses are included and sometimes they're omitted.

Here's how the `isAdolescent` method could be used in a calling module:

```
Mouse pinky = new Mouse();
. . .
if (pinky.isAdolescent() == false)
{
  System.out.println("The mouse's growth is no longer" +
    " being simulated - too old.");
}
```

Do you know how the above `if` statement can be shortened? Here's a functionally equivalent `if` statement with an improved condition:

```
if (!pinky.isAdolescent())
{
  System.out.println("The mouse's growth is no longer" +
    " being simulated - too old.");
}
```

The goal is to print the warning message if `pinky` is old (not an adolescent). If `isAdolescent` returns `false` (indicating an old Pinky), then the `if` statement's condition is `true` (`!false` evaluates to `true`) and the program prints the warning message. On the other hand, if `isAdolescent` returns `true` (indicating a young Pinky), then the `if` statement's condition is `false` (`!true` evaluates to `false`) and the program skips the warning message.

Although the shortened-version `if` statement might be harder to understand initially, experienced programmers would prefer it. Following that lead, we encourage you to use `!` rather than `== false` for similar situations.

6.13 Problem Solving with Simulation (Optional)

In our previous mouse examples, to keep the focus on OOP concepts rather than mouse growth details, we used a simplistic growth formula. In this section we show you how to simulate growth in a way that is much closer to the kind of growth that occurs in the real world. Then we show you a simple trick that can be applied to many simulation problems to greatly improve the program's speed and accuracy.

Previously, we modeled growth by assuming that added weight is proportional to weight, like this:

$$addedWeight = fractionGrowthRate \times weight$$

where

$$fractionGrowthRate = .01 \times percentGrowthRate$$

This kind of growth makes weight increase exponentially and continue to curve upward in time, as indicated by Figure 6.16. This is a good approximation for a young plant or animal, where most of the ingested food energy goes into new growth.

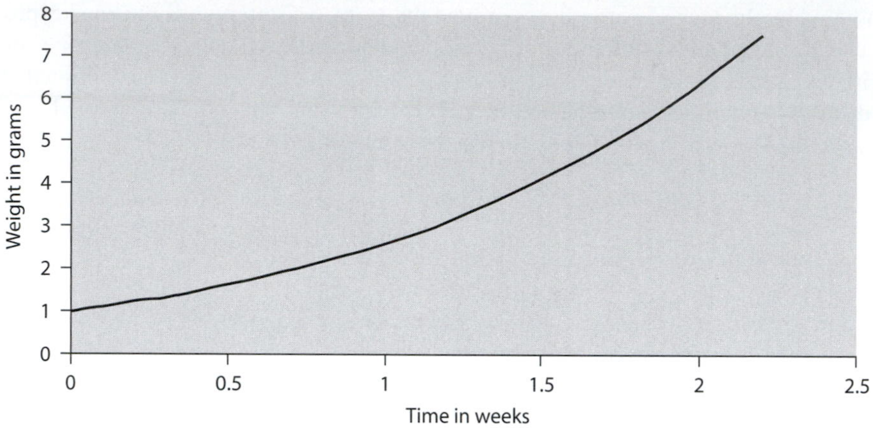

Figure 6.16 Exponential growth

Maturation

But there's a problem with the exponential growth model. Nothing keeps growing forever! After a while, old tissue starts to die, and some of the ingested nutrients must be used to replace the old tissue instead of just adding to it. This slows the growth. As a larger fraction of ingested nutrients go into replacement, the growth curve straightens out, begins to bend the other way, and approaches a maximum. The easiest way to modify the basic exponential growth formula to make it describe maturation is to multiply by another factor to obtain what's called the *logistic equation:*

$$\mathit{addedWeight} = \mathit{fractionGrowthRate} \times \mathit{weight} \times \left(1.0 - \frac{\mathit{weight}}{\mathit{maxWeight}}\right)$$

A quick inspection of this improved growth formula shows that as `weight` approaches `maxWeight`, the quantity in parentheses on the right approaches zero, and therefore the added weight on the left approaches zero. At that point, there's no more growth. This provides a reasonable description of an organism reaching maturity.

Computer simulations rely on approximate mathematical models, like the model provided by the above logistic equation. Such simulation models are sometimes good, sometimes not so good, and it's difficult to know how good they are without comparing them to actual live data. But for the current weight gain problem, we have the luxury of being able to compare the simulation model with an exact mathematical model. Here is a closed form exact mathematical solution that determines the weight of any given time.

$$\mathit{weight} = \frac{1.0}{\frac{1.0}{\mathit{maxWeight}} + e^{-(\mathit{fractionGrowthRate} \times \mathit{time} + g_0)}}$$

This formula contains a growth constant, g_0, which is:

$$g_0 = \log_e\left(\frac{\mathit{minWeight}}{1.0 - \frac{\mathit{minWeight}}{\mathit{maxWeight}}}\right)$$

You can find g_0 by plugging *minWeight* and *maxWeight* values into the second formula. Then find *weight* by plugging g_0 into the first formula.

Simulation

If you can describe it, you can simulate it.

Usually an exact solution is not available, and the only way to solve a problem is with a simulation. But for this weight gain problem, we have both. Let's look at a program that

```
/*********************************************************************
* Growth.java
* Dean & Dean
*
* This provides different ways to calculate growth.
*********************************************************************/

public class Growth
{
  private double startSize;               // initial size
  private double endSize;                 // maximum size
  private double fractionGrowthRate;      // per unit time

  //******************************************************************

  public void initialize(double start, double end, double factor)
  {
    this.startSize = start;
    this.endSize = end;
    this.fractionGrowthRate = factor;
  } // end initialize

  //******************************************************************

  public double getSize(double time)
  {
    double g0 = Math.log(startSize / (1.0 - startSize / endSize));

    return 1.0 / (1.0 / endSize +
      Math.exp(-(fractionGrowthRate * time + g0)));
  } // end getSize

  //******************************************************************

  public double getSizeIncrement(double size, double timeStep)
  {
    return fractionGrowthRate *
      size * (1.0 - size / endSize) * timeStep;
  } // end getSizeIncrement
} // end class Growth
```

Figure 6.17 `Growth` class that implements different ways to evaluate growth

displays time, the exact solution, and the simulated solution together. See the program's `Growth` class in Figure 6.17.

The `Growth` class has three instance variables, `startSize`, `endSize`, and `fractionGrowthRate`, and three methods. The `initialize` method initializes the three instance variables. The `getSize` method uses the closed form mathematical solution formula provided earlier. It returns the size (e.g., current mouse weight) at the given time. Notice that this method's name starts with "get," so it looks like the name of an accessor method, and it returns a `double` value just like our previous `getWeight` method does. But this class does not have any instance variable called "size." So here's an example of a method that is not really an accessor like the accessors described in Section 6.12, even though its name makes it look like an accessor. The point is: any method can return a value, not just an accessor method, and any method can have any name that seems appropriate—`getSize` is simply the most appropriate name we could think of for this method that computes and returns a size.

The `getSizeIncrement` method implements one simulation step. It returns the change in size between the current time and the next time. Notice that the `getSize` and `getSizeIncrement` methods do different things. The first one gives the answer directly. The second one gives an incremental value which must be added to a previous answer to get the next answer.

If you are writing your own class and you want to model the growth of one of your class's entities, you could copy and paste the `Growth` class's variables and methods into your class. Alternatively, you could delegate the work to a `Growth` class object just like you delegate work to `Scanner` class objects. To do this, use `new` to instantiate a `Growth` object, initialize it with the growth-related data in your object, and then ask the `Growth` object to solve the growth problem for you by calling its `getSize` or `getSizeIncrement` method. In your program, you could use code like that in the `main` method of the `GrowthDriver` class in Figure 6.18.

This driver class may seem imposing, but it's not difficult. We start by declaring and initializing local variables, and this includes instantiating and initializing a `Growth` object. Then we ask the user to provide a time increment and the total number of time increments. Finally, we use a `for` loop to print time, the exact solution, and the simulated solution for each time step. If you run the program composed of the code in Figures 6.17 and 6.18 you'll get this result:

<u>Sample session:</u>

```
Enter time increment: 1
Enter total time units to simulate: 15
          exact  simulated
time      size     size
 0.0       1.0      1.0
 1.0       2.6      2.0
 2.0       6.4      3.9
 3.0      13.6      7.3
 4.0      23.3     13.3
 5.0      31.7     22.2
 6.0      36.5     32.1
 7.0      38.6     38.4
 8.0      39.5     39.9
 9.0      39.8     40.0
10.0      39.9     40.0
```

```
11.0    40.0    40.0
12.0    40.0    40.0
13.0    40.0    40.0
14.0    40.0    40.0
15.0    40.0    40.0
```

```
/*******************************************************************
* GrowthDriver.java
* Dean & Dean
*
* This compares exact and simulated solutions for growth.
*******************************************************************/

import java.util.Scanner;

public class GrowthDriver
{
  public static void main(String[] args)
  {
    Scanner stdIn = new Scanner(System.in);
    double timeStep;
    double timeMax;
    Growth entity = new Growth();
    double startSize = 1.0;            // weight in grams
    double endSize = 40.0;             // weight in grams
    double fractionGrowthRate = 1.0;   // per unit time
    double size = startSize;

    entity.initialize(startSize, endSize, fractionGrowthRate);
    System.out.print("Enter time increment: ");
    timeStep = stdIn.nextDouble();
    System.out.print("Enter total time units to simulate: ");
    timeMax = stdIn.nextDouble();
    System.out.println("       exact  simulated");
    System.out.println("time    size    size");

    for (double time=0.0; time<=timeMax; time+=timeStep)
    {
      System.out.printf("%4.1f%8.1f%8.1f\n",
        time, entity.getSize(time), size);
      size += entity.getSizeIncrement(size, timeStep);
    } // end for
  } // end main
} // end class GrowthDriver
```

Instantiate Growth object.

Initialize Growth object.

Figure 6.18 GrowthDriver class that demonstrates the Growth class in Figure 6.17

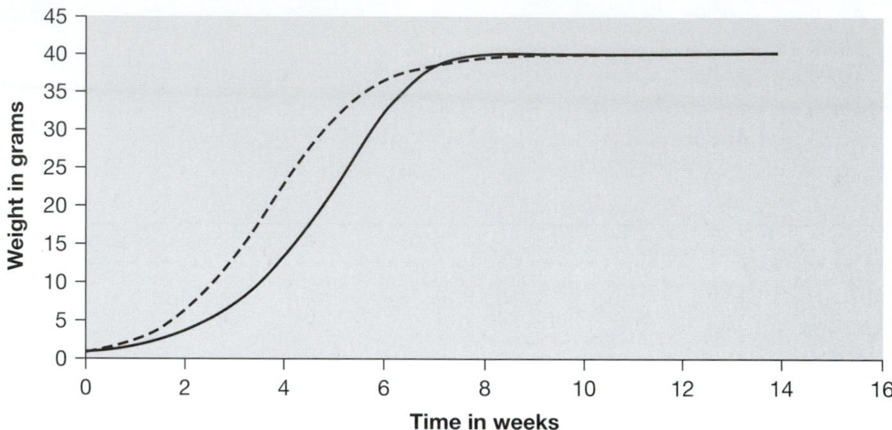

Figure 6.19 Simulated solution with time increment = 1 (solid) compared to exact solution (dashed)

Figure 6.19 shows what this data looks like in a two-dimensional plot. Alas, the simulated solution doesn't agree very well with the exact solution. It doesn't rise quickly enough, and then it overshoots. The reason for this error is actually quite simple. Each size increment is based on the size at the beginning of the increment. But as time passes, the actual size changes, so for all but the first instant in the increment the calculation is using old data.

The most straightforward way to fix this accuracy problem is to use a smaller time step. With this simulation algorithm, the error is proportional to the size of the time step. If you cut the time step in half, this cuts the error in half, if you divide the time step by 10, this divides the error by 10, and so on. In the above output, at four weeks the exact solution says the size is 23.3 grams, but the simulation says it's only 13.3 grams. That's an error of $23.3 - 13.3 = 10$ grams. If we want to reduce this error to less than 1 gram, we need to reduce the time step by a factor of about 10.

If you don't know the exact solution, how do you know your error? Here's a rule of thumb: If you want less than 1% error, make sure the size increment in each time step is always less than about 1% of the average size in that time interval.

This simple algorithm works fine for simple problems. But if you have a tough problem, some things may be sensitive to very small errors, and you may have to take a very large number of very small steps. This might take more time than you can stand. There's also a more insidious problem. Even a double number has limited precision, and when you process many numbers, round-off errors can accumulate. In other words, as you make step sizes smaller, errors initially decrease, but eventually they begin to increase again.

Improved Accuracy and Efficiency Using a Step-with-Midpoint Algorithm[3]

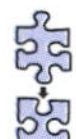

Remove bias.

There's a better way to improve accuracy. It's based on a simple principle: Instead of using the condition(s) (e.g., weight) at the beginning of the interval to estimate the change(s) during the interval, use the condition(s) in the middle of the interval to estimate the change(s) during the interval. But how can you know the conditions in the middle of the interval until you get there? Send out a "scouting party"! In other words, make a tentative half-step forward, and evaluate the

[3] The formal name for this algorithm is: "Second-order Runge-Kutta."

conditions there. Then go back to the beginning and use the condition(s) at the midpoint to determine what the change(s) will be in a full step forward.

At first, this might sound like a hard way to do an easy thing. Why not just cut the step size in half and take two small steps forward? The qualitative answer is: That still leaves a regular bias toward old data. The quantitative answer is: If you use a step-with-midpoint algorithm for your simulation, the size of the error is proportional to the square of the size of the time step. That means that if you reduce the full-step size by a factor of 100, the error goes down by a factor of 10,000. In other words, you can get an extra factor-of-100 accuracy by increasing the computer's work by only a factor of 2.

But what about the work you do? How much harder is it to implement a step-with-midpoint algorithm? Not much. All you have to do is add one simple method. Specifically, to the `Growth` class in Figure 6.17, just add the `getSizeIncrement2` method shown in Figure 6.20.

```
public double getSizeIncrement2(double sizeCopy, double timeStep)
{
  sizeCopy += getSizeIncrement(sizeCopy, 0.5 * timeStep);
  return getSizeIncrement(sizeCopy, timeStep);
} // end getSizeIncrement2
```

No prefix necessary since `getSizeIncrement` and `getSizeIncrement2` are in the same class.

Figure 6.20 Method that implements step-with-midpoint algorithm
Add this method to the code in Figure 6.17 to improve simulation accuracy and efficiency.

How does this little method work? It simply calls the original `getSizeIncrement` method two times. Notice that the `sizeCopy` parameter in Figure 6.20 is just a copy of the `size` variable in the driver class. The first call to `getSizeIncrement` uses the size at the beginning of the time increment, and it goes only half a time step forward. Then, it uses the returned value to increment `sizeCopy` to the size at the midpoint. The second call to `getSizeIncrement` uses this computed midpoint size and a full time step to determine the change from the beginning to the end of the full time interval.

Within the `getSizeIncrement2` method definition, note the calls to `getSizeIncrement`. There's no reference variable dot prefix at the left of `getSizeIncrement`. Here's why: If you call a method that's in the same class as the current class, then you can call the method directly, with no reference variable dot prefix.

The work required to modify the driver is negligible. All you have to do is change the name of the method called to the name of the new method. In our case, all you have to do is change the last statement in the driver in Figure 6.18 to this:

```
size += entity.getSizeIncrement2(size, timeStep);
```

This appended '2' is the only difference!

Figure 6.21 shows what the improved algorithm produces with a full step size equal to the step size used for Figure 6.19. This takes twice as much computer time as what's in Figure 6.19, but it's clearly much

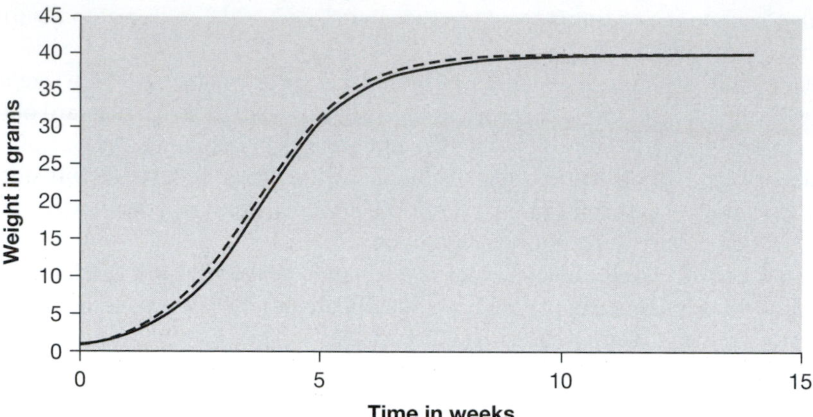

Figure 6.21 Step-with-midpoint simulated solution with time increment = 1 (solid) compared to exact solution (dashed)

more than twice as good. For example, at 4 weeks the error is now only 1.5 grams, instead of the previous 10 grams.

Summary

- An object is a group of related data which identifies the current condition or *state* of the object plus the methods that describe the *behavior* of that object.
- Objects are *instances* of the classes which define them. A class definition specifies the instance variables an object of that class contains, and it defines the methods an object of that class may call. Each object contains its own copy of the instance variables its class defines, and a given instance variable generally has different values in different objects.
- Use the `private` access modifier to specify that a particular variable is encapsulated or hidden. Use the `public` access modifier to make methods accessible to the outside world.
- To make a class as general as possible, drive it from a `main` method in a separate "driver" class. In the driver's `main` method, declare a reference variable of the driven class's type. Then, use Java's keyword `new` to instantiate an object of the driven class, and initialize the reference variable with the object reference returned by `new`.
- Use Java's keyword `this` to refer to the calling object from within one of that object's methods. Use `this` to distinguish an instance variable from a same-named parameter or local variable.
- When you trace an object-oriented program, you need to keep track of which class you're in, which method you're in, which object called that method, parameter and local variable names, and the names of all instance variables in each object.
- A UML class diagram has separate boxes for the class name, a description of the class's variables, and headings for the class's methods. Use a "+" prefix for `public` and a "-" prefix for `private`. Specify variable and method return types and non-default initial values.
- Instance variable default values are zero for numbers, `false` for `boolean` values, and `null` for references. Instance variable values persist for the life of their object. Local variable default values are undefined garbage. Local variables and parameters persist for as long as their method is being executed, and after that, their values are undefined.

- Unless a method's return type is `void`, every path through the method must end with a statement that returns a value of the method's type.
- A method's parameter must have the same type as the method call's argument. What the method gets is a copy of what is in the calling program, so changing a parameter in a method does not change the calling program's value.
- Use `setX` and `getX` methods to modify and retrieve `private` instance variable values. Include filtering in `setX` methods to protect your program from bad input. Use `boolean isX` methods to return `true` or `false` depending on the value of some condition.
- Optionally improve simulation speed and accuracy by computing the next increment with values determined half way between that increment's starting and ending points.

Review Questions

§6.2 Object-Oriented Programming Overview

1. A class is an instance of an object. (T / F)
2. How many objects may there be within a single class?

§6.3 First OOP Class

3. A class's instance variables must be declared outside of all ____, and all instance variable declarations should be located at the ______________________.
4. Methods accessible from outside a class are `public`, but instance variables (even those that an outsider may need to change or read) are usually `private`. Why?

§6.4 Driver Class

5. Where does `main` go—in the driver class or in one of the driven classes?
6. When a program has both driver and driven classes, where should most of the program code reside?
7. How do you retrieve a `private` instance variable's value from within a `main` method?
8. A reference variable holds the __________ of an object.

§6.5 Calling Object, this Reference

9. An instance method might contain a statement like `this.weight = 1.0;` but if that method's class currently has five instantiated objects, there are five different variables called `weight`. How can we determine which one is getting the new value?

§6.6 Instance Variables

10. What are the default values for `int`, `double`, and `boolean` for an object's instance variables?
11. In the Mouse program of Figures 6.4 and 6.5, what is the persistence of `gus`'s `age` variable?

§6.8 UML Class Diagrams

12. After a program is written, a UML class diagram provides a brief outline of each class in the program. It helps other people see what methods are available and what arguments they need. Give some reasons why it might be helpful to have an already created class diagram in front of you while you are implementing the class and writing its methods.

§6.9 Local Variables

13. Assume the `main` method in `Mouse2Driver` had started more simply with only `Mouse mickey;` What would be the value of `mickey` immediately after this statement?

§6.10 The `return` Statement

14. Usually, the use of multiple `return` statements leads to code that is more understandable. (T / F)

§6.11 Argument Passing

15. How is a method parameter like a local variable, and how do they differ?
16. What is the relationship and difference between a method argument and a method parameter?

§6.12 Specialized Methods—Accessors, Mutators, Boolean Methods

17. What is the standard prefix for an accessor method?
18. What is the standard prefix for a mutator method?
19. What is the standard prefix for a Boolean method?

§6.13 Problem Solving with Simulation (Optional)

20. Identify two general ways to reduce the size of the error in a simulation. For a given accuracy, which way is more efficient?

Exercises

1. [after §6.2] Suppose you are asked to model plants using an OOP program. For each of the following plant-related entities, specify the most appropriate item to use for its implementation. For each entity, select one of the following: instance variable, object, method, or class.
   - **a)** plant height
   - **b)** sequence of activities that occur when a seed germinates
   - **c)** an indication of whether the plant contains a vascular system
   - **d)** an individual plant
2. [after §6.3] In Java, how do you encapsulate an instance variable?
3. [after §6.4] Describe the relationship between the `main` method and driver and driven classes. Give an example of a class that runs by itself and does not need a separate driver.
4. [after §6.4] Wrapper objects: The wrapper classes discussed in Chapter 5 also provide you with the ability to instantiate objects that are wrapped versions of primitive variables. For example, to create a wrapped version of the `double` number x, you can do this:

```
double x = 55.0;
Double xWrapped = new Double(x)
```

This instantiates an object of type `Double`, which is a wrapped version of the primitive variable, `x`. Then it assigns a reference to that object to the reference variable, `xWrapped`. The `Double` class has a number of pre-built methods that work with `Double` objects. You can read about these methods in Sun's documentation on the `Double` class. The following program illustrates some of these methods.

```
/****************************************************************
* Wrapper.java
* Dean & Dean
*
* This program exercises some wrapped primitive numbers.
****************************************************************/

public class Wrapper
{
  public static void main(String[] args)
  {
    double x = 44.5;
    double y = 44.5;
```

```
    Double xW = new Double(x);          // the object: wrapped x
    Double yW = new Double(y);          // the object: wrapped y

    System.out.println("object == object? " + (xW == yW));
    System.out.println("value  == value? " +
      (xW.doubleValue() == yW.doubleValue()));
    System.out.println(
      "object.equals(object)? " + xW.equals(yW));
    System.out.println("object.compareTo(object)? " +
      xW.compareTo(yW));

    yW = new Double(y + 3.0);
    System.out.println("object.compareTo(largerObject)? " +
      xW.compareTo(yW));

    yW = new Double(Double.NEGATIVE_INFINITY);
    System.out.println("-infinity isInfinite()? " +
      yW.isInfinite());
  } // end main
} // end Wrapper class
```

Compile and run this program, and display the output. Read about the `Double` class in Sun's documentation, and explain why each of the outputs comes out the way it does.

5. [after §6.4] Suppose you have a `Town` class that describes the demographics of small towns. The vital statistics described by this class are `numberOfAdults` and `numberOfChildren`. These vital statistics are encapsulated and not directly accessible from outside the class.

a) Write the following methods for `class Town`:

i. An `initialize` method that establishes initial values of instance variables. Assume that `initialize` gathers all the data it needs by prompting for and inputting values from a user.

ii. A `simulateBirth` method that simulates the birth of one child.

iii. A `printStatistics` method that prints out the current vital statistics.

b) Write a `main` method for a separate driver class that does the following:

i. Creates a town named `newHome`

ii. Calls `initialize` to establish initial values of instance variables for `newHome`.

iii. Simulates the birth of a pair of twins.

iv. Prints out `newHome`'s vital statistics.

6. [after §6.7] Given this PcDesign program:

```
/*********************************************************
* PcDesignDriver.java
* Dean & Dean
*
* This exercises the PcDesign class.
*********************************************************/

public class PcDesignDriver
{
  public static void main(String[] args)
  {
    PcDesign myPc = new PcDesign();
```

```
    myPc.assignRamSize();
    myPc.assignDiskSize();
    myPc.assignProcessor();
    myPc.calculateCost();
    myPc.printSpecification();
  } // end main
} // end class PcDesignDriver
```

```
/*************************************************************
* PcDesign.java
* Dean & Dean
*
* This class collects specifications for a PC.
*************************************************************/

import java.util.Scanner;

public class PcDesign
{
  private long ramSize = (long) 1000000000.0;
  private long diskSize;
  private String processor;
  private double cost;

  //**********************************************************

  void assignRamSize()
  {
    this.ramSize = (long) 2000000000.0;
  } // end assignRamSize

  //**********************************************************

  void assignDiskSize()
  {
    Scanner stdIn = new Scanner(System.in);
    long diskSize;
    diskSize = stdIn.nextLong();
  } // end assignDiskSize

  //**********************************************************

  void assignProcessor()
  {
    Scanner stdIn = new Scanner(System.in);
    this.processor = stdIn.nextLine();
  } // end assignProcessor

  //**********************************************************

```

```java
  void calculateCost()
  {
    this.cost = this.ramSize / 10000000.0 +
      this.diskSize / 100000000.0;
    if (this.processor.equals("Intel"))
    {
      this.cost += 400;
    }
    else
    {
      this.cost += 300;
    }
  } // end calculateCost

  //*******************************************************

  public void printSpecification()
  {
    System.out.println("RAM = " + this.ramSize);
    System.out.println("Hard disk size = " + this.diskSize);
    System.out.println("Processor = " + this.processor);
    System.out.println("Cost = $" + this.cost);
  } // end printSpecification
} // end class PcDesign
```

Use the following trace setup to trace the PC-design program. Note that we have used abbreviations to keep the trace setup's width as small as possible. Don't forget to specify default and initial values even if they don't impact the final result.

<u>input</u>

```
60000000000
Intel
```

Driver		PcDesign											
	main		aRSize	assignDiskSize		aProc	cCost	printS	obj1				
line#	myPc	*line#*	this	this	diskSize	this	this	this	ramSize	dSize	proc	cost	output

7. [after §6.8]The answer to this exercise is not in the book—you'll need to look elsewhere. Who are UML's "Three Amigos"?

8. [after §6.8] Construct a UML class diagram for files in a computer directory. The class name should be `File`. Include the following methods: `public String getName()`, `public long length()`, and `public boolean isHidden()`. Also include the instance variable associated with the first of these methods. Include indication of whether the member is `public` or `private` and the type of the return value or variable. A `File` class already exists as part of the Java language, and this class also has many other methods, but the API library documentation for this class does not show any instance variables. Does that mean this class has no instance variables?

9. [after §6.9] If an object calls the same method two separate times, in the second execution, the method's local variables begin with the values they had at the end of the previous execution of that method. (T / F)

10. [after §6.9] Trace the Mouse2 program shown in Figures 6.13 and 6.14. Use the following trace setup. Note that we have used abbreviations to keep the trace setup's width as small as possible.

input

2

Mouse2Driver			Mouse												
	main			setPGR		getAge	getWt	grow			obj1				
line#	**mickey**	**days**	*line#*	**this**	**rate**	**this**	**this**	**this**	**days**	**i**	**age**	**wt**	**rate**	**output**

11. [after §6.11] The diagram below shows Mouse2 program methods, with their parameters and local variables indented, and the one instantiated object, with its instance variables indented. Your task is to construct a time line for each method, local variable or parameter, object, and instance variable. Each time line should show that item's persistence (when it starts and ends) relative to the other items. To help you get started we have provided the time lines for the `main` method and one of its local variables. Provide all the other time lines, and show how they align with each other and those already provided. (Assume that the object and its instance variables come into existence simultaneously.)

```
                                 time →
methods:
  main                  |-------------------------|
    mickey               |------------------------|
    days
  setPercentGrowthRate
  getAge
  getWeight
  grow
    days
    i
object:
  mickey
    age
    weight
    percentGrowthRate
```

12. [after §6.12] Complete the following `StudentIdDriver` class skeleton by replacing all six occurrences of *<insert-code-here>* with your own code such that the program operates properly. For details, read the comments above or next to the *<insert-code-here>* insertions. Note the `StudentId` class, which is below the `StudentIdDriver` class. The two classes are in separate files.

```
import java.util.Scanner;

public class StudentIdDriver
{
  public static void main(String[] args)
  {
    Scanner stdIn = new Scanner(System.in);
    StudentId student;
```

```
    String name;
    // Instantiate StudentId object and assign it to student.
    <insert-code-here>

    System.out.print("Enter student name: ");
    name = stdIn.nextLine();

    // Assign name to the student object.
    <insert-code-here>

    System.out.print("Enter student id: ");
    // In a single line, read an int for the id value,
    // and assign it to the student object.
    <insert-code-here>

    // If invalid id, execute the loop.
    // (Use the isValid method in the while loop condition.)
    while (<insert-code-here>)
    {
      System.out.print("Invalid student id - reenter: ");
      // In a single line, read an int for the id value
      // and assign it to the student object.
    <insert-code-here>
    }

    System.out.println("\n" + name +
      ", your new e-mail account is: \n" +
      <insert-code-here>                    // Get email account.
  } // end main
} // end class StudentIdDriver

public class StudentId
{
  private String name;
  private int id;

  //*********************************************************

  public void setName(String n)
  {
    this.name = n;
  }

  public String getName()
  {
    return this.name;
  }
```

```
  public void setId(int id)
  {
    this.id = id;
  }

  public int getId()
  {
    return this.id;
  }

  //*****************************************************

  public String getEmailAccount()
  {
    // Include "" in concatenation to convert to strings.
    return "" + this.name.charAt(0) + this.id +
      "@pirate.park.edu";
  }

  //*****************************************************

  public boolean isValid()
  {
    return this.id >= 100000 && this.id <= 999999;
  }
} // end class StudentId
```

13. [after §6.13] Construct a UML class diagram for the `Growth` class in Figure 6.17, with the `getSizeIncrement2` method of Figure 6.20 included.

Review Question Solutions

1. False. An object is an instance of a class.
2. Any number, including zero.
3. A class's instance variables must be declared outside of all methods, and all instance variable declarations should be located at the top of the class definition.
4. Instance variables are usually `private` to further the goal of encapsulation. That means an object's data is harder to access, and, consequently, harder to mess up. The only way for the data to be accessed from outside of the class is if the data's associated `public` methods are called.
5. The `main` method goes in the driver class.
6. Most of a program's code should be in driven classes.
7. To access a `private` instance variable from within a `main` method, you have to use an instantiated object's reference variable and then call an accessor method. In other words, use this syntax:
   ‹reference-variable›.‹accessor-method-call›
8. A reference variable holds the <u>memory location</u> of an object.
9. Go back to where the method was called, and look at the reference variable which precedes the method name at that point. That reference variable is the one that the method uses whenever `this` is used.

10. For an object's instance variables, the default values are: `int = 0, double = 0.0, boolean = false`.
11. `gus`'s `age` is an instance variable. Instance variables persist for the duration of a particular object. Since the `gus` object is declared in `main`, `gus` and its instance variables (including `age`) persist for the duration of the `main` method.
12. Some reasons to construct a UML class diagram before writing code:
    a) It provides a complete "to do" list. When you are into the details of writing one method, and wondering whether that method should perform a particular function, the diagram reminds you of what other methods might be able to perform that function.
    b) It provides a complete "parts list," like the parts list of a typical user-assembled "kit." This pre-defined list helps you avoid accidentally generating different and conflicting names for variables and parameters as you write your code.
    c) It's a working document that can change as work progresses. Changing the UML class diagram helps identify needed alterations to previous work.
13. Immediately after the statement `Mouse mickey;` the value of `mickey` would be garbage.
14. False. Normally, for a method that returns a value, you should have a single return statement at the end of the method. However, it's also legal to have return statements in the middle of a method. That might be appropriate in a very short method, where an internal `return` is immediately obvious. If the method is relatively long, however, a reader might not notice an internal `return`. With a large method, it's better practice to arrange things so that there is only one `return`, located at the end of the method.
15. Parameters and local variables both have method scope and persistence. The code inside the method treats parameters just like it treats local variables. The method initializes the local variables, while the method call initializes the parameters.
16. Arguments and parameters are two different words describing data that passes into a called method. An arguments is the method call's name for the data, and a parameter is the method's name for the same data. A parameter is just a copy of the method call's argument, however, so if the called method changes the value of one if its parameters, this does not alter the value of the method call's argument.
17. The standard prefix for an accessor method is `get`.
18. The standard prefix for a mutator method is `set`.
19. The standard prefix for a Boolean method is `is`.
20. To reduce the error in a simulation, you can reduce step size or switch to a step-with-midpoint algorithm. For a given accuracy, the step-with-midpoint algorithm is more efficient.

CHAPTER 7

Object-Oriented Programming—Additional Details

Objectives

- Improve your understanding of the relationship between a reference variable and an object.
- Learn what happens when you assign a reference.
- Learn how Java recycles memory space.
- Learn how to compare the equality of two different objects.
- Be able to swap the data in two different objects.
- See how a reference parameter can enhance data transfer to and from a called method.
- Learn how to execute a sequence of several method calls in the same statement.
- Learn how to create alternative variations for a method.
- Learn how to combine object creation and initialization in a constructor.
- Learn how to avoid code redundancy by nesting method and constructor calls.
- Learn how to partition a large problem into several smaller problems with multiple driven classes.

Outline

7.1 Introduction

In Chapter 6, you learned to write simple object-oriented programming (OOP) programs using simple OOP building blocks. In this chapter, you learn to write more advanced OOP programs using more advanced OOP concepts. In particular, you learn the details of what happens behind the scenes when a program instantiates an object and stores its address in a reference variable. That will help you to appreciate and understand what happens when a program assigns one reference variable to another.

One of the OOP concepts you learn about in this chapter is testing objects for equality. It's common to compare primitives for equality (for example, `if (team1Score == team2Score)`), and likewise, it's common to compare references for equality. Comparing references for equality requires a bit more effort, and in this chapter, you learn what that effort entails. Another concept you learn about is what happens behind the scenes when a program passes a reference as an argument. That's important to know because you'll often need to pass references as arguments.

In addition to presenting more advanced OOP concepts, this chapter also presents more advanced applications of what you already know in regard to OOP. For example, you learn to call several methods in succession, all within one statement. That's called *method-call chaining,* and it can lead to more compact and more elegant code. You also learn about *method overloading.* That's when you have different versions of a method and each version operates on different kinds of data. That should sound familiar because you saw it with the `Math` class. Remember the two versions of the `Math.abs` method? One version returns the absolute value of a `double`, and one version returns the absolute value of an `int`.

In the previous chapter, you learned how to instantiate an object in one statement (for example, `Mouse gus = new Mouse();`) and assign a value to the object in a separate statement (for example, `gus.setPercentGrowthRate(10);`). In this chapter you learn how to combine those two tasks into one statement. To do that, you'll use a special kind of method called a *constructor.* Like methods, constructors can be overloaded by using different types of data for the different constructor versions. But unlike methods, constructors are designed specifically for object creation and initialization.

In a final problem-solving section, you learn how to partition large programming problems into several smaller and simpler problems by using multiple driven classes. As this text progresses, the size and complexity of problems gradually increases, and you'll see more and more examples of programs with multiple driven classes.

7.2 Object Creation—A Detailed Analysis

Let's start the chapter with a behind-the-scenes detailed look at what happens when a program instantiates an object and stores its address in a reference variable. Having a clear understanding will help when it comes time to understand other OOP operations, and it will help with some debugging efforts.

Consider the following code fragment:

```
Car car1;              ← reference variable declaration

car1 = new Car();      ← object instantiation
car1.year = 1998;      ← assign 1998 to car1's year instance variable
```

Let's now examine this code in detail one statement at a time.

Statement 1:

The first statement is a variable declaration for the `car1` reference variable. It allocates space in memory for the `car1` reference variable—just the reference variable itself, not an object. Eventually, the `car1` reference variable will hold the address of an object, but since there's no object created for it yet, it doesn't yet hold a legitimate address. What's the default value for a reference variable? It depends. If the reference variable is defined locally within a method (that is, it's a local variable), then it gets garbage initially. If it's defined at the top of a class, above all the method definitions (that is, it's an instance variable), then it gets initialized to `null`. Since Statement 1 doesn't have an access modifier (`private`), we can assume it's a local variable. So `car1` will contain garbage by default, and that's what this picture indicates:

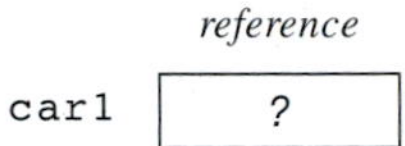

Statement 2:

The second statement's `new` operator allocates space in memory for a new `Car` object. The assignment operator assigns the address (memory location) of the allocated space to the `car1` reference variable. Don't forget this operation. Forgetting to instantiate is a common beginner's error.

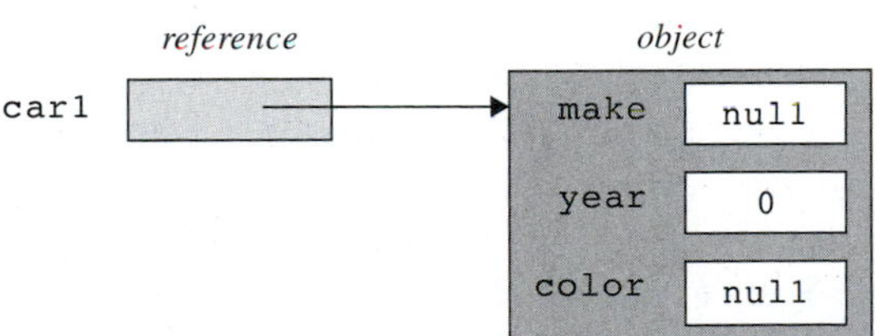

Statement 3:

The third statement uses the `car1` variable's value (the address of a `Car` object) to find a particular `Car` object in memory. Once that `Car` object is found, 1998 is assigned into it. More specifically, 1998 is assigned into the `year` instance variable portion of that `Car` object. Normally, we'd use a method to assign 1998 into `car1`'s `year` instance variable. In the interest of simplification for clarity's sake, we avoided the method call by assuming that `year` is a `public` instance variable.

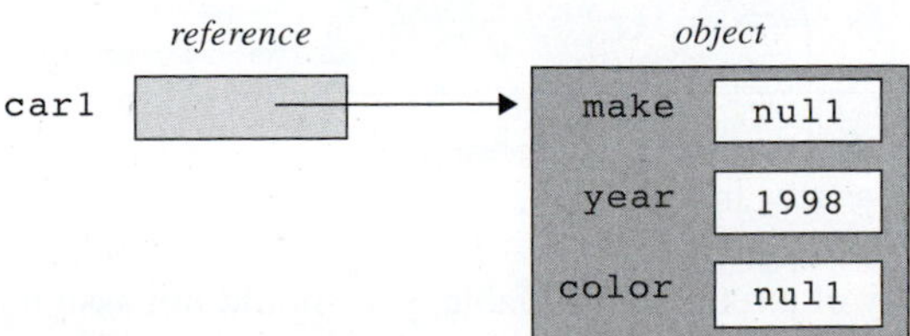

7.3 Assigning a Reference

The result of assigning one reference variable to another is that both reference variables then refer to the same object. Why do they refer to the same object? Since reference variables store addresses, you're actually assigning the right-side reference variable's address into the left-side's reference variable. So after the assignment, the two reference variables hold the same address, and that means they refer to the same object. With both reference variables referring to the same object, if the object is updated using one of the reference variables, then the other reference variable will benefit (or suffer) from that change when it attempts to access the object. Sometimes, that's just what you want, but if it's not, it can be disconcerting.

An Example

Suppose you want to create two `Car` objects that are the same except for their color. Your plan is to instantiate the first car, use it as a template when creating the second car, and then update the second car's `color` instance variable. Will this code accomplish that?

```
Car johnCar = new Car();
Car stacyCar;
johnCar.setMake("Honda");
johnCar.setYear(2003);
johnCar.setColor("silver");
stacyCar = johnCar;
stacyCar.setColor("peach");
```

This makes `stacyCar` refer to the same object as `johnCar`.

The problem with the above code is that the `stacyCar = johnCar;` statement causes the two references to point to the same single `Car` object. Figure 7.1a illustrates what we're talking about.

Later, we'll see that this *aliasing* (using different names for the same object) can be quite useful, but in this case, it's not what we wanted. In the last statement in the code fragment above, when we use the `setColor` method to change Stacy's car to "peach," we're not specifying the color for a new car. What we're doing is repainting the original car. Figure 7.1a depicts the result. Uh oh . . . John may not be pleased to find his car repainted to peach!

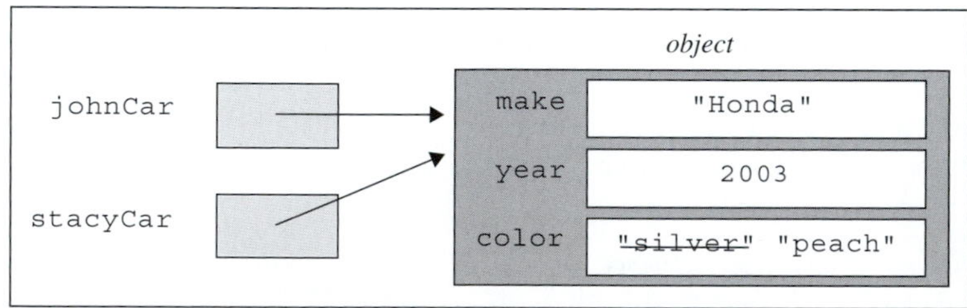

Figure 7.1a Effect of assignment: `stacyCar = johnCar;`
Both reference variables refer to exactly the same object.

If you want to make a copy of a reference variable, you should not assign the reference to another reference. Instead, you should instantiate a new object for the second reference and then assign the two objects' instance variables one at a time. Figure 7.1b shows what we're talking about.

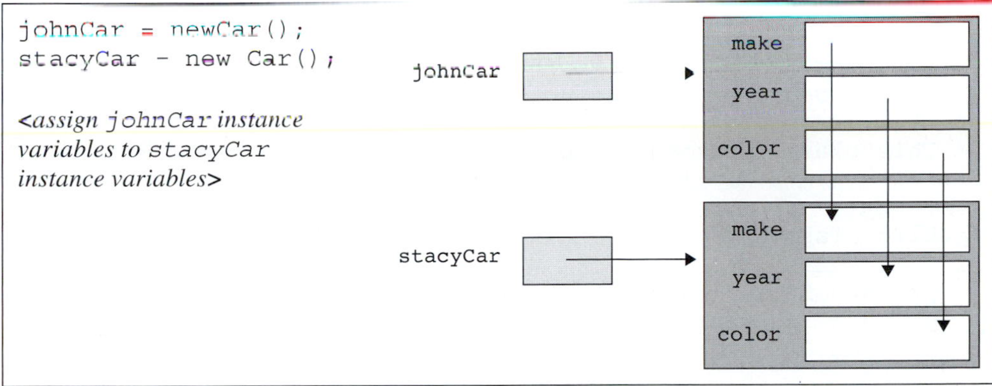

Figure 7.1b Effect of instantiating two separate objects and copying instance variable values from first object into instance variables of second object

To illustrate the strategy outlined in Figure 7.1b, we present the Car program in Figures 7.2 and 7.3. The code includes line numbers to facilitate tracing in an end-of-chapter exercise. Look at the `makeCopy` method in the `Car` class in Figure 7.2. As its name implies, that's the method that's in charge of making a copy of a `Car` object. The `makeCopy` method instantiates a new `Car` object and assigns its reference to a local variable named `car`. Then it copies each of the calling object's instance variable values into `car`'s instance variables. Then it returns `car` to the calling module. By returning `car`, it returns a reference to the newly instantiated `Car` object.

Now look at the driver in Figure 7.3. Note how `main` assigns `makeCopy`'s returned value to `stacyCar`. After `stacyCar` gets the reference to the newly created `Car` object, it calls `setColor` to change the `Car` object's color. Since `stacyCar` and `johnCar` refer to two separate objects, the `stacyCar.setColor("peach")` method call updates only the `stacyCar` object, not the `johnCar` object. Yeah!

Whenever a method finishes, its parameters and locally declared variables are deleted. In our traces, we represent this deletion by drawing a heavy line under all of the terminating method's parameters and local variables. In the `makeCar` method in Figure 7.2, there is one local variable, the reference variable, `car`. When the `makeCar` method finishes, the `car` reference variable is deleted. When a reference variable is deleted, the reference it holds is lost, and if that reference is not saved in a separate variable, the program will have no way of finding the object it referred to. In the `makeCar` method, the `car` reference variable's value does get saved. It gets returned to `main` where it gets assigned to `stacyCar`.

Inaccessible Objects and Garbage Collection

Sometimes, you'll want to instantiate a temporary object inside a method, use it for some purpose in that method, and then abandon that object when the method finishes. At other times you may wish to abandon an object before a method finishes. For example, suppose that in the `main` method in Figure 7.3, after calling `makeCopy` and creating a new `Car` object for `stacyCar`, you want to model John's old car being destroyed in a fire and Stacy volunteering to let him become a co-owner of her new car. You could represent this joint ownership of one car with the statement:

```
johnCar = stacyCar;
```

```
/*****************************************************************
* Car.java
* Dean & Dean
*
* This class implements copy functionality for a car.
*****************************************************************/

public class Car
{
  private String make;     // car's make
  private int year;        // car's manufacturing year
  private String color;    // car's primary color

  //**************************************************************

  public void setMake(String make)
  {
    this.make = make;
  }

  public void setYear(int year)
  {
    this.year = year;
  }

  public void setColor(String color)
  {
    this.color = color;
  }

  //**************************************************************

  public Car makeCopy()
  {
    Car car = new Car();

    car.make = this.make;
    car.year = this.year;
    car.color = this.color;
    return car;
  } // end makeCopy

  //**************************************************************

  public void display()
  {
    System.out.printf("make= %s\nyear= %s\ncolor= %s\n",
    this.make, this.year, this.color);
  } // end display
} // end class Car
```

This instantiates a new object.

This returns a reference to the new object.

Figure 7.2 Car class with `makeCopy` method that returns a reference to copy of calling object

```
/*******************************************************
* CarDriver.java
* Dean & Dean
*
* This class demonstrates copying an object.
*******************************************************/

public class CarDriver
{
  public static void main(String[] args)
  {
    Car johnCar = new Car();
    Car stacyCar;

    johnCar.setMake("Honda");
    johnCar.setYear(2003);
    johnCar.setColor("silver");
    stacyCar = johnCar.makeCopy();
    stacyCar.setColor("peach");
    System.out.println("John's car:");
    johnCar.display();
    System.out.println("Stacy's car:");
    stacyCar.display();
  } // end main
} // end class CarDriver
```

This assigns the returned reference to a reference variable in the calling method.

Output:

```
John's car:
make= Honda
year= 2003
color= silver
Stacy's car:
make= Honda
year= 2003
color= peach
```

Figure 7.3 `CarDriver` class that drives `Car` class in Figure 7.2

Doing this overlays `johnCar`'s previous reference to John's original `Car` object, and that `Car` object becomes inaccessible to the program (abandoned), like `Car` object #1 is in this picture:

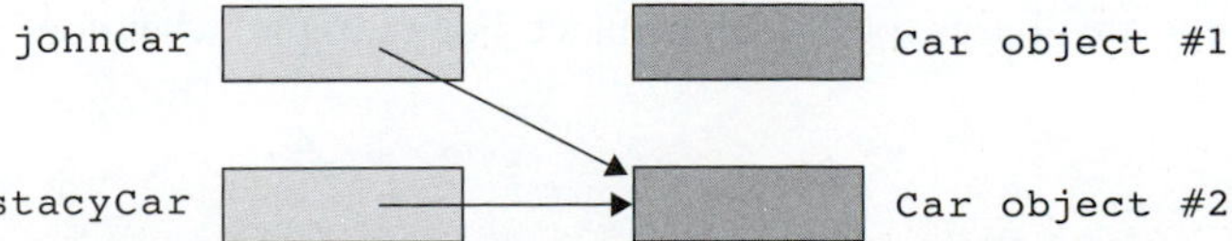

The question is, how does the Java Virtual Machine (JVM) treat abandoned or inaccessible objects? Inaccessible objects can't participate in the program, so there's no need to keep them around. They become "garbage." In fact, it would be bad to keep them around, because they can lead to clogging up the computer's memory. A computer has a finite amount of memory, and each piece of garbage uses up some of that memory. And that means less memory is available for new tasks. If garbage is allowed to accumulate unabated, it would eventually chew up all the *free space* in a computer's memory (free space is the portion of memory that is unused). If there's no free space in memory, there's no space for any new objects, and the computer stops working (until a reboot).

If an inaccessible object is allowed to persist and use up space in a computer's memory, that's called a *memory leak*. Memory leaks can occur in computer programs that allocate memory during execution. When a computer language requires the programmer to do something specific to prevent memory leaks, and the programmer forgets to do that, a nasty bug is born—a bug that is very hard to find. In creating the Java language, James Gosling and the good folks at Sun realized this, and they opted to make the language itself deal with the problem. How? By going into the garbage collection business. Not what Dirk and Lenny do when they pick up the trash at your curb every Tuesday, but Java *garbage collection*! Actually, James Gosling didn't invent garbage collection; it's been around since the dawn of garbage. But Java is the first popular programming language to include it as a standard service.

So what in the heck is garbage collection? It's when a garbage collection program searches for inaccessible objects and recycles the space they occupy by asking the operating system to designate their space in memory as free space. This space might not be used right away, and some computer whiz kid might be able to find some of those old abandoned objects—like wandering through a trash dump, fighting off mean dogs, and looking for furniture—but for practical purposes, you should consider those abandoned objects unrecoverable and gone.

The beauty of Java's automatic garbage collection is that the programmer doesn't have to worry about it—it just happens whenever it's appropriate. And when is it appropriate? Whenever the computer is running low on free space in memory or whenever nothing else is happening, such as when a program is waiting for keyboard input. At that point, the operating system wakes up his buddy the Java garbage collector, and tells him to go earn his keep.

7.4 Testing Objects for Equality

The previous section illustrated returning a reference from a method. This section illustrates passing a reference to a method to allow the method to read the referenced object's data. One of the most common applications of this occurs in testing two objects for equality. Before looking at this application, it's appropriate to look at the simplest way to evaluate equality.

The == Operator

The == operator works the same for primitive variables and for reference variables. It tests if the values stored in these variables are the same. When applied to reference variables, the == operator returns `true` if and only if the two reference variables refer to the same object; that is, the two reference variables contain the same address and thus are aliases for the same object. For example, what does the following code fragment print?

```
Car car1 = new Car();
Car car2 = car1;
```

```
if (car1 == car2)
{
  System.out.println("the same");
}
else
{
  System.out.println("different");
}
```

It prints "the same" because `car1` and `car2` hold the same value—the address of the lone `Car` object. But if you want to see if two different objects have the same instance-variable values, the == operator is not what you want. For example, what does this code print?

```
Car car1 = new Car();
Car car2 = new Car();

car1.setColor("red");
car2.setColor("red");
if (car1 == car2)
{
  System.out.println("the same");
}
else
{
  System.out.println("different");
}
```

The `car1 == car2` expression returns `false`. Why?

This code prints "different" because `car1 == car2` returns `false`. It doesn't matter that `car1` and `car2` contain the same data (red). The == operator doesn't look at the object's data; it just looks at whether the two reference variables point to the same object. In this case, `car1` and `car2` refer to distinct objects, with different storage locations in memory.

The `equals` Method

If you want to see whether two different objects have the same characteristics, you need to compare the contents of two objects rather than just whether two reference variables point to the same object. To do that, you need an `equals` method in the object's class definition that compares the two objects' instance variables. Having such an `equals` method is very common since you often want to test two objects to see whether they have the same characteristics. For Java's API classes, use the classes' built-in `equals` methods. For example, in comparing the contents of two strings, call the `String` class's `equals` method. For classes that you implement yourself, adopt the habit of writing your own `equals` methods.

An `equals` method is a handy utility.

An Example

The following diagram depicts two objects with identical instance variable values. Comparing `nathanCar` to `nickCar` with the == operator generates `false`, because the two reference variables point to different objects. However, comparing `nathanCar` to `nickCar` with a standard `equals` method generates `true`, because a standard `equals` method compares instance variable values, and these two objects have identical instance variable values.

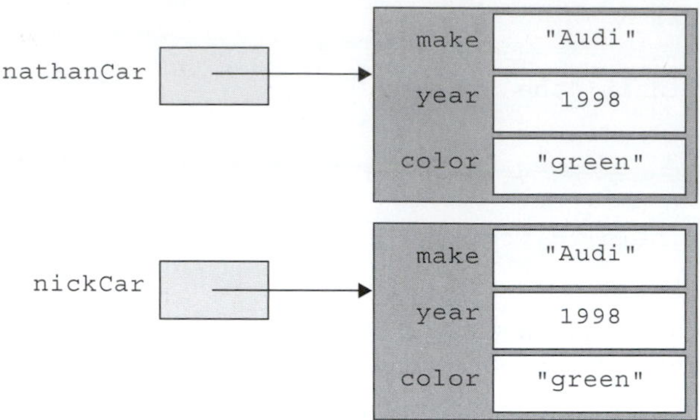

The Car2 program in Figures 7.4 and 7.5 illustrates this example. Figure 7.5's `Car2` class defines an `equals` method, and Figure 7.4's `Car2Driver` class calls the `equals` method while comparing two `Car2` objects. As is common with `equals` method calls, Figure 7.4's `equals` method call is embedded in the condition of an `if` statement. That should make sense when you realize that an `if` statement condition must evaluate to `true` or `false` and an `equals` method does indeed evaluate to `true` or `false`. Typically, an `equals` method evaluates to `true` if the instance variables in two objects contain the same data values, and it evaluates to `false` otherwise. For our Car2 program, the `equals` method evaluates to `true` if `nathanCar` contains the same data (`make`, `year`, and `color`) as `nickCar`. Figure 7.4 shows that `nathanCar` and `nickCar` are assigned the same data. Therefore, the `equals` method returns `true` and the program prints "Cars have identical features."

In the `equals` method call, note how the first `Car2` reference variable, `nathanCar`, appears at the left of the `.equals` and the second `Car2` reference variable, `nickCar`, appears inside the parentheses. Thus, `nathanCar` is the calling object, and `nickCar` is an argument This happens a lot when using two reference variables with a method call—one reference variable will be the calling object and the other one will be the argument.

Let's now examine the `equals` method definition in Figure 7.5. First, note the `equals` method heading. Why is the `return` type `boolean`? Because the `return` type must match the type of the returned value, and `equals` methods always return a Boolean value (either `true` or `false`). Also note that the type of the `otherCar` parameter is `Car2`. That should make sense when you look back at the `equals` method call in Figure 7.4. It shows that the argument being passed into the `equals` method is `nickCar`, and `nickCar` is a `Car2` reference variable.

OK, now it's time to examine the body of the `equals` method. Notice that there is just one statement—the `return` statement. The return value must be a `boolean`, so the expression after the word `return` must evaluate to either `true` or `false`. This expression is an "anding" together of three `boolean` sub-expressions, each of which evaluates to either `true` or `false`. For the overall expression to be `true` all three of the sub-expressions must be `true`.

Each sub-expression checks whether a particular instance variable has the same value in the calling object and the passed-in parameter object. For example, to check whether the `year` instance variable has the same value in the calling object and the passed-in parameter object, we do this:

```
this.year == otherCar.year
```

In this case, we use the == operator to check for equality. That works fine for the `year` instance variable because `year` is an `int`. But the `make` and `color` instance variables are strings, and the == operator is

```
/**********************************************************************
* Car2Driver.java
* Dean & Dean
*
* This class is a demonstration driver for the Car2 class.
**********************************************************************/

public class Car2Driver
{
  public static void main(String[] args)
  {
    Car2 nathanCar = new Car2();
    Car2 nickCar = new Car2();

    nathanCar.setMake("Audi");
    nathanCar.setYear(1998);
    nathanCar.setColor("green");
    nickCar.setMake("Audi");
    nickCar.setYear(1998);
    nickCar.setColor("green");
    if (nathanCar.equals(nickCar))
    {
      System.out.println("Cars have identical features.");
    }
  } // end main
} // end class Car2Driver
```

Note how equals method call is embedded in an if condition.

Figure 7.4 `Car2Driver` class that drives the `Car2` class in Figure 7.5

anathema to strings. We must use the `equals` method for strings! Thus, to check whether the `make` instance variable has the same value in the calling object and the passed-in parameter object, we do this:

```
this.make.equals(otherCar.make)
```

Hmmm . . . . Does it strike you as odd to use the `String` class's `equals` method inside of our `Car2` class's `equals` method? That's perfectly OK—the compiler doesn't care if two methods happen to have the same name as long as they are in different classes. That's part of the beauty of encapsulation!

Can you think of another way to write the body of the `Car2` class's `equals` method? We might have used that `boolean` expression to the right of the `return` keyword as the condition of an `if` statement and then put `return true` in the `if` clause and `return false` in the `else` clause. But that would have been a harder and longer way to do the same thing—and probably more confusing, too, because it would have required more parentheses. Although Figure 7.5's `return` statement might appear at first glance to be a Cerberean rat's nest,[1] most veteran programmers would consider it to be rather elegant.

[1] You probably already know what a "rat's nest" is—a tangled mess. But how about "Cerberean"? In Greek mythology, Cerberus is a vicious three-headed dog creature that guards the entrance to Hades (the world of the dead). We say our `return` statement might appear to be a Cerberean rat's nest because it's complicated and it has three parts. Which would you rather meet in a dark alley—a vicious three-headed dog creature or a complicated `return` statement?

```
/**********************************************************************
* Car2.java
* Dean & Dean
*
* This class implements equals functionality for a car.
*********************************************************************/

public class Car2
{
  private String make;
  private int year;
  private String color;

  //********************************************************************

  public void setMake(String make)
  {
    this.make = make;
  }

  public void setYear(int year)
  {
    this.year = year;
  }

  public void setColor(String color)
  {
    this.color = color;
  }

  //********************************************************************

  // This method tests whether two cars hold the same data.

  public boolean equals(Car2 otherCar)
  {
    return this.make.equals(otherCar.make) &&
           this.year == otherCar.year &&
           this.color.equals(otherCar.color);
  } // end equals
} // end class Car2
```

This compares all instance variables.

Figure 7.5 `Car2` class with `equals` method

Suppose you want uppercase colors to be considered the same as lowercase colors. In other words, you want a silver 2005 Ford to be considered the same as a Silver 2005 Ford. How should you change the code to handle that? Use `equalsIgnoreCase` instead of `equals` when comparing the color strings:

```
this.color.equalsIgnoreCase(otherCar.color)
```

This shows that you can make your `equals` method return `true` when there is only approximate equality, where you define "approximate" however you wish. We'll discuss the `equals` method in more depth in Chapter 13.

7.5 Passing References as Arguments

By now, you should be fairly comfortable with the concept of passing an argument to a method. We've covered all you need to know about passing primitive types as arguments. But you still need to know a bit more about passing references as arguments. In the example in Figure 7.4, we passed the `nickCar` reference as an argument to the `equals` method. The `equals` method assigned the `nickCar` reference to its `otherCar` parameter, and then it used the `otherCar` parameter to read the object's data. In that example, we used a passed-in reference to read an object's data. Now let's use a passed-in reference to update an object's data.

Suppose you pass a reference variable to a method, and inside the method you update the reference variable's instance variables. What happens? Remember that a reference variable holds the address of an object, not the object itself. So in passing a reference variable argument to a method, a copy of the object's address (not a copy of the object itself) is passed to the method and stored in the method's parameter. Since the parameter and the argument hold the same address value, they point to the same object. Thus, if the parameter's instance variables are updated, then the update simultaneously updates the argument's instance variables in the calling module. This is a case where aliasing (using two names for the same thing) is really handy.

Person-Swapping Example

Let's see if you understand all of this reference-passing stuff by putting it in the context of a complete program. See the Person program in Figures 7.6 and 7.7. The Person program swaps names for two `Person` objects. As shown in Figure 7.6's `main` method, the `person1` reference variable starts with the name "Jonathan" and the `person2` reference variable starts with the name "Benji." After the `swapPerson` method call, `person1` has the name "Benji," and `person2` has the name "Jonathan." The `swapPerson` method swaps the names by taking advantage of the phenomenon discussed above—if a reference variable is passed to a method, then the parameter and the argument refer to the same object, and an update to one means an update to the other as well. Bottom line: When you pass a reference to a method, you enable the method to modify the referenced object.

General-Purpose Swapping Algorithm

Before digging deeper into the Person program's code, let's come up with a general-purpose swapping algorithm. Having to swap two values is a very common programming requirement, so you should make sure that you fully understand how to do it.

How do you swap two values?

Suppose you're asked to provide an algorithm that swaps the contents of two variables, x and y. To make the goal more concrete, you are given the following algorithm skeleton. Replace *<Insert swap code here.>* with appropriate pseudocode so that the algorithm prints `x=8, y=3`.

```
x ← 3
y ← 8
<Insert swap code here.>
print "x = " + x + ", y = " + y
```

Note that the algorithm skeleton uses the formal version of pseudocode introduced near the end of Chapter 2. The formal-version pseudocode is more compact and closer to Java than the informal version. For

```
/*************************************************************
* PersonDriver.java
* Dean & Dean
*
* This class is a demonstration driver for the Person class.
*************************************************************/

public class PersonDriver
{
  public static void main(String[] args)
  {
    Person person1 = new Person();
    Person person2 = new Person();

    person1.setName("Jonathan");
    person2.setName("Benji");
    System.out.println(person1.getName() + ", " +
      person2.getName());

    person1.swapPerson(person2);
    System.out.println(person1.getName() + ", " +
      person2.getName());
  } // end main
} // end class PersonDriver
```

This argument allows the called method to modify the referenced object.

Output:

```
Jonathan, Benji
Benji, Jonathan
```

Figure 7.6 Driver for program that implements swapping by passing a reference to a method

example, rather than saying "set x to 3," the formal-version pseudocode uses a backwards arrow and says "x ← 3." We feel that at this point, with several chapters of Java under your belt, the formal-version pseudocode is preferable to the informal version because of its conciseness.

Would the following code work? Would it swap x and y's contents successfully?

```
y ← x
x ← y
```

The first statement puts x's original value into y. The second statement attempts to put y's original value into x. Unfortunately, the second statement doesn't work because y's original value is gone (overwritten by x in the first statement). If you inserted the above code into the above algorithm, the algorithm would print:

```
x = 3, y = 3
```

Swapping requires a temporary variable.

That's not what you want! The trick is to save the value of y before you wipe it out with x's value. How do you save it? Use a temporary variable like this:

```
temp ← y
y ← x
x ← temp
```

```
/*************************************************************
* Person.java
* Dean & Dean
*
* This stores, retrieves, and swaps a person's name.
*************************************************************/

public class Person
{
  private String name;

  //**********************************************************

  public void setName(String name)
  {
    this.name = name;
  }

  public String getName()
  {
    return this.name;
  }

  //**********************************************************

  // This method swaps the names for two Person objects.

  public void swapPerson(Person otherPerson)
  {
    String temp;

    temp = otherPerson.name;
    otherPerson.name = this.name;
    this.name = temp;
  } // end swapPerson
} // end class Person
```


Figure 7.7 `Person` class which implements swapping by passing a reference to a method

Person-Swapping Example—Continued

Now look at the `Person` class in Figure 7.7. In particular, let's examine how the `swapPerson` method implements the swapping algorithm. The swapped items are the passed-in object's name and the calling object's name. The passed-in object is accessed via the `otherPerson` parameter. Note how we access the passed-in object's name with `otherPerson.name`. And note how we access the calling object's name with `this.name`. And finally, note how we use a `temp` local variable as temporary storage for `otherPerson.name`.

7.6 Method-Call Chaining

At this point, you should be fairly comfortable with calling a method. Now it's time to go one step further. In this section, you learn to call several methods in succession, all within one statement. That's called *method-call chaining,* and it can lead to more compact and more elegant code.

If you look back at Figures 7.3 and 7.4, you'll see several instances where we call several methods one after another, and we use a separate statement for each successive method call, like this code fragment from Figure 7.4:

```
nathanCar.setMake("Audi");
nathanCar.setYear(1998);
```

Wouldn't it be nice to be able to chain the method calls together like this?

```
nathanCar.setMake("Audi").setYear(1998);
```

Method-call chaining is an option, not a requirement. So why use it? Because it can often lead to more elegant code—more compact and easier to understand.

Let's look at method-call chaining in the context of a complete program. See the method-call chain (indicated by a callout) in Figure 7.8's `Car3Driver` class. Left-to-right precedence applies, so `car.setMake` executes first. The `setMake` method returns the calling object, which is the `car` object at the left of `car.setMake`. The returned `car` object is then used to call the `setYear` method. The `setYear` method calls the `printIt` method in a similar fashion.

Method call chaining doesn't work by default. If you want to enable method-call chaining for methods from the same class, you need the following two items in each method definition:

1. The last line in the method body should return the calling object by specifying `return this;`
2. In the method heading, the return type should be the method's class name.

```
/*************************************************************
* Car3Driver.java
* Dean & Dean
*
* This drives Car3 to illustrate method-call chaining.
*************************************************************/

public class Car3Driver
{
  public static void main(String[] args)
  {
    Car3 car = new Car3();

    car.setMake("Honda").setYear(1998).printIt();
  } // end main
} // end class Car3Driver
```

Callout: Use dots to chain together method calls.

Figure 7.8 `Car3` program driver which illustrates method-call chaining

We've implemented those items in the Car3 class in Figure 7.9. Verify that setMake and setYear are enabled properly for method-call chaining. Specifically, verify that (1) the last line in each method body is return this;, and (2) in each method heading, the return type is the method's class name, Car3.

Whenever you finish a method with a return this; statement, you're making it possible to use the same object to call the next method in the chain. However, you can also chain methods called by different types of objects. Just arrange the chain so that the reference type returned by each preceding method matches the class of each following method. So, in general, to make a method chainable, do these two things:

1. In the method heading, specify the return type as the class of a potential following method.
2. Finish the method body with:
   return <*reference-to-object-that-will-call-the-following-method*>;

```
/*************************************************************
* Car3.java
* Dean & Dean
*
* This class illustrates methods that can be chained.
*************************************************************/

public class Car3
{
  private String make;
  private int year;

  //**********************************************************

  public Car3 setMake(String make)
  {
    this.make = make;
    return this;
  } // end setMake

  public Car3 setYear(int year)
  {
    this.year = year;
    return this;
  } // end setYear

  //**********************************************************

  public void printIt()
  {
    System.out.println(make + ", " + year);
  } // end printIt
} // end class Car3
```

The return type is the same as the class name.

Return the calling object.

Figure 7.9 Car3 class

Here is a familiar example that illustrates chaining of two methods defined in the Java API:

```
ch = stdIn.nextLine().charAt(0);
```

The `stdIn` variable is a reference to an object of the `Scanner` class. It calls `Scanner`'s `nextLine` method, which returns a reference to an object of the `String` class. Then that object calls `String`'s `charAt` method, which returns a character.

7.7 Overloaded Methods

Up until this point, all of the methods we defined for a given class have had unique names. But if you think back to some of the Java API methods presented in Chapter 5, you'll recall that there were several examples where the same name (`abs`, `max`, `min`) was used to identify more than one method in the same class (the `Math` class). This section will show you how to do this in classes you write.

What Are Overloaded Methods?

Overloaded methods are two or more methods in the same class that use the same name. Since they use the same name, the compiler needs something else besides the name in order to distinguish them. Parameters to the rescue! To make two overloaded methods distinguishable, you define them with different parameters. More specifically, you define them with a different number of parameters or different types of parameters. The combination of a method's name, the number of its parameters, and the types of its parameters is called the method's *signature*. Each distinct method has a distinct signature. Could these three lines be used as headings for three overloaded `findMaximum` methods?

```
int findMaximum(int a, int b, int c)
double findMaximum(double a, double b, double c)
double findMaximum(double a, double b, double c, double d)
```

Yes, they are a legal overloading of the `findMaximum` method name, because each heading is distinguishable in terms of number and types of parameters. How about the next two lines—could the `findAverage` method name be overloaded in this way?

```
int findAverage(int a, int b, int c)
double findAverage(int x, int y, int z)
```

No. These are not distinguishable methods because they have the same signature—same method names and same number and types of parameters. Since these two methods are not distinguishable, if you try to include these two method headings in the same class, the compiler will think you're defining the same method twice. And that will make the compiler irritable. Be prepared for it to snarl back at you with a "duplicate definition" compile-time error message.

Note that the above `findAverage` method headings have different return types. You might think that the different return types indicate different signatures. Not true. The return type is not part of the signature, so you cannot use just a different return type to distinguish overloaded methods.

Benefit of Overloaded Methods

When should you use overloaded methods? When there's a need to perform essentially the same task with different parameters. For example, the methods associated with the above `findMaximum` headings perform essentially the same basic task—they calculate the maximum value from a given list of numbers.

But they perform the task on different sets of parameters. Given that situation, overloaded methods are a perfect fit.

Note that the use of overloaded methods is never an absolute requirement. As an alternative, you can always use different method names to distinguish different methods. So why are the above findMaximum method headings better than the below method headings?

```
int findMaximumOf3Ints(int a, int b, int c)
double findMaximumOf3Doubles(double a, double b, double c)
double findMaximumOf4Doubles(double a, double b, double c, double d)
```

As these examples suggest, using different method names is cumbersome. With only one method name, the name can be simple. As a programmer, wouldn't you prefer to use and remember just one simple name rather than several cumbersome names?

An Example

Look at the class in Figure 7.10. It uses overloaded `setHeight` methods. Both methods assign a `height` parameter to a `height` instance variable. The difference is the technique for assigning the height's units. The first method automatically assigns a hard-coded "cm" (for centimeters) to the `units` instance variable. The second method assigns a user-specified `units` parameter to the `units` instance variable. The second method thus requires two parameters, `height` and `units`, whereas the first method requires only one parameter, `height`. The two methods perform pretty much the same task, with only a slight variation. That's why we want to use the same name and "overload" that name.

Now look at the driver in Figure 7.11 and its two `setHeight` method calls. For each method call, can you tell which of the two overloaded methods is called? Figure 7.11's first method call, `setHeight(72.0, "in")`, calls Figure 7.10's second `setHeight` method because the two arguments in the method call match the two parameters in the second method's heading. Figure 7.11's second method call, `setHeight(180.0)`, calls Figure 7.10's first `setHeight` method because the one argument in the method call matches the one parameter in the first method's heading.

Calling an Overloaded Method from within an Overloaded Method

Suppose you have overloaded methods and you want one of the overloaded methods to call another one of the overloaded methods. Figure 7.12 provides an example that shows how to do that. Figure 7.12's `setHeight` method is an alternative version of Figure 7.10's one-parameter `setHeight` method. Note how it calls the two-parameter `setHeight` method.

The additional method call makes the program slightly less efficient, but some might consider it more elegant because it eliminates code redundancy. In Figure 7.10, `this.height = height;` appears in both methods, and that's code redundancy—albeit trivial code redundancy.

Why is there no reference variable dot at the left of the `setHeight` method call in the body of the method in Figure 7.12? Because if you're in an instance method, and if you call another method that's in the same class, the reference variable dot prefix is unnecessary. And in this case, the two overloaded `setHeight` methods are instance methods and they are indeed in the same class.

With no reference variable dot prefix in Figure 7.12's `setHeight(height, "cm");` method call, you might be thinking that the method call has no calling object. Actually, there is an implied calling object; it's the same calling object that called the current method. Review quiz: How can you access the current method's calling object? Use the `this` reference. If you want to make the `this` reference explicit, you can add it to Figure 7.12's `setHeight` method call as follows:

```
this.setHeight(height, "cm");
```

```
/*************************************************************
* Height.java
* Dean & Dean
*
* This class stores and prints height values.
*************************************************************/

class Height
{
  double height;  // a person's height
  String units;   // like cm for centimeters

  //**********************************************************

  public void setHeight(double height)
  {
    this.height = height;
    this.units = "cm";
  }

  //**********************************************************

  public void setHeight(double height, String units)
  {
    this.height = height;
    this.units = units;
  }

  //**********************************************************

  public void print()
  {
    System.out.println(this.height + " " + this.units);
  }
} // end class Height
```

Figure 7.10 `Height` class with overloaded methods

We point out this alternative syntax not because we want you to use it, but because we want you to get a clearer picture of calling object details.

Program Evolution

The ability to overload a method name promotes graceful program evolution because it corresponds to how natural language regularly overloads the meanings of words. For example, the first version of your program might define just the one-parameter version of its `setHeight` method. Later, when you decide to enhance your program, it's easier for your existing users if you minimize the new things they have to learn. In this case, you let them either keep using the original method or switch to the improved method.

```
/**************************************************************
* HeightDriver.java
* Dean & Dean
*
* This class is a demonstration driver for the Height class.
**************************************************************/

public class HeightDriver
{
  public static void main(String[] args)
  {
    Height myHeight = new Height();

    myHeight.setHeight(72.0, "in");
    myHeight.print();
    myHeight.setHeight(180.0);
    myHeight.print();
  } // end main
} // end class HeightDriver
```

Figure 7.11 `HeightDriver` class that drives the `Height` class in Figure 7.10

```
public void setHeight(double height)
{
  setHeight(height, "cm");
}
```

Do not put a reference variable dot prefix here.

Figure 7.12 Example of method that calls another method in the same class
This helps avoid duplication of code details and possible internal inconsistencies.

When they want to use the improved method, all they have to remember is the original method name and adding a second argument, for units, to the method call. That's an almost obvious variation, and it's easier to remember than a different method name. It's certainly easier than being forced to learn a new method name for the old task—which would be a necessary cost of upgrading if method overloading were not available.

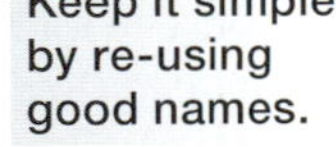

Keep it simple by re-using good names.

7.8 Constructors

Up to this point, we have used mutators to assign values to the instance variables in newly instantiated objects. That works OK, but it requires having and calling one mutator for each instance variable. As an alternative, you could use a single method to initialize all of an object's instance variables as soon as possible after you create that object. For example, in this chapter's `Car` class in Figure 7.2, instead of defining three mutator methods, you could define a single `initCar` method to initialize `Car` objects. Then you could use it like this:

```
Car allexCar = new Car();
allexCar.initCar("Porsche", 2006, "beige");
```

This code fragment uses one statement to allocate space for a new object, and it uses another statement to initialize that object's instance variables. Since the instantiation and initialization of an object is so common, wouldn't it be nice if there were a single statement that could handle both of these operations? There is such a statement, and here it is:

```
Car allexCar = new Car("Porsche", 2006, "beige");
```

This unifies the creation of an object and the initialization of its instance variables in just one call. It guarantees that an object's instance variables are initialized as soon as the object is created. The code that follows the word `new` should remind you of a method call. Both that code and a method call consist of a programmer-defined word (`Car` in this case) and then parentheses around a list of items. You can think of that code as a special method call, but it's so special that it has its own name. It's used to construct objects, so it's called a *constructor.*

What Is a Constructor?

A constructor is a method-like entity that's called automatically when an object is instantiated. The above `new Car("Porsche", 2006, "beige")` object instantiation calls a constructor named `Car` that has three parameters—a `String`, an `int`, and a `String`. Here's an example of such a constructor:

```
public Car(String m, int y, String c)
{
  this.make = m;
  this.year = y;
  this.color = c;
}
```

As you can see, this constructor simply assigns passed-in parameter values to their corresponding instance variables. After the constructor is executed, the JVM returns the address of the newly instantiated and initialized object to the place where the constructor was called. In the above `Car allexCar = new Car("Porsche", 2006, "beige")` declaration, the address of the instantiated `Car` object gets assigned to the `allexCar` reference variable.

There are several constructor details you should know before looking at a complete program example. A constructor's name must be the same as the class it's associated with. Thus, a `Car` class's constructor must be named `Car`, with an uppercase "C."

In the heading of a method, you must include a return type, so you might expect the same requirement for the heading of a constructor. Nope. Return types are not used in constructor headings[2] because a constructor call (with `new`) automatically returns a reference to the object it constructs, and the type of this object is always specified by the constructor name itself. Just specify `public` at the left and then write the class name (which is the name of the constructor).

An Example

Let's now look at a complete program example that uses a constructor. See the Car4 program in Figures 7.13 and 7.14. In Figure 7.13, note that we put the constructor above the `getMake` method. In all class definitions, it's good style to put constructors above methods.

[2] If you try to define a constructor with a return type specification, the compiler will not recognize it as a constructor and will think it is an ordinary method instead.

```
/***********************************************************
* Car4.java
* Dean & Dean
*
* This class stores and retrieves data for a car.
***********************************************************/

public class Car4
{
  private String make;    // car's make
  private int year;       // car's manufacturing year
  private String color;   // car's primary color

  //********************************************************

  public Car4(String m, int y, String c)
  {
    this.make = m;
    this.year = y;
    this.color = c;
  } // end constructor

  //********************************************************

  public String getMake()
  {
    return this.make;
  } // end getMake
} // end class Car4
```

constructor definition

Figure 7.13 `Car4` class, which has a constructor

Accommodating Java's Fickle Default Constructor

Any time you instantiate an object (with `new`), there must be a matching constructor. That is, the number and types of arguments in your constructor call must match the number and types of parameters in a defined constructor. But until recently, we've instantiated objects without any explicit constructor. So were those examples wrong? No. They all used a zero-parameter freebie *default constructor* that the Java compiler automatically provides if and only if there is no explicitly defined constructor. The Employee program in Figures 7.15a and 7.15b illustrates the use of Java's implicit zero-parameter default constructor.

In Figure 7.15a, note how `main`'s `new Employee()` code calls a zero-parameter constructor. But Figure 7.15b does not define a zero-parameter constructor. No problem. Since there are no other constructors, the Java compiler provides the default zero-parameter constructor, and it matches up with the `new Employee()` zero-argument constructor call.

Note that as soon as you define any kind of constructor for a class, Java's default constructor becomes unavailable. So if your class contains an explicit constructor definition, and if `main` includes a zero-argument constructor call, you must also include an explicit zero-parameter constructor in your class definition.

```
/****************************************************************
* Car4Driver.java
* Dean & Dean
*
* This class is a demonstration driver for the Car4 class.
****************************************************************/

public class Car4Driver
{
  public static void main(String[] args)
  {
    Car4 allexCar = new Car4("Porsche", 2006, "beige");
    Car4 latishaCar = new Car4("Saturn", 2002, "red");

    System.out.println(allexCar.getMake());
  } // end main
} // end class Car4Driver
```

constructor calls

Output:

```
Porsche
```

Figure 7.14 `Car4Driver` class which drives the `Car4` class in Figure 7.13

See the Employee2 program in Figures 7.16a and 7.16b. The driven class in Figure 7.16a compiles successfully, but the driver in Figure 7.16b generates a compilation error. As in Figure 7.15a, the driver code in Figure 7.16b calls a zero-parameter constructor. It worked before, so why doesn't it work this time? This time, the driven class in Figure 7.16a explicitly defines a constructor, so Java does not provide a default zero-parameter constructor. And without that constructor, the compiler complains that there's no matching constructor for the zero-parameter constructor call. How can you fix the Employee2 program to get rid of this error? Add the following zero-parameter `Employee2` constructor to your `Employee2` class:

```
public Employee2()
{ }
```

```
public class EmployeeDriver
{
  public static void main(String[] args)
  {
    Employee emp = new Employee();

    emp.readName();
  } // end main
} // end class EmployeeDriver
```

zero-parameter constructor call

Figure 7.15a Driver for Employee program

```
import java.util.Scanner;

public class Employee
{
  private String name;

  //*******************************************

  public void readName()
  {
    Scanner stdIn = new Scanner(System.in);

    System.out.print("Name: ");
    this.name = stdIn.nextLine();
  } // end readName
} // end class Employee
```

Figure 7.15b Driven class for Employee program
This works even though there is no explicitly defined constructor because the Java compiler supplies a matching default zero-parameter constructor.

```
import java.util.Scanner;

public class Employee2
{
  private String name;

  //*****************************************

  public Employee2(String n)
  {
    this.name = n;
  } // end constructor

  //*****************************************

  public void readName()
  {
    Scanner stdIn = new Scanner(System.in);

    System.out.print("Name: ");
    this.name = stdIn.nextLine();
  } // end readName
} // end class Employee2
```

Figure 7.16a Driven class for Employee2 program

```
public class Employee2Driver
{
  public static void main(String[] args)
  {
    Employee2 waitress = new Employee2("Wen-Jung Hsin");
    Employee2 hostess = new Employee2();

    hostess.readName();
  } // end main
} // end class Employee2Driver
```

Zero-parameter constructor call generates a compilation error.

Figure 7.16b Driver for Employee2 program

That's an example of a *dummy constructor*. It's called a dummy constructor because it doesn't do anything other than satisfy the compiler. Note how the braces are on a line by themselves with a blank space between them. That's a style issue. By writing the dummy constructor like that, it makes the empty braces more prominent and clearly shows the intent of the programmer to make the constructor a dummy constructor.

Initializing Named Constants

If you include the `final` modifier in the declaration of an instance variable, that "variable" becomes a named constant. Whenever you use `final`, it's good style to write the variable name in uppercase. In Chapter 3 we used `final` and uppercase to declare and initialize named constants like this:

```
final double FREEZING_POINT = 32.0;
```

At that point, all our named constant declarations were within a method (the `main` method). When a named constant is defined within a method, it's called a *local named constant* and its scope is limited to that one method. If you want an attribute that's constant throughout the life of a particular object, you'll need another kind of named constant, an *instance constant*. You declare this kind of named constant at the beginning of a class, but you normally do not initialize it in the declaration. Instead, you initialize it in a constructor. This allows you to initialize instance constants with different values for different objects. Thus, an instance constant can represent an attribute whose value varies from one object to another, but remains constant throughout the life of any particular object. It represents an inalienable attribute of that object, an attribute which permanently distinguishes that object from all other objects in the same class. Because the `final` modifier keeps a named constant from being changed after it's initialized, it's safe to make an instance constant `public`. This makes it especially easy to determine the value of an object's permanent attributes. Just use this syntax:

<reference-variable>`.`*<instance-constant>*

For example, instead of treating an employee's name as an instance variable, as we did in the `Employee` and `Employee2 classes`, you can treat it as an instance constant, as in the `Employee3` class of Figure 7.17a.

Notice that the `Employee3` class does not include a zero-parameter constructor. Why don't we include one here? Because we want to force use of our one-parameter constructor to make sure `NAME` is initialized with a distinct value that's appropriate for each object. To drive the `Employee3` class, you can use something like what's in Figure 7.17b. Notice how the `public` modifier on the instance constant in Figure 7.17a makes it possible to access this constant value directly from another class.

```
/*************************************************************
* Employee3.java
* Dean & Dean
*
* This gives an employee a permanent name.
*************************************************************/

import java.util.Scanner;

public class Employee3
{
  Scanner stdIn = new Scanner(System.in);
  public final String NAME;   <-- declaration of instance constant

  //*******************************************************

  public Employee3(String name)
  {
    this.NAME = name;   <-- initialization of instance constant
  } // end constructor
} // end class Employee3
```

Figure 7.17a `Employee3` class uses an instance constant

```
/*************************************************************
* Employee3Driver.java
* Dean & Dean
*
* This instantiates an object and prints permanent attribute.
*************************************************************/

import java.util.Scanner;

public class Employee3Driver
{
  public static void main(String[] args)
  {
    Employee3 waitress = new Employee3("Angie Klein");

    System.out.println(waitress.NAME);   <-- direct access to instance constant
  } // end main
} // end class Employee3Driver
```

Output:

```
Angie Klein
```

Figure 7.17b Driver for the `Employee3` class in Figure 7.17a

Elegance

Note that the use of programmer-defined constructors is never an absolute requirement. Although it would defeat their purpose, you could initialize instance constants when you declared them. And you can always instantiate an object with empty parentheses and then call an initialization method to initialize instance variables as we did earlier. So why bother to use programmer-defined constructors? If you want distinctive instance constants, you must initialize them in a constructor—the compiler won't let you do it in a method. Whenever you need to initialize an object's instance variables, it's more elegant to do it with the constructor that instantiates the object. The constructor intimately ties instance constant and instance variable initialization with object creation. Constructors simplify things by avoiding a separate initialization step, and you don't need a separate name for them because they just use the class name. Bravo, constructors!

7.9 Overloaded Constructors

Overloading a constructor is like overloading a method. Constructor overloading occurs when there are two or more constructors with the same name and different parameters. Overloaded constructors are very common (more common than overloaded methods). That's because you'll often want to be able to create objects with different amounts of initialization. Sometimes you'll want to pass in initial values to the constructor. At other times, you'll want to refrain from passing in initial values to the constructor, and rely on assigning values later on. To enable both of those scenarios, you need overloaded constructors—one constructor with parameters and one constructor without parameters.

An Example

Suppose you want to implement a `Fraction` class, which stores the numerator and denominator for a given fraction. The `Fraction` class also stores the fraction's quotient, which is produced by dividing the numerator by the denominator. Normally, you want to instantiate the `Fraction` class by passing a numerator argument and a denominator argument to a two-parameter `Fraction` constructor. But for a whole number, you want to instantiate a `Fraction` class by passing just one argument (the whole number) to a `Fraction` constructor, rather than passing two arguments. For example, to instantiate a 3 whole number as a `Fraction` object, you want to pass in just a 3 to a `Fraction` constructor, rather than a 3 for the numerator and a 1 for the denominator. To handle two-argument `Fraction` instantiations as well as one-argument `Fraction` instantiations, you need overloaded constructors. One way to begin solving a problem is to write a driver that shows how you want the solution to be used. With that in mind, we present a driver in Figure 7.18 that illustrates how the proposed `Fraction` class and its overloaded constructors can be used. The driver's code includes line numbers to facilitate later tracing.

Assume that within the `Fraction` class, `numerator` and `denominator` are `int` instance variables and `quotient` is a `double` instance variable. The two-parameter constructor should look something like this:

```
public Fraction(int n, int d)
{
  this.numerator = n;
  this.denominator = d;
  this.quotient = (double) this.numerator / this.denominator;
}
```

```
/*********************************************************
* FractionDriver.java
* Dean & Dean
*
* This driver class demonstrates the Fraction class.
*********************************************************/

public class FractionDriver
{
  public static void main(String[] args)
  {
    Fraction a = new Fraction(3, 4);
    Fraction b = new Fraction(3);

    a.printIt();
    b.printIt();
  } // end main
} // end class FractionDriver
```

calls to overloaded constructors

Sample session:

```
3 / 4 = 0.75
3 / 1 = 3.0
```

Figure 7.18 `FractionDriver` class which drives Fraction class in Figure 7.19

Why the `(double)` cast? Without it, we'd get integer division and truncation of fractional values. The cast converts `numerator` into a `double`, the `double` numerator promotes the `denominator` instance variable to `double`, floating-point division occurs, and fractional values are preserved. Our cast to double also provides a more graceful response if the denominator is zero. Integer division by zero causes the program to crash. But floating-point division by zero is acceptable. Instead of crashing, the program prints "Infinity" if the numerator is positive or "-Infinity" if the numerator is negative.

Make it robust.

For a whole number like 3, we could call the above two-parameter constructor with 3 as the first argument and 1 as the second argument. But we want our `Fraction` class to be friendlier. We want it to have another (overloaded) constructor which has just one parameter. This one-parameter constructor could look like this:

```
public Fraction(int n)
{
  this.numerator = n;
  this.denominator = 1;
  this.quotient = (double) this.numerator;
}
```

Calling a Constructor from within Another Constructor

The two constructors above contain duplicate code. Duplication makes programs longer. More importantly, it introduces the possibility of inconsistency. Earlier we used overloaded methods to avoid this kind of danger. Instead of repeating code as in Figure 7.10,

Avoid duplicate code.

in Figure 7.12 we inserted a call to a previously written method that already had the code we wanted. You do the same thing with constructors; that is, you can call a previously written constructor from within another constructor. Constructor calls are different from method calls in that they use the reserved word `new`, which tells the JVM to allocate space in memory for a new object. Within the original constructor, you could use the `new` operator to call another constructor. But that would create a separate object from the original object. And most of the time, that's not what you want. Normally, if you call an overloaded constructor, you want to work with the original object, not a new, separate object.

```
/*************************************************************
* Fraction.java
* Dean & Dean
*
* This class stores prints fractions.
*************************************************************/

public class Fraction
{
  private int numerator;
  private int denominator;
  private double quotient;

  //**********************************************************

  public Fraction(int n)
  {
    this(n, 1);
  }

//**********************************************************

  public Fraction(int n, int d)
  {
    this.numerator = n;
    this.denominator = d;
    this.quotient = (double) this.numerator / this.denominator;
  }

  //**********************************************************

  public void printIt()
  {
    System.out.println(this.numerator + " / " +
      this.denominator + " = " + this.quotient);
  } // end printIt
} // end class Fraction
```

This statement calls the other constructor.

Figure 7.19 `Fraction` class with overloaded constructors

To avoid creating a separate object, Java designers came up with special syntax that allows an overloaded constructor to call one of its partner overloaded constructors such that the original object is used. Here is the syntax:

```
this(<arguments-for-target-constructor>);
```

A `this(<arguments-for-target-constructor>)` constructor call may appear only in a constructor definition, and it must appear as the very first statement in the constructor definition. That means you can't use `this` syntax to call a constructor from inside a method definition. It also means you can have only one such constructor call in a constructor definition, because only one call statement could be the "very first statement in the constructor definition."

Now look at the `Fraction` class in Figure 7.19. It has three instance variables—`numerator`, `denominator`, and `quotient`. The `quotient` instance variable holds the floating-point result of dividing the numerator by the denominator. The first constructor is just like the two-parameter constructor we wrote above. But the second constructor is shorter. Instead of repeating code appearing in the first constructor, it calls the first constructor with the `this(...)` command.

Suppose during program development, for debugging purposes, you decided to print "In 1-parameter constructor" from within the `Fraction` class's one-parameter constructor. Where would you put that print statement? Since the `this(n, 1)` constructor call must be the first statement in the constructor definition, you would have to put the print statement below the constructor call.

Tracing with Constructors

Figure 7.20 shows a trace of the Fraction program. In the following discussion of it, you'll need to actively refer to not only the trace figure, but also the `FractionDriver` class (Figure 7.18) and the `Fraction` class (Figure 7.19). Note how line 12 in the `FractionDriver` class passes 3 and 4 to the two-parameter `Fraction` constructor. 3 and 4 are assigned to the constructor's `n` and `d` parameters. As part of the implied constructor functionality, lines 10-12 in the `Fraction` class are executed, and they initialize `Fraction` instance variables with their default values. Then lines 25-27 overwrite those initialized values. Going back to `FractionDriver`, `new` returns an object reference (obj1) to the reference variable `a`. Then on line 13, the driver passes 3 to the one-parameter constructor. After parameter assignment and instance variable initialization, line 18 in the `Fraction` class passes 3 and 1 to the two-parameter constructor. After the two-parameter constructor overwrites the instance variables, control flows back to the one-parameter constructor, and back to `FractionDriver`, where `new` returns an object reference (obj2) to the reference variable `b`. Finally, in lines 15 and 16, the driver prints out the two results.

7.10 Problem Solving with Multiple Driven Classes

We started simply and we are gradually adding complexity. In Chapters 1 through 5, we showed you programs that contain only one class and one method (the `main` method). In Chapters 6 and 7 we've been showing you programs that contain two classes: (1) a driver class, which contains a single `main` method and (2) a driven class, which typically contains several methods.

So far we've used only one driven class to keep things simple, but in the real world, you'll often need more than one driven class. That's because most real-world systems are heterogeneous—they contain mixtures of different types of things. For each different type of thing, it's appropriate to have a different class. Having more than one driven class allows you to partition a complicated problem into several simpler problems. That lets you focus on one type of thing at a time. When you've finished that type of thing, you can move onto another type of thing. In this step-by-step fashion you can gradually build up a large program.

FractionDriver			Fraction											
	main			Fraction		Fraction	printIt	obj1			obj2			
line#	**a**	**b**	***line#***	**n**	**d**	**n**	**this**	**num**	**den**	**quot**	**num**	**den**	**quot**	**output**
12				3	4									
			10					0						
			11						0					
			12							0.00				
			25					3						
			26						4					
			27							0.75				
12	obj1													
13						3								
			10								0			
			11									0		
			12										0.00	
			18	3	1									
			25								3			
			26									1		
			27										3.00	
13		obj2												
15							obj1							
			34											3 / 4 = 0.75
16							obj2							
			34											3 / 1 = 3.00

Figure 7.20 Trace of Fraction program in Figures 7.18 and 7.19

It's no big deal to drive more than one driven class from a single driver. In fact, you already saw us do it back in Chapter 5 when statements in a single `main` method called methods from more than one wrapper class, like `Integer` and `Double`. The only thing to remember is that when you're compiling the driver, the compiler must be able to find all the driven classes. If they are pre-built classes they must be part of the `java.lang` package or you must import them. If they are classes you write, they should be in the same directory as your driver.[3]

Example—Garage Door Opener

As an example, suppose you want to write a program that models the operation of a garage door opener. A typical system contains four control components—a push button, a normally closed up switch, a normally closed down switch, and a controller. The push button starts the door moving, or if the door is moving and has not yet reached the end of its normal travel, the push button stops the door. Whenever the door stops, its travel direction reverses, and the next push-button push makes the door go in the direction opposite to the direction it was going before it stopped. The up switch stops upward travel by opening its contacts and stopping the door at its upper limit. The up switch contacts close again when the door starts to go down.

[3] It's possible to put your own classes in your own packages in separate directories and import them as you import pre-built classes. You can learn how to do this in Appendix 4. However, if all your driven classes are in the same directory as your driver class, it's not necessary to package and import them, and we assume this to be the case throughout the body of this book.

The down switch stops downward travel by opening its contacts and stopping the door at its lower limit. The down switch contacts close again when the door starts to go up.

The controller interprets the information from the various switches, and it operates the motor that raises and lowers the door. The system has four distinct states: Door stopped after going down, which we'll call state #0. Door going up, which we'll call state #1. Door stopped after going up, which we'll call state #2. Door going down, which we'll call state #3.

Here's the kind of thing we want our program to do:

Sample session:

```
Door initially down.
Enter number of operations: 8
Enter 'b' for button or 'e' for end switch: e
Already stopped. Enter 'b': b
Button switch hit. Door moving up.
Enter 'b' for button or 'e' for end switch: e
Upper limit switch hit. Door is up.
Enter 'b' for button or 'e' for end switch: b
Button switch hit. Door moving down.
Enter 'b' for button or 'e' for end switch: b
Button switch hit. Door stopped by button.
Enter 'b' for button or 'e' for end switch: e
Already stopped. Enter 'b': b
Button switch hit. Door moving up.
Enter 'b' for button or 'e' for end switch: e
Upper limit switch hit. Door is up.
Enter 'b' for button or 'e' for end switch: b
Button switch hit. Door moving down.
Enter 'b' for button or 'e' for end switch: e
Lower limit switch hit. Door is down.
```

Now that we've described the problem and said what we want the program to do, let's analyze the problem to see how the program might be organized.

Use a separate class for each type of thing.

The up an down end switches are hard wired, and the push button contains a radio transmitter. But from a modeling viewpoint, we can think of the push button as being hard wired like the end switches. So the two end switches and the push button can be just three instances of a generic thing called a "switch." This suggests that we write a `Switch` class and construct three objects from it—an `upSwitch`, a `downSwitch`, and a `button`.

Although the three switches are similar to each other, they are all different from the controller that gathers information from them and does things to change the state of the door. So it makes sense to use a separate class for the controller—a `GarageDoorController` class. We'll have our driver construct one object from it—a `control`.

There is also the door, which is what we really care about. You can think of the door in the narrow sense as just another component, or you can think of it in the broader sense as the system—the `GarageDoorSystem`. A system is an object that contains other objects (its components), and it knows about its components. In our current example, a `GarageDoorSystem` object contains the door, the controller that moves the door, and the three switches that send signals to the controller.

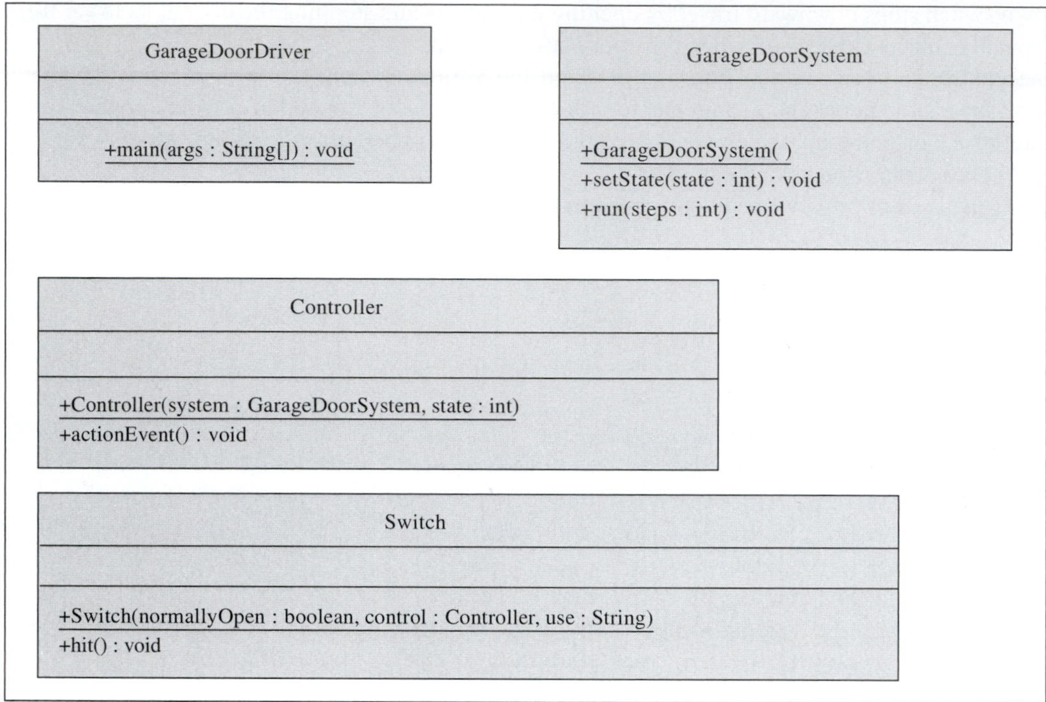

Figure 7.21 First-cut UML diagram for Garage Door program

Figure 7.21 shows a first-cut Unified Modeling Language (UML) class diagram for the program. This first-cut diagram shows `public` methods but no instance variables or instance constants. Each of the driven classes contains a single constructor. Notice that each constructor is underlined. That conforms to UML standards, which suggest that you underline all constructors.

As usual, `GarageDoorDriver` has only a `main` method. Because we plan to do most of the controlling activities in the `GarageDoorSystem` class instead of in the driver class, that `main` method can be very simple. As you can see in Figure 7.22, our driver does just two things. It constructs a `GarageDoorSystem` object, and it runs a test on that object.

Notice that this driver does not construct any of the system's components. It delegates that job to the `GarageDoorSystem` constructor. Since component construction probably depends on what the components are like, let's look at those components next. Figure 7.23 contains the code for the controller.

As we wrote the code in Figure 7.23 we became aware of the need for several instance variables. They expand the UML class diagram for the `Controller` class to this:

Controller
-system : GarageDoorSystem
-state : int
-motorDirection : boolean = false;
+Controller(system : GarageDoorSystem, state : int)
+actionEvent() : void

```
/*************************************************************
* GarageDoorDriver.java
* Dean & Dean
*
* This simulates installation and testing.
*************************************************************/

import java.util.Scanner;

public class GarageDoorDriver
{
  public static void main(String[] args)
  {
    GarageDoorSystem system;
    Scanner stdIn = new Scanner(System.in);

    // Install system
    system = new GarageDoorSystem();

    // Test system
    System.out.print("Enter number of operations: ");
    system.run(stdIn.nextInt());
  } // end main
} // end class GarageDoorDriver
```

Figure 7.22 Driver for Garage Door program

The `system` instance variable gives the controller a reference to the system that includes it. We'll want the constructor to initialize or re-initialize the `system`, `state`, and `motorDirection` instance variables.

The `state` and `motorDirection` instance variables represent electromechanical relays or solid-state flip flops (primitive electronic memory elements). These primitive memory elements keep track of the current state of the controller—its current mode of operation. In the physical controller these primitive memory elements determine what the controller does. The `actionEvent` method changes the values of these primitive memory elements when it's called by a switch. Every time the `actionEvent` method is called, the state increments by one, *modulo four*. Modular four means the value of `state` cycles through four values like this: 0, 1, 2, 3, 0, 1, 2, and so on. Also, whenever the motor stops, it reverses direction. That is, whenever `state` changes to an even value (0 or 2), the `motorDirection` variable toggles to its opposite `boolean` value.

Figure 7.24 contains the code that defines the switches. Each switch is characterized by a named instance constant, `NORMALLY_OPEN`. `NORMALLY_OPEN` is a switch contact property. If `NORMALLY_OPEN` is `true`, when you push the switch, its contacts close. On the other hand, if `NORMALLY_OPEN` is false, when you push the switch, its contacts open. So, when you push on either of the two limit switches, its contacts open and this stops current flow to the motor. The instance variable, `use`, tells how the switch fits into the system. The instance variable, `controller`, is a reference to the controller to which the switch is attached. (If there were two garage door systems, a particular switch might be associated with either

```
/*********************************************************************
* Controller.java
* Dean & Dean
*
* This class models controller with sensors attached.
*********************************************************************/

public class Controller
{
  private GarageDoorSystem system;
  private int state;    // 0=down, 1=goingUp, 2=up, 3=goingDown
  private boolean motorDirection = false;         // true = go up

  //*******************************************************************

  public Controller(GarageDoorSystem system, int state)
  {
    this.system = system;
    this.state = state;
    if (state < 2)
    {
      this.motorDirection = true;
    }
  } // end constructor

  //*******************************************************************

  public void actionEvent()
  {
    this.state++;
    this.state %= 4;
    if (this.state % 2 == 0)
    {
      this.motorDirection = !this.motorDirection;
    }
    system.setState(this.state);
  } // end actionEvent
} // end class Controller
```

Figure 7.23 `Controller` class for the Garage Door program

system's controller.) The constructor initializes these three values. The `hit` method prints a message that identifies which switch was hit. Then it calls `control`'s `actionEvent` method in the `Controller` class.

The instance constant and instance variables in Figure 7.24 expand the UML class diagram for the `Switch` class to this:

Switch
+NORMALLY_OPEN : boolean +use : String -control : Controller
+Switch(normallyOpen : boolean, control : Controller, use : String) +hit() : void

```
/*************************************************************************
* Switch.java
* Dean & Dean
*
* This class models switches.
*************************************************************************/

import java.util.Scanner;

public class Switch
{
  public final boolean NORMALLY_OPEN;       // hit makes connection
  public String use;                        // role in the system
  private Controller control;

  //**********************************************************************

  public Switch(
    boolean normallyOpen, Controller control, String use)
  {
    this.NORMALLY_OPEN = normallyOpen;
    this.control = control;
    this.use = use;
  } // end constructor

  //**********************************************************************

  public void hit()
  {
    System.out.print(this.use + " switch hit. ");
    control.actionEvent();
  } // end hit
} // end class Switch
```

Figure 7.24 `Switch` class for the Garage Door program

Now, we're ready for the `GarageDoorSystem` class, shown in Figures 7.25a and 7.25b. In Figure 7.25a, we declare an instance variable called `state`. Then we declare the four reference variables that refer to the four component objects in the system. The constructor instantiates all of the component objects and initializes all of its instance reference variables with references to those component objects. It initializes `state` to 0, corresponding to the door-down position, and in the `Controller` constructor call, it passes this `state` value to the new `control` object to synchronize that object's state with the state of the complete system. The `setState` method provides a way for the subordinate `control` object to keep the system's state synchronized with the controller's state immediately after the controller takes action that changes the state.

```
/*********************************************************************
* GarageDoorSystem.java
* Dean & Dean
*
* This represents a garage door.
*********************************************************************/

import java.util.Scanner;

public class GarageDoorSystem
{
  private int state;           // 0=down, 1=goingUp, 2=up, 3=goingDn
  private Controller control;
  private Switch upSwitch;     // upper limit switch
  private Switch downSwitch;   // lower limit switch
  private Switch button;       // electronic pushbutton

  //******************************************************************

  public GarageDoorSystem()
  {
    this.state = 0;
    System.out.println("Door initially down.");
    this.control = new Controller(this, this.state);
    this.upSwitch =
      new Switch(false, this.control, "Upper limit");
    this.downSwitch =
      new Switch(false, this.control, "Lower limit");
    this.button = new Switch(true, this.control, "Button");
  } // end constructor

  //******************************************************************

  public void setState(int state)
  {
    this.state = state;
  }

  //******************************************************************
```

Figure 7.25a `GarageDoorSystem` class for the Garage Door program—Part A

```
  public void run(int steps)
  {
    Scanner stdIn = new Scanner(System.in);
    char input;
    boolean OK = false;

    for (int step=0; step<steps; step++)
    {
      System.out.print(
        "Enter 'b' for button or 'e' for end switch: ");
      do
      {
        input = stdIn.nextLine().charAt(0);
        if (input == 'b')
        {
          button.hit();
          switch (state)
          {
            case 0: case 2:
              System.out.println("Door stopped by button.");
              break;
            case 1:
              System.out.println("Door moving up.");
              break;
            case 3:
              System.out.println("Door moving down.");
          } // end switch
          OK = true;
        }
        else
        {
          switch (state)
          {
            case 1:
              upSwitch.hit();
              System.out.println("Door is up.");
              OK = true;
              break;
            case 3:
              downSwitch.hit();
              System.out.println("Door is down.");
              OK = true;
              break;
            default:
              System.out.print("Already stopped. Enter 'b': ");
              OK = false;
          } // end switch
        } // end if
      } while (!OK);
    } // end for
  } // end run
} // end GarageDoorSystem class
```

Figure 7.25b GarageDoorSystem class for the Garage Door program—Part B

The instance variables in Figure 7.25a expand the UML class diagram for the `GarageDoorSystem` class to this:

GarageDoorSystem
-state : int -control : Controller -upSwitch : Switch -downSwitch : Switch -button : Switch
<u>+GarageDoorSystem()</u> +setState(state : int) : void +run(steps : int) : void

Figure 7.25b contains the rest of the `GarageDoorSystem` class. This is all just one big method, the `run` method, which describes the garage-door operation—the system's process. It's a big `for` loop that takes a specified number of steps. At each step, the user specifies one of two types of events, either a button press or an arrival at one of the travel limits. A big `do` loop uses the input value to print out an appropriate message and perhaps ask for data re-entry. Delegating this detail to a subordinate class is more elegant than trying to handle it all in the `main` method of a driver.

Summary

- When you declare a reference variable, the JVM allocates space in memory for holding a reference to an object. At that point, there is no memory allocation for the object itself.
- Assigning one reference variable to another does not clone an object. It just makes both reference variables refer to the same object and gives that object an alternate name—an alias.
- To create a separate object, you must use Java's `new` operator. To make a second object be like a first object, copy the first object's instance variable values into the corresponding instance variables in the second object.
- A method can return an assortment of data originating in a method by returning a reference to an internally instantiated object that contains that data.
- Java's garbage collection program searches for inaccessible objects and recycles the space they occupy by asking the operating system to designate their space in memory as free space.
- If you compare two object references with ==, the result is `true` if and only if the references point to the same object.
- To see whether two different objects contain similar data, you must write an `equals` method that individually compares respective instance variable values.
- To swap two variables' values, you need to store one of the variable's values in a temporary variable.
- If you pass a reference as an argument, and if the reference parameter's instance variables are updated, then the update simultaneously updates the reference argument's instance variables in the calling module.
- If a method returns a reference to an object, you can use what's returned to call another method in the same statement. That's method-call chaining.

- To make a program more understandable, you can *overload* a method name by using the same name again in a different method definition that has a different sequence of parameter types. The combination of method name, number of parameters, and parameter types is called a method's *signature*.
- A constructor enables you to initialize instance variables separately for each object. A constructor's name is the same as its class name, and there is no return value specification.
- For a constructor call to work there must be a matching constructor definition, that is, a definition with the same signature.
- If you define a constructor, the default zero-parameter constructor vanishes.
- Use a constructor to initialize instance constants, which represent permanent attributes of individual objects.
- To call an overloaded constructor from within a constructor, make the first statement in the constructor be: `this(`<*constructor-argument(s)*>`).`
- Partition a large problem into a set of simpler problems by using multiple driven classes.

Review Questions

§7.2 Object Creation—A Detailed Analysis

1. The statement

```
Car car;
```

allocates space in memory for an object. (T / F)

2. What does the `new` operator do?

§7.3 Assigning a Reference

3. Assigning one reference variable to another copies the right-side object's instance variables into the left-side object's instance variables. (T / F)
4. What is a memory leak?

§7.4 Testing Objects for Equality

5. Consider this code fragment:

```
boolean same;
Car carX = new Car();
Car carY = carX;
same = (carX == carY);
```

What is the final value of `same`?

6. What is the return type of an `equals` method?
7. By convention, we use the name `equals` for methods that perform a certain kind of evaluation. What is the difference between the evaluation performed by an `equals` method and the == operator?

§7.5 Passing References as Arguments

8. When you pass a reference to a method, you enable the method to modify the referenced object. (T / F)

§7.6 Method-Call Chaining

9. What two things must be included in a method definition so that it may be called as part of a method-call-chaining statement?

§7.7 Overloaded Methods

10. What is it called when you have two or more methods with the same name in the same class?

11. If you want the current object to call a different method in the same class as the current class, the method call is easy—just call the method directly, with no reference variable dot prefix. (T / F)

§7.8 Constructors

12. What is the return type of a constructor?

13. The name of a constructor must be exactly the same as the name of its class. (T / F)

14. Standard coding conventions suggest that you put constructor definitions after the definitions of all methods. (T / F)

§7.9 Overloaded Constructors

15. If a class's source code contains a single one-parameter constructor, the constructor is overloaded because this one-parameter constructor has the same name as the default zero-parameter constructor. (T / F)

16. Suppose you have a class with two constructors. What are the rules for calling one constructor from the other constructor?

§7.10 Problem Solving with Multiple Driven Classes

17. You can partition a large problem into many smaller problems by using many driven classes. (T / F)

18. How do you give a component object a reference to its container or another component in the same container?

19. What do you do to make one object logically contain another object?

Exercises

1. [after §7.2] Given a Car class with these two instance variables:

```
String make;
int year;
```

Describe all the operations that occur when this statement executes:

```
Car caidenCar = new Car();
```

2. [after §7.3] Trace the Car program shown in Figures 7.2 and 7.3. Use the following trace setup. Note that we have used abbreviations to keep the trace's width as small as possible.

CarDriver			Car																
	main			setMake		setYear		setColor		makeCopy		disp	obj1			obj2			
line#	**jCar**	**sCar**	*line#*	**this**	**make**	**this**	**year**	**this**	**color**	**this**	**car**	**this**	**make**	**year**	**color**	**make**	**year**	**color**	**output**

3. [after §7.3] What is garbage collection?

4. [after §7.5] Suppose a `Computer` class contains, along with other instance variables, a `hardDrive` string instance variable. Complete the following `swapHardDrive` method that swaps the calling object's hard drive value with the passed-in parameter's hard drive value.

```
public void swapHardDrive(Computer otherComputer)
{
  <insert code here>
} // end swapHardDrive
```

5. [after §7.5] Normally, we give each object a unique name by assigning its address to only one reference variable. Assigning the value of one reference variable to another reference variable creates two different names for the same thing, which is ambiguous. Identify a situation where this kind of assignment is useful, even though there is name ambiguity.

6. [after §7.6] Given this automobile-specification program:

```
/***************************************************************
* AutoOptionsDriver.java
* Dean & Dean
*
* This exercises the AutoOptions class.
***************************************************************/

import java.util.Scanner;

public class AutoOptionsDriver
{
  public static void main(String[] args)
  {
    Scanner stdIn = new Scanner(System.in);
    String serial;
    AutoOptions auto = new AutoOptions();

    System.out.print("Enter serial number: ");
    serial = stdIn.nextLine();
    auto.specifyEngine(auto.setSerial(serial).
      specifyFrame().specifyBody().isTight());
    auto.specifyTransmission();
    auto.printOptions();
  } // end main
} // end class AutoOptionsDriver
```

```
/**************************************************************
* AutoOptions.java
* Dean & Dean
*
* This class records options for "custom" automobiles.
**************************************************************/

```

```
import java.util.Scanner;

public class AutoOptions
{
  private String serial;      // automobile serial number
  private char frame = 'x';   // frame type: A,B
  private String body = "";   // body style: 2Door,4Door
  private int hp = 0;         // engine horsepower: 85, 115, 165

  // transmission: false = manual, true = automatic
  private boolean automatic = false;

  //*************************************************************

  public AutoOptions setSerial(String serial)
  {
    this.serial = serial;
    return this;
  } // end setSerial

  //*************************************************************

  public AutoOptions specifyFrame()
  {
    Scanner stdIn = new Scanner(System.in);

    while (this.frame != 'A' && this.frame != 'B')
    {
      System.out.print("Enter frame (A or B): ");
      this.frame = stdIn.nextLine().charAt(0);
    } // end while
    return this;
  } // end specifyFrame

  //*************************************************************

  public AutoOptions specifyBody()
  {
    Scanner stdIn = new Scanner(System.in);

    while (!this.body.equals("2-door")
      && !this.body.equals("4-door"))
    {
      System.out.print(
        "Enter (2-door or 4-door): ");
      this.body = stdIn.nextLine();
    } // end while
    return this;
  } // end specifyBody

```

```
//***********************************************************

public boolean isTight()
{
  boolean tight = false;

  if (this.frame == 'A' && this.body.equals("4-door"))
  {
    tight = true;
  }
  return tight;
} // end isTight

//***********************************************************

public void specifyEngine(boolean tight)
{
  Scanner stdIn = new Scanner(System.in);

  if (tight)
  {
    while (this.hp != 85 && this.hp != 115)
    {
      System.out.print("Enter HP (85 or 115): ");
      this.hp = stdIn.nextInt();
    } // end while
  }
  else
  {
    while (this.hp != 85 && this.hp != 115 && this.hp != 165)
    {
      System.out.print("Enter HP (85, 115, 165): ");
      this.hp = stdIn.nextInt();
    } // end while
  } // end if tight else
  stdIn.nextLine(); // flush \r\n after nextInt
} // end specifyEngine

//***********************************************************

public void specifyTransmission()
{
  Scanner stdIn = new Scanner(System.in);

  System.out.print("Automatic (y/n?): ");
  if (stdIn.nextLine().charAt(0) == 'y')
  {
    this.automatic = true;
  }
} // end specifyTransmission
```

```
  //*****************************************************************

  public void printOptions()
  {
    System.out.printf("serial# %s\n%s frame\n%s\n%-3d HP\n",
      this.serial, this.frame, this.body, this.hp);
    if (automatic)
    {
      System.out.println(" automatic");
    }
    else
    {
      System.out.println("4-speed manual");
    }
  } // end printOptions
} // end class AutoOptions
```

Use the following trace setup to trace the AutoOptions program. Note that we have used abbreviations to keep the trace setup's width as small as possible.

<u>input</u>

X142R
A
4-door
165
115
Y

AutoOptionsDriver			AutoOptions																
	main			setSerial		spec Frame	spec Body	isTight		specEngine		spec Trans	print Opt	obj1					
line#	ser	auto	*line#*	this	ser	this	this	this	tight	this	tight	this	this	ser	frm	body	hp	auto	output

7. [after §7.6] In the following `Time` and `TimeDriver` class skeletons, replace the italicized <*insert . . .*> lines with your own code such that the program operates properly. More specifically:
   a) In the `Time` class, provide a method definition for the `setHours` method such that `setHours` can be called as part of a method-call chain.
   b) In the `TimeDriver` class, provide a single statement that chains calls to the `setHours`, `setMinutes`, `setSeconds`, and `printTime` methods. Use reasonable values for your method-call arguments. If you pass 8 to `setHours`, 59 to `setMinutes`, and 0 to `setSeconds`, then your method-call-chaining statement should print this:

   ```
   08:59:00
   ```

```
public class Time
{
  private int hours;
  private int minutes;
  private int seconds;
```

```
  //**********************************************************

  <insert setHours method definition here>

  public Time setMinutes(int minutes)
  {
    this.minutes = minutes;
    return this;
  } // end setMinutes

  public Time setSeconds(int seconds)
  {
    this.seconds = seconds;
    return this;
  } // end setSeconds

  //************************************************************

  public void printTime()
  {
    System.out.printf("%02d:%02d:%02d\n", hours, minutes, seconds);
  } // end printTime
} // end Time class

public class TimeDriver
{
  public static void main(String[] args)
  {
    Time time = new Time();
    <insert chained-method-calls statement here>
  }
} // end TimeDriver class
```

8. [after §7.7]

a) Modify the two-parameter `setHeight` method in Figure 7.10 to make it test its `units` parameter to see if `units` is equal to one of the following allowable symbols: "m," "cm," "mm," "in," or "ft." If it is equal to one of these, set the instance variables and return `true`. If it is not equal to one of these, return `false`.

b) Does this modification *require* any change to any program that calls the two-argument `setHeight` method? Why or why not?

c) Write a statement that calls the modified method and utilizes the returned information to print an error message "Error: units not recognized" if the units argument is not one of the allowed values.

9. [after §7.8] Provide a standard three-parameter constructor for a class named `JewelryItem`. The class contains three instance variables—`description`, `price`, and `qtyOnHand`. The constructor simply assigns its three parameters to the three instance variables.

10. [after §7.9] Overloaded Constructors:

a) Add a pair of constructors to the `Height` class that implement the initializations provided by the two `setHeight` operations in Figure 7.11. Minimize the total number of statements by having the one-parameter constructor call the one-parameter `setHeight` method and having the two-parameter constructor call the two-parameter `setHeight` method.

b) Provide a complete, rewritten `main` method for the `HeightDriver` class such that the new `main` method uses one of the new constructors from part a) to generate this output:

```
6.0 ft
```

11. [after §7.9] Overloaded Constructors:

Assume that the `Height` class of Figure 7.10 contains only one `setHeight` method—the two-parameter version. Write two constructors for the `Height` class, one with one argument (`double height`), and the other with two arguments (`double height` and `String units`). For the one-argument constructor, use the default of "m" for `units`.

Do not duplicate any internal code. That is, have the one-parameter constructor transfer control to the two-parameter constructor, and have the two-parameter constructor transfer control to the two-parameter `setHeight` method.

12. [after §7.9]: Assume that the following two classes are compiled and run. What is their output?

```
public class SillyClassDriver
{
  public static void main(String[] args)
  {
    SillyClass sc = new SillyClass();
    sc.display();
  }
} // end SillyClassDriver class

public class SillyClass
{
  private int x = 10;

  public SillyClass()
  {
    this(20);
    System.out.println(this.x);
  }

  public SillyClass(int x)
  {
    System.out.println(this.x);
    System.out.println(x);
    this.x = 30;
    x = 40;
  }

  public void display()
  {
    int x = 50;
    display(x);
    System.out.println(x);
  }
```

```
    public void display(int x)
    {
      x += 10;
      System.out.println(x);
    }
} // end SillyClass class
```

Review Question Solutions

1. False. It just allocates memory for a reference variable.
2. The `new` operator allocates memory for an object and returns the address of where that object is stored in memory.
3. False. Assigning a reference variable to another reference variable causes the address in the right side's reference variable to be put into the left side's reference variable. And that makes both reference variables refer to the same object.
4. A memory leak is when an inaccessible object is allowed to persist and use up space in a computer's memory.
5. The final value of `same` is `true`.
6. The return type of an `equals` method is `boolean`.
7. The == operator compares the values of two variables of the same type. If the variables are reference variables, == compares their addresses to see if they refer to the same object. An `equals` method typically compares the values of all the instance variables in the object referred to by its parameter with the values of corresponding instance variables in the object that called it. The `equals` method returns `true` only if all corresponding instance variables have the same values.
8. True. The reference gives the method access to the reference's object.
9. For a method to be called as part of a method-call-chaining statement, include these things:
   - Within the method body, specify `return` <*reference-variable*>;
   - Within the method heading, specify the reference variable's associated class as the return type.
10. If you have two or more methods with the same name in the same class, they're called overloaded methods.
11. True.
12. A constructor does not have a return type and it does not use a `return` statement, but when you call a constructor, `new` returns a reference to the constructed object.
13. True.
14. False. Standard coding conventions suggest that you put constructor definitions <u>before</u> all other method definitions.
15. False. There is only one constructor, because if a class contains a programmer-defined constructor, then the compiler does not provide a default constructor.
16. Use this syntax:

    `this(`<*arguments-for-target-constructor*>`);`
17. True.

18. For the component in question, you declare an instance reference variable for the container or other component you want it to know about. Then when you instantiate the component in question, you pass its constructor a reference to the container or other component, and you have its constructor initialize the corresponding instance reference variable.

19. In your definition of the container class, you declare an instance reference variable for each prospective component. In the container constructor you instantiate each component and assign a reference to it to the corresponding instance reference variable.

CHAPTER 8

Software Engineering

Objectives

- Develop good coding style.
- Learn how to simplify complicated algorithms by encapsulating subordinate tasks.
- Distinguish use of instance variables and local variables.
- Learn when and how to use a top-down design strategy.
- Learn when and how to use a bottom-up design strategy.
- Resolve to use prewritten software whenever feasible.
- Recognize role of prototyping.
- Develop habit of frequent and thorough testing.
- Avoid unnecessary use of the `this` prefix.

Outline

8.1 Introduction

In Chapters 6 and 7, we looked mostly at the "science" of Java programming—how to declare objects, define classes, define methods, and so on. In this chapter, we'll be looking more at the "practice" of Java programming—how to design and develop a program, and how to make it easy to read. The practice of programming is nicely summed up in the term *software engineering,* where software engineering is:[1]

1. The application of a systematic, disciplined, quantifiable approach to the development, operation, and maintenance of software, that is, the application of engineering to software.
2. The study of approaches as in 1.

We start the chapter with an in-depth discussion of coding-style conventions that help make programs more readable. We show how to divide a large task into a set of smaller tasks by delegating some of the work in a method to other methods. We discuss encapsulation, one of the cornerstones of proper OOP design. Next, we describe alternative design strategies—top-down, bottom-up, and case-based. As you work with something, your understanding of it improves, and we suggest that you plan to continuously redesign with more sophistication in an evolutionary process called *iterative enhancement.* We emphasize that you'll be happier and your product will be better if you test thoroughly and frequently as you go along. To facilitate modular testing, we show how you can include a `main` method in each class. Up until now we've made heavy use of `this` to emphasize that each execution of an instance method is uniquely tied to a particular object, but near the end of the chapter we show how you can streamline your code by omitting `this` when there is no ambiguity. In a final optional section, we show how you can use simple graphics to construct a handy organizational tool called CRC cards.

8.2 Coding-Style Conventions

We'll now present some guidelines for coding style. We've mentioned and illustrated many of these style guidelines previously, so much of this section should be review. We'll provide more guidelines later as we describe more Java. For a complete list of all the coding-style guidelines used in this book, refer to Appendix 5, "Java Coding-Style Conventions." The coding-style conventions we use are for the most part a simplified subset of the style conventions presented in Sun's Java Code Conventions Web site.[2] If you have a style question that is not addressed in Appendix 5, refer to Sun's Web site.

We realize there are some style issues where there is legitimate disagreement over the best way to do things. Many different standards exist. Sun attempts to choose the best conventions from among the commonly used conventions. We attempt to do the same. If you're reading this book as part of a course and your teacher disagrees with the book's style conventions or Sun's style conventions, please follow your teacher's guidelines. One thing in particular that your teacher might require is special formatting for class and method documentation. Many professional Java programmers use Java's `javadoc` tool to aid with class and method documentation. The `javadoc` tool extracts specially commented documentation from the source code and displays it in a neatly organized report. Sun uses the javadoc tool to produce its API library documentation. See Appendix 6 for details.

---

[1] Definition taken from Institute of Electrical and Electronics Engineers (IEEE) Standard 610.12.

[2] http://java.sun.com/docs/codeconv

We'll illustrate coding-style conventions by referring to the Student program in Figure 8.1 and Figures 8.2a and 8.2b. This program is a modified version of the Student program at the back of the "Java Coding-Style Conventions" appendix.

Prologue Section

Note the boxed text at the tops of Figures 8.1 and 8.2a. They're called *prologues.* Include a prologue section at the top of each file. The prologue contains these things in this order:

- line of asterisks
- filename
- programmer name(s)
- blank line with one asterisk
- description
- line of asterisks
- blank line

Enclose the prologue in a `/*...*/` comment, and to make the prologue look like a box, insert an asterisk and a space in front of the filename, programmer name, blank line, and description lines.

Named Constants and Instance Variables

Provide a blank line, a line of asterisks, and another blank line after the block of statements that declares and/or initializes all named constants and instance variables.

```
/*************************************************************
* StudentDriver.java
* Dean & Dean
*
* This class acts as a driver for the Student class.
*************************************************************/

public class StudentDriver
{
  public static void main(String[] args)
  {
    Student s1;  // first student
    Student s2;  // second student

    s1 = new Student();
    s1.setFirst("Adeeb");
    s1.setLast("Jarrah");
    s2 = new Student("Heejoo", "Chun");
    s2.printFullName();
  } // end main
} // end class StudentDriver
```

Figure 8.1 `StudentDriver` class

```
/*********************************************************************
* Student.java
* Dean & Dean
*
* This class handles processing of a student's name.
*********************************************************************/

import java.util.Scanner;

public class Student
{
  private String first = ""; // student's first name
  private String last = "";  // student's last name

  //*******************************************************************

  public Student()
  { }

  // This constructor verifies that each passed-in name starts
  // with an uppercase letter and follows with lowercase letters.

  public Student(String first, String last)
  {
    setFirst(first);
    setLast(last);
  }

  //*******************************************************************
```

Figure 8.2a `Student` class—part A

Method Descriptions

Note the descriptions above one of the constructors in Figure 8.2a and the methods in Figure 8.2b. Put things in this order above each method:

- blank line
- line of asterisks
- blank line
- description
- blank line

For short obvious methods, it's OK to omit the method description. Between short constructors and between short accessor and mutator methods, it's also OK to omit the line of asterisks.

```
  // This method verifies that first starts with an uppercase
  // letter and contains lowercase letters thereafter.

  public void setFirst(String first)
  {
    // [A-Z][a-z]* is a regular expression. See API Pattern class.
    if (first.matches("[A-Z][a-z]*"))
    {
      this.first = first;
    }
    else
    {
      System.out.println(first + " is an invalid name.\n" +
        "Names must start with an uppercase letter and have" +
        " lowercase letters thereafter.");
    }
  } // end setFirst

  //*******************************************************************

  // This method verifies that last starts with an uppercase
  // letter and contains lowercase letters thereafter.

  public void setLast(String last)
  {
    // [A-Z][a-z]* is a regular expression. See API Pattern class.
    if (last.matches("[A-Z][a-z]*"))
    {
      this.last = last;
    }
    else
    {
      System.out.println(last + " is an invalid name.\n" +
        "Names must start with an uppercase letter and have" +
        " lowercase letters thereafter.");
    }
  } // end setLast

  //*******************************************************************

  // Print the student's first and last names.

  public void printFullName()
  {
    System.out.println(this.first + " " + this.last);
  } // end printFullName
} // end class Student
```

Figure 8.2b Student class—part B

Blank Lines

In general, use blank lines to separate logical chunks of code. In Figure 8.1's `StudentDriver` class, note the blank lines:

- Between the prologue section and the class definition.
- Right after a method's local variable declarations.

It's not shown in the Student program, but for long methods, it's appropriate to insert blank lines between logically separate chunks of code within the method. Also, when a comment line appears within the body of the code, it's nice to have white space above that comment to make it more visible.

Meaningful Names

Use meaningful names for your classes and variables. For example, `Student` is a good name for the class in Figures 8.2a and 8.2b because the class models a student. Similarly, `setName` would be a good name for a mutator method that sets a student's `first` and `last` name instance variables, and `getLast` would be a good name for an accessor method that returns the last name.

Braces and Indentations

As shown in Figure 8.1 and Figures 8.2a and 8.2b, place opening braces ({) immediately below the first letter of the preceding line. Indent everything that's logically inside the brace. When you're done with a block (that is, when you're ready for the closing brace), "outdent" so the opening and closing braces for a particular block are aligned. By following this indent-outdent scheme, you'll always align opening and closing brace partners in the same column. For example, note how the `Student` class's opening and closing braces are both in the same column.

Our recommendation on where to put the opening brace ({) is different from Sun's recommendation, which is that the opening brace be at the end of the previous line, like this:

```
public void setName(String first, String last) {
  this.first = first;
  this.last = last;
}
```

This is one of the few places where our recommendation differs from Sun's recommendation. Many programmers follow the recommendation we prefer, because it provides better visual bracketing of the block of code that the braces define. However, placing the opening brace at the end of the previous line makes the code a little tighter, and if you or your teacher or your boss wants the opening brace at the end of the previous line, you have our blessing to follow that convention.

Be consistent with your indentations. Any indentation width between two and five is acceptable as long as you're consistent throughout your program. We use two spaces in the book because book page widths are less than computer screen widths, and we don't want to run out of room for programs with deep nesting.

Many novice programmers indent improperly. They either don't indent when they should indent, or they indent when they shouldn't indent, or they use inconsistent widths for their indents. That leads to programs that are unprofessional looking and difficult to read. Some novice programmers postpone entering their indents until the end, after they've finished debugging. Big mistake! Use proper indentation as you enter your program. That should be pretty easy since there are really only two rules to remember:

1. Use braces to surround a block of code that is logically inside something else.
2. Indent the code that is inside the braces.

There is one exception to the first rule:

> Code that follows a `switch` statement's `case` clause is considered to be logically inside the `case` clause, but braces are not used.

Variable Declarations

As shown in Figure 8.1's `main` method, place all local variable declarations at the top of the method (even though that's not required by the compiler). Exception: Unless you need a `for` loop iteration variable to persist beyond the end of the `for` loop, declare it in the initialization field of the `for` loop header.

Normally, specify only one variable declaration per line. Exception: If several variables with obvious meanings are intimately related, it's OK to group them on one line.

Include a comment for every variable whose meaning is not obvious. For example, the cryptic local variable declarations in the `main` method in Figure 8.1 definitely need comments, and we also provide comments for the instance-variable declarations in Figure 8.2a. Note how those comments are aligned—their `//`'s are in the same column. In general, if you have comments that appear at the right side of several nearby lines, try to align those comments.

Line Wrap

If you have a statement that is too long to fit on one line, split it at one or more natural breaking points within the statement. For example, note where we break the long print statement in Figure 8.2b's `setFirst` and `setLast` methods. We consider these to be natural breaking points:

- right after the opening parenthesis
- after a concatenation operator
- after a comma that separates parameters
- at whitespace in expressions

After a break point in a long statement, indent the remaining part of the statement on the next line. In Figure 8.2b, note how we indented the continuation lines with the same standard two-space width that we use for all other indentations.

Rather than simply indenting continuation lines with the standard indentation width, some programmers prefer to align continuation lines with a parallel entity on the previous line. For example, in the aforementioned print statement, they would align the continuation line with `first` like this:

```
System.out.println(first +
                   " is an invalid name.\n" +
                   " Names must start with an uppercase" +
                   " letter and have lowercase letters" +
                   " thereafter.");
```

In our opinion, the above code is pushed too far to the right and is unnecessarily chopped up. That's why we prefer to keep it simple and just indent with the normal indentation width.

Braces That Surround One Statement

For a loop statement or an `if` statement that includes only one subordinate, it's legal to omit the braces around the statement. For example, in Figure 8.2b's `setFirst` method, the if-else statement could be written like this:

```
if (first.matches("[A-Z][a-z]*"))
  this.first = first;
else
  System.out.println(first + " is an invalid name.\n" +
    "Names must start with an uppercase letter and have" +
    " lowercase letters thereafter.");
```

However, we like to use braces for all loop statements and `if` statements, even if there is only one enclosed statement. Why?

- Braces provide a visual cue for remembering to indent.
- Braces help you avoid a logical mistake if you add code later that's supposed to be within the loop statement or the `if` statement.

The second point can best be understood with an example. Assume that a program contains this code:

```
if (person1.isFriendly())
  System.out.println("Hi there!");
```

Assume that a programmer wants to add a second print statement ("How are you?") for a friendly `person1` object. A careless programmer might do it like this:

```
if (person1.isFriendly())
  System.out.println("Hi there!");
  System.out.println("How are you?");
```

Since the second print statement is not within braces, it is executed regardless of whether `person1` is friendly. And do you want to ask an unfriendly person "How are you?" You might get a scowl for a response.

On the other hand, if the program followed our style guidelines, the original code would look like this:

```
if (person1.isFriendly())
{
  System.out.println("Hi there!");
}
```

Then if a programmer wants to add a second print statement ("How are you?") for a friendly `person1` object, it would be harder to make a mistake. Even a careless programmer would probably code the second print statement correctly like this:

```
if (person1.isFriendly())
{
  System.out.println("Hi there!");
  System.out.println("How are you?");
}
```

In our above discussion, we said that "we like to use braces for all loop statements and `if` statements." More formally stated, we like to use a *block* for all loop statements and `if` statements. A block is a set of statements surrounded by braces.

Comments

As shown in Figure 8.1 and Figures 8.2a and 8.2b, for all but the shortest blocks, include a comment after a closing brace in order to specify the block that is being closed. For example, in Figure 8.2b, note this closing brace line for the `setFirst` method:

```
} // end setFirst
```

Why is that good practice? So someone reading the program can quickly identify the block that is being ended without having to scroll to the top of the block to find out. It's OK to omit closing-curly-brace comments for short blocks of less than about five lines. For short blocks, it's easy to tell what block the closing brace is attached to, and the final comment just adds clutter.

Include comments for code segments that would not be obvious to a typical Java programmer. In Figure 8.2b, notice this comment that appears at the tops of the bodies of the `setFirst` and `setLast` methods:

```
// [A-Z][a-z]* is a regular expression. See API Pattern class.
```

Direct reader to more info.

This comment is helpful because the subsequent statement is more obscure than most. The comment should either explain directly or help the programmer find more information on the topic, or both. A comment like this that references an authoritative source is especially important whenever code implements something mysterious—an arbitrary definition like the "regular expression" above, a formula with empirical coefficients, or a mysterious mathematical expression.

Whenever a comment is too long to fit at the right of the line that is being explained, put it on one or more lines by itself above the line that is being explained. The // should be indented the same as the described line. If you put a comment on a line by itself, make sure there is sufficient whitespace above it. In the `setFirst` and `setLast` methods of Figure 8.2b, there's sufficient whitespace above the comments because the prior lines happen to be opening braces for their respective method bodies. In other cases, you'll need to insert a full blank line above the comment. It's optional whether you insert a blank line below it.

Do not add individual comments that just restate what the code already tells you. For example, for the first assignment statement in Figure 8.1's `main` method, this comment would be overkill:

```
s1 = new Student();    // instantiate a Student object
```

Developing readable programs is an important skill and a bit of an art form. Having too few comments is bad because it leads to programs that are difficult to understand. But having too many comments is also bad because it leads to cluttered programs that are difficult to wade through. There's a similar balancing act for blank lines. Having too few blank lines is bad because it leads to programs that are difficult to understand. But having too many blank lines is also bad because it leads to programs with too much dead space.

Blank Spaces

As shown in Figure 8.1 and Figures 8.2a and 8.2b, include blank spaces:

- after the single asterisks in the prologue
- before and after all operators (except for the operators inside a `for` loop header)
- between a closing brace and the //'s for its associated comment
- after the //'s for all comments
- after the `if`, `while`, and `switch` keywords

On the other hand, do not include blank spaces:

- between a method call and its opening parenthesis
- within each of the three components in a `for` loop header

The last point can best be understood with an example. Here is a nicely written `for` loop header:

```
for (int i=0; i<10; i++)
```

Note that there are no spaces surrounding the = operator or the < operator. Why is that good practice? Because the `for` loop header is inherently complex. In order to temper that complexity, we add visual cues to compartmentalize the `for` loop header. More specifically, we consolidate each section (no spaces within each section), and we insert a space after each semicolon to keep the three sections separate.

Grouping Constructors, Mutators, and Accessors

For short, obvious methods, you should omit descriptions. For example, mutators and accessors are short and obvious, so you should omit descriptions for them. Constructors are sometimes short and obvious, but not always. If a constructor simply assigns parameter values to associated instance variables, then it is short and obvious and you should omit a description for it. If, on the other hand, a constructor performs non-obvious input validation on user-entered values prior to assigning them into associated instance variables, then you should include a description for the constructor.

In the interest of grouping similar things together, we recommend omitting the line of asterisks between mutators and accessors and between short obvious constructors. Assuming that a class contains two short, obvious constructors, several mutator and accessor methods, and two short, obvious other methods, here's the framework for such a class:

```
<class-heading>
{
   <instance-variable-declarations>

   //**********************************************************

   <constructor-definition>

   <constructor-definition>

   //**********************************************************

   <mutator-definition>

   <mutator-definition>

   <accessor-definition>

   <accessor-definition>

   //**********************************************************

   <method-definition>

   //**********************************************************

   <method-definition>
}
```

For this case, there are no descriptions for the constructors, the accessors, or the mutators. There is a line of asterisks above the first mutator, but not above the subsequent mutator and accessors. These omissions make the program more readable by grouping similar things together.

8.3 Helper Methods

In the first four chapters, we solved essentially every problem we addressed in just one module—the `main` method in one class. As problems get bigger, however, it becomes more and more necessary to partition them into subproblems, each of which has a manageable size. We started doing this in Chapter 5 when our `main` method called on some of Java's API methods for help. Then in Chapter 6 and Chapter 7, we split our programs into two classes—a driver class, which contained the `main` method, and a driven class, which contained all other methods. At the end of Chapter 7 we introduced the concept of multiple driven classes, each of which contained other methods. Then, part of the partitioning came from splitting the program into two or more classes, and part of the partitioning came from defining multiple methods in each class. This enabled the `main` method in the driver class to delegate most of its work to methods in other classes.

In a broad sense, you could say that all of the other methods called by code in the `main` method are "helper methods"—they help the `main` method do its job. In other words, in a broad sense, any method that is called by another method is a helper method—the called method helps the calling method. The calling method is a *client,* and the called method (the broad-sense helper method) is a *server.*

You can narrow the definition of helper method by restricting it to a called method that happens to be in the same class as the calling method. In the previous section, the `Student` constructor of Figure 8.2a calls two of the same class's methods, `setFirst` and `setLast`, in Figure 8.2b. Presumably, these mutators were written to allow a user to change the instance variables in an object after the object was originally initialized. But once their code is written, why not reuse it? By including calls to these two ordinary methods in the constructor, we avoid duplication of the code in the called methods. Because the `setFirst` and `setLast` mutator methods each include a significant amount of error-checking code that helps the constructor do its job, this organization helps divide the problem into smaller chunks.

You can narrow the definition of helper method even more. Up to this point, all methods we've covered have used the `public` access modifier. These `public` methods are part of the class's *interface,* because they are responsible for the communication between an object's data and the outside world. Sometimes, you'll want to create a method that is not part of the interface; instead it just supports the operation of other methods within its own class. This special type of method—a method that is in the same class and has a `private` access modifier—is often called a *helper method.*

For example, suppose you're asked to write a program that handles order entries for sports-uniform shirts. For each shirt order, the program should prompt the user for a shirt's primary color and its trim color. For each color selection, the program should perform the same input validation. It should verify that the entered color is one of three values—w, r, or y, for white, red, or yellow. That input validation code is nontrivial. It's in charge of:

- Prompting the user for a color entry.
- Checking whether the entry is valid.
- Repeating the prompt if the entry is invalid.
- Converting the single-character color entry to a full-word color value.

These four tasks are a coherent group of activities. Therefore, it's logical to encapsulate them (bundle them together) in a separate module. The fact that the `Shirt` constructor needs to perform this coherent group of activities two separate times provides an additional reason to encapsulate them in a separate module.

Thus, instead of repeating the complete code for these four tasks in the constructor each time color selection is needed, you should put this color-selection code in a separate helper method and then call that method whenever color selection is needed. Study the Shirt program and sample session in Figures 8.3, 8.4a, and 8.4b, especially the `public` constructor, `Shirt`, and the `private` helper method, `selectColor`. Note how the constructor calls the `selectColor` method twice. In this particular case (and in the previous section's `Student` class), the helper method calls are from a constructor. You can also call a helper method from any ordinary method in the same class.

There are two main benefits to using helper methods:

First, by moving some of the details from `public` methods into `private` methods, they enable the `public` methods to be more streamlined. That leads to `public` methods whose basic functionality is more apparent. And that in turn leads to improved program readability.

Second, using helper methods can reduce code redundancy. Why is that? Assume that a particular task (such as color input validation) needs to be performed at several places within a program. With a helper method, the task's code appears only once in the program, and whenever the task needs to be performed, the helper method is called. On the other hand, without helper methods, whenever the task needs to be performed, the task's complete code needs to be repeated each time the task is done.

```
/*****************************************
* ShirtDriver.java
* Dean & Dean
*
* This is a driver for the Shirt class.
*****************************************/

public class ShirtDriver
{
  public static void main(String[] args)
  {
    Shirt shirt = new Shirt();

    System.out.println();
    shirt.display();
  } // end main
} // end ShirtDriver
```

<u>Sample session:</u>

```
Enter person's name: Corneal Conn
Enter shirt's primary color (w, r, y): m
Enter shirt's primary color (w, r, y): r
Enter shirt's trim color (w, r, y): w

Corneal Conn's shirt:
red with white trim
```

Figure 8.3 `ShirtDriver` class and associated sample session

Note that in Figure 8.4a, we call the `selectColor` method without a reference variable prefix:

```
this.primary = selectColor("primary");
```

Why is there no reference variable dot prefix? If you're in a constructor (or an instance method, for that matter), and you want the current object to call another method that's in the same class, the reference variable dot prefix is unnecessary. Since the constructor and the `selectColor` method are in the same class, no reference variable dot prefix is necessary.

```
/*********************************************************
* Shirt.java
* Dean & Dean
*
* This class stores and displays color choices for
* a sports-uniform shirt.
*********************************************************/

import java.util.Scanner;

public class Shirt
{
  private String name;       // person's name
  private String primary;    // shirt's primary color
  private String trim;       // shirt's trim color

  //******************************************************

  public Shirt()
  {
    Scanner stdIn = new Scanner(System.in);

    System.out.print("Enter person's name: ");
    this.name = stdIn.nextLine();

    this.primary = selectColor("primary");
    this.trim = selectColor("trim");
  } // end constructor

  //******************************************************

  public void display()
  {
    System.out.println(this.name + "'s shirt:\n" +
    this.primary + " with " + this.trim + " trim");
  } // end display

  //******************************************************
```

No need for a reference variable dot prefix here.

Figure 8.4a `Shirt` class—part A

Use the `private` access modifier for a helper method.

```
  // Helper method prompts for and inputs user's selection

  private String selectColor(String colorType)
  {
    Scanner stdIn = new Scanner(System.in);
    String color; // chosen color, first a letter, then a word

    do
    {
      System.out.print("Enter shirt's " + colorType +
        " color (w, r, y): ");
      color = stdIn.nextLine();
    } while (!color.equals("w") && !color.equals("r") &&
             !color.equals("y"));

    switch (color.charAt(0))
    {
      case 'w':
        color = "white";
        break;
      case 'r':
        color = "red";
        break;
      case 'y':
        color = "yellow";
    } // end switch

    return color;
  } // end selectColor
} // end class Shirt
```

Figure 8.4b `Shirt` class—part B: `selectColor` helper method

8.4 Encapsulation (With Instance Variables and Local Variables)

We say that a program exhibits encapsulation if its data is hidden; that is, if its data is difficult to access from the "outside world." Why is encapsulation a good thing? Since the outside world isn't able to directly access the encapsulated data, it's more difficult for the outside world to mess things up.

Encapsulation Implementation Guidelines

There are two main techniques for implementing encapsulation:

- First, break a big problem into separate classes where each class defines a set of encapsulated data that describe the current state of an object of that class. Encapsulate this object-state data by using the private access modifier for each such data item. As you already know, a class's object state data items are called instance variables.

- Second, break a class's tasks into separate methods, where each method holds a set of additional encapsulated data it needs to do its job. As you already know, a method's data items are called local variables.

Declaring instance variables within a class is one form of encapsulation, and declaring local variables within a method is another form of encapsulation. Which is the stronger (more hidden) form of encapsulation? All instance methods have access to all instance variables defined in the same class. On the other hand, only the current method has access to one of its local variables. Therefore, a local variable is more encapsulated than an instance variable. Thus, to promote encapsulation, use local variables, not instance variables, whenever possible.

In writing a method, you'll often find the need for more data than what's provided by the current instance variables. The question then becomes—how should you store that data? In another instance variable? Or locally? Try to resist the urge to add another instance variable. You should use instance variables only for storing fundamental attributes of the class's objects, not for storing additional details. If you can store the data locally, then do so. That furthers the goal of encapsulation. Usually when we think of storing data locally, we think of a local variable declared inside a method's body. Be aware that parameters are another way to store data locally. Remember that a parameter is declared in a method's heading—that tells us it has local scope.

Local Variables Versus Instance Variables in The `Shirt` Class

Now let's see how the above philosophy plays out in the `Shirt` class. The fundamental attributes of a shirt are its name, its primary color and its trim color. That's the basis for our declaration of the three instance variables declared in Figure 8.4a:

```
private String name;       // person's name
private String primary;    // shirt's primary color
private String trim;       // shirt's trim color
```

Now let's look at the other variables we need as we write the class's methods. All of these other variables are somehow associated with the `selectColor` method in Figure 8.4b. We need to transfer data in both directions between the calling `Shirt` constructor and the called `selectColor` method.

First, consider transfer of data into the `selectColor` method. If a shirt's primary color is needed, then `selectColor` should print this prompt message:

```
Enter shirt's primary color (w, r, b):
```

If a shirt's trim color is needed, then `selectColor` should print this prompt message:

```
Enter shirt's trim color (w, r, b):
```

We must transfer data into the `selectColor` method that tells the `selectColor` method which query to print. It would be possible to transfer this data by declaring another instance variable called `colorType`, have the `Shirt` constructor write a value to this instance variable, and then have the `selectorColor` method read the value of this instance variable. But this would be bad practice because it would break the encapsulation within the `selectColor` method and add confusing clutter to our nice clean list of object attributes. The proper way to implement this method-to-method communication is the way we did it, with an argument/parameter transfer.

Second, consider transfer of data out of the `selectColor` method. We also have to transfer data back from the `selectColor` method to the `Shirt` constructor. This data is the string representation of the selected color. There are three good ways to transfer data back to the calling method:

1. If there is only a single return value, you can send it back to the calling module as a `return` value.
2. If there is more than one value to return, you can assemble these values into an object, create that object in the helper method, and return a reference to that locally created "communication object."
3. You can pass into the helper method references to "communication objects" instantiated in the calling module and use code in the helper method to write to those objects.

It's also possible to transfer data back to the calling module by declaring other instance variables, having the helper method write values to them, and having the calling module read from them after the helper method terminates its execution. But this would be bad practice, because it would break the encapsulation and add confusing clutter to our nice clean list of object attributes. The proper way to implement this method-to-method communication is the way we did it, with a `return` value. In this case, the `return` value is a reference to a `String` object.

The `Shirt` class has one other variable to consider, the `stdIn` reference to a keyboard communication object. This particular object is used by both the calling constructor and the called helper method, and it is instantiated twice, once in each of those two modules. It is tempting to try to avoid duplicate instantiation by making `stdIn` an instance variable. And it will "work." But we recommend against it, because `stdIn` is clearly not a fundamental attribute of this class's objects. It's not a variable that describes the state of a shirt! In a later version of the program, you might want to change the method of input from the keyboard to something else, like a data file, described later in Chapter 15. You might even want to use one method of input for the name and a different method of input for the other state variables. Then you'd need to change `stdIn`, and you might want to change it in different ways for different methods. Declaring it local makes future modifications local also, and it's better design practice.

An argument used for not making a variable local is "maybe someday we'll need broader scope." If you have a specific plan that truly requires the broader scope you propose, OK. But if it's just "maybe someday," don't provide broader scope until that "someday" actually comes. Then, at that time, modify your program to increase scope only where it's absolutely necessary.

8.5 Design Philosophy

In the next several sections, we discuss alternative strategies for solving problems. That's plural "strategies" because there's not just one cookie-cutter strategy that can be used to solve all problems. If there were just one universal strategy, programming would be easy and anyone could do it. But it's not easy. That's why good programmers are in demand and earn a decent wage.

Simplistic Approach to Design

Here's a simplistic recipe for how to design things:

1. Figure out what you want to do.
2. Figure out how to do it.
3. Do it.
4. Test it.

At first this list seems like obvious common sense. But actually, it works only for very simple problems—problems where everything is easy and you don't need any recipe. What's wrong with this recipe?

First, if a problem is difficult, it's hard to know what its solution will be like. Often we need experience to know even what we want to do. Most clients recognize this and are flexible enough to accept a range of possible solutions. They want to avoid imposing arbitrary specifications that would cause them to miss inexpensive opportunities or incur expensive penalties. With difficult problems, people want to keep their options open.

Second, most problems have several alternate ways in which they can be solved. It takes some experimentation to determine the best way to solve a difficult problem. For very difficult problems, it's impossible to know exactly "how to do it" until we have done it.

Third, when we "do it," we must recognize it will not be perfect. There will be hidden errors. We will discover a better way to do it. The client will discover it would have been better to have asked for something different. And we'll need to do it again.

Fourth, if we defer testing of anything complicated until the end, we are almost sure to fail. The thing might pass its one final "test," but it will probably fail in its ultimate job, because one final test cannot catch all problems.

So, how can you deal with these difficulties?

1. Develop and maintain a sensible compromise between tight specification and flexibility.
2. Perform continuous testing at all levels. This helps you identify problems early when they are easy to fix, and it gives you objective assessment of progress. Suppose you're in charge of a large programming project, and you ask your programmers, "How's it coming?" You don't want them just to say, "fine." You want them to show you—by running tests that demonstrate what their current code actually does.

Testing

It's been said that, on average, experienced programmers make one mistake for every 8 or 10 lines of code.[3] Whew! That's a lot of mistakes. With such a high incidence of mistakes, we hope you're properly convinced about the importance of testing.

Testing has three aspects:

Check most obvious things first.

- First, subject your program to typical input values. If your program doesn't work with typical input values, you're in real trouble. Co-workers and end users may question your competence if your program generates wrong answers for the typical cases.
- Second, subject your program to input values that are at the boundaries of acceptability. These boundary tests often reveal subtle problems that wouldn't show up until later, and such problems might be much harder to fix at that time.
- Third, subject your program to invalid input values. In response to an invalid input value, your program should print a user-friendly message that identifies the problem and prompts the user to try again.

Testing is something that many people envision occurring after a product is finished. That's an unfortunate notion, because a lone test at the end of the production of a complicated product is almost worthless. If the product fails such a test, it may be hard to determine why it failed. If the fix requires many changes, a great deal of work may have been wasted. If the product does not fail a lone final test, you may be lulled into thinking everything is OK even when it's not. Passing a lone final test may actually be worse than failing a lone final test, because passing motivates you to release the product. It's much more costly to fix a problem after a product has been released. (Ray knows about this!) Bottom line—Don't wait until the end to start your testing. Test your program on a regular basis throughout the development process.

Novice programmers sometimes get the idea that it would be "unscientific" to form a pre-conception of what a test result should be before you do the test. That's wrong. It's important that you do have a good idea

[3] Of course, we, John and Ray, never make any mistakes. ☺

of what the test result should be before you perform a test. Before you push the "run" button, say out loud what you think the result should be! This improves your chance of recognizing an error.

Testing keeps you on track. In any development program, you should interleave testing and coding so that you get quick feedback. If an experienced programmer makes a mistake in every 8 or 10 lines of code, a new programmer is well advised to perform some kind of test after every 4 or 5 lines of new code! This makes it easy to identify errors, and it reduces your level of stress. The more frequently you test, the more positive feedback you get, and this helps your attitude—it gives you a "warm-fuzzy feeling." Frequent testing makes programming a more pleasant experience.

There is no practical way to verify all the aspects of a complicated system by looking at it only from the outside. Testing should be performed on each component and on combinations of components, at all levels. As you'll see in subsequent discussion, testing typically requires creation of some kind of extra testing code. Sometimes it's a special driver. Sometimes it's a special driven module. Creating such test code may seem like extra work for something that's to be used only in a test environment and not in an actual runtime environment. Yes, it is extra work, but it is well worth the effort. Writing and using test code will save you time in the long run, and it will lead to a better final product.

8.6 Top-Down Design

The dominant design methodology for large high-performance systems is the top-down design strategy. Top-down design requires the designer to think about the big picture first—that's the "top." After completing the design at the top, the designer works on the design at the next lower level. The design process continues in this iterative manner until the bottom level (the level with the most detail) is reached.

For an object-oriented programming project, top-down design means starting with a problem description and working toward a solution using these guidelines:

1. Decide on the classes that are needed. You should normally include a driver class as one of the classes. To determine the other classes, think of the problem in terms of its component objects. Specify one class for each unique type of object. With large systems that have many classes, pure top-down design defers identification of detailed classes until later, because identifying detail classes is itself a detail.
2. For each class, decide on its instance variables, which should be state variables identifying object attributes. The driver class should not have any instance variables.
3. For each class, decide on its `public` methods. The driver class should contain only one `public` method—`main`.
4. For each `public` method, implement in a top-down fashion. Consider each `public` method to be a "top" method. If it is fairly involved and can be broken into subtasks, have it call `private` helper methods to do the subtask work. Finish writing the top methods before starting to write the lower level helper methods. Initially, implement the helper methods as *stubs*. A stub is a dummy method that acts as a placeholder for an actual method. A stub's body typically consists of a print statement that displays something like "In method x, parameters = a, b, c" where x is the name of the method and a, b, and c are values of passed-in arguments. We'll show an example later in this section.

Start testing right away.

5. Test and debug the program. The suggested stub print messages will help you trace the program's actions.
6. Replace stub methods one at a time with fully implemented helper methods. After each replacement, test and debug the program again.

Top-down design is sometimes referred to as *stepwise refinement*. The term stepwise refinement is used because the methodology encourages programmers to implement solutions in an iterative manner where each solution "step" is a refined version of a previous solution step. After implementing top-level tasks, the programmer goes back and refines the solution by implementing the subtasks at the next lower levels.

Benefits of Using Top-Down Design

In top-down design, the designer doesn't worry initially about the details of subtask implementation. The designer focuses on the "big picture" first. Because it focuses on the big picture first, top-down design is good at getting a project going in the right direction. That helps to ensure that the completed program matches the original specifications.

Top-down design is particularly appropriate when a project involves many programmers. Its early emphasis on the big picture forces the project's programmers to agree on common goals. Its strong organizational emphasis promotes coherence and prevents the project from splintering off in different directions. The top-down design methodology facilitates tight managerial control.

Square Program Example: First-Cut Version

Let's now apply the top-down design methodology to a simple example. We'll implement a `Square` class such that each `Square` object can:

- Initialize the square's width.
- Calculate and return its area.
- Draw itself with asterisks using either an asterisks border or a solid pattern of asterisks. Each time the square is drawn, the user is prompted as to whether he/she would like a border format or a solid format, like one of these:

Devise a way to solve the problem.

```
border-format square      solid-format square
     width = 6                 width = 4

   * * * * * *                 * * * *
   *         *                 * * * *
   *         *                 * * * *
   *         *                 * * * *
   *         *
   * * * * * *
```

Using the above top-down design guidelines, the first step is to decide on the classes. In this simple example, it's easy to identify all the classes right at the start—`SquareDriver` and `Square`. The next step is to decide on the instance variables. They should be a minimum definitive set of object properties—state variables. All you need to specify a square is one number. The typical number that people use is the width. So we'll use `width` as our lone instance variable.

But what about the square's area? Area is a property, but it's a simple function of width: area equals width squared. Since we can easily calculate area from width, it would be redundant to include area as another state variable. In principle, we could use `area` as the only state variable, and calculate `width` as the square root of `area` any time we needed `width`. But computing the square root is more difficult than computing the square, and we would frequently end up with a non-integer value for `width`, which would be hard to display in our prescribed asterisk format. So, for our problem, it's a better strategy to use `width` as the lone instance variable.

What about the solidness of the square? This is a conceptual choice. If you want to think of solidness as an inherent property of `Square`-class objects, it's appropriate to create another instance variable like `boolean solid`. On the other hand, if you want to think of solidness as just a temporary display option, solidness should not have state-variable status and it should

Identify state variables.

not be an instance variable. For our example, we've elected to think of solidness as just a temporary display option, so we do not include it as another instance variable.

Returning to the top-down design guidelines, we see that the next step is to decide on the `public` methods. The problem description often determines what needs to be `public`. Here's what we need:

- a constructor that sets the square's width
- `getArea`—compute the square's area
- `draw`—display the square with asterisks using either an asterisks border or a solid pattern of asterisks

Let's now step back and look at what we've done so far. See Figure 8.5. It presents a first-cut UML class diagram for our solution's classes, instance variables, and constructor and `public` methods.

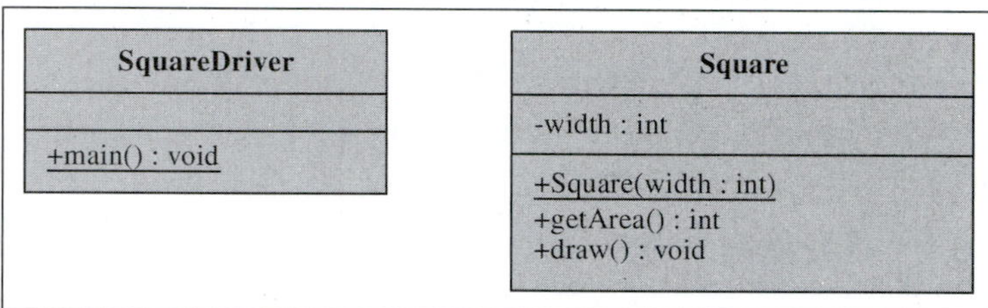

Figure 8.5 Square program's UML class diagrams: first-cut version

The next step in the top-down design process is to implement the `main` method in the top-level class This implementation appears in Figure 8.6. The code in `main` includes calls to the `Square` constructor and

```
/*************************************************************
* SquareDriver.java
* Dean & Dean
*
* This is the driver for the Square class.
*************************************************************/

import java.util.Scanner;

public class SquareDriver
{
  public static void main(String[] args)
  {
    Scanner stdIn = new Scanner(System.in);
    Square square;

    System.out.print("Enter width of desired square: ");
    square = new Square(stdIn.nextInt());
    System.out.println("Area = " + square.getArea());
    square.draw();
  } // end main
} // end class SquareDriver
```

Figure 8.6 `SquareDriver` class

methods identified in Figure 8.5, but it does not yet say anything about how those members of the `Square` class are implemented.

The next step is to implement the public methods in the `Square` class. This implementation appears in Figure 8.7a. The constructor and `getArea` methods are straightforward and do not need explanation. But notice that the "get" in `getArea` makes this method look like an accessor that simply retrieves an instance

```
/*************************************************************
* Square.java
* Dean & Dean
*
* This class manages squares.
*************************************************************/

import java.util.Scanner;

public class Square
{
  private int width;

  //**********************************************************

  public Square(int width)
  {
    this.width = width;
  }

  //**********************************************************

  public int getArea()
  {
    return this.width * this.width;
  }

  //**********************************************************

  public void draw()
  {
    Scanner stdIn = new Scanner(System.in);

    System.out.print("Print with (b)order or (s)olid? ");
    if (stdIn.nextLine().charAt(0) == 'b')
    {
      drawBorderSquare();
    }
    else
    {
      drawSolidSquare();
    }
  } // end draw
```

Figure 8.7a `Square` class: first-cut version—part A

variable. Is it OK to create this "false" impression? Yes, it is, because the instance variable is `private` and therefore hidden from public view. In fact, as noted above, we might actually have used `area` as the lone instance variable! A user of a class does not have to know exactly how it's implemented. Don't worry about the implementation when you pick a method name. It's the effect that matters, and `getArea` accurately describes the effect of calling that method.

The `draw` method prompts the user to choose a border format or a solid format for the square's display. It's now becoming apparent that the `draw` method is not trivial. The `drawBorderSquare` and `drawSolidSquare` method calls are examples of subtasks that we should split off into separate helper methods.

Stubs

Top-down design tells us to implement helper methods initially as stubs. For our Square program, that means implementing `drawBorderSquare` and `drawSolidSquare` as stubs. Note the stubs in Figure 8.7b.

```
  //*********************************************************

  private void drawBorderSquare()                    // a STUB
  {
    System.out.println("In drawBorderSquare");
  }

  //*********************************************************

  private void drawSolidSquare()                     // a STUB
  {
    System.out.println("In drawSolidSquare");
  }
} // end class Square
```

Figure 8.7b `Square` class: first-cut version—part B

As you can probably surmise from the examples, a stub doesn't do much. Its main purpose is to satisfy the compiler so that the program is able to compile and run. Its secondary purpose is to provide an output that confirms that the method was called, and (where appropriate) show values passed into that method. When the stubbed Square program runs, it produces either this sample session:

```
Enter width of desired square: 5
Area = 25.0
Print with (b)order or (s)olid? b
In drawBorderSquare
```

or this sample session:

```
Enter width of desired square: 5
Area = 25.0
Print with (b)order or (s)olid? s
In drawSolidSquare
```

Using stubs lets programmers test their partially implemented programs to determine whether their behavior is correct down to the stub level. Second, it makes debugging easier. After compiling and running the program successfully with stubs, replace the stubs with actual code one method at a time. As each stub is replaced, test and debug the updated program. If a bug appears, it should be easy to find since you know it's probably in the most recently replaced method.

Test one thing at a time.

Square Program Example: Second-Cut Version

The next step in the top-down design process is to replace the helper methods' stub implementations with actual implementations. We have two helper methods to work on—`drawBorderSquare` and `drawSolidSquare`.

Let's start with the `drawBorderSquare` helper method. It prints a horizontal line of asterisks, prints the square's sides, and then prints another horizontal line of asterisks. Here's pseudocode for this algorithm:

```
drawBorderSquare method
   draw horizontal line of asterisks
   draw sides
   draw horizontal line of asterisks
```

All three of `drawBorderSquare`'s draw statements represent non-trivial tasks. Thus, when we translate the `drawBorderSquare` pseudocode into a Java method, we use method calls for each of the draw subtasks:

```
private void drawBorderSquare()
{
  drawHorizontalLine();
  drawSides();
  drawHorizontalLine();
} // end drawBorderSquare
```

Now let's consider the `drawSolidSquare` helper method. It prints a series of horizontal lines of asterisks. Here's pseudocode for its algorithm:

```
drawSolidSquare method
   for (int i=0; i<square's width; i++)
      draw horizontal line of asterisks
```

Once again, the draw statement represents a non-trivial task. Thus, when we translate the `drawSolidSquare` pseudocode into a Java method, we use a repeated method call for the draw subtask:

```
private void drawSolidSquare()
{
  for (int i=0; i<this.width; i++)
  {
    drawHorizontalLine();
  }
} // end drawSolidSquare
```

Notice that the `drawBorderSquare` method and the `drawSolidSquare` method both call the same `drawHorizontalLine` helper method. Being able to share the `drawHorizontalLine` method is a nice reward for our diligent use of helper methods, and it provides a good example for this general principle:

> If two or more methods perform the same subtask, avoid redundant code by having those methods call a shared helper method that performs the subtask.

By writing final code for the `drawBorderSquare` and `drawSolidSquare` methods and writing stub code for the `drawHorizontalLine` and `drawSides` methods, we complete the coding for the Square program's second-cut version. When executed with appropriate print statements in the two stub methods, `drawHorizontalLine` and `drawSides`, the second-cut version produces either this sample session:

```
Enter width of desired square: 5
Area = 25.0
Print with (b)order or (s)olid? b
In drawHorizontalLine
In drawSides
In drawHorizontalLine
```

or this sample session:

```
Enter width of desired square: 5
Area = 25.0
Print with (b)order or (s)olid? s
In drawHorizontalLine
In drawHorizontalLine
In drawHorizontalLine
In drawHorizontalLine
In drawHorizontalLine
```

Square Program Example: Final Version

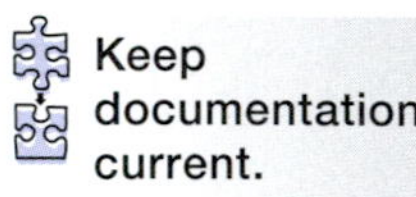

To facilitate management, it's a good idea to formalize your program's design at various points during the design process. The formalization usually takes the form of UML class diagrams. Having up-to-date UML class diagrams helps to ensure project coherence. At a minimum, current UML class diagrams ensure that all members of a project are using the same classes, instance variables, and method headings. See Figure 8.8.

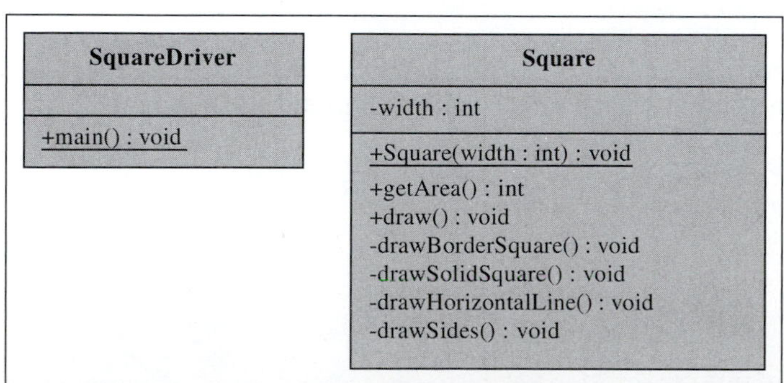

Figure 8.8 Square program's UML class diagram: final version

Figure 8.8 presents a UML class diagram for our complete Square program. It's the same as our earlier UML class diagram except that we've added the helper methods.

```
/**********************************************************
* Square.java
* Dean & Dean
*
* This class manages squares.
**********************************************************/

import java.util.Scanner;

public class Square
{
  private int width;

  //*********************************************************

  public Square(int width)
  {
    this.width = width;
  }

  //*********************************************************

  public double getArea()
  {
    return this.width * this.width;
  }

  //*********************************************************

  public void draw()
  {
    Scanner stdIn = new Scanner(System.in);

    System.out.print("Print with (b)order or (s)olid? ");
    if (stdIn.nextLine().charAt(0) == 'b')
    {
      drawBorderSquare();
    }
    else
    {
      drawSolidSquare();
    }
  } // end draw
```

Figure 8.9a `Square` class: final version—part A (an exact copy of Figure 8.7a.)

```
    //*****************************************************

    private void drawBorderSquare()
    {
      drawHorizontalLine();
      drawSides();
      drawHorizontalLine();
    } // end drawBorderSquare

    //*****************************************************

    private void drawSolidSquare()
    {
      for (int i=0; i<this.width; i++)
      {
        drawHorizontalLine();
      }
    } // end drawSolidSquare

    //*****************************************************

    private void drawHorizontalLine()
    {
      for (int i=0; i<this.width; i++)
      {
        System.out.print("*");
      }
      System.out.println();
    } // end drawHorizontalLine

    //*****************************************************

    private void drawSides()
    {
      for (int i=1; i<(this.width-1); i++)
      {
        System.out.print("*");
        for (int j=1; j<(this.width-1); j++)
        {
          System.out.print(" ");
        }
        System.out.println("*");
      }
    } // end drawSides
  } // end class Square
```

Figure 8.9b `Square` class: final version—part B (a fleshed-out version of Figure 8.7b)

The second-cut version of the Square program contains stub implementations for the `drawHorizontalLine` and `drawSides` methods. Now, we need to replace those stub methods with actual methods. Figures 8.9a and 8.9b contain our final version `Square` class. The only new items are the `drawHorizontalLine` and `drawSides` methods, which are straightforward. We encourage you to study their implementations on your own in Figure 8.9b.

Top-Down-Design Downside

Almost every human-designed project must necessarily include some form of top-down thinking. However, pure top-down design has some undesirable side effects. One such side effect is that subordinate modules tend to be overly specialized. A well-known and particularly egregious example of how the top-down way of thinking can lead to excessive specialization is the case of the $660 Pentagon ashtrays. The Pentagon (headquarters of the United States Department of Defense) hired a large military contractor to manufacture ashtrays for Pentagon use. Since compatibility is important for many military components, the military generally wants faithful adherence to its specifications, and contractors naturally develop procedures and attitudes that promote conformity. However, sometimes there can be too much of a good thing. The ashtrays conformed perfectly to their specification, but each one had a price of $660. Top-down design went to a ridiculous extreme. Even though some of the top-level specifications may have been unconventional, the contractor probably followed the standard operating procedure and tried to match them perfectly. Hypothetical quote from the contractor's marketing manager: "What was specified did not match anything that was available, so we had to make it by hand in the machine shop."

You may be thinking—Interesting story, but how do the $660 ashtrays relate to programming? The top-down philosophy can lead to inefficient development practices. In the extreme case, that philosophy led to the military contractor expending enormous effort on the design and manufacture of something as simple as an ashtray. In general, the top-down design philosophy can motivate people to "reinvent the wheel." This tends to increase overall product cost. It also tends to reduce the reliability of the final product. Why? Because with everything being new or reinvented, there's no past history of testing and debugging to rely on.

8.7 Bottom-Up Design

Now, let's look at the logical opposite of top-down design—bottom-up design. Bottom-up design implements specific low-level tasks first. To apply bottom-up design to the Square program, you might implement a `drawSolidSquare` method first. Next, you might implement a `drawBorderSquare` method. After finishing these bottom-level methods, you would implement higher-level methods, which are in charge of more general tasks, like a `draw` method to draw either type of square—a solid square or a border square.

As you implement each program component, you should test it immediately with a custom driver that's tailored to that particular component. You won't need any stubs, since already-tested lower-level methods will be available to be called by whatever higher-level method you are currently testing.

For simple programs like many of those that appear throughout the body of this book, bottom-up design is an appropriate strategy to use because it allows you to focus quickly on the essence of whatever problem is currently most critical, and it allows you to defer presentation details until later. For an example of bottom up design, look at any program in this book in which we present a driven class before we present a driver for that class. Whenever we do that, we are using a bottom up presentation, and we are inviting you to think about the program being described from the bottom up.

Bottom-up design also makes it easiest for you to use prewritten software, like that in the Java API and described previously in Chapter 5. The Java API is a particularly good source for prewritten software because its code is (1) optimized for high speed and low-memory consumption and (2) highly reliable because it has undergone testing and debugging for years. It's good to use the Java API, but it takes time to learn how to use it. To learn about the Java API, see Sun's Java API Web site at http://java.sun.com/javase/6/docs/api/. There, you'll find several ways to look things up. Here are two techniques:

1. Try guessing the name of a class that seems appropriate. Use the scrollbar in the classes frame to search for the guessed class name. There are about 4000 classes so finding a particular class requires a well-behaved mouse (we recommend proper diet and exercise to keep your mouse running smoothly). When you find a class name that looks promising, click on it and read about its public constants and methods.
2. Related classes are grouped together in about 166 packages. Use the scrollbar in the packages frame to find a package that looks promising. Click on that package and scroll through its classes. Again, when you find a class name that looks promising, click on it and read about its public constants and methods.

Using pre-written software for your low-level modules reduces development time and project cost. It also improves product quality, because presumably the pre-written parts of your program have already been thoroughly tested and debugged. As in the case of Java API code, you'll often find that pre-written low-level software is quite flexible, because it was designed for a broad spectrum of applications. This inherent low-level flexibility will make it easier for you to expand the capabilities of your program when you upgrade it in the future. Using pre-written software can facilitate parallel development. If several different programmers want to use a common subordinate module, they can do it independently. They do not have to coordinate their efforts, because that module's design is already established and stable.

Work on most critical problem first.

Another benefit of bottom-up design is that it provides freedom to implement tasks in the most beneficial order. If there's a significant concern as to whether a particular calculation is feasible, it's important to begin working on that calculation as soon as possible. With bottom-up design, there's no need to wait around to address the concern—just attack it immediately. That way, you can determine at the earliest possible time whether the concern will be a show stopper. Likewise, if there is some low-level task that will take a long time to complete, bottom-up design allows you to begin work on it immediately and avoid a potential bottleneck later.

There are several drawbacks to using bottom-up design, however. As compared to top-down design, bottom-up design provides less structure and guidance. It's often hard to know where to start, and because development is hard to predict, bottom-up programming projects are hard to manage. In particular, with less inherent guidance, it's harder for managers to keep their programmers on track. As a result, programmers might spend significant amounts of time working on code that may not be relevant to the final program. Another drawback in using bottom-up design is that it can lead to difficulties in getting the final product to conform precisely to design specifications. Top-down design facilitates conformity by addressing specifications in detail at the beginning. With bottom-up design, specifications receive only superficial consideration at the beginning.

So, when should you use bottom-up design? When you can use a substantial amount of pre-written and pre-tested low-level software, the bottom-up design process makes it easy for you to design around that software so that it fits naturally into your complete program. When you can use a substantial amount of pre-written software that is open to your inspection and already designed to fit together (like Java API software[4]), bottom-up design simultaneously promotes high quality and low cost. When low-level details are critical, bottom-up design motivates you to deal with the tough problems first it gives you the most time to solve them. Thus, bottom-up design can also help you minimize delivery time.

A familiar example of bottom-up software design is the early development of the Microsoft Windows operating system. The original version of Windows was built on top of the already existing and successful DOS operating system.[5] The next major version of Windows was built on top of a novel low-level software core called "NT" (for New Technology). It's important to note that the component source code in these cases was always open to and under the control of system developers, because it was all owned by the same company.[6]

8.8 Case-Based Design

There is another basic way to solve problems and design things. It's what normal people do most of the time in their everyday lives. Instead of going through a formal top-down or bottom-up sequence of steps, you look around for an already-solved problem that's like the problem at hand. Then you figure out how that problem was solved, and you modify that solution to fit your problem. This approach is holistic. It starts with a whole solution and "bends" that whole solution to a different application.

If you have access to source code and the right to copy it or modify it and then redistribute it in a new context, you can modify an existing program or significant parts of existing code. Sometimes the code you want to borrow is code you wrote yourself for a different application. Such code deserves your consideration, because you'll be intimately familiar with what it does and how it does it. For example, many of this book's projects were designed to show you how to solve a wide range of real-world problems. You can use the algorithms presented in the project assignments to generate Java code that solves particular versions of those problems. Once you have written that code, you'll be completely free to modify it and re-use it in any other context to solve other variations of those problems.

Frequently, the code you'd like to use will be code that somebody else wrote. Would it be theft or plagiarism to use such code? It might be. If the code is copyrighted, and you don't have permission to use it, you shouldn't try to use it. But you might have permission to use it. Whenever you use code that somebody else wrote, be sure to acknowledge and identify your source.

There is a growing body of what's called "free" software[7] that is debugged and maintained by a select body of experts, and it's available to all people to use and modify for their own purposes, provided they conform to certain reasonable rules. Basically, these rules are: acknowledge the source, and don't try to make a profit on resale of the original code. Sometimes this software is low-level code that you can use like Java API software. But sometimes it's a complete program, which you can adapt to a problem you're currently addressing.

[4] Although we have been encouraging you to think of Java API software as being completely encapsulated, Sun does not keep the Java API source code secret. It can be downloaded and is available for inspection by Java developers.

[5] The set of commands you can enter into a Microsoft Windows command-prompt window are essentially DOS commands—they are a software legacy of the IBM PC that came out in the early 1980s.

[6] In principle, it's possible to build software systems out of components that are Commercial-Off-The-Shelf (COTS) programs from different companies. This strategy can be used to avoid "reinventing the wheel" in a big way, and it minimizes new code to the "glue" that provides component interfaces. However, it takes longer to write this glue code than it does to write ordinary code. Moreover, since (in general) the system developer does not have access to component source code and does not have control of component evolution, the development process is relatively risky, and the resulting composite program is relatively brittle. COTS-based system design has a distinctive methodology that is outside the scope of this text.

[7] See http://www.fsf.org. The Free Software Foundation is "dedicated to promoting computer users' rights to use, study, copy, modify, and redistribute computer programs." Two famous examples of this kind of software are the GNU/Linux operating system (GNU stands for "Gnu's Not Unix") and the Apache software that underlies most Web servers (http://www.apache.org).

8.9 Iterative Enhancement

Often, you have to start working on a problem in order to understand how to solve the problem. That leads to a design process that is often iterative in nature. In the first iteration, you implement a bare-bones solution to the problem. In the next iteration, you add features and implement an improved solution. You continue adding features and repeating the design process until you have implemented a solution that does everything you need. This repetitive process is called *iterative enhancement*.

Prototyping—An Optional First Step

A *prototype* is a very "thin" or "bare-bones" implementation or perhaps just a faked "simulation" of a prospective program. Because of a prototype's limited scope, developers can produce prototypes relatively quickly and present them to customers very early in the development process.

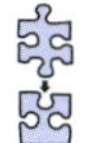

Make sure you are solving the right problem.

A prototype helps end users get an early feel for what it will be like to use the program—well before the program is finished. It helps clients provide early feedback that improves the quality of product specification. Thus, prototyping provides a valuable adjunct to the first part of the top-down design process, and it complements early work in a bottom-up design process. Without a prototype, there's always a risk that you'll solve the wrong problem. Even if you solve the problem with great elegance, if it's the wrong problem, the whole effort is a waste of time.

There are two basic ways to generate a prototype. One way is to write a very limited version of the final program in Java. Since a prototype should be relatively simple, you could use whatever design approach seemed easiest. The other way is to use a computer application that provides nice presentations to simulate the final program's user interface for particular "canned" data or a narrow range of user inputs.

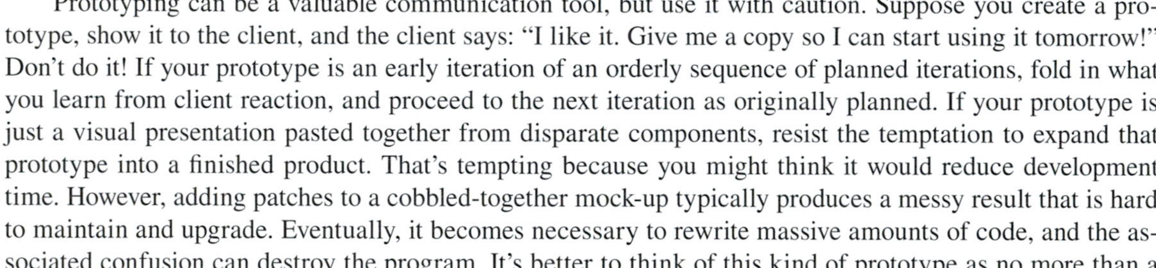

Prototyping can be a valuable communication tool, but use it with caution. Suppose you create a prototype, show it to the client, and the client says: "I like it. Give me a copy so I can start using it tomorrow!" Don't do it! If your prototype is an early iteration of an orderly sequence of planned iterations, fold in what you learn from client reaction, and proceed to the next iteration as originally planned. If your prototype is just a visual presentation pasted together from disparate components, resist the temptation to expand that prototype into a finished product. That's tempting because you might think it would reduce development time. However, adding patches to a cobbled-together mock-up typically produces a messy result that is hard to maintain and upgrade. Eventually, it becomes necessary to rewrite massive amounts of code, and the associated confusion can destroy the program. It's better to think of this kind of prototype as no more than a communication aid that elicits feedback which improves product specification.

Iterating

The first normal design iteration—or the iteration after an optional prototype—should be either a simple adaptation of some already existing program or a bare-bones implementation developed with either the top-down or bottom-up design strategy. Subsequent iterations may or may not continue to use the same design strategy.

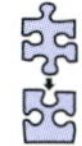

Adjust design strategy to address greatest current need with resources currently available.

How do you decide which strategy to use for each iteration? Select that strategy which best addresses your greatest current need or concern:

- If your greatest current need is to understand what the customer wants, construct a prototype.
- If your greatest concern is on-time delivery, try to use an adaptation of existing software.

- If your greatest current concern is whether some particular functionality can be implemented, use the bottom-up design strategy to implement that functionality as soon as possible.
- If your greatest needs are reliability and low cost, use pre-written software with bottom-up design.
- If your greatest concern is overall performance and managerial control, use the top-down design strategy.

A famous iterated-design example is NASA's man-on-the-moon space program. President Kennedy was thinking top-down when he announced the program. However, the first implementation was a prototype. Using a modified version of the existing Atlas ICBM rocket, "Project Mercury" shot one man a few hundred miles out into the Atlantic Ocean.

Subsequent iterations of Project Mercury used a bottom-up approach to put astronauts into earth orbit. Then, NASA replaced the Atlas booster rocket with the newer and larger Titan ICBM rocket, which carried several people into earth orbit in several iterations of "Project Gemini."

NASA's next iteration was a top-down design plan known as "Project Apollo." Project Apollo originally envisioned the use of a gigantic booster rocket called Nova. After working on that for awhile, NASA realized that a much smaller booster rocket (called Saturn) would suffice if a smaller moon lander was separated from the mother ship orbiting the moon, and the moon lander's return module was separated from its descent mechanism.

Project Apollo was a top-down design, optimized for NASA's requirements, rather than a bottom-up adaptation of existing military equipment. In the end, the top-down plan involving Nova was scrapped and replaced by a radically different top-down plan. This apparently erratic development sequence is a great example of successful real-world design. The history of successful software is the same. Different design cycles often emphasize different design strategies, and sometimes there are major changes.

Maintenance

After a program has been developed and put into operation, you might think there's no more need to work on it. Not so. In the real world, if a program is useful, programmers are often asked to *maintain* it long after that program is first put into operation. On average, 80% of the work on a successful program is done after the program is first put into operation. Maintenance consists of fixing bugs and making improvements. Maintenance is much easier if good software practices are employed at the beginning and throughout the life of the program. This includes writing the code elegantly in the first place, preserving elegance when you make changes, and providing and keeping complete and well organized documentation.

Remember that documentation is more than just comments for programmers reading source code. Documentation is also interface information for programmers who want to use already-compiled classes. Appendix 6 shows how to embed interface information in your source code so that it can be read by `javadoc` and presented like Sun's documentation of the Java API. Documentation also includes information for people who are not programmers at all but need to use a finished program. This type of documentation needs to be even more user-oriented than `javadoc`'s output.

If you are responsible for maintaining an existing program, here are some useful thumb rules:

1. Respect your predecessor. Don't change any piece of code you think is wrong until you have spent as much time thinking about it as some other programmer (or you) spent creating it in the first place. There may have been an important reason for doing something in a certain way, even if there is a problem in how it was done, and you want to understand that reason before you make changes.
2. Respect your successor. Whenever you have trouble figuring out what a particular section of code is doing, after you thoroughly understand the problem, fix the code and documentation so that it is easier to figure out next time.

3. Maintain a "standard" bank of test input data (and the corresponding output data), and use it to verify that any changes you have made affect only the problem you are trying to solve and do not have other unwanted effects that ripple through the program.

8.10 Merging Driver Method into Driven Class

It's legal to include a `main` method in any class. Figure 8.10 contains a simple Time program that includes its own `main` method.

```
/******************************************************************
* Time.java
* Dean & Dean
*
* This class stores time in the form of hours, minutes, and
* seconds. It prints the time using military format.
******************************************************************/

public class Time
{
  private int hours, minutes, seconds;

  //***************************************************************

  public Time(int h, int m, int s)
  {
    this.hours = h;
    this.minutes = m;
    this.seconds = s;
  }

  //***************************************************************

  public void printIt()
  {
    System.out.printf("%02d:%02d:%02d\n",
      hours, minutes, seconds);
  } // end printIt

  //***************************************************************

  public static void main(String[] args)
  {
    Time time = new Time(3, 59, 0);
    time.printIt();
  } // end main
} // end class Time
```

This is a driver for the rest of the code in this class.

Figure 8.10 `Time` class with built-in `main` driver method

Up until now, we've split each of our OOP programs into separate classes—a driver class and one or more driven classes. It's easiest to grasp the concept of an object if it's associated with one class, while the code that instantiates it is associated with another class. Driven classes and driver classes have distinctive roles. A driven class describes a thing that's being modeled. For example, in our Mouse programs, the `Mouse` class describes a mouse. A driver class contains a `main` method, and it drives the separate `Mouse` class. In our Mouse programs, the `MouseDriver` class instantiates `Mouse` objects and performs actions on those objects. Using two or more classes fosters the habit of putting different types of things in different modules.

Although we'll continue to use separate classes for most of our programs, for short programs that don't do much except demonstrate a concept, we'll sometimes merge `main` into the class that implements the rest of the program. It's a matter of convenience—there's one less file to create and there's slightly less code to enter.

Provide each class with a built-in test method.

In a big program that has one driver class in charge of a large number of driven classes, it's sometimes handy to insert an additional `main` method in some or all of the driven classes. The additional `main` method in a driven class serves as a local tester for the code in that class. Whenever you make a change in the code of a particular class, you can use its local `main` method to test that class directly. It's easy. Just execute the class of interest, and the JVM automatically uses that class's `main` method. Once you've verified the changes you've made locally, you can proceed to execute the driver in a higher-level module to test more or all of the program. You don't have to remove the local `main` methods. You can just leave them there for future local testing or demonstration of the features of each particular class. When you execute the overall program's driver class, the JVM automatically uses the `main` method in that driver class, and it ignores any `main` methods that may happen to be in other classes in the program.

Thus, you can add a `main` method to any class, so that the class can be executed directly and act as its own driver. When a multiclass program contains multiple `main` methods (no more than one per class), the particular `main` method that's used is the one in the class that's current when execution starts.

8.11 Accessing Instance Variables Without Using `this`

For a while now, we've used `this` to access the calling object's instance variables from within a method. Here's a formal explanation for when to use `this`:

> Use `this` within an instance method or a constructor to access the calling object's instance variables. The `this` reference distinguishes instance variables from other variables (like local variables and parameters) that happen to have the same name.
>
> However, if there is no name ambiguity, you may omit the `this` prefix when accessing an instance variable.

The code in Figure 8.11 has several places where the `this` prefix is worth mentioning. It's OK to omit `this` in the statement in the `setAge` method, because the instance variable name is different from the parameter name. It's not OK to omit `this` in the statement in the `setWeight` method, because the similarity in instance variable and parameter names would create an ambiguity. It is OK to omit `this` in the statement in the `print` method, because there is no name ambiguity.

Sometimes an instance method is called by one object and has a parameter which refers to a different object in the same class. `String`'s `equals` method is a familiar example of this situation. Inside such a method, there will be code that needs to refer to two different objects, the calling object and the object

```
/***************************************************************
* MouseShortcut.java
* Dean & Dean
*
* This class illustrates uses and omissions of this.
***************************************************************/

public class MouseShortcut
{
  private int age;             // age in days
  private double weight;       // weight in grams

  //***********************************************************

  public MouseShortcut(int age, double weight)
  {
    setAge(age);
    setWeight(weight);
  } // end constructor

  //***********************************************************

  public void setAge(int a)
  {
    age = a;
  } // end setAge

  //***********************************************************

  public void setWeight(double weight)
  {
    this.weight = weight;
  } // end setWeight

  //***********************************************************

  public void print()
  {
    System.out.println("age = " + age +
      ", weight = " + weight);
  } // end print
} // end class MouseShortcut
```

OK to omit `this` before instance variable, `age`, because it's different from parameter, `a`.

Not OK to omit `this` before instance variable, `weight`, because it's same as parameter, `weight`.

OK to omit `this` before `age` and `weight` instance variables.

Figure 8.11 `MouseShortcut` class illustrates the use and omission of `this`

referred to by the parameter. The safest and most understandable way to refer to these two objects is to use the `this` prefix to refer to the calling object and the reference-parameter prefix to refer to the other object. However, it's OK to omit the `this` when referring to the calling object, and you'll see this done quite frequently. It makes the code more compact.

8.12 Problem Solving with the API `Calendar` Class (Optional)

Although textbooks (including ours) ask you to write little programs that manipulate times and dates, if you get serious about times and dates, you will discover it's a hornet's nest of different number bases, different length months, leap years, daylight savings time, different time zones, and many different formatting conventions. For serious time and date work, you should use Java API prewritten software. Unfortunately, it's not always easy to find the right Java class. This is a case in point, because most of the methods in the obvious classes, `Time` and `Date`, are obsolete. Usually, you should use the `Calendar` class instead. Figure 8.12 contains an example program that exercises some of the methods in the `Calendar` class.

Don't reinvent the wheel.

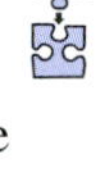

The `Calendar` class is in the `java.util` package. To include it in your program, you could use this `import` statement:

```
import java.util.Calendar;
```

However, since the `Calendar` class is in the same package as the `Scanner` class, which this program also needs, it's easier to make both classes available simultaneously with this one "wildcard" `import` statement:

```
import java.util.*;
```

In the first declaration, the program loads `stdIn` with a reference to an instance of the `Scanner` class. In the second declaration, the program loads `time` with a reference to an instance of the `Calendar` class. Notice, however, that the program creates the `Calendar` object in a strange way. For a reason we'll explain later in Chapter 13, you can't just use `new Calendar()` directly. Instead, you have to use the `getInstance` method. If you look up the `getInstance` method in the Java API documentation for the `Calendar` class, you'll see that this method has a `static` modifier, so it's a class method. How do you invoke a class method? Think back to how you invoked `Math`-class methods in Chapter 5. Instead of using an instance variable before the method name, you use the class name. How does `getInstance` work? We're not supposed to know, because it's an encapsulated module, but it probably internally instantiates a `Calendar` object, initializes it with the current time, and then returns a reference to that object. Although this is not the standard way to instantiate new objects, it works. The Java API includes several examples of this indirect type of object construction.

For the rest of the program, you can forget about how the `time` object was created and use it like you would any other object to call instance methods in its own class. The first print statement uses `Calendar`'s `getTime` method to retrieve the time information, and then it prints it all out as shown in the first line of the sample session.

The next two statements use the object reference with `get` methods to retrieve two particular instance variable values. But wait! There's something wonderfully strange about these two `get` methods. They're not two separate methods like `getDayOfYear` and `getHour` would be. They're both the same method—one method called just plain `get`. Instead of using the method name to identify the instance variable that will be retrieved, the designers of this class decided to use an `int` parameter value to identify that variable. We don't have

Use ID number in argument to select one of many similar variables.

```
/*********************************************************************
* CalendarDemo.java
* Dean & Dean
*
* This program demonstrates how to use the Calendar class.
*********************************************************************/

import java.util.*;                    // for Scanner and Calendar

public class CalendarDemo
{
  public static void main(String[] args)
  {
    Scanner stdIn = new Scanner(System.in);
    Calendar time = Calendar.getInstance();    // initially now
    int day;                                   // day of year
    int hour;                                  // hour of day

    System.out.println(time.getTime());
    day = time.get(time.DAY_OF_YEAR);
    hour = time.get(time.HOUR_OF_DAY);
    System.out.println("day of year= " + day);
    System.out.println("hour of day= " + hour);

    System.out.print("Enter number of days to add: ");
    day += stdIn.nextInt();
    System.out.print("Enter number of hours to add: ");
    hour += stdIn.nextInt();

    time.set(time.DAY_OF_YEAR, day);
    time.set(time.HOUR_OF_DAY, hour);
    System.out.println(time.getTime());
  } // end main
} // end class CalendarDemo
```

Parameters are `int` codes that specify the kind of information desired.

Sample session:

```
Mon Sep 24 16:42:27 CDT 2007
day of year= 267
hour of day= 16
Enter number of days to add: 8
Enter number of hours to add: 13
Wed Oct 03 05:42:27 CDT 2007
```

Figure 8.12 Demonstration program for the `Calendar` class.

to know how the method is implemented, because it's encapsulated, but we can use a plausible guess to shed light on what it does. For example, `get`'s parameter could be a `switch` index that steers the control flow to a particular case, where there's code that returns the value of the instance variable that corresponds to that index number.

The problem with using an index number to identify one of many instance variables is that simple integers don't convey much meaning. But you know a solution to this problem. All you have to do is make each such index number a named constant. Then, for the distinguishing method argument, use the named constant instead of the number. That's how the `Calendar` class implements its generic `get` method. And it's at least as easy for a user to remember one `get` method with different named-constant arguments as it would be to remember different get-method names.

Armed with this concept, you should now be able to see what the rest of the code in our CalendarDemo program is doing. It gets the current day of the year and the current hour of the day. Then it adds a user-input number of days to the current day and a user-input number of hours to the current hour. Then it uses `Calendar`'s generic `set` method (which probably works like `Calendar`'s generic `get` method) to mutate the object's instance variables for day-of-year and hour. Finally, it prints out the mutated time.

The `Calendar` class nicely illustrates the value of using pre-written software. It really is easier to learn to use that class than it is to write a program that does what it does. Moreover, other people's code sometimes illustrates techniques that may be applicable to code you write. However, the `Calendar` class also illustrates the kinds of penalties associated with using pre-written software. The biggest penalty is usually the time you have to spend to locate and figure out what's available. Another penalty is that what you find may not exactly match your immediate needs, and you might have to provide extra code to adapt the pre-written software to your current program. Such penalties motivate many programmers to say, "Oh heck, I'll just write it myself." Sometimes that's the thing to do, but in the long run you'll be ahead if you take time to learn about what others have already developed.

8.13 GUI Track: Problem Solving with CRC Cards (Optional)

When you begin a new design, there's often a period of head-scratching when you're trying to figure out what your classes should be and what they should do. Section 8.6 presented a formal top-down recipe, but sometimes you just need to "muck around" or brainstorm for awhile to get your thinking straight.

Explore your options.

Even when you're just mucking around and brainstorming, it's still helpful to write things down. To provide a minimal structure for this informal activity, several years ago computer scientists Kent Beck and Ward Cunningham[8] suggested using old-fashioned 3" × 5" file cards, with a pencil and eraser. Their idea was to allocate one card to each proposed class, with three kinds of information on each card: (1) At the top, put a class name. (2) Below and on the left, make a list of active verb phrases that described what that class will do. (3) Below and on the right, make a list of other classes with which the current class interacts—either actively as a client or passively as a server. The acronym, CRC, helps you remember the kinds of information each card should have. The first 'C' stands for "Class." The 'R' stands for "Responsibility." The last 'C' stands for "Collaboration."

When several different people are participating in a brainstorming session, pencils, erasers, and little white cards might indeed be the best medium to employ. But when you're the only designer, it might be more fun to use little windows on your computer screen. The program presented in Figure 8.13 sets up simulated CRC cards on your computer screen so you can do just that.

[8] OOPSLA '89 Conference Proceedings.

```
/*********************************************************************
* CRCCard.java
* Dean & Dean
*
* This program creates a GUI display of CRC cards.
*********************************************************************/

import java.util.Scanner;
import javax.swing.*;  // for JFrame, JTextArea, & JSplitFrame

public class CRCCard
{
  public static void main(String[] args)
  {
    Scanner stdIn = new Scanner(System.in);
    String input;

    System.out.print("Enter class name or 'q' to quit: ");
    input = stdIn.nextLine();
    while (!input.equalsIgnoreCase("q"))
    {
      JFrame frame = new JFrame("Class: " + input);
      JTextArea responsibilities =
        new JTextArea("RESPONSIBILITIES:\n");
      JTextArea collaborators =
        new JTextArea("COLLABORATORS:\n");
      JSplitPane splitPane =
        new JSplitPane(JSplitPane.HORIZONTAL_SPLIT,
        responsibilities, collaborators);

      frame.setSize(350, 210);
      frame.add(splitPane);
      frame.setLocationByPlatform(true);
      frame.setVisible(true);
      frame.toFront();
      splitPane.setDividerLocation(0.67);

      System.out.print("Enter class name or 'q' to quit: ");
      input = stdIn.nextLine();
    } // end while
  } // end main
} // end class CRCCard
```

Create a new window.

Create two containers.

Put containers into split panes.

Put split pane in window.

Figure 8.13 Program that puts interactive CRC cards on your computer screen

This program imports the `javax.swing` package to provide access to three classes in the Java API: `JFrame`, `JTextArea`, and `JSplitPane`. In a `main` method, it repeatedly asks the user for another class until a 'q' entry says it's time to quit. After the user enters each class name, the program instantiates a small `JFrame` window that represents one CRC card. The `JFrame` constructor automatically inserts the text, "Class: <*classname*>" in that window's header and thereby implements the first 'C' in CRC. Then the program instantiates two `JTextArea` "panes," which act like little erasable scratch pads, on which you can write any text anywhere. The two `JTextArea` constructor calls automatically write "RESPONSIBILITIES:" and "COLLABORATORS:," respectively, on the first line of each of these two `JTextArea` panes. Then, the program instantiates a `JSplitPane` with a `HORIZONTAL_SPLIT` specification that splits the window into two side-by-side "openings" separated by a moveable vertical partition. The last two `JSplitPane` parameters paste the individual `JTextArea` panes into these two openings.

The `setSize` method call sizes the window to make it about like a 3" × 5" file card. The `add` method call adds the split pane to the window. The `setLocationByPlatform` method call tells the computer to offset each additional card so that you can continue to see the titles and borders of previously created cards as they "pile up" on your desktop. The `setVisible` method makes each new card visible. The `toFront` method moves it to the front of your screen. The `setDividerLocation` method positions the `JSplitPane` divider two-thirds of the way to the right, to provide twice as much space for "responsibilities" text as for "collaboration" text. The specified window dimensions and the location of the split-pane divider are just initial settings, and if you find you need more space, you'll be able to change them interactively on the computer screen at any time while the program is running.

When you run the program in a Windows environment, you'll get a Command Prompt window with a query asking for a class name, like what appears in Figure 8.14.

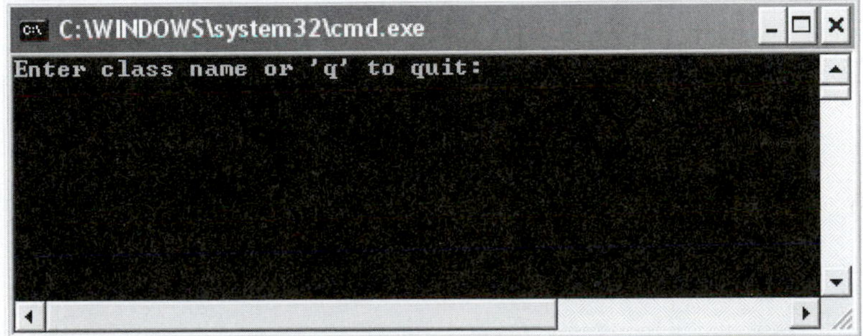

Figure 8.14 Initial Command Prompt display for CRCCards program

After you enter a class name, an additional window appears. This is your first CRC card. If the Command Prompt window is now underneath the new card, drag the Command Prompt window down and to the right, to get it out of the way. Then, move the cursor to the new CRC card, and fill in additional information, like the "run program" entry in the RESPONSIBILITIES pane and the "GarageDoorSystem" entry in the COLLABORATORS pane in Figure 8.15.

Go back to the Command Prompt and enter another class name, and so on. until you have created all the CRC cards you need. They should automatically pile up in a "stack" that looks something like the four cards in the upper left of the computer screen shown in Figure 8.16.

Now, before you enter a 'q' in the Command Prompt window, you can reduce it to an icon and play around with four CRC cards. You can drag them anywhere on the screen to form logical hierarchies or

Class: GarageDoorDriver
RESPONSIBILITIES:
run program
COLLABORATORS:
GarageDoorSystem

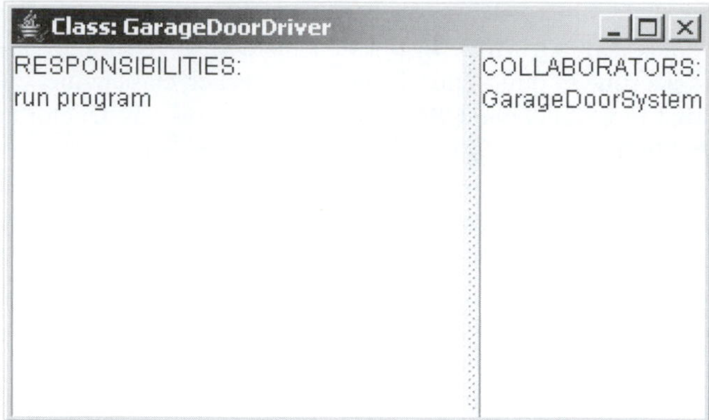

Figure 8.15 First CRC Card after user entries

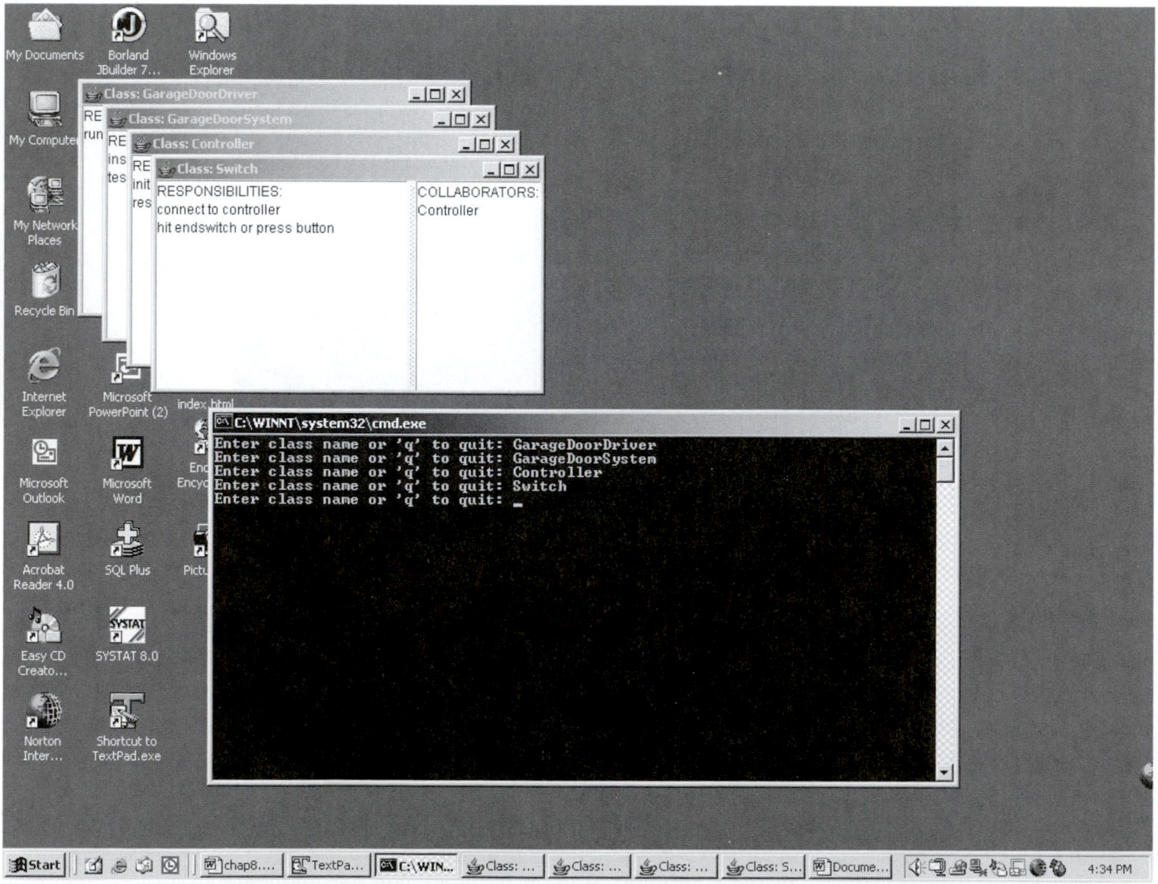

Class: Switch
RESPONSIBILITIES:
connect to controller
hit endswitch or press button
COLLABORATORS:
Controller
C:\WINNT\system32\cmd.exe
Enter class name or 'q' to quit: GarageDoorDriver
Enter class name or 'q' to quit: GarageDoorSystem
Enter class name or 'q' to quit: Controller
Enter class name or 'q' to quit: Switch
Enter class name or 'q' to quit:

Figure 8.16 What you might see after creating four CRC cards

groupings. On any of the cards you can change any of the wordings in either of the two panes. If you decide that one of the classes is no good, you can click on its X box to throw it away, reactivate the Command Prompt window, and create more new CRC cards with different class names. When you're through with everything, use Ctrl-PrtScr to print the screen to record your thinking, and then enter 'q' in the Command Prompt window to terminate the program.

Summary

- Begin every class with a prologue. Include program name, author(s), and a brief description of what the class does.
- Provide a descriptive comment above or after any code that an experienced Java programmer would not understand.
- Use meaningful names for everything. Do not be cryptic.
- Enclose logical blocks of code in braces. The opening and closing braces should be in the same column as the start of the line that precedes the opening brace.
- Supply a `// end` *<block-name>* comment after a block's closing brace to improve readability.
- Declare each variable at the beginning of its class or method, or in its `for` loop header. Normally use one line per variable and follow each declaration with an appropriate descriptive comment.
- Use subordinate helper methods to simplify large methods and reduce code redundancy. Make helper methods `private` to minimize clutter in the class interface.
- Use instance variables for object attributes (state information) only. Use local variables and input parameters for calculations within a method and to transfer data into a method. Use return values and/or input reference parameters to transfer data out of a method.
- Plan to test the software you develop frequently and thoroughly as you go along. Include typical, boundary, and unreasonable cases.
- Top-down design is appropriate for large projects that have well-understood objectives. Proceed from general to specific, using stubs to defer implementation of subordinate methods.
- Bottom-up design allows you to give priority to critical details. It fosters re-use of existing software, which reduces development cost and improves system reliability. But this methodology makes large projects hard to manage.
- Expect to go through several design iterations. Use prototyping to help customers get a clearer understanding of what they want, but avoid the trap of trying to convert a clumsy prototype directly into a final product. In each subsequent iteration, select that design strategy which best addresses the greatest current need or concern. A successful program will require ongoing maintenance, and you can make this easier if you preserve and enhance elegance as the program changes and grows.
- To facilitate modular testing, provide a `main` method with every class.
- If there is no name ambiguity, you may omit the `this` prefix when accessing an instance member.

Review Questions

§8.2 Coding-Style Conventions

1. One should avoid inserting blank lines between different code sections (because that leads to wasted paper when the program is printed). (T / F)
2. In order, list the seven items that we recommend you include in a file prologue.

3. When adding a comment to a variable declaration, always begin the comment one space after the end of the declaration. (T / F)
4. To get the most on each line of code, always break a long line at the point determined by your text editor or IDE. (T / F)
5. For an `if` or `while` that has only one statement in its body, braces for the body are optional. The compiler does not require them, but proper style suggests that you should include them. Give at least one reason why it's a good idea to put braces around the body's single statement.
6. What's wrong with the style of a class description that ends like this?

```
    }
  }
}
```

   What might you do to fix it?
7. What should you use to separate large "chunks" of code?
8. For each, write "yes" or "no" to indicate whether it is good style to include a blank space.
   - after the single asterisks in the prologue
   - between a method call and its opening parentheses
   - within each of the three components in a `for` loop header
   - after the two semicolons in the `for` loop header
   - between a closing brace and the `//`'s for its associated comment
   - after the `//`'s for all comments
   - after the `if`, `while`, and `switch` keywords

§8.3 Helper Methods

9. Which of the following is a legitimate reason for creating a helper method?
   a) You want the method to be hidden from the outside world.
   b) You have a long and complicated method and would like to partition it into several smaller modules.
   c) Your class contains two or more methods where some of the code is the same in both methods.
   d) All of above.
10. Does a class's interface include the names of `private` methods?

§8.4 Encapsulation (with Instance Variables and Local Variables)

11. In the interest of encapsulation, use local variables instead of instance variables whenever possible. (T / F)
12. If a method modifies a particular instance variable, and if a program calls the same method two separate times, the value of the instance variable at the beginning of the second method call is guaranteed to be the same as the value it had at the end of the first method call. (T / F)

§8.5 Design Philosophy

13. Since some of your preliminary code might change in the course of development, do not waste time testing until everything is done. (T / F)
14. When you are testing a program, it's important to not have any preconceived expectations of what your output should look like. (T / F)

§8.6 Top-Down Design

15. The top-down design methodology is good because:
   a) It keeps everyone focused on a common goal. (T / F)
   b) It avoids "reinventing the wheel." (T / F)
   c) It keeps management informed. (T / F)
   d) It minimizes the chances of solving the wrong problem. (T / F)

e) It minimizes overall cost. (T / F)
f) It results in the fewest number of undetected bugs. (T / F)

16. In a top-down design process, which do you decide on first—the classes or the `public` methods?

§8.7 Bottom-Up Design

17. When should you use bottom-up design?

§8.9 Iterative Enhancement

18. If a prototype is successful, what temptation should you resist?
19. Once you select a particular design methodology, keep using that same methodology throughout the entire design process, and do not allow other methodologies to "contaminate" the process originally selected. (T / F)

§8.10 Merging Driver Method into Driven Class

20. You can drive any class from a `main` method within that class, and you can retain that `main` method for future testing of that class even though that class is normally driven from another class in a larger program. (T / F)

Exercises

1. [after §8.2] Describe the way to declare variables that conforms to good style. Include description of when and how to include associated comments.
2. [after §8.2] Correct the style of the following class definition.

```
/*Environment.java This class models the world's environment.
It was written by Dean & Dean and it compiles so it must be OK*/
public class Environment{//instance variables
private double sustainableProduction;private double
initialResources;private double currentResources;private
double yieldFactor = 2.0;public void setSustainableProduction
(double production){this.sustainableProduction = production;}
// Set pre-industrial mineral and fossil resources
public void setInitialResources(double resources){this.
initialResources=resources;}
// Initialize remaining mineral and fossil resources
public void setCurrentResources(double resources){this.
currentResources = resources;}
// Fetch remaining mineral and fossil resources
public double getCurrentResources(){return this.
currentResources;}/*Compute annual combination of renewable
and non-renewable environmental production*/public double
produce(double populationFraction,double extractionExpense){
double extraction;extraction=this.yieldFactor*
extractionExpense*(this.currentResources/this.
initialResources);this.currentResources-= extraction;return
extraction+populationFraction*this.sustainableProduction;}}
```

3. [after §8.3] Given the following shirt-design program, which is the same as the Shirt program in Figures 8.3 and 8.4, except for a slight modification in `main`:

```
/*************************************************************
* ShirtDriver.java
* Dean & Dean
*
* This is a driver for the Shirt class.
*************************************************************/

public class ShirtDriver
{
  public static void main(String[] args)
  {
    Shirt shirt1 = new Shirt();
    Shirt shirt2 = new Shirt();

    System.out.println();
    shirt1.display();
    shirt2.display();
  } // end main
} // end ShirtDriver
```

```
/***********************************************************
* Shirt.java
* Dean & Dean
*
* This class stores and displays color choices for
* a sports-uniform shirt.
***********************************************************/

import java.util.Scanner;

public class Shirt
{
  private String name;      // person's name
  private String primary;   // shirt's primary color
  private String trim;      // shirt's trim color

  //********************************************************

  public Shirt()
  {
    Scanner stdIn = new Scanner(System.in);
    System.out.print("Enter person's name: ");
    this.name = stdIn.nextLine();

    this.primary = selectColor("primary");
    this.trim = selectColor("trim");
  } // end constructor

  //********************************************************

  public void display()
```

```
  {
    System.out.println(this.name + "'s shirt:\n" +
      this.primary + " with " + this.trim + " trim");
  } // end display

  //*******************************************************

  // Helping method prompts for and inputs user's selection

  private String selectColor(String colorType)
  {
    Scanner stdIn = new Scanner(System.in);
    String color; // chosen color, first a letter, then word

    do
    {
      System.out.print("Enter shirt's " + colorType +
        " color (w, r, y): ");
      color = stdIn.nextLine();
    } while (!color.equals("w") && !color.equals("r") &&
             !color.equals("y"));

    switch (color.charAt(0))
    {
      case 'w':
        color = "white";
        break;
      case 'r':
        color = "red";
        break;
      case 'y':
        color = "yellow";
    } // end switch

    return color;
  } // end selectColor
} // end class Shirt
```

Trace the above shirt-design program using either the short form or the long form. To help you get started, here's the trace setup, including the input. For the short form, you won't need the line# column.

<u>input</u>

Corneal
r
w
Jill
w
y

ShirtDriver			Shirt												
	main			Shirt	display	selectColor			obj1			obj2			
line#	**sh1**	**sh2**	*line#*	**this**	**this**	**this**	**cType**	**color**	**name**	**prim**	**trim**	**name**	**prim**	**trim**	**output**

4. [after §8.3] Assume that the `GarageDoorSystem` class in Figures 7.25a and 7.25b has another instance variable:

```
public final String SYSTEM_ID;
```

Rewrite the `GarageDoorSystem` constructor so that it calls a helper method called `initialize` which asks the user to supply a name for `SYSTEM_ID`. In that method, also ask the user if the starting position is to be up. Then, use the user's input to initialize the `state` variable, assuming the only possible starting states are down (0) or up (2).

5. [after §8.4] This exercise demonstrates using a reference parameter to pass data back to the calling method. Suppose you want a `Car5` class to include a method with this heading:

```
public boolean copyTo(Car5 newCar)
```

This method is supposed to be called by an existing `Car5` object with an argument to a new `Car5` object. If any of the calling car's instance variables has not been initialized, the desired method should not try to modify any of the new car's instance variable values, and the method should return `false`. Otherwise, the method should copy all of the calling car's instance variable values into the new car and return `true`. Here's a driver that illustrates the usage:

```
/*****************************************************************
* Car5Driver.java
* Dean & Dean
*
* This class is a demonstration driver for the Car5 class.
*****************************************************************/

public class Car5Driver
{
  public static void main(String[] args)
  {
    Car5 annaCar = new Car5();
    Car5 nickCar = new Car5();

    System.out.println(annaCar.copyTo(nickCar));
    annaCar = new Car5("Porsche", 2006, "beige");
    System.out.println(annaCar.copyTo(nickCar));
  } // end main
} // end class Car5Driver
```

<u>Output:</u>

```
false
true
```

Write the code for the desired `copyTo` method.

6. [after § 8.5] We recommend that you test frequently, even if it means creating special test code that is not used in the final program. Why might it be useful to save such special test code?

7. [after §8.6] Assuming it will be called by the `draw` method in the `Square` class in Figure 8.7a, write a `drawSolidSquare` method that asks the user for the character to print and draws the desired solid square all by itself, without calling any separate `drawHorizontalLine` method.

Sample session:

```
Enter width of desired square: 5
Area = 25
Print with (b)order or (s)olid? s
Enter character to use: #
#####
#####
#####
#####
#####
```

8. [after §8.6] Assuming it will be called by the `draw` method in the `Square` class in Figure 8.7a, write a `drawBorderSquare` method that asks the user for two characters to use to draw a bordered square, one character of the border and a different character for the space in the middle. Notice that using the same character for the border and the middle makes this method draw a solid square, and thus this method makes the `drawSolidSquare` method redundant, although this method requires more user interaction.

Sample session:

```
Enter width of desired square: 5
Area = 25
Print with (b)order or (s)olid? b
Enter character for border: B
Enter character for middle: m
BBBBB
BmmmB
BmmmB
BmmmB
BBBBB
```

9. [after §8.6] Figure 8.2b has two if statement conditions that contain what are called regular expressions. As indicated these are explained in the Java API `Pattern` class. This exercise is intended to help you get a better feeling for Java's regular expressions and their usage. Use your Java API documentation on the `Pattern` class to get the answers to these questions:

a) What is the meaning of the regular expression, `"[A-Z][a-z]*"`, which appears in Figure 8.2b?

b) What is the regular expression for a character string starting with a 'Z' and containing any number of additional characters of any kind except for a space or a tab?

c) What is the regular expression for a string that represents a U.S. long-distance telephone number (three digits, a dash or space, three digits, a dash or space, and four digits)?

10. [after §8.6] Define "stepwise refinement."

11. [after §8.6] Write stubs for all the constructors and methods in the `Student` class of Figures 8.2a and 8.2b. Each stub should print out the method name followed by the initial (passed-in) values of all parameters, like this sample output:

```
in Student
in setFirst, first= Adeeb
in setLast, last= Jarrah
in Student, first= Heejoo, last= Chun
in printFullName
```

12. [after §8.7] Write a generic drawRow method having this heading:

```
private void drawRow(int startCol, int endCol)
```

startCol and endCol are the column numbers of the left and right borders, respectively. Then modify the Square class's draw method in Figure 8.7a to draw either a solid square or a solid triangle whose height and width equal the width of the input width of a square container. What about the area now? Is it a redundant value, or is it a legitimate object attribute? Modify the instance variables and the getArea method accordingly. Then drive your modified Square class (call it Square2) with a Square2Driver whose main method looks like this:

```
public static void main(String[] args)
{
  Scanner stdIn = new Scanner(System.in);
  Square2 square;

  System.out.print("Enter width of square container: ");
  square = new Square2(stdIn.nextInt());
  square.draw();
  System.out.println("Area = " + square.getArea());
} // end main
```

Sample session:

```
Enter width of square container: 5
Print (s)quare or (t)riangle? t
*
**
***
****
*****
Area = 15
```

13. [after §8.9] Write a prototype of the Square program, using just one class called SquarePrototype, with only one method, main. Write the minimum amount of code needed to generate the prescribed output for only the simplest case of a solid square. The sample session should look exactly like it would for the final program described in Figures 8.6, 8.9a, and 8.9b, if the user selects the (s)olid option. If the user selects the (b)order option, however, the prototype should respond by printing a "Not Implemented."

14. [after §8.9] When you design something, you should select the design methodology that is best able to address the greatest current design concern. (T / F)

15. [after §8.10] Write a separate driver program that executes the Time class shown in Figure 8.10 and sets the time for 17 hours, 30 minutes, and zero seconds. Assume that the main method that appears in Figure 8.10 is still there.

16. [after §8.11] Rewrite the Car class in Figure 7.2 to eliminate the use of this.

17. [after §8.12] The Java API Calendar class contains a method called getTimeInMillisec which enables you to retrieve the absolute time (in milliseconds) at which any Calendar object was created. As indicated in Section 8.12, you can get such an object by calling the getInstance class method. You can use this capability to evaluate the runtime of any chunk of code. All you have to do is create a Calendar object before the test code starts, create another Calendar object right after the code ends, and print out the difference in those two object's times. To demonstrate this capability, write a short program called

TestRuntime that asks the user for a desired number of iterations, num. Then have it measure the runtime for a loop of num iterations that executes the single statement:

```
Math.cos(0.01 * i);
```

The variable i is the loop count variable.

Review Question Solutions

1. False. Readability is an important attribute of good computer code. To save printer paper, print on both sides of the page and/or use smaller font.
2. The seven items to include in a file prolog are:
   - line of asterisks
   - filename
   - programmer name(s)
   - blank line with one asterisk
   - description
   - line of asterisks
   - blank line
3. False. That would provide maximum room for each comment, but good programmers make the beginnings of declaration comments line up with each other, and they try to make declaration comments short enough to avoid line wrap.
4. False. Take control, and break a long line at the most logical place(s).
5. Even though it's not necessary, it's a good idea to provide braces with single-statement `if` and `while` statements because
   - Braces provide a visual cue for remembering to indent.
   - Braces help you avoid a logical mistake if you add code later.
6. Unless a block is very short, it may not be immediately obvious which block is being terminated by a particular brace. It's good practice to terminate all but the shortest blocks with a comment, for example,

```
      } // end if
    } // end main
  } // end class Whatever
```

7. Separate large chunks of code with blank lines.
8. Yes means include a space, No means do not.
   - Yes, after the single asterisks in the prologue.
   - No, not between a method call and its opening parentheses.
   - No, not within each of the three components in a `for` loop header.
   - Yes, after the two semicolons in the `for` loop header.
   - Yes, between a closing brace and the `//`'s for its associated comment.
   - Yes, after the `//`'s for all comments.
   - Yes, after the `if`, `while`, and `switch` keywords.
9. d) All of above.
10. No. the interface does not describe `private` members.
11. True. You should generally try to keep things as local as possible, and using local variables instead of instance variables is one way to do this. Instance variables should be reserved for attributes that describe an object's state.

12. False. It's true that an instance variable persists throughout the life of an object, and if the second call of the same method were right after the first call of that method, the final value of the instance variable in the first call would be the same as the initial value in the second call of that method. However, it's possible that some other method could change the value of the instance variable between the two calls of the method in question.

13. False. Test frequently throughout the development process.

14. False. It's important to have a clear idea of what you expect to see before you do a test, so you will have the best chance of recognizing a discrepancy when it occurs.

15. The top-down design methodology is the best because:

- **a)** True.
- **b)** False. It sometimes forces people to re-invent the wheel.
- **c)** True.
- **d)** False. If you're worried about solving the wrong problem, use prototyping.
- **e)** False. To minimize cost, organize the design to reuse existing components.
- **f)** False. To maximize reliability, organize the design to reuse existing components.

16. In top-down design you decide on the classes before the `public` methods.

17. You should use bottom-up design when your program can utilize a substantial amount of prewritten software or when low-level details are critical and require early attention.

18. If a prototype is successful, it's important to resist the temptation of continuing the development by tinkering with that prototype.

19. False. Many problems need benefits of more than one design methodology. It's a good idea to stick with one methodology through one design cycle (planning, implementation, testing and evaluation), but you might need to switch to a different methodology in the next design iteration.

20. True. The particular `main` method used is the one that's current when execution starts.

CHAPTER 9

Classes with Class Members

Objectives

- Learn how and when to use class variables.
- Learn how to write class methods and when to use them.
- Learn how and when to use class constants.
- Practice some of the design approaches suggested in Chapter 8.
- Optionally, learn how to construct a linked list of objects and access them through class methods.

Outline

9.1 Introduction

When you think about an object-oriented solution, what do you envision? Based on what you've learned up to this point, you should see separate objects, each with their own set of data and behaviors (instance variables and instance methods, respectively). That's a valid picture, but you should be aware that in addition to data and behaviors that are specific to individual objects, you can also have data and behaviors that relate to an entire class. Since they relate to an entire class, such data and behaviors are referred to as *class variables* and *class methods,* respectively.

Let's look at an example. Suppose you are charged with keeping track of YouTube videos. You need to instantiate a YouTube object for each YouTube video, and within each object you need to store attributes like the videographer, the video's length, and the video file itself. You should store those attributes in instance variables because they are associated with individual YouTube objects. You also need to store attributes like the number of videos and the most popular video. You should store those attributes in class variables because they relate to the collection of YouTube objects as a whole.

For another example, think about the Math class. Its members, like Math.round and Math.PI, are class members because they are associated with the Math class as a whole. In Chapter 5, you learned how to access and use the Math class's class members. In this chapter, you learn how to implement your own class members.

We start the chapter by showing you how to implement your own class variables. We then show you how to implement class methods, and we use class variables within those methods. Next, we discuss class constants, which are class variables that use the final modifier. After that we present a *utility class*—a class with general-purpose functionality that other classes can easily use. In the last part of the chapter, you'll see different kinds of instance and class members brought together in two complete programs. The second of those programs does more than just provide another example with instance and class members. It implements an important data structure called a *linked list,* which allows you to dynamically create an arbitrarily large number of chained-together objects.

9.2 Class Variables

You already know that class variables are variables that are associated with a class as a whole. In this section, you'll learn more details about class variables such as how to declare them, when to use them, what their default values are, and what their scope is. In the next section, you'll see examples of using class variables from within class methods.

Class Variable Declaration Syntax

To make a variable a class variable, use the static modifier in its declaration. The static modifier is why many programmers use the term "static variable" when talking about class variables. Likewise, since class constants and class methods also use the static modifier, many programmers use the terms static constant and static method. We'll stick with the terms class variable, class constant, and class method since those are the terms that Sun uses.

Here is the syntax for a class variable declaration statement:

<private-or-public> static *<type>* *<variable-name>*;

And here is an example:

```
private static int mouseCount;  // total number of mouse objects
```

Should class variables be public or private? The philosophy on this is the same as it is for instance variables. Since you can always write public get/set class methods, you don't need public class variables any more than you need public instance variables. It's best to keep your variables as private as possible to maintain control over how they are accessed. Therefore, in addition to making instance variables private, you should also make class variables private.

Why the Term "static"?

As you know, when the Java Virtual Machine (JVM) sees the new operator in a program, it instantiates an object for the specified class. In so doing, it allocates memory space for all of the object's instance variables. Later, the garbage collector might deallocate (take away) that memory space before the program stops if all references to that space disappear. That sort of memory management, done while the program runs, is called *dynamic allocation*. Class variables are different. The JVM allocates space for a class variable when the program starts, and that class-variable space remains allocated as long as the program runs. That sort of memory management is called static allocation. That's why class variables are called static.

Class Variable Examples

As you know, each use of new creates a separate copy of all instance variables for each object. Class variables are different. For a particular class, there is only one copy of each class variable, and all objects share that single copy. Thus, you should use class variables to describe properties of a class's objects that need to be shared by all of the objects. For example, consider again the problem of simulating mouse growth. In our previous mouse programs, we kept track of data pertinent to each individual mouse—a mouse's growth rate, a mouse's age, and a mouse's weight. For a more useful simulation program, you'd probably also want to keep track of group data and common environmental data. For example:

`mouseCount` would keep track of the total number of mice.
`youngestMouse` would keep track of which mouse was born last.
`averageLifeSpan` would keep track of the average life span for all of the mice.
`simulationDuration` would limit the number of simulation iterations.
`researcher` would identify a person in charge of an experiment on the group of mice.
`noiseOn` would indicate the presence or absence of a stressful noise heard by all the mice.

If you used instance variables for `mouseCount`, `averageLifeSpan`, and so on, each individual mouse object would have its own copy of that data. So if there were one hundred total mice, each of the one hundred mice would store the value 100 in its own `mouseCount` variable, the average life span value in its own `averageLifeSpan` variable, and so on. This would mean that every time a new mouse was born or died or aged a year, you would have to update 100 separate copies of `mouseCount`, `averageLifeSpan`, and so on—all with exactly the same information. What a waste of effort! Why not just do it once and let everyone write and read the same common data? If `mouseCount`, `averageLifeSpan`, and so on are class variables, all mouse objects can write to and read from a single record of each of these pieces of information. An outsider can access these class properties by just prefixing the class name to an appropriate class method. It's neither necessary nor desirable to go through a particular instance to get to this group information.

The class variable declarations in our enhanced `Mouse` class would look something like the code in Figure 9.1. In the figure, does it strike you as odd that the type of `youngestMouse` is the name of the class in which it is defined? Does that mean there's a mouse within a mouse? No! The `static` modifier in `youngestMouse`'s declaration means that `youngestMouse` is a class variable. As such, it's a property of the collection of all mice. More specifically, it identifies the mouse object that was most recently instantiated. In the next section, we present `youngestMouse` in the context of a complete program, and you'll see how it gets updated every time there's a mouse object instantiation.

```
public class Mouse
{
  private static int mouseCount;
  private static Mouse4 youngestMouse;
  private static double averageLifeSpan = 18;  // months
  private static int simulationDuration = 730; // days
  private static String researcher;
  private static boolean noiseOn;
  ...
```

Initializations are allowed. (averageLifeSpan, simulationDuration)

attributes of the environment (researcher, noiseOn)

Figure 9.1 Class variable declarations in an enhanced `Mouse` class

Default Values

Class variables use the same default values as instance variables:

Class Variable's Type	Default Value
integer	0
floating point	0.0
`boolean`	`false`
reference	`null`

It follows that the default values for Figure 9.1's class variables are:

```
mouseCount = 0
youngestMouse = null
averageLifeSpan = 0.0
simulationDuration = 0
researcher = null
noiseOn = false
```

Presumably, the program updates `mouseCount`, `youngestMouse`, and `averageLifeSpan` as it runs. The default values of `averageLifeSpan` and `simulationDuration` are zero like `mouseCount`, but in Figure 9.1 the defaults don't apply because the declarations include initializations. Even though we expect the program to recompute `averageLifeSpan`, we initialize it to provide documentation of what we think is a reasonable value. We also initialize `simulationDuration` (to 730) even though we expect the program to reassign `simulationDuration` with a user-entered value. Presumably, the program prompts the user to enter the number of days to simulate. With appropriate code, the user might be invited to enter −1 to get a "standard" 730-day simulation.

Scope

Let's now compare class variables, instance variables, and local variables in terms of their scopes. You can access a class variable from anywhere within its class. More specifically, that means you can access class variables from instance methods as well as from class methods. That contrasts with instance variables, which you can access only from instance methods. Thus, class variables have broader scope than instance variables. Local variables, on the other hand, have narrower scope than instance variables. They can be accessed only within one particular method. Here is the scope continuum:

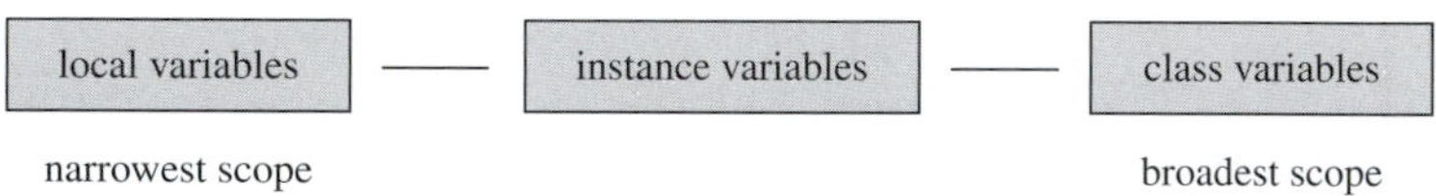

Having narrower scope for local variables might seem like a bad thing because it's less "powerful," but it's actually a good thing. Why? Narrower scope equates to more encapsulation, and as you learned in Chapter 6, encapsulation means you are less vulnerable to inappropriate changes. Class variables, with their broad scope and lack of encapsulation, can be accessed and updated from many different places, and that makes programs hard to understand and debug. Having broader scope is necessary at times, but in general you should try to avoid broader scope. We encourage you to prefer local variables over instance variables and instance variables over class variables.

9.3 Class Methods

Class methods, like class variables, relate to the class as a whole, and they don't relate to individual objects. As such, if you need to perform a task that involves the class as a whole, then you should implement and use a class method. In Chapter 5 you used class methods defined in the Java API `Math` class; for example, `Math.round` and `Math.sqrt`. Now you'll learn how to write your own class methods. Class methods often access class variables, and in writing your own class methods, you'll get an opportunity to see how to access class variables that you've defined.

Class Method Syntax

See Figure 9.2's `Mouse4` class. In particular, look at the `printMouseCount` method. It deals with class-wide information, so it's appropriate to make it a class method. More specifically, it prints the value of `mouseCount`, where `mouseCount` is a class variable that keeps track of the total number of mouse objects.

```
public class Mouse4
{
  private static int mouseCount;
  private static Mouse4 youngestMouse;
  private int age;

  public Mouse4()
  {
    Mouse4.mouseCount++;
    Mouse4.youngestMouse = this;
  }

  public static void printMouseCount()
  {
    System.out.println("Total mice = " + Mouse4.mouseCount);
  }

  public void olderByOneDay()
  {
    this.age++;
  }

  //*************************************************************

  public static void main(String[] args)
  {
    Mouse4 pinky = new Mouse4();
    pinky.olderByOneDay();
    Mouse4.printMouseCount();
  }
} // end class Mouse4
```

class variables

specifies a class method

Normally, to access a class variable, prefix it with *<class-name>* dot.

Normally, to access a class method, prefix it with *<class-name>* dot.

Figure 9.2 A simple mouse program that illustrates class member concepts

To declare a class method, use this syntax for the method heading:

<private-or-public> `static` *<return-type>* *<method-name>*`(`*<parameters>*`)`

Note how Figure 9.2's `printMouseCount` method follows that syntax pattern.

Normally, to access a class member, you should prefix the class member with the class member's class name and then a dot. For example, within the `printMouseCount` method and the `Mouse4` constructor, note how `mouseCount` and `youngestMouse` are accessed with `Mouse4` dot prefixes—`Mouse4.mouseCount` and `Mouse4.youngestMouse`. Also, within the `main` method, see how the `printMouseCount` class method is called with `Mouse4.printMouseCount()`. Prefixing a class member with its class name and then a dot should look familiar. You've done that with `Math` class members for quite a while (e.g., `Math.round()`, `Math.PI`).

Be aware that you don't always have to use the class name dot prefix when accessing a class member. In accessing a class member, you may omit the class name dot prefix if the class member is in the same class as the class from which you're trying to access it. So in the `Mouse4` class, since all the class member accesses and the class members themselves are in the same `Mouse4` class, all the class name dot prefixes can be omitted. But if the program were written with `main` appearing in a separate driver class, then the `Mouse4` dot could not be omitted from `main`'s call to `printMouseCount`.

Although it's often legal to omit the class name dot prefix, we have a slight preference for always including it because it's a form of self documentation. It alerts the person reading the code to the fact that the accessed member is special—it deals with class-wide information.

Calling an Instance Method from within a Class Method

If you're within a class method, you'll get a compilation error if you attempt to access an instance member directly. To access an instance member, you first must have an object, and then you access the object's instance member by prefacing it with the object's reference variable. The reference variable is often referred to as the calling object. Does all that sound familiar? The `main` method is a class method (`main`'s heading includes the `static` modifier), and you've been calling instance methods from `main` for quite a while now. But whenever you do that, you first must instantiate an object and assign the object's reference to a reference variable. Then you call the instance method by prefixing it with the reference variable and a dot. Figure 9.2's `main` method shows what we're talking about:

```
public static void main(String[] args)
{
  Mouse4 pinky = new Mouse4();
  pinky.olderByOneDay();
  Mouse4.printMouseCount();
}
```

Reference variable dot prefix is necessary when calling an instance method from within a class method

If you attempt to access an instance method directly from within a class method, you'll see an error message like this:

`Non-static` *<method-name>* `cannot be referenced from a static context`

That error message is very common (you've probably seen it many times) because it's easy to forget to prefix instance method calls with a reference variable. When veteran programmers see it, they know what to do; they make sure to prefix the instance method call with a calling object's reference variable. But when beginning programmers see the error message, they often compound the error by trying to "fix" the bug inappropriately.

More specifically, when confronted with the non-static method error message, a beginning programmer will often change the offending instance method to a class method, by inserting `static` in the method's heading. (In the Mouse4 program, `olderByOneDay` would be changed to a class method). They then get the non-static member error message for any instance variables within the method. They then compound the problem further by changing the method's instance variables to class variables. (In the Mouse4 program, `olderByOneDay`'s `age` variable would be changed to a class variable). With that change in place, the program compiles successfully and the beginning programmer is happy as a lark, ready to slay the next dragon. Unfortunately, that type of solution leads to a worse problem than a compilation error. It leads to a logic error.

As you know, if a class's member relates to one object rather than to the class as a whole, you should make it an instance member. If you do as described above and "fix" a bug by changing an instance member to a class member, you can get your program to compile and run. And if you have only one object, your program might even produce a valid result. But if you have more than one object, either now or in the future, then with class variables, the objects will share the same data. If you change one object's data, you'll simultaneously change all other objects' data, and normally that would be incorrect.

Aside: Accessing a Class Member from an Instance Method or Constructor

Although you can't access an instance member directly from a class method, you can access a class member from an instance method. In addition, you can access a class variable from a constructor, and Figure 9.2 illustrates that. The relevant code is repeated below for your convenience. It shows how the `mouseCount` and `youngestMouse` class variables are updated automatically with each new instantiation. Note how the `this` reference assigns the constructor's newly instantiated mouse to the `youngestMouse` variable.

```
public Mouse4()
{
  Mouse4.mouseCount++;
  Mouse4.youngestMouse = this;
}
```

When To Use Class Methods

When should you make a method a class method? The general answer is "when you need to perform a task that involves the class as a whole." But let's get more specific. Here are situations where class methods are appropriate:

1. If you have a method that uses class variables and/or calls class methods, then it's a good candidate for being a class method. For example, Figure 9.2's `printMouseCount` is a class method because it prints the `mouseCount` class variable. Warning: If in addition to accessing class members, the method also accesses instance members, then the method must be an instance method, not a class method.
2. If you might need to call a method even when there are no objects from the method's class, then you should make it a class method. For example, during a mouse population simulation, you might call `printMouseCount` when there are no mouse objects (they've all died perhaps). Since it's a class method, you do it like this, without needing a calling object:

   ```
   Mouse4.printMouseCount();
   ```

3. The `main` method is the starting point for all programs and, as such, it gets executed prior to the instantiation of any objects. To accommodate that functionality, you're required to make the `main` method a class method. If your `main` method is rather long and you decide to break it up with helper methods,

then the helper methods (assuming that they don't involve instance members) should be class methods as well. By making them class methods, it's easier for `main` to call them.

4. If you have a general-purpose method that stands on its own, make it a class method. By standing on its own, we mean that the method is not related to a particular object. Such methods are called *utility methods*. You've seen examples of utility methods, like `Math.round` and `Math.sqrt`, in the `Math` class. In Section 9.5, you'll learn how to write your own utility methods.

9.4 Named Constants

Using names instead of hard-coded values makes a program more self-documenting. When a constant value is needed in more than one place in the block of code, establishing the value at one place at the beginning of that block minimizes the chance of inconsistency. In Java, you can define named constants at several levels of scale.

Local Named Constants—A Review from Chapter 3

At the most microscopic level, you can define local named constants. Back in Figure 3.5 of Chapter 3, we defined two local named constants, `FREEZING_POINT`, and `CONVERSION_FACTOR`, to self-document the Fahrenheit-to-Celsius conversion formula in a simple program that did nothing more than make a temperature conversion. Usually, we embed this kind of activity in some larger program by putting it in a helper method like this:

```
private double fahrenheitToCelsius(double fahrenheit)
{
  final double FREEZING_POINT = 32.0;
  final double CONVERSION_FACTOR = 5.0 / 9.0;

  return CONVERSION_FACTOR * (fahrenheit - FREEZING_POINT);
} // end fahrenheitToCelsius
```

The local named constants in this method make the code easier to understand.

Instance Named Constants—A Review from Chapter 7

At the next higher level of scale, sometimes you want a constant that's a permanent property of an object and accessible to all instance methods associated with that object. Those constants are called instance named constants, or, more simply, *instance constants*. Here's an example instance constant declaration that identifies a permanent property of a `Person` object:

```
public final String SOCIAL_SECURITY_NUMBER;
```

An instance constant declaration differs from a local named constant declaration in three ways: (1) An instance constant declaration should appear at the top of the class definition, rather than within a method, (2) An instance constant declaration is preceded by a `public` or `private` access modifier, and (3) Although it's legal to initialize an instance constant in a declaration, it's more common to initialize it in a constructor.

Class Named Constants

At the next higher level of scale, sometimes you want a constant that's the same for all objects in a class. In other words, you want something that's like a class variable, but it's constant. Those constants are called class named constants, or, more simply, *class constants*. In Chapter 5 you learned about two class constants defined in the Java API `Math` class, `PI` and `E`. Now you'll learn how to write your own class constants. To declare a class constant, use this syntax:

<private-or-public> `static final` *<type>* *<variable-name>* = *<initial-value>*;

A class constant declaration differs from an instance constant declaration in two ways: (1) A class constant includes the `static` modifier; and (2) A class constant should be initialized as part of its declaration.[1] If you attempt to assign a value to a class constant later on, that generates a compilation error.

As with an instance constant, a class constant declaration should be preceded by a `public` or `private` access modifier. If the constant is needed only within the class (and not outside the class), you should make it `private`. This allows you to modify the constant without upsetting somebody else who previously elected to use your constant in one of their programs. However, if you want the constant to be available to other classes, it's appropriate to make it `public`. It's safe to do that because the `final` modifier makes it immutable (unchangeable). In the next section, you'll see examples of `public` class constants embedded in a utility class.

The following `Human` class contains a `NORMAL_TEMP` named constant. We make it a class constant (with the `static` and `final` modifiers) because all `Human` objects have the same normal temperature of 98.6° Fahrenheit. We make it a `private` class constant because it is needed only within the `Human` class.

```
public class Human
{
  private static final double NORMAL_TEMP = 98.6;
  private double currentTemp;
  ...
  public boolean isHealthy()
  {
    return Math.abs(currentTemp - NORMAL_TEMP) < 1;
  } // end isHealthy

  public void diagnose()
  {
    if ((currentTemp - NORMAL_TEMP) > 5)
    {
      System.out.println("Go to the emergency room now!");
      ...

} // end class Human
```

Let's summarize when you should use the three different types of named constants. Use a local named constant if the constant is needed within only one method. Use an instance constant if the constant describes a permanent property of an object. And use a class constant if the constant is a property of the collection of all the objects in the class or of the class in general.

Positions of Declarations

Now for some coding-style issues. We recommend putting all class constant declarations above all instance constant declarations. Putting declarations at the top makes them stand out more, and it's appropriate for class constants to stand out the most since they have the broadest scope. Likewise, we recommend putting

[1] Although relatively rare, it's legal to declare a class constant as part of a static initializer block. For details on initializer blocks, see http://java.sun.com/docs/books/tutorial/java/javaOO/initial.html.

all class variable declarations above all instance variable declarations. Here is the preferred sequence of declarations within a given class:

class constants
instance constants
class variables
instance variables
constructors
methods

9.5 Writing Your Own Utility Class

Up to this point, you've implemented methods that solve problems for a particular class. Suppose you want to implement methods that are more general purpose, so that multiple and unforeseen classes can use them. Those types of methods are called *utility methods*. In the past, you've used utility methods from the `Math` class; for example, `Math.round` and `Math.sqrt`. In this section you learn to write your own utility methods as part of a utility class.

See Figure 9.3's `PrintUtilities` class. It contains print-oriented utility constants and methods. The two constants, `MAX_COL` and `MAX_ROW`, keep track of the maximum column and maximum row for a standard-sized piece of paper. If you have multiple classes that print reports, those constants can help to ensure report-size uniformity. The `printCentered` method prints a given string horizontally centered. The `printUnderlined` method prints a given string with dashes underneath it. We put those methods in a utility class because they perform print routines that might be needed by multiple other classes.

In the `PrintUtilities` class, note that the constants and methods all use the `public` and `static` modifiers. That's normal for utility class members. The `public` and `static` modifiers make it easy for other classes to access `PrintUtilities`' members.

9.6 Using Class Members in Conjunction with Instance Members

Now, let's look at a problem that requires a combination of instance members and class members. The goal is to model a collection of penny jars. With each insertion of a penny in any jar, we want the program to print "clink" and increment the penny count for that jar and the total penny count. When the total number of pennies exceeds a fixed goal, the program should print "Time to spend!" Then the program should print the total number of pennies in each jar and the total number of pennies in all jars.

The Primary Class

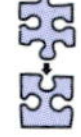

Address the most critical problem as soon as possible.

The most important part of this problem is the usage of instance and class members. So let's address this complexity immediately. We need a class that describes both individual penny jars and the collection of all penny jars. Figure 9.4 has a UML class diagram for a `PennyJar` class that does what we want. To handle the pennies in an individual `PennyJar` object, it uses instance members—`pennies`, `addPenny`, and `getPennies`. To handle the pennies in the collection of all penny jars, it uses class members—`GOAL`, `allPennies`, and `getAllPennies`. In the UML diagram, you can tell that those three members are class members because they are underlined (as you may recall, UML standards suggest that you underline all class members). The UML diagram does not include a `main` method, so this class won't run by itself. In effect, we're starting

```
/*************************************************************************
* PrintUtilities.java
* Dean & Dean
*
* This class contains constants and methods for fancy printing.
*************************************************************************/

public class PrintUtilities
{
  public static final int MAX_COL = 80; // last allowed column
  public static final int MAX_ROW = 50; // last allowed row

  //*******************************************************************

  // Print given string horizontally centered.

  public static void printCentered(String s)
  {
    int startingCol; // starting point for string
    startingCol = (MAX_COL / 2) - (s.length() / 2);

    for (int i=0; i<startingCol; i++)
    {
      System.out.print(" ");
    }
    System.out.println(s);
  } // end printCentered

  //*******************************************************************

  // Print given string with dashes underneath it.

  public static void printUnderlined(String s)
  {
    System.out.println(s);
    for (int i=0; i<s.length(); i++)
    {
      System.out.print("-");
    }
  } // end printUnderlined
} // end class PrintUtilities
```

Figure 9.3 Example utility class that handles special-needs printing

with an implementation view of the problem and developing the program from bottom up, because our current focus is on the details of instance and class members.

See Figure 9.5. It contains an implementation of the `PennyJar` class. Let's first examine `PennyJar`'s constant and variable declarations:

- `GOAL` is the target number of pennies to be saved for all penny jars combined. As such, it's a class member and uses the `static` modifier. Since the goal amount is fixed, `GOAL` is a named constant and uses the `final` modifier and all uppercase letters. The `GOAL` is initialized to `10000`, which amounts

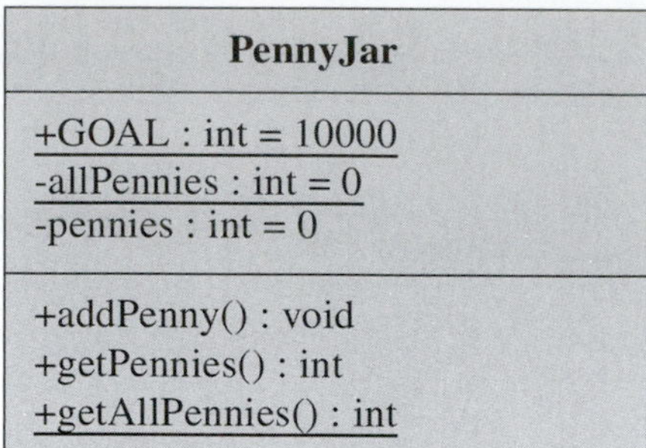

Figure 9.4 Class describing penny jars individually and as a group

to $100.00. Presumably, when the user reaches the `GOAL` amount, he/she will empty all penny jars and spend all the money in a big shopping spree.

- The `allPennies` variable stores the total pennies in all jars. Since `allPennies` is an attribute of all the penny jars, it's a class member and uses the `static` modifier. Although we could just accept the zero default as the initial value, we explicitly initialize to zero to emphasize what we want.
- The `pennies` variable is an ordinary instance variable. Again, although we could just accept the zero default as the initial value, we explicitly initialize to zero to emphasize what we want.

Let's now examine the method definitions:

- The `getPennies` method is a typical accessor method, and it retrieves the value of the `pennies` instance variable. Accessing the `pennies` instance variable means that `getPennies` must be an instance method. You can see that `getPennies` is an instance method because there's no `static` modifier in its heading.
- The `addPenny` method simulates adding a penny to a jar. It updates the `pennies` instance variable for the jar that the penny was added to and updates the `allPennies` class variable for the collection of jars. Accessing the `pennies` instance variable means that `addPenny` must be an instance method, and, as such, there's no `static` modifier in its heading.
- The `getAllPennies` method retrieves the value of the `allPennies` class variable. Since `getAllPennies` deals only with class-wide data, it's appropriate to make it a class method. You can see that `getAllPennies` is a class method because of the `static` modifier in its heading.

Driver

Figure 9.6 contains a driver for the `PennyJar` class. Notice how `main` calls the instance methods `addPenny` and `getPennies` by first creating `PennyJar` objects. It assigns the newly created objects to the reference variables `pennyJar1` and `pennyJar2`. Then it uses those reference variables to call the instance methods.

Notice how `main` uses a different technique for calling `getAllPennies`. Instead of prefixing `getAllPennies` with a reference variable (`pennyJar1` or `pennyJar2`), `main` calls `getAllPennies` by prefixing it with the `PennyJar` class name. That's because `getAllPennies` is a class method, not an instance method. Would it be OK to omit the class name prefix and just call `getAllPennies` directly? No. We cannot omit the class name prefix because `getAllPennies` is in a separate class. If we had merged `main` into the `PennyJar` class to run the program from that class, then we could omit the `PennyJar` prefix from the `getAllPennies` method call. However, it never hurts to include the class name prefix for a class method call. It makes it easier to cut and paste, and it helps make the code more self-documenting.

```java
/****************************************************************
* PennyJar.java
* Dean & Dean
*
* This class counts pennies for individual penny jars and for
* all penny jars combined.
****************************************************************/

public class PennyJar
{
  public static final int GOAL = 10000;
  private static int allPennies = 0;
  private int pennies = 0;

  //*************************************************************

  public int getPennies()
  {
    return this.pennies;
  }

  //*************************************************************

  public void addPenny()
  {
    System.out.println("Clink!");
    this.pennies++;
    PennyJar.allPennies++;

    if (PennyJar.allPennies >= PennyJar.GOAL)
    {
      System.out.println("Time to spend!");
    }
  } // end addPenny

  //*************************************************************

  public static int getAllPennies()
  {
    return PennyJar.allPennies;
  }
} // end class PennyJar
```

class variables

instance variable

instance method

class method

Figure 9.5 A `PennyJar` class that illustrates both instance members and class members

```
/*************************************************************
* PennyJarDriver.java
* Dean & Dean
*
* This class drives the PennyJar class.
*************************************************************/

public class PennyJarDriver
{
  public static void main(String[] args)
  {
    PennyJar pennyJar1 = new PennyJar();
    PennyJar pennyJar2 = new PennyJar();

    pennyJar1.addPenny();
    pennyJar1.addPenny();
    pennyJar2.addPenny();
    System.out.println(pennyJar1.getPennies());
    System.out.println(PennyJar.getAllPennies());
  } // end main
} // end class PennyJarDriver
```

Output:

```
Clink!
Clink!
Clink!
2
3
```

Figure 9.6 Driver for the `PennyJar` class in Figure 9.5

9.7 Problem Solving with Class Members and Instance Members in a Linked List Class (Optional)

The previous PennyJar program is admittedly just a "toy" program, but sometimes toy programs can help you learn new techniques. In this section, you'll use the case-based design approach described in Chapter 8 and turn the PennyJar program into something more practical.

FundRaiser Program

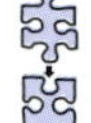

Adapt a previous program to a new purpose.

Each penny jar is an agent in the process of collecting money. Think of the agent as a human solicitor. Then the collection of all penny jars becomes a body of people working in an organized fund-raising activity. The penny jar pennies become donation pledges, and the GOAL of 10,000 pennies becomes a GOAL of 10,000 dollars in donations. Now for the big picture: Replace the `PennyJar` class with a more general `Agent` class. And replace the `PennyJarDriver` class with a `FundRaiser` class.

The `Agent` class should have methods that are similar to the methods in the `PennyJar` class. You can replace the `getPennies` instance method with a `getValue` instance method, the `addPenny` instance method with an addValue instance method, and the getAllPennies class method with getAllValues class method. When you do this, ask yourself if there might be a better way to allocate the work done by these methods.

Since you have turned the passive penny jars into active human agents, you should ask yourself, "Where is the time-to-spend decision made?" This high-level decision should be made in the driver. So as you transition from the PennyJar program to the FundRaiser program, you need to switch the location of the final spending decisions. That means the GOAL constant should be moved up to the FundRaiser class.

Similarly, you should ask yourself, "Where are the decisions made about individual contributions?" Are they made at the level of the manager in the FundRaiser class, or are they made at the level of individual agents in the Agent class? The donors talk to individual agents, so that information should enter the program through an Agent method, probably the addValue method. Since individual contribution decisions are now decentralized, you should coordinate efforts from the top. You should plan to conduct a sequence of centrally directed publicity campaigns. To carry out each campaign, you should define another class method—addAllValues. In an attempt to get multiple donation pledges, the addAllValues method loops through all of the agents and has each agent call addValue. After each campaign, call the getAllValues class method to see if the total value exceeds the GOAL. If it does, print the total value and quit.

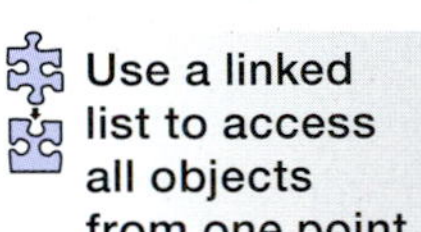
Use a linked list to access all objects from one point.

In a real fund raiser, you can't predict how many donors you'll have. Likewise, in the FundRaiser program, you want to be able to handle an unknown number of donor agents. The trick is to set things up like a "treasure hunt"—a trip in which each intermediate destination gives you the next destination. Each agent tells you where the next agent is, until you get the last agent, who tells you that's all.

You'll use this strategy for the getAllValues method as well as for the addAllValues method. Instead of just reading a previously accumulated value from a class variable like allPennies, the getAllValues method will accumulate values from individual agents. This avoids data duplication and eliminates the need for an allValues class variable. It also frees each individual agent from the task of adding the current contribution to an allValues variable in addition to adding it to its own value.

The Agent class still needs one class variable, however—a reference variable that tells class methods where to start their trips. We'll call this one class reference variable listOfAgents. This variable always contains a reference to the first object to visit. Each object contains an instance reference variable called nextAgent, which refers to the next object to visit. In the last object in the list, the nextAgent reference variable contains null. This says the trip is done. This structure is called a *linked list,* and the single class reference variable, listOfAgents, points to the object at the *head* of the list.

Initially, there are no objects in the list, and the value in the listOfAgents variable is null. The constructor for each new Agent object inserts that object at the head of the Agent class's linked list, using this algorithm:

```
set this agent's nextAgent to listOfAgents
set listOfAgents to this agent
```

This means that the first object visited in a trip through all the objects is the last object constructed, and the last object visited is the first object constructed. In other words, the visitation sequence is opposite to the construction sequence.

Figure 9.7 shows a UML class diagram for the program. As usual, the driver class (FundRaiser) has a main method. It also has a class constant, GOAL, which establishes the stopping criterion. The Agent class has a constructor, two public class methods (getAllValues and addAllValues), and two private instance methods (getValue and addValue). Notice that the two public class methods

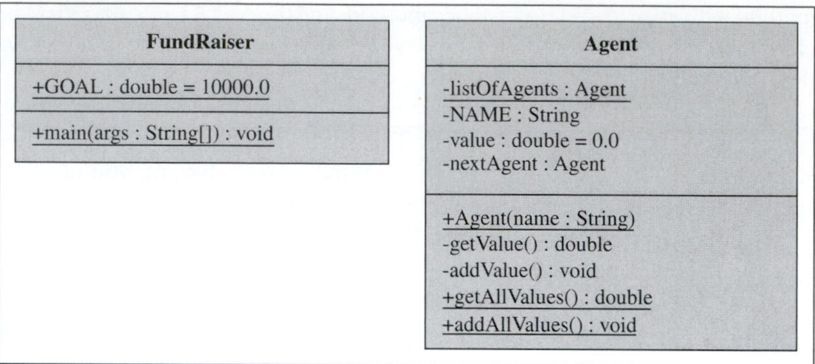

Figure 9.7 UML class diagram for driver of FundRaiser program

provide the only access route to everything else in this class. Do you remember the rule that a class method cannot access an instance member directly? If that rule is valid, and everything else is some kind of instance member, how can these two class methods access everything else? These methods do not access any instance members directly. They directly access the class variable `listOfAgents`. That class variable gives them a reference to an object, and each object gives them the reference to the next object. These object references enable the class members to access everything indirectly.

It's time to look at the implementation code. Figure 9.8 shows the `FundRaiser` driver class. The driver prompts the user to enter a desired number of agents, and the `for` loop steps through a process that inputs each agent's name and instantiates an `Agent` object with that name. The subsequent `do` loop initiates each fund-raising campaign by calling the `addAllValues` method. Then it determines the result of that campaign by calling the `getAllValues` method. Then it prints the cumulative result after that campaign. If the result is still less than `GOAL`, it launches another campaign until the goal is attained. Notice that this driver contains no references to particular `Agent` objects. It does not even contain a reference to the linked list of agents. All access to data in the `Agent` class is controlled by the `Agent` class methods, `addAllValues` and `getAllValues`. The data is well encapsulated—a very good thing indeed!

Figure 9.9a shows the first part of the `Agent` class. The class variable, `listOfAgents`, initially contains `null`, because initially there are no objects in the list. Now look at the constructor. The first instantiation assigns this `null` value to the first object's `nextAgent` reference variable. Then it uses the `this` reference to assign the first object to the `listOfAgents` class variable. The second instantiation assigns the reference now in the `listOfAgents` reference variable (a reference to the first object) to the second object's `nextAgent` instance reference variable. Then it uses the `this` reference to assign the second object to the `listOfAgents` class variable. Thus, the list of linked objects builds up like this:

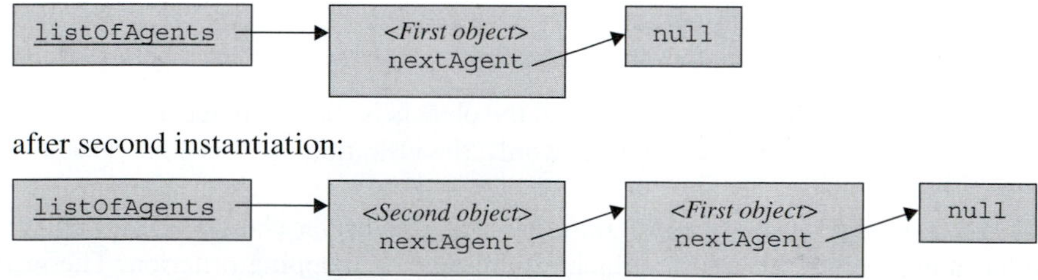

```
/*******************************************************************
* FundRaiser.java
* Dean & Dean
*
* This program manages fund-raising agents.
*******************************************************************/

import java.util.Scanner;

public class FundRaiser
{
  public static final double GOAL = 10000.00;

  //****************************************************************

  public static void main(String[] args)
  {
    Scanner stdIn = new Scanner(System.in);
    int numberOfAgents;
    double totalValue;
    String name;

    System.out.print("Enter total number of agents: ");
    numberOfAgents = stdIn.nextInt();
    stdIn.nextLine();
    for (int i=0; i<numberOfAgents; i++)
    {
      System.out.print("Enter agent name: ");
      name = stdIn.nextLine();
      new Agent(name);
    }
    do
    {
      Agent.addAllValues();
      totalValue = Agent.getAllValues();
      System.out.printf("Total value = $%,.2f\n", totalValue);
    } while (totalValue < GOAL);
    System.out.println("Time to Spend!");
  } // end main
} // end FundRaiser class
```

Notice that this driver does not need to keep track of any object references.

All subsequent access to Agent class is through class methods.

Figure 9.8 Top level of FundRaiser program
This drives the Agent class in Figure 9.9a and 9.9b.

```
/*************************************************************
* Agent.java
* Dean & Dean
*
* Class that describes agents that collect quantitative values.
*************************************************************/

import java.util.Scanner;

public class Agent
{
  private static Agent listOfAgents = null;   // head of list

  private final String NAME;
  private double value = 0.0;
  private Agent nextAgent;                    // next in list

  //**********************************************************

  public Agent(String name)
  {
    this.NAME = name;
    this.nextAgent = listOfAgents;
    listOfAgents = this;
  } // end constructor

  //**********************************************************

  private double getValue()
  {
    return this.value;
  }

  //**********************************************************

  private void addValue()
  {
    Scanner stdIn = new Scanner(System.in);

    System.out.printf("Enter %s's contribution: ", this.NAME );
    this.value += stdIn.nextDouble();
  } // end addValue
```

This inserts each new object at the head of the linked list.

Figure 9.9a First part of `Agent` class of FundRaiser program
This code and the code in 9.9b are driven by the `FundRaiser` class in Figure 9.8.

```
//**************************************************************

public static double getAllValues()
{
  double totalValue = 0.0;
  Agent agent = listOfAgents;
  while (agent != null)
  {
    totalValue += agent.getValue();
    agent = agent.nextAgent;
  }
  return totalValue;
} // end getAllValues

//**************************************************************

public static void addAllValues()
{
  Agent agent = listOfAgents;
  while (agent != null)
  {
    agent.addValue();
    agent = agent.nextAgent;
  }
} // end addAllValues
} // end class Agent
```

This retrieves location of next object in list.

Figure 9.9b Class methods in `Agent` class of FundRaiser program
This code and the code in Figure 9.9a are driven by the `FundRaiser` class in Figure 9.8.

The rest of the code in Figure 9.9a is straightforward. The `getValue` instance method returns the value in the `value` instance variable. The `addValue` instance method assigns a user input to the `value` instance variable.

Figure 9.9b shows the two class methods in the `Agent` class. The `addAllValues` method starts at the object referred to by the class reference variable, `listOfObjects`. It calls that object's `addValue` instance method to retrieve input and add it to that object's `value` instance variable. Then it uses the current object's `nextAgent` instance variable to find the next object in the list, and it repeats the process until `nextAgent` is `null`. The `getAllValues` method initializes local variables, `totalValue` and `agent`. Then it steps through the objects just like the `addAllValues` method did, adding the value returned by the instance method `getValue` to `totalValue`. When the `agent` reference becomes `null`, it stops and returns the accumulated `totalValue`.

The sample session below shows what the program does. Notice that the sequence employed when new objects are added is opposite to the sequence employed when the original objects were created. That's because each new object is inserted at the head of the linked list, rather than at the tail, as you might normally expect. You could append each new object to the tail end of the list and make the sequences the same, but that would require an additional class variable and more code in the constructor.

Sample session:

```
Enter total number of agents: 3
Enter agent name: Bavitha
Enter agent name: Alan
Enter agent name: Rebecca
Enter Rebecca's contribution: 6000
Enter Alan's contribution: 6000
Enter Bavitha's contribution: 6000
Total value = $18,000.00
Time to Spend!
```

`LinkedList` API Class

Sun's API library contains several classes that handle collections of data. Those classes are referred to as the *collections framework* or the *collections API*. We'll discuss one such collection class, the `ArrayList` class, in depth in the next chapter. In this chapter, and this section specifically, you've learned about linked lists. Programmers often implement linked lists from scratch as shown in this section, but as an alternative, they also implement linked lists using the `LinkedList` class, another class from the collections framework. To learn about the `LinkedList` class and all the other collection classes, see http://java.sun.com/javase/6/docs/technotes/guides/collections/.

Summary

- Class variables have a `static` modifier. Use class variables for attributes of the collection of all objects in a class. Use instance variables for the attributes of individual objects.
- Remember that class variables have broader scope than instance variables, and instance variables have broader scope than local variables. To improve encapsulation, you should try to use variables with narrower scope rather than broader scope.
- An instance method can directly access class members as well as instance members.
- A class method can directly access class members, but it cannot directly access instance members. To access a class member from a class method, you need to use a class name dot prefix.
- Use class methods for processes related to the group of all the objects in a class, for processes that must exist before any objects are defined (like `main`), for class method helpers, and for general-purpose utilities.
- Instance constants have a `final` modifier only. Use them for permanent attributes of individual objects.
- Use class constants for permanent data that is not associated with any particular object. Class constants use the `final` and `static` modifiers.
- You can use a class variable to refer to an arbitrarily long linked list of a class's objects. This enables another class to access all of the class's objects through class methods only, and the other class does not need any references to specific objects.

Review Questions

§9.2 Class Variables

1. Normally, you should use the `private` access modifier for class variables. (T / F)
2. When should you declare a variable to be a class variable as opposed to an instance variable?
3. What are the default values for class variables?

§9.3 Class Methods

4. In Figure 9.2's `Mouse4` class, assume you have a method whose heading is `public int getAge()`. Suppose you want to call this method from another class. What's wrong with the following statement?

```
int age = Mouse4.getAge();
```

5. Member access:
   a) It is OK to use `this` in a class method. (T / F)
   b) It is OK to use the class name as a prefix when calling a class method. (T / F)
   c) Within a `main` method, it is OK to omit the class name prefix before the name of another class method being called. (T / F)
6. It is legal to access a class member from an instance method and also from a constructor. (T / F)
7. It is legal to directly access an instance member from a class method. (T / F)
8. What are four common reasons for making a method a class method?

§9.4 Named Constants

9. What keyword converts a variable into a constant?
10. If you want a named constant used by instance methods to have the same value regardless of which object accesses it, the declaration should include the `static` modifier. (T / F)
11. A class constant should be initialized within a constructor. (T / F)
12. Suppose you have a grading program that instantiates multiple exam objects from an `Exam` class. Provide a declaration for a constant minimum passing score. Assume the minimum passing score for all exams is 59.5.

§9.5 Writing Your Own Utility Class

13. A utility class's members should normally use the `private` and `static` modifiers. (T / F)

Exercises

1. [after §9.2] Given a class with a class variable. All of the class's objects get a separate copy of the class variable. (T / F)

2. [after §9.2] In general, why should you prefer local variables over instance variables and instance variables over class variables?

3. [after §9.2] Given a program that keeps track of book details with the help of a `Book` class, for each of the following program variables, specify whether it should be a local variable, an instance variable, or a class variable.

   `bookTitle` (the title of a particular book)
   `averagePrice` (the average price of all of the books)
   `price` (the price of a particular book)
   `i` (an index variable used to loop through all of the books)

4. [after §9.3] If a method accesses a class variable and also an instance variable, the method:
   a) must be a local method
   b) must be an instance method
   c) must be a class method
   d) can be either a class method or an instance method—it depends on other factors

5. [after §9.3] If you attempt to directly access an instance method from within a class method, you'll see an error message like this:

```
Non-static <method-name> cannot be referenced from a static context
```

   Normally, how should you fix the bug?

6. [after §9.3] Consider the following program.

```
public class Test
{
  private int x;
  private static int y;
  public void doIt()
  {
    x = 1;
    y = 2;
  }
  public static void tryIt()
  {
    x = 3;
    y = 4;
  }
  public static void main(String[] args)
  {
    doIt();
    tryIt();
    Test t = new Test();
    t.doIt();
    Test.doIt();
    Test.tryIt();
  }
} // end Test class
```

a) Mark all of the lines of code that have a compilation error.
b) For each compilation-error line, explain why it is incorrect.

Note:

- There are no errors in the variable declarations and there are no errors in the method headings, so don't mark any of those lines as having an error.
- For each compilation error, just provide the reason that the error occurs. In particular, do not solve the problem by fixing the code until you get rid of all the compilation errors.

7. [after §9.4] Why is it safe to declare named constants `public`?

8. [after §9.4] Write appropriate declarations for the following constants. In each case, decide whether to include the keyword, `static`, and whether to include initialization in the declaration. Also, make each constant as easily accessible as possible, consistent with protection from inadvertent corruption.
a) The year of birth of a person.
b) The format string, `"%-25s%,13.2f%,13.2f%(,15.2f\n"`, to use in several `printf` statements in a single method.
c) The "golden ratio" or width/length of a golden rectangle. It's equal to (sqrt(5) − 1) / 2 = 0.6180339887498949.

9. [after §9.5] Write a utility class called `RandomDistribution`, which contains the following four class methods. You should be able to implement all of these methods with calls to `Math` class methods and/or calls to one of the `uniform` methods within the `RandomDistribution` class.
a) Write a method called `uniform` that generates a `double` random number from a continuous distribution that is uniform between `double` values `min` and `max`.
b) Write another (overloaded) method called `uniform` that generates an `int` random number from a discrete distribution that is uniform between `int` values `min` and `max`, including both of these end points.

c) Write a method called `triangular` that generates an `int` random number from a symmetrical discrete triangular distribution that goes between the `int` values `min` and `max`, including both of these end points. (*Hint:* Make two calls to the `int` version of the above `uniform` method.)

d) Write a method called `exponential` that generates a `double` random number from an exponential distribution having an expected time between random arrival events equal to `averageTimeInterval`. Here is the algorithm:

`return ← averageTimeInterval *` $\log_e$(1.0 − `Math.random`)

10. [after §9.6] In the PennyJar program, the `PennyJar` dot prefix is used to access `PennyJar` members. There are four `PennyJar` dot prefixes in the `PennyJar` class and one `PennyJar` dot prefix in the `PennyJarDriver` class. For each such prefix, is it legal to omit it?

11. [after §9.7] PetMouse program:
The program below creates a linked list of objects. The class reference variable, `pets`, refers to the first object in the list, and each subsequent object contains an instance reference variable that refers to the next object, except the instance reference variable in the last object refers to null. Notice that the individual pets are *anonymous objects,* in that they do not have separate names. The class reference variable, `pets`, actually refers to the first object in the list, but conceptually it refers to all the objects in the list. Notice that we use the same word, `next`, for a local variable in a class method and an instance variable, because both variables are really talking about the same things, and it would be unnatural to use different terms.

```
/*************************************************************
* PetMouseDriver.java
* Dean & Dean
*
* This creates & displays a linked list of simple objects.
*************************************************************/

public class PetMouseDriver
{
  public static void main(String[] args)
  {
    new PetMouse();
    new PetMouse();
    new PetMouse();
    PetMouse.list();
  } // end main
} // end class PetMouseDriver
```

```
/*************************************************************
* PetMouse.java
* Dean & Dean
*
* This creates & displays a linked list of simple objects.
*************************************************************/

import java.util.Scanner;

public class PetMouse
{
```

```
  private static PetMouse pets;  // points to list of pets

  private String name;
  private PetMouse next;

  //***************************************************************

  // Insert each new object at beginning of existing list.

  public PetMouse()
  {
    Scanner stdIn = new Scanner(System.in);

    this.next = pets;
    System.out.print("Enter name: ");
    this.name = stdIn.nextLine();
    pets = this;
  } // end constructor

  //***************************************************************

  public static void list()
  {
    PetMouse next = pets;

    while (next != null)
    {
      System.out.print(next.name + "  ");
      next = next.next;
    }
    System.out.println();
  } // end list
} // end class PetMouse
```

Use the following trace setup to trace the PetMouse program. Note how the `pets` class variable is underneath the `PetMouse` header, but separate from the three objects. We've shown `pets`'s initial value, `null`.

input
cutie
sugar
fluffy

Driver	PetMouse									
		static	list	obj1		obj2		obj3		
line#	***line#***	**pets**	**next**	**name**	**next**	**name**	**next**	**name**	**next**	**output**
		null								

Review Question Solutions

1. True.
2. You should declare a variable to be a class variable as opposed to an instance variable if the variable holds data that is associated with the class as a whole. You should use class variables to describe properties of a class's objects that need to be shared by all of the objects.
3. The default values for class variables are the same as they are for instance variables of the same type. Here are the default values:

   integer types get 0
   floating point types get 0.0
   `boolean` types get `false`
   reference types get `null`

4. Because there's no `static` modifier, `getAge` is an instance method. The `Mouse4.getAge()` call uses a `Mouse4` dot prefix. It's illegal to use a class name (`Mouse4`) as a prefix for an instance method call. To call an instance method, you need to use a reference variable dot prefix.
5. Member access:
   a) False. You cannot use `this` in a class method.
   b) True. You can always use the class name as a class method prefix.
   c) True, if the `main` method is "merged" into the same class as the other method.
   False, if the other method is in a different class.
   Including the class name prefix allows you to move the `main` method to another class later.
6. True. You can access a class member from an instance method and also from a constructor—just prefix the class member with the class name.
7. False. You can access an instance member from a class method only if you prefix the method name with a reference to a particular object.
8. You should make a method a class method:
   a) If you have a method that uses class variables and/or calls class methods, then it's a good candidate for being a class method.
   b) If you might need to call a method even when there are no objects from the method's class, then you should make it a class method.
   c) The main method has to be a class method. If a main method uses helper methods that don't involve instance members, then the helper methods should be class methods.
   d) If you have a general-purpose method that stands on its own, make it a class method.
9. The keyword `final` converts a variable into a constant.
10. True. Use `static` to make a constant be the same for all objects.
11. False. A class constant should normally be initialized as part of its declaration. If it is assigned a value later on, including within a constructor, it generates a compilation error.
12. Minimum passing score declaration:

```
private static final double MIN_PASSING_SCORE = 59.5;
```

13. False. A utility class's members should normally use the `public` and `static` modifiers.

CHAPTER 10

Arrays and ArrayLists

Objectives

- Compare an array with other objects.
- Create and initialize arrays.
- Copy values from one array to another.
- Shift data in an array.
- Make histograms.
- Search an array for particular data.
- Sort data.
- Create and use two-dimensional arrays.
- Create and use arrays of objects.
- See how the ArrayList class makes arrays more flexible.
- Store primitives in an ArrayList.
- Pass anonymous objects to and from methods.
- Learn how to use for-each loops.

Outline

10.1 Introduction

In the past, you've seen that objects typically contain more than one data item, and the different data items each have a different name. Now, we'll look at a special kind of object that holds several items of the same type and uses the same name for all of them. Natural language has ways to give a single name to a population: "pack" of wolves, "herd" of cattle, "pride" of lions, "passel" of possum, "fesnying" of ferrets, and so on. Java has a way to do the same thing.

When you have a collection of items of the same type, and you'd like to use the same name for all of them, you can define them all together as an *array*. Each item in the array is more formally called an array *element*. To distinguish the different elements in the array, you use the array name plus a number that identifies the position of the element within the array. For example, if you stored a collection of song titles in an array named `songs`, you'd distinguish the first song title by saying `songs[0]`, and you'd distinguish the second song title by saying `songs[1]`. As evidenced by this example, array elements start at position 0. An array's position numbers (0, 1, 2, and so on) are more formally called *indexes*. We'll have more to say about array indexes in the next section.

There's an important advantage in using one name for all of a group of similar items and distinguishing them only by a number. It can lead to simpler code. For example, if you need to store 100 song titles, you could declare 100 separate variables. But what a pain it would be to have to write 100 declaration statements and keep track of 100 different variable names. The easier solution is to use an array and declare just one variable—a `songs` array variable.

Readers who want an early introduction to arrays have the option of reading Sections 10.1 through 10.6 after completing Chapter 4. The natural connection between Chapter 4 and this chapter is that Chapter 4 describes loops and arrays rely heavily on loops.

Starting with Section 10.7, we present arrays in an object-oriented context, where arrays are members of a class. We discuss techniques for searching an array and sorting an array. We describe different organizational structures for arrays—two-dimensional arrays and arrays of objects. We then present `Array Lists`, which are similar to arrays but provide more flexibility. `ArrayLists` grow dynamically as you add elements, and it's easy to insert or delete elements in the middle of `ArrayLists`. Finally, we describe a special type of `for` loop called a for-each loop, which is particularly useful for processing the elements in an `ArrayList`.

10.2 Array Basics

In this section, we show you how to perform simple operations on an array, such as loading an array with data and printing an array. To illustrate these operations, we'll refer to the `phoneList` array in Figure 10.1. The `phoneList` array holds a list of five speed-dial phone numbers for a cell phone. The first phone number is 8167412000, the second phone number is 2024561111, and so on.

Accessing an Array's Elements

To work with an array, you need to access an array's elements. For example, to print the contents of an array, you need to access the array's first element, print it, access the array's second element, print it, and so on. To access an element within an array, you specify the array's name, followed by square brackets surrounding the

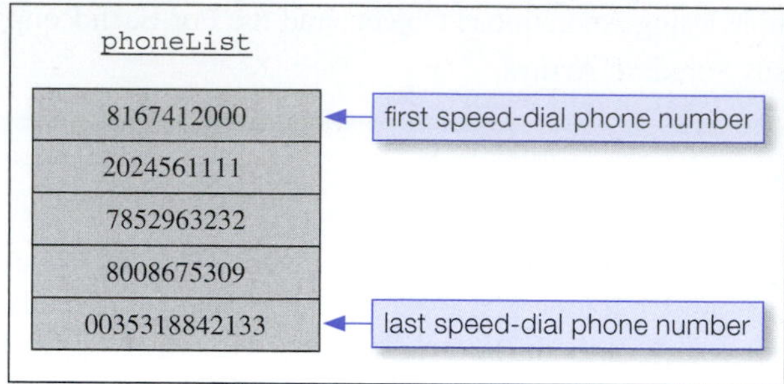

Figure 10.1 Example array—five-element array for holding a list of speed-dial phone numbers

element's index. Figure 10.2 shows how to access the individual elements within the `phoneList` array. The first element's index is 0, so you access the first element with `phoneList[0]`. Why is the first element's index 0 instead of 1? The index is a measure of how far you are from the beginning of the array. If you're right at the beginning, the distance from the beginning is 0. So the first element uses 0 for its index value.

index	phoneList	how to access each element
0	8167412000	phoneList[0]
1	2024561111	phoneList[1]
2	7852963232	phoneList[2]
3	8008675309	phoneList[3]
4	0035318842133	phoneList[4]

5 elements

Figure 10.2 Accessing elements in a `phoneList` array

Beginning programmers often think that the last index in an array is equal to the number of elements in the array. For example, a beginning programmer might think that the last index in the `phoneList` array equals 5 because the `phoneList` array has 5 elements. Not so. The first index is 0, and the last index is 4. Try to remember this important rule: The last index in an array is equal to one less than the number of elements in the array. If you attempt to access an array element with an index that's greater than the last index or less than zero, you'll get a program crash. So if you specify `phoneList[5]` or `phoneList[-1]`, you'll get a program crash. As part of that crash, the Java Virtual Machine (JVM) prints an error message with the word "`ArrayIndexOutOfBoundsException`" in it. `ArrayIndexOutOfBoundsException` is an *exception*. You'll learn about exceptions in Chapter 15, but for now, just think of an exception as a sophisticated type of error that can be used by programmers to determine the source of a bug.

Now that you know how to access an array element, let's put it to use. Here's how you can change the first phone number to 2013434:

```
phoneList[0] = 2013434;
```

And here's how you can print the second phone number:

```
System.out.println(phoneList[1]);
```

Be aware that some people use the term "subscript" rather than "index" because subscripting is the standard English way to represent an element from within a group. In other words, x_0, x_1, x_2, and so on in ordinary writing is the same as `x[0]`, `x[1]`, `x[2]`, and so on in Java.

Example Program

Let's see how arrays are used within the context of a complete program. In Figure 10.3, the SpeedDialList program prompts the user for the number of speed-dial phone numbers that are to be entered, fills up the `phoneList` array with user-entered phone numbers, and prints the created speed-dial list. To fill an array and to print an array's elements, you typically need to step through each element of the array with the help of an index variable that increments from zero to the index of the array's last filled element. Often, the index variable's increment operations are implemented with the help of a `for` loop. For example, the SpeedDialList program uses the following `for` loop header to increment an index variable, `i`:

```
for (int i=0; i<sizeOfList; i++)
```

With each iteration of the `for` loop, `i` goes from 0 to 1 to 2, and so on, and `i` serves as an index for the different elements in the `phoneList` array. Here's how the loop puts a phone number into each element:

```
phoneList[i] = phoneNum;
```

10.3 Array Declaration and Creation

In the previous section, we showed you how to perform simple operations on an array. In so doing, we focused on accessing an array's elements. In this section, we focus on another key concept—declaring and creating arrays.

Array Declaration

An array is a variable and, as such, it must be declared before you can use it. To declare an array, use this syntax:

<element-type>`[]` *<array-variable>*`;`

The *<array-variable>* is the name of the array. The empty square brackets tell us that the variable is defined to be an array. The *<element-type>* indicates the type of each element in the array—`int`, `double`, `char`, `String`, and so on.

Here are some array declaration examples:

```
double[] salaries;
String[] names;
int[] employeeIds;
```

The `salaries` variable is an array whose elements are of type `double`. The `names` variable is an array whose elements are of type `String`. And finally, the `employeeIds` variable is an array whose elements are of type `int`.

Java provides an alternative declaration format for arrays, where the square brackets go after the variable name. Here's what we're talking about:

```
double salaries[];
```

```
/*********************************************************************
* SpeedDialList.java
* Dean & Dean
*
* This program creates a cell phone speed-dial phone number
* list and prints the created list.
*********************************************************************/

import java.util.Scanner;

public class SpeedDialList
{
  public static void main(String[] args)
  {
    Scanner stdIn = new Scanner(System.in);
    long[] phoneList;   // list of phone numbers
    int sizeOfList;     // number of phone numbers
    long phoneNum;      // an entered phone number

    System.out.print(
      "How many speed-dial numbers would you like to enter? ");
    sizeOfList = stdIn.nextInt();
    phoneList = new long[sizeOfList];

    for (int i=0; i<sizeOfList; i++)
    {
      System.out.print("Enter phone number: ");
      phoneNum = stdIn.nextLong();
      phoneList[i] = phoneNum;
    } // end for

    System.out.println("\nSpeed Dial List:");
    for (int i=0; i<sizeOfList; i++)
    {
      System.out.println((i + 1) + ". " + phoneList[i]);
    } // end for
  } // end main
} // end class SpeedDialList
```

Create an array with a user-specified size.
Fill the array.
Print the array.

Sample session:

```
How many speed-dial numbers would you like to enter? 2
Enter phone number: 8167412000
Enter phone number: 2024561111

Speed Dial List:
1. 8167412000
2. 2024561111
```

Figure 10.3 SpeedDialList program that shows how to create, fill, and print an array

The two formats are identical in terms of functionality. Most folks in industry prefer the first format, and that's what we use, but you should be aware of the alternative format in case you see it in someone else's code.

Array Creation

An array is an object, albeit a special kind of object. As with any object, an array holds a group of data items. As with any object, an array can be created/instantiated using the `new` operator. Here's the syntax for creating an array object with the `new` operator and assigning the array object into an array variable:

<array-variable> `= new` *<element-type>*`[`*<array-size>*`];`

The *<element-type>* indicates the type of each element in the array. The *<array-size>* indicates the number of elements in the array. The following code fragment creates a 10-element array of `long`s:

```
long[] phoneList;
phoneList = new long[10];
```


These two lines perform three operations: (1) The first line declares the `phoneList` variable, (2) the boxed code creates the array object, and (3) the assignment operator assigns a reference to the array object into the `phoneList` variable.

It's legal to combine an array's declaration, creation, and assignment operations into one statement. The following example does just that. It reduces the previous two-line code fragment to just one line:

```
long[] phoneList = new long[10];
```

Here, we use a constant (10) for the array's size, but you're not required to use a constant. You can use any expression for the array's size. Figure 10.3's SpeedDialList program prompts the user for the size of the array, stores the entered size in a `sizeOfList` variable, and uses `sizeOfList` for the array creation. Here's the array creation code from the SpeedDialList program:

```
phoneList = new long[sizeOfList];
```

Array Element Initialization

Usually, you'll want to declare and create an array in one place and assign values to your array elements in a separate place. For example, the following code fragment declares and creates a `temperatures` array in one statement, and assigns values to the `temperatures` array in a separate statement, inside a loop.

```
double[] temperatures = new double[5];
for (int i=0; i<5; i++)
{
  temperatures[i] = 98.6;
}
```


On the other hand, sometimes you'll want to declare and create an array, and assign values to your array, all in the same statement. That's called an *array initializer.* Here's the syntax:

<element-type>`[]` *<array-variable>* `= {`*<value1>*`,` *<value2>*`, ...,` *<valuen>*`};`

The code at the left of the assignment operator declares an array variable using syntax that you've seen before. The code at the right of the assignment operator specifies a comma-separated list of values that are assigned into the array's elements. Note this example:

```
double[] temperatures = {98.6, 98.6, 98.6, 98.6, 98.6};
```

Comparing the above statement to the previous `temperatures` code fragment, you can see that it is the same in terms of functionality but different in terms of structure. Key differences: (1) It's one line, rather than five lines. (2) There's no `new` operator. (3) There's no array-size value. With no array-size value, how do you think the compiler knows the size of the array? The size of the array is dictated by the number of values in the element-values list. In the above example, there are five values in the initializer list, so the compiler creates an array with five elements.

We presented two solutions for assigning values to a temperatures array. Which is better—the five-line code fragment or the one-line array initializer? We prefer the array initializer solution because it's simpler. But remember that you can use the array initializer technique only if you know the assigned values when you first declare the array. For the temperatures example, we do know the assigned values when we first declare the array—we initialize each temperature to 98.6, the normal human body temperature in degrees Fahrenheit. You should limit your use of array initializers to situations where the number of assigned values is reasonably small. For the temperatures example, the number of assigned values is reasonably small—it's five. If you need to keep track of a hundred temperatures, it would be legal to use the array initializer solution, but it would be cumbersome:

```
double[] temperatures =
{
  98.6, 98.6, 98.6, 98.6, 98.6, 98.6, 98.6, 98.6, 98.6, 98.6,
  <repeat above line eight times>
  98.6, 98.6, 98.6, 98.6, 98.6, 98.6, 98.6, 98.6, 98.6, 98.6
}
```

Default Values

You now know how to initialize an array's elements explicitly with an array initializer. But what do an array's elements get by default if you don't use an array initializer? An array is an object, and an array's elements are the instance variables for an array object. As such, an array's elements get default values when the array is created, the same as any other instance variables get default values. Here are the default values for array elements:

Array Element's Type	Default Value
integer	0
floating point	0.0
`boolean`	`false`
reference	`null`

So what are the default values for the elements in the arrays below?

```
double[] rainfall = new double[365];
String[] colors = new String[5];
```

The `rainfall` array gets 0.0 for each of its 365 elements. The `colors` array gets `null` for each of its 5 elements.

10.4 Array length Property and Partially Filled Arrays

As illustrated earlier, when working with an array, it's common to step through each element in the array. In doing so, you need to know the size of the array and/or the number of filled elements in the array. In this section, we discuss how to obtain the size of an array and how to keep track of the number of filled elements in an array.

Array length Property

Suppose you have a five-element colors array that's been initialized like this:

```
String[] colors = {"blue", "gray", "lime", "teal", "yellow"};
```

Here's how to print such an array:

hard-coded array size

```
for (int i=0; i<5; i++)
{
  System.out.println(colors[i]);
}
```

That works OK, but suppose you have several other color-related loops in your code, each of them using i<5. If you modify your program to accommodate more colors, and change the five-element array to a ten-element array, you'd have to change all occurrences of i<5 to i<10. To avoid such maintenance work, wouldn't it be nice to replace i<5 or i<10 with something generic, like i < array's size? You can do that by using the color array's length property. Every array object contains a length property that stores the number of elements in the array. The length property is called a "property," but it's actually just an instance variable with public and final modifiers. The public modifier says that length is directly accessible without need of an accessor method. The final modifier makes length a named constant; so you can't update it. Here's how the length property can be used:

number of elements in the array

```
for (int i=0; i<colors.length; i++)
{
  System.out.println(colors[i]);
}
```

Array length Property Versus String length Method

Remember where else you've seen the word length in the Java language? The String class provides a length method to retrieve the number of characters in a string. Remember that String's length is a method, so you must use trailing parentheses when calling it. On the other hand, an array's length is a constant, so you don't use trailing parentheses when accessing it. Figure 10.4's SpeedDialList2 program illustrates these concepts. Note that phoneNum.length() uses parentheses when checking for the length of the phoneNum string as part of input validation. And note that phoneList.length does not use parentheses when checking the number of elements in the phoneList array to make sure that there's room for another phone number.

If you're like us, you might have a hard time remembering when to use parentheses and when not to. Try using the mnemonic acronym ANSY, which stands for Arrays No, Strings Yes. "Arrays No" means that

```
/*************************************************************
* SpeedDialList2.java
* Dean & Dean
*
* This program creates a speed-dial phone number list and
* prints the created list. It uses a partially filled array.
*************************************************************/

import java.util.Scanner;

public class SpeedDialList2
{
  public static void main(String[] args)
  {
    Scanner stdIn = new Scanner(System.in);
    String[] phoneList = new String[100]; // phone numbers
    int filledElements = 0;      // number of phone numbers
    String phoneNum;             // an entered phone number

    System.out.print("Enter phone number (or q to quit): ");
    phoneNum = stdIn.nextLine();
    while (!phoneNum.equalsIgnoreCase("q") &&
           filledElements < phoneList.length)
    {
      if (phoneNum.length() < 1 || phoneNum.length() > 16)
      {
        System.out.println("Invalid entry." +
          " Must enter between 1 and 16 characters.");
      }
      else
      {
        phoneList[filledElements] = phoneNum;
        filledElements++;
      }
      System.out.print("Enter phone number (or q to quit): ");
      phoneNum = stdIn.nextLine();
    } // end while

    System.out.println("\nSpeed Dial List:");
    for (int i=0; i<filledElements; i++)
    {
      System.out.println((i + 1) + ". " + phoneList[i]);
    } // end for
  } // end main
} // end class SpeedDialList2
```

Array length property does not use ()'s.
String length method uses ()'s.
Update number of filled elements.
Use filledElements for printing the array.

Figure 10.4 SpeedDialList2 program that processes a partially filled array, using the array `length` property and the `String length` method

arrays do not use parentheses when specifying length. "Strings Yes" means that strings do use parentheses when specifying length. If you don't like DFLAs,[1] you can try a more analytical approach to remembering the parentheses rule. Arrays are special-case objects that don't have methods; therefore, an array's `length` must be a constant, not a method. And constants don't use parentheses.

Partially Filled Arrays

In Figure 10.4, note how the SpeedDialList2 program declares the `phoneList` array to have 100 elements. The program repeatedly prompts the user to enter a phone number or enter q to quit. Typically, the user will enter fewer than the maximum 100 phone numbers. That results in the `phoneList` array being partially filled. If you have a partially filled array, as opposed to a completely filled array, you have to keep track of the number of filled elements in the array so you can process the filled elements differently from the unfilled elements. Note how the SpeedDialList2 program uses the `filledElements` variable to keep track of the number of phone numbers in the array. `filledElements` starts at zero and gets incremented each time the program stores a phone number in the array. To print the array, the program uses `filledElements` in the following `for` loop header.

```
for (int i=0; i<filledElements; i++)
```

⚠ It's fairly common for programmers to accidentally access unfilled elements in a partially filled array. For example, suppose `SpeedDialList2`'s `for` loop looked like this:

```
for (int i=0; i<phoneList.length; i++)
{
  System.out.println((i + 1) + ". " + phoneList[i]);
} // end for
```

Using `phoneList.length` in the `for` loop header works great for printing a completely filled array, but not so great for printing a partially filled array. In the SpeedDialList2 program, unfilled elements hold `null` (the default value for a string), so the above `for` loop would print `null` for each of the unfilled elements. And that makes for confused and unhappy users. ☹

10.5 Copying an Array

In the previous sections, we focused on array syntax details. In the next several sections, we'll focus less on the syntax and more on the application side of things. In this section, we discuss a general-purpose problem—how to copy from one array to another.

Using Arrays to Hold a Store's Prices

Suppose you use arrays to hold a store's prices, one array for each month's prices. Here's the array for January's prices:

```
double[] pricesJanuary = {1.29, 9.99, 22.50, 4.55, 7.35, 6.49};
```

[1] DFLA = dumb four-letter acronym.

Your intent is to use January's array as a starting point for the other month's arrays. Specifically, you want to copy January's prices into the other months' arrays and modify the other months' prices when necessary. The below statement creates the array for February's prices. Note how `pricesJanuary.length` ensures that February's array is the same length as January's array.

```
double[] pricesFebruary = new double[pricesJanuary.length];
```

Suppose you want the values in February's array to be the same as the values in January's array except for the second entry, which you want to change from 9.99 to 10.99. In other words, you want something like this:

Output:

```
  Jan     Feb
 1.29    1.29
 9.99   10.99
22.50   22.50
 4.55    4.55
 7.35    7.35
 6.49    6.49
```

To minimize re-entry effort and error, it would be nice to have the computer copy the first array's values into the second array and then just alter the one element of the second array that needs changing. Would the following code fragment work?

```
pricesFebruary = pricesJanuary;   <-- Not a good idea.
pricesFebruary[1] = 10.99;
```

An array name is just a reference. It contains the address of a place in memory where the array's data begins. So `pricesFebruary = pricesJanuary;` gets the address of `pricesJanuary`'s data and copies the address into `pricesFebruary`. Then `pricesFebruary` and `pricesJanuary` refer to the same physical data. This picture illustrates the point:

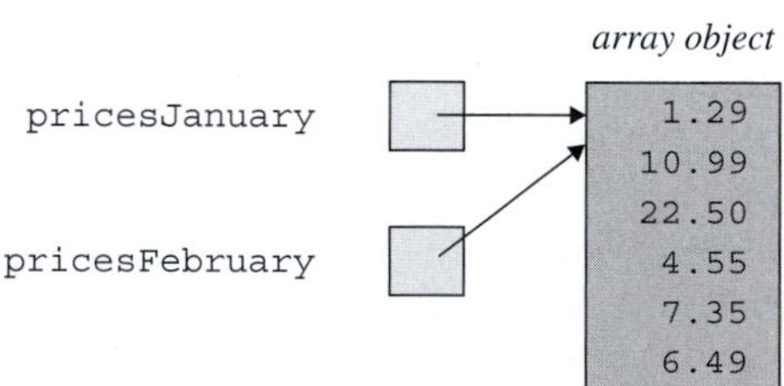

The problem with `pricesFebruary` and `pricesJanuary` referring to the same physical data is that if you change the data for one of the arrays, then you automatically change the data for the other array. For example, the above `pricesFebruary[1] = 10.99;` statement updates not only `pricesFebruary`'s second element, but also `pricesJanuary`'s second element. And that's not what you want.

Usually when you make a copy of an array, you'll want the copy and the original to point to different array objects. To do that, assign array elements one at a time. See Figure 10.5's ArrayCopy program. It uses a `for` loop to assign `pricesJanuary` elements to `pricesFebruary` elements one at a time.

```
/***************************************************************
* ArrayCopy.java
* Dean & Dean
*
* This copies an array and then alters the copy.
****************************************************************/

public class ArrayCopy
{
  public static void main(String[] args)
  {
    double[] pricesJanuary =
      {1.29, 9.99, 22.50, 4.55, 7.35, 6.49};
    double[] pricesFebruary = new double[pricesJanuary.length];

    for (int i=0; i<pricesJanuary.length; i++)
    {
      pricesFebruary[i] = pricesJanuary[i];
    }
    pricesFebruary[1] = 10.99;

    System.out.printf("%7s%7s\n", "Jan", "Feb");
    for (int i=0; i<pricesJanuary.length; i++)
    {
      System.out.printf("%7.2f%7.2f\n",
        pricesJanuary[i], pricesFebruary[i]);
    }
  } // end main
} // end class ArrayCopy
```

Figure 10.5 ArrayCopy program that copies an array and then alters the copy

This is what the code in Figure 10.5 produces:

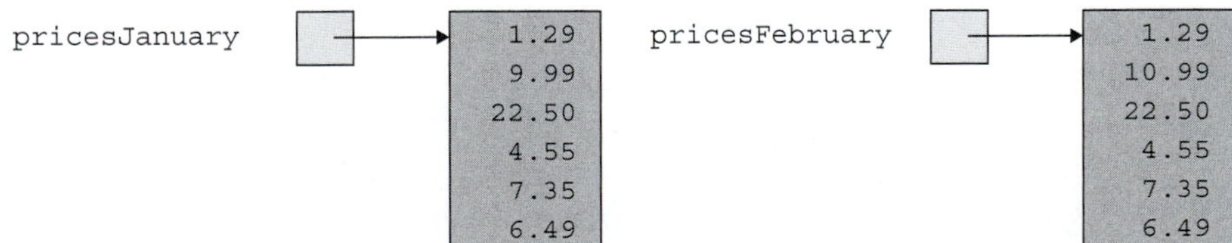

System.arraycopy

Copying data from one array to another is a very common operation, so Java designers provide a special method, `System.arraycopy`, just for that purpose. It allows you to copy any number of elements from any place in one array to any place in another array. Here's how you could use it, copy Figure 10.5's `pricesJanuary` array to the `pricesFebruary` array:

```
System.arraycopy(pricesJanuary, 0, pricesFebruary, 0, 6);
pricesFebruary[1] = 10.99;
```

The first argument is the source array name, that is, the name of the array you're copying from. The second argument is the index of the source array's first element to copy. The third argument is the destination array name, that is, the name of the array you're copying to. The fourth argument is the index of the destination array's first element to replace. The final argument is the total number of elements to copy.

10.6 Problem Solving with Array Case Studies

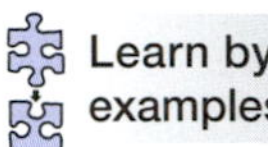

In this section, we present two array-based case studies. For each case study, we present a problem and then examine its solution. The point of these case studies isn't so much that you memorize the details. The point is that you get a feel for how to solve array-oriented problems. Then when you're a programmer in the real world, you'll have a "bag of tricks" that you can draw from. You'll probably have to modify the case-study solutions to make them fit your specific real-world problems, but that's OK. You've got to earn your keep, after all.

Shifting Array-Element Values

Consider the `hours` array in Figure 10.6. The `hours` array contains the scheduled work hours for a person for a 31 day period of time. The first element (`hours[0]`) contains the scheduled work hours for the person for the current day. The last element (`hours[30]`) contains the scheduled work hours for the person for the day that's 30 days in the future. At the beginning of each new day, the work hours need to shift to lower-index positions. For example, the `hours[1]` value needs to shift to the `hours[0]` element. That should make sense when you realize that when you're going to a new day, you need to make what was the next day's scheduled hours, `hours[1]`, become the current day's scheduled hours, `hours[0]`.

index	hours	
0	4	← first day's hours
1	8	
2	0	
	⋮	
30	8	← last day's hours

Figure 10.6 Array that holds scheduled work hours for next 31 days

Now let's look at Java code that performs this shifting operation. We want to shift each `hours` element value to its adjacent lower-indexed element. In other words, we want to copy the second element's value into the first element, copy the third element's value into the second element, and so on. Then we want to assign a user-entered value to the last element. Here's the code:

```
for (int d=0; d<hours.length-1; d++)
{
  hours[d] = hours[d+1];
}

System.out.print("Enter last day's scheduled hours: ");
hours[hours.length-1] = stdIn.nextInt();
```

To shift values to lower-index positions, you must start at the low-index end and work toward the other end.

There are several things to note about this code fragment. It's OK to use an expression inside the [ ]'s—we use `hours[d+1]` to access the element after the `hours[d]` element. Notice how we shift elements at the low-index end first. What would happen if you started the shifting at the high-index end? You'd overwrite the next element you wanted to move and end up filling the entire array with the value that was originally in the highest element. Not good.

Calculating a Moving Average

Let's now borrow code from the above example and apply it to another problem. Suppose you need to present a four-day moving average of the Dow Jones Industrial Average (DJIA) at the end of each business day. Assume you already have a four-element array holding the values of the DJIA at the end of the day on each of the past four days, with four-days-ago's value at index 0, three-days-ago's value at index 1, two-days-ago's value at index 2, and yesterday's value at index 3. For today's four-day moving average, you'll want the sum of the values for the last three days plus the value for today. This means you'll need to shift everything in the array to lower-index positions and insert today's value at the high-index end. Then you'll need to sum up everything in the array and divide by the length of the array. Presumably, you'll save the shifted array somewhere and then do the same thing again at the end of each day in the future. You could do the shifting and summing in separate loops, but it's easier to do both in the same loop as shown in Figure 10.7.

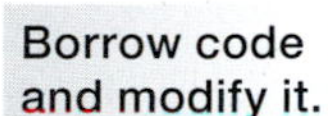
Borrow code
and modify it.

To allow for different lengths of time, it's best not to hard code the array length. Instead, you should always use *<array-name>*`.length`. Think carefully about each boundary. Notice that the index `[d+1]` on the right side of the first statement in the inside `for` loop is one greater than the count variable value `d`. Remember that the highest index value in an array is always one less than the array's length. So the highest value of the count variable should be the array's length minus <u>two.</u> That's why the loop-continuation condition is `d<days.length-1`. Also notice that we insert the new final value for the array after the loop terminates, and then we include this final value in the sum before computing the average. Here's an example of what the program does:

<u>Sample session</u>:

```
Enter number of days to evaluate: 4
Enter next day's value: 9800
Moving average =  9650
Enter next day's value: 9800
Moving average =  9725
Enter next day's value: 9700
Moving average =  9750
Enter next day's value: 9600
Moving average =  9725
```

A moving average is smoother than an instantaneous plot, but notice that its values lag behind.

There's a simpler way to do shifting. Do you remember the API `arraycopy` method mentioned in the previous section? You can use it to implement shifts to lower-index positions with this code fragment:

```
System.arraycopy(days, 1, days, 0, days.length-1);
System.out.print("Enter next day's value: ");
days[days.length-1] = stdIn.nextInt();
```

```
/*********************************************************************
* MovingAverage.java
* Dean & Dean
*
* This program contains an operation that shifts each array
* element to the next lower element and loads a new input
* into the final element.
*********************************************************************/

import java.util.Scanner;

public class MovingAverage
{
  public static void main(String[] args)
  {
    Scanner stdIn = new Scanner(System.in);
    int[] days = {9400, 9500, 9600, 9700}; // rising market
    double sum;
    int samples;

    System.out.print("Enter number of days to evaluate: ");
    samples = stdIn.nextInt();
    for (int j=0; j<samples; j++)
    {
      // shift down and sum
      sum = 0.0;
      for (int d=0; d<days.length-1; d++)
      {
        days[d] = days[d+1];
        sum += days[d];
      }
      System.out.print("Enter next day's value: ");
      days[days.length-1] = stdIn.nextInt();
      sum += days[days.length-1];
      System.out.printf(
        "Moving average = %5.0f\n", sum / days.length);
    }
  } // end main
} // end class MovingAverage
```

This shifts to lower-index positions.
This accumulates the already-shifted values.
This shifts in the latest value.

Figure 10.7 Calculation of a moving average

Conceptually, the `arraycopy` method copies everything from element 1 to the last element into a temporary array, and then copies it from this temporary array back into the original array starting at element 0. This eliminates the inner `for` loop in Figure 10.7. Unfortunately, we also used the inner `for` loop to compute the sum needed for the average. But there's a trick you can use, and it makes a program like this more efficient when the array is very large. If you keep track of the sum of all the elements in the array, each time you shift the array element values, you can just correct the sum, rather than completely re-computing it. To correct the sum, subtract the value shifted out and add the value shifted in, like this:

```
sum -= days[0];
System.arraycopy(days, 1, days, 0, days.length-1);
System.out.print("Enter next day's value: ");
days[days.length-1] = stdIn.nextInt();
sum += days[days.length-1];
```

Histograms

In this subsection, we'll use an array as part of a histogram program. But before we present the program, a histogram overview is in order. A *histogram* is a graph that displays quantities for a set of categories. Typically, it indicates category quantities with bars—shorter bars equate to smaller quantities, longer bars equate to larger quantities. For example, Figure 10.8's histogram shows quantities of frozen desserts produced in the United States in 2003.[2] Histograms are a popular way to present statistical data because they provide a quick and clear representation of the data's distribution.

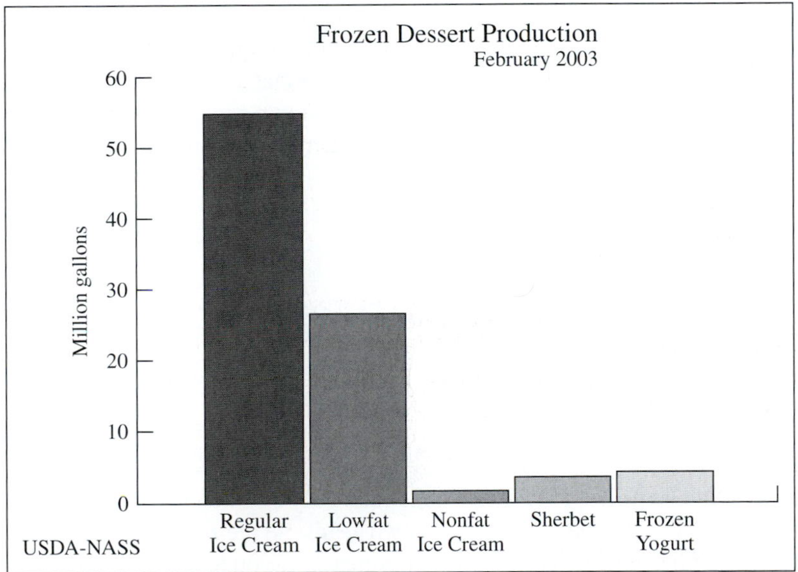

Figure 10.8 Example histogram

Suppose you have three coins. When you flip all three, you're curious how likely it is you'll get zero heads, how likely you'll get one head, how likely you'll get two heads, and how likely you'll get three heads. In other words, you're curious about the frequency distribution for the number of heads.

Approximate a mathematical solution with simulation.

You could calculate the frequency distribution mathematically (with the binomial distribution formula), but, instead, you decide to write a program to simulate the coin flips. If you simulate enough coin flips, then the results will approximate the mathematically calculated result.

In your program, you should simulate flipping the three coins a million times. You should print the simulation results in the form of a histogram. For each of the four cases (zero heads, one head, two heads,

[2] National Agricultural Statistics Service, *Frozen Dessert Production Histogram,* on the Internet at http://www.usda.gov/nass/nasskids/glossary_1.html.

three heads), print a series of *'s where the number of these asterisks is proportional to the number of times the case occurred. Each series of asterisks represents a histogram bar. That should make more sense by looking at this sample output:

```
Number of times each head count occurred:
 0  124960 **************
 1  375127 ******************************************
 2  375261 ******************************************
 3  124652 **************
```

Note the first row of asterisks. That's a horizontal "bar" that pictorially describes the number of times that the zero-heads case occurred. The zero at the left is the label for the zero-heads case. The 124960 is the specific number of times that the zero-heads case occurred. Or said another way, 124960 is the *frequency* of the zero-heads case. Note that the zero-heads and three-heads frequencies (124960 and 124652, respectively) are nearly the same, and the one-head and two-heads frequencies (375127 and 375261, respectively) are also nearly the same. Also note that the zero-heads and three-heads frequencies are each approximately one third of the one-head and two-heads frequencies. It's always a good idea to use some kind of independent calculation to predict what a computer's answer should be like. For this simple problem, it's relatively easy to compute an exact answer. Assuming that "T" means "tails" and "H" means "heads," here are all the possible flipping results:

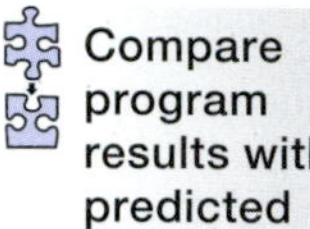

Compare program results with predicted results.

TTT (0 heads)
TTH (1 head)
THT (1 head)
THH (2 heads)
HTT (1 head)
HTH (2 heads)
HHT (2 heads)
HHH (3 heads)

Note that there is only one way to obtain zero heads and only one way to obtain three heads, but there are three ways to obtain one head and three ways to obtain two heads. So the zero-head and three-head frequencies should each be one third of the one-head or two-head frequency. If you look at the numbers and bar lengths in the above sample output, you'll see that the computer result does indeed conform to this expectation.

See Figure 10.9's CoinFlips program. It does what we want. It simulates flipping three coins a million times, and it prints the simulation results in the form of a histogram. It uses a four-element `frequency` array to keep track of the number of times each head-count value occurs. Each element in the frequency array is called a *bin*. In general, a bin contains the number of occurrences of an event. For the CoinFlips program, the `frequency[0]` element is the first bin, and it holds the number of times none of the three coins lands heads up. The `frequency[1]` element is the second bin, and it holds the number of times one of the three coins lands heads up. After each three-coin-flip simulation iteration, the program adds one to the appropriate bin. For example, if a particular iteration generates one head, the program increments the `frequency[1]` bin. And if a particular iteration generates two heads, the program increments the `frequency[2]` bin.

Let's now examine how the CoinFlips program prints the histogram asterisk bars. As specified by the second callout in Figure 10.9, the second large `for` loop prints the histogram. Each iteration of the `for` loop prints the bin label (0, 1, 2, or 3) and then the frequency for that bin. Then it computes the number of asterisks to print by dividing the frequency in the current bin by the total number of repetitions and multiplying by 100. Then it uses an inner `for` loop to display the computed number of asterisks.

```
/*********************************************************************
* CoinFlips.java
* Dean & Dean
*
* This generates a histogram of coin flips.
*********************************************************************/

public class CoinFlips
{
  public static void main(String[] args)
  {
    final int NUM_OF_COINS = 3;       // number of coins
    final int NUM_OF_REPS = 1000000;  // repetitions

    // The frequency array holds the number of times
    // a particular number of heads occurred.
    int[] frequency = new int[NUM_OF_COINS + 1];
    int heads;                // heads in current group of flips
    double fractionOfReps; // head count / repetitions
    int numOfAsterisks;     // asterisks in one histogram bar

    for (int rep=0; rep<NUM_OF_REPS; rep++)
    {
      // perform a group of flips
      heads = 0;
      for (int i=0; i<NUM_OF_COINS; i++)
      {
        heads += (int) (Math.random() * 2);
      }
      frequency[heads]++;    // update appropriate bin
    } // end for
    System.out.println(
      "Number of times each head count occurred:");
    for (heads=0; heads<=NUM_OF_COINS; heads++)
    {
      System.out.print(
        " " + heads + "  " + frequency[heads] + " ");
      fractionOfReps = (float) frequency[heads] / NUM_OF_REPS;
      numOfAsterisks = (int) Math.round(fractionOfReps * 100);

      for (int i=0; i<numOfAsterisks; i++)
      {
        System.out.print("*");
      }
      System.out.println();
    } // end for
  } // end main
} // end class CoinFlips
```

This loop fills up the frequency bins. Each iteration simulates one group of three coin flips.

This loop prints the histogram. Each iteration prints one histogram bar.

Figure 10.9 CoinFlips program that generates a histogram for coin-flips simulation

10.7 Searching an Array

In order to use an array, you need to access its individual elements. If you know the location of the element you're interested in, then you simply access the element by putting the element's index inside square brackets. But if you don't know the location of the element, then you need to search for it. For example, suppose you're writing a program that keeps track of student enrollments for the courses at your school. The program is supposed to be able to add a student, remove a student, view a student's data, and so on. All of those operations require that you first search for the student within a students array (even the add-a-student operation requires a search, to ensure that the student isn't already in the array). In this section, we present two techniques for searching an array.

Sequential Search

If the array is short (has less than about 20 items), the best way to search it is the simplest way: Step through the array sequentially and compare the value at each array element with the searched-for value. When you find a match, do something and return. Here's a pseudocode description of the sequential-search algorithm:

```
i ← 0
while i < number of filled elements
   if list[i] equals the searched-for value
      <do something and stop the loop>
   increment i
```

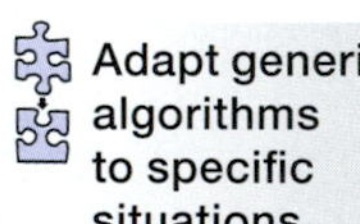

Adapt generic algorithms to specific situations.

Typically, algorithms are more generic than Java implementations. Part of problem solving is the process of adapting generic algorithms to specific situations. In this case, the "do something" code will be different for different cases. The `findStudent` method in Figure 10.10 illustrates one implementation of the sequential-search algorithm. This particular method might be part of a `Course` class that implements an academic course. The `Course` class stores a course's name, an array of student ids for the students enrolled in the course, and the number of students in the course. The `findStudent` method searches for a given student id within the student ids array. If the student id is found, it returns the index of the found id. Otherwise, it returns −1. Note how `findStudent`'s code matches the sequential-search algorithm's logic. In particular, note how `findStudent` implements *<do something and stop the loop>* with a `return i` statement. The `return i` implements "do something" by returning the index of the found student id. It implements "stop the loop" by returning from the method and terminating the loop simultaneously.

In examining the `findStudent` method, you might be asking yourself "What is the practical use for the returned index?" To do anything with an id in the `ids` array, you need to know the id's index. If you don't know the id's index in advance, the `findStudent` method finds the id's index for you. Later in this chapter, you'll see how to call a search method and use the returned index when sorting an array and when adding a new value to an array. Are you still asking yourself "What is the practical use for the returned −1 when the id is not found?" The −1 can be used by the calling module to check for the case of an invalid student id.

Figure 10.11 contains a `CourseDriver` class which drives Figure 10.10's `Course` class. The `CourseDriver` class is fairly straightforward. It creates an array of student ids, stores the array in a `Course` object, prompts the user for a particular student id, and then calls `findStudent` to see whether that particular student is taking the course. To keep things simple, we use an initializer to create the `ids`

```
/**********************************************************************
* Course.java
* Dean & Dean
*
* This class represents a particular course in a school.
**********************************************************************/

public class Course
{
  private String courseName;   // name of the course
  private int[] ids;           // ids for students in the course
  private int filledElements; // number of filled-in elements

  //*******************************************************************

  public Course(String courseName, int[] ids, int filledElements)
  {
    this.courseName = courseName;
    this.ids = ids;
    this.filledElements = filledElements;
  } // end constructor

  //*******************************************************************

  // This method returns index of found id or -1 if not found.

  public int findStudent(int id)
  {
    for (int i=0; i<filledElements; i++)
    {
      if (ids[i] == id)
      {
        return i;
      }
    } // end for

    return -1;
  } // end findStudent
} // end class Course
```

Figure 10.10 Class with sequential search method (`findStudent`)

array. For a more general purpose driver, you might want to replace the initializer with a loop that repeatedly prompts the user to enter a student id or q to quit. If you choose that option, then you'd need to store the number of filled elements in a `filledElements` variable and pass the `filledElements` variable as the third argument in the `Course` constructor call. This is what the constructor call would look like:

```
Course course = new Course("CS101", ids, filledElements);
```

```
/*********************************************************************
* CourseDriver.java
* Dean & Dean
*
* This class creates a Course object and searches for a student
* id within the newly created Course object.
*********************************************************************/

import java.util.Scanner;

public class CourseDriver
{
  public static void main(String[] args)
  {
    Scanner stdIn = new Scanner(System.in);
    int[] ids = {4142, 3001, 6020};
    Course course = new Course("CS101", ids, ids.length);
    int id;         // ID being searched for
    int index;      // index of ID sought or -1 if not found

    System.out.print("Enter 4-digit ID: ");
    id = stdIn.nextInt();
    index = course.findStudent(id);
    if (index >= 0)
    {
      System.out.println("found at index " + index);
    }
    else
    {
      System.out.println("not found");
    }
  } // end main
} // end class CourseDriver
```

Sample session:

```
Enter 4-digit ID: 3001
found at index 1
```

Figure 10.11 Driver for program illustrating a sequential search

Binary Search

If you have an array with a large number of array elements, like 100,000, a sequential search typically takes quite a long time. If such an array has to be searched many times, it's often worthwhile to use a binary search. Binary search gets its name from the way that it bisects a list of values and narrows its search to just half of the bisected list.

For a binary search to work on an array, the array must be sorted so that everything is in some kind of alphabetical or numerical order. The next section describes one of the many available sorting methods. This initial sorting takes more time than a single sequential search, but you have to do it only once.

```
public static int binarySearch(
  int[] array, int filledElements, int value)
{
  int mid;                          // index of middle element
  int midValue;                     // value of middle element
  int low = 0;                      // index of lowest element
  int high = filledElements - 1;    // index of highest element

  while (low <= high)
  {
    mid = (low + high) / 2;         // next midpoint
    midValue = array[mid];          // and the value there
    if (value == midValue)
    {
      return mid;                   // found it!
    }
    else if (value < midValue)
    {
      high = mid - 1;               // next time, use lower half
    }
    else
    {
      low = mid + 1;                // next time, use upper half
    }
  } // end while

  return -1;
} // end binarySearch
```

Figure 10.12 Method that performs a binary search of an array already sorted in ascending order

After the array has been sorted, you can use a binary search to find values in the array very quickly—even when the array is extremely long. A sequential search takes an amount of time proportional to the array length. A binary search takes an amount of time proportional to the logarithm of the array length. When an array is very long, the difference between linear and logarithmic is huge. For example, suppose the length is 100,000. It works out that $\log_2(100{,}000) \approx 17$. Since 17 is about 6,000 times smaller than 100,000, binary search is approximately 6,000 times faster than sequential search for a 100,000-element array.

Note the `binarySearch` method in Figure 10.12, and, in particular, note its `static` modifier. You can use either an instance method or a class method to implement searching. In the previous subsection, we implemented searching with an instance method. This time, we implement searching with a class method, which is appropriate if you want a method to be used generically. To make it generic (that is, to make it usable by different programs), you should put the method in a separate class and make the method a class method. Since it's a class method, different programs can call the `binarySearch` method easily, using `binarySearch`'s class name, rather than using a calling object. For example, if you put the `binarySearch` method in a `Utilities` class, you would call `binarySearch` like this:

```
Utilities.binarySearch(
  <array-name>, <number-of-filled-elements>, <searched-for-value>);
```

In the `binarySearch` method call, note the array argument. Being a class method, `binarySearch` cannot access instance variables. More specifically, it cannot access the searched array as an instance variable. So the searched array must be passed in as an argument. This allows the method to be used from outside its class.

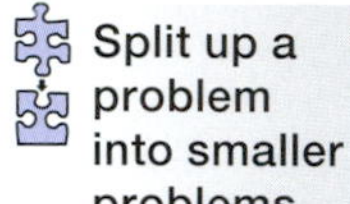
Split up a problem into smaller problems.

Before examining the code details in the `binarySearch` method, let's discuss the basic strategy—*divide and conquer.* You first identify the middle element in the sorted array. You then figure out whether the searched-for value goes before or after the middle element. If it belongs before the middle element, you narrow the search range to the lower half of the array (the half with the smaller-indexed elements). If, on the other hand, the searched-for value belongs after the middle element, you narrow the search range to the upper half of the array. You then repeat the process. In other words, within the narrowed-down half of the array, you identify the middle element, figure out whether the searched-for value belongs before or after the middle element, and narrow the search range accordingly. Every time you do this, you cut the problem in half, and this enables you to zero in quickly on the searched-for value—if it's there at all. Splitting the array in half is the "divide" part of "divide and conquer." Finding the searched-for value within one of the halves is the "conquer" part.

Now let's see how the `binarySearch` method implements the divide-and-conquer algorithm. The method declares `mid`, `low`, and `high` variables that keep track of the indexes for the middle element and the two elements at the ends of the array's search range. For an example, see the left drawing in Figure 10.13. Using a `while` loop, the method repeatedly calculates `mid` (the index of the middle element) and checks whether the `mid` element's value is the searched-for value. If the `mid` element's value is the searched-for value, then the method returns the `mid` index. Otherwise, the method narrows the search range to the low half or the high half of the array. For an example of that narrowing process, see Figure 10.13. The method repeats the loop until either the searched-for value is found or the search range shrinks to the point where `low`'s index is greater than `high`'s index.

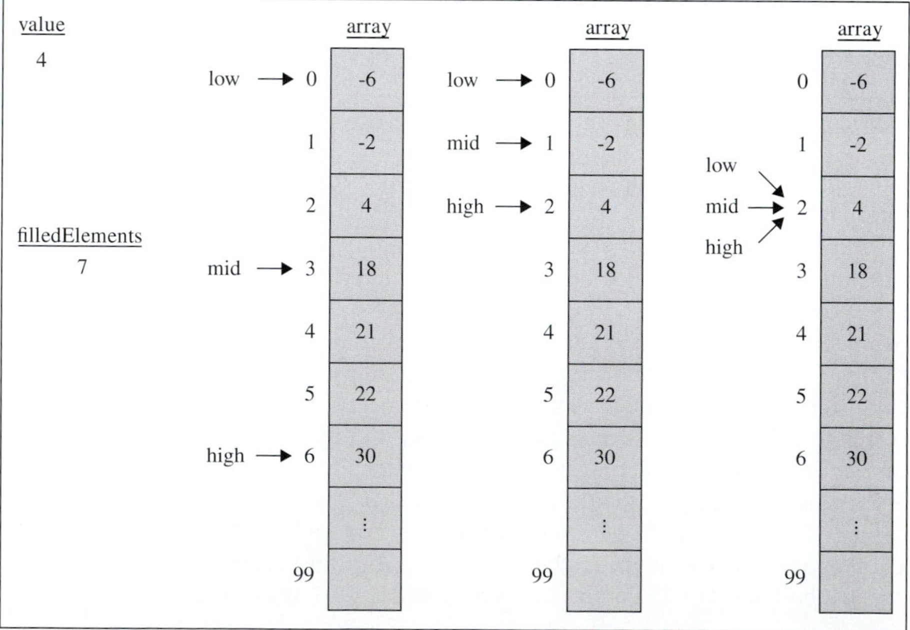

Figure 10.13 Example execution of Figure 10.12's `binarySearch` method

10.8 Sorting an Array

Computers are particularly good at storing large quantities of data and accessing that data quickly. As you learned in the previous section, binary search is an effective technique for finding and accessing data quickly. In order to prepare the data for binary search, the data must be sorted. Sorting data is done not only for binary search purposes. Computers also sort data so that it's easier to display in a user-friendly fashion. If you look at the e-mails in your inbox, aren't they normally sorted by date with the most recent e-mail first? Most e-mail organizers allow you to sort your e-mails using other criteria as well, such as using the "from" person or using the size of the e-mail. In this section, we describe the basics of how sorting is performed. We first present a sorting algorithm, and we then present its implementation in the form of a program that sorts the values in an array.

Selection Sort

There are many different sorting algorithms with varying degrees of complexity and efficiency. Frequently, the best way to solve a problem on a computer is the way a human would naturally solve the problem by hand. To illustrate this idea, we'll show you how to convert one of the common human card-sorting algorithms to a Java sorting program.

If you're sorting cards in a card game, you probably use the *Selection Sort* algorithm. Assume that you're sorting smallest cards first. You search for and select the smallest card and move it to the small-card side of the card group. The small-card side of the card group is where you keep the cards that have been sorted already. You then search for the next smallest card, but in so doing, you look only at cards that are in the unsorted portion of the card group. You move the found card to the second position on the small-card side of the card group. You repeat the search-and-move process until there are no more cards left in the unsorted portion of the card group.

As a first step in implementing the selection sort logic, let's examine a pseudocode solution. Above, we said to "repeat the search-and-move process." Whenever there's a repetition, you should think about using a loop. The following algorithm uses a loop for repeating the search-and-move process. Note how `i` keeps track of where the search starts. The first time through the loop, the search starts at the first element (at index 0). The next time, the search starts at the second position. Each time through the loop, you find the smallest value and move it to the sorted portion of the list (the i tells you where in the list you want the smallest value to go).

```
for (i ← 0; i < list's length; i++)
    find the smallest value in the list from list[i] to the end of the list
    swap the found value with list[i]
```

A picture is worth a thousand words, so we provide a figure (10.14) that shows the Selection Sort algorithm in action. The five pictures show the different stages of a list being sorted using the Selection Sort algorithm. The list's white portions are unsorted. The original list at the left is all white, indicating that it is entirely unsorted. The list's shaded portions are sorted. The list at the right is all shaded, indicating that it is entirely sorted. The bidirectional arrows show what happens after a smallest value is found. The smallest value (at the bottom of the bidirectional arrow) gets swapped up to the top of the unsorted portion of the list. For example, in going from the first picture to the second picture, the smallest value, −3, gets swapped up to 5's position at the top of the unsorted portion of the list.

Now let's implement a Java version of the Selection Sort algorithm. You can use either an instance method or a class method. In the previous section, we implemented binary search with a class method. For additional practice, we'll do the same here for selection sort. By implementing selection sort with a class

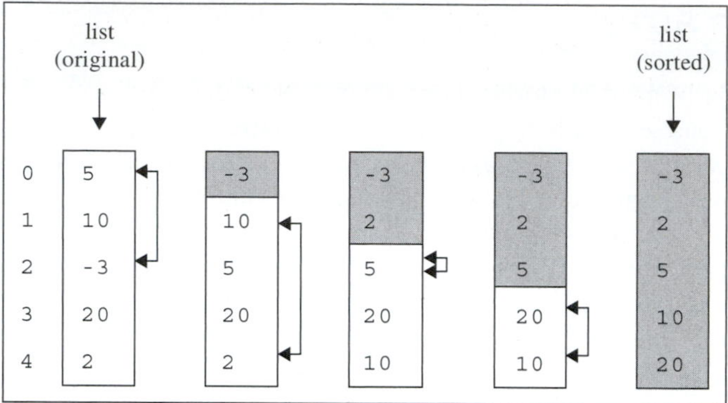

Figure 10.14 Example execution of the Selection Sort algorithm

method, you can easily call it from any program that needs to sort a list of numbers—just prefix the method call with class name dot.

See the `Sort` class in Figure 10.15. Note how the `sort` method body mimics the pseudocode very closely because the sort method uses top-down design. Rather than include the search-for-the-smallest-value code within the `sort` method, the `sort` method calls the `indexOfNextSmallest` helper method. Rather than include the element-swapping code within the `sort` method, the `sort` method calls the `swap` helper method. The only substantive difference between the `sort` method and the sort algorithm is that the `sort` method's `for` loop stops iterating one element before the bottom of the array. That's because there's no need to perform a search when you're at the last element (you already know that the last element is the minimum value for the remainder of the list). We didn't worry about such efficiency details with the algorithm because algorithms are more about basic logic rather than off-by-one details.

Passing Arrays as Arguments

Figure 10.16 contains a driver for Figure 10.15's `Sort` class. Most of the code is fairly straightforward, but please take note of the `studentIds` argument in the `Sort.sort` method call. That's an example of passing an array to a method. An array is an object, and as such, `studentIds` is a reference to an array object. As you may recall from the "Passing References as Arguments" section in Chapter 7, a reference argument (in a method call) and its corresponding reference parameter (in a method heading) point to the same object. So if you update the reference parameter's object from within the method, you simultaneously update the reference argument's object in the calling module. Applying that thinking to the Sort program, when you pass the `studentIds` reference to the `sort` method and sort the array there, there's no need to return the updated (sorted) array with a `return` statement. That's because the `studentIds` reference points to the same array object that is sorted within the `sort` method. Thus, we do not include a `return` statement in the `sort` method, and the method works just fine.

Sorting with a Java API Method

Check for efficient API methods.

When an array has more than about 20 elements, it's better to use an algorithm that's more efficient than the relatively simple Selection Sort algorithm just described. And sure enough, the Java API has a sorting method that uses a more efficient sorting algorithm. It's the `sort` method in the `Arrays` class.

```
/*********************************************************************
* Sort.java
* Dean & Dean
*
* This class uses a selection sort to sort a single array.
*********************************************************************/

public class Sort
{
  public static void sort(int[] list)
  {
    int j;                         // index of smallest value

    for (int i=0; i<list.length-1; i++)
    {
      j = indexOfNextSmallest(list, i);
      swap(list, i, j);
    }
  } // end sort

  //*****************************************************************

  private static int indexOfNextSmallest(
    int[] list, int startIndex)
  {
    int minIndex = startIndex;  // index of smallest value

    for (int i=startIndex+1; i<list.length; i++)
    {
      if (list[i] < list[minIndex])
      {
        minIndex = i;
      }
    } // end for
    return minIndex;
  } // end indexOfNextSmallest

  //*****************************************************************

  private static void swap(int[] list, int i, int j)
  {
    int temp;                      // temporary holder for number

    temp = list[i];
    list[i] = list[j];
    list[j] = temp;
  } // end swap
} // end Sort
```

Figure 10.15 `Sort` class containing a method that sorts an array of integers in ascending order

```
/*************************************************************
* SortDriver.java
* Dean & Dean
*
* This exercises selection sort in class Sort.
*************************************************************/

public class SortDriver
{
  public static void main(String[] args)
  {
    int[] studentIds = {3333, 1234, 2222, 1000};

    Sort.sort(studentIds);
    for (int i=0; i<studentIds.length; i++)
    {
      System.out.print(studentIds[i] + " ");
    }
  } // end main
} // end SortDriver
```

calling the `sort` method

Figure 10.16 Driver that exercises the `sort` method in Figure 10.15

Here's skeleton code for how you might use the `Arrays` class's `sort` method:

```
import java.util.Arrays;
. . .
  int[] studentIds = {...};
  . . .
  Arrays.sort(studentIds);
```

We recommend that you use this API method for heavy-duty sorting. It's an overloaded method, so it also works for arrays of other types of primitive variables.

10.9 Two-Dimensional Arrays

Arrays are good for grouping related data together. Up to this point, we've grouped the data together using standard one-dimensional arrays. If the related data is organized in a table format, consider using a two-dimensional array. In this section, we describe two-dimensional arrays.

Two-Dimensional Array Syntax

Two-dimensional arrays use the same basic syntax as one-dimensional arrays except for a second pair of square brackets (`[]`). Each pair of square brackets contains one index. According to standard programming practice, the first index identifies the row and the second index identifies the column position within a row.

For example, here's a two-row by three-column array named x:

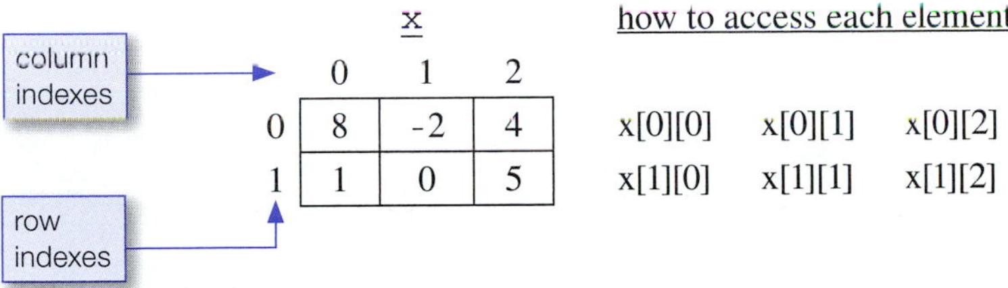

The items at the right, under the "how to access" column heading, show how to access each of the six elements in the array. So to access the value 5, at row index 1 and column index 2, you specify `x[1][2]`.

As with one-dimensional arrays, there are two ways to assign values into a two-dimensional array's elements. You can use an array initializer, where the element assignment is part of the array's declaration. Or you can use standard assignment statements, where the assignment statements are separate from the array's declaration and creation. We'll describe the array initializer technique first. Here's how you can declare the above two-dimensional x array and assign values into its elements, using an array initializer:

```
int[][] x = {{8,-2,4}, {1,0,5}};
```

initializer for a 2-row by 3-column array

Note that the array initializer contains two inner groups, where each inner group represents one row. `{8, -2, 4}` represents the first row. `{1, 0, 5}` represents the second row. Note that elements and groups are separated with commas, and each inner group and the entire set of inner groups are surrounded by braces.

You can use the array initializer technique only if you know the assigned values when you first declare the array. Otherwise, you need to provide array element assignment statements that are separate from the array's declaration and creation. For example, Figure 10.17's code fragment declares and creates the `x` array in one statement, and assigns values to `x`'s elements in a separate statement, inside nested `for` loops.

```
int[][] x = new int[2][3];
for (int i=0; i<x.length; i++)
{
  for (int j=0; j<x[0].length; j++)
  {
    System.out.print("Enter value for row " + i + ", col " + j + ": ");
    x[i][j] = stdIn.nextInt();
  } // end for j
} // end for i
```

Declare and create a 2-row by 3-column array.

Assign a value to the element at row i, column j.

Figure 10.17 Assigning values into a two-dimensional array using nested `for` loops and the `length` property

When working with two-dimensional arrays, it's very common to use nested `for` loops. In Figure 10.17, note the outer `for` loop with index variable `i` and the inner `for` loop with index variable `j`. The outer `for` loop iterates through each row, and the inner `for` loop iterates through each element within a particular row.

Figure 10.17's first line declares `x` to be a 2-row by 3-column array with 6 total elements. So you might expect the first `for` loop's `x.length` property to hold a 6. Not so. Even though it's normal (and useful) to think of `x` as a rectangular box that holds 6 `int` elements, `x` is actually a reference to a

2-element array and each of the two elements is a reference to its own 3-element array of ints. This picture illustrates what were talking about:

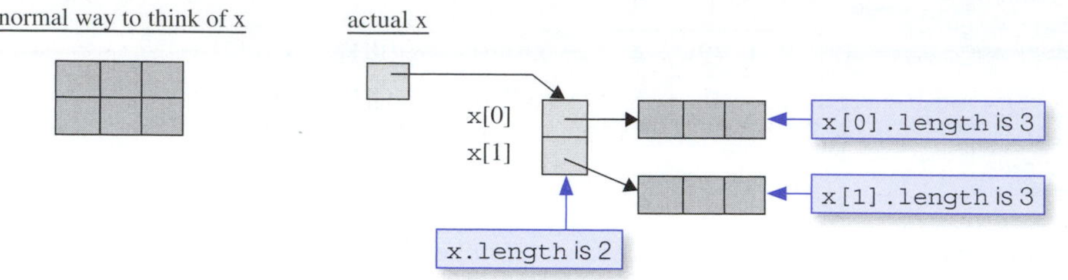

Since x is actually a reference to a 2-element array, x.length holds the value 2. Or thinking about x in the "normal" way (above left picture), x.length holds the number of rows in x. As you can see above, x[0] is a reference to a 3-element array. Thus, x[0].length holds the value 3. Or thinking about x in the "normal" way (above left picture), x[0].length holds the number of columns in x. The point of all this is that the length property can be used for iterating through the elements in a two-dimensional array. In Figure 10.17, note how the first loop uses x.length to iterate through each row in x, and note how the second loop uses x[0].length to iterate through each column in x.

Example

Let's put these two-dimensional array concepts into practice by using a two-dimensional array in the context of a complete program. The program, built for a Kansas and Missouri airline company, tells customers when airplanes are expected to arrive at various Kansas and Missouri airports. It uses a two-dimensional array to store flight times between cities, and it displays output like this:

```
       Wch  Top   KC  Col  StL
Wch      0   22   30   42   55
Top     23    0   14   25   37
 KC     31    9    0   11   28
Col     44   27   12    0   12
StL     59   41   30   14    0
```

It takes 25 minutes to fly from Topeka to Columbia.

Different rows correspond to different cities of origin. Different columns correspond to different cities of destination. The labels are abbreviations for city names: "Wch" stands for Wichita, Kansas. "Top" stands for Topeka, Kansas. "KC" stands for Kansas City, Missouri. "Col" stands for Columbia, Missouri. "StL" stands for St. Louis, Missouri. Thus, for example, it takes 25 minutes to fly from Topeka to Columbia. How long does it take to go the other way, from Columbia to Topeka? 27 minutes. Columbia to Topeka takes longer because the trip goes east to west, and airplanes have to contend with head winds from North America's west-to-east jet stream.

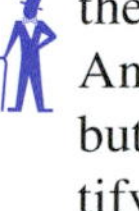

Let's analyze the program by starting with Figure 10.18's FlightTimesDriver class. Note how the main method declares and creates a flightTimes table with a two-dimensional array initializer. And note how the initializer puts each table row on a line by itself. That's not required by the compiler, but it makes for elegant, self-documenting code. It is self-documenting because readers can easily identify each row of table data by looking at a single row of code. After initializing the flightTimes table, main initializes a one-dimensional array of city names and then calls the FlightTimes constructor, the displayFlightTimesTable method, and the promptForFlightTime method. We'll discuss the constructor and those two methods next.

```
/*************************************************************
* FlightTimesDriver.java
* Dean & Dean
*
* This manages a table of intercity flight times.
*************************************************************/

public class FlightTimesDriver
{
  public static void main(String[] args)
  {
    int[][] flightTimes =
    {
      {0, 22, 30, 42, 55},
      {23, 0, 14, 25, 37},
      {31, 9, 0, 11, 28},
      {44, 27, 12, 0, 12},
      {59, 41, 30, 14, 0}
    };
    String[] cities = {"Wch", "Top", "KC", "Col", "StL"};
    FlightTimes ft = new FlightTimes(flightTimes, cities);

    System.out.println("\nFlight times for KansMo Airlines:\n");
    ft.displayFlightTimesTable();
    System.out.println();
    ft.promptForFlightTime();
  } // end main
} // end class FlightTimesDriver
```

<u>Sample session</u>:

```
Flight times for KansMo Airlines:

        Wch   Top    KC   Col   StL
  Wch     0    22    30    42    55
  Top    23     0    14    25    37
  KC     31     9     0    11    28
  Col    44    27    12     0    12
  StL    59    41    30    14     0

1 = Wch
2 = Top
3 = KC
4 = Col
5 = StL
Enter departure city's number: 5
Enter destination city's number: 1
Flight time = 59 minutes.
```

Figure 10.18 Driver of `FlightTimes` class in Figures 10.19a and 10.19b

Figures 10.19a and 10.19b contain the heart of the program—the `FlightTimes` class. In Figure 10.19a, the constructor initializes the `flightTimes` and `cities` instance variable arrays with the data

```
/*********************************************************************
* FlightTimes.java
* Dean & Dean
*
* This manages a table of intercity flight times.
*********************************************************************/

import java.util.Scanner;

public class FlightTimes
{
  private int[][] flightTimes; // table of flight times
  private String[] cities;     // cities in flightTimes table

  //******************************************************************

  public FlightTimes(int[][] ft, String[] c)
  {
    flightTimes = ft;
    cities = c;
  }

  //******************************************************************

  // Prompt user for cities and print associated flight time.

  public void promptForFlightTime()
  {
    Scanner stdIn = new Scanner(System.in);
    int departure;   // index for departure city
    int destination; // index for destination city

    for (int i=0; i<cities.length; i++)
    {
      System.out.println(i+1 + " = " + cities[i]);
    }
    System.out.print("Enter departure city's number: ");
    departure = stdIn.nextInt() - 1;
    System.out.print("Enter destination city's number: ");
    destination = stdIn.nextInt() - 1;
    System.out.println("Flight time = " +
      flightTimes[departure][destination] + " minutes.");
  } // end promptForFlightTime
```

Print the number-city legend.

Figure 10.19a `FlightTimes` class that displays intercity flight times—part A

passed to it by the driver's constructor call. Note that it assigns the passed-in `ft` and `c` array references to the instance variables using the = operator. Previously, you learned to use a `for` loop, not the = operator, to make a copy of an array. Why is the = operator acceptable here? Because there's no need to make a second copy of these arrays. After the constructor's first assignment operation, the `flightTimes` instance variable array reference and the `ft` parameter array reference point to the same array object. And that's appropriate. Likewise, after the constructor's second assignment operation, the `cities` instance variable array reference and the `c` parameter array reference point to the same array object.

Figure 10.19a's `promptForFlightTime` method prompts the user for a departure city and a destination city and prints the flight time for that flight. More specifically, it prints a legend of numbers and their associated city names (1 = Wichita, 2 = Topeka, and so on), it prompts the user to enter numbers for the departure and destination cities, and it prints the flight time between the specified cities. Note how user-entered city numbers start with 1 rather than 0 (1 = Wichita). That makes the program more user-friendly because people usually prefer to start counting at one rather than zero. Internally, the program stores city names in an array. Since all arrays start with a 0 index, the program has to translate between user-entered city numbers (which start at 1) and city array indexes (which start at 0). Note how that's done with `+1` and `-1` in the `promptForFlightTime` method.

```
  //*******************************************************************

  // This method prints a table of all flight times.

  public void displayFlightTimesTable()
  {
    final String CITY_FMT_STR = "%5s";   } <- format strings
    final String TIME_FMT_STR = "%5d";   }

    System.out.printf(CITY_FMT_STR, ""); // empty top-left corner
    for (int col=0; col<cities.length; col++)
    {
      System.out.printf(CITY_FMT_STR, cities[col]);
    }
    System.out.println();

    for (int row=0; row<flightTimes.length; row++)
    {
      System.out.printf(CITY_FMT_STR, cities[row]);
      for (int col=0; col<flightTimes[0].length; col++)
      {
        System.out.printf(TIME_FMT_STR, flightTimes[row][col]);
      }
      System.out.println();
    } // end for
  } // end displayFlightTimesTable
} // end class FlightTimes
```

Figure 10.19b `FlightTimes` class that displays intercity flight times—part B

Figure 10.19b's `displayFlightTimesTable` method displays the flight times table. In doing so, it employs an interesting formatting technique. First look at the two local named constants, which are separately defined format strings. You have been using literal format strings embedded in strings of text for some time now in the arguments of `printf` method calls. But instead of embedding literal format strings, sometimes it's easier to understand if you declare them separately as named constants. If you go back and count the spaces in the six-column table of flight times, you'll see that each column is exactly5 spaces wide. So the labels at the top of the columns and the numbers in the columns must both be formatted to use exactly 5 spaces. Thus, the format string for the labels (CITY_FMT_STR) should be `"%5s"`, and the format string for the integer entries (TIME_FMT_STR) should be `"%5d"`. Using named constants for format strings allows each format string to be used in many places, and it makes it easy and safe to alter them at any later time—just change the values assigned to the named constants at the beginning of the method.

In the `displayFlightTimesTable` method, note the three `for` loop headers. They all use the `length` property for their termination condition. Since length holds 5, the program would run correctly if you replaced the length termination conditions with hardcoded 5's. But don't do it. Using the `length` property makes the implementation more *scalable*. Scalable means it's easy to change the amount of data that the program uses. For example, in the FlightTimes program, using a `cities.length` loop termination condition means that if you change the number of cities in the program, the program will still work properly.

Multi-Dimensional Arrays

Arrays may have more than two dimensions. Arrays with three or more dimensions use the same basic syntax except they have additional `[]`'s. The first pair of brackets corresponds to the largest scale, and each subsequent pair of brackets nests within the previous pair, at progressively smaller levels of scale. For example, suppose the Missouri-Kansas airline company decides to go "green" and expands its fleet with new solar-powered airplanes and wind-powered airplanes that burn hydrogen. The new airplanes have different flight times than the original jet-fuel airplanes. Thus, they need their own flight-times tables. The solution is to create a three-dimensional array where the first dimension specifies the airplane type—0 for the jet-fuel airplanes, 1 for the solar-powered airplanes, and 2 for the wind-powered airplanes. Here's how to declare the new three-dimensional `flightTimes` array instance variable:

```
private int[][][] flightTimes;
```

10.10 Arrays of Objects

You learned in the previous section that a two-dimensional array is actually an array of references where each reference points to an array object. Now let's look at a related scenario. Let's look at an array of references where each reference points to a programmer-defined object. For example, suppose you'd like to store total sales for each sales clerk in a department store. If sales clerk Amanda sells two items for $55.45 and $22.01, then you'd like to store 77.46 for her total-sales value. You can store the sales clerk data in an array, `clerks`, where each element holds a reference to a `SalesClerk` object. Each `SalesClerk` object holds a sales clerk's name and the total sales for that sales clerk. See Figure 10.20 for an illustration of what we're talking about.

The `clerks` array is an array of references. But most folks in industry would refer to it as an array of objects, and that's what we'll do as well. An array of objects isn't that much different from an array of primitives. In both cases, you access each array element with square brackets (e.g., `clerks[0]`, `clerks[1]`). But there are some differences that you should be aware of, and those differences are the main focus of this section.

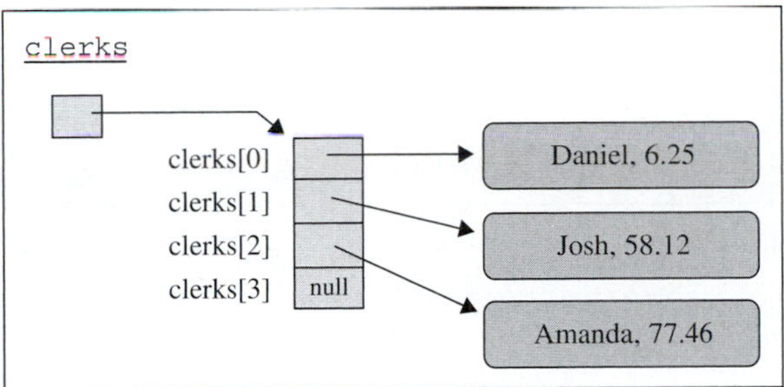

Figure 10.20 An array of objects that stores sales-clerk sales data

Need to Instantiate Array of Objects and the Objects in That Array

With an array of primitives, you perform one instantiation—you instantiate the array object and that's it. But with an array of objects, you have to instantiate the array object, and you must also instantiate each element object that's stored in the array. It's easy to forget the second step, the instantiation of individual element objects. If you do forget, then the elements contain default values of `null`, as illustrated by `clerks[3]` in Figure 10.20. For the empty part of a partially filled array, `null` is fine, but for the part of an array that's supposed to be filled, you need to overlay `null` with a reference to an object. The following is an example of how to create an array of objects—more specifically, how to create the `clerks` array of objects shown in Figure 10.20. Note the separate instantiations, with the `new` operator, for the `clerks` array and for each `SalesClerk` object.

```
SalesClerk[] clerks = new SalesClerk[4];
clerks[0] = new SalesClerk("Daniel", 6.25);
clerks[1] = new SalesClerk("Josh", 58.12);
clerks[2] = new SalesClerk("Amanda", 77.46);
```

Can't Access Array Data Directly

With an array of primitives, you can access the array's data, the primitives, directly. For example, the following code fragment shows how you can assign and print the first rainfall value in a `rainfall` array. Note how the value is directly accessed with `rainfall[0]`.

```
double[] rainfall = new double[365];
rainfall[0] = .8;
System.out.println(rainfall[0]);
```

On the contrary, with an array of objects, you normally cannot access the array's data, the variables inside the objects, directly. Since the variables inside the objects are normally `private`, you normally have to call a constructor or method to access them. For example, the following code fragment shows how you can use a constructor to assign Daniel and 6.25 to the first object in the `clerks` array. It also shows how you can use accessor methods to print the first object's name and sales data.

```
SalesClerk[] clerks = new SalesClerk[4];
clerks[0] = new SalesClerk("Daniel", 6.25);
System.out.println(
  clerks[0].getName() + ", " + clerks[0].getSales());
```

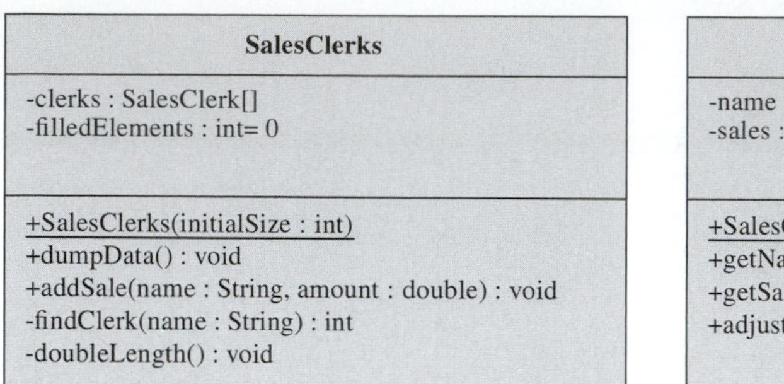

Figure 10.21 UML class diagram for the SalesClerks program

Sales Clerks Program

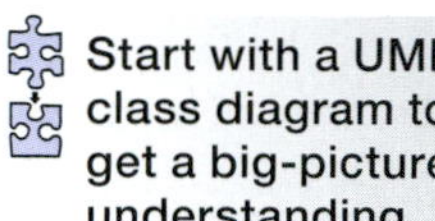

Start with a UML class diagram to get a big-picture understanding.

Let's now implement a complete program that adds sales and prints sales for a group of sales clerks in a department store. As is customary, we'll first get a big-picture view of things by presenting a UML class diagram. Figure 10.21's class diagram shows two classes. The `SalesClerks` class represents sales data for the entire department store, and the `SalesClerk` class represents total sales for one particular sales clerk.

The `SalesClerks` class contains two instance variables—`clerks` and `filledElements`. `clerks` is an array of `SalesClerk` objects. `filledElements` stores the number of elements that have been filled so far in the `clerks` array. For a `filledElements` example, see Figure 10.20, where `filledElements` would be 3. The `SalesClerks`'s constructor instantiates the `clerks` array, using the constructor's `initialSize` parameter for the array's size.

The `SalesClerks` class contains four methods—`dumpData`, `addSale`, `findClerk`, and `doubleLength`. The `dumpData` method is the most straightforward of the four. It prints all the data in the `clerks` array. The term *dump* is a computer term which refers to a simple (unformatted) display of a program's data. See the `dumpData` method in Figure 10.22b and verify that it prints the data in the `clerks` array.

The `addSale` method processes a sale for a particular sales clerk. More specifically, the `addSale` method finds the sales clerk specified by its `name` parameter and updates that sales clerk's total sales with the value specified by its `amount` parameter. To find the sales clerk, the `addSale` method calls the `findClerk` helper method. The `findClerk` method performs a sequential search through the `clerks` array, and returns the index of the found sales clerk or -1 if the sales clerk is not found. If the sales clerk is not found, `addSale` adds a new `SalesClerk` object to the `clerks` array in order to store the new sale transaction in it. In adding a new `SalesClerk` object to the `clerks` array, `addSale` checks to make sure that there is available space in the `clerks` array for the new `SalesClerk` object. If the `clerks` array is all full (that is, `filledElements` equals `clerks.length`), then `addSale` must do something to provide for more elements. That's where the `doubleLength` helper method comes to the rescue.

The `doubleLength` method, as its name suggests, doubles the size of the `clerks` array. To do that, it instantiates a new array, `clerks2`, whose length is twice the length of the original `clerks` arrays. Then it copies all the data from the `clerks` array into the lowest-numbered elements in the `clerks2` array. Finally, it assigns the `clerks2` array to the `clerks` array so the `clerks` array points to the new longer array. See the `addSale`, `findClerk`, and `doubleLength` methods in Figures 10.22a and 10.22b and verify that they do what they're supposed to do.

The `SalesClerk` class, shown on the right side of Figure 10.21, is fairly straightforward. It contains two instance variables, `name` and `sales`, for the sales clerk's name and the sales clerk's total sales. It

```
/*******************************************************************
* SalesClerks.java
* Dean & Dean
*
* This class stores names and sales for sales clerks.
*******************************************************************/

class SalesClerks
{
  private SalesClerk[] clerks;      // contains names and sales
  private int filledElements = 0;   // number of elements filled

  //****************************************************************

  public SalesClerks(int initialSize)
  {
    clerks = new SalesClerk[initialSize];
  } // end SalesClerks constructor

  //****************************************************************

  // Process a sale for the clerk whose name is passed in.
  // If the name is not already in the clerks array,
  // create a new object and insert a reference to it in the
  // next array element, doubling array length if necessary.

  public void addSale(String name, double amount)
  {
    int clerkIndex = findClerk(name);

    if (clerkIndex == -1)           // add a new clerk
    {
      if (filledElements == clerks.length)
      {
        doubleLength();
      }
      clerkIndex = filledElements;
      clerks[clerkIndex] = new SalesClerk(name);
      filledElements++;
    } // end if

    clerks[clerkIndex].adjustSales(amount);
  } // end addSale
```

Figure 10.22a `SalesClerks` class—part A.

```
  //*************************************************************

  // Print all the data - sales clerk names and sales.

  public void dumpData()
  {
    for (int i=0; i<filledElements; i++)
    {
      System.out.printf("%s: %6.2f\n",
        clerks[i].getName(), clerks[i].getSales());
    }
  } // end dumpData

  //*************************************************************

  // Search for the given name. If found, return the index.
  // Otherwise, return -1.

  private int findClerk(String name)
  {
    for (int i=0; i<filledElements; i++)
    {
      if (clerks[i].getName().equals(name))
      {
        return i;
      }
    } // end for
    return -1;
  } // end findClerk

  //*************************************************************

  // Double the length of the array.

  private void doubleLength()
  {
    SalesClerk[] clerks2 = new SalesClerk[2 * clerks.length];
    System.arraycopy(clerks, 0, clerks2, 0, clerks.length);
    clerks = clerks2;
  } // end doubleLength
} // end class SalesClerks
```

Figure 10.22b SalesClerks class—part B

contains two accessor methods, getName and getSales. It contains an adjustSales method that updates the sales clerk's total sales value by adding the passed-in amount to the sales instance variable. See the SalesClerk class in Figure 10.23 and verify that it does what it's supposed to do.

Now look at the main method in the Figure 10.24's SalesClerksDriver class. In a declaration, it instantiates a SalesClerks object, passing an initial array-length value of 2 to the SalesClerks

```
/*******************************************************************
* SalesClerk.java
* Dean & Dean
*
* This class stores and retrieves a sales clerk's data.
*******************************************************************/

public class SalesClerk
{
  private String name;          // sales clerk's name
  private double sales = 0.0;   // total sales for clerk

  //****************************************************************

  public SalesClerk(String name)
  {
    this.name = name;
  }

  //****************************************************************

  public String getName()
  {
    return name;
  }

  public double getSales()
  {
    return sales;
  }

  //****************************************************************

  // Adjust clerk's total sales by adding the passed-in sale.

  public void adjustSales(double amount)
  {
    sales += amount;
  }
} // end class SalesClerk
```

Figure 10.23 SalesClerk class

```
/*******************************************************************
* SalesClerksDriver.java
* Dean & Dean
*
* This drives the SalesClerks class.
*******************************************************************/

import java.util.Scanner;

public class SalesClerksDriver
{
  public static void main(String[] args)
  {
    Scanner stdIn = new Scanner(System.in);
    SalesClerks clerks = new SalesClerks(2);
    String name;

    System.out.print("Enter clerk's name (q to quit): ");
    name = stdIn.nextLine();
    while (!name.equals("q"))
    {
      System.out.print("Enter sale amount: ");
      clerks.addSale(name, stdIn.nextDouble());
      stdIn.nextLine();          // flush newline
      System.out.print("Enter clerk's name (q to quit): ");
      name = stdIn.nextLine();
    } // end while
    clerks.dumpData();
  } // end main
} // end SalesClerksDriver
```

Sample session:

```
Enter clerk's name (q to quit): Daniel
Enter sale amount: 6.25
Enter clerk's name (q to quit): Josh
Enter sale amount: 58.12
Enter clerk's name (q to quit): Amanda
Enter sale amount: 40
Enter clerk's name (q to quit): Daniel
Enter sale amount: -6.25
Enter clerk's name (q to quit): Josh
Enter sale amount: 12.88
Enter clerk's name (q to quit): q
Daniel:   0.00
Josh:  71.00
Amanda:  40.00
```

Figure 10.24 Driver for the SalesClerks program in Figures 10.22a, 10.22b, and 10.23

constructor. Then it repeatedly prompts the user for a sales clerk name and sales value and calls the `addSale` method to insert the input data into the `SalesClerks` object. The looping stops when the user enters a `q` for the next name. Then `main` calls `dumpData` to display the accumulated sales data.

10.11 The `ArrayList` Class

As you've learned throughout this chapter, arrays allow you to work with an ordered list of related data. Arrays work great for many lists, but if you have a list where the number of elements is hard to predict, they don't work so well. If you don't know the number of elements, you have to either (1) start with an array size that's large enough to accommodate the possibility of a very large number of elements or (2) create a new larger array whenever the array becomes full and you need more room for more elements. The first solution is wasteful of computer memory as it requires allocating space for a large array where most of the elements are unused. The second solution is what we did in the SalesClerks program's `doubleLength` method. It works OK in terms of saving memory, but it requires the programmer to do extra work (writing the code that creates a larger array).

To help with lists where the number of elements is hard to predict, the folks at Sun came up with the `ArrayList` class. The `ArrayList` class is built using an array, but the array is hidden in the background, so you can't access it directly. With an array in the background, the `ArrayList` class is able to provide the basic functionality that comes with a standard array. With its methods, the `ArrayList` class is able to provide additional functionality that helps when you don't know the number of elements. In this section, we discuss how to create an `ArrayList` and how to use its methods.

How to Create an `ArrayList`

The `ArrayList` class is defined in the Java API's `java.util` package, so to use the class, you should provide an `import` statement, like this:

```
import java.util.ArrayList;
```

To initialize an `ArrayList` reference variable, use this syntax:

`ArrayList`<*element-type*> *reference-variable* `= new ArrayList`<*element-type*>`();`[3]

Note the angled brackets around *element-type* and *reference-variable*. The angled brackets are part of the required syntax. As indicated by the italics, *element-type* and *reference-variable* are descriptions. Normally, we use angled brackets around such descriptions, but we'll refrain from doing so when describing `ArrayList` syntax because description angled brackets might get confused with the `ArrayList`'s required angled brackets. You should replace *element-type* with the type for the `ArrayList`'s elements. You should replace *reference-variable* with an actual reference variable. For example, suppose you've defined a `Student` class, and you want an `ArrayList` of `Student` objects. Here's how to create such an `ArrayList`, named `students`:

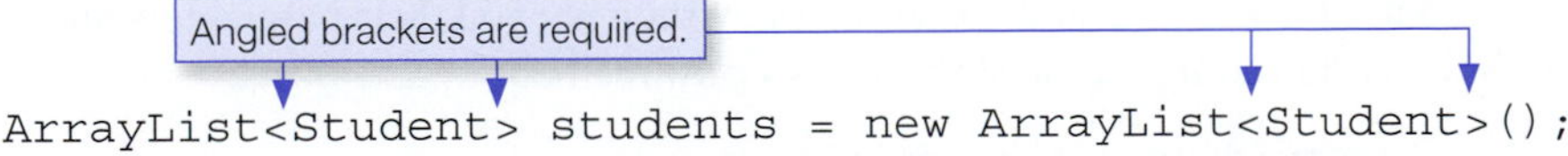
Angled brackets are required.
ArrayList<Student> students = new ArrayList<Student>();

[3] It's legal to omit <*element-type*> when you use `ArrayLists`. If you omit it, then the `ArrayList` can store different types of elements. That may sound exciting, but it's not needed all that often. And there are drawbacks to omitting <*element-type*>:

a) It forces the programmer to use the cast operator when assigning an extracted element into a variable.

b) It eliminates type checking for assigning values into the `ArrayList` (since then it's legal to assign any type).

Besides the angled brackets, there are two additional noteworthy items in the above example. First, there is no size specification. That's because ArrayList objects start out with no elements and they automatically expand to accommodate however many elements are added to them. Second, the element type, Student, is a class name. For ArrayLists, you must specify a class name, not a primitive type, for the element type. Specifying a class name means that ArrayLists can hold only references to objects. They cannot hold primitives, like int or double. That's technically true, but there's an easy way to mimic storing primitives in an ArrayList. We'll discuss how to do that in the next section.

Adding Elements to an ArrayList

To convert an instantiated empty ArrayList into something useful, you need to add elements to it. To add an element to the end of an ArrayList, use this syntax:

ArrayList-reference-variable.add(*item*);

The *item* that's added must be the same type as the element type specified in the ArrayList's declaration. Perhaps the simplest type of element object is a string, so let's start with an ArrayList of strings. Suppose you want to write a code fragment that creates this ArrayList object:

	colors
0	"red"
1	"green"
2	"blue"

Try writing the code on your own before proceeding. When you're done, compare your answer to this:

```
import java.util.ArrayList;
. . .
ArrayList<String> colors = new ArrayList<String>();
colors.add("red");
colors.add("green");
colors.add("blue");
```

The order in which you add elements determines the elements' positions. Since we added "red" first, it's at index position 0. Since we added "green" next, it's at index position 1. Likewise, "blue" is at index position 2.

API Headings

In describing the ArrayList class, we'll use *API headings* to present the ArrayList class's methods. As you may recall from Chapter 5, API stands for application programming interface, and API headings are the source code headings for the methods and constructors in Sun's library of pre-built Java classes. The API headings tell you how to use the methods and constructors by showing you their parameters and return types. For example, here's the API heading for the Math class's pow method:

```
public static double pow(double num, double power)
```

The above line tells you everything you need to know to use the pow method. To call the pow method, pass in two double arguments: one argument for the base and one argument for the power. The static modifier tells you to preface the call with the class name and then a dot. The double return value tells you to embed the method call in a place that can use a double value. Here's an example that calculates the volume of a sphere:

```
double volume = 1.333333333 * Math.PI * Math.pow(radius, 3)
```

How to Access Elements in an ArrayList

With standard arrays, you use square brackets to read and update an element. But with an ArrayList you don't use square brackets. Instead, you use a get method to read an element's value and a set method to update an element's value.

Here's the API heading for the ArrayList's get method:

```
public E get(int index)
```

The index parameter specifies the position of the desired element within the ArrayList calling object. For example, the following method call retrieves the second element in a colors ArrayList:

```
colors.get(1);
```

If the index parameter refers to a nonexistent element, then a runtime error occurs. For example, if colors contains three elements, then this generates a runtime error:

```
colors.get(3);
```

In the get method's API heading, note the E return type:

```
public E get(int index)
```

The E stands for "element." It represents the data type of the ArrayList's elements, whatever that data type happens to be. So if an ArrayList is declared to have string elements, then the get method returns a string value, and if an ArrayList is declared to have Student elements, then the get method returns a Student value. The E in the get method's heading is a generic name for an element type. Using a generic name for a type is an important concept that will come up again with other methods. It's important enough to justify a pedagogical analogy.

Using a generic return type is like saying you're going to the grocery store to get "food." It's better to use a generic term like food rather than a specific term like broccoli. Why? Because you might end up getting *Princess Fruit Chews* at the store instead of broccoli. By specifying generic food as your "return type," you're free to get Princess Fruit Chews rather than broccoli, as your preschooler sees fit.[4]

Using a generic name for a type is possible with ArrayLists because the ArrayList class is defined to be a *generic class*, by using <E> in its class heading:

```
public class ArrayList<E>
```

You don't need to understand generic class details in order to use ArrayLists, but if you want such details, visit http://java.sun.com/docs/books/tutorial/java/generics/index.html.

How to Update an ArrayList Element

Now for the get method's partner, the set method. The set method allows you to assign a value to an ArrayList element. Here is the API heading for ArrayList's set method:

```
public E set(int index, E elem)
```

[4] This analogy is taken from the real-life adventures of preschooler Jordan Dean.

In the set method's API heading, the index parameter specifies the position of the element you're interested in. If index refers to a nonexistent element, then a runtime error occurs. If index is valid, then set assigns the elem parameter to the specified element. Note that elem is declared with E for its type. As with the set method, the E represents the data type of the ArrayList's elements. So elem is the same type as the type of ArrayList's elements. This example illustrates what we're talking about:

```
String mixedColor;
ArrayList<String> colors = new ArrayList<String>();

colors.add("red");
colors.add("green");
colors.add("blue");
mixedColor = colors.get(0) + colors.get(1);
colors.set(2, mixedColor);
```

Note that mixedColor is declared to be a string and colors is declared to be an ArrayList of strings. So in the last statement when we use mixedColor as the second argument in the set method call, the argument is indeed the same type as the type of color's elements.

Can you determine what the colors ArrayList looks like after the code fragment executes? Draw a picture of the colors ArrayList on your own before proceeding. When you're done, compare your answer to this:

	colors
0	"red"
1	"green"
2	"redgreen"

In the set method's API heading, note the return type, E. Most mutator/set methods simply assign a value and that's it. In addition to assigning a value, the ArrayList's set method also returns a value—the value of the specified element prior to the element being updated. Usually, there's no need to do anything with the original value, so you just call set and the returned value dies. That's what happens in the above code fragment. But if you want to do something with the original value, it's easy to get it because set returns it.

Additional ArrayList Methods

We've now explained the most important methods for the ArrayList class. There are quite a few more methods, and Figure 10.25 provides API headings and brief descriptions for five of them. As you read through the figure, we hope that you'll find most of the methods to be straightforward. But some items may need clarification. In searching an ArrayList for the first occurrence of a passed-in elem parameter, the indexOf method declares elem's type to be Object. The Object type means the parameter may be any kind of object. Naturally, if the parameter's actual type is different from the type of elements in the ArrayList, then indexOf's search comes up empty and it returns −1 to indicate that elem was not found. By the way, we'll have lots more to say about the Object type (it's actually an Object class) in Chapter 13. Previously, we covered a one-parameter add method that adds an element at the end of the ArrayList. Figure 10.25's overloaded two-parameter add method adds an element at a specified position within the ArrayList.

public void add(int index, E elem)
Starting with the specified index position, the add method shifts the original elements at and above the index position to next-higher-indexed positions. It then inserts the elem parameter at the specified index position.

public int indexOf(Object elem)
Searches for the first occurrence of the elem parameter within the list and returns the index position of the found element. If the element is not found, the indexOf method returns -1.

public boolean isEmpty()
Returns true if the ArrayList contains no elements.

public int lastIndexOf(Object elem)
Searches for the last occurrence of the elem parameter within the list and returns the index position of the found element. If the element is not found, the indexOf method returns -1.

public E remove(int index)
Removes and returns the element at the specified index position. To handle the removed element's absence, the remove method shifts all higher-indexed elements by one position to lower-indexed positions.

public int size()
Returns the number of elements currently in the ArrayList.

Figure 10.25 API headings and descriptions for some additional ArrayList methods

Survivor Example

To reinforce what you've learned so far, let's take a look at how an ArrayList class is used in a complete working program. See the Survivor[5] program in Figure 10.26. It creates a list of survivor tribesmen by instantiating an ArrayList object and calling add to append tribesmen to the list. It then randomly chooses one of the tribesmen and removes that tribe member from the list. It prints a sorry message for the removed tribe member and a remaining message for the remaining tribesmen.

Note the format of the tribesmen in Figure 10.26's bottom output line—square brackets surrounding a comma-separated list. Can you find the Survivor code that prints that list? If you're looking for square brackets and a loop, forget it, they're not there. So how in the world does the square-bracketed list get printed? In the final println statement at the bottom of the program, the tribe ArrayList gets concatenated to a string. That causes the JVM to do some work behind the scenes. If you attempt to concatenate an ArrayList with a string or print an ArrayList, the ArrayList returns a comma-separated list of ArrayList elements surrounded by square brackets ([]). And that's exactly what happens when Figure 10.26's last statement executes.

[5] Survivor is a trademark of CBS Broadcasting Inc.

```
/*********************************************************************
* Survivor.java
* Dean & Dean
*
* This class creates an ArrayList of survivors.
* It randomly chooses one tribe member and removes him/her.
*********************************************************************/

import java.util.ArrayList;

public class Survivor
{
  public static void main(String[] args)
  {
    int loserIndex;
    String loser;
    ArrayList<String> tribe = new ArrayList<String>();

    tribe.add("Richard");
    tribe.add("Jerri");
    tribe.add("Colby");
    tribe.add("Amber");
    tribe.add("Rupert");
    loserIndex = (int) (Math.random() * tribe.size());
    loser = tribe.remove(loserIndex);
    System.out.println("Sorry, " + loser +
      ". The tribe has spoken. You must leave immediately.");
    System.out.println("Remaining: " + tribe);
  } // end main
} // end Survivor
```

Typical Output:

```
Sorry, Colby. The tribe has spoken. You must leave immediately.
Remaining: [Richard, Jerri, Amber, Rupert]
```

Figure 10.26 Survivor program

10.12 Storing Primitives in an ArrayList

As mentioned earlier, ArrayLists store references. For example, in the Survivor program, tribe is an ArrayList of strings, and strings are references. If you need to store primitives in an ArrayList, you can't do it directly, but if the primitives are wrapped up in wrapper classes,[6] you can store the resulting wrapped objects in an ArrayList. In this section, we show you how to do that.

[6] If you need a refresher on wrapper classes, see Chapter 5.

Stock Average Example

The StockAverage program in Figure 10.27 reads weighted stock values and stores them in an ArrayList. In simplified terms, a weighted stock value is the market price of one stock share times a number that scales that price up or down to reflect the importance of the stock's company in the overall marketplace. After the StockAverage program stores the weighted stock values in an ArrayList, the program calculates the average of all the entered weighted stock values. Why is an ArrayList appropriate for calculating a stock average? An ArrayList's size grows as necessary. That works well for stock averages because there are lots of stock averages (also called stock indexes), and they use different numbers of stocks in their calculations. For example, the Dow Jones Industrial Average uses stock values from 30 companies while the Russell 3000 Index uses stock values from 3,000 companies. Because it uses an ArrayList, the StockAverage program works well for both situations.

The StockAverage program stores stock values in an ArrayList named stocks. The stock values originate from user input in the form of doubles, like 25.6, 36.0, and so on. As you know, ArrayLists can't store primitives; they can store references only. So the StockAverage program wraps up the doubles into Double wrapper objects just prior to storing them in the stocks ArrayList. As you might imagine, a *wrapper object* is an instance of a wrapper class, and each wrapper object stores one "wrapped up" primitive value. You don't have to worry very much about wrapper objects for ArrayLists. For the most part, you can pretend that ArrayLists can hold primitives. Case in point: The following line from the StockAverage program appears to add a primitive (stock) to the stocks ArrayList:

```
stocks.add(stock);
```

What actually happens behind the scenes is that the stock primitive gets automatically converted to a wrapper object prior to its being added to the stocks ArrayList. Really, there is just one thing you have to worry about when working with primitives in an ArrayList. When you create an ArrayList object to hold primitive values, the type you specify in the angled brackets must be the wrapped version of the primitive type, that is, Double instead of double, Integer instead of int, and so on. This line from the StockAverage program illustrates what we're talking about:

```
ArrayList<Double> stocks = new ArrayList<Double>();
```

Autoboxing and Unboxing

In most places, it's legal to use primitive values and wrapper objects interchangeably. The way it works is that the JVM automatically wraps primitive values and unwraps wrapper objects when it's appropriate to do so. For example, if the JVM sees an int value on the right of an assignment statement and an Integer variable at the left, it thinks to itself, hmmm, to make this work, I need to convert the int value to an Integer wrapper object. It then gets out its Styrofoam packing peanuts and duct tape and wraps up the int value into an Integer wrapper object. That process is called *autoboxing*. On the other hand, if the JVM sees an Integer wrapper object on the right of an assignment statement and an int variable at the left, it thinks to itself, hmmm, to make this work, I need to extract the int value from the Integer wrapper object. It then proceeds to tear off the Integer wrapper object's covering, and it gets the int value that's inside. That process is called *unboxing*.

More formally, autoboxing is the process of automatically wrapping a primitive value in an appropriate wrapper class whenever there's an attempt to use a primitive value in a place that expects a reference. Refer to the stocks.add(stock); statement in Figure 10.27. That statement causes autoboxing to occur. The stocks.add method call expects a reference argument. Specifically, it expects the argument to be

```
/*********************************************************************
* StockAverage.java
* Dean & Dean
*
* This program uses an ArrayList to store user-entered stock
* values. It prints the average stock value.
*********************************************************************/

import java.util.Scanner;
import java.util.ArrayList;

public class StockAverage
{
  public static void main(String[] args)
  {
    Scanner stdIn = new Scanner(System.in);
    ArrayList<Double> stocks = new ArrayList<Double>();
    double stock;                          // a stock value
    double stockSum = 0;                   // sum of stock values

    System.out.print("Enter a stock value (-1 to quit): ");
    stock = stdIn.nextDouble();

    while (stock >= 0)
    {
      stocks.add(stock);
      System.out.print("Enter a stock value (-1 to quit): ");
      stock = stdIn.nextDouble();
    } // end while

    for (int i=0; i<stocks.size(); i++)
    {
      stock = stocks.get(i);
      stockSum += stock;
    }

    if (stocks.size() != 0)
    {
      System.out.printf("\nAverage stock value = $%.2f\n",
        stockSum / stocks.size());
    }
  } // end main
} // end class StockAverage
```

This must be a wrapper class, not a primitive type!

Autoboxing takes place here.

Unboxing takes place here.

Figure 10.27 StockAverage program illustrating ArrayList of Double objects

a reference to a Double wrapper object (since stocks is declared to be an ArrayList of Double references). When the JVM sees a primitive value argument (stock), it automatically wraps the argument in a Double wrapper class.

More formally, unboxing is the process of automatically extracting a primitive value from a wrapper object whenever there's an attempt to use a wrapper object in a place that expects a primitive. Refer to the stock = stocks.get(i); statement in Figure 10.27. That statement causes unboxing to occur. Since stock is a primitive variable, the JVM expects a primitive value to be assigned into it. When the JVM sees a wrapper object on the right of the assignment statement (stocks holds Double wrapper objects and get(i) retrieves the ith such wrapper object), it automatically extracts the primitive value from the wrapper object.

Autoboxing and unboxing take place automatically behind the scenes. That makes the programmer's job easier. Yeah!

10.13 ArrayList Example Using Anonymous Objects and the For-Each Loop

Anonymous objects and *for-each loops* are programming constructs that are particularly useful when used in conjunction with ArrayLists. In this section, we present for-each loop details and anonymous object details by showing how they're used in the context of an ArrayList program. But before we get to the program, we provide brief introductions for the two new constructs.

Usually, when you create an object, you immediately store the object's reference in a reference variable. That way, you can refer to the object later on by using the reference variable's name. If you create an object and don't immediately assign the object's reference to a reference variable, you've created an anonymous object. It's called anonymous because it doesn't have a name.

A for-each loop is a modified version of the traditional for loop. It can be used whenever there's a need to iterate through all of the elements in a collection of data. An ArrayList is a collection of data, and, as such, for-each loops can be used to iterate through all of the elements in an ArrayList.

A Bear-Store Example

Suppose you want to model a store which sells customized toy bears. You need a Bear class to represent each bear, a BearStore class to represent the store, and a BearStoreDriver class to "drive" the program. Let's start by examining the Bear class in Figure 10.28. The Bear class defines two instance named constants which represent two permanent properties of a particular bear: (1) MAKER, the bear's manufacturer, such as Gund, and (2) TYPE, the bear's type, such as "pooh bear" or "angry campground bear." A constructor initializes these two instance constants, and a display method displays them.

Now let's examine the first part of the BearStore class, shown in Figure 10.29a. The BearStore class has one instance variable, bears, which is declared to be an ArrayList of Bear references. It holds the store's collection of toy bears. The BearStore class's addStdBears method fills the bears ArrayList with a specified number of standard teddy bears. Here's the statement that adds one standard teddy bear to the ArrayList:

```
bears.add(new Bear("Acme", "brown teddy"));
```

The statement instantiates a Bear object and passes the Bear object's reference to the bears.add method call. The statement does not assign the Bear object's reference to a Bear reference vari-

```
/*************************************************************
* Bear.java
* Dean & Dean
*
* This class models a toy bear.
*************************************************************/

public class Bear
{
  private final String MAKER; // bear's manufacturer
  private final String TYPE;  // type of bear

  //**********************************************************

  public Bear(String maker, String type)
  {
    MAKER = maker;
    TYPE = type;
  }

  //**********************************************************

  public void display()
  {
    System.out.println(MAKER + " " + TYPE);
  }
} // end Bear class
```

Figure 10.28 Class that represents a toy bear

able. Since there's no assignment to a Bear reference variable, that's an example of an anonymous object. As an alternative, the statement could have been written with a Bear reference variable like this:

```
Bear stdBear = new Bear("Acme", "brown teddy");
bears.add(stdBear);
```

But why bother with using two statements instead of one? The new bear's reference gets stored in the bears ArrayList and that's where it's processed. There's no need to store it in a second place (e.g., in the stdBear reference variable), so in the interest of code compactness, don't.

Now let's examine the bottom part of the BearStore class, shown in Figure 10.29b. The BearStore class's getUserSpecifiedBear method prompts the user for a customized bear's maker and type and returns the newly created bear. Here's the return statement:

```
return new Bear(maker, type);
```

Note that there's no reference variable for the new bear. Thus, the new bear is considered to be an anonymous object. The return statement returns the new bear to the addUserSpecifiedBears method, where it gets added to the bears ArrayList.

```
/*********************************************************************
* BearStore.java
* Dean & Dean
*
* This class implements a store that sells toy bears.
*********************************************************************/

import java.util.Scanner;
import java.util.ArrayList;

public class BearStore
{
  ArrayList<Bear> bears = new ArrayList<Bear>();

  //*****************************************************************

  // Fill store with specified number of standard teddy bears.

  public void addStdBears(int num)
  {
    for (int i=0; i<num; i++)
    {
      bears.add(new Bear("Acme", "brown teddy"));
    }
  } // end addStdBears

  //*****************************************************************

  // Fill store with specified number of customized bears.

  public void addUserSpecifiedBears(int num)
  {
    for (int i=0; i<num; i++)
    {
      bears.add(getUserSpecifiedBear());
    }
  } // end addUserSpecifiedBears
```

anonymous object as argument
Returned anonymous object becomes argument in this method call.

Figure 10.29a Class that implements a toy-bear store—part A

When to Use an Anonymous Object

The bear-store program contains several specific examples of using anonymous objects. In general, you'll see anonymous objects being used in two circumstances:

1. When passing a newly created object into a method or constructor. For example:

   `bears.add(new Bear("Gund", "Teddy"));`

2. When returning a newly created object from a method. For example:

   `return new Bear(maker, type);`

```
  //***************************************************************

  // Prompt user for bear's maker and type and return bear.

  private Bear getUserSpecifiedBear()
  {
    Scanner stdIn = new Scanner(System.in);
    String maker, type;

    System.out.print("Enter bear's maker: ");
    maker = stdIn.nextLine();
    System.out.print("Enter bear's type: ");
    type = stdIn.nextLine();
    return new Bear(maker, type);
  } // end getUserSpecifiedBear

  //***************************************************************

  // Print all the bears in the store.

  public void displayInventory()
  {
    for (Bear bear : bears)
    {
      bear.display();
    }
  } // end displayInventory

  //***************************************************************

  public static void main(String[] args)
  {
    BearStore store = new BearStore();
    store.addStdBears(3);
    store.addUserSpecifiedBears(2);
    store.displayInventory();
  } // end main
} // end BearStore class
```

anonymous object as return value

for-each loop

Figure 10.29b Class that implements a toy-bear store—part B

Embedded Driver

At the bottom of the BearStore class, we've embedded the program's driver, main. It instantiates a BearStore object, adds three standard bears to the bear store, adds two user-specified bears to the bear store, and then displays the store's inventory of bears by calling displayInventory. In displaying the store's inventory, the displayInventory method accesses each bear in the bears ArrayList with the help of a for-each loop. In the next subsection, you'll learn about for-each loop details.

For-Each Loop

As mentioned earlier, a for-each loop can be used whenever there's a need to iterate through all the elements in a collection of data. Here is the for-each loop syntax for an `ArrayList`:

```
for (<element-type> <element-name> : <ArrayList-reference-variable>)
{
  ...
}
```

And here is an example for-each loop from Figure 10.29b's `displayInventory` method:

```
for (Bear bear : bears)
{
  bear.display();
}
```

Note how the for-each loop header matches the above syntax: `bears` is an `ArrayList` reference variable, `bear` is the name of an element in the `bears ArrayList`, and `Bear` is the type for each element. It's legal to choose any name for the element, but, as always, you should choose a descriptive name, like `bear` in this example. With each iteration of the for-each loop, you use the element's name to refer to the current element. For example, `bear.display()` calls the `display` method for the current `bear` element.

Are you wondering why the for-each loop is called a for-each loop even though there's no "each" in the syntax? It's because most people say "for each" to themselves when reading a for-each loop's header. For example, in reading `displayInventory`'s for-each loop, most people would say "For each bear in the bears collection, do the following."

Note that, as an alternative, you could implement the `displayInventory` method using a traditional `for` loop rather than a for-each loop. Here's an implementation with a traditional `for` loop:

```
for (int i=0; i<bears.size(); i++)
{
  bears.get(i).display();
}
```

The for-each loop implementation is preferred because it is simpler. There's no need to declare an index variable, and there's no need to calculate and specify the `ArrayList`'s first and last index values.

Be aware that you can use the for-each loop for more than just `ArrayLists`. You can use them for iterating through any collection of elements. More specifically, you can use them for arrays and for any of Java's *collection classes*. `ArrayList` is a collection class, and to learn about the other collection classes, see http://java.sun.com/javase/6/docs/technotes/guides/collections/.

The following code fragment illustrates how to use a for-each loop with a standard array. It prints the numbers in a `primes` array.

```
int[] primes = {1, 2, 3, 5, 7, 11};
for (int p : primes)
{
  System.out.println(p);
}
```

The for-each loop is great, but you should be aware of several issues when using it. (1) It was introduced in Java 5.0, so it won't work with older compilers. (2) The for-each loop doesn't use an index variable to loop through its elements. That can be a benefit in that it leads to less cluttered code. But it's a drawback if there's a need for an index within the loop. For example, suppose you're given a `primes` array, like above, and you want to print this:

```
primes[0] = 1
primes[1] = 2
...
primes[5] = 11
```

The numbers inside the square brackets are index values. So if you implemented a solution with a for-each loop, you'd have to add an index variable to your code and increment it each time through the loop. On the other hand, if you implemented a solution with a traditional for loop, you'd already have an incrementing index variable built in.

10.14 ArrayLists Versus Standard Arrays

There's a lot of overlap in the functionality of an `ArrayList` and a standard array. So how can you tell which one to use? Your answer will be different for different situations. When deciding on an implementation, consider this table:

Benefits of an `ArrayList` Over a Standard Array	Benefits of a Standard Array Over an `ArrayList`
1. It's easy to increase the size of an `ArrayList`—just call `add`.	1. A standard array uses []'s to access array elements (which is easier than using `get` and `set` methods).
2. It's easy for a programmer to insert or remove an element to or from the interior of an `ArrayList`—just call `add` or `remove` and specify the element's index position.	2. A standard array is more efficient when storing primitive values.

In looking at the table's first `ArrayList` benefit, easy to increase the size of an `ArrayList`, think about how much work is required to increase the size of a standard array. For a standard array, the programmer needs to instantiate a larger array and then copy the old array's contents to the new larger array. On the other hand, for an `ArrayList`, the programmer simply needs to call the `add` method. Note that behind the scenes, the JVM has to put forth some effort in implementing the `add` method, but the effort is kept to a minimum. `ArrayLists` are implemented with the help of an underlying standard array. Usually, the underlying array has a greater number of elements than the `ArrayList`, so adding another element to the `ArrayList` is easy—the JVM just borrows an unused element from the underlying array. As a programmer, you don't have to worry about or code those details; the "borrowing" takes place automatically.

The table's second `ArrayList` benefit, easy for a programmer to insert or remove an element to or from the interior of an `ArrayList`, is true, but just because it's easy for programmers doesn't mean it's easy for the JVM. Actually, the JVM has to do quite a bit of work when it adds or removes from the interior of an `ArrayList`. To insert an element, the JVM has to adjust its underlying array by shifting higher indexed elements to make room for the new element. And to remove an element, the JVM has to adjust its underlying array by shifting higher indexed elements to overlay the removed element.

Since ArrayLists and standard arrays are both inefficient when it comes to inserting or removing an element to or from the interior of a list, if you're doing a lot of inserting and removing, you should consider a different structure—a *linked list.* A linked list is a sequence of elements, where each element contains a data item plus a reference (a "link") that points to the next element. You can create a linked list using exactly the same procedures you used to create an ArrayList. Just replace the ArrayList class with the LinkedList class. If you're interested in LinkedList details, look up the LinkedList collection class on Sun's Java API Web site.

The above table says that a standard array is more efficient than an ArrayList when it comes to storing primitive values. Why is that? Remember that before an ArrayList stores a primitive value, it must wrap the primitive in a wrapper object. That wrapping process takes time, and that's the cause of the inefficiency.

Summary

- Arrays facilitate the representation and manipulation of collections of similar data. You access array elements with *<array-name>*[index], where index is a nonnegative integer, starting at zero.
- You can create and completely initialize an array in one statement, like this:
  <element-type>[] *<array-name>* = {*element0*, *element1*, ...};
- Usually, however, it's more useful to defer element initialization and use new to create an array of uninitialized elements, like this:
  <element-type>[] *<array-name>* = new *<element-type>*[*array-size*];
- You can read or write directly to an array element by inserting an appropriate index value in square brackets after the array name at any time after the array has been created.
- Every array automatically includes a public property called length, which you can access directly with the array name. The highest index value is *<array-name>*.length - 1.
- To copy an array, you copy each of its elements individually, or you can use the System.arraycopy method to copy any subset of elements in one array to any location in another array.
- A histogram is an array of elements in which each element's value is the number of occurrences of some event.
- A sequential search is a good way to search for a match in an array whose length is less than about 20, but for long arrays, you should first sort the array with the Arrays.sort method and then use a binary search.
- A two-dimensional array is an array of arrays, declared with two sets of square brackets after the element-type identification. You can instantiate it with an initializer or with new followed by element type and two array-size specifications in square brackets.
- In creating an array of objects, multiple instantiations are required. After instantiating the array, you also need to instantiate the individual element objects within the array.
- If you need to repeatedly insert or delete elements within an array, you should consider using an ArrayList rather than a standard array. When you declare or instantiate an ArrayList for a group of Car elements, you should include the type of elements it will contain in angled brackets, like this:
  ```
  ArrayList<Car> car = new ArrayList<Car>();
  ```
- An ArrayList stores objects only. Java automatically makes necessary conversions between primitives and wrapped primitives, so you don't have to worry about that, but if you want an ArrayList of primitives like int, you must declare it with the wrapped type, like this:
  ```
  ArrayList<Integer> num = new ArrayList<Integer>();
  ```
- You can pass objects to and from methods anonymously.
- Use a for-each loop to iterate through a collection of data items.

Review Questions

§10.2 Array Basics

1. It's legal to store ints and also doubles in a single standard array. (T / F)
2. Given an array that's named myArray, you access the first element in the array using myArray[0]. (T / F)

§10.3 Array Declaration and Creation

3. Provide a declaration for an array of strings called names.
4. Consider the heading for any main method:

```
public static void main(String[] args)
```

   What kind of a thing is args?

5. Suppose you create an array with the statement:

```
char[] choices = new char[4];
```

   What is the default value in a typical element of this array? Is it garbage or something in particular?

§10.4 Array length Property and Partially Filled Arrays

6. The value of an array's length equals the value of the array's largest acceptable index. (T / F)

§10.5 Copying an Array

7. Given

```
String letters = "abcdefghijklmnopqrstuvwxyz";
char alphabet[] = new char[26];
```

   Write a for loop that initializes alphabet with the characters in letters.

8. Write a single statement that copies all the elements in

```
char arr1[] = {'x', 'y', 'z'};
```

   to the last three elements of

```
char arr2[] = new char[26];
```

§10.6 Problem Solving with Array Case Studies

9. In Figure 10.7's MovingAverage program, suppose you want to shift in the other direction. How would you write the inner for loop header, and how would you write the array assignment statement in the inner for loop?
10. What kind of value does a typical histogram "bin" contain?

§10.7 Searching an Array

11. It's possible to search array ids for an element equal to id with nothing more than this:

```
int i;
for (i=0; i<ids.length && id != ids[i]; i++)
{ }
if (<boolean-expression>)
{
  return i;
}
```

   What is the *<boolean-expression>* that indicates that i has been found?

§10.8 Sorting an Array

12. We elected to use class methods to implement our sort algorithm. What is an advantage of that?
13. Java's API `sort` method is in what class?

§10.9 Two-Dimensional Arrays

14. We have said that a two-dimensional array is an array of arrays. Consider the following declaration:

```
double[][] myArray = new double[5][8];
```

In the context of the expression, array of arrays, what does `myArray[3]` mean?

§10.10 Arrays of Objects

15. In creating an array of objects, you have to instantiate the array object, and you must also instantiate each element object that's stored in the array. (T / F)

§10.11 The `ArrayList` Class

16. How is an `ArrayList` more versatile than an array?
17. To avoid runtime errors, you must always specify the size of an `ArrayList` when you declare it. (T / F)
18. What is the return type of the `ArrayList` class's `get` method?
19. If you call the `ArrayList` method, `add(i, x)`, what happens to the element originally at position `i`?

§10.12 Storing Primitives in an `ArrayList`

20. Specifically, under what circumstances does autoboxing take place?
21. Write one statement that appends the `double` value, 56.85, to the end of an existing `ArrayList` called `prices`.
22. Write one statement that displays all of the values in an `ArrayList` of `Doubles` called `prices`. Put the complete list in square brackets and use a comma and a space to separate different values in the list.

§10.13 `ArrayList` Example Using Anonymous Objects and the For-Each Loop

23. What is an anonymous object?
24. You must use a for-each loop, and not a traditional `for` loop, whenever you need to iterate through a collection of elements. (T / F)

§10.14 `ArrayLists` Versus Standard Arrays

25. Given:
    - You have a `WeatherDay` class that stores weather information for a single day.
    - You'd like to store `WeatherDay` objects for a whole year.
    - The primary task of your program is sorting `WeatherDay` objects (e.g., sort by temperature, sort by wind speed, and so on).

    How should you store your `WeatherDay` objects—in an `ArrayList` or in a standard array? Provide a rationale for your answer.

Exercises

1. [after §10.2] The index number of the last element in an array of length 100 is ____.
2. [after §10.3] Declare an array named `scores` that holds `double` values.
3. [after §10.3] Provide a single initialization statement that initializes `myList` to all 1's. `myList` is a 5-element array of `int`'s.

4. [after §10.4] Zoo Animals Program:

As part of your internship at Parkville's new zoo, you've been asked to write a program that keeps track of the zoo animals. You want to make the program general purpose so that when you're done, you can sell your program to zoos worldwide and make millions. Thus, you decide to create a generic `Zoo` class.

Write a `Zoo` class. Your class does not have to do very much—it simply handles the creation and printing of `Zoo` objects. To give you a better idea of the `Zoo` class's functionality, we provide a `main` method:

```
public static void main(String[] args)
{
  Zoo zoo1 = new Zoo();
  String[] animals = {"pig", "possum", "squirrel", "Chihuahua"};
  Zoo zoo2 = new Zoo(animals, "Parkville");
  animals[0] = "white tiger";
  Zoo zoo3 = new Zoo(animals, "San Diego");
  zoo1.display();
  zoo2.display();
  zoo3.display();
}
```

When run, the `main` method should print this:

```
The zoo is vacant.
Parkville zoo: pig, possum, squirrel, Chihuahua
San Diego zoo: white tiger, possum, squirrel, Chihuahua
```

Although it's not required, you're encouraged to write a complete program in order to test your `Zoo` class.

5. [after §10.5] Assume that this code fragment compiles and runs. What is its output? Be precise when showing your output.

```
char[] a = new char[3];
char[] b;
for (int i=0; i<a.length; i++)
{
  a[i] = 'a';
}
b = a;
b[2] = 'b';
System.out.println("a[1]=" + a[1] + ", a[2]=" + a[2]);
System.out.println("b[1]=" + b[1] + ", b[2]=" + b[2]);
```

6. [after §10.5] What needs to be added to the following code fragment so that all values except the first two values (100000.0 and 110000.0) are copied from `allSalaries` to `workerSalaries`?

```
double[] allSalaries = {100000.0, 110000.0, 25000.0, 18000.0,
  30000.0, 9000.0, 12000.0};
double[] workerSalaries;
```

7. [after §10.5] The following program is supposed to reverse the order of the elements in the `simpsons` array. It compiles and runs, but it doesn't work properly.

```
public class Reverse
{
  public static void main(String[] args)
  {
    String[] simpsons = {"Homer", "Flanders", "Apu"};
```

```
    reverse(simpsons);
    System.out.println(
      simpsons[0] + " " + simpsons[1] + " " + simpsons[2]);
  } // end main

  public static void reverse(String[] list)
  {
    String[] temp = new String[list.length];

    for (int i=0; i<list.length; i++)
    {
      temp[i] = list[list.length-i-1];
    }
    list = temp;
  } // end reverse
} // end class Reverse
```

a) What does the program print?

b) Fix the program by providing one or more lines of alternative code for the `list = temp;` line. You are not allowed to change any other code, just provide alternative code for that one line.

8. [after §10.6] Write a program that implements the example described at the beginning of Section 10.6. Your program should shift the array's elements from position x to position x − 1 as described in that section. (Move the value at position 1 to position 0; move the value at position 2 to position 1, and so on).

Start by creating two arrays, `double[] initialHours` and `double[] hours`. In its declaration initialize `initialHours` with the values `{8, 8, 6, 4, 7, 0, 0, 5}`, but don't initialize `hours` when you declare and instantiate it with its 31 elements. Instead, initialize `hours` after its creation by using `System.arraycopy` to copy all the values in `initialHours` into the first elements in hours. Then perform one down-shift operation, and load zero into the (new) highest element.

9. [after §10.7] Write a class method named `allPositive` that receives an array named `arr` of `double` values and returns `true` if all the element values are positive and returns `false` otherwise. Use appropriate access modifiers. Make the method accessible from outside of its class.

10. [after §10.7] Assume that you have already successfully written a class named `Students` that handles student records for the Registrar's office. Assume that the `Students` class:

- Contains a `studentIds` instance variable—an array of `int`s that contains student ID numbers.
- Contains a 1-parameter constructor that initializes the `studentIds` instance variable.
- Contains this `main` method:

```
public static void main(String[] args)
{
  Students s1 = new Students(new int[] {123, 456, 789});
  Students s2 = new Students(new int[] {123, 456, 789, 555});
  Students s3 = new Students(new int[] {123, 456, 789});
  if (s1.equals(s2))
  {
    System.out.println("s1 == s2");
  }
  if (s1.equals(s3))
  {
    System.out.println("s1 == s3");
  }
} // end main
```

Write a `public` method named `equals` for your `Students` class that tests whether two `Students` objects are equal. Your `equals` method should be written such that the above `main` method would produce this output:

```
s1 == s3
```

Only provide code for the asked-for `equals` method; do not provide code for the entire `Students` class.

11. [after §10.8] Given the following list array, use the Selection Sort algorithm to sort the array. Show each step of the selection sort process. Do not provide code; just show pictures of the `list` array after each element swap.

	list (original)
0	12
1	2
2	−4
3	0
4	9

	list (sorted)
0	−4
1	0
2	2
3	9
4	12

12. [after §10.8] The Insertion Sort algorithm provides an alternative to the Selection Sort algorithm for sorting small numbers of items (of order 20 or less). It's not quite as efficient as Selection Sort for arrays, but it is slightly more efficient for other kinds of data collections. The following code implements the Insertion Sort algorithm:

```
10  public static void insertionSort(int[] list)
11  {
12    int temp;
13    int j;
14
15    for (int i=1; i<list.length; i++)
16    {
17      temp = list[i];
18      for (j=i; j>0 && temp<list[j-1]; j--)
19      {
20        list[j] = list[j-1];
21      }
22      list[j] = temp;
23    } // end for
24  } // end insertionSort
```

Note that the scope of the `j` count variable extends beyond the scope of the `for` loop in which it's used. Assume that an array of `int` has been instantiated and the `insertionSort` method has been called with a reference to this array passed in as a parameter. Trace the execution of this method, using the following header and initial entries:

Sort					<arrays>				
	insertionSort				arr1				
line#	**(list)**	**i**	**j**	**temp**	**length**	**0**	**1**	**2**	**3**
					4	3333	1234	2222	1000
10	arr1								

13. [after §10.8] Trace the following code and show the exact output.

```
public class ModifyArray
{
  public static void main(String[] args)
  {
    int sum = 0;
    int[] list = new int[3];

    for (int i=0; i<3; i++)
    {
      list[i] = i + 100;
    }
    modify(list, sum);
    for (int i=0; i<3; i++)
    {
      System.out.print(list[i] + " ");
    }
    System.out.println("\nsum = " + sum);
  }

  public static void modify(int[] list, int sum)
  {
    int temp = list[0];

    list[0] = list[list.length - 1];
    list[list.length - 1] = temp;
    for (int i=0; i<3; i++)
    {
      sum += list[i];
    }
  }
} // end ModifyArray
```

Use the following trace header:

<table>
<tr><td colspan="8">ModifyArray</td><td colspan="4"><arrays></td><td></td></tr>
<tr><td rowspan="2">line#</td><td colspan="3">main</td><td colspan="4">modify</td><td colspan="4">arr1</td><td></td></tr>
<tr><td>i</td><td>sum</td><td>list</td><td>(list)</td><td>(sum)</td><td>temp</td><td>i</td><td>length</td><td>0</td><td>1</td><td>2</td><td>output</td></tr>
</table>

14. [after §10.9] Specify a single statement that initializes an array of `int`'s named `myTable` to all 1's. The array should be a two-dimensional array with 2 rows and 3 columns.

15. [after §10.9] Write a method named `getMask` that receives a single parameter named `table` which is a two-dimensional array of `int`'s. The `getMask` method should create and return an array *mask* for the passed-in table array. The programming term mask refers to an array that is built from another array and it contains all 0's and 1's. For each element in the mask array, if the original array's corresponding element contains a positive number, the mask array's element should contain a 1. And if the original array's corresponding element contains a zero or negative number, the mask array's element should contain a 0. Note this example:

table parameter

5	−2	3	1
0	14	0	6
3	6	−1	4

returned array

1	0	1	1
0	1	0	1
1	1	0	1

Note:

- Your method should not change the content of the passed-in table array.
- Your method should work with any sized table, not just the 3-row, 4-column table shown in the example.
- Use appropriate access modifiers. Assume that the method should be accessible from outside of its class. In deciding whether the method should be a class method or an instance method, note that the method does not access any instance variables (it only accesses a parameter).

16. [after §10.10] Assume you have the following `City` class:

```
public class City
{
  private String name;
  private double north;           // north latitude in degrees
  private double west;            // west longitude in degrees

  //*************************************************************

  public City(String name, double latitude, double longitude)
  {
    this.name = name;
    this.north = latitude;
    this.west = longitude;
  } // end constructor

  //*************************************************************

  public void display()
  {
    System.out.printf("%12s%6.1f%6.1f\n", name, north, west);
  }
} // end class City
```

Write a code fragment that creates an array of `City` objects that contains the name, latitude, and longitude of the following four cities and displays the contents of those arrays like this:

```
New York 41.0  74.0
   Miami 26.0  80.0
 Chicago 42.0  88.0
 Houston 30.0  96.0
```

17. [after §10.11] What does the `ArrayList`'s `remove` method do?

18. [after §10.12] Provide a single statement (an initialization statement) that declares an `ArrayList` named `evenNumbers` and assigns a newly instantiated `ArrayList` to it. The instantiated `ArrayList` should be able to store integers.

19. [after §10.12] Using the `evenNumbers` `ArrayList` created in the previous exercise, provide a code fragment that stores the first 10 even numbers in the `evenNumbers` `ArrayList`. In other words, put 0 in the first `evenNumbers` element, put 2 in the second `evenNumbers` element, . . . , put 18 in the tenth `evenNumbers` element. You must use a standard `for` loop for your code fragment.

20. [after §10.13] Provide a more elegant (but functionally equivalent) version of this code fragment:

```
ArrayList<Car> cars = new ArrayList<Car>();
Car car1 = new Car("Mustang", 2006, "tiger-striped");
cars.add(car1);
Car car2 = new Car("MiniCooper", 2006, "lime green");
cars.add(car2);
```

21. [after §10.13] Suppose you have an `ArrayList` of street addresses that's been initialized and filled as follows:

```
ArrayList<String> addressList = new ArrayList<String>();
addressList.add("1600 Pennsylvania Avenue");
addressList.add("221B Baker Street");
...
addressList.add("8700 N.W. River Park Drive");
```

Provide a for-each loop (<u>not</u> a standard `for` loop) that prints the `addressList`'s addresses, one address per line.

22. [after §10.14] Suppose you wanted to maintain a list of cities described by the `City` class defined in Exercise 16. And suppose you wanted to be able to insert or remove cities at any place in the list to maintain a certain ordering as you added or removed elements. Should you use an array or an `ArrayList`, and why?

Review Question Solutions

1. False. The types of the data elements in a particular array must be the same.

2. True.

3. Declaration for an array of strings called `names`:

```
String[] names;
```

4. The `args` parameter in `main` is an array of strings.

5. The elements of an array are like the instance variables in an object. Array-element default values are not garbage. The default value of a `char[]` element is a special character whose underlying numeric value is `0`.

6. False. The largest acceptable index value is one less than the array's length.

7. This code fragment initializes the character array, alphabet:

```
for (int i=0; i<26; i++)
{
  alphabet[i] = letters.charAt(i);
}
```

8. You can copy:

```
arr1[] = {'x', 'y', 'z'}
```

to the end of:

```
arr2[] = new char[26]
```

with the following statement:

```
System.arraycopy(arr1, 0, arr2, 23, 3);
```

9. In the MovingAverage program, to shift in the other direction, the inner `for` loop header is:

```
for (int d=days.length-1; d>0; d--)
```

The array element assignment statement in this loop is:

```
days[d] = days[d-1];
```

10. A histogram "bin" contains the number of occurrences of an event.
11. The Boolean expression that indicates that `i` has been found is:

```
(ids.length != 0 && i != ids.length)
```

12. The advantage of using class methods is that the sort method can be used with any passed-in array, not just on a specific instance variable array.
13. Java's API `sort` method is in the `Arrays` class.
14. `myArray[3]` refers to the fourth row, which happens to be an array of eight `double` values.
15. True.
16. With an `ArrayList`, you can insert and delete elements anywhere in the sequence, and the list length grows and shrinks dynamically.
17. False. Normally, you specify no size for an `ArrayList` when you declare it.
18. The `get` method's return type is `E`, which refers to the type of each element in the `ArrayList`.
19. The element that is originally at position `i` shifts to the next higher index position.
20. Autoboxing takes place when a primitive is being used in a place that expects a reference.
21. `prices.add(56.85);`
22. `System.out.println(prices);`
23. An anonymous object is an object that's instantiated but it's not stored in a variable.
24. False. You can use a traditional `for` loop (or a for-each loop) to iterate through a collection of elements.
25. You should store your `WeatherDay` objects in a standard array.
Rationale:
    - There's no need for the array to grow or shrink since the size is fixed at 365 (and standard arrays have a fixed size).
    - With sorting, you'll need to access the objects quite often (and access is easier with standard arrays).

CHAPTER 11

Type Details and Alternate Coding Mechanisms

Objectives

- Improve your understanding of relationships and differences among primitive data types and your appreciation for their individual limitations.
- Understand how numerical codes identify characters.
- Learn the rules for automatic type conversions and the risks in explicit type casting.
- Understand embedded postfix and prefix increment and decrement operators.
- Understand embedded assignment expressions.
- Learn where and how conditional operator expressions can shorten code.
- See how short-circuit evaluation helps avoid troublesome operations.
- See how empty statement works.
- Learn how to use `break` statements in loops.
- Optionally, use Unicode characters in GUI applications.

Outline

11.1 Introduction

In Chapters 3 and 4, you learned Java language basics. Among other things, you learned about data types, type conversions, and control statements. This chapter describes some additional data types and additional type conversions. It also describes some alternative control statement coding mechanisms.

Chapter 3 introduced you to some of Java's integer and floating-point types of numbers, and Chapter 5 showed you how to find the limits of their ranges. In this chapter, you'll see two more integer types, and for all of the numerical types you'll learn the amount of storage needed, the precision provided, and how to use range limits. Chapter 3 introduced you to the use of the character type, `char`. In this chapter, you'll see that each character has an underlying numeric value, and you'll learn how to use those values. Chapter 3 introduced you to type conversion with the cast operator. In this chapter, you'll learn more about type conversions. Chapter 3 introduced you to the increment and decrement operators. In this chapter, you'll discover that you can move the positions of these operators (before or after the variable) to control when they act. Chapter 3 introduced you to assignment operators. In this chapter, you'll see how you can embed assignments within expressions to make code more compact.

Chapter 4 introduced you to several kinds of conditional evaluations. In this chapter you'll learn about the conditional operator that can take on either of two possible values depending on a `boolean` condition. You'll also learn about short-circuit evaluation which can prevent errors by stopping a "dangerous" conditional evaluation in certain situations. In addition, you'll learn more about loops. Specifically, you'll see empty-bodied loops and loops that terminate from within the loop's body. And you'll see alternative coding techniques for `for` loop headers.

The material in this chapter will improve your understanding of several Java nuances and subtleties. This will help you avoid problems in the first place, and it will help you create code that is more efficient and easier to maintain. It will also help you debug code that has problems. It might be your code, or it might be someone else's code. As a real-world programmer, you'll have to work with other people's code, and you'll need to understand what that code is doing.

Much of the material in this chapter could have been inserted at various places earlier in the text. However, it was not necessary for anything we did up until now, and we deferred it until now to keep from encumbering earlier presentations. The assembly of these details into one chapter at this point in the book provides an excellent opportunity for review. As you go through this chapter, integrate this new material into what you learned before and see how it enriches your understanding of those topics.

11.2 Integer Types and Floating-Point Types

This section supplements the numeric data types material you studied in Chapter 3, Section 3.13.

Integer Types

Integer types hold whole numbers (whole numbers are numbers without a decimal point). Figure 11.1 shows the four integer types. The types are ordered in terms of increasing memory storage requirements. Type `byte` variables require only 8 bits, so they take up the least amount of storage. If you have a program that's taking too much space in memory, you can use smaller types for variables that hold small values. Using smaller types means less storage is needed in memory. Now that memory has become relatively cheap, types `byte` and `short` are not used very often.

Type	Storage	Wrapper Class's MIN_VALUE	Wrapper Class's MAX_VALUE
byte	8 bits	−128	127
short	16 bits	−32,768	32767
int	32 bits	−2,147,483,648	2,147,483,647
long	64 bits	≈ $-9*10^{18}$	≈ $9*10^{18}$

Figure 11.1 Properties of Java integer data types

To access an integer's minimum and maximum values, use the MIN_VALUE and MAX_VALUE named constants that come with the integer's wrapper class. As you learned in Chapter 5, Integer and Long are the wrapper classes for the int and long data types. And as you might expect, Byte and Short are the wrapper classes for the byte and short data types. So here's how to print the maximum byte value:

```
System.out.println("Largest byte = " + Byte.MAX_VALUE);
```

The default type for an integer constant is int. But you might have a need for an integer constant that is too big for an int. In that case, you can explicitly force an integer constant to be a long by adding an l or L suffix to the integer constant. For example, suppose you're writing a solar system program, and you want to store the age of the earth in a variable named ageOfPlanet. The earth is 4.54 billion years old and 4.54 billion is larger than Integer.MAX_VALUE's 2,147,483,647. This generates a compilation error:

```
long ageOfPlanet = 4540000000;
```

But this, with the L suffix, works just fine:

```
long ageOfPlanet = 4540000000L;
```

makes the int into a long.

When you declare a numeric variable, be sure that the type you select is large enough to handle the largest value that your program might put into it. If a value can't fit in the memory space provided, that's called *overflow*. Overflow errors are dramatic, as the ByteOverflowDemo program in Figure 11.2 illustrates.

Integer overflow reverses the sign, so the ByteOverflowDemo program prints negative 128 rather than the correct result, positive 128. In this example, the magnitude of the error is approximately twice as big as the magnitude of the largest allowable value! Overflow also causes sign reversal for types short, int, and long. In such cases, the compiler does not find the problem, and the Java Virtual Machine (JVM) does not find it either. Java runs the program with no complaints and happily generates a massive error. In the end, it's up to you. Whenever there is any doubt, use a larger type!

Floating-Point Types

As you know, floating-point numbers are real numbers—numbers that allow for non-zero digits to the right of a decimal point. This means you can use floating-point numbers to hold fractional values—values that are smaller than one. Figure 11.3 shows the two floating-point types—float and double.

```
/*********************************************************************
* ByteOverflowDemo.java
* Dean & Dean
*
* This demonstrates integer overflow.
*********************************************************************/

public class ByteOverflowDemo
{
  public static void main(String[] args)
  {
    byte value = 64;

    System.out.println("Initial byte value = " + value);
    System.out.println("Byte maximum = " + Byte.MAX_VALUE);
    value += value;
    System.out.println("Twice initial byte value = " + value);
  } // end main
} // end ByteOverflowDemo class
```

Output:

```
Initial byte value = 64
Byte maximum = 127
Twice initial byte value = -128
```

A very large error!

Figure 11.2 ByteOverflowDemo program illustrates the overflow problem

Type	Storage	Precision	Wrapper Class's `MIN_NORMAL`	Wrapper Class's `MAX_VALUE`
`float`	32 bits	6 digits	$\approx 1.2 * 10^{-38}$	$\approx 3.4*10^{38}$
`double`	64 bits	15 digits	$\approx 2.2 * 10^{-308}$	$\approx 1.8*10^{308}$

Figure 11.3 Properties of Java floating-point data types

Note Figure 11.3's precision column. Precision refers to the approximate number of digits the type can represent accurately. For example, since `float` types have 6 digits of precision, if you attempt to store 1.2345678 in a `float` variable, you would actually store a rounded version—a number like 1.234568. The first six digits (1.23456) are precise, but the rest of the number is imprecise. `double` values have 15 digits of precision—quite a bit better than `float` values with their 6 digits of precision. The relatively low precision of a `float` can lead to significant round-off errors when you subtract two numbers that are close in value. If the numbers are close enough, then the difference is a very small number where the rightmost digits are merely approximations. This round-off error is compounded when you have repetitive calculations. Since memory is now relatively inexpensive, you should consider `float` to be an archaic data type, and you should usually avoid it. An exception is when you specify color. Several methods in the Java API `Color` class employ `float` type parameters and/or return values.

Be aware that floating-point numbers do worse than integer numbers when it comes to precision. For example, when comparing the 32-bit `float` type and the 32-bit `int` type, the floating-point type has less precision. `float` numbers have 6 digits of precision, whereas `int` numbers have 9 digits of precision. Likewise, when comparing the 64-bit `double` type and the 64-bit `long` type, the floating-point type has less precision. `double` numbers have 15 digits of precision, whereas `long` numbers have 19 digits of precision. Why do floating-point numbers lose out on precision? Some of the bits in floating-point numbers are used to specify the exponent that allows these numbers to take on much greater ranges in magnitude than integer numbers can take on. This reduces the bits available to supply precision.

As you learned in Chapter 5, `Float` and `Double` are the wrapper classes for the `float` and `double` data types. To access a floating-point data type's minimum and maximum values, use the `Float` and `Double` classes' `MIN_NORMAL` and `MAX_VALUE` named constants. `MAX_VALUE` is a floating-point data type's largest positive value, and `MIN_NORMAL` is a floating-point data type's smallest full-precision positive value. A floating-point's `MIN_NORMAL` is qualitatively different from an integer's `MIN_VALUE`. Instead of being a large negative value, a floating-point `MIN_NORMAL` is a tiny positive fraction. So what are the limits of negative floating-point numbers? The largest-magnitude negative number a floating-point variable can hold is `-MAX_VALUE`. The smallest-magnitude negative number a floating-point variable can hold safely is `-MIN_NORMAL`, a tiny negative fraction.

Actually, it's possible for a floating-point variable to hold a number whose magnitude is smaller than `MIN_NORMAL`. It can hold a value as small as a floating-point `MIN_VALUE`, which is approximately $1.4 * 10^{-45}$ for `float` and approximately $4.9 * 10^{-324}$ for `double`. But the `MIN_VALUE` of a floating-point number has only one bit of precision, and that could produce a significant error in a computed result—without any explicit indication that an error is present. This is an example of the worst kind of bug, because it can go unrecognized for a long time. Therefore, with floating-point numbers, always use `MIN_NORMAL` instead of `MIN_VALUE`.

The default floating-point constant type is `double`. If you declare a variable to be a `float`, you must append an `f` or `F` suffix to all floating-point constants that go into it, like this:

```
float gpa1 = 3.22f;
float gpa2 = 2.75F;
float gpa3 = 4.0;   ← compilation error, because 4.0 is a double
```

Because of the `f` and `F` suffixes, 3.22f and 2.75F are 32-bit `float` values, so it's legal to assign them into the 32-bit `gpa1` and `gpa2` `float` variables. But 4.0 is a 64-bit `double` value, and attempting to assign it into the 32-bit `gpa3` `float` variable generates a compilation error.

To write a floating-point number in scientific notation, put `e` or `E` before the base-10 exponent value. If the exponent is negative, insert a minus sign between the `e` or `E` and the exponent value. If the exponent is positive, you may use a plus sign after the `e` or `E`, but it's not standard practice. In any event, there must never be any whitespace within the number specification. For example:

```
double x = -3.4e4;   ← equivalent to -34000.0
double y = 5.6E-4;   ← equivalent to 0.00056
```

11.3 `char` Type and the ASCII Character Set

 This section supplements the `char` type material you studied in Chapter 3, Section 3.20.

Underlying Numeric Values

For most programming languages, including Java, each character has an underlying numeric value. For example, the character 'A' has the underlying value of 65 and the character 'B' has the underlying value of 66. Most programming languages, including Java, get character numeric values from the *American Standard Code for Information Interchange* (*ASCII*, pronounced "askee") character set. See the ASCII character set in Figure 11.4's ASCII table and confirm that the character 'A' has an underlying value of 65.

So what's the point of having underlying numeric values for characters? With underlying numeric values, it makes it easier for the JVM to determine the ordering of characters. For example, since 'A' has the value 65 and 'B' has the value 66, the JVM can easily determine that 'A' comes before 'B'. And knowing the order of characters is necessary for string sort operations. For example, suppose a sort method is given the strings "peach", "pineapple", and "apple." The sort method compares the words' first characters 'p', 'p', and 'a', and in doing so, the JVM looks up the characters in the ASCII table. Since 'p' has the value 112 and 'a' has the value 97, "apple" goes first. Then the sort method compares the second characters in "peach" and "pineapple." Since e has the value 101 and i has the value 105, "peach" goes before "pineapple."

Most characters in the ASCII character set represent printable symbols. For example, the 'f' character represents the printable letter *f*. But the first 32 characters and the last character in the ASCII character set are different—they are *control characters*. Control characters perform non-printing operations. For example, the start-of-heading character (ASCII numeric value 1) helps with data being sent from one computer device to another. More specifically, it signals the beginning of transmitted data. When you print a control character, you might be surprised by what appears on the screen. The bell character (ASCII numeric value 7) normally generates a sound and displays nothing, which makes sense, but the start-of-heading character displays something less intuitive. When you print the start-of-heading character, you'll get different results in different environments. For example, in a console window[1] in a Windows environment, a smiley face is displayed. In other environments, a blank square is displayed. Note the following code fragment, with associated output from a console window in a Windows environment:

```
char ch;
for (int code=1; code<=6; code++)
{
  ch = (char) code;
  System.out.print(ch + " ");
}
```

<u>Output:</u>

☺ ☻ ♥ ♦ ♣ ♠

In the above code fragment, the `(char)` cast operator uses the ASCII table to return the character associated with `code`'s numeric value. So if `code` has the value 1, then `(char) code` returns the start-of-heading character.

[1] See Chapter 1's "First Program—Hello World" section for a description of how to run a program in a console window.

numeric value	character	numeric value	char-acter	numeric value	char-acter	numeric value	char-acter
0	null	32	space	64	@	96	`
1	start of heading	33	!	65	A	97	a
2	start of text	34	"	66	B	98	b
3	end of text	35	#	67	C	99	c
4	end of transmission	36	$	68	D	100	d
5	enquiry	37	%	69	E	101	e
6	acknowledge	38	&	70	F	102	f
7	audible bell	39	'	71	G	103	g
8	backspace	40	(	72	H	104	h
9	horizontal tab	41	)	73	I	105	i
10	line feed	42	*	74	J	106	j
11	vertical tab	43	+	75	K	107	k
12	form feed	44	,	76	L	108	l
13	carriage return	45	-	77	M	109	m
14	shift out	46	.	78	N	110	n
15	shift in	47	/	79	O	111	o
16	data link escape	48	0	80	P	112	p
17	device control 1	49	1	81	Q	113	q
18	device control 2	50	2	82	R	114	r
19	device control 3	51	3	83	S	115	s
20	device control 4	52	4	84	T	116	t
21	negative acknowledge	53	5	85	U	117	u
22	synchronous idle	54	6	86	V	118	v
23	end transmission block	55	7	87	W	119	w
24	cancel	56	8	88	X	120	x
25	end of medium	57	9	89	Y	121	y
26	substitute	58	:	90	Z	122	z
27	escape	59	;	91	[	123	{
28	file separator	60	<	92	\	124	|
29	group separator	61	=	93	]	125	}
30	record separator	62	>	94	^	126	~
31	unit separator	63	?	95	_	127	delete

Figure 11.4 ASCII Table
These characters and their code values are the same as the first 128 characters in Unicode, which is discussed in Section 11.13.

The ASCII character set served well in the early years of computer programming, but it's no longer sufficient. Sometimes you'll need characters and symbols that are outside of the ASCII character set. For example, suppose you want to display a check mark (√) or the pi symbol (π). Those two characters don't appear in Figure 11.4. Those characters are part of a newer coding scheme called *Unicode,* which is a superset of ASCII. You can learn about Unicode in the optional section at the end of this chapter (Section 11.13). In that section, we show you how to access the check mark and pi symbols and the many other characters enumerated in the Unicode standard.

Using the + Operator with chars

Remember how you can use the + operator to concatenate two strings together? You can also use the + operator to concatenate a `char` to a string. Note this example:

```
char first = 'J';
char last = 'D';
System.out.println("Hello, " + first + last + '!');
```

Output:

```
Hello, JD!
```

When the JVM sees a string next to a + sign, it concatenates by first converting the operand on the other side of the + sign to a string. So in the above example, the JVM converts the `first` variable to a string and then concatenates the resulting "J" to the end of "Hello, " to form "Hello, J". The JVM does the same thing with each of the next two characters it sees, `last`'s stored character and '!'. It converts each one to a string and concatenates each one to the string at its left.

Be aware that if you apply the + operator to two characters, the + operator does not perform concatenation; instead, it performs mathematical addition using the characters' underlying ASCII values. Note this example:

```
char first = 'J';
char last = 'D';
System.out.println(first + last + ", What's up?");
```

Output:

```
142, What's up?
```

The intended output is: `JD, What's up?` Why does the code fragment print 142 instead of JD? The JVM evaluates + operators (and most other operators as well) left to right, so in evaluating `println`'s argument, it first evaluates `first + last`. Since both `first` and `last` are `char` variables, the JVM performs mathematical addition using the characters' underlying ASCII values. `first` holds 'J' and J's value is 74. `last` holds 'D' and D's value is 68. So `first + last` evaluates to 142.

There are two ways to fix the above code. You can change the first two lines to string initializations like this:

```
String first = "J";
String last = "D";
```

Or you can insert an empty string at the left of `println`'s argument like this:

```
System.out.println("" + first + last + ", What's up?");
```

11.4 Type Conversions

This section supplements the type casting material you studied in Chapter 3, Section 3.19.

Java is a *strongly typed* language, so each variable and each value within a program is defined to have a particular data type. As with all strongly typed languages, you need to be careful when working with more than one data type. In this section, you learn how some, but not all, data types convert to other data types. Java makes some type conversions automatically, and it allows you to force some other type conversions. Either way, be careful. Inappropriate type conversions can cause problems.

To figure out what's allowed in terms of type conversions, learn the ordering scheme in Figure 11.5. Crudely speaking, this picture shows what types can "fit inside" other types. For example, a `byte` value with 8 bits can fit inside a `short` variable that holds 16 bits because an 8-bit entity is "narrower" than a 16-bit entity. We like the terms "narrower" and "wider" to describe type sizes, but be aware that those are not formal terms; other people do not use those terms. Notice that the `boolean` type does not appear in this picture. You cannot convert between numeric types and the `boolean` type.

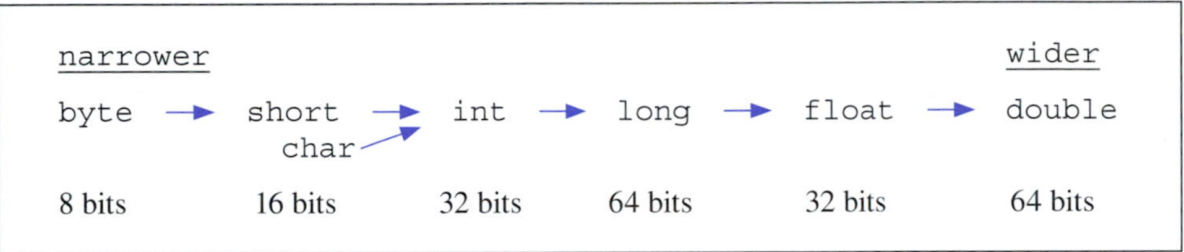

Figure 11.5 Type conversion ordering scheme

Promotion

There are two kinds of type conversion—*promotion* (automatic type conversion) and *type casting* (forced type conversion). You've already seen type casting. We'll revisit it shortly, but let's first discuss promotion.

A promotion is an implicit conversion. It's when an operand's type is automatically converted without having to use a cast operator. It occurs when there's an attempt to use a narrower type in a place that expects a wider type; that is, it occurs when you're going with the flow of the arrows in Figure 11.5. Promotion often occurs in assignment statements. If the expression on the right of an assignment statement evaluates to a type that is narrower than the type of the variable on the left of the assignment statement, then during the assignment the narrower type on the right gets promoted to the wider type on the left. Note these promotion examples:

```
long x = 44;
float y = x;
```

In the first statement, 44 is an `int`. The `int` 44 is narrower than the `long` `x`, so the JVM promotes 44 to a `long`, and then performs the assignment. In the second assignment statement, `x` is a `long`. The `long` `x` is narrower than the `float` `y`, so the JVM promotes `x` to a `float`, and then performs the assignment.

Note these additional promotion examples:

mixed expressions

```
double z = 3 + 4.5;
int num = 'f' + 5;
```

The expressions on the right are *mixed expressions*. A mixed expression is an expression that contains operands of different data types. Within a mixed expression, the narrower operand automatically promotes to the type of the wider operand. In the first statement above, the `int` 3 is narrower than the `double` 4.5, so the JVM promotes 3 to a `double`, before adding it to 4.5. In the second statement above, do you know which operand, 'f' or 5, gets promoted to match the other one? 'f' is a `char` and 5 is an `int`, and Figure 11.5 shows that `char` is narrower than `int`. Thus, the JVM promotes 'f' to an `int`. More specifically, since f's underlying numeric value is 102 (see Figure 11.4), the JVM promotes 'f' to 102. Then the JVM adds 102 to 5 and assigns the resulting 107 to `num`.

Promotions typically occur as part of assignment statements, mixed expressions, and method calls. You've already seen examples with assignment statements and mixed expressions; now let's examine promotions with method calls. As mentioned above, conversions take place any time there's an attempt to use a narrower type in a place that expects a wider type. So if you pass an argument to a method and the method's parameter is defined to be a wider type than the argument's type, the argument's type promotes to match the parameter's type. Figure 11.6's program provides an example of this behavior. Can you determine what promotion takes place within the program? The `x` argument is a `float` and it promotes to a `double`. The `3` argument is an `int` and it promotes to a `double` as well.

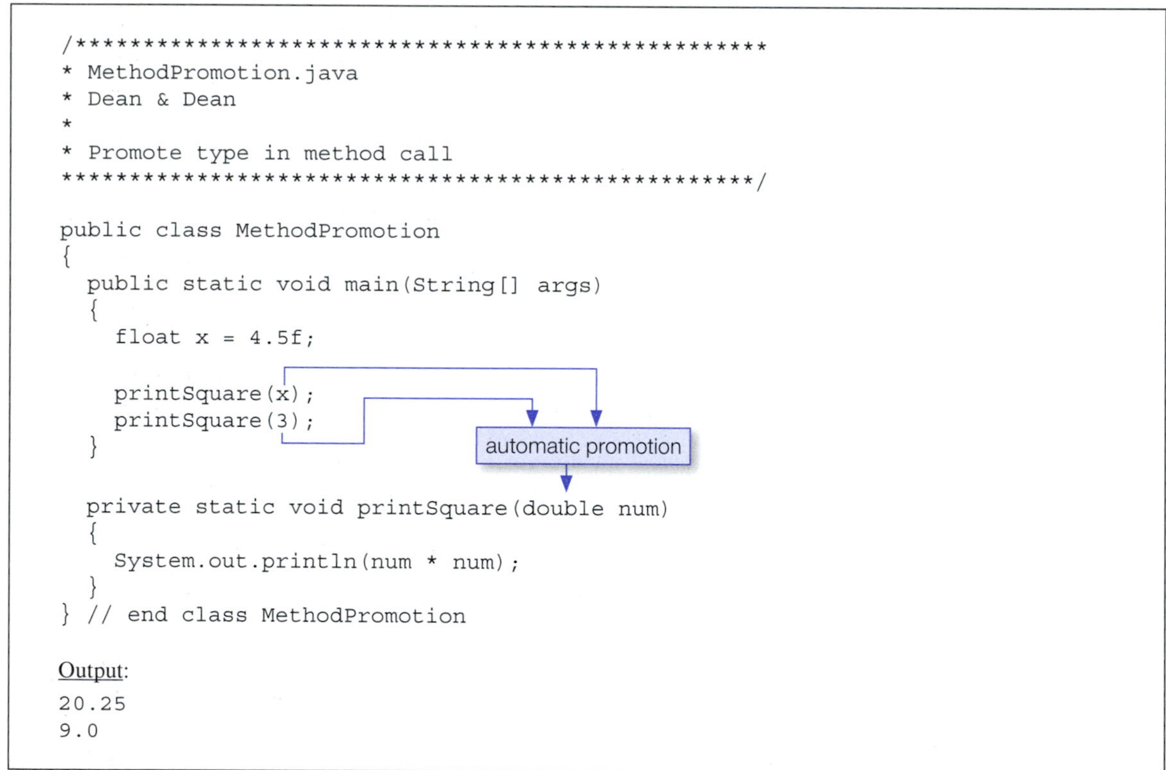

```
/*************************************************
* MethodPromotion.java
* Dean & Dean
*
* Promote type in method call
*************************************************/

public class MethodPromotion
{
  public static void main(String[] args)
  {
    float x = 4.5f;

    printSquare(x);
    printSquare(3);
  }

  private static void printSquare(double num)
  {
    System.out.println(num * num);
  }
} // end class MethodPromotion
```


Output:

```
20.25
9.0
```

Figure 11.6 Program that demonstrates type promotion in method call

Type Casting

Type casting is an explicit type conversion. It occurs when you use a cast operator to convert an expression's type. Here's the syntax for using a cast operator:

(*type*) *expression*

It's legal to use a cast operator to convert any numeric type to any other numeric type; that is, the conversion can go in either direction in Figure 11.5's ordering-scheme diagram. For example, the following code fragment casts the `double` `x` to the `int` `y`.

```
double x = 12345.6;
int y = (int) x;
System.out.println("x = " + x + "\ny = " + y);
```

What happens if you omit the `(int)` cast operator? You'd get a compilation error because you'd be directly assigning a `double` into an `int` and that's forbidden (in Figure 11.5's ordering-scheme diagram, there's no arrow going from the `double` type to the `int` type). Why is it illegal to directly assign a floating-point number into an `int`? Because floating-pointing numbers can have fractions and `int`s can't handle fractions.

Do you know what the above code fragment prints? `x` remains unchanged (even though `(int)` was applied to it), and `y` gets the whole-number portion of `x` with `x`'s fraction truncated, not rounded. So here's the output:

```
x  = 12345.6
y  = 12345
```

The program in Figure 11.7 further illustrates the use of cast operators. It prompts the user to enter an ASCII value (an integer between 0 and 127). Then it prints the character associated with that ASCII value and also the next character in the ASCII table. In the program, what do the two cast operators do? The first one returns the `char` version of `asciiValue`, an `int` variable. The second one returns the `char` version of `asciiValue + 1`. The cast operations are needed to print `ch` and `nextCh` as characters, rather than integers. What would happen if you omitted the cast operators? You'd get compile-time errors because you'd be assigning an `int` directly into a `char`, and that's forbidden according to the ordering scheme in Figure 11.5.

Why is it illegal to assign a number directly into a `char`? You'd think it would be safe to assign a small whole number, like a `byte` with 8 bits, into a `char` with 16 bits. It's illegal to assign a number directly into a `char` because numbers can be negative and a `char` can't handle negativity (a `char`'s underlying value is a positive number between 0 and 65535).

11.5 Prefix/Postfix Modes for Increment/Decrement Operators

This section supplements material you studied in the first part of Chapter 3, Section 3.17 (Increment and Decrement Operators), and it uses techniques you studied in Chapter 3, Section 3.18 (Tracing).

The increment operator has two different modes—the *prefix mode* and the *postfix mode*. The prefix mode is when you put the ++ before the variable that is to be incremented. Using the prefix mode causes the variable to be incremented <u>before</u> the variable's value is used. For example:

```
y = ++x        is equivalent to        x = x + 1;
                                       y = x;
```

The postfix mode is when you put the ++ after the variable that is to be incremented. Using the postfix mode causes the variable to be incremented <u>after</u> the variable's value is used. For example:

```
y = x++        is equivalent to        y = x;
                                       x = x + 1;
```

```
/*************************************************************
* PrintCharFromAscii.java
* Dean & Dean
*
* This illustrates manipulation of ASCII code values.
*************************************************************/

import java.util.*;

public class PrintCharFromAscii
{
  public static void main(String[] args)
  {
    Scanner stdIn = new Scanner(System.in);
    int asciiValue; // user entered ASCII value
    char ch;        // the asciiValue's associated character
    char nextCh;    // the character after ch in the ASCII table

    System.out.print("Enter an integer between 0 and 127: ");
    asciiValue = stdIn.nextInt();
    ch = (char) asciiValue;
    nextCh = (char) (asciiValue + 1);
    System.out.println("Entered number: " + asciiValue);
    System.out.println("Associated character: " + ch);
    System.out.println("Next character: " + nextCh);
  } // end main
} // end class PrintCharFromAscii
```

Note the `(char)` cast operators.

Sample session:

```
Enter an integer between 0 and 127: 67
Entered number: 67
Associated character: C
Next character: D
```

Figure 11.7 Program illustrating use of cast to convert character codes into characters

To get a better feeling for how this works, trace this code fragment:

```
int x, y;

x = 4;
y = ++x;
System.out.println(x + " " + y);
x = 4;
y = x++;
System.out.println(x + " " + y);
```

Here is the trace:

line#	x	y	output
1	?	?	
3	4		
4	5		
4		5	
5			5 5
6	4		
7		4	
7	5		
8			5 4

Here's a review question to help with your debugging skills. What would the outputs have been if the `println` arguments had been `(x + ' ' + y)`? Instead of specifying the string version of a space, this would have specified the character version of a space, and it would make the computer consider the argument to be a mathematical expression rather than a string concatenation. Since `x` and `y` are integers, it would promote the space character to its underlying numeric value, which is 32 (see Figure 11.4). The first print statement would add (5 + 32 + 5) and print 42. The second statement would add (5 + 32 + 4) and print 41.

Pay attention to the quotes.

The decrement operator's prefix and postfix modes work the same as for the increment operator, but they subtract one instead of add one. To get a feeling for how they work, trace this code fragment:

```
1  int a, b, c;
2
3  a = 8;
4  b = --a;
5  c = b-- + --a;
6  System.out.println(a + " " + b + " " + c);
```

line#	a	b	c	output
1	?	?	?	
3	8			
4	7			
4		7		
5	6			
5			13	
5		6		
6				6 6 13

Let's examine line 5 in more depth:

```
c = b-- + --a;
```

As you might have guessed, in executing this statement, the JVM first decrements a. This should make sense when you look at Appendix 2's operator precedence table and confirm that the decrement operator has very high precedence. The JVM also executes b's decrement operator early on, but its execution consists of using b's original value and incrementing b afterwards. The operator precedence table shows that the + operator has higher precedence than the = operator, so the JVM next adds b's original value to a's decremented value. Finally, the JVM assigns the sum to c.

For many people, line 5 is particularly confusing. We showed you this example because you might see this kind of thing in someone else's code, but if you want your code to be understandable, we recommend that you not do this yourself. That is, don't embed ++ or -- expressions within other expressions. Instead of trying to do everything line 5 does in one statement, it would be more understandable to partition line 5 into three separate statements, like this:

```
5a  a--;
5b  c = b + a;
5c  b--;
```

The JVM performs the evaluation in separate steps anyway, so writing it out does not incur any performance penalty. It takes more space on the page, but most people will agree that it's easier to read.

When writing code, how do you decide which mode to use, prefix or postfix? It depends on the rest of your code. Usually, to minimize confusion, you'll put increment and decrement operations on separate lines. Then it doesn't matter which mode you use, but postfix is more common.

11.6 Embedded Assignments

This section supplements material you learned in Chapters 3 and 4. Specifically, it supplements the assignment statements material in Chapter 3, Section 3.11 and the `while` loop material in Chapter 4, Section 4.8.

Embedding an Assignment within Another Assignment

Assignments are sometimes embedded as expressions in larger statements. When that happens, remember that (1) an assignment expression evaluates to the assigned value, and (2) assignment operators exhibit right-to-left associativity. To see these concepts in action, consider this code fragment:

```
1  int a, b = 8, c = 5;
2
3  a = b = c;
4  System.out.println(a + " " + b + " " + c);
```

same as: `a = (b = c);`

Line 3 shows an assignment expression embedded inside a larger assignment statement. Which of the two assignment operators does the JVM execute first? Since assignment operators exhibit right-to-left associativity, the JVM executes the right assignment operation first. What does the b = c expression evaluate to? It evaluates to 5 because the assigned value, c, is 5. In evaluating line 3, replace the b = c part of the statement with 5 to reduce the statement to:

```
a = 5.
```

Here's what the code fragment's trace looks like:

line#	a	b	c	output
1	?	8	5	
3		5		
3	5			
4				5 5 5

Embedding an Assignment within a Loop Condition

Except for a pure multiple assignment like `a = b = c;` it's best to avoid embedding multiple assignments as expressions in other statements, because that makes code hard to understand. Nevertheless, it's fairly common to embed a single assignment as an expression in a loop condition. For example, Figure 11.8 contains a program that averages a set of input scores. Note the `(score = stdIn.nextDouble())`

```
/*******************************************************************
* AverageScore.java
* Dean & Dean
*
* This program averages input scores.
*******************************************************************/

import java.util.Scanner;

public class AverageScore
{
  public static void main(String[] args)
  {
    double score;
    double count = 0;
    double totalScore = 0;
    Scanner stdIn = new Scanner(System.in);

    System.out.print("Enter a score (or -1 to quit): ");
    while ((score = stdIn.nextDouble()) != -1)
    {
      count++;
      totalScore += score;
      System.out.print("Enter a score (or -1 to quit): ");
    }
    if (count > 0)
    {
      System.out.println("Average score = " + totalScore / count);
    }
  } // end main
} // end AverageScore class
```

embedded assignment

Figure 11.8 AverageScore program that demonstrates use of embedded assignments

assignment inside the `while` condition. If, for example, the user responds to the prompt by entering 80, `score` gets the value 80, the assignment expression within the parentheses evaluates to 80, and the `while` loop header becomes:

```
while (80 != -1)
```

Since the condition is true, the JVM executes the body of the loop. If the assignment expression were not embedded in the `while` loop condition, it would have to appear twice—once above the loop header and again at the bottom of the loop. Embedding the assignment in the condition improves the loop's structure.

You will sometimes also see embedded assignments in method arguments and array indices. This makes code more compact. Compactness is often a good thing in that it can lead to code that is less cluttered and therefore easier to understand. But don't go too far in trying to make your code compact because compactness can sometimes lead to code that is harder to understand (i.e., it can lead to code that is more *cryptic*). Some programmers get a kick out of making "clever" programs that are as compact as possible. If that's you, try to redirect your efforts to making programs as understandable as possible. You can still use compact code, but do so in a manner that helps, not hinders, understandability.

11.7 Conditional Operator Expressions

This section supplements the material in Chapter 4, Section 4.3 (`if` Statements).

Syntax and Semantics

When you want a logical condition to determine which of two alternate values applies, instead of using the "if, else" form of the `if` statement, you can use a conditional operator expression. The conditional operator is Java's only *ternary* operator. Ternary means three. The conditional relates three operands with the two symbols, `?` and `:`. The `?` goes between the first and second operands, and the `:` goes between the second and third operands.

Here's the syntax:

<condition> ? *<expression1>* : *<expression2>*

If the condition is `true`, the conditional operator expression evaluates to the value of *expression1,* and it ignores *expression2*. If the condition is `false`, the conditional operator expression evaluates to the value of *expression2,* and it ignores *expression1*. Think of *expression1* as the true part of an "if, else" statement. Think of *expression2* as the false part of an "if, else" statement.

For example, consider this expression:

```
(x>y) ? x : y
```

The parentheses around the condition are not required, because > has higher precedence than the `?:` pair, but we recommend using them because they improve readability. What does the JVM do when it sees this expression?

- It compares `x` with `y`.
- If `x` is greater, it evaluates the expression to `x`.
- If `x` is not greater, it evaluates the expression to `y`.

Do you know what general functionality the expression implements? It finds the maximum between two numbers. You can prove this to yourself by plugging in sample numbers. Suppose x = 2 and y = 5. Here's how the expression evaluates to the maximum, 5:

```
(2>5) ? 2 : 5  ⇒
(false) ? 2 : 5  ⇒
5
```

Using the Conditional Operator

A conditional operator expression cannot appear on a line by itself because it is not a complete statement. It is just part of a statement—an expression. The following code fragment includes two examples of embedded conditional operator expressions:

```
int score = 58;
boolean extraCredit = true;

score += (extraCredit ? 2 : 0);
System.out.println(
  "grade = " + ((score>=60) ? "pass" : "fail"));
```

How does it work? Since `extraCredit` is `true`, the first conditional operator evaluates to 2. `score` then increments by 2 from its initial value of 58 to 60. Since `(score>=60)` evaluates to `true`, the second conditional operator evaluates to "pass". The `println` statement then prints:

```
grade = pass
```

In the above code fragment, we like the parentheses the way they are shown, but in the interest of honing your debugging skills, let's examine what happens if you omit each of the pairs of parentheses. As shown in Appendix 2's operator precedence table, the conditional operator has higher precedence than the += operator. Therefore, it would be legal to omit the parentheses in the += assignment statement. In the `println` statement, the conditional operator has lower precedence than the + operator, so you must keep the parentheses that surround the conditional operator expression. Since the >= operator has higher precedence than the conditional operator, it would be legal to omit the parentheses that surround the `score>=60` condition. Note how we omit spaces in the `score>=60` condition but include spaces around the ? and : that separate the three components of the conditional operator expression. This style improves readability.

You can use the conditional operator to avoid `if` statements. Conditional operator code might look more efficient than `if` statement code because the source code is shorter, but the generated bytecode is typically longer. This is another example of something you might see in someone else's code, but because it's relatively hard to understand, we recommend that you use it with restraint in your own code. For example, the `score += (extraCredit ? 2 : 0);` statement in the above code fragment is rather cryptic. It would be better style to increment the `score` variable like this:

```
if (extraCredit)
{
  score += 2;
}
```

11.8 Expression Evaluation Review

So far in this chapter, you've learned quite a few type details and operator details. Learning such details will help you debug code that has problems, and it will help you avoid problems in the first place. To make sure that you really understand the details, let's do some expression evaluation practice problems.

Hand calculation helps you understand.

Expression Evaluation Practice with Characters and String Concatenation

Note the following three expressions. Try to evaluate them on your own prior to looking at the subsequent answers. While performing the evaluations, remember that if you have two or more operators with the same precedence, use left-to-right associativity (i.e., perform the operation at the left first). So in the first expression, you should perform the + operation in `'1' + '2'` before attempting to perform the second + operation.

1. `'1' + '2' + "3" + '4' + '5'`
2. `1 + 2 + "3" + 4 + 5`
3. `1 + '2'`

Here are the answers:

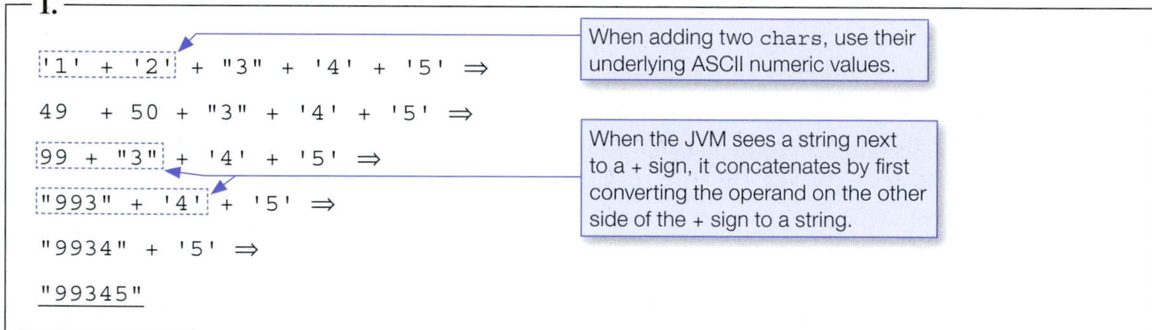

2.

```
1 + 2 + "3" + 4 + 5 ⇒
3 + "3" + 4 + 5 ⇒
"33" + 4 + 5 ⇒
"334" + 5 ⇒
"3345"
```

Left-to-right associativity dictates adding the two numbers at the left.

3.

```
1 + '2' ⇒
1 + 50 ⇒
51
```

Mixed expression—the `char` gets promoted to an `int`, using the underlying ASCII numeric value for '2.'

Expression Evaluation Practice with Type Conversions and Various Operators

Assume:

```
int a = 5, b = 2;
double c = 3.0;
```

Try to evaluate the following expressions on your own prior to looking at the subsequent answers.

1. `(c + a / b) / 10 * 5`
2. `a + b++`
3. `4 + --c`
4. `c = b = a % 2`

Here are the answers:

1.

```
(c + a / b) / 10 * 5 ⇒
(3.0 + 5 / 2) / 10 * 5 ⇒
(3.0 + 2) / 10 * 5 ⇒
5.0 / 10 * 5 ⇒
0.5 * 5 ⇒
2.5
```

Mixed expression—the `int` gets promoted to a `double`.

/ and * have same precedence. Perform left operation first.

2.

```
a + b++ ⇒
5 + 2 ⇒
7
```

Use `b`'s original value of 2 in the expression. Afterwards, `b`'s value increments to 3.

3.

```
4 + --c ⇒
4 + 2.0 ⇒
6.0
```

`c`'s value decrements to 2.0 before using it in the expression.

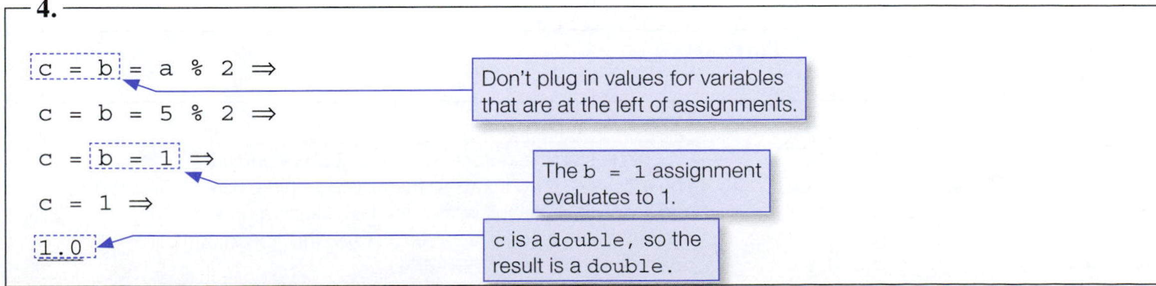

4.
c = b = a % 2 ⇒
c = b = 5 % 2 ⇒
c = b = 1 ⇒
c = 1 ⇒
1.0
Don't plug in values for variables that are at the left of assignments.
The b = 1 assignment evaluates to 1.
c is a double, so the result is a double.

More Expression Evaluation Practice

Assume:

```
int a = 5, b = 2;
double c = 6.6;
```

Try to evaluate the following expressions on your own prior to looking at the subsequent answers.

1. `(int) c + c`
2. `b = 2.7`
3. `('a' < 'B') && ('a' == 97) ? "yes" : "no"`
4. `(a >2) && (c = 6.6)`

Here are the answers:

1.

```
(int) c + c ⇒
6 + 6.6 ⇒
12.6
```

`(int) c` evaluates to 6, which is the truncated version of 6.6, but `c` itself doesn't change, so the second `c` remains 6.6.

2.

```
b = 2.7
```

Compilation error. The `double` value won't fit into the narrower `int` variable without a cast operator.

3.

Look up underlying numeric values in ASCII table.

Mixed types, so `char 'a'` converts to `int` 97 before comparison.

```
('a' < 'B') && ('a' == 97) ? "yes" : "no" ⇒
false && true ? "yes" : "no" ⇒
false ? "yes" : "no" ⇒
"no"
```

4.

```
(a > 2) && (c = 6.6) ⇒
(true) && ...
```

`c = 6.6` is an assignment, not an equality condition. Thus, `c = 6.6` evaluates to the `double` value, `6.6`, and a `double` doesn't work with the `&&` operator, so this generates a compilation error. Probably, the second operand should be `(c == 6.6)`.

11.9 Short-Circuit Evaluation

This section supplements the && logical operator material you studied in Chapter 4, Section 4.4 and the || logical operator material you studied in Chapter 4, Section 4.5.

Consider the program in Figure 11.9. It calculates a basketball player's shooting percentage and prints an associated message. Note the `if` statement's heading, repeated here for your convenience. In particular, note the division operation with `attempted` in the denominator.

```
/*********************************************************************
* ShootingPercentage.java
* Dean & Dean
*
* This program processes a basketball player's shooting percentage.
*********************************************************************/

import java.util.Scanner;

public class ShootingPercentage
{
  public static void main(String[] args)
  {
    int attempted; // number of shots attempted
    int made;      // number of shots made
    Scanner stdIn = new Scanner(System.in);
    System.out.print("Number of shots attempted: ");
    attempted = stdIn.nextInt();
    System.out.print("Number of shots made: ");
    made = stdIn.nextInt();

    if ((attempted > 0) && ((double) made / attempted) >= .5)
    {
      System.out.printf("Excellent shooting percentage - %.1f%%\n",
        100.0 * made / attempted);
    }
    else
    {
      System.out.println("Practice your shot more.");
    }
  } // end main
} // end class ShootingPercentage
```

If `attempted` is zero, division by zero does not occur.

Use `%%` to print a percent sign.

Sample session:

```
Number of shots attempted: 0
Number of shots made: 0
Practice your shot more.
```

Second sample session:

```
Number of shots attempted: 12
Number of shots made: 7
Excellent shooting percentage - 58.3%
```

Figure 11.9 Program that illustrates short-circuit evaluation

```
if ((attempted > 0) && ((double) made / attempted) >= .5)
```

With division, you should always think about, and try to avoid, division by zero. If `attempted` equals zero, will the JVM attempt to divide by zero? Nope! Short-circuit evaluation saves the day.

Short-circuit evaluation means that the JVM stops evaluating an expression whenever the expression's outcome becomes certain. More specifically, if the left side of an `&&` expression evaluates to `false`, then the expression's outcome is certain (`false && ` anything evaluates to `false`) and the right side is skipped. Likewise, if the left side of an `||` expression evaluates to `true`, then the expression's outcome is certain (`true ||` anything evaluates to `true`) and the right side is skipped. So in Figure 11.9's `if` statement condition, if `attempted` equals zero, the left side of the `&&` operator evaluates to `false` and the right side is skipped, thus avoiding division by zero.

So what's the benefit of short-circuit evaluation?

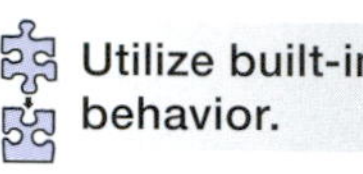
Utilize built-in behavior.

1. Error avoidance: It can help to prevent problems by enabling you to avoid an illegal operation on the right side of an expression.
2. Performance: Since the result is already known, the computer doesn't have to waste time calculating the rest of the expression.

As an aside, note the `%%` in Figure 11.9's `printf` statement. It's a conversion specifier for the `printf` method. Unlike the other conversion specifiers, it is a standalone entity; it doesn't have an argument that plugs into it. It simply prints the percent character. Note the printed % at the end of Figure 11.9's second sample session.

11.10 Empty Statement

This section supplements the loop material you studied in Chapter 4.

It's sometimes possible to put all of a loop's functionality inside of its header. For example:

```
for (int i=0; i<1000000000; i++)
{ }
```

The Java compiler requires that you include a statement for the `for` loop's body, even if the statement doesn't do anything. The above empty braces ({ }) form a compound statement[2] and satisfy that requirement. In this section, you learn about an alternative way to satisfy that requirement. You learn about the empty statement.

Using the Empty Statement

The *empty statement* consists of a semicolon by itself. Use the empty statement in places where the compiler requires a statement, but there is no need to do anything. For example, the below `for` loop can be used as a "quick and dirty" way to add a delay to your program:

```
monster.display();
for (int i=0; i<1000000000; i++)
  ;
monster.erase();
```

Coding convention: Put the empty statement on a line by itself and indent it.

[2] The compound statement, defined in Chapter 4, is a group of zero or more statements surrounded by braces.

Note how the empty statement is appropriate here because all the work is done in the `for` loop header, where `i` counts up to one billion. All that counting takes time. Depending on your computer's speed, it might take anywhere from a fraction of a second to five seconds.

So why would you want to add a delay to your program? Suppose you're writing a game program that needs to have a monster appear for only a certain time interval. To implement that functionality, print the monster, execute the delay loop, and then erase the monster.

You might want to use the above code fragment as part of a first-cut attempt at implementing the delay, but don't use it for your final implementation. Why? Because it introduces delay that is dependent on the speed of the computer that runs the program. With varied delay, slow computers would have monsters that linger too long and fast computers would have monsters that disappear too quickly. In a final implementation, you should use the `Thread` class's `sleep` method to implement the delay. The `sleep` method allows you to precisely specify the amount of delay in milliseconds. To use the `sleep` method, you need to understand exception handling, and we discuss exception handling in Chapter 14.[3]

In the above code fragment, note the coding-convention callout. Can you think of why it's a good idea to put the empty statement on a line by itself? If you put the empty statement on a line by itself and indent it, readers will see it. On the other hand, if you put the empty statement at the end of the previous statement's line, readers probably won't see it. Seeing the code is an important part of making the code understandable. And making code understandable makes it easier to maintain.

Avoid Accidental Misuse of the Empty Statement

It's fairly common for programmers to accidentally create unintended empty statements. Because you enter a semicolon at the end of most lines of Java code, it's easy to get into the habit of hitting the semicolon key at the end of every line of code you write. If you do that at the end of a loop header, it generates an empty statement. Your code might compile and run without a reported error, but it would produce mysterious results. Here is an example:

```
System.out.print("Do you want to play a game (y/n)? ");
while (stdIn.next().equals("y"));
{
  <The code to play the game goes here.>
  System.out.print("Play another game (y/n)? ");
}
```

This semicolon creates an empty statement.

Does the semicolon at the end of the `while` loop header generate a compilation error? No—the semicolon acts as the lone statement (an empty statement) that's inside the `while` loop. The subsequent braces form a compound statement. The compound statement is not part of the `while` loop; it executes after the `while` loop has finished.

So what does the code do? First, suppose the user enters `n`. In the `while` loop header, the JVM compares the entered `n` value to "y." The loop condition is `false`, so the JVM skips the `while` loop's body, the empty statement. The JVM then executes the compound statement and attempts to play a game. That's a logic error: The JVM attempts to play a game even though the user entered `n`.

Now suppose the user enters `y`. In the `while` loop header, the JVM compares the entered `y` value to "y". The loop condition is `true`, so the JVM executes the `while` loop's body, the empty statement. The

[3] This adds a delay of 1000 milliseconds (which equals 1 second):

```
try {Thread.sleep(1000);}
catch (InterruptedException e) { }
```

JVM then returns to the loop header and executes the `stdIn.next()` method call again. The JVM waits for the user to enter another value. But the user won't know he/she is supposed to enter anything because there's no prompt. That's a particularly nasty logic error because the program produces no erroneous output and no error message. That means no help in determining what to do.

You can produce these same types of logic errors by putting semicolons after "if," "else if," or "else" headings. Such semicolons effectively create empty statements, and they're often introduced accidentally during program development or debugging. Be on the alert for empty statements, and whenever you see one, be suspicious and check it out! Better yet, minimize confusion at the end by maximizing care at the beginning.

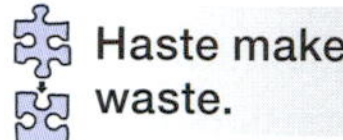

11.11 break Statement within a Loop

This section supplements the loop material you studied in Chapter 4.

In Chapter 4 we introduced you to the use of the `break` statement inside a `switch` statement. It terminates the `switch` statement and transfers control to the next statement after the `switch` statement. In addition, you can use the `break` statement inside a `while`, `do`, or `for` loop. It does the same thing as when it's in a `switch` statement. The `break` terminates the immediately enclosing loop and transfers control to the next statement after the bottom of the loop. We say "immediately enclosing" because you can have a `break` that's nested inside multiple loops. The `break` gets associated with the loop that immediately surrounds it.

The DayTrader program in Figure 11.10 illustrates what's called "day trading." It's a form of gambling in which people buy and sell stock on the stock market every day in hopes of making money off short-term stock movements. This program keeps track of a day trader's stock balance over a three-month period (for day = 1 to 90). The original balance is $1,000. In our simple model, at the beginning of each day, the day trader retains half the initial balance in savings and invests the other half in the stock market. The money returned at the end of the day equals the investment times a random number between 0 and 2. Thus, the money returned ranges anywhere from zero to double the original investment. Each day, the day trader adds the money returned to the balance in savings. If the balance ever goes below $1 or above $5,000, the day trader quits.

Before examining the `break` statement in Figure 11.10, look at the `(day - 1)` argument in the final `printf` statement. This is after the `for` loop, so the scope of `day` needs to be bigger than the scope of the `for` loop. That's why we declared it before the `for` loop with the other local variables. But why did we subtract 1 in the `printf` statement? Because the `day++` operation in the third compartment of the `for` loop header increments `day` one extra time, after the transaction that drives the balance to a terminating value. If we had forgotten to subtract 1 in the `printf` statement, that would be an off-by-one error.

Now look at the DayTrader program's `break` statement. If the balance ever gets outside the $1 to $5,000 range, program control jumps immediately to the next statement below the `for` loop. If you run the program several times, you'll see that sometimes this causes the loop to terminate before `day` reaches 90. You'll get a different result each time you run the program because this program uses `Math.random` to generate a random number in the range between 0.0 and 1.0.

Be aware that you never really have to use a `break` statement to implement this premature loop-termination capability. For example, you can eliminate the DayTrader program's `if` and `break` statements by changing the `for` loop header to this:

```
for (day=1; day<=90 && !(balance < 1.0 || balance > 5000.0); day ++)
```

Don't fall into the trap of using the `break` statement too often. Usually, someone reading your program will look only at the loop header to figure out how the loop terminates. In using a `break` statement, you force

```
/***********************************************************************
* DayTrader.java
* Dean & Dean
*
* This simulates stock market day trading.
***********************************************************************/

public class DayTrader
{
  public static void main(String[] args)
  {
    double balance = 1000.00; // money that's retained
    double moneyInvested;     // money that's invested
    double moneyReturned;     // money that's earned at end of day
    int day;                  // current day, ranges from 1 to 90

    for (day=1; day<=90; day++)
    {
      if (balance < 1.0 || balance > 5000.0)
      {
        break;
      }
      balance = moneyInvested = balance / 2.0;
      moneyReturned = moneyInvested * (Math.random() * 2.0);
      balance += moneyReturned;
    } // end for

    System.out.printf("final balance on day %d: $%4.2f\n",
      (day - 1), balance);
  } // end main
} // end DayTrader
```

Figure 11.10 DayTrader program that illustrates use of the `break` statement

the reader to look inside of the loop for loop termination conditions. And that makes your program harder to understand. Nonetheless, in certain situations, the `break` statement improves readability rather than hinders it. The DayTrader program's `break` statement is an example where the `break` statement improves readability.

11.12 `for` Loop Header Details

This section supplements the `for` loop material you studied in Chapter 4, Section 4.10. 

Omitting One or More of the `for` Loop Header Components

It's legal, although not all that common, to omit the first and/or third components in the `for` loop header. For example, to print a countdown from a user-entered number, you could do this:

```
System.out.print("Enter countdown starting number: ");
count = stdIn.nextInt();
for (; count>0; count--)
{
  System.out.print(count + " ");
}
System.out.println("Liftoff!");
```

no initialization component

Actually, it's legal to omit any of the three `for` loop header components, as long as the two semicolons still appear within the parentheses. For example, you can even write a `for` loop header like this:

```
for (;;)
```

When a `for` loop header's condition component (the second component) is omitted, the condition is considered true for every iteration of the loop. With a permanently true condition, such a loop is often an infinite loop and a logic error. But that's not always the case. You can terminate it by using a `break` statement like this:

```
for (;;)
{
  ...
  if (<condition>)
  {
    break;
  }
}
```

You should understand the above example in case you see similar code in someone else's program. But it's rather cryptic, and, as such, you should avoid writing your own code that way.

Multiple Initialization and Update Components

For most `for` loops, one index variable is all that's needed. But every now and then, two or more index variables are needed. To accommodate that need, you can include a list of comma-separated initializations in a `for` loop header. The caveat for the initializations is that their index variables must be the same type. Working in concert with the comma-separated initializations, you can also include a list of comma-separated updates in a `for` loop header. The following code fragment and associated output show what we're talking about. In the `for` loop header, note the two index variables, `up` and `down`, and their comma-separated initialization and update components.

```
System.out.printf("%3s%5s\n", "Up", "Down");
for (int up=1,down=5; up<=5; up++,down--)
{
  System.out.printf("%3d%5d\n", up, down);
}
```

Output:

```
Up  Down
 1    5
 2    4
 3    3
 4    2
 5    1
```

As with many of the techniques presented in this chapter, using multiple initialization and update components in a `for` loop is a bit of an art. It leads to more compact code, which can be a good thing or a bad thing. If the compact code is more understandable, use it. If the compact code is more cryptic, don't use it.

11.13 GUI Track: Unicode (Optional)

Earlier, you learned that characters get their underlying numeric values from the ASCII character set. That's true for the 128 characters shown in Figure 11.4, but be aware that there are way more than 128 characters in the world. The ASCII character set contains the characters in the Latin alphabet—A through Z—but it does not contain the characters in other alphabets. For example, it does not contain the characters in the Greek, Cyrillic, and Hebrew alphabets. The designers of the Java language wanted Java to be general purpose, so they wanted to be able to produce text output for many different languages using many different alphabets. To handle the additional characters, the Java designers had to use a bigger character set than the ASCII character set. Thus, they adopted the *Unicode* standard. The Unicode standard defines underlying numeric values for a huge set of 65,536 characters.

Why are there 65,536 characters in the Unicode standard? Because the people who designed the Unicode standard (the Unicode Consortium) decided that 16 bits would be sufficient to represent all the characters needed in a computer program.[4] And 16 bits can represent 65,536 characters. Here are the binary representations for the first four characters and the last character:

0000 0000 0000 0000
0000 0000 0000 0001
0000 0000 0000 0010
0000 0000 0000 0011
. . .
1111 1111 1111 1111

Notice that each row is a different permutation of 0's and 1's. If you wrote all such permutations, you'd see 65,536 rows. Thus, with 16 bits, you can represent 65,536 characters. The formula for determining the number of permutations (and consequently the number of rows and the number of characters) is 2 raised to the power of the number of bits. In other words, $2^{16} = 65{,}536$.

You can apply that same reasoning in determining why there are 128 characters in the ASCII character set. Way back in 1963 (when dinosaurs roamed the earth), the people who designed the ASCII character set

[4] We're focusing on the original Unicode standard, which is a subset of the current Unicode standard. The original Unicode standard is good enough for almost all Java programming. The original Unicode standard uses 16 bits for all characters. The current Unicode standard uses additional bits for additional characters that can't fit in the original Unicode set of 65,536 values. For additional details, see http://www.unicode.org/.

decided that 7 bits would be sufficient to represent all the characters needed in a computer program. $2^7 = 128$, so 7 bits can represent 128 unique values.

Since the ASCII table was and is such a popular standard with many programming languages, the Unicode designers decided to use the ASCII character set as a subset of the Unicode character set. They inserted the ASCII character set's characters in the first 128 slots of the Unicode character set. That means programmers can find those characters' numeric values by referring to a simple ASCII table; they don't have to wade through the enormous Unicode character set.

Hexadecimal Numbers

Normal numbers are expressed as powers of 10, but since computers are binary and 16 is a simple power of two ($16 = 2^4$), it's common practice to express computer quantities in base 16 (using powers of 16), rather than base 10 (using powers of 10). Base 10 numbers are called decimal numbers. Base 16 numbers are called *hexadecimal* numbers. The places in decimal numbers are called digits. The places in hexadecimal numbers are sometimes called *hexits,* but more often, they're simply called *hexadecimal digits.* Base 10 numbers use 10 symbols: 0, 1, 2, 3, 4, 5, 6, 7, 8, and 9. Base 16 numbers use the 16 symbols: 0, 1, 2, 3, 4, 5, 6, 7, 8, 9, a, b, c, d, e, and f (uppercase letters A through F are considered to be equivalent to a through f). Thus, hexadecimal numbers frequently include one or more of the first six alphabetic characters as well as one or more of the normal numerical characters.

In Java, any integer can be written in either decimal or hexadecimal. If you want a number to be interpreted as hexadecimal, you must prefix it with the character pair, `0x`. So, if you see something like `0x263A`, for example, you can recognize it as a hexadecimal number. For most of us, hexadecimal numbers are not very intuitive. It's pretty easy to make conversions, however. Just use `Integer`'s two-parameter `toString` method:

```
Integer.toString(<starting-number>, <desired-base>)
```

For example, if you want to see the decimal equivalent of `0x263A`, write this:

```
System.out.println(Integer.toString(0x263A, 10));
```

This generates an output of 9786. Conversely, if you want to see the hexadecimal equivalent of 9786, write this:

```
System.out.println(Integer.toString(9786, 16));
```

This generates an output of `263a`. Notice that this method's output does not include the `0x` prefix, and it uses lowercase letters for the alphabetic hexadecimal digits.

Unicode Escape Sequence

Whenever you write an integer, you can write it in either decimal format or hexadecimal format. Likewise, you can specify a character by writing its numeric value in either decimal format or hexadecimal format and then casting it with the `(char)` cast operator. Java also provides another way to specify a character. You can use the *Unicode escape sequence.* The Unicode escape sequence is `\u` followed immediately by the hexadecimal digits of a hexadecimal number. Here's what we're talking about:

```
'\u####'
```

This is a single character.

Each # stands for one hexadecimal digit. We elected to show this in single quotes, not double quotes, to emphasize that the 6-element escape sequence is just a single character, not a string. It's just like any other escape sequence, however, so you can embed the `\u####` anywhere in a string. The `u` must be lowercase, and there must be exactly four hexadecimal digits.[5]

Using Unicode in Java Programs

If you want to print characters using Unicode escape sequences, you can use `System.out.println` in a text-based environment for the first 128 characters, but for the other characters, `System.out.println` in a text-based environment doesn't work consistently. That's because text-based environments recognize just the ASCII portion of the Unicode table; that is, the first 128 characters. To print all the characters in the Unicode table, you need to use graphical user interface (GUI) commands in a GUI environment.

The program in Figure 11.11 provides a GUI window and uses it to illustrate a small sampling of the many characters that are available. The `codes` array contains `int` code values for the Unicode escape sequences for the first characters in blocks of characters that we choose to display. These Unicode escape sequences automatically promote from type `char` to type `int` in the initializing assignment. The array called `descriptions` contains a simple `String` description for each block of characters.

For the window, we use an instance of the Java API `JFrame` class, which is in the `javax.swing` package. We set the window size at 600 pixels wide and 285 pixels high. We include in the window a single `JTextArea` object called `area`, and we enable its line-wrap capability. We use `JTextArea`'s `append` method to add each new string or character to whatever is already there.

Before looping, we display some general font information. The outer `for` loop displays the value of the first code number in one of the chosen blocks of characters and then a description of that block. The inner `for` loop displays the first 73 characters in that block. In the `append` method's argument, notice how we add the loop count, `j`, to the initial Unicode value to get each individual Unicode value as an `int`. Then we cast that `int` into a `char`. Then the concatenated `"   "` converts that `char` into a `String`, which matches the `append` method's parameter type.

Figure 11.12 shows the GUI output this program generates. The characters in the `codes` array in Figure 11.11 are the Unicode escape sequences for the first character in each block of characters shown in Figure 11.12. The hollow squares indicate code numbers that don't have symbols assigned to them or symbols that are not present in the current computer's software library. Notice that both the Greek and Cyrillic blocks include both upper and lower case characters, and they include some additional characters beyond the normal final values of Ω (ω) and Я (я), respectively. These (and other) additional characters are needed for some of the individual languages in the families of languages using these alphabets. Of course, the characters shown in Figure 11.12 are just a tiny sampling of all the characters in Unicode.

Notice that the different characters shown in Figure 11.12 have generally different widths. To get constant-width characters, you'd have to change the font type to something like Courier New. You could do that—and also change the style to bold and size to 10 points—by inserting a statement like this:

```
area.setFont(new Font("Courier New", Font.BOLD, 10));
```

Suppose you want the Unicode value for ≈. That's the last mathematical operator displayed in Figure 11.12. As indicated by the third `codes` value in the UnicodeDisplay program, the first mathematical operator has

[5] The supplementary Unicode characters have numeric values that require more than 4 hexadecimal digits. To specify one of these supplementary characters, use a decimal or hexadecimal `int` representation of the character, or prefix the \u-representation of the 4 least-significant hexadecimal digits with an appropriate u-representation in the range, `\uD800` through `\uDFFF`. The prefix, called a *surrogate*, has no independent character association. (See documentation on Java's `Character` class and http://www.unicode.org/Public/UNIDATA/Blocks.txt.) There's also another surrogate scheme which represents characters with an 8-bit base value and multiple 8-bit surrogates. This latter scheme is used in communications.

```
/*************************************************************
* UnicodeDisplay.java
* Dean & Dean
*
* This prints unicode characters.
*************************************************************/

import javax.swing.*;
import java.awt.Font;

public class UnicodeDisplay
{
  public static void main(String[] args)
  {
    int[] codes = {'\u0391',
                   '\u0410',
                   '\u2200',
                   '\u2500',
                   '\u2700'};
    String[] descriptions = {"Greek",
                             "Cyrillic (Russian)",
                             "mathematical operators",
                             "box drawing",
                             "dingbats"};
    JFrame window = new JFrame("Some Unicode Characters");
    JTextArea area = new JTextArea();
    Font font = area.getFont();

    window.setSize(600,285);     // pixel width, height
    window.setDefaultCloseOperation(JFrame.EXIT_ON_CLOSE);
    window.add(area);
    area.setLineWrap(true);
    area.append("Font type, style, and size: " +
      font.getFontName() + ", " + font.getSize() + "\n");
    for (int i=0; i<codes.length; i++)
    {
      area.append("0x" + Integer.toString(codes[i], 16) +
        " " + descriptions[i] + ":\n");
      for (int j=0; j<=72; j++)
      {
        area.append((char) (codes[i] + j) + "  ");
      }
      area.append("\n");
    }
    window.setVisible(true);
  } // end main
} // end UnicodeDisplay
```

Figure 11.11 Program that uses GUI to display a sampling of Unicode characters

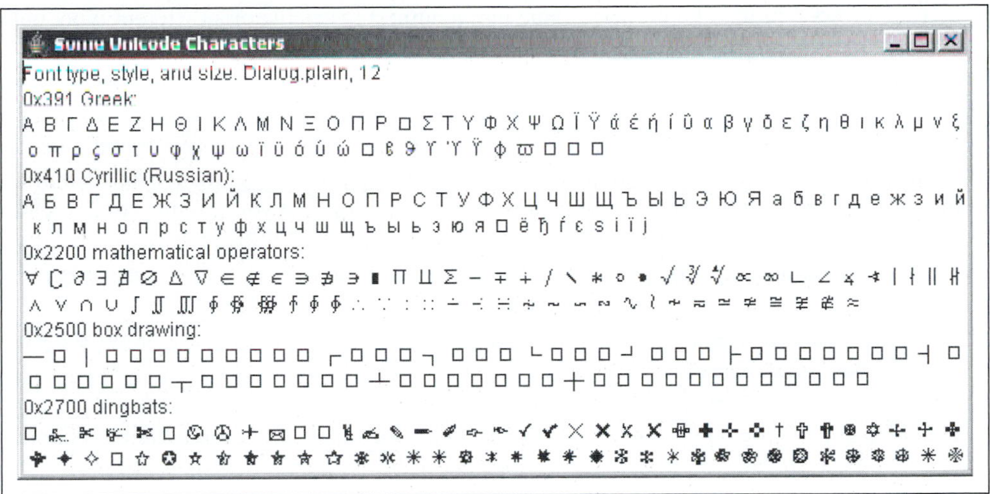

Figure 11.12 Output produced by the program in Figure 11.11

a unicode hexadecimal value of 0x2200. The maximum value of the inner `for` loop in Figure 11.11 is 72. The hexadecimal value of 72 is $4 \times 16 + 8 = 0x0048$. Thus, the Unicode hexadecimal value of the last mathematical operator displayed in Figure 11.12 is 0x2200 + 0x0048 = 0x2248. Sometimes you can use a word processor to help you find the Unicode value of the special symbol you want. For example, in Microsoft Word, select Insert / Symbol / Mathematical Operators, and then select ≈. Then read the Unicode hex value for the selected symbol from the "Character code" field near the bottom of the Symbol window. You'll find this also says the Unicode hexadecimal value for the ≈ character is 0x2248.

Look it up.

You can find everything that Unicode has to offer by browsing through the http://www.unicode.org Web site. If you go there, look for a Code Charts link, and click on it. That should take you to a page that lets you explore the various sub-tables within the huge Unicode table. Try to find the Basic Latin link. That takes you to the Basic Latin sub-table, which is equivalent to the ASCII table. The sub-table is referred to as Latin because it contains the Latin alphabet—a, b, c, and so on. Visit a few of the other sub-tables to get an idea of what's available. In every sub-table, you'll see a set of characters, and for each character, you'll see its equivalent Unicode value.

There are also several other standards for assigning numbers to characters. Computer applications sometimes include translation tables to make conversions between their own character-coding schemes and Unicode. Be warned however. The translations don't always work as you might like, and special characters may change in surprising ways when you transfer text with special characters from one application to another.

Summary

- Numerical overflow creates dramatic errors. Whenever there is any doubt about a particular type's ability to hold a value that might be assigned to it, change to a larger type.
- Floating point numbers have a greater range than integers, but for a given amount of memory, they provide less precision.
- The ASCII character set provides numerical values for the symbols on a standard keyboard.
- Since characters are represented as numbers, `ch1 + ch2` evaluates to the sum of the ASCII values for the `char` variables, `ch1` and `ch2`.

- Type casting allows you to put a numeric value into a numeric variable of a different type, but be careful that you don't get overflow or undesired truncation when you do it.
- When used as a prefix, an increment (++) or decrement (--) operator changes the variable value before that variable participates in other expression operations. When used as a postfix, an increment or decrement operator changes the variable value after it participates in other expression operations.
- If a statement contains multiple assignment operators, the rightmost assignment evaluates first.
- It's sometimes helpful to embed an assignment within a condition, but you should avoid excessive use of embedded increment, decrement and assignment operations.
- A conditional operator expression provides a compact conditional evaluation. If what's before the `?` is `true`, use what's after the `?`. Otherwise, use what's after the `:`.
- Short-circuit evaluation means that the JVM stops evaluating an expression whenever the expression's outcome becomes certain. Use this feature to avoid illegal operations.
- Use a `break` statement sparingly to terminate loops prematurely.
- In its extended form, Unicode provides numerical codes for up to a million different characters. You can specify them as decimal or hexadecimal integers or with a Unicode escape sequence. To see the Unicode characters for codes above 127, you must display them in a GUI window.

Review Questions

§11.2 Integer Types and Floating-Point Types

1. For each integer data type, how many bits of storage are used?
2. How would you write the decimal constant, 1.602×10^{-19}, as a `double`?
3. What is the approximate precision (number of accurate decimal digits) of each of the floating-point types?

§11.3 `char` Type and the ASCII Character Set

4. How many distinct characters are identified by the basic ASCII character set?
5. What number can you add to an uppercase letter `char` variable to convert it to lowercase?

§11.4 Type Conversions

6. Assume the declaration:

```
public final double C = 3.0E10;   // speed of light in cm/sec
```

Write a Java print statement that uses a cast operator to display the value of `C` in this format:

```
30000000000
```

7. Will this statement be OK or will it generate a compile-time error? (OK / error)

```
float price = 66;
```

8. Will this statement be OK or will it generate a compile-time error? (OK / error)

```
boolean done = (boolean) 0;
```

9. Will this statement be OK or will it generate a compile-time error? (OK / error)

```
float price = 98.1;
```

§11.5 Prefix/Postfix Modes for Increment/Decrement Operators

10. What is the value of `z` after these statements execute?

```
int z, x = 3;
z = --x;
z += x--;
```

§11.6 Embedded Assignments

11. Write one Java statement that makes `w`, `x`, and `y` all equal to the current value of `z`.

§11.7 Conditional Operator Expressions

12. Suppose x equals 0.43. Given the following `switch` statement heading, what does the `switch` heading's controlling expression evaluate to?

```
switch (x>0.67 ? 'H' : (x>0.33 ? 'M' : 'L'))
```

§11.8 Expression Evaluation Review

13. Assume this:

```
int a = 2;
int b = 6;
float x = 8.0f;
```

Evaluate each of the following expressions, using these guidelines:

- As shown in Section 11.8, put each evaluation step on a separate line and use the ⇒ symbol between steps.
- Evaluate each expression independently of the other expressions; in other words, use the above assumed values for each expression evaluation.
- Expression evaluation problems can be tricky. We encourage you to check your work by running test code on a computer.
- If there would be a compilation error, specify "compilation error."

a) `a + 25 / (x + 2)`
b) `7 + a * --b / 2`
c) `a * --b / 6`
d) `a + b++`
e) `a - (b = 4) % 7`
f) `b = x = 23`

§11.9 Short-Circuit Evaluation

14. Assume `expr1` and `expr2` are expressions that evaluate to `boolean` values. Assume that `expr1` evaluates to `true`. When the computer evaluates each of the following expressions, will it evaluate `expr2`? If yes, just say "yes." If no, explain why, and use the term "short-circuit evaluation" in your explanation.

a) `expr1 || expr2`
b) `expr1 && expr2`

15. Assume this:

```
int a = 2;
boolean flag = true;
```

Evaluate the following expression:

```
a < 3 || flag && !flag
```

§11.10 Empty Statement

16. Assume that the following code fragment is inside of a program that compiles successfully. What does the code fragment print? Hint: This is a trick question. Study the code carefully.

```
int x = 1;
while (x < 4);
{
  System.out.println(x);
  x++;
}
```

§11.11 break Statement within a Loop

17. Usually, you should avoid using break except in switch statements because using break statements forces readers to look for termination conditions inside loop bodies. (T / F)

§11.12 for Loop Header Details

18. Assume that the following code fragment is inside of a program that compiles successfully. What does the code fragment print?

```
for (int i=0,j=0; ; i++,j++)
{
  System.out.print(i + j + " ");
}
```

§11.13 GUI Track: Unicode (Optional)

19. What is the hexadecimal symbol for the decimal number 13?
20. The Unicode values for characters are the same as the ASCII values in the range 0x00 to 0xFF. (T / F)

Exercises

1. [after §11.2] If an integer overflows, what type of error is produced—compile-time error, runtime error, or logic error?
2. [after §11.4] How many bits are used to store a char value?
3. [after §11.4] What does this print? System.out.println('A' + 2);
4. [after §11.6] Assume a and b are boolean variables. What are their values after this statement executes?

```
a =!((b=4<=5) && (a=4>=5));
```

   Hint: First rewrite the statement to make it more readable.

5. [after §11.7] Assume this:

```
int a = 2;
float x = 8.0f;
boolean flag = true;
```

   Evaluate:

```
(flag) ? (a = (int) (x + .6)) : a
```

6. [after §11.8] Assume this:

```
int a = 10;
int b = 2;
double x = 6.0;
```

   Evaluate each of the following expressions. Follow these guidelines:

- As shown in Section 11.8, put each evaluation step on a separate line and use the ⇒ symbol between steps.
- Evaluate each expression independently of the other expressions; in other words, use the above assumed values for each expression evaluation.
- Expression evaluation problems can be tricky. We encourage you to check your work by running test code on a computer.
- If there would be a compilation error, specify "compilation error."

a) `a - 7 / (x - 4)`
b) `8 + a * ++b / 20`
c) `a + b--`
d) `a + (b = 5) % 9`
e) `a = x = -12`

7. [after §11.8] Assume this:

```
String s = "hi";
int num = 3;
char ch = 'm';
```

Evaluate each of the following expressions. Follow these guidelines:

- As shown in Section 11.8, put each evaluation step on a separate line and use the ⇒ symbol between steps.
- Evaluate each expression independently of the other expressions; in other words, use the above assumed values for each expression evaluation.
- Expression evaluation problems can be tricky. We encourage you to check your work by running test code on a computer.
- If there would be a compilation error, specify "compilation error."

a) `s + (num + 4)`
b) `s + num + 4`
c) `s + '!' + "\""`
d) `num + ch`
e) `'8' + 9`

8. [after §11.9] Consider the following code fragment. Line numbers are at the left.

```
1    int a = 2;
2    boolean b = false;
3    boolean c;
4    c = b && ++a == 2;
5    b = a++ == 2;
6    b = !b;
7    System.out.println(a + " " + b + " " + c);
```

Trace the code using this trace setup:

line#	a	b	c	output

9. [after §11.9] Assume:

```
boolean a = false;
boolean b;
double c = 2.5;
```

Determine the output of the following code fragment:

```
b = a && (++c == 3.5);
a = true || (++c == 3.5);
System.out.println(a + " " + b + " " + c);
```

10. [after §11.10] In the Fibonacci sequence, each successive element is the sum of the two previous elements. Starting with 0 and 1, the next element is 0 + 1 = 1.The element after that is 1 + 1 = 2. The element after that is 1 + 2 = 3, and the one after that is 2 + 3 = 5, and so on. Given this declaration:

```
int p, q;
```

Provide a `for` loop that prints this part of the Fibonacci sequence:

```
1 2 3 5 8
```

Your solution should consist of just a `for` loop header and then an empty statement—nothing else. By the way, we recommend that you avoid code like this for your real programs. This exercise is just for fun (fun for a hacker, anyway ☺).

11. [after §11.10] A common error is to accidentally add a semicolon at the end of a loop header. Run the following `main` method on a computer. What is the output?

```
public static void main(String[] args)
{
  int i;
  int factorial = 1;

  for (i=2; i<=4; i++);
  {
    factorial *= i;
  }
  System.out.println("i = " + i + ", factorial = " + factorial);
} // end main
```

12. [after §11.12] Note the following program. Provide a `for` loop that is functionally equivalent to the given do loop.

```
import java.util.Scanner;

public class Test
{
  public static void main(String[] args)
  {
    Scanner stdIn = new Scanner(System.in);
    String entry;

    do
    {
      System.out.println("Enter 'q' to quit: ");
      entry = stdIn.nextLine();
    } while (!entry.equals("q"));
  } // end main
} // end class Test
```

13. [after §11.13] What is the Unicode hexadecimal value for the "∞" (infinity) symbol? Show or explain how you got your answer.

Review Question Solutions

1. `byte` = 8 bits, `short` = 16 bits, `int` = 32 bits, `long` = 64 bits
2. `1.602E-19` or `1.602e-19`
3. `float` precision ≈ 6 digits, `double` precision ≈ 15 digits
4. The basic ASCII character set describes 128 different characters.
5. To convert uppercase to lowercase, add 32. To go the other way, subtract 32.
6. `System.out.println((long) C);   // (int) isn't big enough!`
7. This statement is OK:

   ```
   float price = 66;
   ```

8. This statement generates a compile-time error because it's illegal to convert between numeric values and `boolean` values:

   ```
   boolean done = (boolean) 0;
   ```

9. This statement generates a compile-time error because floating point constants are `double` by default:

   ```
   float price = 98.1;
   ```

10. `z`'s value is 4. The first decrement uses prefix mode so `x` is first decremented to 2, then 2 is assigned into `z`. The second decrement uses postfix mode so `x` is decremented after its value of 2 is added to `z`.
11. `w = x = y = z;` or any other sequence that has `z` on the right.
12. The `switch` controlling expression evaluates to `'M'`
13. Expression-evaluation practice:

    a)
    ```
    a + 25 / (x + 2) ⇒
    ( 2 + 25 / (8.0 + 2) ⇒
    2 + 25 / 10.0 ⇒
    2 + 2.5 ⇒
    4.5
    ```
    b)
    ```
    7 + a * --b / 2 ⇒
    7 + 2 * --6 / 2 ⇒
    7 + 2 * 5 / 2 ⇒
    7 + 10 / 2 ⇒
    7 + 5 ⇒

    12
    ```
    c)
    ```
    a * --b / 6  ⇒
    2 * --6 / 6 ⇒
    2 * 5 / 6 ⇒
    10 / 6 ⇒
    1
    ```
    d)
    ```
    a + b++ ⇒
    2 + 6 (b is updated to 7 after its value is accessed) ⇒
    8
    ```

e) `a - (b = 4) % 7 ⇒`

`2 - 4 % 7 ⇒`

`2 - 4 ⇒`

`-2`

f) `b = x = 23 ⇒`
`b = 23.0 ⇒`
compilation error (because the `float` 23.0 cannot be assigned to the `int` `b` without a cast operator)

14. Will it evaluate `expr2`?
a) No. Since the left side of the `||` operator is `true`, short-circuit evaluation will cause the right side of the `||` operator (`expr2`) to be ignored (since the result of the entire expression will evaluate to `true` regardless of `expr2`'s value).
b) Yes.

15. Assuming:

```
int a = 2;
boolean flag = true;
```

```
a < 3 || flag && !flag ⇒
2 < 3 || true && !true ⇒
2 < 3 || true && false ⇒
true || true && false ⇒
true      (short circuit evaluation dictates "true or anything" evaluates to true)
```

16. It prints nothing because, due to the empty statement, the `while` loop header executes repeatedly in an infinite loop.

17. True. Normally, you should avoid using `break` other than in `switch` statements.

18. The code fragment generates an infinite loop because the `for` loop header's missing second component is true by default. The output is:

```
0 2 4 6 ...
```

19. The hexadecimal symbol for the decimal number 13 is either `d` or `D`.

20. False. They are the same only in the range from `0x00` to `0x7F`.

CHAPTER 12

Aggregation, Composition, and Inheritance

Objectives

- Understand how things are naturally organized in aggregations and compositions.
- Implement aggregation and composition relationships within a program.
- Understand how inheritance can be used to refine an existing class.
- Implement an inheritance hierarchy within a program.
- Learn how to write constructors for derived classes.
- Learn how to override an inherited method.
- Learn how to prevent overriding.
- Learn how to use a class to represent an association.

Outline

12.1 Introduction

Prior to this chapter, the programs you've created have been relatively simple in terms of their object orientation, so you've been able to describe all the objects in a program with just a single class. But for more complex programs, you should consider implementing multiple classes, one for each different type of object within a program. In this chapter you'll do just that, and you'll focus on the different ways to organize classes in a multiple-class program. First, you'll learn how to organize classes that are parts of a larger containing class. When classes are related like that, where one class is the whole and the other classes are parts of the whole, the classes form an *aggregation.* Then you'll learn how to organize classes where one class, the *base class,* defines common features for a group of objects, and the other classes define specialized features for each of the different types of objects in the group. When classes are related like that, the classes form an *inheritance* hierarchy. It's called an inheritance hierarchy because the specialized classes inherit features from the base class.

In describing inheritance, we present various techniques for working with an inheritance hierarchy's classes. Specifically, we present *method overriding,* which allows you to redefine a method in a specialized class that's already been defined in the base class. We also present the `final` modifier, which allows you to prevent a specialized class from overriding a method defined in the base class.

As a follow-up to the initial presentation of aggregation and inheritance concepts, we describe how the two design strategies can work together. It's sometimes difficult to decide which is the best strategy to use. To give you practice with those decisions, we guide you part way through a program design activity and develop the skeleton for what could be a sophisticated card game program. In a final optional section, we show you how to improve organization by creating an association class, which defines a set of characteristics that belong to a particular relationship between classes.

By showing you how to organize multiple classes, this chapter provides you with important tools necessary to tackle real-world problems. After all, most real-world programming projects are large and involve multiple types of objects. When you organize objects correctly, it makes programs easier to understand and maintain. And that's good for everyone!

12.2 Composition and Aggregation

There are two primary forms of aggregation. As described above, standard aggregation is when one class is the whole and other classes are parts of the whole. The other form of aggregation also defines one class as the whole and other classes as parts of the whole. But it has an additional constraint that says the whole class is the exclusive owner of the parts classes. "Exclusive ownership" means that the parts classes cannot be owned by another class while they are being owned by the whole class. This exclusive-ownership form of aggregation is called *composition.* With composition, the whole class is called the *composite,* the parts classes are called *components,* and the composite contains the components. Composition is considered to be a strong form of aggregation since the composite-component connections are strong (due to each component having only one owner, the composite).

Composition and Aggregation in the Real World

The concept of composition was not created for computer programming; it's frequently used for complex objects in the real world. Every living creature and most manufactured products are made up of parts. Often, each part is a subsystem that is itself made up of its own set of subparts. Together, the whole system forms a composition hierarchy.

Figure 12.1 shows a composition hierarchy for a human body. At the top of this particular composition hierarchy is a whole body. A human body is composed of several organs—brain, heart, stomach, bones, muscles, and so on. Each of these organs is in turn composed of many cells. Each of these cells is composed of many organelles, like the nucleus (a cell's "brain"), and the mitochondria, (a cell's "muscles"). Each organelle is composed of many molecules. And finally, each organic molecule is typically composed of many atoms.

In a composition hierarchy (as well as in an aggregation hierarchy), the relationship between a containing class and one of its part classes is known as a *has-a* relationship. For example, each human body has a brain and has a heart. Remember that with a composition relationship, a component part is limited to just one owner at a time. For example, a heart can be in only one body at a time. Although the ownership is exclusive, it's possible for the ownership to change. With a heart transplant, a heart can switch to a new owner, but it still has just one owner at a time.

Note the diamonds in Figure 12.1. In the Universal Modeling Language (UML), solid diamonds denote a composition relationship. They indicate that a whole has exclusive ownership of a part.

Now let's think about an aggregation example where the parts are not exclusively owned by the whole. You can implement a school as an aggregation by creating a whole class for the school and part classes for the different types of people who work and study at the school. The people aren't exclusively owned by the school because a person can be part of more than one aggregation. For example, a person can attend classes at two different schools and be part of two school aggregations. The same person might even be part of a third aggregation, of a different type, like a household aggregation.

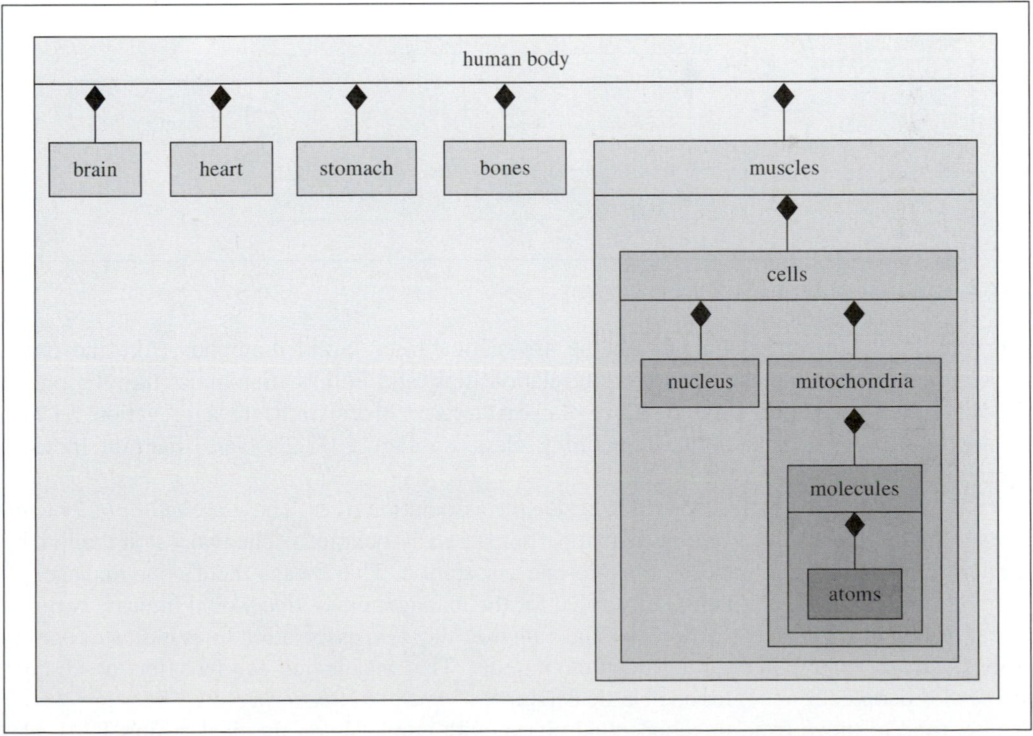

Figure 12.1 Partial representation of a composition hierarchy for a human body

Composition and Aggregation in a Java Program

Let's look at an example that uses both class relationships—composition (where exclusive ownership is required) and standard aggregation (where exclusive ownership is not required). Suppose you're trying to model a car dealership with a computer program. Since the car dealership is made from several distinct non-trivial parts, it's a good candidate for being implemented as an aggregation. The "whole" (the top of the aggregation hierarchy) is the dealership. Typically, a business has two kinds of "parts"– people and property. For simplicity, suppose the only types of people at the car dealership are management and sales people, and suppose the only type of property is cars. The control the dealership has over the people is limited. They may also have other jobs, and they may have family obligations. The dealership does not own its employees exclusively. Therefore, the relationship between the dealership and its employees is just aggregation. But the dealership does own its cars exclusively. So that relationship is composition. Note that the dealership can transfer ownership of its cars to its customers. That's OK because composition permits ownership to be transferred. Using a bottom-up design methodology, you should define three classes—`Car`, `Manager`, and `SalesPerson`—for the three types of component objects. Then, you should define a `Dealership` class for the container object.

Before you see the Dealership program's code, let's focus on the big-picture concepts using a UML class diagram. Figure 12.2's UML class diagram shows the Dealership program's four classes and the relationships among them. Since we're now focusing on just the relationships among classes, in each representation of a class, we include just the class name and omit variables and methods. That's OK—UML is very flexible, and such omissions are allowed by the UML standards. UML indicates class relationships with connecting lines that run from one class to another. Formally, each connecting line is called an *association line*.

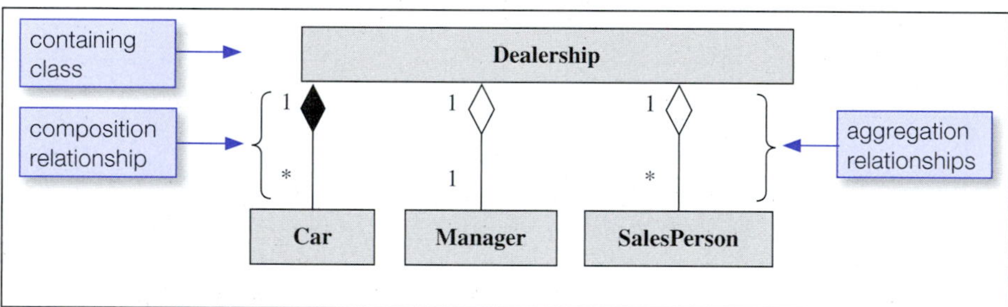

Figure 12.2 Class diagram for Dealership program

In Figure 12.2, note the diamonds on the association lines. Solid diamonds (like the one on the `Dealership-Car` line) indicate composition relationships, and hollow diamonds (like the ones on the `Dealership-Manager` and `Dealership-SalesPerson` lines) indicate aggregation relationships. The diamonds always go next to the containing class, so Figure 12.2's class diagram indicates that `Dealership` is the containing class.

Notice the numbers and asterisks written beside the association lines. These are *multiplicity values* that UML uses to specify the number of objects that participate in associations. The two 1's on the line between `Dealership` and `Manager` indicate a one-to-one association. That means there's one manager for each car dealership. If there were a 2 multiplicity value for the manager class, that would indicate two managers for each car dealership. The combination of 1 and * on the other two association lines indicates one-to-many associations, where "many" implies an indefinite number. That means you can have lots of cars (or none) and lots of sales people (or none) for one car dealership.

It's now time to move from the conceptual phase, with emphasis on the dealership's UML class diagram, to the implementation phase, with emphasis on the Dealership program code. Note the `Dealership` class in Figure 12.3, and in particular, note the `manager`, `people`, and `cars` instance variables declared

```
/****************************************************************
* Dealership.java
* Dean & Dean
*
* This represents an auto retail sales organization.
****************************************************************/

import java.util.ArrayList;

public class Dealership
{
  private String company;
  private Manager manager;
  private ArrayList<SalesPerson> people =
    new ArrayList<SalesPerson>();
  private ArrayList<Car> cars = new ArrayList<Car>();

  //*************************************************************

  public Dealership(String company, Manager manager)
  {
    this.company = company;
    this.manager = manager;
  }

  //*************************************************************

  public void addCar(Car car)
  {
    cars.add(car);
  }

  public void addPerson(SalesPerson person)
  {
    people.add(person);
  }

  //*************************************************************

  public void printStatus()
  {
    System.out.println(company + "\t" + manager.getName());
    for (SalesPerson person : people)
      System.out.println(person.getName());
    for (Car car : cars)
      System.out.println(car.getMake());
  } // end printStatus
} // end Dealership class
```

Containership implemented here.

Figure 12.3 `Dealership` class for Dealership program

inside of the Dealership class. Those instance variable declarations implement the concept of the dealership class containing the other three classes. The general rule is that whenever you have a class that contains another class, declare an instance variable inside the containing class such that the instance variable holds a reference to one or more of the contained class's objects.

Also in the Dealership class, note the use of ArrayLists for the people and cars instance variables. Typically, if you have a class in a UML class diagram with a * multiplicity value, you should use an ArrayList to implement the reference to the asterisked class. ArrayLists are good for implementing * multiplicity values because they can expand to accommodate any number of elements.

Peruse the Car, Manager, and SalesPerson classes in Figures 12.4, 12.5, and 12.6. They simply store and retrieve data. Note the SalesPerson's sales instance variable—it keeps track of the total sales for a sales person for the current year. There are no methods for accessing or updating the sales instance variable. We omitted those methods to avoid code clutter and to maintain focus on the matter at hand, aggregation and composition. In an actual car dealership program, you'd need to provide those methods.

```
/********************************
* Car.java
* Dean & Dean
*
* This class implements a car.
********************************/

public class Car
{
  private String make;

  //*****************************

  public Car(String make)
  {
    this.make = make;
  }

  //*****************************

  public String getMake()
  {
    return make;
  }
} // end Car class
```

Figure 12.4 Car class for Dealership program

See the car dealership program's driver class in Figure 12.7. Most of the code is straightforward. The main method instantiates a Manager object, two SalesPerson objects, and a Dealership object. Then main adds salesPerson and Car objects to the Dealership object. The part of main that merits further attention is the use of local variables for the Manager and SalesPerson objects and the use of anonymous objects for the Car objects. Why the discrepancy? Because Manager and SalesPerson relate to the Dealership class with aggregation, and Car relates to the Dealership class with composition.

```
/*************************************************************
* Manager.java
* Dean & Dean
*
* This class implements a car dealership sales manager.
*************************************************************/

public class Manager
{
  private String name;

  //**********************************************************

  public Manager(String name)
  {
    this.name = name;
  }

  //**********************************************************

  public String getName()
  {
    return name;
  }
} // end Manager class
```

Figure 12.5 `Manager` class for Dealership program

```
/************************************************
* SalesPerson.java
* Dean & Dean
*
* This class implements a car sales person.
************************************************/

public class SalesPerson
{
  private String name;
  private double sales = 0.0; // sales to date

  //*********************************************

  public SalesPerson(String name)
  {
    this.name = name;
  }

  //*********************************************

  public String getName()
  {
    return name;
  }
} // end SalesPerson class
```

Figure 12.6 `SalesPerson` class for Dealership program

```
/*************************************************************
* DealershipDriver.java
* Dean & Dean
*
* This class demonstrates car dealership composition.
*************************************************************/

public class DealershipDriver
{
  public static void main(String[] args)
  {
    Manager ryne = new Manager("Ryne Mendez");
    SalesPerson nicole = new SalesPerson("Nicole Betz");
    SalesPerson vince = new SalesPerson("Vince Sola");
    Dealership dealership =
      new Dealership("OK Used Cars", ryne);

    dealership.addPerson(nicole);
    dealership.addPerson(vince);
    dealership.addCar(new Car("GMC"));
    dealership.addCar(new Car("Yugo"));
    dealership.addCar(new Car("Dodge"));
    dealership.printStatus();
  } // end main
} // end DealershipDriver class
```

For aggregations, pass in copies of references.

For compositions, create anonymous objects.

Output:

```
OK Used Cars        Ryne Mendez
Nicole Betz
Vince Sola
GMC
Yugo
Dodge
```

Figure 12.7 Driver for Dealership program

Here's the general rule for implementing aggregation relationships. Whenever two classes have an aggregation relationship, you should save the contained class's object in a reference variable in the containing class, and you should also save it in another reference variable outside of the containing class. That way, the object can be added to another aggregation and have two different "owners" (having two different owners is allowed by aggregation). Putting this in the context of the Dealership program, `DealershipDriver` uses local variables when it instantiates `Manager` and `SalesPerson` objects. That enables `Manager` and `SalesPerson` objects to exist independently from the dealership, and that mirrors the real world.

Now let's look at the general rule for implementing composition relationships. Whenever two classes have a composition relationship, you should save the contained class's object in a reference variable in the containing class, and you should not save it elsewhere. That way, the object can have only one "owner" (having just one owner is required by composition). Putting this in the context of the Dealership program,

`DealershipDriver` creates anonymous objects when it instantiates cars. That gives the dealership exclusive ownership and complete control over the cars, and that mirrors the real world.

12.3 Inheritance Overview

So far in this chapter, we've focused on aggregation and composition hierarchies, where one class is the whole and other classes are parts of the whole. Now we turn to inheritance hierarchies, which are qualitatively different from composition hierarchies. Whereas a composition hierarchy describes a nesting of things, an inheritance hierarchy describes an elaboration of concepts. The concept at the top is the most general/generic, and the concepts at the bottom are the most specific.

Real-World Inheritance Hierarchies

Before looking at inheritance hierarchy code, let's think about a real-world inheritance hierarchy example. Figure 12.8 describes a few of the many possible characteristics of organisms living on the earth today, with the most general characteristics at the top of the diagram and the most specific characteristics at the bottom of the diagram. Although this chart includes only characteristics of current living organisms, it's helpful to recognize that there was a natural time sequence in the development of these characteristics. The characteristics at the top developed first, and the characteristics at the bottom developed last. The earliest types of life—bacteria—appeared on earth almost 4 billion years ago as single-celled organisms with no internal partitions. About 2.3 billion years ago a nucleus and other components appeared inside cells, creating more sophisticated single-celled organisms called Eukaryotes (true-celled organisms). About 1.3 billion years ago the first animals appeared. They had more than one cell, and they were vascular (had containers and conveyors like arteries and veins). About 510 million years ago some of the animals (vertebrates) developed backbones and braincases. About 325 million years ago, the first reptiles appeared. Then, about 245 million years ago, the first mammals appeared.

Recognizing the natural time sequence in the biological inheritance hierarchy that describes current life is useful for two reasons: (1) We're talking about "inheritance" here. What's at the bottom of the chart "inherits" from what's above it, and in real life descendants inherit from their ancestors. (2) The natural development of life from simple (at the top of the chart) to complex (at the bottom of the chart) provides an excellent model for the engineered development of an object-oriented computer program. It's good design practice to start with a relatively simple and generic implementation and add specializations and complexity in subsequent design cycles. You'll see some examples of this later on.

Start generic. 

With composition, certain classes contain other classes, but with inheritance, there's no such containership. For example, in Figure 12.8, Animal is above Mammal, but an animal does not contain a mammal. Rather, an animal is a generic type, and a mammal is a specialized version of an animal.

Each descendant type of organism inherits some characteristics from its ancestors and adds some new characteristics of its own. In an inheritance hierarchy, the characteristics associated with a type high in the hierarchy are not supposed to be all of the characteristics possessed by any individual living organism. Ideally, the characteristics associated with each type high in the hierarchy should be just those characteristics that are "conserved"—actually inherited by all types descended from that type. Thus, ideally, any type at the bottom of the hierarchy inherits all of the characteristics associated with all types above it. For example, mammals have mammary glands and hair. And, since mammals are vertebrates, they inherit the vertebrate characteristics of having a backbone and a braincase. And, since mammals are also animals, they also inherit the animal characteristics of having more than one cell and being vascular. And, since mammals are also eukaryotes, they also inherit the eukaryote characteristic of having a nucleus in each cell.

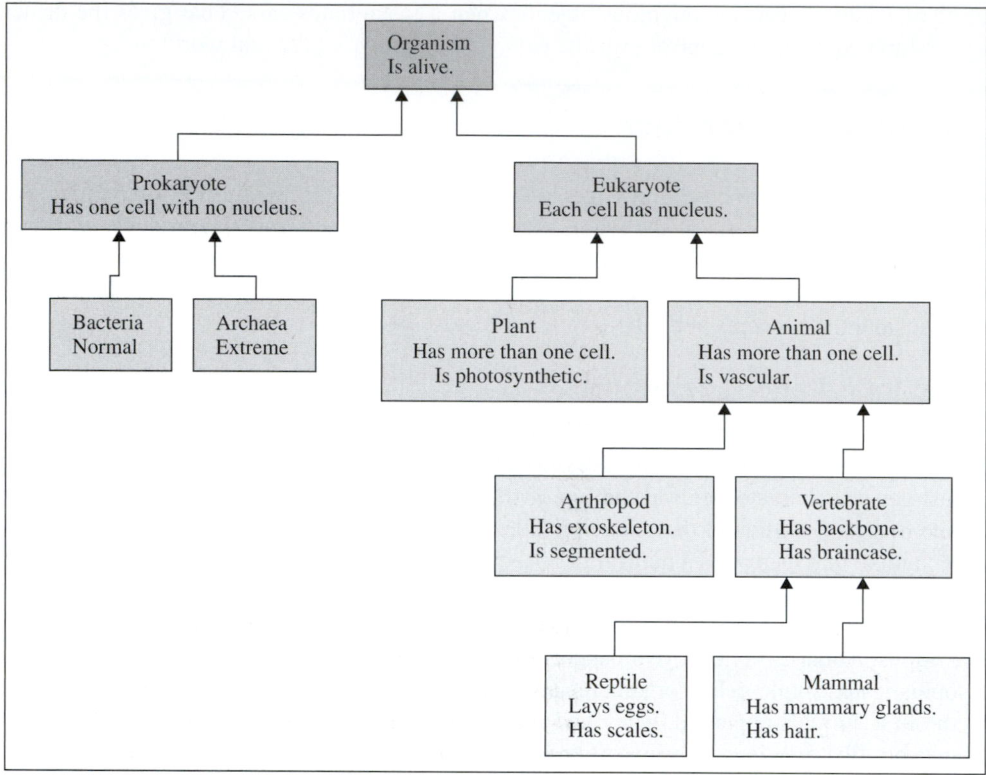

Figure 12.8 Biological example of an inheritance hierarchy

The types at the very bottom of a real-life biological inheritance hierarchy do not appear in Figure 12.8, because the complete hierarchy is too big to display in one figure. What's actually at the bottom are species, like Homo sapiens (human beings). In nature, reproduction is possible only among members of the same species. Similarly, in an ideal OOP computer program, the only *realizable* (instantiable) types are the types at the very bottom of inheritance hierarchies. Organizing an inheritance hierarchy so that all realizable (instantiable) types appear only at the lowest level (the *leaves* of a hierarchical tree) minimizes duplication, and it minimizes maintenance and enhancement labor.

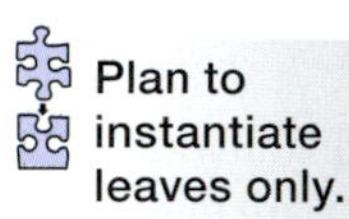

UML Class Diagrams for Inheritance Hierarchies

Figure 12.9 shows a UML class diagram for an inheritance hierarchy that keeps track of people associated with a department store. The top class, `Person`, is generic. It contains data and methods that are common to all classes in the hierarchy. Classes below the top class are more specific. For example, the `Customer` and `Employee` classes describe specific types of people in the department store. Since there are two distinct types of store employees, the `Employee` class has two subordinate classes for the two types—the `FullTime` class for full-time employees and the `PartTime` class for part-time employees.

Within an inheritance hierarchy, lower classes inherit upper classes' members. Thus, the `Employee` and `Customer` classes inherit `name` from the `Person` class. Likewise, the `FullTime` and `PartTime`

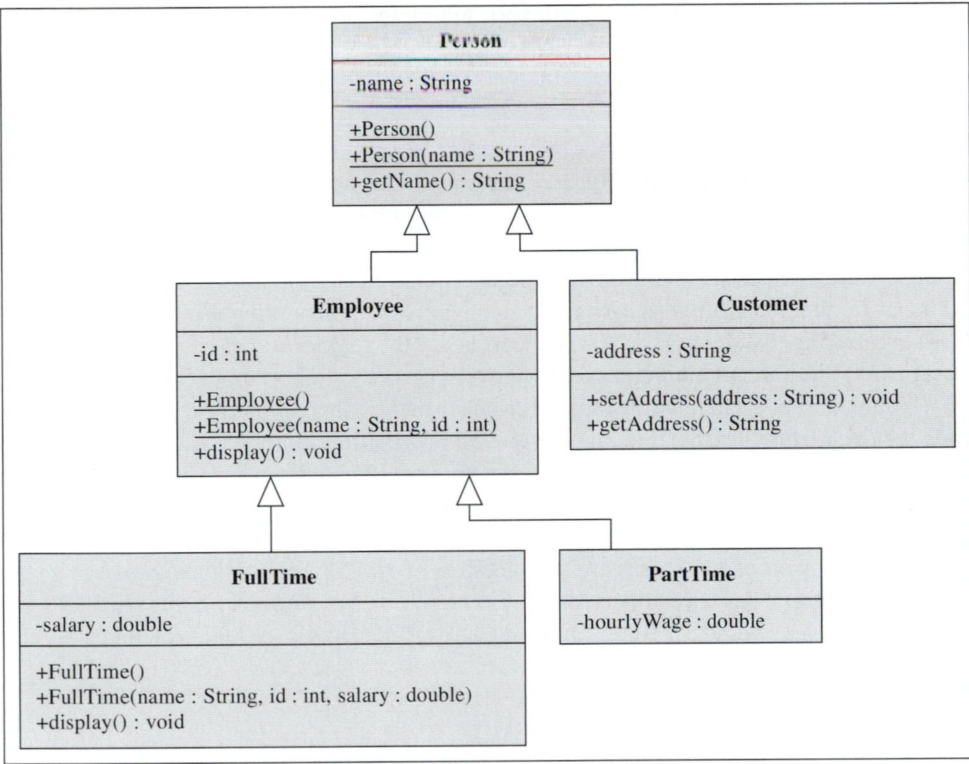

Figure 12.9 UML class diagram for a `Person` class inheritance hierarchy

classes inherit `id` from the `Employee` class. Inheritance travels all the way down the inheritance hierarchy tree, so in addition to inheriting `id` from the `Employee` class, the `FullTime` and `PartTime` classes also inherit `name` from the `Person` class.

Within an inheritance hierarchy, classes are linked in pairs. Can you identify the linked pairs in Figure 12.9? The four pairs of linked classes are `Person-Customer`, `Person-Employee`, `Employee-FullTime`, and `Employee-PartTime`. For each pair of linked classes, the more general class is considered to be the *superclass* and the more specific one is considered to be the *subclass*.

Inheriting a superclass's variables and methods enables a subclass to be a clone of its superclass. But making a subclass that's just a clone would be silly, because you could just use the superclass instead. You always want a subclass to be a more specific version of its superclass. That's achieved by establishing additional variables and/or methods inside the subclass's definition. For example, in Figure 12.9, the `Customer` class defines an address instance variable. That means Customer objects have a name (inherited from the Person class) plus an address. Customer addresses are important in that they enable department stores to mail monthly "Everything-Must-Go Liquidation Sale!" advertisements to their customers.

UML class diagrams usually show superclasses above subclasses. However, that's not always the case. With large projects, you'll have lots of classes and several different types of relationships among the classes. With all that going on, it's sometimes impossible to draw a "clean" class hierarchy picture and preserve the traditional superclass-above-subclass layout. Thus, subclasses sometimes appear at the left, at the right, or even above their superclasses. So how can you tell which is the subclass and which is the superclass? UML class diagrams use a solid line and a hollow arrow for inheritance relationships, with the arrow pointing to the superclass. In Figure 12.9, note how the arrows do indeed point to the superclasses.

Inheritance Terminology

Unfortunately, the terms superclass and subclass can be misleading. The "super" in superclass seems to imply that superclasses have more capability, and the "sub" in subclass seems to imply that subclasses have less capability. Actually, it's the other way around—subclasses have more capability. Subclasses can do everything that superclasses can do, plus more.

For the most part, we'll stick with the terms superclass and subclass since those are the formal terms used by Sun, but be aware that there is alternative terminology. Programmers often use the terms *parent class* or *base class* when referring to a superclass. And they often use the terms *child class* or *derived class* when referring to a subclass. The parent-child relationship between classes is important because it determines inheritance. With a human parent-child relationship, the child normally inherits money from the parent.[1] The class parent-child relationship parallels the human parent-child relationship. But with a class parent-child relationship, the child doesn't inherit money; instead it inherits the variables and methods defined in the superclass.

There are two more inheritance-related terms that you should be aware of. An *ancestor* class refers to any of the classes above a particular class in an inheritance hierarchy. For example, in Figure 12.9's inheritance hierarchy, `Employee` and `Person` are the ancestors of `FullTime`. A *descendant* class refers to any of the classes below a particular class in an inheritance hierarchy. For example, in Figure 12.9's inheritance hierarchy, `Employee`, `Customer`, `FullTime`, and `PartTime` are descendants of `Person`.

Benefits of Inheritance

Long before reading this chapter, you were already convinced of the benefit of modeling your programs with classes, right? (In case you need to be reminded why you love classes so much, it's because classes allow you to encapsulate things.) So you should be able to see the benefit of having a `Customer` class and also an `Employee` class for a department store program. OK, having separate `Customer` and `Employee` classes is good, but why stir up trouble and give them a superclass? If there's no superclass for the `Customer` and `Employee` classes, then the things common to customers and employees would have to be defined in both classes. For example, you'd need a `name` instance variable and a `getName` method in both classes. But redundant code is almost always a bad idea. Why? With redundant code, debugging and upgrading chores are more tedious. After fixing or improving the code in one place, the programmer must remember to fix or improve the code in the other place as well.

In Figure 12.9, notice that classes at different levels in the hierarchy contain different instance variables, and they have different methods (although `Employee` and `FullTime` both have a `display` method, the methods are different; that is, they behave differently). There is no functional duplication, and there is maximal *code reusability*. Code reusability is when you have code that provides functionality for more than one part of a program. Putting common code from two classes into a superclass is one example of code reusability. Code reusability can also take place when you want to add a significant chunk of functionality to an existing class. You might want to implement the functionality by adding code directly to the existing class. But suppose the class works perfectly, and you're scared to touch it for fear of messing it up. Or maybe your know-it-all co-worker wrote the class, and you don't want to risk getting him/her riled up over code modifications. No problem. Extend the class (that is, create a subclass) and implement the new functionality in the extended class.

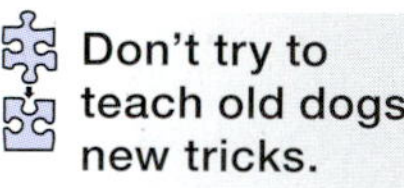
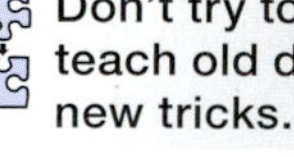

Don't try to teach old dogs new tricks.

[1] Author John hopes that author/father Ray shares this sentence's sentiment.

You've seen that inheritance gives rise to code reusability, and you should now be properly convinced of the benefits of code reusability. Another benefit of inheritance is that it gives rise to smaller modules (because classes are split into superclasses and subclasses). In general, smaller modules are good because there's less code to wade through when searching for bugs or making upgrades.

12.4 Implementation of Person/Employee/FullTime Hierarchy

To explain how to implement inheritance, we'll implement the Person/Employee/FullTime hierarchy shown in Figure 12.9. We'll implement the Person and Employee classes in this section and the FullTime class in Section 12.6.

The Person class

Figure 12.10 contains an implementation of the Person class. It will be a superclass, but there's no special code in the Person class that indicates it will be a superclass. The special code comes later when we define Person's subclasses. That's where we indicate that Person is a superclass for those subclasses.

```
/*********************************************************
* Person.java
* Dean & Dean
*
* The is a base class for an inheritance hierarchy.
*********************************************************/

public class Person
{
  private String name = "";

  //*****************************************************

  public Person()
  { }

  public Person(String name)
  {
    this.name = name;
  }

  //*****************************************************

  public String getName()
  {
    return this.name;
  }
} // end Person class
```

Remember: Once you write your own constructor, the automatic zero-parameter default constructor disappears, and if you want one, you must write it explicitly.

Figure 12.10 Person class, superclass for the Employee class

The Person class doesn't do much. It just stores a name and allows the name to be retrieved with a getName accessor method. The Person class contains one item worth examining—the zero-parameter constructor. Normally, when a driver instantiates a Person class, the driver will assign the person's name by passing a name argument to the one-parameter constructor. But suppose you want to test your program with a Person object, and you don't want to hassle with storing a name in the Person object. The zero-parameter constructor allows you to do that. Do you know what name will be given to a Person object created by the zero-parameter constructor? name is a string instance variable, and the default value for a string instance variable is null. To avoid the ugly null default, note how name is initialized to the empty string.

Quick quiz: Can you achieve the same functionality by omitting the zero-parameter constructor since the compiler automatically provides a default zero-parameter constructor? Nope—remember that once you write any constructor, the compiler no longer provides a default zero-parameter constructor.

The Employee Class

Figure 12.11 contains an implementation of the derived Employee class, which provides an id. Note the extends clause in the Employee class's heading. To enable inheritance, extends *<superclass>* must appear at the right of the subclass's heading. Thus, extends Person appears at the right of the

```
/*******************************************
* Employee.java
* Dean & Dean
*
* The describes an employee.
*******************************************/

public class Employee extends Person
{
  private int id = 0;

  //*****************************************

  public Employee()
  { }

  public Employee(String name, int id)
  {
    super(name);
    this.id = id;
  }

  //*****************************************

  public void display()
  {
    System.out.println("name: " + getName());
    System.out.println("id: " + id);
  }
} // end Employee class
```

This means the Employee class is derived from the Person superclass.

This calls the one-parameter Person constructor.

Since name is in a different class and is private, we must use an accessor to get it. Since getName is inherited, we don't need a referencing prefix for it.

Figure 12.11 Employee class, derived from the Person class

Employee class's heading. Note that the Employee class defines just one instance variable, id. Does that mean that an Employee object has no name? No. Employee objects do have names because the Employee class inherits the name instance variable from the Person superclass. Now you'll learn how to access name from within the Employee class.

The Employee class's display method is in charge of printing an employee's information—name and id. Printing the id is easy because id is declared within the Employee class. Printing name requires a bit more work. Since name is a private instance variable in the Person superclass, the Employee class cannot access name directly (that's the same interpretation of private that we've always had). But the Employee class can access name by calling the Person class's public getName accessor method. Here's the relevant code from the display method:

```
System.out.println("name: " + getName());
```

As you might recall, in an instance method, if you call a method that's in the same class as the class you're currently in, the reference variable dot prefix is unnecessary. Likewise, in an instance method, if you call a method that's in the superclass of the class you're currently in, the reference variable dot prefix is unnecessary. Thus, there's no reference variable dot prefix in the above call to getName.

12.5 Constructors in a Subclass

Let's now examine Figure 12.11's two-parameter Employee constructor. The goal is to assign the passed-in name and id values to the associated instance variables in the instantiated Employee object. Assigning to the id instance variable is easy because id is declared within the Employee class. But assigning to the name instance variable is harder because name is a private instance variable in the Person superclass. There's no setName mutator method in Person, so how does name get set? Read on. . . .

Using super to Call a Superclass Constructor

Employee objects inherit the name instance variable from Person. It follows that Employee objects should use the Person constructor to initialize their inherited name instance variables. But how can an Employee object call a Person constructor? It's easy—once you know how. To call a superclass constructor, use the reserved word super followed by parentheses and a comma-separated list of arguments that you want to pass to the constructor. For example, here's how Figure 12.11's Employee constructor calls the one-parameter Person constructor:

```
super(name);
```

Calls to super are allowed only in one particular place. They're allowed only from within a constructor, and they must be the first line within a constructor. That should sound familiar. In Chapter 7, you learned another usage for the keyword this, a usage that is distinct from using this dot to specify an instance member. The syntax for this other usage of this is:

```
this(<arguments>);
```

This kind of this usage calls another (overloaded) constructor from within a constructor in the same class. And recall that you must make such a call on the first line of your constructor.

By the way, would it be legal to have a this constructor call and a super constructor call within the same constructor? No, because with both constructor calls in the same constructor, that means only one of the constructor calls can be in the first line. The other one would violate the rule that constructor calls must be in the first line.

Default Call to Superclass Constructor

The Java designers at Sun are fond of calling superclass constructors since doing so promotes software reuse. If you write a subclass constructor and don't include a call to another constructor (with `this` or with `super`), the Java compiler sneaks in and inserts a superclass zero-parameter constructor call by default. Thus, although Figure 12.11's `Employee` zero-parameter constructor has an empty body, the Java compiler automatically inserts `super();` in it. So these two constructors are functionally equivalent:

```
public Employee()
{ }

public Employee()
{
  super();
}
```

The explicit `super();` call makes it clear what's going on. Feel free to include it if you wish, to make your code more self-documenting.

Whenever a constructor is called, the JVM automatically runs up the hierarchical tree to the greatest grandparent's constructor, and it executes that greatest grandparent's constructor first. Then it executes the code in the constructor below it, and so on, and finally it executes the rest of the code in the originally called constructor.[2]

12.6 Method Overriding

From Chapter 7, you know about method overloading—that's when a single class contains two or more methods with the same name but a different sequence of parameter types. Now for a related concept—*method overriding*. That's when a subclass has a method with the same name, the same sequence of parameter types, and the same return type as a method in a superclass. The term "overriding" should make sense when you realize that an overriding method overrides/supersedes its associated superclass method. That means, by default, an object of the subclass uses the subclass's overriding method and not the superclass's overridden method.

The concept of a subclass object using the subclass's method rather than the superclass's method falls in line with this general principle of programming: Local stuff takes precedence over global stuff. Can you think of where else this rule applies? If a local variable and an instance variable have the same name, the local variable takes precedence when you're inside the local variable's method. The same reasoning applies to parameters taking precedence over instance variables when you're inside the parameter's method.

Method Overriding Example

To explain method overriding, we'll continue with the implementation of the Person/Employee/FullTime program. We implemented the `Person` and `Employee` classes in Section 12.4. We implement the `FullTime` class in Figure 12.12. Note `FullTime`'s `display` method. It has the same sequence of parameter types as the `display` method in the `Employee` class of Figure 12.11. Since the `FullTime` class

[2] This sequence is the same as the sequence that occurs naturally in the embryonic development of a living creature. The characteristics that develop first are the most ancient ones.

```
/*************************************************************
* FullTime.java
* Dean & Dean
*
* The describes a full-time employee.
*************************************************************/

public class FullTime extends Employee
{
  private double salary = 0.0;

  //**********************************************************

  public FullTime()
  { }

  public FullTime(String name, int id, double salary)
  {
    super(name, id);
    this.salary = salary;
  }

  //**********************************************************

  public void display()
  {
    super.display();
    System.out.printf(
      "salary: $%,.0f\n", salary);
  }
} // end FullTime class
```

This calls the two-parameter Employee constructor.

This method *overrides* the display method defined in the Employee class.

This calls the display method defined in the Employee class.

Figure 12.12 FullTime class, which illustrates method overriding

extends the Employee class, the FullTime class's display method overrides the Employee class's display method.

Using super to Call an Overridden Method

Sometimes, an object of the subclass might need to call the superclass's overridden method. To perform such a call, you need to prefix the method call with super and then a dot. For example, in Figure 12.12's FullTime subclass, note how the display method calls the superclass's display method with super.display();.

Now look again at that super.display() method call in Figure 12.12's FullTime class. What do you suppose would happen if you forgot to prefix that method call with super dot? Without the prefix, display(); would call the display method in the current class, FullTime, not the display method in the superclass. In executing the FullTime class's display method, the JVM would call the FullTime class's display method again. This process would repeat in an infinite loop.

By the way, you can have a series of overriding methods; that is, you can override an overriding method. But it's illegal to have a series of `super` dot prefixes chained together. In other words, in the `Person/Employee/FullTime` inheritance hierarchy, suppose the `Person` class contains a `display` method that's overridden by the `Employee` and `FullTime` classes. In the `FullTime` class, it would be illegal to call the `Person` class's `display` method like this:

```
super.super.display();   ◄── compilation error
```

To call the `Person` class's `display` method from the `FullTime` class, you'd have to call the `Employee` class's `display` method, and rely on the `Employee` class's `display` method to call the `Person` class's `display` method.

Have you noticed that `super` has two different purposes? You can use `super` dot to call an overridden method, and you can also use `super` with parentheses (e.g., `super(name);`) to call a superclass's constructor.

Return Types Must Be the Same

An overriding method must have the same return type as the method that it's overriding. If it has a different return type, the compiler generates an error. Said another way, if a subclass and a superclass have methods with the same name, the same sequence of parameter types, and different return types, the compiler generates an error.

This error doesn't occur all that often because if you've got methods with the same names and sequences of parameter types, you'll usually also want the same return types. But you'll see the error crop up every now and then when you're debugging, so be aware of it. By the way, if a subclass and a superclass have methods with the same name and different sequences of parameter types, it doesn't matter if the return types are the same. Why? Because such methods are not in an overriding relationship. They are different methods entirely.

12.7 Using the `Person/Employee/FullTime` Hierarchy

Now let's reinforce what you've learned about inheritance by looking at what happens when you instantiate an object of the lowest-level derived type and use that object to call overridden methods and inherited methods. Figure 12.13 contains a driver for the `FullTime` class, and the subsequent output shows what it does. This driver instantiates a `fullTimer` object from the `FullTime` class. Then the `fullTimer` object calls its `display` method. As shown in Figure 12.12, this `display` method uses `super` to call the `Employee` class's `display` method, which prints the `fullTimer`'s `name` and `id`. Then `fullTimer`'s `display` method prints the `fullTimer`'s `salary`.

In the final statement in Figure 12.13, the `fullTimer` object calls its `getName` method and prints `fullTimer`'s `name`. But wait a minute! The `FullTime` class does not have a `getName` method, and its superclass, `Employee`, does not have one either. The code seems to be calling a non-existent method. What's going on here? What's going on is inheritance—produced by those wonderful little `extends` clauses. Because there is no explicitly defined `getName` method in its own `FullTime` class, the `fullTimer` object goes up its inheritance hierarchy until it finds a `getName` method, and then it uses that method. In this case, the first `getName` method found is in the `Person` class, so that's the method the `fullTimer` object inherits and uses. There is no need to use `super` dot to access the `getName` method (but using `super` dot would work, in case you're curious). If a method is not in the current class, the JVM automatically goes up the inheritance hierarchy and uses the first definition of that method it finds.

Notice that our driver did not instantiate any `Employee` or `Person` objects. It just instantiated an object from a class at the bottom of the inheritance hierarchy only. This is the way a good inheritance

```
/*************************************************************
* FullTimeDriver.java
* Dean & Dean
*
* The describes a full-time employee.
*************************************************************/

public class FullTimeDriver
{
  public static void main(String[] args)
  {
    FullTime fullTimer = new FullTime("Shreya", 5733, 80000);

    fullTimer.display();
    System.out.println(fullTimer.getName());
  }
} // end FullTimeDriver class
```

Output:

```
name:   Shreya
id:     5733
salary: $80,000
Shreya
```

Figure 12.13 Driver of constructors and methods in an inheritance hierarchy

hierarchy should be used. Ideally, you should just instantiate objects from classes at the bottom of the hierarchy. Ideally, all the classes above the bottom classes are there to make the bottom classes simple. In real life, we often do use classes above the bottom, but using bottom classes only is the ideal situation.

12.8 The `final` Access Modifier

You've used the `final` access modifier for quite a while now to turn a variable into a named constant. In this section, you'll learn how to use `final` to modify a method and modify a class.

If you use the `final` modifier in a method heading, you'll prevent the method from being overridden with a new definition in a subclass. You might want to do this if you think that your method is perfect and you don't want its original meaning to "drift." You might also want to consider using `final` to help speed things up a bit. Methods that use the `final` modifier should run faster since the compiler can generate more efficient code for them. The code efficiency comes from the compiler not having to prepare for the possibility of inheritance. However, the speed improvement is miniscule for adding `final` to a single method, and you probably won't notice it unless you have a large programming project with lots of subclasses and you use `final` a lot.

If you use the `final` access modifer in a class heading, you prevent the class from having any subclasses. You might want to do this if you have a class that's good and reliable, and you want to preserve its quality and protect it from future "feature creep." By the way, if a class is declared to be a `final` class, there's no point in specifying `final` for any of its methods. A `final` class cannot be extended, so overriding methods cannot exist.

Even though it may be difficult to see palpable benefits from the use of `final`, go ahead and use it when appropriate. And even if you don't use it for your own programs, you'll need to understand it because you'll see it quite often in the Java API library classes. For example, the `Math` class is defined with the `final` access modifier, so it's illegal to extend the `Math` class and override any of its methods.

12.9 Using Inheritance with Aggregation and Composition

We have described several ways classes can be related—with aggregation, composition, and inheritance. Now let's consider using all three relationships together.

Aggregation, Composition, and Inheritance Compared

Aggregation and composition both implement a has-a relationship. We call aggregation and composition relationships has-a relationships because one class, the container class, has a component class inside of it. For example, in Section 12.2's Dealership program, a dealership has a sales manager, with non-exclusive ownership rights, and that's why the Dealership program implements the `Dealership-SalesManager` relationship with aggregation. Also, a dealership has an inventory of cars, with exclusive ownership rights, and that's why the Dealership program implements the `Dealership-Car` relationship with composition.

Inheritance implements an *is-a* relationship. We call an inheritance relationship an is-a relationship because one class, a subclass, is a more detailed version of another class. For example, in the Person/Employee/FullTime program, a full-time employee is an employee, and that's why the program implements the `FullTime-Employee` relationship with inheritance. Also, an employee is a person, and that's why the program implements the `Employee-Person` relationship with inheritance as well.

It's important to keep in mind that these are not alternative ways to represent the same relationship. They are ways to represent different relationships. The aggregation and composition relationships are when one class is a whole made up of non-trivial constituent parts defined in other classes. The inheritance relationship is when one class is a more detailed version of another class. More formally, inheritance is when one class, a subclass, inherits variables and methods from another class, a superclass, and then supplements those with additional variables and methods. Since composition and inheritance deal with different aspects of a problem, many programming solutions include a mixture of both paradigms.

Aggregation, Composition, and Inheritance Combined

In the real world, it's fairly common to have aggregation, composition, and inheritance relationships together in the same program. Let's look at an example that uses all three class relationships. Section 12.2's Dealership program uses aggregation and composition, as illustrated by this UML class diagram:

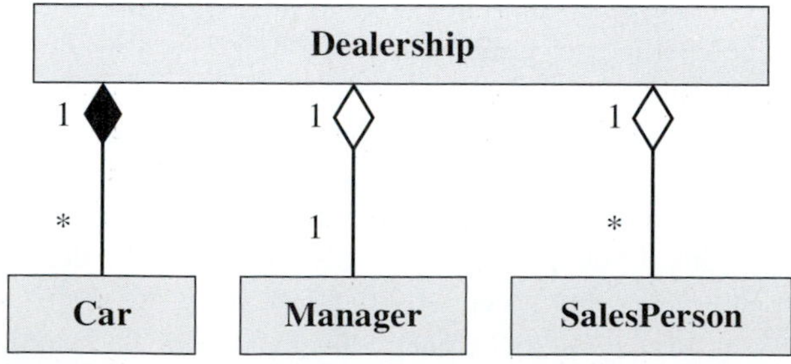

What sort of inheritance relationship could/should be added to the Dealership program? If you look back at Figures 12.5 (Manager class) and 12.6 (SalesPerson class), you'll see that Manager and SalesPerson both declare the same instance variable, name, and they both define the same instance method, getName. That's an example of undesirable duplication, and we can use inheritance to eliminate that duplication. Introducing inheritance into that program does not alter the original whole-parts structure. It just introduces a complementary mechanism that eliminates duplication.

Factor out the common code.

Figure 12.14 shows an improved and expanded UML class diagram for a new Dealership2 program. If you compare this with the previous UML class diagram, you'll see that each class is fleshed out to include

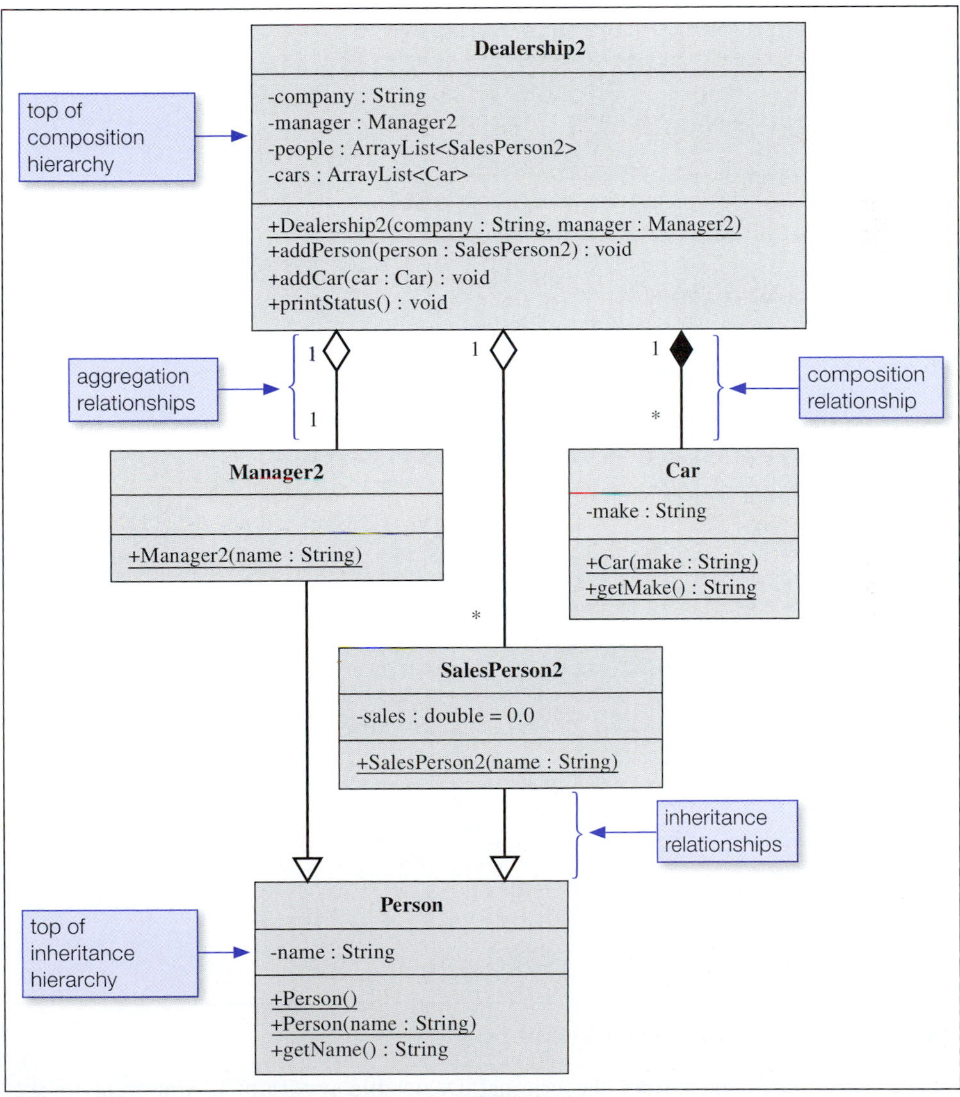

Figure 12.14 Class diagram for revised car dealership program—Dealership2

instance variables and methods. Figure 12.14's diagram also includes a Person class. Our previous Manager and SalesPerson classes now inherit a variable, two constructors and a method from this Person class. The inheritance reduces the Manager and SalesPerson classes to the simpler Manager2 and SalesPerson2 classes. These simpler classes do not need explicit declaration of name and explicit definition of getName because they inherit these members from Person. Read through the code for the shortened Manager2 and SalesPerson2 classes in Figures 12.15 and 12.16.

```
/*******************************************
* Manager2.java
* Dean & Dean
*
* This represents car dealership manager
*******************************************/

public class Manager2 extends Person
{
  public Manager2(String name)
  {
    super(name);
  }
} // end Manager2 class
```

Figure 12.15 Manager2 class for Dealership2 program

```
/********************************************
* SalesPerson2.java
* Dean & Dean
*
* This represents car sales person
********************************************/

public class SalesPerson2 extends Person
{
  private double sales = 0; // sales to date

  //*****************************************

  public SalesPerson2(String name)
  {
    super(name);
  }
} // end SalesPerson2 class
```

Figure 12.16 SalesPerson2 class for Dealership2 program

The Car class is unchanged from the original Dealership program; if you want to see its code, look back at Figure 12.4. The Dealership2 and Dealership2Driver classes are the same as the

Dealership and DealershipDriver classes defined in Figures 12.3 and 12.7, respectively, except Dealership is changed to Dealership2, Manager is changed to Manager2, and SalesPerson is changed to SalesPerson2.

In Figure 12.14, the addition of the Person class makes it look like we made the Dealership2 program bigger by adding another class. But the additional Person class was already defined in another program, the Person/Employee/FullTime program. In borrowing the Person class from that program, we got something for nothing. The borrowed Person class enabled us to shorten two other classes. Being able to borrow classes that have already been written and then inheriting from them in other contexts is an important benefit of OOP. If you look at the prewritten classes in the Java API, you'll see that they do a lot of inheriting from one to another, and in many cases, you have the option of inheriting from them into your own programs, as well.

12.10 Design Practice with Card Game Example

In the previous section, you learned how to use different types of class relationships together in a single program. The way you learned was by adding inheritance to an existing program. In this section, you'll once again use different types of class relationships, but this time you'll design the program from the ground up. And you'll be doing most of the work, rather than just understanding how it's done by someone else.

Learn by doing.

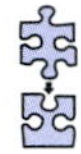

Your Mission (Should You Choose to Accept It)

Your mission is to design and implement a generic card game program. In carrying out this mission, follow these guidelines:

- Assume it's a game like war or gin rummy where you have a deck of cards and two players.
- Decide on appropriate classes. For each class, draw a UML class diagram and write in the class name.
- Look for composition relationships between classes. For each pair of classes related by composition, draw a compositional association line with appropriate multiplicity values.
- For each class, decide on appropriate instance variables.
- For each class, decide on appropriate public methods.
- Look for common instance variables and methods. If two or more classes contain a set of common instance variables and methods, provide a superclass and move the common instance variables and methods to the superclass. The classes originally containing common members now become subclasses of the superclass. For each subclass-superclass pair, draw an association line with an inheritance arrow from the subclass to the superclass to indicate an inheritance relationship.

Now go ahead and use the above guidelines to draw a UML class diagram for a generic card game program. Since this is a non-trivial exercise, you may be tempted to look at our solution before trying to come up with a solution on your own. Please resist that temptation! By implementing your own solution, you'll learn more and make yourself aware of potential problems.

Defining the Classes and the Relationships Between Them

Have you finished your class diagram? If so, then you may continue. . . .

In coming up with a class diagram, the first thing to do is to decide on the classes themselves. Unfortunately, that's a bit of an art. The easy classes are the ones that directly correspond to something you can see.

In visualizing a card game, can you see two people holding cards and taking additional cards from a deck that sits between them? You should be able to see a deck, two hands, individual cards, and two people. For the deck, use a `Deck` class. For the two hands, use a `Hand` class. For the individual cards, use a `Card` class. You may or may not wish to represent the people. If you're implementing an elaborate card game where players have personalities, use a `Person` class. Otherwise, there's no need for a `Person` class. Let's keep things simple and not implement a `Person` class.

In thinking about the big picture, you should ask yourself, "What is a game?" A game is a composition of several parts, so define `Game` as a whole class and define other classes as the parts of the game. A `Game` is composed of three components/parts—a deck and two hands. Thus, `Deck` and `Hand` are parts classes within the `Game` composition class. In Figure 12.17's class diagram, note the association line connecting `Game` to `Deck`. The association line has a solid diamond, which indicates composition, and it has 1-to-1 multiplicity values, which indicate each game has one deck. The `Game` to `Hand` association line also has a solid diamond for composition, but it has 1-to-2 multiplicity values, which indicate each game has two hands.

Coming up with the idea of using a `Game` class is probably more difficult than coming up with the ideas for using `Deck`, `Hand`, and `Card` classes. Why? A game is non-tactile (that is, you can't touch it), so it's hard to see it as a class. Why bother with having a `Game` class? If you omit the `Game` class, you could still implement a card game. Instead of declaring the deck and hand objects inside the `Game` class, you could declare them inside the `main` method. But it's more elegant to put them inside a `Game` class. Why? By putting them inside a `Game` class, it furthers the goal of encapsulation. Also, it enables `main` to be streamlined. As you'll

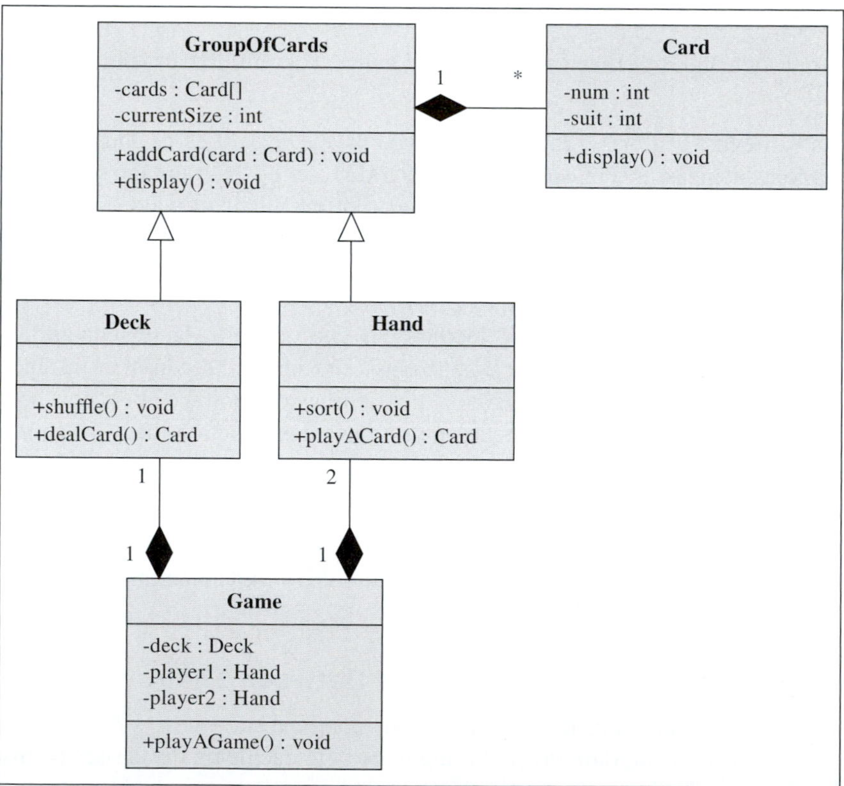

Figure 12.17 Preliminary class diagram for Card Game program

see later on, if you have defined a Game class, the driver's `main` method just needs to instantiate a `Game` object and then call `playAGame` and that's it. You can't get much more streamlined (and elegant) than that.

For each class in the Card Game program, what are its members (that is, instance variables and methods)? Let's tackle the easy classes first—`Game` and `Card`. The `Game` class needs three instance variables—one for the deck and two for the two hands. It needs a method for playing a game. The `Card` class needs two instance variables—one for a number (two through ace) and one for a suit (clubs through spades). It needs a method to display the card's number and suit values. As a sanity check, verify that Figure 12.17's `Game` and `Card` members match what we've described.

The `Deck` class needs an instance variable for an array of cards such that each card is a `Card` object. The `Deck` class also needs an instance variable to keep track of the current size of the deck. The `Deck` class needs methods for shuffling and dealing. To help with debugging, you should probably also include a method to display all the cards in the deck.

The `Hand` class needs instance variables for an array of cards and for a current-size value. It needs methods for displaying all the cards, adding a card to the hand, and playing a card from the hand. For most card games, you'd also want a method to sort the hand. Different card games would use different and/or additional `Hand` methods. We'll keep things simple and not worry about them.

The next step is to try to identify common members and move them to a superclass. The `Deck` and `Hand` classes have three common members—a `cards` array variable, a `currentSize` variable, and a `display` method. In moving those members to a superclass, what would be a good name for such a class? It should be something generic that can be used as the superclass for both `Deck` and `Hand`. `GroupOfCards` or just plain `Cards` both sound pretty good. Let's use `GroupOfCards`. In Figure 12.17's class diagram, note the inheritance association lines connecting `Deck` to `GroupOfCards` and `Hand` to `GroupOfCards`.

We've now examined the members in all five classes in the Card Game program, and we've examined the relationships between four of the classes—`Game`, `Deck`, `Hand`, and `GroupOfCards`. The last piece of the UML-class-diagram puzzle is the relationship between `GroupOfCards` and `Card`. Is it an is-a relationship or a has-a relationship? It's not an is-a relationship because it doesn't make sense to say that a group of cards is a card or a card is a group of cards. Instead, it's a has-a relationship because a group of cards has a card (a group of cards usually has more than one card, but that doesn't negate the has-a relationship). In Figure 12.17, note the has-a composition association line connecting `GroupOfCards` to `Card`. Figure 12.17 suggests implementing the composition as an array called `cards,` but it could be an `ArrrayList`

Note that Figure 12.17's label says "preliminary" class diagram. It's preliminary because for a decent-sized application, it's nearly impossible to get the class diagram 100% right on your first-cut attempt. When you're done coding and testing(!) your prototype program, you should go back and update your class diagram appropriately. The class diagram serves two purposes. Early in the design process, it helps organize ideas and it keeps everybody on the same page. In the post-implementation phase, it serves as documentation so interested parties can quickly get a handle on the application's organization.

Design is an iterative process.

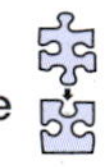

Inheritance Versus Composition

When deciding on the relationship between two classes, it's usually pretty clear whether to use inheritance or composition. For example, in the Dealership program, a `Manager` is a `Person`, so inheritance is used. In the Card Game program, a `Game` has a `Deck`, so composition is used.

However, sometimes it's not so clear-cut. For example, you could make the claim that a `Deck` is a `GroupOfCards`, and you could also make the claim that a `Deck` has a `GroupOfCards`. As a rule of thumb, in cases like this where the inheritance is-a relationship exists and the composition has-a relationship also exists, you're better off going with the inheritance relationship. To see why, we'll compare code for each of the two relationships. See Figure 12.18's `Deck` class, which implements the `Deck-GroupOfCards` relationship with inheritance.

```
public class Deck extends GroupOfCards
{
  public static final int TOTAL_CARDS = 52;

  public Deck()
  {
    for (int i=0; i<TOTAL_CARDS; i++)
    {
      addCard(new Card((2 + i%13), i/13));
    }
  } // end constructor
  ...

} // end class Deck
```

This implements inheritance.
With inheritance, there's no need to prefix the method call with an object reference.

Figure 12.18 Inheritance implementation for the `Deck` class

Also see Figure 12.19's alternative `Deck` class, which implements the `Deck-GroupOfCards` relationship with composition. We feel that Figure 12.18's inheritance code is more elegant than Figure 12.19's composition code. It has one less line, which is a good thing, but more importantly, it isn't cluttered with references to a `groupOfCards` variable. In the composition code, you're required to (1) declare a `groupOfCards` variable, (2) instantiate the `groupOfCards` variable, and (3) prefix the

```
public class Deck
{
  public static final int TOTAL_CARDS = 52;
  private GroupOfCards groupOfCards;

  public Deck()
  {
    groupOfCards = new GroupOfCards();

    for (int i=0; i<TOTAL_CARDS; i++)
    {
      groupOfCards.addCard(new Card((2 + i%13), i/13));
    }
  } // end constructor
  ...

} // end class Deck
```

With composition, declaring a GroupOfCards variable and instantiating it are required.
With composition, you must prefix the method call with an object reference.

Figure 12.19 Composition implementation for the `Deck` class

call to addCard with the groupOfCards calling object. Isn't the inheritance code nicer where you don't have to worry about all that? In particular, you can call addCard directly (no groupOfCards calling object required), and that results in more readable code. By the way, the addCard method is defined in the GroupOfCards class. With inheritance, the fact that it's in a separate class from Deck is transparent. In other words, you call it from the Deck constructor the same way that you would call any other Deck method—without a calling object.

For some class pairs (like Deck and GroupOfCards), it's legal to use either an inheritance or a composition relationship. But it's never OK to use both inheritance and composition for the same feature. What would happen if Deck declared a GroupOfCards local variable and Deck also inherited from a GroupOfCards class? Deck objects would then contain two separate groups of cards and that's wrong!

At this point, you might want to go back to Figure 12.17's preliminary UML class diagram and add some more detail. We didn't bother with constants or constructors in Figure 12.17's class diagram. In working with the Deck class skeleton (see Figure 12.18), it's now clear that there's a need to (1) add a TOTAL_CARDS constant to the Deck class, (2) add a constructor to the Deck class, and (3) add a constructor to the Card class. For practice we encourage you to update Figure 12.17's class diagram with these changes in mind. If you don't feel like it, that's OK; our main point here is to make you aware of the iterative nature of the program design process. Try to organize your thoughts as clearly as possible up front, but be prepared to adjust those thoughts later on.

Designing is a gradual process.

Code to Get You Started

Once you've finished with the card game's class diagram, normally the next step would be to implement the classes with Java code. We won't bother to show class implementation details, but we would like to show you how the suggested classes might be driven by a main method. Having followed proper OOP design guidelines, it's easy to produce an elegant main method—see Figure 12.20. Note how short and understandable the main method is. Yeah!

Another example will further illustrate how the finished classes might be used by the rest of the program. See main's call to playAGame in Figure 12.20. Figure 12.21 shows a partial implementation for the

```
public static void main(String[] args)
{
  Scanner stdIn = new Scanner(System.in);
  String again;
  Game game;

  do
  {
    game = new Game();
    game.playAGame();
    System.out.print("Play another game (y/n)?: ");
    again = stdIn.nextLine();
  } while (again.equals("y"));
} // end main
```

Figure 12.20 Card Game program's main method

`playAGame` method. To shuffle the deck, call `deck.shuffle()`. To deal a card to the first player, call `player1.addCard(deck.dealCard())`. How's that for straightforward?

```
public void playAGame()
{
  deck.shuffle();

  // Deal all the cards to the two players.
  while (deck.getCurrentSize() > 0)
  {
    player1.addCard(deck.dealCard());
    player2.addCard(deck.dealCard());
  }
  ...

} // end playAGame
```

Figure 12.21 Partial implementation for `Game` class's `playAGame` method

We'll leave it to you to finish this program. Two end-of-chapter exercises and a project suggest various elaborations.

12.11 Problem Solving with Association Classes (Optional)

Aggregation, composition, and inheritance implement some of the most common kinds of associations among classes and objects—a has-a association for aggregation and composition, and an is-a association for inheritance. Be aware that there are many other possible kinds of associations, which you can conjure up easily by rattling off a few verb phrases, like: "be next to. . . ," "get. . .from. . . ," "set. . .in. . . ," "make. . . with. . . ," run. . .toward. . . ," "sell. . .to. . . ," and so on. Typically, these other kinds of associations are more complicated than is-a or has-a associations. This section describes a powerful way to model other associations.

As you have seen, you can implement simple aggregation and composition associations by giving the container object a reference to each component object. This reference allows container object code to invoke component object methods. But for other kinds of associations, you may need multiple references and additional variables and methods. In other words, you may need a separate class just to describe the association. Such a class is called an *association class*. An association class defines an association object that represents a relationship among other objects. An association object is like an aggregation/composition container, in that it has instance variables that refer to other objects. But it's different in that the objects it refers to also refer to it, and each cannot contain the other. An association object typically receives references to the objects it associates when it is constructed. Whereas an aggregation/composition container contains its component objects, an association object just "knows about" the objects it associates.

Now let's see how this might apply to our previous Dealership program. What we've done so far with that program isn't much to brag about. We created a company with a sales manager, some sales people, and some cars. But what about customers? What about sales? Suppose we add a customer class to our Dealership program. Then suppose some eager salesperson finally makes a sale to that first customer. The next question is, where should we put the information about that sale? In the Dealership class? In the SalesPerson class (as we seem to be doing in Figure 12.6)? In the Car class? In the Customer class? Technically, we could put that information in any one of these classes, and then put references to that class in whatever classes need access to that information. We could also scatter the information around among the participating classes in some way. No matter which of these alternatives we picked, however, from some points of view, what we did would seem inappropriate.

A more elegant solution is to encapsulate all of the sale information into one association class, and give that class a name that describes the association. That's what we portray in Figure 12.22, which shows an abbreviated class diagram of another version of our previous Dealership program. First, look at the Customer class. Since a customer is a person, just like the sales manager and sales people, we can use inheritance to reduce code and avoid redundancy in the Customer class by making the Customer class extend the Person class. Second, look at the Sale class. The Sale class appears as just another component in the Dealership class diagram. The one-to-many multiplicity suggests that its objects are elements of an ArrayList, perhaps named sales, which is instantiated in an enhanced version of the Dealership constructor. As far as the dealership is concerned, a Sale would be just another type of aggregation or composition component, like a SalesPerson2 or a Car.

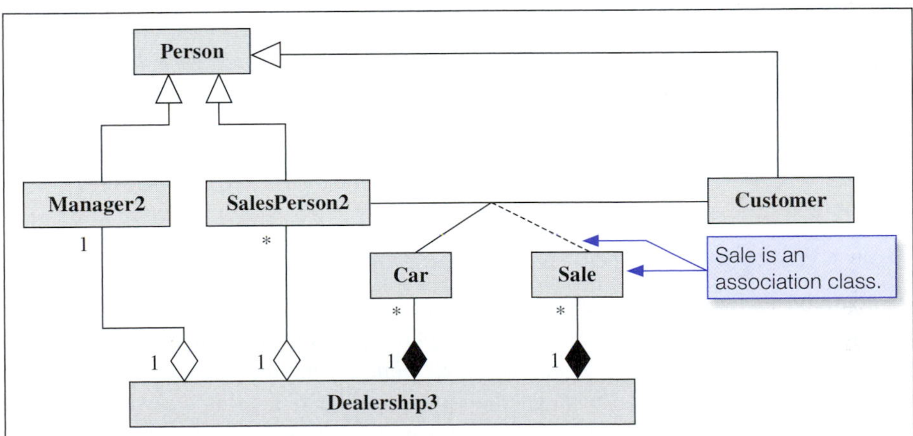

Figure 12.22 Class diagram for another car dealership program with customers and a salesperson-car-customer association

However, a sale is not a physical entity, like an organism or car is. It's a process—or event—that associates a group of entities. So the Sale class needs to be an association class. What types of objects participate in a Sale association? There's a Car, there's a SalesPerson2, and there's a Customer. Notice how the UML class diagram in Figure 12.22 uses simple solid association lines to interconnect all normal classes that participate in an association. The UML standard suggests ways to decorate these association lines with additional symbols and nomenclature, but just the lines shown convey the message—the idea of an association among objects of the Car, SalesPerson2, and Customer classes. The dashed line that connects the Sale class to the solid association lines graphically identifies the Sale class as an association class describing the related association. The code fragment in Figure 12.23 illustrates the Sale constructor.

```
// This class associates SalesPerson2, Car, and Customer classes

public class Sale
{
  private Car car;
  private SalesPerson2 salesperson;
  private Customer customer;
  private double price;
  ...

  //****************************************************************

  public Sale(Car car, SalesPerson2 person,
    Customer customer, double price)
  {
    this.car = car;
    this.salesperson = person;
    this.customer = customer;
    this.price = price;
    ...
  } // end constructor
  ...
```

references to classes being associated

references passed into constructor

Figure 12.23 Partial implementation of Sale class shown in Figure 12.22

Caveat—Don't Try to Inherit from an Association Participant

You might be tempted to try to use inheritance to create an association class, because you might think that would give you "free access" to at least one of the participants in the association. Don't try to do that. All you'd get would be the ability to make an enhanced clone of one of the objects you want to associate, and you'd have to copy all the details between the clone and the real thing—a waste of effort. Treat an association like an aggregation, with references to the participating objects passed into the association constructor.

Summary

- Object-oriented languages help you organize things and concepts into two basic kinds of hierarchies—a has-a hierarchy for components in an aggregation or composition, and an is-a hierarchy for types in an inheritance.
- An aggregation or composition hierarchy exists when one large object contains several smaller (component) objects.
- For a given whole-part class relationship, if the container contains the only reference to a component, the component association is composition. Otherwise, it's aggregation.
- In an inheritance hierarchy, subclasses inherit all the variables and methods of the superclasses above them, and they typically add more variables and methods to what they inherit.

- To minimize descriptive duplication, organize your ideas so that only the concepts at the very bottom of an inheritance hierarchy (the leaves of the upside-down tree) are specific enough to represent real objects.
- To enable class `B` to inherit all the variables and methods in class `A` and all of class `A`'s ancestors, append `extends A` to the end of class `B`'s heading.
- A constructor should initialize the variables it inherits by immediately calling its superclass's constructor with the statement: `super(`*<arguments>*`);`
- You can override an inherited method by writing a different version of the inherited method in the derived class. Overriding occurs automatically if you use the same method name and the same sequence of parameter types, but if you do this, you must also use the same `return` type.
- You can access an overridden method by prefixing the common method name with `super` and then a dot.
- A `final` access modifier on a method keeps that method from being overridden. A `final` access modifier on a class keeps that class from being extended.
- Programmers frequently use combinations of aggregation, composition, and inheritance to deal with different aspects of an overall programming problem. In a UML class diagram, both relationships are represented by solid lines between related classes, and these lines are called associations. In a composition/aggregation association, there is a solid/hollow diamond at the container end of each association line. In a hierarchical association, there is a hollow arrowhead at the superclass end of the association line.
- Inheritance allows you to re-use code that was written for another context.
- When you have a complicated association among objects, it may help to gather references to those objects together into a common association class.

Review Questions

§12.2 Composition and Aggregation

1. In a UML diagram, what does an asterisk (*) indicate?
2. In a UML diagram, what does a solid diamond indicate?

§12.3 Inheritance Overview

3. Explain how using an inheritance hierarchy can lead to code reusability.
4. What are two synonyms for a superclass?
5. What are two synonyms for a subclass?

§12.4 Implementation of `Person/Employee/FullTime` Hierarchy

6. How do you tell the compiler that a particular class is derived from another class?
7. Based on the UML diagram in Figure 12.9, an instance of the `PartTime` class includes the following instance variables: `name` and `id`. (T / F)

§12.5 Constructors in a Subclass

8. In a subclass's constructor, what do you have to do if you want to begin the constructor with a call to the superclass's zero-parameter constructor?

§12.6 Method Overriding

9. If a superclass and a subclass define methods having the same name and the same sequence of parameter types, and an object of the subclass calls the method without specifying which version, Java generates a runtime error. (T / F).

10. If a subclass method overrides a method in the superclass, is it still possible to call the method in the superclass from the subclass?
11. If a superclass declares a variable to be `private`, can you access it directly from a subclass?

§12.7 Using the `Person/Employee/FullTime` Hierarchy

12. If you wish to call a superclass method, you must always prefix the method name with `super.` (T / F)

§12.8 The `final` Access Modifier

13. A `final` method is called "final" because it's allowed to contain only named constants, not regular variables. (T / F)

§12.9 Using Inheritance with Aggregation and Composition

14. Composition and inheritance are alternative programming techniques for representing what is essentially the same kind of real-world relationship. (T / F).

§12.10 Design Practice with Card Game Example

15. A Deck is a group of cards and a Deck has a group of cards. In our example, it's better to choose the is-a relationship and implement inheritance. In this case, why is inheritance a better choice than composition?

§12.11 Problem Solving with Association Classes (Optional)

16. It's possible to support an association with references, variables, and methods in existing classes. What's the advantage of using an association class instead?

Exercises

1. [after §12.2] (This exercise should be used in combination with Exercises 2 and 3.) Write a definition for a `Point` class. Provide two `double` instance variables, `x` and `y`. Provide a two-parameter constructor that initializes `x` and `y`. Provide a `shiftRight` method that shifts the point in the x direction by the value of the method's `double` parameter, `shiftAmount`. Provide a `shiftUp` method that shifts the point in the y direction by the value of the method's `double` parameter, `shiftAmount`. Make each of these methods return values that enable chaining. Provide accessor methods to retrieve the values of the two instance variables.

2. [after §12.2] (This exercise should be used in conjunction with Exercise 1 and 3.) Write a definition for a `Rectangle` class. Provide two `Point` instance variables, `topLeft` and `bottomRight`, which establish the top left and bottom right corners of the rectangle, respectively. Provide a two-parameter constructor that initializes `topLeft` and `bottomRight`. Provide a `shiftRight` method that shifts the rectangle in the x direction by the value of the method's `double` parameter, `shiftAmount`. Provide a `shiftUp` method that shifts the rectangle in the y direction by the value of the method's `double` parameter, `shiftAmount`. Make each of these methods return values that enable chaining. Provide a `printCenter` method that displays the x and y values of the center of the rectangle.

3. [after §12.2] (This exercise should be used in conjunction with Exercise 1 and 2.) Write a definition for a `RectangleDriver` class with a `main` method to do the following: Instantiate a `Point` called `topLeft` at $x = -3.0$ and $y = 1.0$. Instantiate a `Point` called `bottomRight` at $x = 3.0$ and $y = -1.0$. Instantiate a `Rectangle` called `rectangle` using `topLeft` and `bottomRight` as arguments. Call `rectangle`'s `printCenter` method. Use a single chained statement to shift the rectangle right by one and then up by one. Call rectangle's printCenter method again. The output should be:

```
x = 0.0 y = 0.0
x = 1.0 y = 1.0
```

4. [after §12.3] Suppose you have three classes—`Shape` (which defines a shape's position in a coordinate system), `Square` (which defines a square's position in a coordinate system plus the square's width), and `Circle` (which defines a circle's position in a coordinate system plus the circle's radius). Assume that the three classes form an appropriate inheritance hierarchy with two inheritance relationships. For each of the two inheritance relationships, specify the superclass and subclass.

5. [after §12.3] Suppose you want to create a computer description of various kinds of energy sources, including the four classes: `Electrical`, `EnergySource`, `Heat`, `Mechanical`, and the six variables: `firstCost`, `fuelUsed`, `maxRevolutionsPerMinute`, `maxTemperature`, `powerOutput`, `volts`. Decide which class should get each variable, establish inheritance relationships, and draw a UML class diagram with class names, variable names, and inheritance arrows. (You may omit type specifications and methods.)

6. [after §12.4] Ellipse program:
Java's API classes make extensive use of inheritance. For example, Sun's Java API documentation shows that the `java.awt.geom.Ellipse2D` package has a class named `Double` that has these instance variables:[3]

`double`	`height` The overall height of the `Ellipse2D`.
`double`	`width` The overall width of this `Ellipse2D`.
`double`	`x` The x coordinate of the upper left corner of this `Ellipse2D`.
`double`	`y` The y coordinate of the upper left corner of this `Ellipse2D`.

And it has these constructors:

`Double()` Constructs a new `Ellipse2D`, initialized to location (0, 0) and size (0, 0).
`Double(double x, double y, double w, double h)` Constructs and initializes an `Ellipse2D` from the specified coordinates.

It has accessors for the instance variables, and an initializing method, but that's about all. Fortunately, this class `extends` a class called `Ellipse2D`, which has several other useful methods, including:

`boolean`	`contains(double x, double y)` Tests if a specified point is inside the boundary of this `Ellipse2D`.
`boolean`	`contains(double x, double y, double w, double h)` Tests if the interior of this `Ellipse2D` entirely contains the specified rectangular area.
`boolean`	`intersects(double x, double y, double w, double h)` Tests if the interior of this `Ellipse2D` intersects the interior of a specified rectangular area.

[3] These boxed descriptions were copied from Sun's Java API Web site (http://java.sun.com/javase/6/docs/api/).

Write a short program in a class called `EllipseDriver`:

Import `java.awt.geom.Ellipse2D.Double`, and write a `main` method that calls the 4-parameter `Double` constructor to instantiate an ellipse like that shown in the picture below.[4] Then, in `println` statements, call the superclass's 2-parameter `contains` method to show whether the points x=3.5, y=2.5 and x=4.0, y=3.0 are contained within the specified ellipse.

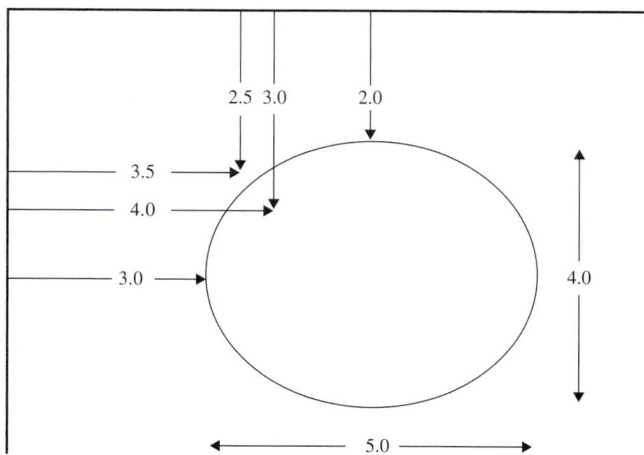

Output:

```
contains x=3.5, y=2.5? false
contains x=4.0, y=3.0? true
```

7. [after §12.5] Define a class named `Circle` that is derived from this API superclass:

```
java.awt.geom.Ellipse2D.Double
```

See Exercise 6 for a brief description of this `Double` superclass. Your subclass should declare the two `private` instance variables, `xCtr` and `yCtr`, initialized to `0.0`. These variables are the x- and y-coordinates of the circle's center. Your class should include a zero-parameter constructor, and it should also include a 3-parameter constructor whose parameters are the x- and y-distances to the circle's center and the circle's diameter. This 3-parameter constructor should not only initialize the new instance variables but also use the 4-parameter constructor of the superclass to initialize the four instance variables in the superclass. Your class should also provide the following accessor methods: `getXCtr`, `getYCtr`, and `getRadius`, where the radius is half the height of the superclass shape. Verify the code you write by compiling it and running it with representative values for x-center, y-center, and diameter.

8. [after §12.6] Suppose you have two classes related by inheritance that both contain a zero-parameter method named `doIt`. Here's the subclass's version of `doIt`:

```
public void doIt()
{
  System.out.println("In subclass's doIt method.");
  doIt();
} // end doIt
```

[4] The program does not actually draw the ellipse, but the `...Ellipse2D.Double` class has a mathematical understanding of it.

The `doIt();` call is an attempt to call the superclass's version of `doIt`.

a) Describe the problem that occurs when another method calls the above `doIt` method and the `doIt` method executes.

b) How should you fix the problem?

9. [after §12.8] What does it mean when you use the `final` modifier for a method?

10. [after §12.8] What does it mean when you use the `final` modifier for a class?

11. [after §12.9] Fill in the blanks:

If thing A "has a" thing B and "has a" thing C, there is a(n) ______ association, and A's class definition will contain declarations for ______ variables. If A "is a" special form of B, there is a(n) _____ association, and the right side of A's class heading will contain the words _____.

12. [after §12.9] Identification of type of association:

Given the following list of word pairs, for each word pair, identify the association between the two words. More specifically, identify whether the two words are related by composition or inheritance. To get you started, we've provided the answers to the first two word pairs. Bicycle and front wheel are related by composition because a bicycle "has a" front wheel. Bicycle and mountain bike are related by inheritance because a mountain bike "is a" bicycle.

		inheritance or composition?
bicycle	front wheel	composition
bicycle	mountain bike	inheritance
structural member	beam	_____
building	floor	_____
company	fixed assets	_____
employee	salesperson	_____
forest	tree	_____
bird	robin	_____
class	method	_____
neurosis	paranoia	_____

13. [after §12.10] Shuffling:

Suppose you are developing the Card Game program suggested by Figure 12.17 in the text. The following partial UML class diagram shows where you are in the developmental process:

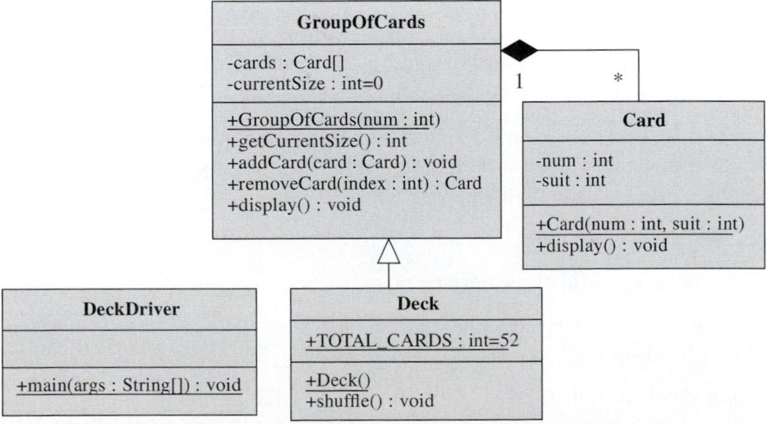

Assume you have written methods for a `Card` class and a `GroupOfCards` class. Assume that the `addCard` method increments `currentSize` after adding the input card to the end of the currently filled part of the `cards` array. Assume that the `removeCard` method retrieves a reference to the card at `index` in the `cards` array, decrements the `currentSize` of the cards array, shifts all array elements above `index` down by one place, and returns the reference to the card originally at `index`.

To shuffle the deck, use a `for` loop that starts with `unshuffled = getCurrentSize()` and steps down to one. In each iteration, use `Math.random` to pick an index in the unshuffled range, remove the card at that index, and then add it to the high end of the array. Include all that functionality in a `Deck.shuffle` method.

Extra credit:
Write Java code that tests your `shuffle` method. To do that, you'll need to implement all of the classes and methods in the above UML class diagram. Your `main` method should instantiate a `deck`, display it, shuffle it, and display it again.

14. [after §12.10] First part of `Game` class for game of Hearts:

The `Game` class introduced in the text contained a deck and exactly two players. Improve that `Game` class by including an array of type `Trick[]` and a `numberOfTricks` variable that keeps track of the number of tricks played so far. Include a `final` instance variable called `PLAYERS`, that will be initialized in a constructor whose parameter value is the number of players participating in the game. Replace the individual `player1` and `player2` instance variables by instances in an array of type `Hand[]`. Include two `boolean` instance variables, `hearts` and `queenOfSpades`, whose values switch from `false` to `true` whenever the first heart or the queen of spades is played.

Write Java code that defines that part of the `Game` class that includes the class heading, the instance variable declarations, and the one-parameter custom constructor whose parameter is the number of players. This constructor should instantiate a `Hand` array with a length equal to the number of players. It should instantiate individual `Hand` objects for each player, using a two-parameter `Hand` constructor. The first parameter is the player number, starting with 0. The second parameter is the maximum number of cards the player will receive, which depends on the total number of cards in the deck and the number of players. The game constructor should also instantiate a `Trick` array, but not populate it with any individual tricks.

Review Question Solutions

1. A * on a UML diagram means the multiplicity can be "any number."
2. In a UML diagram, a solid diamond is placed on an association line next to a containing class in a composition association. It indicates that the containing class exclusively contains the class that's at the other end of the association line.
3. Putting common code from two classes into a superclass is one example of code reusability. Code reusability can also take place when you want to add a significant chunk of functionality to an existing class, and you implement the solution with a new subclass.
4. Two synonyms for a superclass—parent class, base class.
5. Two synonyms for a subclass—child class, derived class.
6. To tell the compiler that a class is derived from another class, you write `extends` *<other-class>* at the end of your new class's heading line.
7. True. An instance of a subclass includes that class's instance variables and its ancestors' instance variables.

8. Nothing. This happens automatically. You can, however, preempt this by writing `super();` as the first line in your derived constructor.

9. False. There is no problem. The JVM selects the method in the subclass.

10. Yes. In the call statement, preface the common method name with `super.`

11. No. If a superclass's instance variable is `private`, you cannot access it directly from a subclass. You can access it by calling an accessor method (assuming the accessor is `public`). In calling the superclass's method, there's no need to prefix the method call with a reference dot.

12. False. The `super.` prefix is only necessary when you want to call a superclass method that has been overridden.

13. False. A `final` method is allowed to contain regular variables. It's called "final" because it's illegal to create an overriding version of the method in a subclass.

14. False. Composition and inheritance are completely different class relationships. Composition is when a class is comprised of non-trivial constituent parts and the parts are defined to be classes. Inheritance is when one class is a more detailed version of another class. More formally, inheritance is when one class, a subclass, inherits variables and methods from another class, a superclass.

15. Because with this example, there's a second class that is also a group of cards. Since there are two classes that share some of the same properties, you should put those common properties in a shared superclass, `GroupOfCards`. Doing this promotes software reuse and avoids code redundancy.

16. You can make a complicated association easier to recognize and understand by organizing the references to all association participants and other association information and methods in a single class that represents the association only.

CHAPTER 13

Inheritance and Polymorphism

Objectives

- Understand the role of the `Object` class.
- Learn why you need to redefine the `equals` and `toString` methods.
- Learn how polymorphism and dynamic binding improve program versatility.
- Understand what the compiler checks and what the JVM does when a reference variable is associated with a method name.
- Understand the constraints affecting assignment of an object of one class to a reference variable of another class.
- See how to use an array of ancestor reference variables to implement polymorphism among descendant methods.
- See how an `abstract` method declaration in an `abstract` superclass eliminates the need for a dummy method definition in the superclass.
- See how you can use an interface to specify common method headings, store common constants, and implement multiple polymorphisms.
- Learn where to use `protected` member access.
- Optionally, learn how to draw a three-dimensional object.

Outline

13.1 Introduction

This is the second of two chapters on inheritance. The previous chapter applied a broad brush stroke to fundamental inheritance concepts. In this chapter, we narrow the focus and describe several inheritance-related topics in depth. We start with the `Object` class, which is the provided-by-Sun superclass of all other classes. We then discuss one of the cornerstones of object-oriented programming (OOP)—polymorphism. *Polymorphism* is the ability for a particular method call to perform different operations at different times. It occurs when you have a reference variable that refers to different types of objects during the course of a program's execution. When the reference variable calls the polymorphic method, the reference variable's object type determines which method is called at that time. Pretty cool, eh? Polymorphism provides programs with a great deal of power and versatility.

After introducing polymorphism, we describe its partner, dynamic binding. *Dynamic binding* is the mechanism used by Java to implement polymorphism. We then provide alternative implementations of polymorphism, using `abstract` classes and interfaces to make coding cleaner and even more versatile. We then describe the `protected` modifier, which simplifies access to inherited code. Finally, in an optional section, we present a three-dimensional graphics problem that illustrates polymorphism with the Java API.

The material in this chapter is relatively difficult, but once you get it, you'll truly understand what OOP is about, and you'll know how to craft elegantly structured programs.

13.2 The `Object` Class and Automatic Type Promotion

The `Object` class is the ancestor of all other classes. It is the primordial ancestor—the root of the inheritance hierarchy. Any class that explicitly extends a superclass uses `extends` in its definition. Whenever anyone creates a new class that does not explicitly extend some other class, the compiler automatically makes it extend the `Object` class. Therefore, all classes eventually descend from the `Object` class. The `Object` class doesn't have many methods, but the ones it has are significant, because they are always inherited by all other classes. In the next two sections you'll see the `Object` class's two most important methods, `equals` and `toString`. Since any class you write automatically includes these two methods, you need to be aware of what happens when these methods are called.

Before diving into the details of these two methods, however, we want to make you aware of a Java process that's very similar to the numerical type promotion you studied in Chapter 3 and Chapter 11. There you saw that in the course of making an assignment or copying an argument into a parameter, the Java Virtual Machine (JVM) automatically promotes a numerical type—provided that the change conforms to a certain numerical hierarchy. For example, when an `int` value is assigned into a `double` variable, the JVM automatically promotes the `int` value to a `double` value.

An analogous automatic promotion also occurs with other types. When an assignment or argument passing operation involves different reference types, the JVM automatically promotes the source reference type to the target reference type if the target reference type is above the source reference type in the inheritance hierarchy. In particular, since the `Object` class is an ancestor of every other class, when the need arises, Java automatically promotes any class type to the `Object` type. The next section describes a situation that stimulates this kind of type promotion.

13.3 The equals Method

Syntax

The `Object` class's `equals` method—which is inherited automatically by all other classes—has this public interface:

```
public boolean equals(Object obj)
```

Because all classes automatically inherit this method, unless a similarly defined method takes precedence, any object, `objectA`, can invoke this method to compare itself with any other object, `objectB`, with a method call like this:

```
objectA.equals(objectB)
```

This method call returns a `boolean` value of either `true` or `false`. Notice that we did not specify the type of either `objectA` or `objectB`. In general, they can be instantiations of any class, and they do not need to be objects of the same class. The only constraint is that `objectA` must be a non-`null` reference. For example, if `Cat` and `Dog` classes exist, this code works correctly:

```
Cat cat = new Cat();
Dog dog = new Dog();

System.out.println(cat.equals(dog));
```

Output:

```
false
```

The `equals` method that is called here is the `equals` method which the `Cat` class automatically inherits from the `Object` class. The parameter in this inherited method is of type `Object`, as specified in the method's public interface above. But the `dog` argument we pass to this method is not of type `Object`. It is of type `Dog`. So what's happening? When we pass the `dog` reference into the inherited `equals` method, the reference type automatically promotes from type `Dog` to type `Object`. Then the inherited `equals` method performs an internal test to see if the passed in `dog` is the same as the calling `cat`. Of course it is not, so the output is `false`, as you can see.

Semantics

Notice that we just said, "performs an internal test." Now let's focus on that mysterious "internal test." How can you tell if two objects are the same or "equal"? When you say "`objectA` equals `objectB`," you could mean this:

1. `objectA` is just an alias for `objectB`, and both `objectA` and `objectB` refer to exactly the same object.

Or you could mean this:

2. `objectA` and `objectB` are two separate objects which have the same attributes.

The `equals` method that all classes inherit from the `Object` class implements the narrowest possible meaning of the word "equals." That is, this method returns `true` if and only if `objectA` and `objectB` refer to exactly the same object (definition 1. above). This meaning of "equals" is exactly the same as the meaning associated with the == operator when it is employed to test the equality of two reference variables. That operator also returns true if and only if both references refer to exactly the same object.

Suppose you have a Car class with three instance variables, make, year, and color, and you have a constructor that initializes these instance variables with corresponding argument values. Suppose this Car class does not define an equals method itself, and the only equals method it inherits is the one it inherits automatically from the Object class. The following code illustrates that the equals method inherited from the Object class does exactly the same thing as the == operator does.

```
Car car1 = new Car("Honda", 2008, "red");
Car car2 = car1;
Car car3 = new Car("Honda", 2008, "red");

System.out.println(car2 == car1);
System.out.println(car2.equals(car1));
System.out.println(car3 == car1);
System.out.println(car3.equals(car1));
```


Output:

```
true
true
false
false
```

This narrow sense of the word "equals" is not always what you want. For example, suppose your spouse decides to buy a new car and goes to a particular auto dealer and orders a red 2008 Honda as suggested by the above car1 instantiation. When you see the brochures your spouse brings home, you're impressed and decide you would like a new car for yourself too. You'd like it to be just like your spouse's car except for the color, which you want to be blue. So you go to the same dealer and say "I want the same car my spouse just ordered, but I want the color to be blue." A month later the dealer calls both you and your spouse at your separate places of work and says to each of you separately, "Your car is ready. Please come in to pick it up at 5:30 PM this afternoon." You both show up as requested, and the dealer takes you outside and proudly exclaims, "Here it is. How do you like it?" You say "Great, it's just like I wanted!" Then your spouse says, "But where is my car?" And the dealer replies, "But I thought you were to be joint owners of the same car, and your spouse told me to change the color of that car to blue." Oops, somebody made a mistake. . . .

The mistake occurred in the communication between you and the dealer when you said, "the same car." You meant the second meaning above: objectA and objectB are two separate objects which have the same attributes. But the dealer heard the first meaning above: objectA is just another name for objectB, and both objectA and objectB refer to exactly the same object.

Defining Your Own equals Method

Now let's see how you can implement the second meaning. To do so, include in your class an explicit version of an equals method that tests for equal attributes. Then, when your program runs, and an instance of your class calls the equals method, your equals method takes precedence over Object's equals method, and the JVM utilizes the equals method you defined. The equals method in Figure 13.1's Car class tests for equal attributes by comparing the values of all three instance variables, that is, the object's attributes. It returns true only if all three instance variables have the same values, and it returns false otherwise. Notice that this equals method includes two subordinate equals method calls—one made by the make

```
/*************************************************
* Car.java
* Dean & Dean
*
* This defines and compares cars.
*************************************************/

public class Car
{
  private String make;  // car's make
  private int year;     // car's listed year
  private String color; // car's color

  //**********************************************

  public Car(String make, int year, String color)
  {
    this.make = make;
    this.year = year;
    this.color = color;
  } // end Car constructor

  //**********************************************

  public boolean equals(Car otherCar)
  {
    return otherCar != null &&
           make.equals(otherCar.make) &&
           year == otherCar.year &&
           color.equals(otherCar.color);
  } // end equals
} // end class Car
```

This overrides the Object class's equals method.

Figure 13.1 Car class which defines equals to mean same instance variable values

instance variable and the other made by the color instance variable. As explained in Chapter 3, these calls to String's equals method check to see if two different strings have the same character sequence.

In the equal method's return expression, notice the otherCar != null subexpression. If this evaluates to false (indicating that otherCar is null), Java's short-circuit evaluation keeps the computer from trying to use a null reference to access the other car's make and color reference variables. Such short-circuit evaluation prevents runtime errors. You should always strive to make your code robust. In this case, that means you should consider the possibility of someone passing in a null value for otherCar. If null gets passed in and there's no test for null, the JVM generates a runtime error when it sees otherCar.make. This is a fairly common error—attempting to access a member from a null reference variable—and you can avoid it easily. Just test for null prior to accessing the member. For our equals method, if otherCar is null, then the otherCar != null subexpression is false, and the return statement returns false. Returning false is appropriate because a null otherCar is clearly not the same as the calling object Car.

Get in the habit of writing equals methods for most of your programmer-defined classes. Writing equals methods is usually straightforward since they tend to look the same. Feel free to use the Car class's equals method as a template.

Remember that any reference variable can call the equals method. even if the reference variable's class doesn't define an equals method. You know what happens in that case, right? When the JVM realizes that there's no local equals method, it looks for the equals method in an ancestor class. If it doesn't find an equals method prior to reaching the Object class at the top of the tree, it uses the Object class's equals method. This default operation often appears as a bug. To fix the bug, make sure that your classes implement their own equals methods.

equals Methods in API Classes

Note that equals methods are built into many API classes.[1] For example, the String class and the wrapper classes implement equals methods. As you'd expect, these equals methods test whether two references point to data that is identical (not whether two references point to the same object).

You've seen the String class's equals method before, so the following example should be fairly straightforward. It illustrates the difference between the == operator and the String class's equals method. What does this code fragment print?

```
String s1 = "hello";
String s2 = "he";

s2 += "llo";
if (s1 == s2)
{
  System.out.println("same object");
}
if (s1.equals(s2))
{
  System.out.println("same contents");
}
```

The above code fragment prints "same contents." Let's make sure you understand why. The == operator returns true only if the two reference variables being compared refer to the same object. In the first if statement, s1 == s2 returns false since s1 and s2 do not refer to the same object. In the second if statement, s1.equals(s2) returns true since the characters in the two compared strings are the same.

Actually, there's another twist to the String class. To minimize storage requirements, the Java compiler makes String references refer to the same String object whenever an assignment refers to a duplicate string literal, That's called *string pooling*. For example, suppose the above code included a third declaration that looked like this:

```
String s3 = "hello";
```

Then, if the if condition were (s1 == s3), the output would say "same object," because s1 and s3 would refer to the same "hello" string object.

[1] To get an idea of how common equals methods are, go to Sun's Java API Web site (http://java.sun.com/javase/6/docs/api/) and search for all occurrences of equals.

13.4 The toString Method

The Object Class's toString Method

Let's now consider another important method that all classes inherit from the Object class. The Object class's toString method returns a string that's a concatenation of the calling object's full class name, an @ sign, and a sequence of digits and letters. For example, consider this code fragment:

```
Object obj = new Object();
Car car = new Car();

System.out.println(obj.toString());
System.out.println(car.toString());
```

When executed, the code fragment produces this:

```
java.lang.Object@601BB1
Car@1BA34F2
```

full class name

These digits and letters form a hashcode.

Note how obj.toString() generates java.lang.Object for the full class name. The full class name consists of the class name prefixed by the package that the class is part of. The Object class is in the java.lang package, so its full class name is java.lang.Object. Note how car.toString() generates Car for the full class name. Since the Car class is not part of a package, its full class name is simply Car.

Note how obj.toString() generates 601BB1 for its *hashcode* value. You can think of an object's hashcode value as its location in memory, but it's really a bit more complicated than that. The JVM translates an object's hashcode value to one or more other values and the last value in the translation chain specifies the object's actual location in memory. In Java, hashcode values, like 601BB1, are written as hexadecimal numbers. We described the hexadecimal number system in the optional Unicode section at the end of Chapter 11. What follows is a review.

Hexadecimal Numbers

Hexadecimal numbers use digits that can have one of sixteen values—0, 1, 2, 3, 4, 5, 6, 7, 8, 9, A, B, C, D, E, and F (lowercase letters a through f are also acceptable). The A through F values represent the numbers 10 through 15. With 16 unique digits, hexadecimal numbers form what is known as a base-16 number system. With the number system that you are used to, base-10 for decimal numbers, suppose you're counting up and you get to the largest digit, 9. To form the next number, 10, you need two digits—a 1 at the left and a 0 at the right and the result is 10. Likewise, suppose you're counting up with hexadecimal numbers and you get to the largest digit, F for 15. To form the next number, 16, you need two digits—a 1 at the left and a zero at the right and the result is 10. In other words, 10 is how you write 16 in hexadecimal. For additional help with hexadecimal counting, see Appendix 1. In it, you'll see a sequence of hexadecimal numbers and their associated decimal numbers, in the context of the Unicode/ASCII character set.

You know that the hexadecimal number A is equivalent to the decimal number 10. What about the 601BB1 value generated by the previous code fragment—what is its equivalent decimal number? Converting large hexadecimal numbers to their decimal equivalents can be done mathematically, but we'll present a shortcut. If you're on a Windows-based computer, select Start / Programs / Accessories / Calculator. In the calculator window, click the Hex button, enter 601BB1, and then click the Dec button. The calculator displays 6298545, which is the decimal number equivalent to 601BB1. Thus, in the previous code fragment, when `obj.toString()` returns a string with 601BB1 at the right of the @ sign, it means the `obj` object's location in memory can be found by going to the 6,298,545[th] position in the object *hash table*. The object hash table is the entity in change of translating hashcode values into actual locations in memory.

Overriding the `toString` Method

Retrieving the class name, an @ sign, and a hashcode is usually worthless, so you'll almost always want to avoid calling the `Object` class's `toString` method and instead call an overriding `toString` method. The reason we're discussing the `Object` class's `toString` method is because it's easy to call it accidentally, and when that happens, we want you to understand what's going on.

Since the `Object` class defines a `toString` method, every class has a `toString` method, even if it does not define one or inherit one through some other class it explicitly `extends`. Many Java API classes define overriding `toString` methods. For example, the `String` class's `toString` method trivially returns the string that's stored in the `String` object. As described in Chapter 10, the `ArrayList` class's `toString` method (inherited from the `AbstractCollection` class) returns a square-bracketed comma-delimited list of strings that represent the individual array elements. The `Date` class's `toString` method returns a `Date` object's month, day, year, hour, and second values as a single concatenated string. In general, `toString` methods should return a string that describes the calling object's contents.

Since retrieving the contents of an object is such a common need, you should get in the habit of providing an explicit `toString` method for most of your programmer-defined classes. Typically, your `toString` methods should simply concatenate the calling object's stored data and return the resulting string. Your `toString` methods should not print the concatenated string value; they should just return it.  We're mentioning this point because novice programmers have a tendency to put print statements in their `toString` methods, and that's wrong. A method should do only what it's supposed to do and nothing more. The `toString` method is supposed to return a string value, and that's it!

For example, look at the `toString` method in the Car2 program in Figure 13.2. It returns a string that describes the calling object's contents.

Implicit `toString` Method Calls

In the Car2 program, the `main` method has no explicit `toString` method call. So how does this program illustrate use of the `toString` method? Whenever a reference appears alone inside a print statement (`System.out.print` or `system.out.println`), the JVM automatically calls the referenced object's `toString` method. In Figure 13.2, this statement generates a call to the `toString` method in the `Car2` class:

```
System.out.println(car);
```

Let's look at another example that uses the `toString` method. See the Counter program in Figure 13.3. Once again, there's a `toString` method and no explicit call to it. So how does it get called? When you concatenate a reference variable and a string (with the + operator), the JVM automatically calls the reference's `toString` method. Thus, in Figure 13.3, this statement's `counter` reference generates a call to the `Counter` class's `toString` method:

```
String message = "Current count = " + counter;
```

```
/*******************************************************
* Car2.java
* Dean & Dean
*
* This instantiates a car and displays its properties.
*******************************************************/

public class Car2
{
  private String make;  // car's make
  private int year;     // car's listed year
  private String color; // car's color

  //****************************************************

  public Car2(String make, int year, String color)
  {
    this.make = make;
    this.year = year;
    this.color = color;
  } // end Car2 constructor

  //****************************************************

  public String toString()
  {
    return "make = " + make + ", year = " + year +
      ", color = " + color;
  } // end toString

  //****************************************************

  public static void main(String[] args)
  {
    Car2 car = new Car2("Honda", 1998, "silver");
    System.out.println(car);
  } // end main
} // end class Car2
```

This overrides the `Object` class's `toString` method.

Figure 13.2 Car2 program that illustrates overriding `toString` method

Note that you'll often see the `toString` method explicitly called with the standard call syntax even when it's not necessary. For example, in the Counter program's `main` method, we might have used this alternative implementation for the `message` assignment statement:

```
String message = "Current count = " + counter.toString();
```

Some programmers would claim that this alternative implementation is better because the code is more self-documenting. Some programmers would claim that the original implementation is better because the code is more compact. We don't have a preference as to which implementation is better—either way is fine.

```
/****************************************************************
* Counter.java
* Dean & Dean
*
* This creates a counter and displays its count value.
****************************************************************/

public class Counter
{
  private int count;

  //*************************************************************

  public Counter(int count)
  {
    this.count = count;
  } // end constructor

  //*************************************************************

  public String toString()
  {
    return Integer.toString(count);
  } // end toString

  //*************************************************************

  public static void main(String[] args)
  {
    Counter counter = new Counter(100);
    String message = "Current count = " + counter;
    System.out.println(message);
  } // end main
} // end class Counter
```

This overrides the `Object` class's `toString` method.

Figure 13.3 Counter program that illustrates implicitly calling the `toString` method

Counter Program's `toString` Method—A Detailed Analysis

Let's revisit the `toString` method in Figure 13.3's Counter program. Since the `Counter` class contains only one piece of data, `count`, there's no need for concatenation code as part of the `toString` implementation. Just return `count`'s value and that's it. So this might have been your first-cut implementation for `toString`:

```
public int toString()
{
  return count;
}
```

But this produces a compile-time error. Do you know why? An overriding method must have the same return type as the method it's overriding. Since the Counter class's toString method is an overriding implementation of the Object class's toString method, the two methods must have the same return type. Since the Object class's return type is a String, the above int return type generates an error. With that in mind, this might have been your second-cut implementation for toString:

```
public String toString()
{
  return count;
}
```

But this also produces an error. Why? Incompatible types. The returned value, count, is an int, and the return type is defined to be a String. The solution is to convert count explicitly to a String before returning it, like this:

```
public String toString()
{
  return Integer.toString(count);
}
```

Do you understand the Integer.toString code? In Chapter 5, you learned that all primitive types have a corresponding wrapper class. Integer is one such class—it wraps up the int primitive. The Integer class's toString method returns a string representation of its passed-in int argument. So if count is 23, then Integer.toString(count) returns the string "23."

Quick quiz: Is the Integer class's toString method a class method or an instance method? Look at the method call's prefix. The method call, Integer.toString, uses a class name for the prefix. When a method call uses a class name for a prefix instead of a reference variable, you know the method is a class method. Thus, Integer's toString is a class method.

Note that all the wrapper classes have toString methods. They all do the same thing—they return a string representation of their passed-in argument. Here are some examples:

```
Double.toString(123.45)     : evaluates to string "123.45"
Character.toString('G')     : evaluates to string "G"
```

String's valueOf Method

There's another way to convert primitive variables to strings. Use the String class's valueOf method. This takes a primitive value, and returns a string. Like the wrapper toString methods described above, it's a class method, so you must use its class name, String, as a prefix. Thus, instead of the previous method calls, you could use these method calls:

```
String.valueOf(123.45)      : evaluates to string "123.45"
String.valueOf('G')         : evaluates to string "G"
```

The valueOf method is useful if you don't know the data type ahead of time. It works with different data types because it's an overloaded method, and the JVM automatically selects that particular method whose parameter type matches the type of the data provided.

In addition to converting primitives to strings, the valueOf method can also be used to convert an array of vowel characters to a string. This code fragment prints the string "aeiou":

```
Char[] vowels = {'a','e', 'i', 'o', 'u'};
System.out.print{String.valueOf(vowels));
```

13.5 Polymorphism and Dynamic Binding

Polymorphism Overview

If you ask an object-oriented programming (OOP) aficionado to name the three most important characteristics of OOP, he or she will probably answer "encapsulation, inheritance, and polymorphism." The previous chapter discussed encapsulation and inheritance. Now it's time to discuss *polymorphism*. The word polymorphism comes from the Greek for "having many forms." In chemistry and mineralogy, polymorphism is when a substance can crystallize in two or more alternative forms. In zoology, polymorphism is when a species has two or more different forms, like the different castes of bees spawned by the same queen to perform different functions in a beehive. In computer science, polymorphism is when different types of objects respond differently to the same method call.

Here's how it works. You declare a general type of reference variable that is able to refer to objects of different types. What is the most general type of reference variable? It's an `Object` reference variable, declared, for example, like this:

```
Object obj;
```

Once you have declared a reference variable of type `Object`, you can use it to refer to any type of object. For example, suppose you define a class named `Dog`, as in Figure 13.4, and another class named `Cat`, as in Figure 13.5. Each of the two derived classes contains a `toString` method that overrides the `toString` method in the `Object` class. Notice that the two `toString` methods shown override `Object`'s `toString` method in different ways. One returns what a dog says, "Woof! Woof!", and the other returns what a cat says, "Meow! Meow!"

The different `toString` method definitions in the `Dog` and `Cat` classes enable the `toString` method to be polymorphic. If you call `toString` with a reference to a `Dog` object, it responds the way a dog would respond, but if you call `toString` with a reference to a `Cat` object, it responds the way a cat would respond. The driver in Figure 13.6 demonstrates this effect. Notice how the `obj` reference variable can contain a reference to either a `Dog` object or a `Cat` object, and that object determines which `toString` method is called.

```
/****************************************
* Dog.java
* Dean & Dean
*
* This class implements a dog.
****************************************/

public class Dog
{
  public String toString()
  {
    return "Woof! Woof!";
  }
} // end Dog class
```

Figure 13.4 Dog class for Pets program driven by code in Figure 13.6

```
/*************************************
* Cat.java
* Dean & Dean
*
* This class implements a cat.
*************************************/

public class Cat
{
  public String toString()
  {
    return "Meow! Meow!";
  }
} // end Cat class
```

Figure 13.5 `Cat` class for Pets program driven by code in Figure 13.6

Why does the program print "Woof! Woof!" twice? There are two print statements. The first one explicitly calls a `toString` method. The second one uses an implicit call to a `toString` method—when a reference variable appears alone in a `String` context, the compiler automatically appends `.toString()` to the bare reference variable. So the last two statements in the `Pets` class are equivalent.

Dynamic Binding

The terms polymorphism and *dynamic binding* are intimately related, but they're not the same. It's helpful to know the difference. Polymorphism is a form of behavior. Dynamic binding is the mechanism for that behavior—how it's implemented. Specifically, polymorphism is when different types of objects respond differently to the exact same method call. Dynamic binding is what the JVM does in order to match up a polymorphic method call with a particular method.

Just before the JVM executes a method call, it determines the type of the method call's actual calling object. If the actual calling object is from class `X`, the JVM *binds* class `X`'s method to the method call. If the actual calling object is from class `Y`, the JVM binds class `Y`'s method to the method call. After the JVM binds the appropriate method to the method call, the JVM executes the bound method. For example, note the `obj.toString` method call in the following statement near the bottom of Figure 13.6:

```
System.out.println(obj.toString());
```

Depending on which type of object is referred to by `obj`, the JVM binds either `Dog`'s `toString` method or `Cat`'s `toString` method to the `obj.toString` method call. After binding takes place, the JVM executes the bound method and prints either "Woof! Woof!" or "Meow! Meow!"

Dynamic binding is referred to as "dynamic" because the JVM performs the binding operation while the program is running. The binding takes place at the latest possible moment, right before the method is executed. That's why dynamic binding is often referred to as *late binding*. By the way, some programming languages bind method calls at compile time rather than at runtime. That type of binding is called *static binding*. Java's designers decided to go with dynamic binding rather than static binding because dynamic binding facilitates polymorphism.

```
/*************************************************************
* Pets.java
* Dean & Dean
*
* This illustrates simple polymorphism.
*************************************************************/

import java.util.Scanner;

public class Pets
{
  public static void main(String[] args)
  {
    Scanner stdIn = new Scanner(System.in);
    Object obj;

    System.out.print("Which type of pet do you prefer?\n" +
      "Enter d for dogs or c for cats: ");
    if (stdIn.next().equals("d"))
    {
      obj = new Dog();
    }
    else
    {
      obj = new Cat();
    }
    System.out.println(obj.toString());
    System.out.println(obj);
  } // end main
} // end Pets class
```

The obj reference variable can contain a reference to either a Dog object or a Cat object.

That object determines which version of the toString method is called here.

These two statements are equivalent.

Sample session:

```
Which type of pet do you prefer?
Enter d for dogs or c for cats: d
Woof! Woof!
Woof! Woof!
```

Figure 13.6 Driver for Pets program that includes classes in Figures 13.4 and 13.5

Compilation Details

In the a Pets program, we illustrated polymorphic behavior by calling `Dog` and `Cat` versions of the `toString` method. Could we have done the same thing with `Dog` and `Cat` versions of a `display` method? In other words, if `Dog` implemented a display method that prints "I'm a dog," would the following code work?

```
Object obj = new Dog();
obj.display());
```

According to our dynamic binding discussion, the code would work just fine. The JVM would see a `Dog` object in the `obj` reference variable and bind the `Dog`'s `display` method to the `obj.display` method call. But it doesn't matter that the code works fine in terms of dynamic binding. The code won't compile successfully because the compiler senses there might be a problem.

When the compiler sees a method call, *<reference-variable>*.*<method-name>*`()`, it checks to see if the reference variable's class contains a method definition for the called method. Note the `obj.toString` and `obj.display` method calls in the examples below. In the left example, the compiler checks to see if `obj`'s class, `Object`, contains a `toString` method. The `Object` class does contain a `toString` method, so the code compiles successfully. In the right example, the compiler checks to see if `obj`'s class, `Object`, contains a `display` method. The `Object` class does not contain a `display` method, so the code produces a compile-time error.

```
Object obj = new Dog();
System.out.println(obj.toString());
```

legal

```
Object obj = new Dog();
obj.display();
```

compile-time error

Wait a second! Does this mean that polymorphism works only for the methods defined in the `Object` class? Fortunately, that's not the case. Later in this chapter, you'll learn how to make polymorphism work for any method.

The `instanceof` Operator

As you've seen, whenever a generic reference calls a polymorphic method, the JVM uses the type of the referenced object to decide which method to call. You might want to do a similar thing explicitly in your code. In particular, you might want to see if a referenced object is an instance of some particular class. You can do this with a special operator called the `instanceof` operator (note that the "o" in `instanceof` is lowercase). Using the Pets example again, suppose you want to print "Wags tail" if `obj`'s object is an instance of class `Dog` or any class descended from class `Dog`. You can do that with the `if` statement at the bottom of the `main` method in Figure 13.8. Thus, the `instanceof` operator provides a simple and direct way to sort out the various object types that might be referred to a by a generic reference variable.

13.6 Assignments Between Classes in a Class Hierarchy

Let's now look at something that's quite common with polymorphic programs—assigning an object to a reference where the object's class and the reference's class are different. In the following code fragment, assume that `Student` is a subclass of `Person`. What does this code fragment do?

```
Person p = new Student();
Student s = new Person();
```

This generates a compile-time error.

The first line assigns a `Student` object (actually a reference to a `Student` object) to a `Person` reference variable. It's assigning a subclass object to a superclass reference variable. That's a legal assignment because a `Student` "is a" `Person`. It's going up the inheritance hierarchy—the direction in which automatic type promotion occurs. The second line tries to assign a `Person` object to a `Student` reference variable. It's trying to assign a superclass object to a subclass reference variable. That's illegal because a `Person` is not necessarily a `Student`. The second line generates a compile-time error.

```
/*************************************************************
* Pets2.java
* Dean & Dean
*
* This illustrates use of instanceof operator.
*************************************************************/

import java.util.Scanner;

public class Pets2
{
  public static void main(String[] args)
  {
    Scanner stdIn = new Scanner(System.in);
    Object obj;

    System.out.print("Which type of pet do you prefer?\n" +
      "Enter d for dogs or c for cats: ");
    if (stdIn.next().equals("d"))
    {
      obj = new Dog();
    }
    else
    {
      obj = new Cat();
    }
    if (obj instanceof Dog)
    {
      System.out.println("Wag tail");
    }
  } // end main
} // end Pets2 class
```

This condition evaluates to `true` if the object referred to is an instance of the `Dog` class or a class descended from the `Dog` class.

Sample session:

```
Which type of pet do you prefer?
Enter d for dogs or c for cats: d
Wag tail
```

Figure 13.7 Demonstration of `instanceof` operator

The "is a" mnemonic can help you remember the rule, but if you're a Curious George,[2] you probably want more. You probably want to understand the true rationale behind the rule. So here goes. It's OK to assign a descendant-class object into an ancestor-class reference variable because all the compiler cares about is whether the assigned-in descendant-class object has all the members that any object of the reference variable's class should have. And if you assign a descendant-class object to a ancestor-class reference variable, it does. Why? Because descendant-class objects always inherit all ancestor-class members!

[2] Curious George is the main character in a series of books written by Margret and H. A. Rey. George is a curious monkey. Author John's toddler, Caiden, is a Curious-George wannabe.

As with primitives, if there is compatibility, you can go the other way by using a cast. In other words, you can use a cast to force an object referred to by a more generic reference variable into a more specific type—a type that's below it in the same inheritance hierarchy. For example, if `p` is a `Person` reference variable, and `Student` inherits from `Person`, the compiler will accept this:

```
Student s = (Student) p;
```

Although the compiler will accept this statement, that does not necessarily mean the program will run successfully. For successful execution, when dynamic binding occurs, the object actually referred to by the `p` reference variable must be at least as specific as a `Student`. That is, the referenced object must be either an instance of the `Student` class or an instance of a descendant of the `Student` class. Why? Because after the assignment of the reference to a `Student` reference variable, the object will be expected to have all of the members that a `Student` has, which is generally more than all the members a `Person` has.

13.7 Polymorphism with Arrays

So far, you've seen polymorphism in the context of code fragments and a simple Pets program. Those examples served their purpose—they illustrated the basics. But they didn't illustrate the real usefulness of polymorphism. The real usefulness of polymorphism comes when you have an array or `ArrayList` of generic reference variables and assign different types of objects to different elements. That allows you to step through the array or `ArrayList` and call a polymorphic method for each element. At runtime, the JVM uses dynamic binding to pick out the particular method that applies to each type of object found.

Polymorphism in an Explicit Inheritance Hierarchy

The Pets program used polymorphic `toString` methods for the `Dog` and `Cat` classes. The compiler accepted the `Object` reference variable with the `toString` method calls because the `Object` class defines its own `toString` method. Recall that polymorphism did not work for `Dog` and `Cat` `display` methods because the `Object` classs does not define its own `display` method. Suppose the method you want to make polymorphic is not defined in the `Object` classs. How can you have polymorphism and still satisfy the compiler? Actually, there are several related ways. One way is to create a superclass for the classes that define the different versions of the polymorphic method, and define the method within the superclass. Then use that superclass name when declaring the polymorphic reference variable(s). Another way to satisfy the compiler is to *declare the method* (specify the method heading only) in an `abstract` ancestor class and then use that ancestor class name for the reference variable type. Still another way to satisfy the compiler is to `implement` an *interface* that declares the method and then use that interface name for the reference variable type. We'll illustrate the first way in this section and the other two ways in subsequent sections.

Payroll Example

To illustrate polymorphism in an explicit inheritance hierarchy, we'll develop a payroll program that uses dynamic binding to select the appropriate method for calculating an employee's pay. Employees that happen to be salaried get dynamically bound to a `Salaried` class's `getPay` method. Employees that happen to be hourly get dynamically bound to an `Hourly` class's `getPay` method.

Let's start with the UML class diagram in Figure 13.8. It describes the Payroll program's class structure. As you can see, `Employee` is a superclass and `Salaried` and `Hourly` are subclasses. The fourth class, `Payroll`, is the program driver. Its `main` method drives the `Salaried` and `Hourly` classes by instantiating them and then calling their methods. What is the association between `Payroll` and the

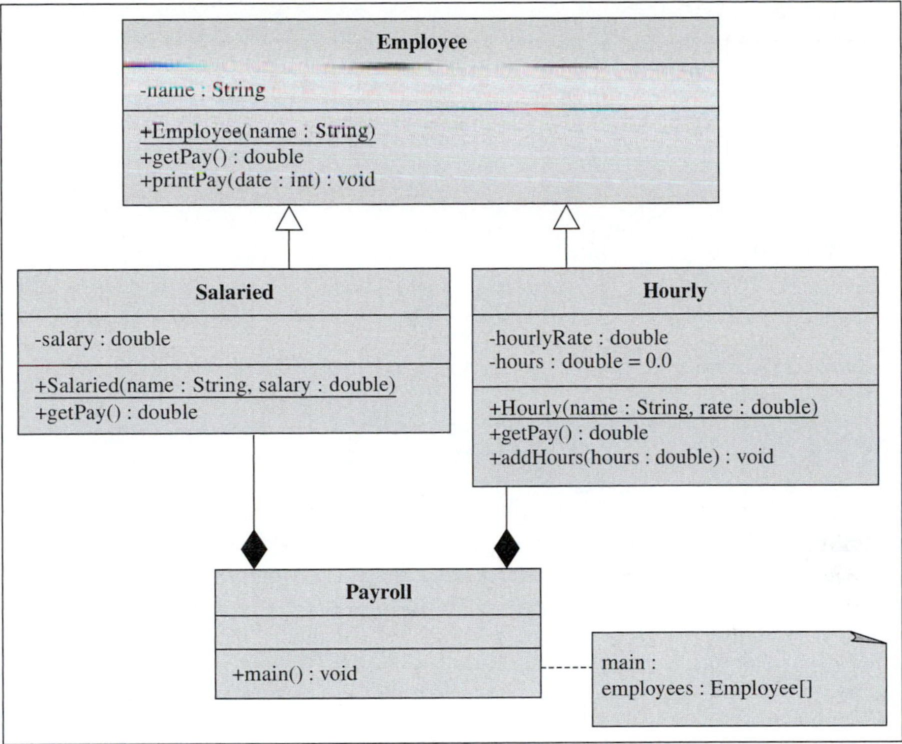

Figure 13.8 Class diagram for Payroll program

other classes—inheritance or composition/aggregation? The UML class diagram's diamonds indicate a composition/aggregation association between the `Payroll` container and the `Salaried` and `Hourly` components. That should make sense when you realize that the `Payroll` class "has a" heterogeneous array of `Salaried` and `Hourly` objects. Assuming the `Payroll` class has exclusive control over these objects, its association with them is a composition, and the diamonds should be solid.

Suppose Anna and Donovan are hourly employees paid at $25 per hour and $20 per hour, respectively, Simon is a salaried employee paid at $4,000 per month, and all three start work at the beginning of the month, which is a Tuesday. When the program runs, it should output the date of the month, the employee name, and the amount paid on the indicated date, like this:

Output:

```
 4      Anna:  800.00
 4   Donovan:  640.00
11      Anna: 1000.00
11   Donovan:  800.00
15     Simon: 2000.00
```

Let's begin implementation with the `main` method in the driver in Figure 13.9. Note `main`'s local variable, `employees`. It's declared to be a 100-element array of `Employee` objects. That's what it's declared as, but that's not exactly what it holds. As you can see from the assignment statements, the first three `employees` elements are an `Hourly`, a `Salaried`, and another `Hourly`. This is a heterogeneous array. All of the elements in the array are instances of classes derived from the array's class, and none of them is an instance

```
/*************************************************************
* Payroll.java
* Dean & Dean
*
* This class hires and pays employees.
*************************************************************/

public class Payroll
{
  public static void main(String[] args)
  {
    Employee[] employees = new Employee[100];
    Hourly hourly;
    employees[0] = new Hourly("Anna", 25.0);
    employees[1] = new Salaried("Simon", 48000);
    employees[2] = new Hourly("Donovan", 20.0);

    // This arbitrarily assumes that the payroll's month
    // starts on a Tuesday (day = 2), and it contains 30 days.
    for (int date=1,day=2; date<=15; date++,day++,day%=7)
    {
      for (int i=0;
        i<employees.length && employees[i] != null; i++)
      {
        if (day > 0 && day < 6
          && employees[i] instanceof Hourly)
        {
          hourly = (Hourly) employees[i];
          hourly.addHours(8);
        }
        if ((day == 5 && employees[i] instanceof Hourly) ||
          (date%15 == 0 && employees[i] instanceof Salaried))
        {
          employees[i].printPay(date);
        }
      } // end for i
    } // end for date
  } // end main
} // end class Payroll
```

This selects appropriate elements.

This casts elements into their native class.

This selects the appropriate time to print each different type.

Figure 13.9 Driver for simple Payroll program

of the `Employee` class itself. Even though there may be no instances of the array's class in the array, the array's type is the right type to use because it is able to accommodate instances of all classes descended from the array's class.

Continuing with the `main` method, the outer `for` loop steps through 30 days, keeping track of two variables. Notice how the first compartment in the `for` loop header declares more than one variable of the specified type. The `date` variable represents the date of the month. It determines when salaried employees are paid. For simplicity, this program assumes 30 days per month. If you want to learn how to get the actual number of days in each month, go to Sun's Java API Web site and read up on the `Calendar` class.[3] The `day` variable represents the day of the week. It determines when hourly employees are paid. Assuming that day 1 is a Monday, since the initial value of `day` is 2, the program's month starts on a Tuesday. Notice how the third compartment of the `for` loop header executes more than one operation. It increments both `date` and `day` and then uses `day%=7` to make the `day` variable roll over to 0 whenever it reaches 7.

The inner `for` loop steps through the heterogeneous array of employees. The for loop header's second component employs a compound continuation condition. The `i<employees.length` condition alone would allow looping through all 100 elements of the `employees` array. What's the point of the for loop header's `employees[i] != null` condition? The program instantiates only three objects for this array, and 97 elements still contain the default value of `null`. If the program tries to call a method with a `null` reference, it crashes. More specifically, it generates a `NullPointerException` error the first time it tries to use the `null` reference. The `employees[i] != null` condition avoids that by stopping the loop when it gets to the first `null` element.

Inside the inner `for` loop, the first `if` statement accumulates hours for hourly workers. It checks to see if `day` is a week day (not 0 or 6). It also checks to see if the object referenced by the current array element is an instance of the `Hourly` class. This enables the program to accumulate hours only during working days of the week and only for hourly workers. Once we know that the actual object is an instance of the `Hourly` class, it's safe to cast the generic reference into an `Hourly` reference. So we proceed to cast that reference into type `Hourly`, assign it to an `Hourly` reference variable, then use that specific type of reference variable to call the `addHours` method. Why did we jump through those hoops? Suppose we tried to call the `addHours` method with our generic reference in a statement like this:

```
employees[i].addHours(8);
```

The compiler would generate the error message:

```
cannot find symbol
symbol  : method addHours(int)
```

Because there is no `addHours` method in the `Employee` class, but there is one in the `Hourly` class, we must cast the array element explicitly into an `Hourly` type of reference and use that reference to call the method we need.

Now look at the second `if` statement in the inner `for` loop. Instead of accumulating hours, its purpose is generating output for a payroll report. This `if` statement executes if either of two or'd conditions is `true`. The first condition is `true` if it's Friday (`day` = 5) and if the calling object is an instance of the `Hourly` class. The second condition is `true` if it's the middle of the month and if the calling object is not an instance of the `Hourly` class. If either of these conditions is satisfied, the raw array element calls the method, like this:

```
employees[i].printPay(date);
```

This strategy wouldn't have worked with the `addHours` method in the first `if` statement, but it does work with the `printPay` method in the second `if` statement. Why? Look at the UML specification of the `Employee` class in Figure 13.8. This time, the method being called, `printPay`, is supposed to be defined in the array's class.

[3] Here's an example of how the last day in the current month can be found:

```
int lastDayInCurrentMonth =
  Calendar.getInstance().getActualMaximum(Calendar.DAY_OF_MONTH);
```

Now let's work on implementation of that printPay method in the Employee class. In Figure 13.10 note how printPay prints the date and the employee's name and then calls getPay. The getPay method is supposed to calculate an employee's pay. But the Employee class's getPay method simply returns 0.0. What's up with that? Are employees really paid nothing? Certainly not! The Employee class's getPay method is simply a dummy method that's never executed. The "real" getPay methods (i.e., the ones that are executed) are the overriding definitions in the Salaried and Hourly subclasses. These overriding definitions make the getPay method polymorphic! How does the JVM know to use those methods and not the dummy method in the Employee class? When it performs dynamic binding, the JVM looks at the method's calling object. For the getPay case, the calling object is an instance of either the Salaried class or the Hourly class. Can you see why?

```
/*************************************************
* Employee.java
* Dean & Dean
*
* This is a generic description of an employee.
*************************************************/

public class Employee
{
  private String name;

  //**********************************************

  public Employee(String name)
  {
    this.name = name;
  }

  //**********************************************

  public void printPay(int date)
  {
    System.out.printf("%2d %10s: %8.2f\n",
      date, name, getPay());
  } // end printPay

  //**********************************************

  // This dummy method satisfies the compiler.

  public double getPay()
  {
    System.out.println("error! in dummy");
    return 0.0;
  } // end getPay
} // end class Employee
```

Figure 13.10 Employee class

Go back to Figure 13.9's `main` method and note the assignment of an `Hourly` object into `employees[0]`. When `employees[i].printPay()` gets called with `i` equal to 0, the calling object is an `Hourly` object. Within the `printPay` method, when `getPay` is called, the calling object is still an `Hourly` object. Therefore, the JVM uses the `Hourly` class's `getPay` method. And that's what we want—the `employees[0]` object is an `Hourly`, so it uses the `Hourly` class's `getPay` method. The same argument can be applied to the `employees[1]` object. Since it's a `Salaried` object, it uses the `Salaried` class's `getPay` method. Thanks to polymorphism and dynamic binding, life is good.

The really cool thing about polymorphism and dynamic binding is being able to program generically. In the `main` method, we can call `printPay` for all the objects in the array and not worry about whether the object is an `Hourly` or a `Salaried`. We just assume that `printPay` works appropriately for each employee. This ability to program generically enables programmers to think about the big picture without getting bogged down in details.

In the `Employee` class, were you bothered by the dummy `getPay` method? Were you thinking "Why include a `getPay` method in the `Employee` class even though it's never executed?" It's needed because if there were no `getPay` method in the `Employee` class, the compiler would generate an error. Why? Because when the compiler sees a method call with no dot prefix, it checks to make sure that the method can be found within the current class. The `getPay()` method call (within the `printPay` method) has no dot prefix, so the compiler requires the `Employee` class to have a `getPay` method.

Now it's time to implement the "real" `getPay` methods. See Figures 13.11 and 13.12. The methods

```
/***********************************************************
* Salaried.java
* Dean & Dean
*
* This class implements a salaried employee.
***********************************************************/

public class Salaried extends Employee
{
  private double salary;      // per year

  //*******************************************************

  public Salaried(String name, double salary)
  {
    super(name);
    this.salary = salary;
  } // end constructor

  //*******************************************************

  public double getPay()
  {
    return this.salary / 24;  // per half month
  } // end getPay
} // end class Salaried
```

Figure 13.11 Salaried class

```
/*************************************************************
* Hourly.java
* Dean & Dean
*
* This class implements an employee paid by the hour.
*************************************************************/

public class Hourly extends Employee
{
  private double hourlyRate;
  private double hours = 0.0;

  //**********************************************************

  public Hourly(String name, double rate)
  {
    super(name);
    hourlyRate = rate;
  } // end constructor

  //**********************************************************

  public double getPay()
  {
    double pay = hourlyRate * hours;
    hours = 0.0;
    return pay;
  } // end getPay

  //**********************************************************

  public void addHours(double hours)
  {
    this.hours += hours;
  } // end addHours
} // end class Hourly
```

Figure 13.12 `Hourly` class

in these two classes are both simple, but they are different. To keep the JVM from selecting the dummy `getPay` method in the base class during dynamic binding, all derived classes should override that method.

13.8 `abstract` Methods and Classes

The dummy `getPay` method in Figure 13.10 is an example of a *kludge* (pronounced "klooj"). Kludgy code is ugly inelegant code that provides a workaround for a problem. Usually, inelegant code is hard to understand. And hard-to-understand code is hard to maintain. So try to avoid kludges. Sometimes that's not possible, but in this case we can indeed avoid the dummy-method kludge. Here's how. . . .

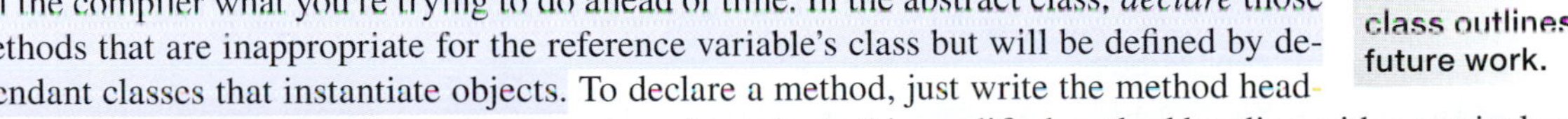

If you find yourself writing a dummy method that will be overridden by methods defined in all instantiable descendant classes, stop and reconsider. There's a better way. Use an *abstract class* to tell the compiler what you're trying to do ahead of time. In the abstract class, *declare* those methods that are inappropriate for the reference variable's class but will be defined by descendant classes that instantiate objects. To declare a method, just write the method heading with the additional modifier `abstract`, and terminate this modified method heading with a semicolon. For example, note the `abstract` modifier in the `Employee2` class heading in Figure 13.13.

An abstract class outlines future work.

An `abstract` declaration doesn't contain enough information to define the method. It just specifies its outside-world interface and says that definition(s) will exist somewhere else. Where? In all instantiable descendant classes! Using an `abstract` method avoids the inelegant dummy method definition, and it's a better way to implement polymorphism.

The `abstract` modifier is well named. Something is abstract if it is general in nature, not detailed in nature. An `abstract` method declaration is general in nature. It doesn't provide method details. It just serves notice that the method exists and that it must be fleshed out by "real" method definitions in all instantiable descendant classes. Have we followed this rule for our program? In other words, do we have

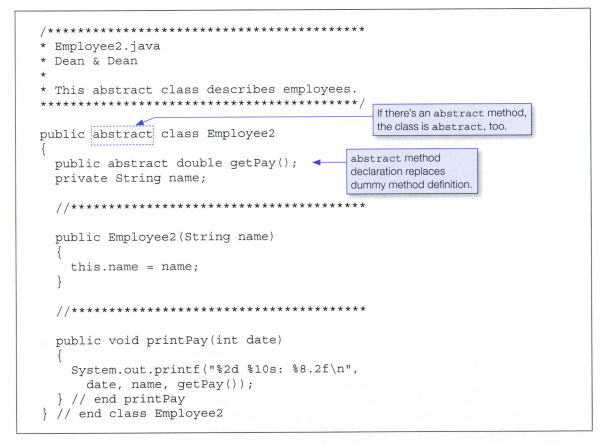

```
/*******************************************
* Employee2.java
* Dean & Dean
*
* This abstract class describes employees.
*******************************************/

public abstract class Employee2
{
  public abstract double getPay();
  private String name;

  //*****************************************

  public Employee2(String name)
  {
    this.name = name;
  }

  //*****************************************

  public void printPay(int date)
  {
    System.out.printf("%2d %10s: %8.2f\n",
      date, name, getPay());
  } // end printPay
} // end class Employee2
```

If there's an `abstract` method, the class is `abstract`, too.

`abstract` method declaration replaces dummy method definition.

Figure 13.13 `Employee2` class, using the `abstract` modifier to replace a dummy method definition with simpler method declaration

definitions of the `getPay` method in all of the `Employee2` descendant classes? Yes, the `Salaried` and `Hourly` classes in Figures 13.11 and 13.12 already contain the required `getPay` method definitions. However, we need to revise the `Salaried`, `Hourly`, and `Payroll` classes by making these replacements:

```
Employee → Employee2
Salaried → Salaried2
Hourly → Hourly2
Payroll → Payroll2
```

Then the `Salaried2`, `Hourly2`, and `Payroll2` classes will start out looking like this:

```
public class Salaried2 extends Employee2
{
  ...

public class Hourly2 extends Employee2
{
  ...

public class Payroll2
{
  public static void main(String[] args)
  {
    Employee2[] employees = new Employee2[100];
    ...
```

Here's another thing to note when declaring an `abstract` method. Since an `abstract` method declaration does not provide a definition for that method, the class definition is incomplete. Since the class definition is incomplete, it can't be used to construct objects. The compiler recognizes this and complains if you don't recognize it in your code. To satisfy the compiler, you must add an `abstract` modifier to the class heading whenever you have a class that contains one or more `abstract` methods. For example, note the `abstract` modifier in the `Employee2` class heading in Figure 13.13.

Adding an `abstract` modifier to a class heading makes it impossible to instantiate an object from that class. If a program attempts to instantiate an `abstract` class, the compiler generates an error. For example, since `Employee2` is an `abstract` class, we'd get a compilation error if we had a `main` method like this:

```
public static void main(String[] args)
{
  Employee2 emp = new Employee2("Benji");
}
```

Because `Employee2` is `abstract`, this generates a compilation error.

Sometimes you don't want a child class to define a method that was declared to be `abstract` in its parent. Instead you want to defer the method definition to the next generation. It's easy to do this. In the child class, just ignore that method and declare the child class `abstract` also (since at least that method is still undefined). You can defer method definitions like this as far as you want, provided you ultimately define them all in any non-abstract descendant class you use to instantiate objects.

We have said that if any method in a class is `abstract`, that class must be `abstract`. But this does not mean all methods in an `abstract` class must be `abstract`. It's frequently useful to include one or more non-abstract method definitions in an abstract class. Thus, classes descended from an abstract class can inherit non-abstract methods from that class and are not required to redefine those non-abstract methods.

Illegal to Use `private` or `final` with `abstract`

An `abstract` method declaration cannot be `private`, and the definitions of the method that appear in descendant classes cannot be `private` either. Why? An `abstract` method declaration provides a minimum kludge-free way for the compiler to accept a polymorphic method call. If a method is polymorphic, versions of it appear in more than one class, so at least one of the polymorphic methods is inevitably outside the class that calls it. You can't access an outside method that's `private`, and since all definitions of a polymorphic method must have identical outside-world interfaces, none of the polymorphic definitions can be `private`. Since the `abstract` declaration in the `abstract` ancestor class is supposed to describe correctly what the method is like to the outside world (and to the compiler), the access modifier that appears in the `abstract` declaration cannot be `private` either.

An `abstract` class or method cannot be `final`. The `final` modifier keeps a class from being extended and keeps a method from being overridden. But an `abstract` class is supposed to be extended and an `abstract` method is supposed to be overridden, so it's illegal to use `final` with `abstract`.

13.9 Interfaces

Java interfaces can do lots of different things, and one of those things is help implement polymorphism. But before we get into that, we'd like to mention a couple of other uses of a Java interface.

Using Interfaces to Standardize Inter-Class Communication

The most obvious use of a Java interface is what its name implies—to specify the headings for a set of methods that a class must implement. A Java interface is a contract between a program designer and program implementers that standardizes communication among different classes. This use of interfaces is essential to the success of large programming projects.

Establish communication protocols early.

Suppose, for example, that you are designing an accounting system, and you're currently focusing on "asset" accounts, which keep track of the value of things the company owns or has rights to. Typical asset accounts are: Cash, Accounts Receivable, Inventory, Furniture, Manufacturing Equipment, Vehicles, Buildings, and Land. These things are different from each other, so it would not be natural for classes representing them to be in a single inheritance hierarchy. Some of these accounts (Furniture, Manufacturing Equipment, Vehicles, and Buildings) describe long-term or "fixed" assets whose values depreciate gradually over time. Each year, an accountant prepares a set of financial statements, like the Balance Sheet and a Profit and Loss Statement. This preparation requires access to the objects representing the depreciating assets to get information like original cost, date of acquisition, and depreciation rate.

To facilitate this access, it would be nice to have references to these objects in a common array or `ArrayList`. Then a program could step through that array or `ArrayList` and call identically named polymorphic "get" methods to retrieve values of the `originalCost`, `acquisitionDate`, and `depreciationRate` instance variables in each object that represents a depreciating asset. Suppose that different programmers are writing the classes for different accounts. The best way to assure that all programmers are "reading from the same page" is to require that all the classes that access a certain set of data `implement` the same Java *interface*. In our accounting system example, the interface for the "get" methods that access `originalCost`, `acquisitionDate`, and `depreciationRate` instance variables might be called the `AssetAging` interface. The `AssetAging` interface would contain declarations/headings for its methods, but not definitions.

If a particular class includes a definition of all of the methods declared in some interface (like `AssetAging`), you can tell the world (and the Java compiler) that that class provides such definitions by appending an `implements` clause to its class heading, like this:

```
public <class-name> implements <interface-name>
{
  ...
```

For multiple interfaces, separate their names with commas, like this:

```
public <class-name> implements <interface-name1>, <interface-name2>, ...
{
  ...
```

For inheritance and an interface, do it like this:

```
public <class-name> extends <parent-class-name> implements <interface-name>
{
  ...
```

A given class can extend only one superclass, but it can `implement` any number of interfaces. A Java interface is like a "pure" `abstract` class. It's pure in that it never defines any methods. It's less versatile than an `abstract` class, however. It can't declare any `static` methods, it can't declare any variables, and it can't declare any instance constants. In other words, it provides only `public static final` named constants and only `public abstract` method declarations. Here's the syntax for an interface definition:

```
interface <interface-name>
{
  <type> <CONSTANT_NAME> = <value>;
  ...
  <return-type> <method-name>(<type> <parameter-name> ...);
  ...
}
```

You begin the definition of an interface with the keyword, `interface`, just like you begin the definition of a class with the keyword, `class`. You define named constants in an interface the same way you define named constants in a class, and you declare methods in an interface by appending a semicolon to the method headings. Note that the keyword `public` does not appear anywhere in our syntax template. You may include the `public` modifier, but it's not necessary, and it's standard practice to omit it, since it simply does not make sense for an interface or any of its components to be anything but `public`. Also note that the keyword `abstract` does not appear anywhere in our syntax template. You may include an `abstract` modifier in any method declaration, and you may include the `abstract` modifier in the interface heading, but again, it's not necessary, and it's standard practice to omit it, since it simply does not make sense to have an interface that is not completely `abstract`. Also note that the keyword `static` does not appear anywhere in our syntax template. It's understood that any constant is `static`, and it's understood that any method is not `static`. Finally, note that the keyword `final` does not appear in our syntax template. It's understood that all constants are `final`, and since no methods are defined, it's understood that any method declaration is not `final`.

Using an Interface to Store Universal Constants

In addition to telling the world that your class defines a certain minimum set of methods, implementing an interface also gives your class free access to all the named constants which that interface defines. Putting common named constants into an interface and then giving multiple classes access to those named constants by having them implement that interface is a handy way to provide easy access to a large set of common physical constants and/or empirical factors or constants. You avoid duplicate definitions of those constants, and you don't have to use a class-name dot prefix to access those constants. In principle, you could use an inheritance hierarchy to provide direct access to common constants, but that would be bad practice, because it would waste your one inheritance opportunity on nothing more than a bunch of constants. If you use an interface to do this, you're still free to use inheritance and/or additional interfaces for other purposes.

Using Interfaces to Implement Additional Polymorphisms

Now suppose you have already created an inheritance hierarchy, and you are already using it to implement some particular polymorphism, as we did in our Payroll program. Then suppose you want to add another polymorphism that doesn't fit the structure of the original inheritance hierarchy. For example, you might want a method to be polymorphic among only some of the classes in the original hierarchy, and/or you might want a polymorphism to include classes that are outside that hierarchy. A Java class cannot participate in more than one inheritance—it can extend only one other class. Thus, you cannot use `abstract` classes to support polymorphisms that span more than one inheritance hierarchy. But as the previous accounting system example suggests, you can span more than one inheritance hierarchy with a Java interface. And one of the principle reasons to use Java interfaces is to implement multiple polymorphisms.

Make it polymorphic without distorting inheritance.

To illustrate this, we'll enhance the previous Payroll program by adding two classes of commissioned employees.[4] One of those classes gets a "straight" commission. The other class gets a salary plus a commission. In either case, the commission is based on a common fixed percentage of sales. Figure 13.14 contains the code for an interface that defines this fixed percentage as a named constant and declares a method that must be defined in all classes that implement the interface.

Figure 13.15 shows the code for a `Commissioned` class, which describes a class of employees who work on a straight commission. The `Commissioned` class extends Figure 13.13's `Employee2` class. `Employee2` is an `abstract` class, and as such, the `Commissioned` subclass must define all of `Employee2`'s `abstract` methods. The only `abstract` method in the `Employee2` class is the `getPay` class, so the `Comissioned` class must define the `getPay` method, and yes, it does. This increases the total number of polymorphic `getPay` methods to three. In the `commissioned` class's heading, note the clause, `implements interface Commission`. This provides direct access to the `COMMISSION_RATE` named constant, which the `Commissioned` class's `getPay` method uses to do its job. When it implements the `Commission` interface, the `Commissioned` class also takes on an obligation. It must define all the methods declared in that interface. The only method declared in the `Commission` interface is the `addSales` method, and yes, the `Commissioned` class defines this method, too.

[4] See Appendix 7 for a complete UML diagram of the enhanced Payroll program developed in this subsection.

```
/*************************************************************
* Commission.java
* Dean & Dean
*
* This inteface specifies a common attribute
* and declares common behavior of commissioned employees.
*************************************************************/

interface Commission
{
  double COMMISSION_RATE = 0.10;

  void addSales(double sales);
} // end interface Commission
```

Figure 13.14 An interface for use with an enhanced version of the Payroll program

```
/*********************************************************************
* Commissioned.java
* Dean & Dean
*
* This class represents employees on straight commission.
*********************************************************************/

public class Commissioned extends Employee2 implements Commission
{
  private double sales = 0.0;

  //******************************************************************

  public Commissioned(String name)
  {
    super(name);
    this.sales = sales;
  } // end constructor

  //******************************************************************

  public void addSales(double sales)
  {
    this.sales += sales;
  } // end addSales

  //******************************************************************

  public double getPay()
  {
    double pay = COMMISSION_RATE * sales;

    sales = 0.0;
    return pay;
  } // end getPay
} // end class Commissioned
```

The interface requires this method definition.

The interface supplies this constant value.

Inheritance from an `abstract` class requires this method definition.

Figure 13.15 Class defining straight-commission employees in enhanced Payroll program

```
/*************************************************************
* SalariedAndCommissioned.java
* Dean & Dean
*
* This class represents salaried and commissioned employees.
*************************************************************/

public class SalariedAndCommissioned
  extends Salaried2 implements Commission
{
  private double sales;

  //**********************************************************

  public SalariedAndCommissioned(String name, double salary)
  {
    super(name, salary);
  } // end constructor

  //**********************************************************

  public void addSales(double sales)
  {
    this.sales += sales;
  } // end addSales

  //**********************************************************

  public double getPay()
  {
    double pay =
      super.getPay() + COMMISSION_RATE * sales;

    sales = 0.0;    // reset for next pay period
    return pay;
  } // end getPay
} // end class SalariedAndCommissioned
```

The interface requires this method definition.

The interface supplies this constant value.

This method overrides the method defined in the parent class.

Figure 13.16 Class defining salary-and-commission employees in enhanced Payroll program

Figure 13.16 shows the code for a `SalariedAndCommissioned` class. This class extends the `Salaried2` class. The `Salaried2` class is like the `Salaried` class in Figure 13.11, except for one difference: whereas the `Salaried` class `extends Employees`, the `Salaried2` class `extends Employee2`. The `SalariedAndCommissioned` class describes a class of employees that earn a salary and a commission. The `Salaried2`'s class defines a `getPay` method, so the compiler does not insist that the `SalariedAndCommissioned` class also define a `getPay` method, but logically we need to override `Salaried2 getPay` method. Notice how the overriding method uses the `super` prefix to call the method it overrides. This additional `getPay` method definition increases the total number of polymorphic `getPay` methods to four.

The `SalariedAndCommissioned` class also implements the `Commission` interface. This provides direct access to the `COMMISSION_RATE` named constant, which the `getPay` method uses to do its job. Because it implements the `Commission` interface, the `SalariedAndCommissioned` class must define all methods declared in that interface, and yes, it does define the `addSales` method.

To execute these additional classes, we need a `Payroll3` class like that shown in Figure 13.17. The `Payroll3` class adds two more objects (Glen and Carol) to the array. Then it uses those objects to call the `addSales` methods in the new classes. To make these method calls, we cast the array elements into the interface type. The compiler requires a cast because the `addSales` method does not appear in the

```
/*************************************************************
* Payroll3.java
* Dean & Dean
*
* This class hires and pays four different types of employees.
*************************************************************/

public class Payroll3
{
  public static void main(String[] args)
  {
    Employee2[] employees = new Employee2[100];
    Hourly2 hourly;
    employees[0] = new Hourly2("Anna", 25.0);
    employees[1] = new Salaried2("Simon", 48000);
    employees[2] = new Hourly2("Donovan", 20.0);
    employees[3] = new Commissioned("Glen");
    employees[4] = new SalariedAndCommissioned("Carol", 24000);

    ((Commission) employees[3]).addSales(15000);
    ((Commission) employees[4]).addSales(15000);

    // This arbitrarily assumes that the payroll's month
    // starts on a Tuesday (day = 2), and it contains 30 days.
    for (int date=1,day=2; date<=15; date++,day++,day%=7)
    {
      for (int i=0;
        i<employees.length && employees[i] != null; i++)
      {
        if (day > 0 && day < 6
          && employees[i] instanceof Hourly2)
        {
          hourly = (Hourly2) employees[i];
          hourly.addHours(8);
        }
        if ((day == 5 && employees[i] instanceof Hourly2) ||
          (date%15 == 0 &&
            (employees[i] instanceof Salaried2 ||
            employees[i] instanceof Commissioned)))
        {
          employees[i].printPay(date);
        }
      } // end for i
    } // end for date
  } // end main
} // end class Payroll3
```

Figure 13.17 Driver for third version of Payroll program

Employee2 class. Note that we need an extra set of parentheses surrounding the (Commission) cast operator and the calling object. We could have used more specific casts like this:

```
((Commissioned) employees[3]).addSales(15000);
((SalariedAndCommissioned) employees[4]).addSales(15000);
```

But it's more elegant to cast into the more generic Commission interface type and let the JVM select among the polymorphic alternatives as it does its dynamic binding. Using either type of casting, here's what the Payroll3 driver generates:

Output:

```
 4       Anna:     800.00
 4    Donovan:     640.00
11       Anna:    1000.00
11    Donovan:     800.00
15      Simon:    2000.00
15       Glen:    1500.00
15      Carol:    2500.00
```

In our coded examples, notice the similarity between the use of an interface name and the use of a class name! It's not possible to instantiate an interface because it's inherently abstract, but you can use it like any ordinary class to specify type. For example, you can declare an array of elements whose type is an interface name, you can populate that array with instances of classes that implement that interface, and then you can pull objects out of that array and cast them into any type (class or interface) that those objects conform to. The Payroll4 driver in Figure 13.18 and the subsequent output illustrate these possibilities.

The trick is to think about what the compiler needs and what the JVM does. For example, you can create an array of interface references because the elements in the array are just references, not instantiated objects. The compiler lets you populate that array with references to objects from classes that implement that interface because it knows those objects can call any method the interface declares. In a method call, the compiler lets you cast a reference into the type of any class that declares or defines any version of that method because it knows the JVM can find at least one method to bind. At runtime, the JVM selects the most appropriate method to bind.

13.10 The protected Access Modifier

So far, we've discussed only two modes of accessibility for a class's members—public and private; public members can be accessed from anywhere; private members can be accessed only from inside the members' class. There is another access modifier that is a limited form of the public access modifier—the protected access modifier. It specifies an accessibility that's between public and private. Members that are protected can be accessed only from within the same package[5] or from within the member's *subtree*. What's a subtree? It's a class hierarchy that consists of a class plus all of its descendant classes.

[5] If you want to learn more about packages and how to group your classes into a programmer-defined package, see Appendix 4.

```
/*************************************************************
* Payroll4.java
* Dean & Dean
*
* This class hires and pays employees some kind of commission.
*************************************************************/

public class Payroll4
{
  public static void main(String[] args)
  {
    Commission[] people = new Commission[100];

    people[0] = new Commissioned("Glen");
    people[1] = new SalariedAndCommissioned("Carol", 24000);

    people[0].addSales(15000);
    people[1].addSales(15000);
    for (int i=0; i<people.length && people[i] != null; i++)
    {
      ((Employee2) people[i]).printPay(15);
    }
  } // end main
} // end class Payroll4
```

Although you can't instantiate an interface itself, you can declare interface references.

The compiler accepts this cast because `Employee2` defines a `printPay` method, but the JVM binds the objects to methods in classes descended from `Employee2`.

Output:

```
15    Glen:   1500.00
15   Carol:   2500.00
```

Figure 13.18 Demonstration of class-like properties of an interface

When should you use the `protected` modifier? The general rule is that you should use it when you want easy access to a member, but you don't want to advertise it to the general public. In other words, you want it to have more exposure than a `private` member, but less exposure than a `public` member.[6] Hmmm . . . that's still kind of vague. Let's elaborate with an example.

Payroll Program with a `protected` Method

Suppose you want to enhance the Payroll program so that it includes calculation of FICA taxes (FICA stands for Federal Insurance Contribution Act, and it funds America's Social Security program). This tax calculation is best done in a separate method. Where should that method go? The only time this calculation will be done is when employees are paid. So, logically, it's a helper method called by the `getpay` method.

[6] Because a `protected` member can be accessed from any class descended from the class that defines the `protected` member, anyone could extend the class that defines the `protected` member and thereby gain direct access to it. In other words, the `protected` modifier doesn't actuallyprovide much protection. If you're an outsider, stay away from someone else's `protected` members. Consider them to be non-standard products that are not guaranteed.

Where is the `getPay` method? It's a polymorphic method that apperars in all classes that directly and indirectly extend the `Employee` class—`Commissioned`, `Salaried`, `Hourly`, and `SalariedAndCommissioned`. But hey! This set of classes together with the `Employee` class itself is the Employee subtree. So instead of repeating the definition of the FICA calculation in all classes that have a `getPay` method, it's more logical and more efficient to put this common calculation in the subtree's root class `Employee` and make it `protected`.

To avoid trampling on previous versions of the program, we use new class names in our new FICA enhanced Payroll program. See Figure 13.19. It shows the program's UML diagram with the new class names—`Payroll5`, `Employee3`, `Commissioned2`, `Salaried3`, `Hourly3`, and `SalariedAndCommissioned2`.

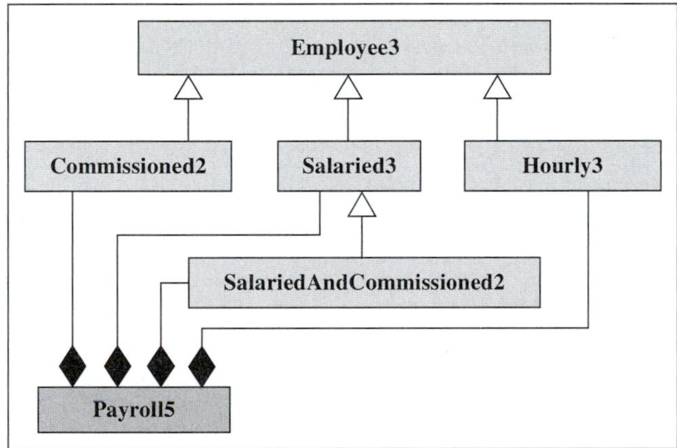

Figure 13.19 Abbreviated class diagram for an enhanced Payroll program

Figure 13.20 shows the definition of `Employee3`, which includes this additional common helper method, `getFICA`. `Employee3` also includes some named constants used in the FICA calculation. The details of this calculation are not relevant to the present discussion, so to save space, we implement it in a fairly cryptic form using the conditional operator. What this little `getFICA` method does is a reasonable representation of what actually happens to people's paychecks. So if you're curious, you might want to expand the cryptic code into a more readable form. (An end-of-chapter exercise asks you to do this.)

Each of the polymorphic `getPay` methods includes a call to this new `getFICA` method. The code for this call is essentially the same in each of the `getPay` methods, so we'll show it just once, in the `Salaried3` class in Figure 13.21.

For the most part, the `SalariedAndCommissioned2` class that extends the `Salaried3` class is like what's shown in Figure 13.16, with appropriate changes in the version numbers at the ends of the class names. However, in the `getPay` method we cannot use `super.getPay()` to access `salary` in the `Salaried3` class, because the FICA tax makes the value returned by `Salaried3`'s `getPay` method different from the value of `salary`.

With the FICA tax, there must be another way to access `salary`. Although `Salaried3` could include a `getSalary` accessor method, the code would be simpler if `salary` were `public`. But would you want everybody's salary to be `public`? The most appropriate thing to do here is to elevate the accessibility of the `salary` variable in the `Salaried3` class from `private` to `protected`. This gives descendant classes direct access to the `salary` variable, but it does not expose it as much as a `public` modifier would. Because the `SalariedAndCommissioned2` class `extends Salaried3`, if there is

```
/*************************************************************
* Employee3.java
* Dean & Dean
*
* This abstract class describes employees and it includes
* social-security tax calculation.
*************************************************************/

public abstract class Employee3
{
  public abstract double getPay();
  private String name;
  private final static double FICA_TAX_RATE = 0.08; // fraction
  private final static double FICA_MAX = 90000;     // dollars
  private double ytdIncome;        // total year-to-date income

  //***********************************************************

  public Employee3(String name)
  {
    this.name = name;
  }

  //***********************************************************

  public void printPay(int date)
  {
    System.out.printf("%2d %10s: %8.2f\n",
      date, name, getPay());
  } // end printPay

  //***********************************************************

  protected double getFICA(double pay)
  {
    double increment, tax;

    ytdIncome += pay;
    increment = FICA_MAX - ytdIncome;
    tax = FICA_TAX_RATE *
      (pay < increment ? pay : (increment > 0 ? increment : 0));
    return tax;
  } // end getFICA
} // end class Employee3
```

This limits accessibility to classes in subtree or in same package.

Figure 13.20 `Employee3` class which includes `protected getFICA` method

```
/*******************************************************
* Salaried3.java
* Dean & Dean
*
* This class represents salaried employees.
*******************************************************/

public class Salaried3 extends Employee3
{
  protected double salary;

  //*****************************************************

  public Salaried3(String name, double salary)
  {
    super(name);
    this.salary = salary;
  } // end constructor

  //*****************************************************

  public double getPay()
  {
    double pay = salary;

    pay -= getFICA(pay);
    return pay;
  } // end getPay
} // end class Salaried3
```

This allows direct access from descendant classes.

This calls protected method at top of subtree.

Figure 13.21 Enhanced version of Salaried class that includes tax deduction

a protected modifier on the salary variable in Salaried3, you can define the getPay method in the SalariedAndCommissioned2 class like this:

```
public double getPay()
{
  double pay = salary + COMMISSION_RATE * sales;

  pay -= getFICA(pay);
  sales = 0.0;    // reset for next pay period
  return pay;
} // end getPay
```

protected in Salaried3

protected in Employee3

So there you have it. Polymorphism enables you to put heterogeneous objects into generic arrays whose type is either a class the objects' classes descend from or an interface the objects' classes implement. Then you can cast array elements into subclass or interface types, so the array elements can make method calls that are specific to their subclass or interface. The JVM finds the method that best matches the calling object and executes that method. The `protected` modifier allows direct access to variables and methods from anywhere in the `protected` member's subtree.

13.11 GUI Track: Three-Dimensional Graphics (Optional)

Now that you know how inheritance and interface-based polymorphism work, you should be able to follow some of the subtleties that make graphical painting work. This section provides a typical illustration of polymorphism in Java API usage.

The Java API provides several classes which together enable you to draw and color many two-dimensional shapes. In addition, the `Graphics2D` class includes two methods (`draw3DRect` and `fill3DRect`) that enable you to portray a simple three-dimensional shape. They draw a rectangle with shading that makes it look like the rectangle is either raised slightly above the page or depressed slightly below the page. In Chapters 16 and 17 we'll show you how you can use these two methods to simulate an un-pressed or pressed button. But that's about the extent of the help you can get from the Java API in the creation of what appear to be three-dimensional images.

Portraying a general three-dimensional image in Java requires consideration of geometry and trigonometric calculations. In this section we'll give you a taste of this by portraying an arbitrarily oriented solid cylinder. Figure 13.22 shows a driver for a class that displays such an object. In the declarations section, the `JFrame` constructor instantiates a window called `frame`. The subsequent method calls, `setSize` and `setDefaultCloseOperation`, establish that window's size in pixels and what should happen when the user clicks the **x** box in its upper-right corner.

Now look at the two user prompts. This program uses a spherical coordinate system. In this kind of coordinate system, elevation is an angle that's like latitude. A zero elevation input says the cylinder should lie flat, with its axis pointing at the equator. A plus or minus 90 degree elevation input says the cylinder should stand up, with its axis pointing at either the north pole or the south pole. Azimuth is an angle that's like east longitude. With elevation at zero, a zero azimuth input says the cylinder axis should point right at the viewer. A positive azimuth input says it should point to the right, and a negative azimuth input says it should point to the left. The `Cylinder` constructor call instantiates the `Cylinder` object, and the subsequent `add` method call puts that object in the window. The `setVisible` method call makes the window's contents visible. Figure 13.23 shows the resulting display for the input $-15°$ elevation and $+60°$ azimuth angles.

The class that defines this shape and describes how to paint it appears in Figures 13.24a, 13.24b, and 13.24c. In Figure 13.24a, notice that our `Cylinder` class extends the `JPanel` class, which is imported from the Java API. The instance variables include the basic attributes of the object—its height (`cylH`) and diameter (`cylD`). These are pixel values, which are inherently integers, but we declare them to be `double`. Why do we use `double` instead of `int`? Three-dimensional graphics typically involves a considerable amount of calculation. Declaring variables to be `double` forces automatic promotion of any `int` factors that might appear in expressions. This keeps track of fractional information and provides the best possible visual display.

The other instance variables describe attributes of the displayed image—its orientation angles and its illumination extremes. For simplicity, the program uses "white" illumination, which contains identical values for red, green, and blue components. The `c1` and `c2` variables represent the intensity of these components for shaded and directly illuminated surfaces, respectively. The program declares these variables to be of type `float` because that's the type of the parameters in the Java API `Color` constructor. Zero corresponds to pitch black, and unity corresponds to pure white, so the specified `c1` and `c2` values correspond to two different shades of gray—the darkest and lightest shades seen on the curved sides of the cylinder in Figure 13.23.

```
/*************************************************************
* CylinderDriver.java
* Dean & Dean
*
* This drives the Cylinder class.
*************************************************************/

import java.util.Scanner;
import javax.swing.*;     // for JFrame and JPanel

public class CylinderDriver
{
  public static void main(String[] args)
  {
    Scanner stdIn = new Scanner(System.in);
    JFrame frame = new JFrame("Three-Dimensional Cylinder");
    Cylinder cylinder;
    double elev;     // cylinder axis elevation angle in degrees
    double azmuth;   // cylinder axis azmuth angle in degrees

    frame.setSize(600, 600);
    frame.setDefaultCloseOperation(JFrame.EXIT_ON_CLOSE);
    System.out.print("Enter axis elevation (-90 to +90): ");
    elev = stdIn.nextDouble();
    System.out.print("Enter axis azmuth (-90 to +90): ");
    azmuth = stdIn.nextDouble();
    cylinder = new Cylinder(elev, azmuth);
    frame.add(cylinder);
    frame.setVisible(true);
  } // end main
} // end CylinderDriver class
```

Sample session:

```
Enter axis elevation (-90 to +90): -15
Enter axis azmuth (-90 to +90): 60
```

Figure 13.22 Driver for `Cylinder` class in Figures 13.24a, 13.24b, and 13.24c

Note the `Cylinder` constructor in Figure 13.24a. This transforms the input elevation and azimuth angles from degrees to radians, and it also constrains the magnitudes of the input angles to less than 90 degrees. This avoids spurious results. It lets the user see only one end of the cylinder, but since the other end is the same, the program still portrays everything of interest.

Now look at Figure 13.24b. This contains the first part of a large `paintComponent` method. The JVM automatically calls the `paintComponent` method when the program first runs and whenever a user does something to alter the contents of the program's window. (For example, if a user maximizes a window, the JVM calls the program's `paintComponent` method.) The `paintComponent` method defined here overrides a `paintComponent` method defined in the `JComponent` class, which is the superclass of the `JPanel` class and therefore an ancestor of the `Cylinder` class. To ensure that graphical components

Figure 13.23 Three-dimensional portrayal of a solid cylinder

get painted properly, if you ever implement an overriding `paintComponent` method, you should always call the `paintComponent` method the superclass defines or inherits as the first line in your overriding `paintComponent` method. Here's the relevant code from Figure 13.24b:

```
super.paintComponent(g);
```

By definition, when a method overrides another method, the two methods must have the exact same signature (same name and same sequence of parameter types). Since the `PaintComponent` method in `JComponent` declares a `Graphics` object parameter, the `PaintComponent` method in `Cylinder` also declares a `Graphics` object parameter, named `g`. Even though `g` is declared as a `Graphics` object, the JVM actually passes a `Graphics2D` argument to the `g` parameter. That's a good thing because the `Cylinder` class relies on the `g` parameter to perform sophisticated graphics operations found only in the `Graphics2D` class. The `Graphics2D` class is a subclass of `Graphics`. As you may recall from ear-

```
/*****************************************************************
* Cylinder.java
* Dean & Dean
*
* This displays a cylinder illuminated from viewing direction.
*****************************************************************/

import javax.swing.JPanel;
import java.awt.*;              // for Graphics, Graphics2D, Color
import java.awt.Rectangle;
import java.awt.geom.*;         // for Ellipse2D and GeneralPath
import java.awt.GradientPaint;

public class Cylinder extends JPanel
{
  private double cylElev;      // cylinder axis elevation radians
  private double cylAzm;       // cylinder axis azimuth radians
  private double cylH = 400;   // cylinder height in pixels
  private double cylD = 200;   // cylinder diameter in pixels
  private float c1 = 0.3f;     // minimum illumination brightness
  private float c2 = 0.7f;     // maximum illumination brightness

  //**************************************************************

  public Cylinder(double elev, double azimuth)
  {
    cylElev = Math.toRadians(elev);
    if (Math.abs(cylElev) >= Math.PI / 2.0)
    {
      cylElev = Math.signum(cylElev) * Math.PI / 2.0001;
    }
    cylAzm = Math.toRadians(azimuth);
    if (Math.abs(cylAzm) >= Math.PI / 2.0)
    {
      cylAzm = Math.signum(cylAzm) * Math.PI / 2.0001;
    }
  }
```

inheritance from the API `JPanel` class

Figure 13.24a `Cylinder` class—part A

lier in the chapter, it's always legal to pass a descendant-class argument into a ancestor-class parameter. Also you may recall that to call descendant-class methods with the ancestor-class parameter, first you need to assign the ancestor-class parameter into a descendant-class variable. Here's the relevant code from Figure 13.24b:

```
Graphics2D g2d = (Graphics2D) g;
```

Notice that everything in Figure 13.24b is some kind of declaration. As before, the program uses `double` for the `MIDX` and `MIDY` pixel positions to preserve fractional information. For use later, it casts the incoming

```
//*************************************************************
public void paintComponent(Graphics g)
{
  super.paintComponent(g);
  final double MIDX = 0.5 * getWidth();
  final double MIDY = 0.5 * getHeight();
  Graphics2D g2d = (Graphics2D) g;
  double imageRotAngle;                 // image rotation angle
  GeneralPath shape;                    // curved cylinder side
  float c;                              // current color level

  // Apparent tipping of cylinder
  double tipCosine = Math.cos(cylAzm) * Math.cos(cylElev);
  double tipSine = Math.sqrt(1.0 - tipCosine * tipCosine);
  double frontEndAngle =
    Math.acos(tipCosine) * 2.0 / Math.PI;

  // Minor diameter of end ovals & apparent cylinder height
  double minorD = cylD * tipCosine;
  double apparentH = cylH * tipSine;

  // Shapes of curved sides and oval ends
  Rectangle rectangle = new Rectangle(
    (int) Math.round(MIDX - cylD / 2),
    (int) Math.round(MIDY - apparentH / 2),
    (int) Math.round(cylD),
    (int) Math.round(apparentH));
  Ellipse2D.Double frontEllipse = new Ellipse2D.Double(
    (int) Math.round(MIDX - cylD / 2),
    (int) Math.round(MIDY - apparentH / 2 - minorD / 2),
    (int) Math.round(cylD),
    (int) Math.round(minorD));
  Ellipse2D.Double backEllipse = new Ellipse2D.Double(
    (int) Math.round(MIDX - cylD / 2),
    (int) Math.round(MIDY + apparentH / 2 - minorD / 2),
    (int) Math.round(cylD),
    (int) Math.round(minorD));

  // Color for sides of cylinder
  GradientPaint gradientPaint = new GradientPaint(
    (float) (MIDX - cylD / 2), 0.0f, new Color(c1, c1, c1),
    (float) (MIDX), 0.0f, new Color(c2, c2, c2), true);
```

Passed in object's class must be in `Graphics2D` subtree.

Figure 13.24b `Cylinder` class—part B

`Graphics` parameter into a more specific `Graphics2D` reference. After declaring the working variables, `imageRotAngle`, `shape`, and `c`, it begins a sequence of initialized declarations. These declarations actually implement most of the method's calculations. Using declarations to implement sequential steps in a calculation provides self-documentation. It makes a long tedious calculation easier to understand by giving intermediate variables understandable names.

```
    // Rotate image from vertical around center
    if (cylElev == 0.0)
    {
      imageRotAngle =
        Math.signum(Math.sin(cylAzm)) * Math.PI / 2.0;
    }
    else
    {
      imageRotAngle =
        Math.atan(Math.sin(cylAzm) / Math.tan(cylElev));
      if (Math.tan(cylElev) < 0)
      {
        imageRotAngle += Math.PI;
      }
    }
    g2d.rotate(imageRotAngle, MIDX, MIDY);

    // Define and paint curved sides of cylinder
    shape = new GeneralPath(rectangle);
    shape.append(backEllipse, false);
    g2d.setPaint(gradientPaint);
    g2d.fill(shape);

    // Paint visible end of cylinder
    c = c2 - (float) ((c2 - c1) * frontEndAngle);
    g2d.setColor(new Color(c, c, c));
    g2d.fill(frontEllipse);
  } // end paint
} // end Cylinder class
```

Parameter type is `interface Shape`, which `Rectangle` implements.

Parameter type is `interface Paint`, which `GradientPaint` implements.

Figure 13.24c `Cylinder` class—part C

You can use your understanding of geometry and trigonometry to verify the calculation of the apparent angle, apparent cylinder height, and minor diameter of the elliptical ends of a cylinder that's oriented as the input specifies. The declarations under "// Shapes of curved sides and oval ends" use these values to define a rectangle and two ellipses. The `rectangle` and `backEllipse` objects will help configure the cylinder's sides in a `GeneralPath` object called `shape`, and the `frontEllipse` object will enable the program to paint the cylinder's visible end.

The last declaration in Figure 13.24b instantiates a `GradientPaint` object. This establishes a color gradation that makes the sides of the cylinder appear to be round. In the range between x = (`MIDX` − `clyD/2`) and x = (`MIDX`), this creates 16 narrow vertical stripes with color varying linearly from an intensity given by `c1` on the left to an intensity given by `c2` on the right. The `true` argument makes the method ramp the shading back down again in the range between x = (`MIDX`) and x = (`MIDX` + `clyD` / 2).

Notice that the rectangle and both ellipses are defined in a vertical orientation, but the cylinder in Figure 13.23 is not vertical! It is oriented at an angle sloping down and to the right. This requires a rotation. Now look at Figure 13.24c. The subordinate statement in the `else` part of the `if` statement computes the amount of rotation. The call to `Graphics2D`'s `rotate` method after the `else` clause tells the computer how to perform this rotation around the window's midpoint. But the rotation doesn't actually occur until after the object is painted.

The next step is instantiating a GeneralPath object and assigning it to the reference variable called shape. Initially this shape is nothing more than our previously defined rectangle. Then shape's append method adds the backEllipse component, so that shape now includes everything in either the rectangle or the back-side ellipse.

Before it actually paints, the program must specify the coloring scheme with a setPaint method call. The setPaint parameter must be a reference to an object that implements the Paint interface. If you look up the API documentation for the GradientPaint class, you'll see that, yes, it implements the Paint interface. Since our gradientPaint object is an instance of the GradientPaint class, and since the GradientPaint class implements the Paint interface, the program can call setPaint with a reference to the gradientPaint object as the argument. At this point, the program is ready to paint the sides of the cylinder with the fill(shape) method call. This tells the computer to perform the previously specified method of painting in the previously specified shape, and then rotate the result as previously specified.

The last three statements in the program paint the visible end of the cylinder. The first statement calculates intensity based on the angle of the visible end—using a lighter shade when we're looking directly at the end and a darker shade when we see it at a grazing angle. The setColor method call changes the paint mode from the previously established gradient painting to a flat gray having the just-computed intensity. The final fill(frontEllipse) method call tells the computer to paint the front ellipse shape and then rotate the result as previously specified.

Figure 13.24c contains several examples where API input parameter types are interfaces rather than classes. The GeneralPath constructor's parameter is of type Shape, where Shape is an interface. The object called rectangle conforms to this because its class, Rectangle, implements the Shape interface. The first parameter in GeneralPath's append method and the parameter in Grahpics2D's fill method are also of type Shape. The objects called backEllipse, shape and frontEllipse all conform because their classes, Ellipse2D and GeneralPath, both implement the Shape interface, too. Graphics2D's setPaint method receives a parameter of type Paint, where Paint is another interface. The object called gradientPaint conforms to this because its class, GradientPaint, implements the Paint interface. These are all polymorphic references!

Summary

- The Object class is the ancestor of all other classes.
- To avoid using the Object class's equals method, for each of your classes, you should define an equals method that compares instance variable values.
- To avoid the Object class's mysterious response to a toString method call, for each of your classes, you should define a toString method that outputs a string concatenation of instance variable values.
- At compile time, the compiler confirms that a reference variable's class is able to handle each of the reference variable's method calls in some way. At runtime, the JVM looks at the particular type of the object referred to by the reference variable to determine which one of several alternative polymorphic methods should actually be called, and it binds the object to that method.
- The instanceof operator enables you to determine explicitly whether the object referred to by a reference variable is an instance of a particular class or descended from that class.
- You can always assign an object to a more generic reference variable, because the object's methods include methods inherited from the reference variable's class.

- You can safely cast a more generic reference into a more specific type only if you know the actual object referred to will be as specific as or more specific than the cast.
- You can implement polymorphism in an array of heterogeneous objects by declaring the array elements to be instances of a common inheritance ancestor. To satisfy the compiler, you can write a dummy method in that ancestor class and override it in all classes instantiated in the array. Or you can declare the method in an `abstract` ancestor class and then define overriding methods in all descendant classes instantiated in the array. Or you can declare the method in an interface and implement that interface in all classes instantiated in the array.
- A class can extend one inherited superclass and/or implement any number of interfaces.
- An interface provides simple access to common constants.
- The `protected` access modifier provides direct access to members of classes in the same package or in the inheritance subtree whose root is the class in which the protected member is declared.
- With the aid of explicit trigonometric calculations, you can use Java API classes to draw what appear to be three-dimensional objects.

Review Questions

§13.2 The `Object` Class and Automatic Type Promotion

1. If you want a class you define to inherit methods from the `Object` class, you must append the suffix, `extends Object`, to your class's heading. (T / F)

§13.3 The `equals` Method

2. When used to compare reference variables, the == operator works the same as the `Object` class's `equals` method. (T / F)
3. What does the `equals` method defined in the `String` class compare?

§13.4 The `toString` Method

4. What is returned by the `Object` class's `toString` method?
5. What's wrong with replacing the `println` statement in Figure 13.2's `main` method with these two statements?

```
String description = car.toString();
System.out.println(description);
```

6. The return type of an overriding method must be the same as the return type of the overridden method. (T / F)

§13.5 Polymorphism and Dynamic Binding

7. In Java, polymorphic method calls are bound to method definitions at compile time (not runtime). (T / F)

§13.6 Assignments Between Objects in a Class Hierarchy

8. Assume one reference variable's class is descended from another reference variable's class. To be able to assign one reference variable to the other one (without using a cast operator), the left-side variable's class must be a(n) ____________ of the right-side reference variable's class.

§13.7 Polymorphism with Arrays

9. A given array may contain elements of varying type. (T / F)

§13.8 `abstract` Methods and Classes

10. What are the syntax features of an `abstract` method?
11. Any class that contains an `abstract` method must be declared to be an `abstract` class. (T / F)
12. You cannot instantiate an abstract class. (T / F)

§13.9 Interfaces

13. You can use an interface to provide direct access to a common set of constants from many different classes. (T/F)
14. You can declare reference variables to have an interface type and use them just like you would use reference variables declared to be the type of a class in an inheritance hierarchy. (T / F)

§13.10 The `protected` Access Modifier

15. Describe the access provided by the `protected` modifier.
16. It's illegal to use `private` for any method that overrides an abstract method. (T/F)

Exercises

1. [after §13.3] Write a `sameColorAs` method for the `Car` class in Figure 13.1. It should return `true` if the compared cars' colors are the same, regardless of their other attributes.
2. [after §13.4] Write the output produced by the program in Figure 13.2.
3. [after §13.4] What does the following program output? For each dog's output, describe how the output is generated (be specific).

```
public class Animal
{
  public static void main(String[] args)
  {
    Animal sparky = new Dog();
    Animal lassie = new Animal();

    System.out.println(
      "sparky = " + sparky + "\tlassie = " + lassie);
  } // end main
} // end Animal

class Dog extends Animal
{
  public String toString()
  {
    return "bark, bark";
  }
} // end class Dog
```

4 [after §13.4] What happens if you add an object of a class that does not define a `toString` method to an `ArrayList`, and then you try to print the `ArrayList`? (Assume the object's class is a programmer-defined class that does <u>not</u> have an `extends` phrase in its heading.)

5. [after §13.5] Why is dynamic binding often called *late binding*?
6. [after §13.6] Given: `Animal` = superclass, `Dog` = subclass.

Identify all compilation errors in this code fragment. Provide a compilation error message if you like, but it's not required.

```
Animal animal;
Dog fido, sparky = new Dog();
animal = sparky;
fido = new Animal();
```

7. [after §13.6] Suppose you have an object called `thing`, but you are not sure what type it is, and you would like to have your program print that type out. The `Object` class (and therefore any class!) has another method, `getClass`, that returns a special object of type `Class` that contains information about the class of the object calling the `getClass` method. The `Class` class has a method called `getName` which returns the name of the class described by its calling object. Write a statement that prints the name of `thing`'s class.

8. [after §13.7] Given: `Animal` = superclass, `Dog` = subclass, `Cat` = subclass.
In the following code fragment, the bottom two lines generate compile-time errors. Provide corrected versions of those two lines. Preserve the spirit of the original code. For example, the bottom line should assign the second `animals` element into the `fluffy` variable.

```
Animal[] animals = new Animal[20];
animals[0] = new Dog();
animals[1] = new Cat();
Dog lassie = animals[0];
Cat fluffy = animals[1];
```

9. [after §13.8] Each `abstract` method in a superclass must be overridden by a corresponding method in every non-`abstract` class descended from it. (T/F).

10. [after §13.8] Given the Pets3 program below, write an `abstract Animal2` class that contains just one item—an `abstract` declaration for a `speak` method. Write `Dog2` and `Cat2` classes that extend `Animal2`, so that when you run the Pets3 program and input either a 'c' or a 'd,' the program prints either "Meow! Meow!" or "Woof! Woof."

```
import java.util.Scanner;

public class Pets3
{
  public static void main(String[] args)
  {
    Scanner stdIn = new Scanner(System.in);
    Animal2 animal;

    System.out.print("Which type of pet do you prefer?\n" +
      "Enter c for cats or d for dogs: ");
    if (stdIn.nextLine().charAt(0) == 'c')
    {
      animal = new Cat2();
    }
    else
    {
      animal = new Dog2();
    }
    animal.speak();
  } // end main
} // end Pets3 class
```

11. [after §13.9] Rewrite the `Commission` interface shown in Figure 13.14 to explicitly show the `abstract`, `public`, `static`, and `final` modifiers in every place where they apply. (Your elaborated interface definition should compile.)

12. [after §13.9] Change the `Pets3` class in Exercise 10, above, as follows: Replace all instances of `Pets3` by `Pets4`, and replace `Animal2` by `Animal3`. Then, write an `Animal3` interface and `Dog3` and `Cat3` classes that implement `Animal3`, so that when you run the Pets4 program and input either a 'c' or a 'd,' the program prints either "Meow! Meow!" or "Woof! Woof."

13. [after §13.10] Expand the cryptic code in the `getFICA` method of the `Employee3` class in Figure 13.20 into "if else" statements so that the algorithm is easier to understand.

Review Question Solutions

1. False. Every class is a descendant of the `Object` class, so specifying `extends Object` is not necessary. In fact it is undesirable, because it prevents extension of some other class.
2. True.
3. The `equals` method defined in the `String` class compares a string's characters.
4. The `Object` class's `toString` method returns a string concatenation of these three text components:
   - full classname
   - @ character
   - a hexadecimal hashcode value
5. Nothing. It's just a matter of style—whether you want more compactness or more self-documentation.
6. True.
7. False. At runtime. The JVM determines which method is called.
8. To be able to assign one reference variable to the other one (without using a cast operator), the left-side variable's class must be a(n) superclass/ancestor of the right-side reference variable's class.
9. True, if each element's type is either the type defined in the array declaration or a descendant of that type (or conforms to the interface that defines the array's type—see Section 13.9).
10. The syntax features of an `abstract` method are:
    - The method heading contains the `abstract` modifier.
    - There is a semicolon at the end of the heading.
    - There is no method body.
11. True.
12. True.
13. True
14. True.
15. It is legal to access a `protected` member:
    - from within the same class as the `protected` member
    - from within a class descended from the `protected` member
    - from within the same `package`
16. True. An `abstract` method must be `public` or `protected` (it cannot be `private`). An overriding method must be no more restrictive than its overridden method. Therefore, if a method overrides an `abstract` method, it cannot be `private`.

CHAPTER 14

Exception Handling

Objectives

- Understand what an exception is.
- Use `try` and `catch` blocks for numeric input validation.
- Understand how `catch` blocks catch an exception.
- Explain the difference between checked and unchecked exceptions.
- Look up exception details on Sun's Java API Web site.
- Catch exceptions with the generic `Exception` class.
- Use the `getMessage` method.
- Catch exceptions with multiple `catch` blocks.
- Understand exception messages.
- Propagate exceptions back to the calling module with the help of a `throws` clause.

Outline

14.1 Introduction

As you know, programs sometimes generate errors. Compile-time errors deal with incorrect syntax, like forgetting parentheses around an `if` statement condition. Runtime errors deal with code that behaves inappropriately, like trying to divide by zero. In previous chapters, we fixed compile-time errors by correcting the erroneous syntax, and we fixed runtime errors by making code more robust. In this chapter, we deal with errors using a different technique—exception handling. We'll describe exceptions more formally later on, but for now, think of an exception as an error, or simply something that goes wrong with a program. Exception handling is an elegant way to deal with such problems.

We start this chapter by looking at a common problem—making sure that users enter a valid number when they are asked for a numeric input. You'll learn how to implement such input validation using `try` and `catch` blocks, two of the key exception handling constructs. There are different types of exceptions, and you'll learn how to deal with the different types appropriately. In the chapter's final section, you'll use exception handling as part of a GUI line-plot program.

To understand this chapter, you need to be familiar with object-oriented programming, arrays, and inheritance basics. As such, you need to have read up through Chapter 12. This chapter does not depend on material covered in Chapter 13.

We realize that readers may want to read different amounts of this chapter (*Exception Handling*) and the next chapter (*Files*). If you plan to read the next chapter, then you'll need to read this chapter in its entirety since the topic addressed in the next chapter, file manipulation, relies heavily on exception handling. On the other hand, if you plan to skip the next chapter and go directly to Chapters 16 and 17 (GUI programming), then you'll need to read only the first part of this chapter, Sections 14.1 through 14.7.

14.2 Overview of Exceptions and Exception Messages

As defined by Sun,[1] an *exception* is an event that disrupts the normal flow of instructions during the execution of a program. *Exception handling* is a technique for handling such exceptions gracefully.

The first exceptions we'll look at deal with invalid user input. Have you ever crashed a program (made it terminate ungracefully) due to invalid input? If a program calls the `Scanner` class's `nextInt` method and a user enters a non-integer, the Java Virtual Machine (JVM) generates an exception, displays a big, ugly error message, and terminates the program. Here's a sample session that illustrates what we're talking about:

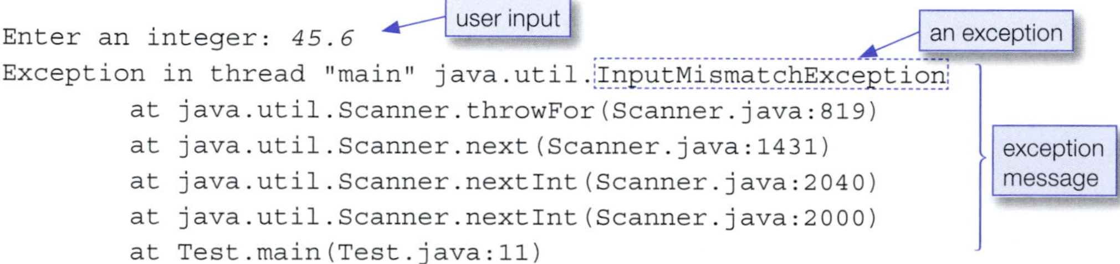

```
Enter an integer: 45.6
Exception in thread "main" java.util.InputMismatchException
        at java.util.Scanner.throwFor(Scanner.java:819)
        at java.util.Scanner.next(Scanner.java:1431)
        at java.util.Scanner.nextInt(Scanner.java:2040)
        at java.util.Scanner.nextInt(Scanner.java:2000)
        at Test.main(Test.java:11)
```


[1] Sun Microsystems, "The Java Tutorial, Handling Errors with Exceptions," which can be found on the Internet at http://java.sun.com/docs/books/tutorial/essential/exceptions/.

Note the `InputMismatchException` above. That's the type of exception that's generated when a user enters a non-integer in response to a `nextInt` method call. Note the *exception message*. Exception messages can be annoying, but they serve a useful purpose. They provide information about what's gone wrong. Toward the end of this chapter, we cover exception message details. But first a more important issue—how to avoid getting ugly exception messages in the first place. Let us begin.

14.3 Using `try` and `catch` Blocks to Handle "Dangerous" Method Calls

Some method calls, like `nextInt`, are dangerous in that they can lead to exceptions, and exceptions can lead to program crashes. By the way, "dangerous" is not a standard exception handling term, but we'll use it because it helps with explanations. In this section, we describe how to use `try` and `catch` blocks to fend off exception messages and program crashes. Use a `try` block to "try" out one or more dangerous method calls. If there's a problem with the dangerous method call(s), the JVM jumps to a `catch` block and the JVM executes the `catch` block's enclosed statements. Drawing an analogy, a `try` block is like a circus trapeze act. A trapeze act contains one or more dangerous stunts (e.g., a triple flip, a triple twist). The dangerous stunts are like dangerous method calls. If something goes wrong with one of the stunts and an acrobat falls, there's a net to catch the acrobat. Likewise, if something goes wrong with one of the dangerous method calls, control passes to a `catch` block. If nothing goes wrong with the trapeze stunts, the net isn't used at all. Likewise, if nothing goes wrong with the dangerous method calls, the `catch` block isn't used at all.

Syntax and Semantics

Here's the syntax for `try` and `catch blocks`:

```
try
{
  <statement(s)>
}
catch (<exception-class> <parameter>)
{
  <error-handling-code>
}
```

Normally, one or more of these statements will be a "dangerous" API method call or constructor call.

The exception class should match the type of exception that the `try` block might throw.

As shown above, a `try` block and its associated `catch` block (or multiple `catch` blocks, which we'll address later) must be contiguous. You can put other statements before the `try` block or after the (last) `catch` block, but not between them. Note the parameter in the `catch` block's heading. We'll explain `catch` block parameters in the context of the following example program.

See Figure 14.1's LuckyNumber program. Note how the `try` and `catch` blocks follow the syntax pattern shown above. Within the `try` block, the `nextInt` method call tries to convert a user entry to an integer. For the conversion to work, the user entry must contain only digits and an optional preceding minus sign. If the user entry conforms to that format, the JVM assigns the user entry to the `num` variable, skips the `catch` block, and continues with the code below the `catch` block. If the user entry does not conform to that format, an exception occurs. If an exception occurs, the JVM immediately exits from the `try` block and instantiates an *exception object*—an object that contains information about the exception event.

```
/*************************************************************
* LuckyNumber.java
* Dean & Dean
*
* This program reads the user's lucky number as an int.
*************************************************************/

import java.util.Scanner;
import java.util.InputMismatchException;

public class LuckyNumber
{
  public static void main(String[] args)
  {
    Scanner stdIn = new Scanner(System.in);
    int num; // lucky number
    try
    {
      System.out.print("Enter your lucky number (an integer): ");
      num = stdIn.nextInt();
    }
    catch (InputMismatchException e)
    {
      System.out.println(
        "Invalid entry. You'll be given a random lucky number.");
      num = (int) (Math.random() * 10) + 1;    // between 1-10
    }
    System.out.println("Your lucky number is " + num + ".");
  } // end main
} // end LuckyNumber class
```

Import `InputMismatchException` for use below.

The e parameter receives an `InputMismatchException` object.

Sample session 1:

```
Enter your lucky number (an integer): 27
Your lucky number is 27.
```

Sample session 2:

```
Enter your lucky number (an integer): 33.42
Invalid entry. You'll be given a random lucky number.
Your lucky number is 8.
```

Figure 14.1 LuckyNumber program that uses `try` and `catch` blocks for numeric user entry

In this example, the JVM instantiates an `InputMismatchException` object. The JVM then passes the `InputMismatchException` object to the `catch` block heading's `e` parameter. Since `e` is declared to be an `InputMismatchException` and `InputMismatchException` is not part of the core Java language, at the top of the program we need to include:

```
import java.util.InputMismatchException;
```

After passing the exception object to the catch block, the JVM executes the catch block's body. In this example, the catch block prints an "Invalid entry . . ." message and assigns a random number to the num variable. Then execution continues with the code below the catch block.

Throwing an Exception

When the JVM instantiates an exception object, we say that the JVM *throws an exception*. We'd prefer to say "throws an exception object" rather than "throws an exception" since the thing that's being thrown is an exception object. But most programmers don't worry about the difference between an exception, which is an event, and an exception object. No big deal. We'll go with the flow and use the standard terminology—throwing an exception.

When the JVM throws an exception, the JVM looks for a matching catch block. If it finds a matching catch block, it executes it. If it does not find a matching catch block, the JVM prints the exception object's exception message and terminates the program. What is a "matching catch block"? A catch block is "matching" if the catch heading's parameter type is the same as the type of the thrown exception.[2] For example, in the LuckyNumber program, the InputMismatchException parameter matches the InputMismatchException object thrown by the nextInt method call. So the InputMismatchException parameter's catch block is a matching catch block if and when the nextInt method call throws an InputMismatchException.

An exception object contains information about the error, including the error's type and a list of the method calls that led to the error. We'll use some of the exception object's information later on, but for now, all we need the exception object for is its ability to match up with the proper catch block.

14.4 Line Plot Example

Now let's see how try and catch are used in the context of a more complicated program. We start by presenting a program without try and catch blocks. Then we analyze the program and determine how it can be improved by adding try and catch blocks.

First-Cut LinePlot Program

The program in Figure 14.2 plots a line by reading in coordinate positions for a series of points. The best way to get a handle on what the LinePlot program does is to show a sample session. Below, the user chooses to plot a line that goes from the origin (the default starting point) to point (3,1) to point (5,2):

Sample session:

```
Enter x & y coordinates (q to quit): 3 1
New segment = (0,0)-(3,1)
Enter x & y coordinates (q to quit): 5 2
New segment = (3,1)-(5,2)
Enter x & y coordinates (q to quit): q
```

[2] Actually, as you'll see in Section 14.9, a catch block is also considered matching if the catch heading's parameter type is a superclass of the thrown exception's class.

```
/*******************************************************************
* LinePlot.java
* Dean & Dean
*
* This program plots a line as a series of user-specified
* line segments.
*******************************************************************/

import java.util.Scanner;

public class LinePlot
{
  private int oldX = 0;  // oldX and oldY save previous point
  private int oldY = 0;  // starting point is the origin (0,0)

  //****************************************************************

  // This method prints description of a line segment from the
  // previous point to the current point.

  public void plotSegment(int x, int y)
  {
    System.out.println("New segment = (" + oldX + "," + oldY +
      ")-(" + x + "," + y + ")");
    oldX = x;
    oldY = y;
  } // end plotSegment

  //****************************************************************

  public static void main(String[] args)
  {
    Scanner stdIn = new Scanner(System.in);
    LinePlot line = new LinePlot();
    String xStr, yStr;   // coordinates for point in String form
    int x, y;            // coordinates for point

    System.out.print("Enter x & y coordinates (q to quit): ");
    xStr = stdIn.next();
    while (!xStr.equalsIgnoreCase("q"))
    {
      yStr = stdIn.next();
      x = Integer.parseInt(xStr);
      y = Integer.parseInt(yStr);
      line.plotSegment(x, y);
      System.out.print("Enter x & y coordinates (q to quit): ");
      xStr = stdIn.next();
    } // end while
  } // end main
} // end class LinePlot
```

These could generate runtime errors.

Figure 14.2 LinePlot program that plots a line—first draft

As you can see, the program's display is very primitive—it uses text to represent each line segment. In a real line-plotting program, you'd use Java's `lineDraw` method to display the line. That's what we do in the GUI section at the end of this chapter. But for now, we'll keep it simple and use a text-based display rather than a GUI-based display. That way, we can maintain focus on this chapter's primary topic, exception handling.

Using "q" as a Sentinel Value

In the past, when you entered numbers inside a loop, you often terminated the loop with a numeric sentinel value. This program employs a more elegant solution because it allows a non-numeric "q" as the sentinel value. How can you read in numbers and the string "q" with the same input statement? Use strings for both types of input—for the "q" and also for the numbers. For each number input, the program converts the number string to a number by calling the `Integer` class's `parseInt` method.

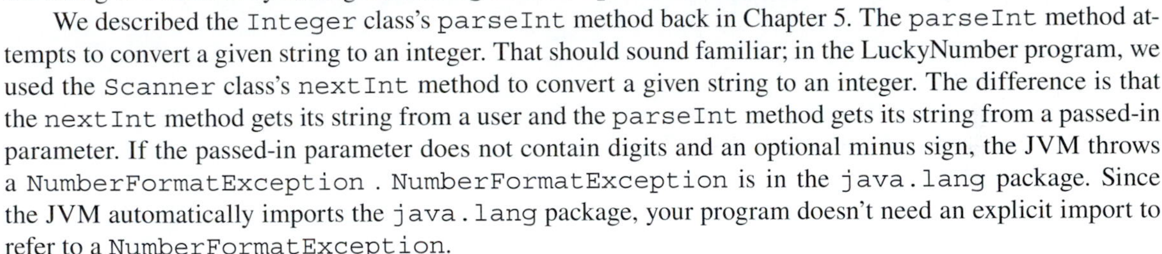

We described the `Integer` class's `parseInt` method back in Chapter 5. The `parseInt` method attempts to convert a given string to an integer. That should sound familiar; in the LuckyNumber program, we used the `Scanner` class's `nextInt` method to convert a given string to an integer. The difference is that the `nextInt` method gets its string from a user and the `parseInt` method gets its string from a passed-in parameter. If the passed-in parameter does not contain digits and an optional minus sign, the JVM throws a `NumberFormatException` . `NumberFormatException` is in the `java.lang` package. Since the JVM automatically imports the `java.lang` package, your program doesn't need an explicit import to refer to a `NumberFormatException`.

Input Validation

Note how the LinePlot program calls `stdIn.next` to read x coordinate and y coordinate values into `xStr` and `yStr`, respectively. Then the program attempts to convert `xStr` and `yStr` to integers by calling `Integer.parseInt`. The conversions work fine as long as `xStr` and `yStr` contain digits and an optional minus sign. But what happens if the user enters a non-integer for `xStr` or `yStr`? With invalid input, the program crashes, like this:

<u>Sample session</u>:

```
Enter x & y coordinates (q to quit): 3 1.25
Exception in thread "main" java.lang.NumberFormatException: For
input string: "1.25"
...
```

To deal with this possibility, let's rewrite the `while` loop in the `main` method of Figure 14.2 so that it includes input validation using a `try-catch` mechanism. The first step is to identify the dangerous code. Can you find the dangerous code? The two `parseInt` method calls are dangerous in that they might throw a `NumberFormatException`. So let's put those two statements into a *try* block and add a matching `catch` block, as shown in Figure 14.3.

Look for potential problems.

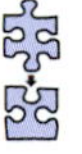

Do you see any logic errors in Figure 14.3's `while` loop? What happens if there's invalid input? A `NumberFormatException` object is thrown and caught, and then an error message is printed. Then `line.plotSegment` executes. But you wouldn't want to print the line segment if the input values were messed up. To avoid that possibility, move the `line.plotSegment(x, y);` line to the last line in the `try` block. This way, it gets executed only if the two `parseInt` method calls work properly. Figure 14.4 shows the final version of the LinePlot program's `while` loop.

```
while (!xStr.equalsIgnoreCase("q"))
{
  yStr = stdIn.next();
  try
  {
    x = Integer.parseInt(xStr);
    y = Integer.parseInt(yStr);
  }
  catch (NumberFormatException nfe)
  {
    System.out.println("Invalid entry: " + xStr + " " + yStr
      + "\nMust enter integer space integer.");
  }

  line.plotSegment(x, y);
  System.out.print("Enter x & y coordinates (q to quit): ");
  xStr = stdIn.next();
} // end while
```

These statements should be inside a `try` block.

Figure 14.3 First attempt at improving the LinePlot program's `while` loop

```
while (!xStr.equalsIgnoreCase("q"))
{
  yStr = stdIn.next();
  try
  {
    x = Integer.parseInt(xStr);
    y = Integer.parseInt(yStr);
    line.plotSegment(x, y);
  }
  catch (NumberFormatException nfe)
  {
    System.out.println("Invalid entry: " + xStr + " " + yStr
      + "\nMust enter integer space integer.");
  }
  System.out.print("Enter x & y coordinates (q to quit): ");
  xStr = stdIn.next();
} // end while
```

This statement should be inside the `try` block, not after the `try-catch` structure.

Figure 14.4 Final version of the LinePlot program's `while` loop

14.5 try Block Details

Now that you know the basic idea behind `try` blocks, it's time to flesh out some subtle `try` block details.

try Block Size

Deciding on the size of your `try` blocks is a bit of an art. Sometimes it's better to use small `try` blocks, and sometimes it's better to use larger `try` blocks. It's legal to surround an entire method body with a `try` block, but that's usually counterproductive because then dangerous code is harder to identify. In general, you should make your `try` blocks small enough so that your dangerous code is easily identified.

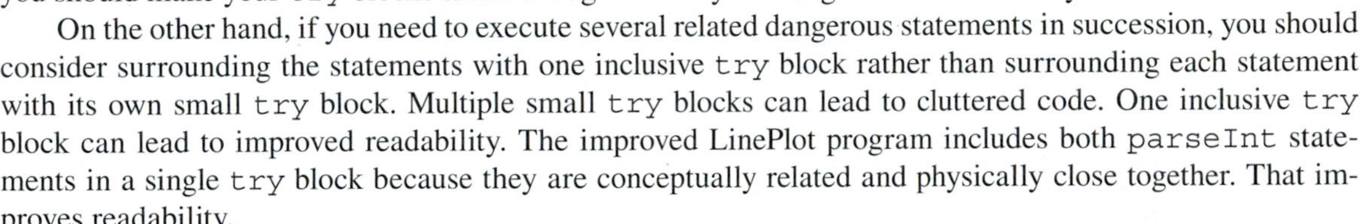

On the other hand, if you need to execute several related dangerous statements in succession, you should consider surrounding the statements with one inclusive `try` block rather than surrounding each statement with its own small `try` block. Multiple small `try` blocks can lead to cluttered code. One inclusive `try` block can lead to improved readability. The improved LinePlot program includes both `parseInt` statements in a single `try` block because they are conceptually related and physically close together. That improves readability.

Assume That try Block Statements Are Skipped

If an exception is thrown, the JVM immediately jumps out of the current `try` block. The immediacy of the jump means that if there are statements in the `try` block after the exception-throwing statement, those statements get skipped. The compiler is a pessimist. It knows that statements inside a `try` block might possibly be skipped, and it assumes the worst; that is, it assumes that all statements inside a `try` block get skipped. Consequently, if there's a `try` block that contains an assignment to x, the compiler assumes that the assignment is skipped. If there's no assignment to x outside of the `try` block and x's value is needed outside of the `try` block, you'll get this compile-time error:

```
variable x might not have been initialized
```

If you get that error, usually you can fix it by initializing the variable prior to the try block. Let's look at an example. . . .

Your goal is to implement a `getIntFromUser` method that performs robust input for an `int` value. Your method should prompt the user for an integer, read the entered value as a string, and then convert the string to an `int`. If the conversion fails, your method should reprompt the user for an integer. If the user eventually enters a valid integer value, `getIntFromUser` should return it to the calling module.

Figure 14.5 is a first-cut attempt at implementing the `getIntFromUser` method. It does a good job with the logic, but it contains compile-time errors that are due to the initializations inside the `try` block. We'll fix the `try` block's errors soon enough, but let's first explain the `try` block's logic.

The `try` block contains these three lines:

```
valid = false;
x = Integer.parseInt(xStr);
valid = true;
```

Note how the three-line code fragment assigns `valid` to `false` and then turns around and assigns it back to `true`. Strange, eh? Actually, it's a fairly common strategy to assume one thing, try it out, and then change the assumption if it's proven wrong. And that's what's happening here. This code starts by assuming that the user entry is invalid. It calls `parseInt` to test whether it's actually valid; that is, it checks to see if the user entry is an integer. If it is valid, the next statement executes, and `valid` gets set to `true`. But what happens if the `parseInt`

Assume one thing, then change as required.

```
public static int getIntFromUser()
{
  Scanner stdIn = new Scanner(System.in);
  String xStr;    // user entry
  boolean valid; // is user entry a valid integer?
  int x;          // integer form of user entry

  System.out.print("Enter an integer: ");
  xStr = stdIn.next();

  do
  {
    try
    {
      valid = false;
      x = Integer.parseInt(xStr);
      valid = true;
    }
    catch (NumberFormatException nfe)
    {
      System.out.print("Invalid entry. Enter an integer: ");
      xStr = stdIn.next();
    }
  } while (!valid);

  return x;
} // end getIntFromUser
```

compile-time error: `valid` might not have been initialized

compile-time error: `x` might not have been initialized

Figure 14.5 A method that illustrates the problem with initializing inside a `try` block

conversion fails? The `valid` variable never gets set to `true` because an exception is thrown and the JVM immediately jumps out of the `try` block. So this code seems reasonable. Unfortunately, "seems reasonable" isn't good enough this time.

Can you figure out the compile-time errors? If not, don't feel bad; we didn't see them until after the compiler helped us. As shown by the callouts in Figure 14.5, the compiler complains that the `valid` and `x` variables might not have been initialized. Why all the fuss? Can't the compiler see that `valid` and `x` are assigned values in the `try` block? Yes, the compiler can see the assignments, but remember that the compiler is a pessimist. It assumes that all statements inside a `try` block are skipped. Even though we know that the `valid = false;` statement is in no actual danger of being skipped (it's a simple assignment, and it's the first line in the `try` block), the compiler still assumes that it gets skipped.

What's the solution? (1) Move the `valid = false;` assignment up to `valid`'s declaration line. (2) Initialize `x` to `0` as part of `x`'s declaration line. Figure 14.6 contains the corrected implementation.

14.6 Two Categories of Exceptions—Checked and Unchecked

Exceptions fall into two categories—*checked* and *unchecked*. Checked exceptions must be checked with a `try-catch` mechanism. Unchecked exceptions can optionally be checked with a `try-catch` mechanism, but it's not a requirement.

```
public static int getIntFromUser()
{
  Scanner stdIn = new Scanner(System.in);
  String xStr;              // user entry
  boolean valid = false; // is user entry a valid integer?
  int x = 0;               // integer form of user entry

  System.out.print("Enter an integer: ");
  xStr = stdIn.next();

  do
  {
    try
    {
      x = Integer.parseInt(xStr);
      valid = true;
    }
    catch (NumberFormatException nfe)
    {
      System.out.print("Invalid entry. Enter an integer: ");
      xStr = stdIn.next();
    }
  } while (!valid);

  return x;
} // end getIntFromUser
```

These initializations before the `try` block meet the compiler's demands.

Figure 14.6 Corrected version of the `getIntFromUser` method

Identifying an Exception's Category

How can you tell whether a particular exception is classified as checked or unchecked? An exception is an object, and as such, it is associated with a particular class. To find out if a particular exception is checked or unchecked, look up its associated class on Sun's Java API Web site.[3] Once you find the class, look at its ancestors. If you find that it's a descendant of the `RuntimeExeption` class, then it's an unchecked exception. Otherwise, it's a checked exception.

For example, if you look up `NumberFormatException` on Sun's Java API Web site, you'll see this:

```
java.lang.Object
 └java.lang.Throwable
    └java.lang.Exception
       └java.lang.RuntimeException
          └java.lang.IllegalArgumentException
             └java.lang.NumberFormatException
```

If you see this class in the hierarchy, the exception is unchecked.

This shows that the `NumberFormatException` class is a descendant of the `RuntimeException` class, so the `NumberFormatException` class is an unchecked exception.

[3] http://java.sun.com/javase/6/docs/api/

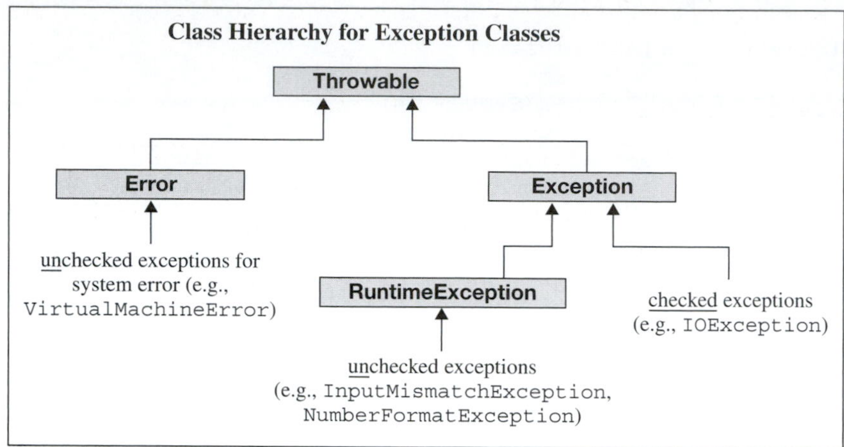

Figure 14.7 Exception class hierarchy

Figure 14.7 shows the class hierarchy for all exceptions. It reiterates the point that unchecked exceptions are descendants of the `RuntimeException` class. It also shows that some unchecked exceptions are descendants of the `Error` class. In the interest of keeping things simple, we didn't mention the `Error` class above. You probably won't encounter its exceptions.

Programmer-Defined Exception Classes

It's possible for programmers to define their own exception classes. Such programmer-defined exception classes must be derived from the `Exception` class or from a subclass of the `Exception` class. Generally speaking, you should limit yourself to predefined exception classes, because programmer-defined exception classes tend to fragment error-handling activities, and that makes programs harder to understand.

14.7 Unchecked Exceptions

As you learned in the previous section, unchecked exceptions need not be checked with a `try-catch` mechanism. However, at runtime, if the JVM throws an unchecked exception and there's no `catch` block to catch it, the program will crash.

Strategies for Handling Unchecked Exceptions

If your program contains code that might throw an unchecked exception, there are two alternate strategies for dealing with it:

1. Use a `try-catch` structure.

or

2. Don't attempt to catch the exception, but write the code carefully so as to avoid the possibility of the exception being thrown.

In the `getIntFromUser` method in Figure 14.6, we employed the first strategy—we used a `try-catch` structure to handle the dangerous `parseInt` method call. Normally, you should use a `try-catch` structure for parse method calls (`parseInt`, `parseLong`, `parseDouble`, and so on) because that leads to cleaner solutions. In the next example, the preferred strategy isn't so clear cut. We'll use both strategies and compare the results.

StudentList Example

Figure 14.8 presents a StudentList class that manages a list of student names. The class stores student names in an ArrayList named students. The class contains a constructor for initializing the students list, a display method for printing the students list, and a removeStudent method that removes a specified student from the students list. We'll focus on the removeStudent method.

```
/*******************************************************
* StudentList.java
* Dean & Dean
*
* This class manages an ArrayList of students.
*******************************************************/

import java.util.ArrayList;

public class StudentList
{
  ArrayList<String> students = new ArrayList<String>();

  //****************************************************

  public StudentList(String[] names)
  {
    for (int i=0; i<names.length; i++)
    {
      students.add(names[i]);
    }
  } // end constructor

  //****************************************************

  public void display()
  {
    for (int i=0; i<students.size(); i++)
    {
      System.out.print(students.get(i) + " ");
    }
    System.out.println();
  } // end display

  //****************************************************

  public void removeStudent(int index)
  {
    students.remove(index);     ◄── This is a dangerous method call.
  } // end removeStudent
} // end StudentList
```

Figure 14.8 First draft of StudentList class which maintains a list of students

The students.remove method call is dangerous because it might throw an unchecked exception, IndexOutOfBoundsException. If its index argument holds the index of one of the students' elements, then that element is removed from the students ArrayList. But if its index argument holds an invalid index, then an IndexOutOfBoundsException is thrown. This occurs, for example, if we use Figure 14.9's StudentListDriver class as the driver. Note how the StudentListDriver class uses an index value of 6 even though there are only four students in the student list. The StudentListDriver and StudentList classes compile just fine, but when run, the students.remove method call throws an exception and the JVM terminates the program and prints the error message shown at the bottom of Figure 14.9.

```
/*************************************************************
* StudentListDriver.java
* Dean & Dean
*
* This is the driver for the StudentList class.
*************************************************************/

public class StudentListDriver
{
  public static void main(String[] args)
  {
    String[] names = {"Caleb", "Izumi", "Mary", "Usha"};
    StudentList studentList = new StudentList(names);

    studentList.display();
    studentList.removeStudent(6);
    studentList.display();
  } // end main
} // end StudentListDriver
```

This argument value generates a runtime error.

Output:

```
Caleb Izumi Mary Usha
Exception in thread "main" java.lang.IndexOutOfBoundsException: Index: 6,
Size: 4
        at java.util.ArrayList.RangeCheck(ArrayList.java:547)
        at java.util.ArrayList.remove(ArrayList.java:390)
        at StudentList.removeStudent(StudentList.java:43)
        at StudentListDriver.main(StudentListDriver.java:17)
```

Figure 14.9 Driver of StudentList class

Improve the removeStudent Method

Let's now make the removeStudent method more robust by gracefully handling the case where it's called with an invalid index. Figures 14.10a and 14.10b show two different robust implementations for the removeStudent method. The first implementation uses a try-catch mechanism and the second implementation uses careful code. These are the two strategies mentioned earlier for handling unchecked exceptions.

```
public void removeStudent(int index)
{
  try
  {
    students.remove(index);
  }
  catch (IndexOutOfBoundsException e)
  {
    System.out.println("Can't remove student because " +
      index + " is an invalid index position.");
  }
} // end removeStudent
```

Figure 14.10a Using a `try-catch` structure for the `removeStudent` method

```
public void removeStudent(int index)
{
  if (index >= 0 && index < students.size())
  {
    students.remove(index);
  }
  else
  {
    System.out.println("Can't remove student because " +
      index + " is an invalid index position.");
  }
} // end removeStudent
```

Figure 14.10b Using a careful-code strategy for the `removeStudent` method

Which solution is better—a `try-catch` mechanism or careful code? The solutions are about the same in terms of readability. With things being equal in terms of readability, go with the careful-code implementation because it's more efficient. Exception handling code is less efficient because it requires the JVM to instantiate an exception object and find a matching `catch` block.

14.8 Checked Exceptions

Let's now look at checked exceptions. If a code fragment has the potential of throwing a checked exception, the compiler forces you to associate that code fragment with a `try-catch` mechanism. If there is no associated `try-catch` mechanism, the compiler generates an error. With unchecked exceptions, you have a choice of how to handle them—a `try-catch` mechanism or careful code. With checked exceptions, there's no choice—you must use a `try-catch` mechanism.

CreateNewFile Program

In Figure 14.11, the CreateNewFile program attempts to create an empty file with a user-specified name. We cover files in detail in the next chapter. Since this example views files only "from the outside," at this point you don't need to understand file details. So why did we decide to use a file example prior to the files chapter? Because we wanted a good checked exception example and file programs provide for that. It would make more sense to use previously covered material for our checked exception example, but that wasn't really an option. Our previously covered commands don't throw checked exceptions.

The CreateNewFile program prompts the user for the name of a file that is to be created. If the file exists already, the program prints a "Sorry, file already exists." message. If the file does not exist, it creates the file. In doing all that, the program uses the `File` class and its application programming interface (API). More

```
/*********************************************************
* CreateNewFile.java
* Dean & Dean
*
* This creates a new file.
*********************************************************/

import java.util.Scanner;
import java.io.File;
import java.io.IOException;

public class CreateNewFile
{
  public static void main(String[] args)
  {
    Scanner stdIn = new Scanner(System.in);
    String fileName; // user-specified file name
    File file;

    System.out.print("Enter file to be created: ");
    fileName = stdIn.nextLine();
    file = new File(fileName);        // API constructor call

    if (file.exists())                // API method call
    {
      System.out.println("Sorry, file already exists.");
    }
    else
    {
      file.createNewFile();           // API method call
      System.out.println(fileName + " created.");
    }
  } // end main
} // end CreateNewFile class
```

Figure 14.11 Draft of CreateNewFile program which is supposed to create a new file

specifically, the program calls a `File` constructor, it calls `File`'s `exists` method, and it calls `File`'s `createFile` method. As with many file-related API calls, those calls all have the potential of throwing an exception. So how should you deal with that? Read on. . . .

Using API Documentation When Writing Exception Handling Code

Whenever you want to use a method or constructor from one of the API classes and you're not sure about it, you should look it up in the API documentation so you know whether to add exception handling code. On the API documentation page for the method or constructor of interest, look for a "throws" section, which identifies specific types of exceptions that might be thrown. To handle the exceptions, you need to understand them. To understand a particular exception, click on its link in the throws section. That should take you to the API documentation for the exception's class.

On the exception class's API page, scroll down a bit and read the exception class's description. Then scroll back up and look at the class's class hierarchy. As mentioned previously, if `RuntimeException` is an ancestor, the exception is an unchecked exception. Otherwise, it's a checked exception.

Back to the CreateNewFile Program

If you apply the above API-lookup strategy to the CreateNewFile program, you'll find that:

- The `File` constructor call throws a `NullPointerException` if its argument is `null`. The `NullPointerException` class is derived from the `RuntimeException` class, so it's an unchecked exception. The code is written so that there's no danger of the `File` constructor's argument being `null`, so there's no need to add any code for the `File` constructor call.
- The `exists` method call throws a `SecurityException` if a security manager exists. The `SecurityException` class is derived from the `RuntimeException` class, so it's an unchecked exception. If you don't have a security manager, there's no need to add any code for the `exists` method call.
- The `createNewFile` method call throws an `IOException` if there's an I/O problem like a corrupt hard disk or an invalid directory name. The `IOException` class is derived from the `Exception` class but not from the `RuntimeException` class, so it is a checked exception. Thus, we're required to add `try-catch` code to handle this exception.

Because of the `createNewFile` method call, Figure 14.11's CreateNewFile program doesn't compile successfully. What's the solution? Suppose you simply surround the `createNewFile` method call with a `try` block like this:

```
else
{
  try
  {
    file.createNewFile();
  }
  catch (IOException ioe)
  {
    System.out.println("File I/O error");
  }
  System.out.println(fileName + " created.");
}
```

That results in a program that compiles successfully and runs. But is it a good program? Novice programmers often solve problems by trying something out without thoroughly thinking it through, and if it leads to reasonable results, they quickly move on. Try to resist that urge. Although the above code compiles and runs, it doesn't behave appropriately when an `IOException` is thrown. Can you identify the inappropriate behavior? If an `IOException` is thrown, the `catch` block prints its `"File I/O error"` message. But then it also prints the `fileName + " created."` message, even though no file was created. Remember—just because a program runs, that doesn't mean it's right.

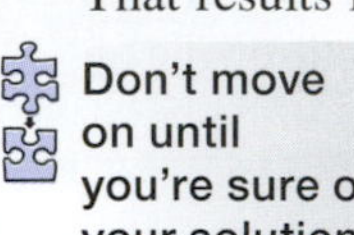

Don't move on until you're sure of your solution.

Here's the preferred solution:

```
else
{
  try
  {
    file.createNewFile();
    System.out.println(fileName + " created.");
  }
  catch (IOException ioe)
  {
    System.out.println("File I/O error");
  }
}
```

This statement is now in a better location.

Now the program prints the "created" message only if the file is actually created. Yeah!

14.9 The `Exception` Class and Its `getMessage` Method

So far, our examples have been relatively simple. Each `try` block has thrown only one type of exception. In that case, the `catch` logic is straightforward—catch the type of exception that's being thrown. For cases where you have a `try` block that might throw more than one type of exception, the `catch` logic can be a bit more complicated. You have to choose between these two techniques: (1) provide a generic `catch` block that handles every type of exception that might be thrown, or (2) provide a sequence of specific `catch` blocks, one for each type of exception that might be thrown. In this section, we describe the generic-`catch`-block technique, and in the next section we describe the sequence-of-`catch`-blocks technique.

Generic `catch` Block

To provide a generic `catch` block, define a `catch` block with an `Exception` type parameter. Then, inside the `catch` block, call the `Exception` class's `getMessage` method, like this:

```
catch (Exception e)
{
  System.out.println(e.getMessage());
}
```

If a `catch` block uses an `Exception` parameter, it will match all thrown exceptions. Why? Because when an exception is thrown, it looks for a `catch` parameter that's either identical to the thrown exception or a superclass of the thrown exception. The `Exception` class is the superclass of all thrown exceptions, so all thrown exceptions consider an `Exception catch` parameter to be a match.

The `Exception` class's `getMessage` method returns a text description of the thrown exception. For example, if you attempt to open a file using a new `FileReader(String` *<filename>*`)` constructor call and you pass in a filename for a file that doesn't exist, the JVM throws an exception and the `getMessage` call returns this:

<filename> `(The system cannot find the file specified)`

The message displays the specified filename where it says *<filename>*. This message is helpful, but be aware that sometimes `getMessage` returns messages that are not particularly helpful.

PrintLineFromFile Example

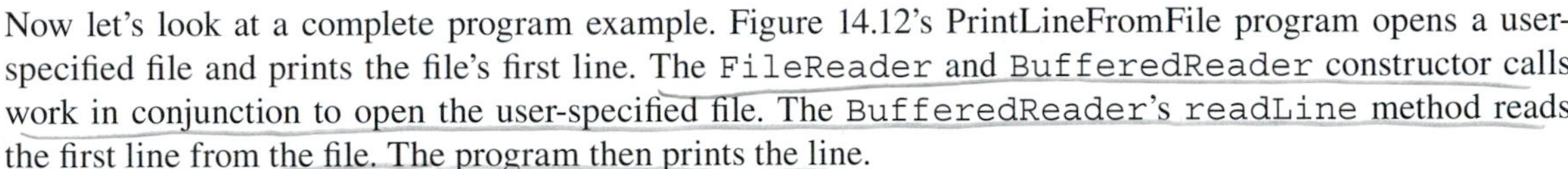

Now let's look at a complete program example. Figure 14.12's PrintLineFromFile program opens a user-specified file and prints the file's first line. The `FileReader` and `BufferedReader` constructor calls work in conjunction to open the user-specified file. The `BufferedReader`'s `readLine` method reads the first line from the file. The program then prints the line.

Both the `FileReader` constructor and the `readLine` method throw checked exceptions, so if we had not put them in a `try` block, the compiler would have complained and identified the checked exceptions that needed to be caught. In particular, if the user inputs a filename for a file that doesn't exist, the `FileReader` constructor throws a `FileNotFoundException`. If the file is corrupted and unreadable, the `readLine` method throws an `IOException`. Our generic `catch` block catches either of these exceptions, and we use the `getMessage` method to print a description of the thrown exception.

In the first sample session in Figure 14.12, the user enters input that tells the program to read the `PrintLineFromFile.java` source file. Since the program's first line is a line of `*`'s, the program prints a line of `*`'s.

In the second sample session in Figure 14.12, the user specifies a nonexistent file. The bad filename causes the `FileReader` constructor to throw a `FileNotFoundException` object, and the `getMessage` call generates the error message shown.

Now you've seen an example of the `FileReader` constructor throwing an exception, but you haven't seen an example of the `readLine` method throwing an exception. That's because it's harder to produce an exception with the `readLine` method call. It occurs only if you have a corrupted file that can be opened, but not read, and we can't generate such a file intentionally. Even though the `readLine` method call rarely throws an exception, you must put it inside of a `try-catch` structure because the compiler knows it might throw a checked exception.

14.10 Multiple `catch` Blocks

When you have a `try` block that throws more than one type of exception, you can provide a generic `catch` block or you can provide a sequence of specific `catch` blocks—one for each type of exception that might be thrown. Now let's look at the sequence-of-`catch`-blocks technique.

PrintLineFromFile Example Revisited

Figure 14.13 shows PrintLineFromFile2, a modified version of the previous PrintLineFromFile program. Instead of using one generic `catch` block, PrintLineFromFile2 uses a sequence of `catch` blocks, one `catch` block for the `FileNotFoundException` and one `catch` block for the `IOException`. Note that because this new program specifically names the types of exceptions that might be thrown, it must import their classes. If you run the program with a valid filename for input, you get a printout of the first line

```
/*************************************************************
* PrintLineFromFile.java
* Dean & Dean
*
* This opens existing text file and prints a line from it.
*************************************************************/

import java.util.Scanner;
import java.io.BufferedReader;
import java.io.FileReader;

public class PrintLineFromFile
{
  public static void main(String[] args)
  {
    Scanner stdIn = new Scanner(System.in);
    String fileName;        // name of target file
    BufferedReader fileIn;  // target file
    String line;            // first line from fileIn

    System.out.print("Enter a filename: ");
    fileName = stdIn.nextLine();

    try
    {
      fileIn = new BufferedReader(new FileReader(fileName));
      line = fileIn.readLine();
      System.out.println("Line 1:\n" + line);
    } // end try

    catch (Exception e)
    {
      System.out.println(e.getMessage());
    }
  } // end main
} // end PrintLineFromFile class
```

Sample session #1:

```
Enter a file name: PrintLineFromFile.java
Line 1:
/*************************************************************
```

Sample session #2:

```
Enter a filename: garbage
garbage (The system cannot find the file specified)
```

Figure 14.12 PrintLineFromFile program—a simple file-reader

```
/*************************************************************
* PrintLineFromFile2.java
* Dean & Dean
*
* This opens an existing text file and prints a line from it.
*************************************************************/

import java.util.Scanner;
import java.io.BufferedReader;
import java.io.FileReader;
import java.io.FileNotFoundException;
import java.io.IOException;

public class PrintLineFromFile2
{
  public static void main(String[] args)
  {
    Scanner stdIn = new Scanner(System.in);
    String fileName;         // name of target file
    BufferedReader fileIn;   // target file
    String line;             // first line from fileIn

    System.out.print("Enter a filename: ");
    fileName = stdIn.nextLine();

    try
    {
      fileIn = new BufferedReader(new FileReader(fileName));
      line = fileIn.readLine();
      System.out.println("Line 1:\n" + line);
    } // end try

    catch (FileNotFoundException e)
    {
      System.out.println("Invalid filename: " + fileName);
    }
    catch (IOException e)
    {
      System.out.println("Error reading from file: " + fileName);
    }
  } // end main
} // end PrintLineFromFile2 class
```

Sequence of catch blocks

Sample session with input of an invalid filename:

```
Enter a filename: garbage
Invalid filename: garbage
```

Figure 14.13 PrintLineFromFile2 program—an improved file-reader

of that file, just as before. But if you supply an invalid filename for input, you get something like the sample session at the bottom of Figure 14.13.

catch Block Ordering—The Order Matters

If there are multiple catch blocks, the first catch block that matches the type of the exception thrown is the one that's executed. Then the other catch blocks are skipped. This behavior is similar to the behavior of a switch statement. But there is a slight difference. With a switch statement, after a matching case block is found and executed, control continues to the next case unless there happens to be a break statement. With catch blocks, after a matching catch block is found and executed, the subsequent catch blocks are automatically skipped.

Whenever you use more than one catch block after a given try block, and one catch block's exception class is derived from another catch block's exception class, you must arrange the catch blocks with the more general exception classes at the bottom. For example, if you look up the FileNotFoundException on Sun's Java API Web site, you'll see this hierarchy:

```
java.lang.Object
 └java.lang.Throwable
    └java.lang.Exception
       └java.io.IOException
          └java.io.FileNotFoundException
```

If you choose to have a FileNotFoundException catch block and an IOException catch block in the same catch-block sequence, then you must put the IOException catch block at the bottom because the IOException class is a more general version of the FileNotFoundException class. If you put the IOException catch block first, it would match both types of exceptions, and the FileNotFoundException catch block would always be skipped. And that's not good. As long as you understand this principle, there's no need to memorize the hierarchical relationships among all types of exceptions, because the compiler will tell you in a compile-time error if you arrange multiple catch blocks in the wrong order.

Generic catch Block Versus Multiple catch Blocks

In the previous section, we looked at the generic-catch-block technique. In this section we looked at the sequence-of-catch-blocks technique. Which one is better? The generic-catch-block technique is slightly easier to code, so if you're interested in simplicity, use that technique. The sequence-of-catch-blocks technique allows you to handle different exceptions differently, so if you're interested in having more control over your exception handling and more control over your error messages, use that technique.

14.11 Understanding Exception Messages

Unless you're incredibly careful, you've probably written programs that have generated runtime error messages. But prior to this chapter, you weren't properly prepared to thoroughly understand those error messages. Now you are. In this section, we describe exception messages by showing exception message details in the context of a complete program.

NumberList Program

The program in Figures 14.14a and 14.14b reads in a list of numbers and calculates the mean. The program compiles and runs successfully most of the time, but it's not very robust. There are three types of entries that make the program crash. We'll describe those three entry types, but before you read about them, first try to determine them on your own.

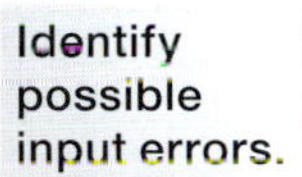
Identify
possible
input errors.

```
/***************************************************
* NumberListDriver.java
* Dean & Dean
*
* This is the driver for the NumberList class.
***************************************************/

public class NumberListDriver
{
  public static void main(String[] args)
  {
    NumberList list = new NumberList();
    list.readNumbers();
    System.out.println("Mean = " + list.getMean());
  } // end main
} // end class NumberListDriver
```

Figure 14.14a NumberList program driver that drives class in Figure 14.14b

User Enters a Non-Integer

In the `readNumbers` method, note the `parseInt` call. If the user enters a *q,* the `while` loop terminates and `parseInt` is not called. But if the user enters something other than q, `parseInt` is called. If `parseInt` is called with a non-integer argument, then `parseInt` throws a `NumberFormatException`. And since there's no `try-catch` structure the JVM prints a detailed error message and then terminates the program. For example, if the user enters `hi`, the JVM prints a detailed error message and terminates the program, like this:[4]

Sample session:

```
Enter a whole number (q to quit): hi
Exception in thread "main" java.lang.NumberFormatException:
For input string: "hi"
    at java.lang.NumberFormatException.forInputString(
      NumberFormatException.java:48)
    at java.lang.Integer.parseInt(Integer.java:447)
    at java.lang.Integer.parseInt(Integer.java:497)
    at NumberList.readNumbers(NumberList.java:28)
    at NumberListDriver.main(NumberListDriver.java:13)
```

thrown exception

call stack trace

[4] The formatting of the error message may be slightly different, but the information will be similar.

```
/*************************************************************
* NumberList.java
* Dean & Dean
*
* This inputs numbers and calculates their mean value.
*************************************************************/

import java.util.Scanner;

public class NumberList
{
  private int[] numList = new int[100]; // array of numbers
  private int size = 0;                 // number of numbers

  //***********************************************************

  public void readNumbers()
  {
    Scanner stdIn = new Scanner(System.in);
    String xStr;    // user-entered number (String form)
    int x;          // user-entered number

    System.out.print("Enter a whole number (q to quit): ");
    xStr = stdIn.next();

    while (!xStr.equalsIgnoreCase("q"))
    {
      x = Integer.parseInt(xStr);
      numList[size] = x;
      size++;
      System.out.print("Enter a whole number (q to quit): ");
      xStr = stdIn.next();
    } // end while
  } // end readNumbers

  //***********************************************************

  public double getMean()
  {
    int sum = 0;

    for (int i=0; i<size; i++)
    {
      sum += numList[i];
    }
    return sum / size;
  } // end getMean
} // end class NumberList
```

Figure 14.14b `NumberList` class that computes mean of input numbers

Let's analyze the error message. First the JVM prints the exception that was thrown, `NumberFormatException`. Then it prints a *call stack trace*. A call stack trace is a listing of the methods that were called prior to the crash, in reverse order. What methods were called? First `main`, then `readNumbers`, then `parseInt`. Note the numbers at the right side of the call stack trace. They are the line numbers in the source code for where the methods are called. For example, the 13 in the bottom line says that `main`'s 13th line is a call to the `readNumbers` method.

User Immediately Enters q to Quit

At the bottom of the `getMean` method, note the division operation. Whenever you perform integer division, you should always be sure to avoid division by zero. In the NumberList program, it's not avoided. The `size` instance variable is initialized to zero, and if the user immediately enters `q` to quit, `size` stays at zero and getMean performs division by zero. Integer division by zero causes the JVM to throw an `ArithmeticException`. Since there's no `try-catch` mechanism, the JVM prints a detailed error message and terminates the program, like this:

Sample session:

```
Enter a whole number (q to quit): q
Exception in thread "main"
    java.lang.ArithmeticException: / by zero
    at NumberList.getMean(NumberList.java:47)
    at NumberListDriver.main(NumberListDriver.java:14)
```

Note that if you perform floating-point division with a denominator of zero, there is no exception. If the numerator is a positive number, division by 0.0 returns the value `Infinity`. If the numerator is a negative number, division by 0.0 returns the value `-Infinity`. If the numerator is also 0.0, division by 0.0 returns the value `NaN` (for not a number).

User Enters More Than 100 Numbers

In the NumberList program's instance-variable declarations, note that `numList` is a 100 element array. In the `readNumbers` method, note how this statement assigns user-entered numbers into the `numList` array:

```
numList[size] = x;
```

If the user enters 101 numbers, then the `size` variable increments to 100. That's bigger than the maximum index (99) in the instantiated array. If you access an array element with an index that's greater than the maximum index or less than zero, the operation throws an `ArrayIndexOutOfBoundsException`. Since there are no `try` and `catch` blocks, the JVM prints a detailed error message and then terminates the program, like this:

Sample session:

```
...
Enter a whole number (q to quit): 32
Enter a whole number (q to quit): 49
Enter a whole number (q to quit): 51
Exception in thread "main"
  java.lang.ArrayIndexOutOfBoundsException: 100
  at NumberList.readNumbers(NumberList.java:29)
  at NumberListDriver.main(NumberListDriver.java:13)
```

We've now finished our description of the NumberList program's three runtime errors. Normally, when you see such errors, you should fix your code so as to avoid the runtime errors in the future. So for the NumberList program, you should add fixes for the three runtime errors. One of the chapter exercises asks you to do just that.

14.12 Using `throws` *<exception-type>* to Postpone the `catch`

In all of the examples so far, we've handled thrown exceptions locally; that is, we've put the `try` and `catch` blocks in the method that contains the dangerous statement. But sometimes that's not feasible.

Moving `try` and `catch` Blocks Back to the Calling Method

When it's not feasible to use local `try` and `catch` blocks, you can move the `try` and `catch blocks` out of the dangerous statement's method and back to the calling method. If you do that and the dangerous statement throws an exception, the JVM immediately jumps out of the dangerous statement's method and passes the exception back to the `try` and `catch` blocks in the calling method.[5]

So when should you put `try` and `catch blocks` in the calling method as opposed to in the dangerous statement's method? Most of the time, you should put your `try` and `catch blocks` in the dangerous statement's method because that promotes modularization, which is a good thing. But sometimes it's hard to come up with an appropriate `catch` block when you're inside the dangerous statement's method. For example, suppose you've written a utility method that's called from lots of different places, and the method sometimes throws an exception. When an exception is thrown, you'd like to have an error message that's customized to the calling method. It's hard to do that if the `catch` block is in the utility method. The solution is to move the `try` and `catch blocks` to the calling methods.

Consider another example. Suppose you've written a method with a non-`void` return type that sometimes throws an exception. With a non-`void` return type, the compiler expects the method to return a value. But when an exception is thrown, you normally don't want to return a value because there's no appropriate value to return. So how can you have a non-`void` method and not return a value? Move the `try` and `catch` blocks to the calling method. Then when an exception is thrown, the JVM returns to the calling method without returning a value. The calling method's `try` and `catch` blocks handle the thrown exception, most likely with an error message. Let's see how this works in a Java program.

StudentList Program Revisited

Figure 14.15 contains a modified version of Figure 14.8's `StudentList` class. The main difference is that the `removeStudent` method now returns the name of the student it removes. This enables the calling method to do something with the removed element.

In the `removeStudent` method, note the `return` statement. The `students.remove` method call attempts to remove the element at the position indicated by `index`. If `index` is less than zero or greater than the index of the last element, then the JVM throws an `IndexOutOfBoundsException`. In our previous `StudentList` class, we handled the exception locally, within the `removeStudent` method.

[5] Actually, the jump to the calling method is not immediate if there's a `finally` block below the `try` block(s). In that case, the JVM jumps to the `finally` block prior to jumping to the calling method. We describe the `finally` block at the end of this section.

```
/*******************************************************************
* StudentList2.java
* Dean & Dean
*
* This program manages an ArrayList of students.
*******************************************************************/

import java.util.ArrayList;

public class StudentList2
{
  private ArrayList<String> students = new ArrayList<String>();

  //*****************************************************************

  public StudentList2(String[] names)
  {
    for (int i=0; i<names.length; i++)
    {
      students.add(names[i]);
    }
  } // end constructor

  //*****************************************************************

  public void display()
  {
    for (int i=0; i<students.size(); i++)
    {
      System.out.print(students.get(i) + " ");
    }
    System.out.println();
  } // end display

  //*****************************************************************

  public String removeStudent(int index)
    throws IndexOutOfBoundsException
  {
    return students.remove(index);
  } // end removeStudent
} // end StudentList2
```

Throw the error-handling job to the calling method.

Figure 14.15 `StudentList2` class which is driven by the class in Figure 14.16

This time, since we're returning a value, it's more convenient to transfer the exception handling work back to the calling method. We do that by putting `try` and `catch blocks` in the calling method and by putting a `throws` clause in the `removeStudent` method's heading. Here's the heading:

```
public String removeStudent(int index)
  throws IndexOutOfBoundsException
```

Adding the `throws` clause reminds the compiler that the method might throw an unhandled exception. The `throws` clause is required if the unhandled exception is a checked exception, and it's just recommended if the unhandled exception is an unchecked exception. Since the `IndexOutOfBoundsException` is an unchecked exception, it's legal to omit the above `throws` clause. But it's good style to include it because it provides valuable self-documentation. If a programmer later on wants to use the `removeStudent` method, the `throws` clause warns the programmer to provide a "remote" `try-catch` mechanism to handle the `IndexOutOfBoundsException` when calling `removeStudent`.

To see how to implement this "remote" `try-catch` mechanism, look at the `StudentList2Driver` class in Figure 14.16. It displays a list of students, asks the user which student should be removed, and attempts to remove that student. If the `removeStudent` method call fails, the `catch` block handles the thrown exception, and the program asks the user again which student should be removed.

The `finally` Block

In implementing an exception handler, you'll sometimes want to provide "cleanup code" that's executed regardless of whether an exception is thrown. Suppose you open a file and attempt to write to it. The write operation may or may not throw an exception. Either way, you should close the file when you're done. If you forget to close the file, then system resources remain tied up servicing the open file, and that causes system performance to degrade. Closing a file is an example of cleanup code. If you handle the cleanup locally (e.g., the write and close operations are in the same method), then the cleanup is straightforward. Just place the cleanup code below the `try` and `catch` blocks, and the JVM executes it regardless of whether an exception is thrown. But if you transfer the exception handling work with a `throws` clause, the cleanup is slightly more involved.

If you handle an exception with a `throws` clause, and you need to provide clean-up code regardless of whether an exception is thrown, use a `finally` block. A `finally` block is associated with a particular `try` block and, as such, it should be placed immediately after a `try` block.[6] If the JVM throws an exception within the `try` block, the JVM immediately jumps to the `finally` block, executes it, and then throws the exception back to the calling module. If the JVM does not throw an exception within the `try` block, the JVM finishes the `try` block and then executes the `finally` block.

The `writeToFile` method in Figure 14.17 illustrates the `finally` block. The method opens a file and writes a test message to the file. Specifically, the `PrintWriter` constructor call opens a file named `testFile.txt`. The `fileOut.printf` call writes "This is a test." to the opened file. Then the file is closed by `fileOut.close`. Since the `fileOut.close` call is within a `finally` block, it executes regardless of whether an exception is thrown.

[6] It's legal to insert a `catch` block(s) between the `try` and `finally` blocks, but that can lead to confusing code. We recommend that you keep things simple. Use a `try` block with a `catch` block(s) or `try` block with a `finally` block, but not all three together.

```
/*************************************************************
* StudentList2Driver.java
* Dean & Dean
*
* This drives StudentList2 class.
*************************************************************/

import java.util.Scanner;

public class StudentList2Driver
{
  public static void main(String[] args)
  {
    Scanner stdIn = new Scanner(System.in);
    String[] names = {"Caleb", "Izumi", "Mary", "Usha"};
    StudentList2 studentList = new StudentList2(names);
    int index;
    boolean reenter;

    studentList.display();

    do
    {
      System.out.print("Enter index of student to remove: ");
      index = stdIn.nextInt();
      try
      {
        System.out.println(
          "removed " + studentList.removeStudent(index));
        reenter = false;
      }
      catch (IndexOutOfBoundsException e)
      {
        System.out.print("Invalid entry. ");
        reenter = true;
      }
    } while (reenter);

    studentList.display();
  } // end main
} // end StudentList2Driver
```

If there is no error, this method returns name of student removed.

If exception is thrown in removeStudent method, this catch block catches it.

Sample session:

```
Caleb Izumi Mary Usha
Enter index of student to remove: 6
Invalid entry. Enter index of student to remove: 1
removed Izumi
Caleb Mary Usha
```

Figure 14.16 Driver for StudentList2 class

```
public void writeToFile() throws IOException
{
  PrintWriter fileOut = new PrintWriter("testFile.txt");
  try
  {
    fileOut.printf("%s", "This is a test.");
  }
  finally
  {
    fileOut.close();
  }
} // end writeToFile
```

Figure 14.17 Method that uses a `finally` block to close an output file

14.13 GUI Track and Problem Solving: Line Plot Example Revisited (Optional)

Problem Description

Earlier in the chapter, we implemented a LinePlot program that plotted a line defined by a sequence of user-specified points. The line plot's display was less than ideal. It "displayed" the line as a text description of line segments. For example, this is what the program produces for a five-segment line that goes from point (0,0) to (1,3) to (2,1) to (3,2) to (4,2) to (5,1):

(0,0)–(1,3), (1,3)–(2,1), (2,1)–(3,2), (3,2)–(4,2), (4,2)–(5,1)

Figure 14.18 shows how LinePlotGUI, an improved version of the LinePlot program, displays the above (0,0) to (1,3) to … to (5,1) line. In the interest of simplicity, there are no interval hash marks on the x and y axes. As you can perhaps guess, the shown x axis has six implied hash marks for the values 0, 1, 2, 3, 4, and 5. And the shown y axis has four implied hash marks for the values 0, 1, 2, and 3.

Pre-Written Software and the `drawPolyLine` Method

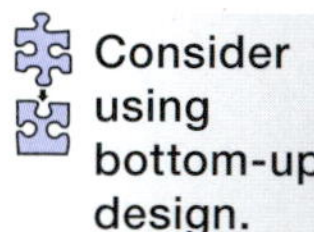
Consider using bottom-up design.

In solving problems, it's fairly common to take a top-down approach: Write the driver method first (`main`), then write the `public` methods that provide an interface to the outside world, then write the `private` helping methods. That approach frequently works fine, but it can sometimes lead to reinventing the wheel. If you used a pure top-down approach to implement the LinePlotGUI program, you'd probably implement the line display as a sequence of `drawLine` method calls, one for each segment of the line (for a discussion of the `drawLine` method, see Chapter 5). Using `drawLine` would work, but it would require a loop and probably some debugging effort. The better approach is to dust off your Java API tome (http://java.sun.com/javase/6/docs/api/) and search for alternative line-drawing methods.

Lo and behold, there's a line drawing method that does exactly what you want. The `drawPolyline` method draws a line by connecting a sequence of points. More specifically, the `Graphic` class's `drawPolyline` method receives three parameters—`xPixels`, `yPixels`, and `numOfPoints`. The `numOfPoints` parameter holds the number of points in the line. The `xPixels` parameter holds an array

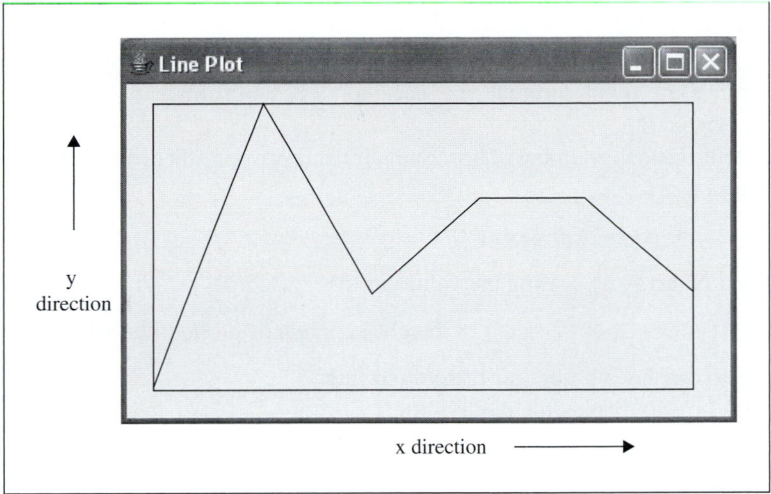

Figure 14.18 Sample output for the LinePlotGUI program

of the horizontal pixel positions for each of the points. The `yPixels` parameter holds an array of the vertical pixel positions for each of the points. For example, `xPixels[0]` and `yPixels[0]` hold pixel positions for the first point, `xPixels[1]` and `yPixels[1]` hold pixel positions for the second point, and so on. Figure 14.19's `drawPolyline` method call displays a line that connects four points in the shape of an N.

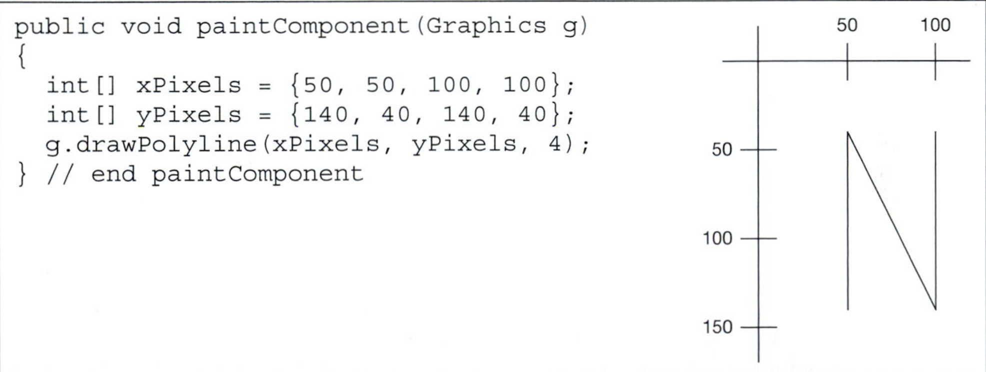

```
public void paintComponent(Graphics g)
{
  int[] xPixels = {50, 50, 100, 100};
  int[] yPixels = {140, 40, 140, 40};
  g.drawPolyline(xPixels, yPixels, 4);
} // end paintComponent
```


Figure 14.19 An example `drawPolyline` method call that displays a line in the shape of an N

Algorithm Development

Once you learn about the `drawPolyline` method, the LinePlotGUI program's basic algorithm becomes clear: Fill up the `xPixels` and `yPixels` arrays with pixel values for a sequence of points. Then use those arrays to call `drawPolyline`.

Before fleshing out that basic algorithm with more details, you need to be aware of an important assumption. The plotted line's points are evenly spaced along the x axis. More specifically, the points occur at positions x=0, x=1, x=2, and so on. So when the program prompts the user for a point, only a y value is needed, not an x value (because x's value is already known: x=0, x=1, x=2, and so on).

Here's a high-level description of the algorithm:

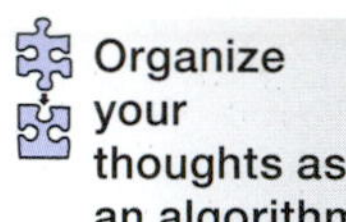
Organize your thoughts as an algorithm.

1. Prompt the user for the number of points and the maximum y value (`maxY`).
2. For each point, prompt the user for a y coordinate value and store the value in `yCoords`.
3. Determine the number of horizontal pixels between adjacent points (`pixelInterval`).
4. Fill up the `xPixels` array:

   `xPixels[i] ← i * pixelInterval`

5. Fill up the `yPixels` array by scaling the values in the `yCoords` array:

   `yPixels[i] ← (yCoords[i]/maxY) *` height in pixels of plotted line's border

6. Call `drawRect` to display a border for the plotted line.
7. Call `drawPolyline` to display the plotted line.

Program Structure

Now that you have a high-level description of the algorithm, you might be tempted to immediately translate it into source code. First, you should determine where the different parts of the program should go. As is customary for a non-trivial program like this one, you should implement the solution with two classes—a `LinePlotGUI` class for driving the program and a `LinePlotPanel` class for drawing the pictures. Clearly, the `drawRect` and `drawPolyline` method calls should go in the `LinePlotPanel` class., since they involve drawing. But what about the code that prompts the user for y coordinate values, and what about the code that calculates the `xPixels` and `yPixels` values? It's important to have the code in the right class to ensure that each class has a clearly defined role. That helps with program development, readability, and maintainability. The `LinePlotGUI` class drives the program and input plays a big role in that effort. Therefore, you should put the user-prompt code in the `LinePlotGUI` class. The `LinePlotPanel` class draws the pictures, and calculations play a big role in that effort. Therefore, you should put the drawing-calculations code in the `LinePlotPanel` class.

Modularity

Now it's time to look at the LinePlotGUI program's source code. Note the modular nature of the `LinePlotGUI` class in Figures 14.20a, 14.20b, and 14.20c. The `JFrame` calls (`setSize`, `setTitle`, `setDefaultCloseOperation`) are in their own module, the `LinePlotGUI` constructor. The user-prompt code is in its own module, the `readYCoordinates` method. The `readYCoordinates` method prompts the user for the number of points. It also prompts the user for the maximum value on the y axis. The two inputs both need to undergo the same type of input validation. To avoid redundant code, the input validation code is in a common helping method, `getIntFromUser`. The `readYCoordinates` method also prompts the user for the y value of each point, which can be anywhere in the range between zero and the maximum y value.

Note the `paintComponent` method in Figure 14.21b. The `paintComponent` method is called automatically by the JVM when the program starts up and whenever a user does something to alter the program's window (e.g., when the user resizes the window, or moves another window off of the window). The `paintComponent` method is in charge of drawing the window's pictures. You could put the drawing-calculations code and the drawing graphics code together in the `paintComponent` method, but as shown in Figures 14.21a and 14.21b, the drawing-calculations code is in its own module, the `LinePlotPanel`

```
/*****************************************************************
* LinePlotGUI.java
* Dean & Dean
*
* This program plots a line as a sequence of connected,
* user-specified points.
*****************************************************************/

import javax.swing.*;  // for JFrame, JOptionPane

public class LinePlotGUI extends JFrame
{
  private static final int FRAME_WIDTH = 400;
  private static final int FRAME_HEIGHT = 250;
  private static final int MARGIN = 20; // space between frame
                                        // and line plot

  int numOfPoints       // points go from N=0 to N=numOfPoints-1
  int maxY;             // y coordinate values go from y=0 to y=maxY
  double[] yCoords;     // y coordinate values for all the points

  //**************************************************************

  public LinePlotGUI()
  {
    setSize(FRAME_WIDTH, FRAME_HEIGHT);
    setTitle("Line Plot");
    setDefaultCloseOperation(JFrame.EXIT_ON_CLOSE);
  } // end LinePlotGUI

  //**************************************************************

  int getMargin()
  {
    return MARGIN;
  }

  int getMaxY()
  {
    return maxY;
  }

  double[] getYCoords()
  {
    return yCoords;
  }
```

Figure 14.20a `LinePlotGUI` class—part A

```
//*************************************************************

// This method prompts the user for y coordinates for points
// at positions x=0, x=1, etc.

public void readYCoordinates()
{
  String yStr;  // user's entry for a point's y coordinate
  numOfPoints = getIntFromUser("Enter number of points: ");
  maxY = getIntFromUser("Enter maximum point value: ");
  yCoords = new double[numOfpoints];

  for (int i=0; i<=maxX; i++)
  {
    yStr = JOptionPane.showInputDialog(
      "At x = " + i + ", what is y's value?\n" +
      "Enter an integer between 0 and " +
      maxY + " inclusive:");
    try
    {
      yCoords[i] = Integer.parseInt(yStr);
      if (yCoords[i] < 0 || yCoords[i] > maxY)
      {
        JOptionPane.showMessageDialog(null,
          "Invalid entry. Value must be between 0 and " + maxY);
        i--;
      }
    }
    catch (NumberFormatException e)
    {
      JOptionPane.showMessageDialog(null,
        "Invalid entry. Must enter an integer.");
      i--;
    }
  } // end for
} // end readYCoordinates
```

These initializations use a helper method.

Figure 14.20b `LinePlotGUI` class—part B

constructor. That's a good idea for several reasons. One, it furthers the goal of modularization in that separate tasks are performed in separate modules. Two, it improves program speed. The `LinePlotPanel` constructor executes only one time, when the `LinePlotPanel` object is instantiated in `main`. The `paintComponent` method executes every time the user does something to alter the program's window. There's no need to redo the drawing calculations every time that happens, so moving that code to the `LinePlotPanel` constructor works well.

For a line plot with a small number of points it would be no big deal if we'd made the mistake of putting all the drawing calculations code in the `paintComponent` method. But if there are many points, the

```
  //***************************************************************

  // This method prompts the user for an integer, performs input
  // validation, and returns the entered integer.

  private static int getIntFromUser(String prompt)      helper method
  {
    String entry;           // user entry
    boolean valid = false; // is user entry a valid integer?
    int entryInt = 0;       // integer form of user entry

    entry = JOptionPane.showInputDialog(prompt);
    do
    {
      try
      {
        entryInt = Integer.parseInt(entry);
        valid = true;
      }
      catch (NumberFormatException e)
      {
        entry = JOptionPane.showInputDialog(
          "Invalid entry. Enter an integer:");
      }
    } while (!valid);

    return entryInt;
  } // end getIntFromUser

  //***************************************************************

  public static void main(String[] args)
  {
    LinePlotGUI linePlotGUI = new LinePlotGUI();
    linePlotGUI.readYCoordinates();
    LinePlotPanel linePlotPanel = new LinePlotPanel(linePlotGUI);
    linePlotGUI.add(linePlotPanel);
    linePlotGUI.setVisible(true);
  } // end main
} // end class LinePlotGUI
```

Figure 14.20c `LinePlotGUI` class—part C

```
/*************************************************************
* LinePlotPanel.java
* Dean & Dean
*
* This class displays a line as a sequence of connected points.
*************************************************************/

import javax.swing.*; // for JPanel
import java.awt.*;    // for Graphics

public class LinePlotPanel extends JPanel
{
  private int[] xPixels; // holds x value for each plotted point
  private int[] yPixels; // holds y value for each plotted point

  // Line plot is surrounded by a rectangle with these specs:
  private int topLeftX, topLeftY;
  private int rectWidth, rectHeight;

  //**********************************************************

  // Calculate dimensions for the line-plot rectangle, using the
  // passed-in frame, which contains the frame's dimensions and
  // coordinate values. Fill in xPixels and yPixels arrays.

  public LinePlotPanel(LinePlotGUI frame)
  {
    int numOfPoints = frame.getYCoords().length;
    int pixelInterval;   // distance between adjacent points

    topLeftX = topLeftY = frame.getMargin();

    // getInsets works only if setVisible is called first
    frame.setVisible(true);
    rectWidth =
      frame.getWidth() - (2 * topLeftX +
      frame.getInsets().left + frame.getInsets().right);
    rectHeight =
      frame.getHeight() - (2 * topLeftY +
      frame.getInsets().top + frame.getInsets().bottom);
```

Figure 14.21a `LinePlotPanel` class—part A

window-resizing slowdown might be noticeable. Slow is acceptable for some things, like initially loading a program, but not for graphical user interface things, like resizing a window. Users are an impatient bunch. Have you ever thumped your mouse in a fit of haste?

```
    // Calculate integer pixel interval between adjacent points
    pixelInterval = rectWidth / (numOfPoints - 1);

    // Make rectangle's actual width = multiple of pixelInterval
    rectwidth = (numOfPoints - 1) * pixelInterval;

    xPixels = new int[numOfPoints];
    yPixels = new int[numOfPoints];

    for (int i=0; i<numOfPoints; i++)
    {
      xPixels[i] = topLeftX + (i * pixelInterval);
      yPixels[i] = topLeftY + rectHeight - (int) Math.round(
        (frame.getYCoords()[i] / frame.getMaxY()) * rectHeight);
    }
  } // end LinePlotPanel constructor

  //***********************************************************

  // This class displays line as sequence of connected points.

  public void paintComponent(Graphics g)
  {
    super.paintComponent(g);
    g.drawRect(topLeftX, topLeftY, rectWidth, rectHeight);
    g.drawPolyline(xPixels, yPixels, xPixels.length);
  } // end paintComponent
} // end class LinePlotPanel
```

precomputed parameters

Figure 14.21b `LinePlotPanel` class—part B

Scalability

A program is *scalable* if it's able to support larger or smaller amounts of data and more or fewer users. The support for more data and more users might require changes to the software, but the changes should be cost-effective incremental add-ons, not massive rewrites.

A professional-grade line-plotting program should be able to handle large quantities of data and different types of data. Our LinePlotGUI program may not achieve that level of scalability (it handles only one type of data, and all the data must fit in one window), but it's not too bad, considering that we needed to keep it reasonably short to fit in an introductory textbook. The LinePlotGUI program is scalable in that its scope is constrained primarily by user input and a few named constants, not by hard-to-change coding constructs. Case in point: The user specifies the number of points and the maximum y value for each point; named constants specify the window size and the window margin.

Robustness and the `getInsets` Method

In the `LinePlotPanel` constructor in Figure 14.21a, note how `frame` (the program's output window) calls the `getInsets` method. The `getInsets` method returns a window's `Insets` object. The `Insets` object stores the thicknesses of the window's four borders. For example, `frame.getInsets().left` returns the width (in pixels) of the `frame` window's left border and `frame.getInsets().top` returns the height (in pixels) of the `frame` window's top border. The top border includes the height of the title bar.

If you don't want to bother with the `getInsets` method, you might be tempted to use hard-coded guesses for the border sizes. Don't do it. Different Java platforms (e.g., Windows, UNIX, and Macintosh platforms) have different window border sizes. So even if you guess right for your current Java platform, your guesses won't necessarily work for alternative Java platforms. Moral of the story: Be robust and use `getInsets`. Don't use hard-coded guesses.

Summary

- An exception is an event that occurs during the execution of a program that disrupts the normal flow of instructions during the execution of a program.
- Exception handling is a technique for handling exceptions gracefully.
- Use a `try` block to "try" out one or more dangerous method calls. If there's a problem with the dangerous method calls, the JVM throws an exception and looks for a "matching" `catch` block.
- A `catch` block is matching if the `catch` heading's parameter type is the same as or an ancestor of the type of the thrown exception.
- If an exception is thrown, the JVM immediately jumps out of the current `try` block. That means that if there are statements in the `try` block after the exception-throwing statement, those statements get skipped.
- Checked exceptions must be checked with a `try-catch` mechanism.
- Unchecked exceptions may optionally be checked with a `try-catch` mechanism, but it's not a requirement.
- Unchecked exceptions are descendants of the `RuntimeException` class.
- To implement a simple, general-purpose exception handler, define a `catch` block with an `Exception` type parameter, and inside the `catch` block, call the `Exception` class's `getMessage` method.
- To define an exception handler with more specificity, define a sequence of catch blocks. Arrange the `catch` blocks with the more general exception classes at the bottom.
- If a program crashes, the JVM prints a call stack trace. A call stack trace is a listing of the methods that were called prior to the crash, in reverse order.
- Use a `throws` clause to propagate an exception back to the calling module.
- If you handle an exception with a `throws` clause, and you need to provide clean up code regardless of whether an exception is thrown, use a `finally` block.

Review Questions

§14.3 Using `try` and `catch` Blocks to Handle "Dangerous" Method Calls

1. If your program contains an API method call, you should put it inside a `try` block. To be fully compliant with proper coding practice, you should apply this rule for all your API method calls. (T / F)

2. A `try` block and its associated `catch` block(s) must be contiguous. (T / F)

§14.5 `try` Block Details

3. Usually, you should try to aggregate related dangerous statements in the same `try` block to minimize clutter. (T / F)
4. Where should you put safe statements that use the results of dangerous operations?
5. If an exception is thrown, the JVM jumps to a matching `catch` block, and after executing the `catch` block, it returns to the `try` block at the point where the exception was thrown. (T / F)
6. In checking for compile-time errors, the compiler takes into account that all statements inside a `try` block might get skipped. (T / F)

§14.6 Two Categories of Exceptions—Checked and Unchecked

7. If an exception is derived from the `RuntimeException` class it is a(n) ________________ exception.
8. Checked exceptions are exceptions that are in or derived from the ________________ class, but not in or derived from the ____________________ class.

§14.7 Unchecked Exceptions

9. In the following list, indicate whether each option is a viable option for an unchecked exception that you know your program might throw:
   a) Ignore it.
   b) Rewrite the code so that the exception never occurs.
   c) Put it in a `try` block, and catch it in a following `catch` block.

§14.8 Checked Exceptions

10. When a statement might throw a checked exception, you can keep the compiler from complaining if you put that statement in a `try` block and follow the `try` block with a `catch` block whose parameter type is the same as the exception type. (T / F)
11. You can determine whether a particular statement contains a checked exception and the type of that exception by attempting to compile with no `try-catch` mechanism. (T / F)

§14.9 The `Exception` Class and Its `getMessage` Method

12. Is it OK to include code that can throw both unchecked and checked exceptions in the same `try` block?
13. What type of exception matches all checked exceptions and all unchecked exceptions except those derived from the `Error` class?
14. What does the `getMessage` method return?

§14.10 Multiple `catch` Blocks

15. For each distinct type of exception that might be thrown, there must be a separate `catch` block. (T / F)
16. The compiler automatically checks for out-of-order `catch` blocks. (T / F)

§14.11 Understanding Exception Messages

17. What are the two types of information displayed by the JVM when it encounters a runtime error that terminates execution?

§14.12 Using `throws` *<exception-type>* to Postpone the `catch`

18. Suppose you want to postpone catching of a `NumberFormatException`. What should you append to the heading of a method to alert the compiler and a potential user that something in the method might throw that type of exception?

19. Given a non-`void` method that contains no `try` and `catch blocks`. If the method throws an exception, we know that the JVM transfers the thrown exception back to the calling method. But does the JVM return a value (with a `return` statement) to the calling module?

Exercises

1. [after §14.3] Given the below program, what is the output if the user enters "one" in response to the prompt?

```
/*************************************************************
* FantasyFootball.java
* Dean & Dean
*
* This prints out names of football players.
*************************************************************/

import java.util.Scanner;
import java.util.ArrayList;

public class FantasyFootball
{
  public static void main(String[] args)
  {
    Scanner stdIn = new Scanner(System.in);
    ArrayList<String> players = new ArrayList<String>();
    String indexStr;
    int index = 0;

    players.add("Peyton Manning");
    players.add("Ladanian Tomlinson");
    players.add("Reggie Bush");
    System.out.print("Enter a number between 1 and 3: ");
    indexStr = stdIn.nextLine();
    try
    {
      index = Integer.parseInt(indexStr);
      System.out.println("Entered index OK.");
    }
    catch (NumberFormatException e)
    {
      System.out.println("Entered index wasn't an integer");
    }
    try
    {
      System.out.println(players.get(index - 1));
    }
    catch (IndexOutOfBoundsException e)
    {
      System.out.println(
        "Can't access players[" + (index - 1) + "]");
    }
```

```
    System.out.println("done");
  } // end main
} // end class FantasyFootball
```

2. Given the above program. What is the output if the user enters 1 in response to the prompt?

3. [after §14.4] Add a `try-catch` structure to the following program to make it compile and execute correctly, even when the divisor is zero. Note that division by zero throws an `ArithmeticException`.

```
import java.util.Scanner;

public class Division
{
  public static void main(String[] args)
  {
    Scanner stdIn = new Scanner(System.in);
    int n, d, q;

    System.out.print("Enter numerator: ");
    n = stdIn.nextInt();
    System.out.print("Enter divisor: ");
    d = stdIn.nextInt();
    q = n / d;
    System.out.println(q);
  } // end main
} // end Division class
```

To help you out, we've provided the `catch` block, below:

```
catch (ArithmeticException e)
{
  System.out.println("Error, but keep going anyway.");
}
```

There's no need to check for correct input; you may assume that the user enters two properly formatted `int` values for input.

4. [after §14.5] Program Improvement:

The following program performs division and does not throw an exception when you input a zero for the denominator. It also does not detect input number format exceptions. Minimize the total lines of code required to meet the requirements.

```
/*************************************************************
* Division2.java
* Dean & Dean
*
* This attempts to prevent division by zero.
*************************************************************/

import java.util.Scanner;

public class Division2
{
  public static void main(String[] args)
  {
    Scanner stdIn = new Scanner(System.in);
```

```
      double n;
      int d;

      System.out.print("Enter numerator: ");
      n = stdIn.nextDouble();
      System.out.print("Enter divisor: ");
      d = stdIn.nextInt();
      System.out.println(n / d);
    } // end main
  } // end Division2 class
```

a) First, rewrite the program so that it still employs a `double` numerator and `int` denominator, but if the value input for the denominator is zero, it refuses to perform the division operation, and keeps asking for the denominator until the user supplies something other than zero.

b) Next, rewrite the program of part a so that if the user inputs an improper format for either numerator or denominator, the entire input query repeats until both formats are OK. Hint: Put `try` and `catch blocks` in a loop that executes `while (OK == false)`, and set `OK = true` after all of the critical operations in the `try` block have succeeded. Note: If the scanned format is bad, you'll get infinite looping unless you re-instantiate `stdIn` in each iteration, or use a two-step operation for each input (input a string and then parse it).

5. [after §14.7] What happens if an unchecked exception is thrown and never caught?

6. [after §14.9] WebPageReader program:

In addition to testing your exception handling prowess, this exercise also tests your ability to use online help and/or reference books. The following program attempts to read in a Web address and print the contents of the Web page at that address.

In the given program:

For each class that's used, add an `import` statement for it, if it's necessary.

For each method call and constructor call:

If it throws an unchecked exception, ignore it.

If it throws a checked exception:

Specify the specific exception in a `throws` clause.

Within a `catch` block in `main`, catch the exception and print the exception's message using its `getMessage` method.

Assume that the following code works except for the items mentioned above.

```
/*************************************************************
* WebPageReader.java
* Dean & Dean
*
* This reads a Web page.
*************************************************************/

import java.util.Scanner;

public class WebPageReader
{
  BufferedReader reader;

  public WebPageReader(String webAddress)
  {
```

```
    URL url = new URL(webAddress);
    URLConnection connection = url.openConnection();
    InputStream in = connection.getInputStream();

    reader = new BufferedReader(new InputStreamReader(in));
  } // end constructor

  //***********************************************************

  public String readLine()
  {
    return reader.readLine();
  } // end readLine

  //***********************************************************

  public static void main(String[] args)
  {
    Scanner stdIn = new Scanner(System.in);
    String url, line;

    System.out.print("Enter a full URL address: ");
    url = stdIn.nextLine();
    WebPageReader wpr = new WebPageReader(url);

    while ((line = wpr.readLine()) != null)
    {
      System.out.println(line);
    }
  } // end main
} // end WebPageReader
```

Be aware that your program might be correct, but it might not be able to access Web pages successfully. To access Web pages, your computer needs to have Internet access capabilities. If your firewall asks if it's OK for Java to access the Internet, click "yes" and continue. Here are three sample sessions:

First sample session:

```
Enter a full URL address: http://www.park.edu
unknown protocol: htp
```

Second sample session:

```
Enter a full URL address: http:/www.park.edu
Connection refused: connect
```

Third sample session:

```
Enter a full URL address: http://www.park.edu


<!DOCTYPE html PUBLIC "-//W3C//DTD XHTML 1.0 Transitional//EN"
"http://www.w3.org/TR/xhtml1/DTD/xhtml1-transitional.dtd">

<html xmlns="http://www.w3.org/1999/xhtml">
<head>
<title>Park University Home Page</title>
<meta name="TITLE" content="Park University Home Page:
Bachelor's, Master's and Online Degree Programs" />
```

```
<meta name="ROBOTS" content="INDEX,FOLLOW" />
<meta name="Description" content="Park University offers
undergraduate, graduate, and online degree programs at campuses
nationwide. Park is accredited by the Higher Learning Commission
of the North Central Association of Colleges and Schools." />
...
```

7. [after §14.10] Multiple `catch` Blocks:

Suppose the code in a `try` block might throw any of the following exceptions:

a) `Exception`
b) `IllegalArgumentException`
c) `IOException`
d) `NumberFormatException`
e) `RuntimeException`

Identify an acceptable sequence for multiple `catch` blocks of these types.

8. [after §14.11] Correcting Problems:

Fix the problems in the NumberList program without making any changes to the `NumberListDriver` class.

If a user immediately enters "q" to quit, print "NaN" by making a small program correction that utilizes `double`'s `NaN` value, and avoid using the `try-catch` mechanism to catch the `int` arithmetic exception.

Sample session:

```
Enter a whole number (q to quit): q
Mean = NaN
```

If the entry is not a "q," and if it is not a legal integer, catch the exception, and in the `catch` block use the `getClass` method inherited from the `Object` class to print the name of the exception class followed by the error message with the statement:

```
System.out.println(e.getClass() + " " + e.getMessage());
```

Avoid the possibility of an `ArrayIndexOutOfBoundsException` by adding to the `while` condition `size < numList.length`, and perform the query and entry at the end of the `while` loop only if `size < numList.length`.

9. [after §14.12] TestExceptions:

What does this program output? Since this program converts between string and numeric values, use quotes to denote string values.

```
/*************************************************************
* TestExceptions.java
* Dean & Dean
*
* This looks up the value at a calculated index.
*************************************************************/

public class TestExceptions
{
  private double[] value =
    new double[] {1.0, 0.97, 0.87, 0.7, 0.47, 0.17};
  private int num;
```

```
  //***********************************************************

  public double eval(String n1, String n2)
    throws IndexOutOfBoundsException
  {
    try
    {
      num = Integer.parseInt(n1) / Integer.parseInt(n2);
    }
    catch (NumberFormatException nfe)
    {
      num++;
      System.out.println("in first catch");
    }
    catch (ArithmeticException ae)
    {
      num++;
      System.out.println("in second catch");
    }
    return value[num];
  }

  //***********************************************************

  public static void main(String[] args)
  {
    TestExceptions te = new TestExceptions();
    try
    {
      System.out.println(te.eval("5.0", "4"));
      System.out.println(te.eval("5", "0"));
      System.out.println(te.eval("22", "5"));
      System.out.println(te.eval("33", "5"));
    }
    catch (Exception e)
    {
      System.out.println("in main's catch");
    }
    System.out.println("Bye");
  } // end main
} // end TestExceptions class
```

Review Question Solutions

1. False. Many API method calls are safe, and there's no need to put those method calls inside a `try` block.
2. True. You cannot put any statements between associated `try` and `catch` blocks.
3. True.
4. Put safe statements that use the results of dangerous operations inside the `try` block and after those dangerous operations.

5. False. After executing the `catch` block, the JVM continues downward; it does not jump back to the `try` block. Consequently, `try`-block statements get skipped if they follow an exception-throwing statement.
6. True.
7. If an exception is derived from the `RuntimeException` class, it is an unchecked exception.
8. Checked exceptions are exceptions that are in or derived from the `Exception` class, but not in or derived from the `RuntimeException` class.
9. Viable options for an unchecked exception that you know might be thrown:
   a) Not viable! You don't want your program to crash at runtime.
   b) Viable.
   c) Viable.
10. True.
11. True. If the statement contains a checked exception, the compiler will say so and identify the exception type.
12. Yes.
13. The `Exception` exception.
14. The `Exception` class's `getMessage` method returns a text description of the thrown exception.
15. False. You can use a generic `catch` block to catch different kinds of exceptions.
16. True. The compiler complains if an earlier more generic `catch` block preempts a later more specific `catch` block.
17. The two types of information displayed by the JVM when it encounters a runtime error are:
   a) Identification of the particular exception thrown.
   b) A call-stack trace, which is a reverse-order listing of the methods called just prior to the crash, along with the line numbers where the error occurred in each method.
18. You must append `throws NumberFormatException` to the end of the method heading.
19. No. When an exception is thrown back to the calling method, the JVM does not return a value (with a `return` statement) to the calling module.

CHAPTER 15

Files

Objectives

- Become acquainted with classes in the `java.io` package.
- Learn how to write text and data to a text file.
- Learn how to read text and data from a text file.
- Use text file I/O in a data translation activity.
- Understand the differences between text and binary file formats.
- Learn how to write and read primitive values to and from binary files.
- Learn the use of a data file header.
- Learn how to write and read objects to and from Java object files.
- Use the API `File` class to gather information about a specified file.
- Implement GUI file chooser functionality with the API `JFileChooser` class.

Outline

15.1 Introduction

Up until now, all program input has come from the keyboard and all output has gone to the computer screen. But that type of input/output (I/O) is temporary. When you send output to the computer screen, it's not saved. A day later, if you want to display it again, you have to run the program again. Likewise, when you enter input from the keyboard, the input is not saved. A day later, if you want to use the same input, you have to enter it again.

For permanent or re-usable I/O, you can store input or output data in a *file*. A file is a group of related data that is typically stored in a contiguous block on a non-volatile storage device (such as a hard disk). Data files are fundamentally the same as the `.java` and `.class` program files that you have been using all along to hold your java programs. But instead of holding programs, data files hold data that programs read from for input or write to for output. To keep from confusing yourself or your computer, for your data files, you should name them with an extension that identifies them as data, like `.txt` or `.data`.

In this chapter you'll learn how to write code that creates output data files and stores data in those files, and you'll learn how to write code that reads data from pre-existing input files. You'll learn how to do these things with simple *text files,* which hold their data as text characters. You'll learn how to do these things more efficiently with *binary files,* which hold data in *native* format—the format your computer uses when it processes data during program execution. And you'll learn how to store complete objects in *object files.*

15.2 Java API Classes You Need to Import

In programs that manipulate files, you will use several of Java's pre-built classes. To access these classes, you need to `import` the packages that contain them. Figure 15.1 shows the subset of Java API classes we'll discuss in this chapter. You'll recognize the `Scanner` class because you've been using it to get input from a keyboard. In this chapter, you'll learn how to use it to get input from a file, too. As you know, you can import it with this statement:

```
import java.util.Scanner;
```

All the rest of the classes in Figure 15.1 are in the `java.io` package. Usually, you'll need more than one of them, and you can import any combination with this wildcard statement:

```
import java.io.*;
```

The three groupings that appear in Figure 15.1, that is, "text," "binary," and "object," identify three different I/O strategies. Each has its place. Text I/O is a handy way to store primitive data types. It's relatively easy to read or write text files in Java, and you can use almost any other kind of computer program (like word processors and spreadsheets) to read or write text files. Binary files hold data more efficiently than either text files or object files. When the data to be stored is complex—involves objects or a combination of objects and primitives—object files are easiest to use. Be aware that it's hard to inspect a binary file or object file because you can't read such files with text processing programs. To read a binary file, you must know how it's organized. To read an object file, you must know the types of objects it holds, but you can ignore their internal structure because structural information inserted by the JVM when you write an object file tells the JVM how the file is organized when you read it.

In addition to the classes that appear in Figure 15.1, there are also many other classes that deal with file I/O, and their operations overlap. In other words, some classes handle the same sort of file operation as other classes do. Why are there so many classes? Each class has different features, so certain classes work better in certain situations. There's also an historical reason. File I/O classes were added to the Java language incrementally. Whenever the Java designers realized that the file I/O classes were deficient in some way, they didn't want to modify the existing classes because that would mess up existing code that depended on those classes. So they added new classes. Unfortunately, the result is that there are many file I/O classes, and it's hard to remember what they all do. We'll discuss only those that are the most useful and most straightforward.

Text file I/O. For primitive data. Easy to understand.
Computer transforms primitive data from native format into readable text format for files.
You can create or view text files with almost any text editor.

for output to a text file:
```
PrintWriter
FileWriter
```
for input from a text file:
```
Scanner
FileReader
```

Binary file I/O. For primitive data. Efficient.
Files get primitive data in native format.
You cannot create or view binary files with a text editor, but binary files are very compact.

for output to a binary file:
```
DataOutputStream
FileOutputStream
```
for input from a binary file:
```
DataInputStream
FileInputStream
```

Object file I/O. For complete objects. Easy to use.
Computer decomposes objects into primitive data for files, which also get descriptive headers.
You cannot create or view object files with a text editor, but your coding is minimized.

for output to an object file:
```
ObjectOutputStream
FileOutputStream        <same as for binary output>
```
for input from an object file:
```
ObjectInputStream
FileInputStream         <same as for binary input>
```

Figure 15.1 Classes we recommend using for file I/O
The `Scanner` class is in the `java.util` package. The others are in the `java.io` package.

The simplest way to store text and/or text representations of numbers is in text files. In text files, everything is represented in terms of ASCII characters, which we described in Chapter 11. As shown in Figure 11.4, each ASCII character is coded in an eight-bit sequence of 0's and 1's. We'll discuss this coding scheme in more depth later in this chapter, in Section 15.6. To write text to a text file, we recommend that you use the `PrintWriter` class, which has `println`, `print`, and `printf`, methods. Those methods parallel the same-named methods that you've called from `System.out` for quite a while. The `System.out` methods print to the computer monitor. The `PrintWriter` methods print to a file. To read text from a text file, we recommend that you use the `Scanner` class, which has the `nextLine`, `next`, `nextInt`, `nextLong`, `nextFloat`, and `nextDouble` methods that you've used for quite a while. But now you'll use those methods to get input from a file rather than from a keyboard. The `Scanner` class works in conjunction with the `FileReader` class. You instantiate the `Scanner` constructor with a `FileReader` argument. We present text-file examples that use `PrintWriter`, `Scanner`, and `FileReader` in Sections 15.3 and 15.4.

The most efficient way to store homogeneous arrays of primitive data is in binary files. To write primitive data to a binary file, you instantiate an object of the `DataOutputStream` class with an argument that refers to an object of the `FileOutputStream` class. (A *stream* is a sequential flow of data.) To read primitive data from a binary file, you instantiate an object of the `DataInputStream` class with an argument that refers to an object of the `FileInputStream` class. We illustrate use of `DataOutputStream`, `FileOutputStream`, `DataInputStream`, and `FileInputStream` in Section 15.7.

If you have a substantial amount of data in object form that you need to transfer to other Java programs, you'll want to use object files. To write objects (and any combination of primitives) to an object file, you instantiate an object of the `ObjectOutputStream` class with an argument that refers to an object of the `FileOutputStream` class. To read objects from an object file, you instantiate an object of the `ObjectInputStream` class with an argument that refers to an object of the `FileInputStream` class. We present examples that use `ObjectOutputStream`, `FileOutputStream`, `ObjectInputStream`, and `FileInputStream` in Section 15.8.

If you're interested in the alternative Java API file I/O classes, see Sun's Java API Web site at http://java.sun.com/javase/6/docs/api/.

15.3 Text-File Output

Readers who want to use file I/O early have the option of reading this section and the next section after completing Chapter 3, Section 3.23. If you elect to jump from Chapter 3 to here, you should be aware that some of the material in Sections 15.3 and 15.4 won't make sense. But if you treat Figure 15.2's program as a recipe, it will show you how to output to a file anything you can output to the computer screen. Likewise, if you treat Figure 15.5's program as a recipe, it will show you how to input from a file anything you can input from the keyboard.

In this section, we show you how to use a `PrintWriter` object to output text to a file. In Section 15.4, we show you how to use a `Scanner` object to input text from a file. For all file I/O, there are three basic steps:

- Open the file by instantiating the appropriate class(es).
- Write to or read from the file by calling the appropriate method.
- Close the file by calling the `close` method.

Let's now consider these three steps in relation to the `PrintWriter` class.

Opening a Text File for Output

To open a text file for output, instantiate the `PrintWriter` class like this:

```
PrintWriter <reference-variable>;
. . .
<reference-variable> = new PrintWriter(<filename>);
```

Note that there is no explicit "open" command in this statement. You just instantiate a `PrintWriter` object and that automatically opens the file specified by the `PrintWriter` constructor's filename argument.

If the filename is invalid, the JVM throws a `FileNotFoundException`. There are several ways for the filename to be invalid: (1) The filename might contain an invalid filename character, like an asterisk, (2) The filename might specify a directory rather than a file, (3) The filename might specify a nonexistent directory followed by a filename (e.g., `javaFiles/Mouse.java`). The `FileNotFoundException` is a checked exception, so the `PrintWriter` constructor call must be in a `try` block, and the corresponding `catch` block's parameter must match the `FileNotFoundException`.

To open a file for text output, all you need to do is write the statement specified above. You don't have to know how it works. But if you're curious, here's an explanation: Whenever you instantiate a `PrintWriter` object, you also automatically get a `FileWriter` object. That `FileWriter` object uses one of the `write` methods it inherits from its parent, `OutputStreamWriter`, to transform a *stream* (or sequence) of Unicode characters into a stream of bytes—the file's natural data format. In addition, `FileWriter` provides a *buffer* for that final stream of bytes. A buffer is a variable-length array that absorbs data-flow variations, so that the flow of data out of the processor (where the program is) does not have to be perfectly synchronized with the flow of data into memory (where the file is). Suppose the hardware that services memory is busy. If there were no buffer, the program would have to stop and wait until that hardware became available. But with a buffer, the processor can simply put the data into the buffer and let it pile up there. Then when the memory-servicing hardware becomes free, it can scoop up everything that has accumulated in the buffer and transfer it into memory in a relatively large chunk. Because of its ability to absorb variations in data flow rates, a buffer is a great performance enhancer—it makes a program run faster. So you can see that opening a file is a big operation. It builds a substantial "infrastructure" to carry data from the processor to the file whenever needed.

Example Program

See the WriteTextFile program in Figure 15.2. It illustrates how to use the `PrintWriter` class for text-file output. The `PrintWriter` constructor call causes the JVM to open the user-specified file as just described. If the specified file does not exist, the program creates a new one. If the specified file exists already, the program clears the contents of that file before writing the new data.

Because the `PrintWriter` constructor throws a checked exception, the WriteTextFile program embeds the `PrintWriter` constructor call in a `try` block, and it provides a corresponding `FileNotFoundException` `catch` block.[1] The `catch` block calls `e.getMessage`, which returns the exception's automatically generated error message.

To write to the opened text file, the program calls `PrintWriter`'s `println` method. As indicated earlier, it works like `System.out.println`, which automatically appends a line terminator. The `PrintWriter` class also has `print` and `printf` methods, which work like `System.out`'s `print` and `printf` methods. These latter two methods do not supply line terminators automatically, so if you want new lines with them, be sure to supply explicit `\n` characters. All these methods accept `String` arguments and convert those strings into streams of characters. The `FileWriter` object in the background transforms the streams of characters into streams of bytes for the file.

To close the opened text file, the program calls `PrintWriter`'s `close` method using this format:

```
<PrintWriter-reference-variable>.close();
```

This flushes out any partially filled streams and disassembles the outputting "infrastructure." Remember to close a file after you're done. If you write to a `PrintWriter` file and forget to close the file, all the data in

[1] As indicated in the previous chapter, it's possible to remove `try` and `catch` blocks from a method by adding a `throws` clause to the method header. But we recommend against this practice, because it unnecessarily separates exception handling from the point where the exception occurs, and that makes programs harder to understand and debug.

```
/*******************************************************
* WriteTextFile.java
* Dean & Dean
*
* This writes a string to a text file.
*******************************************************/

import java.util.Scanner;
import java.io.*;

public class WriteTextFile
{
  public static void main(String[] args)
  {
    Scanner stdIn = new Scanner(System.in);
    PrintWriter fileOut;
    String text = "Hello, world!";

    try
    {
      System.out.print("Enter filename: ");
      fileOut = new PrintWriter(stdIn.nextLine());   // Open the file.
      fileOut.println(text);   // Write to the file.
      fileOut.close();   // Close the file.
    }
    catch (FileNotFoundException e)   // for PrintWriter constructor call
    {
      System.out.println("Error: " + e.getMessage());
    }
  } // end main
} // end WriteTextFile class
```

Figure 15.2 WriteTextFile program for writing text to a new file or overwriting an old file

the file's write operation(s) might not be saved to the file. Also, if you forget to close a file, system resources remain allocated to the open file, and that causes system performance to degrade.

Appending Data to an Existing File

Suppose you already have data in an existing file and you would like to add data to it. To append new data to an existing file, you call a `PrintWriter` constructor, as before, but you have to get some help from a `FileWriter` object. Specifically, you have to pass a `FileWriter` object to the `PrintWriter` constructor. To see what we're talking about, examine the `PrintWriter` instantiation code in Figure 15.3.

To open a file for text output in append mode, all you need to do is write the `fileOut =` statement shown in Figure 15.3. You don't have to know why it is the way it is. But if you're curious, here's an explanation: None of the various overloaded `PrintWriter` constructors includes an `append` parameter,

```
/*************************************************************
* WriteTextFile2.java
* Dean & Dean
*
* This appends data to an existing text file.
*************************************************************/

import java.util.Scanner;
import java.io.*;

public class WriteTextFile2
{
  public static void main(String[] args)
  {
    Scanner stdIn = new Scanner(System.in);
    PrintWriter fileOut;
    String text = "Hello, world!";

    try
    {
      System.out.print("Enter filename: ");
      fileOut =
        new PrintWriter(new FileWriter(stdIn.nextLine(), true));
      fileOut.println(text);
      fileOut.close();
    }
    catch (IOException e)
    {
      System.out.println("IO: " + e.getMessage());
    }
  } // end main
} // end WriteTextFile2 class
```

value passed to boolean append parameter
IOException needed for FileWriter also catches FileNotFoundException.

Figure 15.3 WriteTextFile2 program for appending text to an existing file

but there is a `FileWriter` constructor that does. So instead of using the `PrintWriter` constructor which automatically instantiates a `FileWriter` object that never appends, you can explicitly construct a `FileWriter` object that can append. Then you can pass it to an overloaded `PrintWriter` constructor which has a `Writer` parameter type. Since the `FileWriter` class is a descendant of the `Writer` class, this other `PrintWriter` constructor accepts a `FileWriter` object as its argument.

The second parameter in the `FileWriter` constructor is a `boolean` which tells the computer whether you want to append or not. Using `true` says you want to append. If you wanted, you could use this more elaborate file opening statement to create a new file or completely overwrite an existing output file by using `false` for the second argument in the `FileWriter` constructor. Note that this alternate way of opening a text file for output requires a more generic `catch` to catch either `PrintWriter`'s `FileNotFoundException` or an `IOException` thrown by the `FileWriter` constructor. (The `PrintWriter` constructor used in Figure 15.2 catches `FileWriter`'s `IOException` internally.)

Figure 15.3's explicit `FileWriter` performs the same basic streaming activity that Figure 15.2's implicit `FileWriter` performs. In either case, here's what the text output process looks like:[2]

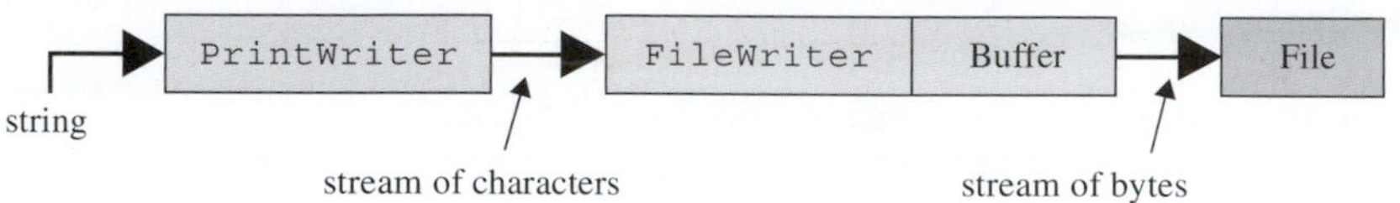

There's one additional item worth mentioning in Figure 15.3. Notice the `fileOut` assignment, repeated here for your convenience:

```
fileOut = new PrintWriter(new FileWriter(stdIn.nextLine(), true));
```

anonymous object

The `new FileWriter` code, embedded in `PrintWriter`'s constructor call, is an example of an anonymous object. Anonymous objects are very common when working with files because file constructors often use other file objects as arguments. In those cases, there's no need to save the newly instantiated argument file in a separate variable. Just use it anonymously.

15.4 Text-File Input

Suppose you have a large amount of input data that you need to use more than once. Instead of entering it directly from the keyboard repeatedly, it's more efficient and more reliable to enter it into a file just once. You can create a Java-readable text file with almost any text editor or word processor, provided you save it as "Plain Text." Then read the data from the file each time you need it. In this section, we show you how to read input from a text file.

Opening a Text File for Input

It's possible to open a file for input using an instance of the `FileReader` class with a filename argument. That enables you to read in one character at a time. Sometimes that's what you want to do. But usually you would rather read a whole line, a whole word, or some type of number. `Scanner` has methods that perform these other operations. So, to open a text file for string input, we recommend that you instantiate the `FileReader` and `Scanner` classes together in a single statement, as shown below:

```
Scanner <reference-variable>;
...
<reference-variable> = new Scanner(new FileReader(<filename>));
```

If the file specified by the `FileReader` constructor's filename argument is invalid, the JVM throws a `FileNotFoundException`. That should sound familiar—we said the same thing about the `PrintWriter` constructor for text-file output. But there is an important difference. The `PrintWriter` constructor allows the filename argument to specify a non-existent file. The `FileReader` constructor

[2] Optionally, you can speed up execution by inserting a `BufferedWriter` object between the `PrintWriter` and `FileWriter` objects.

requires the filename argument to specify an existing file. The `FileNotFoundException` is a checked exception, so unless you want to use a `throws` clause, you must put the `FileReader` constructor call in a `try` block, and the corresponding `catch` block's parameter must match the `FileNotFoundException`.

To open a file for text input, all you need to do is use `new Scanner(new FileReader(`*<filename>*`))` as shown above. You don't have to know why it is the way it is. But if you're curious, here's an explanation: None of the various `Scanner` constructors accepts a filename argument like the `PrintWriter` constructor in Figure 15.2 does.[3] So if you want to use `Scanner`, you must use it in combination with another class that does accept a filename argument and also matches the parameter type in one of the available `Scanner` constructors. One of `Scanner` constructors has a `Readable` parameter type. Since the `FileReader` class implements the `Readable` interface, you can instantiate a `FileReader` object and supply it as an argument in this `Scanner` constructor.

The `FileReader` object buffers input from the file and transforms the file's bytes into characters. The `Scanner` object converts the stream of characters into strings and numbers. Here's what the text input process looks like:[4]

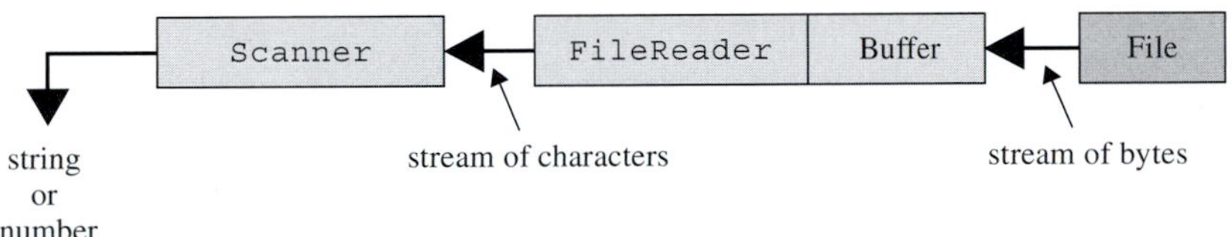

Example Program

Let's now see how text-file input works in the context of a complete program. Suppose you have a text file named `markAntony.txt` that contains the quotation from Shakespeare's play *Julius Caesar* shown in Figure 15.4a. Also, suppose you have a text file named `randomNumbers.txt` that contains the list of random numbers shown Figure 15.4b.

```
Friends, Romans, countrymen,
Lend me your ears;
I come to bury Caesar,
not to praise him.
```

Figure 15.4a Contents of `markAntony.txt` text file

```
0.9709900750891582  0.3874009922012617  0.1262329780823327
0.7782696919307651  0.15480236215303655  0.9756100238518657
```

Figure 15.4b Contents of `randomNumbers.txt` text file

[3] The `Scanner` constructor with a `String` parameter reads a plain old string, not a file.

[4] Optionally, you can speed up execution by inserting a `BufferedReader` object between the `Scanner` and `FileReader` objects.

Figure 15.5 contains a ReadTextFile program that can read the data in either of those files. Be aware that the numbers appearing in Figure 15.4b do not go into the program as numbers. They go into the program as string representations of numbers. The ReadTextFile program prompts the user for a filename (such as `markAntony.txt` or `randomNumbers.txt`), reads the specified file, and prints the file's contents. Most of the program's code is straightforward, but some of it deserves attention. . . .

You've used the `Scanner` class for keyboard input for quite a while now. When using the `Scanner` class for file input, you can still use your old friends, `nextInt`, `nextDouble`, `nextLine`, and so on the same way that you did for keyboard input. But with file input, you should be aware of several additional `Scanner` methods. When you're done reading from the `Scanner` file, call its `close` method. See `fileIn.close()` in Figure 15.5. Also, when reading a series of lines from a file, you'll often want to use `Scanner`'s `hasNextLine` method in a `while` loop header, as we do in Figure 15.5.

```
/****************************************************************
* ReadTextFile.java
* Dean & Dean
*
* This reads data from a text file.
****************************************************************/
import java.util.Scanner;
import java.io.*;

public class ReadTextFile
{
  public static void main(String[] args)
  {
    Scanner stdIn = new Scanner(System.in);
    Scanner fileIn;
    String line;

    try
    {
      System.out.print("Enter filename: ");
      fileIn = new Scanner(new FileReader(stdIn.nextLine()));
      while (fileIn.hasNextLine())
      {
        line = fileIn.nextLine();
        System.out.println(line);
      }
      fileIn.close();
    }
    catch (FileNotFoundException e)
    {
      System.out.println("Error: " + e.getMessage());
    }
  } // end main
} // end ReadTextFile class
```

Open the file.

Read a line from the file and print it.

Close the file.

Figure 15.5 ReadTextFile program that reads text from the keyboard and also from a text file

Scanner's hasNextLine method provides a convenient loop-termination signal when you're reading data with Scanner's nextLine method. Looping stops automatically at the end of the file when there are no more lines to read. You can use the program in Figure 15.5 to read either the text in Figure 15.4a or the numbers in Figure 15.4b. It works for the numbers as well as the text because the program just prints the numbers and spaces between them as it reads them—as sequences of characters—without bothering to interpret the meanings of those sequences of characters.

Instead of reading a full line at a time, you could use Scanner's hasNext method as a loop termination signal and then read data with Scanner's next method. The next method reads one *token* at a time. A token is a sequence of characters separated from preceding and subsequent sequences by whitespace. Said another way, a token is an isolated word or number. Whether you read a line at a time or a token at a time, it's hard to fail at reading pure text!

It's a different story, however, if the program needs to know the numerical values of numbers in a text file. If the text file has whitespace between adjacent numbers, the computer can read those numbers and simultaneously *parse* them (determine their numerical values) by using Scanner methods like nextInt or nextDouble. These methods throw unchecked exceptions if parsing errors occur. If you want to enhance the program in Figure 15.5 to include numerical parsing, you might want to catch the unchecked exceptions thrown by parsing errors.

Reading Formatted Data in a Text File

Use knowledge of format.

If you want to use Scanner's nextInt or nextDouble to parse numerical data as it is input, you must use whitespace to make each number a separate token. It is not absolutely necessary, however, to use whitespace to separate items in a text file. Instead, you can keep track of the character position of the start and end of each item. That's what was done in the days of old. For example, suppose each line in the file is formatted into three fields, like this:

columns 0–20 hold a String that might contain more than one word

columns 21–28 hold the text representation of an int

columns 30–42 hold the text representation of a double.

To read the three fields, you should declare these three variables:

```
String text;
int iNum;
double dNum;
```

Read each line in as pure text, and then parse it, like this:

```
...
line = in.nextLine();
text = line.substring(0,21);
iNum = Integer.parseInt(line.substring(21,29).trim());
dNum = Double.parseDouble(line.substring(30,43).trim());
```

As you might recall, substring's second argument is one greater than the index of the last character in the substring that is to be extracted. So in the above code fragment's third statement, 29 is one greater than the int field's last column.

15.5 HTML File Generator

Now let's look at an example that illustrates both input from a text file and output to a text file. The program in Figures 15.6a and 15.6b reads the contents of a user-specified text file. It translates that data into a Web page format. Then, it outputs the translation to a newly generated HTML file.

```
/**********************************************************
* HTMLGenerator.java
* Dean & Dean
*
* This program copies the contents of a user-specified
* file and pastes it into a newly generated HTML file.
**********************************************************/

import java.util.Scanner;
import java.io.*;

public class HTMLGenerator
{
  public static void main(String[] args)
  {
    Scanner stdIn = new Scanner(System.in);
    String filenameIn;     // original file's name
    Scanner fileIn;        // input file connection
    int dotIndex;          // position of dot in filename
    String filenameOut;    // HTML file's name
    PrintWriter fileOut;   // HTML file connection
    String line;           // a line from the input file

    System.out.print("Enter file's name: ");
    filenameIn = stdIn.nextLine();

    try
    {
      fileIn = new Scanner(new FileReader(filenameIn));

      // Compose the new filename
      dotIndex = filenameIn.lastIndexOf(".");
      if (dotIndex == -1) // no dot found
      {
        filenameOut = filenameIn + ".html";
      }
      else // dot found
      {
        filenameOut =
          filenameIn.substring(0, dotIndex) + ".html";
      }
      fileOut = new PrintWriter(filenameOut);
```

This opens a file for input.

This opens a file for output.

Figure 15.6a HTMLGenerator program—part A

In Figure 15.6a, the program starts by reading a user-specified filename into the `filenameIn` variable. Then it uses the entered filename to open the input file and create a `Scanner` object named `fileIn` to manage file reading operations.

The name of the output file should be the same as the name of the input file except for the extension, which should be `.html`. To compose the name of the output file, the `String` method `lastIndexOf` finds the index of the last dot in `filenameIn`. If there is no dot, the `lastIndexOf` method returns a value of `-1`, and the program simply appends `.html` to the original filename. If there is a dot, `String`'s `substring` method returns the part of the string up to the character immediately before the dot, and the program adds `.html` to that. This process replaces the original filename's extension with a `.html` extension, and it assigns the result to `filenameOut`.

Before examining the rest of the program, let's digress by providing a brief overview of HTML (the computer language used to create Internet Web pages). This book is not about HTML, but the following overview will help you understand the HTMLGenerator program. Also, it's worth learning a little about HTML because Internet Web pages are what got the Java language going.

HTML overview:

- HTML *tags* are surrounded by angled brackets, and they describe the purpose of their associated text.
- Tags without slashes (like `<html>`, `<head>`, and `<title>` tags) are called *start tags*. Tags with slashes (like `</title>`, `</head>`, and `</html>` tags) are called *end tags*.
- `<html>` and `</html>` tags surround the entire Web page.
- The content between `<head>` and `</head>` tags is the heading for an HTML page. The heading contains information that describes the HTML page. This information is used by the browser and by search engines, but it is not visible on the HTML page.
- `<title>` and `</title>` tags surround the text that appears in a Web page's title bar. Internet search engines use the `<title>` content to find Web pages.
- The content between `<body>` and `</body>` tags is the body for the HTML page. The body contains the text that's displayed on the HTML page.
- `<h1>` and `</h1>` tags surround the text that appears as a heading within a Web page. Web browsers use large fonts to display text that's surrounded by `<h1>` tags.
- `<p>` tags indicate the beginning of a new paragraph. Web browsers generate a blank line for each `<p>` tag, and this helps set paragraphs apart.

Now let's analyze Figure 15.6b, the second half of the HTMLGenerator program. The code starts by checking for an empty input file. If it's empty, it prints a warning message. Otherwise, it does the following. It prints `<html>` and `<head>` tags to the output file. It prints the input file's first line to the output file, surrounded by `<title>` and `</title>` tags. Then it ends the Web page's head section by printing `</head>` to the output file, and it begins the Web page's body section by printing `<body>` to the output file. Then it re-uses the input file's first line and prints it to the output file, surrounded by `<h1>` and `</h1>` tags. Then it loops through the subsequent lines in the input file. For each blank line, it prints a `<p>` tag to the output file, indicating a new paragraph. It prints each line that's not blank to the output file as is.

To see how the HTMLGenerator program works when applied to an actual input file, study the input file and resulting output file in Figure 15.7. If you'd like to verify that the HTMLGenerator program generates a working Web page, create Figure 15.7's `family.txt` file, and then run the HTMLGenerator program with `family.txt` as input. That should generate Figure 15.7's `family.html` file. Open a browser window, and within that browser window, open the `family.html` file. For example, open a Microsoft Internet Explorer browser window and perform a File / Open command. Voila—you should see the `family.html` displayed as a Web page!

```
        // First line used for title and header elements
        line = fileIn.nextLine();
        if (line == null)
        {
          System.out.println(filenameIn + " is empty.");
        }
        else
        {
          // Write the top of the HTML page.
          fileOut.println("<html>");
          fileOut.println("<head>");
          fileOut.println("<title>" + line + "</title>");
          fileOut.println("</head>");
          fileOut.println("<body>");
          fileOut.println("<h1>" + line + "</h1>");

          while (fileIn.hasNextLine())
          {
            line = fileIn.nextLine();

            // Blank lines generate p tags.
            if (line.isEmpty())
            {
              fileOut.println("<p>");
            } // end if
            else
            {
              fileOut.println(line);
            }
          } // end while

          // Write ending HTML code.
          fileOut.println("</body>");
          fileOut.println("</html>");
        } // end else
        fileIn.close();
        fileOut.close();
      } // end try

      catch (FileNotFoundException e)
      {
        System.out.println("Error: " + e.getMessage());
      } // end catch
    } // end main
  } // end class HTMLGenerator
```

Figure 15.6b HTMLGenerator program—part B

Example input file, `family.txt`:

```
Our Family

We have a dog, Barkley. Barkley is a good dog. She sleeps a lot
and digs up the grass. We feed her twice a day.

We have two kids, Jordan and Caiden. They're girls. They like to
eat, cry, and play. We like them a lot.
```

Resulting output file, `family.html`:

```
<html>
<head>
<title>Our Family</title>
</head>
<body>
<h1>Our Family</h1>
<p>
We have a dog, Barkley. Barkley is a good dog. She sleeps a lot
and digs up the grass. We feed her twice a day.
<p>
We have two kids, Jordan and Caiden. They're girls. They like to
eat, cry, and play. We like them a lot.
</body>
</html>
```

First line of input file appears twice in output file.

This works, but to conform to strict HTML standards, Web pages should have a </p> at the end of each paragraph.

Figure 15.7 Example input file for the HTMLGenerator program and its resulting output file

Note Figure 15.7's second callout. To conform to strict HTML standards, you should insert a `</p>` tag at the end of each paragraph. However, many current Web pages conform only to loose HTML standards, not to strict HTML standards. Current browsers handle both strict and loose Web pages, but future browsers will probably handle only strict Web pages. An end-of-chapter exercise asks you to improve the HTMLGenerator program so that it generates `</p>` end tags at the end of every paragraph.

15.6 Text File Data Format Versus Binary File Data Format

This section compares the text format used in text files with the native binary format used in binary files and object files.

Text Format

Text file data is stored using eight-bit American Standard Code for Information Interchange (ASCII) values. Since the ASCII character set is a universal standard, ASCII characters can be read by almost any text editor[5] or word processor, and they can be read by programs written in any language, not just Java.

[5] Exception: Microsoft Notepad recognizes only `\r\n` as a line terminator. Thus if Notepad tries to read a Java text file that uses `\n` for line termination, it displays each `\n` as an unrecognized character (□) and does not generate a new line.

Text files are line oriented. When writing to a text file, `PrintWriter`'s `println` method automatically inserts an end-of-line symbol at the end of the line. In Microsoft Windows, it inserts `\r\n`. (`\r` is the carriage return symbol, and `\n` is the new line symbol.) In UNIX , it inserts `\n` only. When reading from a text file, `Scanner`'s `nextLine` method reads an entire line of characters, and it accepts either `\r\n` or `\n` by itself as a line terminator, but it does not include the terminator in the retrieved string. Since `\n` by itself is simpler, we'll use it in our illustrations. Now let's see what a text file looks like. Suppose you have this data:

```
Bob 2222
Paul5555
```

Figure 15.8 shows how it's stored in a text file.

B	o	b		2	2	2	2	\n	P
01000010	01101111	01100010	00100000	00110010	00110010	00110010	00110010	00001010	01010000
a	u	l	5	5	5	5	\n		
01100001	01110101	01101100	00110101	00110101	00110101	00110101	00001010		

Figure 15.8 Raw form of text format
ASCII characters are shown in blue above each byte. Each logical line is terminated by the `\n` character, but in a file everything is strung together in one continuous sequence. Here the sequence wraps around so that everything fits within the available page width.

Now let's analyze the actual storage for characters in this text file. The ASCII code value for 'B' is decimal 66. (B's value, along with all the other ASCII code values can be found in Figure 11.4.) To find the equivalent binary value, identify the powers of two that add up to 66. 2^6 and 2^1 are the powers of two that add up to 66 ($2^6 = 64$, $2^1 = 2$, and $64 + 2 = 66$). For each identified power of two, use its exponent as a place marker for a 1 in the equivalent binary value. For the 66 example, the powers of two, 2^6 and 2^1, have 6 and 1 exponents, so the 6 and 1 bit positions are 1 in the following binary representation of 66. Note that bit positions start at 0 from the right side.

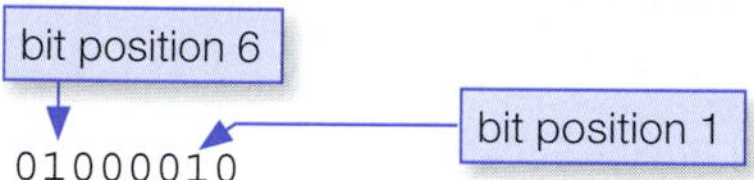

Here's the mathematical explanation of why decimal 66 is equivalent to binary 01000010:

$$66 = (64 + 2) = (2^6 + 2^1) = (0*2^7 + 1*2^6 + 0*2^5 + 0*2^4 + 0*2^3 + 0*2^2 + 1*2^1 + 0*2^0)$$
$$= (01000010)$$

The ASCII code value for a space character is decimal 32. The binary value is:

$$32 = (2^5) = (0*2^7 + 0*2^6 + 1*2^5 + 0*2^4 + 0*2^3 + 0*2^2 + 0*2^1 + 0*2^0) = (00100000)$$

The ASCII code value for '2' is decimal 50. The binary value is:

$$50 = (32 + 16 + 2) = (2^5 + 2^4 + 2^1) =$$
$$(0*2^7 + 0*2^6 + 1*2^5 + 1*2^4 + 0*2^3 + 0*2^2 + 1*2^1 + 0*2^0) = (00110010)$$

The ASCII code value for the new line character is decimal 10. The binary value is:

$$10 = (8 + 2) = (2^3 + 2^1) = (0*2^7 + 0*2^6 + 0*2^5 + 0*2^4 + 1*2^3 + 0*2^2 + 1*2^1 + 0*2^0) = (00001010)$$

Note that a new line character does not put the data on a separate "line" in a file. `Bob 2222` and `Paul5555` print on separate lines, but within a file the data is stored sequentially—one byte after another.

Binary Format

When writing primitive values to a binary file or an object file, Java uses each data type's native storage format. We don't like the name "binary file" because it implies that binary files use binary numbers and text files do not. Actually, all computer file information is "binary" in the sense that everything on a computer is represented with 1's and 0's. We'd prefer that "binary files" be called "native storage files," but alas, "binary" is the term everyone uses. So when we talk about a binary format, we mean the native storage format recognized by the processor. For example, in a binary file, a `char` uses *16-bit Unicode,* an `int` uses *32-bit 2's complement,* a `double` uses the standard *64-bit IEEE floating-point,* and so on. See Chapter 11 for a discussion of Unicode. 2's complement means:[6] if (binaryValue >= 2^{bits-1}) then value = binaryValue − 2^{bits}. IEEE stands for Institute of Electrical and Electronic Engineers.

Binary files are not line oriented. Binary file read methods do not recognize end-of-line characters as having any special function. These characters may be present—just like any other characters—but they do not affect the extent of what's read, and methods that write to binary files never append end-of-line characters automatically. Therefore, programs that access primitive data in binary files do not read or write whole lines. That is, they do not use `nextLine` and `println` methods to read a line or print a line. Instead, they use methods like `readChar`, `writeChar`, `readInt`, `writeInt`, `readDouble`, `writeDouble`, and so on to read and write individual primitive variable values.

For example, suppose you have this data:

```
Bob2147483647
```

Figure 15.9 shows how it's stored in a binary or object file.

B		o		b		2147483647			
00000000	01000010	00000000	01101111	00000000	01100010	01111111	11111111	11111111	11111111

Figure 15.9 Raw form of binary format
Unicode characters and `int` number are shown in blue above 16-bit character and 32-bit number sequences.

Characters in a Java program use the 16-bit Unicode storage scheme. Therefore, a 'B' is usually stored in a binary file using the 16-bit Unicode storage scheme. In this scheme, the first byte has eight 0's, and the second byte's bit sequence matches the ASCII value for 'B' shown in Figure 15.8. The left eight bits for 'B', 'o', and 'b' are all zeros and that doesn't provide any useful information. So why are these extra eight bits there? As described in Chapter 11, they're there to handle Unicode characters that are not in the ASCII character set. Those other characters need the extra eight bits on the left to hold their full code values.

How is the `2147483647` stored? If it were a text file, the digits would be stored as 10 separate ASCII characters, which would take 10 bytes. But with a binary file, `2147483647` is stored as a single `int` number. Since an `int` takes 32 bits, binary files use 32 bits to store `int`'s, and that takes only 4 bytes. The most significant bit indicates the sign of the number. A 0 in the most significant position says the number is positive. A 1 in the most significant position says the number is negative. The number `2147483647`

[6] Here's an `int` example (where bits = 32): If binaryValue = (10000000000000000000000000000000) = 2^{31} = 2147483648, then value = 2147483648 − 4294967296 = −2147483648. For a more extensive explanation of 2's complement, see http://en.wikipedia.org/wiki/Two's_complement.

happens to be the largest positive number an `int` can hold. Since it's a positive number, the most significant bit must be 0. Since it's the largest positive number, all the other bits are 1. Sure enough, if you punch it out on your hand calculator, you'll find that:

$$(01111111\ 11111111\ 11111111\ 11111111) =$$
$$(0*2^{31} + 1*2^{30} + 1*2^{29} + 1*2^{28} + 1*2^{27} + 1*2^{26} + 1*2^{25} + 1*2^{24} +$$
$$1*2^{23} + 1*2^{22} + 1*2^{21} + 1*2^{20} + 1*2^{19} + 1*2^{18} + 1*2^{17} + 1*2^{16} +$$
$$1*2^{15} + 1*2^{14} + 1*2^{13} + 1*2^{12} + 1*2^{11} + 1*2^{10} + 1*2^{9} + 1*2^{8} +$$
$$1*2^{7} + 1*2^{6} + 1*2^{5} + 1*2^{4} + 1*2^{3} + 1*2^{2} + 1*2^{1} + 1*2^{0}) =$$

```
2147483647
```

Trade-Offs

Benefits of text files:

- Independent creation—using UNIX vi, Microsoft Notepad, Wordpad, Word Text File, and so on.
- Independent viewing—using almost any word processor or other computer language.

Benefits of binary files or object files:

- Can handle all Unicode characters
- More efficient number storage
- Can store complex objects

15.7 Binary File I/O

In Java it's straightforward to store primitive data in binary files. From a hardware perspective, it's the most efficient storage strategy.

Output

To open a binary file for primitive data output, instantiate a `FileOutputStream` object. This sends a stream of bytes to the file. To transform primitive data types into bytes, instantiate a `DataOutputStream` object. The `FileOutputStream` class descends from the `OutputStream` class, and the only `DataOutputStream` constructor has an `OutputStream` type of parameter, so you can pass the new `FileOutputStream` object directly into the `DataOutputStream` constructor as an argument like this:[7]

```
DataOutputStream fileOut;
...
fileOut =
  new DataOutputStream(new FileOutputStream(stdIn.nextLine(), true));
...
```

[7] Optionally, you can speed up execution by inserting a `BufferedOutputStream` object between the `DataOutputStream` and `FileOutputStream` objects.

This looks rather like the fileOut = statement in Figure 15.3. The FileOutputStream instantiation here is like the FileWriter instantiation in Figure 15.3 in that it opens the file and implements a buffer. As in Figure 15.3, the second argument says whether to append or overwrite an existing file. This object is different from FileWriter object in that it does not perform any fundamental data-type transformation. It just receives raw bytes or an array of raw bytes, and it passes those bytes on to the file unchanged. The data transformation is done by the DataOutputStream object, which uses one of its write methods to convert primitive data or a string into an appropriate sequence of char's. To write an individual char, int, double, or String to a file, you could use one of these DataOutputStream methods:

```
void writeChar(int ch)
void writeInt(int i)
void writeDouble(double x)
void writeChars(String s)
```

For example, suppose you had an array of double values called doubleValues. In a try block after the above file-opening statement, you could write these values to the binary file using code like this:

```
for (int i=0; i<doubleValues.length; i++)
{
  fileOut.writeDouble(doubleValues[i]);
}
```

The writeChars method writes a string "as is"—it does not append any line-termination character(s). However, the original String object could include any number of '\n' characters at any places. Thus, you could refer to a multi-line document with just one String variable, and you could write that whole document to a binary file with a single for loop that contains just one writeChars statement.

Input

To open a binary file for primitive data input, instantiate a FileInputStream and a DataInputStream like this:[8]

```
DataInputStream fileIn;
...
fileIn =
  new DataInputStream(new FileInputStream(stdIn.nextLine()));
...
```

This looks rather like the fileIn = statement in Figure 15.5. The FileInputStream instantiation here is like the FileReader instantiation in Figure 15.5 in that it opens the file and provides a buffer. FileInputStream is different from FileReader object, however, in that it does not perform a data-type transformation. It just receives raw bytes from the file and passes them on. All data transformation is done by the DataInputStream object, which uses one of its read methods to convert the bytes it receives into primitive variables. To read an individual char, int, or double to a file, you could use one of these DataInputStream methods:

[8] Optionally, you can speed up execution by inserting a BufferedInputStream object between the DataInputStream and FileInputStream objects.

```
char readChar()
int readInt()
double readDouble()
```

For example, suppose you had declared an array of `double` values called `doubleData`. In a `try` block after the above file-opening statement, you could fill this array with data from the binary file using code like this:

```
for (int i=0; i<doubleData.length; i++)
{
  doubleData[i] = fileIn.readDouble();
}
```

Common Properties

The `FileOutputStream` and `FileInputStream` constructors throw `FileNotFoundExceptions`, and the methods in the `DataOutputStream` and `DataInputStream` classes throw `IOExceptions`. So you can use an `IOException catch` block to catch them all. Of course, you should close each file when you're finished with it, and you can use `close` methods inherited by the `DataOutputStream` and `DataInputStream` classes to perform this operation. It's easiest to include the `close` statement with the opening and transfer statements in the same `try` block.

The `DataInputStream` class does not include a viable line-input method. Although such a method does exist,[9] it's often better to read through `'\n'` characters and accumulate text input in larger chunks than lines. To do this, use the two-byte `null` character whose code value is zero to terminate a string-reading operation. You can append this character to your string when writing to a binary file with this statement:

```
fileOut.writeChar(0);
```

Then in your file-reading program, you can check each character as it comes in to see whether its code value equals zero. When it does, you're at the end of the string.

Structured Binary Files

Binary file I/O is easiest when file data is all one type. With some work, however, you can mix data types and put structure into a binary file. Doing this gives you a sense of what Java's built-in code does in the next section's object I/O. So let's look at a simple example of a structured binary file. Suppose you have a binary file that contains some entries from a database table. To read this information, you need to know how that file is structured. Let's say you know it has this relatively simple organization:

1. The first data block is for a text title and/or description. It is composed of an unspecified number of 2-byte `char`'s. This text block is terminated by the `null` character, whose code value is a sequence of two zero bytes.
2. The second data block is a single 4-byte `int`. It gives the number of sub-blocks in the third block.
3. The third block contains a number of identical sub-blocks. Each of these sub-blocks has two fields:
   a) The first field is a 4-byte `int`.
   b) The second field is an 8-byte `double`.

In your file-reading program, suppose you want to put the two values in each sub-block into the two instance variables of a new object of type `Record`. And suppose `Record` has a two-parameter constructor that initializes these two variables.

[9] If your binary file contains only text, instead of a `DataInputStream`, it's better to use a `BufferedReader`, and the `BufferedReader` class includes a `readLine` method.

The following code fragment shows what you might see in a program that reads data from a binary file having the above organization. After opening the file for binary input, the code stores the first block's characters into a StringBuffer called table. (The API StringBuffer class implements a flexible kind of String.) Notice how the while loop condition looks for a null character that signals the end of the incoming stream of characters. After the character-reading operation terminates, the code reads the second block's integer and stores it in an int called numRecords. Finally, the code instantiates Record objects to hold the pairs of values in the sub-blocks, and it adds those objects to an ArrayList called table.

```
Scanner stdIn = new Scanner(System.in);
DataInputStream fileIn;
char ch = 0;
int numRecords = 0;
ArrayList<Record> table = new ArrayList<Record>();
StringBuffer tableName = new StringBuffer();

System.out.print("Enter filename: ");
try
{
  fileIn = new DataInputStream(new FileInputStream(
    stdIn.nextLine()));
  while((ch = fileIn.readChar()) != 0)
  {
    tableName = tableName.append(ch);
  }
  numRecords = fileIn.readInt();
  for (int i=0; i<numRecords; i++)
  {
    table.add(new Record(
      fileIn.readInt(), fileIn.readDouble()));
  }
  fileIn.close();
} // end try
...
```

a flexible "array"

a flexible "string"

Accumulate characters in a StringBuffer.

Accumulate objects in an ArrayList.

A StringBuffer is more flexible than a String because it has append and insert methods that append to the end or insert anywhere in the middle. The above code uses the append method to accumulate characters as they stream in from the file. Of course, StringBuffer also has a toString method which allows you to convert a StringBuffer into a String at any later time.

The argument of the Record constructor in the table.add method call near the end of this example tells how each object's instance-variable values are arranged in the file. They are lined up in a sequence, one after another. Notice that our file-reading code had to know the basic file-formatting scheme ahead of time, but some of the file-format detail—the number of records the file contained—is embedded in the file itself. The file-reading code determines this formatting detail at the very last instant, as the data streams in. This combination of a standard *protocol* (formal agreement on how something should be done) plus an embedded variation is typical of formatting in real-world binary files. The difference is that real-world protocols and their embedded variations are a hundred times more complicated than our simple example. Programmers often employ some kind of pre-written software to perform the data transformations needed for binary file I/O.

15.8 Object File I/O

When you can remain within a Java programming environment, that is, use Java programs for all file writing and all file reading, you have an advantage. You can use software that's built into the Java language to perform the structural conversion between program objects and primitive data streams. This section explains how to use that built-in software.

Enabling Java Objects to be Stored in a File

The java language has built-in software that *serializes* each object's data as it goes into a file and *unserializes* that data as it comes out of a file and goes back into object form. Whenever a program writes serialized data into a file, it also writes the recipe it used to serialize that data. That recipe includes the type of the object, the type of each data item, and the sequence in which the data items are stored. When another program reads serialized data from a file, it also reads the recipe to learn how to reconstruct the object from the serialized data. To enable a class to use Java's built-in serializing software you must append the following clause to that class's heading:

```
implements Serializable
```

This makes it look like your class is implementing an interface. But this interface doesn't define any named constants, and it doesn't require that the class implement any particular methods. It just *tags* (identifies) the class's objects as objects needing serialization services. For example, look at the `TestObject` class in Figure 15.10. Notice that this class `implements` the `Serializable` interface.

Writing a `Serializable` Object to a File

Figure 15.11 contains a simple program that writes a `TestObject` object to a user-specified file. The first `try` block statement uses `ObjectOutputStream` and `FileOutputStream` instantiations to open the file. Notice that the `FileOutputStream` constructor has only one parameter. This constructor either creates a new file or over-writes an existing file. There is no append option. (One of this chapter's projects shows how to append objects to data already in an existing object file.) The second `try` block statement writes an object to the opened file. The object written is an instance of the class in Figure 15.10. The third statement closes the file.

The `catch` parameter is an `IOException` because the `ObjectOutputStream` constructor and `ObjectOutputStream`'s `writeObject` and `close` methods all throw an `IOException`. As indicated earlier, the `FileOutputStream` constructor throws a `FileNotFoundException`, but this exception is derived from `IOException`. Therefore, using `IOException` as the `catch` parameter enables the `catch` block to catch all of the exceptions that might be thrown from the `try` block.

Reading a `Serializable` Object from a File

Figure 15.12's ReadObject program tries to read data for two objects of the `TestObject` class from a user-specified file. The program's code should look familiar since it parallels Figure 15.11's WriteObject program. However, instead of using `FileOutputStream` and `ObjectOutputStream` constructors and the `writeObject` method, it uses `FileInputStream` and `ObjectInputStream` constructors and the `readObject` method. The only tricky thing is you must include a cast like `(TestObject)` to convert the reference returned by the `readObject` method to the specific type that defines the methods you want to use. That cast might throw a `ClassNotFoundException`, so we include an extra `catch` block for that exception.

```
/****************************************************
* TestObject.java
* Dean & Dean
*
* This is a typical heterogeneous object.
****************************************************/

import java.io.*;

public class TestObject implements Serializable
{
  private int id;
  private String text;
  public double number;

  //*************************************************

  public TestObject(int id, String text, double number)
  {
    this.id = id;
    this.text = text;
    this.number = number;
  } // end constructor

  //*************************************************

  public void display()
  {
    System.out.print(this.id + "\t");
    System.out.print(this.text + "\t");
    System.out.println(this.number);
  } // end display
} // end TestObject class
```

To be writable to and readable from a file, an object must be an instance of a class that implements this interface.

Figure 15.10 Typical definition of a `Serializable` object

Notice the second output in Figure 15.12's sample session. Can you figure out what happened? The WriteObject program outputs only one object to the `objectFile.data` file, but the ReadObject program tries to read two objects from that file. Since it cannot find a second object, the JVM throws an `IOException`, which generates the print statement in the last output line.

If a class is `Serializable`, all classes derived from it are automatically `Serializable`, too. Suppose your `Serializable` class has instance variables that refer to other objects. Those objects' classes also must be `Serializable`. This must be true through all levels in a composition hierarchy. Does this sound like a pain? It's not, really. Just be sure to include `implements Serializable` in the definition of all classes that define objects you'd like to store as objects. The alternative would be a pain, though. If you couldn't store a whole object, you'd have to provide explicit code to write and read each primitive data item

```
/*******************************************************************
* WriteObject.java
* Dean & Dean
*
* This writes an object to a binary file.
*******************************************************************/

import java.io.*;
import java.util.Scanner;

public class WriteObject
{
  public static void main(String[] args)
  {
    Scanner stdIn = new Scanner(System.in);
    ObjectOutputStream fileOut;
    TestObject testObject = new TestObject(1, "test", 2.0);
    String filename;

    System.out.print("Enter filename: ");
    filename = stdIn.nextLine();
    try
    {
      fileOut = new ObjectOutputStream(        } Open the file.
        new FileOutputStream(filename));       }
      fileOut.writeObject(testObject);         <- Write an object to the file.
      fileOut.close();                         <- Close the file.
    } // end try
    catch (IOException e)
    {
      System.out.println("Error: " + e.getMessage());
    }
  } // end main
} // end WriteObject class
```

Sample session:

```
Enter filename: objectFile.data
```

Figure 15.11 WriteObject program that writes a `Serializable` object to a file

in the container object, and each primitive data item in all component objects in that container object, and so on, down the composition tree to all the primitive leaves.

Outputting an Updated Version of a Previously Output Object

If you ask `ObjectOutputStream`'s `writeObject` method to output exactly the same object again while the file is still open, the serializing software recognizes the repetition and outputs just a reference to the previously output object. This is like what happens when you instantiate a new `String` that is exactly

```
/*************************************************************
* ReadObject.java
* Dean & Dean
*
* This reads two objects from a binary file.
*************************************************************/

import java.io.*;
import java.util.Scanner;

public class ReadObject
{
  public static void main(String[] args)
  {
    Scanner stdIn = new Scanner(System.in);
    ObjectInputStream fileIn = null;
    TestObject testObject;

    System.out.print("Enter filename: ");
    try
    {
      fileIn = new ObjectInputStream(
        new FileInputStream(stdIn.nextLine()));
      testObject = (TestObject) fileIn.readObject();
      testObject.display();
      testObject = (TestObject) fileIn.readObject();
      testObject.display();
      fileIn.close();
    }
    catch (IOException e)
    {
      System.out.println("IO Error: " + e.getMessage());
    }
    catch (ClassNotFoundException e)
    {
      System.out.println("ClassNotFound " + e.getMessage());
    }
  } // end main
} // end ReadObject class
```


<u>Sample session</u>:

```
Enter filename: objectFile.data
1    test    2.0
IO Error: null
```

Figure 15.12 ReadObject program that tries to read two objects from a file

the same as a previously instantiated `String`. This is a nice space-saving feature, but it can be a problem if you're simulating the behavior of a particular object, and you want a file to accumulate a record of that object's changing state as the simulation progresses. To see this problem, replace the `writeObject` statement in Figure 15.11's WriteObject program with these three statements:

```
fileOut.writeObject(testObject);
testObject.number *= 1.1;
fileOut.writeObject(testObject);
```

Then execute the revised WriteObject program and the ReadObject program, and this is what you'll get:

```
Enter filename: objectFile.data
1        test    2.0
1        test    2.0
```

The second record of the object's state is just a copy of the first record. It doesn't reflect the change in the value of the `number` variable. To make Java store the latest state of an object instead of just a reference to the original state, you need to invoke `ObjectOutputStream`'s `reset` method sometime before you output the updated version of the object. To see how this works, replace the above three statements with these four statements:

```
fileOut.writeObject(testObject);
fileOut.reset();
testObject.number *= 1.1;
fileOut.writeObject(testObject);
```

This allows an updated version of the same object to be output.

Then execute the revised WriteObject program and the ReadObject program, and you'll get the result you want:

```
Enter filename: objectFile.data
1        test    2.0
1        test    2.2
```

15.9 The `File` Class

This section describes the `File` class. It's different from the other classes in this chapter in that it doesn't deal with a file's contents. It deals with the file itself, and it describes the file's environment—where the file is in the computer.

Instantiating a `File` Object

To use the `File` class, you first need to instantiate an object that represents a file. Here's the API heading for the `File` constructor:

```
public File(String filename)
```

For example, to instantiate a `File` object for a file named `dalaiLamaEssay.doc`, do this:

```
File paper = new File("daliLamaEssay.doc");
```

A File object is not a file itself. It is just a container for information about a file. If you want to see whether a file with a particular name actually exists, you need to instantiate a file object with the filename you care about and then use that object to call File's exists method, like this:

```
File paper = new File("daliLamaEssay.doc");
if (paper.exists())
{
  System.out.println("Yes it exists.");
}
```

The paper object above represents a file in the *current directory*. The current directory is the directory where the currently running program resides. To specify a file in a directory that's different from the current directory, include the file's *path* as part of the filename argument. A path is the location of a file within the computer's directory structure. More specifically, a path is a series of one or more forward-slash-separated directory names that lead to a particular file. Optionally, you may use backslashes on Windows machines, but backslashes are messier than forward slashes because in Java a backslash is the escape character, and you'd need to have two backslashes wherever you meant to have just one. So we recommend that you use forward slashes in your pathnames. There are two types of path—*relative path* and *absolute path*. A relative path goes from the current directory to the specified file. An absolute path goes from the root directory to the specified file. The *root directory* is the directory at the top of the computer's directory structure. An initial slash represents the root directory.

Suppose that a dalaiLamaEssay.doc file is in a re101 directory and the re101 directory is in the root directory. To instantiate a File object for the dalaiLamaEssay.doc file, use an absolute path like this:

```
File paper = new File("/re101/daliLamaEssay.doc");
```

Suppose that a checkers.class file is in a checkers subdirectory of the current directory. To instantiate a File object for the checkers.class, use a relative path like this:

```
File paper = new File("checkers/checkers.class");
```

File Methods

Once you have a reference to a File object, you can use it to call any of the File class's several useful methods. As indicated above, the boolean exists method returns true if the calling object's file is present. The boolean isfile method returns true if the calling object's file is a normal file. The boolean isDirectory method returns true if the calling object's file is a directory. (A directory is considered to be a file, albeit a special kind of file.) The boolean delete method deletes the calling object's file. The boolean mkdir method creates a new directory and gives it the name specified by the argument you give it. The boolean renameTo method changes the name to the pathname specified by the argument you give it. The delete, mkdir, and renameTo methods return true if they succeed.

When you want to transfer data to and from files, it's often helpful to see what files already exist, and it's sometimes helpful to see how big they are. The program in Figure 15.13 displays this kind of information.

In the FileSizes program, note the "." argument in the File constructor call. The dot is a special symbol that represents the computer's current directory. So new File(".") instantiates a File object for the current directory. Similarly, new File("..") instantiates a File object for the parent directory.

Note this statement in the FileSizes program:

```
File[] files = currentDirectory.listFiles();
```

```
/************************************************
* FileSizes.java
* Dean & Dean
*
* This program displays the names and sizes of
* files in the current directory.
*************************************************/

import java.io.*;

public class FileSizes
{
  public static void main(String[] args)
  {
    File currentDirectory = new File(".");
    File[] files = currentDirectory.listFiles();

    for (int i=0; i<files.length; i++)
    {
      System.out.printf("%-25s%6d bytes\n",
        files[i].getName(), files[i].length());
    }
  } // end main
} // end FileSizes class
```

Sample output:

```
.classpath                  226 bytes
.project                    384 bytes
FileSizes.class            1135 bytes
FileSizes.java              645 bytes
FileSizesGUI.class         2058 bytes
FileSizesGUI.java          2185 bytes
HTMLGenerator.class        2182 bytes
HTMLGenerator.java         2659 bytes
```

Figure 15.13 `FileSizes` program with sample output

The `currentDirectory.listFiles` call returns an array of `File` objects, with one `File` object for each file in the current directory. Also note this statement:

```
System.out.printf("%-25s%6d bytes\n",
  files[i].getName(), files[i].length());
```

The format string says to print a left-aligned string in 25 spaces and then print a (right-aligned) floating point number in 6 spaces. The `files[i]` variable identifies file `i` in the current directory. The `getName` call returns the name of file `i`. The `length` call returns the size of file `i` in bytes.

15.10 GUI Track: The JFileChooser Class (Optional)

In the previous section's FileSizes program, we displayed the filenames and file sizes for all the files in the current directory. But suppose what you're looking for is in another directory. Wouldn't it be nice to display filenames and file sizes for any directory, not just the current directory? This section presents a program that does just that. It uses a GUI format to display filenames and file sizes for a user-specified directory. The program gets the user's directory selection with the help of the JFileChooser dialog box. Before looking at the program, let's consider the JFileChooser dialog box defined in the Java API.

User Interface

A file-chooser dialog box allows the user to select a file or a directory from a graphical, interactive directory structure. File choosers are ubiquitous in modern software. For example, a word processor employs a file chooser whenever the user selects Open from the File menu. Figure 15.14 shows how a user selects a file with the help of a JFileChooser dialog box.

JFileChooser Usage

The JFileChooser class is defined in the javax.swing package, so you must import that package to access this class. To create a JFileChooser dialog box, call the JFileChooser constructor like this:

```
JFileChooser chooser = new JFileChooser(<current-directory>);
```

The *current-directory* argument specifies the name of the directory that initially appears at the top of the file-chooser dialog box. That's the file chooser's current directory. This statement shows how we created Figure 15.14's file chooser:

```
JFileChooser chooser = new JFileChooser(".");
```

As mentioned previously, the "." argument represents the computer's current directory. Be aware that the file chooser's current directory and the computer's current directory aren't always the same. If you called the JFileChooser constructor with a "C:/spreadsheets" argument, file chooser's current directory would be C:/spreadsheets, but the computer's current directory would be unaffected.

The JFileChooser class has many methods. We'll look at just three of them—the setFileSelectionMode, showOpenDialog, and getSelectedFile methods. Here are their API headings and descriptions:

```
public void setFileSelectionMode(int mode)
```

Specifies the type of file the user can choose—a file, a directory, or either one.

```
public int showOpenDialog(null)
```

Displays a file-chooser dialog box. Returns a named constant, which indicates whether the user selected Open or Cancel.

```
public File getSelectedFile()
```

Returns the selected file or directory.

Initial display when the file chooser's current directory is `filePgms`:

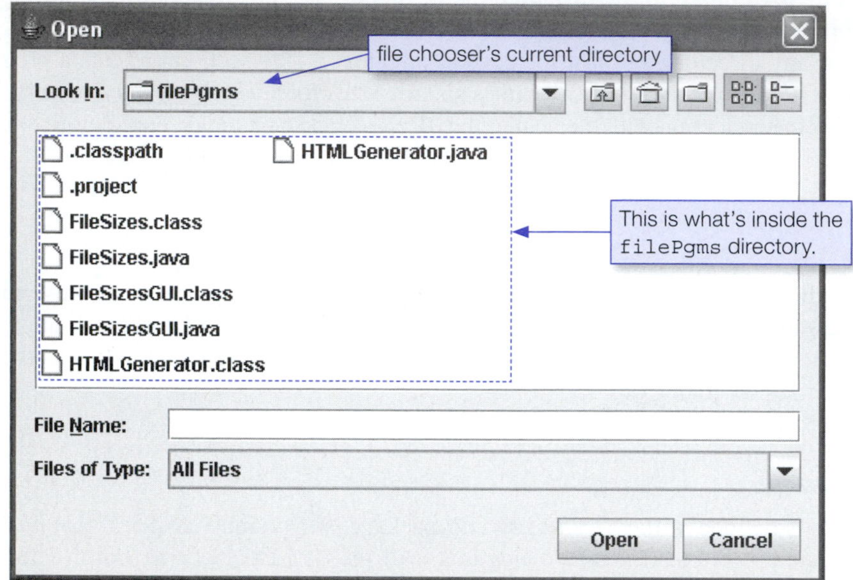

Display that appears after user selects the `FileSizes.java` file:

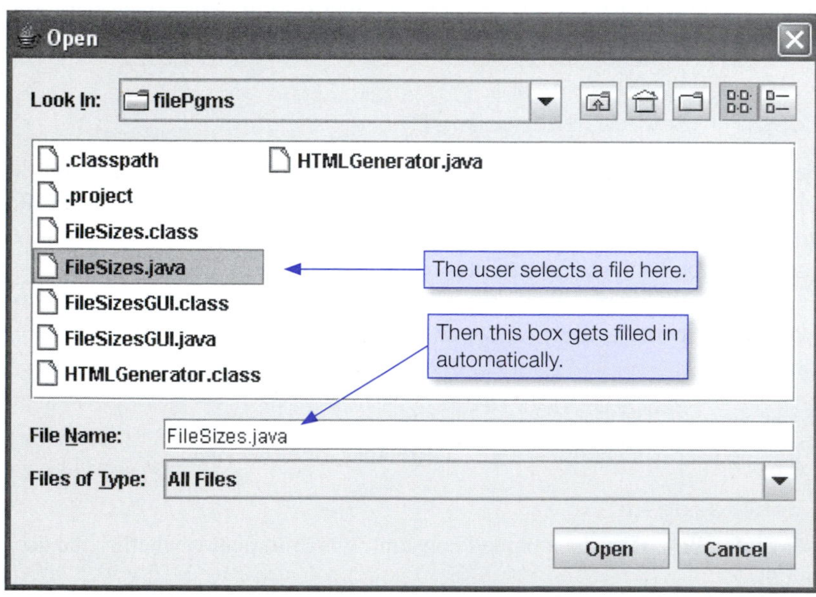

Figure 15.14 Selecting a file with a `JFileChooser` component

When you call setFileSelectionMode, you pass in a mode argument to specify the type of file the user can choose. If the mode is JFileChooser.FILES_ONLY, the user is allowed to choose only a file. If the mode is JFileChooser.DIRECTORIES_ONLY, the user is allowed to choose only a directory. If the mode is JFileChooser.FILES_AND_DIRECTORIES, the user is allowed to choose either a file or a directory.

You call showOpenDialog to display a file-chooser dialog box. After the dialog box displays, if the user clicks the file chooser's **Open** button, the showOpenDialog method call returns the JFileChooser.APPROVE_OPTION named constant. If the user clicks the file chooser's **Cancel** button, the showOpenDialog method call returns the JFileChooser.CANCEL_OPTION named constant.

After a user selects a file with the JFileChooser dialog box, the program calls getSelectedFile to retrieve the selected file or directory. At that point, the program will probably want to do something with the file or directory. But before it does, it should use File's exists method to determine if the user's entry is valid, and it should use File's isFile or isDirectory method to determine the selected file's type.

JOptionPane Usage

You may need to use some of the methods of the JOptionPane class also. This class is also in the javax.swing package, so if you imported this package for the JFileChooser class, you'll have access to the JOptionPane class too. The JOptionPane class provides many useful class methods, which you can access directly with the class name. We'll look at just two of them—the showConfirmDialog method and the showMessageDialog method. Here are the API headings and descriptions:

```
public static int showConfirmDialog(Component parentComponent,
  Object message, String title, int optionType)
```

This brings up a dialog box in which the number of choices is determined by optionType.

```
public static void showMessageDialog(Component parentComponent,
  Object message, String title, int messageType)
```

This brings up a dialog box that displays a message.

When you call showConfirmDialog, you can use a reference to another frame within which you want the box displayed, or you can use just a null to position it relative to the whole screen. In addition, you may supply a text message, and you must supply a text title. For the optionType parameter, enter either JOptionPane.YES_NO_OPTION or JOptionPane.YES_NO_CANCEL_OPTION. The value returned is the option selected by the user, like JOptionPane.YES_OPTION or JOptionPane.NO_OPTION.

When you call showMessageDialog, you can use a reference to another frame within which you want the box displayed, or you can use just a null to position it relative to the whole screen. In addition, you may supply a text message, and you must supply a text title. For the messageType parameter, enter either JOptionPane.ERROR_MESSAGE, JOptionPane.INFORMATION_MESSAGE, JOptionPane.WARNING_MESSAGE, JOptionPane.QUESTION_MESSAGE, or JOptionPane.PLAIN_MESSAGE.

FileSizesGUI Program

We're now ready to incorporate these ideas in that improved FileSizes program we mentioned earlier. Our FileSizesGUI program uses a JFileChooser dialog box to retrieve a user-specified file or directory. If the user selects a file, the program displays the file's name and size. If the user selects a directory, the program displays the filenames and sizes for all of the files in the directory. To get a better idea of how the program will operate, see the sample session in Figure 15.15. The program itself is in Figure 15.16.

When you run the program, a `JOptionPane.showConfirmDialog` method call displays this:

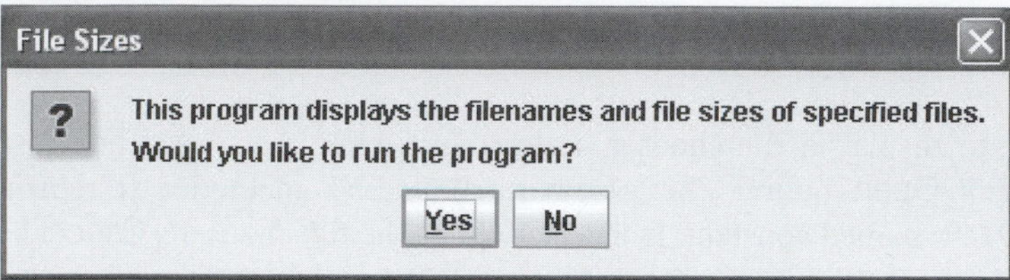

Clicking Yes causes a call to `JFileChooser`'s `showOpenDialog` method to display another window, and after you select filePgms, it looks like this:

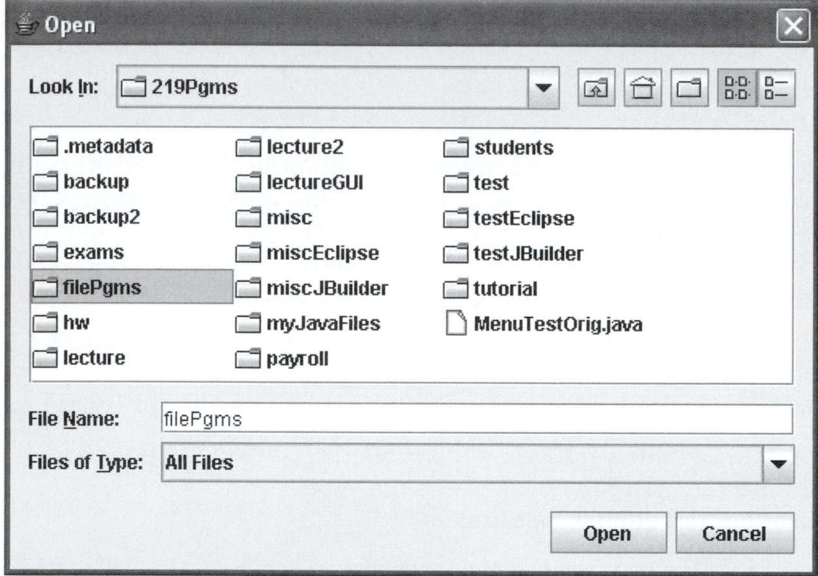

Clicking Open causes a call to `JOptionPane`'s `showMessageDialog` method to display this:

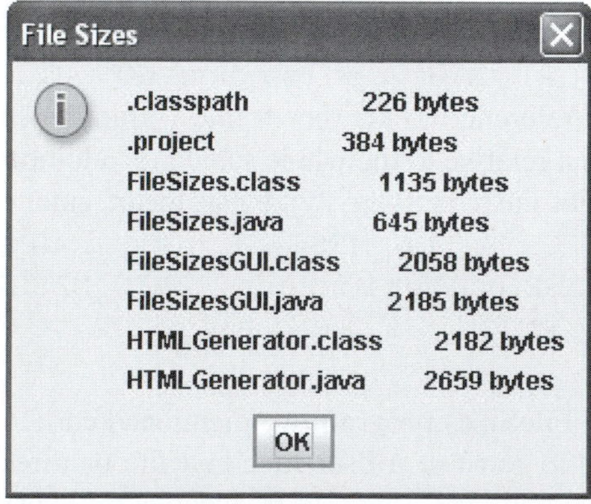

And clicking OK terminates the program.

Figure 15.15 Sample session for the `FileSizesGUI` program

```
import java.io.File;
import javax.swing.*;    // for JFileChooser and JOptionPane;

public class FileSizesGUI
{
  public static void main(String[] args)
  {
    File fileDir;          // user-specified file or directory
    int response;          // user's response to GUI prompts
    File[] files;          // array of files in specified directory
    String output = ""; // list of filenames and sizes
    JFileChooser chooser = new JFileChooser(".");

    response = JOptionPane.showConfirmDialog(null,
      "This program displays the filenames and file sizes of" +
      " specified files.\nWould you like to run the program?",
      "File Sizes", JOptionPane.YES_NO_OPTION);
    if (response == JOptionPane.YES_OPTION)
    {
      chooser.setFileSelectionMode(
        JFileChooser.FILES_AND_DIRECTORIES);
      response = chooser.showOpenDialog(null);
      if (response == JFileChooser.APPROVE_OPTION)
      {
        fileDir = chooser.getSelectedFile();
        if (fileDir.isFile())
        {
          output += String.format("%-25s%12s%n",
            fileDir.getName(), fileDir.length() + " bytes");
        }
        else if (fileDir.isDirectory())
        {
          files = fileDir.listFiles();
          for (int i=0; i<files.length; i++)
          {
            output += String.format("%-25s%12s%n",
              files[i].getName(), files[i].length() + " bytes");
          } // end for
        } // end else
        else
        {
          output = "Invalid entry. Not a file or directory.";
        }
        JOptionPane.showMessageDialog(null, output,
          "File Sizes", JOptionPane.INFORMATION_MESSAGE);
      } // end if
    } // end if
  } // end main
} // end FileSizesGUI class
```

Figure 15.16 FileSizesGUI program

In Figure 15.16, look for each of the following operations:

- A `JFileChooser` constructor call.
- A call to `JOptionPane`'s `showConfirmDialog` method, and use of the value returned.
- A call to `JFileChooser`'s `setFileSelectionMode` method.
- A call to `JFileChooser`'s `showOpenDialog` method, and use of the value returned.
- A call to `JFileChooser`'s `getSelectedFile` method, and use of the value returned.
- A call to `JOptionPane`'s `showMessageDialog` method.

After calling `getSelectedFile`, the program needs to determine the type of the user's selection—file or directory. The `isFile` and `isDirectory` calls take care of that. Within the directory-processing code, note how `fileDir`, a `File` object, calls `listFiles`. The `listFiles` method returns the files and directories that are in the `fileDir` directory. The returned files and directories are stored as `File` objects in an array named `files`. After filling the `files` array, the program loops through each of its `File` elements. For each element, it prints filename and file size by calling `getName` and `length`, respectively.

In the FileSizesGUI program, note the `String.format` method calls. The `String.format` method works the same as the `printf` method except that instead of printing a formatted value, it returns a formatted value. We use the `String.format` method calls in an attempt to display values with uniform widths. Specifically, we want to display the filenames and file sizes with uniform widths, so that the file-size values display in an aligned fashion. But the bottom dialog box in Figure 15.15 shows that the file-size values are not aligned. The problem is that with GUI output, different characters print with different widths. For example, you can see that the "HTML" in `HTMLGenerator.class` is wider than the "File" in `FileSizesGUI.java`. Thus, the `HTMLGenerator.class` line is longer. Having different characters print with different widths is stylish most of the time, but in our FileSizesGUI program, it's annoying. To fix this problem, you could embed a `JTextArea` component into the `JOptionPane` dialog box and set the `JTextArea` component's font to a monospaced font (with a monospaced font, every character prints with the same width). You'll learn about the `JTextArea` component in Chapter 17.

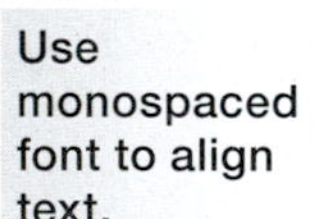
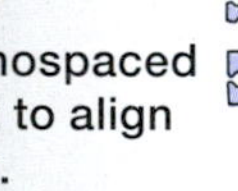
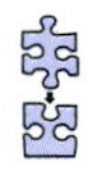

Use monospaced font to align text.

Summary

- You can find most of the file-transfer classes you'll need in the `java.io` package.
- To output text to a new file, open the file by instantiating a `PrintWriter` object with a `String` filename as the constructor argument. Write to the file by calling `PrintWriter`'s `println`, `print`, or `printf` method, and close the file by calling `PrintWriter`'s `close` method.
- To append text to an existing file, open the file by instantiating a `PrintWriter` object with an anonymous `FileOutputStream` object as the constructor argument. Use filename and `true` for the `FileOutputStream` constructor arguments.
- To input text from a file, open the file by instantiating a `Scanner` object with an anonymous `FileReader` object as the constructor argument. Use the filename for the `FileReader` constructor argument. Read from the file by calling one of `Scanner`'s methods, and close the file by using Scanner's `close` method.
- You can use text file I/O to translate plain-text information into HTML format for a Web page.
- The data in a text file appears as a sequence of bytes, where each byte corresponds to one character, and lines are delimited by `\r\n` or `\n` symbols. You can use a text editor or word processor with Plain Text

storage to create a text file that a Java program can read. You can use a word processor to read any text file written by a Java program.

- The data in a binary file appears as a sequence of data items, each encoded in the computer's native format for that type of data. You cannot create or read binary files with text editors or word processors. However, binary files can store a much greater variety of characters, and they can store high-precision numbers more efficiently.
- To output (or input) primitives to (or from) a binary file, open the file by instantiating a `DataOutputStream` (or `DataInputStream`) object with an anonymous `FileOutputStream` (or `FileInputStream`) object as the constructor argument. Use the filename for the `FileOutputStream` (or `FileInputStream`) argument. Then use methods like `writeInt` or `readInt` to write or read primitive values.
- You can store whole objects in a file in binary format, provided those objects and all their component objects `implement` the `Serializable` interface.
- To output (or input) objects to a file, open the file by instantiating an `ObjectOutputStream` (or `ObjectInputStream`) object with an anonymous `FileOutputStream` (or `FileInputStream`) object as the constructor argument. Use the filename for the `FileOutputStream` (or `FileInputStream`) constructor argument. Then use `writeObject` and `readObject` methods to transfer complete objects to and from the file.
- The `File` class manipulates whole files and describes their environments.
- Optionally, with Java's `JFileChooser` class, you can enable a user of one of your programs to find any file in his or her computer by interacting with a familiar graphical user interface.

Review Questions

§15.2 Java API Classes You Need to Import

1. You can create or view the contents of binary or object files with many text editors. (T / F)
2. Write an import statement that provides access to any of the classes in the `java.io` package.

§15.3 Text-File Output

3. What are the three basic steps to performing file I/O?
4. Using a `PrintWriter` method, write a Java statement that outputs a `String` called `name` followed by a space and an `int` called `id`, so that a later file-input `nextLine` operation will recognize the combination as a distinct string.
5. Write a single statement that opens an existing text file called `mydata.txt` for output, such that new output data is appended to the data already in the file.

§15.4 Text-File Input

6. Assuming `fileName` is a `String` that correctly identifies a text file in the current directory, what's wrong with this file-opening statement?

```
Scanner fileReader = new Scanner(fileName);
```

7. Assume you have a text file with these two lines of data:

```
55.6 hi
there
```

Assume you have successfully opened this text file for input and given the connection the name `fileIn`. Assume the next lines of code are:

```
double num = fileIn.nextDouble();
String name = fileIn.nextLine();
```

What is the length of the final string in `name`? Explain.

8. Given this array:

```
int[] number = new int[] {2, 3, 4};
```

Suppose you use the following code to write the three elements of the `number` array into a text file:

```
for (i=0; i<3; i++)
{
  fileOut.print(Integer.toString(number[i]));
}
```

Then, if you used the ReadTextFile program modified to read `int` values, what value would `number[0]` have?

§15.5 HTML File Generator

9. Assuming the object that manages output will be called `writer`, write a statement that opens a text file called `dogs.html` for output by `println` statements.
10. Where do the `<h1>` and `</h1>` tags go in an HTML file?
11. Write a statement that breaks a file-output connection called `writer`.

§15.6 Text File Data Format Versus Binary File Data Format

12. In a text file, each character consumes only one byte (8 bits) of memory. (T / F)
13. In a binary file, each character normally consumes two bytes (16 bits) of memory. (T / F)

§15.7 Binary File I/O

14. Write a statement that opens a new binary file for output and assigns a reference to the connection to `binaryOut`. Put the file in the current directory, with the name `windSpeed.data`.

§15.8 Object File I/O

15. Write a statement that opens a file for input of objects and assigns a reference to the connection to `objectIn`. Assume the file is in the current directory, with the name `automobiles.data`.

§15.9 The `File` Class

16. Write a code fragment that lists all the files in the directory that contains the currently executing program.

Exercises

1. [after §15.2] What is the principal advantage of each of the three types of file I/O—text, binary, and object?
2. [after §15.3] If you forget to close an input file, it may cause your computer's system performance to degrade. (T / F)

3. [after §15.3] Provide the missing code fragments in the following Java program so that it successfully writes the indicated `churchill` string to a file called `elAlamein.txt`. Create `fileOut` so that the new data overwrites any previous data in an existing file having the specified name.

```
/*************************************************************
* TextWriter.java
* Dean & Dean
*
* This writes two lines of text to a text file.
*************************************************************/

<fragment>

public class TextWriter
{
  public static void main(String[] args)
  {
    String[] churchill =
      {"Before Alamein we never had a victory.",
      "After Alamein we never had a defeat."};
    PrintWriter fileOut;

    try
    {
      <fragment>
      for (String line : churchill)
      {
        <fragment>
      }
      <fragment>
    }
    catch (FileNotFoundException e)
    {
      System.out.println(e.getMessage());
    }
  } // end main
} // end TextWriter class
```

4. [after §15.3] Modify the code in the previous exercise so that it appends to the text already in the `elAlamein.txt` file the year in which the battle took place, 1942. In the program, create this additional piece of information as an integer, like this:

```
int year = 1942;
```

In the file, put this additional piece of information on the next line, after the previous text.

5. [after §15.4] The program below is supposed to open a file whose full pathname is provided by the user in a keyboard entry. Then it is supposed to count the number of words in the file, where any kind of whitespace is a word delimiter. The program is complete except for a code fragment of several lines in the `try` block. Provide the missing code fragment. Use an anonymous `File` object as the `Scanner` argument when you instantiate the `fileIn` object. Of course, you can use the same `Scanner`-class `hasNext` and `next` methods for the `fileIn` object that you used before with the `stdIn` object when reading from the keyboard.

```
/*************************************************************
* WordsInFile.java
* Dean & Dean
*
* This counts the words in a text file.
*************************************************************/
import java.io.*;
import java.util.*;

public class WordsInFile
{
  public static void main(String[] args)
  {
    Scanner stdIn = new Scanner(System.in);
    Scanner fileIn;
    int numWords = 0;

    try
    {
      <fragment>
    } // end try
    catch (FileNotFoundException e)
    {
      System.out.println("Invalid filename.");
    }
    catch (Exception e)
    {
      System.out.println("Error reading from the file.");
    }
  } // end main
} // end WordsInFile class
```

If the file is the `family.txt` file displayed in the following exercise, you should get something like this:

Sample session:

```
Enter full pathname of file:
e:/myJava/problems/chapter15/family.txt
Number of words = 63
```

6. [after §15.5] As explained in the text, strict HTML standards require all `p` start tags (`<p>`) to have an accompanying `p` end tag (`</p>`). Edit the `HTMLGenerator.java` program given in the text so that `p` end tags (`</p>`) are inserted properly in the generated HTML file. The `p` end tags should be inserted at the bottom of each paragraph.

Note:

- In the `family.txt` file below, assume that there is a newline character at the end of each line.
- Do not allow a `p` end tag to be generated when there's no accompanying `p` start tag (start and end tags must always be partnered).

- Your program should be robust (that is, handle the weird cases). In particular, it should handle the case where there's only a title and no paragraphs at all.

`family.txt` (the input file):

```
Our Family

We are Stacy and John and we live in a camper
down by the river.

We have a dog, Barkley.
Barkley is a good dog.
She sleeps a lot and digs up the grass.
We feed her twice a day.

We have two kids, Jordan and Caiden.
They're girls. They like to eat, cry, and play.
We like them a lot.
```

`family.html` (the output file):

```
<html>
<head>
<title>Our Family</title>
</head>
<body>
<h1>Our Family</h1>
<p>
We are Stacy and John and we live in a camper
down by the river.
</p>
<p>
We have a dog, Barkley.
Barkley is a good dog.
She sleeps a lot and digs up the grass.
We feed her twice a day.
</p>
<p>
We have two kids, Jordan and Caiden.
They're girls. They like to eat, cry, and play.
We like them a lot.
</p>
</body>
</html>
```

7. [after §15.6] Assume that each of the following two lines (records) consists of 9 viewable characters each. Assuming they are written to a text file by `println` statements by a Windows computer, show the bit pattern for this data in a file.

```
Nik:  x88
Josh: x24
```

8. [after §15.6] In Windows the text new-line symbol is __________. In UNIX the text new-line symbol is __________.

9. [after §15.7] In a binary file, carriage-return and new-line characters have no special function in reading or writing operations—they are just like any other characters. (T / F).

10. [after §15.8] Grocery Store Inventory:

Enhance the grocery-store Inventory program created in a Chapter 13 project by providing a `FileHandler` class that contains write and read methods to write an object to a file in the local directory or read an object from a file in the local directory. Complete the following skeleton by providing the needed code fragments. You don't actually need the Chapter 13 grocery store Inventory program to do this exercise. You can test this new class with any appropriately instantiated object. The class that defines that object must, however, include a certain special feature. How would you modify the `Inventory` class to incorporate that special feature?

```
/*************************************************************
* FileHandler.java
* Dean & Dean
*
* This stores and retrieves an object.
*************************************************************/

import java.util.*;
import java.io.*;

public class FileHandler
{
  public static void write(Object object, String filename)
  {
    ObjectOutputStream fileOut;

    try
    {
      <provide code fragment here>
    }
    catch (IOException e)
    {
      System.out.println(e.getMessage());
    }
  } // end write

  //**********************************************************

  public static Object read(String filename)
  {
    ObjectInputStream fileIn;
    Object object;

    try
    {
      <provide code fragment here>
    }
```

```
    catch (Exception e)
    {
      System.out.println(e.getMessage());
      return new Object();                    // to satisfy compiler
    }
  } // end read
} // end FileHandler class
```

Now, with the FileHandler class added to the slightly modified grocery-store Inventory program, the following driver shows how you can wipe out unwanted modifications by restoring previously saved data:

```
/*************************************************************
* InventoryDriver2.java
* Dean & Dean
*
* This demonstrates filing of grocery inventory.
*************************************************************/

public class InventoryDriver2
{
  public static void main(String[] args)
  {
    Inventory store = new Inventory("groceries");

    store.newItem("bread", 15, 9.99);
    store.newItem("SunnyDale", "milk", 2, 2.00);
    store.newItem("eggs", 3, 1.50);
    store.newItem("bread", 2, 1.25);        // warning: in stock
    store.stockReport();
    FileHandler.write(store, "Inventory.data");

    store.update("SunnyDale", "milk", .25); // raise price 25%
    store.update("eggs", -1);               // lower quantity by 1
    store.update("beer", 3);                // warning: not stocked
    store.newItem("BrookSide", "milk", 4, 1.95);
    store.stockReport();

    store = (Inventory) FileHandler.read("Inventory.data");
    store.stockReport();
  } // end main
} // end InventoryDriver2 class
```

Output:

```
Item already exists - bread
bread - in stock: 15, price: $9.99
SunnyDale milk - in stock: 2, price: $2.00
eggs - in stock: 3, price: $1.50
Total value: $158.35

Cannot find specified item - beer
bread - in stock: 15, price: $9.99
```

```
SunnyDale milk - in stock: 2, price: $2.50
eggs - in stock: 2, price: $1.50
BrookSide milk - in stock: 4, price: $1.95
Total value: $165.65

bread - in stock: 15, price: $9.99
SunnyDale milk - in stock: 2, price: $2.00
eggs - in stock: 3, price: $1.50
Total value: $158.35
```

11. [after §15.9] Suppose you used a program like Microsoft's Notepad or UNIX's vi to create a text file, `alphabet.txt`, that contains this single line of text: "abcdefg." Provide the missing code fragments in the following Java program so that it successfully reads and displays the data in that file.

```
/*************************************************************
* TextReader.java
* Dean & Dean
*
* This reads a line of text from a text file.
*************************************************************/

<fragment>

public class TextReader
{
  public static void main(String[] args)
  {
    File file = <fragment>;
    Scanner fileIn;

    try
    {
      fileIn = <fragment>;
      System.out.println(fileIn.nextLine());
      <fragment>                    // close the file
    }
    catch (FileNotFoundException e)
    {
      System.out.println(e.getMessage());
    }
  } // end main
} // end TextReader class
```

12. [after §15.9] Suppose a text file called `myDates.txt` contains this line of text:

```
1999 2000 2001 2002
```

Modify the program in the previous exercise so that it reads the data from this file as integers and immediately prints them out onto the screen, like this:

Output:

```
1999
2000
```

```
2001
2002
```

13. [after §15.9] Look at the text example in Figure 15.13 and Sun's Java documentation for the `File` class, and explain what the following constructor and methods do:
    a) `File(".")`
    b) `getAbsoluteFile()`
    c) `getParentFile()`
    d) `list()`

Review Question Solutions

1. False. You cannot view the contents of binary or object files with text editors.
2. `import java.io.*;`
3. (1) Open the file. (2) Make the transfer and transform the data format. (3) Close the file.
4. Use the `println` method to put the distinct string on a separate line, like this:

```
fileOut.println(name + " " + id);
```

5.
```
fileOut = new PrintWriter(
  new FileOutputStream("mydata.txt", true));
```

6. The `String`-parameter `Scanner` constructor operates on the input string itself, not on the file it identifies.
7. The final value of `name.length() = 3`. The `nextDouble` method reads everything up through the last numerical digit. The `nextLine` method reads the following space plus the two characters in "hi."
8. `number[0] equals 234` Writing integers without a following space combines the separately output numbers into what looks like one number in the file, and a subsequent read interprets the combination as one number.
9. `writer = new PrintWriter("dogs.html");`
10. The `<h1>` and `</h1>` tags enclose the visible Web page header.
11. `writer.close;`
12. True. In a text file, each character consumes only one byte of memory.
13. True. In a binary file, each character normally consumes two bytes (16 bits) of memory.
14.
```
DataOutputStream binaryOut = new DataOutputStream(
  new FileOutputStream("windSpeed.data"));
```

15.
```
ObjectInputStream objectIn = new ObjectInputStream(
  new FileInputStream("automobiles.data"));
```

16. This lists all the files in the currently executing program's current directory:

```
String[] listing =
  (new File(".")).getAbsoluteFile().getParentFile().list();
for (int i=0; i<listing.length; i++)
{
  System.out.println(listing[i]);
}
```

CHAPTER 16

GUI Programming Basics

Objectives

- Understand the event-driven programming paradigm. In particular, understand what it means to fire an event, and understand the terms listener and event handler.
- Use the `JFrame` class to implement window functionality.
- Create and use `JLabel`, `JTextField`, and `JButton` components.
- Implement a listener for the `JTextField` and `JButton` components.
- Understand what an interface is and implement the `ActionListener` interface.
- Understand what an inner class is and implement a listener as an inner class.
- Know the difference between an anonymous inner class and a standard inner class.
- Create and use `JOptionPane` dialog boxes.
- Be able to distinguish between multiple events.
- Describe the primary GUI packages.
- Describe the difference between lightweight and heavyweight components.

Outline

16.1 Introduction

Hopefully, you've been on the edge of your seat in reading the prior chapters. If not, be prepared to be on the edge of your seat now. It's time for the really good stuff, *graphical user interface* (*GUI*) programming.

You've probably heard the term GUI, and you probably know that it's pronounced "gooey." But do GUI's three words, Graphical User Interface, make sense? "Graphical" refers to pictures, "user" refers to a person, and "interface" refers to communication. Thus, GUI programming employs pictures—like windows, text boxes, buttons, and so on—to communicate with users. For example, Figure 16.1 shows a window with a text box and a button. We'll describe windows, text boxes, and buttons in detail later on.

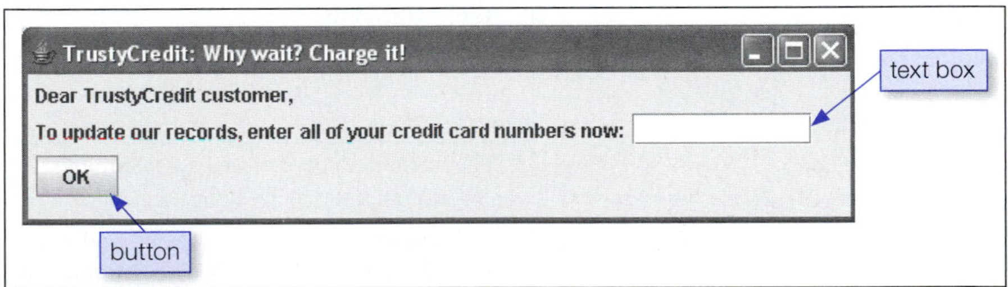

Figure 16.1 Example window that uses a text box and a button

In the old days, program interfaces consisted of just text. Programs would prompt the user with a text question, and users would respond with a text answer. That's what we've been using for all of our programs so far. Text input/output (I/O) works well in many situations, but you can't get around the fact that some people consider text display to be boring. Many of today's users expect programs to be livelier. They expect windows, buttons, colors, and so on for input and output. They expect GUI.

Although companies still write many text-based programs for internal use, they normally write GUI-based programs for programs that are to be used externally. It's important for external programs to be GUI based because external programs go to customers, and customers typically won't buy programs unless they are GUI based. So if you want to write programs that people will buy, you'd better learn GUI programming.

We start this chapter with an overview of basic GUI concepts and terminology. We then move on to a bare-bones program where we introduce basic GUI syntax. We next cover listeners, inner classes, and several rudimentary *GUI components,* which are objects that sit inside a window, including `JLabel`, `JTextField`, and `JButton`. Finally, we cover the `JOptionPane` class (for generating a dialog box) and the `Color` class (for generating a color).

You may have noticed optional GUI-track sections at the end of about half of the prior chapters. The GUI material in this chapter and the next is different from the GUI material in the earlier chapters, and it does not depend on the earlier chapters' GUI material. So if you skipped the earlier GUI material, no worries.

To understand this chapter, you need to be familiar with object-oriented programming, arrays, inheritance, and exception handling. As such, you need to have read up through Chapter 14. This chapter does not depend on material covered in Chapter 15.

16.2 Event-Driven Programming Basics

GUI programs usually use *event-driven programming* techniques. The basic idea behind event-driven programming is that the program waits for events to occur and the program responds to events if and when they occur.

Terminology

So what is an event? An *event* is a message that tells the program that something has happened. For example, if the user clicks a button, then an event is generated, and it tells the program that a particular button was clicked. More formally, when the user clicks a button, we say that the button object *fires an event*. Note these additional event examples:

User Action	What Happens
Pressing the Enter key while the cursor is inside a text box.	The text box object fires an event, and it tells the program that the Enter key was pressed within the text box.
Clicking a menu item.	The menu item object fires an event, and it tells the program that the menu item was selected.
Closing a window (clicking on the window's top-right corner "X" button).	The window object fires an event, and it tells the program that the window's close button was clicked.

If an event is fired, and you want your program to handle the fired event, then you need to create a *listener* for the event. For example, if you want your program to do something when the user clicks a particular button, you need to create a listener for the button. For now, think of a listener as an ear. If an event is fired and there's no ear listening to it, then the fired event is never "heard" and there's no response to it. On the other hand, if there is an ear listening to a fired event, then the ear "hears" the event and the program then responds to the fired event. The way the program responds is by executing a chunk of code known as an *event handler*. See Figure 16.2. It depicts a button being pressed (see the mouse pointer), an event being fired (see the sound waves), a listener hearing the event (see the ear), and an event handler being executed (see the arrow going down the event-handler code). This system of using listeners for event handling is known as the *event-delegation model*—event handling is "delegated" to a particular listener.

The Event-Driven Programming Framework

Based on the above description, event-driven programming may feel like an altogether new type of programming. Particularly the part about firing an event and listening for a fired event. Many people are fine with the idea of event-driven programming being a new type of programming. But the truth of the matter is that it's really just object-oriented programming with window dressing. Make that lots of window dressing. Sun provides an extensive collection of GUI classes that, together, form a framework on which to build GUI applications. And that framework is comprised of classes, methods, inheritance, and so on; that is, it's comprised of OOP components. As a programmer, you don't have to understand all the details of how the framework

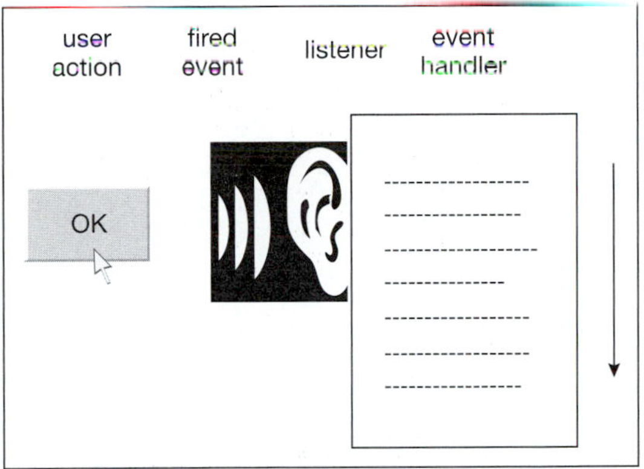

Figure 16.2 What happens when a button is pressed

works; you just have to understand it well enough to use it. For example, you have to know how to plug in your event handlers properly. Figure 16.3 provides a high-level, graphic illustration of what we're talking about.

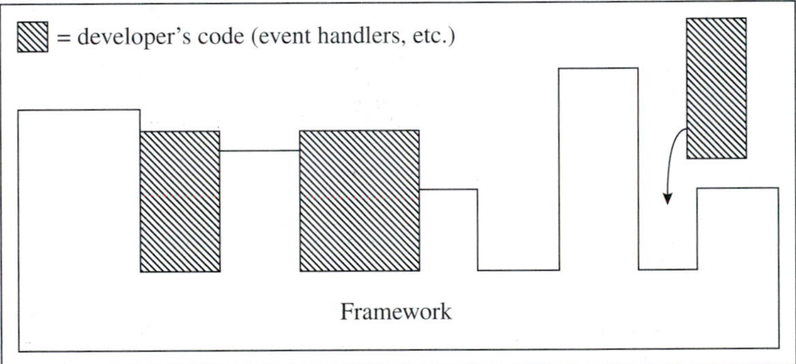

Figure 16.3 Event-driven programming framework

Why did Sun bother to provide the event-driven programming framework? It satisfies the goal of getting maximum benefit from minimum code. With the help of the framework, Java programmers can get a GUI program up and running with a relatively small amount of effort. Initially, the effort might not seem so small, but when you consider all that the GUI program does (automatic event firing, listening for fired events, and so on), you'll find that your return on investment is quite good.

16.3 A Simple Window Program

OK. Enough talk about concepts. Time to roll up your sleeves and get your hands dirty with some code. To get a feel for the big picture, let's start with a simple GUI program and discuss the GUI commands at a high level. Later, we'll cover the GUI commands in greater detail.

In Figure 16.4, we present a SimpleWindow program that displays a line of text inside a window. Note the two `import` statements at the top of the program. They import the `javax.swing` and `java.awt` packages. In writing GUI programs, you'll use many of Java's pre-built GUI classes from Sun's API library.

```
/*************************************************************
* SimpleWindow.java
* Dean & Dean
*
* This program displays a label in a window.
*************************************************************/

import javax.swing.*; // for JFrame, JLabel
import java.awt.*;    // for FlowLayout

public class SimpleWindow extends JFrame
{
  private static final int WIDTH = 250;
  private static final int HEIGHT = 100;

  //**********************************************************

  public SimpleWindow()
  {
    setTitle("Simple Window");
    setSize(WIDTH, HEIGHT);
    setLayout(new FlowLayout());
    setDefaultCloseOperation(EXIT_ON_CLOSE);
    createContents();
    setVisible(true);
  } // end SimpleWindow constructor

  //**********************************************************

  private void createContents()
  {
    JLabel label = new JLabel("Hi! I'm Larry the label!");
    add(label);   <-- This adds the label to the window.
  } // end createContents

  //**********************************************************

  public static void main(String[] args)
  {
    new SimpleWindow();   <-- This instantiates an anonymous window object.
  } // end main
} // end class SimpleWindow
```

Simple Window

Hi! I'm Larry the label!

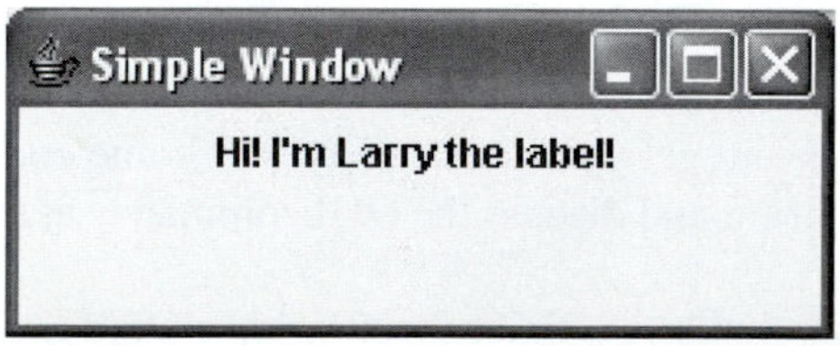

Figure 16.4 SimpleWindow program and its output

To use the pre-built GUI classes, you'll need to import them into your GUI programs. You could import the classes individually, but there's a better way. Recall that a package is a collection of pre-built classes. Since most of the critical pre-built GUI classes come from the javax.swing and java.awt packages, import those two packages and you'll import most of the critical pre-built GUI classes. Get used to importing those two packages in every one of your GUI programs. Recall that to import a package, you need to use an asterisk; that is, import javax.swing.*;. The * is a wildcard, and it allows you to import all the classes within a particular package.

In SimpleWindow's class heading, note the extends JFrame clause. The JFrame class is part of the GUI framework mentioned above. The JFrame class provides standard Windows features such as a title bar, a minimize button, and so on. Below the class heading, note the WIDTH and HEIGHT named constants. They're used by the setSize method call to specify the dimensions of the window.

Let's now examine the main method. GUI programs typically create a window with GUI components, and then they just sit around waiting for the user to do something like click a button, select a menu option, and so on. Thus, main is very short—it just instantiates the window and that's it. In this simple example, we don't even bother to assign the instantiated window object to a reference variable. Review: What do you call an object that isn't stored in a reference variable? An anonymous object.

In performing the anonymous-object instantiation, main calls the SimpleWindow constructor. The SimpleWindow constructor (1) calls setTitle to assign the window's title, (2) calls setSize to assign the window's size, (3) calls setLayout to assign the window's layout scheme, and (4) calls setDefaultCloseOperation to enable the *close-window button* (the "X" in the top-right corner) to work properly.

In the interest of modularization, the SimpleWindow constructor then calls a helper method, createContents, to create the components that go inside the window. The createContents method contains only two lines. With only two lines, there's really no need for a helper method, but we want you to form good habits. For this trivial example, there's only one component and there's no event handler for the component. Thus, two lines are all that's needed. But normal GUI programs have multiple components and multiple event handlers. For that, quite a few lines are needed. If you stick those lines in the constructor, you'd have a long constructor. Better to break things up and stick them in a helper method.

The createContents method instantiates a JLabel component and then calls the add method to add the JLabel component to the window. A JLabel component is the simplest type of GUI component. It's a piece of text that the user can read but cannot change.

After executing createContents, the JVM returns to the SimpleWindow constructor. The SimpleWindow constructor then calls setVisible to make the window visible.

16.4 JFrame Class

In the previous section, we introduced you to the JFrame class. In this section, we describe the JFrame class in more depth. More specifically, we cover its characteristics and its methods.

JFrame Basics

These days, most purchasable software is windows-based. When you load such software, you'll see a window and that window will have a title bar, a border, a minimize button, a close-window button, the ability to resize the window, and so on. You could implement all those features from scratch in your own classes, but why "reinvent the wheel"? The JFrame class implements the standard windows features that you've come to know and love. To get all that cool windows functionality for free, just implement your classes by extending the JFrame class. What a deal!

The `JFrame` class should be the superclass for most of your GUI application windows, so a programmer-defined window will normally have `extends JFrame` in its class heading. For the `extends JFrame` to work, you must import the `JFrame` class or import `JFrame`'s package, `javax.swing`. As explained above, it's common to import the `javax.swing` package for all GUI programs.

The `JFrame` class is called a *container* because it contains components (like labels, buttons, menus, and so on). It inherits the ability to contain components from its superclass, the `Container` class.

`JFrame` Methods

By extending the `JFrame` class, you automatically get the standard windows functionality mentioned above. In addition, you inherit a host of windows-related methods. In the SimpleWindow program, we use these inherited methods—`setTitle`, `setSize`, `setLayout`, `setDefaultCloseOperation`, `add`, and `setVisible`. The `setLayout` and `setDefaultCloseOperation` methods come directly from the `JFrame` class. The other methods come from ancestors of the `JFrame` class—`setTitle` from the `Frame` class, `add` from the `Container` class, `setSize` and `setVisible` from the `Component` class.

The `setTitle` method displays a specified string in the current window's title bar. If `setTitle` is not called, then the window's title bar is empty.

The `setSize` method assigns the width and height of the current window. See Figure 16.4 and note how the SimpleWindow program assigns the width to 300 and the height to 200. The width and height values are specified in terms of *pixels*. A pixel is a computer monitor's smallest displayable unit, and it displays as a dot on the screen. If you call `setSize` with a width of 300 and a height of 200, then your window will consist of 200 rows where each row contains 300 pixels. Each pixel displays with a certain color. The pixels form a picture by having different colors for the different pixels. For example, the window depicted in Figure 16.4 might contain blue pixels on the perimeter (for the window's border), and black pixels in the center (for the window's message).

To give you perspective on how big a 300-by-200 pixel window is, you need to know the dimensions, in pixels, of an entire computer screen. The dimensions of a computer screen are referred to as the screen's *resolution*. Resolution settings are adjustable. Two common resolution settings are 800-by-600 and 1024-by-768. The 800-by-600 setting displays 600 rows where each row contains 800 pixels.

If you forget to call the `setSize` method, your window will be really small. It will display only the beginning of the title and the three standard window-adjustment buttons—minimize, maximize, and close-window. It won't display the window's contents unless you manually resize the window. Here's what the SimpleWindow program displays if you omit the `setSize` method call:

The `setLayout` method assigns a specified *layout manager* to the current window. The layout manager is pre-built software from Sun that determines the positioning of components. In the SimpleWindow program's `setLayout` call, we specify the `FlowLayout` manager, and the `FlowLayout` manager causes components to be positioned in the top-center position. The `FlowLayout` class is defined in the `java.awt` package, so don't forget to import that package. In the next chapter, we describe the `FlowLayout` manager and other layout managers in more detail. We're using the `FlowLayout` manager (as opposed to other layout managers) in this chapter because the `FlowLayout` manager is the easiest to use, and we're trying to keep things simple for now.

By default, a program's close-window button (the X in the top-right corner) doesn't work very nicely. When the user clicks it, the window closes, but the program still runs in the background. To remedy this situation, call `setDefaultCloseOperation(EXIT_ON_CLOSE)`. Then when the user clicks the close-window button, the window closes and the program terminates. Having a closed program run in the background is usually unnoticeable, and that's why many programmers have a hard time remembering to call `setDefaultCloseOperation(EXIT_ON_CLOSE)`. Nonetheless, you should try to remember to call it. If you forget to call it, and a user's computer has limited memory and there are many programs running in the background, the computer's performance will degrade.

The `add` method adds a specified component to the current window. Once the component is added, it stays with the window for the life of the program. We mention this so that you're comfortable using a local variable declaration for a component. In the following example, even though `label` is defined locally within `createContents`, the instantiated `JLabel` component stays with the window after `createContents` finishes:

```
private void createContents()
{
  JLabel label = new JLabel("Hi! I'm Larry the label!");
  add(label);
} // end createContents
```

Windows are invisible by default. To make a window and its contents visible, add the components to the window and then call `setVisible(true)`. Do it in that order—add components first, then call `setVisible`. Otherwise, the added components won't display. To make a window invisible, call `setVisible(false)`.

The `JFrame` class contains many additional methods, too many to mention here. If you've got some time on your hands, we encourage you to find out what's available by looking up the `JFrame` class on Sun's Java API Web site—http://java.sun.com/javase/6/docs/api/.

16.5 Java Components

Now let's consider the objects that sit inside a window—the components. Here are some examples of Java components:

- `JLabel`, `JTextField`, `JButton`,
- `JTextArea`, `JCheckBox`, `JRadioButton`, `JComboBox`
- `JMenuBar`, `JMenu`, `JMenuItem`

These aren't all of the Java components, just some of the more commonly used ones. We'll describe the first three components in this chapter and the other components in the next chapter.

All of the above component classes are in the `javax.swing` package, so you must import that package to use them. But remember that you're already importing the `javax.swing` package to access the `JFrame` class. There's no need to import it twice.

Component classes typically are derived from the `JComponent` class, which supports many useful inheritable features. Along with many other methods, the `JComponent` class contains methods that handle these component features:

- foreground and background colors
- text font

- border appearance
- tool tips
- focus

For detailed information on the above features, look up the `JComponent` class on Sun's Java API Web site.

16.6 JLabel Component

User Interface

The `JLabel` component doesn't do much. It simply displays a specified single line of text. It's considered to be a read-only component because the user can read it, but the user cannot interact with it.

Normally, the `JLabel` component displays a single line of text, not multiple lines. If you want to display multiple lines, use the `JTextArea` component, which is covered in the next chapter.

Implementation

To create a `JLabel` object, call the `JLabel` constructor like this:

```
JLabel <JLabel-reference> = new JLabel(<label-text>);
```

optional

The *label-text* is the text that appears in the `JLabel` component. If the label-text argument contains a newline character, `\n`, it's ignored (remember, the `JLabel` component only displays a single line of text). If the label-text argument is omitted, then the `JLabel` component displays nothing. Why instantiate an empty label? So you can fill it in later on with text that's dependent on some condition.

To add a `JLabel` object to your `JFrame` window, use this syntax:

```
add(<JLabel-reference>);
```

JLabel-reference comes from the above initialization statement

The `JLabel` class needs the `javax.swing` package, but that should be available already, since it's needed for the `JFrame` class.

Methods

The `JLabel` class, like all the GUI component classes, has quite a few methods. We'll just mention two of them—the `getText` and `setText` accessor and mutator methods. Here are their API headings and descriptions:

`public String getText()`

Returns the label's text.

`public void setText(String text)`

Assigns the label's text. Note that the programmer can update the label's text even though the user cannot.

16.7 JTextField Component

User Interface

The *JTextField* component displays a rectangle and allows the user to enter text into the rectangle. Here's an example:

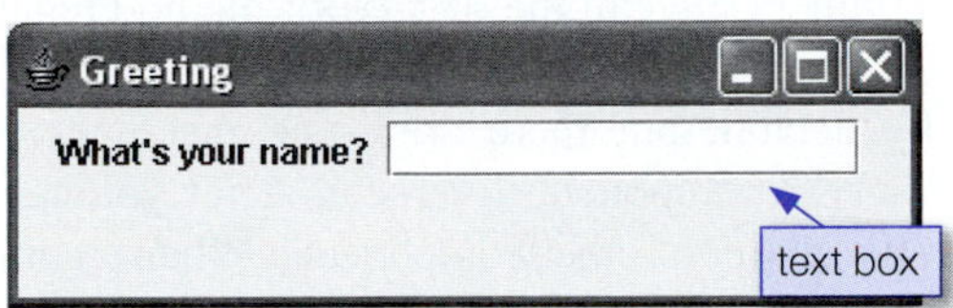

Implementation

To create a JTextField object, call the JTextField constructor like this:

```
JTextField <JTextField-reference> = new JTextField(<default-text>, <width>);
```

optional

The *default-text* is the text that appears in the text box by default. The *width* is the number of characters that can display in the text box at one time. If the user enters more characters than can display at one time, then the leftmost characters scroll off the display. If the default-text argument is omitted, then the empty string is used as the default. If the width argument is omitted, then the box's width is slightly greater than the width of the default text.

To add a JTextField object to your JFrame window, use this syntax:

```
add(<JTextField-reference>);
```

The JTextField class needs the javax.swing package, but that should be available already, since it's needed for the JFrame class.

Methods

The JTextField class has quite a few methods. Here are API headings and descriptions for some of the more useful ones:

```
public String getText()
```

Returns the text box's contents.

```
public void setText(String text)
```

Assigns the text box's contents.

```
public void setEditable(boolean flag)
```

Makes the text box editable or non-editable.

```
public void setVisible(boolean flag)
```

Makes the text box visible or invisible.

```
public void addActionListener(ActionListener listener)
```
Adds a listener to the text box.

Text boxes are editable by default, which means that users can type inside them. If you want to prevent users from editing a text box, call `setEditable` with an argument value of `false`. Calling `setEditable(false)` prevents users from updating a text box, but it does not prevent programmers from updating a text box. Programmers can call the `setText` method regardless of whether the text box is editable or non-editable.

Components are visible by default, but there are some instances where you might want to call `setVisible(false)` and make a component disappear. After you calculate a result, you might want just the result to appear without the clutter of other components. When a component is made to disappear, its space is automatically reclaimed by the window so other components can use it.

When a `JTextField` component calls `addActionListener`, the JVM attaches a listener object to the text box, and that enables the program to respond to the user pressing Enter within the text box. We'll cover listeners in more detail soon enough, but first we're going to step through an example program that puts into practice what you've learned so far. . . .

16.8 Greeting Program

In Figures 16.5a and 16.5b, we present a Greeting program that displays a personalized greeting. It reads the user's name from a text box (a `JTextField` component) and displays the entered name in a label (a `JLabel` component).

Most of the code in the Greeting program should look familiar since it closely parallels the code in the SimpleWindow program. For example, note the short `main` method with the anonymous object instantiation. Note the constructor that contains calls to `setTitle`, `setSize`, `setLayout`, `setDefaultCloseOperation`, and `setVisible`. Finally, note the `createContents` helper method that creates the components and adds them to the window. Now let's focus on what's new about the Greeting program—a text box and an event handler.

The `Greeting` program uses a text box, `nameBox`, to store the user's name. Note how the `createContents` method instantiates `nameBox` with a width of 15. Note how the `createContents` method calls the `add` method to add `nameBox` to the window. That code is straightforward. But something that's not so straightforward is `nameBox`'s declaration. It's declared as an instance variable at the top of the class. Why an instance variable instead of a `createContents` local variable? Aren't local variables preferred? Yes, but in this case, we need to access `nameBox` not only in `createContents`, but also in the `actionPerformed` event handler (which we'll get to next). It's possible to use a local variable within `createContents` and still access it from the event handler, but that's a bit of a pain.[1] For now, we'll keep things simple and declare `nameBox` as an instance variable. The same rationale applies to the `greeting` label. We need to access it in `createContents` and also in the `actionPerformed` event handler, so we make it an instance variable.

The Greeting program's `actionPerformed` event handler specifies what happens when the user presses Enter within the text box. Note that the `actionPerformed` method is inside our `Listener` class. We cover listeners and event-handler mechanics in the next section.

[1] If you declare a variable locally within `createContents`, you can retrieve it from an event handler by calling `getSource`. The `getSource` method is covered in Section 16.14.

```
/*************************************************************
* Greeting.java
* Dean & Dean
*
* This program demonstrates text boxes and labels.
* When the user presses Enter after typing something into the
* text box, the text box value displays in the label below.
*************************************************************/

import javax.swing.*;    // for JFrame, JLabel, JTextField
import java.awt.*;       // for FlowLayout
import java.awt.event.*; // for ActionListener, ActionEvent

public class Greeting extends JFrame
{
  private static final int WIDTH = 325;
  private static final int HEIGHT = 100;
  private JTextField nameBox; // holds user's name
  private JLabel greeting;    // personalized greeting

  //**********************************************************

  public Greeting()
  {
    setTitle("Greeting");
    setSize(WIDTH, HEIGHT);
    setLayout(new FlowLayout());
    setDefaultCloseOperation(EXIT_ON_CLOSE);
    createContents();
    setVisible(true);
  } // end constructor

  //**********************************************************

  // Create components and add them to window.
  private void createContents()
  {
    JLabel namePrompt = new JLabel("What's your name?");
    nameBox = new JTextField(15);
    greeting = new JLabel();
    add(namePrompt);
    add(nameBox);
    add(greeting);
    nameBox.addActionListener(new Listener());
  } // end createContents
```

4. Import this package for event handling.

3. Register a listener.

Figure 16.5a Greeting program—part A

```
  //*************************************************************

  // Inner class for event handling.

  private class Listener implements ActionListener
  {
    public void actionPerformed(ActionEvent e)
    {
      String message; // the personalized greeting
      message = "Glad to meet you, " + nameBox.getText()+ "!";
      nameBox.setText("");
      greeting.setText(message);
    } // end actionPerformed
  } // end class Listener

  //*************************************************************

  public static void main(String[] args)
  {
    new Greeting();
  } // end main
} // end class Greeting
```

1. listener class heading

2. event handler

Greeting

What's your name?

Greeting

What's your name? Azad Ahmed

After pressing **Enter** in the text box:

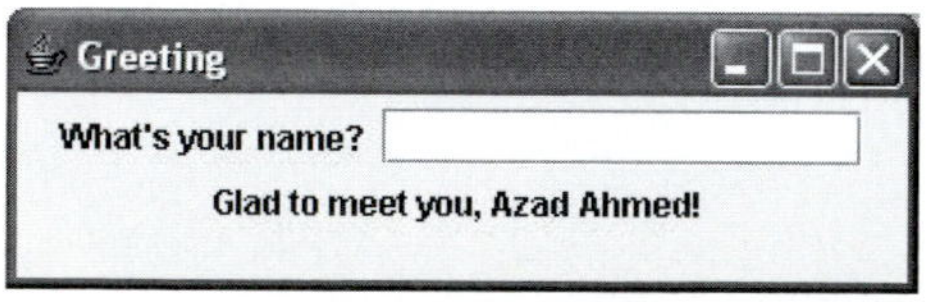

Greeting

What's your name?

Glad to meet you, Azad Ahmed!

Figure 16.5b Greeting program—part B, and its associated output

16.9 Component Listeners

When the user interacts with a component (e.g., when the user clicks a button or presses Enter while in a text box), the component fires an event. If the component has a listener attached to it, the fired event is "heard" by the listener. Consequently, the listener handles the event by executing its `actionPerformed` method. In this section, you'll learn how to make all that work by creating a listener and an associated `actionPerformed` method.

How to Implement a Listener

Below, we show the steps needed to implement a listener for a text box. These steps correspond to the numbered callouts in Figures 16.5a and 16.5b:

1. Define a class with an `implements ActionListener` clause appended to the right of the class's heading. To see an example, look at callout 1 in Figure 16.5b. The `implements ActionListener` clause means that the class is an implementation of the `ActionListener` interface. We discuss interfaces in the next subsection.

2. Include an `actionPerformed` event handler method in your listener's class. Here's a skeleton of an `actionPerformed` method inside a listener class:

```
private class Listener implements ActionListener
{
  public void actionPerformed(ActionEvent e)
  {
    <do-something>
  }
}
```

   Even if your `actionPerformed` method doesn't use the `ActionEvent` parameter (e, above), you still must include that parameter in the method heading to make your method conform to the requirements of a listener.

   To see an example of a complete `actionPerformed` method, look at callout 2 in Figure 16.5b. It refers to a listener class that's named `Listener`. `Listener` is not a reserved word—it's just a good descriptive name we picked for the listener class in the Greeting program.

3. *Register* your listener class. More specifically, that means adding your listener class to a text box component by calling the `addActionListener` method. Here's the syntax:

   <text-box-component>`.addActionListener(new` *<listener-class>*`());`

   To see an example, look at callout 3 in Figure 16.5a.

   The point of the registration process is so your text box can find a listener when an *enter event* is fired. An enter event is fired whenever the user presses Enter from within the text box.

   Registering a listener is like registering your car. When you register your car, nothing much happens at that point. But later, when some event occurs, your car registration comes into play. What event would cause your car registration to be used? If you get caught speeding, the police can use your registration number as part of a traffic citation. If you get into a wreck, your insurance company can use your registration number to raise your insurance rates.

4. Import the `java.awt.event` package. Event handling requires the use of the `ActionListener` interface and the `ActionEvent` class. Those entities are in the `java.awt.event` package, so that package must be imported for event handling to work. To see the `import` statements within a complete program, look at callout 4 in Figure 16.5a.

The `ActionListener` Interface

In the Greeting program, we specified `implements ActionListener` in the listener's class heading. `ActionListener` is an *interface*. You might recall interfaces from Chapter 13. An interface is somewhat like a class in that it contains variables and methods. But unlike a class, its variables must be constants (i.e., `final` variables), and its methods must be empty (i.e., method headings). If a programmer uses an interface to derive a new class, the compiler requires the new class to implement methods for all of the interface's method headings.

So what's the point of having an interface with all empty methods? The answer is that it can be used as a template or pattern when creating a class that falls into a certain category. More specifically, what's the point of the `ActionListener` interface? Since all action-event listeners must implement it, it means that all action-event listeners will be similar and therefore understandable. It means that all action-event listeners will implement the `ActionListener`'s one method, the `actionPerformed` method. And in implementing that method, they'll be forced to use this prescribed heading:

```
public void actionPerformed(ActionEvent e)
```

By using the prescribed heading, it ensures that fired action events will be received properly by the listener.

16.10 Inner Classes

Here's a reprint of the Greeting program, in skeleton form:

```
public class Greeting extends JFrame
{
  ...
  private class Listener implements ActionListener
  {
    public void actionPerformed(ActionEvent e)
    {
      String message; // the personalized greeting
      message = "Glad to meet you, " + nameBox.getText();
      nameBox.setText("");
      greeting.setText(message);
    } // end actionPerformed
  } // end class Listener
  ...
} // end class Greeting
```

Do you notice anything odd about the position of the `Listener` class in the `Greeting` program? See how the `Listener` class is indented and how its closing brace is before the `Greeting` class's closing brace? The `Listener` class is inside of the `Greeting` class!

If a class is limited in its scope such that it is needed by only one other class, you should define the class as an *inner class* (a class inside of another class). Since a listener is usually limited to listening to just one class, listeners are usually implemented as inner classes.

It's not required by the compiler, but inner classes should normally be `private`. Why? Because the main point of using an inner class is to further the goal of encapsulation and using `private` means the outside world won't be able to access the inner class. Note the `private` modifier in the above `Listener` class heading.

Besides furthering the goal of encapsulation, there's another reason to use an inner class as opposed to a *top-level* class (top-level class is the formal term for a regular class—a class not defined inside of another class). An inner class can directly access its enclosing class's instance variables. Since listeners normally need to access their enclosing class's instance variables, this is an important benefit.

16.11 Anonymous Inner Classes

Take a look at the GreetingAnonymous program in Figures 16.6a and 16.6b. It's virtually identical to the previous Greeting program. Can you identify the difference between the GreetingAnonymous program and the Greeting program?

```
/*************************************************************
* GreetingAnonymous.java
* Dean & Dean
*
* This program demonstrates an anonymous inner class.
*************************************************************/

import javax.swing.*;     // for JFrame, JLabel, JTextField
import java.awt.*;        // for FlowLayout
import java.awt.event.*; // for ActionListener, ActionEvent

public class GreetingAnonymous extends JFrame
{
  private static final int WIDTH = 325;
  private static final int HEIGHT = 100;
  private JTextField nameBox; // holds user's name
  private JLabel greeting;    // personalized greeting

  //*********************************************************

  public GreetingAnonymous()
  {
    setTitle("Greeting Anonymous");
    setSize(WIDTH, HEIGHT);
    setLayout(new FlowLayout());
    setDefaultCloseOperation(EXIT_ON_CLOSE);
    createContents();
    setVisible(true);
  } // end constructor
```

Figure 16.6a GreetingAnonymous program that has an anonymous inner class—part A

```
  //***********************************************************

  // Create components and add them to window.

  private void createContents()
  {
    JLabel namePrompt = new JLabel("What's your name?");
    nameBox = new JTextField(15);
    greeting = new JLabel();
    add(namePrompt);
    add(nameBox);
    add(greeting);
    nameBox.addActionListener(

      // anonymous inner class for event handling
      new ActionListener()
      {
        public void actionPerformed(ActionEvent e)
        {
          String message; // the personalized greeting
          message = "Glad to meet you, " + nameBox.getText();
          nameBox.setText("");
          greeting.setText(message);
        } // end actionPerformed
      } // end anonymous inner class
    ); // end addActionListener call
  } // end createContents

  //***********************************************************

  public static void main(String[] args)
  {
    new GreetingAnonymous();
  } // end main
} // end class GreetingAnonymous
```

Figure 16.6b GreetingAnonymous program that has an anonymous inner class—part B

In the Greeting program, we implemented a listener class named `Listener`, using this code:

```
private class Listener implements ActionListener
{
```

That code is omitted in the GreetingAnonymous program—there's no class named `Listener`. But we still need a listener object so that the text box's enter event is detected and acted upon. This time, instead of declaring a listener class with a name (e.g., `Listener`), we implement a listener class anonymously (without a name).

We've discussed anonymous objects previously. That's where you instantiate an object without storing its reference in a variable. In our previous Greeting program, we instantiated an anonymous `Listener` object with this line:

```
nameBox.addActionListener(new Listener());
```

The point of using an anonymous object is to avoid cluttering the code with a variable name when an object needs to be used only one time. The same idea can be applied to classes. The point of using an *anonymous inner class* is to avoid cluttering up the code with a class name when a class needs to be used only one time. For example, if a particular listener class listens to just one object, then the listener class needs to be used only one time as part of an `addActionListener` method call. Therefore, to unclutter your code, you may want to use an anonymous inner class for the listener.

Using an anonymous inner class is not a compiler requirement. It's an elegance issue. In industry, you'll find some people who say anonymous inner classes are elegant and you'll find other people who say anonymous inner classes are confusing. Do as you see fit. Better yet, do as your teacher sees fit.

Below, we show the syntax for an anonymous inner class. Naturally, there's no class name. But there is an interface name. So anonymous inner classes aren't built from scratch; they're built with the help of an interface.[2] Note the `new` operator. Formally speaking, the `new` operator isn't part of the anonymous inner class. But practically speaking, since there's no point in having an anonymous inner class without instantiating it, you can think of the `new` operator as being part of the anonymous inner class syntax.

```
new <interface-name> ()
{
 <class-body>
}
```

Here's an example of an anonymous inner class, taken from the GreetingAnonymous program:

```
nameBox.addActionListener(
  new ActionListener()
  {
    public void actionPerformed(ActionEvent e)
    {
      ...
    } // end actionPerformed
  } // end inner-class constructor
);
```

`ActionListener` is an interface

For comparison purposes, here's an example of a named (non-anonymous) inner class. It's taken from the Greeting program:

```
private void createContents()
{
  ...
  nameBox.addActionListener(new Listener());
} // end createContents

private class Listener implements ActionListener
{
  public void actionPerformed(ActionEvent e)
  {
    ...
  } // end actionPerformed
} // end class Listener
```

[2] As an alternative, it's legal to define an anonymous class with a superclass instead of an interface. Details are beyond the scope of this textbook.

There are only two syntactic differences between the two code fragments—the `addActionListener` call and the listener class heading. There are no semantic differences between the two code fragments, so the Greeting program and the GreetingAnonymous program behave the same.

16.12 `JButton` Component

It's now time to learn another GUI component—a button component.

User Interface

If you press a button on an electronic device, something usually happens. For example, if you press the power button on a television, the television turns on or off. Likewise, if you press/click a GUI *button* component, something usually happens. For example, in Figure 16.1's TrustyCredit window, if you click the OK button, then the entered credit card numbers get processed by the TrustyCredit company.

Implementation

To create a button component, call the *`JButton`* constructor like this:

```
JButton helloButton = new JButton("Press me");
```

(callout pointing to "Press me": button label's text)

When this button is displayed, it says "Press me" in the center of the button. The label argument is optional. If it's omitted, the label gets the empty string by default and the button displays with a blank face (no writing or icons on it).

After you have created the `helloButton`, add it to your window, like this:

```
add(helloButton);
```

To make the button useful, you'll need to implement a listener. As with the text box listeners, button listeners must implement the `ActionListener` interface. The `ActionListener` interface dictates that you must have an `actionPerformed` event handler method. The code skeleton looks like this:

```
private class Listener implements ActionListener
{
  public void actionPerformed(ActionEvent e)
  {
    <do-something>
  }
}
```

We're using `private` instead of `public` for the listener class because a listener normally is implemented as an inner class, and inner classes are normally `private`. We're using a named inner class instead of an anonymous inner class because named inner classes are slightly more flexible. They allow you to create a listener that's used on more than one component. We'll provide an example in an upcoming program.

To register the above listener with our `helloButton` component, do this:

```
helloButton.addActionListener(new Listener());
```

The JButton class needs the javax.swing package, but that should be available already, since it's needed for the JFrame class. The ActionListener interface and the ActionEvent class need the java.awt.event package, so import that package.

Methods

Here are API headings and descriptions for some of the more useful JButton methods:

```
public String getText()
```
Returns the button's label.

```
public void setText(String text)
```
Assigns the button's label.

```
public void setVisible(boolean flag)
```
Makes the button visible or invisible.

```
public void addActionListener(ActionListener listener)
```
Adds a listener to the button. The listener "listens" for the button being clicked.

FactorialButton Program

It's time to put all this JButton syntax into practice by showing you how it's used within a complete program. We've written a FactorialButton program that uses a JButton component to calculate the factorial for a user-entered number.[3] To give you a better idea of how the program operates, see the sample session in Figure 16.7.

Figures 16.8a and 16.8b contain the FactorialButton program listing. Most of the code should already make sense since the program's structure parallels the structure in our previous GUI programs. We'll skip the more familiar code and focus on the more difficult code.

We declare most of our GUI variables locally within createContents, but we declare the two text box components as instance variables at the top of the program. Why the difference? As discussed earlier, normally you should declare components as local variables to help with encapsulation. But if a component is needed in createContents and also in an event handler, it's fine to declare it as an instance variable where it can be shared more easily. In the FactorialButton program, we declare the two text boxes as instance variables because we need to use them in createContents and also in the actionPerformed event handler.

Note this line from the createContents method:

```
xfBox.setEditable(false);
```

This causes the factorial text box, xfBox, to be non-editable (i.e., the user won't be able to update the text box). That should make sense since xfBox holds the factorial, and it's up to the program (not the user) to generate the factorial. Note in Figure 16.7 that the factorial text box is grayed out. You get that visual cue free of charge whenever you call setEditable(false) from a text box component. Cool!

[3] The factorial of a number is the product of all positive integers less than or equal to the number. The factorial of n is written as n! Example: The factorial of 4 is written as 4!, and 4! is equal to 24 because 1 times 2 times 3 times 4 equals 24.

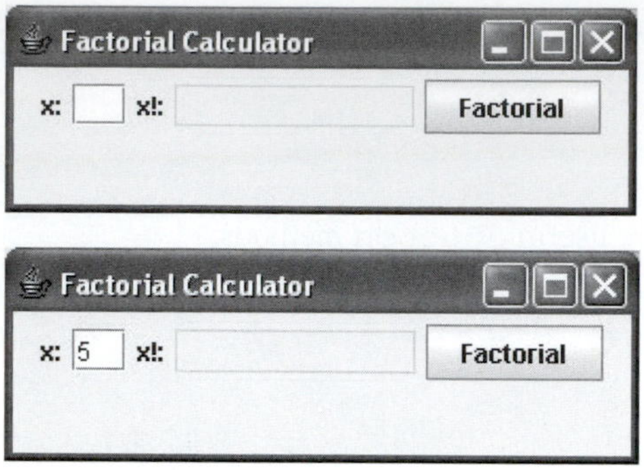

After pressing **Enter** in the x box or clicking the **Factorial** button:

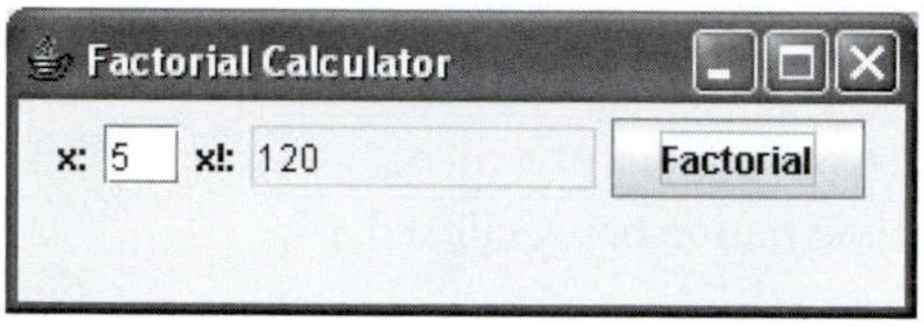

Figure 16.7 Sample session for the FactorialButton program

Again from the `createContents` method:

```
Listener listener = new Listener();
...
xBox.addActionListener(listener);
btn.addActionListener(listener);
```

Note that we're registering the same listener with two different components. By doing this, we give the user two ways to trigger a response. The user can press **Enter** when the cursor is in the input text box (`xBox`) or the user can click on the button (`btn`). Either way causes the listener to react. Whenever you register the same listener with two different components, you need to have a name for the listener. That's why we use a named inner class for this program (an anonymous inner class wouldn't work).

Figure 16.8b's `actionPerformed` method is chock full of interesting code. Of greatest importance is the `Integer.parseInt` method call. If you ever need to read numbers or display numbers in a GUI program, you have to use string versions of the numbers. Thus, to read a number from the input text box, we first read it in as a string, and then we convert the string to a number. To accomplish this, we read the string using `xBox.getText()`, and we convert it to a number using `Integer.parseInt`.

Ideally, you should always check user input to make sure it's valid. In the `actionPerformed` method, we check for two types of invalid input—a non-integer input and a negative number input. Those inputs are invalid because the factorial is mathematically undefined for those cases. The negative number case is easier, so we'll start with it. Note this code in the middle of the `ActionPerformed` method:

```
if (x < 0)
{
  xfBox.setText("undefined");
}
```

```
/*************************************************************
* FactorialButton.java
* Dean & Dean
*
* When user clicks button or presses Enter in input text box,
* entered number's factorial displays in the output text box.
*************************************************************/

import javax.swing.*;
import java.awt.*;
import java.awt.event.*;

public class FactorialButton extends JFrame
{
  private static final int WIDTH = 300;
  private static final int HEIGHT = 100;
  private JTextField xBox;  // holds user entry
  private JTextField xfBox; // holds generated factorial

  //**********************************************************

  public FactorialButton()
  {
    setTitle("Factorial Calculator");
    setSize(WIDTH, HEIGHT);
    setLayout(new FlowLayout());
    setDefaultCloseOperation(EXIT_ON_CLOSE);
    createContents();
    setVisible(true);
  } // end FactorialButton constructor

  //**********************************************************

  private void createContents()
  {
    JLabel xLabel = new JLabel("x:");
    JLabel xfLabel = new JLabel("x!:");
    JButton btn = new JButton("Factorial");
    Listener listener = new Listener();

    xBox = new JTextField(2);
    xfBox = new JTextField(10);
    xfBox.setEditable(false);
    add(xLabel);
    add(xBox);
    add(xfLabel);
    add(xfBox);
    add(btn);
    xBox.addActionListener(listener);
    btn.addActionListener(listener);
  } // end createContents
```

Here we register the same listener with two different components.

Figure 16.8a FactorialButton program—part A

```
  //***************************************************

  // Inner class for event handling.

  private class Listener implements ActionListener
  {
    public void actionPerformed(ActionEvent e)
    {
      int x;          // numeric value for user-entered x
      int xf;         // x factorial

      try
      {
        x = Integer.parseInt(xBox.getText());
      }
      catch (NumberFormatException nfe)
      {
        x = -1;   // indicates an invalid x
      }

      if (x < 0)
      {
        xfBox.setText("undefined");
      }
      else
      {
        if (x == 0 || x == 1)
        {
          xf = 1;
        }
        else
        {
          xf = 1;
          for (int i=2; i<=x; i++)
          {
            xf *= i;
          }
        } // end else

        xfBox.setText(Integer.toString(xf));
      } // end else
    } // end actionPerformed
  } // end class Listener

  //***************************************************

  public static void main(String[] args)
  {
    new FactorialButton();
  } // end main
} // end class FactorialButton
```

Convert user-entered number from a string to a number.

Figure 16.8b FactorialButton program—part B

x is the user's entry after it's been converted to an integer. If x is negative, the program displays undefined in the xfBox component.

Now for the non-integer input case. Note this code near the top of the ActionPerformed method:

```
try
{
  x = Integer.parseInt(xBox.getText());
}
catch (NumberFormatException nfe)
{
  x = -1;    // indicates an invalid x
}
```

The Integer.parseInt method attempts to convert xBox's user-entered value to an integer. If xBox's user-entered value is a non-integer, then parseInt throws a NumberFormatException. To handle that possibility, we put the Integer.parseInt method call inside a try block, and we include an associated catch block. If parseInt throws an exception, we want to display undefined in the xfBox component. To do that, we could call xfBox.setText("undefined") in the catch block, but then we'd have redundant code—xfBox.setText("undefined") in the catch block and also in the subsequent if statement. To avoid code redundancy and its inherent maintenance problems, we assign −1 to x in the catch block. That causes the subsequent if statement to be true and that in turn causes xfBox.setText("undefined") to be called.

After validating the input, the actionPerformed method calculates the factorial. It first takes care of the special case when x equals 0 or 1. It then takes care of the x ≥ 2 case by using a for loop. Study the code. It works fine, but do you see a way to make it more compact? You can omit the block of code that starts with if (x == 0 || x == 1) because that case is handled by the else block. More specifically, you can delete the six lines above the second xf = 1; line.

Write compact code.

16.13 Dialog Boxes and the JOptionPane Class

A *dialog box*—often referred to simply as a *dialog*—is a specialized type of window. The primary difference between a dialog box and a standard window is that a dialog box is more constrained in terms of what it can do. While a standard window usually remains on the user's screen for quite a while (often for the duration of the program) and performs many tasks, a dialog box remains on the screen only long enough to perform one specific task. While a standard window is highly customizable, a dialog box typically is locked into one particular format.

User Interface

There are three types of JOptionPane dialogs—a *message dialog,* an *input dialog,* and a *confirmation* dialog. Each type performs one specific task. The message dialog displays output. The input dialog displays a question and an input field. The confirmation dialog displays a yes/no question and yes/no/cancel button options. See what the different types look like in Figure 16.9. In this chapter, we'll focus on just one of the three dialogs—the message dialog. If you want to learn about the input dialog, see the GUI track section in Chapter 3. If you want to learn about the confirmation dialog, refer to Sun's Java API Web site.

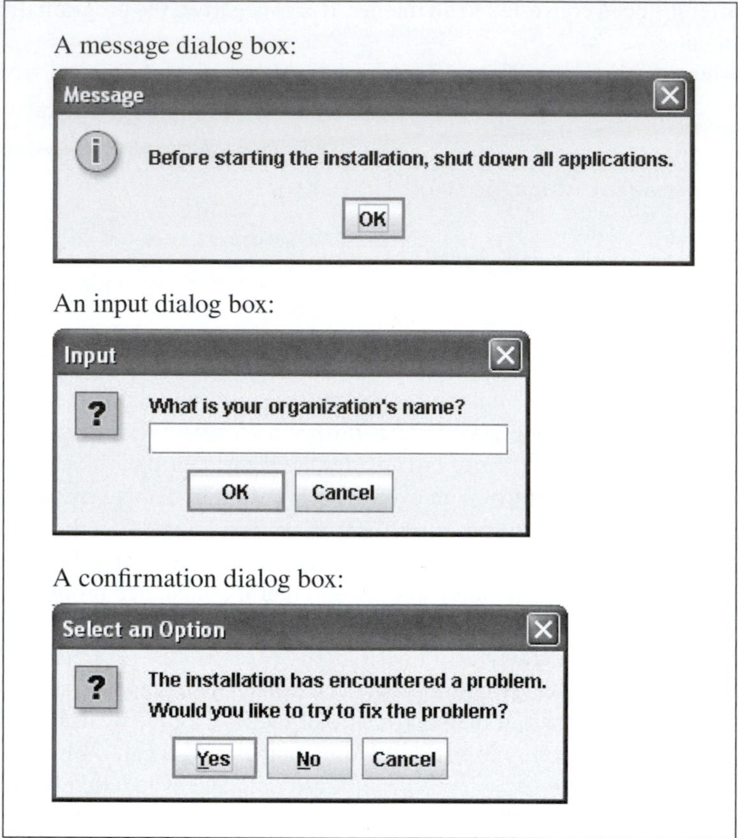

Figure 16.9 Three types of `JOptionPane` dialog boxes

Implementation

To create a message dialog box, call the `showMessageDialog` method like this:

`JOptionPane.showMessageDialog(`*<container>*`,` *<message>*`);`

You need to prefix the `showMessageDialog` call with "`JOptionPane` dot" because `showMessageDialog` is a class method in the `JOptionPane` class. Remember—call instance methods using "*<reference-variable>* dot" syntax, and call class methods using "*<class-name>* dot" syntax.

In the above `showMessageDialog` call, the message argument specifies the text that appears in the dialog box. The container argument specifies the container that surrounds the dialog box. The dialog box displays in the center of that container.

Note the `showMessageDialog` call in Figure 16.10's HelloWithAFrame program. We use `helloFrame` for `showMessageDialog`'s container argument. What type of container is it? As you can see from the code, `helloFrame` is an instance of the `HelloWithAFrame` class, and the `HelloWithAFrame` class extends the `JFrame` container. Therefore, by inheritance, `helloFrame` is a `JFrame` container. And consequently, the dialog box displays in the center of the program's `JFrame` container. Verify this by looking at Figure 16.10's output.

```
import javax.swing.*;
public class HelloWithAFrame extends JFrame
{
  public HelloWithAFrame()
  {
    setTitle("Hello");
    setSize(400, 200);
    setDefaultCloseOperation(EXIT_ON_CLOSE);
    setVisible(true);
  } // end HelloWithAFrame constructor

  //**************************************************************

  public static void main(String[] args)
  {
    HelloWithAFrame helloFrame = new HelloWithAFrame();
    JOptionPane.showMessageDialog(helloFrame, "Hello, world!");
  } // end main
} // end class HelloWithAFrame
```

Hello

Message

Hello, world!

OK

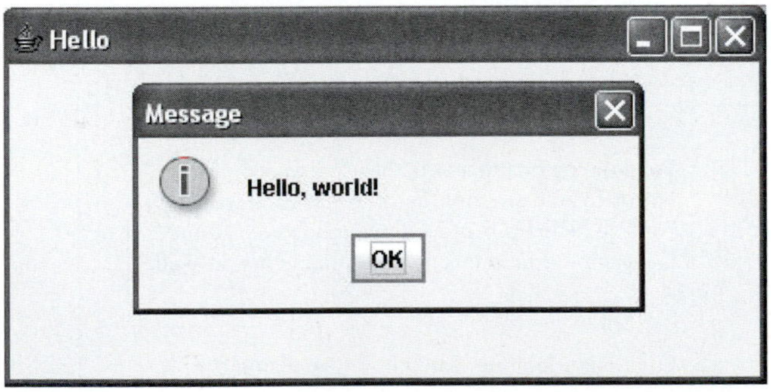

Figure 16.10 HelloWithAFrame program and its output

Suppose you don't want to bother with centering the dialog box within a particular container. In that case, use `null` for `showMessageDialog`'s container argument. That causes the dialog box to display in the center of the screen. For example, this code fragment generates a screen-centered dialog box:

```
JOptionPane.showMessageDialog(
  null, "Before starting the installation,\n" +
  "shut down all applications.");
```

By the way, it's very common to use `null` for `showMessageDialog`'s container argument, probably more common than using a non-`null` value.

The `JOptionPane` class needs the `javax.swing` package. If you've imported the `javax.swing` package for the `JFrame` class already, there's no need to import it again.

Method Details

In Figure 16.10, note the message dialog box's title-bar message—it's "Message." Kinda boring, eh? To liven things up, add a third argument to the `showMessageDialog` call that specifies the dialog box's title. Also in Figure 16.10, note the message dialog box's icon—it's an **i** inside a circle. That's the default icon. To explicitly specify an icon, add a fourth argument to the `showMessageDialog` call that specifies one of the named constants in Figure 16.11.

`JOptionPane` Named Constants (for Specifying a Dialog Box's Icon)	Icon	When to Use
INFORMATION_MESSAGE	(i)	For a dialog box that provides informational text.
WARNING_ MESSAGE	⚠	For a dialog box that warns the user about a problem.
ERROR_MESSAGE	X	For a dialog box that warns the user about an error. Normally, an error is considered to be more serious than a warning.
QUESTION_MESSAGE	?	For a dialog box that asks the user a question. Normally, the question-mark icon is used with a confirm dialog box or an input dialog box. But it is legal to use it with a message dialog box as well.
PLAIN_MESSAGE	no icon	For a plain-looking dialog box. The dialog box contains a message, but no icon.

Figure 16.11 Icon options within a `JOptionPane` dialog box

Here's how to call the four-parameter version of `showMessageDialog`:

```
JOptionPane.showMessageDialog(
  <null-or-container>, <message>, <title>, <icon_constant>);
```

Here's an example four-argument `showMessageDialog` call and the resulting dialog box:

```
JOptionPane.showMessageDialog(null, "A virus has been detected.", "Warning",
  JOptionPane.WARNING_MESSAGE);
```

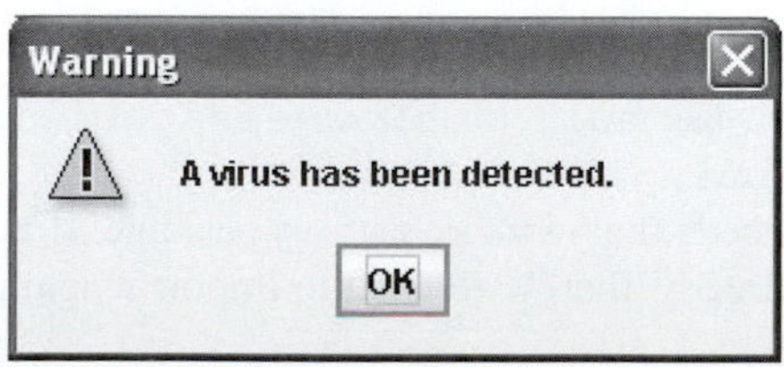

16.14 Distinguishing Between Multiple Events

Now that you understand the basic building blocks of GUI programming (`JFrame` and `JOptionPane` windows; `JLabel`, `JTextField`, and `JButton` components), you're prepared to consider more complex situations that GUI programmers encounter. In this section, you'll learn how to use a single listener to distinguish between two different component events.

The `getSource` Method

Suppose you register a listener with two components. When the listener hears an event, you'll probably want to determine which component fired the event. That way, you can customize your event handling: Do one thing if component X fired the event, and do another thing if component Y fired the event.

From within a listener, how can you determine the source of an event? In other words, how can you identify the component that fired an event? Call `getSource`, of course! More specifically, within the `actionPerformed` method, use the `actionPerformed` method's `ActionEvent` parameter to call `getSource`. The `getSource` method returns a reference to the component whose event was fired. To see which component that was, use == to compare the returned value with the components in question. For example, in the below code fragment, we compare the returned value to a button component named `okButton`.

```
public void actionPerformed(ActionEvent e)
{
  if (e.getSource() == okButton)
  {
    ...
```

Improved FactorialButton Program

Remember the FactorialButton program from Figure 16.8? It calculated the factorial of a user-entered number. The calculations were triggered by the user clicking the factorial button or the user pressing Enter in the input text box. With our simple first-cut FactorialButton program, we didn't bother to distinguish between the button-click event and the text-box-enter event. Let's now improve the program by having the different events trigger different results. The button click will still display the factorial, but the text box enter will display this dialog-box message:

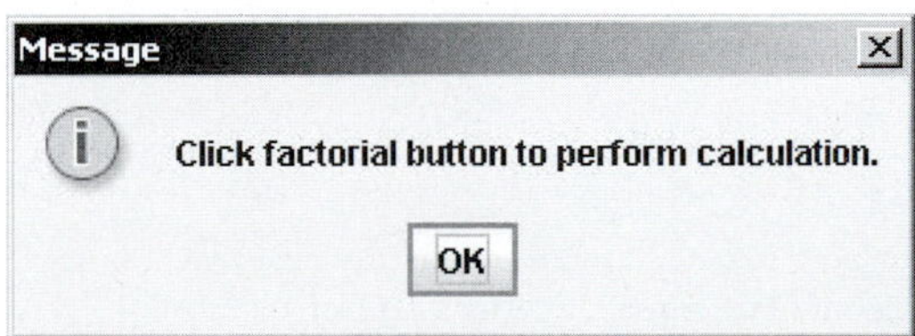

See Figure 16.12. It shows the `Listener` class for our new and improved FactorialButton program. We're only showing the `Listener` class because the rest of the program hasn't changed. If you want to see the rest of the program, refer back to Figure 16.8. In our new `Listener` class, note how we call `getSource` and compare its returned value to `xBox`. `xBox` is the text box component that holds the user's entry for `x`. If `getSource` returns `xBox`, we call `showMessageDialog` and display the above dialog-box message.

```
private class Listener implements ActionListener
{
  public void actionPerformed(ActionEvent e)
  {
    int x;    // numeric value for user entered x
    int xf;   // x factorial

    if (e.getSource() == xBox)
    {
      JOptionPane.showMessageDialog(null,
        "Click factorial button to perform calculation.");
    }

    else // the button must have been clicked
    {
      try
      {
        x = Integer.parseInt(xBox.getText());
      }
      catch (NumberFormatException nfe)
      {
        x = -1;    // indicates an invalid x
      }

      if (x < 0)
      {
        xfBox.setText("undefined");
      }
      else
      {
        if (x == 0 || x == 1)
        {
          xf = 1;
        }
        else
        {
          xf = 1;
          for (int i=2; i<=x; i++)
          {
            xf *= i;
          }
        } // end else

        xfBox.setText(Integer.toString(xf));
      } // end else
    } // end else button was clicked
  } // end actionPerformed
} // end class Listener
```

This is the input text box.

Figure 16.12 Modified `Listener` class for the FactorialButton program

16.15 Using getActionCommand to Distinguish Between Multiple Events

In this section, we continue our discussion of distinguishing between multiple events. But instead of calling getSource, this time we call getActionCommand.

getSource Is Somewhat Limited

In Figure 16.12's Listener class, we call getSource to identify the component whose event was fired. That works fine most of the time, but not always. Note the following cases where calling getSource is inadequate:

1. If the event-firing components are in a different class from the listener class.

   The listener class's getSource method can successfully retrieve the component responsible for the fired event, but there is no way to identify the type of the returned component because that requires comparing the returned component with the original components (using ==). If the original components are in a different class and private, using them in the listener class generates a compile-time error.

2. If there's a need to have a *modal* component.

   A modal component is a component with more than one state or status. For example, suppose there's a button whose label toggles between "Show Details" and "Hide Details." The two labels correspond to two different modes of operation—in one mode details are shown, and in another mode details are hidden. If a modal button is clicked, getSource can retrieve the button, but it cannot retrieve the button's mode. In the show details/hide details example, getSource cannot directly determine whether the button's mode is show details or hide details.

getActionCommand to the Rescue

If you need to identify an event from within a listener and getSource is inadequate, try getActionCommand. The getActionCommand method returns the "action command" associated with the component whose event was fired. Typically, the action command is the component's label. For example, the default action command for a button is the button's label.

Let's revisit the case where a button's label toggles between "Show Details" and "Hide Details." In the following code fragment, assume that instructions is a label component, detailedInstructions and briefInstructions are string local variables, and btn is the "Show Details/Hide Details" button. Note how getActionCommand determines the button's mode by retrieving the button's label.

```
public void actionPerformed(ActionEvent e)
{
  if (e.getActionCommand().equals("Show Details"))
  {
    instructions.setText(detailedInstructions);
    btn.setText("HideDetails");
  }
  else
  {
```

```
        instructions.setText(briefInstructions);
        btn.setText("ShowDetails");
      }
    } // end actionPerformed
```

16.16 Color

So far in this chapter, all of our components have been simple in terms of color—black text on white background or black text on light-gray background. It's time to add some color. You should get used to adding color to most of your GUI applications. After all, color can enhance a user's experience with a program by providing visual cues and visual appeal. Remember, color is fun!

Color Methods

Most GUI components are composed of two colors. The *foreground color* is the color of the text, and the *background color* is the color of the area behind the text. Let's jump right into an example that shows you how to set the colors. This code fragment creates a blue button with white text:

```
JButton btn = new JButton("Click Me");
btn.setBackground(Color.BLUE);
btn.setForeground(Color.WHITE);
```

And here's what the blue-white button looks like:

Click Me

The `setBackground` and `setForeground` methods are mutator methods. Here are the API headings and descriptions for their associated accessor methods:

`public Color getBackground()`
  Returns the component's background color.

`public Color getForeground()`
  Returns the component's foreground color.

Here's an example that uses the `getBackground` and `getForeground` methods with a text box:

```
JTextField nameBox = new JTextField();
Color originalBackground = nameBox.getBackground();
Color originalForeground = nameBox.getForeground();
```

Why might you want to save a text box's original colors? As a visual cue, you might want to change a text box's colors when the user enters something invalid. And when the user fixes the entry, you'd change back to the original colors. In order to do that, you need to retrieve and save the original colors when the window is first loaded.

You've now seen color examples with a button and a text box. Color works the same way for most other components. An exception is the `JLabel` component. Its background is transparent by default, so if you apply color to it, you won't see the color. To change a label's background color, you first have to make it opaque by calling `label.setOpaque(true)`. After that, if you call `setBackground(`*<color>*`)`, you'll see the specified color.

Color Named Constants

Let's now talk about color values. You can specify color values with named constants or with instantiated Color objects. We'll start with named constants.

The Color class defines this set of named constants:

```
Color.BLACK        Color.GREEN        Color.RED
Color.BLUE         Color.LIGHT_GRAY   Color.WHITE
Color.CYAN         Color.MAGENTA      Color.YELLOW
Color.DARK_GRAY    Color.ORANGE
Color.GRAY         Color.PINK
```

As is customary, the named constants are class members. As with all class members, they are accessed using *<class name>* dot syntax. In other words, they are accessed with a "Color." prefix.

The Color class is in the java.awt package, so don't forget to import that package when working with colors.

Color Objects

To obtain a color that is not in the Color class's list of named constant colors, instantiate a Color object with a specified mixture of red, green, and blue. Here's the Color constructor call syntax:

new Color(*<red 0–255>*, *<green 0–255>*, *<blue 0–255>*)

Each of the three Color constructor arguments is an int value between 0 and 255. The int value represents an amount of color, with 0 indicating no color and 255 indicating the maximum amount of color. For example, this line sets a button's background color to a dark magenta:

```
button.setBackground(new Color(128, 0, 128));
```

The instantiated Color object uses half the maximum for red (128), no green (0), and half the maximum for blue (128). In the brightest magenta, increase the red and blue values from 128 to 255.

White light is the combination of all colors,[4] so new Color(255, 255, 255) produces white. Black is the absence of all colors, so new Color(0, 0, 0) produces black.

This technique of creating a color by mixing specified amounts of red, green, and blue is used by many programming languages. The red, green, blue 3-tuple is commonly referred to as an *RGB value*. When coming up with RGB values for your programs, it's perfectly acceptable to use trial and error, but to save time, you may want to visit an RGB color table online. For example—http://www.pitt.edu/~nisg/cis/web/cgi/rgb.html.

JFrame Background Color

Setting the background color for a JFrame window is slightly trickier than setting it for a component. First you have to get the JFrame's *content pane*, and then you have to apply the background color to it. As shown below, the content pane is the inner part of the JFrame.

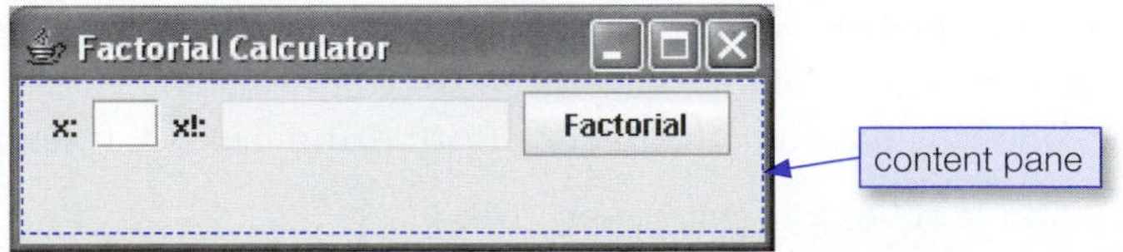

[4] In 1666, Isaac Newton discovered that white light is composed of all of the colors of the color spectrum. He showed that when white light is passed through a triangular prism, it separates into different colors. And when the resulting colors are passed through a second triangular prism, they are brought back together to form the original white light.

While the `JFrame` class handles perimeter features such as window dimensions, the title bar, and the close-out button, the content pane handles interior features such as components, layout, and background color. So when you add components, set the layout, and set the background color, you do it to the content pane, not the `JFrame`. These three statements illustrate what we're talking about:

```
getContentPane().add(btn);
getContentPane().setLayout(new FlowLayout());
getContentPane().setBackground(Color.YELLOW);
```

In versions of Java prior to Java 5.0, `JFrame`'s `getContentPane` method was required for all three tasks—adding a component, setting the layout, and setting the window's background color. With the advent of Java 5.0, the folks at Sun made things easier for the first two tasks. Now, if you want to add a component or set the layout, you may optionally omit the call to `getContentPane`. In other words, this works:

```
add(btn);
setLayout(new FlowLayout());
```

The reason that code works is that with the current version of Java, `JFrame`'s `add` and `setLayout` methods automatically get the content pane behind the scenes. And the retrieved content pane is used for the ensuing `add` and `setLayout` operations. So which is better—`add(btn)` or `getContentPane().add(btn)`? They are functionally equivalent, but the first one is generally preferred since it's less cluttered. Ditto for the `setLayout` method call.

For setting the window's background color, the current version of Java still requires that you call `getContentPane` before calling `setBackground`. If you call `setBackground` without calling `getContentPane`, it sets the `JFrame`'s background color, not the content pane's background color. And since the content pane sits on top of the `JFrame`, the `JFrame`'s color is covered up and not seen.

Now you know that setting a window's background color requires `getContentPane`. Similarly, getting a window's background color requires `getContentPane`. For example:

```
Color saveColor = getContentPane().getBackground();
```

ColorChooser Program

Let's put what you've learned about color into practice by using it within a complete program. In our ColorChooser program, we implement light gray and light blue buttons that set the window's background color to gray or blue, respectively. See Figure 16.13 to get an idea of what we're talking about.

See the ColorChooser program listing in Figures 16.14a and 16.14b. Most of the code should already make sense since its structure mirrors the structure in our previous GUI programs. We'll focus on the new code—the color code.

Note the difference between the `setBackground` calls in the `createContents` method and the `setBackground` calls in the `actionPerformed` method. In `createContents`, we're dealing with the gray and blue button components, so it is not necessary to call `getContentPane` prior to calling `setBackground`. In `actionPerformed`, we're dealing with the `JFrame` window, so it is necessary to call `getContentPane` prior to calling `setBackground`.

Note the following line from the `createContents` method. It sets the blue button color to light blue:

```
blueButton.setBackground(new Color(135, 206, 250));
```

There is no named constant for light blue so we have to instantiate a light-blue `Color` object by using an RGB value. We use almost the maximum amount of blue (250) as well as a substantial amount of red (135) and green (206). Are you curious why we're using so much red and green? To achieve a light shade, you

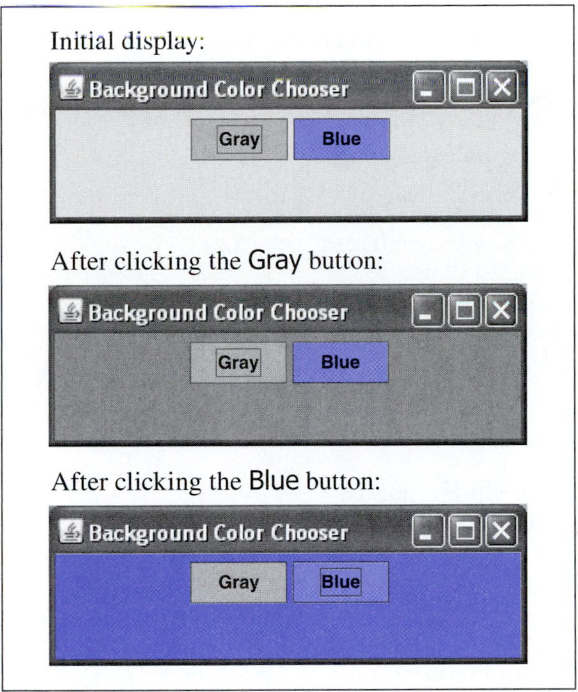

Figure 16.13 Sample session for the ColorChooser program

need to use a substantial amount of all three color values. That should make sense when you realize that white is `Color(255, 255, 255)`.

```
/*************************************************************
* ColorChooser.java
* Dean & Dean
*
* This program's buttons allow the user to set the window's
* background color to gray or blue.
*************************************************************/

import javax.swing.*;      // for JFrame & JButton
import java.awt.*;         // for FlowLayout, Color, & Container
import java.awt.event.*;   // for ActionListener & ActionEvent

public class ColorChooser extends JFrame
{
  private static final int WIDTH = 300;
  private static final int HEIGHT = 100;

  private JButton grayButton;  // changes background to gray
  private JButton blueButton;  // changes background to blue
```

Figure 16.14a ColorChooser program—part A

```
//**********************************************************

public ColorChooser()
{
  setTitle("Background Color Chooser");
  setSize(WIDTH, HEIGHT);
  setLayout(new FlowLayout());
  setDefaultCloseOperation(EXIT_ON_CLOSE);
  createContents();
  setVisible(true);
} // end ColorChooser constructor

//**********************************************************

private void createContents()
{
  grayButton = new JButton("Gray");
  grayButton.setBackground(Color.LIGHT_GRAY);
  grayButton.addActionListener(new ButtonListener());
  add(grayButton);

  blueButton = new JButton("Blue");
  blueButton.setBackground(new Color(135,206,250));
  blueButton.addActionListener(new ButtonListener());
  add(blueButton);
} // end createContents

//**************************************************************

// Inner class for event handling.

private class ButtonListener implements ActionListener
{
  public void actionPerformed(ActionEvent e)
  {
    Container contentPane = getContentPane();
    if (e.getSource() == grayButton)
    {
      // Change the window background color to gray.
      contentPane.setBackground(Color.GRAY);
    }
    else
    {
      // Change the window background color to blue.
      contentPane.setBackground(Color.BLUE);
    }
  } // end actionPerformed
} // end class ButtonListener
```

This sets the Gray button's color.

This sets the Blue button's color.

These lines change the window's background color.

Figure 16.14b ColorChooser program—part B

```
    //*************************************************************

    public static void main(String[] args)
    {
      new ColorChooser();
    }
  } // end class ColorChooser
```

Figure 16.14c ColorChooser program—part C

16.17 How GUI Classes Are Grouped Together

Throughout this chapter, you've used Java's pre-built GUI classes from Sun's API library. For example, you used the `JFrame` class for creating a window, the `JButton` class for creating a button, and the `Color` class for creating a color. In this section, we describe how Sun's pre-built GUI classes are grouped and organized.

Subpackages

The Java API is a huge class library that adds functionality to the core Java language. To simplify things, the classes are organized into a hierarchy of packages where each package contains a group of classes. To avoid having too many classes in one package, packages are often split into *subpackages*. A subpackage is a group of classes from within a larger group of classes. For example, rather than putting all the GUI classes (and there are lots of them!) within the `java.awt` package, the folks at Sun split off the GUI event-handling classes and put them in their own subpackage, `java.awt.event`. To import all the classes in the `java.awt` package and the `java.awt.event` subpackage, do this:

```
import java.awt.*;
import java.awt.event.*;
```

Since the `java.awt.event` subpackage contains `java.awt` in its name, is it OK to omit the `java.awt.event import` statement and do just the following?

```
import java.awt.*;
```

This imports classes in the `java.awt` package only.

No, you must import `java.awt` and `java.awt.event` separately. Think of the `java.awt` package and the `java.awt.event` subpackage as completely separate entities. The fact that they share the common name "java.awt" is irrelevant as far as the compiler is concerned. The compiler treats them as separate packages. So then why the shared name? The shared name helps programmers remember that the classes in `java.awt.event` are conceptually related to the classes in `java.awt`.

We've been referring to `java.awt.event` as a "subpackage." It's just as common to refer to it as a "package." We'll use both terms since both are valid.

The AWT and Swing Libraries

In Sun's first Java compiler, all GUI classes were bundled into one library known as the Abstract Windowing Toolkit (AWT). The AWT's GUI commands generate GUI components that look different on different platforms. In other words, if your program instantiates an AWT button component, the button will have a

Macintosh look and feel if the program is run on a Macintosh computer, but a Windows look and feel if the program is run on a Windows computer.[5] That leads to portability issues. Your programs are still portable in the sense that they'll run on different platforms. But they'll run differently on different platforms. If you have a persnickety customer who demands one precise appearance on all platforms, then AWT components probably won't be satisfactory.

One of Java's strongest selling points was (and is) its portability, so soon after Java's initial release, the folks at Sun set out to develop a set of more portable GUI components. They put their new, more-portable components in a brand new library named Swing. To make the relationship clear between the new Swing components and the AWT components, they used the same component names except that they prefaced the new Swing components with a "J." For example, the AWT has a `Button` component, so Swing has a `JButton` component.

The AWT GUI components are known as *heavyweight components,* while the Swing GUI components are known as *lightweight components.* The AWT components are heavyweight because they are built with graphics commands that are part of the computer's platform. Being part of the computer's platform, they're too "heavy" to move to other platforms. Swing components are lightweight because they're built with Java code. Being built with Java code means that they're "light" enough to move to different platforms.

The Swing library includes quite a bit more than just GUI component classes. It adds lots of functionality to the AWT, but it does not replace the AWT entirely. Today, Java GUI application programmers use both libraries—the AWT and Swing.[6] The primary AWT packages are `java.awt` and `java.awt.event`. The primary Swing package is `javax.swing`. The "x" in `javax` stands for "extension" because the `javax` packages (`javax.swing` is one of several `javax` packages) are considered to be a major extension to the core Java platform.

16.18 Mouse Listeners and Images (Optional)

Sun provides several different types of listeners. Earlier in this chapter, you learned about the most common listener—the `ActionListener`. You should use the `ActionListener` for events where the user does something to a component, such as clicking a button or pressing Enter within a text box. In this section, you'll learn about mouse listeners. As the name implies, you should use mouse listeners for events where the user does something with the mouse. Also in this section, you'll learn about images (pictures). You'll learn how to display an image and drag an image with your mouse.

Mouse Listeners

In creating a mouse listener, you use the same basic steps that you use for the `ActionListener`—you define a listener class, you define an event handler method(s) within the listener class, and you register your listener class with a component. Although the same basic steps are used, mouse listeners are slightly more complicated than the `ActionListener`. There are several different types of mouse listeners, and each type of mouse listener handles multiple types of mouse events.

We describe two mouse listener types, and they are defined by their two interfaces—`MouseListener` and `MouseMotionListener`. Figure 16.15 shows the API headings and descriptions for the methods

[5] *Look and feel* is a standard GUI term, and it refers to the appearance of something and the way in which the user interacts with it.

[6] Java applet programmers typically use the AWT only, even for GUI components, and do not use the Swing library at all. Why? Because applets rely on browsers and, sadly, many of today's browsers use old versions of Java, versions that don't include Swing.

`MouseListener` Interface Event Handlers
`public void mouseClicked(MouseEvent event)` Called when the user presses and releases the mouse button while the mouse cursor is stationary on a `MouseListener`-registered component.
`public void mouseEntered(MouseEvent event)` Called when the mouse cursor enters the bounds of a `MouseListener`-registered component.
`public void mouseExited(MouseEvent event)` Called when the mouse cursor exits from the bounds of a `MouseListener`-registered component.
`public void mousePressed(MouseEvent event)` Called when the user presses the mouse button while the mouse cursor is on a `MouseListener`-registered component.
`public void mouseReleased(MouseEvent event)` Called when the user releases the mouse button, but only if the prior mouse press was on a `MouseListener`-registered component.

`MouseMotionListener` Interface Event Handlers
`public void mouseDragged(MouseEvent event)` Called when the user holds the mouse button down while moving the mouse cursor, but only if the initial mouse press was on a `MouseMotionListener`-registered component.
`public void mouseMoved(MouseEvent event)` Called when the user moves the mouse while the mouse cursor is on a `MouseMotionListener`-registered component.

Figure 16.15 API headings and descriptions for the methods in the `MouseListener` and `MouseMotionListener` interfaces

defined by the two interfaces. Read through the API headings and descriptions to get an idea of what's possible in terms of mouse event handling.

As a programmer, you don't have to worry about calling the mouse event handler methods. They're called automatically when their associated mouse events occur. For example, if the user presses the mouse button while the mouse cursor is on a `MouseListener`-registered component, the JVM automatically calls the `mousePressed` event handler.

In the upcoming program, the goal is to enable a user to drag an image across a window using the mouse. To do that, you need to detect the mouse being pressed and moved (i.e., dragged) while the mouse cursor is on the image. And to do that, you need to register a mouse listener. But you can register a mouse listener only with a component, not with an image. So what's the solution? You're already familiar with some components—`JLabel`, `JTextField`, and `JButton` components. Those classes are component classes because they are descendants of the `Component` class. There's another component class that's a bit different. It doesn't feel like a component in the normal sense of the word, but it's a Java component nonetheless (because it's a descendant of the `Component` class), and it works great for handling mouse events. So what is the mystery component? `JPanel`!

Think of a `JPanel` object as a generic storage area for other objects. More formally, the `JPanel` class is a descendant of the `Container` class, and as such, it's a container and you can add objects to it. In the next chapter, you'll add Swing components (`JLabel`, `JTextField`, and so on) to `JPanel` containers. In the upcoming program example, you add an image object to a `JPanel` container. By surrounding the image with a `JPanel` container, you provide a platform that mouse listeners can attach to. In the upcoming program example, the `JPanel` listeners allow you to detect mouse events on the image object.

The DragSmiley Program

See Figure 16.16. It contains a driver class and a sample session for a DragSmiley program. As indicated in the sample session, the program initially displays a smiley face in the top-left corner of the program's window. If the user presses the mouse button, the smiley image changes to a scared image (presumably because the smiley is apprehensive of what the user might do to it). When the user releases the mouse button, the scared image changes back to the smiley image. If the mouse cursor resides on the image and the user drags the mouse, the image follows the mouse cursor.

Study Figure 16.16's `DragSmiley` constructor. In it, the following two statements instantiate a `JPanel` container named `smileyPanel` and add the `JPanel` container to `DragSmiley`'s window.

```
smileyPanel = new SmileyPanel();
add(smileyPanel);
```

See the `SmileyPanel` class in Figures 16.17a and 16.17b. The `SmileyPanel` class is where the bulk of the program's logic is. We'll describe the `SmileyPanel` class by first focusing on the listeners. Note how the `SmileyPanel` constructor creates the mouse listeners and adds them to the `JPanel` container. Note the mouse listener class headings, repeated here for your convenience:

```
private class ClickListener extends MouseAdapter
private class DragListener extends MouseMotionAdapter
```

The `extends` clauses indicate inheritance from the `MouseAdapter` and `MouseMotionAdapter` classes. For each event handling interface with more than one method, Sun provides an associated class that already implements the interface's methods for you. Those classes are called *adapter classes*. The `MouseAdapter` class implements the `MouseListener` interface's methods, and the `MouseMotionAdapter` class implements the `MouseMotionListener` interface's methods. Adapter classes don't do much. They simply implement their associated interface's methods as dummy methods, like this:

```
public void mousePressed(MouseEvent event)
{ }
```

To implement a listener that detects the mouse being pressed, you extend the `MouseAdapter` class and provide an overriding `mousePressed` method. For an example, see Figure 16.17a. As an alternative, you can implement a listener using an interface rather than an adapter. But remember that an interface is a contract, and when you implement an interface, you're required to provide methods for all of the interface's methods. So if you wanted to replace the `SmileyPanel` class's adapters with interfaces, you'd have to provide dummy methods for the methods that you don't use.

```
/************************************************************
* DragSmiley.java
* Dean & Dean
*
* This program displays a smiley face image.
* When the user presses the mouse, the image changes to a
* scared image. The user can drag the image.
************************************************************/

import javax.swing.*;

public class DragSmiley extends JFrame
{
  private static final int WIDTH = 250;
  private static final int HEIGHT = 250;
  private SmileyPanel smileyPanel;      // drawing panel

  //*******************************************************

  public DragSmiley()
  {
    setTitle("Drag Smiley");
    setSize(WIDTH, HEIGHT);
    setDefaultCloseOperation(EXIT_ON_CLOSE);
    smileyPanel = new SmileyPanel();
    add(smileyPanel);
    setVisible(true);
  } // end DragSmiley constructor

  //****************************************

  public static void main(String[] args)
  {
    new DragSmiley();
  }
} // end class DragSmiley
```

Initial display: While dragging smiley: After releasing mouse button:

Figure 16.16 Driver class and sample output for the DragSmiley program

```
/*************************************************************
* SmileyPanel.java
* Dean & Dean
*
* This class contains a smiley image and listeners
* that enable image dragging and image swapping.
*************************************************************/

import javax.swing.*;
import java.awt.*;
import java.awt.event.*;

public class SmileyPanel extends JPanel
{
  private final ImageIcon SMILEY = new ImageIcon("smiley.gif");
  private final ImageIcon SCARED = new ImageIcon("scared.gif");
  private final int WIDTH = SMILEY.getIconWidth();
  private final int HEIGHT = SMILEY.getIconHeight();

  private Point imageCorner;  // image's top-left corner location
  private Point prevPt;       // mouse location for previous event
  private ImageIcon image;    // toggles between smiley and scared

  //**********************************************************

  public SmileyPanel()
  {
    image = SMILEY;
    imageCorner = new Point(0, 0); // image starts at top left
    ClickListener clickListener = new ClickListener();
    DragListener dragListener = new DragListener();
    this.addMouseListener(clickListener);
    this.addMouseMotionListener(dragListener);
  } // end SmileyComponent constructor

  //**********************************************************

  private class ClickListener extends MouseAdapter
  {
    // When mouse pressed, change to scared image.

    public void mousePressed(MouseEvent e)
    {
      image = SCARED;
      prevPt = e.getPoint();  // save current position
      repaint();
    } // end mousePressed
```

Add mouse listeners to the `JPanel` container.

Figure 16.17a The DragSmiley program's `SmileyPanel` class—part A

```
    // When mouse released, return to smiley image.

    public void mouseReleased(MouseEvent e)
    {
      image = SMILEY;
      repaint();
    } // end mouseReleased
  } // end class ClickListener

  //*********************************************************

  private class DragListener extends MouseMotionAdapter
  {
    // Enable image to be dragged by mouse.

    public void mouseDragged(MouseEvent e)
    {
      Point currentPt = e.getPoint(); // current position

      // Make sure mouse was pressed within the image.
      if (currentPt.getX() >= imageCorner.getX() &&
          currentPt.getX() <= imageCorner.getX() + WIDTH &&
          currentPt.getY() >= imageCorner.getY() &&
          currentPt.getY() <= imageCorner.getY() + HEIGHT)
      {
        imageCorner.translate(
          (int) (currentPt.getX() - prevPt.getX()),
          (int) (currentPt.getY() - prevPt.getY()));
        prevPt = currentPt;  // save current position
        repaint();
      }
    } // end mouseDragged
  } // end class DragListener

  //*********************************************************

  // Draw the window, including the updated image.

  public void paintComponent(Graphics g)
  {
    super.paintComponent(g);
    image.paintIcon(this, g,
      (int) imageCorner.getX(), (int) imageCorner.getY());
  } // end paintComponent
} // end class SmileyPanel
```

Call `paintIcon` to display the image.

Figure 16.17b The DragSmiley program's `SmileyPanel` class—part B

Displaying an Image

It's now time to see how the SmileyPanel class draws its images. At the top of the class, the SMILEY and SCARED named constants are initialized as follows:

```
final private ImageIcon SMILEY = new ImageIcon("smiley.gif");
final private ImageIcon SCARED = new ImageIcon("scared.gif");
```

The ImageIcon constructor creates an image object from its passed-in filename parameter. So in the above code fragment, two image objects are created from the smiley.gif and scared.gif files, respectively.[7]

In the SmileyPanel constructor, the mousePressed event handler, and the mouseReleased event handler, note how SMILEY and SCARED get assigned into the image instance variable. Those assignments are what cause the image to change when the user presses the mouse button and releases it.

The JPanel class has a paintComponent method that's in charge of drawing Swing components (e.g., text boxes and buttons) within the JPanel container. But it doesn't handle drawing lines, shapes, or images. To draw those things, you need to provide an overriding paintComponent method with calls to graphics methods. For example, here is SmileyPanel's overriding paintComponent method:

```
public void paintComponent(Graphics g)
{
  super.paintComponent(g);
  image.paintIcon(this, g,
    (int) imageCorner.getX(), (int) imageCorner.getY());
} // end paintComponent
```

Note the paintComponent method's g parameter. It's a Graphics object, and it's used to call graphics methods within the paintComponent method. For example, the image.paintIcon method call draws image (a smiley face or a scared face), and it requires a Graphics object, g, for its second argument. In calling the paintIcon method, you provide three arguments in addition to the Graphics argument: (1) the window in which the image is displayed (in the above example, the this reference refers to the JPanel's window, (2) the x coordinate of the image's top-left corner, and (3) the y coordinate of the image's top-left corner. Note the super.paintComponent(g) method call. You should always include that call as the first statement within an overriding paintComponent method. Without it, the background for paintComponent's associated object might be displayed improperly.

Notice that there's no explicit call to the DragSmiley program's paintComponent method. You should never call the paintComponent method directly. Instead, you should call the repaint method and let the repaint method call the paintComponent method for you. The repaint method waits until the program's window is properly prepared to handle the paintComponent method. Note in the SmileyPanel class how repaint is called at the bottom of the three event handlers. That's where there's a need to redraw the image. By the way, in addition to calling paintComponent whenever repaint is called, the JVM calls paintComponent automatically when the program starts up and whenever a user does something to alter the program's window (e.g., when the user resizes the window, or moves another window off of the window).

[7] *gif* stands for Graphics Interchange Format. It's used for an exact representation of a simple drawn image.

Summary

- The JFrame class should be used as the superclass for most of your GUI application windows.
- The JFrame class implements all the standard window features such as a border, a title bar, a minimize button, a close-window button (the "X"), the ability to resize the window, and so on.
- JLabel is a read-only component; the user simply reads the label's message.
- The JTextField component allows the user to enter text into a text box.
- When the user interacts with a component (e.g., when the user clicks a button or presses enter while in a text box), the component fires an event.
- If a component has a listener attached to it, the fired event is "heard" by the listener and consequently handled by the listener.
- A listener handles an event by executing its actionPerformed event-handler method.
- Listeners often are implemented with the ActionListener interface. An interface is a class-like entity whose methods are all empty. If a programmer uses an interface to derive a new class, the compiler requires the new class to implement methods for all of the interface's methods.
- If a class is limited in its scope such that it is only needed by one other class, then you should define the class as an inner class (a class inside of another class).
- An anonymous inner class is an inner class without a name.
- To display a simple window with a message, call JOptionPane's showMessageDialog method.
- To identify the component whose event was fired, use the actionPerformed method's ActionEvent parameter to call getSource or getActionCommand.
- To adjust a GUI component's text color, call setForeground. To adjust the color behind the text, call setBackground.
- To adjust a window's background color, call the content pane's setBackground method.
- To detect and handle mouse events, use the MouseAdapter and MouseMotionAdapter classes, which implement the MouseListener and MouseMotionListener interfaces, respectively.

Review Questions

§16.2 Event-Driven Programming Basics

1. What is a listener?
2. What is an event handler?

§16.3 A Simple Window Program

3. Write a statement that adds functionality to a program's close-window button such that when the close-window button is clicked, it causes the program to terminate.

§16.4 JFrame Class

4. What is the name of the superclass for classes that contain components?

§16.5 Java Components

5. What package are JButton and many other J-prefixed components defined in?

§16.6 JLabel Component

6. Provide an initialization statement that declares a JLabel reference variable named hello and assigns "Hello World" to the reference variable.

§16.7 `JTextField` Component

7. Provide an initialization statement that instantiates a 10-character-wide text box object. As part of the initialization, assign the text box object to a reference variable named `input`.

§16.9 Component Listeners

8. Write a statement that registers a listener reference variable named `responder` with a component named `component`.
9. If you want a class to handle an event, what clause must be added to the right side of the class's heading?
10. What is the heading of the one method specified by the `ActionListener` interface?

§16.10 Inner Classes

11. If a class is limited in scope such that it is only needed internally within another class, you should define the class to be an ____________.

§16.11 Anonymous Inner Classes

12. If you want to implement an event handler with an anonymous inner class, what argument do you give to the `addActionListener` method to register the listener?

§16.12 `JButton` Component

13. In the `createContents` method of the FactorialButton program in Figure 16.8a, what type of object calls the `add` methods?
14. In the FactorialButton program in Figures 16.8a and 16.8b, what component fires the event that the listener handles?

§16.13 Dialog Boxes and the `JOptionPane` Class

15. What package contains the `JOptionPane` class?
16. Write a statement that displays a dialog box in the center of the screen. The dialog box should display "This is only a test." in the message area, "TEST" in the title area, and no icon.

§16.14 Distinguishing Between Multiple Events

17. Suppose you have several components registered with the same listener, and the components and listener are defined within the same class. Within the listener, what `ActionEvent` method should you call to determine which component fires an event?

§16.15 Using `getActionCommand` to Distinguish Between Multiple Events

18. Assume there's a listener that's been registered for several different buttons. Assume the listener uses an `actionPerformed` method with an `ActionEvent` parameter named `action`. Assume that the user clicks one of the registered buttons. Provide a statement that retrieves the text label from the clicked button and assigns the retrieved label to a `String` variable named `buttonLabel`.

§16.16 Color

19. Write a statement that sets the text color to blue for a `JButton` object named `button1`.
20. How do you get a reference to the container that surrounds all of the components in a `JFrame` object?

§16.17 How GUI Classes Are Grouped Together

21. If your program needs the `java.awt.event` subpackage, you can implicitly import it by importing the `java.awt` package. (T / F)

Exercises

1. [after §16.2] Give three examples of how a user might cause an event to be fired.

2. [after §16.3] For each of the following, what Java API package must you import?
   a) `JFrame` and `JLabel`
   b) `FlowLayout`

3. [after §16.4] For our previous GUI programs, we've done set-up work (setting the title, adding components, and so on) within a constructor. That's generally preferred, but it's not a compiler requirement. For practice purposes, write a minimal, but fully functional, program that displays this:

   Your program should not include a constructor. It should include only one method—a `main` method with only five statements (or four statements if you find a shortcut for setting the frame's title).

4. [after §16.6] Provide a complete program that displays this `Hello World` message:

   Note these label characteristics: (1) raised bevel border, (2) italics, (3) large font size (30 points), (4) tool tip that says "Life is Great!" Use this program skeleton as a starting point:

```
import javax.swing.*;
import java.awt.*;

//***********************************************************

public class BigHello extends JFrame
{
  public BigHello()
  {
    JLabel label = <instantiation> ;
    setSize(200, <height> );
    setLayout(new FlowLayout());
    add(label);

    <3-statement code fragment>

    setVisible(true);
  } // end constructor

  //*********************************************************

  public static void main(String[] args)
```

```
  {
    BigHello hello = new BigHello();
  } // end main
} // end BigHello class
```

To figure out how to do this, in Java's API, look up the `setFont`, `setBorder`, and `setToolTipText` methods that `JLabel` inherits from `JContainer`. For the `setFont` argument, use `JContainer`'s `getFont` to get the default font, and then alter it by using `Font`'s two-parameter `deriveFont` method in which the first parameter specifies an italic font style and the second parameter specifies a 30-point size. Use `JContainer`'s `setBorder` method, and for its `Border` argument use the appropriate class method from the `BorderFactory` class.

5. [after §16.7] The width parameter in the `JTextField` constructor specifies the width of the text box in pixels. (T / F)
6. [after §16.7] What can you do to prevent users from updating a `JTextField` component?
7. [after §16.9] Write the heading for the method you must define in a class that implements an `ActionListener`.
8. [after §16.9] The `ActionListener` interface and the `ActionEvent` class are in what Java API package?
9. [after §16.9] An interface is a class-like thing whose methods are all empty. If an interface is applied to a class, then the interface acts like a template that the class must conform to. (T / F)
10. [after §16.10] An inner class can directly access its enclosing class's instance variables. (T / F)
11. [after §16.12] It's appropriate to use an anonymous inner class if you are going to use the class only once. In the Factorial program in Figures 16.8a and 16.8b, we use the `listener` object twice, so that `listener` object needed to have a name. However, we used that object's class only once, to instantiate that one object. Therefore, that object's class did not need to have a name, and we could have used an anonymous class to create our `listener` object. For this exercise, modify the Factorial program to use an anonymous `ActionListener` class instead of the named `Listener` class. [Hint: The program is already set up to facilitate this change—it's mostly cut-and-paste.]
12. [after §16.13] Do you have to create a `JFrame` window to use a `JOptionPane` dialog box?
13. [after §16.13] To answer this question, you may need to look up `JOptionPane`'s `showInputDialog` and `showConfirmDialog` methods on Sun's Java API Web site. What does this program do?

```
import javax.swing.JOptionPane;
public class UncertainHello
{
  public static void main(String[] args)
  {
    String name;
    int response;
    do
    {
      name = JOptionPane.showInputDialog("What's your name? ");
      response = JOptionPane.showConfirmDialog(null, "Are you sure?");
      if (response == JOptionPane.NO_OPTION)
      {
        name = "there";
```

```
        break;
      }
    } while (response == JOptionPane.CANCEL_OPTION);

    System.out.println("Hello " + name);
  } // end main
} // end class UncertainHello
```

14. [after §16.14] By calling `setEnabled(false)`, you can disable a button and give it a muted appearance and make its listener unresponsive to clicks on it. Modify Figure 16.12's program so that the factorial button is initially disabled. Enable it only after the user enters a character in the `xBox` text box. To enable it, create a *key listener* for the `xBox` text box, and have the key listener's `keyTyped` event handler call `setEnabled(true)`. Use the following key listener code skeleton:

```
private class KeyListener extends KeyAdapter
{
  public void keyTyped(KeyEvent e)
  {
    ...
  }
} // end class KeyListener
```

Note `extends KeyAdapter` in the above class heading. An *adapter* class implements an interface by providing an empty-bodied method for each method in the interface. In this case, the `KeyAdapter` API class implements the `KeyListener` API interface.

15. [after §16.16] To set a `JFrame`'s background color, what method should you call right before calling `setBackground`?

16. [after §16.17] What do the letters in "awt" stand for?

Review Question Solutions

1. A listener is an object that waits for events to occur.
2. An event handler is a method that responds to an event.
3. `setDefaultCloseOperation(EXIT_ON_CLOSE);`
4. The superclass for objects that contain other objects is the `Container` class.
5. Many J-prefixed components are defined in the `javax.swing` package.
6. `JLabel hello = new JLabel("Hello World!");`
7. `JTextField input = new JTextField(10);`
8. `component.addActionListener(responder);`
9. For a class to handle an event, add this to the right side of the class's heading:
   `implements ActionListener`
10. The heading of the method specified by the `ActionListener` interface is:
   `public void actionPerformed(ActionEvent e)`

11. If a class is limited in scope such that it is only needed internally within another class, you should define the class to be an inner class.

12. The argument to give to the `addActionListener` method to register an anonymous listener class is:

```
new ActionListener()
{
  <implementation-of-ActionListener-interface>
}
```

13. The object that calls the `add` methods is a `JFrame` object.

14. It's ambiguous. It could be either `xBox` or `btn`.

15. The package that contains the `JOptionPane` class is the `javax.swing` package.

16. This code generates the asked-for dialog box:

```
JOptionPane.showMessageDialog(null,
  "This is only a test.", "TEST", JOptionPane.PLAIN_MESSAGE);
```

17. To identify the firing component, call the `getSource` method.

18. `buttonLabel = action.getActionCommand();`

19. `button1.setForeground(Color.BLUE);`

20. Call `JFrame`'s `getContentPane` method.

21. False. The `java.awt` and `java.awt.event` packages contain separate classes. To import classes from `java.awt.event`, you must import that package explicitly like this:

```
import java.awt.event.*;
```

CHAPTER 17

GUI Programming—Component Layout, Additional GUI Components

Objectives

- Know GUI design basics.
- Know the benefits of using layout managers.
- Understand FlowLayout manager details.
- Understand BorderLayout manager details.
- Be able to use the SwingConstants interface.
- Understand GridLayout manager details.
- Use embedded layout managers and JPanels for windows that have a substantial number of components.
- Implement JTextArea components for text that spans more than one line.
- Implement a JCheckBox component for yes/no user input.
- Implement JRadioButton and JComboBox components when the user needs to choose a value from among a list of predefined values.
- Become familiar with additional Swing components such as menus, scroll panes, and sliders.

Outline

17.1 Introduction

This is the second chapter in our two-chapter sequence on GUI programming. In the previous chapter, you learned GUI basics. You learned about windows, components, and listeners. Almost all GUI programs need those things. In this chapter, you'll learn how to make your GUI programs more functional and more visually appealing. You'll improve the functionality by implementing some additional GUI components—`JTextArea`, `JCheckBox`, `JRadioButton`, and `JComboBox`. You'll improve the visual appeal by applying various layout techniques to your windows' components. More specifically, you'll learn how to apply these layout managers—`FlowLayout`, `BorderLayout`, and `GridLayout`. And you'll learn how to apply different layout managers to different areas of your windows.

For an example of what you'll be learning, see Figure 17.1. Note the combo box, radio button, and check box components. Also, note how the radio buttons are grouped in the center, the check buttons are grouped at the right, and the Next and Cancel buttons are grouped at the bottom center. In this chapter, you'll learn how to make such groupings, and you'll learn how to position them appropriately.

17.2 GUI Design and Layout Managers

With text-based programs, it's relatively easy to tell users what to do. As a programmer, you just provide text instructions and the user enters input when prompted to do so. With GUI programs, it's more difficult to tell users what to do. As a programmer, you display a window with various components, set up listeners, and then wait for the user to do something. It's important that your display be easy to understand; otherwise your users won't know what to do. To make your display easy to understand, follow these guidelines:

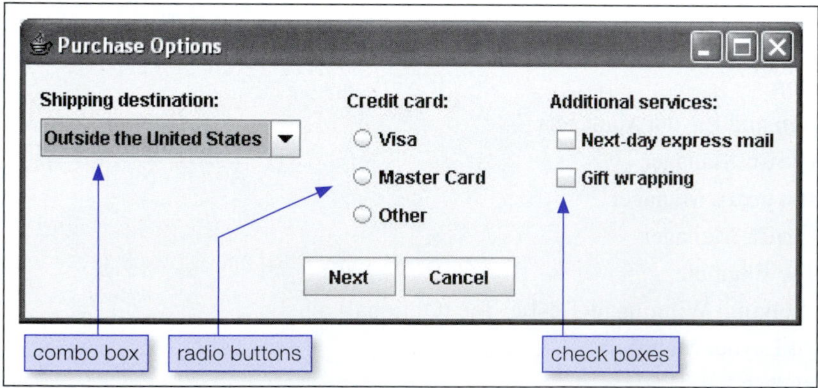

Figure 17.1 Example window that uses radio buttons, check boxes, and a combo box

- Choose the right components.
- Be consistent.
- Position components appropriately.

GUI Design Basics

In Figure 17.1, note the small circles next to Visa, MasterCard, and Other. Those circles are radio button components (we describe radio buttons in section 17.13). Using radio buttons for the credit card options is an example of choosing the right component. Radio buttons provide implicit instructions to the user about how to proceed. Most users recognize small circles as radio buttons, and when they see them, they know to click one of them with their mouse.

In Figure 17.1, note the Next and Cancel buttons at the bottom center of the window. Assume that the window is one of several windows in a purchasing application. Assume that other windows in the application also display Next and Cancel buttons in the bottom center position. Placing Next and Cancel buttons in the same position is an example of being consistent. Consistency is important because users are more comfortable with things they've seen before. As another example, be consistent with color schemes. In a given application, if you choose red for a warning message, use red for all your warning messages.

In Figure 17.1, note how the three radio button components (Visa, MasterCard, and Other) and the "Credit card:" label component are positioned together as a group. More specifically, they're aligned in a vertical column and they're physically close together. That's an example of positioning components appropriately. Positioning them together as a group provides a visual cue that they're logically related. As another example of appropriate positioning, note that there are sizable gaps separating the left, center, and right component groups. Finally, note how the "Shipping destination:", "Credit card:", and "Additional services:" labels are aligned in the same row. That alignment, the aforementioned gaps, and the aforementioned component groupings all lead to a more appealing and understandable display.

Layout Managers

As you now know, positioning components appropriately is an important part of GUI design. In the old days, positioning components was a tedious, manual process. Programmers would spend hours calculating the space needed for each component and the pixel coordinate positions for each component. Today, programmers are freed from that tedium by having layout managers do those calculations for them. As you may recall from the previous chapter, a *layout manager* is an object that controls the positioning of components within a container. In general, the layout manager's goal is to arrange components neatly. Usually, the neatness goal equates to making sure components are aligned and making sure components are appropriately spaced within the layout manager's container. For example, in Figure 17.1, layout managers are responsible for aligning the left components, aligning the middle components, aligning the right components, and spacing the three component groups across the width of the window.

If a user adjusts a window's size, the Java Virtual Machine (JVM) consults with the layout manager and the layout manager then recalculates the pixel coordinate positions for each component. All this takes place automatically without any intervention on the programmer's part. How convenient! Hail to the layout manager!

There are different types of layout managers and they have different strategies for positioning components within a container. See the table in Figure 17.2. It describes several layout managers from Sun's API library.

Layout Manager	Description
`BorderLayout`	Splits container into five regions—north, south, east, west, and center. Allows one component per region.
`BoxLayout`	Allows components to be arranged in either a single column or a single row.
`FlowLayout`	Allows components to be added left to right, flowing to next row as necessary.
`GridLayout`	Splits container into a rectangular grid of equal-sized cells. Allows one component per grid cell.
`GridBagLayout`	A more flexible and complex version of `GridLayout`. Allows grid cells to vary in size.

Figure 17.2 Several of the more popular layout managers

In the previous chapter, we used the simplest type of layout manager—the `FlowLayout` manager. The `FlowLayout` manager is useful for some situations, but we'll often need alternative layout managers for other situations. In this chapter, we'll describe the `FlowLayout` manager in more detail, and we'll also describe the `BorderLayout` and `GridLayout` managers. Those are the three most popular layout managers, so you should know them well.

Assigning a Layout Manager

To assign a particular layout manager to a `JFrame` window from within a class that extends `JFrame`, call the `setLayout` method as follows:

```
setLayout(new <layout-manager-class>());
```

In this code template, replace *<layout-manager-class>* by one of the layout manager classes (e.g., `FlowLayout`, `BorderLayout`, `GridLayout`). If `setLayout` is not called, then the `BorderLayout` manager is used, because that's the default layout manager for a `JFrame` window.

Layout manager classes are in the `java.awt` package, so that package must be imported. Of course, if you've already imported it for something else, then there's no need to import it again.

17.3 `FlowLayout` Manager

In the previous chapter, we wanted to present GUI basics without getting bogged down in layout manager details. So we chose a simple layout manger, `FlowLayout`, that didn't require much explanation. We just used it and didn't dwell on particulars. Now it's time to explain the particulars, so you can take advantage of its functionality more fully.

Layout Mechanism

The `FlowLayout` class implements a simple one-compartment layout scheme that allows multiple components to be inserted into the compartment. When a component is added to the compartment, it is placed to the right of any components that were previously added to the compartment. If there is not enough room to add a component to the right of the previously added components, the new component is placed on the next line (i.e., it "flows" to the next line). Note the following example.

Assume you've implemented a program that prompts the user to enter his/her name and prints a personalized greeting after the user presses enter. We'll show you a sample session that starts with a wide window and a short name. Here's what the program displays after the user types Tom:

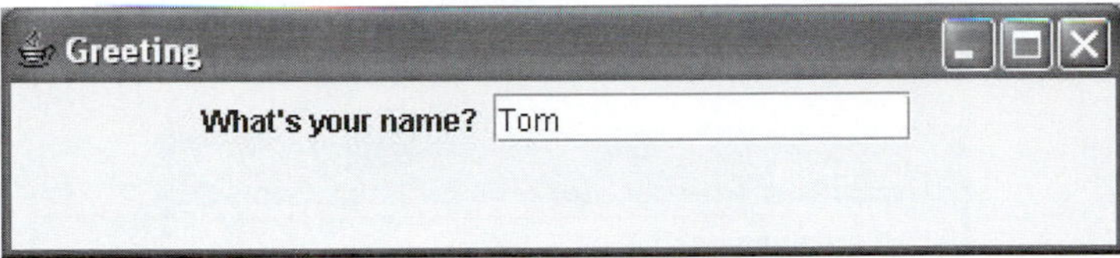

And here's what the program displays after the user presses enter:

If the user enters a longer name, like Fidelis Kiungua, the greeting label can't fit on the first line, so it wraps to the next line:

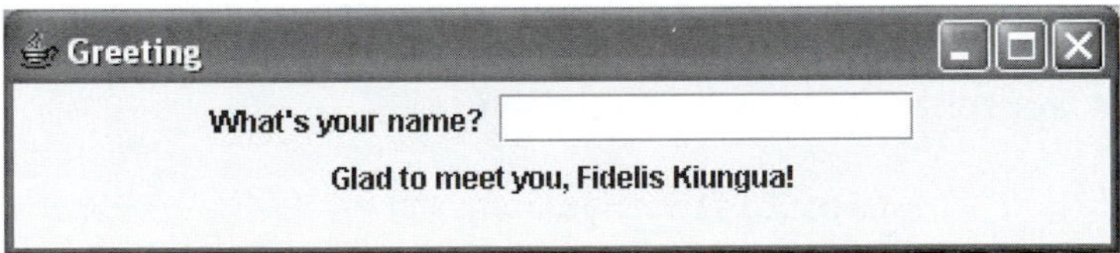

If the user manually resizes the window to make it narrower, the text box can no longer fit on the first line, so it wraps to the next line:

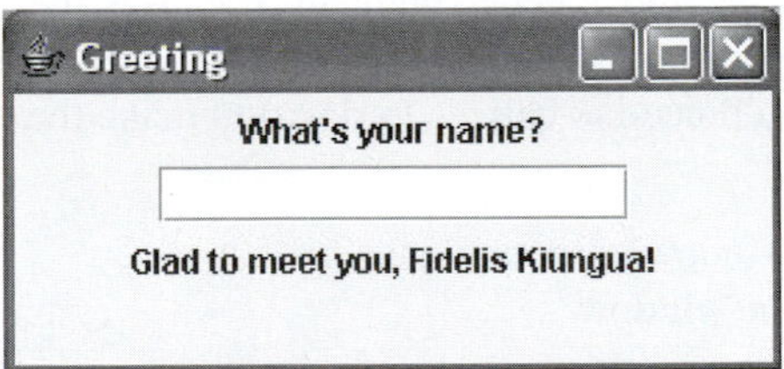

Alignment

By default, the `FlowLayout` manager positions its components using center alignment. For example, in the above window, note how the "What's your name" label is centered between the left and right borders. If you'd like to change the `FlowLayout` manager's alignment, insert one of the `FlowLayout` alignment constants (`FlowLayout.LEFT`, `FlowLayout.CENTER`, `FlowLayout.RIGHT`) in the `FlowLayout` constructor call. For example, here's how to specify left alignment:

```
setLayout(new FlowLayout(FlowLayout.LEFT));
```

Here's what our Greeting program displays when left alignment is used:

Layout Changes

Normally, `setLayout` is called just once in a program—when the program initially lays out its components. But if there's a need to dynamically adjust the layout scheme, call `setLayout` again. For example, if you want the user to be able to adjust text alignment, add Align Left, Align Center, and Align Right buttons. Add a listener to each button. In each listener, call `setLayout`. This would be the listener for the Align Left button:

```
private class Listener implements ActionListener
{
  public void actionPerformed(ActionEvent e)
  {
    setLayout(new FlowLayout(FlowLayout.LEFT));
    validate();
  } // end actionPerformed
} // end class Listener
```

Note the validate method in the above code fragment. It causes the layout manager to regenerate the component layout. If your window is visible (i.e., you've called `setVisible(true)`), and you attempt to change its layout in some way, you'll need to call `validate` to make the change take effect. These method calls attempt to change the layout:

- `setLayout`—Change the window's layout manager.
- `add`—Add a component to the window.
- `setSize`—Change the window's size.

If your window is already visible and you call one of those methods, don't forget to call `validate` afterwards. If you have a series of such calls, there's no need to have separate `validate` method calls. Putting one `validate` method call at the end works fine.

17.4 `BorderLayout` Manager

The `FlowLayout` manager is popular because it's easy to use. Just add components to its container and that's it. Sometimes all you need is something simple. But be aware that the `FlowLayout` manager doesn't provide much control over where components are positioned. Using a `FlowLayout` manager, you can position components horizontally (left, right, or center), but you can't position components vertically. If you need to position components along both dimensions (horizontal and vertical), you need to use one of the other layout managers. In this section, we discuss the BorderLayout manager, which does allow you to position components along both dimensions.

BorderLayout Regions

The BorderLayout manager is particularly useful for windows that need components near their edges. It's common to put a title near the top edge of a window. It's common to put a menu near the left edge of a window. It's common to put buttons near the bottom edge of a window. The BorderLayout manager accommodates all those situations by splitting up its container into five *regions,* or compartments. Four of the regions are near the edges and one is in the center. You access the four edge regions with geographical names—north, south, east, and west. Note the regions' positions in Figure 17.3.

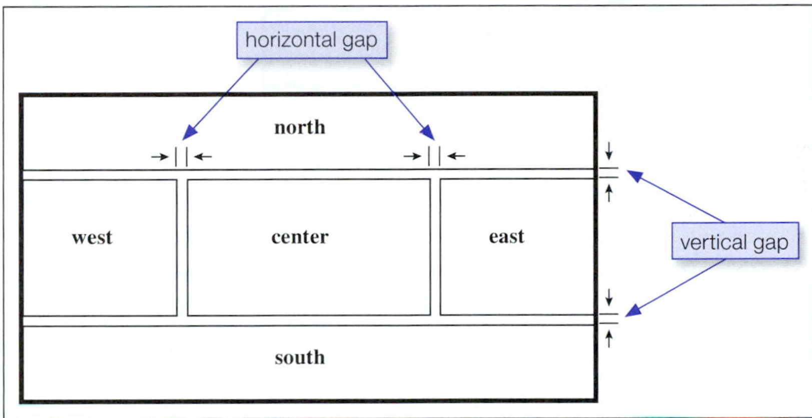

Figure 17.3 BorderLayout regions

Assume that you're inside a container class. To assign a BorderLayout manager to the container, call the setLayout method like this:

setLayout(new BorderLayout(<*horizontal-gap*>, <*vertical-gap*>));

The *horizontal-gap* argument specifies the number of pixels of blank space that separate the west, center, and east regions. Figure 17.3 illustrates this. The *vertical-gap* argument specifies the number of pixels of blank space that separate the north region from the other regions and the south region from the other regions. Once again, Figure 17.3 illustrates this. If you omit the gap arguments, the gap values are zero by default. In other words, if you call the BorderLayout constructor with no arguments, there will be no gaps between the regions.

The sizes of the five regions are determined at runtime, and they're based on the contents of each region. Thus, if the west region contains a long label, the layout manager attempts to widen the west region. Likewise, if the west region contains a short label, the layout manager attempts to narrow the west region.

If an outer region is empty, it collapses so that it does not take up any space. But what exactly happens during the collapse? Each outer region controls only one dividing line, so only one dividing line moves for each collapsed region. Figure 17.4 shows you that the west region's dividing line is the boundary between west and center, the north region's dividing line is the boundary between north and below, and so on. So if the north region is empty, the north dividing line moves all the way up to the top border, and the west, center, and east regions all expand upward. What happens if the east and south regions are both empty? The east region being

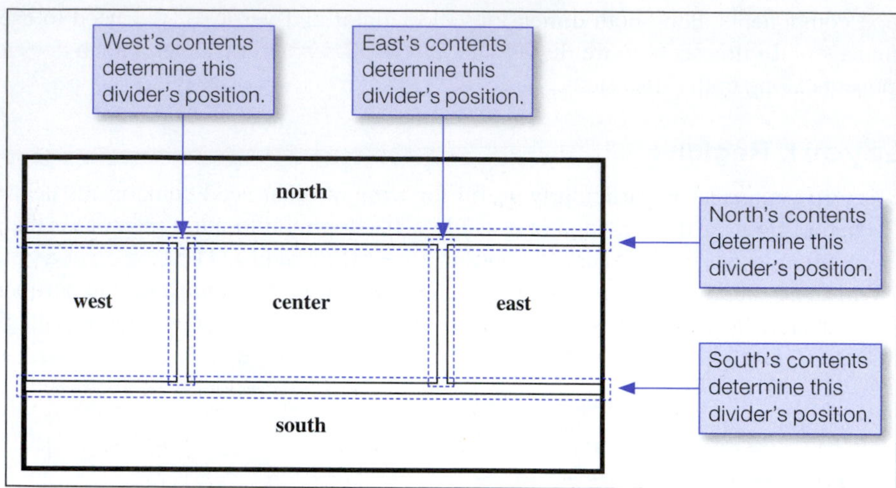

Figure 17.4 `BorderLayout` regions

empty causes the east dividing line to move all the way to the right border. The south region being empty causes the south dividing line to move all the way down to the bottom border. Here's the resulting layout:

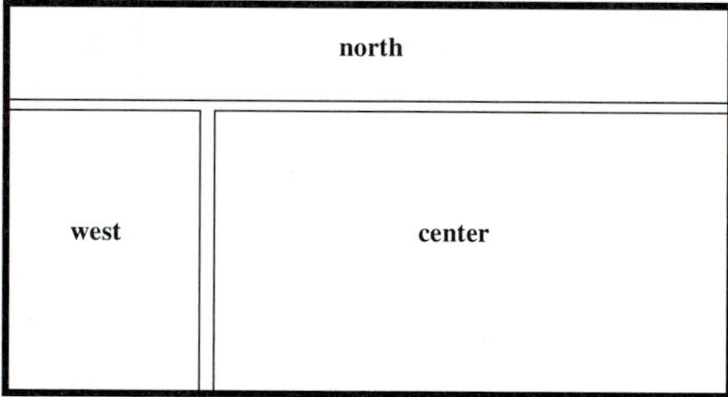

What happens if the center region is empty? The center region doesn't control any of the dividing lines, so nothing happens.

Adding Components

Suppose you have a container class that uses a `BorderLayout` manager. To add a component to one of the container's `BorderLayout` regions, call the container's `add` method like this:

```
add(<component>, <region>);
```

Replace *<component>* by a component (a `JLabel` object, a `JButton` object, and so on) and replace *<region>* by one of these named constants: `BorderLayout.NORTH`, `BorderLayout.SOUTH`, `BorderLayout.WEST`, `BorderLayout.EAST`, or `BorderLayout.CENTER`. For example, here's how to add a Tunisia button to the north region:

```
add(new JButton("Tunisia"), BorderLayout.NORTH);
```

If you call the `add` method with no region argument, the center region is used by default. Thus, to add a Central African Republic button to the center region, you can use either of these two statements:

```
add(new JButton("Central African Republic"), BorderLayout.CENTER);
add(new JButton("Central African Republic"));
```

Which statement is better? We prefer the first statement because it makes the code easier to understand. More formally, we say that the first statement is self-documenting.

With a `FlowLayout` container, you can add as many components as you like. With a `BorderLayout` container, you can add only five components total, one for each of the five regions. If you add a component to a region that already has a component, then the new component overlays the old component. Thus, in executing the following lines, the Somalia button overlays the Djibouti button:

```
add(new JButton("Djibouti"), BorderLayout.EAST);
add(new JButton("Somalia ", BorderLayout.EAST));
```

If you need to add more than one component to a region, it's easy to make the mistake of calling `add` twice for the same region. After all, there's no compile-time error to warn you of your misdeed. But what you really need to do is add a `JPanel` component. We'll discuss the `JPanel` component later in the chapter. It allows you to store multiple components in a place where only one component is allowed.

AfricanCountries Program with Buttons

Let's put this `BorderLayout` material into practice by using it within a complete program. In our AfricanCountries program, we add African-country buttons to the five regions of a `BorderLayout` window. See the program's output window at the bottom of Figure 17.5. The five rectangles you see are the five regions, but they're also the five buttons. The buttons are the same size as the regions because, with a `BorderLayout` manager, components automatically expand to fill their entire region. Note how the outer four regions' sizes conform nicely to their contents. In other words, the west region is wide enough to show "Western Sahara," the south region is tall enough to show "South Africa," and so on. In contrast, note how the center region is unable to display its full "Central African Republic" content. This is because the outer regions control the dividing lines. The center region gets whatever room is left over.

Skim through the AfricanCountries program listing in Figure 17.5. Most of the code is straightforward. But this statement is rather quirky:

```
add(new JButton("<html>South<br>Africa</html>"), BorderLayout.SOUTH);
```

Let's review briefly what those angled-bracket commands are that you see—<html>, <br>, and </html>. As you may recall from the HTMLGenerator program in Chapter 15, the angled bracket elements are called tags. The `<html>` tag indicates the start of an HTML file, the `<br>` tag indicates a line break (i.e., a new line), and the `</html>` tag indicates the end of an HTML file. Normally, you insert tags into an HTML file. But here we're inserting them into component text in order to produce a new line. When used in `JLabel` and `JButton` text, the `<html>` and `</html>` tags tell the Java compiler that the enclosed text (the text between the `<html>` and `</html>` tags) should be interpreted as HTML text. And the `<br>` tag tells the Java compiler to insert a newline character in the text.[1]

We'd like to mention one additional item in the AfricanCountries program. The `setLayout` method call can be omitted. As we said previously, the `BorderLayout` is the default layout manager for `JFrame` windows. Therefore, if you omit the `setLayout` method call, the program works just fine. But we prefer to keep the `setLayout` call because it makes the program easier to understand.

[1] It may have occurred to you to insert the newline character, `\n`, into the component's text. Unfortunately, that doesn't work for `JButton` and `Jlabel` components. However, it does work for the `JtextArea` component. We'll describe the `JtextArea` component later in the chapter.

```
/*************************************************************
* AfricanCountries
* Dean & Dean
*
* This program shows component layout for BorderLayout manager.
*************************************************************/

import javax.swing.*;
import java.awt.*;

public class AfricanCountries extends JFrame
{
  private static final int WIDTH = 325;
  private static final int HEIGHT = 200;

  public AfricanCountries()
  {
    setTitle("African Countries");
    setSize(WIDTH, HEIGHT);
    setDefaultCloseOperation(EXIT_ON_CLOSE);
    setLayout(new BorderLayout());
    add(new JButton("Tunisia"), BorderLayout.NORTH);
    add(new JButton("<html>South<br>Africa</html>"),
      BorderLayout.SOUTH);
    add(new JButton("Western Sahara"), BorderLayout.WEST);
    add(new JButton("Central African Republic"),
      BorderLayout.CENTER);
    add(new JButton("Somalia"), BorderLayout.EAST);
    setVisible(true);
  } // end AfricanCountries constructor

  //**********************************************************

  public static void main(String[] args)
  {
    new AfricanCountries();
  } // end main
} // end class AfricanCountries
```

African Countries
Tunisia
Western Sahara
Central Afri...
Somalia
South
Africa

Figure 17.5 AfricanCountries program and its output

AfricanCountries Program with Labels

You might have noticed the dividing lines in Figure 17.5's output window. Those come from the buttons' borders, not from the `BorderLayout` manager. If we used label components instead of button components, you would see no dividing lines. Likewise in Figure 17.5, the margins around the words come from the button components. If we used label components instead of button components, you would see no margins around the words. Below, we show what the AfricanCountries program displays when the button components are replaced with label components. Be aware that the dashed lines don't appear on the actual window. We've drawn them in to show you the region boundaries.

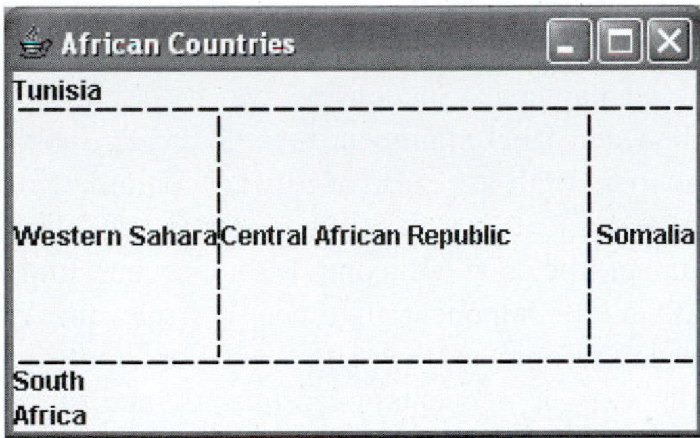

The regions are much the same as before except that the west and east regions are narrower. That's because there are no margins around the words. Narrower west and east regions means there's more room for the center region. Thus, the center region displays its entire "Central African Republic" text.

Note that the African-country labels are left aligned. That's the default for a label in a `BorderLayout` region. If you want a different alignment than the default, instantiate the label with an alignment constant like this:

```
new JLabel(<label's-text>, <alignment-constant>)
```

Replace *<alignment-constant>* by one of these named constants: `SwingConstants.LEFT`, `SwingConstants.CENTER`, or `SwingConstants.RIGHT`. Here's an example that adds a center-aligned label to a `BorderLayout` north region:

```
add(new JLabel("Tunisia", SwingConstants.CENTER), BorderLayout.NORTH);
```

If we apply that line of code to our AfricanCountries program and we apply similar center-alignment code to our center and south regions, the program displays this:

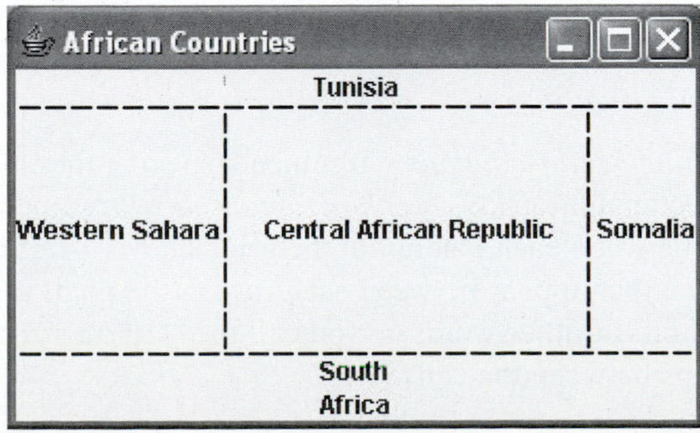

Once again, the dashed lines don't appear on the actual window. We've drawn them to show you the region boundaries. There's no point in applying center alignment to the west and east labels. For these labels, the alignment is irrelevant because the west and east labels have no room to move. As evidenced by the dashed lines, they're already aligned with both their left and right boundaries.

Now back to the alignment constants—`SwingConstants.LEFT`, `SwingConstants.CENTER`, `SwingConstants.RIGHT`. You might think that `SwingConstants` is a class since its first letter is capitalized. If it were a class, then it would describe an object. But it doesn't describe an object, and it's not a class. Actually, `SwingConstants` is an interface, defined in the `javax.swing` package. Sun provides the `SwingConstants` interface as a repository for various GUI-related named constants. To access a named constant in the `SwingConstants` interface, preface the named constant with the interface name. For example, to access the `LEFT` alignment constant, use `SwingConstants.LEFT`. If you want additional details about interfaces, see Chapter 13, Section 13.9.

It's easy to get confused between label alignment for a `BorderLayout` container and label alignment for a `FlowLayout` container. With a `BorderLayout` container, if you want to specify a label's alignment, you need to specify a `SwingConstants` value as part of the label's instantiation. If you do that with a `FlowLayout` container, the code will compile, but it won't impact the label's alignment. With a `FlowLayout` container, individual component alignment is irrelevant. What matters is the container's alignment. If the container uses left alignment, then all of its components are left aligned; if the container uses center alignment, then all of its components are center aligned; and so on. To set the container's alignment, insert one of the `FlowLayout` alignment constants (`FlowLayout.LEFT`, `FlowLayout.CENTER`, `FlowLayout.RIGHT`) in the `FlowLayout` constructor call. Here's how to specify left alignment for all the components in a `FlowLayout` container:

```
setLayout(new FlowLayout(FlowLayout.LEFT));
```

17.5 GridLayout Manager

The `BorderLayout` manager's partitioning scheme (north, south, east, west, center) works well for many situations, but not for all situations. Often, you'll need to display information using a table format; that is, you'll need to display information that's organized by rows and columns. The `BorderLayout` manager doesn't work well for table formats, but the `GridLayout` manager works great!

GridLayout Cells

The `GridLayout` manager lays out a container's components in a rectangular grid. The grid is divided into equal-sized cells. Each cell can hold only one component.

Assume that you're inside a container class. To assign a `GridLayout` manager to the container, call the `setLayout` method like this:

```
setLayout(new GridLayout(<number-of-rows>, <number-of-columns>,
 <horizontal-gap>, <vertical-gap>));
```

The *<number-of-rows>* and *<number-of-columns>* arguments specify the number of rows and number of columns, respectively, in the rectangular grid. The *<horizontal- gap>* argument specifies the number of pixels of blank space that appear between each column in the grid. The *<vertical-gap>* argument specifies the number of pixels of blank space that appear between each row in the grid. If you omit the gap arguments, the gap values are zero by default. In other words, if you call the `GridLayout` constructor with only two arguments, there will be no gaps between the cells.

Adding Components

Assume that you're inside a GridLayout container class. To add a component to one of the container's cells, call the add method like this:

```
add(<component>);
```

Note the simplicity of the add method call. In particular, note that there's no mention of the cell that the component plugs into. So how does the GridLayout manager know which cell to plug the component into? The GridLayout manager positions components within the container using left-to-right, top-to-bottom order. The first added component goes in the top-left-corner cell, the next added component goes in the cell to the right of the first component, and so on.

The code fragment below generates a two-row, three-column table with six buttons. The code fragment specifies gaps of 5 pixels between the rows and columns.

```
setLayout(new GridLayout(2, 3, 5, 5));
add(new JButton("1"));
add(new JButton("2"));
add(new JButton("3"));
add(new JButton("4"));
add(new JButton("5"));
add(new JButton("6"));
```

Assume the above code fragment is part of a complete, working program. Here's what the program displays:

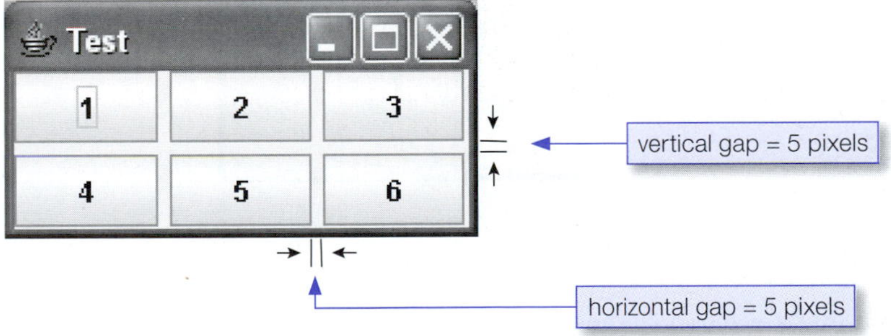

The six rectangles you see are the six cells, but they're also the six buttons. The buttons are the same size as the cells because, with a GridLayout manager, components expand to fill their cells. That should sound familiar; BorderLayout components do the same thing.

Specifying Number of Rows and Number of Columns

When creating a GridLayout manager, you call the GridLayout constructor with a number-of-rows argument and a number-of-columns argument. Those two arguments require some explanation. To help with the explanation, consider three different cases.

Case one:

If you know the number of rows and columns in your table and the table will be completely filled in (i.e., there are no empty cells), call the GridLayout constructor with the actual number of rows and the actual number of columns. That's what we did in our previous example. We knew we wanted a 2-row by 3-column table with six buttons, so we specified 2 for the rows argument and 3 for the columns argument.

Case two:

Sometimes, you might want a row-oriented display. In other words, you want a certain number of rows displayed, and you don't care about or aren't sure about the number of columns. If that's the case, call the `GridLayout` constructor with the actual number of rows for the rows argument and 0 for the columns argument. A 0 for the columns argument indicates that you're leaving it up to the `GridLayout` manager to determine the number of columns.

The code fragment below generates a two-row `GridLayout` with five buttons. Since the `setLayout` call does not specify gap values, the `GridLayout` displays no gaps between the buttons.

```
setLayout(new GridLayout(2, 0));
add(new JButton("1"));
add(new JButton("2"));
add(new JButton("3"));
add(new JButton("4"));
add(new JButton("5"));
```

Assume the above code fragment is part of a complete, working program. Here's what the program displays:

Test

1	2	3
4	5	

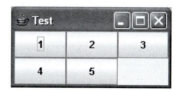

Case three:

Sometimes, you might want a column-oriented display. In other words, you want a certain number of columns displayed, and you don't care about or aren't sure about the number of rows. If this is the case, call the `GridLayout` constructor with the actual number of columns for the columns argument and 0 for the rows argument. A 0 for the rows argument indicates that you're leaving it up to the `GridLayout` manager to determine the number of rows.

The code fragment below generates a four-column `GridLayout` with five buttons.

```
setLayout(new GridLayout(0, 4));
add(new JButton("1"));
add(new JButton("2"));
add(new JButton("3"));
add(new JButton("4"));
add(new JButton("5"));
```

Assume the above code fragment is part of a complete, working program. Here's what the program displays:

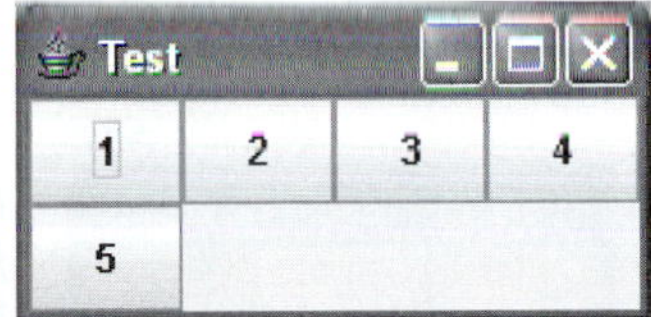

Now for a couple of things to watch out for. As you know, there's special significance when you call the `GridLayout` constructor with rows = 0 or columns = 0. It puts the `GridLayout` manager in charge of choosing the number of rows or the number of columns. But it only works if you have one 0-value argument, not two. If you call the `GridLayout` constructor with two 0-value arguments, you'll get a compile-time error.

What about the opposite case—when you call the `GridLayout` constructor with two non-0 values for the rows and columns arguments. That's fine as long as your table is completely filled. If it's not completely filled, you might get unexpected results. For example, the above four-column window is not completely filled. Suppose you accidentally specify a value for the rows argument:

```
setLayout(new GridLayout(2, 4));
```

Here's what the program displays:

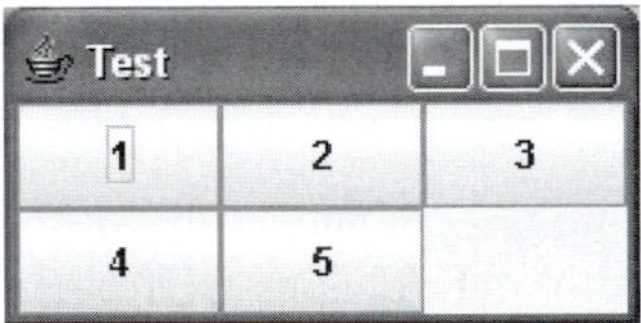

Now that's strange! There are three columns even though we specified four. Moral of the story: Call the `GridLayout` constructor with two non-0 values only if your table is completely filled.[2]

17.6 Tic-Tac-Toe Example

In this section, we present a simple tic-tac-toe program. We've chosen tic-tac-toe because we wanted to illustrate `GridLayout` details. And tic-tac-toe, with its three-row by three-column board, provides the perfect opportunity for that.

User Interface

The program initially displays a three-row, three-column grid of blank buttons. Two users, player X and player O, take turns clicking blank buttons. Player X goes first. When player X clicks a button, the button's label changes from blank to X. When player O clicks a button, the button's label changes from blank to O.

[2] Here's the inside skinny. If you call the `GridLayout` constructor with two non-0 values for the rows and columns arguments, the columns argument is ignored and the `GridLayout` manager determines the number of columns on its own. For the case where you have two non-0 values and the table is completely filled, the `GridLayout` manager still determines the number of columns on its own. But the determined number of columns works out perfectly (that is, the determined number of columns matches the specified number of columns).

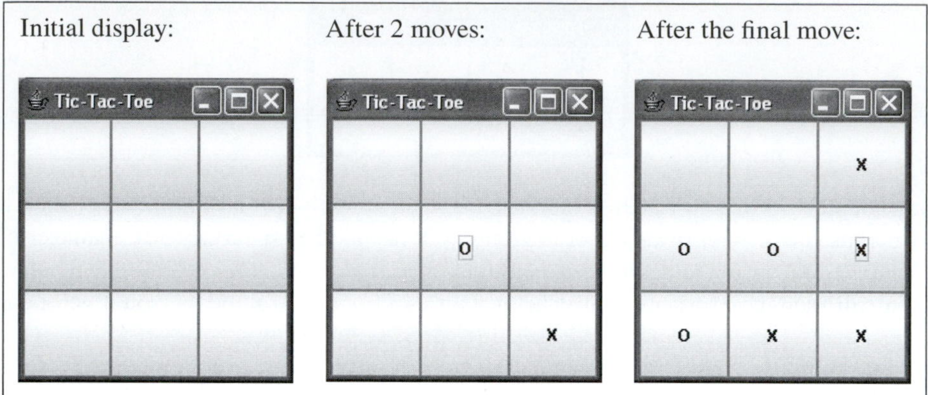

Figure 17.6 Sample session for the TicTacToe program

Player X wins by getting three X's in a row, 3 X's in a column, or 3 X's in a diagonal. Player O wins in the same manner except that O's are looked at instead of X's. To get a better handle on all this, see the sample session in Figure 17.6.

Program Details

See the TicTacToe program listing in Figures 17.7a and 17.7b. Most of the code should make sense already since its structure parallels the structure in our previous GUI programs. We'll skip the familiar code and focus on the more difficult code.

Note the `setLayout` method call in Figure 17.7a. It contains a `GridLayout` constructor call that specifies three rows and three columns. The constructor call does not include horizontal-gap and vertical-gap arguments, so the tic-tac-toe buttons display with no gaps between them.

Now let's take a look at the `Listener` class in Figure 17.7b. In particular, note the statement where we get the clicked button and save it in a local variable:

```
JButton btn = (JButton) e.getSource();
```

The `(JButton)` cast operator is used because if there were no cast operator, the compiler would generate an error. Why? Because the compiler would see an `Object` at the right being assigned into a `JButton` at the left (it sees an `Object` at the right because `getSource` is defined with an `Object` return type). In this case, since `getSource` really returns a `JButton`, it's legal to cast its returned value to `JButton`, and that satisfies the compiler and eliminates the error.

Let's examine the `Listener` class's `if` statement:

```
if (btn.getText().isEmpty())
{
  btn.setText(xTurn ? "X" : "O");
  xTurn = !xTurn;
}
```

We first check to ensure that the button is a blank button. We then reassign the button's label by using a conditional operator. If `xTurn` holds `true`, then X is assigned to the button label. Otherwise, O is assigned to the button label. We then change the value of `xTurn` by assigning its negated value into it. More

```
/**************************************************************
* TicTacToe.java
* Dean & Dean
*
* This program implements the game of tic-tac-toe.
* When the first blank button is clicked, its label changes
* to an X. Subsequent clicked blank buttons change their labels
* to O and X in alternating sequence.
**************************************************************/

import javax.swing.*;
import java.awt.*;
import java.awt.event.*;

public class TicTacToe extends JFrame
{
  private boolean xTurn = true; // keeps track of whether
                                // it's X's turn or O's turn

  //***********************************************************

  public TicTacToe()
  {
    setTitle("Tic-Tac-Toe");
    setSize(200, 220);
    setDefaultCloseOperation(EXIT_ON_CLOSE);
    createContents();
    setVisible(true);
  } // end TicTacToe constructor

  //***********************************************************

  // Create components and add to window.

  private void createContents()
  {
    JButton button; // re-instantiate this button and use
                    // to fill entire board
    setLayout(new GridLayout(3, 3));

    for (int i=0; i<3; i++)
    {
      for (int j=0; j<3; j++)
      {
        button = new JButton();
        button.addActionListener(new Listener());
        add(button);
      } // end for j
    } // end for i
  } // end createContents
```

Figure 17.7a TicTacToe program—part A

```
  //**************************************************************

  // If user clicks a button, change its label to "X" or "O".

  private class Listener implements ActionListener
  {
    public void actionPerformed(ActionEvent e)
    {
      JButton btn = (JButton) e.getSource();
      if (btn.getText().isEmpty())
      {
        btn.setText(xTurn ? "X" : "O");
        xTurn = !xTurn;
      }
    } // end actionPerformed
  } // end class Listener

  //**************************************************************

  public static void main(String[] args)
  {
    new TicTacToe();
  }
} // end class TicTacToe
```

Figure 17.7b TicTacToe program—part B

specifically, if `xTurn` is `false`, we assign `true` into `xTurn`. And if `xTurn` is `true`, we assign `false` into `xTurn`.

17.7 Problem Solving: Winning at Tic-Tac-Toe (Optional)

As you might have noticed, the previous section's TicTacToe program doesn't check for a winning move. As a problem-solving exercise, let's now discuss how to add that functionality. Rather than provide you with a Java solution, we'll provide you with the thought process for coming up with a solution. We'll codify the thought process using pseudocode. One of chapter's projects asks you to finish the job by implementing a complete Java program solution.

Iterate to enhance.

To check for a win (i.e., to check for three in a row, three in a column, or three in a diagonal), the listener needs to access multiple buttons. As it stands now, the `TicTacToe` listener can access only one button—the button that was clicked. It gets that button by calling `getSource`. So how should you change the program so the listener can access multiple buttons?

To access multiple buttons, you need to declare multiple buttons. You could declare nine separate buttons, but the more elegant solution is to declare a three-row, three-column, two-dimensional array of buttons. The next question is, where should you declare the array? Do you declare it as a local variable inside the listener or as an instance variable at the top of the program? In general, local variables are preferred, but in this case, a local variable won't work. Local variables don't persist. You need to be able to update a button from within the listener and have that update be remembered the next time the listener is called. Thus, you need to declare the buttons array as an instance variable.

You need to check for a win only when the user clicks a button. So add check-for-a-win code to the `actionPerformed` method inside the button's listener. In adding the code, use top-down design. In other words, don't worry about the low-level details; just assume they work. Here's the updated `actionPerformed` method. The added code is in pseudocode:

```
public void actionPerformed(ActionEvent e)
{
  JButton btn = (JButton) e.getSource();
  if (btn.getText().isEmpty())
  {
    btn.setText(xTurn ? "X" : "O");
    if win()
    {
      print winning player
      prepare for new game
    }
    else
    {
      xTurn = !xTurn;
    }
  }
} // end actionPerformed
```

pseudocode

The pseudocode contains three tasks—checking for a win, printing the winner, and preparing for a new game. Checking for a win requires the most thought, so we'll postpone that task for now. Let's discuss the other two tasks first.

Printing the winner should be straightforward. Just call `JOptionPane.showMessageDialog` with a congratulatory message. The message should include the player's name, X or O, which can be obtained by re-using the conditional operator code, `xTurn ? "X" : "O"`.

Preparing for a new game should be straightforward as well. Just assign the empty string to the board's button labels and assign `true` to the `xTurn` variable (X always goes first).

Feel free to implement the print-winning-player and prepare-for-new-game tasks as embedded code inside the `if` statement or as separate helper methods. Either way is fine. But the checking-for-a-win task should definitely be implemented as a separate helper method. Why? Note how cleanly `win` is called in the above pseudocode. You can retain that clean look in the final Java code only if you implement the checking-for-a-win task as a method, not as embedded code.

In implementing the win method, you need to check the two-dimensional buttons array for three in a row, three in a column, or three in a diagonal. Normally, when you access a group of elements in an array, you should use a `for` loop. So you might want to use a `for` loop to access the elements in the first row, use another `for` loop to access the elements in the second row, and so on. But that would require eight `for` loops:

```
for loop for first row
for loop for second row
...
for loop for second diagonal
```

Yikes! That's a lot of `for` loops! Is there a better way? How about taking the opposite approach and using no `for` loops? Use one big `if` statement like this:

```
if (btns[0][0] = X && btns[0][1] = X && btns[0][2] = X) ||
   (btns[1][0] = X && btns[1][1] = X && btns[1][2] = X) ||
   ...
   (btns[0][2] = X && btns[1][1] = X && btns[2][0] = X)
  return true
else
  return false
end-if
```

That works fine, but if you're bothered by the length of the `if` condition (eight lines long), you might want to try the following. Use one `for` loop for all the rows, one `for` loop for all the columns, and one `if` statement for the two diagonals:

```
for (i=0; i<3; i++)
  if (btns[i][0] = X && btns[i][1] = X && btns[i][2] = X)
    return true
  end-if
end-for

for (j=0; j<3; j++)
  if (btns[0][j] = X && btns[1][j] = X && btns[2][j] = X)
    return true
  end-if
end-for

if (btns[0][0] = X && btns[1][1] = X && btns[2][2] = X) ||
   (btns[0][2] = X && btns[1][1] = X && btns[2][0] = X)
  return true
end-if

return false
```

Of the three solutions, we prefer the last one because we feel its code is the most understandable.

To make the tic-tac-toe program more "real world," you'd probably want to provide additional functionality. In particular, you'd want to check for a "cat's game," which is when the board is filled and no one has won. You're asked to implement that functionality in one of the chapter's projects.

17.8 Embedded Layout Managers

Suppose you'd like to implement this math-calculator window:

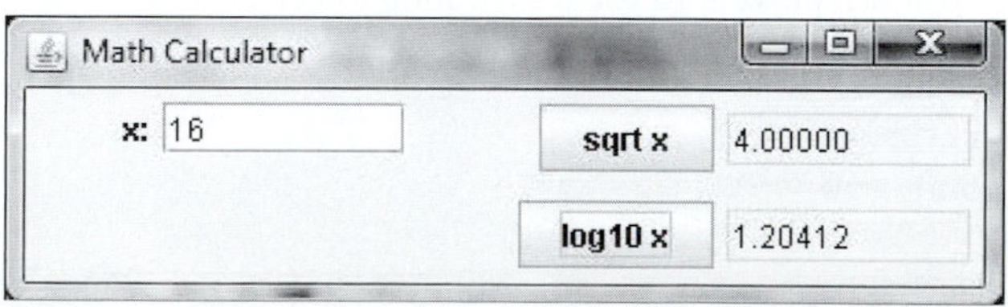

What type of layout scheme should you use? Coming up with a good layout scheme often requires creativity. We'll walk you through the creative process for this math-calculator example.

Trying Out the Different Layout Managers

The math-calculator window appears to have two rows and four columns. So is a two-row by four-column `Gridlayout` scheme appropriate? The `GridLayout` manager is usually adequate for positioning components in an organized tabular fashion, but it's limited by one factor—each of its cells must be the same size. If we use a two-row by four-column `GridLayout` scheme for the math-calculator window, then we'll have eight same-sized cells. That's fine for most of the cells, but not for the top-left cell. The top left cell would hold the x: label. With such a small label, we would want a relatively small cell for it. But with a `GridLayout` scheme, a "relatively small cell" is not an option.

Since the `GridLayout` manager is less than ideal, you might want to think about the `FlowLayout` manager. That could sort of work if you use right-aligned components. But then you'd be at the mercy of the user to not resize the window. If the user widens the window, then the log10 x button would flow up to the top line, and you don't want that. So the `FlowLayout` manager is also less than ideal. The `BorderLayout` manager isn't even close. So what's the solution?

Using an Embedded Layout Scheme

Delegate. 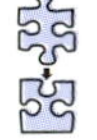

In coming up with layouts for more complex windows, the key is often to embed layout managers inside other layout managers. Let's first tackle the outer layout manager. For the math-calculator window, we want the input at the left and the output at the right. Those two entities are approximately the same width, so it makes sense to consider using a two-column `GridLayout` for them. The left column would contain the input components—the x label and the input text box. The right column would contain the output components—the square root's button and output text box and the logarithm's button and output text box. We'd like to organize the output components so that the square root's items are above the logarithm's items. That means using two rows for our `GridLayout`. See the two-row by two-column `GridLayout` scheme in Figure 17.8.

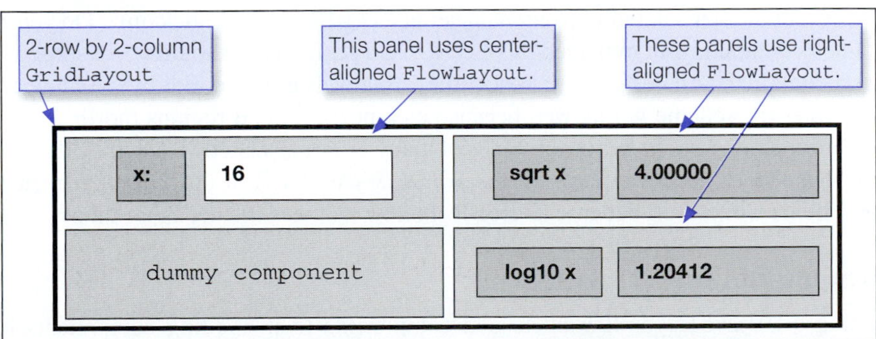

Figure 17.8 `GridLayout` with embedded `FlowLayout` panels in three of the cells

As you know, `GridLayout` managers only allow one component per cell. But Figure 17.8 shows two components in the top-left cell and two components in the top-right cell. To implement that organization scheme, you'll need to group each of the two-component pairs into their own separate containers. And to achieve the proper layout, you'll need to apply layout managers to each of those containers. The top-left cell's container uses a center-aligned `FlowLayout` manager. The right cells' containers use right-aligned `FlowLayout` managers. Voila, layout managers inside a layout manager. Pretty cool, eh?

When you have a non-trivial window, it's very common to have embedded layout managers. And when that happens, it can take a considerable amount of tweaking to get your windows to look right. Despite the tweaking, using embedded layout managers is still a lot easier than having to manually position components with pixel values like in the old days. The next section provides details on the containers for the embedded layout managers.

17.9 `JPanel` class

Before continuing with the implementation of the math-calculator program, we need to discuss the `JPanel` class. A `JPanel` container object is a generic storage area for components. If you have a complicated window with many components, you might want to compartmentalize the components by putting groups of components in `JPanel` containers. `JPanel` containers are particularly useful with `GridLayout` and `BorderLayout` windows because each compartment in those layouts can store only one component. If you need a compartment to store more than one component, let that one component be a `JPanel` container, and put multiple components into the `JPanel` container.

Implementation

As you may recall, GUI classes that begin with *J* come from the `javax.swing` package. So that's where the `JPanel` container class comes from, and you need to import the `javax.swing` package in order to use `Jpanel`.

To instantiate a `JPanel` container, use this syntax:

```
JPanel <JPanel-reference> = new JPanel(<layout-manager>);
```

The *layout-manager* argument is optional. If it's omitted, then the default is to have a center-aligned `FlowLayout` manager.

So the `JPanel` container's default layout manager is `FlowLayout`. Quick quiz: Do you remember the `JFrame` container's default layout manager? It's `BorderLayout`. That should make sense when you realize that `JFrame` containers are designed to handle the window as a whole. For the window as a whole, the default `BorderLayout` scheme works well because its report-oriented regions (north for a header, south for a footer, center for a main body) match the needs of many program windows. On the other hand, `JPanel` containers are designed to handle compartments within a window. For such compartments, the default `FlowLayout` scheme works well because its free-form flow matches the needs for many compartments.

Adding Components to a `JPanel`

After instantiating a `JPanel`, you'll want to add components to it. Adding components to a `JPanel` is the same as adding components to a `JFrame`. Call the `add` method. As you know, the `add` method works differently for the different layout managers. If your `JPanel` uses a `FlowLayout` manager or a `GridLayout` manager, call the `add` method like this:

```
<JPanel-reference>.add(<component>);
```

If your `JPanel` uses a `BorderLayout` manager, you should add a second argument to specify the component's region:

<*JPanel-reference*>.add(<*component*>, <*BorderLayout-region*>);

Adding JPanel to a Window

After adding components to a JPanel, you'll need to add the JPanel to a window. If your window uses a FlowLayout manager or a GridLayout manager, call the add method like this:

add(<*JPanel-reference*>);

If your window uses a BorderLayout manager, you'll want to add a second argument to specify the component's region:

add(<*JPanel-reference*>, <*BorderLayout-region*>);

In the next section, we return to the math-calculator program. That will give us an opportunity to see how JPanel works in the context of a complete program.

17.10 MathCalculator Program

See the MathCalculator program listing in Figures 17.9a, 17.9b, and 17.9c. You should peruse the entire program on your own, but we'll focus primarily on the panel-related code.

From the MathCalculator program's createContents method, here's the code that creates the top-left cell's panel:

```
xPanel = new JPanel(new FlowLayout(FlowLayout.CENTER));
xPanel.add(xLabel);
xPanel.add(xBox);
```

The first statement instantiates the JPanel container. Since the JPanel constructor uses a center-aligned FlowLayout by default, you can write the first statement like this and get the same result:

```
xPanel = new JPanel();
```

But we prefer the original statement since it's self-documenting. The second and third statements add the **x:** label and the input text box to the panel.

Further down in the createContents method, here's the code that adds the panels to the window:

```
add(xPanel);
add(xSqrtPanel);
add(new JLabel()); // dummy component
add(xLogPanel);
```

The first, second, and fourth statements add the three panels to the window's top-left, top-right, and bottom-right cells, respectively. The third statement adds a dummy component (a blank label) to the bottom-left cell. The dummy component is necessary because without it, the xLogPanel would go into the bottom-left cell, and that's not what you want.

There's one additional item worth mentioning in this program. Note the String.format method call in Figure 17.9c's actionPerformed method. The String.format method works the same as the printf method except that instead of printing a formatted value, it returns a formatted value. In the actionPerformed method, we call String.format to retrieve a formatted version of the calculated

```
/***************************************************************
* MathCalculator.java
* Dean & Dean
*
* This program uses embedded layout managers to display
* the square root and logarithm of a user-entered number.
***************************************************************/

import javax.swing.*;
import java.awt.*;
import java.awt.event.*;

public class MathCalculator extends JFrame
{
  private static final int WIDTH = 380;
  private static final int HEIGHT = 110;

  private JTextField xBox;     // user's input value
  private JTextField xSqrtBox; // generated square root
  private JTextField xLogBox;  // generated logarithm

  //************************************************************

  public MathCalculator()
  {
    setTitle("Math Calculator");
    setSize(WIDTH, HEIGHT);
    setDefaultCloseOperation(EXIT_ON_CLOSE);
    createContents();
    setVisible(true);
  } // end MathCalculator constructor

  //************************************************************

  // Create components and add to window.

  private void createContents()
  {
    JPanel xPanel;     // holds x label and its text box
    JPanel xSqrtPanel; // holds "sqrt x" label and its text box
    JPanel xLogPanel;  // holds "log x" label and its text box
    JLabel xLabel;
    JButton xSqrtButton;
    JButton xLogButton;
    Listener listener;

    setLayout(new GridLayout(2, 2));
```

Figure 17.9a MathCalculator program—part A

```
    // Create the x panel:
    xLabel = new JLabel("x:");
    xBox = new JTextField(8);
    xPanel = new JPanel(new FlowLayout(FlowLayout.CENTER));
    xPanel.add(xLabel);
    xPanel.add(xBox);

    // Create the square-root panel:
    xSqrtButton = new JButton("sqrt x");
    xSqrtBox = new JTextField(8);
    xSqrtBox.setEditable(false);
    xSqrtPanel = new JPanel(new FlowLayout(FlowLayout.RIGHT));
    xSqrtPanel.add(xSqrtButton);
    xSqrtPanel.add(xSqrtBox);

    // Create the logarithm panel:
    xLogButton = new JButton("log10 x");
    xLogBox = new JTextField(8);
    xLogBox.setEditable(false);
    xLogPanel = new JPanel(new FlowLayout(FlowLayout.RIGHT));
    xLogPanel.add(xLogButton);
    xLogPanel.add(xLogBox);

    // Add panels to the window:
    add(xPanel);
    add(xSqrtPanel);
    add(new JLabel()); // dummy component
    add(xLogPanel);

    listener = new Listener();
    xSqrtButton.addActionListener(listener);
    xLogButton.addActionListener(listener);
  } // end createContents

  //**************************************************************

  // Inner class for math calculations.

  private class Listener implements ActionListener
  {
    public void actionPerformed(ActionEvent e)
    {
      double x;       // numeric value for user entered x
      double result; // calculated value
```

Add dummy component so bottom-left cell gets filled in.

Figure 17.9b MathCalculator program—part B

```
        try
        {
          x = Double.parseDouble(xBox.getText());
        }
        catch (NumberFormatException nfe)
        {
          x = -1;    // indicates an invalid x
        }

        if (e.getActionCommand().equals("sqrt x"))
        {
          if (x < 0)
          {
            xSqrtBox.setText("undefined");
          }
          else
          {
            result = Math.sqrt(x);
            xSqrtBox.setText(String.format("%7.5f", result));
          }
        } // end if

        else // calculate logarithm
        {
          if (x < 0)
          {
            xLogBox.setText("undefined");
          }
          else
          {
            result = Math.log10(x);
            xLogBox.setText(String.format("%7.5f", result));
          }
        } // end else
      } // end actionPerformed
    } // end class Listener

    //*************************************************************

    public static void main(String[] args)
    {
      new MathCalculator();
    } // end main
  } // end class MathCalculator
```

Figure 17.9c MathCalculator program—part C

logarithm value. Specifically, the `%7.5f` conversion specifier returns a floating-point value with 5 decimal places and 7 total characters.

17.11 JtextArea Component

In the previous chapter, we introduced you to a few GUI components—`JLabel`, `JTextField`, `JButton`, and `JOptionPane`—that provide basic input/output functionality. Now we'll introduce you to a few more GUI components—`JTextArea`, `JCheckBox`, `JRadioButton`, and `JComboBox`—that provide more advanced input/output functionality. We'll start with the `JTextArea` component.

User Interface

The `JLabel` component works great for displaying a single line of text. As described in Chapter 16, you can use a `JLabel` component to display multiple lines of text, but achieving multiple lines requires cluttering up your code with HTML `<br>` line-break tags. The preferred technique for displaying multiple lines of text is to use a `JTextArea` component. The large white area in Figure 17.10 is a `JTextArea` component. By the way, the small shaded area at the bottom of Figure 17.10 is a `JCheckBox` component. We'll describe `JCheckBox` components in the next section.

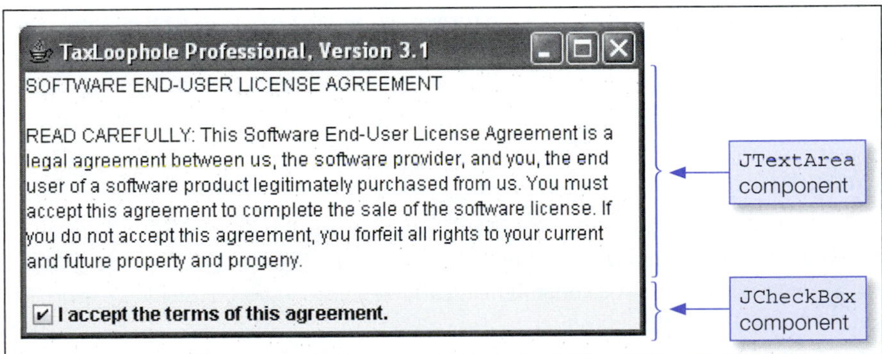

Figure 17.10 A window with a `JTextArea` component and a `JCheckBox` component

Implementation

To create a `JTextArea` component, call the `JTextArea` constructor like this:

```
JTextArea <JTextArea-reference> = new JTextArea(<display-text>);
```

The *display-text* is the text that appears in the `JTextArea` component. If the display-text argument is omitted, then the `JTextArea` component displays nothing.

Methods

The `JTextArea` class, like all the GUI component classes, has quite a few methods. Here are the API headings and descriptions for the more popular `JTextArea` methods:

```
public String getText()
```

Returns the text area's text.

```
public void setText(String text)
```
Assigns the text area's text.

```
public void setEditable(boolean flag)
```
Makes the text box editable or non-editable.

```
public void setLineWrap(boolean flag)
```
Turns line wrap on or off.

```
public void setWrapStyleWord(boolean flag)
```
Specifies whether word boundaries are used for line wrapping.

`JTextArea` components are editable by default, which means users are allowed to type inside them. If you want to prevent users from editing a `JTextArea` component, call `setEditable` with an argument value of `false`. Doing so prevents <u>users</u> from updating the text area, but it does not prevent <u>programmers</u> from updating the text area. Programmers can call the `setText` method regardless of whether the text area is editable or non-editable.

`JTextArea` components have line wrap turned off by default. Normally, you'll want to turn line wrap on by calling `setLineWrap(true)`. That way, long lines automatically wrap to the next row, instead of disappearing when they reach the text area's right boundary.

For `JTextArea` components with line wrap turned on, the default is to perform line wrap at the point where the text meets the text area's right boundary, regardless of whether that point is in the middle of a word. Normally, you'll want to avoid that draconian[3] default behavior and have line wrap occur only at word boundaries. To change to a word-boundary line-wrap policy, call `setWrapStyleWord(true)`.

License-Agreement Example

Look back at the license-agreement `JText Area` component in Figure 7.10. Figure 17.11 contains the code associated with that component. Let's now examine Figure 17.11's code. Note the `\n\n` in the `JTextArea` constructor call. As you might recall, `\n`'s are ignored inside `JLabel` text. But they work fine inside `JTextArea` text. Note the `setEditable(false)`, `setLineWrap(true)`, and `setWrapStyleWord(true)` calls. Those calls are common for `JTextArea` components.

Take a look at the background color for the license-agreement `JTextArea` component in Figure 17.10. It's white. That's in contrast to the rest of the window. If you want your text area to stand out, then the white background color is appropriate, but if you want it to blend in, then it's inappropriate. How can you change its background color so that it blends in? More specifically, how can you change the code so that the window looks like Figure 17.12? The solution requires the use of a few methods not mentioned in the above API method list. But we've used the methods in the past for other GUI needs. Try to figure this out on your own before reading on.

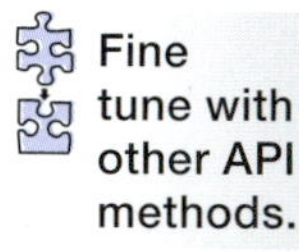
Fine tune with other API methods.

To change a component's background color, call setBackground(<*color*>). For our license-agreement component, we want its color to match the window's color, so we need to call `setBackground` with a color value equal to the window's background color. To get the window's background color, call `getContentPane().getBackground()`. Here's the solution:

```
license.setBackground(getContentPane().getBackground());
```

[3] A draconian policy is a policy that is harsh or severe. Draconion comes from Draco, a 7th century B.C. government official from Athens who was in charge of codifying local law. Draco's laws were exceedingly severe. For example, even minor offenses were punishable by the death penalty.

```
private void createContents()
{
  JTextArea license;
  JCheckBox confirmBox;

  setLayout(new BorderLayout());
  license = new JTextArea(
    "SOFTWARE END-USER LICENSE AGREEMENT\n\n" +
    "READ CAREFULLY: This Software End-User License Agreement" +
    " is a legal agreement between us, the software provider," +
    " and you, the end user of a software product legitimately" +
    " purchased from us. You must accept this agreement to" +
    " complete the sale of the software license. If you do not" +
    " accept this agreement, you forfeit all rights to your" +
    " current and future property and progeny.");
  license.setEditable(false);
  license.setLineWrap(true);
  license.setWrapStyleWord(true);
  confirmBox = new JCheckBox(
    "I accept the terms of this agreement.", true);

  add(license, BorderLayout.CENTER);
  add(confirmBox, BorderLayout.SOUTH);
} // end createContents
```

Figure 17.11 The code that created figure 17.10's display

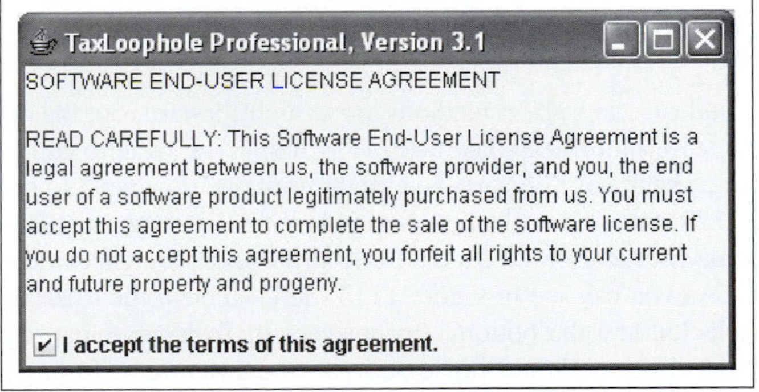

Figure 17.12 Modified background color for license-agreement `JTextArea` component

17.12 `JcheckBox` Component

User Interface

Look at the *check box* component at the bottom of Figure 17.12. Use a check box component if you want to present an option. A check box component displays a small square with a label to its right. When the square is blank, the check box is unselected. When the square contains a check mark, the check box is selected. Users click on the check box in order to toggle between selected and unselected.

Implementation

To create a check box component, call the `JCheckBox` constructor like this:

```
JCheckBox <JCheckBox-reference> = new JCheckBox(<label>, <selected>);
```

The *label* argument specifies the text that appears at the right of the check box's square. If the label argument is omitted, then no text appears at the right of the check box's square. The *selected* argument specifies whether the check box is selected initially—`true` means selected, `false` means unselected. If the selected argument is omitted, then the check box is initially unselected.

Here's how the check box was created in the license-agreement window:

```
confirmBox = new JCheckBox("I accept the terms of this agreement.", true);
```

Methods

Here are the API headings and descriptions for the more popular `JCheckBox` methods:

`public boolean isSelected()`

Returns `true` if the check box is selected and `false` otherwise.

`public void setVisible(boolean flag)`

Makes the check box visible or invisible.

`public void setSelected(boolean flag)`

Makes the check box selected or unselected.

`public void setEnabled(boolean flag)`

Makes the check box enabled or disabled.

`public void addActionListener(ActionListener listener)`

Adds a listener to the check box.

The `isSelected` and `setVisible` methods are straightforward, but the other three methods need further explanation. Let's start with `setSelected`. Why might you want to call `setSelected` and adjust the selection status of a check box? Because you might want one user input to impact another user input. For example, in Figure 17.13, the user's selection of standard versus custom[4] should impact the check box selections. More specifically, if the user selects the Standard option, the check box selections should go to their "standard" settings. As you can see in Figure 17.13's left window, the standard settings for the check boxes are the top two selected and the bottom two unselected. To have your program select the top two check boxes, those two check boxes should call `setSelected(true)`. To have your program unselect the bottom two check boxes, those two check boxes should call `setSelected(false)`.

To have your program disable a check box, the checkbox should call `setEnabled(false)`. Why might you want to call `setEnabled(false)` and disable a check box? Because you might want to keep the user from modifying that box's value. For example, if the user selects the Standard option as shown in Figure 17.13's left window, the check box selections should be set to their standard settings (as explained above), and then each check box should call `setEnabled(false)`. That way, the user cannot make

[4] The Standard and Custom circles at the top of Figure 17.13 are called radio buttons. We'll describe `JradioButton` components in the next section.

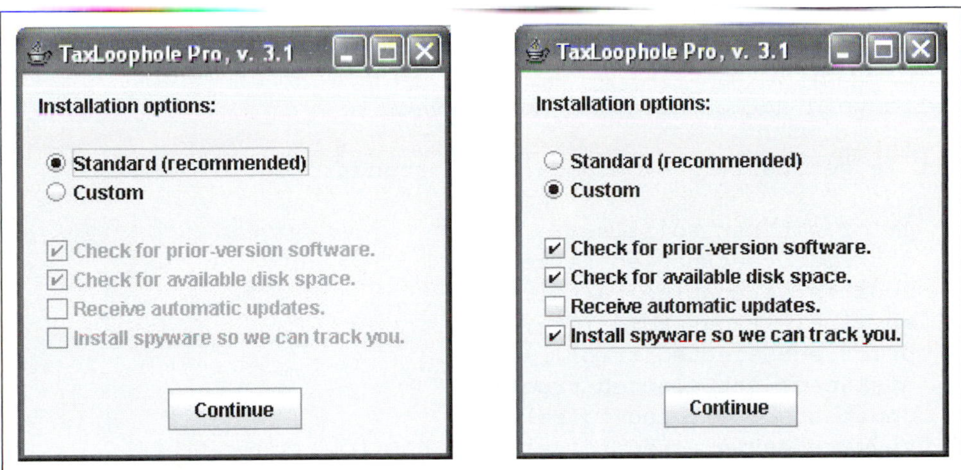

Figure 17.13 Example that illustrates `JCheckBox`'s `setSelected` and `setEnabled` methods

changes to the standard-configuration check box values. In Figure 17.13's left window, note that the check boxes are gray. We say that they're *grayed out*. That's the standard GUI way of telling the user that something is disabled.

Check Box Listeners

With a `JButton` component you'll almost always want an associated listener. But with a `JCheckBox` component, you may or may not want an associated listener. If you have a check box with no listener, then the check box simply serves as an input entity. If that's the case, then the check box's value (checked or unchecked) would typically get read and processed when the user clicks a button. On the other hand, if you want something to happen immediately, right when the user selects a check box, then add a listener to the check box component. Suppose you have a Green Background check box. If you want the window's background color to change to green right when the user clicks the check box, add a listener to the check box. The syntax for adding a listener to a `JCheckBox` component is the same as the syntax for adding a listener to a `JButton` component. Provide a listener that implements the `ActionListener` interface and then add the listener to the `JCheckBox` component by calling `addActionListener`.

Be aware that Sun provides an alternative listener interface for the `JCheckBox` component—the `ItemListener` interface. An `ActionListener` listens for the user clicking on a check box. An `ItemListener` listens for a *state change*; that is, it listens for a check box changing from selected to unselected or vice versa. A check box state change is triggered when a user clicks the check box or when a program calls `setSelected` with a value that's different from the current value. Since the `ActionListener` interface is the preferred interface for most situations, we'll stick with it when implementing `JCheckBox` listeners. When we get to the `JRadioButton` and `JComboBox` components in the next sections, we'll continue to use the `ActionListener` interface, not the `ItemListener` interface.

Installation-Options Example

It's now time to put these check box concepts into practice by showing you some code. Look back at the installation-options windows in Figure 17.13. In Figure 17.14, we provide the listener code associated with those windows. Let's walk through the code. In the `if` statement's condition, we check

```
private class Listener implements ActionListener
{
  public void actionPerformed(ActionEvent e)
  {
    if (e.getSource() == standard) // standard option chosen
    {
      prior.setEnabled(false);
      diskSpace.setEnabled(false);
      updates.setEnabled(false);
      spyware.setEnabled(false);
      prior.setSelected(true);
      diskSpace.setSelected(true);
      updates.setSelected(false);
      spyware.setSelected(false);
    }
    else                           // custom option chosen
    {
      prior.setEnabled(true);
      diskSpace.setEnabled(true);
      updates.setEnabled(true);
      spyware.setEnabled(true);
    }
  } // end actionPerformed
} // end Listener
```

Figure 17.14 Listener code for figure 17.13's installation-options windows

to see whether the standard option was selected. If that's the case, we disable the check boxes by calling `setEnabled(false)` for each check box. We then assign the check boxes to their standard settings by calling `setSelected(true)` or `setSelected(false)` for each check box. In the `else` block, we handle the custom option being selected. We enable the check boxes by having each box call `setEnabled(true)`. This enables the user to control whether the box is selected or not.

17.13 `JradioButton` Component

User Interface

Look at the circles in the windows in Figure 17.13. They're called *radio buttons*. A `JRadioButton` component displays a small circle with a label to its right. When the circle is blank, the radio button is unselected. When the circle contains a large dot, the radio button is selected.

According to the description so far, radio buttons sound a lot like check boxes. They display a shape and a label, and they keep track of whether something is on or off. The key difference between radio buttons and check boxes is that radio buttons almost always come in groups. And within a radio button group, only one radio button can be selected at a time. If a user clicks an unselected radio button, the clicked button becomes selected, and the previously selected button in the group becomes unselected. If a user clicks a selected radio button, no change occurs (i.e., the clicked button remains selected). In contrast, if a user clicks a selected check box, the check box changes its state from selected to unselected.

Implementation

To create a `JRadioButton` component, call the `JRadioButton` constructor like this:

```
JRadioButton <JRadioButton-reference> =
 new JRadioButton(<label>, <selected>);
```

The *label* argument specifies the text that appears at the right of the radio button's circle. If the label argument is omitted, then no text appears at the right of the radio button's circle. The *selected* argument specifies whether the radio button is initially selected—`true` means selected, `false` means unselected. If the selected argument is omitted, then the radio button is initially unselected.

This example shows how we created the `standard` and `custom` radio buttons in the installation-options program:

```
standard = new JRadioButton("Standard (recommended)", true);
custom = new JRadioButton("Custom");
```

To enable the only-one-button-selected-at-a-time functionality of a radio button group, create a `ButtonGroup` object and add individual radio button components to it. Here's how:

```
ButtonGroup <ButtonGroup-reference> = new ButtonGroup();
<ButtonGroup-reference>.add(<first-button-in-group>);
. . .
<ButtonGroup-reference>.add(<last-button-in-group>);
```

The following example shows how we created the radio button group for the `standard` and `custom` radio buttons in the installation-options program:

```
ButtonGroup rbGroup = new ButtonGroup();
rbGroup.add(standard);
rbGroup.add(custom);
```

After adding radio buttons to a radio button group, you still have to add them to a container. Radio buttons work the same as other components in terms of adding them to a container. Call the container's `add` method like this:

```
add(<first-button-in-group>);
. . .
add(<last-button-in-group>);
```

That's a lot of adding. You need to add each radio button twice—once to a radio button group and once to a container. If you like shortcuts, you might be thinking, Why does Java make you add the individual radio buttons to the container? Why are they not added automatically when the radio button group is added? Adding the buttons separately from the button group gives you freedom in positioning the buttons. If you wanted to, you could even put them in different panels.

Since the `JRadioButton` class begins with a *J*, you can correctly assume that it's defined in the `javax.swing` package. But what about the `ButtonGroup` class? Even though it doesn't begin with a *J*, it's also defined in the `javax.swing` package.

Methods

Here are the API headings and descriptions for the more popular `JRadioButton` methods:

`public boolean isSelected()`

Returns `true` if radio button is selected and `false` otherwise.

`public void setSelected(boolean flag)`

Makes radio button selected if argument is true. Does nothing if argument is `false`.

`public void setEnabled(boolean flag)`

Makes radio button enabled or disabled. If enabled, it responds to mouse clicks.

`public void addActionListener(ActionListener listener)`

Adds a listener to the radio button.

We described these same methods in the `JCheckBox` section. Only one of them needs further attention—the `setSelected` method. To understand how `setSelected` works, you first need to understand fully how a user interacts with a radio button group. To select a radio button, a user clicks it. That causes the radio button to become selected and all other radio buttons in the group to become unselected. To programmatically select a radio button, you have the radio button call `setSelected(true)`. That causes the radio button to become selected and all other radio buttons in the group to become unselected. As mentioned above, there is no way for a user to unselect a button. Likewise, there is no way for a program to unselect a button. That's why calling `setSelected(false)` doesn't do anything. It compiles and runs, but it doesn't cause any buttons to change their selected status.

17.14 `JcomboBox` Component

User Interface

A *combo box* allows a user to select an item from a list of items. Combo boxes are sometimes called *drop-down lists* because if a user clicks a combo box's down arrow, a list of selection items drops down from the original display. Then, if a user clicks a selection from the drop-down list, the list disappears and only the selected item remains displayed. To get a better idea of what we're talking about, see the select-a-day combo box in Figure 17.15.

Combo boxes and radio button groups are similar in that they both allow the user to select one item from a list of items. But a combo box takes up less space on the window. So if you have a long list of items to choose from, and you want to save space, use a combo box rather than a group of radio buttons.

Implementation

Creating a combo box component is a two-step process. First, instantiate an array of list options. Then, use the array as part of a `JComboBox` instantiation. Here's the syntax for a `JComboBox` instantiation:

`JComboBox` *<JComboBox-reference>* `= new JComboBox(`*<array-of-list-options>*`);`

The following example shows how we created the combo box in Figure 17.15:

```
String[] days =
  {"Monday", "Tuesday", "Wednesday", "Thursday", "Friday"};
daysBox = new JComboBox(days);
```

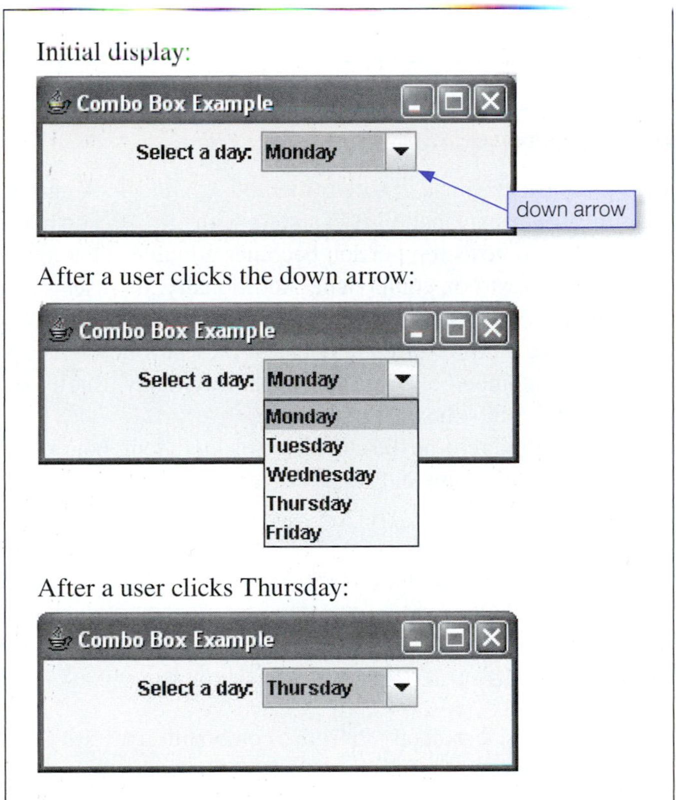

Figure 17.15 Select-a-day combo box example

When a combo box first displays, the first item in its array is selected. So in the above example, Monday is selected when the combo box first displays.

Methods

Here are the API headings and descriptions for the more popular `JComboBox` methods:

`public void setVisible(boolean flag)`
Makes the combo box visible or invisible.

`public void setEditable(boolean flag)`
Makes the combo box's top portion editable or non-editable.

`public Object getSelectedItem()`
Returns the item that is currently selected.

`public void setSelectedItem(Object item)`
Changes the currently selected item to the item that's passed in.

`public int getSelectedIndex()`
Returns the index of the item that is currently selected.

```
public void setSelectedIndex(int index)
```

Changes the currently selected item to the item at the given index position.

```
public void addActionListener(ActionListener listener)
```

Adds a listener to the combo box.

The `setVisible` and `addActionListener` methods should look familiar by now. The other methods are new and require further explanation. Let's start with `setEditable`. If a combo box calls `setEditable(true)`, the combo box's top portion becomes editable. That means that a user can enter text into it the same as if it were a text box component. Additionally, the user still can use the pull-down portion of the combo box the same as always. Combo boxes are named "combo" for "combination" because they are capable of implementing a mixture of components—part pull-down list, part text box. But most programmers don't bother with the combo box's text-box capability. They usually stick with the default behavior, where the top portion of the combo box is not editable.

The `getSelectedItem` method returns the currently selected item. For example, here's how you can retrieve the currently selected `daysBox` item and store it in a `favoriteDay` variable:

```
String favoriteDay = (String) daysBox.getSelectedItem();
```

What's the point of the `(String)` cast operator? The `getSelectedItem` method is defined to have a return type of `Object`. Therefore, if there were no cast operator, the compiler would see an `Object` at the right being assigned into a `String` at the left, and that would generate a compile-time error. But there is a cast operator, so the compiler sees a `String` at the right being assigned into a `String` at the left. And that makes the compiler happy.

If you'd like to programmatically select an option from a combo box, call `setSelectedItem` and pass in the item that you want to select. For example, to select `Friday` from the `daysBox` component, do this:

```
daysBox.setSelectedItem("Friday");
```

Normally, you'll call `setSelectedItem` with an argument that matches one of the combo box's items. But that's not always the case. If you'd like to clear a combo box so that no options are selected, call `setSelectedItem(null)`. If you call `setSelectedItem` with a different item (not null and not a combo box item), then nothing happens. Well, actually, nothing happens if it's a standard combo box. But if it's an editable combo box, then the passed-in item gets put into the editable top portion of the combo box.

There are two ways to access items in a combo box—use item names or use item indexes. The `getSelectedItem` and `setSelectedItem` methods use item names. The `getSelectedIndex` and `setSelectedIndex` methods use item indexes. For example, note how this code fragment calls `setSelectedIndex` with an index value of 2:

```
String[] days =
  {"Monday", "Tuesday", "Wednesday", "Thursday", "Friday"};
daysBox = new JComboBox(days);
daysBox.setSelectedIndex(2);
```

Since combo boxes store their items in arrays, combo box item indexes are 0-based. Therefore, in the above code fragment, Monday is 0, Tuesday is 1, and Wednesday is 2. Thus, `daysBox.setSelectedIndex(2)` changes the selected item to Wednesday.

Indexing helps you process data.

Now for a short brain-teaser. Given the above code fragment, how can you change the currently selected day to the next day? Do arithmetic with the index, like this:

```
daysBox.setSelectedIndex(daysBox.getSelectedIndex() + 1);
```

17.15 Job Application Example

In this section, we put into practice what you've learned in the previous three sections. We present a complete program that uses check boxes, radio buttons, and a combo box. The program implements a job application form. If the user enters values that are indicative of a good employee, the program displays an encouraging message ("Thank you for your application submission. We'll contact you after we process your information."). Study the sample session in Figure 17.16 to get a better idea of what we're talking about.

See the JobApplication program listing in Figures 17.17a, 17.17b, and 17.17c. You should peruse the entire program on your own, particularly the listener code, but we'll focus only on the most difficult part—the layout design.

We spent quite a bit of time on the `JobApplication`'s layout in order to get things to look right. Initially, we thought a simple one-column `GridLayout` manager would work. We added one component per cell, and we added three filler components (empty `JLabel`s) to create gaps between the four different input areas. We thought that plan would yield the layout shown in Figure 17.18's left picture. Unfortunately, when we entered the code, the actual program yielded the layout shown in Figure 17.18's right picture. There are three problems with the actual layout—the Submit button is too wide, the top two gaps are missing, and the components are touching the left boundary. We'll now discuss how to fix those problems.

If at first you don't succeed, try again.

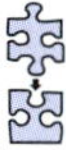

Problem 1: Submit Button is Too Wide

As you may recall from earlier in the chapter, buttons expand if they're added directly to a `GridLayout` cell. That explains the wide Submit button. You can fix the problem by embedding a `FlowLayout` panel into the Submit button's area, and then adding the Submit button to the `FlowLayout` panel. With a `FlowLayout` manager, buttons don't expand; they keep their natural size.

Embed another manager.

Problem 2: Top Two Gaps are Missing

In our first cut of the program, we used this code to implement the filler components:

```
JLabel filler = new JLabel();
...
add(filler);
...
add(filler);
...
add(filler);
```

We instantiated only one label and reused it three times. You like to reuse, right? Well, the layout manager doesn't. The layout manager sees only one object and so it makes only one cell. It does not make cells for the first two `add(filler)` calls; it only makes a cell for the last `add(filler)` call. You can fix the problem by using three anonymous `JLabel` objects like this:

Use separate objects.

```
add(new JLabel());
...
add(new JLabel());
...
add(new JLabel());
```

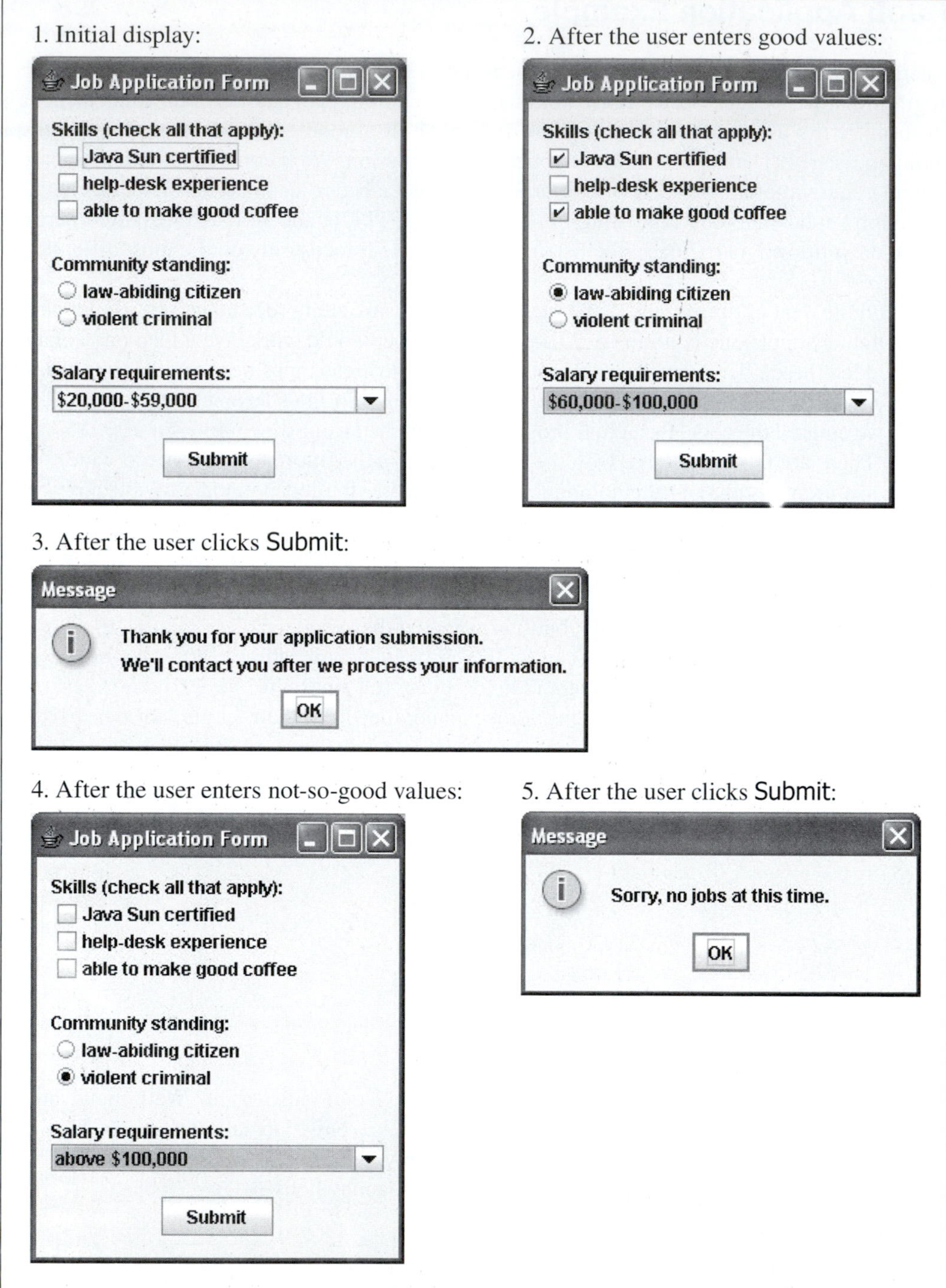

Figure 17.16 Sample session for the JobApplication program

```
/*************************************************************
* JobApplication.java
* Dean & Dean
*
* This program implements job application questions
* with check boxes, radio buttons, and a combo box.
*************************************************************/

import javax.swing.*;
import java.awt.*;
import java.awt.event.*;
import javax.swing.border.*;    // for EmptyBorder

public class JobApplication extends JFrame
{
  private static final int WIDTH = 250;
  private static final int HEIGHT = 300;

  private JCheckBox java;        // Java Sun certified?
  private JCheckBox helpDesk;    // help-desk experience?
  private JCheckBox coffee;      // good coffee maker?
  private JRadioButton goodCitizen, criminal;
  private JComboBox salary;
  private String[] salaryOptions =
    {"$20,000-$59,000", "$60,000-$100,000", "above $100,000"};
  private JButton submit;        // submit the application

  //**********************************************************

  public JobApplication()
  {
    setTitle("Job Application Form");
    setSize(WIDTH, HEIGHT);
    setDefaultCloseOperation(EXIT_ON_CLOSE);
    createContents();
    setVisible(true);
  } // end JobApplication constructor

  //**********************************************************

  // Create components and add to window.
```

Figure 17.17a JobApplication program—part A

Problem 3: Components Are Touching Left Boundary

By default, containers have no margins. So if a container has left-aligned components, those components touch the container's left boundary. That explains the left-boundary ugliness in Figure 17.18's right picture. You can add a margin by calling `setBorder` like this:

<container>`.setBorder(new EmptyBorder(`*<top>*`, `*<left>*`, `*<bottom>*`, `*<right>*`));`

In calling `setBorder`, you'll need to pass a border object as an argument. There are several different types of border classes. You should use the `EmptyBorder` class because an empty border produces a margin,

```
private void createContents()
{
  ButtonGroup radioGroup;

  // Note:
  // The most straightforward implementation is to use a
  // GridLayout manager for the JFrame and add all components
  // to its cells. That doesn't work well because:
  // 1) Can't apply a margin to JFrame.
  // 2) The button panel is taller than the other components.

  // Need windowPanel for south-panel separation & outer margin
  JPanel windowPanel = new JPanel(new BorderLayout(0, 10));
  windowPanel.setBorder(new EmptyBorder(10, 10, 10, 10));

  // centerPanel holds all components except button
  JPanel centerPanel = new JPanel(new GridLayout(11, 1));

  // Need a panel for button so it can be center aligned
  JPanel southPanel = new JPanel(new FlowLayout());

  java = new JCheckBox("Java Sun certified");
  helpDesk = new JCheckBox("help-desk experience");
  coffee = new JCheckBox("able to make good coffee");
  goodCitizen = new JRadioButton("law-abiding citizen");
  criminal = new JRadioButton("violent criminal");
  radioGroup = new ButtonGroup();
  radioGroup.add(goodCitizen);
  radioGroup.add(criminal);
  salary = new JComboBox(salaryOptions);
  submit = new JButton("Submit");
  submit.addActionListener(new ButtonListener());

  centerPanel.add(new JLabel("Skills (check all that apply):"));
  centerPanel.add(java);
  centerPanel.add(helpDesk);
  centerPanel.add(coffee);
  centerPanel.add(new JLabel());  // filler
  centerPanel.add(new JLabel("Community standing:"));
  centerPanel.add(goodCitizen);
  centerPanel.add(criminal);
  centerPanel.add(new JLabel());  // filler
  centerPanel.add(new JLabel("Salary requirements:"));
  centerPanel.add(salary);

  windowPanel.add(centerPanel, BorderLayout.CENTER);
  southPanel.add(submit);
  windowPanel.add(southPanel, BorderLayout.SOUTH);
  add(windowPanel);
} // end createContents
```

Figure 17.17b JobApplication program—part B

```
//*************************************************************

// Read entered values and display an appropriate message.

private class ButtonListener implements ActionListener
{
  public void actionPerformed(ActionEvent e)
  {
    if (
      (java.isSelected() || helpDesk.isSelected()
                         || coffee.isSelected()) &&

      (goodCitizen.isSelected()) &&
      (!salary.getSelectedItem().equals("above $100,000")))
    {
      JOptionPane.showMessageDialog(null,
        "Thank you for your application submission.\n" +
        "We'll contact you after we process your information.");
    }
    else
    {
      JOptionPane.showMessageDialog(null,
        "Sorry, no jobs at this time.");
    }
  } // end actionPerformed
} // end class ButtonListener

//*************************************************************

public static void main(String[] args)
{
  new JobApplication();
}
} // end class JobApplication
```

Figure 17.17c JobApplication program—part C

which is what you want. In calling the `EmptyBorder` constructor, you'll need to pass in pixel values for the widths of the border's top, left, bottom, and right sides. For example, this constructor call passes in 10-pixel values for all four of the border's sides:

```
windowPanel.setBorder(new EmptyBorder(10, 10, 10, 10));
```

Be aware that the `EmptyBorder` class is in the `javax.swing.border` package. So import that package if you want to create an empty border.

You might think that the `setBorder` method works for all containers. Not so. It works for the `JPanel` container, but not the `JFrame` container. Therefore, you need to add a `JPanel` container to the `JobApplication` `JFrame` window and call `setBorder` from the `JPanel` container.

Use a panel.

What type of layout manager is appropriate for the new `JPanel` container? If you use a `GridLayout` manager, that works OK, but not great. With a `GridLayout`, all rows are the same height. In Figure 17.16,

Intended layout:

Intended layout:
Skills (check all that apply):
Java Sun certified
help-desk experience
able to make good coffee
<filler>
Community standing:
law-abiding citizen
violent criminal
<filler>
Salary requirements:
$20,000-$59,000
<filler>
Submit

Actual layout:
Skills (check all that apply):
Java Sun certified
help-desk experience
able to make good coffee
Community standing:
law-abiding citizen
violent criminal
Salary requirements:
$20,000-$59,000
<filler>
Submit

Figure 17.18 Intended versus actual layouts with 13-row by 1-column `GridLayout` scheme

note how the Submit button is slightly taller than the other components. The Submit button's added height provides a visual cue for the button's importance. To accommodate the button being taller than the other components, use a `BorderLayout` manager. Add the button panel to the south region and add all the other components to the center region. Actually, since the center region allows for only one component, you need to add the components to a `GridLayout` panel and then add the `GridLayout` panel to the center region.

Document Difficult Code

The JobApplication program's layout design is rather complicated and somewhat non-intuitive. If you ever write complicated and non-intuitive code, you should document it with detailed comments. If you don't, then someone (maybe you) might waste time later in trying to figure it out. See all the comments for the panel declarations in Figure 17.17b. Those comments help to clarify the layout-design code.

17.16 More Swing Components

In this chapter and the previous chapter, you've learned quite a bit about the Swing library. Enough to get up and running for most basic GUI needs. If you decide you want to know more, refer to Sun's Java API Web site. In particular, refer to this Web page within Sun's Java API Web site:

http://java.sun.com/docs/books/tutorial/uiswing/components/componentlist.html

It contains picture examples of all the standard Swing components and links to more detailed information. By perusing that Web page now, you'll know what's available.

Menus and Scroll Panes

As a first attempt at learning Swing components on your own, we recommend that you look up the `JMenuBar`, `JMenu`, and `JMenuItem` classes on Sun's Web site. Those classes allow you to add a *menu bar* and *menus* to the top of a window. Also look up the `JScrollPane` class. It allows you to create a scrollable container. See Figure 17.19. It shows a window with a menu bar and a scroll bar. The menu bar contains two menus—one allows the user to adjust the brightness of the window's background color and one

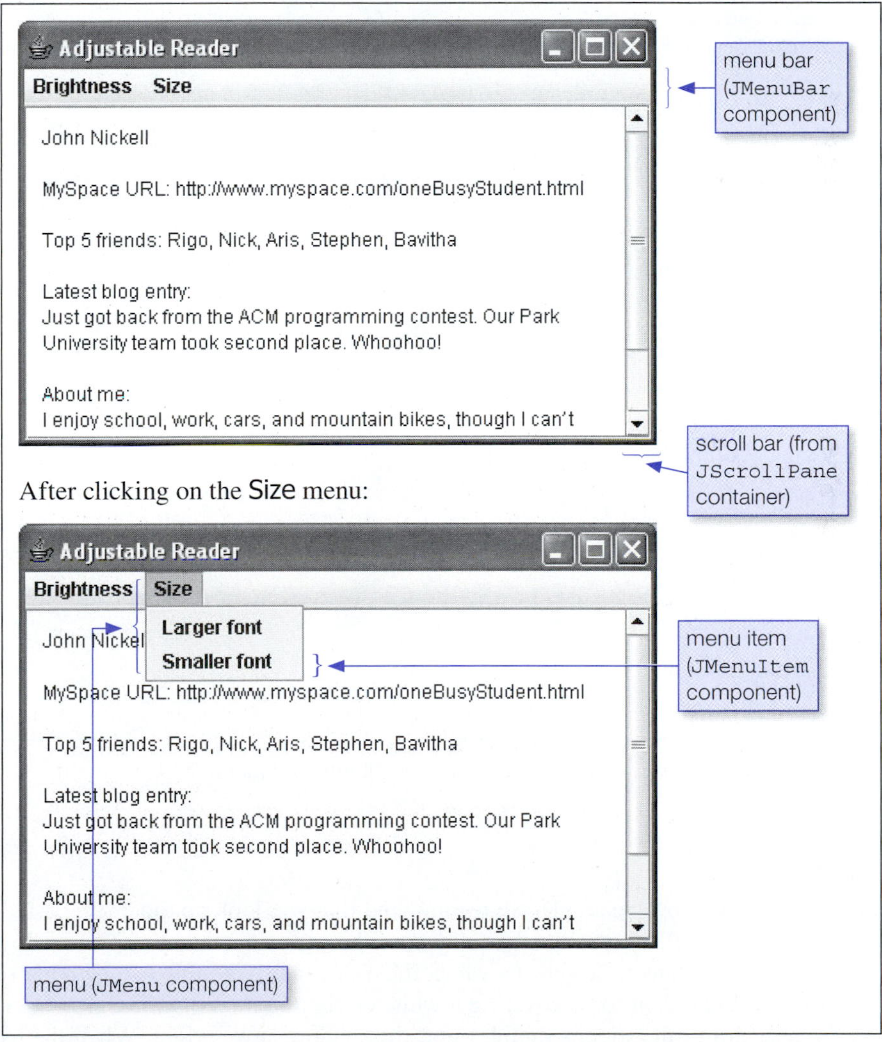

Figure 17.19 A reader program that uses a menu bar and a scroll bar to adjust the view

allows the user to adjust the font size of the window's text. The scroll bar is part of what is known as a *scroll pane*. The scroll bar allows the user to scroll up and down and view the contents of the entire window.

If you'd like to see Figure 17.19's program in its entirety, view the `ReaderMenu.java` file on the book's Web site. Figure 17.20 shows a portion of that program—the portion that creates the menu bar, menus, and menu items. And the following statement shows the portion of the program that creates the scroll pane. More specifically, the following statement creates a scroll pane for a text area component and then adds the scroll pane to the window.

```
add(new JScrollPane(textArea));
```

```
private JMenuBar mBar;                      // the menu bar
private JMenu menu1, menu2;                 // the two menus
private JMenuItem mi1, mi2, mi3, mi4; // the four menu items
⋮
menu1 = new JMenu("Brightness");
menu2 = new JMenu("Size");

mi1 = new JMenuItem("Lighter background");
mi2 = new JMenuItem("Darker background");
mi3 = new JMenuItem("Larger font");
mi4 = new JMenuItem("Smaller font");

mi1.addActionListener(new BrightnessListener());
mi2.addActionListener(new BrightnessListener());
mi3.addActionListener(new SizeListener());
mi4.addActionListener(new SizeListener());

menu1.add(mi1);
menu1.add(mi2);
menu2.add(mi3);
menu2.add(mi4);

mBar = new JMenuBar();
mBar.add(menu1);
mBar.add(menu2);
setJMenuBar(mBar);
```

Figure 17.20 Code that creates menu bar, menus, and menu items for Figure 17.19's program

Sliders

For another learn-on-your-own example, we recommend that you look up the `JSlider` class on Sun's Web site. The `JSlider` class allows you to add a *slider* component to a window. A slider allows the user to select a value from a range of values. To select a value, the user drags a "thumb" along a bar of values. See Figure 17.21. It mimics a lunar eclipse by covering a white circle (the moon) with a gray circle (the earth's shadow). When the user drag's the slider's thumb right, the shadow moves right. When the user drag's the slider's thumb left, the shadow moves left. The slider uses an event handler to adjust the shadow's position.

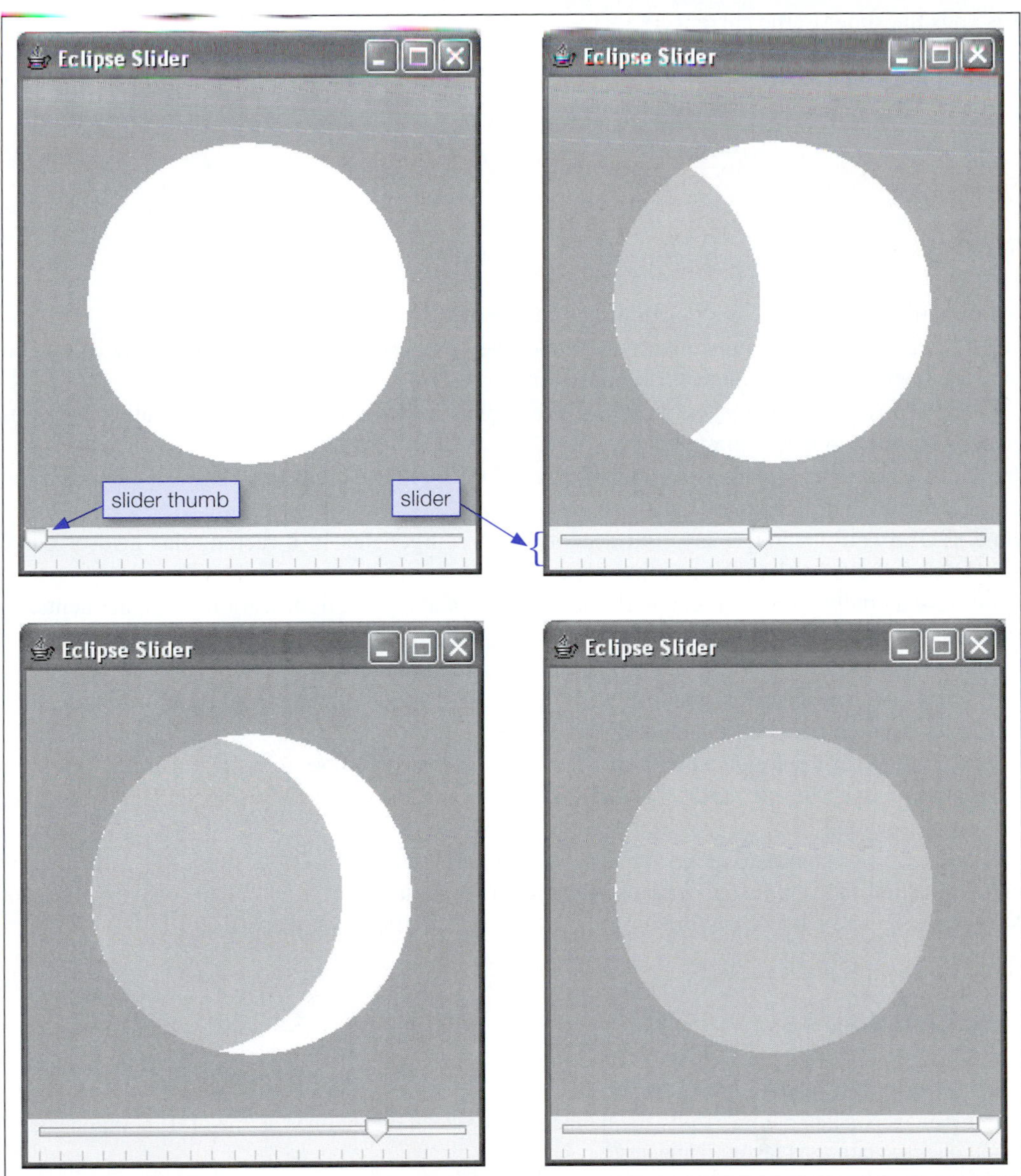

Figure 17.21 Four displays of a window that uses a slider to mimic an eclipse

The following code from the lunar eclipse program shows how to instantiate a slider, set properties, and add a listener:

```
slider = new JSlider(SwingConstants.HORIZONTAL, 0, 100, 0);
slider.setMajorTickSpacing(5);
slider.setPaintTicks(true);
slider.addChangeListener(new Listener());
```

This adds the slider to the current `JFrame`:

```
add(slider, BorderLayout.SOUTH);
```

If you'd like to see Figure 17.21's program in its entirety, view the `EclipseSlider.java` file on the book's Web site.

Summary

- Layout managers automate the positioning of components within containers.
- The `FlowLayout` class implements a simple one-compartment layout scheme that allows multiple components to be inserted into the compartment.
- The `BorderLayout` manager provides five regions/compartments—north, south, east, west, and center—in which to insert components.
- The `SwingConstants` interface stores a set of GUI-related constants that are commonly used by many different GUI programs.
- The `GridLayout` manager lays out a container's components in a rectangular grid of equal-sized cells. Each cell can hold only one component.
- If you have a complicated window with many components, you might want to compartmentalize them by storing groups of components in `JPanel` containers.
- To display multiple lines of text, use a `JTextArea` component.
- A `JCheckBox` component displays a small square with an identifying label. Users click the check box in order to toggle it between selected and unselected.
- A `JRadioButton` component displays a small circle with a label to its right. If an unselected button is clicked, the clicked button becomes selected, and the previously selected button in the group becomes unselected.
- A `JComboBox` component allows the user to select an item from a list of items. `JComboBox` components are called "combo boxes" because they are a combination of a text box (normally, they look just like a text box) and a list (when the down arrow is clicked, they look like a list).

Review Questions

§17.2 GUI Design and Layout Managers

1. Layout managers adapt automatically to changes in the size of a container or one of its components. (T / F)
2. Which package contains layout managers?

§17.3 `FlowLayout` Manager

3. How does the `FlowLayout` manager arrange components?
4. Write a single statement that gives the current container a flow layout with right alignment.

§17.4 `BorderLayout` Manager

5. What are the five regions established by the `BorderLayout` manager?
6. The sizes of the five regions in a border layout are determined at runtime based on the contents of the four outer regions. (T / F)
7. By default, how many components can you put in any one region of a border layout?
8. Write a single statement that adds a new `JLabel` with the text "Stop" to the center region of a `BorderLayout` manager. The label should be centered within the center region.

§17.5 `GridLayout` Manager

9. When you instantiate a `GridLayout` manager, you should always specify both the number of rows and the number of columns. (T / F)
10. In a grid layout, all cells are the same size. (T / F)

§17.6 Tic-Tac-Toe Example

11. What happens to the `xTurn` variable in the Tic-Tac-Toe program if you click the same cell twice?

§17.9 `JPanel` Class

12. Why are `JPanel` containers particularly useful with `GridLayout` and `BorderLayout` windows (as opposed to `FlowLayout` windows)?

§17.10 `MathCalculator` Program

13. In the MathCalculator program's `createContents` method, what's the purpose of the `add(new JLabel());` statement?

§17.11 `JTextArea` Component

14. JTextArea components are editable by default. (T / F).
15. JTextArea components employ line wrap by default. (T / F).

§17.12 `JCheckBox` Component

16. What happens if you click a check box that's already selected?
17. Provide a statement that creates a check box named `attendance`. The check box should be pre-selected, and it should have an "I will attend" label.

§17.13 `JRadioButton` Component

18. What happens if you click a radio button that is already selected?
19. What happens if you click an initially unselected radio button that is a member of a `RadioGroup`?

§17.14 `JComboBox` Component

20. How are combo boxes and radio button groups similar?
21. What two methods can be called to determine the current selection for a combo box?

§17.15 Job Application Example

22. The JobApplication program contains the following code fragment. What happens to the program if the code fragment is omitted?

```
radioGroup = new ButtonGroup();
radioGroup.add(goodCitizen);
radioGroup.add(criminal);
```

23. Provide a statement that adds a 20-pixel blank margin to a `JPanel` container named `panel`.

§17.16 More Swing Components

24. Provide a `JSlider` constructor call where the minimum value is 0, the maximum value is 50, and the initial value is 10. Hint: Look up the answer on Sun's Java API Web site.

Exercises

1. [after §17.2] What is the default layout manager for a `JFrame` window?
2. [after §17.3] With a `FlowLayout` manager, a button component expands so that it completely fills the size of the region in which it is placed. (T / F)

3. [after §17.4] Provide a complete program that is a modification of Chapter 16's Greeting program. Your new program should use a `BorderLayout` manager (instead of a `FlowLayout` manager), and it should generate the following display after a name has been entered. Make the frame size 300 pixels wide and 80 pixels high.

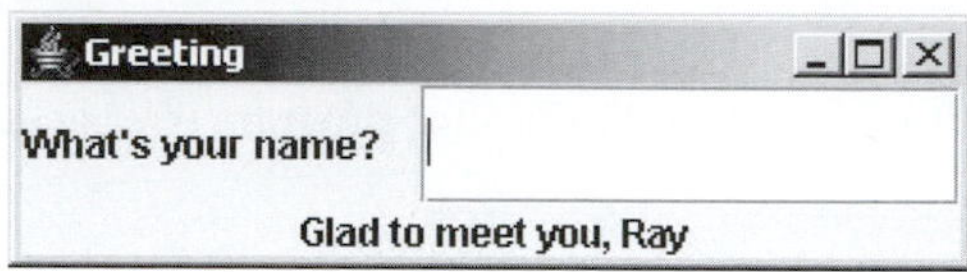

4. [after §17.4] With a `BorderLayout`, what happens if the east region is empty? Said another way, which region(s), if any, expand(s) if the east region is empty?

5. [after §17.4] Assume you have this program:

```
import javax.swing.*;
import java.awt.*;

public class BorderLayoutExercise extends JFrame
{
  public BorderLayoutExercise()
  {
    setTitle("Border Layout Exercise");
    setSize(300, 200);
    setDefaultCloseOperation(EXIT_ON_CLOSE);
    setLayout(new BorderLayout());
    add(new JLabel("Lisa the label"), BorderLayout.NORTH);
    add(new JLabel("LaToya the label"), BorderLayout.CENTER);
    add(new JLabel("Lemmy the label"), BorderLayout.SOUTH);
    setVisible(true);
  } // end BorderLayoutExercise constructor

  //*****************************************************

  public static void main(String[] args)
  {
    new BorderLayoutExercise();
  }
} // end class BorderLayoutExercise
```

(a) Specify the changes you would make to the above code to produce this output:

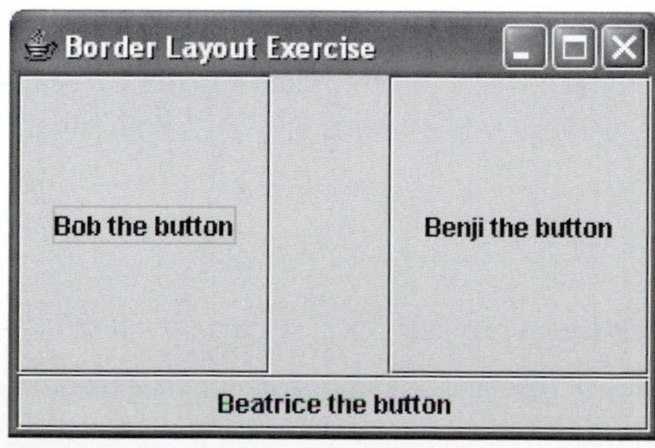

(b) Specify the changes you would make to the above code to produce this output:

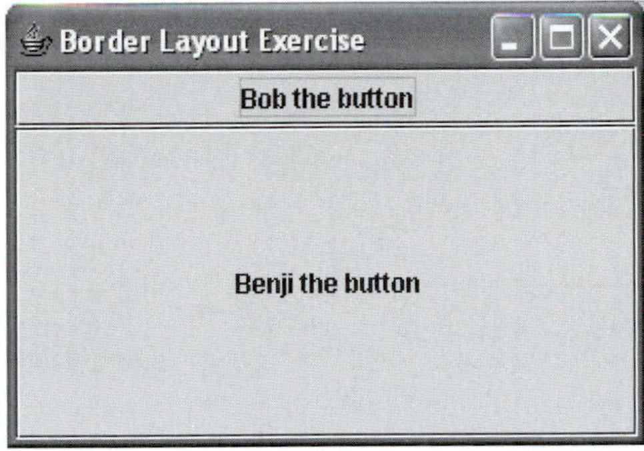

6. [after §17.5] If a `JButton` component is directly added to a `GridLayout` cell, it expands so that it completely fills the size of its cell. (T / F)

7. [after §17.5] Given the following code fragment, draw a picture that illustrates the buttons' positions within the program's window.

```
setLayout(new GridLayout(0, 3));
add(new JButton("1"));
add(new JButton("2"));
add(new JButton("3"));
add(new JButton("4"));
add(new JButton("5"));
add(new JButton("6"));
add(new JButton("7"));
```

8. [after §17.9] What kind of container should you put into an individual grid layout cell or an individual border layout region to allow that cell or region to contain more than one component?

9. [after §17.11] Suppose you're given a window with two `JTextArea` components, named `msg1` and `msg2`, and a `JButton` component. When clicked, the button swaps the contents of the two text areas. Provide the code that performs the swap operation. More specifically, provide the code that goes inside the below `actionPerformed` method:

```
private class Listener implements ActionListener
{
  public void actionPerformed(ActionEvent e)
  {
    ...
  }
}
```

10. [after §17.12] Provide a statement that creates a check box named `bold`. The check box should be unselected, and it should have a "boldface type" label.

11. [after §17.12] How can your code determine whether a check box is selected or not?

12. [after §17.13] Provide a `createContents` method for a program that displays this window:

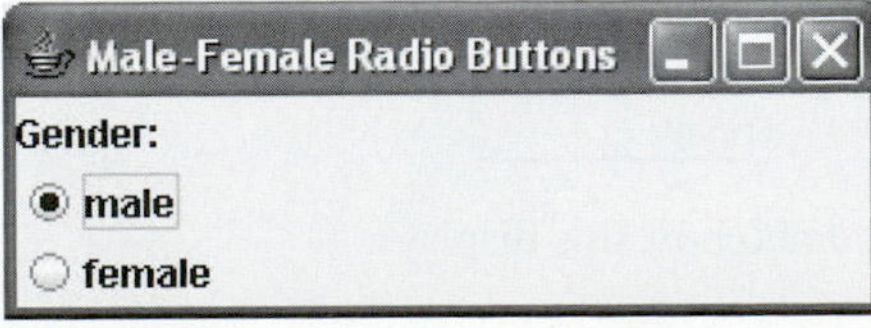

The male and female radio buttons should behave in the normal fashion—when one is selected, the other is unselected. Note that the male button is selected when the window initially displays. Your `createContents` method must work in conjunction with this program skeleton:

```
import javax.swing.*;
import java.awt.*;

public class MaleFemaleRadioButtons extends JFrame
{
  private JRadioButton male;
  private JRadioButton female;

  public MaleFemaleRadioButtons()
  {
    setTitle("Male-Female Radio Buttons");
    setSize(275, 100);
    setDefaultCloseOperation(EXIT_ON_CLOSE);
    createContents();
    setVisible(true);
  } // end MaleFemaleRadioButtons constructor

  <The createContents method goes here.>

  public static void main(String[] args)
  {
    new MaleFemaleRadioButtons();
  }
} // end class MaleFemaleRadioButtons
```

13. [after §17.14] The `JCheckBox`, `JRadioButton`, and `JComboBox` components are defined in what package?

14. [after §17.14] Provide a `createContents` method for a program that initially displays this window:

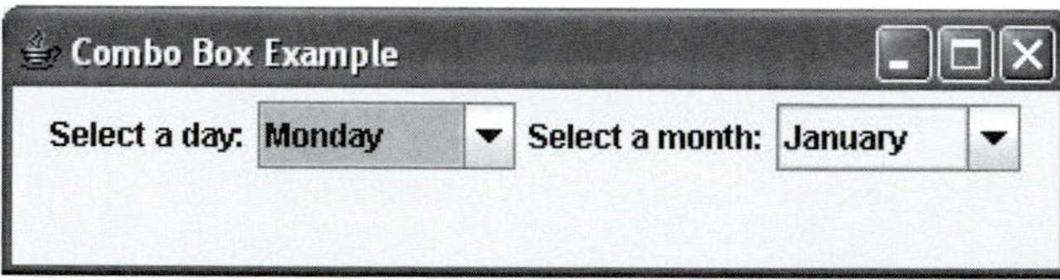

When the user clicks the left combo box, this displays:

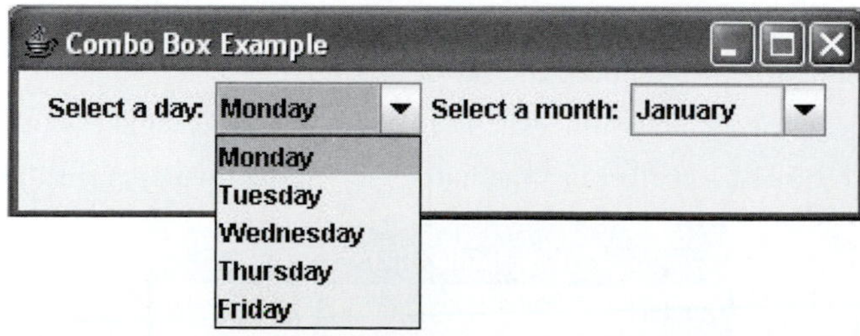

When the user clicks the right combo box, this displays:

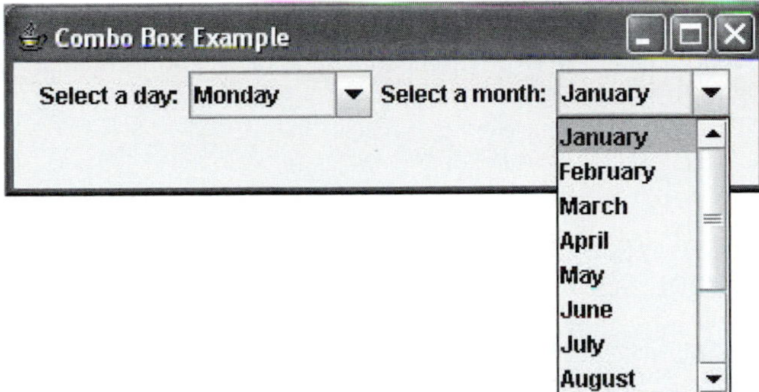

Your `createContents` method must work in conjunction with this program skeleton:

```
import javax.swing.*;
import java.awt.*;
public class ComboBoxExample extends JFrame
{
  private JComboBox daysBox;
  private JComboBox monthsBox;
  private String[] days =
    {"Monday", "Tuesday", "Wednesday", "Thursday", "Friday"};
  private String[] months =
    {"January", "February", "March", "April", "May", "June",
     "July", "August", "September", "October", "November",
     "December"};

  public ComboBoxExample()
  {
    setTitle("Combo Box Example");
    setSize(400, 100);
    setDefaultCloseOperation(EXIT_ON_CLOSE);
    createContents();
    setVisible(true);
  } // end ComboBoxExample constructor

  <The createContents method goes here.>

  public static void main(String[] args)
  {
    new ComboBoxExample();
  }
} // end class ComboBoxExample
```

Review Question Solutions

1. True.
2. Layout managers are in the `java.awt` package.
3. The `FlowLayout` manager places components left-to-right in a row until it runs out of space, and then it goes to the next row and does the same thing, and so on.

4. `setLayout(new FlowLayout(FlowLayout.RIGHT));`

5. The five regions of a border layout are North at the top, South at the bottom, and West, Center, and East in a row between them.

6. True.

7. Zero or one.

8. `add(new JLabel("Stop", SwingConstants.CENTER),`
   `BorderLayout.CENTER);`
   or
   `add(new JLabel("Stop", SwingConstants.CENTER));`

9. False. Specify both values, for rows and columns, only if you know the number of rows and columns in your table and the table is completely filled in (i.e., there are no empty cells). Otherwise, specify just one dimension that you're sure of and specify zero for the other dimension.

10. True.

11. Nothing. It does not change value.

12. `JPanel` containers are particularly useful with `GridLayout` and `BorderLayout` windows because each compartment in those layouts can store only one component. If you need a compartment to store more than one component, let that one component be a `JPanel` container, and put multiple components into the `JPanel` container.

13. The `add(new JLabel());` statement adds a dummy component (a blank label) to the bottom-left cell. The dummy component is necessary because, without it, the `xLogPanel` would go into the bottom-left cell, and that's inappropriate.

14. True. `JTextArea` components are editable by default.

15. False. `JTextArea` components do not employ line wrap by default.

16. If you click a check box that's already selected, the check box becomes unselected.

17. The following code creates a check box named `attendance`. The check box is pre-selected, and it has an "I will attend" label.

```
JCheckBox attendance = new JCheckBox("I will attend", true);
```

18. Nothing. It stays selected.

19. The clicked button becomes selected and all other buttons in the group become unselected.

20. Combo boxes and radio button groups are similar in that they both allow the user to select one item from a list of items.

21. To determine the current selection for a combo box, call either `getSelectedItem` or `getSelectedIndex`.

22. If the `radioGroup` code is omitted from the JobApplication program, the program still compiles and runs, but the radio buttons operate independently. In other words, clicking one radio button will not cause the other one to be unselected.

23. This statement adds a 20-pixel blank margin to a `JPanel` container named `panel`:

```
panel.setBorder(new EmptyBorder(20, 20, 20, 20));
```

24. `JSlider` constructor call:

```
new JSlider(0, 50, 10);
```

APPENDIX 1

Unicode/ASCII Character Set with Hexadecimal Codes

Java assigns a unique two-byte numerical code value to each character in accordance with the Unicode standard. Since two bytes contain a total of 16 bits, this provides a total of $2^{16} = 65{,}536$ different codes. Chapter 11's Figure 11.4 describes or shows those characters whose code values lie in the range 0 to decimal 127. In this particular range of code values, Unicode code values coincide exactly with ASCII code values. (ASCII = American Standard Code for Information Interchange.)

Hexadecimal numbers use digits that can have one of 16 values. The allowed values are 0 through 9 and A through F. The A through F values represent the numbers 10 through 15. Figure 11.4 used decimal numbers to represent Unicode (and ASCII) code values in the range 0 through decimal 127. However, sometimes in this numerical range, and especially at higher numerical values, it's more convenient to use hexadecimal numbers to represent Unicode values as well as memory locations. To give you a better feeling for how hexadecimal counting works, and to help you find the hexadecimal values for characters in the important ASCII Character Set, Figure A1.1a displays the ASCII characters with hexadecimal numbers shown alongside the corresponding decimal numbers.

Notice that the hexadecimal code values for the numerical characters '1' through '9' are hexadecimal 31 through hexadecimal 39. Now look at the rest of the ASCII characters in Figure A1.1b. Notice that the code value for the first uppercase letter, `A`, is hexadecimal 41, and the code value for the first lowercase letter, `a`, is hexadecimal 61. To change case, you can simply add or subtract hexadecimal 20. The people who assigned these codes were "thinking" in hex!

In the columns under "Unicode," Figures A1.1a and A1.1b also show the Unicode escape sequence for each character. These are what you use if you want to embed within a `String` any character or symbol that cannot be typed in directly. Each of these Unicode escape sequences puts a `\u` prefix on a four-place hexadecimal version of the code number. (If necessary, we pad the raw hexadecimal number left with zeros to increase the total number of hexadecimal digits to four.) This format enables the standard Unicode escape sequence to accommodate up to a total of $16^4 = 65{,}536$ distinct characters or symbols.

Of course there are many other characters and symbols. For more discussion and information, read the material in optional Section 11.12, GUI Track: Unicode. Figure 11.12 displays a sampling of some of the other available characters and symbols. That display was generated by the program in Figure 11.11, and you can modify that program to display the characters for any other range of codes. For all the details on the Unicode standard, see:

http://www.unicode.org/

code value			character
dec	hex	Unicode	
0	0	\u0000	null
1	1	\u0001	start of heading
2	2	\u0002	start of text
3	3	\u0003	end of text
4	4	\u0004	end of transmission
5	5	\u0005	enquiry
6	6	\u0006	acknowledge
7	7	\u0007	audible bell
8	8	\u0008	backspace
9	9	\u0009	horizontal tab (\t)
10	A	\U000A	line feed (\n)
11	B	\U000B	vertical tab
12	C	\U000C	form feed
13	D	\u000D	carriage return (\r)
14	E	\u000E	shift out
15	F	\u000F	shift in
16	10	\u0010	data link escape
17	11	\u0011	device control 1
18	12	\u0012	device control 2
19	13	\u0013	device control 3
20	14	\u0014	device control 4
21	15	\u0015	negative acknowledge
22	16	\u0016	synchronous idle
23	17	\u0017	end transmission block
24	18	\u0018	cancel
25	19	\u0019	end of medium
26	1A	\u001A	substitute
27	1B	\u001B	escape
28	1C	\u001C	file separator
29	1D	\u001D	group separator
30	1E	\u001E	record separator
31	1F	\u001F	unit separator

code value			character
dec	hex	Unicode	
32	20	\u0020	space
33	21	\u0021	!
34	22	\u0022	"
35	23	\u0023	#
36	24	\u0024	$
37	25	\u0025	%
38	26	\u0026	&
39	27	\u0027	'
40	28	\u0028	(
41	29	\u0029	)
42	2A	\U002A	*
43	2B	\U002B	+
44	2C	\U002C	,
45	2D	\u002D	-
46	2E	\u002E	.
47	2F	\u002F	/
48	30	\u0030	0
49	31	\u0031	1
50	32	\u0032	2
51	33	\u0033	3
52	34	\u0034	4
53	35	\u0035	5
54	36	\u0036	6
55	37	\u0037	7
56	38	\u0038	8
57	39	\u0039	9
58	3A	\u003A	:
59	3B	\u003B	;
60	3C	\u003C	<
61	3D	\u003D	=
62	3E	\u003E	>
63	3F	\u003F	?

Figure A1.1a Unicode/ASCII character codes—part A

code value			character
dec	hex	Unicode	
64	40	\u0040	@
65	41	\u0041	A
66	42	\u0042	B
67	43	\u0043	C
68	44	\u0044	D
69	45	\u0045	E
70	46	\u0046	F
71	47	\u0047	G
72	48	\u0048	H
73	49	\u0049	I
74	4A	\U004A	J
75	4B	\U004B	K
76	4C	\U004C	L
77	4D	\u004D	M
78	4E	\u004E	N
79	4F	\u004F	O
80	50	\u0050	P
81	51	\u0051	Q
82	52	\u0052	R
83	53	\u0053	S
84	54	\u0054	T
85	55	\u0055	U
86	56	\u0056	V
87	57	\u0057	W
88	58	\u0058	X
89	59	\u0059	Y
90	5A	\u005A	Z
91	5B	\u005B	[
92	5C	\u005C	\
93	5D	\u005D	]
94	5E	\u005E	^
95	5F	\u005F	_

code value			character
dec	hex	Unicode	
96	60	\u0060	`
97	61	\u0061	a
98	62	\u0062	b
99	63	\u0063	c
100	64	\u0064	d
101	65	\u0065	e
102	66	\u0066	f
103	67	\u0067	g
104	68	\u0068	h
105	69	\u0069	i
106	6A	\U006A	j
107	6B	\U006B	k
108	6C	\U006C	l
109	6D	\u006D	m
110	6E	\u006E	n
111	6F	\u006F	o
112	70	\u0070	p
113	71	\u0071	q
114	72	\u0072	r
115	73	\u0073	s
116	74	\u0074	t
117	75	\u0075	u
118	76	\u0076	v
119	77	\u0077	w
120	78	\u0078	x
121	79	\u0079	y
122	7A	\u007A	z
123	7B	\u007B	{
124	7C	\u007C	|
125	7D	\u007D	}
126	7E	\u007E	~
127	7F	\u007F	delete

Figure A1.1b Unicode/ASCII character codes—part B

This Web site contains two one-page charts that categorize the world's major alphabets, symbols, and punctuation. You can select the alphabet or type of symbol you want and obtain pictures and code numbers for all the characters in that category.

In addition to the `\u` Unicode escape sequence prefix, there are two other hexadecimal annotations you should know. Sometimes you'll want to use the hexadecimal form of a literal number in a declaration or mathematical formula, because it might be easier or more self-documenting than the decimal form. To do this, just apply `0x` as a prefix to the raw hexadecimal number. For example, to tell the compiler you are writing a hexadecimal number rather than a decimal number, you would write `0x41` to specify the number whose decimal value is 65. If you want to display the hexadecimal form of an integer constant or variable using the `printf` method, use `%x` for the number's placeholder in the format string. If what you are representing is a literal, its form in the data list doesn't matter. It could be either a decimal or a hexadecimal with the `0x` prefix. For example, suppose you want an output like this:

Output:

```
The hexadecimal value for 10 is a
```

You could generate it with this code:

```
System.out.printf("The hexadecimal value for 10 is %x\n", 10);
```

Notice that the hexadecimal output happens to be a lowercase 'a.' Case doesn't matter.

APPENDIX 2

Operator Precedence

The operator groups at the top of the table have higher precedence than the operator groups at the bottom of the table. All operators within a particular precedence group have equal precedence. If an expression has two or more same-precedence operators, then within that expression, those operators execute from left to right or right to left as indicated in the group heading.

1. grouping and access (left to right):

(*<expression>*)	expressions
(*<list>*)	arguments or parameters
[*<expression>*]	indices
<type-or-member> . *<type-or-member>*	member access

2. unary operations (right to left):

`x++`	post increment
`x--`	post decrement
`++x`	pre increment
`--x`	pre decrement
`+x`	plus
`-x`	minus
`!x`	logical inversion
`~`	bit inversion
`new` *<classname>*	object instantiation
(*<type>*) `x`	cast

3. multiplication and division (left to right):

`x * y`	multiplication
`x / y`	division
`x % y`	remainder

4. addition and subtraction; concatenation (left to right):

`x + y`	addition
`x - y`	subtraction
`s1 + s2`	string concatenation

5. bit shift operations (left to right):

`x << n`	arithmetic shift left ($*2^{n}$)
`x >> n`	arithmetic shift right ($*2^{-n}$; same MS bit)
`x >>> n`	logical shift right (MS bit = 0)

Figure A2.1a Operator precedence—part A

5. range comparisons (left to right):

`x < y`	less than
`x <= y`	less than or equal to
`x >= y`	greater than or equal to
`x > y`	greater than
<object> `instanceof` *<class>*	conforms to

6. equality comparisons (left to right):

`x == y`	equal
`x != y`	not equal

7. unconditional `boolean` or bit AND (left to right):

`x & y`	both

8. unconditional `boolean` or bit EXCLUSIVE OR (left to right):

`x ^ y`	either but not both

9. unconditional `boolean` or bit OR (left to right):

`x | y`	either or both

10. conditional `boolean` AND (left to right):

`x && y`	both (if not resolved)

11. conditional `boolean` OR (left to right):

`x || y`	either or both (if not resolved)

12. terniary conditional evaluation (right to left):

`x ? y : z`	if `x` is `true`, `y`, else `z`

13. assignment (right to left):

`y = x`	`y ← x`
`y += x`	`y ← y + x`
`y -= x`	`y ← y - x`
`y *= x`	`y ← y * x`
`y /= x`	`y ← y / x`
`y %= x`	`y ← y % x`
`y <<= n`	`y ← y << n`
`y >>= n`	`y ← y >> n`
`y >>>= n`	`y ← y >>> n`
`y &= x`	`y ← y & x`
`y ^= x`	`y ← y ^ x`
`y |= x`	`y ← y | x`

Figure A2.1b Operator precedence—part B

APPENDIX 3

Java Reserved Words

Java reserved words are words you cannot use for the name of anything you define because they already have special meanings. Most of these words are *keywords*—they play particular roles in a Java program. An asterisk indicates that the word in question is not used in the body of this text.

`abstract`—not realizable. This is a modifier for classes and methods and an implied modifier for interfaces. An `abstract` method is not defined. An `abstract` class contains one or more `abstract` methods. All of an interface's methods are abstract. You cannot instantiate an interface or `abstract` class.

`assert`*—claim something is true. Anywhere in a program, you can insert statements saying `assert` *<boolean-expression>*`;` Then if you run the program with the option, `enableassertions`, the JVM throws an `AssertionError` exception when it encounters an `assert` that evaluates to `false`.

`boolean`—a logical value. This primitive data type evaluates to either `true` or `false`.

`break`—jump out of. This command causes execution in a `switch` statement or loop to jump forward to the first statement after the end of that `switch` statement or loop.

`byte`—8 bits. This is the smallest primitive integer data type. It is the type stored in binary files.

`case`—a particular alternative. The `byte`, `char`, `short`, or `int` value immediately following the `case` keyword identifies one of the `switch` alternatives.

`catch`—capture. A `catch` block contains code that is executed when code in a preceding `try` block `throws` an exception, which is a special object that describes an error.

`char`—a character. This is a primitive data type that contains the integer code number for a text character or any other symbol defined in the Unicode standard.

`class`—a complex type. This block of Java code defines the attributes and behavior of a particular type of object. Thus, it defines a data type that is more complex than a primitive data type.

`const`*—a constant. This archaic term is superceded by `final`.

`continue`*—skip to end. This command causes execution in a loop to skip over the remaining statements in the loop's code and go directly to the loop's continuation condition.

Figure A3.1a Reserved words—part A

`default`—otherwise. This is usually the last case in a `switch` statement. It represents all other cases (cases not identified in previous `case` blocks).

`do`—execute. This is the first keyword in a do-while loop. The continuation condition appears in parentheses after the `while` keyword at the end of the loop.

`double`—twice as much. This primitive floating-point data type requires twice as much storage, 8 bytes, as the older floating-point data type, `float`, which requires only 4 bytes.

`else`—otherwise. This keyword may be used in a compound `if` statement as the header (or part of the header) of a block of code that executes if the previous `if` condition is not satisfied.

`enum`*—enumeration. This special type of `class` defines a set of named constants, which are implicitly `static` and `final`.

`extends`—derives from. This class heading extension specifies that the class being defined will inherit all members of the class named after the `extends` keyword.

`false`—no. This is one of the two possible `boolean` values.

`final`—last form or value. This modifier keeps classes and methods from being redefined, and it says a named value is a constant.

`finally`—last operation. This may be used after `try` and `catch` blocks to specify operations that need to be performed after a `catch` processes an exception.

`float`—floating point. This is an older floating-point data type. It requires 4 bytes.

`for`—the most versatile type of loop. This keyword introduces a loop whose header specifies and controls the range of iteration.

`goto`*—jump to. This deprecated command specifies an unconditional branch. Don't use it.

`if`—conditional execution. This keyword initiates execution of a block of code if an associated condition is satisfied.

`implements`—defines. This class heading extension specifies that the class being defined will define all methods declared by the `interface` named after the `implements` keyword.

`import`—bring in. This tells the compiler to make subsequently identified classes available for use in the current program.

Figure A3.1b Reserved words—part B

`inner`—internal. When followed by the keyword `class`, this specifies that the class defined in the subsequent code block be nested inside the current class.

`instanceof`—conforms to. This `boolean` operator tests whether the object on the left is an instance of the class on the right or an ancestor of that class.

`int`—integer. This is the standard integer data type. It requires 4 bytes.

`interface`—what an outsider sees. A Java interface declares a set of methods but does not define them. A class that `implements` an `interface` must define all the methods declared in that `interface`. An `interface` can also define `static` constants. Another kind of interface just conveys a particular message to the compiler.

`long`—long integer. This is the longest integer data type. It requires 8 bytes.

`native`—indigenous. Native code is code that has been compiled into the (low-level) language of the local processor. Sometimes called machine code.

`new`—fresh instance of. This Java command calls a class constructor to create a new object at runtime.

`null`—nothing. This is the value in a reference variable that does not refer to anything.

`package`—an associated group. In Java, this is a container for a group of related classes that a programmer can `import`.

`private`—locally controlled. This modifier of methods and variables makes them accessible only from within the class in which they are declared.

`protected`—kept from public exposure. This is a modifier for methods and variables that makes them accessible only from within the class in which they are declared, descendants of that class, or other classes in the same `package`.

`public`—accessible to everyone. This modifier of classes, methods, and variables makes them accessible from anywhere. A Java `interface` is implicitly `public`.

`return`—go and perhaps send back to. This command causes program control to leave the current method and go back to the point that immediately follows the point from which the current method was called. A value or reference may be sent back too.

`short`—small integer. This integer data type requires only 2 bytes.

`static`—always present. This modifier for methods and variables gives them class scope and continuous existence.

Figure A3.1c Reserved words—part C

strictfp*—strict floating point. This modifier for a class or method restricts floating-point precision to the Java specification and keeps calculations from using extra bits of precision that the local processor might provide.

super—parent or progenitor. This is a reference to a constructor or method that would be inherited by the object's class if it were not overridden by a new definition in that class.

switch—select an alternative. This causes program control to jump forward to the code following the `case` that matches the condition supplied immediately after the `switch` keyword.

synchronized*—This modifier for methods prevents simultaneous execution of a particular method by different threads. It avoids corruption of shared data in a multithreading operation.

this—the current object's. The `this` dot reference distinguishes an instance variable from a local variable or parameter, or it says the object calling another method is the same as the object that called the method in which the calling code resides, or it yields initiation of object construction to another (overloaded) constructor in the same class.

throw*—generate an exception. This command followed by the name of an exception type causes an exception to be `thrown`. It enables a program to throw an exception explicitly.

throws—might throw an exception. This keyword followed by the name of a particular type of exception may be appended to a method heading to transfer the `catch` responsibility to the method that called the current method.

transient*—may be abandoned. This variable modifier tells Java serializing software that the value in the modified variable should not be saved to an object file.

true—yes. This is one of the two `boolean` values.

try—attempt. A `try` block contains code that might throw an exception plus code that would be skipped if an exception were thrown.

void—nothing. This describes the type of a method that does not return anything.

volatile*—erratic. This keyword keeps the compiler from trying to optimize a variable that might be asynchronously altered.

while—as long as. This keyword plus a `boolean` condition heads a `while` loop, or it terminates a do-while loop.

Figure A3.1d Reserved words—part D

APPENDIX 4

Packages

As you may recall, a package is a group of related classes. In this appendix, we describe the packages Sun created for organizing its library of Java API classes. We then show you how to create your own packages for programmer-defined classes. Finally, we introduce you to some nifty advanced options.

Java API Packages

When you download a version of Java from Sun, you get the API package hierarchies as part of the Java 2 Software Development Kit (SDK). Installation of that "kit" automatically makes the Java API packages part of your Java environment.

Java API classes are organized in package hierarchies. Figure A4.1 shows part of these Java API package hierarchies. Notice that this shows two hierarchies, one with the `java` package at its root, and another

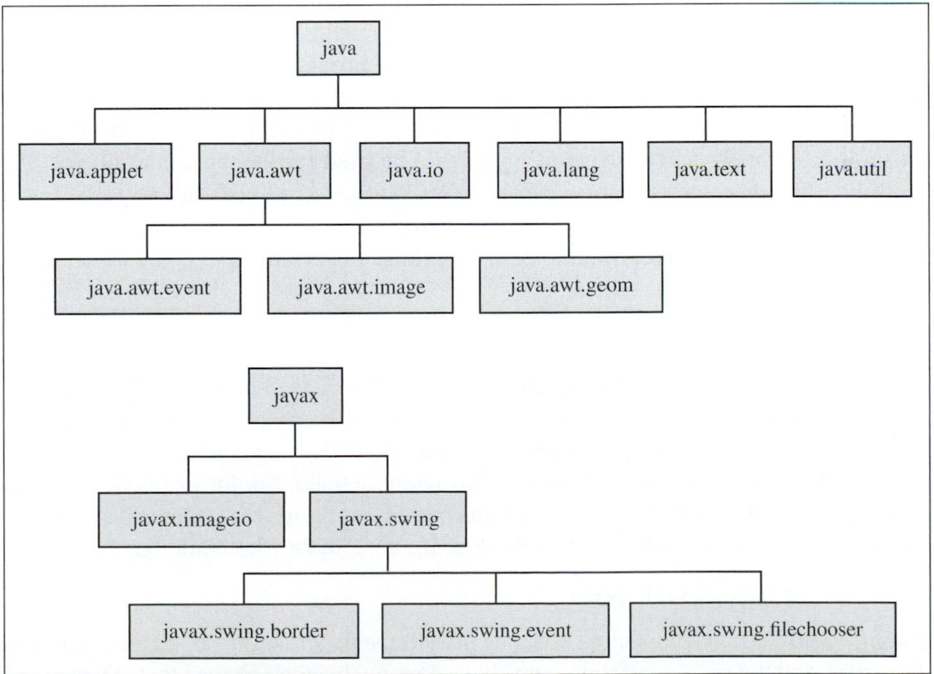

Figure A4.1 Abbreviated Java API package hierarchies

with the javax package at its root. This picture includes all of the API packages we import at some point in this book, but the packages shown in Figure A4.1 are only a small fraction of all the packages in the API package hierarchies.

This hierarchical organization helps people locate particular classes they need to use. It's OK for several different classes to have the same class name if they are all in different packages. So encapsulating small groups of classes into individual packages allows a given class name to be reused in different contexts. Also, each package protects the protected members of the classes it includes from access from outside that package.

To make the classes in a particular package available to a program you are writing, you import that package, as in these statements, which import the java.util and java.awt packages:

```
import java.util.*;
import java.awt.*;
```

Figure A4.1 includes some packages at a third level down from the top. Consider, for example, the java.awt.event package under java.awt in the java tree. When we import the java.awt package in the statement above, this provides access to all classes in the java.awt package itself, but it does not also provide access to packages under it. In other words it does not also import the java.awt.event package. If you also need access to classes in the java.awt.event package, you also must import that package explicitly by adding this third import statement:

```
import java.awt.event.*;
```

Custom Packages

The Java language permits you to create your own packages for organizing programmer-defined classes into package hierarchies. This involves the following steps:

First, design a package structure that makes sense for the program you are creating. Then create a directory structure that corresponds exactly to that package structure. (Later, we'll show how to create this directory structure automatically, but the manual process we're describing now is easier to understand.) Figure A4.2a shows part of a package structure that could be used for this book's examples. Figure A4.2b shows the corresponding directory structure. Note "IPWJ" at the top of both figures. IPWJ is an acronym for our book's title, *Introduction to Programming with Java.*

Whenever you compile a class you want to be in a package, insert this line at the top of the class, above all statements, even the import statements:

package <*package-path*>

The *package path* is a sub-directory path, except it uses a dot (.) instead of a slash (/ or \). The first name in the package path should be the name of the root of the package hierarchy and the name of the highest directory in the part of the directory structure that corresponds to it. The last name in the package path should be the name of the directory that will contain the class being defined. So, for example, if you are defining a Car class and you intend for the Car.class bytecode file to be in the IPWJ.chapter13.things package shown in Figure A4.2a, the first statement in your Car.java file should be:

```
package IPWJ.chapter13.things;
```

When you compile your Car.java source code, by default the generated Car.class bytecode goes into the current directory, and the package statement above does not by itself change that. Thus, if you choose to write your source code in the ...IPWJ/chapter13/things directory, the Car.class file goes immediately into this directory also. If you want this directory to include both source code and bytecode, you're

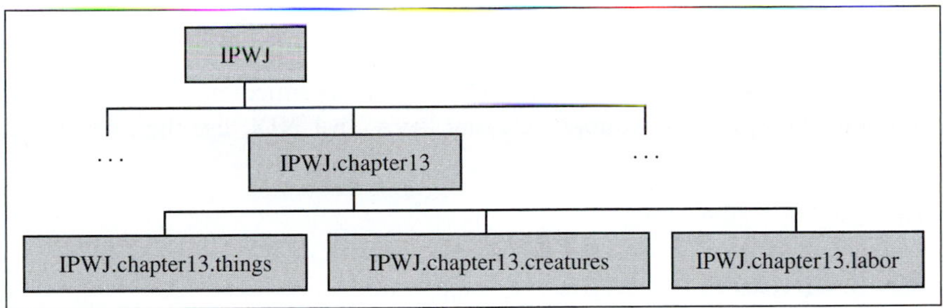

Figure A4.2a A typical programmer-defined package structure

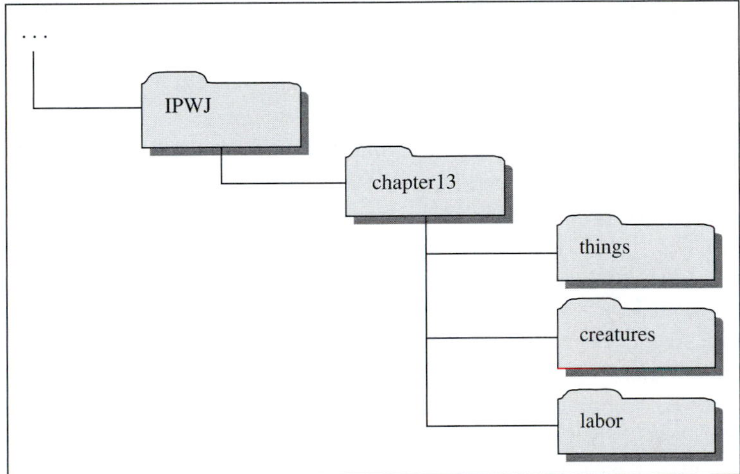

Figure A4.2b Directory structure that corresponds to package structure in Figure A4.2a

done. If you want source code and bytecode to be in separate directories, you'll probably decide to write your source code in a separate source-code directory and then move the generated bytecode to the directory that matches its specified package. (Later, we'll show how you can ask the compiler to move it for you.)

For the Java compiler to import a class that's in a separate package, that class must be accessible through a *class path* that has been established previously in your operating system's environment. There may be more than one class path. On a Windows machine, you can see all registered `CLASSPATH`'s by opening a command prompt window and entering the command, `set`. (In UNIX, the command is `env`.) After `CLASSPATH`, you'll see a list of several class path specifications, with semicolons between them. (In UNIX the separators are colons.) Typically, the first class path in the list is a single dot. That means "current directory." Suppose `myJava` is a root directory in the `C:` drive, and suppose the `IPWJ` directory shown in Figure A4.2b above is in the `myJava` directory. To make classes in the `IPWJ` package hierarchy accessible to the Java compiler, your computer's `CLASSPATH` must include the following path:

```
C:/myJava.
```

Thus, the full pathname of the `Car.class` file in the `things` directory shown in Figure A4.2b would be:

```
C:/myJava/IPWJ/chapter13/things/Car.class
```

In a Windows environment, the appropriate way to add a class path to the operating system's environment is to go to the Control Panel icon and click System. Then under the Advanced tab click Environment Variables. . . .Then select CLASSPATH and click Edit. . . .Add a semicolon to the end of the list, and then enter your desired new class path, for example, `C:/myJava`. In UNIX, use the `setenv` command, like this:

```
setenv classpath .:/myJava
```

Some Advanced Options

Optionally, you can ask the Java compiler to put the compiled `.class` file into your desired destination directory automatically. To do this, invoke the compiler from a command prompt with the `-d` option, like this:

`javac -d` *<class-path>* *<source-code>*

For our `Car` example, this would be:

```
javac -d E:/myjava Car.java
```

The full pathname of the directory that gets the compiled code is *<class-path>*/*<package-path>*. If the destination directory exists already, the generated `.class` file goes into that directory. If it does not exist, the compiler automatically creates the required directory and then inserts the generated `.class` file into it. Thus, if you plan to use this option, you do not need to create the directory structure in Figure A4.2b explicitly. You can let the compiler do it for you as you go along. Typical IDE's also provide ways to do this.

If you are developing a Java application for use by others, you'll probably want to organize your application's classes into a package structure and store the `.class` files in a corresponding directory structure, as previously described. When you have finished developing your application, it's straightforward to use a program like WinZip to compress all your application's files into a single file, perhaps called `IPWJ.zip`. After downloading this `.zip` file, your customer can insert this `.zip` file anywhere in his or her directory structure and then establish a class path to that `.zip` file which includes the name of the `.zip` file itself as the final element in the class path. For example, if the `IPWJ.zip` file is in your customer's `C:/myJava` directory, your customer's `CLASSPATH` should include this class path:

```
C:/myJava/IPWJ.zip
```

This enables your customer's Java compiler to access all of your package classes while they are still in their compressed form. Notice that the class path to a `.zip` file should include the `.zip` file itself, but if you unzip the file, the class path should go only to the containing directory.

Of course, this also works the other way. If you acquire a Java application developed by someone else, it will probably have its classes pre-packaged and compressed into a `.zip` file (or some other type of *archive*). In that case, you may be able to put that compressed `.zip` file wherever you want in your computer's directory structure, and then just add a class path to that `.zip` file, with the `.zip` filename as the final element in that class path.

APPENDIX 5

Java Coding-Style Conventions

This appendix describes Java coding-style conventions. Most of these guidelines are widely accepted. However, alternative guidelines do exist in certain areas. The coding conventions presented in this document are for the most part a simplified subset of the coding conventions presented on Sun's Java Code Conventions Web page:

http://java.sun.com/docs/codeconv/

If you have a style question that is not addressed in this document, refer to Sun's Web page.

While reading the following sections, refer to the example program in the last section. You can mimic the style in that example.

Prologue

1. Put this prologue section at the top of the file:

```
/*********************************************
* <filename>
* <programmer's name>
*
* <file description>
*********************************************/
```

2. Include a blank line below the prologue section.

Section Delimiting

1. After state variable definitions and between constructor and method definitions, enter a line of stars, like this:

```
//*********************************************************
```

Leave a blank line above and below this line of stars.

2. Within a large constructor or method, insert blank lines between logical sections of code. For example, unless the loops are small and intimately related, enter a blank line between the end of one loop and the beginning of another loop.

Embedded Comments

1. Provide comments for code that might be confusing to someone reading your program for the first time. Assume the reader understands Java syntax.
2. Do not comment code that is obvious. For example, this comment is unnecessary and therefore exhibits poor style:

This comment just adds clutter.

```
for (int i=0; i<10; i++)    // for loop header
```

3. Write your programs with clear, self-documenting code in order to reduce the need for comments. For example, use mnemonic (descriptive) identifier names.
4. Always include a single space between the // and the comment text.
5. The comment's length determines its format.

   - If the comment will occupy more than one line, use complete lines, like this:

```
// This is a block comment. Use it for comments that
// occupy more than one line. Note the alignment for /'s
// and words.
```

   - If a comment is to reside on a line by itself, position it above the line of code it describes. Indent the // the same as the described line of code. Include a blank line above the comment line. Here's an example:

```
// Display error if invalid file name.
if (fileName == null || filename.getName().equals(""))
{
  JOptionPane.showMessageDialog(this, fileErrorMsg);
}
```

   - Many comments are small enough to fit in space to the right of the code they describe. Whenever possible, all such comments should start in the same column, as far to the right as possible. The following example demonstrates proper positioning for short comments.

```
float testScores = new float[80]; // index is student number
int student;

...
while (testScores[student] >= 0)   // negative index quits
{
  testScores[student] = score;
  ...
```

6. Provide an end comment for each closing brace that is a significant number of lines (five or more?) down from its matching opening brace. For example, note the `// end for row` and `// end getSum` comments below:

```
public double getSum(float table[][], int rows, int cols)
{
  double sum = 0.0;

  for (int row=0; row<rows; row++)
  {
    for (int col=0; col<cols; col++)
    {
      sum += table[row][col];
    } // end for col
  } // end for row

  return sum;
} // end getSum
```

Variable Declarations

1. Normally, you should declare only one variable per line. For example:

```
float avgScore;        // average score on the test
int numOfStudents;     // number of students in the class
```

   Exception:
   If several variables are intimately related, it is acceptable to declare them together on one line. For example:

```
int x, y, z;           // coordinates for a point
```

2. Normally, you should include a comment for each variable declaration line.

   Exception:
   Don't include a comment for names that are obvious (i.e., `studentId`) or standard (i.e., `i` for a `for` loop index variable, `ch` for a character variable).

Braces That Surround One Statement

1. For `if`, `else`, `for`, `while`, and `do` constructs that execute only one statement, it's good practice to treat that one statement as though it were a compound statement and enclose it in braces, like this:

```
for (int i=0; i<scores.length; i++)
{
  sumOfSquares += scores[i] * scores[i];
}
```

2. Exception:
   If it would be illogical to add another statement to the construct at a later time, you may omit the curly braces when the omission improves readability. For example, this is acceptable for an experienced programmer:

```
for (; num>=2; num--)
  factorial *= num;
```

Placement of Braces

1. Place opening and closing braces on lines by themselves such that the braces are aligned with the line above the opening brace. For `do` loops, put the `while` condition on the same line as the closing brace.

2. Examples:

```
public class Counter
{
  <field-and-method-declarations>
}

if (...)
{
  <statements>
}
else if (...)
{
  <statements>
}
else
{
  <statements>
}

for/while (...)
{
  <statements>
}

do
{
  <statements>
} while (...);

switch (...)
{
  case ... :
    <statements>
    break;
  case ... :
    <statements>
    break;
    ...
  default:
    <statements>
}
```

```
int doIt()
{
  <statements>
}
```

3. Brace alignment is a contentious issue. Sun's Java Code Conventions Web site recommends putting the opening curly brace at the end of the previous line. This is one place where this document's conventions diverge from Sun's conventions. We recommend that you put the opening curly brace on its own line because that helps make compound statements stand out.

4. For empty-bodied constructors, place the opening and closing braces on the same line and separate them with a space, like this:

```
public Counter()
{ }
```

The `else if` Construct

1. If the body of an `else` is just another `if`, form an `else if` construct (put the `else` and the `if` on the same line). See the above brace placement section for an example of a proper `else if` construct.

Alignment and Indentation

1. Align all code that is logically at the same level. See the above brace placement section for examples of proper alignment.

2. Indent all code that is logically inside other code. That is, for nested logic, use nested indentation. For example:

```
for (...)
{
  while (...)
  {
    <statements>
  }
}
```

3. You may use an indentation width of two to five spaces. Once you choose an indentation width, you should stick with it. Use the same indentation width throughout your program.

4. When a statement is too long to fit on one line, write it on multiple lines such that the continuation lines are indented appropriately. If the long statement is followed by a single statement that is logically inside of the long statement, use braces to enclose the single statement. Use either of the following techniques to indent continuation lines:

   - Indent to a column position such that similar entities are aligned. In the example below, the entities that are aligned are the three method calls:

```
while (bucklingTest(expectedLoad, testWidth, height) &&
       stressTest(expectedLoad, testWidth) &&
       slendernessTest(testWidth, height))
{
  numOfSafeColumns++;
}
```

- Indent the same number of spaces as all other indents. For example:

```
while (bucklingTest(expectedLoad, testWidth, height) &&
  stressTest(expectedLoad, testWidth) &&
  slendernessTest(testWidth, height))
{
  numOfSafeColumns++;
}
```

Multiple Statements on One Line

1. Normally, each statement should be put on a separate line.

   Exception:
   If statements are intimately related and very short, it is acceptable (but not required) to put them together on one line. For example:

   ```
   a++; b++; c++;
   ```

2. For assignment statements that are intimately related and use the same assigned value, it is acceptable (but not required) to combine them into one assignment statement. For example:

   ```
   x = y = z = 0;
   ```

Spaces within a Line of Code

1. Never put a space at the left of a semicolon.
2. Parentheses:

   - Never enter a space on the inside of enclosing parentheses.
   - If the entity to the left of a left parenthesis is an operator or a construct keyword (`if`, `switch`, etc.), then precede the parenthesis with a space.
   - If the entity to the left of a left parenthesis is a method name, then do not precede the parenthesis with a space.

   For example:

   ```
   if ((a == 10) && (b == 10))
   {
     printIt(x);
   }
   ```

3. Operators:

   - Normally, an operator should be surrounded by spaces. For example:

   ```
   if (response == "avg")
   {
     y = (a + b) / 2;
   }
   ```

- Special cases:
  - o Complex expressions:
    - —Within an inner component of a complex expression, do not surround the inner component's operators with spaces.
    - —Two common occurrences of complex expressions are conditional expressions and `for` loop headers. See the examples below.
  - o Dot operator—no spaces at its left or right.
  - o Comma operator—no space at its left.
  - o Unary operators—no space between unary operator and its associated operand.

For example:

```
if (zeroMinimum)
{
  x = (x<0 ? 0 : x);
}

while (list1.row != list2.row)
{
  <statements>
}

for (int i=0,j=0; i<=bigI; i++,j++)
{
  <statements>
}
```

Shortcut Operators

1. Use increment and decrement operators instead of their equivalent longer forms. For example:

Do not use	Use this
`x = x + 1`	`x++ or ++x` (depending on the context)
`x = x - 1`	`x-- or --x` (depending on the context)

2. Use compound assignments instead of their equivalent longer forms. For example:

Do not use	Use this
`x = x + 5`	`x += 5`
`x = x * (3 + y)`	`x *= 3 + y`

Naming Conventions

1. Use meaningful names for your identifiers.

2. For named constants, use all uppercase letters. If there are multiple words, use underscores to separate the words. For example:

```
public static final int SECONDS_IN_DAY = 86400;
private final int ARRAY_SIZE;
```

3. For class names (and their associated constructors), use uppercase for the first letter and lowercase for all other letters. If there are multiple words in the class name, use uppercase for the first letter of all words. For example:

```
public class InnerCircle
{
  public InnerCircle(radius)
  {
     <constructor-body>
  }
```

4. For all identifiers other than constants and constructors, use all lowercase letters. If there are multiple words in the identifier, use uppercase for the first letter of all words that follow the first word. For example:

```
float avgScore;       // average score on the test
int numOfStudents;    // number of students in the class
```

Methods and Constructor Organization

1. Normally, each method definition should be preceded by a prologue section. The method prologue contains:

   - a blank line
   - a line of *'s
   - a blank line
   - a description of the purpose of the method
   - a blank line
   - parameter descriptions (for non-obvious parameters)
   - a blank line

   Ideally, all method parameters should use descriptive enough names so that the purpose of each parameter is inherently obvious. However, if this is not the case, then include a list of parameters and their descriptions in a method prologue above the method heading. For example, in a tic-tac-toe program, a method that handles a player's move would be relatively complicated and would require a method prologue like this:

```
//*****************************************************

// This method prompts the user to enter a move, validates the
// entry, and then assigns that move to the board. It also checks
// whether that move is a winning move.
//
// Parameters: board - the tic-tac-toe board/array
//             player - holds the current player ('X' or 'O')

public void handleMove(char[][] board, char player)
{
```

   Assuming you describe instance and class variables when you declare them, you should not provide prologues for "trivial" accessors, mutators, and constructors that just read or write instance and class variables. On the other hand, if a mutator performs validation on a parameter prior to assigning it to its associated instance variable, then it is not trivial, and you should include a prologue with it. The same reasoning applies to a constructor. A simple-assignment constructor should not have a prologue. A validation constructor should have a prologue.

2. In the interest of grouping similar things together, you should omit asterisk lines between trivial constructors, and you should omit asterisk lines between mutators and accessors.
   Assume that a class contains two trivial constructors, several mutator and accessor methods, and two other simple methods. Here's the framework for such a class:

```
<class-heading>
{
  <instance-variable-declarations>

  //********************************************************

  <trivial-constructor-definition>

  <trivial-constructor-definition>

  //********************************************************

  <mutator-definition>

  <mutator-definition>

  <accessor-definition>

  <accessor-definition>

  //********************************************************

  <simple-method-definition>

  //********************************************************

  <simple-method-definition>
}
```

   In the above framework, note that there are no descriptions for trivial constructors, accessors, or mutators, or for simple methods. Note also that there is a line of asterisks above the first mutator, but not above the subsequent mutator and accessors. Those omissions help to make a program more readable by grouping similar things together. Also note that there are no comments above each of the two simple methods at the bottom of the class, but there are lines of asterisks.

3. Place local variable declarations immediately below the method heading. Do not place local variable declarations within the executable code.
   Exception: Declare a `for` loop index variable within its `for` loop header.

Class Organization

1. Each of your classes may contain the following items (in the following order):
   a) class prologue section
   b) `import` statements
   c) constant class variables
   d) non-constant class variables
   e) instance variables
   f) abstract methods
   g) constructors
   h) instance methods
   i) class methods
2. Normally you should place a `main` method and any of its helper methods in its own separate driver class. But it's sometimes appropriate to include a short `main` method within the class it drives as an embedded testing tool. Put such a method at the end of the class definition.

Sample Java Program

```
/*******************************************************************
* Student.java
* Dean & Dean
*
* This class handles processing of a student's name.
*******************************************************************/

import java.util.Scanner;

public class Student
{
  private String first = ""; // student's first name
  private String last = "";  // student's last name

  //***************************************************************

  public Student()
  { }

  // This constructor verifies that each passed-in name starts
  // with an uppercase letter and follows with lowercase letters.

  public Student(String first, String last)
  {
    setFirst(first);
    setLast(last);
  }
```

Figure A5.1a `Student` class, used to illustrate coding conventions—part A

```
//*****************************************************************

// This method verifies that first starts with an uppercase
// letter and contains lowercase letters thereafter.

public void setFirst(String first)
{
  // [A-Z][a-z]* is a regular expression. See API Pattern class.
  if (first.matches("[A-Z][a-z]*"))
  {
    this.first = first;
  }
  else
  {
    System.out.println(first + " is an invalid name.\n" +
      "Names must start with an uppercase letter and have" +
      " lowercase letters thereafter.");
  }
} // end setFirst

//*****************************************************************

// This method verifies that last starts with an uppercase
// letter and contains lowercase letters thereafter.

public void setLast(String last)
{
  // [A-Z][a-z]* is a regular expression. See API Pattern class.
  if (last.matches("[A-Z][a-z]*"))
  {
    this.last = last;
  }
  else
  {
    System.out.println(last + " is an invalid name.\n" +
      "Names must start with an uppercase letter and have" +
      " lowercase letters thereafter.");
  }
} // end setLast

//*****************************************************************

// Print the student's first and last names.

public void printFullName()
{
  System.out.println(first + " " + last);
} // end printFullName
} // end class Student
```

Figure A5.1b `Student` class, used to illustrate coding conventions—part B

```
/***************************************************
* StudentDriver.java
* Dean & Dean
*
* This class acts as a driver for the Student class.
***************************************************/

public class StudentDriver
{
  public static void main(String[] args)
  {
    Student s1;  // first student
    Student s2;  // second student

    s1 = new Student();
    s1.setFirst("Adeeb");
    s1.setLast("Jarrah");
    s2 = new Student("Heejoo", "Chun");
    s2.printFullName();
  } // end main
} // end class StudentDriver
```

Figure A5.2 `StudentDriver` class, used with the `Student` class in Figures A5.1a and A5.1b.

APPENDIX 6

Javadoc

Appendix 5 describes a programming style that's optimized for code presentation in an introductory textbook and students writing relatively simple programs. Most of the suggestions there carry over to professional programming practice. But there are some notable exceptions. In professional programming you need to provide interface information about already-compiled classes like the documentation Sun provides for its Java API classes. This appendix shows how to embed interface information in your Java source code so that a special program called `javadoc` can extract it, convert it into HTML, and display it like Sun displays its description of the Java API.

The `javadoc` executable comes in the same directory as the `javac` and `java` executables, so if you can run `javac` and `java`, you can run `javadoc` also. To run `javadoc`, at a command prompt, enter this command:

`javadoc -d` *<output-directory>* *<source-files>*

The `-d` *<output-directory>* option ("d" means "destination") causes the output to go to another directory. If you omit this `-d` option, by default the output goes to the current directory, but that's not a good idea, because `javadoc` creates many files that would clutter up the current directory. You can put documentation for more than one class in the same directory. Use spaces to separate multiple source-file names with spaces.[1]

Suppose you want to generate interface documentation on the `Student` class whose source code is presented in Figure A5.1 in Appendix 5. Assuming you are currently in the directory that contains the source code, and assuming that you want `javadoc`'s output to go to a subdirectory called `docs`, here's what the command would look like:

```
javadoc -d docs Student.java
```

To see the output, open a Web browser like Windows Explorer, navigate to the `docs` file, and click on `index.html`. Figures A6.1 shows the top part of the interface document that `javadoc` creates—the "Summary" information. This interface document contains an impressive amount of information—but not quite everything we need. For example, it doesn't include the comment in the last line of the prologue that describes the class in general, it doesn't include the comment that describes the two-parameter constructor, and it doesn't include the comments that describe the three methods.

To enable `javadoc` to extract this other information from source code, we need for all interface information to be located immediately above the heading of whatever it is describing. Also, we need for this

[1] To see other options and other argument possibilities, enter `javadoc` by itself.

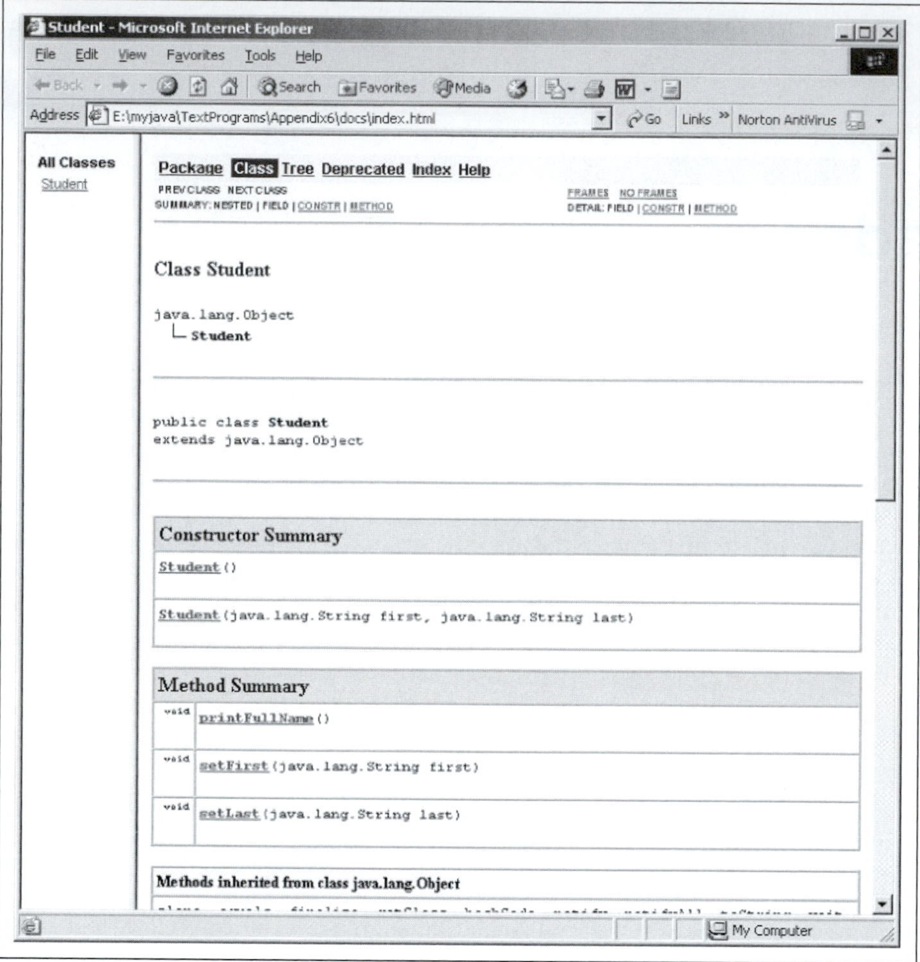

Figure A6.1 Top part of `javadoc` output for `Student` class defined in Figure A5.1

information to be enclosed in a *`javadoc` block comment* that begins with a single forward slash followed by two asterisks and ends with a single asterisk followed by a single forward slash, like this:

/** *<extractable-information>* */

Since Figure A5.1 has an `import` statement between the general prologue and the class heading, we must move our general comment out of the general prologue and put it into a `javadoc` block comment located just above the class heading. Similarly, we must put individual constructor and method interface information into `javadoc` block comments located just above their respective headings. There is some flexibility. The extractable information in one of these `javadoc` block comments does not need to be on just one line. Also, if you wish, you may put the opening `/**` and the closing `*/` on lines above and below the text, as shown in Figure A6.2.

```
/*******************************************************************
* Student_jd.java
* Dean & Dean
*******************************************************************/

import java.util.Scanner;

/** This class handles processing of a student's name. */

public class Student_jd
{
  private String first = ""; // student's first name
  private String last = "";  // student's last name

  //****************************************************************

  public Student_jd()
  { }

  /**
  This constructor verifies that each passed-in name starts with
  an uppercase letter and follows with lowercase letters.
  */

  public Student_jd(String first, String last)
  {
    setFirst(first);
    setLast(last);
  }
```


Figure A6.2 Top part of Figure A5.1's `Student` class, modified to accommodate `javadoc`

With these changes implemented in the `Student.java` code, Figure A6.3 shows the top part of what `javadoc` generates. If you compare this with Figure A6.1, you'll see that Figure A6.3 includes the general comment for the whole class and the special comment for the two-parameter constructor. We also changed the rest of the code so that `Student_jd` has `/** ... */` `javadoc` block comments above the method headings too. Therefore, the `javadoc` output also includes special comments for each method. The constructor and method comments also appear in the "Detail" parts of the output display, which is below what you see in Figures A6.1 and A6.3.

Within a `/** ... */` `javadoc` comment block, `javadoc` also recognizes several special *tags,* which enable it to extract other kinds of information. For a complete description, see:

http://java.sun.com/j2se/javadoc/

Figure A6.4 contains an abbreviated list of `javadoc` tags.

The most important tags are the `@param` and the `@return` tags. Figure A6.5 shows a class originally defined in Figure 13.11 but with its comments modified for `javadoc`. The functionality of this class is

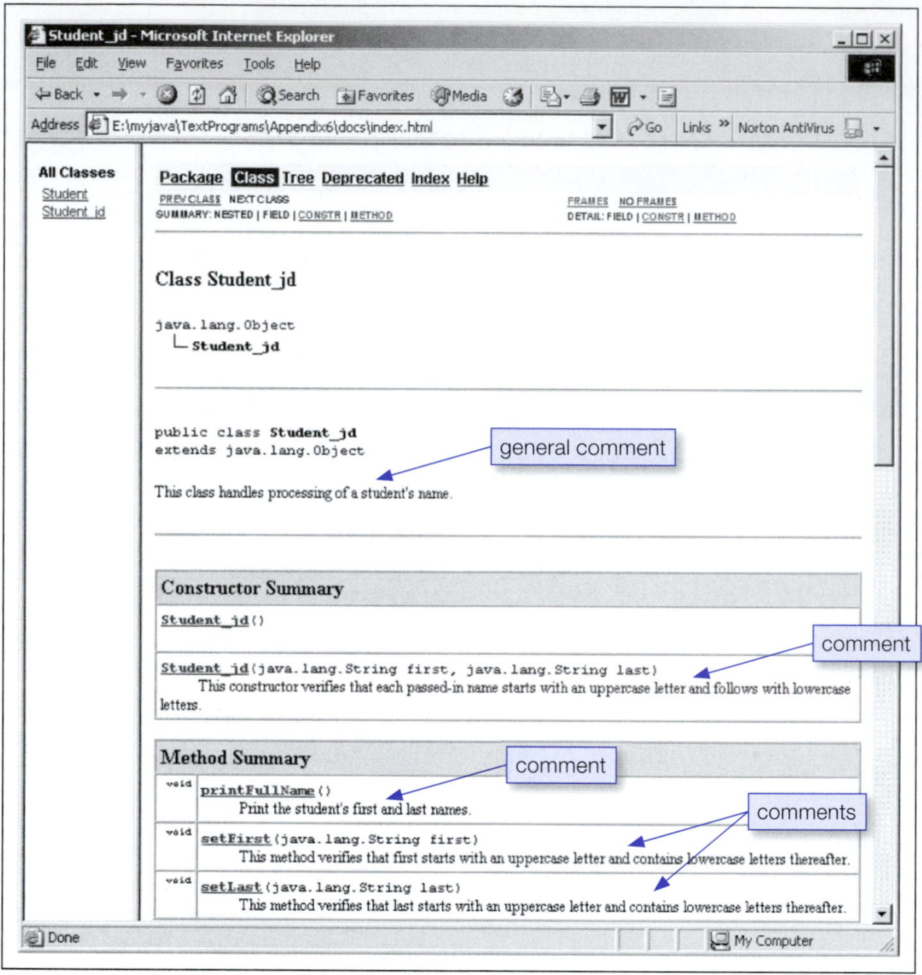

Figure A6.3 Top part of `javadoc` output for modified `Student` class

Description of a constructor or method parameter:
`@param` *<parameter-name>* *<explanation>*

Description of a return value:
`@return` *<explanation>*

Description of an exception that might be thrown:
`@throws` *<exception_type>* *<explanation>*

Hyperlink reference to another documented item:
`@see` *<package-name>*`.`*<class-name>*
`@see` *<package-name>*`.`*<class-name>*`#`*<method-name>*`(`*<type1>*`, ...)`
`@see` *<package-name>*`.`*<class-name>*`#`*<variable-name>*

Figure A6.4 Abbreviated list of `javadoc` tags

```
/*************************************************************
* Salaried_jd.java
* Dean & Dean
*************************************************************/

/**
This class implements a salaried employee.
It has same functionality as the Salaried class in Chapter 13.
*/

public class Salaried_jd extends Employee
{
  private double salary;

  //**********************************************************

  /**
  @param name    person's name
  @param salary  annual salary in dollars
  */

  public Salaried_jd(String name, double salary)
  {
    super(name);
    this.salary = salary;
  } // end constructor

  //**********************************************************

  /** @return    half month's pay in dollars  */

  public double getPay()
  {
    return this.salary / 24;
  } // end getPay
} // end class Salaried_jd
```


Figure A6.5 `Salaried` class from Figure 13.11 modified to enable `javadoc`

exactly the same as that defined in Figure 13.11. But this version enables several `javadoc` features. Notice how the general class description has been moved from the prologue into a separate `javadoc` comment block immediately above the class heading. In the `javadoc` comment block above the constructor there are two tagged parameter descriptions. In the `javadoc` comment block above the method there is a tagged `return` value description.

Suppose that the current directory contains source code for the `Employee` class copied from Figure 13.10, and it also contains the source code for the `Salaried_jd` class shown in A6.5. Then suppose we open a Command Prompt window and enter the following command:

```
javadoc -d docs Employee.java Salaried_jd.java
```

This creates interface documentation for both classes and outputs that combined documentation to the `docs` subdirectory. Figure A6.6a shows what you'll see if you open a web browser, navigate to the `docs` directory, click on `index.html`, and select `Salaried_jd` in the left panel under "All Classes."

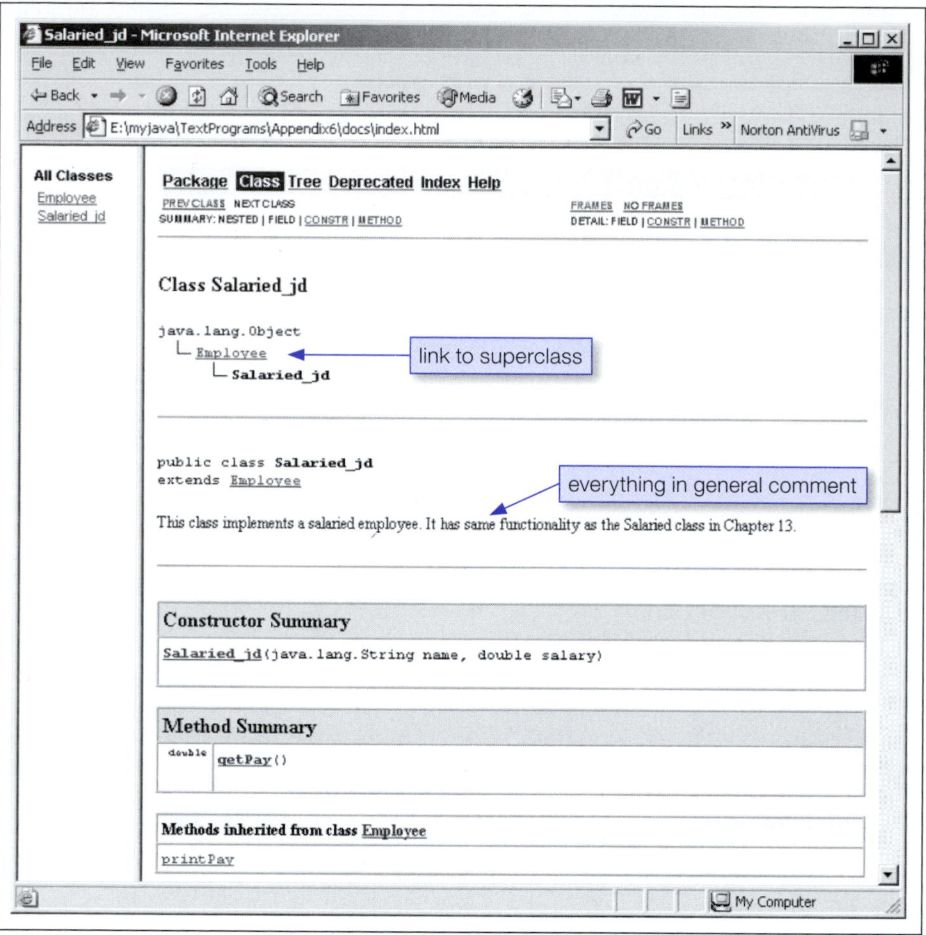

Figure A6.6a `javadoc` output for `javadoc`-commented `Salaried` class—part A

In the right panel, near the top, you can see the documentation of `Salaried_jd`'s inheritance from `Employee`. In the `Salaried_jd` documentation, `Employee` is colored and underlined in several places. These are links, and if you click on any of them, the display switches immediately to the `Employee` class's documentation. In Figure A6.5, our general comment had two sentences, and both of these sentences appear in the general comment in Figure A6.6a. Notice that the constructor and method summary blocks do not contain any comments. The `@param` and `@return` tags do not produce any summary-block output. If we had included text in the `javadoc` comment block above the constructor or method heading in Figure A6.5, only the first sentence of that text (the "summary" sentence) would appear in the corresponding summary block in Figure A6.6a.

Now suppose you use the scroll bar on the right to scroll down. This displays what you see in Figure A6.6b. Notice that the "Detail" blocks do display the tagged parameter and return information supplied in `javadoc` comment blocks above the constructor and method headings in Figure A6.5. If you had included text in a `javadoc` comment block preceding the constructor or method heading in Figure A6.5, all of this text would appear in the corresponding "Detail" block in Figure A6.6b. Finally, notice that `javadoc` also tells us that the `getPay` method defined in `Salaried_id` overrides a `getPay` method defined in `Employee`.

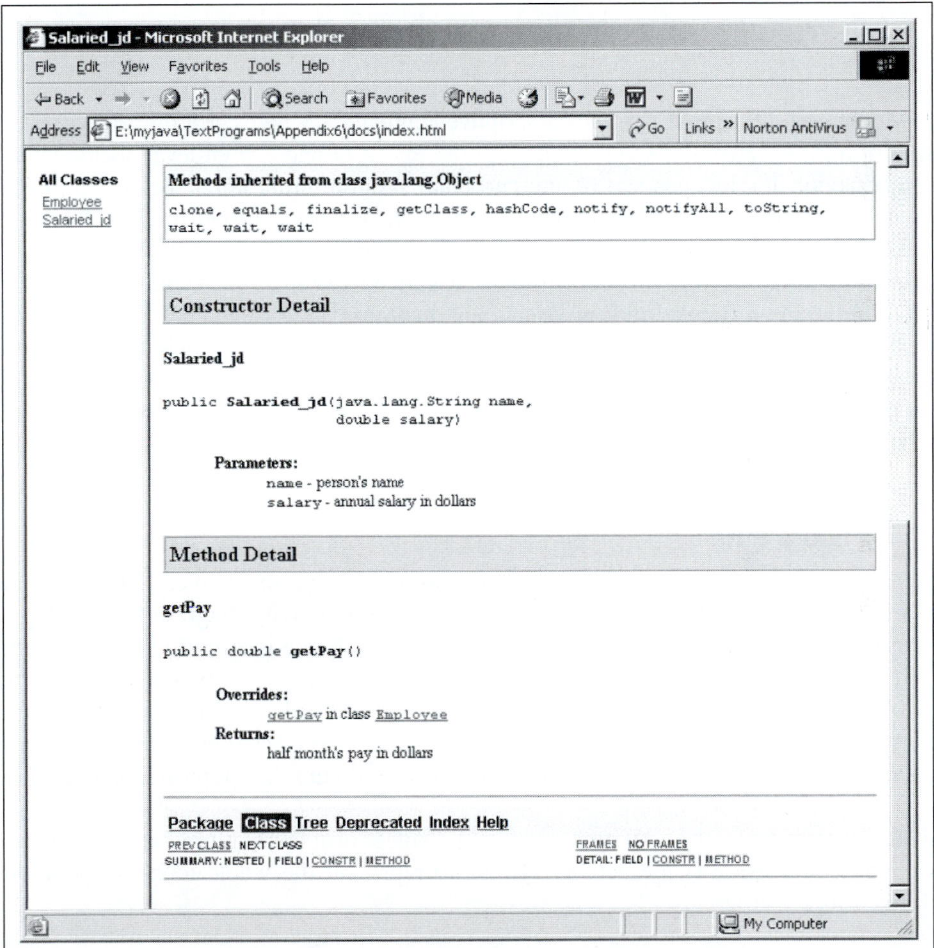

Figure A6.6b `javadoc` output for `javadoc`-commented `Salaried` class—part B

APPENDIX 7

UML Diagrams

The Unified Modeling Language (UML) is a descriptive language that helps program designers organize the subject matter of a prospective object-oriented program, and it provides high-level documentation of both structure and behavior. It's independent of any particular programming language, and it doesn't compile into an executable program. It's just an organizational tool. It was developed by the "Three Amigos"—Grady Booch, James Rumbaugh, and Ivar Jacobson, at Rational Software Corp, which is now part of IBM. Currently it is maintained by the non-profit Object Management Group (OMG) consortium.

UML specifies many different kinds of visualizing diagrams.[1] In this appendix, we'll focus on just two of them—*activity diagrams* (which depict behavior) and *class diagrams* (which depict structure). When UML describes behavior, arrows point to what happens next. When UML describes structure, arrows point to what provides support, and this is opposite to the direction of "information flow." So in the following discussion, be prepared for a switch in arrow directionality as we move from activity diagrams to class diagrams.

UML Activity Diagrams

Activity diagrams are UML's version of the flowcharts we introduced in Chapter 2. They portray an algorithm's flow of control. Figure A7.1 shows an example of a UML activity diagram for the Happy Birthday algorithm presented as a flowchart in Figure 2.9. The solid black circle is an *initial state,* and the black dot in a white circle is a *final state.* The oval boxes represent *action states* or *activities.* They contain informal descriptions of coherent actions. The arrows are *transitions.* The labels in square brackets next to some of the transitions are `boolean` conditions called *guards*—a particular transition occurs if and only if the adjacent guard value is `true`. The actions or activities shown in Figure A7.1 represent low-level or primitive operations.

At a higher level of scale, the activity described in a single oval could represent a whole set of actions. For example, you could use a single activity symbol to represent the whole looping operation shown in Figure A7.1, like this:

print "Happy birthday!"
100 times

[1] The full UML specification is a thousand pages long. For a simple 20-page introduction to the UML specification, see: ftp://ftp.software.ibm.com/software/rational/web/whitepapers/2003/intro_rdn.pdf. For a more complete description, see: Sinan Si Alhir, *UML In a Nutshell,* O'Reilly, 1998. Also see: Ivar Jacobson, Grady Booch, and James Rumbaugh, *The Unified Software Development Process,* Addison-Welsey, 2005.

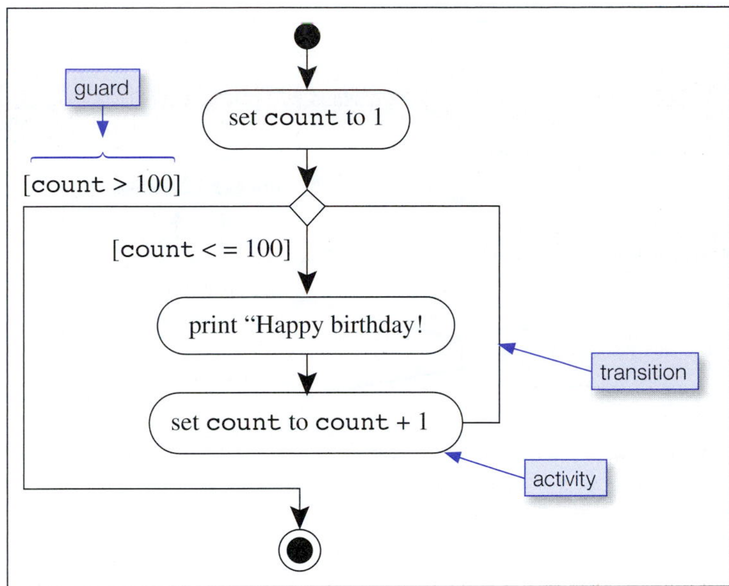

Figure A7.1 UML activity diagram for Happy Birthday algorithm in Figure 2.9

Or you could use a single activity symbol to represent all the actions performed by a complete method. An activity symbol is not supposed to represent code itself. It's supposed to represent the code's "activity." Thus, it's appropriate to repeat an activity symbol that represents a complete method when you call that method more than once.

When there is more than one class and perhaps several objects, UML suggests that you organize the activities into columns, such that all the activities for any one class or object are in a single column dedicated to that class or object. UML calls these separate columns *swimlanes.* Vertical dashed lines separate adjacent swimlanes. At the top of the diagram over appropriate swimlane(s), write the class name for the lane or lanes below. Precede each class name with a colon and put it into a separate rectangular box. When you mean to instantiate an object, write that object's name followed by a colon and its class name. Underline it and put it into a separate rectangular box located just after the activity that creates it.

Figure A7.2 shows the UML activity diagram for the Mouse2 program defined in Figures 6.14 and 6.15. Notice how each activity (oval) is aligned under its own class and (if applicable) its own object. Activities for the lowest-level objects typically represent complete methods. Activities for higher level objects typically represent code fragments. Solid black arrows represent control flow. They always go from one activity to another activity. Notice how the control flow moves continuously downward.

Dashed black arrows represent data flow associated with each activity. They go from an activity to an object or from an object to an activity but never from one activity to another activity. These dashed lines are often omitted to reduce clutter, but you can see how they help to show what the activities do. For example, notice how the dashed line from the "mickey : Mouse2" object to the "print mickey's attributes" activity helps explain what happens and allows us to suppress the two "get" method calls embedded in the print statement:

```
System.out.printf("Age = %d, weight = %.3f\n",
  mickey.getAge(), mickey.getWeight());
```

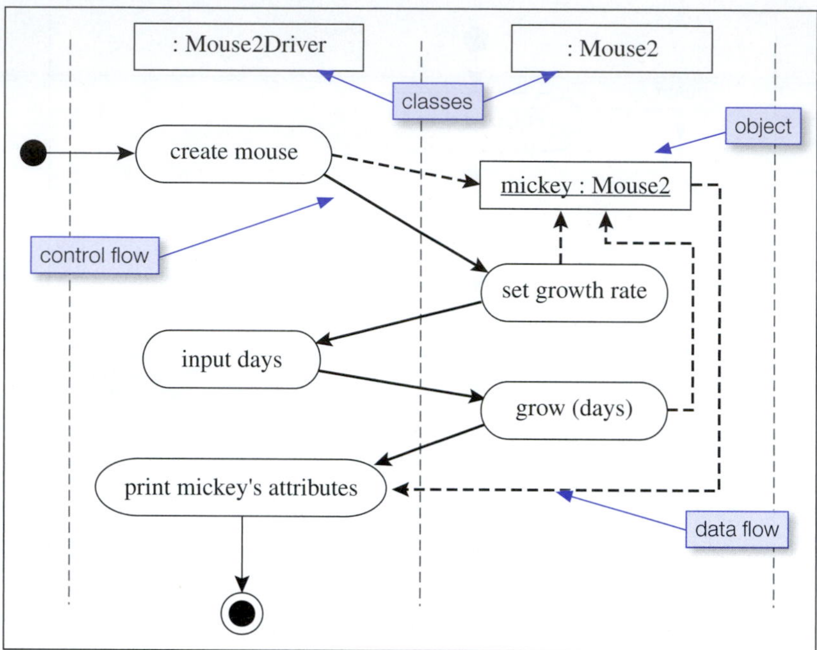

Figure A7.2 UML activity diagram for Mouse2 program in Figures 6.14 and 6.15
Ovals are activities. Rectangles are classes or objects—objects are underlined. Dashed gray vertical lines separate adjacent *swimlanes*, with one lane for each class or object. Solid black arrows represent control flow. Dashed black arrows represent data flow.

The introduction of constructors in Chapter 7 makes it possible to include the "set growth rate" activity within the "create mouse" activity. This would replace the top two swimlane-crossing transitions with a single transition from the "create mouse" activity to the "input days" activity in the same left-side swimlane. Minimizing swimlane crossings is a good design goal.

UML Class and Object Diagrams

Starting in Chapter 6 we gradually introduced you to various features of UML class diagrams. UML object diagrams are similar, except the title (object name followed by a colon followed by class name) is underlined—as in the UML activity diagram in A7.2. An object block does not include a methods compartment, and only those variables of current interest should be listed in the attribute compartment. Object diagrams are context-dependent snapshots, with attribute values being current values rather than initial values. Class diagrams have more general application, and from now on we'll restrict our attention to them.

We'll use a comprehensive example to summarize most of the features of UML class diagrams presented throughout the main part of the book. The example we'll use is the Payroll3 program described in Section 13.9. Figure A7.3 portrays a first-cut class diagram in which each class is represented by a simple one-compartment rectangle that contains nothing more than the class name. The solid lines drawn between related classes are simple association lines. A simple (unadorned) association line implies bi-directional knowledge—the class at each end knows about the class at the other end. Thus a simple line says dependencies are mutual, but it says nothing else about the nature of the relationship between connected classes.

As you progress in your design thinking, you'll flesh out class descriptions, perhaps deciding to make some of the classes `abstract` or converting them to interfaces. In addition, you'll modify many of the

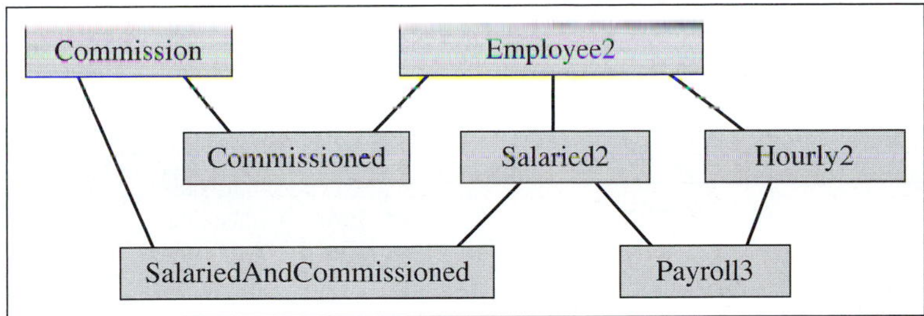

Figure A7.3 First-cut UML class diagram for Payroll3 program in Section 13.9

association lines by adding special symbols that describe particular types of relationships. In addition, you might add barbed arrowheads to convert associations from bi-directional to unidirectional and make dependencies go just one way. Unidirectional dependencies are preferable to bi-directional dependencies because they simplify software management—software changes to one class are less likely to require changes to other classes.

Figure A7.4 contains a fleshed-out and modified version of the first-cut UML class diagram in Figure A7.3. Notice that we italicize the `Commission` and `Employee2` class names. That means they have at least one `abstract` method and cannot be instantiated. We also italicize all the `abstract` methods they contain. Next, look at the hollow arrowheads, which indicate inheritance. Inheritance arrowheads on solid lines indicate extension of a class. Inheritance arrowheads on dashed lines indicate implementation of an interface. The arrowheads point in the direction of generalization—toward the more general entity. The more specific entities know about the more general entities and depend on them. Because of this dependency, changes to ancestor classes or interfaces can force changes to descendant or implementing classes. On the other hand, since an ancestral class or interface does not know about its descendants, changes in descendants or implementations never force changes in ancestors or interfaces. Inheritance is automatically a unidirectional association.

Now look at the composition indicators.[2] We chose to show them as (solid diamond) compositions rather than (hollow diamond) aggregations because the class that instantiates the components (`Payroll3`) inserts anonymous components into its containing array. All the composition lines have multiplicities. These indicate that there is always exactly one payroll and there could be any number of employees of any of the four types. Since `Hourly2`, `Salaried2`, `Commissioned`, and `SalariedAndCommissioned` all descend from the `Employee2` class, we can put instances of all four of these classes into a common `Employees2` array, as we do in the `Payroll3` class definition in Figure 13.17.

Finally, look at the barbed arrowheads we have added to the composition association lines. As we said, all association lines are bidirectional by default, and one design objective is to convert bidirectional associations into unidirectional associations. The barbed arrowheads on the non-diamond ends of the four composition lines do that. They say the composition's components have no knowledge of their container. That's appropriate in this case, because this container is just a driver, and many drivers are ephemeral—here today and gone tomorrow.

Figure A7.4 also includes a dashed association line with a barbed arrow that points to the `abstract` class, `Employee2`. This acknowledges that the local variable called `employees` "depends on" the `Employee2` class because the type of its elements is `Employees2`. The barbed arrow at the `Employees2`

[2] Notice how the association line between `Payroll3` and `Commissioned` arcs over the association line between `SalariedAndCommissioned` and `Salaried2`. This UML detail helps distinguish a cross-over from a junction.

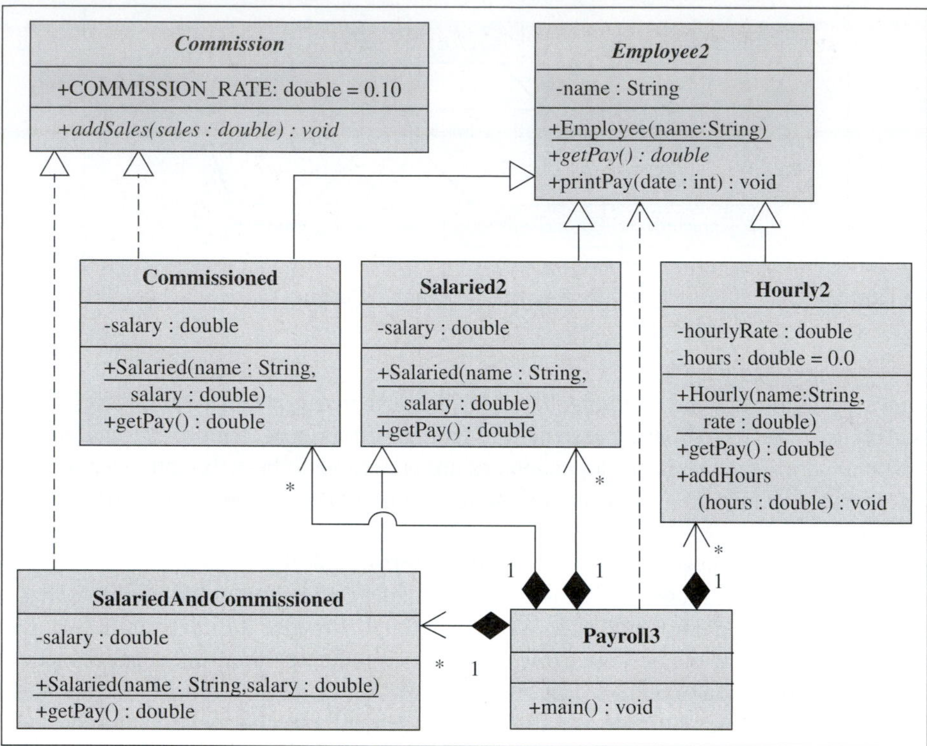

Figure A7.4 UML Class diagram for the Payroll3 program
This shows inheritance from classes and implementation of an interface. It also shows composition. Since every association line in this figure has some kind of arrowhead, all its associations are unidirectional. The dashed association between `Payroll3` and `Employee2` is a simple dependence. That means the `Employee2` type appears in the declaration of a parameter or local variable somewhere in `Payroll3`'s code.

end of this dashed association line indicates that the association is unidirectional. `Payroll3` knows about `Employees2`, but `Employees2` does not know about `Payroll3`. Thus, changes to `Employees2` might require changes to `Payroll3`, but changes to `Payroll3` would never require changes to `Employees2`. UML uses dashed association lines for parameter and local variable dependencies, and it uses solid association lines for instance and class variable dependencies.

As described in the optional section at the end of Chapter 12, UML also uses dashed association lines to connect an association class to an association between or among other classes. Figure 12.22 shows an association line connecting the three classes, `SalesPerson2`, `Customer`, and `Car`. Although we did not discuss this detail in Chapter 12, the fact that this association line is solid and has no barbed arrowheads at its ends suggests that each of these three classes has instance variables that refer to particular instances of the other two classes.

The association class called `Sales` makes these additional references unnecessary, because the `Sales` class can hold all these references itself—in one place. Thus, this extra association class reduces the number of reference variables. More importantly, it eliminates the need to alter the definition of the `SalesPerson2` and `Car` classes when we add a `Customer` class and a `Sale` association to the program. To reflect the fact that the `SalesPerson2`, `Car`, and `Customer` classes do not need any references to instances of other

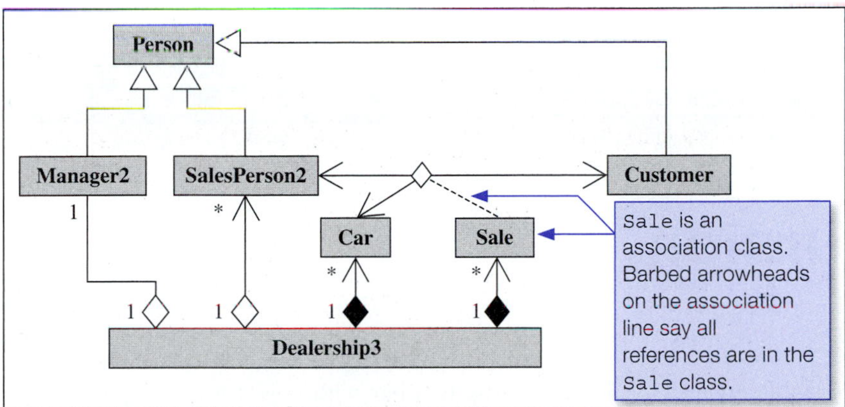

Figure A7.5 Improved version of class diagram in Figure 12.22
An arrowhead on an association line means the adjacent class does not have references to the other classes in that association.

classes in the common association, we put barbed arrowheads on the three ends of the association line that connects them. This changes Figure 12.22 to what appears in Figure A7.5.[3]

Notice that Figure A7.5 also includes a composition association between `Dealership3` and `Sale`. The barbed arrowheads at the `Sale` and `Car` ends of their respective composition lines and at the `SalesPerson2` end of its aggregation line say that `Dealership3` depends on these other classes. In other words, `Dealership3` has references to instances of the `Sale`, `Car` and `SalesPerson2` classes, but not vice versa. In contrast, the aggregation association between `Dealership3` and `Manager2` does not have any arrowheads. This says each has a reference to the other.

[3] Notice the small diamond at the intersection of the `Sale` association lines. This UML detail helps distinguish a junction from a cross-over.

APPENDIX 8

Recursion

To understand this appendix, you need to be familiar with object-oriented programming and arrays. As such, you need to have read up through Chapter 10.

Recursion is when a method calls itself. What follows is a general approach to solving a task with a recursive implementation.

First, identify a way to make the problem progressively simpler, and identify a condition, called the "stopping condition," that is associated with the simplest version of the problem. Use an `if` statement to check for the stopping condition. The `if` body should contain the solution to the simplest version of the problem. The `else` body should contain a call(s) to the same method with an argument value(s) that makes the problem progressively simpler. Once the method is called, it automatically continues to call itself with progressively simpler conditions, until its stopping condition is satisfied.

When the stopping condition is satisfied, the method solves the simplest version of the problem. Then it returns the simplest problem's solution to the previous method execution at the next higher level of difficulty. That method execution generates the solution to its version of the problem. This process of returning simpler solutions to previous method executions continues back up to the original method execution, which generates the solution to the original problem.

Recursion does not add unique functionality—all recursive algorithms can be converted to loop programs that don't use recursion. So why use recursion? Because with some problems, a recursive solution is more straightforward than a looping solution. For example, some mathematical concepts, like the factorial of a number and the Fibonacci sequence, are defined recursively, and they lend themselves well to programmatic solutions that use recursion. And some games, like the towers of Hanoi and maze traversals, can be solved best with recursive thinking, and they also lend themselves well to programmatic solutions that use recursion.

Be aware that there is a downside to recursion. Recursive programs tend to be slow because they generate lots of function calls and function calls have lots of *overhead*. Overhead is work that the computer has to do. For each function call, the computer has to: (1) save the calling module's local variables, (2) find the method, (3) make copies of call-by-value arguments, (4) pass the arguments, (5) execute the method, (6) find the calling module, and (7) restore the calling module's local variables. Whew! All that work takes time. That's why some recursive implementations can be prohibitively slow. For such cases, you should consider rewriting the solution with a loop implementation.

Find the Factorial of a Number

The factorial of a number n is n! = n * (n-1) * (n-2) * . . . * 2 * 1. This is an easy problem, and we were able to solve it entirely within the header of an empty `for` loop in Figure 11.9. So, it's not really a good candidate for recursion in practice. But because it is easy, it provides a nice introductory illustration of how recursion works. The way to make this problem simpler is to reduce the value of n, and the stopping condition is when n = 1. At that point, n! = 1. For any other value of n, we have the relationship:

```
n! = n * (n-1)!
```

This formula is the *recursive relationship* in the calculation of a factorial.

Figure A8.1 contains a Java implementation of the recursive calculation of a factorial. The recursive method, `factorial`, is an "if-else" statement. The `if` condition is the stopping condition, and the `else` body includes a recursive method call, in which the method calls itself. When `factorial` is first called from `main`, its parameter value is `5`, so the stopping condition is not satisfied, and the method calls itself from within the `else` body with the argument value 5 minus 1, which equals 4. This recursive method calling continues until the method parameter equals 1. At that point, the method returns 1 to the previous

```
/****************************************************
* Factorial.java
* Dean & Dean
*
* This program computes the factorial of an integer.
****************************************************/

public class Factorial
{
  public static void main(String[] args)
  {
    System.out.println(factorial(5));
  } // end main

  //************************************************

  private static int factorial(int n)
  {
    int nF; // n factorial

    if (n == 1)  // stopping condition
    {
      nF = 1;
    }
    else
    {
      nF = n * factorial(n-1);
    }
    return nF;
  } // end factorial
} // end Factorial class
```

recursive method call

work on returned value

Output:

```
120
```

Figure A8.1 Use of recursion to calculate the factorial of an integer

	Factorial										
	factorial		factorial		factorial		factorial		factorial		
line#	**n**	**nF**	**n**	**nF**	**n**	**nF**	**n**	**nF**	**n**	**nF**	**output**
12	5	?									
27			4	?							
27					3	?					
27							2	?			
27									1	?	
23										1	
27								2			
27						6					
27				24							
27		120									
12											120

Figure A8.2 Trace of Factorial program in Figure A8.1

method execution, where the parameter value was 2. That method execution returns 2 * 1 = 2 to the previous method execution, where the parameter value was 3, etc., until it gets back to the original method execution, which returns 5 * 24 = 120, as the value for the argument in the `println` method called in `main`.

Figure A8.2 shows a trace of the execution of the program in Figure A8.1. The first call to the `factorial` method is on line 12 in the `main` method with an argument of 5. The next four calls to the factorial method is from within the factorial method on line 27 with arguments of 4, 3, 2, and 1. When the parameter equals one, the stopping condition is satisfied, and `nF` gets assigned the value 1 on line 23. Then, the returning process commences. The 1 from the fifth `factorial` call returns to the fourth `factorial` call, which on line 27 multiplies it by 2 and returns 2. This value returns to the third `factorial` call, which on line 27 multiplies it by 3 and returns 6. This value returns to the second `factorial` call, which on line 27 multiplies it by 4 and returns 24. This value returns to the first `factorial` call, which on line 27 multiplies it by 5 and returns 120. This value returns to the argument of the `println` statement in the `main` method on line 12, and this statement prints out the computed value. In this problem, all the useful work is done in the return sequence, after the stopping condition is reached.

We included the local variable `nF` in the program in Figure A8.1 just to give this trace some substance. Hopefully, it helps you visualize the recursive calling that drills down to the simplest case and the subsequent result accumulation as the nested methods return. In practice, however, experienced programmers would not include the local `nF` variable. Instead, they would probably write the `factorial` method like that shown in Figure A8.3.

Notice that Figure A8.3's implementation extends the stopping condition to `n == 0` to include the case of `0!`, which is also equal to unity.

```
private static int factorial(int n)
{
  if (n == 0)   // stopping condition
  {
    return 1;
  }
  else
  {
    return n * factorial(n-1);
  }
} // end factorial
```

Figure A8.3 Cleaner implementation of `factorial` method

Binary Search of an Ordered Array

Now let's look at another example that is a little harder to implement with loops and makes a better case for recursion. In this case, you'll see that all the useful work is done while the algorithm is drilling down to the stopping condition and the returns just pass the answer back.

Here's the problem: Suppose you want to find the location of a particular value in an array. This is a common database operation. If the array is not sorted, the best you can do is use a sequential search and look at each item, individually. If the array is very short, a sequential search is also the fastest way to search, because a sequential search is very simple. If the array is long, however, and if it's relatively stable, it's often faster to sort the array and then use a *binary* search. (Chapter 10 describes sorting algorithms.)

Why is a binary search faster than a sequential search? The number of steps required for a sequential search equals *<array>*`.length`, but the number of steps required in a binary search equals only $\log_2$(*<array>*`.length`). For example, if there are one million items in the array, that's one million steps for a sequential search but only about 20 steps for a binary search. Even if a typical binary-search step is more complicated than a typical sequential-search step, the binary search will still be significantly faster when the array is very long.

It's appropriate to use recursion to implement a binary search. The way to make the problem simpler is to divide the array into two nearly equally sized arrays, and continue dividing until each half contains no more than one element, which is the stopping condition. Figure A8.4 shows our implementation of this algorithm. We have included shaded print statements at appropriate places in the code to show what the code is doing when it executes. After debugging the program, you would want to remove all of these shaded print statements.

Figure A8.5 shows a driver that demonstrates the binary search algorithm implemented in Figure A8.4. In the output section, the shaded areas are outputs generated by the shaded print statements in Figure A8.4. In this recursion the real work is done while the process is drilling down to the stopping condition. Notice how the `first` and `last` values converge on the match or the place where the match would be if it were there. The answer is generated at the point when the stopping condition is reached. The nested returns just pass this answer back. When you remove the shaded print statements from Figure A8.4, the only output you will see is the un-shaded parts of the output.

```
/*************************************************************
* BinarySearch.java
* Dean & Dean
*
* This uses recursion to find the index of a target value in
* an ascending sorted array. If not found, the result is -1.
*************************************************************/

public class BinarySearch
{
  public static int binarySearch(
    int[] arr, int first, int last, int target)
  {
    int mid;
    int index;

    System.out.printf("first=%d, last=%d\n", first, last);
    if (first == last)                // stopping condition
    {
      if (arr[first] == target)
      {
        index = first;
        System.out.println("found");
      }
      else
      {
        index = -1;
        System.out.println("not found");
      }
    }
    else                              // continue recursion
    {
      mid = (last + first) / 2;
      if (target > arr[mid])
      {
        first = mid + 1;
      }
      else
      {
        last = mid;
      }
      index = binarySearch(arr, first, last, target);
      System.out.println("returnedValue=" + index);
    }
    return index;
  } // end binarySearch
} // end BinarySearch class
```

Do some work.

Then drill down.

Figure A8.4 Implementation of binary search algorithm

```
/*************************************************************
* BinarySearchDriver.java
* Dean & Dean
*
* This drives the BinarySearch class.
*************************************************************/

public class BinarySearchDriver
{
  public static void main(String[] args)
  {
    int[] array = new int[] {-7, 3, 5, 8, 12, 16, 23, 33, 55};

    System.out.println(BinarySearch.binarySearch(
      array, 0, (array.length - 1), 23));
    System.out.println(BinarySearch.binarySearch(
      array, 0, (array.length - 1), 4));
  } // end main
} // end BinarySearchDriver class
```

Output:

```
first=0, last=8
first=5, last=8
first=5, last=6
first=6, last=6
found
returnedValue=6
returnedValue=6
returnedValue=6
6
first=0, last=8
first=0, last=4
first=0, last=2
first=2, last=2
not found
returnedValue=-1
returnedValue=-1
returnedValue=-1
-1
```

Reduce range and drill down.

Just return the answer.

Figure A8.5 Driver for `BinarySearch` class in Figure A8.4

Towers of Hanoi Problem

Now it's time for a problem that would be very hard to solve with loops—where recursion is unquestionably the best way to go. Imagine you are a medieval lord who oversees a group of bored monks. To keep them busy on rainy days, you have them solve the Towers of Hanoi problem. There are three locations "A," "B," and "C." Initially, there is a stack of disks at location "A." The smallest disk is on the top, and disk diameter increases as you go down toward the base of the "tower." Locations "B" and "C" are initially empty. Figure A8.6 shows what it looks like when the 4-disk-high tower sits at location "A":

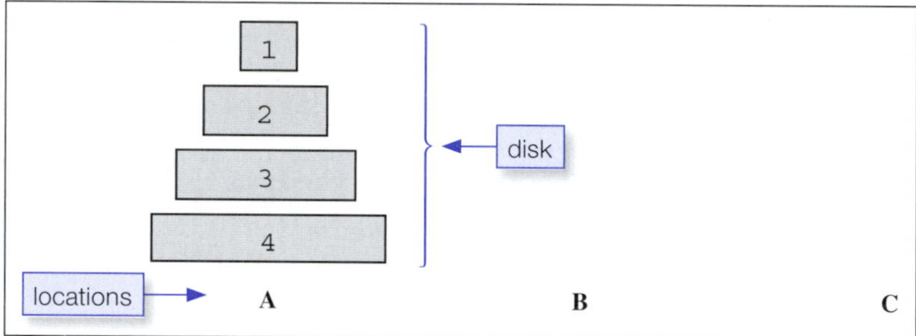

Figure A8.6 Setup for Towers of Hanoi problem

Your monks are to move the tower of disks from location `A` to location `C`, always obeying these rules:

- Move only one disk at a time.
- Never place any disk on top of a smaller disk.

Your task is to come up with a simple algorithm for how to solve this problem. If you had to do it with loops, it would be a mess. But if you use recursion, it's reasonably simple. Whenever you want to make a move, you have a source location, `s`, you have a destination location, `d`, and you have a temporary location, `t`. For our overall goal, `s` is `A`, `d` is `C`, and `t` is `B`. As you progress toward the final solution, you'll have subordinate goals, with different locations for `s`, `d`, and `t`. Here is the general algorithm. It applies to any subset of disks from disk `n` down to disk 1, where `n` is any number from the maximum number of disks down to 1:

- Move the group of disks above disk `n` from `s` to `t`.
- Move disk `n` to `d`.
- Move the group of disks previously above disk `n` from `t` to `d`.

Figure A8.7 shows an example of this algorithm in action. (This particular example happens to be the last few steps in the final solution.) The configuration on the left is a condition that exists shortly before the goal is attained. The configuration on the right is the final condition. The dashed arrows indicate each of the three operations described above for the simplest non-trivial case where there is only one disk above disk 2. The trivial case is the stopping condition. It's when you move the top disk, disk 1, from a source location to a destination location. An example of this appears as the last step in Figure A8.7. This happens to be the final stopping condition, but as you'll see, a program that solves the Towers of Hanoi problem will hit the stopping condition and automatically re-start many times during its execution.

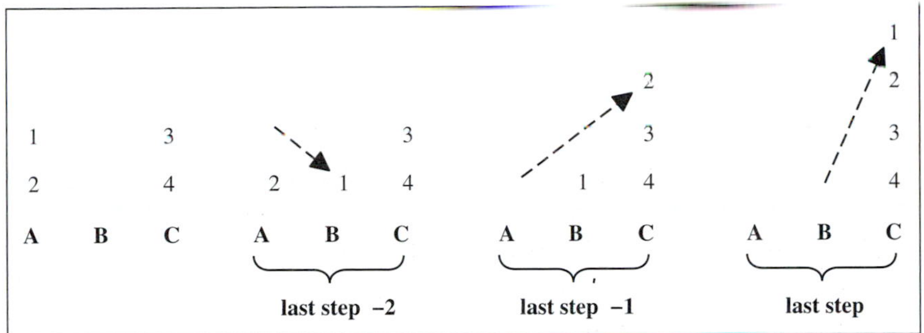

Figure A8.7 Illustration of Towers of Hanoi algorithm in action

Assume the evaluation process is currently in the left frame of Figure A8.7. The next operation calls the following move method with arguments (2, 'A', 'C', 'B'). Within this method, the else clause's first subordinate move method call uses arguments (1, 'A', 'B', 'C') to implement Figure A8.7's "last step-2." The subsequent printf statement implements Figure A8.7's "last step−1." The else clause's second subordinate move method call uses arguments (1, 'B', 'C', 'A') to implement Figure A8.7's "last step."

```
private static void move(int n, char s, char d, char t)
{
  if (n == 1)                 // recursive stopping condition
  {
    System.out.printf("move %d from %s to %s\n", n, s, d);
  }
  else
  {
    move(n-1, s, t, d);   // source to temporary
    System.out.printf("move %d from %s to %s\n", n, s, d);
    move(n-1, t, d, s);   // temporary to destination
  }
}
```

The initial call to the recursive method should establish the overall goal, which is to move the entire tower from location A to location C. To get the largest disk to the new location first, you should start with the maximum possible n. The algorithm says you can do this by moving the subordinate set of disks, 1, 2, and 3 from the source location, A, to the temporary location, B. Then you move disk 4 from the source location, A, to the destination location C. Then you move the subordinate set of disks 1, 2, and 3 from the temporary location, B, to the destination location, C, thereby putting them on top of the largest disk, 4. The problem with this is that the rules don't permit moving more than one disk at a time. So, to move the subordinate set of disks, 1, 2, and 3, you must call the same method recursively to move just disks 1 and 2. To do that, you must call the same method recursively again to move just disk 1.

Of course, the first disk to move is disk 1, but it's hard to know where to put it. Should you move it to location B or to location C? The purpose of the program is to tell you exactly how to proceed. The program is displayed in Figure A8.8. The shaded print statements are not part of the solution, and they should be omitted from a finished product. We inserted them just to help you trace the torturous recursive activity—if you want to. For each method invocation, they print right after the method is called and just before it returns to show you the details of what's happening.

```
/*************************************************************
* Towers.java
* Dean & Dean
*
* This uses a recursive algorithm for Towers of Hanoi problem.
*************************************************************/

public class Towers
{
  public static void main(String[] args)
  {
    move(4, 'A', 'C', 'B');
  }

  // Move n disks from source s to destination d using temporary t.
  private static void move(int n, char s, char d, char t)
  {
    System.out.printf(
      "call n=%d, s=%s, d=%s, t=%s\n", n, s, d, t);
    if (n == 1)              // recursive stopping condition
    {
      System.out.printf("move %d from %s to %s\n", n, s, d);
    }
    else
    {
      move(n-1, s, t, d);  // source to temporary
      System.out.printf("move %d from %s to %s\n", n, s, d);
      move(n-1, t, d, s);  // temporary to destination
    }
    System.out.println("return n=" + n);
  }
} // end class Towers
```

two return points

Figure A8.8 Solution to Towers of Hanoi problem
Shaded statements are for diagnostic tracing. Remove them for final implementation.

Figure A8.9 displays the output. The shaded lines are lines printed by the shaded print statements in Figure A8.8. As we said, they are just to help you see what happened and are not part of the solution. The solution is given by the un-shaded outputs. The most difficult part of tracing a recursive algorithm like this is keeping track of the place from which a call was made and therefore where execution resumes after a return. As our note in Figure A8.8 indicates, sometimes the call is made from the "source to temporary" statement, and sometimes the call is made from the "temporary to destination" statement. Fortunately, if you define a recursive algorithm correctly, you can ignore the details of how it plays out during program execution.

We recommend that you cut out four little paper disks of different sizes, number them 1 through 4 from smallest to largest, and build a tower at location "A" on your left. Then move the disks one at a time as the un-shaded outputs in Figure A8.9 say. You'll see that the tower does in fact get moved from location "A" to location "C" in precise conformity with the specified rules. This works because the eventual moves are informed by goal information in earlier method calls.

Output:

```
call n=4, s=A, d=C, t=B
call n=3, s=A, d=B, t=C
call n=2, s=A, d=C, t=B
call n=1, s=A, d=B, t=C
move 1 from A to B
return n=1
move 2 from A to C
call n=1, s=B, d=C, t=A
move 1 from B to C
return n=1
return n=2
move 3 from A to B
call n=2, s=C, d=B, t=A
call n=1, s=C, d=A, t=B
move 1 from C to A
return n=1
move 2 from C to B
call n=1, s=A, d=B, t=C
move 1 from A to B
return n=1
return n=2
return n=3
move 4 from A to C
call n=3, s=B, d=C, t=A
call n=2, s=B, d=A, t=C
call n=1, s=B, d=C, t=A
move 1 from B to C
return n=1
move 2 from B to A
call n=1, s=C, d=A, t=B
move 1 from C to A
return n=1
return n=2
move 3 from B to C
call n=2, s=A, d=C, t=B
call n=1, s=A, d=B, t=C
move 1 from A to B
return n=1
move 2 from A to C
call n=1, s=B, d=C, t=A
move 1 from B to C
return n=1
return n=2
return n=3
return n=4
```

Figure A8.9 Output from program in Figure A8.8.
Unshaded statements are the solution. Shaded ones provide a trace.

APPENDIX 9

Multithreading

To understand this appendix, you need to be familiar with object-oriented programming, inheritance, exception handling, and files. As such, you need to have read up through Chapter 15.

This appendix introduces a feature, *multithreading,* that helps Java programs take advantage of the parallel processing capabilities contained in many modern computers. By taking advantage of parallel processing capabilities, multithreading can lead to faster programs. And that in turn leads to more user-friendly programs.

Threads

A *thread* is a "lightweight process."[1] Think of it as a coherent code fragment. Ideally, once it has a certain minimum amount of initial information, a thread can run all the way to completion without any more information from the outside world. Ideally, different threads are independent.

A thread is an object derived from a class that `extends` the predefined `Thread` class, and you must override the `Thread` class's `run` method to specify what you want your thread to do. You can call an object's `run` method only once, and you must do it indirectly by calling the `public void start()` method, which your class inherits from the `Thread` class. The `start` method asks the JVM to call your `run` method.[2]

This operation makes the newly started thread run in parallel with the software that called it. After thus starting one thread, your software could start another thread, and you would have three chunks of code running in parallel. You could continue like this to obtain as many parallel operations as you might want. Your computer automatically takes advantage of these relatively independent chunks of code to keep its various parallel hardware components as busy as possible. The driver in Figure A9.1 shows how easy it is to launch new threads.

[1] A "lightweight process" has its own "program counter" and its own "stack," but otherwise it has normal access to the rest of the program in which it exists. A thread's program counter keeps track of where the execution is, and the stack remembers how to return from function calls. Whenever a thread temporarily stops, the computer takes a snapshot of that thread's program counter and stack, and this enables the execution to re-start exactly where it left off when the thread starts running again.

[2] If your class already implements some other class, you can make it work like a thread by also implementing the `Runnable` interface. To start the `run` method of a class that `implements Runnable` but does not `extend Thread`, your class should also include a `start` method that does this:

```
public void start()
{
  new Thread(this).start();
}
```

For simplicity, we restrict our discussion to classes that implement the `Thread` class.

```
/*************************************************************
* Ecosystem.java
* Dean & Dean
*
* Driver for a simple predator/prey (consumer/producer) system.
* The predator and prey objects are separate threads, and
* encounter is an object that describes their relationship.
*************************************************************/

public class Ecosystem
{
  public static void main(String[] args)
  {
    Prey prey = new Prey();                       // producer thread
    Predator predator = new Predator();           // consumer thread
    Encounter encounter = new Encounter(prey, predator);

    // start threads
    prey.start();
    predator.start();
  } // end main
} // end Ecosystem class
```

Figure A9.1 Top level of a program that simulates a simple ecosystem
This class drives the classes in Figures A9.2, A9.3, and (A9.4 or A9.5a and A9.5b).

The class in Figure A9.1 is the top level of a program that describes the interaction of a predator like a fox and prey like a group of field mice. In this example, the prey gets its food continuously from ever-present vegetation, while the predator gets its food intermittently by eating prey when predator and prey happen to meet. The prey is one thread. The predator is another thread. Notice how this driver starts both `prey` and `predator` threads. These threads represent the parallel lives of these creatures in their ecosystem.

The `prey` and `predator` threads are objects. There is also another object, called `encounter`. This object represents an ongoing intermittent relationship between the predator and the prey. In this relationship, some of the prey come into the presence of the predator, and the predator eats them. Presumably the predator eats only part of the prey in each particular encounter, and in the interim the prey continuously replenish by reproducing and eating vegetation. In the encounter relationship, the prey provides food, and the predator consumes food. So computer folks like us might say the prey thread is a *producer* thread, and the predator thread is a *consumer* thread. Of course, the prey also "consume" vegetation, so if our model included a relationship between the field mice and the vegetation they eat, in that context we could call our `prey` thread a "consumer" thread. So the terms "producer" and "consumer" should not be associated absolutely to any one thread.

Any relationship between threads violates the ideal of "thread independence." It complicates the lives of real creatures, and it complicates a program that simulates them.

Figure A9.2 shows the class that describes `prey` threads. Notice that it does extend the `Thread` class. There is just one instance variable, a reference to the `encounter` relationship—field mice are undoubtedly aware of their unpleasant relationship with a fox. The zero-parameter constructor assigns a default name to all

```
/*************************************************************
* Prey.java
* Dean & Dean
*
* This models prey (producers), who avoid encounters.
*************************************************************/

public class Prey extends Thread
{
  private Encounter encounter;

  //***********************************************************

  public Prey()
  {
    super ("prey");
  } // end constructor

  //***********************************************************

  public void setEncounter(Encounter encounter)
  {
    this.encounter = encounter;
  } // end setEncounter

  //***********************************************************

  public void run()
  {
    int number;

    do
    {
      number = encounter.beApart();
    } while (number < encounter.EVENTS - 1);
    System.out.println(getName() + " run finished. ");
  } // end run
} // end Prey class
```

Figure A9.2 Class describing prey (producers) who want to escape from predators
This is driven by the class in Figure A9.1.

objects of the class. That's sufficient for our example, because our driver creates only one such object, but you could also provide a one-parameter constructor to assign different names to different thread instances. The `public setEncounter` method allows the outside world to set the `encounter` reference at any time after `Prey` thread instantiation. The `run` method is the heart of a thread's definition. In this case, it's pretty simple. What prey want is to "be apart," so the `run` method calls the relationship's `beApart` method.

Figure A9.3 shows the class that describes `Predator` threads. It also extends the `Thread` class. It also has an instance variable that refers to the `encounter` relationship—a fox is certainly aware of its pleasant relationship with field mice. It also has a zero-parameter constructor, and it also has a `setEncounter` method.

Notice that `Predator` also declares an array of delay times. With appropriate cross referencing, we could have put this program's time-delay information in any of the classes. But because the predator is the primary "cause" of encounters, we elected to put it in `Predator`'s definition and implement it in the `Predator`'s `run` method. This time-delay implementation makes `Predator`'s `run` method more complicated than `Prey`'s `run` method. We implement each delay by passing an integer number to the prewritten `sleep` method, which is in the `Thread` class in the always-available `java.lang` package:

```
public static void sleep(long millis)
    throws InterruptedException
```

What does this `sleep` method do? It makes the currently executing thread cease its execution for a number of milliseconds equal to the parameter value. In our example, the first element in the `DELAY` array is 2347, so when you run the program, you will experience a pause of 2.347 seconds between the first and second screen outputs.

Notice that the `sleep` method can throw an `InterruptedException`. If you look up `InterruptedException`, you'll find that it's derived directly from the `Exception` class, so it is a checked exception. Therefore, the method call that might throw this exception must be in a `try` block, and that's where we put it. Our program never does anything that might cause this exception to be thrown,[3] so we use an *empty* `catch` block. For better debugging feedback, you could put something like `e.printStackTrace()` in the `catch` block.

Now let's look at a first crude attempt to implement the `Encounter` class, which appears in Figure A9.4. In the lives of a single predator and a group of its prey (our chosen threads), encounters occur several times. We might have written our `Encounter` class so that each `encounter` object represented one *discrete event*, but it's easier to keep track of time and space relationships if you group related events together. Thus, one of our `encounter` objects represents a complete sequence of encounters between our `predator` thread and our `prey` thread. In simulation programming, this kind of on-going relationship is usually called a *process*.

The instance variables in the `encounter` object keep track of the total number of events, the sequence number of the current event, and references to the `prey` and `predator` threads. If you look back at Figure A9.1, you'll see that we call the `Encounter` constructor after we call the `Prey` and `Predator` constructors. This calling sequence enables us to pass `predator` and `prey` references to the `encounter` object when we instantiate it. Then, in the `Encounter` constructor we reciprocate by sending an `encounter` reference to the to the `predator` and `prey` objects.

Now look at the `beApart` and `beTogether` methods. These represent the two phases of the ongoing encounter relationship. The `beApart` method describes a long quiescent period in which the predator rests and hunts. It's called by the `Prey` class in Figure A9.2. The `beTogether` method describes a short violent period in which the predator finds prey, attacks, and eats part of the prey. It's called by the `Predator` class in Figure A9.3.

As they appear in Figure A9.4, these two methods don't do very much. The `beApart` method updates the cycle number. Then it prints the name of the thread that called it and the cycle number's current value.

[3] An `InterruptedException` is thrown when the current thread is sleeping and another thread prematurely wakes it by calling its `interrupt` method, but our program never uses the `interrupt` method.

```
/****************************************************************
* Predator.java
* Dean & Dean
*
* This models predators (consumers), who desire encounters.
****************************************************************/

public class Predator extends Thread
{
  // delay times in milliseconds
  public final long[] DELAY = {2347, 1325, 1266, 3534};
  private Encounter encounter;

  //**************************************************************

  public Predator ()
  {
    super ("predator");
  } // end constructor

  //**************************************************************

  public void setEncounter(Encounter encounter)
  {
    this.encounter = encounter;
  } // end setEncounter

  //**************************************************************

  public void run()
  {
    int i;

    for (i=0; i<DELAY.length; i++)
    {
      try
      {
        Thread.sleep(DELAY[i]);          // rest & hunt
      }
      catch (Exception e) { }
      encounter.beTogether();            // eat prey
    }
    System.out.println(getName() + " run finished.");
  } // end run
} // end Predator class
```

Figure A9.3 Class describing a predator (consumer) which seeks prey
This is driven by the class in Figure A9.1.

```
/****************************************************************
* Encounter.java
* Dean & Dean
*
* This describes predator/prey (consumer/producer) interaction.
****************************************************************/

public class Encounter
{
  public final int EVENTS;
  private int number = -1;
  private Prey prey;
  private Predator predator;

  //*************************************************************

  public Encounter(Prey prey, Predator predator)
  {
    this.prey = prey;
    this.predator = predator;
    prey.setEncounter(this);
    predator.setEncounter(this);
    EVENTS = predator.DELAY.length;
  } // end constructor

  //*************************************************************

  public int beApart()
  {
    // prey has access, so go apart
    number++;
    System.out.println(Thread.currentThread().getName() +
      " start beApart " + number);
    return number;
  } // end beApart

  //*************************************************************

  public int beTogether()
  {
    // predator has access, so come together
    System.out.println(Thread.currentThread().getName() +
      " finish beTogether " + number);
    return number;
  } // end beTogether
} // end Encounter class
```

WARNING!
This implementation does **not** work!

Figure A9.4 Inadequate implementation of `Encounter` class
Because the `prey` and `predator` threads run in parallel but only the `predator` thread contains delays, they do not interleave properly. The `prey` thread finishes quickly, whereas even the first output of the predator method is delayed until much later.

The beTogether method prints the name of the thread that called it and the cycle number's current value. In a more complete model, the beTogether method would also call Predator and Prey methods to change the masses of these objects for the time they were apart. Then it would calculate the change in weights in the violent together period.

If you run the program in Figures A9.1, A9.2, A9.3, and A9.4, this is what you'll get:

Output:

```
prey start beApart 0
prey start beApart 1
prey start beApart 2
prey start beApart 3
prey run finished.
predator finish beTogether 3
predator finish beTogether 3
predator finish beTogether 3
predator finish beTogether 3
predator run finished.
```

Is this what you want? No! Because the prey and predator threads run in parallel but only the predator thread contains delays, they do not interleave properly. The prey thread finishes quickly, whereas even the first output of the predator thread does not occur until much later.

Synchronization

When different threads access a common object, they should be *synchronized*. We synchronize them relative to the common object by including the synchronized modifier in the heading of any common-object method that might be called by a thread that must be synchronized. In addition, we use a *semaphore* to give access to only one thread at a time—and *block* (temporarily stop) all other threads.

Figure A9.5a contains a corrected version of the first part of the Encounter class of Figure A9.4. In this part of the corrected class definition, the only thing different is the addition of another instance variable, a boolean semaphore that indicates which thread currently has access to the common object. This additional declaration appears in bold-face type.

Figure A9.5b contains a corrected version of the second part of the Encounter class of Figure A9.4. All the new code appears in bold-face type. This shows what you do to synchronize multiple threads. First, include the synchronized modifier in the heading of those methods you want to synchronize. Then, at the start of each of those methods, put a while loop with a try block that contains the simple statement:

```
wait();
```

This statement blocks access to the rest of that method, so you should make the while condition true when you want to block access. Finally, insert a pair of special statements right before the return. The first of these special statements should set the phase of the semaphore to make the preceding while condition true. The second of these statements should be:

```
notifyAll();
```

In both cases the while loop's condition is the phase of the semaphore that blocks the calling thread. If this condition is true when an external thread calls the method, flow goes immediately to the wait

```
/*************************************************************
* Encounter.java
* Dean & Dean
*
* This describes predator/prey (consumer/producer) interaction.
*************************************************************/

public class Encounter
{
  public final int EVENTS;
  private int number = -1;
  private Prey prey;
  private Predator predator;
  private boolean predatorHasAccess = false; // access semaphore

  //**********************************************************

  public Encounter(Prey prey, Predator predator)
  {
    this.prey = prey;
    this.predator = predator;
    prey.setEncounter(this);
    predator.setEncounter(this);
    EVENTS = predator.DELAY.length;
  } // end constructor
```

Figure A9.5a Corrected version of the `Encounter` class—Part A

statement[4], and this blocks the execution of the calling thread at that point in its execution. That thread stays in this blocked state until it receives a "wake-up" system call initiated by another thread's execution of the `notifyAll` method, at which time it starts running again—from the place where it was blocked. If the program is written correctly, the condition in the `while` loop of exactly one of the synchronized methods is `false`. When this particular method is called, flow jumps over the `while` loop to the subsequent executable code.

For example, when in Figure A9.2 the `prey` thread first calls `encounter.beApart`, Figure A9.5a's `predatorHasAccess` semaphore is `false`. So in the `beApart` method in Figure A9.5b, `prey` thread execution jumps over the `while` loop and prints the output:

```
prey start beApart 0
```

Then the execution changes the `predatorHasAccess` semaphore to `true`, calls `notifyAll`, and returns. The next time the `prey` thread calls `encounter.beApart`, the `true` value of the `while` condition causes execution of the `wait` statement, and this blocks the `prey` thread at that point.

[4] The `wait` method is inherited by all objects from the `Object` class, and it `throws` an `InterruptedException` (just like the `sleep` method) if the waiting thread is interrupted while it's waiting. We must put the `wait` call in a `try` block because (as indicated previously) the exception it might throw is a checked exception, even though we never create the condition that throws that exception.

```
  //*****************************************************************

  public synchronized int beApart()
  {
    while (predatorHasAccess)
    {
      try
      {
        wait();         // Prey thread waits here until notified
      }
      catch (Exception e) { }
    }
    // prey has access, so go apart
    number++;
    System.out.println(Thread.currentThread().getName() +
      " start beApart " + number);
    predatorHasAccess = true;
    notifyAll();
    return number;
  } // end beApart

  //*****************************************************************

  public synchronized int beTogether()
  {
    while (!predatorHasAccess)
    {
      try
      {
        wait();    // Predator thread waits here until notified
      }
      catch (Exception e) { }
    }
    // predator has access, so come together
    System.out.println(Thread.currentThread().getName() +
      " finish beTogether " + number);
    predatorHasAccess = false;
    notifyAll();
    return number;
  } // end beTogether
} // end Encounter class
```

Figure A9.5b Corrected version of the `Encounter` class—Part B

Meanwhile (as soon as it is started), the `predator` thread begins running in parallel with the `prey` thread. When in Figure A9.3 the `predator` thread first calls its `sleep` method, it stops execution for 2.347 seconds. During most of this time delay, both threads are blocked, and neither is executing. When the 2.347-second time delay expires, the `predator` thread automatically wakes up, jumps over the `catch`, and calls `encounter.beTogether`. Long before this time, the `prey` thread changed the predatorHasAccess semaphore in Figure A9.5a to true, so in Figure A9.5b the predator thread execution jumps over beTogether's while loop and prints the output:

```
predator finish beTogether 0
```

Then the execution changes the predatorHasAccess semaphore to false, calls notifyAll, and returns. Back in the run method of Figure A9.3, the predator thread enters the second iteration of the for loop and goes to sleep again in its second time delay.

Meanwhile, the previous predator thread's notifyAll call re-activates the waiting prey thread and allows it to continue with the while loop in the beApart method in Figure A9.5b. This time, when execution returns to the while condition, it finds that the predatorHasAccess semaphore value is false. This allows it to escape from the while loop and print the output:

```
prey start beApart 1
```

Then, as before, it changes the predatorHasAccess semaphore to true, calls notifyAll, and returns.

This alternation between being apart and being together continues until (in the run method of Figure A9.2) number == encounter.EVENTS - 1, which terminates the prey thread. A little later (in the run method of Figure A9.3) i == DELAY.length, which terminates the predator thread. Using the corrected version of the Encounter class that appears in Figures A9.5a and A9.5b, the program output looks like this:

Output:

```
prey start beApart 0
predator finish beTogether 0
prey start beApart 1
predator finish beTogether 1
prey start beApart 2
predator finish beTogether 2
prey start beApart 3
prey run finished.
predator finish beTogether 3
predator run finished.
```

We encourage you to run this program yourself to get a physical sense of the interaction between the time-delay and wait operations.

Index

B

C

J

K

L

T

U